W9-BZM-558

Criminological Theory

Criminological Theory: Past to Present

ESSENTIAL READINGS

FOURTH EDITION

FRANCIS T. CULLEN
University of Cincinnati

ROBERT AGNEW
Emory University

New York   Oxford
OXFORD UNIVERSITY PRESS
2011

Oxford University Press, Inc., publishes works that further Oxford University's
objective of excellence in research, scholarship, and education.

Oxford   New York
Auckland   Cape Town   Dar es Salaam   Hong Kong   Karachi
Kuala Lumpur   Madrid   Melbourne   Mexico City   Nairobi
New Delhi   Shanghai   Taipei   Toronto

With offices in
Argentina   Austria   Brazil   Chile   Czech Republic   France   Greece
Guatemala   Hungary   Italy   Japan   Poland   Portugal   Singapore
South Korea   Switzerland   Thailand   Turkey   Ukraine   Vietnam

Copyright © 2011, 2006, 2000, 1995, 1991 by Oxford University Press, Inc.

Published by Oxford University Press, Inc.
198 Madison Avenue, New York, New York 10016
http://www.oup.com

Oxford is a registered trademark of Oxford University Press

All rights reserved. No part of this publication may be reproduced,
stored in a retrieval system, or transmitted, in any form or by any means,
electronic, mechanical, photocopying, recording, or otherwise,
without the prior permission of Oxford University Press.

Library of Congress Cataloging-in-Publication Data
Criminological theory : past to present : essential readings / [edited and
selected by] Francis T. Cullen, Robert Agnew. — 4th ed.
p.   cm.
ISBN 978-0-19-538955-5 (pbk.)
1. Criminology.   I. Cullen, Francis T.   II. Agnew, Robert, 1953–
HV6025.C85 2011
364.01—dc22

2010006056

Printing number: 9   8   7   6   5   4   3   2   1

Printed in the United States of America
on acid-free paper

Dedication

For their continuing love and presence,
which gives meaning to our lives,
we dedicate this book to our families –
to Paula Dubeck and Jordan Cullen
and to Mary, Willie, and Jenny Agnew.

About the Editors

FRANCIS T. CULLEN is Distinguished Research Professor in the School of Criminal Justice at the University of Cincinnati, where he also holds a joint appointment in sociology. He received his Ph.D. (1979) in sociology and education from Columbia University. Professor Cullen has published over 200 works in the areas of criminological theory, corrections, white-collar crime, public opinion, and the measurement of sexual victimization. He is author of *Rethinking Crime and Deviance Theory: The Emergence of a Structuring Tradition* and is co-author of *Reaffirming Rehabilitation, Corporate Crime Under Attack: The Ford Pinto Case and Beyond, Criminology, Combating Corporate Crime: Local Prosecutors at Work, Criminological Theory: Context and Consequences, and Unsafe in the Ivory Tower: The Sexual Victimization of College Women.* He also has co-edited *The Origins of Criminological Theory, The Encyclopedia of Criminological Theory, Contemporary Criminological Theory,* and *Offender Rehabilitation: Effective Correctional Intervention.* Professor Cullen has served as president of the Academy of Criminal Justice Sciences and of the American Society of Criminology.

ROBERT AGNEW is Samuel Candler Dobbs Professor of Sociology in the Department of Sociology at Emory University. He received his Ph.D. in sociology from the University of North Carolina at Chapel Hill in 1980. He is noted for his development of "general strain theory," a perspective that has attracted considerable theoretical and empirical attention. His publications include *Pressured into Crime: An Overview of General Strain Theory, Why Do Criminals Offend? A General Theory of Crime and Delinquency, Juvenile Delinquency: Causes and Control* (now in its third edition), and *The Future of Anomie Theory.* Professor Agnew has served on the editorial boards of *Criminology, Journal of Research in Crime and Delinquency, Justice Quarterly, Social Forces,* and *Youth and Society* and is an associate editor of *Theoretical Criminology.* In recognition of his scholarly accomplishments, he was honored as a Fellow of the American Society of Criminology (ASC). He also was elected to serve as an executive counselor of ASC and as president of the Georgia Sociological Association.

Acknowledgments

Criminological Theory was initially conceptualized over a decade ago. Since that time, we have enjoyed a collaboration that has seen our theoretical knowledge and friendship grow. With each edition—now the Fourth—we have endeavored to fashion a volume that retains the wisdom of the past and the excitement found in the fresh criminological contributions of the present. We also have learned that in lives that occasionally are flooded with obligations, finding space to carefully design and write each edition is a source of some strain. We are fortunate, however, that during these times, we have had an amazing amount of social support that has made each edition, including this one, not only possible but also a rewarding experience.

Our most constant source of support has been from our families. Their love, patience, and good humor have sustained us in so many ways across the years. As with past editions, we dedicate this book to them: to Paula Dubeck and Jordan Cullen and to Mary, Willie, and Jenny Agnew.

Criminological Theory would never have come to fruition if it were not for Julia Teweles, who not only owned Roxbury Press but also served as its chief editor. But the world of publishing is dynamic, not stable, and now our volume has moved to Oxford University Press. We approached this new relationship with trepidation, fully aware of Oxford's prestige but also wary of what misery a new editor might bring into our lives! Our apprehension, however, proved groundless. Indeed, we have been deeply grateful for the opportunity to work with Sherith Pankratz, our new editor, who has proven not only welcoming but also inordinately wise. We hope that we will continue to enjoy a lengthy partnership with Sherith, along with Whitney Laemmli and Marianne Paul, who have labored diligently to guide the Fourth Edition to press.

We also wish to take advantage of this opportunity to highlight our appreciation for the continuing support we have received from our academic homes, the School of Criminal Justice at the University of Cincinnati and the Department of Sociology at Emory University. We will refrain from naming the numerous colleagues and students who helped us in diverse ways as we authored past editions, but we will pause to give them a collective expression of our gratitude. For the Fourth Edition of *Criminological Theory*, however, we wish to single out for her special assistance Cheryl Lero Jonson of the University of Cincinnati, who, we suspect, will soon be making her own mark on the field of criminology.

In revising each edition of *Criminological Theory*, we rely not only on our own analysis of changes in the criminological imagination but also on reviews from scholars who, in quite detailed ways, identify essential readings for us to consider. We study these reviews carefully and, where a consensus in recommendations emerges, often follow this collective advice. For the Fourth Edition, we thus are pleased to be able to thank the following scholars for their thoughtful reviews and helpful guidance:

- Leana A. Bouffard, Washington State University
- James J. Chriss, Cleveland State University
- Roger Dunham, University of Miami
- Shannon McAllister, University of Missouri, St. Louis
- Cynthia Perez McCluskey, University of Texas, San Antonio
- Lisa R. Muftic, University of North Texas

- Travis Pratt, Arizona State University
- Wendy C. Regoeczi, Cleveland State University

Jennifer Goode and John Laub deserve our thanks not only for detecting an error in a table in the previous edition but also for bringing it to our attention independently. In fact, this glitch was present from the first edition onward and might have long remained in the pages of *Criminological Theory* if not for their perceptiveness and generosity in contacting us.

Finally, we are most pleased to express our heartfelt gratitude to our fellow criminologists—now hopefully reading this page—who have honored us by using *Criminological Theory* in your research and in your courses. Editing a book is a daunting challenge that demands wisdom in selecting readings and care in writing informative introductory sections. These efforts, however, become meaningful only if the resulting book merits acceptance by one's scholarly peers. So, again, your continued support is much appreciated. We hope that the current edition of *Criminological Theory* again lives up to your expectations and can inspire in your students the fascination for the criminological enterprise that we all share.

Changes Made in the Fourth Edition

As with past editions, the Fourth Edition of *Criminological Theory: Past to Present— Essential Readings* was carefully revised. It is difficult to prune some readings that continue to have value. But every book faces space limitations, and our commitment is to include the most essential theoretical contributions. Indeed, criminology is a dynamic field, and our obligation as authors is to develop new sections that capture these developments. Beyond general editing and updating of our introductory sections, below we detail the main changes made to the previous edition. We trust that these additions and alterations make the Fourth Edition of *Criminological Theory* up to date and able to provide students with a valuable learning experience.

- The inclusion of an entirely new part, "Theories of White-Collar Crime," including a general introduction and introductions to three new readings.

- The inclusion of an entirely new part, "Putting Theory to Work: Guiding Crime Control Policy," including a general introduction and introductions to three new works.

- Eight readings are new or replaced (all new readings have individual introductions).

- A comprehensive instructor's manual and test bank, including learning objectives, key words, discussion topics and exercises, a test bank with multiple choice and essay questions, and PowerPoints, prepared by Pamela Wilcox of the University of Cincinnati and Cheryl Lero Jonson of Northern Kentucky University, is now available on CD-ROM (contact Oxford University Press).

Contents

Criminological Theory

INTRODUCTION

Understanding *Criminological Theory:*
A Guide for Readers

Criminology is a field rich in theoretical imagination. To an extent, this diversity of theorizing reflects the discipline's immaturity—its inability as of yet to develop a single paradigm that is so empirically superior to its competitors that it earns the allegiance of most scholars. In biology, for example, Charles Darwin's theory of evolution provides the organizing framework that virtually all serious scientists embrace. Economists as a field share the assumption that human behavior is self-interested and based on rational choice—the pursuit of benefits over costs. Both biologists and economists disagree among themselves a great deal and develop different ideas about how the world operates, but they tend to do so within the parameters of an overriding paradigm.

Criminology, however, is structured in a different way. There are many theories or "schools of thought." Again, the fact that criminologists do not agree on "why crime occurs" can be seen as a limitation of the field. But the richness in thinking within criminology also is a manifestation of the complexity of its subject matter. Like much social behavior, crime is multifaceted and potentially shaped by a range of factors that operate inside and outside individuals, that exist on the macro level and the micro level, and that have effects across various points in the life cycle. Illuminating what causes crime is thus a daunting

task that benefits from efforts to view its origins from many angles and through different colored lenses.

The purpose of this volume is to capture the diversity of thinking on crime causation that now prevails within criminology. As we surveyed the large and growing body of theoretical criminology, it became apparent that a surplus of worthy contributions was available; this reader could easily have doubled in size. The practicalities of editing a single volume of manageable length and appropriate for classroom use, however, required that we make tough choices as to what to include and what, regrettably, to omit. In doing so, we attempted to select the most *essential readings*—that is, works that have had or are now having the largest impact on criminological theory and research. These writings either were instrumental in creating a theoretical tradition or subsequently extended an existing perspective in noteworthy ways.

However, using and learning from a book of readings—a "reader"—can be challenging. There is a certain comfort in a traditional textbook in which the authors summarize the knowledge in a clear and convenient way. In contrast, edited readers require that you return to the original writings. These writings were authored at different times, for different audiences, and, of course, in different voices. There is much value in revisiting the originals—of not relying exclusively on someone else's retelling of the theory. But it is also not always easy to keep all the ideas straight and to understand fully what is being said.

In this collection, however, we take steps to guide readers along their excursion through criminological theory. This introductory essay is our first effort to tell readers how to use this book and what the Fourth Edition of *Criminological Theory: Past to Present* "is all about." We invite you, therefore, to take a few moments to consider the rest of this "guide." We trust that the investment will make our collection of essays more accessible, understandable, and rewarding.

How to Use This Book

The Fourth Edition of *Criminological Theory* is like two books in one. Most important, the book presents 50 selections from scholars who have sought to explain the origins of criminal behavior. These are arranged from Chapter 1 to Chapter 50. Taken together, these writings provide remarkable insights into why people break the law.

The "second book" is comprised of the introductory material that we, as editors, have written and inserted throughout the book. *Criminological Theory* is divided into 15 parts. These are labeled Part I to Part XV. Each "part" represents a distinct theoretical approach to the explanation of crime. To guide readers on their adventure across time (from past to present) and across theories, each of the volume's parts is preceded by a general introduction that places its readings in their scholarly context. For a given part, the introduction conveys the central thrust of a perspective; that is, it addresses what makes the theory unique or different from other explanations of crime. It also attempts to show how specific readings "fit into" the theoretical paradigm covered in that part of the book. In many ways, these introductions—when taken together—are much like a separate textbook on theories of crime. Again, each introduction is tied to a distinct part and to the selections therein. But they could virtually be

read by themselves as a fairly comprehensive summary of criminological theory.

Beyond the overviews leading into the book's 15 parts, we have also written separate introductions for each of the 50 selections (which are arranged as "chapters" in this volume). These article introductions should make the excerpts more understandable by pointing out the key issues that readers should attend to as they study each selection.

We also divide the book one further way, grouping chapters into Sections 1 to 5. Chapters are placed together into a section based on some commonality, such as a similar time of origin, longstanding rivalry or integration, and shared theoretical or political assumptions. Later in this Introduction, we will return to these five sections and show how they help to organize the book and help you to understand the development of criminological theory.

Given the way we have organized the book, we suspect that the most effective way to understand each theoretical selection is to proceed in four steps:

First, read the introduction to the part in which the selection appears. Again, this material will provide an overview of (1) the principles of the general school of criminological thought examined in the part and (2) the specific selections in that school included in the volume.

Second, before reading a given individual selection, be sure to read the introduction written specifically for that chapter. After doing so, you should have a reasonably solid understanding of both the general theoretical framework and the specific content of the selection you are about to read.

Third, now turn your attention to the original work authored by the criminological theorist(s) in question. Ideally, you will have the foundation to comprehend not only the content of the theory—what the theory is saying—but also how it "fits" in with the school of thought in that part of the book.

Fourth, if you become confused in any way, you might then revisit either the part or the chapter introduction where we have reviewed the materials. As will be explained, we also provide a table here that summarizes the main schools of thought. This chart might also be employed to refresh your thinking.

In short, we have attempted to provide an integrated learning experience. Traditional textbooks are useful, but again, they deprive readers of the opportunities to hear theorists in their own voices. Books of edited readings supply the original works, but many include only cursory introductions, which leave readers to their own devices to "figure out" what the theories mean and how all the information "fits together." Our goal, by contrast, is to furnish both the originals and the kind of detailed but clear commentary that will make reading these primary materials an enriching rather than a mystifying experience. For this reason, we urge readers to take advantage of the introductory essays and to use them to make the primary materials in the individual chapters more accessible and meaningful.

Finally, at the close of each reading, we list several "Discussion Questions." These queries are designed to test your knowledge of the theories, to encourage you to critically evaluate the theories, and to guide class discussions on the theories.

Central Theme: Past to Present

Criminological Theory is not just an endless roster of one reading after another. Already, we have explained that the book is divided into 15 major parts, with each area representing a major theoretical perspective or "school of criminology." In making the selections of which readings to place into each of these 15 parts, we focused—as we have said—on theoretical writings that were essential or "must reads" for anyone wishing to be literate in criminology.

However, our book is organized around another theme that also is represented in its subtitle: *Past to Present*. Within each part, we thus start with one or more "classic" works that were responsible for, in essence, finding or establishing

the school of thought. Then, we include one or more selections from more contemporary criminologists. In this way, readers see how the theoretical perspective covered in the part has evolved from "past to present." This approach makes sense to us because, as we have seen in our joint careers, criminological theory is dynamic, not static.

Studying the past—the classic works—is important for two reasons. First, collectively, they help us to learn about the history of the discipline and to learn in detail how scholars first set forth distinct, competing ways of viewing crime causation. Second, the writings of today's scholars typically are not created anew; they come from someplace. Understanding why a theorist makes certain claims today is difficult without some insight into where his or her ideas first originated. In short, the past provides the context for understanding the present.

But classic works, although due their respect, should not be enshrined as having conveyed sacred truths that are beyond criticism and revision. Knowledge grows, and as this process unfolds new ideas develop that extend earlier statements of a theory. As Robert K. Merton observed, however farsighted the "giants" in the field have been, those who stand "on the shoulders of giants" can see even farther. Contemporary theories thus represent our latest insights into the causes of crime. They also have the largest influence in directing the empirical research of today's scholars. As a result, *Criminological Theory* includes a good deal of material on contemporary explanations of crime.

In short, in arranging this book, our goal was to select works that not only were essential readings but also revealed the development of criminological theory from past to present. In approaching each part, the reader should be aware that selections are arranged with the classic works first and the more contemporary works second. Although the writings within each part can be read in different orders, they are placed in a sequence that we believe best shows the development of ideas within the school of thought represented in the part.

We emphasize this structure of the book—repeated within each individual part—so that readers will not simply read one selection after another without thinking about how each of these chapters are *interconnected*. These theoretical interconnections, moreover, are discussed in the introductions to each part. In this way, readers will be alerted as to how early writings laid a school's theoretical foundation and then how, specifically, later works built upon these classic statements.

The excitement, then, is not simply in knowing what each school of criminology—or each contribution within each school—has said. Admittedly, learning the content of the theoretical works is part of the job, so to speak. But for those of us who make criminological theory not only our livelihood but also our passion, the challenge and fascination come from figuring out *how ideas about crime develop*. As this puzzle is completed one step at a time—that is, as readers master one school of thought after another—it is as though a giant mosaic is being revealed before one's eyes. It is a wonderful experience that the arrangement of our book hopefully makes possible.

Keeping Theories Straight

As authors, our challenge is how to take the many important writings on crime and to whittle them down to the 50 most noteworthy contributions. But to readers, such a lengthy roster of writings might well produce an opposite reaction: "How am I supposed to keep all these readings straight?"

We have given part of the answer already. Thus, we have alerted you that the readings in this book are not simply a continuous list of 50 separate chapters that should be seen as distinct entities. Rather, criminological theory is *organized into schools of thought*, and our book reflects this theoretical landscape. Accordingly, the first "cognitive framework" to employ is to ask yourself what school or general theory a

reading "falls into." Once this fact is known, you are likely to have a good sense or clue as to what the reading is about. Furthermore, the book is arranged by a second "cognitive framework": the readings *within each school* are organized from "past to present"—from original or foundational statements of the theory to more contemporary statements. As a result, readings can be "placed" as being earlier or later in a theory's development.

This ability to *locate* each reading (1) into a general criminological school and then (2) into a particular's school's development is one strategy for "keeping theories straight." As any given work is reviewed, it might be helpful to envision where in the "scheme of things" this reading "fits." For example, when reading about Travis Hirschi's "social bond theory," one would make a "mental note" that this work is in the part on "control theory." This categorization means that Hirschi is going to link crime to some sort of absence or breakdown of control. Now, given the date of publication of Hirschi's work (1969), you would also know that it is a fairly early control theory. This fact makes it likely that later theories would, at least in part, build upon the social bond perspective. With this information "in mind," Hirschi's theory is not an isolated reading but exists within an intellectual context. Making these linkages increases the chance that the details of his theory will be more easily recalled.

Another strategy that you might use to keep theories straight is to think about the *names of the theories*. Criminologists do not select names for their theories randomly. Instead, they take a great deal of time to pick out terms that capture the essence of their theory. Not all titles of theories or of the works listed in this book contain explanatory terms, but many do. For example, Hirschi's work is called "Social Bond Theory." Immediately, as a reader, you should have a good idea what his central thesis is: If people have social bonds, they will not go into crime; if social bonds are weak, they will go into crime. Or, take Sutherland and Cressey's "A Theory of

Differential Association." Any idea of what these theorists propose is the key cause of crime? If you answered "differential association" with criminal definitions, then you already know their central premise. What about "strain theory"? Right! People under strain are more likely to become criminal. Of course, theories are much more complicated than this, and it is important. (and fun!) to learn their nuances. But knowing the names of theories is an effective device to sensitize yourself to recalling the theory's main message; it is then but a small step to fill in the details on the theory in question.

Another way of keeping theories straight is to understand that each theory "says something new and/or different about crime." For a theory to make its mark on criminology—and to be included in a book like this on "essential readings"—it must make a point that other writings have not made previously. Again, theories tend to build upon one another and thus typically are not completely novel. Still, each theory tries to carve out its own special niche—to make the case that previous works either were mistaken, omitted a key cause of crime, and/or can be interpreted in a new way. Thus, when trying to remember a reading, it might be helpful to ask: What is this author saying that makes his or her work different?

For example, James Messerschmidt argues that men commit crime as a way of showing that they are "masculine"—as a way of "doing gender." Two features, then, are unique about his work. First, like other feminist writers, he says that theories that do not take gender into account have omitted a key factor of social life and thus are bound to be incomplete, if not wrong. Second, he says that feminist writers who focused on *female* crime did not pay attention to what it means to be *male*. Yet, if males commit a disproportionate share of crime, it is logical to assume that something about *being a man* might be involved in causing crime. In this context, understanding Messerschmidt's work— "keeping it straight"—is easier if the reader thinks about what makes his work different: his focus on what it means to be male or on "masculinities." Of course, this task is made easier by reading the introductions we have written to his article and to the part of the book in which his selection appears.

Finally, to aid in readers having a sense of where theories fit, we have developed Table 1, which is a brief *reader's guide* to criminological theory. This table lists the general theories of crime, which part of the book each theory appears in, each theory's main authors, and each theory's central thesis. We must caution that this chart does not take the place of actually reading the introductions and selections. It is *not* the *Classic Comics of Criminology*! In fact, the table will make the least sense to those who have done the least amount of reading. However, for those who have studied the book in detail, this table can serve as a handy guide to remind you of how the various theories, theorists, and themes fit together.

How Criminological Theory Developed

As with other scholarly fields, criminology as a discipline has its unique history. The most important ideas about crime have not occurred all at once but rather have developed at particular points in time. We have already alluded to this time dimension when we noted that the readings in each part of the book are arranged from "past to present." But beyond the development of ideas *within each theoretical perspective.* (e.g., control theory), there is also the issue of when different schools of thought first came on the scene and/or became major influences within criminology (e.g., social disorganization theory before labeling theory). This development of criminological schools is not easy to diagram because perspectives have waxed and waned in popularity, and many have overlapped for many years despite beginning at different times. That is, the world of ideas does not always arrange itself in a nice, neat package. Still, it is important to know that the 15 parts in the Fourth Edition of *Criminological Theory* are generally arranged in a

Table 1
A Brief Readers' Guide to Criminological Theory

Theory of Crime	Part of Book	Main Theorists in This Book	Central Thesis of the Theory
Classical	I	Beccaria	Crime occurs when the benefits outweigh the costs—when people pursue self-interest in the absence of effective punishments. Crime is a free-willed choice.
Positivist	I	Lombroso	Crime is caused or determined. Lombroso placed more emphasis on biological deficiencies, whereas later scholars would emphasize psychological and sociological factors (among others).
Individual Trait	II	Ellis and Walsh Rowe Caspi, Moffitt, et al. Lahey, Waldman, and McBurnett	Criminals differ from non-criminals on a number of biological and psychological traits. These traits cause crime either directly or indirectly (i.e., in interaction with the social environment).
Social Disorgani- zation/ Chicago School	III	Shaw and McKay Sampson and Wilson Sampson, Raudenbush, and Earls	Disorganized communities cause crime because informal social controls break down and criminal cultures emerge. They lack the "collective efficacy" to fight crime and disorder.
Differential Association/ Social Learning	IV	Sutherland and Cressey Akers Anderson	Crime is learned through associations with criminal definitions. Interacting with antisocial peers is a major cause of crime. Criminal behavior will be repeated and become chronic if reinforced. When criminal subcultures exist, many individuals can learn to commit crime in one location, and crime rates—including violence—may become very high.
Anomie/ Institutional- Anomie	V	Merton Rosenfeld and Messner	The gap between the American Dream's goal of economic success and the opportunity to obtain this goal creates structural strain. Norms weaken, and "anomie" ensues, thus creating high crime rates. When other social institutions (such as the family) are weak to begin with or are also weakened by the American Dream, the economic institution is dominant. When such an institutional imbalance exists—as in the United States—then crime rates are very high.

(continued) |

Table 1
A Brief Readers' Guide to Criminological Theory (*continued*)

Theory of Crime	Part of Book	Main Theorists in This Book	Central Thesis of the Theory
Strain/General Strain	V	Cohen Agnew	When individuals cannot obtain success goals, (e.g., money, status in school), they experience strain or pressure. Under certain conditions, they are likely to respond to this strain through crime. The strains leading to crime, however, may be linked not only to goal blockage (or deprivation of valued stimuli) but also to the presentation of noxious stimuli and the taking away of valued stimuli.
Control	VI	Sykes and Matza Hirschi Gottfredson	Ask the question, "Why don't people commit crime?" They assume that criminal motivation is widespread. The key factor in crime causation is thus the presence or absence of control. This control or containment might be rooted in relationships (e.g., social bonds) or be internal (e.g., self-control). Further, when normative controls exist, crime might still be possible through the use of "techniques of neutralization" that justify breaking the law under specific circumstances.
Labeling/ Shaming	VII	Lemert Braithwaite Sherman	People become stabilized in criminal roles when they are labeled as criminals, are stigmatized, develop criminal identities, are sent to prison, and are excluded from conventional roles. Reintegrative responses are less likely to create defiance and a commitment to crime.
Critical	VIII	Bonger Currie Colvin	Inequality in power and material well-being creates conditions that lead to street crime and corporate crime. Capitalism and its market economy are especially criminogenic because they create vast inequality that impoverishes many. More generally, coercive experiences in the workplace, family, and justice system are conducive to criminal involvement.
Peacemaking	VIII	Quinney	Crime is caused by suffering, which is linked to injustice rooted in inequality and daily personal acts of harm. Making "war on crime" will not work. Making peace is the solution to crime. (*continued*)

Table 1
A Brief Readers' Guide to Criminological Theory (*continued*)

Theory of Crime	Part of Book	Main Theorists in This Book	Central Thesis of the Theory
Feminist	IX	Adler Chesney-Lind Heimer and De Coster Messerschmidt Steffensmeier and Allan	Crime cannot be understood without considering gender. Crime is shaped by the different social experiences of and power exercised by men and women. Patriarchy is a broad structure that shapes gender-related experiences and power. Men may use crime to exert control over women and to demonstrate their masculinity—that is, to show that they are "men" in a way consistent with societal ideals of masculinity.
Deterrence/ Rational Choice	X	Stafford and Warr Cornish and Clarke	Building on classical theory, crime is seen as a choice that is influenced by its costs and benefits—that is, by its "rationality." Crime will be more likely to be deterred if its costs are raised (e. g., more effort required, more punishment applied), especially if the costs are certain and immediate.
Environmental/ Routine Activity	XI	Cohen and Felson Clarke Wilson and Kelling	Crime occurs when there is an intersection in time and space of a motivated offender, an attractive target, and a lack of capable guardianship. People's daily routine activities affect the likelihood they will be an attractive target, who encounters an offender in a situation where no effective guardianship is present. Changes in routine activities in society (e.g., women working) can affect crime rates. The best way to lower crime is through situational crime prevention in which the focus is not on changing offenders but on reducing the opportunity to commit a crime in a given place. Police can help reduce crime in inner-city neighborhoods by enforcing order—a practice called "fixing broken windows."
Developmental/ Life-Course	XII	Glueck and Glueck Moffitt Laub and Sampson Giordano, Cernkovich, and Rudolph	Crime causation is a developmental process that starts before birth and continues throughout the life course. Individual factors interact with social factors to determine the onset, length, and end of criminal careers. The key theoretical issues involve continuity and change in crime. Some theories predict continuity across the life course; others predict continuity for some offenders and change

(continued)

Table 1
A Brief Readers' Guide to Criminological Theory (*continued*)

Theory of Crime	Part of Book	Main Theorists in This Book	Central Thesis of the Theory
			for other offenders; and some predict continuity and change for the same offenders. Desistance from crime is due to opportunities for change and to offenders experiencing a cognitive transformation.
Theories of White-Collar Crime	XIII	Sutherland Benson Shover and Hochstetler	These theories address why "respectable" people in high-status jobs nonetheless commit crime. Organizational and occupational settings provide rich criminal opportunities and expose workers to pressures and attitudes conducive to crime. These offenders often neutralize their "guilty mind" through techniques or "accounts" that justify their action.
Integrated	XIV	Thornberry Tittle Cullen Agnew	These theories use components from other theories—usually strain, control, and social learning—to create a new theory that explains crime. They often are life-course theories, arguing that causes of crime occur in a sequence across time.
Theory and Policy	XV	Clear Felson Farrington and Welsh	Ideas have consequences. By illuminating the sources of crime, theories also guide efforts to reduce lawbreaking. Theories may show the wisdom of some approaches, such as early intervention and situational crime prevention, and the limits of other approaches, such as the mass incarceration of inner-city minority males.

sequential order, with earlier schools of thought presented first and more recently developed perspectives placed later in the book. We thus pause briefly to review how criminological theory has developed and how this development is reflected in the structure of our book.

In a way, then, our goal is to try to *tell you a story* about the evolution of scholars' thinking about crime. As noted earlier, we have tried to capture this development of criminological theory by grouping the 15 parts into five sections.

To borrow John Laub's term, each section is devoted to a major "turning point" in theoretical criminology—a juncture when a different way of seeing crime emerged and reoriented the direction of the field. Again, many existing theories did not vanish. But during these turning points, existing paradigms were fundamentally challenged and criminology was fundamentally transformed.

Below, we review these five sections of the book and, in so doing, attempt to provide a brief historical account of the criminological enterprise.

Section 1. In Search of the Criminal 'Man'

Criminological Theory begins in Part I with two general perspectives—the Classical and Positivist Schools—that laid the foundation for the field of criminology. The Classical School was rooted in an attempt during the Enlightenment to reform criminal laws that were unfair and cruel. Based on the noble vision that all humans were endowed with free will and equal rights, it suggested that crime was a rational choice based on the pleasures of an illegal act outweighing its pains. The criminal law could deter crime if it was certain and just harsh enough that the choice of crime would not "pay." The focus thus was not on the offender but on finding ways to finely calibrate the criminal law so that it would make crime an unattractive choice.

In contrast, the Positivist School rejected these views as wishful philosophy. Instead, Lombroso and those who followed in his footsteps argued that crime, like illness, was *caused*, not chosen, and that the role of criminology was to use science to detect the sources of criminality. Lombroso's theory, which essentially used the principles of Charles Darwin to argue that criminals were not sufficiently "evolved" biologically, would prove controversial and be rejected by later scholars. But Lombroso's paradigm—his basic approach of studying offenders to see what made them different from non-offenders—would become the main strategy of modern criminology. That is, we could not simply assume that all offenders were the same but would have to search for the origins of the criminal "man" (women would not be studied systematically until many years later).

The readings in Part II follow in the Lombrosian tradition of searching for the criminal "man"—of trying to discover what is peculiar about individuals that makes them criminal. These approaches are said to be searching for *individual differences* or *criminogenic traits*. Some scholars prefer to use the term *heterogeneity*; that is, people's traits—whether eye color, height, weight, or criminal propensity—are not homogeneous but heterogeneous. So, the key to criminology is in asking: What is it about criminals that makes them different? Scholars in the individual-trait paradigm typically answer that offenders have biological or psychological deficiencies. Some of the more sophisticated approaches argue that individual traits do not lead directly to crime but rather interact with the social environment to create a person-situation nexus that is criminogenic (e.g., a temperamental child is more likely to be spanked and rejected by parents, which in turn makes the child develop conduct problems).

Individual trait theories were popular in early American criminology (in the beginning part of the 1900s) and have reemerged in popularity in the last decade. This is especially true because of the revolution within genetics that has made tracing biological influences more feasible. For much of the twentieth century, however, scholars rejected such approaches for failing to incorporate *sociological* causes of crime. During this lengthy period, American criminology was largely sociological criminology. The debate among scholars was not over whether crime was a social product, but rather over which set of social factors was the main source of criminal behavior. These ideas tended to fall into three schools of thought—differential association, control, and strain theories—that have earned the status of the "Big Three" in criminological theory. We turn to these next.

Section 2. The Rise and Growth of American Criminology

Although earlier commentaries and studies existed, the origins of modern American criminology—today's criminology—can be traced most fully to the investigations of Clifford Shaw and Henry D. McKay. Using juvenile court records, Shaw and McKay mapped the distribution of delinquency in pre-1940 Chicago, finding that crime rates were highest in neighborhoods located closest to the center of the city. They rejected the idea that crime in inner-city communities was due to the individual traits of the people who had moved to these areas. (This is sometimes called a "compositional effect.") Instead, they argued that crime was a product of the *characteristics of the community.* (This is sometimes called a "contextual effect.") They thus made a powerful case that crime was a sociological phenomenon—a theme that would dominate American criminology for the rest of the twentieth century.

To be specific, Shaw and McKay set forth a social disorganization perspective that linked crime to the breakdown of informal social control in the neighborhoods. They also argued that as control waned, cultural values supportive of delinquency emerged that were transmitted from one generation to the next (e.g., through gangs). There is a long tradition that, even today, studies how characteristics of communities, rather than of residents, causes crime (see Part III).

Because of the location of their study and the fact that scholars were linked to the University of Chicago, this perspective became known as the "Chicago School" of criminology. Importantly, beyond their own social disorganization model, Shaw and McKay's approach eventually gave rise to two distinct theories that, ironically, have become vigorous rivals in contemporary criminology. These are "differential association/social learning theory" (Part IV) and "control theory" (Part VI).

First, Edwin Sutherland borrowed Shaw and McKay's idea that crime would occur if criminal values were transmitted. Later joined by Donald Cressey, Sutherland formalized this insight into his theory of differential association. His key contention was that learning definitions favorable to crime would precipitate illegal conduct. Other theorists would follow who would document the content of criminal "subcultures" and show how these pro-criminal and pro-violent beliefs were conducive to wayward behavior. Later, Ronald Akers would formalize these views still further in his social learning theory that applied modern learning principles to explain the

initiation and continuation of criminal behavior (see Part IV).

Second, the emphasis of social disorganization theory on the weakening of controls led to the development of a variety of "control theories" (Part VI). Walter Reckless, a member of the Chicago School, developed an influential perspective that he called "containment theory." He was interested in how there could be "good boys" in the "delinquency areas" studied by Shaw and McKay. His answer was that these youngsters had "containments" that insulated them against the pushes and pulls of crime. The general principle of control theory is that crime is more likely when controls are weak but that the lure of crime will be resisted when controls or "containments" are strong.

Perhaps the most famous control theorist has been Travis Hirschi. Hirschi popularized the notion that the motivation or propensity to commit crime was virtually universal. Humans by nature pursued self-gratification in the easiest and most immediate way possible. The attraction of crime, said Hirschi, resided in the fact that such acts were gratifying, readily within reach, and not difficult to commit. The key question thus was not why people committed crime but why they did *not* gratify their desires and commit crime. The answer, of course, was that individuals do not commit crime because *controls* are present.

In his career, Hirschi has promoted two different explanations as to which controls are most important in restraining criminal desires. Early on, in his 1969 book *Causes of Delinquency*, he proposed "social bond theory," which argued that control rested in the relationships or bonds that individuals had with conventional society. Later, in his 1990 book *A General Theory of Crime*, which he coauthored with Michael Gottfredson, he suggested that restraint was more of an internal process. He argued that the key causal factor was "self-control."

Hirschi was also consequential because, in *Causes of Delinquency*, he used data to argue that his control theory was superior to two other theories: "differential association theory" (or what he called "cultural deviance" theory), which we have just discussed, and "strain theory," a perspective developed by the famous Columbia University sociologist Robert K. Merton. Hirschi sought to carve up the field into *three dominant theoretical paradigms*. His project was then to show that the other two perspectives were flawed logically and empirically, and thus that his social bond theory should be the reigning theory of crime.

The third perspective, strain theory (Part V), actually has two different dimensions—one showing how strain produces the societal condition of "anomie"and another focusing on what happens when individuals personally experience strain. In brief, Merton set out to explain why the United States has a high crime rate. He observed that American society is marked by a fundamental contradiction. On the one hand, people are taught to embrace the "American Dream"— the idea that *everyone* should want the goal of economic success. On the other hand, due to an unequal class structure, only some Americans have the legitimate means or opportunity to achieve this goal. This contradiction, contended Merton, created structural strain or a pressure on the *norms* governing the means that should be used to pursue success (i.e., the prescription to "work hard" or "go to school"). Ideally, individuals should use legitimate means, but the constant strain caused by the mean-goal contradiction caused the regulatory norms to lose their vitality and seem less relevant. In turn, as the norms weakened—as "anomie" (or normlessness) set in—people were freer to use "whatever means necessary," including crime, to try to be successful. High rates of crime in America— and in certain deprived segments of the United States—were the result.

Other scholars—most notably Albert Cohen and coauthors Richard Cloward and Lloyd Ohlin— applied this thinking to explain delinquent acts. They focused more on what happens when individuals are blocked from achieving success goals and experience feelings of strain or "status frustration."

The adaptation to this strain, they asserted, was delinquency and, when conditions were correct, the formation of delinquent subcultures. Later, Robert Agnew would broaden this theory into his "general strain theory." He noted that blocked opportunity was only one type of strain; other strains could also be a source of criminal behavior. Agnew further specified the conditions under which strains are most likely to result in crime as opposed to some other behavioral outcome.

Now let us return to Travis Hirschi. He did not fully succeed in eliminating his two theoretical rivals, although he did stir up much debate. Regardless, Hirschi was able to clearly demarcate how American criminological theory was dominated by these three main perspectives—control, differential association, and strain theories. We refer to these as the "Big Three," because they remain—even today—the three most significant and long-standing theories in criminology. Sociological theories that have emerged in the last three decades either have borrowed elements of these perspectives (see the integrated theories in Part XIV) or have been developed in oppositional or "critical" theories that our attention briefly turns.

Section 3. Rethinking Criminology

What goes on in the larger society often influences what goes on inside criminology. Similar to other citizens, criminologists live in and are affected by the prevailing social context. Events of the day show how they see the world. When the social context changes in significant ways, it is likely that old ways of thinking will be challenged and fresh ways of thinking will emerge. This is precisely what occurred in the late 1960s and into the 1970s. At this time, criminologists were moved by the events of their day to ask what role the state (or government) and power played in causing crime. A turning point in the development of criminology thus occured.

As readers may recall, this was a period of remarkable social turmoil in the United States— a time marked by the Civil Rights movement, the Vietnam War and the related protest movement, the state's killings of students at Kent State and inmates and guards at Attica, government scandals highlighted by Watergate, and so on. Taken together, these events prompted many in American society—including criminologists—to become deeply mistrustful of the government's power and to question whether American society was arranged in an equitable way. Theories that resonated with these sentiments emerged and quickly won adherents. The "Big Three" theories were often singled out as examples of how criminology had ignored the role of the state and of unjust social arrangements in crime causation. There was a call for a "new criminology"—a different way of seeing the world.

Labeling theory was one of the earliest of these new perspectives (Part VII). Rather than focus on how societal conditions generate unlawful conduct, this model argued that continued involvement in crime is caused by "societal reaction" initiated by the state's labeling of people as criminals. Crime was depicted as a transitory or experimental stage that would vanish if "left alone." But when the state pulled individuals into the criminal justice system and placed them in prison, it set in motion social processes that ensnared people in crime. Thus, a central theme of theories in this tradition is that publicly stigmatizing offenders, imprisoning them, and excluding them from conventional social roles will have the unanticipated consequences of deepening their criminality.

At the core of the "new criminology" was a diverse group of writings united under the term "critical criminology" (Part VIII). Often informed by the writings of Karl Marx and other radical commentators, these works reflected the growing sentiment in the United States that the nation was racked by social injustices. A central organizing theme was that "capitalism caused crime." A largely unfettered market economy was seen to create vast economic inequality, which in turn fostered conditions ripe for crimes by the rich and poor alike. Thus, the poor were driven to break the law by the suffering inherent in a harsh life of socioeconomic disadvantage, whereas the rich were able to use their corporate positions to exploit workers, "rip off" the public, and despoil the environment in the pursuit of even greater wealth. Inequality was also reproduced within the criminal (in)justice system. The poor who dared to violate the law would feel the heavy hand of the state and be imprisoned, while the rich would visit their immense harms on society without fear of ever being charged with a crime. Jeffery Reiman captured the prevailing sentiment of the day when he stated that "the rich get richer and the poor get prison."

Meanwhile, the growing Women's Movement sensitized criminologists, especially female scholars, to the way in which another form of social injustice—gender inequality—was implicated in crime. For many years, criminologists—who were almost exclusively men—felt free to limit their studies almost exclusively to male offenders. But feminist scholars—led by Freda Adler among others—brought attention both to females as criminals and then to females as victims of men (Part IX). As this paradigm evolved, scholars such as Meda Chesney-Lind illuminated the role of patriarchy—men's dominance over women—as a structure of inequality that shaped the nature of female criminality. Much research and theorizing were conducted on how crime was a reflection of gender inequality of power and used by men to control women (e.g., domestic violence, sexual violence). Later, James Messerschmidt would attempt to show how crime was a means through which men attempted to demonstrate their "masculinity."

Section 4. Choice, Opportunity, and Crime

Over the last two decades, other models have emerged that, although different, share a common link: the depiction of offenders as making choices (Part X and XI). In the late 1970s, Lawrence Cohen and Marcus Felson argued, in essence, that criminologists had erred in focusing mainly on what motivates offenders to break the law and not on how the distribution of opportunities in society shape the amount and nature of crime. Of course, a "motivated offender" is needed for a crime to occur. But Cohen and Felson built on the commonsensical observation that without access to criminal opportunity, no amount of motivation would produce a criminal act.

Cohen and Felson made an important conceptual leap, however, in dividing the general concept of opportunity into two components: "target attractiveness" and "capable guardianship." They then proposed that crime occurred when motivated offenders came into contact with attractive targets (e.g., property, person) in the absence of capable guardianship. They further noted that substantial changes in people's daily routines in American society—such as women entering the workforce in record numbers—could result in more crime, even if the pool of motivated offenders remained unchanged. This might occur because changes in daily routines could increase offenders' access to attractive targets and reduce guardianship (e.g., as women worked, they were more vulnerable to assaults, and houses—now left vacant during the day—were more vulnerable to burglary). Because of this focus, their perspective is referred to as "routine activity theory."

Implicit in Cohen and Felson's theory was the idea that offenders make choices as to which targets are attractive and as to when guardianship is present. This view was accentuated by theorists who sought to revitalize the Classical School's focus on crime as a rational choice. Some of these neo-classical criminologists were human capital economists who used economic thinking to explain a range of social behavior, including crime. Other scholars provided a more sophisticated analysis. They did not contend that crime was completely rational, but only that crime was a choice and that the likelihood of making this choice was influenced by the costs and benefits crime would bring forth.

Routine activity and rational choice theories were tied together—especially in the work of Ronald Clarke—because they encouraged a similar, practical approach to decreasing criminal behavior: situational crime prevention through opportunity reduction. In this model, the goal is to make crime more difficult to commit essentially by making potential targets less attractive and by increasing guardianship—or, if one prefers the language of rational choice theorists, by making crime less beneficial. For example, a house that once was easily burgled could be made less vulnerable—that is, less "rational" to victimize—by installing an alarm system, purchasing a dog, and cutting down bushes so that the prime entry points could be seen by neighbors close by.

A more controversial development is whether legal punishments—increasing the certainty and severity of legal punishments—have a meaningful effect in *deterring* crime. Given the amazing growth of the U.S. state and federal prison system—from near 200,000 inmates in 1970 to over 1.5 million today—research into and theorizing about deterrence has gained increasing attention from criminologists in recent years. Again, the issue revolves around whether crime is mainly a matter of rational choice and whether the calculus used by offenders to make this choice is influenced by legal punishments and the related consequences that flow from being arrested and sanctioned by the state.

Traditionally, criminologists had been skeptical that crime could be lowered by the actions taken by the criminal justice system, including mass incarceration. They believed that the "root causes" of crime were located in social ills such as concentrated disadvantage, blocked opportunities, and disorganized communities—all problems that were beyond the power of the criminal justice system to fix. Criminals raised in these conditions would develop strains, criminal values, and weak social bonds that would make them inclined to enter crime. Unless they were rehabilited—their wayward orientations changed—they would hardly be thwarted from breaking the law by some distant threat of being arrested and sentenced to prison. Labeling theorists even warned that stigmatizing and sanctioning offenders would increase their criminality.

Most criminologists continue to hold these views—and with good reason. But some, more conservative scholars, such as James Q. Wilson, have boldly challenged the discipline's accepted wisdoms. For one thing, they do not believe that deprivation and other "root causes" lead to crime. If there is a root cause, it is not economic poverty but moral poverty—a breakdown of morality and in our ability to teach decent values to children. In their view, bad communities do not produce bad individuals; instead, bad individuals—those not socialized to govern their lives by virtuous morals—produce bad communities.

This perspective helps to explain why these criminologists believe that our best strategies for reducing crime must involve the criminal justice system. In their view, calling for more social welfare programs to address root causes is utopian at best (it will not work) and counterproductive at worst (it teaches offenders that they are "victims" of society rather than responsible for their own choices). Instead, offenders must be sent a different message. In the community, police must teach them that even minor indiscretions—hassling pedestrians, hopping turnstiles at train stations to avoid paying fares, disturbing the peace—will not be tolerated. This is the idea of "fixing broken windows" discussed by James Q. Wilson and George Kelling. In the courts, stern punishment should be meted out to teach offenders that crime does not pay. And for those who are not educable—for those who prove to be "super-predators" or incurably "wicked"—there is a foolproof way to keep the community safe: incapacitate them in prisons for years on end.

When taken together, why were these ideas about choice, opportunity, and punishment a turning point in criminology? As suggested, the key organizing idea is that offenders are not mindless but make choices that include breaking the law. These theorists thus reject the criminological project originally defined by Lombroso: the task to search for the criminal "man" and to find out what makes him (or her) different. By contrast, scholars in Section 4 downplay the importance of this kind of behavioral investigation. They believe that we can safely assume that offenders are rational and, in turn, that we can change the choices they make by restructuring the environment in which they live and behave. In particular, regardless of their individual traits and differences, offenders will be less likely to choose crime if we make doing so harder (e.g., put locks on windows), increase the risks of getting detected, and, if detected, raise the punishment that is forthcoming. Further, there is the ultimate method to take away the opportunity to victimize society: place the offender behind bars.

Section 5. Key Developments in Criminology

What will be the main theoretical developments in criminology in the first decades of the twenty-first century? Prognosticating a discipline's evolution is risky business, because shifts in thinking can occur suddenly and in unanticipated ways. Still, there are at least four areas that we are confident will occupy much theoretical attention in the time ahead.

First, there is a continuing, if not growing, interest in *theoretical integration* (Part XIV). Some scholars believe in theoretical competition, with individual theories squaring off against one another to see which one will win the explanatory contest (e.g., is control theory better than social learning theory?). The other view, however, is that criminal behavior is a complex phenomenon with complex causes and will only be understood if scholars draw from diverse theories to create models capable of addressing crime's multifaceted causes. This controversy—integration versus competition—has not been settled. Even so, it seems virtually certain that efforts to synthesize knowledge about crime remain an important approach to formulating new criminological theories.

Second, perhaps the most important theoretical invention over the past decade or so is "developmental criminology" or—as it is also called—"life-course criminology" (Part XII). Although these insights have long been present in the writings of individual trait theorists (Part II), throughout much of the history of American criminology, scholars simply ignored the fact that humans have a childhood. Of course, these scholars knew that offenders were not "born" at, say, age 14, but they did not give this observation any theoretical weight. Because crime rates spiked upwards in adolescence and into early adulthood, most of the dominant theories focused on what might be happening during this particular segment of the life course to cause criminal involvement. But researchers eventually were confronted with a stubborn empirical finding: Most serious, chronic offenders first started to manifest problem behavior not in the teenage years but in childhood. There was, in short, continuity in problem behavior over time. If this was indeed the case, then the origins of crime must begin—if not substantially lie—early in life.

This realization pushed criminology back into the early years of life. Scholars have now started to trace what occurs from the prenatal period onward to set an individual on a trajectory either toward or away from a life in crime. They also have begun to theorize about what causes continuity in offending and what might cause offenders to change and abandon a criminal life course. These are exciting theoretical developments that are likely to exert an increasing influence on the field of criminology in the years ahead.

Third, there is increasing interest in white-collar crime, a topic introduced in 1940 by Edwin Sutherland but often neglected until more recently. Highly publicized scandals, such as at Enron and the Ponzi scheme of Bernard Madoff, show the enormous costs the lawlessness in the upperworld can exact. Scholars have detailed how employment, including in high-status positions, can induce rather than insulate against criminal involvement. These work settings can expose people both to the lure of lucrative illegal opportunities and to strains and subcultural socialization conductive to crime. Contemporary scholars are thus likely to

continue to illuminate the extent, costs, and sources of white-collar crime.

Fourth, criminologists have become concerned with policy interventions. In part, this focus is due to the seemingly intractable expansion in imprisonment over the past four decades that has consumed vast sums of the public treasury—with, many criminologists would argue, only modest increments in public safety to show for it. Facing this "elephant" in the policy room, many scholars feel compelled to offer alternative strategies for confronting lawlessness. However, a prerequisite for reducing crime is understanding its origins. Criminological theories are thus integral to developing sound crime prevention policies.

In this regard, exciting policy developments are being based on the insights of life-course and environmental criminology. As noted, life-course theories direct attention to the sources of antisocial conduct found in the early stages of development. These insights open up the possibility of using "early intervention programs" to treat these risk factors and save children from a criminal career. Similarly, environmental criminology illuminates how criminal acts can be diverted by eliminating opportunities for offending. Based on this theoretical approach, situational crime prevention is emerging as a significant strategy for making people and places less vulnerable to victimization.

The Criminological Adventure Begins

It is now time to begin your excursion through criminological theory—from past to present, and across its diverse theoretical paradigms. Our purpose in offering this guide has been to facilitate your travels by providing a detailed roadmap to the Fourth Edition of *Criminological Theory*. First, we wanted to explain how the selections of readings were made, how the book was organized, and the importance of consulting the introductory materials we have included. Second, we attempted to provide insights on the best way to use this book, including how to keep theories straight. Third, we believed it would be instructive to furnish an initial overview of the development of criminological theory and to reveal how this development was reflected in the sequencing of writings within the book. Now we are optimistic that you are prepared to learn from the readings and materials that lie ahead. We wish you all our best on your intellectual journey into the study of crime!

PART I

The Origins of Modern Criminology

For much of Western history the dominant theory of crime was the "demonic perspective" (Einstadter and Henry, 1995; Pfohl, 1985). Crime was said to be the result of supernatural forces. People engaged in crime because they succumbed to the temptations of evil forces, such as Satan, or because they were possessed by evil forces. As Pfohl (1985) points out, this perspective can be summed up using the language of comedian Flip Wilson: "The devil made me do it." Although no longer the dominant explanation of crime, this perspective can still be seen today. Many people, for example, argue that certain individuals engage in crime because they are "evil."

According to the demonic perspective, crime is sinful behavior or an offense against God (or the gods). It is not surprising, then, that this perspective inspired very harsh reactions to crime. Brutal methods were often used to determine whether people were possessed or had given into evil forces, with many of these methods involving torture. And those found guilty were often brutally punished. For example, they might be burned alive or otherwise slowly tortured to death in a public ceremony. These punishments were designed "to purge the body of a sinner of traces of the devil and thereby restore the body of the community as a whole to its proper relation to God" (Pfohl, 1985: 25).

The demonic perspective was dominant through the 1700s, when it was challenged during the Age of Enlightenment by a group of individuals who came to be known as the "classical" criminologists. Cesare Beccaria was the first and most prominent of these criminologists, and selections from his book, *An Essay on Crimes and Punishments*, are reprinted here. This book, first published in 1764 in Italy, was immensely popular and had a profound impact on criminology and the Western legal system.

The essential ideas of "classical theory" are quite simple. Individuals are rational beings who pursue their own interests, trying to maximize their pleasure and minimize their pain. And unless they are deterred by the threat of swift, certain, and appropriately severe punishments, they may commit crimes (harm others) in their pursuit of self-interest (for overviews, see Bernard et al., 2009; Martin et al., 1990; Pfohl, 1985).

This simple theory differs from the demonic perspective in a fundamental way. Rather than arguing that crime is caused by *supernatural* or "other-wordly" forces, classical theory argues that crime is caused by natural forces or forces of this world—such as the absence of effective punishments. Supernatural forces cannot be observed, which means that the demonic perspective cannot be tested to determine whether it is true or false—there is no way to definitively test whether crime is caused by demonic possession. As such, the demonic perspective is not a scientific theory of crime. Classical theory focuses on natural forces that can be observed. For example, we can observe how swift and certain punishments are. As a consequence, we can test classical theory and thus it is seen as the first of the modern theories of crime.

Classical theory dominated criminology from the late 1700s until the late 1800s. It then came under heavy attack, with Cesare Lombroso being one of its primary opponents. Lombroso's own theory, first proposed in 1876, soon replaced classical theory as the dominant explanation of crime. Drawing on Darwin's theory of evolution, Lombroso argued that many criminals are "genetic throwbacks," or primitive people in the midst of modern society. Their primitive, savage state is what leads them to engage in crime. Criminals, then, are *not* normal, rational individuals who choose to engage in crime to maximize their pleasure and minimize their pain. Rather, they are fundamentally different than noncriminals, and these differences compel them to engage in crime.

Although Lombroso's theory differs from classical theory in important ways, it too argues that crime is caused by natural forces. Lombroso developed his theory after conducting extensive examinations of criminals and noncriminals. He emphasized that theories must be based on or tested against observations of the world; in fact, he attacked the "armchair theorizing" of classical criminologists. Lombroso is sometimes called the "father" of modern criminology in part because of his emphasis on scientifically testing theories. Brief selections from a book summarizing Lombroso's theory of crime are presented here.

It is important to examine the theories of Beccaria and Lombroso because of their enormous impact on contemporary theories of crime. Many modern theories of crime continue to argue that people are motivated to engage in crime through the pursuit of their self-interests and that what determines whether they engage in crime are the constraints they face, such as the threat of punishment (see the discussions of control theory in Part VI and of deterrence, rational choice, and routine activity in Parts X and XI). Other theories of crime draw more heavily on the tradition established by Lombroso, arguing that individuals differ greatly in their motivation for crime, with such differences being determined by

forces largely beyond their control, including biological factors and the social environment.

Classical Theory

Classical theory was developed in reaction to the harsh, corrupt, and often arbitrary nature of the legal system in the 1700s. Classical theorists were mainly interested in critiquing this system and offering proposals for its reform, but embedded in their arguments is a theory of criminal behavior.

Laws in the 1700s were frequently vague and open to interpretation. Judges, who held great power, would often interpret these laws to suit their own purposes. So the punishment for a particular crime might vary widely, with some people receiving severe penalties and others not being punished at all. Poor people, who could not afford to bribe the judges, were at a special disadvantage. Further, the punishments for many crimes were quite harsh, often involving torture and death.

Beccaria and other classical theorists thought that this system was both unjust and ineffective at controlling crime. They based their critique on the work of several philosophers, particularly Thomas Hobbes. Hobbes argued that people naturally pursue their own interests and that this pursuit of self-interest frequently leads people to harm one another. People, being rational, agree to give up some of their freedom to the state in order to prevent this harm from occurring. That is, people essentially enter into a social contract with one another, agreeing to accept certain limits on the pursuit of their self-interests so as to prevent a "war of all against all." The state enforces this social contract, establishing laws that place limits on the pursuit of self-interest and punishing people who violate these laws.

Beccaria and other classical theorists applied these ideas to the legal system. Like Hobbes, they assume that people act in a rational manner, choosing those actions that result in the greatest pleasure and least pain. Given this assumption, how should crime be controlled?

Classical theorists argue that people will be deterred from crime if the pain associated with punishment outweighs the pleasure associated with crime. But if such punishments are to be effective, they must be well known, swift, and certain. The system will break down if the laws are unknown or obscure, if punishments are delayed, or if judges apply the laws in an arbitrary or discriminatory manner so that only some offenders are punished. Individuals must believe that if they commit a particular crime they will quickly suffer the punishment defined in the law.

For that reason, Beccaria favors clearly defined laws, public punishments, and the elimination of judicial discretion. In his view, the role of judges should be to determine guilt or innocence, not to decide on the punishment to be administered.

Crime, then, stems from the pursuit of self-interest in the absence of effective punishments. Beccaria did not fully explain why some individuals in a particular society are more likely than others to engage in crime, but he offered certain suggestions. He states, for example, that theft

> is commonly the effect of misery and despair; the crime of that unhappy part of mankind, to whom the right of exclusive property...has left but a bare existence. (1983: 36)

The circumstances of some individuals, then, may lead them to evaluate the potential pains of punishment and pleasures of crime differently than other individuals. Poor people, for example, may be less deterred by the pains of punishment and more attracted by the pleasures of crime. These arguments, however, are only briefly mentioned and do not form a central part of classical theory.

Beccaria's book was quite popular and formed the basis for the legal systems in the United States, France, and other countries. The classical idea that offenders are rational individuals who choose to engage in crime is at the foundation of our legal system. It is the reason that we feel it is proper and just to punish offenders. The idea that

the law should be applied equally to everyone (blind justice) also derives from classical theory. In particular, we tend to base punishments on the crimes committed by the offender rather than on the characteristics of the offender. Finally, current proposals to control crime by increasing the certainty and severity of punishment derive from classical theory. People, being rational, should reduce their criminal behavior in response to increases in the certainty and (perhaps) severity of punishment. Beccaria, however, argues that the certainty of punishment is more important than the severity. He states that overly harsh punishments are unnecessary, are unjust, and frequently backfire. For example, "if punishments are very severe, men are naturally led to the perpetration of other crimes; to avoid the punishment due to the first" (1983: 43).

Even though classical theory has had a large effect on our legal system and on contemporary theories of crime, its central assumptions have been challenged. First, classical theory assumes that everyone is motivated to engage in crime through the pursuit of their self-interests. That is, everyone experiences situations where engaging in crime might help them better satisfy their interests, such as monetary interests. While this remains a central assumption of certain control and deterrence theories, most modern theories of crime argue that individuals and groups differ greatly in the motivation for crime (for example, see Parts II, IV, and V of this book).

Second, classical theory assumes that people are rational and engage in crime to minimize their pain and maximize their pleasure. Some criminologists, however, argue that many offenders are not rational and that crime is not in their self-interest. Rather, they engage in crime because of forces beyond their control and they often suffer greatly because of their behavior (see the critique of deterrence and rational choice theories in Part X). The legal system has partly recognized the validity of this challenge by changing the law so that punishments are based not simply on the offense committed but also to some extent on the characteristics and circumstances of the offender. In particular, certain categories of offenders, such as juveniles and the insane, are treated differently because they are seen as being less rational or having less control over their behavior than other offenders. And judges now have more discretion in determining the punishments to be administered, so they can take into account those circumstances that influence the commission of crimes (see Bernard et al., 2009, on the "neoclassical" school).

Third, classical theorists state that whether people engage in crime is largely dependent on the swiftness, certainty, and appropriateness of the punishments they face. Almost all criminologists now recognize that other factors have a larger impact on the likelihood of crime than the punishments administered by the legal system. Those other factors are described throughout this text. Nevertheless, classical theory was the first of the modern scientific theories of crime and, as you will see in subsequent sections, many of its ideas live on today.

Lombroso and the 'Positive School' of Criminology

Although classical theory was the dominant theory of crime for close to 100 years, it came under heavy attack in the late 1800s. One reason for this was that crime rates appeared to be increasing despite changes in the legal system inspired by classical theory. There was also some evidence that punished offenders were more, rather than less, likely to continue offending (see Bernard et al., 2009). Further, the image of the offender suggested by classical theory—a rational, self-interested person who chooses to engage in crime—was challenged by the biological sciences, particularly the work of Darwin. While several criminologists challenged classical theory during this time, the work of Lombroso attracted the most attention.

Lombroso first presented his theory of crime in 1876. He challenged the idea that criminals are

normal, rational people who choose crime in order to maximize their pleasure and minimize their pain. In the initial version of his theory, Lombroso argued that criminals are anything but normal. Rather, they are "genetic throwbacks," primitive people in the midst of modern society, and their primitive or savage state compels them to engage in crime. Lombroso, a physician who worked in the military and at an asylum, based his theory on extensive examinations of criminals and noncriminals. These examinations led him to develop a list of traits that could be used to determine whether a person is one of these throwbacks or "born criminals." These traits included a large jaw and cheekbones, swollen or protruding lips, an arm span greater than the individual's height, excessive wrinkling, and a prehensile foot.

If you imagine what someone with these traits might look like, you will likely think of the stereotypical "caveman." It should be noted that Lombroso increasingly came to recognize that environmental factors also play an important role in the causation of crime, and he later argued that there were several different types of criminals, with the "born criminals" making up about one third of all criminals (see Gibson and Rafter, 2006).

Lombroso's work helped lay the foundation for what is known as the "positive school" of criminology, which now dominates the field. The positive school argues that crime is due to forces beyond the individual's control—biological, psychological, or social forces. The positive school is distinguished by its search for these forces or causes of crime and by its reliance on the "scientific method" in this search. That is, the positive school argues that the theories we develop must be tested against our observations of the world. The positive school is often contrasted with the classical school.

It is said that the classical school argues that individuals *freely choose* to engage in crime, whereas the positive school implies that criminals have no choice in their actions. This difference between the schools, however, has been exaggerated. As Beirne (1991) argues, classical criminologists did *not* place as much emphasis on free choice as is commonly portrayed. In fact, they point to several factors, such as the pursuit of self-interest and the nature of punishments, that strongly influence or determine whether individuals engage in crime. For this reason, Beirne contends that Beccaria's theory might better be viewed as a forerunner of positive criminology. Nevertheless, there is a clear difference in the theories; although both describe the causes or determinants of crime, they focus on rather different causes.

What does the evidence say about Lombroso's theory? His theory and other early biological theories were rather simplistic: they pointed to gross biological features that were said to distinguish criminals from noncriminals, and they argued that biological factors often lead directly to crime. These theories were rigorously evaluated during the early to middle 1900s, with researchers comparing the traits of criminals to those of carefully matched samples of noncriminals (similar in age, class, race, and so on to the criminals being studied). Such comparisons provided little support for the early biological theories. This finding, along with a concern for the policy implications of these theories (e.g., selective breeding and sterilization, justification for racist policies), led to the decline of biological theories of crime (see Bernard et al., 2009; Brennan et al., 1995; Gibson, 2002; Horn, 2003; Rafter, 1997, 2004; Raine, 1993 for excellent overviews of early biological theories).

There has, however, been a recent resurgence of interest in biological theories of crime. The new biological theories are, of course, much more sophisticated than Lombroso's theory. They consider a range of biological factors, argue that these factors increase the likelihood that individuals will develop traits conducive to crime (biological factors do *not* lead directly to crime), and recognize that the impact of biological factors on crime is influenced by the social environment. These theories are described in Part II.

References

Beccaria, Cesare. 1983 [1775]. *An Essay on Crimes and Punishments*. Brookline Village, MA: Branden Press.

Beirne, Piers. 1991. "Inventing Criminology: The 'Science of Man' in Cesare Beccaria's *Dei Delitti E Delle Pene* (1764)." *Criminology* 29: 777–820.

Bernard, Thomas J., Jeffrey B. Snipes, and Alexander L. Gerould. 2009. *Vold's Theoretical Criminology*. New York: Oxford.

Brennan, Patricia A., Sarnoff A. Mednick, and Jan Volavka. 1995. "Biomedical Factors in Crime." In James Q. Wilson and Joan Petersilia (eds.), *Crime*, pp. 65–90. San Francisco: ICS Press.

Einstadter, Werner and Stuart Henry. 1995. *Criminological Theory*. Fort Worth, TX: Harcourt Brace.

Gibson, Mary. 2002. *Born to Crime: Cesare Lombroso and the Origins of Biological Criminology*. Westport, CT: Praeger.

Gibson, Mary and Nicole Hahn Rafter. 2006. *Cesare Lombroso, Criminal Man*. Durham, NC: Duke University Press.

Horn, David G. 2003. *The Criminal Body: Lombroso and the Anatomy of Deviance*. London: Routledge.

Martin, Randy, Robert J. Mutchnick, and W. Timothy Austin. 1990. *Criminological Thought: Pioneers Past and Present*. New York: Macmillan.

Newman, Grame and Pietro Marongiu. 1990. "Penological Reform and the Myth of Beccaria." *Criminology* 28: 325–346.

Pfohl, Stephen J. 1985. *Images of Deviance and Social Control*. New York: McGraw-Hill.

Rafter, Nicole. 1997. *Creating Born Criminals*. Urbana: University of Illinois Press.

——. 2004. "Earnest A. Hooton and the Biological Tradition in American Criminology." *Criminology* 42: 735–771.

Raine, Adrian. 1993. *The Psychopathology of Crime*. San Diego: Academic Press.

1. An Essay on Crimes and Punishments

Cesare Beccaria

Beccaria's book, An Essay on Crimes and Punishments, *presents the first of the modern or scientific theories of crime. The book, first published in 1764, became the foundation for the classical theory of criminology, which dominated explanations of crime for close to 100 years. According to classical theory, people are rational and concerned with minimizing their pain and maximizing their pleasure. Their efforts to do so often lead them to engage in crime, unless they are deterred by the threat of punishment.*

Beccaria's book is primarily concerned with criticizing the legal system in the 1700s and offering proposals for its reform, but he presents the classical theory of crime in the process. Beccaria draws heavily on Thomas Hobbes's theory of society in critiquing the legal system, and his book opens with a brief summary of that theory, reprinted in the opening paragraph here. Hobbes noted that the pursuit of self-interest often leads people to harm one another and that individuals must give up some of their liberty for the sake of "peace and security." In particular, they form nations and such nations establish laws and administer punishments to deter people from harming one another in their pursuit of their interests or "passions." However, to be effective, punishments must meet certain conditions. Beccaria describes the characteristics of effective punishments in the remainder of this selection, noting that such punishments should be set by the "sovereign" or representative of the state (not decided by judges), clearly stated, proportionate to the crime, swift, and certain.

Beccaria's theory is reflected in modern deterrence theories, which focus on the impact of official punishments on crime. Such theories and the evidence on their validity are discussed in Part X. Briefly, some evidence shows that the certainty of punishment influences the likelihood of crime, but it is probably not among the most important causes of crime. The swiftness of punishment appears to have little impact on crime. Not much research has been done on the other characteristics of punishment listed by Beccaria, primarily because they are difficult to measure with existing data.

———————————

Of the Origin of Punishment

Laws are the conditions, under which men, naturally independent, united themselves in society. Weary of living in a continual state of war, and of enjoying a liberty which became of little value, from the uncertainty of its duration, they sacrificed one part of it, to enjoy the rest in peace and security. The sum of all these portions of the liberty of each individual constituted the sovereignty of a nation; and was deposited in the hands of the sovereign, as the lawful administrator. But it was not sufficient only to establish this deposite; it was also necessary to defend it from the

Excerpted from *An Essay on Crimes and Punishments,* by Cesare Beccaria. Copyright © 1983 by Branden Press (ISBN: 0-8283-1800-X; orig. published 1775), pp. 1, 4–8, 18, 31–33, 42–43, 78. Permission courtesy of Branden Books, Boston.

usurpation of each individual, who will always endeavour to take away from the mass, not only his own portion, but to encroach on that of others. Some motives, therefore, that strike the senses, were necessary to prevent the despotism of each individual from plunging society into its former chaos. Such motives are the punishments established against the infractors of the laws. I say, that motives of this kind are necessary; because, experience shows, that the multitude adopt no established principle of conduct; and because, society is prevented from approaching to that dissolution, (to which, as well as all other parts of the physical, and moral world, it naturally tends) only by motives, that are the immediate objects of sense, and which being continually presented to the mind, are sufficient to counterbalance the effects of the passions of the individual, which oppose the general good. Neither the power of eloquence, nor the sublimest truths, are sufficient to restrain, for any length of time, those passions, which are excited by the lively impressions of present objects. . . .

Of the Interpretation of Laws

Judges, in criminal cases, have no right to interpret the penal laws, because they are not legislators. . . . The laws receive their force and authority from an oath of fidelity, either tacit, or expressed, which living subjects have sworn to their sovereign, in order to restrain the intestine fermentation of the private interests of individuals. From hence springs their true and natural authority. Who then is their lawful interpreter? The sovereign, that is, the representative of society, and not the judge, whose office is only to examine, if a man have, or have not committed an action contrary to the laws. . . .

Of the Obscurity of Laws

If the power of interpreting laws be an evil, obscurity in them must be another. . . . Crimes will be less frequent, in proportion as the code of laws is more universally read and understood:

for there is no doubt, but that the eloquence of the passions is greatly assisted by ignorance, and uncertainty of punishments. . . .

Of the Proportion Between Crimes and Punishments

. . . *It* is not only the common interest of mankind, that crimes should not be committed, but that crimes of every kind should be less frequent, in proportion to the evil they produce to society. Therefore, the means made use of by the legislature to prevent crimes, should be more powerful, in proportion as they are destructive of the public safety and happiness, and as the inducements to commit them are stronger. Therefore there ought to be a fixed proportion between crimes and punishments.

It is impossible to prevent entirely all the disorders which the passions of mankind cause in society. These disorders increase in proportion to the number of people, and the opposition of private interests. . . . That force, which continually impels us to our private interest, like gravity, acts incessantly, unless it meets with an obstacle to oppose it. . . . Punishments, which I would call political obstacles prevent the fatal effects of private interests. . . .

Of the Intent of Punishments

The end of punishment . . . is no other, than to prevent the criminal from doing further injury to society, and to prevent others from committing the like offence. Such punishments, therefore, and such a mode of inflicting them, ought to be chosen, as will make the strongest and most lasting impressions on the minds of others, with the least torment to the body of the criminal. . . .

Of the Advantage of Immediate Punishment

The more immediately after the commission of a crime a punishment is inflicted, the more just and useful it will be. . . . *The degree of the punishment, and the consequences of a crime, ought be so contrived, as to have the greatest possible effect on others, with the least possible pain to the delinquent.* If there be any society in which this is not a fundamental principle, it is an unlawful society; for mankind, by their union, originally intended to subject themselves to the least evils possible.

An immediate punishment is more useful; because the smaller the interval of time between the punishment and the crime, the stronger and more lasting will be the association of the two ideas of *Crime and Punishment;* so that they may be considered, one as the cause, and other as the unavoidable and necessary effect. It is demonstrated, that the association of ideas is the cement which unites the fabric of the human intellect; without which, pleasure and pain would be simple and ineffectual sensations. . . .

It is, then, of the greatest importance, that the punishment should succeed the crime as immediately as possible, if we intend, that in the rude minds of the multitude, the seducing picture of the advantage arising from the crime, should instantly awake the attendant idea of punishment. Delaying the punishment serves only to separate these two ideas . . .

Of the Mildness of Punishments

Crimes are more effectually prevented by the *certainty,* than the *severity* of punishment. . . . The certainty of a small punishment will make a stronger impression, than the fear of one more severe, if attended with the hopes of escaping; for it is the nature of mankind to be terrified at the approach of the smallest inevitable evil, whilst hope, the best gift of heaven, hath the power of dispelling the apprehension of a greater; especially if supported by examples of impunity, which weakness or avarice too frequently afford. . . .

That a punishment may produce the effect required, it is sufficient that the *evil* it occasions should exceed the *good* expected from the crime; including in the calculation the certainty of the punishment, and the privation of the expected advantage. All severity beyond this is superfluous, and therefore tyrannical. . . .

Conclusion

From what I have written results the following general theorem. . . .

That a punishment may not be an act of violence, of one, or of many against a private member of society, it should be public, immediate and necessary; the least possible in the case given; proportioned to the crime, and determined by the laws.

Discussion Questions

1. According to Beccaria, why is it necessary for the state to sometimes punish people?
2. Beccaria assumes that offenders are rational individuals pursuing their self-interest. Do you think this is an accurate view of all or most offenders?
3. Do you think Beccaria would favor the death penalty? Why or why not? (He discusses this issue in some detail in his *Essay on Crimes and Punishments.*)
4. Evaluate our current system of punishing offenders using the criteria for effective punishments listed by Beccaria. In particular, do we satisfy the criteria listed by Beccaria?
5. Beccaria states that the "end of punishment is no other than to prevent the criminal from doing further injury to society." Do you agree or do you feel that there are other purposes for punishment? Defend your answer.

2. The Criminal Man

Cesare Lombroso

As Summarized by Gina Lombroso Ferrero

Lombroso's theory is the most prominent of the early biological theories of crime; it replaced classical theory as the dominant explanation of crime in the late 1800s. Lombroso first presented his ideas in 1876 and then revised and expanded on them several times over the next three and a half decades. The selection that follows describes the key features of his theory, as summarized by his daughter.

Lombroso argued that crime is the result of biological differences between criminals and "normal individuals." Drawing on Darwin's evolutionary theory, he claimed that criminals are not as evolved as other individuals: they are savages in the midst of modern society (he discribed such people as "atavistic"). It is their savage or primitive state that causes their criminal behavior. As indicated in the following selection, Lombroso came to this conclusion while working as a physician in the army and at an asylum. His examinations of criminals convinced him of their biological inferiority, and through such examinations he developed a list of traints that could be used to distinguish "born criminals" from others. Many of these traits are listed in the selection (for excellent overviews of Lombroso's work, see Bernard et al., 2009; Gibson, 2002; Gibson and Rafter, 2006; Horn, 2003; Martin et al., 1990; Rafter, 1997).

Lombroso's later research convinced him that environmental factors also play an important role in crime. Further, he came to the conclusion that there are actually several different types of criminals.

"Born criminals," or the genetic throwbacks he first described, made up only about one-third of all criminals, but the savagery of their crimes made them an especially important class of criminals. Subsequent research discredited Lombroso's arguments regarding biology, as most of the traits he listed failed to distinguish criminals from carefully matched samples of noncriminals (see Bernard et al., 2009).

Lombroso's research is important, however, because it helped establish what is known as the "positive school" of criminology. The positive school is distinguished by its search for the causes of crime, whether biological, psychological, or sociological. Positivism is also distinguished by its reliance on the scientific method: Theories must be tested against observations of the world. So even though Lombroso's theory was discredited in the early to middle part of the 1900s, his influence on criminology lives on.

References

Bernard, Thomas J., Jeffrey B. Snipes, and Alexander L. Gerould. 2009. *Vold's Theoretical Criminology.* New York: Oxford.

Gibson, Mary. 2002. *Born to Crime: Cesare Lombroso and the Origins of Biological Criminology.* Westport, CT: Praeger.

Gibson, Mary and Nicole Hahn Rafter. 2006. *Cesare Lombroso, Criminal Man.* Durham, NC: Duke University Press.

Reprinted from Cesare Lombroso, *Criminal Man.* Copyright © 1911 by G.P. Putnam's Sons. Reprinted by permission.

Horn, David G. 2003. *The Criminal Body: Lombroso and the Anatomy of Deviance.* London: Routledge.

Martin, Randy, Robert J. Mutchnick, and W. Timothy Austin. 1990. *Criminological Theory: Pioneers Past and Present.* New York: Macmillan.

Rafter, Nicole Hahn. 1997. *Creating Born Criminals.* Urbana: University of Illinois Press.

The Classical School based its doctrines on the assumption that all criminals, except in a few extreme cases, are endowed with intelligence and feelings like normal individuals, and that they commit misdeeds consciously, being prompted thereto by their unrestrained desire for evil. The offence alone was considered, and on it the whole existing penal system has been founded, the severity of the sentence meted out to the offender being regulated by the gravity of his misdeed.

The Modern, or Positive, School of Penal Jurisprudence, on the contrary, maintains that the anti-social tendencies of criminals are the result of their physical and psychic organisation, which differs essentially from that of normal individuals; and it aims at studying the morphology and various functional phenomena of the criminal with the object of curing, instead of punishing him. . . .

If we examine a number of criminals, we shall find that they exhibit numerous anomalies in the face, skeleton, and various psychic and sensitive functions, so that they strongly resemble primitive races. It was these anomalies that first drew my father's attention to the close relationship between the criminal and the savage and made him suspect that criminal tendencies are of atavistic origin.

When a young doctor at the Asylum in Pavia, he was requested to make a postmortem examination on a criminal named Vilella, an Italian Jack the Ripper, who by atrocious crimes had spread terror in the Province of Lombardy. . . . "At the sight of that skull," says my father, "I seemed to see all at once, standing out clearly illumined as in a vast plain under a flaming sky, the problem of the nature of the criminal, who reproduces in civilised times characteristics, not only of primitive savages, but of still lower types as far back as the carnivora."

Thus was explained the origin of the enormous jaws, strong canines, prominent zygomae, and strongly developed orbital arches which he had so frequently remarked in criminals, for these peculiarities are common to carnivores and savages, who tear and devour raw flesh. Thus also it was easy to understand why the span of the arms in criminals so often exceeds the height, for this is a characteristic of apes, whose fore-limbs are used in walking and climbing. The other anomalies exhibited by criminals—the scanty beard as opposed to the general hairiness of the body, prehensile foot, diminished number of lines in the palm of the hand, cheek-pouches, enormous development of the middle incisors and frequent absence of the lateral ones, flattened nose and angular or sugar-loaf form of the skull, common to criminals and apes; the excessive size of the orbits, which, combined with hooked nose, so often imparts to criminals the aspect of birds of prey, the projection of the lower part of the face and jaws (prognathism) found in negroes and animals, and supernumerary teeth (amounting in some cases to a double row as in snakes) and cranial bones (epactal bone as in the Peruvian Indians): all these characteristics pointed to one conclusion, the atavistic origin of the criminal, who reproduces physical, psychic, and functional qualities of remote ancestors.

Subsequent research on the part of my father and his disciples showed that other factors besides atavism come into play in determining the criminal type. These are: disease and environment. Later on, the study of innumerable offenders led them to the conclusion that all law-breakers cannot be classed in a single species, for their ranks include very diversified types, who differ not only in their bent towards a particular form of crime, but also in the degree of tenacity and intensity displayed by them in their perverse propensities, so that, in reality, they form a graduated scale leading from the born criminal to the normal individual.

Born criminals form about one third of the mass of offenders, but, though inferior in numbers, they constitute the most important part of the whole criminal army, partly because they are constantly appearing before the public and also because the crimes commited by them are of a peculiarly monstrous character; the other two thirds are composed of criminaloids (minor offenders), occasional and habitual criminals, etc., who do not show such a marked degree of diversity from normal persons. . . .

Discussion Questions

1. The positive school of criminology, which Lombroso helped found, argues that crime is not the result of free will; rather, it is due to factors over which the individual often has little or no control. As such, this school focuses less on the punishment of the offender and more on "curing" the offending. To what extent do you think crime is an act of free will or one caused by forces beyond the individual's control?

2. What policy recommendations might an adherent of Lombroso's theory make for controlling crime? (A consideration of these recommendations will help you understand one of the reasons why the theory was later attacked.)

3. List those factors said to distinguish "born criminals" from others. How would one go about providing a good test of Lombroso's theory?

PART II

Individual Traits and Crime

Cesare Lombroso's perspective was the dominant theory of crime in the early 1900s. As indicated in Part I, a central part of the theory argues that many criminals are less evolved than noncriminals, as evidenced by such physical features as large jaws and cheekbones, swollen or protruding lips, and an arm span greater than the individual's height. The primitive or savage state of such criminals is what causes them to engage in crime. Among other things, they are said to be impulsive, vengeful, and unconcerned with the welfare of others.

Lombroso's theory was discredited when subsequent research failed to find that criminals differ from noncriminals in terms of the physical features he listed. And biological theories fell into decline for many years.

Sociological theories came to dominate criminology by the mid-1900s and continue to be dominant today (see Ellis et al., 2008; Laub and Sampson, 1991). Such theories explain crime not in terms of differences between individuals but in terms of differences in the social environments to which individuals are exposed. Certain types of environments, including family, school, peer group, and community, are said to increase the likelihood of crime. Most of the theories covered in the remaining parts of this text are sociological: They describe those social environments most conductive to crime and the reasons these environments foster crime. These theories typically make little or no mention of individual differences, with several explicitly stating that there are no individual differences between criminals and noncriminals. Criminals are said to be much like noncriminals except that they are in environments conducive to crime. Most criminologists have been quite reluctant to acknowledge the role of biological factors and individual traits in explaining crime (see Chapter 5 and the discussions in Andrews and Bonta, 2006; Andrews and Wormith, 1989; Fishbein, 1998; Wright et al., 2008a).

In recent years, however, some criminologists have begun to criticize the *exclusive* focus of many crime theories on the social environment. Like Lombroso, they argue that individuals may differ from one another in ways that influence the likelihood of crime and that these differences may be in part biologically based. The theories advanced by these criminologists, however, are much more sophisticated than Lombroso's. First, they focus on a broader range of biological factors, including genetic inheritance and "biological harms" such as head injury, exposure to toxins such as lead, and birth complications. Second, they better specify how these biological factors lead to crime. They do not argue that biological factors lead directly to crime; for example, no one argues that there is a gene that leads directly to crime. Rather, biological factors are said to affect the central and autonomic nervous systems in ways that contribute to traits conducive to crime, such as impulsivity, sensation seeking, and irritability. Third, most biological theories now recognize that the social environment influences whether biological factors lead to the development of certain traits and whether these traits lead to crime. Birth complications, for example, may be more likely to result in crime among children in disrupted versus intact families. Modern biological theories, then, recognize the importance of both psychological and sociological variables.

It is important for criminologists to consider biological factors and individual traits for two fundamental reasons. First, they may *interact* with the social environment to produce crime. In particular, traits may influence *how* individuals respond to their environment. Even though the social environment has an important influence on crime, we know that individuals often respond to the same environment in different ways. This difference in response may be due to differences in individual traits (see Chapter 37 in Part XII). A child with an irritable disposition or a low IQ, for example, may be more likely to respond to stressors with crime. Second, individual traits may influence the social environment in ways that increase the likelihood of crime. In particular, individuals with traits such as impulsivity and risk seeking may shape their environment in ways conducive to crime. For example, impulsive children may evoke hostile responses from family members, teachers, and peers. Also, certain traits may cause individuals to seek out or sort themselves into environments conducive to crime. Individuals who like risky activities, for example, may chose to associate with delinquent peers (see Chapter 38 in Part XII). (Environmental factors may also influence individual traits, as we will see.) A complete understanding of crime, then, requires a consideration of biological factors, individual traits, and the social environment.

Chapters 3 and 4 focus on those biological factors that may influence traits conducive to crime, although both readings note that such factors work with the social environment to produce these traits. Chapter 5 describes certain individual traits that contribute to crime. Chapter 6 then presents an integrated theory that assigns a central role to biological factors, individual traits, and the social environment. Several other such theories have been developed (see Chapters 38 and 47 as well as Brennan and Raine, 1997; Farrington, 2005; Moffitt, 2006; Raine et al., 1997; Robinson, 2004; Thornberry and Krohn, 2005). At the most general level, these theories state that (1) biological and environmental factors influence the development of traits conducive to crime; (2) traits conducive to crime influence the social environment in ways that increase the likelihood of crime; and (3) crime is most likely among individuals who possess traits conducive to crime *and* are in aversive environments (e.g., troubled families, delinquent peer groups).

Biological Influences on Traits Conducive to Crime

Evidence suggests that there may be a genetic component to those traits conducive to crime and that such traits may also stem from "biological harms" of a nongenetic nature, such as head injury, exposure to certain toxic substances, and some types of birth complications.

Genetic Influences on Crime

Researchers have tried to estimate the extent to which crime is inherited using three major methods: twin studies, adoption studies, and molecular genetic studies (for excellent overviews, see Baker et al., 2006; Brennan, Mednick, and Volavka, 1995; Dick and Todd, 2006; Ellis and Walsh, 2006; Fishbein, 2001; Raine, 1993; Rhee and Waldman, 2007; Rowe, 2002; Tehrani and Mednick, 2000; Wright et al., 2008b). Twin studies compare identical twins to fraternal twins. Identical twins are genetically identical, while fraternal twins are about 50 percent genetically alike on those genes that vary among people (see Raine, 1993). It is assumed that twins—whether identical or fraternal—are exposed to the same environmental influences. If crime is genetically inherited, we would expect identical twins to be more similar in crime than fraternal twins. Most studies indicate that this is the case. Twin studies, however, suffer from certain problems. Most notably, some evidence suggests that identical twins—because of their more similar appearance and traits—are more likely to spend time together and be treated alike than fraternal twins. These factors, rather than their identical genes, may explain their greater similarity in crime.

Adoption studies overcome this problem to some extent, although such studies are not problem-free. Adoption studies focus on children who were separated from their biological parents early in life. The traits of these children are compared to the traits of their biological parents. If crime is inherited, we would expect more crime among adopted children whose biological parents are criminal than among adopted children whose biological parents are not criminal. Most data suggest that this is the case. For example, one large study in Denmark found that when neither adopted nor biological parents were criminal, 13.5 percent of the adopted boys had criminal convictions; when adoptive parents were not criminal and biological parents were, 20 percent of the adopted boys had criminal convictions (Raine, 1993). (Crime was most likely when both biological and adoptive parents were criminal—reinforcing the point that crime is a function of both biological factors and the social environment.)

Twin and adoption studies suggest that there is some genetic basis for crime, but they do not identify those genes that may influence the predisposition for crime. The field of molecular genetics examines variations in genes and relates these variations to body functions and behavioral traits. Recent research in this area has discovered several genes that may be related to traits conducive to crime, such as hyperactivity and impulsivity. We can expect much more research in this area in coming years (see Baker et al., 2006; Dick and Todd, 2006; Rowe, 2002).

In sum, evidence suggests that crime is inherited to some degree. While it is difficult to precisely specify the extent to which crime is inherited, genetic factors *may* be as important as environmental factors for some types of crime and offenders. At the same time, certain cautions are in order (see Brennan et al., 1995; Raine, 1993; Rowe, 2002; Tehrani and Mednick, 2000). Most notably, there is some evidence that genetic factors—and biological and psychological factors more generally—are most relevant to the explanation of what has been called "life-course persistent" offending (see Chapter 38 by Moffitt). That is, these factors help us understand why some individuals offend at high rates over much of their lives. These high-rate, chronic offenders make up a small percentage of the population, but they account for a large share of all crime—including a majority of serious crime. Biological and psychological factors are said to be less relevant to the explanation of what has been called "adolescence-limited" offending. Most individuals commit a range of largely minor offenses during their adolescent years, and this adolescence-limited offending is said to be more strongly influenced by the social environment (see Chapter 38). However, biological factors have also been used to help explain such offending. Data indicate that the prefrontal cortex of the brain is still developing during adolescence. As a consequence, adolescents are less able than adults to control their behavior and emotions. This fact, in combination with the increased freedom and demands experienced by adolescents, may help explain adolescence-limited offending (Ishikawa and Raine, 2003; Wright et al., 2008b).

The fact that there appears to be some genetic predisposition for crime raises a major question: Why is it that some individuals have genes that predispose them for crime? Several gene-based evolutionary theories have attempted to answer this question. These theories all argue that genes have an effect on traits conducive to crime and that *under some conditions* individuals with such traits "might be able to reproduce at fairly high rates," thereby passing their genes on to others. That is to say, certain traits conducive to crime may sometimes provide an evolutionary advantage.

Ellis and Walsh (Chapter 3) provide an overview of gene-based evolutionary theories used to explain crime. Certain of these theories attempt to explain particular types of crime, such as rape, while others attempt to explain crime in general. All try to explain how people with genes promoting traits such as "pushiness" and "deception" may reproduce at high rates in certain circumstances. For example, "pushy" males, including those who rape, may be more likely to mate with multiple sex partners, particularly in large, impersonal societies where the likelihood of punishment for rape is low. Such males thus gain a reproductive advantage and are successful in passing their genes on to others. None of these theories has been fully tested. Ellis and Walsh derive several predictions or hypotheses about crime from these theories (e.g., crime will be more prevalent in men than women, criminals will be unusually promiscuous), and they note that much data support certain of these predictions. In many cases, however, nonevolutionary theories make the same predictions. And there are certain facts about crime that the evolutionary theories have trouble explaining. For example, young children are disproportionately likely to be raped, and many rapes involve oral and anal sex; rape in these cases clearly does not increase the chances of reproducing. The status of these theories, therefore, is still somewhat uncertain (also see Coyne, 2000; Daly and Wilson, 1994; de Waal, 2000; Duntley and Shackleford, 2008; Ellis and Walsh, 2006; Fishbein, 2001; Raine, 1993; Rowe, 1996, 2002; Thornhill and Palmer, 2000).

'Biological Harms' and Crime

Evidence suggests that crime is also influenced by biological factors of a nongenetic origin, such as (1) the mother's poor health habits during pregnancy, including poor nutrition and alcohol and drug use; (2) certain types of delivery complications; (3) exposure to toxic substances such as lead; (4) poor diet; and (5) head injury (see Brennan et al., 1995, 2003; Denno, 1990; Ellis and Walsh, 2006; Raine, 1993, 2002; Scarpa and Raine, 2007; Wright

et al., 2008b). One study, for example, found that the children of mothers who smoke during the third trimester of their pregnancy are more likely to engage in crime as adults (Brennan et al., 1999).

The Central and Autonomic Nervous Systems

Most researchers suggest that genetic inheritance and biological harms contribute to traits and crime through their effect on the central nervous system (the brain and the spinal cord) and the autonomic nervous system (which controls the heart rate and gland secretions, among other things, and influences the emotional reaction to stimuli). (For overviews, see Agnew, 2009; Brennan et al., 1995; Ellis and Walsh, 2006; Farrington, 1996; Fishbein, 2001; Hollin, 1992; Ishikawa and Raine, 2003; Patrick and Verona, 2007; Raine, 1993, 2002; Rowe, 2002; Scarpa and Raine, 2007; Wilson and Herrnstein, 1985; Wright et al., 2008b).

A number of possible effects have been explored. Genetic factors and biological harms may contribute to dysfunctions in the frontal lobe of the brain—which is involved in abstract thinking, planning, self-monitoring of behavior, and behavioral inhibition. Such dysfunctions, in turn, may contribute to such traits as hyperactivity, impulsivity, irritability, the reduced ability to learn from punishment, insensitivity/low empathy, difficulties in problem solving, and immature moral reasoning. Genetic factors and biological harms may also contribute to dysfunctions in the left hemisphere of the brain that have been linked to low verbal IQ scores. And biological factors may affect the autonomic nervous system, with data suggesting that criminals are underaroused. That is, criminals show less emotional response to stimuli (they are "physiologically 'drowsy'" in the words of Bartol and Bartol, 1986: 69). This underarousal is reflected in their lower skin conductance (criminals sweat less in response to stimuli), lower resting heart rate, and slower alpha brain waves. This underarousal may contribute to such traits as impulsivity, sensation seeking, the inability to learn from punishment, and hyperactivity. Individuals who are underaroused are less affected by punishment and require more to stimulate them—which may cause them to become easily distracted, overly active, and in greater need of thrills/excitement.

Researchers are now investigating the ways in which genetic inheritance and biological harms may affect the central and autonomic nervous systems. For example, recent data suggest that some of these factors may result in reduced levels of the neurotransmitter serotonin. Neurotransmitters allow for communication between brain cells and underlie all human behavior, thoughts, perceptions, and emotions. Reduced serotonin may lower one's level of inhibition, contributing to traits such as impulsivity and the reduced ability to learn from punishment.

Chapter 4 by David Rowe summarizes much of the research on the central and autonomic nervous systems, traits, and crime. He notes that genes and biological harms such as exposure to toxic substances may affect neurotransmitters like serotonin, hormones such as testosterone, psycho-physiological factors like heart rate and skin conductance, and brain function abnormalities. And these effects sometimes lead to traits conducive to crime, such as impulsivity and irritability. Much of the research in this area is likely to strike criminologists as difficult, particularly given the unfamiliar terminology. Nevertheless, the Rowe chapter provides a good overview of the work in this rapidly growing area. (For further information, see Brennan et al., 1995; Ellis and Walsh, 2006; Fishbein, 2001; Lahey et al., 2003; Patrick and Verona, 2007; Raine, 1993, 2002; Raine et al., 1997; Rowe, 2002; Rutter, Giller, and Hagell, 1998; Scarpa and Raine, 1997, 2007; Yaralian and Raine, 2001).

Environmental Influences on Traits

It should be kept in mind that traits conducive to crime are also influenced by the individual's social environment (see Agnew, 1997; Caspi et al., 1994;

Colvin, 2000; Gottfredson and Hirschi, 1990; Lahey and Waldman, 2003, 2005, 2007; Rowe, 2002; Wade and Cairney, 2006; Wilson and Herrnstein, 1985; Wright et al., 1999; Wright et al., 2008a). Whether individuals develop such traits depends on the socialization efforts of parents and others; for example, it depends on the extent to which parents try to teach or "instill" such traits as self-restraint and concern for others (as suggested above, biological factors influence the likelihood that individuals will successfully learn such traits). It may also depend on such things as the adversity of the individual's environment. Some have suggested, for example, that poor, inner-city residents who are mistreated on a regular basis are more likely to develop irritable dispositions (see Anderson, 1999; Bernard, 1990). Crime-related traits, then, are a function of the environment as well as biological factors.

It is often difficult to separate out the effects of environmental and biological factors in a precise manner. Many types of biological harm are a function of the social environment—such as one's social class. Lower-class individuals, for example, are more likely to be exposed to lead and have poor prenatal care (Denno, 1990). Also, certain social factors, such as poverty and abuse, may directly affect the individual's biological state—including brain development (Wright et al., 2008b; also see Rutter et al., 2006). At the same time, biological factors can shape one's social environment. Children with dysfunctions in their central and autonomic nervous systems, for example, may be more difficult for parents to raise. As such, they may be more likely to elicit negative reactions from their parents, including harsh discipline and abusive behavior. Further, it has been suggested that environmental and biological factors condition the effect of each other on such traits. For example, biological factors such as genetic inheritance and birth complications may be *more* likely to lead to the crime-related traits if the individual is in a poor family environment. Likewise, a poor family environment may be more likely to lead to such traits if the individual has a genetic predisposition for them or has experienced certain types of biological harm. The important point to remember is that there is evidence suggesting that most of these traits are a function of both biological and environmental factors (see especially Brennan and Raine, 1997; Lahey and Waldman, 2005; Raine, 2002; Raine et al., 1997; Rowe, 2002; Rutter, 1997; Rutter et al., 1998, 2006; Wade and Cairney, 2006; Wright et al., 2008b).

Individual Traits and Crime

Biological and environmental factors, then, may lead to traits conducive to crime. Several such traits have already been mentioned. Traits are "relatively stable ways of perceiving, thinking about, and behaving toward the environment and oneself" (Blackburn, 1993). For example, if a person regularly acts without thinking, we say that this person possesses the trait of impulsivity. Data suggest that several individual traits increase the likelihood of crime, including low verbal IQ, attention deficit/hyperactivity, impulsivity, risk seeking, irritability, insensitivity to others/low empathy, and poor social and problem-solving skills (see Agnew, 2009; Andrews and Bonta, 2006; Dodge, 2003; Ellis and Walsh, 2006; Farrington, 1994; Farrington and Welsh, 2007; Lahey and Waldman, 2007; Lynam and Miller, 2004; Miller and Lynam, 2001; and Rutter et al., 1998 for overviews). Individuals with such traits are more likely to engage in crime in a particular situation, are more likely to elicit negative responses from others (which may foster crime), and are more likely to sort themselves into negative environments (which may foster crime). For example, irritable individuals may be more likely to respond to mild slights with aggression, provoke insults and challenges from others, associate with other criminals, and have poor employment histories.

Psychologists and others have argued that many of these specific traits are related to one another and that they often cluster in the same individuals. Several researchers have developed lists of related traits, with some researchers arguing that most of these traits cluster together into one "super-trait." Perhaps the best-known example is the collection of traits that characterize the "psychopath," which include impulsivity, sensation seeking, an inability to learn from punishment, irritability, and insensitivity/low empathy (see Blackburn, 1993; Lykken, 1995, 1996; many researchers now distinguish between different types of psychopaths, most notably primary and secondary psychopaths). Another well-known example is provided in Gottfredson and Hirschi's (1990) description of individuals who are low in self-control (see Chapter 19 in Part VI). The super-trait of low self-control also includes many of the specific traits listed above.

Data increasingly suggest, however, that those traits related to crime cluster into a few super-traits. One such trait refers to the individual's cognitive abilities, especially verbal abilities. This trait is often measured by the individual's verbal IQ score, and it influences such things as the individual's social and problem-solving skills, academic performance, and ability to communicate with others (Lahey and Waldman, 2005, 2007; Nigg and Huang-Pollock, 2003). Other traits refer to the individual's temperament. Chapter 5 by Caspi et al. draws on the description of traits provided by Tellegen (1985), who proposed that the human personality can be described in terms of three super-traits: negative emotionality, constraint, and positive emotionality. This conception is well grounded in research and is widely accepted in psychology. As the Caspi et al. chapter demonstrates, there is good reason to believe that the super-traits of negative emotionality and low constraint increase the likelihood of crime. Several other studies also support this conclusion—although they sometimes use different terms to describe these traits or they refer to closely related traits (e.g., Andrews and Bonta, 2006; Colder and Stice, 1998; Farrington and Welsh, 2007; Henry et al., 1996; Lahey and Waldman, 2005, 2007; Lynam and

Miller, 2004; Miller and Lynam, 2001; Pratt and Cullen, 2000; Rothbart and Bates, 1998).

Individuals high in negative emotionality are more likely than others to experience events as aversive; to attribute these events to the malicious behavior of others; to experience intense emotional reactions such as anger to these events; and to respond to these events in an aggressive or antisocial manner. Individuals low in constraint are more likely to act on their impulses, including impulses of a criminal nature. Such individuals tend to be impulsive, are risk-taking/ sensation seeking, reject conventional norms, and are unconcerned with the feelings or rights of others. It is not difficult to understand why they would be more likely to engage in crime.

The Interactive Effect of Biological Factors, Traits, and the Social Environment on Crime

Whether individuals with a biological predisposition to crime or with the traits we have described actually engage in crime is often said to depend on the social environment. For example, individuals with a biological predisposition may engage in little crime if they are raised in a loving, supportive family environment but may engage in much crime if they are rejected and abused. Many argue that crime is most likely when individuals who are biologically predisposed to crime (or have crime-related traits) are in environments conducive to crime (the "dual hazard" prediction). Such environments might include families where parents reject their children and treat them in a harsh manner, or poor, inner-city communities plagued by a host of social problems, such as gangs and limited job opportunities. There are several reasons for the dual hazard prediction. For example, one popular argument states that traits such as IQ and negative emotionality influence the ability of individuals to learn how to behave in a noncriminal manner (Brennan and Raine, 1997; Nigg and Huang-Pollock, 2003). That is,

some individuals have an easier time learning how to conform than others. But whether they learn how to conform also depends on their social environment. For example, do their parents and others make a good effort to teach them to conform? Crime, then, is most likely when individuals are biologically disposed to crime or have traits conducive to crime *and* are in unfavorable environments. Another popular argument states that these traits influence how individuals respond to temptations and provocations. For example, individuals low in constraint are more likely to take advantage of tempting opportunities for crime, while individuals high in negative emotionality are more likely to respond to provocations like insults with violence (Agnew et al., 2002; Dodge and Sherill, 2007; Lahey and Waldman, 2005, 2007). Crime, then, is most likely among individuals who possess these traits and in environments where the temptations and provocations for crime are abundant.

The dual hazard prediction has received a fair degree of support (see Agnew et al., 2002; Brennan and Raine, 1997; Dodge and Sherill, 2007; Fishbein, 2001; Keenan and Shaw, 2003; Lahey and Waldman, 2003; Raine et al., 1997; Rutter et al., 1998; Scarpa and Raine, 2007; Wright et al., 2001). For example, a recent study by Tibbetts and Piquero (1999) found that males with low birth weights were more likely to start offending at an early age if they came from low socioeconomic status families. Not all studies find evidence for biosocial interactions, however. And some studies find that biological factors are most likely to lead to crime in advantaged rather than disadvantaged environments. For example, one study found that low heart rate was most likely to lead to crime among those from intact homes versus homes broken by divorce or separation (Wadsworth, 1976; also see Raine, 2002; Scarpa and Raine, 2007). Such findings are usually explained by arguing that biological factors are most important when the "social push" for crime is minimal (i.e., when individuals come from environments where there is little pressure to engage in crime). Overall, however, the evidence tends to favor the proposition that crime is most likely when individuals are biologically predisposed to crime (or have traits conducive to crime) *and* are in environments favorable to crime.

Chapter 6 by Lahey et al. presents an integrated theory that reflects these ideas. This theory states that crime is influenced by cognitive and temperamental traits, such as intelligence and irritability. These traits, in turn, are a function of both genetic and environmental factors. Crime is also influenced by the social environment, including the family and peer environment. Further, individual traits and environmental factors affect one another; most notably, those with traits such as irritability are more likely to evoke negative responses from others and sort themselves into environments that are conducive to crime. Finally, crime is most likely when individuals possess traits such as low intelligence and irritability *and* are in environments such as troubled families and antisocial peer groups. This combination of negative traits and environments often leads to early, frequent, and serious offending (see Chapters 38 and 47 for similar theories).

In sum, biological factors and the individual traits influenced by such factors play a central role in the explanation of crime. They influence the social environments in which people find themselves and play a major role in determining how people respond to such environments. In particular, they help us understand why only some of the individuals exposed to aversive environments, such as abusive families or antisocial peer groups, turn to crime. Nevertheless, most of the sociological theories you will read about in the following chapters do not devote any consideration to biological factors and individual traits. Sociological criminologists, however, are starting to devote much more attention to the role of biological factors and individual traits in their theories. And when reading the sociological theories presented in Parts III through XIV of this book, you should ask yourself what role biological factors and individual traits might play in these theories.

References

Agnew, Robert. 1997. "Stability and Crime Over the Life Course: A Strain Explanation." In Terence P. Thornberry (ed.), *Developmental Theories of Crime and Delinquency: Advances in Criminological Theory*, Volume 7, pp. 101–132. New Brunswick, NJ: Transaction.

——. 2009. *Juvenile Delinquency: Causes and Control*, 3rd edition. New York: Oxford.

Agnew, Robert, Timothy Brezina, John Paul Wright, and Francis T. Cullen. 2002. "Strain, Personality Traits, and Delinquency: Extending General Strain Theory." *Criminology* 40: 43–72.

Anderson, Elijah. 1999. *Code of the Street*. New York: W.W. Norton.

Andrews, D. A. and James Bonta. 2006. *The Psychology of Criminal Conduct*, 4th edition. Cincinnati: Anderson.

Andrews, D. A. and J. Stephen Wormith. 1989. "Personality and Crime: Knowledge Destruction and Construction in Criminology." *Justice Quarterly* 6: 289–309.

Baker, Laura A., Serena Bezdjian, and Adrian Raine. 2006. "Behavioral Genetics: The Science of Antisocial Behavior." *Law and Contemporary Problems* 69: 7–46.

Bartol, Curt R. and Anne M. Bartol. 1986. *Criminal Behavior: A Psychosocial Approach*. Englewood Cliffs, NJ: Prentice-Hall.

Bernard, Thomas J. 1990. "Angry Aggression Among the 'Truly Disadvantaged.'" *Criminology* 28: 73–96.

Blackburn, Ronald. 1993. *The Psychology of Criminal Conduct*. Chichester, England: John Wiley and Sons.

Brennan, Patricia A., Emily R. Grekin, and Sarnoff A. Mednick. 1999. "Maternal Smoking During

Pregnancy and Adult Male Criminal Outcomes."
Archives of General Psychiatry 56(3): 215–219.

——. 2003. "Prenatal and Perinatal Influences on
Conduct Disorder and Serious Delinquency." In
Benjamin B. Lahey, Terrie E. Moffitt, and
Avshalom Caspi (eds.), *Causes of Conduct
Disorder and Juvenile Delinquency*, pp. 319–341.
New York: Guilford.

Brennan, Patricia A., Sarnoff A. Mednick, and Jan
Volavka. 1995. "Biomedical Factors in Crime." In
James Q. Wilson and Joan Petersilia (eds.), *Crime*,
pp. 65–90. San Francisco: ICS Press.

Brennan, Patricia A. and Adrian Raine. 1997. "Biosocial
Bases of Antisocial Behavior: Psychophysiological,
Neurological and Cognitive Factors." *Clinical
Psychology Review* 17: 589–604.

Caspi, Avshalom, Terrie E. Moffitt, Phil A. Silva,
Magda Stouthamer-Loeber, Robert F. Krueger,
and Pamela S. Schmutte. 1994. "Are Some People
Crime-Prone: The Personality-Crime Relationship
Across Countries, Genders, Races and Methods."
Criminology 32: 163–195.

Colder, Craig R. and Eric Stice. 1998. "A Longitudinal
Study of the Interactive Effects of Impulsivity and
Anger on Adolescent Problem Behavior." *Journal
of Youth and Adolescence* 27: 255–274.

Colvin, Mark. 2000. *Crime and Coercion*. New York:
St. Martin's Press.

Coyne, Jerry A. 2000. "Of Vice and Men." *New
Republic*, April 30, 27–34.

Daly, Martin and Margo Wilson. 1994. "Evolutionary
Psychology of Male Aggression." In J. Archer
(ed.), *Male Violence*, pp. 253–288. London:
Routledge.

de Waal, Frans B. M. 2000. "Survival of the Rapist."
New York Times, April 2, Section 7, p. 24.

Denno, Deborah W. 1990. *Biology and Violence*.
Cambridge, England: Cambridge University Press.

Dick, Danielle M. and Richard D. Todd. 2006. "Genetic
Contributions." In Robert T. Ammerman (ed.),
*Comprehensive Handbook of Personality and
Psychopathology*, pp. 16–28. New York: Wiley.

Dodge, Kenneth A. 2003. "Do Social Information-
Processing Patterns Mediate Aggressive
Behavior?" In Benjamin B. Lahey, Terrie E.
Moffitt, and Avshalom Caspi (eds.), *Causes of
Conduct Disorder and Juvenile Delinquency*, pp.
254–274. New York: Guilford.

Dodge, Kenneth A. and Michelle R. Sherrill. 2007.
"The Interaction of Nature and Nature in
Antisocial Behavior." In Daniel J. Flannery,
Alexander T. Vazsonyi, and Irwin D. Waldman
(eds.), *The Cambridge Handbook of Violent
Behavior and Aggression*, pp. 215–242. New
York: Cambridge University Press.

Duntley, Joshua D. and Todd K. Shackleford. 2008.
"Darwinian Foundations of Crime and Law."
Aggression and Violent Behavior 13: 373–382.

Ellis, Lee, Jonathon A. Cooper, and Anthony Walsh.
2008. "Criminologists' Opinions about Causes
and Theories of Crime and Delinquency: A
Follow-Up." *The Criminologist* 33(3): 23–26.

Ellis, Lee and Anthony Walsh. 2006. *Criminology*.
Needham Heights, MA: Allyn.

Farrington, David P. 1994. *Psychological Explanations
of Crime*. Aldershot, England: Dartmouth.

——. 1996. "The Explanation and Prevention of Youthful Offending." In J. David Hawkins (ed.), *Delinquency
and Crime: Current Theories*, pp. 68–148. Cambridge,
England: Cambridge University Press.

——. 2005. "The Integrated Cognitive Antisocial
Potential (ICAP) Theory." In David P.
Farrington (ed.), *Integrated Development and
Life-Course Theories of Offending*, pp. 73–92.
New Brunswick, NJ: Transaction.

Farrington, David P. and Brandon C. Welsh. 2007.
Saving Children from a Life of Crime. New York:
Oxford University Press.

Fishbein, Diana. 1998. "Building Bridges." *Academy of
Criminal Justice Sciences ACJS Today* 17(2): 1, 3–5.

——. 2001. *Biobehavioral Perspectives in Criminology*. Belmont, CA: Wadsworth.

Gottfredson, Michael R. and Travis Hirschi. 1990.
A General Theory of Crime. Stanford, CA:
Stanford University Press.

Henry, Bill, Avshalom Caspi, Terrie Moffitt, and Phil
A. Silva. 1996. "Temperamental and Familial
Predictors of Violent and Nonviolent Criminal
Convictions: Age 3 to Age 18." *Developmental
Psychology* 32: 614–623.

Hollin, Clive. 1992. *Criminal Behaviour: A Psychological Approach to Explanation and Prevention*. London: Falmer Press.

Ishikawa, Sharon S. and Adrian Raine. 2003. "Prefrontal Deficits and Antisocial Behavior." In Benjamin B. Lahey, Terrie E. Moffitt, and Avshalom Caspi (eds.), *Causes of Conduct Disorder and Juvenile Delinquency*, pp. 277–303. New York: Guilford.

Keenan, Kate and Daniel S. Shaw. 2003. "Starting at the Beginning." In Benjamin B. Lahey, Terrie E. Moffitt, and Avshalom Caspi (eds.), *Causes of Conduct Disorder and Juvenile Delinquency*, pp. 153–181. New York: Guilford.

Lahey, Benjamin B., Terrie E. Moffitt, and Avshalom Capsi. 2003. *Causes of Conduct Disorder and Juvenile Delinquency*. New York: Guilford.

Lahey, Benjamin B. and Irwin D. Waldman. 2003. "A Developmental Propensity Model of the Origins of Conduct Problems during Childhood and Adolescence." In Benjamin B. Lahey, Terrie E. Moffitt, and Avshalom Caspi (eds.), *Causes of Conduct Disorder and Juvenile Delinquency*, pp. 77–117. New York: Guilford.

——. 2005. "A Developmental Model of the Propensity to Offend during Childhood and Adolescence." In David P. Farrington (ed.), *Integrated Developmental and Life-Course Theories of Offending*, pp. 15–50. New Brunswick, NJ: Transaction.

——. 2007. "Personality Dispositions and the Development of Violence and Conduct Problems." In Daniel J. Flannery, Alexander T. Vazsonyi, and Irwin D. Waldman (eds.), *The Cambridge Handbook of Violent Behavior and Aggression*, pp. 260–287. New York: Cambridge University Press.

Laub, John H. and Robert J. Sampson. 1991. "The Sutherland-Glueck Debate: On the Sociology of Criminal Knowledge." *American Journal of Sociology* 96: 1402–40.

Lykken, David T. 1995. *The Antisocial Personalities*. Hillsdale, NJ: Lawrence Erlbaum.

——. 1996. "Psychopathy, Sociopathy, and Crime." *Society* 34(1): 29–38.

Lynam, Donald R. and Joshua Miller. 2004. "Personality Pathways to Impulsive Behavior and Their Relations to Deviance." *Journal of Quantitative Criminology* 20: 319–341.

Miller, Joshua D. and Donald Lynam. 2001. "Structural Models of Personality and their Relation to Antisocial Behavior: A Meta-Analytic Review." *Criminology* 39: 765–798.

Moffitt, Terrie E. 2006. "A Review of the Research on the Taxonomy of Life-Course Persistent Versus Adolescence-Limited Antisocial Behavior." In Francis T. Cullen, John Paul Wright, and Kristie R. Blevins (eds.), *Taking Stock: The Status of Criminological Theory*, pp. 277–312. New Brunswick, NJ: Transaction.

Nigg, Joel T. and Cynthia L. Huang-Pollack. 2003. "An Early-Onset Model of the Role of Executive Functions and Intelligence in Conduct Disorder/Delinquency." In Benjamin B. Lahey, Terrie E. Moffitt, and Avshalom Caspi(eds.), *Causes of Conduct Disorder and Juvenile Delinquency*, pp. 227–253. New York: Guilford.

Patrick, Christopher J. and Edelyn Verona. 2007. "The Psychophysiology of Aggression: Auto-nomic, Electrocortial, and Neuro-Imaging Findings." In Daniel J. Flannery, Alexander T. Vazsonyi, and Irwin D. Waldman (eds.), *The Cambridge Handbook of Violent Behavior and Aggression*, pp. 111–150. New York: Cambridge University Press.

Pratt, Travis C. and Francis T. Cullen. 2000. "The Empirical Status of Gottfredson and Hirschi's General Theory of Crime." *Criminology* 38: 931–964.

Raine, Adrian. 1993. *The Psychopathology of Crime*. San Diego: Academic Press.

——. 2002. "The Biological Basis of Crime." In James Q. Wilson and Joan Petersilia (eds.), *Crime*, pp. 43–74. Oakland, CA: ICS Press.

Raine, Adrian, Patricia A. Brennan, David P. Farrington, and Sarnoff A. Mednick. 1997. *Biosocial Bases of Violence*. New York: Plenum.

Rhee, Soo Hyun and Irwin D. Waldman. 2007. "Behavior-Genetics of Criminality and Aggression." In Daniel J. Flannery, Alexander T. Vazsonyi, and Irwin D. Waldman (eds.), *The Cambridge Handbook of Violent Behavior and Aggression*, pp. 77–90. New York: Cambridge University Press.

Robinson, Matthew B. 2004. *Why Crime? An Integrated Systems Theory of Antisocial Behavior*. Upper Saddle River, NJ: Prentice-Hall.

Rothbart, Mary K. and John E. Bates. 1998. "Temperament." In Nancy Eisenberg (ed.), *Handbook of Child Psychology, Volume 3: Social, Emotional, and Personal Development*, pp. 105–176. New York: John Wiley and Sons.

Rowe, David C. 1996. "An Adaptive Theory of Crime and Delinquency." In J. David Hawkins (ed.), *Delinquency and Crime: Current Theories*, pp. 268–314. Cambridge, England: Cambridge University Press.

——. 2002. *Biology and Crime*. Los Angeles: Roxbury.

Rutter, Michael L. 1997. "Nature–Nurture Integration." *American Psychologist* 52: 390–398.

Rutter, Michael, Henri Giller, and Ann Hagell. 1998. *Antisocial Behavior by Young People*. London: Cambridge.

Rutter, Michael, Terrie E. Moffitt, and Avshalom Caspi. 2006. "Gene-Environment Interplay and Psychopathology: Multiple Varieties But Real Effects." *Journal of Child Psychology and Psychiatry* 47: 226–261.

Scarpa, Angela and Adrian Raine. 1997. "Biology of Wickedness." *Psychiatric Annuals* 27: 624–629.

Scarpa, Angela and Adrian Raine. 2007. "Biosocial Bases of Violence." In Daniel J. Flannery, Alexander T. Vazsonyi, and Irwin D. Waldman (eds.), *The Cambridge Handbook of Violent Behavior and Aggression*, pp. 151–169. New York Cambridge University Press.

Tehrani, Jasmine A. and Sarnoff A. Mednick. 2000. "Genetic Factors and Criminal Behavior." *Federal Probation* 64 (2): 24–27.

Tellegen, Auke. 1985. "Structures of Mood and Personality and Their Relevance to Assessing Anxiety, With an Emphasis on Self-Report." In A. Hussain Tuba and Jack Maser (eds.), *Anxiety and the Anxiety-Disorders*, pp. 681–706. Hillsdale, NJ: Erlbaum.

Thornberry, Terence P. and Marvin D. Krohn. 2005. "Applying Interactional Theory to the Explanation of Continuity and Change in Antisocial Behavior." In David P. Farrington (ed.), *Integrated Developmental and Life-Course Theories of Offending*, pp. 183–210. New Brunswick, NJ: Transaction.

Thornhill, Randy and Craig T. Palmer. 2000. *A Natural History of Rape: Biosocial Bases of Sexual Coercion*. Cambridge, MA: MIT Press.

Tibbetts, Stephen G. and Alex R. Piquero. 1999. "The Influence of Gender, Low Birth Weight, and Disadvantaged Environment in Predicting Early Onset of Offending: A Test of Moffitt's Interactional Hypothesis." *Criminology* 37: 843–878.

Wade, Terrance J. and John Cairney. 2006. "Sociological Contributions," In Robert T. Ammerman (ed.), Comprehensive Handbook of Personality and Psychopathology, pp. 47–63. New York:Wiley.

Wadsworth, M. E. J. 1976. "Delinquency, Pulse Rate, and Early Emotional Deprivation." *British Journal of Criminology* 16: 245–256.

Wilson, James Q. and Richard J. Herrnstein. 1985. *Crime and Human Nature*. New York: Touchstone.

Wright, Bradley R. Entner, Avshalom Caspi, Terrie E. Moffitt, and Phil A. Silva. 2001."The Effects of Social Ties on Crime Vary by Crime Propensity: A Life-Course Model of Interdependence." *Criminology* 39: 321–352.

Wright, John P., Kevin M. Beaver, Matt DeLisi, Michael G. Vaughn, Danielle Boisvert, and Jamie Vaske. 2008a. "Lombroso's Legacy: The Miseducation of Criminologists." *Journal of Criminal Justice Education* 19: 325–338.

Wright, John Paul, Stephen G. Tibbetts, and Leah E. Daigle. 2008b. *Criminals in the Making*. Los Angeles: Sage.

Yaralian, Pauline S. and Adrian Raine. 2001. "Biological Approaches to Crime: Psycho-physiology and Brain Dysfunction." In Raymond Paternoster and Ronet Bachman (eds.), *Explaining Criminals and Crime*, pp. 57–72. Los Angeles: Roxbury Publishing.

3. Gene-Based Evolutionary Theories in Criminology

Lee Ellis and Anthony Walsh

Data suggest that crime is inherited to some extent. Although it is quite unlikely that there is a gene for crime, genes likely contribute to the development of individual traits such as "pushiness" and "deception" that are conducive to crime. The Ellis and Walsh selection draws on gene-based evolutionary theories to explain why individuals with such traits are able to reproduce at relatively high rates and thereby pass their genes on to others. We usually think of crime as maladaptive, but the theories described argue that certain genetically based traits conductive to crime may provide a reproductive advantage in some circumstances.

After providing a brief overview of gene-based evolutionary theory, Ellis and Walsh present five gene-based theories focusing on crime; some attempt to explain particular types of crime, such as rape, while others attempt to explain crime in general. None of the theories have been fully tested, and, indeed, it is not possible to fully test them at this time. Ellis and Walsh do, however, derive predictions or hypotheses about crime from each theory and then discuss whether the evidence supports such predictions. They argue that many of the predictions are supported, including certain predictions made only by gene-based evolutionary theories. Although this does not mean that such theories are correct, it does increase our confidence in them.

Other researchers have been somewhat more critical of these theories and have pointed to facts about crime that the theories have trouble explaining—such as the fact that young girls who have not yet reached reproductive age are disproportionately likely to be raped (see the discussions in Coyne, 2000; de Waal, 2000; Raine, 1993; Rowe, 2002). So, although there is some indirect support for these theories, their ultimate status is still in doubt.

Many people hold strong feelings about gene-based theories of crime. Such feelings may stem in part from the view that such theories imply that we cannot change criminal behavior, that the social environment has little or no effect on crime, or that racial or other group differences in crime may have a biological basis. Also, such theories are still connected in the minds of many people with such crime-control policies as selective breeding and sterilization. Raine (1993) challenges many of these beliefs, although see Akins and Griffin (2000) and Rafter (1997).

References

Akins, Scott and Robert Griffin. 2000. "Multiple Birth Rates and Racial Type: A Research Note Regarding r/K Theory." *Deviant Behavior* 21: 15–22.

Coyne, Jerry A. 2000. "Of Vice and Men." *New Republic*, April 3, pp. 27–34.

Excerpted from "Gene-Based Evolutionary Theories in Criminology," by Lee Ellis and Anthony Walsh, *Criminology* 35(2), May 1997. Reprinted by permission of the American Society of Criminology.

De Waal, Frans B. M. 2000. "Survival of the Rapist." *New York Times*, April 2, Section 7, p. 24.

Rafter, Nicole Hahn. 1997. *Creating Born Criminals.* Urbana: University of Illinois Press.

Raine, Adrian. 1993. *The Psychopathology of Crime.* San Diego: Academic Press.

Rowe, David. 2002. *Biology and Crime.* Los Angeles: Roxbury.

———————●———————

According to modern (or gene-based) evolutionary theory, natural selection can operate on traits only if the traits are genetically influenced (Daly and Wilson, 1983:341) and only if the genes are not universally present in a population (Browne, 1995:985). In the case of behavior, nearly all of the effects of genes are quite indirect because they are mediated through complex chains of events occurring in the brain. This means that there are almost certainly no genes for somethings as complex as criminal behavior. Nevertheless, many genes may affect brain functioning in ways that either increase or reduce the chances of individuals learning various complex behavior patterns, including behavior patterns that happen to be so offensive to others that criminal sanctions have been instituted to minimize their recurrence (Ellis, 1990d).

This review may not appeal to most criminologists because it rests on the assumption that genetic factors influence criminal behavior. A survey found that only about 20 percent of criminologists are receptive to the notion that genetic factors have important influences on criminal behavior (Ellis and Hoffman, 1990). For those who are open to persuasion on this point, several recent reviews may be consulted for supportive evidence (Bock and Goode, 1996; Carey, 1992; Eysenck and Gudjonsson, 1989:108; Lykken, 1995:92; Mealey, 1995:526; Raine, 1993; Walters, 1992:604). The evidence is particularly strong in the case of offenders who exhibit antisocial behavior prior to puberty and persist in doing so throughout adolescence and early adulthood (Cadoret and Stewart, 1991; Cadoret et al., 1995; Moffitt, 1993; Willerman et al., 1992). Evidence of genetic influences on serious and persistent criminal and antisocial behavior has now come from general family studies (Jones et al., 1980), twin studies (Cloninger and Gottesman, 1987; Rowe, 1990), adoption studies (Carey, 1992; Cadoret et al., 1995; Raine and Dunkin, 1990:638; Willerman et al., 1992), and one study of twins reared apart (Grove et al., 1990).

One reason most criminologists are skeptical about genetic influences on criminal behavior is that it seems improbable that behavior that is defined differently in every society could have a genetic foundation (see Walsh, 1995a:174). In other words, why would genes affect behavior that is circumscribed by laws that vary from one society to another? Much of the answer lies in the fact that in nearly all societies with written criminal statutes, there are a fairly standard set of "core behavior patterns" that are criminalized (Ellis, 1990a:19; Eysenck and Gudjonsson, 1989:1). These criminalized acts have in common the fact that they directly harm other society members, either physically or by damaging or confiscating property. While most societies go on to criminalize numerous other "peripheral" acts, the core offenses remain almost universally criminalized. This means that as long as one focuses on so-called *victimful offenses* (i.e., violent and property crimes), it is possible to maintain that there is little variation from one society to another in what constitutes criminal behavior (Ellis, 1990a). . . .

If genetic factors influence people's varying probabilities of criminal behavior, as current evidence suggests, why would such genes exist? Obviously, environmental theories cannot address this question because they assume that there are no such genes. For those willing to set aside environmental theories as incomplete (but not necessarily incorrect), a fascinating possibility presents itself: Perhaps some evolutionary forces are responsible for the existence of genes that promote criminal behavior. In other words, persons who are highly disposed toward crime might be able to reproduce at fairly high rates, at least under certain conditions, such as when the chances of being identified or punished are fairly low (e.g., in large cities as opposed to small communities).

As this review will show, recent explorations of this possibility have gone far beyond Lombroso's (1896) suggestion that criminals are atavistic throwbacks to some primitive human life form. Not only did Lombroso know nothing of genetics, he also thought criminals were poorly adapted to life in complex industrial societies. Recently, several evolutionary theorists have argued that criminals may actually be better adapted for living in large modern societies than for living in small foraging or horticultural communities.

It is important to emphasize that the concept of *genetic influence* is not equivalent to genetic determinism and that genetic influence does not mean that a behavior pattern is unlearned. Breeding experiments with various animal species have shown that genes can and do influence learning (Gould and Marler, 1987). More precisely, the ability to learn and the disposition to learn some things more readily than others appears to have genetic foundations, and the responsible genes can respond to natural selection pressure (Kenrick, 1987). Presumably, varying capacities and dispositions to learn are present in animal populations to the extent these capacities and dispositions facilitate reproduction relative to animals whose behavior is more instinctually motivated. Especially in large mammals such as ourselves, numerous genetic programs appear to exist that affect how our brains function in ways that facilitate general tendencies to learn as well as tendencies to learn some things more readily than others.

Recently, a "Swiss army knife" model of how genes may influences brain functioning has been advocated (Cosmides and Tooby, 1992). According to this model, humans (and other animals) have evolved special modules and networks in their brains that incline them to learn certain behavioral responses readily. Thus, depending upon the particular environment to which humans are exposed, much of human behavior could be differentially channeled in particular directions by genes that modify small behavior-control modules in the brain. All of this learning could have been shaped by natural selection forces to which numerous generations of ancestors were exposed.

Whether this "Swiss army knife" model of the brain proves to be true or not, everything in the theories that we are about to review is entirely compatible with the assumption that criminal behavior is largely learned behavior. Nevertheless, these theories all share the assumption that for both genetic and environmental reasons, people will vary in the ease with which they learn some behavior rather than others, including criminal behavior. As one evolutionary criminologist put it,

> Genes do not code themselves for jimmying a lock or stealing a car—criminal acts must be acquired by socialization and learning because the genome does not waste precious DNA encoding the specifics. (Rowe, 1996:285)

Modern Evolutionary Theory

Two scientific breakthroughs from the nineteenth century are at the heart of modern biology: One was Charles Darwin's theory of evolution, which never dealt with the concept of genes. The other was Gregor Mendel's discoveries, which eventually led to the field of genetics. Especially after these two monumental discoveries were combined in the 1920s to give rise to the so-called *Modern Synthesis*, they became enormously useful for understanding how life on earth arose and how life has been transformed into millions of species over billions of years (Blackburn and Schneider, 1994:233; Degler, 1991:230; Lopreato, 1984:16). Out of the Modern Synthesis arose various versions of gene-based (neo-Darwinian) evolutionary theory (Dawkins, 1976:v; Grene, 1982:1, Lewin, 1982:718). All versions of this gene-based theory of evolution have converged on a simple but powerful idea: To the degree a particular characteristic is prevalent in a population, it is likely to have contributed to the reproductive success of the ancestors of the individuals currently living. Increasingly, this fundamental principle has been applied to the study of behavior (e.g., Buss, 1994; Wright, 1995), including criminal behavior (Ellis, 1990c).

A term that has come to be widely used in the applications of gene-based evolutionary theory in the study of criminal behavior is *kin selection*. Kin selection refers to the idea that individuals can often help ensure the representation of their genes in subsequent generations not simply by having offspring of their own, but also by helping other close genetic relatives to have offspring. Of course, the best way to pass on one's genes to the next generation is to have offspring of one's own who go on to do likewise.

Imbedded in the concept of kin selection is the realization that often one cannot identify close genetic relatives with certainty. As we will discuss, this opens the door to numerous social strategies and counterstrategies that animals, including ourselves, may use that that affect not only one's own reproduction, but that of others with whom one has contact.

Applications of Gene-Based Evolutionary Thinking to the Study of Criminality

Two concepts that have received a great deal of attention from those who are applying gene-based evolutionary theory to the study of criminal and antisocial behavior are those of *deception* and *cheating*. Arguments have been made that such behavior could often be advantageous to reproduction (e.g., Harpending and Sobus, 1987; Mealey, 1995; Rowe, 1996:278). The reasoning is as follows: If genes promoting altruistic and cooperative behavior can evolve by natural selection, as some

evidence suggests (Rushton et al., 1986), genes could also evolve that predispose organisms to take advantage of the altruistic and cooperative behavior of others without reciprocating (Badcock, 1986; Thompson, 1980; Thornhill, 1979). This in turn could favor the evolution of attempts by altruists to detect and punish (or ostracize) nonreciprocators. Through this escalating set of social relationships may evolve reproductive strategies rooted in deception and cheating (Cosmides and Tooby, 1992; Ellis, 1990b). If tendencies to learn deceptive and cheating tactics are genetically influenced, so too may be the tendencies to be vigilant against the use of such tactics by others (Bond and Robinson, 1988:296).

Several evolutionary theorists have argued that the best way for cheaters to avoid detection is for them to go so far as to even virtually deceive themselves. Thus, self-deception may have evolved as a character trait that helps cheaters fool others (Beahrs, 1991; Beckstrom, 1989:81; Dugatkin, 1992; Trivers, 1991). In a number of social species, an "arms race" of deception/cheating, and attempts to detect and foil such tactics, may have given rise to the evolution of retaliatory tactics, which may exert pressures for the evolution of even more subtle forms of deception and cheating (Clutton-Brock and Parker, 1995). The human ability to communicate linguistically (especially in writing) may have evolved in part because it facilitates the detection of cheaters and victimizers (Ellis 1990b).

As this review will show, these arguments have allowed evolutionary social scientists to deduce a number of novel hypotheses, several of which are extremely relevant to criminology. The theories to be reviewed all assume that for genetic reasons, if people (or other animals) are going to be altruistic, they are most likely to be so toward close genetic relatives and/or toward others who are willing to reciprocate. The theories also assume that most people are genetically capable of at least occasionally being deceptive, and that a significant minority of human beings (and other animals) may be genetically prone to be extremely deceptive and otherwise prone to take advantage of others, sometimes even close relatives and friends. When human deception and victimizing behavior reach high levels of harm, the term *criminal* is often applied to the behavior, and when offenders are sufficiently chronic in these activities, they are said to be *antisocial* or *psychopathic* (or *sociopathic*).

We now describe each of the five specific gene-based evolutionary theories of criminal and antisocial behavior with a focus on identifying testable hypotheses that may be derived from each theory. Many of the hypotheses derived from these theories overlap ones that can be derived from strictly social environmental theories, although we show that they go beyond them in some intriguing directions.

Evolutionary Theories of Specific Types of Crimes

Two types of gene-based evolutionary theories of criminal behavior can be identified. One type focuses on specific crimes, such as rape, spousal assault, and child abuse, and the other type is applied generally to criminal and antisocial behavior. We discuss each of these two types in turn.

Rape (and Sexual Assault)

Since the early 1980s, numerous theorists have proposed that sexual assault may have been favored by natural selection (Ellis, 1989b; 1991b, in press; Lalumiere and Quinsey, 1996; Shields and Shields, 1983; Thiessen, 1986; Thornhill and Thornhill, 1983, 1987, 1992; van der Dennen, 1992). These proposals basically assert that sexual aggression has been naturally selected to be exhibited predominantly by the sex that invests the least in each offspring conceived. In nearly all species, but especially among mammals, males are not directly involved in gestating offspring, nor do they invest nearly as much time and energy in their offspring after birth as do females. Successfully reproducing females, on

the other hand, rarely escape making high parental investments.

Being relatively free of parenting responsibilities, males have more to gain in reproductive terms from having multiple sex partners than do females (Browne, 1995:995). Since males who succeed in having multiple sex partners generally reproduce more prolifically than males who have just one, it is important to consider the sort of tactics that may have evolved to assist males in securing multiple sex partners.

According to the evolutionary theory of rape, the male reproductive advantage derived from having multiple sex partners has resulted in natural selection favoring genes promoting brain patterns for "pushiness" in pursuit of sexual intercourse. In some males, genes may carry pushiness to the point of actual force, especially after less violent tactics fail to yield results. In other words, over generations, pushy males will probably be more successful at passing on their genes, including any genes coding for readily learning pushy sexual behavior, than will less pushy males. While these ideas may not be pleasant to contemplate, proponents of the evolutionary theory of rape contend that the dynamics of rape cannot be fully understood without taking into account its reproductive consequences. Further insight into the evolutionary theory of rape can come from considering various hypotheses derived from it.

Hypothesis 1: Males should predominate in the commission of rape and sexual assault. Even though females could at least occasionally gain in reproductive terms from being sexually assertive, especially with high-status males (Belsky et al., 1991), there is little doubt that males have the most to gain from sexual assertiveness. Because of the minimal investment of time and energy males must make in each offspring compared to what females must make, they always stand to gain more than females in reproductive terms from becoming pushy when it comes to sex, at least when other tactics are unsuccessful. Thus, evolutionary theory predicts that most sexual assaults will be committed by males, and this is clearly the case throughout the world (reviewed by Cohn, 1993; Ellis, 1989b:82, in press).

Strictly environmental theories make the same prediction, but they posit that differential socialization accounts for the gender difference in propensity to rape and that if each gender was identically socialized it would be equally likely (or unlikely) to rape. As explained more below, one problem with this explanation is that it fails to predict that forced copulations occur in numerous nonhuman species in which nothing akin to differential gender socialization exists, and in all of these species also, most of the assailants are males. Nonevolutionary theories may also point to gender differences in physical strength and aggressiveness to explain the gender difference in propensity to sexually assault. For evolutionary theorists, this begs the question of why these differences exist in the first place (i.e., What reproductive advantages do they confer?), and they would point out that strength and aggressiveness (sexual and otherwise) may be more pronounced in males due in part to these traits facilitating sexual intimidation.

Hypothesis 2: Sexual assaults should not be exclusively a human phenomenon; males of other species should have evolved similar genetically promoted tendencies. The two main alternative theories of rape are the feminist theory and the social learning theory (Ellis, 1989b). As noted above, these theories usually account for why nearly all rapists are males by invoking differential socialization, which implies that sexual assault is a unique human phenomenon, an argument made by Brownmiller (1975:3) in her classic defense of the feminist theory. The evolutionary theory, on the other hand, leads to the opposite hypothesis: If genes contributing to rape have evolved in males because they can reproductively (and thus genetically) benefit from multiple matings more than females can, there is no reason to think that similar genes would not have evolved in other species. The evidence on the matter is

clearly on the side of the evolutionary hypothesis. Forced corpulations have been documented in numerous nonhuman species, and in all cases, males are almost always the assailants (Ellis, 1989b:45; Palmer, 1989; Thornhill and Thornhill, 1992:364). This is even true of some species of monogamous birds in which no significant sex differences exist in terms of size or physical strength (McKinney et al., 1983).

Hypothesis 3: Rape should be strongly resisted by female victims because it denies them the opportunity to choose sex partners who are most likely to help care for offspring. Feminist and social learning theories of rape both assume that females want control over deciding with whom they have sex (Ellis, 1989b). However, these theories do not explain why such control would be important. Evolutionary theory offers an explanation for this desire by postulating that it has been strongly favored by natural selection. Females who tend to withhold copulating with a male until they are relatively confident that the male will help care for any offspring that are produced will be evolutionarily favored over females who copulate simply on the basis of sexual attraction (Townsend, 1995:175). . . .

Supporting this reasoning, research throughout the world has indicated that females are much more cautious in choosing sex partners than is true for males (Buss and Schmitt, 1993) and much more interested in personality traits that suggest loyalty, commitment, and love of children than males are when identifying an ideal mate (Buss, 1994:32; Townsend, 1995). . . .

Hypothesis 4: Victims of sexual assault should primarily be females of reproductive age. According to evolutionary theory, rape victimization should be strongly associated with age. Specifically, the victims should be primarily of reproductive age. The evolutionary theory of rape would be seriously undercut by evidence of no correlation between age and rape victimization or by the discovery of even one society in which most sexual assault victims are not of reproductive age. . . .

Hypothesis 5: In some societies, males who engage in forced copulations may not only reproduce relatively well, they could even out-reproduce males who only mate with voluntary sex partners. A criticism lodged against the evolutionary theory of rape has been that the probability of rape victims becoming pregnant is too low for sexual assault to have been naturally selected (Harding, 1985:51). While additional research is in order, this criticism does not appear to be well founded. Most studies place the probability of becoming pregnant from rape at only slightly below the rate from voluntary intercourse (reviewed by Ellis, 1989b:47; also see Krueger, 1988:24; Winston, 1987). In addition, several studies have found that when all sexual outlets are considered (i.e., both voluntary and forced), rapists have more active sex lives than do males who only engage in voluntary copulations (Abel et al., 1989; Byers, 1988; Koss et al., 1985; Malamuth, 1986). This suggests that any genes inclining males to fall back on force and deception when voluntary copulatory tactics do not succeed would increase the representation of their genes in a population unless fairly effective counter measures were instituted. . . .

Hypothesis 6: Penalties for rape will be severe to prevent genes conducive to rape from overtaking a population. Even if rape is part of a genetically influenced, evolved reproductive strategy, the complex behavior surrounding the offense is still learned. As such, the probability that someone will act on urges to commit a sexual assault is certainly subject to environmental influences, including the threat of punishment. Most criminal justice sanctions may be thought of as a set of evolved strategies whereby generally altruistic people collectively protect their reproductive interests against invasion by people who are minimally altruistic (Boyd and Richerson 1992; Clutton-Brock and Parker, 1995; Ellis, 1990b). The typically severe penalties for rape may be a reflection of these efforts.

There is considerable evidence that many male would-be rapists are deterred by the punitive sanctions imposed on rapists. While studies have found that only about 10 percent to 20 percent of males admit to ever having committed rape (Yegidis, 1986), up to 70 percent admit to at least using deceptive and/or pushy tactics in order to achieve sexual intimacy in dating situations (reviewed by Ellis, 1996). Also, 25 percent to 50 percent of males concede that they might use forceful tactics if somehow assured that they would never be caught and punished for doing so (reviewed by Ellis, 1989b:6). About the only "natural" conditions that ever approximate such assurances come under warfare conditions. Numerous historical accounts have suggested that large proportions of males commit rape when the ability of victims and/or their relatives to retaliate is greatly diminished (Brownmiller, 1975:80; Ellis, 1989b:47; Shields and Shields, 1983).

Spousal and 'Romantic Triangle' Assault

Several evolutionary theorists have proposed that spousal abuse, assault, and homicide (here collectively called *spousal assault*) may have evolutionary underpinnings (Buss, 1994:156; Daly and Wilson, 1988:295; Ellis, 1990c; Weir 1992:353). Spousal assaults cover offenses ranging from occasional slapping and threatening bodily harm to repeated attacks, and even murder. *Romantic triangle assaults* are assaults directed by one individual toward another person (usually of the same sex) in order to prevent the victim from gaining (or retaining) sexual access to a third individual (usually of the opposite sex).

Basically, the evolutionary theory of spousal assault asserts that such behavior will, in one way or another, have a great deal to do with propriety over sexual access. And the theory suggests that the sex that runs the greatest risk of misidentifying its progeny will be particularly prone to resort to assaultive tactics to ensure exclusivity in sexual access. Accordingly, the following hypotheses may be derived from the theory.

Hypothesis 1: Males should be the main offenders in the case of spousal assaults and romantic triangle assaults. Studies have repeatedly shown that except for minor forms of spousal abuse—for which male and female assault rates are nearly equal (Arias et al., 1987:88, Stratus et al., 1980)—males are far more abusive toward their spouses and dating partners than are females (Browne and Williams, 1989, 1993; Roberts et al., 1993; Zawitz et al., 1993:25). This would be consistent with the fact that males have much more to lose reproductively from partner infidelity than do females. As explained below, while females whose partners are unfaithful can still accurately identify their offspring for the purpose of making parental investments, males cannot.

Hypothesis 2: Jealousy and suspicion of infidelity should be a key cause of spousal and dating assaults. As noted in hypothesis 1, the evolutionary explanation of spousal assault rests heavily on evidence that males are more likely than females to be the abusers, especially in the case of serious assaults and homicides. The evolutionary concept most often used to explain this pattern is that of cuckoldry (which refers to unwittingly helping to rear an offspring that is not one's own genetic descendant). Males can only infer that offspring are their genetic descendants by associating the offspring with the female(s) with whom they have had sex. To the degree a male's mate copulates with other males, he risks cuckoldry and thereby having his genes culled from the gene pool.

According to evolutionary theory, assaultive tendencies toward spouses and dating and cohabitating partners have been favored by natural selection as tactics for helping to maintain a mate's sexual fidelity (Smuts, 1992:11). If this is true, jealousy and suspicions of infidelity should be major causes of spousal assaults and homicides. Evidence from many countries indicates that the single most important motivation behind spousal and romantic triangle assault is sexual jealousy and suspicions of infidelity (Crawford and Gartner, 1992; Laner, 1990; Lepowsky, 1994).

Hypothesis 3: "Spousal assaults" should not be an exclusively human phenomenon. Unlike strictly environmental theories of spousal assaults, nothing in evolutionary theory excludes the possibility of similar tactics existing outside the human species. In fact, it would be surprising to find that only humans had evolved violent tactics for discouraging mates from copulating with other partners. Males have been observed attacking females who show interest in other males and/or fail to be sexually receptive towards the assailant in at least four other primate species....

Hypothesis 4: Spousal assault should be highest in human populations that have fewer stable marriages, greater promiscuous sexual intercourse, and more children who do not receive the family name of the father.... Human males still risk cuckoldry to a substantial degree. In some countries, between 1 percent and 3 percent of children appear to have been fathered by someone other than the male claiming fatherhood (Brock and Shrimpton, 1991; Sasse et al., 1994), while in other countries rates of misidentified paternity are estimated at between 10 percent and 30 percent (Birkhead and Moller, 1992; Hirsch et al., 1980). It can hardly be doubted that natural selection has severely disfavored males who make little effort to ensure the sexual fidelity of the female with whom they share parental responsibilities.

Assuming that spousal assault for infidelity is a relatively desperate measure for preventing cuckoldry, the following predictions can be made: Cultures (or subcultures) in which spousal assaults are relatively high should be those in which (a) marriage is uncommon or unstable, (b) prohibitions against pre- and extramarital intercourse are lax, and/or (c) children infrequently receive their father's family name. We were able to locate no scientific evidence specifically undertaken to test these predictions.

Hypothesis 5: Spousal assault may prevent infidelity and/or pregnancy resulting from infidelity. In order for spousal assault to evolve by natural selection, there must be some way that such action at least occasionally benefits the assailant reproductively. There are at least two possibilities in this regard. First, victims could be so frightened and intimidated by threats of being beaten that they avoid the sort of activities that provoke it. In this connection, several researchers have identified what has been called *trauma-induced bonding and dependency* (or *traumatic bonding*) as an emotional response to extreme fear (reviewed by Ellis 1989b:48). This concept has been invoked to help explain why battered wives often do not leave their husbands, even after repeated assaults (Dutton, 1995:189; Painter and Dutton, 1985).

Spousal assault could also serve the reproductive interests of the offender by causing the victim to suffer such severe emotional stress as to disrupt reproductive functioning (reviewed by Ellis, 1995). This disruption appears to include suppression of ovulation (Dunbar, 1984:67) and even the prevention of implantation of fertilized eggs onto the uterine wall (Huck et al., 1988). Perhaps spousal assault by men is sometimes part of an insidious evolved strategy that helps them avoid being cuckolded when mates have been unfaithful. (Keep in mind that evolutionary strategies are rarely conscious strategies.)

Hypothesis 6: Women who become pregnant as a result of sexual infidelity may be subjected to such severe badgering by the men with whom they live that their pregnancy may be aborted. Assaults on women by their spouses or lovers occur at alarming frequencies during pregnancy—estimates range from 4 percent to 20 percent (Helton et al., 1987; Norton et al., 1995; Parker et al., 1994). . . . .

This hypothesis could be tested by determining if unfaithful women experience higher rates of spousal assault *during pregnancy* than faithful women. To our knowledge, this hypothesis has never been tested among humans, although it would be consistent with evidence that domestic assaults during pregnancy are higher for unmarried teenage women than for women in general (Parker et al., 1994).

Overall, several hypotheses can be reasonably derived from the evolutionary theory of spousal (and romantic triangle) assault. Of the hypotheses

tested thus far, they have been fairly well supported. Although we cannot exclude hypotheses derived from cultural theories for spousal assault, evolutionary theories, by documenting analogous behavior in other species, take the issue beyond cultural learning to suggest that such behavior is part of a general evolved strategy that humans share with other mammals.

Child Abuse and Neglect

Child abuse and neglect (including infanticide) is another type of crime that has received a great deal of attention from evolutionists in recent years (Belsky, 1993:42; Burgess and Draper, 1988; Daly and Wilson, 1985, 1987, 1994; Gelles and Lancaster, 1987). At first glance, neglecting or intentionally injuring one's own offspring appears totally incongruent with evolutionary logic. However, there are a few conditions under which abusive actions toward one's offspring could be favored by natural selection (Buss, 1995:8; Daly and Wilson, 1980:284; Ellis, 1990c:65). These conditions are specified by the following four hypotheses.

Hypothesis 1: Parents who have more children than they have resources needed to rear them should abuse and even abandon their children more than parents who have sufficient resources. Thus, when a family is large, poor, and/or has children who are closely spaced, child abuse and neglect should be particularly high. . . . .

Child abuse among humans has been shown to be significantly greater in large families than in small families (Daly and Wilson, 1985; Straus et al., 1980; Wolfner and Gelles, 1993; Zuravin, 1991). Also, child abuse and neglect has been found to be inversely correlated with family income (Walsh and Beyer, 1987; Whipple and Webster-Stratton, 1991; Wolfner and Gelles, 1993).

Hypothesis 2: A parent who lacks the assistance of the other parent in caring for offspring should be more prone toward child abuse, neglect, and abandonment than a parent who has the other parent cooperating in providing child care. If one parent finds the other parent failing to assist either directly or indirectly in caring for their offspring, that parent may be favored for doing likewise. This would be especially true of parents who are young and have a reasonably high probability of attracting a new mate who will be more cooperative. . . .

Among humans, studies have shown that child abuse (including infanticide) by parents is unusually common among couples who have never married or are separated or divorced (Daly et al., 1982; Walsh 1991) and in families marked by excessive marital discord (Green, 1976; Reid et al., 1981). . . .

Hypothesis 3: Children who are less viable from a reproductive standpoint are likely to experience more abuse and neglect from parents than other children. Evolutionary theory leads to the hypothesis that parental investments will not always be equally distributed to all offspring. Theoretically, parents should behave toward each child in ways that roughly correspond to the child's chances of eventually reproducing. If the chances are low, the parents should invest less in a particular offspring than if the chances are high.

Consistent with this deduction, human parents appear to discriminate in favor of offspring who are the most promising from the standpoint of their reproductive potential (Borgerhoff Mulder, 1987:30). For example, children with serious physical and mental handicaps typically receive less care and/or more abuse than their nonhandicapped siblings (Frodi, 1981; Lightcap et al., 1982). . . .

Hypothesis 4: Children will be subjected to more abuse and neglect when no close genetic relationship exists between the child and the parent/guardian. Evolutionary theory posits that parental care has evolved because it contributes to the survival of the caregiver's genes. Hence, there is less genetic advantage in rearing someone else's offspring than in rearing one's own (Daly and Wilson, 1994). Thus, one can expect that child abuse and neglect will be experienced more by adopted children and stepchildren than by children raised by their biological parents. This expectation has been consistently borne out by research (Daly and Wilson, 1985, 1988:89, 1994; Lightcap et al., 1982).

General Gene-Based Evolutionary Theories of Criminal and Antisocial Behavior

In addition to being applied to the study of specific offenses, gene-based evolutionary theories have been applied quite broadly in criminology (Ellis, 1987, 1990c; Harpending and Draper, 1988:313; McGuire et al., 1994:313; Raine, 1993:27). The possibility that evolutionary forces are behind general tendencies to victimize others does not mean that the most victimizing individuals will reproduce at unusually high rates under all conditions. There may be constraints upon which genes for such behavior can infiltrate a population's gene pool, and these constraints might vary from one set of environmental conditions to another.

Consider what might happen if, in a small foraging society, a mutant gene arose that inclined one of its members to be unusually aggressive toward other group members and/or to be disrespectful of other people's property rights. In a small society, this individual would probably be ousted unless he or she quickly learned to restrain his or her impulses. In a large society, however, this same individual might be able to act upon his or her antisocial impulses repeatedly without detection or ill consequences. Not only would he or she be able to find many more unwary victims in a large society, but the chances of being identified and punished would be less. This sort of reasoning has led to two distinguishable gene-based evolutionary theories of criminal and antisocial behavior: the cheater and *r/K* selection theories. Each is described below.

The Cheater (or Cad vs. Dad) Theory of Criminal and Antisocial Behavior

In regard to sexual assault, we noted above that the sex that is not directly involved in gestating offspring can potentially have many more offspring than the sex that is. The time and energy males do not spend gestating offspring can be utilized in other reproductively significant ways, such as competing in various ways with other males for access to females. In response to this strategy, females often seem to evolve tendencies to choose mates who appear willing and able to help them care for the offspring. Males respond by competing with other males to furnish evidence of their ability and inclination to provide parental care. Parental investment by males can be quite general and indiscriminate, such as providing protection to the group in which the mother and her offspring reside, or may be specific, such as provisioning food and shelter for his mate and her offspring.

Unfortunately for females, appearances can be deceiving, and it is often to the male's reproductive advantage to orchestrate this deception. In many species of animals, males have evolved what are broadly called *alternative reproductive strategies* (Bass, 1996; West-Eberhard, 1986); that is, within a species males have evolved the ability to reproduce in two or more distinctive ways. The most frequent alternative reproductive strategy yet documented involves males who minimize their parental investment in any specific offspring. Depending on the species involved these extremely "low investing" males are called *cheaters, floaters, sneakers,* and *satellites* (Bass, 1996; Grahn et al., 1993; Katano, 1990). In some species these males are also referred to as *cads*, thereby allowing the term *dads* to be used to describe males who assist females in caring for offspring and with whom females preferentially mate (Buss, 1994:23; Cashdon, 1993; Draper and Harpending, 1982).

According to the cheater (or cad) theory of criminal and antisocial behavior, a subpopulation of men has evolved with genes that incline them toward an extremely low parental investment reproductive strategy (Belsky et al., 1991; Burgess, 1991; Kofoed, 1988; Mealey, 1995; Raine, 1993:33). Since women will be favored for avoiding mating with these men, their cad strategy requires considerable deception or stealth. Much of this stealth takes the form of mimicking high investing (noncheater) males up to the point of the impregnation. Additional stealthy tactics include devious techniques for acquiring resources quickly

and for gaining sexual access through almost any means that works (Raine, 1993:40).

According to the cheater theory, criminal and antisocial behavior is the human version of a low parental investment reproductive strategy. If this theory is true, criminals should be deceptive, irresponsible, and opportunistic in almost everything they do, and if genes are a major cause of this behavior, it would likely begin to manifest itself early in life. Theoretically, cad males will use just about any tactic that works to coax, trick, and/or force numerous females to copulate, including thievery to acquire resources quickly, and will then shirk all long-term investments in offspring.

In a recent review of evidence pertaining to the cheater theory, Mealey (1995) argued that males may come to a cheater strategy in one of two ways: Either they have genes that more or less compel them to adopt the strategy, or they may learn the strategy. She called those who are genetically inclined toward a life of cheating and crime *primary sociopaths*, and those who largely learned the strategy because of their rearing and circumstances *secondary sociopaths*. Lykken (1995) made the same distinction, but called the first category *psychopaths* and the second category *sociopaths*.

Whatever the source, Mealey contended that the cheater strategy will flourish in a population as long as the number of cheaters does not overwhelm the number of noncheaters in the population. This idea is similar to the fact that the number of predators in an ecosystem is always constrained by the availability of prey. Among the specific hypotheses that may be derived from the cheater theory are the following.

Hypothesis 1: Criminality and psychopathy should be more prevalent among men than among women.... Consistent with this hypothesis, in all societies yet studied, men are more prone toward criminal and antisocial behavior than women, and the more serious and persistent the antisocial tendencies, the stronger the disparity is (reviewed by Ellis, 1988:535). A number of strictly environmental theories also have been offered to explain why males are more criminal and antisocial than females (reviewed by Ellis, 1989/90:19). However, these explanations all imply that environmental conditions *could* exist in which female crime rates will equal or exceed male rates. The fact that no such societies have yet been identified offers some support for the cheater theory.

Hypothesis 2: Criminals and psychopaths should be unusually promiscuous. According to the cheater theory, persistent criminals and psychopaths should be unusually prone to seek to have multiple sex partners (Belsky et al., 1991; Burgess, 1991:20; Kofoed, 1988). Consistent with this prediction, several studies have linked criminality and psychopathy with early onset of promiscuous sexual behavior (e.g., Elliott and Morse, 1987; Weiher et al., 1991) and unstable marriages (Robins, 1966:103).

Hypothesis 3: Criminals and psychopaths should be more inclined to commit sexual assaults than males in general. The cheater theory would predict that cheater males would experiment with any method that seems to work for the purpose of copulating frequently with numerous sex partners. Accordingly, cads should resort more often than dads to more desperate and forceful copulatory tactics. The evidence to date is generally supportive of this hypothesis in the sense that rapists do not appear to be a special type of criminal. Rather, they generally exhibit all of the other major criminal and antisocial behavioral traits (Hall and Proctor, 1987; Knight et al., 1983; Rice et al., 1990).

Hypothesis 4: The cad strategy should be more pronounced among males in the prime of their reproductive careers than in later life. Evolutionary theorists have referred to the tendency for animals to adjust their reproductive strategies according to their age as an *ontogenetic shift* (Wilson, 1993). The assumption is that genetically regulated neurohormonal factors operate to affect the learning of these shifts.

The cheater theory does not assert that males will be either a cad or a dad across the entire lifespan. In some species in which the cad and the dad strategies are exhibited by different males, one finds many young cads gradually switching to a dad strategy as they age. . . .

The cad strategy may offer greater reproductive payoff for young males than for older males in many species, including humans, presumably because young males do not have access to the sort of resources needed to attract stable sex partners. Consequently, they specialize in opportunistic matings and the sort of risky, devious tactics that make such matings successful. As they accumulate resources in later life, many males would be expected to shift to a more dad-oriented reproductive strategy.

The above reasoning would offer an evolutionary explanation for what has been called *burnout* among criminals and psychopaths. Burnout refers to the well-documented tendency for criminals and psychopaths to gradually relinquish their antisocial tendencies as they enter middle age (see Ellis 1988:534; Hirschi and Gottfredson, 1983, 1987; Mealey, 1995; Wilson and Herrnstein, 1985:126). If the cheater theory is applicable to the study of criminality, burnout should be essentially a universal phenomenon. No strictly environmental theory would make such a broad-ranging prediction.

Hypothesis 5: The cheater strategy should be more prevalent in the lower than in the upper social strata. As already noted, two fairly distinct subpopulations of males have evolved in many species. One subpopulation provides mates and offspring with resources, the other has few resources to offer and resorts to alternative strategies for securing mates (Dixson, 1993:563; Grahn et al., 1993:93; Hews et al., 1994:96; Katano, 1990). In these species, females are most attracted to the males who have resources and who engage in elaborate courtship and form long-term cooperative relationships (Grahn et al., 1993; Katano, 1990; Trivers, 1985:408); males controlling fewer resources are more inclined to mate opportunistically (sometimes forcefully) and to avoid parental investment (Hews et al., 1994:96; Jones, 1959).

Some evolutionary theorists have argued that significant proportions of human males, particularly those of low social status, will be genetically inclined to readily learn a cad strategy

(Harpending and Draper, 1988; Harpending and Sobus, 1987; Raine, 1993;40). As one proponent recently stated, males "who are the least likely to outcompete other males in a status hierarchy... are the ones most likely to adopt a cheating strategy" (Mealey 1995:527). It is important to emphasize that evolutionary theory is not positing that social status is itself necessarily genetically determined. It simply asserts that males who find themselves lacking in resources, for whatever reason, will be more likely than high-status males to adopt a cheater strategy to obtain copulation opportunities....

The *r/K* Theory of Criminal and Antisocial Behavior

The concept of an *r/K* continuum has been widely used in evolutionary biology for the past 20 years to describe a theoretical continuum along which all organisms are postulated to exist (e.g., Daly and Wilson, 1983:199; MacArthur and Wilson, 1967; Pianka, 1970). Organisms near the *r* end of the continuum reproduce rapidly and prolifically whenever environmental opportunities allow, but they do so without investing much time or energy in their offspring. Organisms near the *K* end reproduce slowly and cautiously even when environmental opportunities would allow them to be considerably more prolific, and they invest great amounts of time and energy in each of the few offspring they have. Theoretically, *r* strategists will usually begin reproducing at an earlier stage of development, will have numerous offspring per pregnancy as well as over the life course, and will spend less time gestating, protecting, feeding, and training each offspring relative to *K* strategists (Chisholm, 1988:81; Relethford, 1990:498). Several *r/K* theorists assume that there is both intra- and interspecies variability along the *r/K* continuum (Bereczkei, 1993; Ellis, 1987; Gadgil and Solbrig, 1972; Jolly, 1985:42, Menge, 1974: 84, Rushton, 1995).

Basically, *r/K* theory is similar to proposals that both quantitative (*r*) and qualitative (*K*) approaches to reproduction can be successful and that trade-offs are inherent in both strategies (Kaplan, 1994; Smith and Fretwell, 1974). Another way of making the same distinction is to stipulate that reproductive potential can be realized by emphasizing either mating (*r*) or parenting (*K*) (Lalumiere and Quinsey, 1996:33; Rowe, 1996:270). Theoretically, the trade-offs between mating effort versus parenting effort will manifest themselves in various ways, both behaviorally and physiologically. Organisms reproducing in large numbers, for example, cannot spend as much time caring for their offspring as organisms reproducing in small numbers. Traits useful in the pursuit of a *K* strategy would include kin-directed altruism and long-term nurturing of young; traits useful to the *r* strategy would include aggressive competitiveness and a strong sex drive.

Those who have applied the *r/K* concept to the study of criminal and antisocial behavior have contended that antisocial behavior is favored most among *r* strategists. This is partly because deceptive/victimizing approaches to reproduction would frustrate the cooperation among parents required for intense, long-term parental investments. Stated another way, because *K* strategists must invest extensive time and energy in each offspring, they are favored for evolving long-term cooperative, altruistic relationships between parents. Ultimately, parental cooperation leads to the evolution of cooperation among extended relatives and within communities of even more distantly related group members as a result of general inclusive fitness forces. Criminal and antisocial behavior would be contrary to such long-term cooperation arrangements.

Proponents of *r/K* theory have repeatedly noted that males should be more prone toward the *r* approach to reproduction than females (Ellis, 1989/90; Gould, 1982:459; Gross, 1992:246, Masters, 1983). This deduction follows from nothing that males have a higher reproductive potential without the necessity of making as much parental investment as females must make....

Hypothesis 1: Criminality and psychopathy should be more prevalent among men than among women....

Hypothesis 2: Persons with the greatest tendencies toward criminal and antisocial behavior should exhibit at least most of the physiological traits associated with an r strategy, such as low birth weights, high rates of premature birthing, births in fairly rapid succession, and frequent twinning. While the evidence is still sketchy, it generally supports this hypothesis. Specifically, compared to persons in general, criminals are more likely to have been born prematurely and of low birth weight (reviewed by Ellis, 1987:156)....

Hypothesis 3: Parents of criminals and psychopaths should begin having children earlier in life and should have larger numbers of children than parents in general. Studies have consistently found a positive correlation between criminality in offspring and the size of the family in which they were reared (Ellis, 1988:520; West, 1969:73). While this is consistent with *r/K* theory, it is also readily explainable in terms of some strictly environmental theories, such as self-control theory (Gottfredson and Hirschi, 1995:36)....

Hypothesis 4: Biological parents of criminals and psychopaths should themselves be criminal and psychopathic. Since the *r/K* theory assumes that genetic factors underlie tendencies to learn deceptive/victimizing behavior, the biological parents of persons who exhibit high rates of criminal and anti-social behavior should themselves exhibit such behavior. The evidence supporting this deduction is substantial (Nagin and Farrington, 1992; Raine, 1993:245; Robins et al., 1975; Rutter and Giller, 1984:182; West and Farrington, 1973:125).

While there are certainly environmental explanations for why criminality runs in families (e.g., bad example, poor supervision), environmental theories would not predict that the tendency would be any different for genetically intact compared to adoptive families. The *r/K* theory would predict that intergenerational links in criminal tendencies would be substantially reduced in the case of adoptive families. One study was located that

seemed to bear directly on this hypothesis; it found a lower intergenerational correlation for criminality in adoptive families than in genetically intact families (Hutchings and Mednick, 1977:130)....

Discussion and Conclusions

... All of the modern evolutionary theories share only a faint resemblance to the first evolutionary theory in criminology proposed over a century ago by Lombroso. The dissimilarities are understandable in part because Lombroso knew nothing of the concept of genetics, nor did he have the benefit of the vast store of research on evolutionary principles developed over the past century or a modern understanding of how brain functioning controls behavior, including learned behavior. As a result, nothing resembling the concept of atavism is found in modern evolutionary theories of criminal behavior. In fact, rather than considering criminals throwbacks to some primitive human form, most modern evolutionary theories of criminality imply the opposite: that criminal behavior may mark a special adaptation to life in large impersonal societies. If so, criminal and antisocial behavior may have only been adaptive over roughly the past 10,000 years at most, and only then primarily in urbanized environments....

As this review has shown, numerous hypotheses may be derived from each of the five evolutionary theories of criminal behavior discussed. While several of these hypotheses are identical (or almost so) to ones derived from strictly environmental criminological theories, several others are quite unique to the evolutionary perspective. Since most of these hypotheses have not been fully tested, the evidence is currently inadequate for passing judgement on the overall merit of these relatively new theories.

Possible Proximate Mechanisms

Before bringing this review to a close, it is worth nothing that evolutionary theorists often distinguish two categories of causal variables: ultimate causes and proximate causes (Browne, 1995:1003; Thornhill and Thornhill, 1983:137). *Ultimate causes* refer to the natural selection forces that have favored genes for various combinations of traits, both physical and behavioral. *Proximate causes* (or *proximate mechanisms*) pertain to the detailed physiological events that mediate any genetic effects, especially on behavior. Even though the focus of this article has been on possible ultimate causes, it is important to think of these two categories of variable as complementary, not contradictory. Accordingly, we briefly identify some of the possible proximate mechanisms that may affect the probability of criminal behavior.

As noted above, it is naive to believe that there are actual genes directly coding for criminality. Nevertheless, there could still be numerous genes that influence how the brain works in ways that increase (or decrease) the probability of criminal behavior under various environmental conditions. One promising lead in this respect involves the sex hormone testosterone and its effects on brain functioning. Studies of various animal species have shown that the combination of high perinatal testosterone and high postpubertal testosterone increases the probability of aggression (especially dominance-related aggression) (reviewed by Ellis and Coontz, 1990). This high testosterone regimen is typical of male mammals, as opposed to female mammals (Ellis and Coontz, 1990). Thereby, genes functioning on the Y chromosome as well as on the autosomes early in fetal development may eventually help to explain sex differences in criminal behavior (especially violent criminal behavior) (Sluyter et al., 1996; Walsh, 1995b). Consistent with this reasoning are studies indicating modest correlations among males between circulating testosterone and persistent involvement in criminality (Christiansen and Knussmann, 1987; Dabbs and Morris, 1990; Mazur, 1995; Thiessen, 1990; Windle and Windle, 1995) and other forms of socially disruptive activities (Dabbs et al., 1996; Scerbo and Kolko, 1994).

Another promising lead for elucidating the genetic foundation for criminality involves an enzyme that is active in the brain, monoamine oxidase (MAO). This enzyme, which comes in two forms (MAO-A and MAO-B), helps regulate the chemical breakdown of various neurotransmitters, most notably serotonin and dopamine (Zuckerman, 1994:295) and its activity is almost entirely under genetic control (Ellis, 1991a: 230; Zuckerman, 1994:297). Again, among the genes that are involved in regulating MAO activity are those on the Y chromosome that help control the formation of testes and thereby the production of testosterone during fetal development (and consequently later in life).

When testosterone levels are high, MAO enzyme activity is depressed (Ellis, 1991b:231), which is the basic reason males have lower MAO activity than females, especially following the onset of puberty. Within each sex (but especially among males), studies have found MAO activity to be low for individuals with histories of serious antisocial behavior and with problems of alcoholism and drug abuse (reviewed by Ellis, 1991a:235; Zuckerman, 1994:299).

Research still needs to determine why low MAO enzyme activity contributes to antisocial (and related) behavior, but it is not unreasonable to suspect that various neurotransmitters (especially serotonin) are involved. Supporting this view is evidence that low serotonin brain activity has been associated with impulsive, and sometimes violent combative behavior—both in humans (Virkkunen et al., 1989) and in other animals (Kostowski et al., 1984; Vergnes et al., 1988).

Something that is particularly interesting about the link between serotonin and aggression is that this neurotransmitter has also been found to be affected by the positions animals assume in social hierarchies—serotonin levels generally are positively linked to high rank (Brammer et al., 1994; Yeh et al., 1996). Criminologists should explore the possibility that serotonin may be one of the proximate mechanisms whereby genes influence the relationship between criminality and social status.

Yet another way genes could be affecting criminality is through their effects on alcoholism. This would coincide with evidence that genes are responsible for much of the variation in susceptibility to alcohol abuse (reviewed by Koopmans and Boomsma, 1996) and that alcohol abuse is a major behavioral correlate of criminality and antisocial behavior (Greenfield and Weisner, 1995).

The main point being made with this brief coverage of some proximate physiological mechanisms (see Fishbein, 1990, for a more extensive review) is that evolutionary theories are in no way in opposition to the idea that other variables, both biological and social, contribute to criminal behavior. In the final analysis, the explanations for criminal behavior are likely to involve complex interplays among learning and genetic, hormonal, and neurochemical factors, all operating within a complex evolved social system.

In Closing

In bringing this review to a close, we wish to emphasize that there is no fundamental difference between gene-based evolutionary theories and strictly environmental theories of criminal behavior on whether learning is responsible for variations in criminal behavior. For both theories, learning is important. The main difference is that gene-based evolutionary theories assume that learning is ultimately a neurological process highly influenced by genes, an assumption environmental theories do not make. If evolutionary (and other biosocial) theorists are correct on this point, criminologists in the future must not only know how the environment impacts the learning of criminal tendencies, but also how genes, the brain and other biological factors interact with the environment to affect such learning. This article suggests that these interactions get played out in a time-worn evolutionary theater that may have had, and may continue to have, reproductive consequences.

Many believe that evolutionary theorizing in criminology is a thing of the past, all but abandoned in the early part of this century. This article shows that evolutionary theories of criminal and antisocial behavior have in fact reemerged during the past two decades in forms that the 19th century theorists would scarcely recognize. These new theories show promise in offering new explanations for established observations as well as for generating new hypotheses. Decades of careful empirical testing will be required to assess the merit of many of these hypotheses.

Discussion Questions

1. How are the theories presented by Ellis and Walsh similar to and different from Lombroso's theory of "the criminal man" (described in Part I, Chapter 2)?
2. What are the major assumptions or arguments made by gene-based evolutionary theories (for example, one such assumption is that traits are genetically influenced)?
3. How does the "cheater" theory differ from the r/K selection theory?
4. Ellis and Walsh state that "genetic influence is not equivalent to genetic determinism." What do they mean?

5. According to evolutionary theories, why are males more likely than females to rape, engage in spousal assault, and engage in crime in general?
6. Can you think of any "facts" about crime that gene-based evolutionary theories would have trouble explaining?
7. Do you think that gene-based evolutionary theories apply more to some types of crime than others or to some types of offenders than others?
8. What are the policy or crime-control implications of gene-based evolutionary theories?
9. What do Ellis and Walsh mean when they state that "biological factors interact with the environment" to affect the learning of "criminal tendencies"?

4. Does the Body Tell? Biological Characteristics and Criminal Disposition

David Rowe

Studies suggest that genetic factors and "biological harms" of a nongenetic nature, like head injury and exposure to toxic substances, may increase the likelihood that individuals develop traits conducive to crime—such as impulsivity and sensation seeking. A central question, however, involves the mechanisms by which genes and biological harms affect personality traits. As Rowe argues in this chapter, genetic factors and biological harms affect individual traits through their impact on the central nervous system and autonomic nervous system (which includes the sympathetic and parasympathetic nervous systems). There has been much research in this area in recent years.

Certain aspects of this research focus on the chemical messengers, or neurotransmitters, that transmit signals between neurons in the brain (e.g., serotonin) and the hormones that help regulate such things as sex drive and responses to stressors (e.g., testosterone). Other research has focused on such indicators or correlates of nervous system activity as heart rate, skin conductance, level of brain activity, and brain anatomy. All of these factors may reflect or cause dysfunctions in the nervous system and, in doing so, may contribute to traits conductive to crime.

It is important to note that the chapter below does not summarize all of the research in this area, but rather is designed to introduce you to certain areas of more promising research (for more complete overviews, see Fishbein, 2001; Lahey et al., 2003; Patrick and Verona, 2007; Raine, 1993, 2002; Rowe, 2002; Scarpa and Raine, 2007; Wright et al., 2008). This reading will make you aware of how far biological theories of crime have progressed since Lombroso, who focused on the gross physical features of the person and devoted little attention to the mechanisms by which these features might contribute to crime.

References

Fishbein, Diana. 2001. *Biobehavioral Perspectives in Criminology.* Belmont, CA: Wadsworth.

Lahey, Benjamin B., Terrie E. Moffitt, and Avshalom Caspi. 2003. *Causes of Conduct Disorder and Juvenile Delinquency.* New York: Guilford.

Patrick, Christopher J. and Edelyn Verona. 2007. "The Psychophysiology of Aggression: Autonomic, Electrocortial, and Neuro-Imaging Findings." In Daniel J. Flannery, Alexander T. Vazsonyi, and Irwin D. Waldman (eds.), *The Cambridge Handbook of Violent Behavior and Aggression,* pp. 111–150. New York: Cambridge University Press.

Raine, Adrian. 1993. *The Psychopathology of Crime.* New York: Academic Press.

——. 2002. "The Biological Basis of Crime." In James Q. Wilson and Joan Petersilia (eds.), *Crime,* pp. 43–74. Oakland, CA: ICS Press.

Copyright © 2002. Reprinted by permission of Roxbury Publishing Company.

Rowe, David C. 2002. *Biology and Crime.* Los Angeles: Roxbury Publishing Company.

Scarpa, Angela and Adrian Raine. 2007. "Biosocial Bases of Violence." In Daniel J. Flannery, Alexander T. Vazsonyi, and Irwin D. Waldman (eds.), *The Cambridge Handbook of Violent Behavior and Aggression*, pp. 151–169. New York: Cambridge University Press.

Wright, John Paul, Stephen G. Tibbetts, and Leah E. Daigle. 2008. *Criminals in the Making.* Los Angeles: Sage.

———

Two medical cases have been studied by the neurologist Antonio Damasio and his colleagues that illustrate a possible neurological underpinning for psychopathy (Anderson et al. 1999). Their subjects, a man and a woman, had both suffered injuries to the prefrontal cortex during infancy. The prefrontal cortex, located just behind the eye sockets and above the bridge of the nose, is involved in planning a sequence of actions and in anticipating the future. The female subject was run over by a car when she was 15 months old. The male subject had a brain tumor removed from his prefrontal area when he was 3 months old. Both subjects grew up in stable, middle-class families with college-educated parents and had normal biological siblings, but neither made a satisfactory social adjustment; neither had friends and both were dependent on support from their parents. Neither subject had any plans for the future. The woman was a compulsive liar; she stole from her parents and shoplifted; her early and risky sexual behavior led to a pregnancy by age 18. By age 9, the male subject had committed minor theft and aggressive delinquent acts; he had no empathy for others.

The researchers tested the two subjects on a computerized gambling test used to detect how people respond to the uncertainty of rewards and punishments. The task is designed so that payoffs to the "bad" card deck are high and immediate while payoffs to the "good" card deck are low immediately but better in the long term. Most people quickly learn to draw cards from the "good" deck that offers the better long-term payoff. Neither subject was able to learn to use the long-term payoff deck.

Most surprisingly, these brain-injured victims failed to understand the difference between right and wrong; they lacked a sense of social norms and of how to act in social situations. Their moral blindness contrasts with the thought processes of adults who have brain damage in the same region and who display symptoms of psychopathy but understand without any difficulty the moral difference between right and wrong.

Finding the Physiological Basis of Criminal Disposition

The prefrontal cortex could mediate genetic influence on criminal dispositions if genes affect the functioning of this brain region. In a prominent theory of attention deficit hyperactivity disorder, the same brain region has been implicated (Barkley 1997). Deficits in the prefrontal cortex may reduce the executive function—that is, the ability to plan and to reflect on one's actions. Impaired executive function implies impulsive and disorganized behavior, a focus on the present rather than on the future. Tests involving specific tasks that require executive function can distinguish between psychopaths and control individuals. One is the classic delay-of-gratification task. In one version, a computer screen presents a signal for a 40 percent probability of winning a nickel; the subject can take the nickel or wait 14 seconds for an 80 percent probability of a win (and better long-term winnings). Psychopathic offenders pick the immediate reward more often than non-psychopathic offenders (Newman, Kosson, and Patterson 1992). Notice that this task presents the same basic situation as Damasio's card deck task: to work for a long-term payoff in the presence of immediate payoffs. . . .

Blood and Saliva Tests of Criminal Disposition

Could we detect criminal disposition with a simple saliva or blood test? There is some positive evidence that a test can be done for some hormones and metabolites of neurotransmitters that circulate in the blood.

Testosterone is the hormone that is responsible for the fetus carrying a Y chromosome to develop into a male. It is a biochemical that is simple in structure and that is derived from a substance feared by dieters: cholesterol. *T* attaches to receptors on the surface of specific cells and triggers a cascade of biological events within these cells that ultimately change gene expression in the cell's nucleus; that is, it can turn genes off and on. Testosterone circulates in the blood, a portion free and another portion bound to a carrier protein. Free *T*-levels are inexpensively detectable in saliva (Dabbs et al. 1995). With its powerful physiological effects and its strong connection to masculinity, it is no wonder that men revel in the power of testosterone.

Two studies have reported on interactions between social integration and the strength of the association between testosterone level and crime in Vietnam veterans; this association was stronger when men's social integration was weaker—that is, when they were of lower social class, were unmarried, or had an unstable work history (Booth and Osgood 1993; Dabbs and Morris 1990). To illustrate, Dabbs and Morris used data on crime and testosterone level in 4,462 Vietnam-era veterans. In their study, higher *T*-level predicted a variety of antisocial behaviors, including aggressive ones. The association was stronger in lower-class men than in middle-class men. Table 4.1 shows the percentage of high-testosterone (upper 10 percent, N = 202) versus low-testosterone (90th percentile and below; N = 1,294) men who were classified as delinquent. Among lower-class men, a higher testosterone level almost doubled the risk of crime, but among the upper-class men, it hardly

Table 4.1
Percentage of Sample Exhibiting Delinquent Behavior in World War II

Veterans by Testosterone Level		
	Normal *T* % Delinq.	High *T* % Delinq.
Low Social Class	14.7	30.7
High Social Class	4.5	4.1

Note: *T* = Testosterone. 90 percent of the sample fell into the normal *T* category; 10 percent into the high *T* category.

changed their already low rate of crime. Dabbs and Morris's finding suggests that *T*-level interacts with the social context; it may be a more potent cause of criminal disposition in a lower-class environment. Another possibility is that men who become lower class carry additional genetic risk factors that amplify the effects of testosterone. This second theory gains some credence because the men's class attainment was used, not the social class of their parents.

Other studies of the link between testosterone and crime have been reviewed by Jacobson and Rowe (2000). They noted that the association between testosterone and aggression was more consistent for adults than for adolescents, possibly because of the profound influence of puberty on hormone levels. One study also found the hormone estradiol, a close chemical relative, to be related to females' aggression. Only one research group has examined the association of hormones and female crime, a part of the general neglect of females in studies of crime.

In adult men, testosterone concentration in saliva has another quite different association that is more appealing than delinquency: a bass voice (Dabbs and Mallinger 1999). The strength of relationship of testosterone level to criminal disposition is about the same as it is to possessing a deep voice. A choir director would not, of course, take blood or saliva samples to find a man ready to sing the bass line in Handel's

Messiah—the director would audition men to sing instead. Many biological risk factors do not have the specificity to allow them to be used in a strong predictive way to forecast whether a particular individual will in the future commit delinquent acts.

Serotonin Levels

Serotonin is a chemical involved in neurotransmission in the brain. When nerve signals are relayed between sending and receiving nerve cells, serotonin crosses a small gap (the synapse) between one cell and the other and binds to receptor proteins on the surface of the receiving cell. This binding process sets off a biochemical chain reaction that modulates the receiving cell's ability to send further nerve impulses to its target cells. Another molecule, the serotonin transporter protein, has the job of recycling serotonin back into a sending cell for reuse. Serotonin is made from one of the essential amino acids, tryptophan, which is abundant in the American diet, especially in meat. Serotonin originates in cells in a particular region deep in the brain. Like long wires in an electrical circuit, axons from the serotonin-producing nerve cells extend widely throughout the brain, including into the frontal cortex, where they may modulate higher thought processes (Spoont 1992).

Serotonin levels cannot be measured directly by biological test without risking brain damage to the subject. Two indirect methods are thus used; the first involves measuring the level of a serotonin metabolite (SM) in a biochemical pathway that breaks down serotonin in cerebral spinal fluid; the second measures the level of serotonin itself inside blood platelet cells.

A consistent association has been found between low cerebral spinal fluid SM levels and suicidal impulses, suicide attempts, and completed suicides (Asberg 1997). Spinal fluid SM levels are also lower in violent criminals (Fuller 1996). Furthermore, people with suicidal ideation are sometimes impulsively aggressive, and their aggression is associated with lower SM levels.

The serotonin system is the target of a class of antidepressant drugs first discovered about 1975: the serotonin reuptake inhibitors. The most famous of these drugs, fluoxetine, goes under the trade name Prozac. The ability of the drug to relieve major depressive disorder, and seemingly to modify many other personality problems, led to the publication of a best-selling book, *Listening to Prozac* (Kramer 1997). The mechanism of Prozac's action lends further support to the hypothesis linking psychopathology with low serotonin levels. Prozac binds to and thereby blocks the action of the serotonin transporter protein; it is therefore likely that Prozac relieves depression partly by increasing the availability of serotonin in the synapses between cells. On the other hand, this account is certainly an oversimplification of how Prozac works. Prozac also binds to and thereby activates one class of serotonin receptor proteins, and it may have many unknown metabolic effects. In the last chapter, we consider ways in which the antidepressant drugs have become a treatment intervention for criminals.

Unlike most previous researchers, Moffitt and her colleagues (1998) used a general population sample instead of a sample of psychiatric patients. They also measured serotonin levels in blood platelet cells. The sample consisted of 781 21-year-old men and women, all born in the same year in New Zealand. Violence was measured by using criminal convictions and self-reports of violence. In males, higher levels of platelet serotonin were found to be associated with violence. This effect also held up to statistical controls for possibly related factors such as drug use, platelet count, body mass, psychiatric disorder, social class, nonviolent crime, and family relations.

The two measures of serotonin levels, (in spinal fluid versus in platelets) have opposite relationships to behavior disorders. However, the studies of spinal fluid measure the amount of metabolite after serotonin has been released into the synapse between nerve cells and then used. If the metabolite is low, it means that less serotonin has been available for communicating between nerve cells. The platelet serotonin studies measure the amount of serotonin still stored inside the platelet—the amount that has not yet been released for communication. Thus, if communication between cells is poor, this effect would theoretically result in *high* concentrations of serotonin stored (in neurones or platelet cells) and *low* concentrations released to be converted into a serotonin metabolite (by synapse or muscle), conceptually resolving the opposite direction of the associations found with the two assays.

Heart Rate Tests of Criminal Disposition

Heart rate is a physiological activity that is exquisitely sensitive to many environmental demands. Although the heart is a peripheral organ from the brain, the activity of the brain, including a psychological appraisal of situations, determines heart rate through the nervous system. Heart rate depends on the balance of the activity of the sympathetic and parasympathetic nervous systems; the former increases heart rate while the latter decreases it. Stimuli that grab one's attention first accelerate heart rate in an orienting response. The mental exertion of a game of chess makes the heart beat more rapidly—perhaps chess qualifies as a sport after all. Imagine that you are stepping into a doctor's office or are about to receive a medical exam from a survey interviewer. Unconsciously you will appraise the situation; if it seems mildly threatening, your heart rate may increase—but not by much, if you are someone with a greater criminal disposition than the average person.

In his book on crime as a clinical disorder, Raine (1993) summarized 14 studies of the relationship between resting heart rate and crime. All 14 studies found a lower resting heart rate to be associated with a greater rate of crime. Heart rate was measured from simple pulse counting to sophisticated electrical measurements. Definitions of crime included criminal records, teacher ratings, self-reports on personality tests, and a psychiatric diagnosis of conduct disorder. The association between low heart rate and criminal disposition was found in both American and English samples and in

both males and females. The statistical association was also upheld in subsequent studies (Raine et al. 1997). In sum, this finding was particularly robust because it held across samples drawn from different populations and over the various types of heart rate measures.

This association has also been found in studies that follow the same individuals through their lives, with a low heart rate measured well before the onset of criminal behaviors (Farrington 1997; Raine, Venables, and Mednick 1997). Raine et al. examined the association between heart rate when children were age 3 and the same children's antisocial behaviors when they were 11. The study took place on an island of Mauritius in the Indian Ocean, known for its excellent scuba diving. An amazing 100 percent cooperation rate was gained with the local Indian, Creole, and other descent populations by offering mothers two bags of flour, a candy for their children, and a free health screening. Heart rate was measured with a one-minute recording of the pulse. Aggressive and nonviolent antisociality were assessed by parental reports when the children were 11 years old. Those children with lower heart rates were rated as more aggressive than those with higher rates. . . . Children with low heart rates at age 3 had about twice the prevalence of aggression at age 11, versus those children with high heart rates at age 3. Considered from another vantage, the high-aggression group averaged about seven fewer heartbeats per minute than the low aggression group. Heart rate predicted aggressive acts more strongly than nonaggressive forms of delinquency, and this association also held when statistical controls were introduced for body size and social class.

Farrington's Cambridge Study in Delinquent Development also found a prospective association between low resting heart rate at age 18 and criminal convictions from ages 19 to 40. Among men with very low heart rates (fewer than 60 beats per minute), 17 percent had convictions, versus 5 percent of the men with very high heart rates (81 beats or more per minute). This association held when other variables were statistically controlled, including low verbal IQ, unstable job record, risk taking between the ages of 8 and 10, and parental convictions. Thus, this biological measure improved the prediction of crime.

Skin Conductance Tests of Criminal Disposition

Unlike heart rate, which assesses the interaction between the excitatory sympathetic nervous system and the inhibitory parasympathetic nervous system, skin conductance (SC) reflects only the central nervous system's stimulation of the sympathetic nervous system. In the central nervous system, skin conductance can reflect the diversion of attentional resources to a particular stimuli, as when orienting to that stimuli.

Skin conductance is measured by recording how much the fingers sweat. As fluids leak from pores in the skin, they carry ions (charged particles) of chloride and sodium that permit an electrical current to flow; skin conductance is then measured by testing the electrical resistance across wires attached to two fingers.

Associations have been found between a weak skin conductance response and criminal disposition (Raine 1993). However, the research literature on SC response is more mixed than that on resting heart rate. Psychopaths and antisocial individuals tend to be characterized by a weaker resting skin conductance response—measured in the absence of any provoking stimuli, such as a loud noise or speech. Not every study finds this relationship, and the exact reason that some studies are failures and others successful may depend on subtle changes in the test conditions. Criminally disposed individuals also show a stronger skin conductance half-recovery time. The half-recovery time is the time it takes for skin conductance to return halfway to baseline after a stimulus, but its physiological basis is not well understood.

One underlying factor for both a weaker skin conductance and lower resting heart rate may be a lower state of arousal in the brain. This idea, that lower brain arousal leads to crime, was one of the first physiological hypotheses for criminal behavior (Eysenck and Gudjonsson 1989). Because individuals with a criminal disposition would be in a state of low mental arousal, the mildly threatening situation of a medical test would fail to raise their heart rates. This theory holds that to compensate for a low level of arousal, these individuals seek out activities that are intrinsically arousing. Crimes, such as getting into a bruising fight or threatening someone in a robbery, are physically arousing acts. For a person with a normal level of brain arousal, such acts would increase mental arousal to such an intolerable level that the acts would become psychologically aversive. But for a person with a low level of arousal, the same increase of arousal would be pleasantly stimulating and rewarding. In this case, crime is a self-medication for a chronically underaroused brain.

Another interpretation of these physiological findings is an underlying personality characteristic of fearlessness. A lack of fear may account for heart rate and resting skin conductance remaining low in a mildly threatening situation. A lack of fear could also predispose toward crime because fearless children would be more difficult to socialize than fearful ones—punishment would arouse a less intense emotion, and the lesson inadequately learned. It is also better not to be afraid when breaking into a house or threatening violence. As Clint Eastwood intoned in the movie *The Unforgiven*, it is fearlessness that lets the gunslinger shoot straight, not his speed of draw.

Of these two explanations, I favor low arousal over fearlessness. One of my graduate students, Bo Cleveland (1998), included both measures of fearlessness and stimulation seeking in a study of delinquency and sexual coercion. The measure of fearlessness gave uniformly disappointing findings; it correlated neither with crime nor with other measures of criminal disposition. In contrast, the measures that best fit the underarousal theory, scales of impulsiveness and sensation seeking, correlated with crime. My reading of the overall research literature is that impulsivity and sensation seeking are more strongly associated with crime than either anxiety or fearlessness.

On the other hand, the low arousal theory has its limitations. It is hardly an argument for linking physiology specifically to criminal disposition. Low arousal can be relieved through many socially acceptable activities. The NASCAR racer, the high-altitude mountain climber, and the diver exploring an undersea canyon, all have sensation-seeking traits. The low arousal theory is incomplete because it does not indicate why a particular individual turns to crime rather than to adventure. Ideally, a physiological basis of crime would distinguish between these two groups, a level of specificity that has yet to be achieved.

Tests of Brain Anatomy and Function

A technological revolution has made it possible to view the anatomy and function of the living brain with tremendous precision. A variety of brain imaging techniques have opened a whole new window on the mind. One form of brain imaging is *positron emission tomography* (PET) scanning. These scans show which part of the brain is most active during cognitive tasks.

To be PET scanned, you must first be injected with a form of sugar with a radioactive label attached to it. Sugar fuels the brain. The most active regions of the brain draw the most sugar-fuel from the bloodstream, while the less active areas draw in less sugar. This process is dynamic, with sugar utilization rapidly following changes in the level of brain metabolic activity. After receiving your injection of radioactive-labeled sugar, in the typical experiment you would be asked to work on a cognitive task for about half an hour. During this task, the most active brain regions, down to volumes a few millimeters square, would absorb the greatest amount of radioactive sugar.

After completing the task, you would lie down with your head placed in a PET scanner. The radioactively labeled sugar molecules would now be in your brain cells. Their released high-energy positrons can then be detected by the PET scanner and these data would be used by a sophisticated computer program to create a picture of your brain regions according to the intensity of their sugar uptake; this picture thus shows which sections of the brain were most physiologically active. This method of imaging the brain, because it uses a radioactive-labeled sugar and complex equipment, is quite expensive for research use.

In comparison to a PET scan, a *magnetic resonance imaging* (MRI) scan shows brain anatomy more than brain function. As with the PET scanner, the subject lies down inside a large MRI machine and holds his head steady. A powerful magnetic field then rushes through the subject's head, causing hydrogen nuclei, like small spinning tops, to spin in one orientation. The MRI most strongly affects protons in hydrogen atoms. Hydrogen is one of the most abundant elements in the brain, a component of water (H_2O) and of most organic molecules. Once the magnetic field is switched off, the protrons immediately reorient and give off energy in the radio spectrum that is picked up by coils in the MRI machine and translated by a computer program into an exquisitely detailed three-dimensional picture of brain anatomy—one that can be sliced along any plane, as though the brain were cut by a sharp knife and the sections held up for viewing. A modification of the MRI machine, called functional MRI, also provides information about brain activity. These marvelous technologies have greatly aided medical diagnosis and have opened to research the relationship between the mind—mental activity—and the brain, its physical organ.

Raine and his colleagues have explored the relationship between brain images and criminal disposition for more than a decade. Their general finding is that the prefrontal lobes—the brain region most involved in higher thought processes and in the integration of emotions and thought—may malfunction in the brain of criminally disposed individuals. Their earliest work was conducted with PET scanning technology. In their 1993 study, the subjects were 22 California murderers, 20 men and two women; 19 controls were normal subjects matched to the murderers on age and sex. In the murderer group, three individuals were schizophrenic; their matched controls were schizophrenic patients without a history of violence. All subjects completed a PET scan to detect their brain's sugar metabolism and thus its active regions. In the half-hour testing procedure, the subjects identified numerical targets on a computer screen. After the test was completed, they were placed into the PET scanner, and high-energy positrons were used to locate the brain areas of strongest sugar metabolism.

Results from the PET scan are relative ones. Activity in one brain area is expressed relative to activity in all other brain areas. The deficit in murderers, such that their brain activity was lower than the control group's, was relatively specific to the most forward prefrontal areas of the brain, the region behind the forehead. Schizophrenics showed lower than normal activity in the parietal lobe (upper half of the brain above the ear) and temporal lobe (behind the ear). Unlike them, the murderers were no different from controls in their parietal and temporal lobe activity levels. One murderer did not fit the overall pattern. This man was a serial killer with approximately 45 victims over the years. Raine and his colleague speculated that this man planned his crimes—otherwise, he would have been caught long before the 45th victim—and hence he needed normal prefrontal activity for planning and foresight. Raine, Buchsbaum, and LaCasse (1997) extended and replicated these PET scan findings with about twice the number of murderers and controls. They again found a reduced activity level in the prefrontal cortex, as well as abnormal activity levels in deeper brain structures related to aggression.

Why would sugar metabolism be lower in the prefrontal lobes of murderers? One possibility is that the nerve cells themselves differ in the prefrontal region. Perhaps they are less efficient metabolizers of sugar. An alternative hypothesis is that there are fewer nerve cells to uptake sugar, so lower metabolism of sugar would occur in the prefrontal region than in other brain regions.

Raine and his colleagues conducted an MRI study that supported this second hypothesis that individuals with criminal disposition differed from controls in their brain anatomy.

In the MRI study, Raine and his colleagues recruited subjects through temporary employment agencies in Los Angeles (Raine et al. 2000). Some employment seekers were diagnosed with antisocial personality disorder (APD) on the basis of a psychiatric interview and a self-report violence scale. Three control groups were constructed from other employment seekers. Subjects in the normal control group had an absence of drug use or psychiatric illness. Those in the drug use control group abused illegal drugs and alcohol but were not antisocial. This control group was included to deal with the high frequency of substance use in the APD group, as Raine wanted to eliminate the possibility that drug abuse had caused brain abnormalities in the APD group. A third control group was created of individuals diagnosed with other psychiatric disorders. In this first brain-imaging study of a nonimprisoned sample of offenders, the subjects were all scanned in an MRI machine.

. . . At the surface of the brain, a thin layer of gray matter surrounds a larger layer of white matter. The gray layer consists of nerve cell bodies; the white area, of axons from those nerve cells that, like wires, carry signals to other parts of the brain and body. The MRI findings were extremely specific: The antisocial personality disorder group had lower prefrontal gray matter volumes than any of the three control groups. There was no difference in the volume of the prefrontal white matter. Relative to the normal controls, the APD group had an 11 percent reduction in gray-matter volume. Although this anatomical difference is too subtle to be observed in a cursory radiological examination—only a thickness difference of .5 mm—it is still a substantial statistical effect. The correlation of the ratio, prefrontal gray matter volume to whole brain volume, with APD was about .40.

Conclusions About Biological Tests of Crime

This short chapter can only sample from the many advances in the physiological testing of criminal disposition. Among the omitted topics were the association between crime and electrical activity in the brain (as measured with the electroencephalogram, or EEG); brain evoked potentials; cortisol; and other measures (Fishbein et al. 1989; Susman, Dorn, and Chrousos 1991; see reviews in Raine 1993).

This work on the biological basis of crime differs from that of the nineteenth-century phrenologists. Those scientists sought distinctive physical stigmata that could be used to unequivocally identify criminal individuals and distinguish them from noncriminal ones. The phrenologists looked to physical features, such as large jaws and protrusions on the skull, that would absolutely classify a person as criminal. Their chosen physical markers of criminality turned out not to be associated with criminal disposition. The biologically oriented scientists in this chapter would readily admit that the goal of the phrenologists was an unrealistic one. The criminal mind, and its biology, falls on a continuum with the minds of normal, law-abiding individuals. Some noncriminals will have low resting heart rates, nonsweating hands, and thin gray matter in their prefrontal cortexes, along with other biological markers of criminal disposition. With any single biological test, the identification of criminally disposed individuals is likely to be poor. With a set of biological measures, identification can be improved, but it will still be imperfect. In their MRI study, Raine and his colleagues (2000) also tested their subjects' resting heart rate and skin conductance levels. They could predict whether someone had antisocial personality disorder with 77 percent accuracy, a 27 percent improvement over guessing.

Although much less than the phrenologists had hoped for, this level of accuracy is still a considerable accomplishment with biological tests. Biological tests predict criminal disposition with about the same strength as the best measures of individuals' environmental circumstances—correlations on the order of .20 to .40. Indeed, the biological tests perform considerably better than some environmental indicators, such as social class. Combining biological and social measures may further improve our understanding about who is at risk of becoming criminal.

A more fascinating outcome of biological research, though, is that it pinpoints a type of biological deficit that is involved in criminal dispositions. The deficit appears to lie in impaired functioning of the frontal cortex. This conclusion is consistent with Damasio's stroke victims, Raine's brain imaging, Barkley's theories of hyperactivity, and skin conductance and heart rate findings. Perhaps the nineteenth-century phrenologists were right in one sense. An enlargement of the prefrontal cortex is one of the most distinctive anatomical differences between *Homo sapiens* and our evolutionary kissing cousin, the chimpanzee. The prefrontal cortex may create our knowledge of mind—that other people are themselves thinking about us—and allow us to adjust our behavior to the needs and concerns of other. The prefrontal cortex is also the physiological basis of the executive functions of planning, of delaying the enticing impulses of the present for better outcomes in the future, and of evaluating many behavioral choices instead of just one. The phrenologists may be approximately right: What is disrupted in a criminal disposition are those abilities of the mind that make us most distinctively human.

Discussion Questions

1. List one of the biological factors discussed by Rowe (e.g., serotonin level, heart rate, skin conductance) and describe how it might increase the likelihood of crime.

2. High levels of testosterone are more likely to lead to crime in some types of environments than

others. Describe the types of environments where testosterone is most likely to lead to crime.

3. Are there are any circumstances where it would be appropriate to use biological factors, such as testosterone levels and resting heart rate, to predict whether people will commit criminals acts in the future? Defend your response.

4. How do PET and MRI scans work and what do they tell us about the brain activity and anatomy of criminals and noncriminals?

5. Personality and Crime: Are Some People Crime Prone?

Avshalom Caspi, Terrie E. Moffitt, Phil A. Silva, Magda Stouthamer-Loeber, Robert F. Krueger, and Pamela S. Schmutte

Researchers do not argue that biological factors lead directly to crime. Rather, they argue that such factors, in combination with the environment, lead to traits that are conducive to crime. And data suggest that several specific traits are associated with crime, including impulsiveness, a desire for thrills and excitement, irritability, and a low concern for the welfare of others. Psychologists and others argue that many of these traits are associated with one another and often appear together in the same person. Thus, we have what might be called "super-traits." Psychologists have made much progress over the last two decades in identifying those super-traits that make up the human personality, although there is still some debate over whether there are three, four, or five super-traits (see Block, 1995; Caspi, 1998; Lahey and Waldman, 2005; Lilienfeld, 1999; Miller and Lynam, 2001; Watson et al., 1994).

This chapter draws on one of the leading psychological theories of human personality, which argues that there are three super-traits: constraint, negative emotionality, and positive emotionality. The article briefly describes these super-traits—including the specific traits that compose them—and then examines their relation to crime, using data from two rather different samples in New Zealand and Pittsburgh. Two of the traits, negative emotionality and constraint, are related to Gottfredson and Hirschi's concept of self-control (see Chapter 19 in Part VI), but they claim that the concept of self-control is too simple: Crime-proneness is defined by more than a single dimension. You should keep their work in mind when reading the Gottfredson and Hirschi selection. At the end of this chapter, Caspi et al. discuss the origins of negative emotionality and constraint, stating that both super-traits are influenced by biological and environmental factors.

The research described here is important because it suggests that some individuals are crime-prone. That is, some individuals are more likely than others to engage in crime in a given environment. As Caspi et al. state, individuals high in negative emotionality and low in constraint are more likely to interpret events as threatening and to act on their impulses; that is, they are "quick on the draw." Also, as others have argued, such individuals often influence their environment in ways that increase the likelihood of crime; for example, they often provoke others

Excerpted from "Personality and Crime: Are Some People Crime Prone? Replications of the Personality-Crime Relationship Across Countries, Genders, Races, and Methods," by Avshalom Caspi, Terrie E. Moffitt, Phil A. Silva, Magda Stouthamer-Loeber, Robert F. Krueger, and Pamela S. Schmutte, *Criminology* 32(2), May 1994. Reprinted by permission of the American Society of Criminology.

*and they select themselves into negative environ-
ments, such as delinquent peer groups and bad jobs.
Yet, as Caspi et al. state near the start of their selection,
many criminologists have dismissed the importance
of personality traits. This attitude is starting to
change, however, as additional evidence for the
importance of such traits mounts (for overviews, see
Agnew, 2009; Andrews and Bonta, 2006; Ellis and
Walsh, 2006; Farrington, 1996; Farrington and
Welsh, 2007; Lahey and Waldman, 2005; Miller
and Lynam, 2001; Pratt and Cullen, 2000).*

References

Agnew, Robert. 2009. *Juvenile Delinquency: Causes
and Control*. New York: Oxford.

Andrews, D. A. and James Bonta. 2006. *The Psychology
of Criminal Conduct*, 4th edition. Cincinnati:
Anderson.

Block, Jack. 1995. "A Contrarian View of the Five-
Factor Approach to Personality Description."
Psychological Bulletin 117: 187–215.

Caspi, Avshalom. 1998. "Personality Development
Across the Life Course." In Nancy Eisenberg (ed.),
*Handbook of Child Psychology, Volume 3: Social,
Emotional, and Personality Development*, pp. 311–
318. New York: John Wiley and Sons.

Ellis, Lee and Anthony Walsh. 2006. *Criminology*.
Needham Heights, MA: Allyn & Bacon.

Farrington, David. 1996. "The Explanation and
Prevention of Youthful Offending." In J. David
Hawkins (ed.), *Delinquency and Crime: Current
Theories*, pp. 68–148. Cambridge, England:
Cambridge University Press.

Farrington, David P. and Brandon C. Welsh. 2007.
Saving Children from a Life of Crime. New York:
Oxford University Press.

Lahey, Benjamin B. and Irwin D. Waldman. 2005. "A
Developmental Model of the Propensity to Offend
During Childhood and Adolescence." In David P.
Farrington (ed.), *Integrated Developmental and Life-
Course Theories of Offending*, pp. 15–50. New
Brunswick, NJ: Transaction.

Lilienfeld, Scott O. 1999. "Anxiety Sensitivity and the
Structure of Personality." In Steven Taylor (ed.),
Anxiety Sensitivity, pp. 149–180. Mahwah, NJ:
Lawrence Erlbaum Associates.

Miller, Joshua D. and Donald Lynam. 2001. "Structural
Models of Personality and Their Relation to
Antisocial Behavior: A Meta-Analytic Review."
Criminology 39: 765–798.

Pratt, Travis C. and Francis T. Cullen. 2000. "The
Empirical Status of Gottfredson and Hirschi's
General Theory of Crime." *Criminology* 38: 931–964.

Watson, David, Lee Anna Clark, and Allan Harkness.
1994. "Structures of Personality and Their
Relevance to Psychopathology." *Journal of
Abnormal Psychology* 103: 18–31.

———

Are some people crime-prone? Is there a
criminal personality? Psychologists and
criminologists have long been intrigued by the
connection between personality and crime. . . .

We have studied personality and crime by
using a two-pronged approach. First, we have
studied individuals in different developmental
contexts. Second, we have used multiple and
independent measures of their personality and
their criminal involvement. In New Zealand we
have studied 18-year-olds from an entire birth
cohort; the New Zealand study permits us to
make detailed comparisons between males and
females. In the United States we have studied an
ethnically diverse group of 12- and 13-year-old
boys; the American study permits us to make
detailed comparisons between blacks and
whites. By studying different age cohorts in different nations, boys and girls, blacks and whites,
and by collecting in each of our studies multiple
and independent measures of behavior, we can
ascertain with relative confidence the extent to
which personality differences are linked to crime.

Personality and Crime

Personality psychologists have proposed numerous well-articulated theories linking personality
to crime and other antisocial outcomes. For
example, Eysenck (1977) associates crime with

extreme individual values on three personality factors: extroversion, neuroticism, and psychoticism. Zuckerman (1989) regards criminality as the sine qua non of individuals high on a factor he calls P-ImpUSS, which is characterized by impulsivity, aggressiveness, and lack of social responsibility. Cloninger (1987), using his three-factor biosocial model of personality, suggests that persons high in novelty seeking and low in harm avoidance and reward dependence are likely to be today's delinquents and tomorrow's violent, antisocial adults. In addition, a group of psychologists have proposed a link between antisocial behavior and theoretical physiological systems within the brain that are presumed to modulate impulse expression (Gray, 1977). Deficiencies in these neural systems have been suggested as the source for aggression in adults (Fowles, 1980; Gorenstein and Newman, 1980), as well as for conduct problems in children (Quay, 1986).

Many of these theories rely on trait-based personality models. In the past, the existence of traits was viewed as controversial (Mischel, 1968). In the last 20 years, however, researchers have amassed solid evidence documenting the cross-situational consistency (Epstein and O'Brien, 1985) and the longitudinal stability (Caspi and Bem, 1990) of traits, and psychology has witnessed a renaissance of the trait as an essential personality construct (Kenrick and Funder, 1988; Tellegen, 1991). Traits represent consistent characteristics of individuals that are relevant to a wide variety of behavioral domains, including criminality (see Eysenck, 1991).

Advances in personality theory and assessment, however, have had little influence on research conducted by criminologists (Gottfredson and Hirschi, 1990). Reviews of research on personality and crime appearing in mainstream criminology have identified numerous methodological problems with previous research (e.g., Schuessler and Cressey, 1950; Tennenbaum, 1977; Waldo and Dinitz, 1967), leading most criminologists to dismiss personality as a fruitless area of inquiry....

Methodological Problems in Linking Personality to Crime

Although some researchers already are convinced that personality variables are essential to understanding crime (e.g., Eysenck and Gudjonsson, 1989), the criminological reviews cited above suggest that this belief is far from universal. In particular, critics of empirical efforts to link personality to crime have pointed to problems in *measurement of personality, measurement of delinquency,* and *sampling.* In our research we have attempted to redress each of these problems.

Measurement of Personality

. . . In our studies of personality and crime we have used assessment instruments . . . that measure a comprehensive variety of personality traits; they were designed to blanket the human personality. These instruments allowed us to identify a constellation of personality traits, not merely a single trait, that might be linked to criminal involvement.

Previous studies of personality and delinquency also have been criticized for employing delinquency and personality questionnaires that included virtually identical items (Tennenbaum, 1977). For example, both the MMPI and the CPI include such items as "I have never been in trouble with the law" and "Sometimes when I was young I stole things." Similarities between legally defined offenses and the wording of items on personality inventories may inflate correlations between these two theoretically distinct constructs. In our studies we maintained sensitivity to this issue by evaluating each personality item in terms of its potential semantic overlap with any actual illegal acts.

Measurement of Delinquency

In previous studies of personality and crime, the most commonly used delinquency measure was the subject's conviction record or his presence in a correctional facility. A fundamental problem with official measures, however, is that "hidden criminals," offenders who commit crimes but are not caught, escape empirical attention and may slip into "control" samples (Schuessler and Cressey, 1950). Because only the tip of the deviance iceberg is reflected by official statistics (Hood and Sparks, 1970), many criminologists have turned to less strongly biased measures—specifically, self-reported delinquency questionnaires (Hindelang et al., 1979, 1981; Hirschi et al., 1980).

Yet self-report measures are not faultless. They have been criticized for including trivial items that query about acts which are unlikely to result in official intervention, such as skipping school or defying parental authority (Hindelang et al., 1979; Hirschi et al., 1980). Similarly, infrequent offenders may tend to report trivial events such as sibling fisticuffs in response to questions about "assault," or taking the family car without permission in response to questions about "auto theft" (Elliott and Huizinga, 1989). In contrast, frequent offenders may tend to underreport their delinquent behavior because the individual acts are so commonplace that they are not salient in the offenders' memories (Hirschi et al., 1980). Because both official records and self-report delinquency questionnaires have unique benefits and shortcomings, the use of the two measures in tandem is the most effective empirical strategy (Hirschi et al., 1980).

In our studies of personality and crime, we have collected multiple and independent measures of delinquent behavior: police records of contact, court records of conviction, self-reports, and reports from independent informants, parents, and teachers. These multiple measures have allowed us to identify robust personality correlates of crime that replicate across different measurement strategies.

Sampling

In previous studies of personality and crime, the most commonly used samples were drawn from incarcerated populations. These samples are not representative of offenders as a whole; they represent only the subset of offenders who actually are caught and subsequently are sent to jail (Hood

and Sparks, 1970; Klein, 1987). Moreover, adjudicated offenders may differ systematically from non-adjudicated offenders; offenders who are white, middle class, or female may be overlooked inadvertently (e.g., Taylor and Watt, 1977). In addition, the offenders' personal characteristics may influence official responses to their aberrant behavior; for example, some offenders may have enough poise to talk their way out of an arrest. Finally, incarceration itself may contribute to personality aberrations (Schuessler and Cressey, 1950; Wilson and Herrnstein, 1985). Thus, nonrepresentative sampling has clouded interpretation of observed differences between captive offenders and comparison groups.

In our studies of personality and crime, we have surveyed two different age cohorts whose members' level of involvement in illegal behaviors ranges from complete abstinence to a wide variety of delinquent violations. Therefore, our results are not limited to a selected minority of adolescent offenders who have been caught and convicted of their crimes.

The results of our studies are presented in two parts. Study 1 explores the personality-crime relationship in a birth cohort of 18-year-old males and females living in New Zealand. Study 2 attempts to replicate these findings among 12- and 13-year-olds living in a large American city.

Study 1: Personality and Crime Among Males and Females: Evidence From a New Zealand Birth Cohort

Study 1 explores the personality-crime relationship in a longitudinal-epidemiological sample (Krueger et al., in press). Members of this sample have been studied since birth. At age 18 they were administered an omnibus self-report personality inventory that assesses individual differences in several focal personality dimensions. In addition to this personality assessment, we gathered information about their delinquency using multiple

Table 5.1
MPQ Scale Descriptions and Internal Consistency Coefficients

MPQ Scale	Alpha	Description of a High Scorer
Constraint		
Traditionalism	.63	Desires a conservative social environment; endorses high moral standards.
Harm Avoidance	.71	Avoids excitement and danger; prefers safe activities even if they are tedious.
Control	.79	Is reflective, cautious, careful, rational, planful.
Negative Emotionality		
Aggression	.78	Hurts others for own advantage; will frighten and cause discomfort for others.
Alienation	.76	Feels mistreated, victimized, betrayed, and the target of false rumors.
Stress Reaction	.80	Is nervous, vulnerable, sensitive, prone to worry.
Positive Emotionality		
Achievement	.69	Works hard; enjoys demanding projects and working long hours.
Social Potency	.76	Is forceful and decisive; fond of influencing others; fond of leadership roles.
Well-Being	.67	Has a happy, cheerful disposition; feels good about self and sees a bright future.
Social Closeness	.75	Is sociable; likes people and turns to others for comfort.

and independent data sources: self-reports, informant reports, and official records. . . .

Measurement of Personality

As part of the age-18 assessment, 862 subjects completed a modified version (Form NZ) of the Multidimensional Personality Questionnaire (MPQ; Tellegen, 1982). The MPQ is a self-report personality instrument designed to assess a broad range of individual differences in affective and behavioral style. The 177-item version of the MPQ (Form NZ) yields 10 different personality scales (Tellegen, 1982:7–8). . . .

The 10 scales constituting the MPQ can be viewed at the higher-order level as defining three superfactors: Constraint, Negative Emotionality, and Positive Emotionality (Tellegen, 1985; Tellegen and Waller, in press). *Constraint* is a combination of the Traditionalism, Harm Avoidance, and Control scales. Individuals high on this factor tend to endorse conventional social norms, to avoid thrills, and to act in a cautious and restrained manner. *Negative Emotionality* is a combination of the Aggression, Alienation, and Stress Reaction scales. Individuals high on this dimension have a low general threshold for the experience of negative emotions such as fear, anxiety, and anger, and tend to break down under stress (Tellegen et al., 1988). *Positive Emotionality* is a combination of the Achievement,

Social Potency, Well-Being, and Social Closeness scales. Individuals high on Positive Emotionality have a lower threshold for the experience of positive emotions and for positive engagement with their social and work environments, and tend to view life as essentially a pleasurable experience (Tellegen et al., 1988)....

Results

Higher-Order Personality Factors and Delinquency

To summarize the personality correlates of delinquent behavior across the three independent data sources, we examined correlations between the MPQ's three higher-order factors and each measure of delinquent activity....

Among both males and females, Constraint and Negative Emotionality emerged as robust correlates of delinquent behavior across the three different data sources. *Positive Emotionality* was not associated significantly with any measure of delinquent behavior.... [M]ale and female delinquents exhibited convergent personality profiles characterized by impulsivity, danger seeking, a rejection of traditional values, aggressive attitudes, feelings of alienation, and an adversarial interpersonal attitude....

Criminologists would be persuaded more fully by evidence linking personality traits to crime if personality traits could be shown to relate to serious criminal behavior. To address this issue, we examined the higher-order personality scores of three groups of persons: (1) persons who self-reported having committed multiple (two or more) index offenses in the past year, (2) persons who were identified through court conviction records as repeat offenders, and (3) persons who had been convicted for a violent offense. We restricted this examination to males because relatively few females were involved in serious criminal acts, as defined above....

Persons involved in serious criminal behavior scored significantly lower on MPQ Constraint and significantly higher on Negative Emotionality....

In sum, the results from our analyses of the personality correlates of serious crime are very similar to the results from our analyses of the personality correlates of other antisocial activities. Apparently the same personality traits are implicated in antisocial acts of varying severity.

The results have revealed robust personality correlates of delinquency. Among both males and females, three personality scales were correlated with all three independent sources of delinquency data (self-reports, informant reports, and official reports): Delinquency was associated negatively with the MPQ scales' Traditionalism and Control, and positively with Aggression. These results suggest that young men and women who engaged in delinquency preferred rebelliousness to conventionality, behaved impulsively rather than cautiously, and were likely to take advantage of others.

Two additional personality scales showed consistent patterns. Among males, all three data sources correlated with the MPQ scale Alienation, and two data sources correlated with the MPQ scale Stress Reaction; among females, two data sources correlated with both Alienation and Stress Reaction. These results suggest that young men and women who engaged in delinquency were also likely to feel betrayed and used by their friends and to become easily upset and irritable. At the higher-order factor level, greater delinquent participation was associated with a unique trait configuration: greater negative emotionality *and* less constraint.

These findings were not compromised by problems inherent in measuring delinquency; the personality correlates were robust across different methods of measuring delinquency. Moreover, the interpretation of these data was not compromised by predictor-criterion overlap because we eliminated any content overlap between the personality items and the delinquency measures. These findings, however, were observed in a single sample. We now turn to a replication of these findings in a different context.

Study 2: Personality and Crime Among Blacks and Whites: Evidence from an American Metropolis

Study 1 reported on mostly white adolescents who live in a mid-sized city with little social decay in comparison with America's largest cities. It is possible that the racial or ecological composition of this sample may have distorted the relation between personality and crime. For example, it may be that relations between personality characteristics and crime may be attenuated among inner-city youths who experience many contextual pressures to engage in illegal behavior. Will negative emotionality and constraint predict delinquent behavior in individuals from different environments and during different developmental stages?

We address these generalizability issues in Study 2 by exploring the personality-crime relationship in a separate sample of American inner-city youths age 12 and 13. At that age, caregivers provided extensive personality descriptions of the youths. In addition, we gathered information about the youths' delinquency using multiple and independent data sources: self-reports, teachers' reports, and parents' reports.

Method

Measurement of Personality

Because the MPQ is not appropriate for younger adolescents, we used a different personality assessment instrument to describe the personalities of the boys in Pittsburgh. Specifically, the caregivers completed the "Common-Language" version of the California Child Q-sort (CCQ), a language-simplified personality assessment procedure intended for use with lay observers (Caspi et al., 1992).... The CCQ contains 100 statements written on individual cards that describe a wide range of personality attributes (e.g., "He plans ahead; he thinks before he does something," "He is determined in what he does; he does not give up easily," "He tries to see what and how much he can get away with"). The caregiver's task was to sort these item cards into a forced nine-category distribution along a continuum ranging from "most like this boy" to "most *unlike* this boy.".. .

Results

To assess the relation between personality characteristics and delinquency, we computed correlations between the CCQ measures of Constraint, Negative Emotionality, and Positive Emotionality with measures of delinquency drawn from the three independent data sources: self-reports, teachers' reports, and parents' reports....

Across all three data sources, Constraint and Negative Emotionality emerged as robust correlates of delinquency among both black and white adolescents. The positive correlations with Negative Emotionality suggested that delinquent adolescents were prone to respond to frustrating events with strong negative emotions, to feel stressed or harassed, and to approach interpersonal relationships with an adversarial attitude. The negative correlations with Constraint suggested that delinquent adolescents were likely to be impulsive, danger-seeking, and rejecting of conventional values. Positive emotionality was not associated robustly with delinquent behavior....

Discussion

Our studies have revealed that individual differences in personality are correlated consistently with delinquency. Although we performed many analyses, the significant correlations were not scattered randomly across variables; rather, the same pattern of personality correlations was repeated consistently. We obtained these correlations in different countries, in different age cohorts, across gender, and across race. We also obtained these correlations when we measured delinquent involvement with self-reports, teachers' reports, parents' reports, informants' reports, and official records, and when we measured serious crime and less serious delinquency. Finally, we obtained these correlations when we measured personality both with self-reports and with parents' reports. The personality correlates of delinquency were robust: Greater delinquent participation was associated with greater negative emotionality and less constraint.

Gottfredson and Hirschi (1990) have suggested that individual differences in "self-control" predispose some people to criminal behavior; this single stable individual difference is said to define a propensity or proneness to crime. Our findings support this theory somewhat, but they also suggest that it is simplistic psychologically. Crime-proneness is defined not by a single tendency (such as self-control or impulsivity) but by multiple psychological components. Across different samples and different methods, our studies of personality and crime suggest that crime-proneness is defined both by high negative emotionality and by low constraint.

How Might Negative Emotionality and Constraint Lead to Crime?

Negative emotionality is a tendency to experience aversive affective states such as anger, anxiety, and irritability (Watson and Clark, 1984). It is likely that individuals with chronically high levels of such negative emotions perceive interpersonal events differently than other people. They may be predisposed to construe events in a biased way, perceiving threat in the acts of others and menace in the vicissitudes of everyday life.

This situation may be aggravated when negative emotionality is accompanied by weak constraint—that is, great difficulty in modulating impulses. In low-constraint individuals, negative emotions may be translated more readily into action. Such volatile individuals should be, in the vernacular of the Wild West, "quick on the draw." Theoretically, antisocial behavior should be likely among individuals who are high in negative emotionality and low in constraint.

What Are the Origins of Negative Emotionality and Constraint?

Our findings may be placed into a developmental context by considering theories about the environmental and biological origins of negative emotionality and constraint.

The family environment has a pervasive influence on children's lives and personality development, particularly on the development of antisocial behavior (e.g., Patterson, 1982). Harsh, inconsistent disciplinary practices and a chaotic home environment have been shown to predict later aggression (Loeber and Stouthamer-Loeber, 1986). Living under the constant threat of emotional or physical harm makes negative affect more than simply a perceptual bias for these youths; negative affect is rooted in the realities of their everyday lives. Constraint also may be affected by family dynamics. For example, parental conflict has been found to predict children's scores on constraint at age 18 (Vaughn et al., 1988). Thus, a personality configuration involving high levels of negative affect and low levels of constraint may develop when children grow and learn in a discordant family environment where parent-child interactions are harsh or inconsistent.

Negative affectivity and constraint also are considered to have specific neurobiological underpinnings. Recent research has pointed to a possible connection between the rate at which the brain expends its neurotransmitter substances and dimensions of personality (Cloninger, 1987). For example, abnormally low levels of a metabolite by-product from the neurotransmitter called serotonin have been found in the cerebro-spinal fluid of prison inmates whose offense history is habitually violent and impulsive (Linnoila et al, 1983; Virkunnen et al., 1987). This finding has led theorists to outline the neural mechanisms by which low serotonin levels in the brain could simultaneously produce impulsivity *and* greater negative affectivity (Depue and Spoont, 1986; Spoont, 1992).

Theories linking personality traits to the primary neurotransmitters also may have important implications for research on the link between crime and genetics. Some adoption and twin studies have demonstrated a significant heritability for criminal behavior (see DiLalla and Gottesman, 1989; Mednick et al., 1986; Plomin et al., 1990), but these findings remain controversial in criminology (Walters and White, 1989). If future behavior genetic studies should document significant heritability for criminal behavior, how should we interpret this finding? Clearly, behavior itself cannot be inherited. Low serotonin levels, however, may be a heritable diathesis for a personality style involving high levels of negative affect and low levels of constraint, which generates in turn a vulnerability to criminal behavior. Indeed, negative affect and constraint themselves appear to be highly heritable; a study of twins reared together versus twins reared apart (Tellegen et al., 1988) found that more than 50 percent of the observed variance in both Negative Emotionality and Constraint (assessed by the MPQ) could be attributed to genetic factors. . . .

Discussion Questions

1. Caspi et al. state that many criminologists have been critical of previous research linking personality traits to crime, citing certain methodological problems with such research. What are these problems? How do Caspi et al. overcome them?
2. A researcher finds that certain personality traits are more common among prison inmates than among people in the general population. Does this mean that such traits *cause* crime? If not, why not?
3. Describe the super-traits of negative emotionality and constraint. List two questions you might ask respondents in a survey to measure each trait (or dimensions of each trait).
4. Why did Caspi et al. explore the relationship between personality traits and crime using two samples?
5. Describe all the ways that negative emotionality and low constraint might increase the likelihood of crime.

6. The Development of Antisocial Behavior: An Integrative Causal Approach

Benjamin B. Lahey, Irwin D. Waldman, and Keith McBurnett

It has become increasingly clear that biological factors, individual traits, and social factors all have an important role to play in the explanation of crime. Several theories have been constructed to describe that role. These theories list the key biological, trait, and social factors that contribute to crime. They describe the complex relationships between these factors. Biological factors, for example, influence the development of traits conducive to crime, such as low intelligence and impulsivity. These traits, in turn, influence the social environments to which individuals are exposed. Impulsive individuals, for example, often provoke harsh reactions from their parents and seek out other impulsive individuals as friends. At the same time, the social environment influences biological factors. Individuals in supportive and stimulating environments, for example, may experience enhanced brain development (Wright et al., 2008). Further, such individuals may not "express" any genetic predisposition they might have for traits such as impulsivity and irritability (Rutter et al., 2006). In addition, individual traits and the social environment work together to influence crime. Individuals with traits such as impulsivity and irritability are most likely to engage in crime when they are in environments favorable to crime, such as troubled families. It is important to note, however, that the relative importance of biological, trait, and environmental factors varies across individuals. Biological factors and individual traits are said to be most important in explaining the behavior of those individuals who offend at high rates from an early age.

This chapter describes one of the most sophisticated attempts to construct an integrated theory involving biological, trait, and social factors. Lahey et al. begin by arguing that some individuals have a stronger propensity to engage in antisocial behavior than others (antisocial behavior substantially overlaps with crime). This propensity is a function of several cognitive and temperamental traits, including low intelligence, irritability, low inhibition, and a lack of sympathy for others. Such traits are quite similar to those described by Caspi et al. in Chapter 5, although Lahey et al. sometimes describe them in different terms (e.g., low harm avoidance instead of low constraint). These cognitive and temperamental traits are in part genetically based. And they are said to play an especially important role in explaining the behavior of individuals who start offending at an early age.

Offending is also a function of the social environment, including harsh parental discipline, poor parental supervision, antisocial parental

Excerpted from "The Development of Antisocial Behavior: An Integrative Causal Model," by Benjamin B. Lahey, Irwin D. Waldman, and Keith McBurnett, *J. Child Psychol. Psychiat.* 40(5), 1999.

attitudes, and association with antisocial peers. It is critical to note, however, that individuals with those traits conducive to offending are more likely to be in such environments. This is partly because traits such as irritability have a genetic component, so juveniles with these traits are more likely to have parents with the same traits. And these traits undermine effective parenting. Also, juveniles with these traits are more likely to provoke negative responses from others. For example, they are more likely to frustrate and overwhelm their parents, who respond with overly harsh discipline. Also, these juveniles frequently sort or select themselves into environments conducive to crime. For example, they are rejected by conventional peers, and they choose to associate with antisocial peers. Offending, especially long-term, frequent, and serious offending, is said to be most likely among those individuals who have traits conducive to crime and are in these types of negative environments.

The overlap between these negative traits and environments, however, is far from perfect. Some individuals with negative traits are in loving, supportive families. These individuals may be able to avoid antisocial behavior. Further, some individuals without negative traits may encounter environments conducive to crime. This often happens during adolescence, when juveniles are exposed to antisocial peers and sometimes experience family problems. And Lahey et al. argue that environmental factors largely explain the mostly minor offending that many juveniles exhibit during the adolescent years. Lahey et al., in sum, have developed an integrated theory focusing on a range of biological, trait, and social factors; although the relative importance of these factors depends on whether we are explaining the behavior of those who offend at high rates from an early age or those whose offending is largely limited to minor offenses during the adolescent years. Their theory has not yet been fully tested, but it is compatible with much existing evidence about offending (see Lahey and Waldman, 2005, 2007).

References

Lahey, Benjamin B. and Irwin D. Waldman. 2005. "A Developmental Model of the Propensity to Offend During Childhood and Adolescence." In David P. Farrington (ed.), *Integrated Developmental & Life-Course Theories of Offending*, pp. 15–50. New Brunswick, NJ: Transaction.

Lahey, Benjamin B. and Irwin D. Waldman. 2007. "Personality Dispositions and the Development of Violence and Conduct Problems." In Daniel J. Flannery, Alexander T. Vazsonyi, and Irwin D. Waldman (eds.), *The Cambridge Handbook of Violent Behavior and Aggression*, pp. 260–287. New York: Cambridge University Press.

Rutter, Michael, Terrie E. Moffitt, and Avshalom Caspi. 2006. "Gene-Environment Interplay and Psychopathology: Multiple Varieties But Real Effects." *Journal of Child Psychology and Psychiartry* 47: 226–261.

Wright, John Paul, Stephen G. Tibbetts, and Leah E. Daigle. 2008. *Criminals in the Making*. Los Angeles: Sage.

This [chapter] presents an integrative model of the origins and development of antisocial behavior during childhood and adolescence.... We use the term *antisocial* to refer to behaviors that violate important norms or laws....

Antisocial Propensity: Causal Factors and Causal Sequences

We propose that individual differences in antisocial behavior can be explained by a single latent construct of antisocial propensity. Youths with greater antisocial propensity are more likely to engage in antisocial behavior, to engage in a greater variety of antisocial behaviors (including physical aggression), to have an earlier age of onset, and to be more likely to continue to engage in antisocial behavior at least through adolescence. That is, we propose that the prevalence, variety, onset, and persistence of antisocial behavior are correlated because they share causal influences.

Many factors contribute to antisocial propensity through multiple causal sequences. As discussed below, these causal sequences overlap and influence one another in fundamentally important ways. The same causal sequences apply to youths whose antisocial behavior emerges at all ages from early childhood through late adolescence, but the relative strength of the influences changes with age. For youths with earlier ages of onset of antisocial behavior, antisocial propensity is the net result of multiple aspects of genetically influenced temperament and cognitive ability that are transformed into antisocial behavior through successive transactions with the social experiment. The causal role played by heritable temperamental and cognitive predisposition declines with the age of onset of the earliest antisocial behavior. With the decline of genetic influences, environmental factors become more influential. Thus, peer influences are more influential at older ages of onset of antisocial behavior.

Temperamental Contributions to Antisocial Propensity

Like others, we hypothesize that temperament influences antisocial propensity through transactions with the social environment. The term temperament refers to substantially heritable individual differences in global aspects of socioemotional response that emerge early in life (Buss and Plomin, 1975). We use the term more broadly than most, however, to encompass the term "oppositional temperament."

Oppositional temperament. The person variable that contributes most strongly to antisocial behavior, particularly when it emerges early in life, is *oppositional temperament.* This dimension evolves somewhat during infancy and early childhood. During infancy, what we refer to as

oppositional temperament has usually been defined as difficult temperament (Bates et al., 1991). During infancy, difficult temperament is characterized by irritability, resistance to control, temper tantrums, and anger. By early childhood, maladaptive interactions with parents and others often have transformed difficult infant temperament into arguing, defiance, vindictiveness, intentionally annoying others, and blaming others for misbehavior (Sanson, Smart, Prior, and Oberklaid, 1993).

Harm avoidance. Cloninger (1987) identified a dimension of temperament and personality that he termed *harm avoidance.* Persons high in harm avoidance are cautious, apprehensive, shy, and inhibited. During infancy and early childhood, this construct also has been reffered to as "behavioral inhibition." ... We hypothesize that high levels of inhibitory harm avoidance protect children from the development of antisocial behavior, whereas low levels of harm avoidance predispose children to antisocial behavior. ...

Callousness. We propose the term *callousness* to refer to a dimension of temperament characterized by lack of sympathy for others, lack of helpfulness, selfishness, diminished guilt, reduced need for friends and social approval, and dampened displays of some emotions. In extreme cases, this dimension may include enjoyment of dominating, intimidating, embarrassing, and hurting others. Much work is needed to define and study the callousness dimension, but there is promising evidence that its key components are associated with antisocial behavior. ...

It is possible that the sensation-seeking aspects of Cloninger's dimension of novelty seeking is a fourth dimension of temperament that predisposes children to antisocial behavior. There is some evidence that children and adolescents who report a preference for adventurous and thrill-seeking activities over routine and safe activities are more likely to meet criteria for conduct disorder (Russo et al., 1991), and Farrington and West (1993) found that children rated as "daring" are more likely to be chronic offenders during adolescence and adulthood. . . .

Higher Intelligence Protects Against Antisocial Behavior

Better-developed cognitive skills, particularly verbal abilities, protect against the development of antisocial behavior. Although the mechanisms of this effect are unclear, we suspect that there are at least two kinds of contributions of cognitive skills to antisocial propensity. In early childhood, individual differences in intelligence are manifested partly as differences in the development of communication skills. Following Keenan and Shaw (1997), we posit that toddlers with better communication skills are easier to socialize and less frustrating to parents. Thus, lower verbal ability interferes with parents' early efforts to socialize their children. At later ages, youths with greater cognitive ability may be better able to anticipate the consequences of antisocial behavior and adopt appropriate alternative strategies. . . .

Parental Factors

Parental Antisocial Behavior

Youths who engage in high levels of antisocial behavior are much more likely than other youths to have a biological parent who also engages in chronic antisocial behavior (Farrington, 1995; Lahey et al., 1988). We hypothesize that this association reflects both the genetic transmission of predisposing temperament and the maladaptive parenting of antisocial parents.

Parenting and Antisocial Behavior in the Young

Variations in parenting behavior are hypothesized to play causal roles in the development of antisocial behavior. The importance of some aspects of parenting may differ at different ages, however. For example, lax supervision apparently plays a stronger role in late

childhood and adolescence than in early childhood (Reid and Patterson, 1989). As discussed below, we posit that parenting effects and child temperament are inter-related in a variety of highly important ways.

Harsh physical discipline. There is evidence from many studies that parental use of corporal punishment may play a causal role in the development of antisocial behavior. . . .

Parental supervision. In longitudinal studies, higher levels of parental supervision during childhood have been found to predict less antisocial behavior during adolescence, controlling for childhood antisocial behavior. . . .

Antisocial parent attitudes. Gottfredson and Hirschi (1990), West and Farrington (1973), and others have pointed to the fact that parents of antisocial youths often do not define antisocial behavior as something that should be discouraged. For example, some parents of youths who hit other children (in toddlerhood) or bully (in childhood) or shoplift (in adolescence) consider these to be normal and appropriate child behaviors. Thus, even if they supervise their child's behavior well enough to know that he or she engages in these behaviors, they would not attempt to discourage them.

Interplay of Child Characteristics and Parenting

Like Patterson (1982), Loeber (1991), and others, we hypothesize that parenting is an important factor because it plays a key role in the developmental transformation of predisposition into antisocial behavior. Cognitively and temperamentally disposed children are unlikely to develop antisocial behavior if they are raised in adaptive social environments (Reid and Patterson, 1989). It is unfortunate, then, that predisposing child temperament and lower intellectual ability are hypothesized to evoke exactly the kinds of coercive, harsh, nonresponsive, inconsistent, and negative parenting behaviors that transform temperament into antisocial behavior (Anderson, Lytton, and Romney, 1986;

Loeber and Tengs, 1986; Patterson, 1982). The reciprocal effects of (a) child behavior on the parent, and (b) parenting on the child's behavior often lead to escalation in child antisocial behavior and to escalation in parental harshness and the parent's abandonment of efforts to supervise (Patterson, 1982). In addition, temperamental differences that predispose youths to antisocial behavior evoke negative interactions with siblings (Loeber and Tengs, 1986; Patterson et al., 1989), which foster antisocial behavior.

Thresholds for parenting behaviors. Parents do not all respond to child behavior in the same way, however. We hypothesize that parents differ in their *thresholds* for reacting adversely to the child's difficult and challenging behavior (Lahey, Conger, Atkeson, and Treiber, 1984). These postulated differences in threshold lead one parent to respond harshly to a provocative misbehavior that another parent with a higher threshold would respond to adaptively. Such differences in thresholds for adverse reactions to child misbehavior are hypothesized to reflect both stable individual differences and fluctuations over time within individuals (Lahey et al., 1984). Antisocial and/or depressed parents are posited to have chronically low thresholds for responding adversely to challenging child behaviors. Therefore, they often react to the child's oppositional behaviors with coercive and harsh parenting behaviors (Lahey et al., 1984; Leadbeater, Bishop, and Raver, 1996; Patterson, DeBaryshe, and Ramsey, 1989). In addition, time-limited factors such as intoxication or daily hassles temporarily lower parental thresholds for adverse reactions to child misbehavior (Patterson et al., 1989). Parents whose thresholds are low, therefore, are more likely to react to challenging behaviors in ways that foster, rather than discourage, the development of their children's antisocial behavior. Although less is known about positive aspects of parenting, it also seems likely that parents differ in their thresholds for reacting positively to adaptive child behaviors.

Peer Influences

Like others, we hypothesize that peers influence one another to engage in antisocial behavior (Keenan, Loeber, and Zhang, 1995). Children with earlier ages of onset of antisocial behavior tend to have fewer well-behaved friends than other youths, but they often have friendships with other oppositional, aggressive children (Cairns and Cairns, 1994; Tremblay, Masse, Vitaro, and Dobkin, 1995). This is probably both because oppositional-aggressive children alienate themselves from their well-behaved peers and because they are attracted to one another (Cairns and Cairns, 1994). Data from two longitudinal studies suggest, however, that friendships with antisocial peers during elementary school do not influence the likelihood of engaging in antisocial behavior in the future among children who already display antisocial behavior (Bartusch, Lynam, Moffitt, and Silva, 1997; Tremblay et al., 1995). Antisocial children with earlier ages of onset undoubtedly teach one another new antisocial behaviors, and gang membership clearly leads to increases in severity of antisocial behavior (Thornberry, Krohn, Lizotte, and Chard-Wierschem, 1993), but friendships with antisocial peers during childhood do not increase their already high likelihood of continuing to engage in antisocial behavior.

The influence of delinquent peers on later-onset antisocial behavior appears to be much stronger. Bartusch et al. (1997) and Fergusson et al. (1996) found that association with antisocial peers was related to the later emergence of new antisocial behavior during adolescence among youths who had not exhibited behavior problems as children. Based on this evidence, delinquent peer influence is hypothesized to play a causal role in the development of antisocial behavior, but the strength of its influence increases with the age of onset of antisocial behavior....

We would not be surprised if temperamental characteristics of the child that predispose to antisocial behavior are eventually shown to interact with peer influences. Youths with very *low* levels of predisposition (i.e., low levels of oppositionality and callousness and high levels of harm avoidance and intelligence) might be *unlikely* to be influenced by peers to engage in antisocial behavior, however. That is, it is possible that very low levels of predisposition protect against peer influence throughout childhood and adolescence. . . .

Genetic Influences on Temperament and Antisocial Behavior

Many twin and adoption studies suggest that child and adolescent antisocial behavior is influenced by both genetic and environmental factors (Edelbrock, Rende, Plomin, and Thompson, 1995; Mason and Frick, 1994; Miles and Carey, 1997; Rowe, 1983; Rutter, 1997; Rutter et al., 1997). We hypothesize that genetic factors directly influence (1) cognitive and temperamental predispositions to antisocial behavior, and (2) the environments in which antisocial behavior is socialized. These predisposing child factors and socializing environments, in turn, influence antisocial behavior, but genetic influences are hypothesized to have no direct impact on antisocial behavior.

Many twin studies suggest that harm avoidance/behavior inhibition is moderately heritable among infants and children. . . . Similarly, twin studies of infants, children, and adults consistently suggest that empathy (the inverse of the key component of callousness) is moderately heritable (Davis, Luce, and Kraus, 1994; Emde et al., 1992; Rushton et al., 1986; Zahn-Waxler, Robinson, and Emde, 1992). Aspects of temperament very similar to oppositional temperament have been found to be moderately heritable in infants and toddlers (Cyphers et al., 1990; Goldsmith et al., 1997), and oppositional behavior itself has been found to be moderately to substantially heritable in 3-year-old children (van den Oord, Verhulst, and Boomsma, 1996) and adolescents (Eaves et al., 1997). Thus, there is reason to believe that the temperamental predispositions to antisocial behavior are moderately to highly heritable. . . .

Antisocial youths with earlier ages of onset tend to be highly oppositional and to engage in all three types of antisocial behavior (physical aggression, property crimes, and status offenses). For these youths, we hypothesize that genetic factors strongly influence the temperamental predispositions, particularly oppositional temperament, that drive the adverse social interactions that transform predisposition into antisocial behavior. Genetic factors contribute less to antisocial behavior that emerges later in childhood or adolescence. Antisocial youths with ages of onset in later childhood lack the high levels of oppositionality that are the foundation for physical aggression and are more likely to exhibit nonaggressive antisocial behaviors than physical aggression. These nonaggressive antisocial behaviors are posited to be primarily the result of shared environmental influences. At the oldest ages of onset of antisocial behavior, genetic factors are hypothesized to play little role. We suggest that such youths engage mostly in status offenses primarily because of peer influences and lapses in parenting. Heredity may continue to influence the onset of antisocial behavior even in adolescence, however. It seems likely that very low levels of temperamental and cognitive predisposition may protect against delinquent social influences at all ages . . . .

Genotype–Environment Interactions and Covariances

The second indirect route of genetic influence on antisocial behavior is through the social environment. Elaborating on the model of Reid and Patterson (1989), we hypothesize that the degree to which heritable early predisposition results in later antisocial behavior depends on the nature of the child's social environment. That is, highly adaptive parenting can do much to moderate temperamental predisposition in children who are genetically predisposed to antisocial behavior. The genetic and environmental contributions to the origins of antisocial behavior are not independent, however. Following others (Plomin,

DeFries, and Loehlin, 1977; Rutter et al., 1997), we hypothesize that there is common genetic variance underlying children's predisposition to antisocial behavior, their parents' antisocial behavior and parenting styles, and their sibling's temperament and behavior. This means that the temperament that the child brings to the family in early childhood and the nature of the family environment in which the child is raised are substantially correlated for genetic reasons. As a result, young children with the highest degree of temperamental and cognitive predisposition are usually raised in families that are ill-prepared to provide childrearing that could prevent the development of antisocial behavior. The developmental progression from predisposition to antisocial behavior is more likely because children with a genetic predisposition to antisocial behavior often have absent antisocial fathers and are raised by mothers who exhibit antisocial behavior, depression, and substance abuse (Lahey et al., 1988; Lahey, Russo, Walker, and Piacentini, 1989; Wahler and Hann, 1987; Wickramaratne and Weissman, 1998). Similarly, there is evidence that having friends who engage in delinquent behavior is influenced partly by genetics (Rowe and Osgood, 1984). Thus, we hypothesize that genotype–environment covariances that are *passive* (having parents with characteristics that are incompatible with adaptive parenting), *evocative* (displaying behavior that evokes maladaptive parenting), and *active* (seeking out delinquent peers for friendships) are involved in the development of antisocial behavior (Plomin et al., 1977; Rutter, 1997; Rutter et al., 1997).

Consistent with the present model, a number of adoption studies suggest that the likelihood of antisocial behavior in the adopted-away offspring of antisocial parents is significantly lower if they are raised by well-adjusted adoptive parents than by adoptive parents with mental health problems like those of their biological parents (Bohman, 1996; Cadoret, Yates, Troughton, Woodward, and Stewart, 1995). We suggest that the parenting responses of well-adjusted adoptive parents to the child's predisposing temperament

are more adaptive, largely because better-adjusted parents are less susceptible to maladaptive child effects (because their thresholds for adverse parenting reactions are higher), but also because well-adjusted adoptive parents bring more adaptive child-rearing attitudes and skills to parent–child transactions.

Gender Differences

From about 4 years of age on, boys are more likely than girls to engage in both aggressive and nonaggressive antisocial behavior (Keenan and Shaw, 1997; Lahey, Schwab-Stone, et al., 1998a; Tremblay et al., 1996). Much remains to be learned about the causes of gender differences in antisocial behavior, but based on what is known, we hypothesize that there are at least gender differences in the *levels* of the same causal variables that influence both girls and boys. For example, Keenan and Shaw (1997) reviewed evidence that shows that communication skills develop earlier in girls than boys. They suggested that this is one reason that girls are easier to socialize and that these differences in socialization play a role in creating gender differences in antisocial behavior. Although we assume that the development of communication skills plays the same role in girls and boys, boys tend to display lower levels of communication skills during the toddler years, which interferes with their socialization.

Similarly, there is some evidence that female toddlers and preschoolers show higher levels of empathy and guilt than males (Kochanska, De Vet, Goldman, Murray, and Putnam, 1994; Zahn-Waxler et al., 1992). We posit that callousness/lack of empathy plays the same role in the development of antisocial behavior in girls and boys, but that from an early age, boys display higher levels of callousness. This difference may reflect inherent gender differences in empathy, early gender differences in socialization that create differences in callousness, or both. A third example of differences in the factors that cause antisocial behavior can be found in gender differences in parenting. Parental disciplinary responses to difficult child temperament are hypothesized to play the same role in girls and boys, but there is evidence that parents respond differently to evocative temperament in girls and boys (Keenan and Shaw, 1997)....

Summary

In this paper we have described an integrative causal model of the development of antisocial behavior in children and adolescents....We believe that stable individual differences in propensity to antisocial behavior reflect variations in a number of dimensions of predisposing temperament and cognitive ability, each with its own genetic and environmental influences. The dimensions of predisposing temperament include oppositionality, harm avoidance, and callousness. Genetic influences are predicted to have only indirect effects on antisocial behavior via their influence on predisposition and on the youth's social environment. Environmental influences are expected to be important contributors to antisocial propensity, but these environmental influences reflect, in part, the genetic influences on the dimensions of predisposition (i.e., genotype–environment covariance). We also hypothesize that the levels of influence of the factors that determine individual differences in antisocial propensity change with development, such that genetic influences are of greater magnitude in early childhood and social influences contribute more strongly during later childhood and adolescence (both through independent effects and genotype–environment covariance). However, low levels of heritable predisposing child characteristics may protect against peer influences at all ages.

Discussion Questions

1. What major temperamental traits contribute to the propensity to engage in antisocial behavior? How are these traits similar to and different from those listed by Caspi et al. in Chapter 5?
2. Why does higher intelligence protect against antisocial behavior?
3. What major environmental factors contribute to antisocial behavior?
4. What do Lahey et al. mean by the "interplay of child characteristic and parenting"? More generally, how do temperamental and cognitive traits affect the social environments to which juveniles are exposed?
5. What do Lahey et al. mean when they state that temperamental traits and the social environment "interact" with environmental factors in affecting antisocial behavior? Give an example of such an interaction.
6. What do Lahey et al. mean by a "passive genotype–environment covariance"?
7. A sociologist states that crime can be fully explained in terms of the social environment. Develop an argument that will convince this sociologist that she is mistaken. You should list those non-environmental factors that impact crime and describe all the reasons why it is important to consider them (e.g., they influence crime, they influence the social environments to which people are exposed).

SECTION 2

The Rise and Growth of American Criminology

PART III

The Chicago School: The City, Social Disorganization, and Crime

PART IV

Learning to Be a Criminal: Differential Association, Subcultural, and Social Learning Theories

PART V

Anomie/Strain Theories of Crime

PART VI

Varieties of Control Theory

PART III

The Chicago School: The City, Social Disorganization, and Crime

As the United States proceeded into the 20th century, individualistic theories of crime enjoyed substantial popularity (Gould, 1981). Cesare Lombroso's biological theory, for example, was widely read and accepted (Lindesmith and Levin, 1937). In 1939, Harvard anthropologist E. A. Hooton not only claimed boldly that "criminals are organically inferior," but also proposed that "the elimination of crime can be effected only by the extirpation of the physically, mentally, and morally unfit; or by their complete segregation in a social aseptic environment" (quoted in Vold and Bernard, 1986: 6). Hooton's work may have been extreme, even for its time (see Merton and Montagu, 1940), but it represented a way of thinking that persists more than six decades later: The seeds of crime lie within people and the only way to protect public safety is to incapacitate this dangerous class (see Herrnstein and Murray, 1994; compare with Cullen et al., 1997 and Gordon, 1994).

Other social observers in the early part of the century, however, criticized these individualistic theories for their myopia. While criminal anthropologists like Lombroso and Hooton focused their attention on discerning whether criminals had larger foreheads or more tattoos than non-criminals, they ignored the larger changes in society that were occuring around them. The United States was rapidly moving into the modern era, transforming itself from a land

sprinkled with small, stable farming communities into a land dominated by crowded cities that were centered around booming industries and whose residents were constantly in flux. For these social observers, it defied common sense not to see how these vast changes were intimately implicated in the cause of crime. In fact, they claimed that our understanding of the origins and prevention of criminal conduct depended on a careful study of how the forces *outside* individuals prompted their willingness to break the law.

Social Disorganization in the City

Perhaps nowhere was social change more rapid and more dramatic than in the city of Chicago. When first incorporated in 1833, Chicago had a population of just over 4,000. By 1890, this number had climbed to 1 million, and in just 20 years, the population had doubled to 2 million (Palen, 1981). Sheer numbers, however, capture only part of the changes that were taking place. Like other large cities, Chicago was the settling place for virtually every racial and ethnic group, as African Americans traveled to the North in search of a better life and immigrants from Europe ended their journey in the "windy city" that butted up against Lake Michigan. These urban newcomers typically secured work at and settled in the shadows of factories erected in the center of the city. Their lives were hard—they worked long hours in the factories and lived in overcrowded tenements dirtied by industrial pollution. Upton Sinclair captured the social reality of these inner-city neighborhoods in the title of his book, *The Jungle* (1905).

In this context, it may not be surprising that scholars at the University of Chicago believed that the key to understanding crime lay not in studying the traits of individuals but in studying the traits of neighborhoods. Did it make a difference, they asked, if a child grew up in an inner-city community that was characterized by poverty, a mixing together of diverse peoples (i.e., "heterogeneity"), and by people constantly moving in and, when able, moving out (i.e., "transiency")? And if so, might not the solution to crime lay more in changing neighborhoods than in changing people?

This line of inquiry was developed most clearly by Clifford Shaw and Henry McKay (1942 [Chapter 7 in this volume]), who worked at the Institute for Social Research in Chicago and who were deeply influenced by the thinking of sociologists at the University of Chicago. To explain how cities such as Chicago develop, Ernest Burgess (1967[1925]) had theorized that urban areas grow through a process of continual expansion from their inner core toward outer areas. As this growth process matures, we find cities that have a central business or industrial area. Just outside this area is the "zone in transition." It is here that impoverished newcomers settle, attracted by factory jobs and inexpensive housing. In a series of concentric circles, three more zones exist outside the inner city; Burgess called these the "zone of workingmen's homes," the "residential zone," and the "commuters' zone." These areas are settled by people who have adjusted to city life and have accumulated the resources to leave the zone in transition.

Shaw and McKay believed that Burgess's theory of the city might help direct their investigations of juvenile delinquency. If Burgess was correct, then rates of delinquency should be higher in the inner-city areas. In these locations, the intersection of persistent poverty, rapid population growth, heterogeneity, and transiency combined to disrupt the core social institutions of society such as the family; that is, these conditions caused *social disorganization*. They hypothesized that delinquency would be higher in these communities and lower in neighborhoods that were more affluent and stable (i.e., "organized").

But how would they test these ideas? In an innovative and enormous effort in data collection, whose results were published in *Juvenile Delinquency and Urban Areas* (1942), Shaw and McKay analyzed how measures of crime—such as youths referred to the juvenile court, truancy, and recidivism—were distributed in the zones of the city. By hand, they mapped the addresses of each delinquent, which they then compiled to compute rates of delinquency by census track and then by city zone. They discovered that over time, rates of crime by *area* remained relatively the same—regardless, that is, of which ethnic group resided there. This finding suggested that characteristics of the area, not of the individuals living in the area, regulated levels of delinquency. They also learned, as their theory predicted, that crime rates were pronounced in the zone of transition and became progressively lower as one moved away from the inner city toward the outer zones. This finding supported their contention that social disorganization was a major cause of delinquency (Bursik and Grasmick, 1993: 30–31).

Just how did social disorganization cause delinquency? Unfortunately, Shaw and McKay did not supply a refined discussion of this concept in which they systematically explored the dimensions of disorganization and how each one was criminogenic (Bursik and Grasmick, 1993). Even so, they broadly suggested that social disorganization referred to the breakdown of the social institutions in a community. In the inner city, then, families would be disrupted, schools would be marked by disorder, adult-run activities for youths would be sparse, churches would be poorly attended, and political groups would be ineffectual. When such a pervasive breakdown occurred, adults would be unable to control youths or to stop competing forms of criminal organization from emerging (e.g., gangs, vice activities). This combination was highly criminogenic. Freed from adult control, youths roamed the streets, where they came into contact with older juveniles who transmitted to them criminal values and skills (see also Thrasher, 1927).

Shaw and McKay gained many of their insights on the process by which youths become embedded in delinquency from in-depth interviews—"life histories"—that they conducted with wayward adolescents (see, e.g., Shaw, 1966 [1930]). In *The Natural History of a Delinquent Career* (1976 [1931]), for example, Shaw compiled the story of Sidney Blotzman, who by age 16 had engaged in numerous crimes, including robbery and sexual assault. Shaw recorded that Sidney had begun his "career in delinquency" by age 7, a career that persisted and grew more serious as he matured. Referring to Sidney's story, Shaw noted that due to his associations with older delinquents and adult criminals, the boy "began to identify himself with the criminal world and to embody in his own philosophy of life the moral values which prevailed in the criminal groups with which he had contact" (p. 228).

But why was Sidney exposed to these criminogenic influences? Here, Shaw reminds the reader that Sidney "lived in one of the most deteriorated and disorganized sections of the city" (p. 229). In these communities, continued Shaw, "the conventional traditions, neighborhood institutions, and public opinion, through which neighborhoods usually effect a control over the behavior [of the] child, were largely disintegrated" (p. 229). The community, however, "was not only disorganized and thus ineffective as a unit of control"; in addition, "various forms of stealing and many organized delinquent and criminal gangs were prevalent in the area" (p. 229). These criminal groups competed for the lives, in effect, of the area's children. "These groups," observed Shaw, "exercised a powerful influence and

tended to create a community spirit which not only tolerated but actually fostered delinquent and criminal practices" (p. 229).

In Parts IV and VI, we will discuss two theoretical traditions whose roots extend to the work of Shaw and McKay: differential association/social learning theory and control theory. Thus, the work of Edwin Sutherland (Chapter 10) draws directly on Shaw and McKay's contentions that social areas have different mixes of criminal and conventional influences, and that the exposure to and learning of criminal values, mainly by associating with others in the same neighborhood, is a key source of crime. Sutherland captures these ideas in his "theory of differential association," which is an effort to systematize the insights of Shaw and McKay and of other Chicago School theorists (see, e.g., Thrasher's 1927 work, *The Gang*). Similarly, early statements of control theory, such as that by Reckless (1961) and that by Reiss (1951)—both of whom studied at the University of Chicago—build directly from Shaw and McKay's observations and helped to lay the foundation for today's control theories.

It is ironic that in contemporary criminology, these two traditions, which branched off from Shaw and McKay, now are seen as rival theories of crime (compare Akers, 1998, and Matsueda, 1988, with Costello, 1997, Gottfredson and Hirschi, 1990, and Kornhauser, 1978). Although some efforts have been made to *integrate* these two perspectives (see Part XIV), most often advocates of learning and control theories see themselves as advancing incompatible perspectives, only one of which can be correct.

Revitalizing Social Disorganization Theory

Although Shaw and McKay's work was read by subsequent generations of criminologists, by the 1960s their theory of social disorganization had lost its appeal and its ability to direct research. Instead, other theories, advocating new ways of thinking and identifying new questions to be answered, ascended and captured scholars' attention (see Cole, 1975; Pfohl, 1985). Beginning in the 1980s, however, Shaw and McKay's disorganization perspective earned renewed interest—an interest that has remained until this day.

In part, criminologists reconsidered the value of disorganization theory because of a more general interest in the "ecology" of crime. This approach analyzes how crime rates vary by *ecological units*, such as neighborhoods, cities, countries, states, or nations. (Recall that Shaw and McKay examined how delinquency rates varied by zones of the city.) This approach is often seen as being on the "macro-level." In *micro*-level theories, the concern is with identifying how characteristics of *individuals* (e.g., personality, how much strain a person feels) are related to their involvement in criminal behavior. In *macro*-level theories, however, individuals and their traits are not studied; the concern is only with how the characteristics of geographical areas, such as whether they are disorganized, influence crime rates.

In 1982, Judith and Peter Blau published an article that captured the attention of criminologists. Examining 125 of the largest metropolitan areas in the United States, they found that violence was more pronounced in urban areas marked by socioeconomic inequality, especially by a wide gap in riches between African Americans and whites. Indeed, "high rates of criminal violence," concluded the Blaus, "are apparently the price of racial and economic inequalities" (p. 126). This analysis showed the important insights that a macro-level study could uncover. It also was a reminder that governmental policies that increased inequality—such as those embraced in the administration of President Reagan—might make our streets less safe (see also Currie, 1985). At a time when individualistic theories were gaining in prominence (recall that Wilson and Herrnstein's *Crime and Human Nature* was published in 1985), the Blaus' research spoke to the continuing relevance of community characteristics in understanding the roots of crime in America.

Beyond the general interest in ecological research (see Bursik and Grasmick, 1993; Byrne and Sampson, 1986; Reiss and Tonry, 1986), Robert Sampson was most responsible for specifically showing the relevance of using Shaw and McKay's theory to illuminate crime in today's society (see also Bursik, 1988; Pratt and Cullen, 2005). Sampson (1986) argued that crime was high in inner cities because the residents had lost the capacity to exercise "informal social control." Especially in neighborhoods where most families were "broken," the adult resources needed to supervise youths and involve them in wholesome activities were depleted. Coming from a broken home per se was not the key issue, said Sampson. Rather, it was living in a neighborhood where a high proportion of families were headed by a single parent that created a context in which control could not be exercised effectively. Like Shaw and McKay, Sampson stressed that independent of the traits of individuals, communities varied in their capacity to regulate conduct and suppress criminal behavior.

With W. Byron Groves, Sampson (1989) extended this research. Using data from the British Crime Survey, the authors tested Shaw and McKay's idea that in communities marked by poverty, heterogeneity, residential transiency, and family disruption, informal relations and controls would be weakened and, as a result, crime would be high. Previously, empirical tests of Shaw and McKay's perspective had only measured the structural "antecedents" or causes of social disorganization and then examined whether these factors were related to crime (e.g., do communities with more residential mobility have higher rates of crime). These studies took for granted that the social condition in between these structural factors (on the "left" side of the causal chain) and illegal conduct (on the "right" side of the causal chain) was social disorganization. In large part, scholars did not measure social disorganization directly because the existing data sets did not contain information on the extent to which community members were socially integrated and able to exercise social control over wayward conduct. Instead, they were able to compile data on structural factors from the U.S. Census and data on crime rates from the FBI's Uniform Crime Reports. Meanwhile, they had no direct measures of the "black box" that lay in between structural factors and crime rates. Again, they merely assumed that this "black box" was a weak or "disorganized" community.

The special value of Sampson and Groves's study was that the British Crime Survey included questions that could be combined to measure whether community members were willing to supervise rowdy teenagers, had friends locally, and participated in neighborhood voluntary organizations. The more these conditions were present, hypothesized Sampson and Groves, the greater the level of social organization; the less these conditions were present, the greater the level of social disorganization. When Sampson and Groves conducted their statistical analysis, they discovered that, to a large extent, the structural factors predicted their measures of social disorganization and, in turn, that weakly organized areas did indeed have higher crime rates. In short, their data lent support to Shaw and McKay's conclusion that social disorganization was a significant cause of community rates of crime (see also Bursik and Grasmick, 1993; Sampson and Lauritsen, 1994).

It is possible, of course, that other community factors, such as the presence of delinquent subcultures, could also intervene between structural factors such as poverty and transiency and crime (Veysey and Messner, 1999). Still, subsequent research has replicated Sampson and Groves's research with data drawn a decade later from the British Crime Survey, thus indicating that Sampson and Groves's results have proven to be consistent over time (Lowenkamp et al., 2003; see also Taylor, 2001). More generally, Sampson and Groves's article furnished persuasive evidence that the social disorganization perspective had a measure of validity and warranted further empirical and theoretical investigation. Indeed, this article generated considerable excitement and did much to revitalize Shaw and McKay's theory. It was not a theory tied to a particular historical juncture—pre-World War II America—but could provide insights into community differences in rates of crime in contemporary times.

Extending Social Disorganization Theory

Theories of crime, however, are not sacred icons to be worshiped at the altar of criminology. No matter how persuasive and elegantly stated, theoretical paradigms should be viewed as provisional understandings of social reality—important in what they allow us to see but not sacrosanct. The challenge is to illuminate how such works might be reconsidered and their explanatory power improved. In this regard, Robert Sampson has recently engaged in two lines of inquiry that have extended Shaw and McKay's social disorganization theory in noteworthy ways.

First, in an important essay coauthored with William Julius Wilson, he extends social disorganization theory by placing it within the realities of contemporary America (see Chapter 8 in this part). Sampson and Wilson (1995) accept the basic thesis of disorganization theory that a breakdown of community controls, rooted in structural conditions, is criminogenic. They argue, however, that the Chicago school was incorrect in seeing social disorganization as a "natural" part of the process by which cities grow. Instead, variations in disorganization across communities are intimately linked to *racial inequality* (see Blau and Blau, 1982; Currie, 1985; Peterson et al., 2006; Pfohl, 1985).

Independent of their individual socioeconomic status, African Americans are much more likely to reside in neighborhoods where there is a *concentration* of severe poverty and widespread family disruption ("broken homes")—conditions that spawn disorganization (Sampson and Bean, 2006; Wilson, 2009). Why is this so? According to Sampson and

Wilson, "macrostructural factors"—some economic, some conscious political decisions—are responsible for disproportionately consigning African Americans to these inner-city neighborhoods. These factors include, for example, the loss of jobs due to the deindustrialization of the American economy; the departure of middle-class blacks—who provided the social glue that helped to hold neighborhoods together—to more affluent areas; policies that channeled blacks into dense, high-rise public housing; the lack of investment in keeping up the housing stock in inner-city neighborhoods; and urban renewal that displaced African Americans from their homes and disrupted their communities (see Wilson, 1987, 1996, 2009).

Sampson and Wilson also rekindle the cultural side of social disorganization theory. Although their argument differs somewhat from Shaw and McKay's, they follow these early Chicago theorists in proposing that structural conditions affect the content of the culture in communities. For Sampson and Wilson, the near apartheid conditions in which many African Americans live (see Massey and Denton, 1993) create intense "social isolation—defined as the lack of contact or of sustained interaction with individuals and institutions that represent mainstream society" (1995: 51). In response, cultural values emerge that do not so much approve of violence and crime but rather define such actions as an unavoidable part of life in the ghetto (see Anderson, Chapter 12 in Part IV; Sampson and Bean, 2006).

In the end, state Sampson and Wilson (1995: 53), the "intersection of race, place, and poverty goes to the heart of our theoretical concerns with society and community organization." The result is that race-based inequality in urban areas fosters the breakdown of the conventional institutions and cultural values needed to restrain criminal conduct. The cost of this inequality is borne most fully by African Americans, who must live in communities where one in 21 black males will be murdered in his lifetime (the rate for white males is 1 in 131) (Sampson and Wilson, 1995: 36).

Second, in conjunction with Stephen Raudenbush and Felton Earls, Robert Sampson (1997) attempts to further elaborate the social disorganization approach in a study that examines rates of violence across 343 Chicago neighborhoods (see Chapter 9 in this part). These authors show that "concentrated disadvantage"—a combined measure of a community's poverty, race and age composition, and family disruption—is related to neighborhood rates of violence, even controlling for the characteristics of the people surveyed. Importantly, they reveal that the effects of concentrated disadvantage are largely mediated by—that is, occur through—the degree of "collective efficacy" in the neighborhood.

But what is this concept of "collective efficacy"? As envisioned by Sampson and his coauthors, collective efficacy is a concept that includes the willingness of community residents both to exercise informal control (e.g., telling youths to quiet down) and to trust and help one another. In a way, the concept of efficacy seems like the opposite of social disorganization (Taylor, 2001: 128). If so, nothing much would be new theoretically, because Sampson et al. would merely be describing the opposite end of the continuum—that is, what an organized community looks like in contrast to a disorganized community. Clearly, there is theoretical overlap between the concepts of "social disorganization" and "collective efficacy," but Sampson and his colleagues are also offering something fresh. Although their ideas are rooted in social disorganization theory, they enrich this perspective in two important ways.

First, whereas Shaw and McKay largely envisioned social organization (as opposed to disorganization) as the presence of *control*, Sampson et al. have added a second component: the notion that neighbors *mutually trust or support one another* (Sampson et al., 1999: 635). Trust or social support is important because it provides a basis on which neighbors might expect others to collaborate with them—to stand behind them—when it becomes necessary to exercise social support (see also Cullen, 1994—Chapter 46 in this volume). Indeed, empirically, trust and the willingness to engage in informal control are highly intercorrelated. As Sampson et al. found, in reality, control and trust are coterminous; that is, "you don't get one without the other."

Second, social disorganization is typically portrayed as a "condition"—as a state of being into which a person moves or is born. In this sense, it is a *static* factor, or something that more or less constantly surrounds those in a neighborhood. In contrast, Sampson and his colleagues envision collective efficacy as a *dynamic* factor. It is a resource that can be mobilized when the need arises—such as when teenagers become unruly on a street corner or when drug dealers brazenly establish a "crack house" in the neighborhood.

Collective efficacy thus is not simply being organized and having close social ties, but rather is the "*process* of activating or converting social ties to achieve desired outcomes" (Sampson et al., 1999: 635, emphasis in the original). Communities with weak collective efficacy lack the closeness and trust—sometimes called "social capital"—to mobilize as a group and rid their street of troublemakers and disorder (e.g., by personally confronting people, by forming crime watches, by pressuring politicians and the police to "do something" about the problems they face). In contrast, communities high on collective efficacy can amass a unified front to make life for the wayward in their neighborhood uncomfortable by watching them closely, telling them to go elsewhere, and, if necessary, exerting political pressure and getting the police involved (Sampson, 2006).

Although Sampson and his colleagues' recent writings offer important ideas and promise to generate new lines of empirical research, their thinking and findings reinforce the essential truth of Shaw and McKay's theorizing: that is, that strong communities can act to quell disorder while communities weakened by structural problems will be fertile soil for the growth of crime. This general theoretical orientation reminds us that individuals are not islands free from outside influences, but rather are enmeshed in a web of social relations that increase or decrease one's power to influence what transpires in one's neighborhood. Those with the misfortune of residing in isolated, impoverished, disorganized communities have the double difficulty of being exposed to conditions that might permit their criminal involvement and of being less able to do anything about crime when it occurs around them. Thus, they are at risk of being drawn into a criminal lifestyle on the one hand and on the other of being unable to prevent the disorder and victimization they witness, if not personally experience. The vitality and efficacy of community life and relations, as Shaw and McKay understood, matter greatly; this is an insight that must be included in any systematic explanation of the uneven distribution of crime in American society.

References

Akers, Ronald L. 1998. *Social Learning and Social Structure: A General Theory of Crime and Deviance*. Boston: Northeastern University Press.

Blau, Judith R. and Peter M. Blau. 1982. "The Cost of Inequality: Metropolitan Structure and Violent Crime." *American Sociological Review* 47: 114–129.

Burgess, Ernest W. 1967 [originally published in 1925]. "The Growth of the City: An Introduction to a Research Project." In Robert E. Park and Ernest W. Burgess (eds.), *The City*, pp. 47–62. Chicago: University of Chicago Press.

Bursik, Robert J., Jr. 1988. "Social Disorganization and Theories of Crime and Delinquency." *Criminology* 26: 519–551.

Bursik, Robert J., Jr. and Harold G. Grasmick. 1993. *Neighborhoods and Crime: The Dimensions of Effective Community Control*. New York: Lexington.

Byrne, James M. and Robert J. Sampson, eds. 1986. *The Social Ecology of Crime*. New York: Springer-Verlag.

Cole, Stephen. 1975. "The Growth of Scientific Knowledge: Theories of Crime as a Case Study." In Lewis A. Coser (ed.), *The Idea of Social Structure: Papers in Honor of Robert K. Merton*, pp. 175–220. New York: Harcourt Brace Jovanovich.

Costello, Barbara. 1997. "On the Logical Adequacy of Cultural Deviance Theories." *Theoretical Criminology* 1: 403–428.

Cullen, Francis T. 1994. "Social Support as an Organizing Concept for Criminology: Presidential Address to the Academy of Criminal Justice Sciences." *Justice Quarterly* 11: 527–559.

Cullen, Francis T., Paul Gendreau, G. Roger Jarjoura, and John Paul Wright. 1997. "Crime and the Bell Curve: Lessons From Intelligent Criminology." *Crime and Delinquency* 43: 387–411.

Currie, Elliott. 1985. *Confronting Crime: An American Challenge*. New York: Pantheon.

Gordon, Diana R. 1994. *The Return of the Dangerous Classes: Drug Prohibition and Policy Politics*. New York: Norton.

Gottfredson, Michael G. and Travis Hirschi. 1990. A *General Theory of Crime*. Stanford, CA: Stanford University Press.

Gould, Stephen Jay. 1981. *The Mismeasure of Man*. New York: Norton.

Herrnstein, Richard J. and Charles Murray. 1994. *The Bell Curve: Intelligence and Class Structure in American Life*. New York: The Free Press.

Kornhauser, Ruth Rosner. 1978. *Social Sources of Delinquency: An Appraisal of Analytic Models*. Chicago: University of Chicago Press.

Lindesmith, Alfred and Yale Levin. 1937. "The Lombrosian Myth in Criminology." *American Journal of Sociology* 42: 653–671.

Lowenkamp, Christopher T., Francis T. Cullen, and Travis C. Pratt. 2003. "Replicating Sampson and Groves's Test of Social Disorganization Theory: Revisiting a Criminological Classic." *Journal of Research in Crime and Delinquency* 40: 351–373.

Massey, Douglas S. and Nancy A. Denton. 1993. *American Apartheid: Segregation and the Making of the Underclass*. Cambridge, MA: Harvard University Press.

Matsueda, Ross L. 1988. "The Current State of Differntial Association Theory". *Crime and Delinquency* 34: 277–306.

Merton, Robert K. and M. F. Ashley Montagu. 1940. "Crime and the Anthropologist." *American Anthropologist* 42: 384–408.

Palen, John J. 1981. *The Urban World*, 3rd edition. New York: McGraw-Hill.

Peterson, Ruth D., Lauren J. Krivo, and Christopher R. Browning. 2006. "Segregation and Race/Ethnic Inequality in Crime: New Directions." In Francis T. Cullen, John Paul Wright, and Kristie R. Blevins (eds.), *Taking Stock: The Status of Criminological Theory—Advances in Criminological Theory*, Volume 15, pp. 169–187. New Brunswick, NJ: Transaction.

Pfohl, Stephen J. 1985. *Images of Deviance and Social Control: A Sociological History*. New York: McGraw-Hill.

Pratt, Travis C. and Francis T. Cullen. 2005. "Assessing Macro-Level Predictors and Theories of Crime: A Meta-Analysis." In Michael Tonry (ed.), *Crime and Justice: A Review of Research*, Volume 32, pp. 373–450. Chicago: University of Chicago Press.

Reckless, Walter C. 1961. *The Crime Problem*, 3rd edition. New York: Appleton-Century-Crofts.

Reiss, Albert J., Jr. 1951. "Delinquency as the Failure of Personal and Social Controls." *American Sociological Review* 16: 196–207.

Reiss, Albert J., Jr. and Michael Tonry (eds.), 1986. *Communities and Crime*. Chicago: University of Chicago Press.

Sampson, Robert J. 1986. "Crime in Cities: The Effects of Formal and Informal Social Control." In Albert J. Reiss, Jr. and Michael Tonry (eds.), *Communities and Crime*, pp. 271–311. Chicago: University of Chicago Press.

——. 2006. "Collective Efficacy Theory: Lessons Learned and Directions for Future Inquiry." In Francis T. Cullen, John Paul Wright, and Kristie R. Blevins (eds.), *Taking Stock: The Status of Criminological Theory—Advances in Criminological Theory*, Volume 15, pp. 149–167. New Brunswick, NJ: Transaction.

Sampson, Robert J. and Lydia Bean. 2006. "Cultural Mechanisms and Killing Fields: A Revised Theory of Community-Level Racial Inequality." In Ruth D. Peterson, Lauren J. Krivo, and John Hagan (eds.), *The Many Colors of Crime*, pp. 8–36. New York: New York University Press.

Sampson, Robert J. and W. Byron Groves. 1989. "Community Structure and Crime: Testing Social-Disorganization Theory." *American Journal of Sociology* 94: 774–802.

Sampson, Robert J. and Janet Lauritsen. 1994. "Violent Victimization and Offending: Individual, Situational, and Community-Level Risk Factors. "In Albert J. Reiss, Jr. and Jeffrey A. Roth (eds.), *Understanding and Preventing Violence: Social Influences* Vol. 3, pp. 1–114. Washington, DC: National Academy Press.

Sampson, Robert J., Jeffrey D. Morenoff, and Felton Earls. 1999. "Beyond Social Capital: Spatial Dynamics of Collective Efficacy for Children." *American Sociological Review* 64: 633–660.

Sampson, Robert J., Stephen W. Raudenbush, and Felton Earls. 1997. "Neighborhoods and Violent Crime: A Multilevel Study of Collective Efficacy." *Science* 277 (August 15): 918–924.

Sampson, Robert J. and William Julius Wilson. 1995. "Toward a Theory of Race, Crime, and Urban Inequality." In John Hagan and Ruth D. Peterson (eds.), *Crime and Inequality*, pp. 36–54. Stanford, CA: Stanford University Press.

Shaw, Clifford R. 1966 [originally published in 1930]. *The Jack-Roller: A Delinquent Boy's Own Story.* Chicago: University of Chicago Press.

Shaw, Clifford R. and Henry D. McKay. 1942. *Juvenile Delinquency and Urban Areas.* Chicago: University of Chicago Press.

Shaw, Clifford R., with Maurice E. Moore. 1976. [originally published in 1931]. *The Natural History of a Delinquent Career.* Chicago: University of Chicago Press.

Sinclair, Upton. 1905. *The Jungle.* New York: Signet.

Taylor, Ralph B. 2001. "The Ecology of Crime, Fear, and Delinquency: Social Disorganization Versus Social Efficacy." In Raymond Paternoster and Ronet Bachman (eds.), *Explaining Criminals and Crime: Essays in Contemporary Criminological Theory*, pp. 124–139. Los Angeles: Roxbury.

Thrasher, Frederic M. 1927. *The Gang: A Study of 1,313 Gangs in Chicago.* Chicago: University of Chicago Press.

Veysey, Bonita M. and Steven F. Messner. 1999 "Further Testing of Social Disorganization Theory: An Elaboration of Sampson and Groves' 'Community Structure and Crime.'" *Journal of Research in Crime and Delinquency* 36: 156–174.

Vold, George B. and Thomas J. Bernard. 1986. *Theoretical Criminology*, 3rd edition. New York: Oxford University Press.

Wilson, William Julius. 1987. *The Truly Disadvantaged: The Inner City, the Underclass, and Public Policy.* Chicago: University of Chicago Press.

——. 1996. *When Work Disappears: The World of the New Urban Poor.* New York: Alfred A. Knopf.

——. 2009. *More Than Just Race: Being Black and Poor in the Inner City.* New York: W.W. Norton.

7. Juvenile Delinquency and Urban Areas

Clifford R. Shaw and Henry D. McKay

"Delinquency," observed Shaw and McKay in their classic book Juvenile Delinquency in Urban Areas, *"has its roots in the dynamic life of the community" (1942: 435). Theories that focus only on personality or biological traits ignore that youths are surrounded by a community that they interact with over many years. These daily experiences, claimed Shaw and McKay, shape patterns of behavior.*

Not all communities, however, are the same. Surveying the urban landscape, Shaw and McKay noted that in more affluent communities, "the similarity of attitudes and values as to social control is expressed in institutions and voluntary associations designed to perpetuate and protect these values" (p. 165). But in areas wracked by poverty and constant social change, the conventional institutions become weak and a value system supportive of crime is nurtured. Shaw and McKay recognized that even in disorganized inner-city communities, parents and other adults try to inculcate children with moral values. However, they must compete against a range of criminal influences—gangs, adult criminals, ongoing illegal enterprises—that simply are not present in organized communities. Further, these influences are difficult to uproot; once delinquent traditions take hold, they are transmitted from one generation to the next, typically through interactions in neighborhood peer groups.

One criticism of Shaw and McKay's theory is that it paints too rosy a picture of communities outside the inner city. Although serious predatory crimes are more pronounced in ghetto areas, delinquency is commonplace among youths in all communities. It is possible that social disorganization and cultural values supportive of crime are more evenly spread across communities than Shaw and McKay anticipated.

Finally, Shaw and McKay's perspective has important policy implications: If community disorganization is the main source of delinquency, then the solution to crime is to organize communities. Toward this end, in the early 1930s Shaw took steps to put theory into practice by initiating the Chicago Area Project, called the "first systematic challenge to the dominance of psychology and psychiatry in public and private programs for the prevention and treatment of juvenile delinquency" (Schlossman et al., 1984). The Project involved such activities as creating recreational programs, sprucing up the physical appearances of the neighborhood so as to reduce signs of disorder, working with school or criminal justice officials to see how problem youths might be helped, and using community residents to counsel the neighborhood's youngsters. The precise effectiveness of the Chicago Area Project is not known, although some evidence exists that it helped to reduce delinquency (Schlossman et al., 1984). Regardless, the Project illuminates an insight that has relevance to today: Interventions—whether by the police or by correctional officials—that ignore

Reprinted from Clifford R. Shaw and Henry D. McKay, *Juvenile Delinquency and Urban Areas*. Copyright ©1942 by the University of Chicago Press. Reprinted by permission of the University of Chicago Press.

community dynamics will be limited in their ability to prevent the onset of criminal conduct.

Reference

Schlossman, Steven, Gail Zellman, and Richard Shavelson, with Michael Sedlak and Jane Cobb. 1984. *Delinquency Prevention in South Chicago: A Fifty-Year Assessment of the Chicago Area Project.* Santa Monica, CA: RAND.

It is clear from the data included in this volume that there is a direct relationship between conditions existing in local communities of American cities and differential rates of delinquents and criminals. Communities with high rates have social and economic characteristics which differentiate them from communities with low rates. Delinquency—particularly group delinquency, which constitutes a preponderance of all officially recorded offenses committed by boys and young men—has its roots in the dynamic life of the community.

. . . It may be observed, in the first instance, that the variations in rates of officially recorded delinquents in communities of the city correspond very closely with variations in economic status. The communities with the highest rates of delinquents are occupied by those segments of the population whose position is most disadvantageous in relation to the distribution of economic, social, and cultural values. Of all the communities in the city, these have the fewest facilities for acquiring the economic goods indicative of status and success in our conventional culture. Residence in the community is in itself an indication of inferior status, from the standpoint of persons residing in the more prosperous areas. It is a handicap in securing employment and in making satisfactory advancement in industry and the professions. Fewer opportunities are provided for securing the training, education, and contacts which facilitate advancement in the fields of business, industry, and the professions.

The communities with the lowest rates of delinquents, on the other hand, occupy a relatively high position in relation to the economic and social hierarchy of the city. Here the residents are relatively much more secure; and adequate provision is offered to young people for securing the material possessions symbolic of success and the education, training, and personal contacts which facilitate their advancement in the conventional careers they may pursue. . . .

Differential Systems of Values

In general, the more subtle differences between types of communities in Chicago may be encompassed within the general proposition that in the areas of low rates of delinquents there is more or less uniformity, consistency, and universality of conventional values and attitudes with respect to child care, conformity to law, and related matters; whereas in the high-rate areas systems of competing and conflicting moral values have developed. Even though in the latter situation conventional traditions and institutions are dominant, delinquency has developed as a powerful competing way of life. It derives its impelling force in the boy's life from the fact that it provides a means of securing economic gain, prestige, and other human satisfactions and is embodied in delinquent groups and criminal organizations, many of which have great influence, power, and prestige.

In the areas of high economic status where the rates of delinquents are low there is, in general, a similarity in the attitudes of the residents with reference to conventional values, as has been said, especially those related to the welfare of children. This is illustrated by the practical unanimity of opinion as to the desirability of education and constructive leisure-time activities and of the need for a general health program. It is shown, too, in the subtle, yet easily recognizable, pressure exerted upon children to keep them engaged in conventional activities, and in the resistance offered by the community to behavior which threatens the conventional values. It does not follow that all the activities participated in by members of the community are lawful; but, since any unlawful pursuits are likely to be carried out in other parts of the city, children living in the low-rate communities are, on the whole, insulated from direct contact with these deviant forms of adult behavior.

In the middle-class areas and the areas of high economic status, moreover, the similarity of attitudes and values as to social control is expressed in institutions and voluntary associations designed to perpetuate and protect these values. Among these may be included such organizations as the parent-teachers associations, women's clubs, service clubs, churches, neighborhood centers, and the like. Where these institutions represent dominant values, the child is exposed to, and participates in a significant way in one mode of life only. While he may have knowledge of alternatives, they are not integral parts of the system in which he participates.

In contrast, the areas of low economic status, where the rates of delinquents are high, are characterized by wide diversity in norms and standards of behavior. The moral values range from those that are strictly conventional to those in direct opposition to conventionality as symbolized by the family, the church, and other institutions common to our general society. The deviant values are symbolized by groups and institutions ranging from adult criminal gangs engaged in theft and the marketing of stolen goods, on the one hand, to quasi-legitimate businesses and the rackets through which partial or complete control of legitimate business is sometimes exercised, on the other. Thus, within the same community, theft may be defined as right and proper in some groups and as immoral, improper, and undesirable in others. In some groups wealth and prestige are secured through acts of skill and courage in the delinquent or criminal world, while in neighboring groups any attempt to achieve distinction in this manner would result in extreme disapprobation. Two conflicting systems of economic activity here present roughly

equivalent opportunities for employment and for promotion. Evidence of success in the criminal world is indicated by the presence of adult criminals whose clothes and automobiles indicate unmistakably that they have prospered in their chosen fields. The values missed and the greater risks incurred are not so clearly apparent to the young.

Children living in such communities are exposed to a variety of contradictory standards and forms of behavior rather than to a relatively consistent and conventional pattern. More than one type of moral institution and education are available to them. A boy may be familiar with, or exposed to, either the system of conventional activities or the system of criminal activities, or both. Similarly, he may participate in the activities of groups which engage mainly in delinquent activities, those concerned with conventional pursuits, or those which alternate between the two worlds. His attitudes and habits will be formed largely in accordance with the extent to which he participates in and becomes identified with one or the other of these several types of groups.

Conflicts of values necessarily arise when boys are brought in contact with so many forms of conduct not reconcilable with conventional morality as expressed in church and school. A boy may be found guilty of delinquency in the court, which represents the values of the larger society, for an act which has had at least tacit approval in the community in which he lives. It is perhaps common knowledge in the neighborhood that public funds are embezzled and that favors and special consideration can be received from some public officials through the payment of stipulated sums; the boys assume that all officials can be influenced in this way. They are familiar with the location of illegal institutions in the community and with the procedures through which such institutions are opened and kept in operation; they know where stolen goods can be sold and the kinds of merchandise for which there is a ready market; they know what the rackets are; and they see in fine clothes, expensive cars, and other lavish expenditures the evidences of wealth among those who openly engage in illegal activities. All boys in the city have some knowledge of these activities; but in the inner-city areas they are known intimately, in terms of personal relationships, while in other sections they enter the child's experience through more impersonal forms of communication, such as motion pictures, the newspaper, and the radio.

Other types of evidence tending to support the existence of diverse systems of values in various areas are to be found in the data on delinquency and crime. . . . [V]ariations by local areas in the number and rates of adult offenders were presented. When translated into its significance for children, the presence of a large number of adult criminals in certain areas means that children there are in contact with crime as a career and with the criminal way of life, symbolized by organized crime. In this type of organization can be seen the delegation of authority, the division of labor, the specialization of function, and all the other characteristics common to well-organized business institutions wherever found.

Similarly, the delinquency data presented graphically on spot maps and rate maps in the preceding pages give plausibility to the existence of a coherent system of values supporting delinquent acts. In making these interpretations it should be remembered that delinquency is essentially group behavior. A study of boys brought into the Juvenile Court of Cook Country during the year 1928 revealed that 81.8 percent of these boys committed the offenses for which they were brought to court as members of groups. And when the offenses were limited to stealing, it was found that 89 percent of all offenders were taken to court as group or gang members. In many additional cases where the boy actually committed his offense alone, the influence of companions was, nevertheless, apparent. This point is illustrated in certain cases of boys charged with stealing from members of their own families, where the theft clearly reflects the influence and instigation of companions, and in instances where the problems of the boy charged with incorrigibility reveal conflicting values, those of the family competing with those of the delinquent group for his allegiance.

The heavy concentration of delinquency in certain areas means, therefore, that boys living in these areas are in contact not only with individuals who engage in proscribed activity but also with groups which sanction such behavior and exert pressure upon their members to conform to group standards. Examination of the distribution map reveals that, in contrast with the areas of concentration of delinquents, there are many other communities where the cases are so widely dispersed that the chances of a boy's having intimate contact with other delinquents or with delinquent groups are comparatively slight.

The importance of the concentration of delinquents is seen most clearly when the effect is viewed in a temporal perspective. The maps representing distribution of delinquents at successive periods indicate that, year after year, decade after decade, the same areas have been characterized by these concentrations. This means that delinquent boys in these areas have contact not only with other delinquents who are their contemporaries but also with older offenders, who in turn had contact with delinquents preceding them, and so on back to the earliest history of the neighborhood. This contact means that the traditions of delinquency can be and are transmitted down through successive generations of boys, in much the same way that language and other social forms are transmitted . . .

The way in which boys are inducted into unconventional behavior has been revealed by large numbers of case studies of youths living in areas where the rates of delinquents are high. Through the boy's own life-story the wide range of contacts with other boys has been revealed. These stories indicate how at early ages the boys took part with older boys in delinquent activities, and how, as they themselves acquired experience, they initiated others into the same pursuits. These cases reveal also the steps through which members are incorporated into the delinquent group organization. Often at early ages boys engage in malicious mischief and simple acts of stealing. As their careers develop, they become involved in more serious offenses, and finally become skilled workmen or specialists in some particular field of criminal activity. In each of these phases the boy is supported by the sanction and the approbation of the delinquent group to which he belongs . . .

Taken together, these studies indicate that most delinquent acts are committed by boys in groups, that delinquent boys have frequent contact with other delinquents, that the techniques for specific offenses are transmitted through delinquent group organization, and that in his officially proscribed activity the boy is supported and sustained by the delinquent group to which he belongs.

Differential Social Organization

Other subtle differences among communities are to be found in the character of their local institutions, especially those specifically related to the problem of social control. The family, in areas of high rates of delinquents, is affected by the conflicting systems of values and the problems of survival and conformity with which it is confronted. Family organization in high-rate areas is affected in several different ways by the divergent systems of values encountered. In the first place, it may be made practically impotent by the existing interrelationships between the two systems. Ordinarily, the family is thought of as representing conventional values and opposed to deviant forms of behavior. Opposition from families within the area to illegal practices and institutions is lessened, however, by the fact that each system may be contributing in certain ways to the economic well-being of many large family groups. Thus, even if a family represents conventional values, some member, relative, or friend may be gaining a livelihood through illegal or quasi-legal institutions—a fact tending to neutralize the family's opposition to the criminal system.

Another reason for the frequent ineffectiveness of the family in directing the boys' activities along

conventional lines is doubtless the allegiance which the boys may feel they owe to delinquent groups. A boy is often so fully incorporated into the group that it exercises more control than does the family. This is especially true in those neighborhoods where most of the parents are European-born. There the parents' attitudes and interests reflect an Old World background, while their children are more fully Americanized and more sophisticated, assuming in many cases the role of interpreter. In this situation the parental control is weakened, and the family may be ineffective in competing with play groups and organized gangs in which life, though it may be insecure, is undeniably colorful, stimulating, and enticing.

A third possible reason for ineffectiveness of the family is that many problems with which it is confronted in delinquency areas are new problems, for which there is no traditional solution. An example is the use of leisure time by children. This is not a problem in the Old World or in rural American communities, where children start to work at an early age and have a recognized part in the system of production. Hence, there are no time-honored solutions for difficulties which arise out of the fact that children in the city go to work at a later age and have much more leisure at their disposal. In the absence of any accepted solution for this problem, harsh punishment may be administered; but this is often ineffective, serving only to alienate the children still more from family and home.

Other differences between high-rate and low-rate areas in Chicago are to be seen in the nature of the existing community organization. Thomas and Znaniecki have analyzed the effectively organized community in terms of the presence of social opinion with regard to problems of common interest, identical or at least consistent attitudes with reference to these problems, the ability to reach approximate unanimity on the question of how a problem should be dealt with, and the ability to carry this solution into action through harmonious co-operation.

Such practical unanimity of opinion and action does exist, on many questions, in areas where the rates of delinquents are low. But, in the high-rate areas, the very presence of conflicting systems of values operates against such unanimity. Other factors hindering the development of consistently effective attitudes with reference to these problems of public welfare are the poverty of these high-rate areas, the wide diversity of cultural backgrounds represented there, and the fact that the outward movement of population in a city like Chicago has resulted in the organization of life in terms of ultimate residence. Even though frustrated in his attempts to achieve economic security and to move into other areas, the immigrant, living in areas of first settlement, often has defined his goals in terms of the better residential community into which he hopes some day to move. Accordingly, the immediate problems of his present neighborhood may not be of great concern to him. . .

Briefly summarized, it is assumed that the differentiation of areas and the segregation of population within the city have resulted in wide variation of opportunities in the struggle for position within our social order. The groups in the areas of lowest economic status find themselves at a disadvantage in the struggle to achieve the goals idealized in our civilization. These differences are translated into conduct through the general struggle for those economic symbols which signify a desirable position in the larger social order. Those persons who occupy a disadvantageous position are involved in a conflict between the goals assumed to be attainable in a free society and those actually attainable for a large proportion of the population. It is understandable, then, that the economic position of persons living in the areas of least opportunity should be translated at times into unconventional conduct, in an effort to reconcile the idealized status and their practical prospects of attaining this status. Since, in our culture, status is determined largely in economic terms, the differences between contrasted areas in terms of economic status become the most important differences. Similarly, as might be expected, crimes against property are most numerous.

The physical, economic, and social conditions associated with high rates of delinquents in local communities occupied by white population exist in exaggerated form in most of the Negro areas. Of all the population groups in the city, the Negro people occupy the most disadvantageous position in relation to the distribution of economic and social values. Their efforts to achieve a more satisfactory and advantageous position in the economic and social life of the city are seriously thwarted by many restrictions with respect to residence, employment, education, and social and cultural pursuits. These restrictions have contributed to the development of conditions within the local community conducive to an unusually large volume of delinquency. . . .

The development of divergent systems of values requires a type of situation in which traditional conventional control is either weak or nonexistent. It is a well-known fact that the growth of cities and the increase in devices for transportation and communication have so accelerated the rate of change in our society that the traditional means of social control, effective in primitive society and in isolated rural communities, have been weakened everywhere and rendered especially ineffective in large cities. Moreover, the city, with its anonymity, its emphasis on economic rather than personal values, and its freedom and tolerance, furnishes a favorable situation of the development of devices to improve one's status, outside of the conventionally accepted and approved methods. This tendency is stimulated by the fact that the wide range of secondary social contacts in modern life operates to multiply the wishes of individuals. The automobile, motion picture, magazine and newspaper advertising, the radio, and other means of communication flaunt luxury standards before all, creating or helping to create desires which often cannot be satisfied with the meager facilities available to families in areas of low economic status. The urge to satisfy the wishes and desires so created has helped to bring into existence and to perpetuate the existing system of criminal activities.

It is recognized that in a free society the struggle to improve one's status in terms of accepted values is common to all persons in all social strata. And it is a well-known fact that attempts are made by some persons in all economic classes to improve their positions by violating the rules and laws designed to regulate economic activity. However, it is assumed that these violations with reference to property are most frequent where the prospect of thus enhancing one's social status outweighs the chances for loss of position and prestige in the competitive struggle. It is in this connection that the existence of a system of values supporting criminal behavior becomes important as a factor in shaping individual life-patterns, since it is only where such a system exists that the person through criminal activity may acquire the material goods so essential to status in our society and at the same time increase, rather than lose, his prestige in the smaller group system of which he has become an integral part.

Discussion Questions

1. What does it mean to say that a community is socially "disorganized"? Why is crime less likely to occur in an organized community?

2. Why do Shaw and McKay take special pains to point out that delinquency usually occurs in groups? How do they believe that peer groups in the inner city contribute to the causation of crime?

3. Although written several decades ago, how might Shaw and McKay's theory help to explain the occurence of street violence in today's inner-city communities?

4. Would Shaw and McKay favor efforts to fight crime by "getting tough" and locking up more offenders, including juveniles, in prison?

8. A Theory of Race, Crime, and Urban Inequality

Robert J. Sampson and William Julius Wilson

Conservative commentators on public policy are fond of attributing crime in the inner cities to the faulty culture of community residents. "If youths only had good values, respected the law, dressed the right way, and saw the value of schooling," so the argument goes, "they would stay out of trouble, get good jobs, and achieve the American Dream."

Many criminologists reject such thinking not only because it is simplistic, but also because it conveniently ignores the harsh lives that inner-city people face—from birth through adulthood. If culture is to blame, then there is no need to pay attention to the potential "root causes" of lawlessness—conditions such as poverty, inadequate health care, disrupted families, schools in shambles, and the depletion of economic opportunity as jobs move to the suburbs and to other nations. The focus on culture also masks the fact that many of these harsh conditions do not simply emerge naturally but are the result of political choices by elected officials who do little or nothing about them. In short, scholars see attributing crime to "bad culture" as dangerous because it obscures the role of "bad structures" in causing criminal behavior.

Although the position of structural criminologists is understandable, Sampson and Wilson suggest that ignoring the prevailing culture in urban areas results in an incomplete understanding of why crime takes place. They see culture not as the simple internalization of antisocial values but as the acquisition of "cognitive landscapes." Consider the case of violence. Inner-city residents do not espouse "hurting others" as a cherished value. But what if children grow up in a community in which they witness bullet-ridden bodies lying in public spaces or perhaps see older youths brandishing weapons? In this context, using lethal violence enters the mind as a potential choice to be made and, in some circumstances, as an unavoidable thing to do (such as when one's honor is challenged). In neighborhoods bereft of such experiences, however, youths are unlikely even to consider pulling out a gun as a realistic option to settle disputes. Such extreme violence is not seen, cannot be modeled, and just is not part of their "congnitive landscape"; it is virtually "inconceivable." When it does occur, the violence is so shocking and so unexpected that it becomes newsworthy and is plastered all over the evening news.

Sampson and Wilson understand, however, that a purely cultural explanation of inner-city crime and violence has limited merit. Identifying the content of cultures that generate crime is an important task. But, a complete explanation of

Excerpted from Robert J. Sampson and William Julius Wilson, "Toward a Theory of Race, Crime, and Urban Inequality," in *Crime and Inequality,* edited by John Hagan and Ruth D. Peterson. Copyright ©1990 by the Board of Trustees of the Leland Stanford Junior University. With the permission of Stanford University Press, www.sup.org.

criminal conduct must explain what initially causes and then sustains the influence of criminogenic cultures.

In a somewhat complex analysis, Sampson and Wilson single out a critical factor that underlies the crime-inducing cognitive landscapes that flourish in inner cities: social isolation or, in their words, "the lack of contact or of sustained interaction with individuals and institutions that represent mainstream society." They observe that a peculiar reality of American society is the extreme racial segregation of African Americans residing in many major cities (see also Massey and Denton, 1993; Peterson et al., 2006). In disadvantaged urban communities, youths live in segregated housing, attend schools in which virtually every student is a minority, and rarely travel outside the boundaries of their immediate neighborhood. These youths are cut off from the kind of daily routines that kids in more affluent areas witness, take for granted, and implicitly learn from. In many well-to-do suburbs, for example, youngsters see parents go off to nice jobs each day, the children are exposed to an array of enriching cultural experiences (including "taking lessons"), they "summer" at the country club and the beach house, they know that their friends are all going to college, and so on. The American Dream is not really a "dream" but a cognitive expectation. This is not the case for many inner-city youths, whose landscape is devoid of daily examples of how to participate in and profit from such conventional social roles (Sampson and Bean, 2006).

Finally, Sampson and Wilson do not view this social isolation as a "bad choice" made by inner-city residents but rather as the result of persisting racial inequality. Racial inequality is the product both of conscious political decisions—such as permitting racial discrimination in home purchases and "ghettoizing" minorities in high-rise public housing erected in geographically isolated areas—and of broad macro-sociological changes—such as the massive movement of jobs out of the inner city. In the end, these structural forces have isolated minorities in neighborhoods marked by extreme poverty and social disorganization, and they have effectively cut off residents from mainstream American society. In this structural context, cultural values or "cognitive landscapes" conducive to crime emerge and are only weakly rivaled by alternative ways of understanding the broader social world and the possibilities it holds (Wilson, 2009).

References

Massey, Douglas S. and Nancy A. Denton. 1993. *American Apartheid: Segregation and the Making of the Underclass.* Cambridge, MA: Harvard University Press.

Peterson, Ruth D., Lauren J. Krivo, and Christopher R. Browning. 2006. "Segregation and Race/Ethnic Inequality in Crime: New Directions." In Francis T. Cullen, John Paul Wright, and Kristie R. Blevins (eds.), *Taking Stock: The Status of Criminological Theory—Advances in Criminological Theory,* Volume 15, pp. 169–187. New Brunswick, NJ: Transaction.

Sampson, Robert J. and Lydia Bean. 2006. "Cultural Mechanisms and Killing Fields: A Revised Theory of Community-Level Racial Inequality." In Ruth D. Peterson, Lauren J. Krivo, and John Hagan (eds.), *The Many Colors of Crime,* pp. 8–36. New York: New York University Press.

Wilson, William Julius. 2009. *More Than Just Race: Being Black and Poor in the Inner City.* New York: W. W. Norton.

Our purpose in this chapter is to address one of the central yet difficult issues facing criminology—race and violent crime....

[W]e advance in this chapter a theoretical strategy that incorporates both structural and cultural arguments regarding race, crime, and inequality in American cities. In contrast to psychologically based relative deprivation theories and the subculture of violence, we view the race and crime linkage from contextual lenses that highlight the very different ecological contexts that blacks and whites reside in—regardless of individual characteristics. The basic thesis is that macro-social patterns of residential inequality give rise to the social isolation and ecological concentration of the truly disadvantaged, which in turn leads to structural barriers and cultural adaptations that undermine social organizations and hence the control of crime. This thesis is grounded in what is actually an old idea in criminology that has been overlooked in the race and crime debate—the importance of communities.

The Community Structure of Race and Crime

Unlike the dominant tradition in criminology that seeks to distinguish offenders from nonoffenders, the macrosocial or community level of explanation asks what it is about community structures and cultures that produces differential rates of crime (Bursik, 1988; Byrne and Sampson, 1986; Short, 1985). As such, the goal of macrolevel research is not to explain individual involvement in criminal behavior but to isolate characteristics of communities, cities, or even societies that lead to high rates of criminality (Byrne and Sampson, 1986; Short, 1985)....

The Ecological Concentration of Race and Social Dislocations

Having demonstrated the similarity of black-white variations by ecological context, we turn to the second logical question. To what extent are blacks as a group differentially exposed to criminogenic structural conditions?...

The combination of urban poverty and family disruption concentrated by race is particularly severe....In not one city over 100,000 in the United States do blacks live in ecological equality with whites when it comes to these basic features of economic and family organization. Accordingly, racial differences in poverty and family disruption are so strong that the "worst" urban contexts

in which whites reside are considerably better than the average context of black communities (Sampson, 1987: 354).

Taken as a whole, these patterns underscore what W. J. Wilson (1987) has labeled "concentration effects," that is, the effects of living in a neighborhood that is overwhelmingly impoverished. These concentration effects, reflected in a range of outcomes from degree of labor force attachment to social deviance, are created by the constraints and opportunities that the residents of inner-city neighborhoods face in terms of access to jobs and job networks, involvement in quality schools, availability of marriageable partners, and exposure to conventional role models.

The social transformation of the inner city in recent decades has resulted in an increased concentration of the most disadvantaged segments of the urban black population—especially poor, female-headed families with children. Whereas one of every five poor blacks resided in ghetto or extreme poverty areas in 1970, by 1980 nearly two out of every five did so (W. J. Wilson et al., 1988: 131). This change has been fueled by several macrostructural forces. In particular, urban minorities have been vulnerable to structural economic changes related to the deindustrialization of central cities (e.g., the shift from goods-producing to service-producing industries; increasing polarization of the labor market into low-wage and high-wage sectors; and relocation of manufacturing out of the inner city). The exodus of middle-and upper-income black families from the inner city has also removed an important social buffer that could potentially deflect the full impact of prolonged joblessness and industrial transformation. This thesis is based on the assumption that the basic institutions of an area (churches, schools, stores, recreational facilities, etc.) are more likely to remain viable if the core of their support comes from more economically stable families in inner-city neighborhoods (W. J. Wilson, 1987: 56). The social milieu of increasing stratification among blacks differs significantly from the environment that existed in inner cities in previous decades (see also Hagedorn, 1988)....

In short, the foregoing discussion suggests that macrostructural factors—both historic and contemporary—have combined to concentrate urban black poverty and family disruption in the inner city. These factors include but are not limited to racial segregation, structural economic transformation and black male joblessness, class-linked out-migration from the inner city, and housing discrimination. It is important to emphasize that when segregation and concentrated poverty represent structural constraints embodied in public policy and historical patterns of racial subjugation, notions that individual differences (or self-selection) explain community-level effects on violence are considerably weakened (see Sampson and Lauritsen, 1994)....

The consequences of these differential ecological distributions by race raise the substantively plausible hypothesis that correlations of race and crime may be systematically confounded with important differences in community contexts....

More specifically, we posit that the most important determinant of the relationship between race and crime is the differential distribution of blacks in communities characterized by (1) *structural social disorganization* and (2) *cultural social isolation,* both of which stem from the concentration of poverty, family disruption, and residential instability....

The Structure of Social (Dis)organization

In their original formulation Shaw and McKay held that low economic status, ethnic heterogeneity, and residential mobility led to the disruption of community social organization, which in turn accounted for variations in crime and delinquency rates (1942; 1969). As recently extended by Kornhauser (1978), Bursik (1988), and Sampson and Groves (1989), the concept of social disorganization may be seen as the inability of a community structure to realize the common values of its residents and maintain effective social controls. The *structural* dismensions of community social disorganization refer to the prevalence and interdependence of social networks in a community—both informal (e.g., the density of acquaintanceship; intergenerational kinship ties; level of anonymity) and formal (e.g., organizational participation; institutional stability)—and in the span of collective supervision that the community directs toward local problems.

This social-disorganization approach is grounded in what Kasarda and Janowitz (1974: 329) call the "systemic" model, where the local community is viewed as a complex system of friendship and kinship networks, and formal and informal associational ties are rooted in family life and ongoing socialization processes (see also Sampson, 1991). From this view social organization and social *dis*organization are seen as different ends of the same continuum of systemic networks of community social control. As Bursik (1988) notes, when formulated in this way, social disorganization is clearly separable not only from the processes that may lead to it (e.g., poverty, residential mobility), but also from the degree of criminal behavior that may be a result. This conceptualization also goes beyond the traditional account of community as a strictly geographical or spatial phenomenon by focusing on the social and organizational networks of local residents (see Leighton, 1988).

Evidence favoring social-disorganization theory is available with respect both to its structural antecedents and to mediating processes....

Boiled down to its essentials, then, our theoretical framework linking social-disorganization theory with research on urban poverty and political economy suggests that macrosocial forces (e.g., segregation, migration, housing discrimination, structural transformation of the economy) interact with local community-level factors (e.g., residential turnover, concentrated poverty, family disruption) to impede social organization. This is a distinctly sociological viewpoint, for it focuses attention on the proximate structural characteristics and mediating processes of community social organization that help explain crime, while also recognizing the larger historical, social, and political forces shaping local communities.

Social Isolation and Community Culture

Although social-disorganization theory is primarily structural in nature, it also focuses on how the ecological segregation of communities gives rise to what Kornhauser (1978: 75) terms *cultural* disorganization—the attenuation of societal cultural values. Poverty, heterogeneity, anonymity, mutual distrust, institutional instability, and other structural features of urban communities are hypothesized to impede communication and obstruct the quest for common values, thereby fostering cultural diversity with respect to nondelinquent values. For example, an important component of Shaw and McKay's theory was that disorganized communities spawned delinquent gangs with their own subcultures and norms perpetuated through cultural transmission.

Despite their relative infrequency, ethnographic studies generally support the notion that structurally disorganized communities are conducive to the emergence of cultural value systems and attitudes that seem to legitimate, or at least provide a basis of tolerance for, crime and deviance. . . .

[C]ommunity contexts seem to shape what can be termed *cognitive landscapes* or ecologically structured norms (e.g., normative ecologies) regarding appropriate standards and expectations of conduct. That is, in structurally disorganized slum communities it appears that a system of values emerges in which crime, disorder, and drug use are less than fervently condemned and hence expected as part of everyday life. These ecologically structured social perceptions and tolerances in turn appear to influence the probability of criminal outcomes and harmful deviant behavior (e.g., drug use by pregnant women). . . .

A renewed appreciation for the role of cultural adaptations is congruent with the notion of *social isolation*—defined as the lack of contact or of sustained interaction with individuals and institutions that represent mainstream society (W. J. Wilson, 1987: 60). According to this line of reasoning, the social isolation fostered by the ecological concentration of urban poverty deprives residents not only of resources and conventional role models, but also of cultural learning from mainstream social networks that facilitate social and economic advancement in modern industrial society (W. J. Wilson, 1991). Social isolation is specifically distinguished from the culture of poverty by virtue of its focus on adaptations to constraints and opportunities rather than internalization of norms.

As Ulf Hannerz noted in his seminal work *Soulside,* it is thus possible to recognize the importance of macrostructural constraints—that is, avoid the extreme notions of the culture of poverty or culture of violence, and yet see the "merits of a more subtle kind of cultural analysis" (1969: 182). One could hypothesize a difference, on the one hand, between a jobless family whose mobility is impeded by the macrostructural constraints in the economy and the larger society but nonetheless lives in an area with a relatively low rate of poverty, and on the other hand, a jobless family that lives in an inner-city ghetto neighborhood that is influenced not only by these same constraints but also by the behavior of other jobless families in the neighborhood (Hannerz, 1969: 184; W. J. Wilson, 1991). The latter influence is one of culture—the extent to which individuals follow their inclinations as they have been developed by learning or influence from other members of the community (Hannerz, 1969).

Ghetto-specific practices such as an overt emphasis on sexuality and macho values, idleness, and public drinking are often denounced by those who reside in inner-city ghetto neighborhoods. But because such practices occur much more frequently there than in middle-class society, largely because of social organizational forces, the transmission of these modes of behavior by precept, as in role modeling, is more easily facilitated (Hannerz, 1969). For example, youngsters are more likely to see violence as a way of life in inner-city ghetto neighborhoods. They are more likely to witness violent acts, to be taught to be violent by exhortation, and to have role models who do not adequately control their own violent impulses or restrain their own anger. Accordingly, given the availability of and easy access to firearms, knives, and other weapons, adolescent experiments with macho behavior often have deadly consequences (Prothrow-Stith, 1991).

The concept of social isolation captures this process by implying that contact between groups of different class and/or racial backgrounds either is lacking or has become increasingly intermittent, and that the nature of this contact enhances effects of living in a highly concentrated poverty area. Unlike the concept of the culture of violences, then, social isolation does not mean that ghetto-specific practices become internalized, take on a life of their own, and therefore continue to influence behavior no matter what the contextual environment. Rather, it suggests that reducing structural inequality would not only decrease the frequency of these practices; it would also make their transmission by precept less efficient. So in this sense we advocate a renewed appreciation for the ecology of culture, but not the monolithic and hence noncontextual culture implied by the subculture of poverty and violence.

Discussion

Rejecting both the "individualistic" and "materialist" fallacies, we have attempted to delineate a theoretical strategy that incorporates both structural and cultural arguments regarding race, crime, and urban inequality in American cities. Drawing on insights from social-disorganization theory and recent research on urban poverty, we

believe this strategy provides new ways of thinking about race and crime. First and foremost, our perspective views the link between race and crime through contextual lenses that highlight the very different ecological contexts in which blacks and whites reside—regardless of individual characteristics. Second, we emphasize that crime rates among blacks nonetheless vary by ecological characteristics, just as they do for whites. Taken together, these facts suggest a powerful role for community context in explaining race and crime.

Our community-level explanation also departs from conventional wisdom. Rather than attributing to acts of crime a purely economic motive springing from relative deprivation—an individual-level psychological concept—we focus on the mediating dimensions of community social organization to understand variations in crime across areas. Morever, we acknowledge and try to specify the macrosocial forces that contribute to the social organization of local communities. Implicit in this attempt is the incorporation of the political economy of place and the role of urban inequality in generating racial differences in community structure. As Wacquant observes, American urban poverty is "preeminently a *racial poverty* . . . rooted in the *ghetto* as a historically specific social form and mechanism of racial domination" (1991: 36, emphasis in original). This intersection of race, place, and poverty goes to the heart of our theoretical concern with societal and community organization.

Furthermore, we incorporate culture into our theory in the form of social isolation and ecological landscapes that shape perceptions and cultural patterns of learning. This culture is not seen as inevitably tied to race, but more to the varying structural contexts produced by residential and macroeconomic change, concentrated poverty, family instability, and intervening patterns of social disorganization. Perhaps controversially, then, we differ from the recent wave of structuralist research on the culture of violence (for a review see Sampson and Lauritsen 1994). In an interesting methodological sleight of hand, scholars have dismissed the relevance of culture based on the analysis of census data that provide no measures of culture whatsoever (see especially Blau and Blau 1982). We believe structural criminologists have too quickly dismissed the role of values, norms, and learning as they interact with concentrated poverty and social isolation. In our view, macrosocial patterns of residential inequality give rise to the social isolation and concentration of the truly disadvantaged, engendering cultural adaptations that undermine social organization.

Finally, our conceptualization suggests that the roots of urban violence among today's 15- to 21-year-old cohort may stem from childhood socialization that took place in the late 1970s and early 1980s. Consider that this cohort was born between 1970 and 1976 and spent its childhood in the context of a rapidly changing urban environment unlike that of any previous point in U.S. history. As documented in detail by W. J. Wilson (1987), the concentration of urban poverty and other social dislocations began increasing sharply in about 1970 and continued unabated through the decade and into the 1980s. As but one example, the proportion of black families headed by women increased by over 50 percent from 1970 to 1984 alone (W. J. Wilson 1987: 26). Large increases were also seen in the ecological concentration of ghetto poverty, racial segregation, population turnover, and joblessness. These social dislocations were, by comparison, relatively stable in earlier decades. Therefore, the logic of our theoretical model suggests that the profound changes in the urban structure of minority communities in the 1970s may hold the key to understanding recent increases in violence....

Discussion Questions

1. What is a "cognitive landscape"? How might such a landscape make crime more likely in some neighborhoods and less likely in other neighborhoods?
2. What do Sampson and Wilson mean by the concept of "social isolation"? Describe what life might be like in an isolated inner-city neighborhood. How would it differ from or be similar to your life growing up? From your life now?
3. Can you see any dangers in "blaming" individuals who live in inner-cities for their own problems, including crime? When you consider the broader social context that is implicated in the "choice" of crime, why might focusing exclusively on "bad individuals" seem to be a limited way of understanding the causes of crime in inner cities? That is, do communities matter in the causation of criminal behavior?
4. Let's say that you are attending an American Society of Criminology meeting, and Sampson and Wilson are giving an address on their theory of crime. After their talk, they ask if there are any questions. You rise and ask, "Well, in light of your theory, what three policies or interventions might be undertaken to help solve crime in inner-city neighborhoods?" What do you think their answer would be?

9. Collective Efficacy and Crime

Robert J. Sampson, Stephen W. Raudenbush, and Felton Earls

Crime, including violent crime, is not evenly distributed in the United States. Some cities, for example, are safer than others and, within urban areas, some neighborhoods are safer than other neighborhoods. As we have seen in Part III of this book, Shaw and McKay and their intellectual descendants have confronted this daunting task of explaining why some places are more dangerous than other places.

One strategy for distinguishing communities with high and low crime rates has been to focus on structural characteristics. In general, this approach has involved listing conditions that might be undesirable—such as poverty, residential instability, and the prevalence of broken homes— and seeing if these factors might be related to high crime rates (see also Pratt and Cullen, 2005). These "structural antecedents," as they are sometimes called, are important to identify. But they leave one question unanswered: In between the undesirable structural conditions and crime, what actually goes on to make people break the law at such a high rate?

Robert Sampson, Stephen Raudenbush, and Felton Earls set out to solve this mystery. They based their research on data from a remarkable longitudinal six-year survey recently concluded in Chicago, Illinois (called the Project on Human Development in Chicago Neighborhoods). In their particular study, they relied on data collected

in 1995 from 8,782 residents in 343 Chicago neighborhoods. This information allowed them to do two important things.

First, because the project actually surveyed individuals (as opposed to using census information), Sampson et al. could control for characteristics of people that might potentially account for crime in a neighborhood. For example, it could be argued that crime is higher in certain neighborhoods not because of some feature of the neighborhood, but because people who are prone to commit crime have moved into and now reside in the neighborhood. This is called a "compositional effect"; crime is high because individuals with criminal traits "compose" the area's population. Second, Sampson and his colleagues could take the answers that individuals in each neighborhood gave to questions and aggregate them (i.e., total them up and take the average for each neighborhood). In this way, they could create measures for each neighborhood on how the residents, as a group or collective, differed from one another. This would allow them to assess what is called the "contextual effect" of a community on crime. "Collective efficacy," the key concept of Sampson et al., was constructed in this way and is a contextual effect in their theory. The authors examined whether, beyond the compositional effects of individual traits, collective efficacy explained neighborhood differences in crime.

Excerpted with permission from Robert J. Sampson, Stephen W. Raudenbush, and Felton Earls, "Neighborhoods and Violent Crime: A Multilevel Study of Collective Efficacy," *Science*, 227, 15 August 1997. Copyright ©1997 by the American Association for the Advancement of Science.

Originally, Sampson et al. identified two separate contextual factors—features of the neighborhood— that they believed would explain "what went on" between the structural conditions, which they called "concentrated disadvantage" and crime rates. Drawn from Sampson's earlier work (see, e.g., Sampson and Groves, 1989), one factor was "informal social control" or the willingness of neighbors to intervene if they saw wrongdoing going on. The second factor was "social cohesion and trust," or how closely people in an area were tied to and supported each other. When they undertook their empirical analysis, however, Sampson et al. discovered that informal social control and social cohesion and trust were highly intercorrelated. This finding meant that these two factors were not separate conditions but part of some broader underlying construct.

What might this construct be? Sampson and his colleagues then invented the idea of "collective efficacy." They hypothesized that when people in a neighborhood trusted and supported one another, they had a basis for binding together to control disorderly and criminal behavior. This did not mean that people went about fighting crime on a daily basis. Rather, collective efficacy implied that when distruptive conduct arose, the people in these neighborhoods had the cohesiveness to act in an "effective" way to solve the problem. Collective efficacy is thus a resource that is activated in crucial situations (see also Sampson, Morenoff, and Earls, 1999; Sampson and Raudenbush, 1999).

In contrast, when neighborhoods are racked by concentrated disadvantage (e.g., poverty, disrupted families), residential instability, and large populations of immigrants, the residents often are less able to forge close ties, to trust one another, and to exercise informal social control. Lacking collective efficacy, in short, causes disorder and crime to emerge and to spiral out of control. This is what Sampson et al. believed was occurring in Chicago neighborhoods with high crime rates.

Sampson et al. were able to show that spatial differences in collective efficacy—even controlling statistically for compositional effects—helped to account for neighborhood differences in crime rates. In doing so, they provided important evidence that collective efficacy might be the key community-level condition that lies in between structural factors and crime rates (see also Sampson, 2006).

Still, more theorizing and research needs to be done. Sampson et al. need to flesh out more clearly what they mean by collective efficacy: to define its components more systematically, to specify the conditions under which it is activated, and to describe what precisely happens when collective efficacy is exerted. Furthermore, the true explanatory power of collective efficacy will not be known until it squares off against competing theories (e.g., social disorganization, institutional-anomie, conflict) in an empirical test. It seems likely, however, that macro-level theorizing about crime rates will be influenced by the model of collective efficacy for some time to come.

References

Pratt, Travis C. and Francis T. Cullen. 2005. "Assessing Macro-Level Predictors and Theories of Crime: A Meta-Analysis." In Michael Tonry (ed.), *Crime and Justice: A Review of Research*, Volume 32, pp. 373–450. Chicago: University of Chicago Press.

Sampson, Robert J. 2006. "Collective Efficacy Theory: Lessons Learned and Directions for Future Inquiry." In Francis T. Cullen, John Paul Wright, and Kristie R. Blevins (eds.), *Taking Stock: The Status of Criminological Theory—Advances in Criminological Theory*, Volume 15, pp. 149–167. New Brunswick, NJ: Transaction.

Sampson, Robert J. and W. Byron Groves. 1989. "Community Structure and Crime: Testing Social-Disorganization Theory." *American Journal of Sociology* 94: 774–802.

Sampson, Robert J., Jeffery D. Morenoff, and Felton Earls. 1999. "Beyond Social Capital: Spatial Dynamics of Collective Efficacy for Children." *American Sociological Review* 64: 633–660.

Sampson, Robert J. and Stephen W. Raudenbush. 1999. "Systematic Social Observation in Public Spaces: A New Look at Disorder in Urban Neighborhoods." *American Journal of Sociology* 105: 603–651.

Sampson, Robert J. and Stephen W. Raudenbush, and Felton Earls. 1997. "Neighborhoods and Violent Crime: A Multilevel Study of Collective Efficacy." *Science* 277 (August 15): 918–924.

For most of this century, social scientists have observed marked variations in rates of criminal violence across neighborhoods of U.S. cities. Violence has been associated with the low socioeconomic status (SES) and residential instability of neighborhoods. Although the geographical concentration of violence and its connection with neighborhood composition are well established, the question remains: why? What is it, for example, about the concentration of poverty that accounts for its association with rates of violence? What are the social processes that might explain or mediate this relation? In this article, we report results from a study designed to address these questions about crime and communities.

Our basic premise is that social and organizational characteristics of neighborhoods explain variations in crime rates that are not solely attributable to the aggregated demographic characteristics of individuals. We propose that the differential ability of neighborhoods to realize the common values of residents and maintain effective social controls is a major source of neighborhood variation in violence. Although social control is often a response to deviant behavior, it should not be equated with formal regulation or forced conformity by institutions such as the police and courts. Rather, social control refers generally to the capacity of a group to regulate its members according to desired principles—to realize collective, as opposed to forced, goals. One central goal is the desire of community residents to live in safe and orderly environments that are free of predatory crime, especially interpersonal violence.

In contrast to formally or externally induced actions (for example, a police crackdown), we focus on the effectiveness of informal mechanisms by which residents themselves achieve public order. Examples of informal social control include the monitoring of spontaneous play groups among children, a willingness to intervene to prevents acts such as truancy and street corner "hanging" by teenage peer groups, and the confrontation of persons who are exploiting or disturbing public space. Even among adults, violence regularly arises in public disputes, in the context of illegal markets (for example, prostitution and drugs), and in the company of peers. The capacity of residents to control group-level processes and visible signs of social disorder is thus a key mechanism influencing opportunities for interpersonal crime in a neighborhood.

Informal social control also generalizes to broader issues of import to the well-being of neighborhoods. In particular, the differential ability of communities to extract resources and respond to cuts in public services (such as police patrols, fire stations, garbage collection, and housing code enforcement) looms large when we consider the known link between public signs of disorder (such as vacant housing, burned-out buildings, vandalism, and litter) and more serious crime.

Thus conceived, neighborhoods differentially activate informal social control. It is for this reason that we see an analogy between individual efficacy and neighborhood efficacy: both are activated processes that seek to achieve an intended effect. At the neighborhood level, however, the willingness of local residents to intervene for the common good depends in large part on conditions of mutual trust and solidarity among neighbors. Indeed, one is unlikely to intervene in a neighborhood context in which the rules are unclear and people mistrust or fear one another. It follows that socially cohesive neighborhoods will prove the most fertile contexts for the realization of informal social control. In sum, it is the linkage of mutual trust and the willingness to intervene for the common good that defines the neighborhood context of collective efficacy. Just as individuals vary in their capacity for efficacious action, so too do neighborhoods vary in their capacity to achieve common goals. And just as individual self-efficacy is situated rather than global (one has self-efficacy relative to a particular task or type of task), in this paper we view neighborhood efficacy as existing relative to the tasks of supervising children and maintaining public order. It follows that the collective efficacy of residents is a critical means by which urban neighborhoods inhibit the occurrence of personal violence, without regard to the demographic composition of the population.

What Influences Collective Efficacy?

As with individual efficacy, collective efficacy does not exist in a vacuum. It is embedded in structural contexts and a wider political economy that stratifies places of residence by key social characteristics. Consider the destabilizing potential of rapid population change on neighborhood social organization. A high rate of residential mobility, especially in areas of decreasing population, fosters institutional disruption and weakened social controls over collective life. A major reason is that the formation of social ties takes time. Financial investment also provides homeowners with a vested interest in supporting the commonweal of neighborhood life. We thus hypothesize that residential tenure and homeownership promote collective efforts to maintain social control.

Consider next patterns of resource distribution and racial segregation in the United States. Recent decades have witnessed an increasing geographical concentration of lower income residents, especially minority groups and female-headed families. This neighborhood concentration stems in part from macroeconomic changes related to the deindustrialization of central cities, along with the out-migration of middle-class residents. In addition, the greater the race and class segregation in a metropolitan area, the smaller the number of neighborhoods absorbing economic shocks and the more severe the resulting concentration of poverty will be. Economic stratification by race and place thus fuels the neighborhood concentration of cumulative forms of disadvantage, intensifying the social isolation of lower income, minority, and single-parent residents from key resources supporting collective social control.

Perhaps more salient is the influence of racial and economic exclusion on perceived powerlessness. Social science research has demonstrated, at the individual level, the direct role of SES in promoting a sense of control, efficacy, and even biological health itself. An analogous process may work at the community level. The alienation, exploitation, and dependency wrought by resource deprivation act as a centrifugal force that stymies collective efficacy. Even if personal ties are strong in areas of concentrated disadvantage, they may be weakly tethered to collective actions.

We therefore test the hypothesis that concentrated disadvantage decreases and residential stability increases collective efficacy. In turn, we assess whether collective efficacy explains the association of neighborhood disadvantage and residential instability with rates of interpersonal violence. It is our hypothesis that collective efficacy mediates a substantial portion of the effects of neighborhood stratification.

Research Design

This article examines data from the Project on Human Development in Chicago neighborhoods (PHDCN). Applying a spatial definition of neighborhood—a collection of people and institutions occupying a subsection of a larger community—we combined 847 census tracts in the city of Chicago to creat 343 "neighborhood clusters" (NCs).

The overriding consideration in formation of NCs was that they should be as ecologically meaningful as possible, composed of geographically contiguous census tracts, and internally homogeneous on key census indicators. We settled on an ecological unit of about 8,000 people, which is smaller than the 77 established community areas in Chicago (the average size is almost 40,000 people) but large enough to approximate local neighborhoods. Geographic boundaries (for example, railroad tracks, parks, and freeways) and knowledge of Chicago's neighborhoods guided this process.

The extensive racial, ethnic, and social-class diversity of Chicago's population was a major criterion in its selection as a research site. At present, whites, blacks, and Latinos each represent about a third of the city's population. Although there are no low-SES white neighborhoods and no high-SES Latinos neighborhoods, there are black neighborhoods in all three cells of SES, and many heterogeneous neighborhoods vary in SES . . . .

To gain a complete picture of the city's neighborhoods, 8,782 Chicago residents representing all 343 NCs were interviewed in their homes as part of the community survey (CS). The CS was designed to yield a representative sample of households within each NC, with sample sizes large enough to create reliable NC measures. Henceforth, we refer to NCs as "neighborhoods," keeping in mind that other operational definitions might have been used.

Measure of Collective Efficacy

"Informal social control" was represented by a five-item Likert-type scale. Residents were asked about the likelihood ("Would you say it is very likely, likely, neither likely nor unlikely, unlikely, or very unlikely?") that their neighbors could be counted on to intervene in various ways if (i) children were skipping school and hanging out on a street corner, (ii) children were spray-painting graffiti on a local building, (iii) children were showing disrespect to an adult, (iv) a fight broke out in front of their house, and (v) the fire station closest to their home was threatened with budget cuts. "Social cohesion and trust" were also represented by five conceptually related items. Respondents were asked how strongly they agreed (on a five-point scale) that "people around here are willing to help their neighbors," "this is a close-knit neighborhood," "people in this neighborhood generally don't get along with each other," and "people in this neighborhood do not share the same values" (the last two statements were reverse coded).

Responses to the five-point Likert scales were aggregated to the neighborhood level as initial measures. Social cohesion and informal social control were closely associated across neighborhoods ($r = 0.80$, $P < .001$), which suggests that the two measures were tapping aspects of the same latent construct. Because we also expected that the willingness and intention to intervene on behalf of the neighborhood would be enhanced under conditions of mutual trust and cohesion, we combined the two scales into a summary measure labeled collective efficacy. . . .

Discussion and Implications

The results imply that collective efficacy is an important construct that can be measured reliably at the neighborhood level by means of survey research strategies. In the past, sample surveys have primarily considered individual-level relations. However, surveys that merge a cluster sample design with questions tapping collective properties lend themselves to the additional consideration of neighborhood phenomena.

Together, three dimensions of neighborhood stratification—concentrated disadvantage, immigration concentration, and residential stability—explained 70 percent of the neighborhood variation in collective efficacy. Collective efficacy in turn mediated a substantial portion of the association of residential stability and disadvantage with multiple measures of violence, which is consistent with a major theme in neighborhood theories of social organization.

After adjustment for measurement error, individual differences in neighborhood composition, prior violence, and other potentially confounding social processes, the combined measure of informal social control and cohesion and trust remained a robust predictor of lower rates of violence.

There are, however, several limitations of the present study. Despite the use of decennial census data and prior crime as lagged predictors, the basic analysis was cross-sectional in design; causal effects were not proven. Indicators of informal control and social cohesion were not observed directly but rather inferred from informant reports. Beyond the scope of the present study, other dimensions of neighborhood efficacy (such as political ties) may be important, too. Our analysis was limited also to one city and did not go beyond its official boundaries into a wider region. Finally, the image of local residents working collectively to solve their own problems is not the whole picture. As shown, what happens within neighborhoods is in part shaped by socioeconomic and housing factors linked to the wider political economy. In addition to encouraging communities to mobilize against violence through "self-help" strategies of informal social control, perhaps reinforced by partnerships with agencies of formal social control (community policing), strategies to address the social and ecological changes that beset many inner-city communities need to be considered. Recognizing that collective efficacy matters does not imply that inequalities at the neighborhood level can be neglected.

Discussion Questions

1. How does the concept of collective efficacy differ from the concept of social disorganization?
2. Think back to when you were growing up. Was the level of collective efficacy high or low in your neighborhood? Can you give examples of when collective efficacy was or was not activated to deal with public disorder? How might collective efficacy apply to crime on college campuses, including residence halls?
3. Collective efficacy involves informal social control and mutual trust. Why do you think that these two social conditions are so closely related? Why would residents be more willing to help neighbors exercise informal social control if they trusted one another?
4. What are the policy implications of collective efficacy? What might Sampson and his colleagues say would be some key ways to increase collective efficacy and reduce crime rates in a community? Given their perspective, what type of policing or community corrections might Sampson et al. endorse?

PART IV

Learning to Be a Criminal: Differential Association, Subcultural, and Social Learning Theories

The theories in this section argue that people *learn* to engage in criminal behavior, in much the same way that they learn to engage in other sorts of behavior. Certain learning theories are at the micro or individual level: They attempt to explain how individuals learn to engage in crime. Others are at the macro or group level: They attempt to explain why certain groups, like Southerners or young people, have higher rates of certain types of crime.

Micro-Level Learning Theories

While learning theories of crime have been advanced by many theorists over the years, Sutherland's theory of differential association was the first and most prominent formal statement of micro-level learning theory (see Chapter 10 in this part). Sutherland first provided a complete statement of the theory in the 1939 edition of his criminology textbook, and presented the final version of the theory in the 1947 edition. The theory is presented in the form of nine propositions. In brief, it states that criminal behavior is learned in interaction with others, particularly intimate others like friends and family. Through such interaction, we learn techniques of committing crime and "definitions" (motives, drives, rationalizations,

attitudes) favorable and unfavorable toward violation of the law. An individual becomes criminal "because of an excess of definitions favorable to violation of law over definitions unfavorable to violation of law." Individuals are most likely to engage in crime if they are exposed to definitions favorable to law violation (1) early in life, (2) on a relatively frequent basis, (3) over a long period of time, and (4) from sources they like and respect. Recent versions of Sutherland's textbook address some common misconceptions about and criticisms of the theory (see Sutherland et al., 1992; see also Akers, 1998; Akers and Sellers, 2008; Kubrin et al., 2009; Matsueda, 1988; and Warr, 2001).

One major criticism of the theory is that Sutherland does not present a good description of definitions favorable and unfavorable to crime. Several theorists have tried to more precisely define the nature of these definitions. In certain cases, it has been said that individuals hold values that unconditionally approve of crime (Cohen, 1955; Topalli, 2005). In other cases, it has been claimed that individuals hold values that do not directly approve of crime, but are conducive to crime: values such as seeking excitement or thrills, toughness, and the desire for quick, easy success (Agnew, 2000; Matza and Sykes, 1961; Miller, 1958; Mullins, 2006; Wilkinson, 2003).

More commonly, however, it is argued that individuals hold beliefs that approve of, justify, or excuse crime *in certain situations* (see Agnew, 2000; Akers, 1998; Akers and Sellers, 2008; Bandura, 1990; Kubrin et al., 2009; Maruna and Copes, 2005). Sykes and Matza (1957) have written the key article in this area (see Chapter 17 in Part VI). They begin their article by attacking those who claim that delinquents unconditionally approve of crime (they especially attack Cohen, whose theory of the origin of the delinquent subcultures is described in Part V). They then present five "techniques of neutralization" that delinquents commonly use to justify or excuse their delinquency. While these techniques may be used as after-the-fact rationalizations, Sykes and Matza claim that they are also used before crime occurs and that they make crime possible by neutralizing one's belief that crime is bad. The individual essentially says that although crime in general is bad, it is justifiable or excusable in their particular case because the victim has it coming, the behavior will not really hurt anyone, and so on. (It should be noted that Sykes and Matza's theory is sometimes treated as a learning theory, since individuals often learn these justifications and excuses from others; and it is sometimes treated as a control theory, since these justifications and excuses do not positively motivate crime but rather "free" individuals to satisfy their impulses and desires in a criminal manner [see Part VI of this book]).

A number of studies have examined the nature of definitions favorable to delinquency. These studies suggest that few people unconditionally approve of crime (with the exception of minor forms of crime like marijuana use and gambling; also, see Topalli, 2005). More commonly, some individuals are close to amoral in their view of crime. That is, they neither approve of nor condemn crime. This amoral orientation is probably best explained in terms of social control theory, which argues that some individuals are not properly socialized (see Part VI; Warner, 2003). Also, some individuals hold values conducive to crime

(as stated above, thrills or excitement, toughness, quick or easy success). Further, some individuals approve of, justify, or excuse crime *under certain conditions*. These types of individuals are more likely to engage in crime (see Agnew, 1994, 2000; Akers, 1998; Akers and Sellers, 2008; Brezina et al., 2004; Heimer, 1997; Kubrin et al., 2009; Maruna and Copes, 2005).

A second criticism of differential association theory is that it fails to fully describe the process by which crime is learned. The theory simply says we learn definitions favorable (or unfavorable) to crime through our association with others. Burgess and Akers (1966) and Akers (1985, 1998) drew on behavioral and social learning theory in psychology to more fully describe the process by which individuals learn to engage in crime (also see Akers and Jensen, 2003, 2006; Akers and Sellers, 2008, Bandura 1973, 1986; Snyder et al., 2003). In brief, Akers argues that crime is learned through three processes (see Chapter 11 in this part). First, individuals learn beliefs that define crime as desirable, justifiable, or excusable in certain situations. This portion of the theory is very compatible with the emphasis of Sutherland on definitions, although Akers more precisely describes the beliefs that lead to crime. Second, individuals engage in crime because they are differentially reinforced for criminal behavior. This reinforcement may be positive, such as when one receives rewards for engaging in crime (e.g., the social approval of friends, money from a robbery); it may also be negative, such as when the commission of a crime allows one to avoid or escape from unpleasant stimuli (e.g., friends stop taunting you after you use the illicit drugs they offer). Third, individuals engage in crime because they imitate the criminal behavior of others, especially valued others whose own criminal behavior is reinforced (e.g., imitating the successful drug dealers in one's neighborhood).

Differential association and social learning theory are usually tested by examining the relationship between delinquency and association with delinquent peers. Although one may learn to engage in delinquency from both criminals and conventional people, it is felt that delinquent friends are the major source of such learning. Much data indicate that individuals with delinquent friends are more likely to engage in delinquency. In fact, association with delinquent friends emerges as the strongest correlate of delinquency in most studies. Some people have questioned the meaning of this correlation. Most notably, they claim that it is due to fact that delinquents pick other delinquents as friends ("birds of a feather flock together"), rather than to the fact that associating with delinquents *causes* one to engage in delinquency. Several recent studies which have examined adolescents *over time* suggest that association with delinquent friends does have a causal effect on delinquency, although delinquency also increases the likelihood of association with delinquent friends (see Agnew, 2009; Akers, 1998; Gordon et al., 2004; Haynie, 2001; Haynie and Osgood, 2005; Krohn et al., 2007; Kubrin et al., 2009; Matsueda and Anderson, 1998; Thornberry et al., 2003; Warr, 2002).

The above data are usually taken as support for differential association and social learning theory, because it is assumed that delinquent friends cause delinquency by presenting definitions favorable to delinquency, reinforcing delinquency, and modeling delinquency. Several recent studies have tried to determine *why* associating with delinquent friends increases the likelihood of delinquency. The data from these studies are somewhat mixed, but they tend to suggest that the effect of delinquent friends on delinquency is only *partly* explained by delinquent attitudes, the reinforcement of delinquency, and the modeling of delinquency. This may be because these variables are poorly measured. Other researchers, however, suggest that delinquent friends may cause delinquency for reasons related to control and strain theories (see Parts V and VI). For example, associating with delinquent friends may make one less fearful of punishment (see the discussions in Agnew, 2009; Akers, 1998; Akers and Sellers, 2008;

Krohn, 1999, Krohn et al., 2007; Kubrin et al., 2009; Sampson, 1999; Warr, 2002; Warr and Stafford, 1991). Overall, however, the data provide some support for Sutherland's differential association theory and the extension of that theory by Akers. And these are among the leading explanations of crime.

Macro-Level Learning Theories

The macro-level versions of learning theory most commonly argue that there are certain groups in the United States with values that are conducive to crime or that approve of or justify crime in certain circumstances. Such values explain the higher rates of crime in these groups.

Some theorists have argued that members of the lower class or that certain segments of the lower class hold such values. Miller (1958), for example, proposes that there is a lower-class culture whose members sometimes emphasize values like trouble, toughness, smartness (the ability to outsmart or con others), and excitement. Such values are said to explain the allegedly higher rate of crime in the lower class (see Tittle and Meier, 1990). The "subculture of violence" thesis developed by Wolfgang and Ferracuti (1982) has its origins in an attempt to explain the high rate of homicide among young African-American males in the inner city. They assert that in this group violence is seen as an appropriate, even expected response to a wide range of insults and provocations. They state, for example, that

> a male is expected to defend the name and honor of his mother, the virtue of womanhood . . . and to accept no derogation about his race (even from a member of his own race), his age, or his masculinity. (1982: 153)

Chapter 12 by Anderson provides a contemporary account of the subculture of violence thesis. Anderson (1994, 1999) describes the "code of the street," and argues that this code pressures African-American youth in the inner city to respond to shows of disrespect with violence. (The theories of Cohen [1955] and Cloward and Ohlin [1960], described in Part V, also argue that certain segments of the lower class have values conducive to crime.)

Other theorists have argued that young people constitute a deviant subculture. In particular, young people are said to approve of certain minor forms of crime, like gambling and underage drinking, and to hold values that are conducive to crime—like an emphasis on thrills and excitement (this "youth subculture" is a popular subject for movies and TV shows). Still other theorists have argued that many Southerners hold values that are conducive to the use of lethal violence. Such values have been used to explain the higher rate of homicide in the South. Finally, it has been argued that executives in certain corporations approve of select forms of crime, like price fixing and consumer fraud (see Agnew, 2000; Bernard et al., 2009 for brief overviews of these theories).

The origin of these deviant subcultures has been explained in several ways (see Agnew, 2000; Bernard, 1990; Brezina et al., 2004; Curtis, 1975; Heimer, 1997; Nisbett and Cohen, 1996; Stewart and Simons, 2006). The most common explanation draws on strain theory, which is described in Part V of this book. According to one version of this theory, individuals who are unable to achieve valued goals through legitimate channels may attempt to achieve them through illegitimate channels. In the process, they may come to justify or approve of their illegal behavior. Individuals who cannot achieve monetary success through conventional means, for example, may come to justify illegitimate means of goal achievement like theft and drug selling. A second version of strain theory argues that when individuals cannot achieve conventional goals through legitimate channels, they may substitute alternative goals which they are capable of achieving in their place. These alternative goals may sometimes involve crime. For example, individuals who cannot achieve middle-class status may reject this goal, and instead define status in

terms of whether or not one is a good fighter. Elements of these strain explanations can be found in the Anderson article (also see Curtis, 1975; the Cohen and the Cloward and Ohlin selections in Part V). And they are prominent in the British work on youth subcultures (Tanner, 1978; Young, 2009).

Surprisingly, there has not been much research on these macro-level learning theories. The few studies that have been done suggest that all groups—regardless of income, age, race, gender, or area of residence—condemn crime. There may, however, be differences in the degree to which crime is condemned. Also, groups may differ in the extent to which they hold values conducive to crime (e.g., toughness, excitement or thrills) and in the extent to which they approve of, justify, or excuse crime under varying conditions. Although several studies have been conducted in this area, their findings are often suspect due to various methodological problems—like the use of questionable measures of values. Recent evidence from observational studies and survey research, however, tentatively suggests that young people, males, certain Southerners, and possibly urban residents and lower-class people are more likely to hold certain types of values favorable to crime (for overviews and selected studies, see Brezina et al., 2004; Cao et al., 1997; Dixon and Lizotte, 1987; Ellison, 1991; Heimer, 1997; Heimer and De Coster, 1999; Lee et al., 2007; Luckenbill and Doyle, 1989; Markowitz and Felson, 1998; Hayes and Lee, 2005; Messner, 1988; Mullins, 2006; Nisbett and Cohen, 1996; Sampson and Bartusch, 1999; Stewart and Simons, 2006). Rural, white Southerners, for example, appear more likely to approve of violence for defensive purposes and to avenge insults against their honor. Most evidence suggests that blacks are no more likely to approve of crime than whites, with a few studies finding that whites are more likely to hold certain types of values favorable to crime. The "code of the street" described by Elijah Anderson in Chapter 12 may be more strongly related to residence in severely disadvantaged neighborhoods than it is to race (see Brezina et al., 2004; Mullins, 2006; Sampson and Bartusch, 1999; Stewart and Simons, 2006; Wilkinson, 2003). Data also suggest that smaller groups, like certain students within a school, gang members, and members of hate groups, often hold values that are conducive to crime or that approve of, justify, or excuse crime under certain conditions (Agnew, 2009; Blazak, 2001; Felson et al., 1994).

These macro-level learning theories, then, have some limited support. It is important to emphasize, however, that most people in most groups condemn crime. The members of certain groups, however, may be somewhat more likely than the members of other groups to hold values conducive to crime (e.g., toughness) or to approve of, justify, or excuse crime under certain conditions.

Akers (1998) has recently extended macro-level learning theories of crime. In particular, his theory of "social structure and social learning" argues that group differences in crime rates are more than a function of group differences in values or beliefs conducive to crime. As described in Chapter 11, he argues that features of the larger social environment affect crime by influencing *all* of the mechanisms by which individuals learn to engage in crime—including association with criminal others, the differential reinforcement for crime, exposure to criminal models, and the adoption of beliefs favorable to crime. Akers describes several features of the larger social environment that affect the likelihood that individuals will learn to engage in crime. Certain of these features are associated with other macro-level theories of crime, like the extent to which communities are socially disorganized (see Part III). Akers argues that individuals in disorganized communities are more likely to associate with criminal others, such as gang members, are less likely to be punished and more likely to be reinforced for crime, are more likely to be exposed to criminal models, and are more likely to learn beliefs favorable to crime. Related to this, Akers argues that one's position in the larger social environment, as indexed by socio-demographic characteristics such as age and gender, also influences all of the mechanisms by which individuals learn to engage in crime. Akers' theory, then, is much broader than most macro-level learning theories, which focus on group differences in values or beliefs regarding crime.

Akers' macro-level theory has not yet been extensively tested, but a few preliminary studies provide some support for it (see Akers and Jensen, 2003, 2006, Haynie et al., 2006; Jensen, 2007). For example, Bellair et al. (2003) found that adolescent violence is higher in communities where few residents have professional and managerial jobs. They further found that part of the reason for this is that the adolescents in such communities are less likely to be exposed to positive role models, are more likely to join delinquent peer groups, are less likely to anticipate they will be reinforced for conventional activities, and are more likely to learn values conducive to crime. Akers' work, then, holds some promise for substantially expanding the scope of macro-level learning theories.

References

Agnew, Robert. 1994. "The Techniques of Neutralization and Violence." *Criminology* 32: 555–580.

——. 2000. "Sources of Criminality: Strain and Subcultural Theories." In Joseph F. Sheley (ed.), *Criminology: A Contemporary Handbook*, 2nd edition, pp. 349–371. Belmont, CA: Wadsworth.

——. 2009. *Juvenile Delinquency: Causes and Control*, 2nd edition. New York: Oxford University Press.

Akers, Ronald L. 1985. *Deviant Behavior: A Social Learning Approach*. Belmont, CA: Wadsworth.

——. 1998. *Social Learning and Social Structure: A General Theory of Crime and Deviance*. Boston: Northeastern University Press.

Akers, Ronald L. and Gary F. Jensen, eds. 2003. *Social Learning Theory and the Explanation of Crime*. New Brunswick, NJ: Transaction.

——. 2006. "The Empirical Status of Social Learning Theory of Crime and Deviance: Past, Present, and Future." In Francis T. Cullen, John Paul Wright, and Kristie R. Belvins (eds.), *Taking Stock: The Status of Criminological Theory— Advances in Criminological Theory*, Volume 15, pp. 37–176. New Brunswick, NJ: Transaction.

Akers, Ronald L. and Christine S. Sellers. 2008. *Criminological Theories*, 5th edition. New York: Oxford University Press.

Anderson, Elijah. 1994. "The Code of the Streets." *Atlantic Monthly* 273 (May): 81–94.

——. 1999. *Code of the Street*. New York: W. W. Norton.

Bandura, Albert. 1973. *Aggression: A Social Learning Analysis*. Englewood Cliffs, NJ: Prentice Hall.

——. 1986. *Social Foundations of Thought and Action: A Social Cognitive Theory*. Englewood Cliffs, NJ: Prentice Hall.

——. 1990. "Selective Activation and Disengagement of Moral Control." *Journal of Social Issues* 46: 27–46.

Bellair, Paul E., Vincent J. Roscigno, and Marcia B. Velez. 2003. "Occupational Structure, Social Learning, and Adolescent Violence." In Ronald L. Akers and Gary F. Jensen (eds.), *Social Learning Theory and the Explanation of Crime*, pp. 197–225. New Brunswick, NJ: Transition.

Bernard, Thomas J. 1990. "Angry Aggression Among the 'Truly Disadvantaged.'"*Criminology* 28: 73–96.

Bernard, Thomas, J., Jeffrey B. Snipes, and Alexander L. Gerould. 2009. *Vold's Theoretical Criminology*. New York: Oxford University Press.

Blazak, Randy. 2001. "White Boys to Terrorist Men." *American Behavioral Scientist* 44: 982–1000.

Brezina, Timothy, Robert Agnew, Francis T. Cullen, and John Paul Wright. 2004. "The Code of the Street." *Youth Violence and Juvenile Justice* 2: 303–328.

Burgess, Robert L. and Ronald L. Akers. 1966. "A Differential Association-Reinforcement Theory of Criminal Behavior." *Social Problems* 14: 128–147.

Cao, Liqun, Anthony Adams, and Vickie J. Jensen. 1997. "A Test of the Black Subculture of Violence Thesis: A Research Note." *Criminology* 35: 367–379.

Cloward, Richard A. and Lloyd Ohlin. 1960. *Delinquency and Opportunity: A Theory of Delinquent Gangs*. New York: Free Press.

Cohen, Albert K. 1955. *Delinquent Boys: The Culture of the Gang*. New York: Free Press.

Curtis, Lynn A. 1975. *Violence, Race, and Culture*. Lexington, MA: Heath.

Dixon, Jo and Alan J. Lizotte. 1987. "Gun Ownership and the 'Southern Subculture of violence.'" *American Journal of Sociology* 93: 383–405.

Ellison, Christopher G. 1991. "An Eye for an Eye ? A Note on the Southern Subculture of Violence Thesis." *Social Forces* 69: 1223–1239.

Felson, Richard B., Allen E. Liska, Scott J. South, and Thomas L. McNulty. 1994. "The Subculture of Violence and Delinquency: Individual vs. School Context Effects." *Social Forces* 73: 155–173.

Gordon, Rachel A., Benjamin B. Lahey, Eriko Kawai, Role Loeber, Magda Stouthamer-Leober, and David P. Farrington. 2004. "Anti-social Behavior and Youth Gang Membership: Selection and Socialization." *Criminology* 42: 55–87.

Hayes, Timothy C. and Matthew R. Lee. 2005. "The Southern Subculture of Honor and Violent Attitudes." *Sociological Spectrum* 25: 593–617.

Haynie, Dana L. 2001. "Delinquent Peers Revisited: Does Network Structure Matter?" *American Journal of Sociology* 106: 1013–1057.

Haynie, Dana L. and D. Wayne Osgood. 2005. "Reconsidering Peers and Delinquency: How Do Peers Matter." *Social Forces* 84: 1109–1130.

Haynie, Dana E., Eric Silver, and Brent Teasdale. 2006. "Neighborhood Characteristics, Peer Networks, and Adolescent Violence." *Journal of Quantitative Criminology* 22: 147–169.

Heimer, Karen. 1997. "Socioeconomic Status, Subcultural Definitions, and Violent Delinquency." *Social Forces* 75: 799–833.

Heimer, Karen and Stacey De Coster. 1999. "The Gendering of Violent Delinquency." *Criminology* 37: 277–318.

Jensen, Gary F. 2007. "Social Learning and Violent Behavior." In Daniel J. Flannery, Alexander T. Vazsonyi, and Irwin D. Waldman (eds.), *The Cambridge Handbook of Violent Behavior and Aggression*, pp. 636–646. New York: Cambridge University Press.

Krohn, Marvin D. 1999. "Social Learning Theory: The Continuing Development of a Perspective." *Theoretical Criminology* 3: 462–476.

Krohn, Marvin, Charis Kubrin, and Thomas Stuckey. 2007. *Measuring Theories of Crime and Deviance.* Los Angeles: Roxbury Publishing.

Kubrin, Charis E., Thomas D. Stucky, and Marvin D. Krohn, 2009. *Researching Theories of Crime and Deviance.* New York: Oxford University Press.

Lee, Matthew R., William B. Bankston, Timothy C. Hayes, and Shaun A. Thomas. 2007. "Revisiting the Southern Subculture of Violence." *The Sociological Quarterly* 48: 253–275.

Luckenbill, David F. and Daniel P. Doyle. 1989. "Structural Position and Violence: Developing a Cultural Explanation." *Criminology* 27: 419–436.

Markowitz, Fred E. and Richard B. Felson. 1998. "Socio-Demographic Differences in Attitudes and Violence." *Criminology* 36: 117–138.

Maruna, Shadd and Heith Copes. 2005. "What Have We Learned from Five Decades of Neutralization Research?" *Crime and Justice* 32: 221–320.

Matsueda, Ross L. 1988. "The Current State of Differential Association Theory." *Crime and Delinquency* 34: 277–306.

Matsueda, Ross L. and Kathleen Anderson. 1998. "The Dynamics of Delinquent Peers and Delinquent Behavior." *Criminology* 36: 269–309.

Matza, David and Gresham M. Sykes. 1961. "Juvenile Delinquency and Subterranean Values." *American Sociological Review* 26: 712–719.

Messner, Steven F. 1988. "Research on Criminal and Socioeconomic Factors in Criminal Violence." *The Psychiatric Clinics of North America* 11: 511–525.

Miller, Walter B. 1958. "Lower Class Culture as a Generating Milieu of Gang Delinquency." *Journal of Social Issues* 14: 5–19.

Mullins, Christopher W. 2006. *Holding Your Square: Masculinities, Streetlife, and Violence.* Portland, OR: Willan.

Nisbett, Richard E. and Doc Cohen. 1996. *Culture of Honor: The Psychology of Violence in the South.* Boulder, CO: Westview.

Sampson, Robert J. 1999. "Techniques of Research Neutralization." *Theoretical Criminology* 3: 438–451.

Sampson, Robert J. and Dawn Jeglum Bartusch. 1999. *Attitudes Toward Crime, Police, and the Law: Individual and Neighborhood Differences.* Washington, DC: National Institute of Justice Research Preview.

Snyder, James, John Reid, and Gerald Patterson. 2003. "A Social Learning Model of Child and Adolescent Antisocial Behavior." In Benjamin B. Lahey, Terrie E. Moffit, and Avshalom Caspi (eds.), *Causes of Conduct Disorder and Juvenile Delinquency*, pp. 27–48. New York: Guilford Press.

Stewart, Eric A. and Ronald L. Simons. 2006. "Structure and Culture in African American Adolescent Violence: A Partial Test of the 'Code of the Street' Thesis." *Justice Quarterly* 23: 1–33.

Sutherland, Edwin H., Donald R. Cressey, and David F. Luckenbill. 1992. *Principles of Criminology.* Dix Hills, NY: General Hall.

Sykes, Gresham M. and David Matza. 1957. "Techniques of Neutralization." *American Sociological Review* 22: 664–670.

Tanner, Julian. 1978. "New Directions for Subcultural Theory." *Youth & Society* 9: 343–372.

Thornberry, Terence P., Marvin D. Krohn, Alan J. Lizotte, Carolyn A. Smith, and Kimberly Tobin. 2003. *Gangs and Delinquency in Developmental Perspective.* Cambridge, England: Cambridge University Press.

Tittle, Charles R. and Robert F. Meier. 1990. "Specifying the SES/Delinquency Relationship." *Criminology* 28: 271–299.

Topalli, Volkan. 2005. "When Being Good Is Bad: An Expansion of Neutralization Theory." *Criminology* 43: 797–836.

Warner, Barbara D. 2003. "The Role of Attenuated Culture in Social Disorganization Theory." *Criminology* 41: 73–97.

Warr, Mark. 2001. "The Social Origins of Crime: Edwin Sutherland and the Theory of Differential Association." In Raymond Paternoster and Ronet Bachma (eds.), *Explaining Crime and Criminals*, pp. 182–191. Los Angeles: Roxbury Publishing.

——. 2002. *Companions in Crime*. Cambridge, England: Cambridge University Press.

Warr, Mark and Mark Stafford. 1991. "The Influence of Delinquent Peers: What They Think or What They Do?" *Criminology* 4: 851–866.

Wilkinson, Deanna L. 2003. *Guns, Violence, and Identity Among African American and Latino Youth*. New York: LFB Scholarly Publishing.

Wolfgang, Marvin E. and Franco Ferracuti 1982. *The Subculture of Violence: Towards an Integrated Theory in Criminology*. Beverly Hills, CA: Sage.

Young, Jock. 2009. "Sub-Cultural Theory: Virtues and Vices." http://www.malcolmread.co.uk/Jock Young/subculture.htm

10. A Theory of Differential Association

Edwin H. Sutherland and Donald R. Cressey

Before Sutherland developed his theory, crime was usually explained in terms of multiple factors—like social class, broken homes, age, race, urban or rural location, and mental disorder. Sutherland developed his theory of differential association in an effort to explain why these various factors were related to crime. In doing so, he hoped to organize and integrate the research on crime up to that point, as well as to guide future research.

Sutherland's theory is stated in the form of nine propositions. He argues that criminal behavior is learned by interacting with others, especially intimate others. Criminals learn both the techniques of committing crime and the definitions favorable to crime from these others. The sixth proposition, which forms the heart of the theory, states that "a person becomes delinquent because of an excess of definitions favorable to law violation over definitions unfavorable to violation of law." According to Sutherland, factors such as social class, race, and broken homes influence crime because they affect the likelihood that individuals will associate with others who present definitions favorable to crime.

Sutherland's theory has had a tremendous influence on crime research and it remains one of the dominant theories of crime. Studies on the causes of crime routinely attempt to determine whether individuals are associating with delinquent or criminal others. Although one can learn definitions favorable to crime from law-abiding individuals, one is most likely to learn such definitions from delinquent

friends or criminal family members. These studies typically find that association with delinquent others is the best predictor of crime, and that these delinquent others partly influence crime by leading the individual to adopt beliefs conducive to crime (see Agnew, 2000; Akers, 1998; Akers and Sellers, 2008; Kubrin et al., 2009; Warr, 2001 for summaries of such studies).

Sutherland's theory has also inspired much additional theorizing in criminology. Theorists have attempted to better describe the nature of those definitions favorable to violation of the law (see Chapter 17 by Sykes and Matza). They have attempted to better describe the processes by which we learn criminal behavior from others (see the description of social learning theory by Akers in Chapter 11). And they have drawn on Sutherland in an effort to explain group differences in crime rates (see the Anderson selection in this part). Sutherland's theory of differential association, then, is one of the enduring classics in criminology (for excellent discussions of the current state of differential association theory, see Matsueda, 1988, and Warr, 2001).

References

Agnew, Robert. 2000. "Sources of Criminality: Strain and Subcultural Theories." In Joseph F. Sheley (ed.), *Criminology: A Contemporary Handbook*, 3rd edition, pp. 349–371. Belmont, CA: Wadsworth.

Reprinted from Edwin H. Sutherland and Donald R. Cressey, "A Theory of Differential Association" in *Principles of Criminology*, 6th edition. Copyright ©1960 by Elaine S. Cressey. Reprinted by permission of Elaine S. Cressey.

Akers, Ronald L. 1998. *Social Learning and Social Structure: A General Theory of Crime and Deviance.* Boston: Northeastern University Press.

Akers, Ronald L. and Christine S. Sellers. 2004. *Criminological Theories: Introduction and Evaluation,* 4th edition. Los Angeles: Roxbury Publishing.

Kubrin, Charis E., Thomas D. Stucky, and Marvin D. Krohn. 2009. *Researching Theories at Crime and Deviance.* New York: Oxford University Press.

Matsueda, Ross L. 1988. "The Current State of Differential Association Theory." *Crime and Delinquency* 34: 277–306.

Warr, Mark. 2001. "The Social Origins of Crime: Edwin Sutherland and the Theory of Differential Association." In Raymond Paternoster and Ronet Bachman (ed.), *Explaining Criminals and Crime,* pp. 182–191. Los Angeles: Roxbury Publishing.

The following statement refers to the process by which a particular person comes to engage in criminal behavior.

1. *Criminal behavior is learned.* Negatively, this means that criminal behavior is not inherited, as such; also, the person who is not already trained in crime does not invent criminal behavior, just as a person does not make mechanical inventions unless he has had training in mechanics.

2. *Criminal behavior is learned in interaction with other persons in a process of communication.* This communication is verbal in many respects but includes also "the communication of gestures."

3. *The principal part of the learning of criminal behavior occurs within intimate personal groups.* Negatively, this means that the impersonal agencies of communication, such as movies and newspapers, play a relatively unimportant part in the genesis of criminal behavior.

4. *When criminal behavior is learned, the learning includes (a) techniques of committing the crime, which are sometimes very complicated, sometimes very simple; (b) the specific direction of motives, drives, rationalizations, and attitudes.*

5. *The specific direction of motives and drives is learned from definitions of the legal codes as favorable or unfavorable.* In some societies an individual is surrounded by persons who invariably define the legal codes as rules to be observed, while in others he is surrounded by persons whose definitions are favorable to the violation of the legal codes. In our American society these definitions are almost always mixed, with the consequence that we have culture conflict in relation to the legal codes.

6. *A person becomes delinquent because of an excess of definitions favorable to violation of law over definitions unfavorable to violation of law.* This is the principle of differential association. It refers to both criminal and anti-criminal associations and has to do with counteracting forces. When persons become criminal, they do so because of contacts with criminal patterns and also because of isolation from anti-criminal patterns. Any person inevitably assimilates the surrounding culture unless other patterns are in conflict; a Southerner does not pronounce "r" because other Southerners do not pronounce "r." Negatively, this proposition of differential association means that associations which are neutral so far as crime is concerned have little or no effect on the genesis of criminal behavior. Much of the experience of a person is neutral in this sense, e.g., learning to brush one's teeth. This behavior has no negative or positive effect on criminal behavior except as it may be related to associations which are concerned with the legal codes. This neutral behavior is important especially as an occupier of the time of a child so that he is not in contact with criminal behavior during the time he is so engaged in the neutral behavior.

7. *Differential associations may vary in frequency, duration, priority, and intensity.* This means that associations with criminal behavior and also associations with anti-criminal behavior vary in those respects. "Frequency" and "duration" as modalities of associations are obvious and need no explanation. "Priority" is assumed to be important in the sense that lawful behavior developed in

early childhood may persist throughout life, and also that delinquent behavior developed in early childhood may persist throughout life. This tendency, however, has not been adequately demonstrated, and priority seems to be important principally through its selective influence. "Intensity" is not precisely defined but it has to do with such things as the prestige of the source of a criminal or anti-criminal pattern and with emotional reactions related to the associations. In a precise description of the criminal behavior of a person these modalities would be stated in quantitative form and a mathematical ratio be reached. A formula in this sense has not been developed, and the development of such a formula would be extremely difficult.

8. *The process of learning criminal behavior by association with criminal and anti-criminal patterns involves all of the mechanisms that are involved in any other learning.* Negatively, this means that the learning of criminal behavior is not restricted to the process of imitation. A person who is seduced, for instance, learns criminal behavior by association, but this process would not ordinarily be described as imitation.

9. *While criminal behavior is an expression of general needs and values, it is not explained by those general needs and values since non-criminal behavior is an expression of the same needs and values.* Thieves generally steal in order to secure money, but likewise honest laborers work in order to secure money. The attempts by many scholars to explain criminal behavior by general drives and values, such as the happiness principle, striving for social status, the money motive, or frustration, have been and must continue to be futile since they explain lawful behavior as completely as they explain criminal behavior. They are similar to respiration, which is necessary for any behavior but which does not differentiate criminal from non-criminal behavior.

It is not necessary, at this level of explanation, to explain why a person has the associations which he has; this certainly involves a complex of many things. In an area where the delinquency rate is

high, a boy who is sociable, gregarious, active, and athletic is very likely to come in contact with the other boys in the neighborhood, learn delinquent behavior from them, and become a gangster; in the same neighborhood the psychopathic boy who is isolated, introverted, and inert may remain at home, not become acquainted with the other boys in the neighborhood, and not become delinquent. In another situation, the sociable, athletic, aggressive boy may become a member of a scout troop and not become involved in delinquent behavior. The person's associations are determined in a general context of social organization. A child is ordinarily reared in a family; the place of residence of the family is determined largely by family income; and the delinquency rate is in many respects related to the rental value of the houses. Many other aspects of social organization affect the kinds of associations a person has.

The preceding explanation of criminal behavior purports to explain the criminal and non-criminal behavior of individual persons. As indicated earlier, it is possible to state sociological theories of criminal behavior which explain the criminality of a community, nation, or other group. The problem, when thus stated, is to account for variations in crime rates and involves a comparison of the crime rates of various groups or the crime rates of a particular group at different times. The explanation of a crime rate must be consistent with the explanation of the criminal behavior of the person, since the crime rate is a summary statement of the number of persons in the group who commit crimes and the frequency with which they commit crimes. One of the best explanations of crime rates from this point of view is that a high crime rate is due to social disorganization. The term "social disorganization"is not entirely satisfactory and it seems preferable to substitute for it the term "differential social organization." The postulate on which this theory is based, regardless of the name, is that crime is rooted in the social organization and is an expression of that social organization. A group may be organized for criminal behavior or organized against criminal behavior. Most communities are organized both for criminal and anti-criminal behavior and in that sense the crime rate is an expression of the differential group organization.

Differential group organization as an explanation of variations in crime rates is consistent with the differential association theory of the processes by which persons become criminals.

Discussion Questions

1. What does Sutherland mean by "definitions favorable to violation of law"? Give examples of such definitions.
2. According to Sutherland, our associations do not carry equal weight; some are more influential than others. What types of associations carry the greatest weight in influencing our behavior?
3. Strain theorists, described in the next section, argue that frustration is a major cause of crime. How would Sutherland respond to this argument?
4. What policy recommendations might Sutherland have made for controlling crime?

11. A Social Learning Theory of Crime

Ronald L. Akers

As Akers points out in this selection, his social learning theory is a reformulation and extension of Sutherland's differential association theory. Differential association theory argues that criminal behavior is learned in interaction with others, but it does not specify the mechanisms by which such behavior is learned. Burgess and Akers (1966) and Akers (1985, 1998; Akers and Sellers, 2008) draw on several theories of learning, particularly behavioral theory and social learning theory in psychology, to more precisely describe how crime is learned.

Akers's theory is compatible with Sutherland's theory. Like Sutherland, Akers argues that we learn to engage in crime through exposure to and the adoption of definitions favorable to crime. Akers, however, more fully describes the nature of such definitions. In doing so, he draws heavily on Sykes and Matza's description of the techniques of neutralization—although he also argues that the definitions favorable to crime include more than neutralization techniques (i.e., he argues that there are both positive and neutralizing definitions favorable to crime).

At the same time, Akers extends differential association theory. He argues that crime may also be learned through imitation and differential reinforcement. Akers's theory, then, is much broader than that of Sutherland. In fact, Akers (1985, 1998) has argued that his theory is capable of subsuming most of the major sociological theories of crime. As Akers points out in this selection, his theory has received much empirical support. As a consequence, social learning theory is one of the leading theories of why individuals engage in crime. Further, Akers (1998) has recently extended social learning theory to the macro-level, with the theory being used to explain group differences in crime rates, including differences between sociodemographic groups (e.g., class and gender groups), communities, and societies. As described in this selection, features of the larger social environment, as well as the individual's position in the larger environment, affect crime partly through their effect on the individual's "exposure to criminal associations, models, definitions, and reinforcement." Preliminary data provide some support for this argument (see Akers and Jensen, 2003; Akers and Sellers, 2008; Haynie et al., 2006).

References

Akers, Ronald L. 1985. *Deviant Behavior: A Social Learning Approach.* Belmont, CA: Wadsworth.

——. 1998. *Social Learning and Social Structure: A General Theory of Crime and Deviance.* Boston: Northeastern University Press.

Akers, Ronald L. and Gary F. Jensen, eds. 2003. *Social Learning Theory and the Explanation of Crime.* New Brunswick, NJ: Transaction.

Akers, Ronald L. and Christine S. Sellers. 2008. *Criminological Theories,* 4th edition. Los Angeles: Roxbury Publishing.

Burgess, Robert L. and Ronald L. Akers. 1966. "A Differential Association-Reinforcement Theory of Criminal Behavior." *Social Problems* 14: 128–147.

Copyright © 1994. Reprinted with permission from Roxbury Publishing Company.

Haynie, Dana E., Eric Silver, and Brent Teasdale. 2006. "Neighborhood Characteristics, Peer Networks, and Adolescent Violence." *Journal of Quantitative Criminology* 22: 149–169.

Development of the Theory

Sutherland asserted in the eighth statement of his theory that all the mechanisms of learning are involved in criminal behavior. However, beyond a brief comment that more is involved than direct imitation (Trade, 1912), he did not explain what the mechanisms of learning are. These learning mechanisms were specified by Burgess and Akers (1966b) in their "differential association-reinforcement" theory of criminal behavior. Burgess and Akers produced a full reformulation that retained the principles of differential association, combining them with, and restating them in terms of, the learning principles of operant and respondent conditioning that had been developed by behavioral psychologists. Akers followed up his early work with Burgess to develop social learning theory, applying it to criminal, delinquent, and deviant behavior in general. He has modified the theory, provided a fully explicated presentation of its concepts, examined it in light of the critiques and research by others, and carried out his own research to test its central propositions (Akers, 1973; 1977; 1985; 1998).

Social learning theory is not competitive with differential association theory. Instead, it is a broader theory that retains all the differential association processes in Sutherland's theory (albeit clarified and somewhat modified) and integrates it with differential reinforcement and other principles of behavioral acquisition, continuation, and cessation (Akers, 1985:41). Thus, research findings supportive of differential association also support the integrated theory. But social learning theory explains criminal and delinquent behavior more thoroughly than does the original differential association theory (see, for instance, Akers et al., 1979; Warr and Stafford, 1991).

Burgess and Akers (1966b) explicity identified the learning mechanisms as those found in modern behavioral theory. They retained the concepts of differential association and definitions from Sutherland's theory, but conceptualized them in more behavioral terms and added concepts from behavioral learning theory. These concepts include differential reinforcement, whereby "operant" behavior (the voluntary actions of the individual) is conditioned or shaped by rewards and punishments. They also contain classical or "respondent" conditioning (the conditioning of involuntary reflex behavior); discriminative stimuli (the environmental and internal stimuli that provides cues or signals for behavior), schedules of reinforcement (the rate and ratio in which rewards and punishments follow behavioral responses), and other principles of behavior modification.

Social learning theory retains a strong element of the symbolic interactionism found in the concepts of differential association and definitions from Sutherland's theory (Akers, 1985:39–70). Symbolic interactionism is the theory that social interaction is mainly the exchange of meaning and symbols; individuals have the cognitive capacity to imagine themselves in the role of others and incorporate this into their conceptions of themselves (Ritzer, 1992). This, and the explicit inclusion of such concepts as imitation, anticipated reinforcement, and self-reinforcement, makes social learning "soft behaviorism" (Akers, 1985:65). As a result, the theory is closer to cognitive learning theories, such as Albert Bandura's (1973; 1977; 1986; Bandura and Walters, 1963), than to the radical or orthodox operant behaviorism of B. F. Skinner (1953; 1959) with which Burgess and Akers began.

The Central Concepts and Propositions of Social Learning Theory

The word *learning* should not be taken to mean that the theory is only about how novel criminal behavior is acquired. "Behavioral principles are not limited to learning but are fundamental principles of performance [that account for] ... the acquisition, maintenance, and modification of human behavior" (Andrews and Bonta, 1998: 150). Social learning theory offers an explanation of crime and deviance which embraces variables that operate both to motivate and control criminal behavior, both to promote and undermine conformity. The probability of criminal or conforming behavior occurring is a function of the balance of these influences on behavior.

> The basic assumption in social learning theory is that the same learning process in a context of social structure, interaction, and situation, produces both conforming and deviant behavior. The difference lies in the direction ... [of] the balance of influences on behavior.

> The probability that persons will engage in criminal and deviant behavior is increased and the probability of their conforming to the norm is decreased when they differentially associate with others who commit criminal behavior and espouse definitions favorable to it, are relatively more exposed in-person or symbolically to salient criminal/deviant models, define it as desirable or justified in a situation discriminative for the behavior, and have received in the past and anticipate in the current or future situation relatively greater reward than punishment for the behavior. (Akers, 1998:50)

As these quotations show, while referring to all aspects of the learning process, Akers' development of the theory has relied principally on four major concepts: *differential association, definitions, differential reinforcement*, and *imitation* (Akers et al., 1979; Akers, 1985; Akers, 1998).

Differential association. Differential association refers to the process whereby one is exposed to normative definitions favorable or unfavorable to illegal or law-abiding behavior. Differential association has both behavioral interactional and normative dimensions. The interactional dimension is the direct association and interaction with others who engage in certain kinds of behavior, as well as the indirect association and identification with more distant reference groups. The normative dimension is the different patterns of norms and values to which an individual is exposed through this association.

The groups with which one is in differential association provide the major social contexts in which all the mechanisms of social learning operate. They not only expose one to definitions, they also present them with models to imitate and with differential reinforcement (source, schedule, value, and amount) for criminal or conforming behavior. The most important of these groups are the primary ones of family and friends, though they may also be secondary and reference groups. Neighbors, churches, school teachers, physicians, the law and authority figures, and other individuals and groups in the community (as well as mass media and other more remote sources of attitudes and models) have varying degrees of effect on the individual's propensity to commit criminal and delinquent behavior. Those associations that occur earlier (priority), last longer and occupy more of one's time (duration), take place most often (frequency), and involve others with whom one has the more important or closer relationship (intensity) will have the greater effect on behavior.

Definitions. Definitions are one's own attitudes or meanings that one attaches to given behavior. That is, they are orientations, rationalizations, definitions of the situation, and other evaluative and moral attitudes that define the commission of an act as right or wrong, good or bad, desirable or undesirable, justified or unjustified.

In social learning theory, these definitions are both general and specific. General beliefs include religious, moral, and other conventional values and norms that are favorable to conforming behavior and unfavorable to committing any deviant or criminal acts. Specific definitions orient the person to particular acts or series of acts. Thus, one may believe that it is morally wrong to steal and that laws against theft should be obeyed, but at the same time one may see little wrong with smoking marijuana and rationalize that it is all right to violate laws against drug possession.

The greater the extent to which one holds attitudes that disapprove of certain acts, the less one is likely to engage in them. Conventional beliefs are negative toward criminal behavior. Conversely, the more one's own attitudes approve of a behavior, the greater the chances are that one will do it. Approving definitions favorable to the commission of criminal or deviant behavior are basically positive or neutralizing. Positive definitions are beliefs or attitudes which make the behavior morally desirable or wholly permissible. Neutralizing definitions favor the commission of crime by justifying or excusing it. They view the act as something that is probably undesirable but, given the situation, is nonetheless all right, justified, excusable, necessary, or not really bad to do. The concept of neutralizing definitions in social learning theory incorporates then notions of verbalizations, rationalizations, techniques of neutralizations, accounts, disclaimers, and moral disengagement (Cressey, 1953; Sykes and Matza, 1957; Lyman and Scott, 1970; Hewitt and Stokes, 1975; Bandura, 1990). Neutralizing attitudes include such beliefs as, "Everybody has a racket," "I can't help myself, I was born this way," "I am not at fault," "I am not responsible," "I was drunk and didn't know what I was doing," "I just blew my top," "They can afford it," "He deserved it," and other excuses and justification for committing deviant acts and victimizing others. These definitions favorable and unfavorable to criminal and delinquent behavior are developed through imitation and differential reinforcement. Cognitively, they provide a mind-set that makes one more willing to commit the act when the opportunity occurs. Behaviorally, they affect the commission of deviant or criminal behavior by acting as internal discriminative stimuli. Discriminative stimuli operate as cues or signals to the individual as to what responses are appropriate or expected in a given situation.

Some of the definitions favorable to deviance are so intensely held that they almost "require" one to violate the law. For instance, the radical ideologies of revolutionary groups provide strong motivation for terrorist acts, just as the fervent moral stance of some anti-abortion groups justifies in their minds the need to engage in civil disobedience. For the most part, however, definitions favorable to crime and delinquency do not "require" or strongly motivate action in this sense. Rather, they are conventional beliefs so weakly held that they provide no restraint or are positive or neutralizing attitudes that facilitate law violation in the right set of circumstances.

Differential reinforcement. Differential reinforcement refers to the balance of anticipated or actual rewards and punishments that follow or are consequences of behavior. Whether individuals will refrain from or commit a crime at any given time (and whether they will continue or desist from doing so in the future) depends on the past, present, and anticipated future rewards and punishments for their actions. The probability that an act will be committed or repeated is increased by rewarding outcomes or reactions to it, e.g., obtaining approval, money, food, or pleasant feelings—positive reinforcement. The likelihood that an action will be taken is also enhanced when it allows the person to avoid or escape aversive or unpleasant events—negative reinforcement. Punishment may also be direct (positive), in which painful or unpleasant consequences are attached to a behavior; or indirect (negative), in which a reward or pleasant consequence is removed. Just as there are modalities of association, there are modalities of reinforcement— amount, frequency, and probability. The greater the value or amount of reinforcement for the person's behavior, the more frequently it is reinforced, and the higher the probability that it will be reinforced (as balanced against alternative behavior), the greater the likelihood that it will occur and be repeated. The reinforcement process does not operate in the social environment in a simple either/or fashion. Rather, it operates according to a "matching function" in which the occurence of, and changes in, each of several different behaviors correlate with the probability and amount of, and changes in, the balance of reward and punishment attached to each behavior (Herrnstein, 1961; Hamblin, 1979; Conger and Simons, 1995).

Reinforcers and punishers can be nonsocial; for example, the direct physical effects of drugs and alcohol. However, whether or not these effects are experienced positively or negatively is contingent upon previously learned expectations. Through social reinforcement, one learns to interpret the effects as pleasurable and enjoyable or as frightening and unpleasant. Individuals can learn without contact, directly or indirectly, with social reinforcers and punishers. There may be a physiological basis for the tendency of some individuals (such as those prone to sensation-seeking) more than others to find certain forms of deviant behavior intrinsically rewarding (Wood et al., 1995). However, the theory proposes that most of the learning in criminal and deviant behavior is the result of social exchange in which the words, responses, presence, and behavior of other persons directly reinforce behavior, provide the setting for reinforcement (discriminative stimuli), or serve as the conduit through which other social rewards and punishers are delivered or made available.

The concept of social reinforcement (and punishment) goes beyond the direct reactions of others present while an act is committed. It also includes the whole range of actual and anticipated, tangible and intangible rewards valued in society or subgroups. Social rewards can be highly symbolic. Their reinforcing effects can come from their fulfilling ideological, religious, political, or other goals. Even those rewards which we consider to be very tangible, such as money and material possessions, gain their reinforcing value from the prestige and approval value they have in society. Nonsocial reinforcement, therefore, is more narrowly confined to unconditioned physiological and physical stimuli. In self-reinforcement the individual exercises self-control, reinforcing or punishing one's own behavior by taking the role of others, even when alone.

Imitation. Imitation refers to the engagement in behavior after the observation of similar behavior in others. Whether or not the behavior modeled by others will be imitated is affected by the characteristics of the models, the behavior observed, and the observed consequences of the behavior (Bandura, 1977). The observation of salient models in primary groups and in the media affects both pro-social and deviant behavior (Donnerstein and Linz, 1995). It is more important in the initial acquisition and performance of novel behavior than in the maintenance or cessation of behavioral patterns once established, but it continues to have some effect in maintaining behavior.

The Social Learning Process: Sequence and Feedback Effects

These social learning variables are all part of an underlying process that is operative in each individual's learning history and in the immediate situation in which an opportunity for a crime occurs. Akers stresses that social learning is a complex process with reciprocal and feedback effects. The reciprocal effects are not seen as equal, however. Akers hypothesizes a typical temporal sequence or process by which persons come to the point of violating the law or engaging in other deviant acts (Akers, 1998).

This process is one in which the balance of learned definitions, imitation of criminal or deviant models, and the anticipated balance of reinforcement produces the initial delinquent or deviant act. The facilitative effects of these variables continue in the repetition of acts, although imitation becomes less important than it was in the first commission of the act. After initiation, the actual social and non-social reinforcers and punishers affect whether or not the acts will be repeated and at what level of frequency. Not only the behavior itself, but also the definitions are affected by the consequences of the initial act. Whether a deviant act will be committed in a situation that presents the opportunity depends on the learning history of the individual and the set of reinforcement contingencies in that situation.

> The actual social sanctions and other effects of engaging in the behavior may be perceived differently, but to the extent that they are more rewarding than alternative behavior, then the deviant behavior will be repeated under similar circumstances. Progression into more frequent or sustained patterns of deviant behavior is promoted [to the extent] that reinforcement, exposure to deviant models, and definitions are not offset by negative formal and informal sanctions and definitions. (Akers, 1985:60)

The theory does not hypothesize that definitions favorable to law violation only precede and are unaffected by the initiation of criminal acts. Acts in violation of the law can occur in the absence of any thought given to right and wrong. Furthermore, definitions may be applied by the individual retroactively to excuse or justify an act already committed. To the extent that such excuses successfully mitigate others' negative sanctions or one's self-punishment, however, they become cues for the repetition of deviant acts. At that point they precede the future commission of the acts.

Differential association with conforming and non-conforming others typically precedes the individual's committing the acts. Families are included in the differential association process, and it is obvious that association, reinforcement of conforming or deviant behavior, deviant or conforming modeling, and exposure to definitions favorable or unfavorable to deviance occurs within the family prior to the onset of delinquency. On the other hand, it can never be true that the onset of delinquency initiates interaction in the family (except in the unlikely case of the late-stage adoption of a child who is already delinquent who is drawn to and chosen by deviant parents). This is also hypothesized as the typical process within peer groups. While one may be attracted to deviant peer groups prior to becoming involved in delinquency, associations with peers and others are most often formed initially around attractions, friendships, and circumstances, such as neighborhood proximity, that have little to do directly with co-involvement in some deviant behavior. However, after the associations have been established and the reinforcing or punishing consequences of the deviant behavior are experienced, both the continuation of old and the seeking of new associations (over which one has any choice) will themselves be affected. One may choose further interaction with others based, in part, on whether they too are involved in similar deviant or criminal behavior. But the theory proposes that the sequence of events, in which deviant associations precede the onset of delinquent behavior, will occur more frequently than the sequence of events in which the onset of delinquency precedes the beginning of deviant associations.

Social Structure and Social Learning

Akers has proposed a SSSL (social structure and social learning) model in which social structural factors are hypothesized to have an indirect effect on the individual's conduct. They affect the social learning variables of differential association, differential reinforcement, definitions, and imitation which, in turn, have a direct impact on the individual's conduct. The social learning variables are proposed as the main ones in the process by which various aspects of the social structure influence individual behavior (see Figure 11.1).

> The social structural variables are indicators of the primary distal macro-level and meso-level causes of crime, while the social learning variables reflect the primary proximate causes of criminal behavior that mediate the relationship between social structure and crime rates. Some structural variables are not related to crime and do not explain the crime rate because they do not have a crime-relevant effect on the social learning variables. (Akers, 1998:322)

Figure 11.1
Social Structure and Social Learning

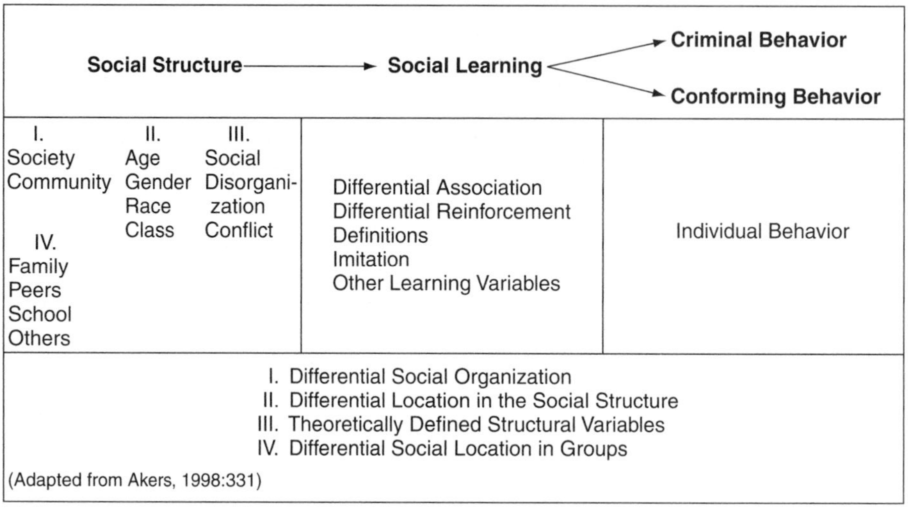

| Social Structure ⟶ Social Learning ⟵ | ⟶ Criminal Behavior |
| | ⟶ Conforming Behavior |

(Adapted from Akers, 1998:331)

As shown in Figure 11.1, Akers (1998) identifies four dimensions of social structure that provide the contexts within which social learning variables operate:

(I) *Differential Social Organization* refers to the structural correlates of crime in the community or society that affect the rates of crime and delinquency including age composition, population density, and other attributes that lean societies, communities, and other social systems "toward relatively high or relatively low crime rates" (Akers, 1998:332).

(II) *Differential Location in the Social Structure* refers to sociodemographic characteristics of individuals and social groups that indicate their niches within the larger social structure. Class, gender, race and ethnicity, marital status, and age locate the positions and standing of persons and their roles, groups, or social categories in the overall social structure.

(III) *Theoretically Defined Structural Variables* refer to anomie, class oppression, social disorganization, group conflict, patriarchy, and other concepts that have been used in one or more theories to identify criminogenic conditions of societies, communities, or groups.

(IV) *Differential Social Location* refers to individuals' membership in and relationship to primary, secondary, and reference groups such as the family, friendship/peer groups, leisure groups, colleagues, and work groups.

The differential social organization of society and community, as well as the differential location of persons in the social class, race, gender, religion, and other structures in society, provides the general learning contexts for individuals that increase or decrease the likelihood of their committing crime. The differential location in family, peer, school, church, and other groups provides the more immediate contexts that promote or discourage the criminal behavior of the individual. Differences in the societal or group rates of criminal behavior are a function of the extent to which their cultural traditions, norms, and social control systems provide socialization, learning environments, and immediate situations conducive to conformity or deviance. The structural conditions identified in macro-level theories can affect one's exposure to criminal associations, models, definitions, and reinforcement to induce or retard criminal actions in individuals. It is possible, therefore, to integrate these structural theories with social learning. Although this has not yet been accomplished, the SSSL model is a step in that direction.

Empirical Validity of Social Learning Theory

Critiques and Research on Social Learning Variables

The testability of the basic behavioral learning principles incorporated in social learning theory has been challenged because they may be tautological. The way in which the principle of reinforcement is often stated by behavioral psychologists makes the proposition true by definition. That is, they define reinforcement by stating that it occurs when behavior has been strengthened, that is, its rate of commission has been increased. If reinforcement is defined this way, then the statement "If behavior is reinforced, it will be strengthened" is tautological. If reinforcement means that behavior has been strengthened, then the hypothesis states simply, "If behavior is reinforced, it is reinforced." If the behavior is not strengthened, then by definition it has not been reinforced; therefore, no instance of behavior that is not being strengthened can be used to falsify the hypothesis.

Another criticism of social learning has to do with the temporal sequence of differential peer association and delinquency. Some have argued that youths become delinquent first then seek out other delinquent youths. Rather than delinquent associations causing delinquency, delinquency causes delinquent associations. If there is a relationship between one's own delinquency and one's association with delinquent peers, then it is simply a case of "birds of a feather flocking together" rather than a bird joining a flock and changing its feathers. Differential peer associations with delinquent friends is almost always a consequence rather than a cause of one's own behavior. Association with delinquent peers takes place only or mainly after peers have already independently established patterns of delinquent involvement. No deviance-relevant learning takes place in peer groups. From this point of view, any association with delinquent youths has no direct effect on an adolescent's delinquent behavior. Therefore, association with delinquent friends has an effect on neither the onset nor acceleration, the continuation nor cessation, of delinquent behavior (Hirschi, 1969; Gottredson and Hirschi, 1990; Sampson and Laub, 1993).

These criticisms, however, may be off the mark. Burgess and Akers (1966a) identified this tautology problem and offered one solution to it. They separated the definitions of reinforcement and other behavioral concepts from nontautological, testable propositions in social learning theory and proposed criteria for falsifying those propositions. Others as well have proposed somewhat different solutions (Liska, 1969; Chadwick-Jones, 1976). Moreover, the variables in the process of reinforcement are always measured separately (and hence nontautologically) from measures of crime and deviance in research on social learning theory. The theory would be falsified if it is typically the case that positive social approval or other rewards for delinquency (that are not offset by punishment) more often reduce than increase its recurrence. Also, as shown above, feedback effects are built into the reinforcement concept with both prior and anticipated reward/punishment influencing present behavior.

Furthermore, the reciprocal relationship between one's own conduct and one's definitions and association with friends is clearly recognized in social learning theory. Therefore, the fact that delinquent behavior may precede the association with delinquent peers does not contradict this theory.

"Social learning admits that birds of a feather do flock together, but it also admits that if the birds are humans, they also will influence one another's behavior, in both conforming and deviant directions" (Akers, 1991:210). It would contradict the theory if research demonstrated that the onset of delinquency always or most often predates interaction with peers who have engaged in delinquent acts and/or have adhered to delinquency-favorable definitions. It would not support the theory if the research evidence showed that whatever level of delinquent behavioral involvement preceded association with delinquent peers stayed the same or decreased rather than increased after the association. Research has not yet found this to be the case. Instead, the findings from several studies favor the process proposed by social learning theory, which recognizes both direct and reciprocal effects. That is, a youngster associates differentially with peers who are deviant or tolerant of deviance, learns definitions favorable to delinquent behavior, is exposed to deviant models that reinforce delinquency, then initiates or increases involvement in that behavior, which then is expected to influence further associations and definitions (Kandel, 1978; Andrews and Kandel, 1979; Krohn et al., 1985; Sellers and Winfree, 1990; Empey and Stafford, 1991; Elliott and Menard, 1991; 1996; Kandel and Davies, 1991; Warr, 1993b; Esbensen and Huizinga, 1993; Thornberry et al., 1994; Menard and Elliott, 1994; Winfree et al., 1994a; Akers and Lee, 1996; Esbensen and Deschenes, 1998; Battin et al., 1998). Kandel and Davies (1991:442) note that

> although assortive pairing plays a role in similarity among friends observed at a single point in time, longitudinal research that we and others have carried out clearly documents the etiological importance of peers in the initiation and persistence of substance use.

Warr (1993b) also refers to the considerable amount of research evidence showing that peer associations precede the development of deviant patterns (or increase the frequency and seriousness of deviant behavior once it has begun) more often than involvement in deviant behavior precedes associations with deviant peers. The reverse sequence also occurs and Warr proposes that the process is

> ... a more complex, sequential, reciprocal process: Adolescents are commonly introduced to delinquency by their friends and subsequently become more selective in their choices of friends. The "feathering" and "flocking" ... are not mutually exclusive and may instead be part of a unified process. (Warr, 1993b:39)

This is, of course, completely consistent with the sequential and feedback effects in the social learning process spelled out above. Menard and Elliott (1990; 1994; Elliott and Menard, 1996) also support the process as predicted by social learning theory. Reciprocal effects were found in their research, but:

> [I]n the typical sequence of initiation of delinquent bonding and illegal behavior, delinquent bonding (again, more specifically, association with delinquent friends) usually precedes illegal behavior for those individuals for whom one can ascertain the temporal order.... [S]imilarly ... weakening of belief typically preceded the initiation of illegal behavior. (Elliott and Menard, 1994:174)

> These results are strong enough to indicate that serious forms of delinquent behavior such as index offending rarely, if ever, precede exposure to delinquent friends. Instead, in the vast majority of cases, exposure precedes index offending. (Elliott and Menard, 1996:43)

> We were *not* able to reject the learning theory hypothesis that the onset of exposure to delinquent others typically precedes the onset of delinquent behavior. Instead, we found that exposure to delinquent peers preceded minor delinquent behavior in a majority of cases, and serious delinquency in nearly all cases where some order could be determined.... Having delinquent friends and being

involved in delinquent behavior may influence one another, but the influence is not symmetric; the influence of exposure on delinquency begins earlier in the sequence, and remains stronger throughout the sequence, than the influence of delinquency on exposure. (Elliott and Menard, 1996:61–62)

The preponderance of findings thus far shows a stronger effect of peer associations on the individual's delinquent behavior. However, some research finds stronger effects running in the other direction and some shows the relationship to be about equal depending on the measures and methods employed (Kandel, 1996; Krohn et al., 1996; Matsueda and Anderson, 1998).

Another criticism of the theory is that the strong relationship between self-reported delinquency and peer associations is entirely due to the fact that associations are often measured by the individual's report of the delinquency of his or her peers; they are the same thing measured twice. One is measuring the same underlying delinquent tendency, whether youngsters are asked about the delinquency of their friends or about their own delinquency. But research shows that the two are not the same and that the respondent's reports of friends' behavior is not simply a reflection of one's own delinquent behavior (Menard and Elliott, 1990; 1991; Agnew, 1991b; Warr, 1993b; Thornberry et al., 1994; Elliott and Menard, 1996; Bartusch et al., 1997).

Almost all research conducted on social learning theory has found strong relationships in the theoretically expected direction between social learning variables and criminal, delinquent, and deviant behavior. When social learning theory is tested against other theories using the same data collected from the same samples, it is usually found to account for more variance in the dependent variables or have greater support than the theories with which it is being compared (for instance, see Akers and Cochran, 1985; Matsueda and Heimer, 1987;

White et al., 1986; Kandel and Davies, 1991; McGee, 1992; Benda, 1994; Burton et al., 1994). When social learning variables are included in integrated or combined models that incorporate variables from different theories, it is the measures of social learning concepts that have the strongest main and net effects (Elliott et al., 1985; Kaplan et al., 1987; Thornberry et al., 1994; Kaplan, 1996; Catalano et al., 1996).

There is abundant evidence to show the significant impact on criminal and deviant behavior of differential association in primary groups such as family and peers. The role of the family is usually as a conventional socializer against delinquency and crime. It provides anticriminal definitions, conforming models, and the reinforcement of conformity through parental discipline; it promotes the development of self-control. But deviant behavior may be the outcome of internal family interaction (McCord, 1991b). It is directly affected by deviant parental models, ineffective and erratic parental supervision and discipline in the use of positive and negative sanctions, and the endorsement of values and attitudes favorable to deviance. Patterson has shown that the operation of social learning mechanisms in parent-child interaction is a strong predictor of conforming/deviant behavior (Patterson, 1975; 1995; Snyder and Patterson, 1995). Ineffective disciplinary strategies by parents increase the chances that a child will learn behavior in the early years that is a precursor to his or her later delinquency. Children learn conforming responses when parents consistently make use of positive reward for proper behavior and impose moderately negative consequences for misbehavior (Capaldi et al., 1997). In some cases, parents directly train their children to commit deviant behavior (Adler and Adler, 1978). And in general, parental deviance and criminality is predictive of the children's future delinquency and crime (McCord, 1991a). Moreover, youngsters with delinquent siblings in the family are more likely to be delinquent, even when parental and other family characteristics are taken into account (Rowe and Gulley, 1992; Lauritsen, 1993; Rowe and Farrington, 1997).

Delinquent tendencies learned in the family may be exacerbated by differential peer association (Simons et al., 1994; Lauritsen, 1993). Other than one's own prior deviant behavior, the best single predictor of the onset, continuance, or desistance of crime and delinquency is differential association with conforming or law-violating peers (Loeber and Dishion, 1987; Loeber and Stouthamer-Loeber, 1986). More frequent, longer-term, and closer association with peers who do not support deviant behavior is strongly correlated with conformity, while greater association with peers who commit and approve of delinquency is predictive of one's own delinquent behavior. It is in peer groups that the first availability and opportunity for delinquent acts are typically provided. Virtually every study that includes a peer association variable finds it to be significantly and usually most strongly related to delinquency, alcohol and drug use and abuse, adult crime, and other forms of deviant behavior. There is a sizable body of research literature that shows the importance of differential associations and definitions in explaining crime and delinquency. The impact of differential peer association on delinquent behavior is among the most fully substantiated and replicated findings in criminology. Only the well-known relationships of crime rates to basic socio-demographic variables like age and sex are as consistently reported in the literature.

One special context of peer association is participation in delinquent gangs. Delinquent gangs and subcultures have received a great deal of attention in criminology for a long time. And research continues to find the strong influence of gang membership on serious delinquency. Battin et al. (1998) found that, controlling for prior delinquency, adolescents with delinquent friends are more likely to engage in delinquent conduct and come before the juvenile court on

delinquency charges, even if they are not part of a gang. But they are even more likely to do so if they and their friends are members of an identified delinquent gang. Whatever the frequency and seriousness of one's previous delinquency, joining a gang promotes an even higher level of his or her delinquent involvement, in large part because

> group processes and norms favorable to violence and other delinquency within gangs subsequently encourage and reinforce participation in violent and delinquent behavior. (Battin et al., 1998:108)

These findings suggest that, compared to having one or more non-gang delinquent friends, gang membership produces more frequent, intense, and enduring association with delinquent friends, exposure to delinquent models and definitions, and reinforcement for delinquent behavior. Other research from the GREAT (Gang Resistance Education And Training) project by Winfree et al. (1994a; 1994b) shows that both gang membership itself and delinquency (gang-related as well as non-gang delinquency) are explained by social learning variables (attitudes, social reinforcers/punishers, and differential association). This is true even controlling for "personal-biographical characteristics, including ethnicity, gender, and place of residence" (Winfree et al., 1994a: 167). The processes specified in social learning theory are

> nearly identical to those provided by qualitative gang research. Gang members reward certain behavior in their peers and punish others, employing goals and processes that are indistinguishable from those described by Akers. (Winfree et al., 1994a:149)

Later research from the GREAT project by Esbensen and Deschenes (1998) found that while neither is especially strong, social learning models do a better job than social bonding models of distinguishing between gang and non-gang members among both boys and girls in the eighth grade.

Many studies using direct measures of one or more of the social learning variables of differential association, imitation, definitions, and differential reinforcement find that the theory's hypotheses are upheld (Elliott et al., 1985; Dembo et al., 1986; White et al., 1986; Sellers and Winfree, 1990; McGee, 1992; Winfree et al., 1993; 1994a; 1994b; Mihalic and Elliott, 1997; Skinner and Fream, 1997; Esbensen and Deschenes, 1998). The relationships between the social learning variables and delinquent, criminal, and deviant behavior found in the research are typically strong to moderate, and there has been very little negative evidence reported in the literature.

Akers' Research on Social Learning Theory

In addition to the consistently positive findings by other researchers, support for the theory comes from research conducted by Akers and his associates in which all of the key social learning variables are measured (Akers, 1998). These include tests of social learning theory by itself and tests that directly compare its empirical validity with other theories. The first of these, conducted with Marvin D. Krohn, Lonn Lanza-Kaduce, and Marcia J. Radosevich, was a self-report questionnaire survey of adolescent substance abuse involving 3,000 students in grades 7 through 12 in eight communities in three Midwestern states (Akers et al., 1979; Krohn et al., 1982; Krohn et al., 1984; Lanza-Kaduce et al., 1984; Akers and Cochran, 1985; Akers and Lee, 1999). The second, conducted with Marvin Krohn, Ronald Lauer, James Massey, William Skinner, and Sherilyn Spear, was a five-year longitudinal study of smoking among 2,000 students in junior and senior high school in one midwest community (Lauer et al., 1982; Krohn et al., 1985; Spear and Akers 1998; Akers, 1992a; Akers and Lee, 1996). The third project, conducted with Anthony LaGreca, John Cochran, and

Christine Sellers, was a four-year longitudinal study of conforming and deviant drinking among elderly populations (1,400 respondents) in four communities in Florida and New Jersey (Akers et al., 1989; Akers and La Greca, 1991; Akers, 1992a). The fourth and fifth studies were the master's and doctoral research of Scot Boeringer, conducted under Akers' supervision, on rape and sexual coercion among samples of 200 and 500 college males (Boeringer et al., 1991; Boeringer, 1992). The dependent variables in these studies ranged from minor deviance to serious criminal behavior.

The findings in each of these studies demonstrated that the social learning variables of differential association, differential reinforcement, imitation, and definitions, singly and in combination, are strongly related to the various forms of deviant, delinquent, and criminal behavior studied. The social learning model produced high levels of explained variance, much more than other theoretical models with which it was compared.

The combined effects of the social learning variables on adolescent alcohol and drug use and abuse are very strong. High amounts (from 31 to 68 percent) of the variance in these variables are accounted for by the social learning variables. Social bonding models account for about 15 percent and anomie models account for less than 5 percent of the variance.

Similarly, adolescent cigarette smoking is highly correlated with the social learning variables. These variables also predict quite well the maintenance of smoking over a three-year period. They fare less well, however, when predicting which of the initially abstinent youngsters will begin smoking in that same period. The social learning variables do a slightly better job of predicting the onset of smoking over a five-year period. The sequencing and reciprocal effects of social learning variables and smoking behavior over the five-year period are as predicted by the theory. The onset, frequency, and quantity of elderly drinking is highly correlated with social learning, and the theory also successfully accounts for problem drinking among the elderly.

The social learning variables of association, reinforcement, definitions, and imitation explain the self-perceived likelihood of using force to gain sexual contact or committing rape by college men (55 percent explained variance). They also account for the actual use of drugs or alcohol, non-physical coercion, and physical force by males to obtain sex (20 percent explained variance). Social bonding, self-control, and relative deprivation (strain) models account for less than 10 percent of the variance in these variables.

The research by Akers and others has also included some evidence on the hypothesized relationship between social structure and social learning. This research has found that the correlations of adolescent drug use and smoking, elderly alcohol abuse, and rape to socio-demographic variables of age, sex, race, and class are reduced toward zero when the social learning variables are taken into account. Also, differences in levels of marijuana and alcohol use among adolescents in four types of communities (farm, rural-non-farm, suburban, and urban), and the differences in overall levels of drinking behavior among the elderly in four types of communities, are mediated by the social learning process. These and other findings from other research show some support for the SSSL theory (Warr, 1998; Mears et al., 1998; Akers and Lee, 1999). However, at this time there has not been enough research to confirm that social learning is the principal process mediating the relationship of social structure and crime as expected by the theory.

Summary

Akers' social learning theory combines Sutherland's original differential association theory of criminal behavior with general behavioral learning principles. The theory proposes that criminal and delinquent behavior is acquired, repeated, and changed by the same process as conforming behavior. While referring to all parts of the learning process, Akers's social learning theory in criminology has focused on the four major concepts of differential association, definitions, differential reinforcement, and imitation. That process will more likely produce behavior that violates social and legal norms than conforming behavior when persons differentially associate with those who expose them to deviant patterns, when the deviant behavior is differentially reinforced over conforming behavior, when individuals are more exposed to deviant than conforming models, and when their own definitions favorably dispose them to commit deviant acts.

This social learning explanation of crime and delinquency has been strongly supported by the research evidence. Research conducted over many years, including that by Akers and associates, has consistently found that social learning is empirically supported as an explanation of individual differences in delinquent and criminal behavior. The hypothesis that social learning processes mediate the effects of socio-demographic and community variables on behavior has been infrequently studied, but the evidence so far suggests that it will also be upheld.

Discussion Questions

1. Much data indicate that associating with delinquents increases one's own level of delinquency. According to social learning theory, why might this be so?
2. Drawing on social learning theory, describe and give an example of the major types of "definitions" favorable to crime.
3. How does positive reinforcement differ from negative reinforcement?
4. Describe the social learning *process*—note how this process changes after the initiation into deviance and describe the feedback effects in this process.
5. How might Akers explain the fact that males have higher rates of crime than females?

12. The Code of the Street

Elijah Anderson

In this selection, Anderson provides a contemporary account of a "subculture of violence." Drawing on his field research in inner-city communities (e.g., Anderson, 1990, 1999), he argues that there exists a "code of the street" in poor, inner-city African-American communities. While most people do not accept the values underlying this code, the code places all young African-American men under much pressure to respond to certain situations—shows of disrespect—with violence.

Anderson's account is perhaps the best description of a subculture of violence now available, and it is important because it makes us aware of the complexity of this subculture. While most people are opposed to the subculture, the subculture nevertheless shapes the behavior of most community residents. Further, the influence of the subculture is pervasive, affecting one's behavior in a wide range of situations and most especially affecting how one interprets and responds to challenges. Anderson's description of the socialization of "street kids"—those most immersed in the subculture—is especially compelling and sheds much light on the violent behavior of such youths.

It should be noted, however, that much data suggest that blacks are no more likely than whites to endorse values that justify or approve of violence (e.g., Brezina et al., 2004; Cao et al., 1997). One recent study, however, found that values favorable to violence are more common in disadvantaged neighborhoods (Sampson and Bartusch, 1999).

Anderson limited his study to a largely black, inner-city community, but the "code of the street" may also be present in disadvantaged Latino and white communities (whites, however, are much less likely than blacks to live in disadvantaged communities). The code, then, may be more a function of neighborhood disadvantage than race.

Anderson argues that the threat of violence is high in many disadvantaged communities and that it is often the case that one cannot count on the police for protection. In such circumstances, some individuals follow the Code to discourage others from victimizing them. That is, individuals act "tough" and respond to disrespectful treatment with violence as a way of letting others know that they are not to be "messed with." Stewart et al. (2006), however, found that individuals who followed the Code were more likely to be victimized, even after taking account of such things as their past history of victimization and the level of violence in their community. There are a few possible reasons for this; most notably, people who follow the Code may be more likely to engage in behaviors that provoke others (see Stewart et al., 2006). The Code of the Street, then, may partly arise out of a desire to protect oneself in a dangerous environment, but it does not appear to serve this function.

Data suggest that certain of the other factors discussed by Anderson also contribute to the adoption of the code. In particular, individuals are more likely to adopt the code if they are male,

Reprinted from Elijah Anderson, "The Code of the Streets" in *Code of the Street*. Originally in the *Atlantic Monthly* 273, no. 5 (May 1994). Copyright © 1994 by Elijah Anderson. Reprinted with the permission of Elijah Anderson.

poor, are poorly supervised and harshly disciplined by parents, believe their opportunities for success are limited, have experienced discrimination, have been the victims of violence, have engaged in violence, and—especially—associate with violent peers (see especially Baron et al., 2001; Brezina et al., 2004; Heimer and De Coster, 1999; Markowitz and Felson, 1998; Mullins, 2006; Stewart and Simons, 2006; Wilkinson, 2003).

References

Anderson, Elijah. 1990. *Streetwise*. Chicago: University of Chicago Press.

——. 1999. *Code of the Street*. New York: W.W. Norton.

Baron, Stephen W., Leslie W. Kennedy, and David R. Forde. 2001. "Male Street Youths' Conflict: The Role of Background, Subcultural, and Situational Factors." *Justice Quarterly* 18: 759–789.

Brezina, Timothy, Robert Agnew, Francis T. Cullen, and John Paul Wright. 2004. "The Code of the Street." *Youth Violence and Culture* 2: 303–328.

Cao, Liqun, Anthony Adams, and Vickie J. Jensen. 1997. "A Test of the Black Subculture of Violence Thesis: A Research Note." *Criminology* 35: 367–379.

Heimer, Karen, and Stacy De Coster. 1999. "The Gendering of Violent Delinquency." *Criminology* 37: 277–312.

Markowitz, Fred E. and Richard B. Felson. 1998. "Socio-demographic Differences in Attitudes and Violence." *Criminology* 36: 117–138.

Mullins, Christopher W. 2006. *Holding Your Square: Masculinities, Streetlife, and Violence*. Portland, OR: Willan.

Sampson, Robert J. and Dawn Jeglum Bartusch. 1999. *Attitudes Toward Crime, Police, and the Law: Individual and Neighborhood Differences*. Washington, DC: U.S. Department of Justice, National Institute of Justice.

Stewart, Eric A., Christopher J. Schreck, and Ronald L. Simons. 2006. "'I Ain't Gonna Let No One Disrepect Me': Does the Code of the Street Reduce or Increase Violent Victimization Among African American Adolescents." *Journal of Research in Crime and Delinquency* 43: 427–458.

Stewart, Eric A. and Ronald L. Simons. 2006. "Structure and Culture in African American Adolescent Violence: A Partial Test of the 'Code of the Street' Thesis." *Justice Quarterly* 23: 1–33.

Wilkinson, Deanna L. 2003. *Guns, Violence, and Identity Among African American and Latino Youth*. New York: LFB Scholarly Publishing.

Of all the problems besetting the poor inner-city black community, none is more pressing than that of interpersonal violence and aggression. It wreaks havoc daily with the lives of community residents and increasingly spills over into downtown and residential middle-class areas. Muggings, burglaries, carjackings, and drug-related shootings, all of which may leave their victims or innocent bystanders dead, are now common enough to concern all urban and many suburban residents. The inclination to violence springs from the circumstances of life among the ghetto poor—the lack of jobs that pay a living wage, the stigma of race, the fallout from rampant drug use and drug trafficking, and the resulting alienation and lack of hope for the future.

Simply living in such an environment places young people at special risk of falling victim to aggressive behavior. Although there are often forces in the community which can counteract the negative influences, by far the most powerful being a strong, loving, "decent" (as inner-city residents put it) family committed to middle-class values, the despair is pervasive enough to have spawned an oppositional culture, that of "the streets," whose norms are often consciously opposed to those of mainstream society. These two orientations—decent and street—socially organize the community, and their coexistence has important consequences for residents, particularly children growing up in the inner city. Above all, this environment means that even youngsters whose home lives reflect mainstream values—and the majority of homes in the community do—must be able to handle themselves in a street-oriented environment.

This is because the street culture has evolved what may be called a code of the streets, which amounts to a set of informal rules governing interpersonal public behavior, including violence. The rules prescribe both a proper comportment and a proper way to respond if challenged. They regulate the use of violence and so allow those who are inclined to aggression to precipitate violent encounters in an approved way. The rules have been established and are enforced mainly by the street-oriented, but on the streets the distinction between street and decent is often irrelevant; everybody knows that if the rules are violated, there are penalties. Knowledge of the code is thus largely defensive; it is literally necessary for operating in public. Therefore, even though families with a decency orientation are usually opposed to the values of the code, they often reluctantly encourage their children's familiarity with it to enable them to negotiate the inner-city environment.

At the heart of the code is the issue of respect—loosely defined as being treated "right," or granted the deference one deserves. However, in the troublesome public environment of the inner city, as people increasingly feel buffeted by forces beyond their control, what one deserves in the way of respect becomes more and more problematic and uncertain. This in turn further opens the issue of respect to sometimes intense interpersonal negotiation. In the street culture, especially among young people, respect is viewed as almost an external entity that is hard-won but easily lost, and so must constantly be guarded. The rules of the code in fact provide a framework for negotiating respect. The person whose very appearance—including his clothing, demeanor, and way of moving—deters transgressions feels that he possesses, and may be considered by others to possess, a measure of respect. With the right amount of respect, for instance, he can avoid "being bothered" in public. If he is bothered, not only may he be in physical danger but he

has been disgraced or "dissed" (disrespected). Many of the forms that dissing can take might seem petty to middle-class people (maintaining eye contact for too long, for example), but to those invested in the street code, these actions become serious indications of the other person's intentions. Consequently, such people become very sensitive to advances and slights, which could well serve as warnings of imminent physical confrontation.

This hard reality can be traced to the profound sense of alienation from mainstream society and its institutions felt by many poor inner-city black people, particularly the young. The code of the streets is actually a cultural adaptation to a profound lack of faith in the police and the judicial system. The police are most often seen as representing the dominant white society and not caring to protect inner-city residents. When called, they may not respond, which is one reason many residents feel they must be prepared to take extraordinary measures to defend themselves and their loved ones against those who are inclined to aggression. Lack of police accountability has in fact been incorporated into the status system: the person who is believed capable of "taking care of himself" is accorded a certain deference, which translates into a sense of physical and psychological control. Thus the street code emerges where the influence of the police ends and personal responsibility for one's safety is felt to begin. Exacerbated by the proliferation of drugs and easy access to guns, this volatile situation results in the ability of the street-oriented minority (or those who effectively "go for bad") to dominate the public spaces.

Decent and Street Families

Although almost everyone in poor inner-city neighborhoods is struggling financially and therefore feels a certain distance from the rest of America, the decent and the street family in a real sense represent two poles of value orientation, two contrasting conceptual categories. The labels "decent" and "street," which the residents themselves use, amount to evaluative judgments that confer status on local residents. The labeling is often the result of a social contest among individuals and families of the neighborhood. Individuals of the two orientations often coexist in the same extended family. Decent residents judge themselves to be so while judging others to be of the street, and street individuals often present themselves as decent, drawing distinctions between themselves and other people. In addition, there is quite a bit of circumstantial behavior—that is, one person may at different times exhibit both decent and street orientations, depending on the circumstances. Although these designations result from so much social jockeying, there do exist concrete features that define each conceptual category.

Generally, so-called decent families tend to accept mainstream values more fully and attempt to instill them in their children. Whether married couples with children or single-parent (usually female) households, they are generally "working poor" and so tend to be better off financially than their street-oriented neighbors. They value hard work and self-reliance and are willing to sacrifice for their children. Because they have a certain amount of faith in mainstream society, they harbor hopes for a better future for their children, if not for themselves. Many of them go to church and take a strong interest in their children's schooling. Rather than dwelling on the real hardships and inequities facing them, many such decent people, particularly the increasing number of grandmothers raising grandchildren, see their difficult situation as a test from God and derive great support from their faith and from the church community.

Extremely aware of the problematic and often dangerous environment in which they reside, decent parents tend to be strict in their child-rearing practices, encouraging children to respect authority and walk a straight moral line. They have an almost obsessive concern about trouble of any kind and remind their children to be on the lookout for people and situations that might lead to it. At the same time, they are themselves polite and considerate of others, and teach their children to be the same way. At home, at work, and in church, they strive hard to maintain a positive mental attitude and a spirit of cooperation.

So-called street parents, in contrast, often show a lack of consideration for other people and have a rather superficial sense of family and community. Though they may love their children, many of them are unable to cope with the physical and emotional demands of parenthood, and find it difficult to reconcile their needs with those of their children. These families, who are more fully invested in the code of the streets than the decent people are, may aggressively socialize their children into it in a normative way. They believe in the code and judge themselves and others according to its values.

In fact the overwhelming majority of families in the inner-city community try to approximate the decent-family model, but there are many others who clearly represent the worst fears of the decent family. Not only are their financial resources extremely limited, but what little they have may easily be misused. The lives of the street-oriented are often marked by disorganization. In the most desperate circumstances people frequently have a limited understanding of priorities and consequences, and so frustrations mount over bills, food, and at times, drink, cigarettes, and drugs. Some tend toward self-destructive behavior; many street-oriented women are crack-addicted ("on the pipe"), alcoholic, or involved in complicated relationships with men who abuse them. In addition, the seeming intractability of their situation, caused in large part by the lack of well-paying jobs and the persistence of racial discrimination, has engendered deep-seated bitterness and anger in many of the most desperate and poorest blacks, especially young people. The need both to exercise a measure of control and to lash out at somebody is often reflected in the adults' relations with their children. At the least, the frustrations of persistent poverty shorten the fuse in such people contributing to a lack of patience with anyone, child or adult, who imitates them.

In these circumstances a woman—or a man, although men are less consistently present in children's lives—can be quite aggressive with children, yelling at and striking them for the least little infraction of the rules she has set down. Often little if any serious explanation follows the verbal and physical punishment. This response teaches children a particular lesson. They learn that to solve any kind of interpersonal problem one must quickly resort to hitting or other violent behavior. Actual peace and quiet, and also the appearance of calm, respectful children conveyed to her neighbors and friends, are often what the young mother most desires, but at times she will be very aggressive in trying to get them. Thus she may be quick to beat her children, especially if they defy her law, not because she hates them but because this is the way she knows to control them. In fact, many street-oriented women love their children dearly. Many mothers in the community subscribe to the notion that there is a "devil in the boy" that must be beaten out of him or that socially "fast girls need to be whupped." Thus much of what borders on child abuse in the view of social authorities is acceptable parental punishment in the view of these mothers.

Many street-oriented women are sporadic mothers whose children learn to fend for themselves when necessary, foraging for food and money any way they can get it. The children are sometimes employed by drug dealers or become addicted themselves. These children of the street, growing up with little supervision, are said to "come up hard." They often learn to fight at an early age, sometimes using short-tempered adults around them as role models. The street-oriented home may be fraught with anger, verbal disputes, physical aggression, and even mayhem. The children observe these goings-on, learning the lesson that might makes right. They quickly learn to hit those who cross them, and the dog-eat-dog

mentality prevails. In order to survive, to protect oneself, it is necessary to marshal inner resources and be ready to deal with adversity in a hands-on way. In these circumstances physical prowess takes on great significance.

In some of the most desperate cases, a street-oriented mother may simply leave her young children alone and unattended while she goes out. The most irresponsible women can be found at local bars and crack houses, getting high and socializing with other adults. Sometimes a troubled woman will leave very young children alone for days at a time. Reports of crack addicts abandoning their children have become common in drug-infested inner-city communities. Neighbors or relatives discover the abandoned children, often hungry and distraught over the absence of their mother. After repeated absences, a friend or relative, particularly a grandmother, will often step in to care for the young children, sometimes petitioning the authorities to send her, as guardian of the children, the mother's welfare check, if the mother gets one. By this time, however, the children may well have learned the first lesson of the streets: survival itself, let alone respect, cannot be taken for granted; you have to fight for your place in the world.

Campaigning for Respect

These realities of inner-city life are largely absorbed on the streets. At an early age, often even before they start school, children from street-oriented homes gravitate to the streets, where they "hang"—socialize with their peers. Children from these generally permissive homes have a great deal of latitude and are allowed to "rip and run" up and down the street. They often come home from school, put their books down, and go right back out the door. On school nights eight- and nine-year-olds remain out until nine or ten o'clock (and teenagers typically come in whenever they want to). On the streets they play in groups that often become the source of their primary social bonds. Children from decent homes tend to be more carefully supervised and are thus likely to have curfews and to be taught how to stay out of trouble.

When decent and street kids come together, a kind of social shuffle occurs in which children have a chance to go either way. Tension builds as a child comes to realize that he must choose an orientation. The kind of home he comes from influences but does not determine the way he will ultimately turn out—although it is unlikely that a child from a thoroughly street-oriented family will easily absorb decent values on the streets. Youths who emerge from street-oriented families but develop a decency orientation almost always learn those values in another setting—in school, in a youth group, in church. Often it is the result of their involvement with a caring "old head" (adult role model).

In the street, through their play, children pour their individual life experiences into a common knowledge pool, affirming, confirming, and elaborating on what they have observed in the home and matching their skills against those of others. And they learn to fight. Even small children test one another, pushing and shoving, and are ready to hit other children over circumstances not to their liking. In turn, they are readily hit by other children, and the child who is toughest prevails. Thus the violent resolution of disputes, the hitting and cursing, gains social reinforcement. The child in effect is initiated into a system that is really a way of campaigning for respect.

In addition, younger children witness the disputes of older children, which are often resolved through cursing and abusive talk, if not aggression or outright violence. They see that one child succumbs to the greater physical and mental abilities of the other. They are also alert and attentive witnesses to the verbal and physical fights of adults, after which they compare notes and share their interpretations of the event. In almost every case the victor is the person who physically won the altercation, and this person often enjoys the esteem and respect of onlookers. These experiences reinforce the lessons the children have learned at home: might makes right, and toughness is a virtue, while humility is not. In effect they learn the social meaning of fighting. When it is left virtually unchallenged, this understanding becomes an ever more important part of the child's working conception of the world. Over time the code of the streets becomes refined.

Those street-oriented adults with whom children come in contact—including mothers, fathers, brothers, sisters, boyfriends, cousins, neighbors, and friends—help them along in forming this understanding by verbalizing the messages they are getting through experience: "Watch your back." "Protect yourself." "Don't punk out." "If somebody messes with you, you got to pay them back." "If someone disses you, you got to straighten them out." Many parents actually impose sanctions if a child is not sufficiently aggressive. For example, if a child loses a fight and comes home upset, the parent might respond,

> Don't you come in here crying that somebody beat you up; you better get back out there and whup his ass. I didn't raise no punks! Get back out there and whup his ass. If you don't whup his ass, I'll whup your ass when you come home.

Thus the child obtains reinforcement for being tough and showing nerve.

While fighting, some children cry as though they are doing something they are ambivalent about. The fight may be against their wishes, yet they may feel constrained to fight or face the consequences—not just from peers but also from caretakers or parents, who may administer another beating if they back down. Some adults recall receiving such lessons from their own parents and justify repeating them to their children as a way to toughen them up. Looking capable of taking care of oneself as a form of self-defense is a dominant theme among both street-oriented and decent adults who worry about the safety of their children. There is thus at times a convergence in their child-rearing practices, although the rationales behind them may differ.

Self-Image Based on "Juice"

By the time they are teenagers, most youths have either internalized the code of the streets or at least learned the need to comport themselves in accordance with its rules, which chiefly have to do with interpersonal communication. The code revolves around the presentation of self. Its basic requirement is the display of a certain predisposition to violence. Accordingly, one's bearing must send the unmistakable if sometimes subtle message to "the next person" in public that one is capable of violence and mayhem when the situation requires it, that one can take care of oneself. The nature of this communication is largely determined by the demands of the circumstances but can include facial expressions, gait, and verbal expressions—all of which are geared mainly to deterring aggression. Physical appearance, including clothes, jewelry, and grooming, also plays an important part in how a person is viewed; to be respected, it is important to have the right look.

Even so, there are no guarantees against challenges, because there are always people around looking for a fight to increase their share of respect—or "juice," as it is sometimes called on the street. Moreover, if a person is assaulted, it is important, not only in the eyes of his opponent but also in the eyes of his "running buddies," for him to avenge himself. Otherwise he risks being "tried" (challenged) or "moved on" by any number of others. To maintain his honor he must show he is not someone to be "messed with" or "dissed." In general, the person must "keep himself straight" by managing his position of respect among others; this involves in part his self-image, which is shaped by what he thinks others are thinking of him in relation to his peers.

Objects play an important and complicated role in establishing self-image. Jackets, sneakers, gold jewelry, reflect not just a person's taste, which tends to be tightly regulated among adolescents of all social classes, but also a willingness to possess things that may require defending.

A boy wearing a fashionable, expensive jacket, for example, is vulnerable to attack by another who covets the jacket and either cannot afford to buy one or wants the added satisfaction of depriving someone else of his. However, if the boy forgoes the desirable jacket and wears one that isn't "hip," he runs the risk of being teased and possibly even assaulted as an unworthy person. To be allowed to hang with certain prestigious crowds, a boy must wear a different set of expensive clothes—sneakers and athletic suit—every day. Not to be able to do so might make him appear socially deficient. The youth comes to covet such items especially when he sees easy prey wearing them.

In acquiring valued things, therefore, a person shores up his identity—but since it is an identity based on having things, it is highly precarious. This very precariousness gives a heightened sense of urgency to staying even with peers, with whom the person is actually competing. Young men and women who are able to command respect through their presentation of self—by allowing their possessions and their body language to speak for them—may not have to campaign for regard but may, rather, gain it by the force of their manner. Those who are unable to command respect in this way must actively campaign for it—and are thus particularly alive to slights.

One way of campaigning for status is by taking the possessions of others. In this context, seemingly ordinary objects can become trophies imbued with symbolic value that far exceeds their monetary worth. Possession of the trophy can symbolize the ability to violate somebody—to "get in his face," to take something of value from him, to "dis" him, and thus to enhance one's own worth by stealing someone else's. The trophy does not have to be something material. It can be another person's sense of honor, snatched away with a derogatory remark. It can be the outcome of a fight. It can be the imposition of a certain standard, such as a girl's getting herself recognized as the most beautiful. Material things, however, fit easily into the pattern. Sneakers, a pistol, even somebody else's girlfriend, can become a trophy. When a person can take something from another and then flaunt it, he gains a certain regard by being the owner, or the controller, of that thing. But this display of ownership can then provoke other people to challenge him. This game of who controls what is thus constantly being played out on inner-city streets, and the trophy—extrinsic or intrinsic, tangible or intangible—identifies the current winner.

An important aspect of this often violent give-and-take is its zero-sum quality. That is, the extent to which one person can raise himself up depends on his ability to put another person down. This underscores the alienation that permeates the inner-city ghetto community. There is a generalized sense that very little respect is to be had, and therefore everyone competes to get what affirmation he can of the little that is available. The craving for respect that results gives people thin skins. Shows of deference by others can be highly soothing, contributing to a sense of security, comfort, self-confidence, and self-respect. Transgressions by others which go unanswered diminish these feelings and are believed to encourage further transgressions. Hence one must be ever vigilant against the transgressions of others or even *appearing* as if transgressions will be tolerated. Among young people, whose sense of self-esteem is particularly vulnerable, there is an especially heightened concern with being disrespected. Many inner-city young men in particular crave respect to such a degree that they will risk their lives to attain and maintain it.

The issue of respect is thus closely tied to whether a person has an inclination to be violent, even as a victim. In the wider society people may not feel required to retaliate physically after an attack, even though they are aware that they have been degraded or taken advantage of. They may feel a great need to defend themselves during an attack, or to behave in such a way as to deter aggression (middle-class people certainly can and do become victims of street-oriented youths), but they are much more likely than street-oriented people to feel that they can walk away from a possible altercation with their self-esteem intact. Some people may even have the strength of character to flee, without any thought that their self-respect or esteem will be diminished.

In impoverished inner-city black communities, however, particularly among young males and perhaps increasingly among females, such flight would be extremely difficult. To run away would likely leave one's self-esteem in tatters. Hence people often feel constrained not only to stand up and at least attempt to resist during an assault but also to "pay back"—to seek revenge—after a successful assault on their person. This may include going to get a weapon or even getting relatives involved. Their very identity and self-respect, their honor, is often intricately tied up with the way they perform on the streets during and after such encounters. This outlook reflects the circumscribed opportunities of the inner-city poor. Generally people outside the ghetto have other ways of gaining status and regard, and thus do not feel so dependent on such physical displays.

By Trial of Manhood

On the street, among males these concerns about things and identity have come to be expressed in the concept of "manhood." Manhood in the inner city means taking the prerogatives of men with respect to strangers, other men, and women—being distinguished as a man. It implies physicality and a certain ruthlessness. Regard and respect are associated with this concept in large part because of its practical application: if others have little or no regard for a person's manhood, his very life and those of his loved ones could be in jeopardy. But there is a chicken-and-egg aspect to this situation: one's physical safety is more likely to be jeopardized in public *because* manhood is associated with respect. In other words, an existential link has been created between the idea of manhood and one's self-esteem, so that it has become hard to say which is primary. For many inner-city youths, manhood and respect are flip sides of the same coin; physical and psychological well-being are inseparable, and both require a sense of control, of being in charge.

The operating assumption is that a man, especially a real man, knows what other men know—the code of the streets. And if one is not a real man, one is somehow diminished as a person, and there are certain valued things one simply does not deserve. There is thus believed to be a certain justice to the code, since it is considered that everyone has the opportunity to know it. Implicit in this is that everybody is held responsible for being familiar with the code. If the victim of a mugging, for example, does not know the code and so responds "wrong," the perpetrator may feel justified even in killing him and may feel no remorse. He may think, "Too bad, but it's his fault. He should have known better."

So when a person ventures outside, he must adopt the code—a kind of shield, really—to prevent others from "messing with" him. In these circumstances it is easy for people to think they are being tried or tested by others even when this is not the case. For it is sensed that something extremely valuable is at stake in every interaction, and people are encouraged to rise to the occasion, particularly with strangers. For people who are unfamiliar with the code—generally people who live outside the inner city—the concern with respect in the most ordinary interactions can be frightening and incomprehensible. But for those who are invested in the code, the clear object of their demeanor is to discourage strangers from even thinking about testing their manhood. And the sense of power that attends the ability to deter others can be alluring even to those who know the code without being heavily invested in it—the decent inner-city youths. Thus a boy who has been leading a basically decent life can, in trying circumstances, suddenly resort to deadly force.

Central to the issue of manhood is the widespread belief that one of the most effective ways of gaining respect is to manifest "nerve." Nerve is shown when one takes another person's possessions (the more valuable the better), "messes with" someone's woman, throws the first punch, "gets in someone's face," or pulls a trigger. Its proper display helps on the spot to check others who would violate one's person and also helps to build a reputation that works to prevent future challenges. But since such a show of nerve is a forceful expression of disrespect toward the person on the receiving end, the victim may be greatly offended and seek to retaliate with equal or greater force. A display of nerve, therefore, can easily provoke a life-threatening response, and the background knowledge of that possibility has often been incorporated into the concept of nerve.

True nerve exposes a lack of fear of dying. Many feel that it is acceptable to risk dying over the principle of respect. In fact, among the hardcore street-oriented, the clear risk of violent death may be preferable to being "dissed" by another. The youths who have internalized this attitude and convincingly display it in their public bearing are among the most threatening people of all, for it is commonly assumed that they fear no man. As the people of the community say, "They are the baddest dudes on the street." They often lead an existential life that may acquire meaning only when they are faced with the possibility of imminent death. Not to be afraid to die is by implication to have few compunctions about taking another's life. Not to be afraid to die is the quid pro quo of being able to take somebody else's life—for the right reasons, if the situation demands it. When others believe this is one's position, it gives one a real sense of power on the streets. Such credibility is what many inner-city youths strive to achieve, whether they are decent or street-oriented, both because of its practical defensive value and because of the positive way it makes them feel about themselves. The difference between the decent and the street-oriented youth is often that the decent youth makes a conscious decision to appear tough and manly; in another setting—with teachers, say, or at his part-time job—he can be polite and deferential. The street-oriented youth, on the other hand, has made the concept of manhood a part of his very identity; he has difficulty manipulating it—it often controls him.

Girls and Boys

Increasingly, teenage girls are mimicking the boys and trying to have their own version of "manhood." Their goal is the same—to get respect, to be recognized as capable of setting or maintaining a certain standard. They try to achieve this end in the ways that have been established by the boys, including posturing, abusive language, and the use of violence to resolve disputes, but the issues for the girls are different. Although conflicts over turf and status exist among the girls, the majority of disputes seem rooted in assessments of beauty (which girl in a group is "the cutest"), competition over boyfriends, and attempts to regulate other people's knowledge of and opinions about a girl's behavior or that of someone close to her, especially her mother.

A major cause of conflicts among girls is "he say, she say." This practice begins in the early school years and continues through high school. It occurs when "people," particularly girls, talk about others, thus putting their "business in the streets." Usually one girl will say something negative about another in the group, most often behind the person's back. The remark will then get back to the person talked about. She may retaliate or her friends may feel required to "take up for" her. In essence this is a form of group gossiping in which individuals are negatively assessed and evaluated. As with much gossip, the things said may or may not be true, but the point is that such imputations can cast aspersions on a person's good name. The accused is required to defend herself against the slander, which can result in arguments and fights, often over little of real substance. Here again is the problem of low self-esteem, which encourages youngsters to be highly sensitive to slights and to be vulnerable to feeling easily "dissed." To avenge the dissing, a fight is usually necessary.

Because boys are believed to control violence, girls tend to defer to them in situations of conflict. Often if a girl is attacked or feels slighted, she will get a brother, uncle, or cousin to do her fighting for her. Increasingly, however, girls are doing their own fighting and are even asking their male relatives to teach them how to fight. Some girls form groups that attack other girls or take things from them. A hard-core segment of inner-city girls inclined toward violence seems to be developing. As one thirteen-year-old girl in a detention center for youths who have committed violent acts told me, "To get people to leave you alone, you gotta fight. Talking don't always get you out of stuff." One major difference between girls and boys: girls rarely use guns. Their fights are therefore not life-or-death struggles. Girls are not often willing to put their lives on the line for "manhood." The ultimate form of respect on the male-dominated inner-city street is thus reserved for men.

"Going for Bad"

In the most fearsome youths such a cavalier attitude toward death grows out of a very limited view of life. Many are uncertain about how long they are going to live and believe they could die violently at any time. They accept this fate; they live on the edge. Their manner conveys the message that nothing intimidates them, whatever turn the encounter takes, they maintain their attack—rather like a pit bull, whose spirit many such boys admire. The demonstration of such tenacity "shows heart" and earns their respect.

This fearlessness has implications for law enforcement. Many street-oriented boys are much more concerned about the threat of "justice" at the hands of a peer than at the hands of the police. Moreover, many feel not only that they have little to lose by going to prison but that they have something to gain. The toughening-up one experiences in prison can actually enhance one's reputation on the streets. Hence the system loses influence over the hard core who are without jobs, with little perceptible stake in the system. If mainstream society has done nothing *for them*, they counter by making sure it can do nothing to them.

At the same time, however, a competing view maintains that true nerve consists in backing down, walking away from a fight, and going on with one's business. One fights only in self-defense. This view emerges from the decent philosophy that life is precious, and it is an important part of the socialization process common in decent homes. It discourages violence as the primary means of resolving disputes and encourages youngsters to accept nonviolence and talk as confrontational strategies. But "if the deal goes down," self-defense is greatly encouraged. When there is enough positive support for this orientation, either in the home or among one's peers, then nonviolence has a chance to prevail. But it prevails at the cost of relinquishing a claim to being bad and tough, and therefore sets a young person up as at the very least alienated from street-oriented peers and quite possibly a target of derision or even violence.

Although the nonviolent orientation rarely overcomes the impulse to strike back in an encounter, it does introduce a certain confusion and so can prompt a measure of soul-searching, or even profound ambivalence. Did the person back down with his respect intact or did he back down only to be judged a "punk"—a person lacking manhood? Should he or she have acted? Should he or she have hit the other person in the mouth? These questions beset many young men and women during public confrontations. What is the "right" thing to do? In the quest for honor, respect, and local status—which few young people are uninterested in—common sense most often prevails, which leads many to opt for the tough approach, enacting their own particular versions of the display of nerve. The presentation of oneself as rough and tough is very often quite acceptable until one is tested. And then that presentation may help the person pass the test, because it will cause fewer questions to be asked about what he did and why. It is hard for a person to explain why he lost the fight or why he backed down. Hence many will strive to appear to "go for bad," while hoping they will never be tested. But when they are tested, the outcome of the situation may quickly be out of their hands, as they become wrapped up in the circumstances of the moment.

An Oppositional Culture

The attitudes of the wider society are deeply implicated in the code of the streets. Most people in inner-city communities are not totally invested in the code, but the significant minority of hard-core street youths who are have to maintain the code in order to establish reputations, because they have—or feel they have—few other ways to assert themselves. For these young people the standards of the street code are the only game in town. The extent to which some children—particularly those who through upbringing have become most alienated and those lacking in strong and conventional social support—experience, feel, and internalize racist rejection and contempt from mainstream society may strongly encourage them to express contempt for the more conventional society in turn. In dealing with this contempt and rejection, some youngsters will consciously invest themselves and their considerable mental resources in what amounts to an oppositional culture to preserve themselves and their self-respect. Once they do, any respect they might be able to garner in the wider system pales in comparison with the respect available in the local system; thus they often lose interest in even attempting to negotiate the mainstream system.

At the same time, many less alienated young blacks have assumed a street-oriented demeanor as a way of expressing their blackness while really embracing a much more moderate way of life; they, too, want a nonviolent setting in which to live and raise a family. These decent people are trying hard to be part of the mainstream culture, but the racism, real and perceived, that they encounter helps to legitimate the oppositional culture. And so on occasion they adopt street behavior. In fact, depending on the demands of the situation, many people in the community slip back and forth between decent and street behavior.

A vicious cycle has thus been formed. The hopelessness and alienation many young inner-city black men and women feel, largely as a result of endemic joblessness and persistent racism, fuels the violence they engage in. This violence serves to confirm the negative feelings many whites and some middle-class blacks harbor toward the ghetto poor, further legitimating the oppositional culture and the code of the streets in the eyes of many poor young blacks. Unless this cycle is broken, attitudes on both sides will become increasingly entrenched, and the violence, which claims victims blacks and white, poor and affluent, will only escalate.

Discussion Questions

1. Describe the central values and norms (or rules) that form the "code of the streets."
2. How does Anderson explain the origin of the code of the streets?
3. Describe the socialization of "street kids," noting how this socialization increases the likelihood that they will resort to violence in various situations. In your description, draw on both Sutherland's differential association and Akers's social learning theory.
4. Why do individuals who oppose the code of the streets nevertheless conform to its rules on occasion?
5. To what extent does the code of the streets affect the behavior of girls?

PART V

Anomie/Strain Theories of Crime

Anomie and strain theory are distinct but related theories of crime (see Agnew, 1997a; Agnew and Passas, 1997; Baumer and Gustafson, 2007; Bernard, 1987; Burton and Cullen, 1992; Messner, 1988, for discussions of the relationship between these theories). Contemporary versions of these theories trace their origins to the work of Merton (1938) and to the revisions in Merton's theory made by Cohen (1955) and Cloward and Ohlin (1960). Messner and Rosenfeld's (2007) institutional-anomie theory of crime now represents the leading version of anomie theory (also see Messner and Rosenfeld, 2006; Messner et al., 2008; Rosenfeld and Messner, 1995), while Agnew's (1992, 2005, 2006a, b, 2009) general strain theory represents the leading version of strain theory.

Anomie Theory

Anomie theory has focused on explaining why some societies, such as the United States, have higher crime rates than others. According to Merton's (1938) version of the theory, the United States places a relatively strong emphasis on the goal of monetary success, but a weak emphasis on the legitimate norms for achieving this goal, like education and hard work. As a consequence, the goal-seeking behavior of individuals is subject to less regulation. Individuals are more likely to pursue monetary success using whatever means are necessary—including crime. Societies that fail to adequately regulate goal-seeking behavior are said to be characterized by a state of "anomie" or normlessness.

Merton's arguments in this area were largely neglected until the 1980s. Most attention instead focused on his version of strain theory (see below). During the 1980s and 1990s, however, several scholars called attention to Merton's anomie theory and began to suggest refinements to it (Bernard, 1987; Burton and Cullen, 1992; Cullen, 1984; Messner, 1988; Passas, 1997; Rosenfeld, 1989). Messner and Rosenfeld (2006) drew heavily on the theory when they developed their institutional-anomie theory of crime (see Chapter 15 in this part). Like Merton, they attempt to explain why the United States has such a high crime rate (although, like Merton, their arguments are applicable to other societies). And they begin their explanation by drawing on Merton's argument that the higher crime rate in the United States stems from a cultural system that encourages everyone to strive for monetary success but places little emphasis on the legitimate norms for achieving such success. This emphasis on the unrestrained pursuit of monetary success is what they refer to as the "American Dream."

Messner and Rosenfeld, however, go on to argue that the American Dream is only part of the explanation for the higher crime rate in the United States. In particular, they argue that the cultural emphasis on money is paralleled by an institutional structure that is dominated by the economy. The other major institutions in the United States—the family, school, and political system—are all subservient to economic institutions. Noneconomic goals and roles are devalued. For example, little value is placed on the role of education for its own sake or on the role of home-maker. Noneconomic institutions must accommodate themselves to the demands of the economy (e.g., parents struggle to arrange child-care so they can work). And economic norms have come to penetrate these other institutions (e.g., the school system, like the economic system, is based on the individualized competition for rewards). As a result, institutions such as the family, school, and political system are less able to effectively socialize or train individuals and to effectively sanction deviant behavior. For example, it is more difficult for parents to effectively socialize and supervise their children when parents must devote the bulk of their time and energy to work.

There have been several recent efforts to test institutional-anomie theory (for overviews, see Messner and Rosenfeld, 2006, 2007; Kubrin et al., 2009; Pratt and Cullen, 2005; for selected studies, see Baumer and Gustafson, 2007; Bjerregard and Cochran, 2008; Chamlin and Cochran, 1995; Jensen and Akers, 2003; Maume and Lee, 2003; Messner and Rosenfeld, 1997; Piquero and Piquero, 1998; Savolainen, 2000). The central prediction of the theory is that high crime rates stem from the dominance of the economy over other institutions, such as the family, school, and political system. If this is true, crime rates should be higher in those countries or areas where economic institutions are relatively strong and lower in those areas where noneconomic institutions are relatively strong. Researchers have measured the strength of noneconomic institutions in terms of such factors as the ratio of marriages to divorces, levels of religious participation (church membership), levels of political participation (voter turnout), and the strength of social welfare programs (e.g., family support, social security, unemployment insurance programs). Most studies suggest that crime rates are lower in societies and areas that are not dominated by the economy; that is, crime rates are lower in societies and areas with stronger families, schools, religious institutions, and political systems. Further, most studies suggest that the effect of economic stressors on crime is lower in societies and areas where noneconomic institutions are stronger. In particular, economic stressors such as poverty and high rates of income inequality have a lower effect on crime rates in areas where welfare spending is higher and noneconomic institutions such as the family and religion are stronger.

It has been more difficult to test the prediction that crime is higher in the United States because of the strong emphasis placed on the unrestrained pursuit of money. This is because we lack good information on the extent to which people in different societies place great value on monetary success, but little value on the legal methods of obtaining such success. Nevertheless, two studies using data from the World Values survey report that people in the United States do *not* place a relatively strong emphasis on the unrestrained pursuit of money (Cao, 2004; Jensen, 2002; also see Jensen and Akers, 2003). This challenges a core argument of institutional anomie theory, although Messner and Rosenfeld (2006) argue that it is difficult to accurately measure the values of people in different societies and that more research is needed in this area (also see Konty, 2005; Messner et al., 2008). A recent study by Baumer and Gustafson (2007), however, found that crime is higher in areas in the U.S. where people express a high commitment to monetary success *and* a low commitment to the legitimate means for achieving such success (e.g., many people agree that "there are no right or wrong ways to make money, only hard or easy ways").

In sum, institutional anomie theory has some support, particularly that part of the theory which states that crime is most likely in those societies and areas where economic institutions are relatively strong and noneconomic institutions such as the family and polity are relatively weak.

Strain Theory

Classic Strain Theory
Strain theory has focused on explaining why some individuals and groups *within* a society are more likely to engage in crime than

others. According to the theory, individuals are pressured into crime. Most commonly, it has been argued that they are pressured into crime when they are prevented from achieving cultural goals like monetary success or middle-class status through legitimate channels. This is the central argument of the "classic" strain theories of Merton (1938), Cohen (1955), and Cloward and Ohlin (1960) (see Chapters 13 and 14 in this part). These theorists argue that everyone in the United States is encouraged to pursue the goals of monetary success or middle-class status. Lower-class individuals, however, are often prevented from achieving such goals through legitimate channels. Their parents do not equip them with the skills and values necessary to do well in school, they attend inferior schools and grow up in troubled neighborhoods, they cannot afford college, and they may face discrimination in the job market. Our society, then, encourages everyone to pursue certain goals but then prevents large segments of the population from achieving these goals through legitimate channels. Individuals experiencing such goal blockage are under a great deal of strain or pressure, and they *may* respond by engaging in crime.

They may attempt to achieve their goals through illegitimate channels, such as theft, drug selling, and prostitution. They may reject the goals of monetary success and middle-class status and substitute new goals that they can achieve. Their hostility toward the society that frustrates them, among other things, may lead them to emphasize goals that are conducive to crime (e.g., being a good fighter). Or they may simply reject cultural goals and norms, retreating into drug use. Strain theorists are careful to emphasize that only some strained individuals turn to crime, and they have tried to specify the factors that determine whether strain leads to crime (see Agnew, 1997a, 2000; Baumer and Gustafson, 2007; Cullen, 1984). Cohen (1955) and Cloward and Ohlin (1960) argue that strained individuals are unlikely to engage in crime unless they first form or join a delinquent subculture whose values are conducive to crime. These theorists describe the conditions under which strained individuals are likely to form delinquent subcultures, and their accounts represent the dominant explanations for the origin of delinquent subcultures.

The classic strain theories dominated research on the causes of crime during the 1950s and 1960s, and had a major impact on public policy (see Burton and Cullen, 1992; Clinard, 1964; Cole, 1975; Empey et al., 1999). Strain theory, in particular, was one of the inspirations for the "War on Poverty" that was launched during the 1960s. The War on Poverty was designed to increase opportunities for low-income and minority individuals to achieve success through legitimate channels. Many of the programs associated with the War on Poverty have since been dismantled, but some—like Project Headstart and Job Corps—remain.

Classic strain theory came under heavy attack during the late 1960s and 1970s, and it no longer dominates criminology as it once did (see Agnew, 2000; Agnew and Passas, 1997; Akers and Sellers, 2008; Bernard, 1984; Burton and Cullen, 1992; Cole, 1975; Rosenfeld, 1989). Among other things, a number of empirical studies failed to provide support for the theory (see Agnew, 2000; Akers and Sellers, 2008; Hirschi, 1969; Jensen, 1995; Kornhauser, 1978). Classic strain theory was most commonly tested by examining the disjunction between aspirations (the goals one ideally would like to achieve) and expectations (the goals one realistically expects to achieve). If the theory is true, we would expect people with high aspirations and low expectations to be most delinquent (that is, people who say they ideally want a lot, but expect very little). The research, however, did not support this prediction. Crime is highest among those with both low aspirations and low expectations (a finding most commonly explained in terms of social control theory—see Part VI). Further, a series of self-report studies during the 1960s and 1970s revealed that delinquency was not concentrated among lower-class individuals. Middle-class delinquency was quite common, perhaps as common as lower-class delinquency (see Akers and Sellers, 2008; Tittle and Meier, 1990). This was taken as further evidence against classic strain theory (since the pressure for delinquency should be greatest in the lower classes).

Several researchers, however, have recently challenged the evidence against classic strain theory. Among other things, they argue that there are better ways to measure strain than by the disjunction between aspirations and expectations. Aspirations or ideal goals have something of the utopian in them and so are not taken seriously. The failure to achieve such goals, then, is not an important source of strain (see Agnew, 1992, 2000; Agnew and Passas, 1997; Bernard, 1984; Burton and Cullen, 1992; Burton et al., 1994; Burton and Dunaway, 1994; Cullen, 1984; 1988; Hoffman and Ireland, 1995; Kubrin et al., 2009; Menard, 1995; Messner, 1988; Passas and Agnew, 1997, for other criticisms). A few recent studies have attempted to provide better tests of classic strain theory (Agnew et al., 1996; Baron, 2004; Baumer and Gustafson, 2007; Burton et al., 1994; Burton and Dunaway, 1994; Cernkovich et al., 2000; Hagan and McCarthy, 1997; Kubrin et al., 2009; Menard, 1995, 1997). These studies tend to provide more support for the theory. Agnew et al. (1996), for example, attempt to directly measure strain by asking individuals how satisfied they are with their financial situation. This measure is related to crime, with the more dissatisfied being more criminal. Additional tests are needed before we can reach any definitive conclusions about classic strain theory, but the theory does seem to be experiencing a minor revival (see Adler and Laufer, 1995; Baumer and Gustafson, 2007; Passas and Agnew, 1997).

In addition, classic strain theory has increasingly been used to explain group differences in crime rates, particularly differences between communities and societies. Many studies find that the strongest predictor of community differences in crime rates in the United States is economic deprivation

(Agnew, 2005; Baumer and Gustafson, 2007; Land et al., 1990; Pratt and Cullen, 2005). That is, poorer communities have much higher crime rates than wealthier communities. The effect of economic deprivation on crime can be explained in terms of several theories. Social disorganization theorists, for example, argue that such deprivation leads to a breakdown in social control (see Part III). But economic deprivation can also be taken as a measure of the strain experienced by community members (see Agnew, 1999; Pratt and Cullen, 2005).

While economic deprivation is strongly related to community differences in crime rates in the United States, it is unrelated or only weakly related to societal differences in crime rates. One reason for this may be that societies differ in the emphasis they place on economic success. So deprivation, in and of itself, may not lead to crime. Following Merton, deprivation may only lead to crime in those societies where most people strongly desire economic success. It has not been possible to directly test this idea. However, this idea has been indirectly tested by examining the effect of economic inequality on societial crime rates. Certain societies are characterized by high levels of economic inequality, with some people being very rich and others very poor. The existence of such "poverty in the midst of plenty" may lead poor people to increase their desire for economic success—since they see that others around them have achieved such success. Most studies support this argument, with economic inequality being perhaps the strongest predictor of societal differences in crime rates (Agnew, 2006a; LaFree, 1999; Messner, 2003; Neapolitan, 1997; Pratt and Godsey, 2003). The effect of economic inequality on crime rates is especially strong when such inequality is due to discrimination against racial/ethnic or religious groups—perhaps because inequality is more likely to be seen as unjust in such circumstances (Messner, 1989, 2003; also see Blau and Blau, 1982). (Note: Messner and Rosenfeld's institutional anomie theory has been criticized for neglecting the effects of economic deprivation and inequality on crime rates (Bernburg, 2002). Messner and Rosenfeld (2006, 2007) acknowledge this criticism, and state that they intend to better incorporate such effects into their theory (also see Pratt and Godsey, 2003).

Classic strain theory, then, has some support—although several problems with the theory have been identified, including its limited ability to explain middle-class crime.

Revisions in Classic Strain Theory

The criticisms against classic strain theory spurred several efforts to revise the theory (see Adler and Laufer, 1995; Agnew, 2000; Bernard, 1990; Burton and Cullen, 1992; Clinard, 1964; Cohen, 1965; Elliott et al., 1979; Greenberg, 1977; Merton, 1968; Passas and Agnew, 1997; Simon and Gagnon, 1976). Certain of the revisions attempt to apply the theory to the explanation of middle-class crime and delinquency. One major revision, for example, argues that strain is a function of *relative deprivation*. That is, one's level of strain or frustration is not dependent on the absolute amount of money one has, but is dependent on how much money one has *relative* to those in one's "reference group" (see Burton et al., 1994; Burton and Dunaway, 1994; Cohen, 1965, 1997; Passas, 1997). Wealthy individuals, as a consequence, may experience much strain if they compare themselves to even wealthier people around them. Limited data provide some support for this argument (Burton et al., 1994; Burton and Dunaway, 1994; although see Baron, 2004).

Another revision argues that adolescents pursue a variety of goals in addition to middle-class status and monetary success. Such goals include popularity with peers and potential romantic partners, athletic success, positive relations with parents and others, and good grades. The achievement of these goals is said to be a function of several factors in addition to social class—factors like intelligence, personality characteristics, and physical appearance and ability. As a result, middle-class adolescents may also experience strain quite frequently. This version of strain theory has not been well tested, although preliminary tests have not been encouraging (see Agnew, 2000, for an overview).

General Strain Theory

Most of the revisions in classic strain theory continue to argue that the major source of strain or frustration is the failure to achieve positively valued goals. They simply argue that goal achievement should be measured relative to others or they broaden the number of goals under consideration. Agnew's (1992, 2006a, b) general strain theory, however, points to additional sources of strain.

According to Agnew (1992:50), strain results from negative relationships with others: "relationships in which others are not treating the individual as he or she would like to be treated." There are three major types of negative relations: relations where others (1) prevent or threaten to prevent the achievement of positively valued goals (e.g., monetary success, popularity with peers), (2) remove or threaten to remove positively valued stimuli (e.g., the loss of a romantic partner, the death of a parent), or (3) present or threaten to present negatively valued stimuli (e.g., insults, physical assault). Such negative relationships increase the likelihood that individuals will experience a range of negative emotions, such as anger and frustration. These emotions create pressure for corrective action, with crime being one possible response. Crime may be a method for alleviating strain (e.g., running away from home, assaulting those who insult), seeking revenge, or managing the negative emotions that the individual experiences (e.g., through illicit drug use). Like previous theorists, Agnew argues that only some strained individuals turn to crime, and he discusses those factors that influence whether one reacts to strains with crime.

Agnew, then, significantly broadens the focus of strain theory. Studies provide some support for Agnew's general strain theory (see the overviews in Agnew, 2001a, 2006a, b, 2009; for selected studies see

Aseltine et al., 2000; Baron, 2004; DeCoster and Kolt-Butler, 2006; Hay and Evans, 2000; Hoffmann and Cerbone, 1999; Mazerolle, 1998; Paternoster and Mazerolle, 1994). In one such test (Agnew and White, 1992), delinquency was found to be higher among individuals experiencing a variety of negative life events (e.g., assault, theft, parental divorce, parental unemployment) and various relational problems with teachers, parents, friends, and others (e.g., teachers talk down to and embarrass them, parents get angry over little things, classmates do not like them). Researchers, however, have only examined certain of the strains described by Agnew. Further, more research is needed on those factors that influence whether individuals react to strains with crime. Here the data are mixed, although recent studies find some support for certain of the predictions made by Agnew (Agnew et al., 2002; Mazerolle and Maahs, 2000). For example, some data suggest that strains are more likely to lead to crime among individuals with certain personality traits, such as negative emotionality and low constraint (see Chapter 5 in this book), and among those who associate with delinquent peers.

Agnew and others continue to refine general strain theory. Recent papers use general strain theory to explain the relationship between age and crime (Agnew, 1997b), gender and crime (Broidy and Agnew, 1997; Jang, 2007), offending over the life-course (Agnew, 1997b; Slocum et al., 2005), community characteristics and crime (Agnew, 1999), and race and crime (Kaufman, 2005, Kaufman et al., 2008). Agnew (2001b) has tried to predict which strains will be most strongly related to crime. Hundreds of specific strains fall under the three broad categories of strains listed by GST, but data suggest that only some of these specific strains are related to crime. Drawing on research in several areas, Agnew argues that strains are most likely to result in crime when they are (1) seen as unjust, (2) seen as high in magnitude, (3) associated with low social control (see Part VI in this text), and (4) create some pressure or incentive for criminal coping. Several strains that meet these conditions are listed. Agnew (2002) has argued that vicarious and anticipated strains, as well as experienced strains, may sometimes lead to crime. Finally, Agnew (2006a) has better described the reasons why strains increase the likelihood of crime. While strains affect crime primarily by increasing negative emotions such as anger, they may also reduce social control (see Part VI), foster the social learning of crime (see Part IV), and contribute to personality traits conducive to crime (see Part II).

Strain and anomie theory no longer dominate the research on the causes of crime as they once did, but they are experiencing a major revival and are among the most influential theories of crime. The readings that follow present the classic anomie and strain theories of Merton (1938), Cohen (1955), and Cloward and Ohlin (1960), as well as the new institutional-anomie theory of Messner and Rosenfeld (2001, 2007) and Agnew's (1992, 2005, 2006a, 2009) general strain theory.

References

Adler, Freda and William J. Laufer, eds. 1995. *The Legacy of Anomie Theory: Advances in Criminological Theory*, Volume 6. New Brunswick, NJ: Transaction.

Agnew, Robert. 1992. "Foundation for a General Strain Theory of Crime and Delinquency." *Criminology* 30: 47–87.

——. 1997a. "The Nature and Determinants of Strain: Another Look at Durkheim and Merton," In Nikos Passas and Robert Agnew (eds.), *The Future of Anomie Theory*, pp. 27–51. Boston: Northeastern University Press.

——. 1997b. "Stability and Change in Crime Over the Life Course: A Strain Theory Explanation." In Terence P. Thornberry (ed.), *Developmental*

Theories of Crime and Delinquency: Advances in Criminological Theory, Volume 7, pp. 101–132. New Brunswick, NJ: Transaction.

——. 1999. "A General Strain Theory of Community Differences in Crime Rates." *Journal of Research in Crime and Delinquency* 36: 123–155.

——. 2000. "Sources of Criminality: Strain and Subcultural Theories." In Joseph F. Sheley (ed.), *Criminology: A Contemporary Handbook*, pp. 349–371. Belmont, CA: Wadsworth.

——. 2001a. "An Overview of General Strain Theory." In Raymond Paternoster and Ronet Bachman (eds.), *Explaining Criminals and Crime*, pp. 161–174. Los Angeles: Roxbury Publishing.

——. 2001b. "Building on the Foundation of General Strain Theory: Specifying the Types of Strain Most Likely to Lead to Crime and Delinquency." *Journal of Research in Crime and Delinquency* 38: 319–361.

——. 2002. "Experienced, Vicarious, and Anticipated Strain." *Justice Quarterly* 19: 603–632.

——. 2005. *Juvenile Delinquency: Causes and Control*, 2nd edition. Los Angeles: Roxbury.

——. 2006a. *Pressured Into Crime: An Overview of General Strain Theory*. Los Angeles: Roxbury.

——. 2006b. "General Strain Theory: Current Status and Directions for Further Research." In Francis T. Cullen, John Paul Wright, and Kristie R. Blevins (eds.), *Taking Stock: The Status of Criminological Theory—Advances in Criminological Theory*, Volume 15, pp. 101–123. New Brunswick, NJ: Transaction.

——. 2009. "General Strain Theory." In Marvin D. Krohn, Alan J. Lizotte, and G. P. Hall (eds.), *Handbook on Crime and Delinquency*. New York: Springer.

Agnew, Robert, Timothy Brezina, John Paul Wright, and Francis T. Cullen. 2002. "Strain, Personality Traits, and Delinquency: Extending General Strain Theory." *Criminology* 40: 43–72.

Agnew, Robert, Francis T. Cullen, Velmer S. Burton, Jr., T. David Evans, and R. Gregory Dunaway. 1996. "A New Test of Classic Strain Theory." *Justice Quarterly* 13: 681–704.

Agnew, Robert and Nikos Passas, eds. 1997. "Introduction." In *The Future of Anomie Theory*, pp. 1–26. Boston: Northeastern University Press.

Agnew, Robert and Helene Raskin White. 1992. "An Empirical Test of General Strain Theory." *Criminology* 30: 475–499.

Akers, Ronald L. and Christine S. Sellers. 2008. *Criminological Theories: Introduction, Evaluation, and Application*. New York: Oxford University Press.

Aseltine, Robert H., Jr., Susan Gore, and Jennifer Gordon. 2000. "Life Stress, Anger and Anxiety, and Delinquency: An Empirical Test of General Strain Theory." *Journal of Health and Social Behavior* 41: 256–275.

Baron, Stephen W. 2004. "General Strain, Street Youth and Crime: A Test of Agnew's Revised Theory." *Criminology* 42: 457–484.

Baumer, Eric P. and Regan Gustafson. 2007. "Social Organization and Instrumental Crime: Assessing the Empirical Validity of Classic and Contemporary Anomie Theories." *Criminology* 45: 617–664.

Bernard, Thomas J. 1984. "Control Criticisms of Strain Theories: An Assessment of Theoretical and Empirical Adequacy." *Journal of Research in Crime and Delinquency* 21: 353–372.

——. 1987. "Testing Structural Strain Theories." *Journal of Research in Crime and Delinquency* 24: 262–280.

——. 1990. "Angry Aggression Among the 'Truly Disadvantaged.'" *Criminology* 28: 73–109.

Bernburg, Jon Gunnar. 2002. "Anomie, Social Change and Crime: A Theoretical Examination of Institutional-Anomie Theory." *British Journal of Criminology* 42: 729–742.

Bjerregaard, Beth and John K. Cochran. 2008. "A Cross-National Test of Institutional Anomie Theory." *Western Criminology Review* 9: 31–48.

Blau, Judith R. and Peter M. Blau. 1982. "The Cost of Inequality: Metropolitan Structure and Violent Crime." *American Sociological Review* 47: 114–129.

Broidy, Lisa and Robert Agnew. 1997. "Gender and Crime: A General Strain Theory Perspective." *Journal of Research in Crime and Delinquency* 34: 275–306.

Burton, Velmer S., Jr. and Francis T. Cullen. 1992. "The Empirical Status of Strain Theory." *Journal of Crime and Justice* 15: 1–30.

Burton, Velmer S., Jr., Francis T. Cullen, T. David Evans, and R. Gregory Dunaway. 1994. "Reconsidering Strain Theory: Operationalization, Rival Theories, and Adult Criminality." *Journal of Quantitative Criminology* 10: 213–239.

Burton, Velmer S., Jr. and R. Gregory Dunaway. 1994. "Strain, Relative Deprivation, and Middle-Class Delinquency." In Greg Barak (ed.), *Varieties of Criminology: Readings From a Dynamic Discipline*, pp. 79–95. Westport, CT: Praeger.

Cao, Liqun. 2004. "Is American Society More Anomic? A Test of Merton's Theory With Cross-National Data." *International Journal of Comparative and Applied Criminal Justice* 28: 17–31.

Cernkovich, Stephen A., Peggy C. Giordano, and Jennifer L. Rudolph. 2000. "Race, Crime, and the American Dream." *Journal of Research in Crime and Delinquency* 37: 131–170.

Chamlin, Mitchell B. and John K. Cochran. 1995. "Assessing Messner and Rosenfeld's Institutional Anomie Theory: A Partial Test." *Criminology* 33: 411–429.

Clinard, Marshall B. 1964. *Anomie and Deviant Behavior*. New York: Free Press.

Cloward, Richard A. and Lloyd Ohlin. 1960. *Delinquency and Opportunity: A Theory of Delinquent Gangs*. New York: Free Press.

Cohen, Albert K. 1955. *Delinquent Boys: The Culture of the Gang*. New York: Free Press.

——. 1965. "The Sociology of the Deviant Act: Anomie Theory and Beyond." *American Sociological Review* 30: 5–14.

——. 1997. "An Elaboration of Anomie Theory." In Nikos Passas and Robert Agnew (eds.), *The Future of Anomie Theory*, pp. 52–61. Boston: Northeastern University Press.

Cole, S. 1975. "The Growth of Scientific Knowledge: Theories of Deviance as a Case Study." In Lewis A. Coser (ed.), *The Idea of Social Structure*, pp. 175–220. New York: Harcourt Brace Jovanovich.

Cullen, Francis T. 1984. *Rethinking Crime and Deviance: The Emergence of a Structuring Tradition*. Totowa, NJ: Rowman and Allanheld.

——. 1988. "Were Cloward and Ohlin Strain Theorists?: Delinquency and Opportunity Revisited." *Journal of Research in Crime and Delinquency* 25: 214–241.

DeCoster, Stacy and Lisa Kort-Butler. 2006. "How General Is General Strain Theory?" *Journal of Research in Crime and Delinquency* 43: 297–325.

Elliott, Delbert S., Suzanne S. Ageton, and Rachelle Canter. 1979. "An Integrated Theoretical Perspective on Delinquent Behavior." *Journal of Research in Crime and Delinquency* 16: 3–27.

Empey, LaMar T., Mark Stafford, and Carter H. Hay. 1999. *American Delinquency: Its Meaning and Construction*. Belmont, CA: Wadsworth.

Greenberg, David F. 1977. "Delinquency and the Age Structure of Society." *Contemporary Crises* 1: 189–223.

Hagan, John and Bill McCarthy. 1997. *Mean Streets*. New York: Cambridge University Press.

Hay, Carter, and Michael M. Evans. 2006. "Violent Victimization and Involvement in Delinquency: Examining Predictions from General Strain Theory." *Journal of Criminal Justice* 34: 261–274.

Hirschi, Travis. 1969. *Causes of Delinquency*. Berkeley: University of California Press.

Hoffmann, John P. and Felice Gray Cerbone. 1999. "Stressful Life Events and Delinquency Escalation in Early Adolescence." *Criminology* 37: 343–374.

Hoffman, John P. and Timothy Ireland. 1995. "Cloward and Ohlin's Strain Theory Re-examined: An Elaborated Theoretical Model." In Freda Adler and William S. Laufer (eds.), *The Legacy of Anomie Theory: Advances in Criminological Theory*, Volume 6, pp. 247–270. New Brunswick, NJ: Transaction.

Jang, Sung Joon. 2007. "Gender Differences in Strain, Negative Emotions, and Coping Behaviors: A General Strain Theory Approach." *Justice Quarterly* 24: 523–553.

Jensen, Gary F. 1995. "Salvaging Structure Through Strain: A Theoretical and Empirical Critique." In Freda Adler and William S. Laufer (eds.), *The Legacy of Anomie Theory: Advances in*

Criminological Theory, Volume 6, pp. 139–158. New Brunswick, NJ: Transaction.

——. 2002. "Institutional Anomie and Societal Variations in Crime: A Critical Appraisal." *International Journal of Sociology and Social Policy* 22: 45–74.

Jensen, Gary and Ronald L. Akers. 2003. "Taking Social Learning 'Global': Micro-Macro Transitions in Criminological Theory." In Ronald L. Akers and Gary F. Jensen (eds.), *Social Learning Theory and the Explanation of Crime: Advances in Criminological Theory*, Volume 11, pp. 9–38. New Brunswick, NJ: Transaction Books.

Kaufman, Joanne M. 2005. "Explaining the Race/Ethnicity-Violence Relationship: Neighborhood Context and Social Psychological Processes." *Justice Quarterly* 22: 224–251.

Kaufman, Joanne M., Cesar J. Rebellon, Sherod Thaxton, and Robert Agnew. 2008. "A General Strain Theory of Racial Differences in Offending." *The Australian and New Zealand Journal of Criminology* 41: 421–437.

Konty, Mark. 2005. "Microanomie: The Cognitive Foundations of the Relationship Between Anomie and Deviance." *Criminology* 43: 107–132.

Kornhauser, Ruth, 1978. *Social Sources of Delinquency*. Chicago: University of Chicago Press.

Kubrin, Charis E., Thomas D. Stucky, and Marvin D. Krohn. 2009. *Researching Theories of Crime and Deviance*. New York: Oxford University Press.

LaFree, Gary. 1999. "A Summary and Review of Cross-National Comparative Studies of Homicide." In Dawyne Smith and Margaret A. Zahn (eds.), *Homicide: A Sourcebook of Social Research*, pp. 124–148. Thousand Oaks, CA: Sage.

Land, Kenneth C., Patricia McCall, and Lawrence Cohen. 1990. "Structural Covariates of Homicide Rates." *American Journal of Sociology* 95: 922–963.

Maume, Michael O. and Matthew R. Lee. 2003. "Social Institutions and Violence: A Sub-National Test of Institutional Anomie Theory." *Criminology* 41: 1137–1172.

Mazerolle, Paul. 1998. "Gender, General Strain, and Delinquency: An Empirical Examination." *Justice Quarterly* 15: 65–91.

Mazerolle, Paul and Jeff Maahs. 2000. "General Strain Theory and Delinquency: An Alternative Examination of Conditioning Influences." *Justice Quarterly* 17: 753–778.

Menard, Scott. 1995. "A Developmental Test of Mertonian Anomie Theory." *Journal of Research in Crime and Delinquency* 32: 136–174.

——. 1997. "A Developmental Test of Cloward's Differential Opportunity Theory." In Nikos Passas and Robert Agnew (eds.), *The Future of Anomie Theory*, pp. 142–186. Boston: Northeastern University Press.

Merton, Robert K. 1938. "Social Structure and Anomie." *American Sociological Review* 3: 672–682.

——. 1968. *Social Theory and Social Structure*. New York: Free Press.

Messner, Steven F. 1988. "Merton's 'Social Structure and Anomie': The Road Not Taken." *Deviant Behavior* 9: 33–53.

——. 1989. "Economic Discrimination and Societal Homicide Rates: Further Evidence of the Cost of Inequality." *American Sociological Review* 54: 597–611.

——. 2003. "Understanding Cross-National Variation in Criminal Violence." In W. Heitmeyer and John Hagan (eds.), *International Handbook of Violence Research*, pp. 701–716. New York: Kluwer Academic.

Messner, Steven F. and Richard Rosenfeld. 1997. "Political Restraint of the Market and Levels of Criminal Homicide: A Cross-National Application of Institutional-Anomie Theory." *Social Forces* 75: 1393–1416.

——. 2001. "An Institutional-Anomie Theory of Crime." In Raymond Paternoster and Ronet Bachman (eds.), *Explaining Crime and Criminals*, pp. 151–160. Los Angeles: Roxbury Publishing.

——. 2006. "The Present and Future of Institutional-Anomie Theory." In Francis T. Cullen, John Paul Wright, and Kristie R. Blevins (eds.), *Taking Stock: The Status of Criminological Theory— Advances in Criminological Theory*, Volume 15, pp. 127–148. New Brunswick, NJ: Transaction.

——. 2007. *Crime and the American Dream*, 4th edition. Belmont, CA: Wadsworth.

Messner, Steven F., Helmut Thorne, and Richard Rosenfeld. 2008. "Institutions, Anomie, and Violent Crime: Clarifying and Elaborating Institutional-Anomic Theory." *International Journal of Conflict and Violence* 2: 163–181.

Neapolitan, Jerome L. 1997. *Cross-National Crime.* Westport, CT: Greenwood Press.

Passas, Nikos. 1997. "Anomie and Relative Deprivation." In Nikos Passas and Robert Agnew (eds.), *The Future of Anomie Theory,* pp. 62–94. Boston: Northeastern University Press.

Passas, Nikos and Robert Agnew, eds. 1997. *The Future of Anomie Theory.* Boston: Northeastern University Press.

Paternoster, Raymond and Paul Mazerolle. 1994. "General Strain Theory and Delinquency: A Replication and Extension." *Journal of Research in Crime and Delinquency* 31: 235–263.

Piquero, Alex and Nicole Leeper Piquero. 1998. "On Testing Institutional Anomie Theory With Varying Specifications." *Studies on Crime and Crime Prevention* 7: 61–84.

Pratt, Travis C. and Francis T. Cullen. 2005. "Assessing Macro-Level Predictors and Theories of Crime: A Meta-Analysis." *Crime and Justice* 32: 373–450.

Pratt, Travis C. and Timothy W. Godsey. 2003. "Social Support, Inequality, and Homicide: A Cross-National Test of an Integrated Theoretical Model." *Criminology* 41: 611–643.

Rosenfeld, Richard. 1989. "Robert Merton's Contribution to the Sociology of Deviance." *Sociological Inquiry* 59: 453–466.

Rosenfeld, Richard and Steven F. Messner. 1995. "Crime and the American Dream: An Institutional Analysis." In Freda Adler and William S. Laufer (eds.), *The Legacy of Anomie Theory: Advances in Criminological Theory,* Volume 6, pp. 159–181. New Brunswick, NJ: Transaction.

Savolainen, Jukka. 2000. "Inequality, Welfare State, and Homicide: Further Support for the Institutional Anomie Theory." *Criminology* 38: 1021–1042.

Simon, William and John H. Gagnon. 1976. "The Anomie of Affluence: A Post-Mertonian Conception." *American Journal of Sociology* 82: 356–378.

Slocum, Lee Ann, Sally S. Simpson, and David A. Smith. 2005. "Strained Lives and Crime: Examining Intra-Individual Variation in Strain and Offending in a Sample of Incarcerated Women." *Criminology* 43: 827–854.

Tittle, Charles R. and Robert F. Meier. 1990. "Specifying the SES/Delinquency Relationship." *Criminology* 28: 271–299.

13. Social Structure and Anomie

Robert K. Merton

It has been said that the following article by Merton, "Social Structure and Anomie," is the most widely read article in sociology (Cole, 1975). Merton opens his 1938 article by challenging certain biologically based theories of crime that were popular at the time. Such theories view crime as the result of "biological drives" which are not adequately restrained by society. Merton instead argues that the motivation for crime frequently derives from society. His theory is in two parts.

The first part of the article presents what may be termed his "anomie" theory, which seeks to explain why some societies have higher rates of crime than others. This theory focuses on the relative emphasis placed on cultural goals and the institutionalized norms for achieving these goals. Societies that place a high relative emphasis on goals (like monetary success) and a low relative emphasis on the norms or rules for goal achievement have higher crime rates. Such societies are characterized by a state of anomie or normlessness, where the goal-seeking behavior of individuals is subject to little regulation. As a consequence, individuals employ the most expedient means—including crime—to achieve their goals. The United States is said be such a society, in which the goal of monetary success is stressed for everyone, but in which there is little emphasis on the norms regulating the achievement of this goal.

The second part of the article describes what may be termed Merton's "strain" theory. He argues that some individuals and groups within

a society are subject to special pressure for crime. While everyone is urged to strive for monetary success, lower-class individuals are frequently prevented from achieving such success through legitimate channels. As a result, they are under considerable strain or pressure. They may adapt to their strain in any one of the five ways listed by Merton. Certain of these adaptations involve crime, and Merton briefly discusses why some types of individuals are more likely to respond to strain with crime than others.

Merton's theory, particularly his strain theory, has been the subject of extensive commentary and research (for summaries, see Agnew, 1997, 2000; Akers and Sellers, 2008, Baumer and Gustafson, 2007; Burton and Cullen, 1992; Kornhauser, 1978; Kubrin et al., 2009). The evidence on his strain theory is mixed, although certain recent tests of this theory are promising (see Agnew, 2000; Agnew et al., 1996; Agnew and Passas, 1997; Baron, 2004; Cernkovich et al., 2000; Pratt and Cullen, 2005). Merton's anomie theory has never received an adequate test, although it is the direct inspiration for Messner and Rosenfeld's recent institutional-anomie theory, described in Chapter 15.

References

Agnew, Robert. 1997. "The Nature and Determinants of Strain: Another Look at Durkheim and Merton." In Nikos Passas and Robert Agnew

Reprinted with permission from Robert K. Merton, "Social structure and Anomie" in the *American Sociological Review* 3 (October). Copyright © 1938 by the American Sociological Review.

(eds.), *The Future of Anomie Theory*, pp. 27–51. Boston: Northeastern University Press.

———. 2000. "Sources of Criminality: Strain and Subcultural Theories of Criminality." In Joseph F. Sheley (ed.), *Criminology: A Contemporary Handbook*, 3rd edition, pp. 349–371. Belmont, CA: Wadsworth.

Agnew, Robert, Francis T. Cullen, Velmer S. Burton, Jr., T. David Evans, and R. Gregory Dunaway. 1996. "A New Test of Classic Strain Theory." *Justice Quarterly* 13: 681–704.

Agnew, Robert and Nikos Passas, eds. 1997. "Introduction." In *The Future of Anomie Theory*, pp. 1–26. Boston: Northeastern University Press.

Akers, Ronald L. and Christine Sellers. 2008. *Criminological Theories: Introduction and Evaluation*. New York: Oxford University Press.

Baron, Stephen W. 2004. "General Strain, Street Youth and Crime: A Test of Agnew's Revised Theory." *Criminology* 42: 457–483.

Baumer, Eric P. and Regan Gustafson. 2007. "Social Organization and Instrumental Crime: Assessing the Empirical Validity of Classic and Contemporary Anomie Theories." *Criminology* 45: 617–664.

Burton, Velmer S. and Francis T. Cullen. 1992. "The Empirical Status of Strain Theory." *Journal of Crime and Justice* 15: 1–30.

Cernkovich, Stephen A., Peggy C. Giordano, and Jennifer L. Rudolph. 2000. "Race, Crime, and the American Dream." *Journal of Research in Crime and Delinquency* 37: 131–170.

Cole, Stephen. 1975. "The Growth of Scientific Knowledge: Theories of Deviance as a Case Study." In Lewis A. Coser (ed.), *The Idea of Social Structure: Papers in Honor of Robert K. Merton*, pp. 175–220. New York: Harcourt Brace Jovanovich.

Kornhauser, Ruth. 1978. *Social Sources of Delinquency*. Chicago: University of Chicago Press.

Kubrin, Charis E., Thomas D. Stucky, and Marvin D. Krohn. 2009. *Researching Theories of Crime and Deviance*. New York: Oxford University press.

Pratt, Travis C. and Francis T. Cullen. 2005. "Assessing Macro-Level Predictors and Theories of Crime: A Meta-Analysis." *Crime and Justice* 32: 373–450.

———

There persists a notable tendency in sociological theory to attribute the malfunctioning of social structure primarily to those of man's imperious biological drives which are not adequately restrained by social control. In this view, the social order is solely a device for "impulse management" and the "social processing" of tensions. These impulses which break through social control, be it noted, are held to be biologically derived. Nonconformity is assumed to be rooted in original nature. Conformity is by implication the result of an utilitarian calculus or unreasoned conditioning. This point of view, whatever its other deficiencies, clearly begs one question. It provides no basis for determining the nonbiological conditions which induce deviations from prescribed patterns of conduct. In this paper, it will be suggested that certain phases of social structure generate the circumstances in which infringement of social codes constitutes a "normal" response.

The conceptual scheme to be outlined is designed to provide a coherent, systematic approach to the study of sociocultural sources of deviate behavior. Our primary aim lies in discovering how some social structures *exert a definite pressure* upon certain persons in the society to engage in nonconformist rather than conformist conduct. The many ramifications of the scheme cannot all be discussed; the problems mentioned outnumber those explicitly treated.

Among the elements of social and cultural structure, two are important for our purposes. These are analytically separable although they merge imperceptibly in concrete situations. The first consists of culturally defined goals, purposes, and interests. It comprises a frame of aspirational reference. These goals are more or less integrated and involve varying degrees of prestige and sentiment. They constitute a basic, but not the exclusive, component of what Linton aptly has called "designs for group living." Some of these cultural aspirations are related to the original drives of man, but they are not determined by them. The second phase of the social structure defines, regulates, and controls the acceptable modes of achieving these goals. Every social group invariably couples its scale of desired ends with moral or institutional regulation of permissible and required procedures for attaining these ends. These regulatory norms and moral imperatives do not necessarily coincide with technical or efficiency norms. Many procedures which from the standpoint of *particular individuals* would be most efficient in securing desired values, e.g., illicit oil-stock schemes, theft, fraud, are ruled out of the institutional area of permitted conduct. The choice of expedients is limited by the institutional norms.

To say that these two elements, culture goals and institutional norms, operate jointly is not to say that the ranges of alternative behaviors and aims bear some constant relation to one another. The emphasis upon certain goals may vary independently of the degree of emphasis upon institutional means. There may develop a disproportionate, at times, a virtually exclusive, stress upon the value of specific goals, involving relatively slight concern with the institutionally appropriate modes of attaining these goals. The limiting case in this direction is reached when the range of alternative procedures is limited only by technical rather than institutional considerations. Any and all devices which promise attainment of the all important goal would be permitted in this hypothetical polar case. This constitutes one type of cultural malintegration. A second polar type is found in groups where activities originally conceived as instrumental are transmuted into ends in themselves. The original purposes are forgotten and ritualistic adherence to institutionally prescribed conduct becomes virtually obsessive. Stability is largely ensured while change is flouted. The range of alternative behaviors is severely limited. There develops a tradition-bound, sacred society characterized by neophobia. The occupational psychosis of the bureaucrat may

be cited as a case in point. Finally, there are the intermediate types of groups where a balance between culture goals and institutional means is maintained. These are the significantly integrated and relatively stable, though changing, groups.

An effective equilibrium between the two phases of the social structure is maintained as long as satisfactions accrue to individuals who conform to both constraints, viz., satisfactions from the achievement of the goals and satisfactions emerging directly from the institutionally canalized modes of striving to attain these ends. Success, in such equilibrated cases, is twofold. Success is reckoned in terms of the product and in terms of the process, in terms of the outcome and in terms of activities. Continuing satisfactions must derive from sheer *participation* in a competitive order as well as from eclipsing one's competitors if the order itself is to be sustained. The occasional sacrifices involved in institutionalized conduct must be compensated by socialized rewards. The distribution of statuses and roles through competition must be so organized that positive incentives for conformity to roles and adherence to status obligations are provided *for every position* within the distributive order. Aberrant conduct, therefore, may be viewed as a symptom of dissociation between culturally defined aspirations and socially structured means.

Of the types of groups which result from the independent variation of the two phases of the social structure, we shall be primarily concerned with the first, namely, that involving a disproportionate accent on goals. This statement must be recast in a proper perspective. In no group is there an absence of regulatory codes governing conduct, yet groups do vary in the degree to which these folkways, mores, and institutional controls are effectively integrated with the more diffuse goals which are part of the culture matrix. Emotional convictions may cluster about the complex of socially acclaimed ends, meanwhile shifting their support from the culturally defined implementation of these ends. As we shall see, certain aspects of the social structure may generate countermores and antisocial behavior precisely because of differential emphases on goals and regulations. In the extreme case, the latter may be so vitiated by the goal-emphasis that the range of behavior is limited only by considerations of technical expediency. The sole significant question then becomes, which available means is most efficient in netting the socially approved value. The technically most feasible procedure, whether legitimate or not, is preferred to the institutionally prescribed conduct. As this process continues, the integration of the society becomes tenuous and anomie ensues.

Thus, in competitive athletics, when the aim of victory is shorn of its institutional trappings and success in contests becomes construed as "winning the game" rather than "winning through circumscribed modes of activity," a premium is implicitly set upon the use of illegitimate but technically efficient means. The star of the opposing football team is surreptitiously slugged; the wrestler furtively incapacitates his opponent through ingenious but illicit techniques; university alumni covertly subsidize "students" whose talents are largely confined to the athletic field. The emphasis on the goal has so attenuated the satisfactions deriving from sheer participation in the competitive activity that these satisfactions are virtually confined to a successful outcome. Through the same process, tension generated by the desire to win in a poker game is relieved by successfully dealing oneself four aces, or, when the cult of success has become completely dominant, by sagaciously shuffling the cards in a game of solitaire. The faint twinge of uneasiness in the last instance and the surreptitious nature of public delicts indicate clearly that the institutional rules of the game *are known* to those who evade them, but that the emotional supports of these rules are largely vitiated by cultural exaggeration of the success-goal. They are microcosmic images of the social macrocosm.

Of course, this process is not restricted to the realm of sport. The process whereby exaltation of the end generates a *literal demoralization*, i.e., a deinstitutionalization, of the means is one which

characterizes many groups in which the two phases of the social structure are not highly integrated. The extreme emphasis upon the accumulation of wealth as a symbol of success in our own society militates against the completely effective control of institutionally regulated modes of acquiring a fortune. Fraud, corruption, vice, crime, in short, the entire catalogue of proscribed behavior, becomes increasingly common when the emphasis on the *culturally induced* success-goal becomes divorced from a coordinated institutional emphasis. This observation is of crucial theoretical importance in examining the doctrine that antisocial behavior most frequently derives from biological drives breaking through the restraints imposed by society. The difference is one between a strictly utilitarian interpretation which conceives man's ends as random and an analysis which finds these ends deriving from the basic values of the culture.

Our analysis can scarcely stop at this juncture. We must turn to other aspects of the social genesis of the varying rates and types of deviate behavior characteristic of different societies. Thus far, we have sketched three ideal types of social orders constituted by distinctive patterns of relations between culture ends and means. Turning from these types of *culture patterning*, we find five logically possible, alternative modes of adjustment or adaptation *by individuals* within the culture-bearing society or group. These are schematically presented in Table 13.1, where (+) signifies "acceptance," (−) signifies "elimination" and (±) signifies "rejection and substitution of new goals and standards."

Our discussion of the relation between these alternative responses and other phases of the social structure must be prefaced by the observation that persons may shift from one alternative to another as they engage in different social activities. These categories refer to role adjustments in specific situations, not to personality *in toto*. To treat the development of this process in various spheres of conduct would introduce a complexity unmanageable within the confines of this paper. For this reason, we shall be concerned primarily

Table 13.1
Typology of Adaptations

	Culture Goals	Institutionalized Means
I. Conformity	+	+
II. Innovation	+	−
III. Ritualism	−	+
IV. Retreatism	−	−
V. Rebellion	±	±

with economic activity in the broad sense, "the production, exchange, distribution and consumption of goods and services" in our competitive society, wherein wealth has taken on a highly symbolic cast. Our task is to search out some of the factors which exert pressure upon individuals to engage in certain of these logically possible alternative responses. This choice, as we shall see, is far from random.

In every society, Adaptation I (conformity to both culture goals and means) is the most common and widely diffused. Were this not so, the stability and continuity of the society could not be maintained. The mesh of expectancies which constitutes every social order is sustained by the modal behavior of its members falling within the first category. Conventional role behavior oriented toward the basic values of the group is the rule rather than the exception. It is this fact alone which permits us to speak of a human aggregate as comprising a group or society.

Conversely, Adaptation IV (rejection of goals and means) is the least common. Persons who "adjust" (or maladjust) in this fashion are, strictly speaking, in the society but not *of it*. Sociologically, these constitute the true "aliens." Not sharing the common frame of orientation, they can be included within the societal population merely in a fictional sense. In this category are *some* of the activities of psychotics, psychoneurotics, chronic autists, pariahs, outcasts, vagrants, vagabonds,

tramps, chronic drunkards and drug addicts. These have relinquished, in certain spheres of activity, the culturally defined goals, involving complete aim-inhibition in the polar case, and their adjustments are not in accord with institutional norms. This is not to say that in some cases the source of their behavioral adjustments is not in part the very social structure which they have in effect repudiated nor that their very existence within a social area does not constitute a problem for the socialized population.

This mode of "adjustment" occurs, as far as structural sources are concerned, when both the culture goals and institutionalized procedures have been assimilated thoroughly by the individual and imbued with affect and high positive value, but where those institutionalized procedures which promise a measure of successful attainment of the goals are not available to the individual. In such instances, there results a two-fold mental conflict insofar as the moral obligation for adopting institutional means conflicts with the pressure to resort to illegitimate means (which may attain the goal) and inasmuch as the individual is shut off from means which are both legitimate and effective. The competitive order is maintained, but the frustrated and handicapped individual who cannot cope with this order drops out. Defeatism, quietism, and resignation are manifested in escape mechanisms which ultimately lead the individual to "escape" from the requirements of the society. It is an expedient which arises from continued failure to attain the goal by legitimate measures and from an inability to adopt the illegitimate route because of internalized prohibitions and institutionalized compulsives, *during which process the supreme value of the success-goal has as yet not been renounced.* The conflict is resolved by eliminating both precipitating elements, the goals and means. The escape is complete, the conflict is eliminated and the individual is socialized.

Be it noted that where frustration derives from the inaccessibility of effective institutional means for attaining economic or any other type of highly valued "success," that Adaptations II, III and V (innovation, ritualism and rebellion) are also possible. The result will be determined by the particular personality, and thus, the *particular* cultural background, involved. Inadequate socialization will result in the innovation response whereby the conflict and frustration are eliminated by relinquishing the institutional means and retaining the success-aspiration; an extreme will lead to ritualism wherein the goal is dropped as beyond one's reach but conformity to the mores persists; and rebellion occurs when emancipation from the reigning standards, due to frustration or to marginalist perspectives, leads to the attempt to introduce a "new social order."

Our major concern is with the illegitimacy adjustment. This involves the use of conventionally proscribed but frequently effective means of attaining at least the simulacrum of culturally defined success—wealth, power, and the like. As we have seen, this adjustment occurs when the individual has assimilated the cultural emphasis on success without equally internalizing the morally prescribed norms governing means for its attainment. The question arises, Which phases of our social structure predispose toward this mode of adjustment? We may examine a concrete instance, effectively analyzed by Lohman, which provides a clue to the answer. Lohman has shown that specialized areas of vice in the near north side of Chicago constitute a "normal" response to a situation where the cultural emphasis upon pecuniary success has been absorbed, but where there is little access to conventional and legitimate means for attaining such success. The conventional occupational opportunities of persons in this area are almost completely limited to manual labor. Given our cultural stigmatization of manual labor, and its correlate, the prestige of white collar work, it is clear that the result is a strain toward innovational practices. The limitation of opportunity to unskilled labor and the resultant low income can not compete *in terms of conventional standards of achievement* with the high income from organized vice.

For our purposes, this situation involves two important features. First, such antisocial behavior is in a sense "called forth" by certain conventional values of the culture and by the class structure involving differential access to the approved opportunities for legitimate, prestige-bearing pursuit of the culture goals. The lack of high integration between the means-and-end elements of the cultural pattern and the particular class structure combine to favor a heightened frequency of antisocial conduct in such groups. The second consideration is of equal significance. Recourse to the first of the alternative responses, legitimate effort, is limited by the fact that actual advance toward desired success-symbols through conventional channels is, despite our persisting open-class ideology, relatively rare and difficult for those handicapped by little formal education and few economic resources. The dominant pressure of group standards of success is, therefore, on the gradual attenuation of legitimate, but by and large ineffective, strivings and the increasing use of illegitimate, but more or less effective, expedients of vice and crime. The cultural demands made on persons in this situation are incompatible. On the one hand, they are asked to orient their conduct toward the prospect of accumulating wealth and on the other, they are largely denied effective opportunities to do so institutionally. The consequences of such structural inconsistency are psychopathological personality, and/or antisocial conduct, and/or revolutionary activities. The equilibrium between culturally designated means and ends becomes highly unstable with the progressive emphasis on attaining the prestige-laden ends by any means whatsoever. Within this context, Capone represents the triumph of amoral intelligence over morally prescribed "failure," when the channels of vertical mobility are closed or narrowed *in a society which places a high premium on economic affluence and social accent for all its members.*

This last qualification is of primary importance. It suggests that other phases of the social structure besides the extreme emphasis on pecuniary success, must be considered if we are to understand the social sources of antisocial behavior. A high frequency of deviate behavior is not generated simply by "lack of opportunity" or by this exaggerated pecuniary emphasis. A comparatively rigidified class structure, a feudalistic or caste order, may limit such opportunities far beyond the point which obtains in our society today. It is only when a system of cultural values extols, virtually above all else, certain *common* symbols of success *for a considerable part of the same population*, that antisocial behavior ensues on a considerable scale. In other words, our egalitarian ideology denies by implication the existence of noncompeting groups and individuals in the pursuit of pecuniary success. The same body of success-symbols is held to be desirable for all. These goals are held to *transcend class lines*, not to be bounded by them, yet the actual social organization is such that there exist class differentials in the accessibility of these *common* success-symbols. Frustration and thwarted aspiration lead to the search for avenues of escape from a culturally induced intolerable situation; or unrelieved ambition may eventuate in illicit attempts to acquire the dominant values. The American stress on pecuniary success and ambitiousness for all thus invites exaggerated anxieties, hostilities, neuroses and antisocial behavior.

This theoretical analysis may go far toward explaining the varying correlations between crime and poverty. Poverty is not an isolated variable. It is one in a complex of interdependent social and cultural variables. When viewed in such a context, it represents quite different states of affairs. Poverty as such, and consequent limitation of opportunity, are not sufficient to induce a conspicuously high rate of criminal behavior. Even the often mentioned "poverty in the midst of plenty" will not necessarily lead to this result. Only insofar as poverty and associated disadvantages in competition for the culture values approved for all members of the society is linked with the assimilation of a cultural emphasis on monetary accumulation as a symbol of success

is antisocial conduct a "normal" outcome. Thus, poverty is less highly correlated with crime in southeastern Europe than in the United States. The possibilities of vertical mobility in these European areas would seem to be fewer than in this country, so that neither poverty *per se* nor its association with limited opportunity is sufficient to account for the varying correlations. It is only when the full configuration is considered, poverty, limited opportunity and a commonly shared system of success symbols, that we can explain the higher association between poverty and crime in our society than in others where rigidified class structure is coupled with *differential class symbols of achievement*.

In societies such as our own, then, the pressure of prestige-bearing success tends to eliminate the effective social constraint over means employed to this end. "The-end-justifies-the-means" doctrine becomes a guiding tenet for action when the cultural structure unduly exalts the end and the social organization unduly limits possible recourse to approved means. Otherwise put, this notion and associated behavior reflect a lack of cultural coordination. In international relations, the effects of this lack of integration are notoriously apparent. An emphasis upon national power is not readily coordinated with an inept organization of legitimate, i.e., internationally defined and accepted, means for attaining this goal. The result is a tendency toward the abrogation of international law, treaties become scraps of paper, "undeclared warfare" serves as a technical evasion, the bombing of civilian populations is rationalized just as the same societal situation induces the same sway of illegitimacy among individuals.

The social order we have described necessarily produces this "strain toward dissolution." The pressure of such an order is upon outdoing one's competitors. The choice of means within the ambit of institutional control will persist as long as the sentiments supporting a competitive system, i. e., deriving from the possibility of outranking competitors and hence enjoying the favorable response of others, are distributed throughout the entire system of activities and are not confined merely to the final result. A stable social structure demands a balanced distribution of affect among its various segments. When there occurs a shift of emphasis from the satisfactions deriving from competition itself to almost exclusive concern with successful competition, the resultant stress leads to the breakdown of the regulatory structure. With the resulting attenuation of the institutional imperatives, there occurs an approximation of the situation erroneously held by utilitarians to be typical of society generally wherein calculations of advantage and fear of punishment are the sole regulating agencies. In such situations, as Hobbes observed, force and fraud come to constitute the sole virtues in view of their relative efficiency in attaining goals—which were for him, of course, not culturally derived.

It should be apparent that the foregoing discussion is not pitched on a moralistic plane. Whatever the sentiments of the writer or reader concerning the ethical desirability of coordinating the means-and-goals phases of the social structure, one must agree that lack of such coordination leads to anomie. Insofar as one of the most general functions of social organization is to provide a basis of social organization is to provide a basis for calculability and regularity of behavior, it is increasingly limited in effectiveness as these elements of the structure become dissociated. At the extreme, predictability virtually disappears and what may be properly termed cultural chaos or anomie intervenes.

This statement, being brief, is also incomplete. It has not included an exhaustive treatment of the various structural elements which predispose toward one rather than another of the alternative responses open to individuals; it has neglected, but not denied the relevance of, the factors determining the specific incidence of these responses; it has not enumerated the various concrete responses which are constituted by combinations of specific values of the analytical variables; it has omitted, or included only by implication, any consideration of the social functions performed by illicit responses; it has not tested the full explanatory power of the analytical scheme by examining a large number of group variations in the frequency of deviate and conformist behavior; it has not adequately dealt with rebellious conduct which seeks to refashion the social framework radically; it has not examined the relevance of cultural conflict for an analysis of culture-goal and institutional-means malintegration. It is suggested that these and related problems may be profitably analyzed by this scheme.

Discussion Questions

1. Describe the "cultural goals" and "institutional norms" that exist at your school. Are these goals and norms in "balance"?
2. Describe the "adaptations" that individuals might employ when they cannot achieve the cultural goals emphasized at your school.
3. What factors determine whether individuals will choose adaptations that may involve crime, like innovation?
4. Would Merton argue that poverty, in and of itself, is a cause of crime?
5. What policy recommendations might Merton make for controlling crime?

14. Delinquent Boys: The Culture of the Gang

Albert K. Cohen

Cohen was a student of both Robert Merton and Edwin Sutherland. Like Sutherland, Cohen was interested in delinquent subcultures, particularly the lower-working-class urban gangs that were the subject of much attention during the 1950s. While a student of Sutherland, Cohen posed a question for which Sutherland did not have an adequate answer: How can we explain the origin and content of delinquent subcultures? Cohen drew heavily on Merton's strain theory to provide his own answer to this question, which is outlined in the following selection from his book: Delinquent Boys: The Culture of the Gang. *In the first part of the selection, Cohen provides a general explanation for the origin of deviant subcultures. In the second part of the selection, Cohen applies this theory to explain the origin and content of male, working-class urban gangs.*

In reading the selection, note the similarities and differences with Merton's strain theory. Like Merton, Cohen argues that delinquency is ultimately caused by goal blockage. Cohen, however, argues that lower-class and working-class boys are not simply concerned with the goal of monetary success. Rather, they want to achieve the broader goal of middle-class status, which involves respect from others as well as financial success. This difference in goals is crucial. One can achieve financial success through illegitimate channels like theft (Merton's adaptation of innovation). One cannot, however, achieve middle-class status through the same channels (one cannot steal middle-class status). As a consequence, lower-class and working-class boys often adapt to their goal blockage by setting up an alternative status system in which they can achieve success (this is similar to Merton's adaptation of rebellion, in which new goals and means are substituted for the old ones). The hostility of lower-class and working-class boys toward the middle class, among other things, leads them to set up a status system that values everything the middle class rejects. The middle class values private property and respect for the individual, for example, while the delinquent gang values the destruction and theft of property and aggression against others. Cohen thus explains the origin and content of the delinquent subculture.

Certain features of Cohen's theory have been criticized (see Akers and Sellers, 2008). Theorists such as Cloward and Ohlin (1960) and Sykes and Matza (Chapter 17) claim that the values of delinquents are not as opposed to conventional values as Cohen claims. The data tend to support this argument (see Agnew, 2000). Nevertheless, Cohen's use of strain theory to explain the origin of deviant subcultures is a fundamental contribution to the crime literature.

Reprinted with the permission of The Free Press, a division of Simon & Schuster, from *Delinquent Boys: The Culture of the Gang* by Albert K. Cohen. Copyright © 1955 by The Free Press; copyright renewed 1983 by Albert K. Cohen.

References

Agnew, Robert. 2000. "Sources of Criminality: Strain and Subcultural Theories." In Joseph F. Sheley (ed.), *Criminology: A Contemporary Handbook*, 3rd edition, pp. 349–371. Belmont, CA: Wadsworth.

Akers, Ronald L. and Christine Sellers. 2008. *Criminological Theories: Introduction and Evaluation*, 5th edition. New York: Oxford University Press.

Cloward, Richard A. and Lloyd E. Ohlin. 1960. *Delinquency and opportunity*. Glencoe, IL: Free Press.

———————————————————

When we speak of a delinquent subculture, we speak of a way of life that has somehow become traditional among certain groups in American society. These groups are the boys' gangs that flourish most conspicuously in the "delinquency neighborhoods" of our larger American cities. The members of these gangs grow up, some to become law-abiding citizens and others to graduate to more professional and adult forms of criminality, but the delinquent tradition is kept alive by the age-groups that succeed them. This book is an attempt to answer some important questions about this delinquent subculture. . . .

Why is there such a subculture? Why is it "there" to be "taken over"? Why does it have the particular content that it does and why is it distributed as it is within our social system? Why does it arise and persist, as it is within our social system? Why does it arise and persist, as it does, in such dependable fashion in certain neighborhoods of our American cities? Why does it not "diffuse" to other areas and to other classes of our population. . . .

Action Is Problem-Solving

Our point of departure is the "psychogenic" assumption that all human action—not delinquency alone—is an ongoing series of efforts to solve problems. By "problems" we do not only mean the worries and dilemmas that bring people to the psychiatrist and the psychological clinic.

Whether or not to accept a proffered drink, which of two ties to buy, what to do about the unexpected guest or the "F" in algebra are problems too. They all involve, until they are resolved, a certain tension, a disequilibrium and a challenge. We hover between doing and not doing, doing this or doing that, doing it one way or doing it another. Each choice is an act, each act is a choice. Not every act is a *successful* solution, for our choice may leave us with unresolved tensions or generate new and unanticipated consequences which pose new problems, but is at least an attempt at a solution. On the other hand, not every problem need imply distress, anxiety, bedevilment. Most problems are familiar and recurrent and we have at hand for them ready solutions, habitual modes of action which we have found efficacious and acceptable both to ourselves and to our neighbours. Other problems, however, are not so readily resolved. They persist, they nag, and they press for novel solutions. . . .

We seek, if possible, solutions which will settle old problems and not create new ones. A first requirement, then, of a wholly acceptable solution is that it be acceptable to those on whose cooperation and good will we are dependent. This immediately imposes sharp limits on the range of creativity and innovation. Our dependence upon our social milieu provides us with a strong incentive to select our solutions from among those already established and known to be congenial to our fellows. . . .

We see then why, both on the levels of overt action and of the supporting frame of reference, there are powerful incentives not to deviate from the ways established in our groups. Should our problems be not capable of solution in ways acceptable to our groups and should they be sufficiently pressing, we are not so likely to strike out on our own as we are to shop around for a group with a different subculture, with a frame of reference we find more congenial. One fascinating aspect of the social process is the continual realignment of groups, the migration of individuals from one group to another in the unconscious quest for a social milieu favorable to the resolution of their problems of adjustment.

How Subcultural Solutions Arise

Now we confront a dilemma and a paradox. We have seen how difficult it is for the individual to cut loose from the culture models in his milieu, how his dependence upon his fellows compels him to seek conformity and to avoid innovation. But these models and precedents which we call the surrounding culture are ways in which other people think and other people act, and these other people are likewise constrained by models in *their* milieux. *These models themselves, however, continually change.* How is it possible for cultural innovations to emerge while each of the participants in the culture is so powerfully motivated to conform to what is already established? This is the central theoretical problem of this book.

The crucial condition for the emergence of new cultural forms is the existence, *in effective interaction with one another, of a number of actors with similar problems of adjustment.* These may be the entire membership of a group or only certain members, similarly circumstanced, within the group. Among the conceivable solutions to their problems may be one which is not yet embodied in action and which does not therefore exist as a cultural model. This solution, except for the fact that it does not already carry the social criteria of validity and promise the social rewards of consensus, might well answer more neatly to the problems of this group and appeal to its members more effectively than any of the solutions already institutionalized. For each participant, this solution would be adjustive and adequately motivated provided that he could anticipate a simultaneous and coresponding transformation in the frames of reference of his fellows. Each would welcome a sign from the others that a new departure in this direction would receive approval and support. But how does one *know* whether a gesture toward innovation will strike a responsive and sympathetic chord in others or whether it will elicit hostility, ridicule and punishment? *Potential* concurence is always problematical

and innovation or the impulse to innovate a stimulus for anxiety.

The paradox is resolved when the innovation is broached in such a manner as to elicit from others reactions suggesting their receptivity; and when, at the same time, the innovation occurs by increments so small, tentative and ambiguous as to permit the actor to retreat, if the signs be unfavorable, without having become identified with an unpopular position. Perhaps all social actions have, in addition to their instrumental, communicative and expressive functions, this quality of being *exploratory gestures*. For the actor with problems of adjustment which cannot be resolved within the frame of reference of the established culture, each response of the other to what the actor says and does is a clue to the directions in which change may proceed further in a way congenial to the other and to the direction in which change will lack social support. And if the probing gesture is motivated by tensions common to other participants it is likely to initiate a process of *mutual* exploration and *joint* elaboration of new solution. My exploratory gesture functions as a cue to you; your exploratory gesture as a cue to me. . . .

The final product, to which we are jointly committed, is likely to be a compromise formation of all the participants to what we may call a cultural process, a formation perhaps unanticipated by any of them. . . .

Subcultural Solutions to Status Problems

One variant of this cultural process interests us especially because it provides the model for our explanation of the delinquent subculture. Status problems are problems of achieving respect in the eyes of one's fellows. Our ability to achieve status depends upon the criteria of status applied by our fellows, that is, the standards or norms they go by in evaluating people. These criteria are an aspect of their cultural frames of reference. If we lack the characteristics or capacities which give status in terms of these criteria, we are beset by one of the most typical and yet distressing of human problems of adjustment. One solution is for individuals who share such problems to gravitate toward one another and jointly to establish new norms, new criteria of status which define as meritorious the characteristics they *do* possess, the kinds of conduct of which they *are* capable. It is clearly necessary for each participant, if the innovation is to solve his status problem, that these new criteria be shared with others, that the solution be a group and not a private solution. If he "goes it alone" he succeeds only in further estranging himself from his fellows. Such new status criteria would represent new subcultural values different from or even antithetical to those of the larger social system. . . .

Insofar as the new subculture represents a new status system sanctioning behavior tabooed or frowned upon by the larger society, the acquisition of status within the new group is accompanied by a loss of status outside the group. To the extent that the esteem of outsiders is a value to the members of the group, a new problem is engendered. To this problem the typical solution is to devalue the good will and respect of those whose good will and respect are forfeit anyway. The new subculture of the community of innovators comes to include hostile and contemptuous images of those groups whose enmity they have earned. Indeed, this repudiation of outsiders, necessary in order to protect oneself from feeling concerned about what they may think, may go so far as to make nonconformity with the expectations of the outsiders a positive criterion of status within the group. Certain kinds of conduct, that is, become reputable precisely because they are disreputable in the eyes of the "out-group. . . ."

In these chapters, in conformity with the model we have proposed, we shall try to demonstrate that certain problems of adjustment tend, in consequence of the structure of American society, to occur most typically in those role sectors where the delinquent subculture is endemic.

Then we shall try to show how the delinquent subculture provides a solution appropriate to those particular problems and to elaboration and perpetuation by social groups. . . .

Growing Up in a Class System

In summary, it may confidently be said that the working-class boy, particularly if his training and values be those we have here defined as working-class, is more likely than his middle-class peers to find himself at the bottom of the status hierarchy whenever he moves in a middle-class world, whether it be of adults or of children. To the degree to which he values middle-class status, either because he values the good opinion of middle-class persons or because he has to some degree internalized middle-class standards himself, he faces a problem of adjustment and is in the market for a "solution."

What the Delinquent Subculture Has to Offer

The delinquent subculture, we suggest, is a way of dealing with the problems of adjustment we have described. These problems are chiefly status problems: certain children are denied status in the respectable society because they cannot meet the criteria of the respectable status system. The delinquent subculture deals with these problems by providing criteria of status which these children *can* meet. . . .

The hallmark of the delinquent subculture is the explicit and wholesale repudiation of middle-class standards and the adoption of their very antithesis. . . .

It is precisely here, we suggest, in the refusal to temporize, that the appeal of the delinquent subculture lies. Let us recall that it is characteristically American, not specifically working-class or middle-class, to measure oneself against the widest possible status universe, to seek status against "all comers," to be "as good as" or "better than" anybody—anybody, that is, within one's own age and sex category.

As long as the working-class corner-boy clings to a version, however attenuated and adulterated, of the middle-class culture, he must recognize his inferiority to working-class and middle-class college-boys. The delinquent subculture, on the other hand, permits no ambiguity of the status of the delinquent relative to that of anybody else. In terms of the norms of the delinquent subculture, defined by its negative polarity to the respectable status system, the delinquent's very nonconformity to middle-class standards sets him above the most exemplary college boy.

Another important function of the delinquent subculture is the legitimation of aggression. We surmise that a certain amount of hostility is generated among working-class children against middle-class persons, with their airs of superiority, disdain or condescension and against middle-class norms, which are, in a sense, the cause of their status-frustration. . . .

Discussion Questions

1. How is Cohen's use of strain theory similar to and different from Merton's version of strain theory?
2. Describe the conditions necessary for a deviant subculture to emerge.
3. Describe the major "problem of adjustment" faced by working-class boys.
4. How does the delinquent subculture solve the problem of adjustment described above?

15. Crime and the American Dream

Richard Rosenfeld and Steven F. Messner

Merton's (1938) theory of "Social Structure and Anomie" is in two parts: The first part tries to explain why the United States has such a high rate of crime and the second tries to explain why some groups within the United States are more likely to engage in crime. Until Messner and Rosenfeld (2007) developed their institutional-anomie theory of crime, researchers largely neglected the first part of Merton's theory. Like Merton, Messner and Rosenfeld seek to explain the high rate of crime in the United States. They draw heavily on Merton's theory, arguing that our high crime rate stems partly from the fact that we encourage everyone to pursue the goal of monetary success, but place little emphasis on the legitimate norms for achieving such success (as they state, "it's not how you play the game; it's whether you win or lose").

They also extend Merton's theory in a fundamental way. They argue that the cultural emphasis on monetary success is paralleled by the fact that the economy dominates the major institutions in our society, including the family, school, and polity. As Rosenfeld and Messner indicate in the following selection, the domination of the economy interferes with the effective functioning of these other institutions. As a result, these institutions are not able to adequately socialize or train individuals and sanction deviance. This further contributes to our high crime rate.

Messner and Rosenfeld's theory is important because it redirects our attention to the explanation of societal differences in crime rates. It also forces us to confront some very difficult issues: are the basic values and organization of our society responsible for our high crime rate, and if so, what is to be done (see Messner and Rosenfeld, 2007, for a discussion of crime control strategies)?

References

Merton, Robert K. 1938. "Social Structure and Anomie." *American Sociological Review* 3: 672–673.

Messner, Steven F. and Richard Rosenfeld. 2007. *Crime and the American Dream*, 4th edition. Belmont, CA: Wadsworth.

The obsession with crime in the United States cannot be dismissed as an irrational feature of the American character or as a peculiarly American penchant for inventing crime waves or using crime as a stage for enacting other social dramas. Rather, the American obsession with crime is rooted in an objective social reality. Levels of crime in the United States, and more specifically levels of serious crime, are in fact very high in comparative perspective....

We maintain that the comparatively high level of serious criminal behavior in the United States is one of the more important facts about crime to be

Reprinted by permission of Transaction Publishers. "Crime and the American Dream" from *The Legacy of Anomie Theory*, vol. 6., Richard Rosenfeld and Steven F. Messner. Copyright © 1995 by Transaction Publishers.

explained by criminological theory (cf. Braithwaite 1989). Curiously, however, criminologists have devoted relatively little attention to this issue for at least two interrelated reasons: the dominance of individual-level perspectives in contemporary criminology and a corresponding deemphasis on serious forms of criminal behavior. Nonetheless, we propose that the foundations for an explanation of the distinctively high levels of crime in the United States can be found in the arguments advanced by Robert Merton in his classic essay "Social Structure and Anomie" (1938, 1968; hereafter SS&A).

Merton proposes that the sources of crime in the United States lie in the same cultural commitments and social arrangements that are conventionally regarded as part of the American success story. High rates of crime are thus not simply the "sick" outcome of individual pathologies, such as defective personalities or aberrant biological structures. Nor are they the "evil consequence" of individual moral failings. Instead, crime in America derives in significant measure from highly prized cultural and social conditions—indeed, from the American Dream itself.

In this chapter, we offer an explanation of American crime rates that is based on an expanded version of Merton's theory. We amplify the theory in two ways. First, we restore the original macro-level intent and orientation to SS&A that were removed in the conversion of "anomie theory" into "strain theory." We then extend anomie theory by considering the connections between core elements of the American Dream, which Merton discussed in some detail, and an aspect of social structure to which he devoted little attention: the interrelationships among social institutions. Our basic thesis is that the anomic tendencies inherent in the American Dream both produce and are reproduced by an *institutional balance of power* dominated by the economy. The result of the interplay between the basic cultural commitments of the American Dream and the companion institutional arrangements is widespread anomie, weak social controls, and high levels of crime. . . .

The Anomie Tendencies of the American Dream

In SS&A, Merton advances the provocative argument that there are inherent features of American culture, of the American Dream itself, that ultimately contribute to the high rates of crime and deviance observed in the United States. Although Merton does not provide a formal definition of "the American Dream," it is possible to formulate a reasonably concise characterization of this cultural orientation on the basis of his discussion of American culture in general and his scattered references to the American Dream. The American Dream refers to a commitment to the goal of material success, to be pursued by everyone in society, under conditions of open, individual competition.

Merton proposes that the American Dream has been highly functional for society in certain respects. This cultural ethos is particularly effective in satisfying motivational requirements because it encourages high levels of "ambition" (Merton 1968: 200). At the same time, there is a dark side to the American Dream. It tends to promote an anomic imbalance wherein the importance of using the legitimate means is deemphasized relative to the importance of attaining the desired cultural goals.

Merton explains that this anomic tendency derives ultimately from the very same basic value commitments upon which the American Dream rests. One such commitment is a strong *achievement orientation*. In American society, personal worth tends to be evaluated on the basis of what people have achieved rather than who they are or how they relate to others in social networks. "Success" is to a large extent the ultimate measure of social worth. Quite understandably, then, there are pervasive cultural pressures to achieve at any cost. A strong achievement orientation, at the level of basic cultural values, thus cultivates and sustains a mentality that "it's not how you play the game; it's whether you win or lose."

A second basic value orientation that contributes to the anomic imbalance in American culture is *individualism*. In the pursuit of success, people are encouraged to "make it" on their own. Fellow members of society are thus competitors in the struggle for achievement and the ultimate validation of personal worth. This intense, individual competition to succeed further encourages a tendency to disregard normative restraints on behavior when these restraints interfere with the realization of goals. Andrew Hacker (1992: 29) offers a cogent description of this distinctive feature of American culture:

> America has always been the most competitive of societies. It poises its citizens against one another, with the warning that they must make it on their own. Hence the stress on moving past others, driven by a fear of failing behind. No other nation so rates its residents as winners or losers.

A third component of American culture that is conductive to anomic imbalance is its *universalism*. Everyone is encouraged to aspire to social ascent, and everyone is susceptible to evaluation on the basis of individual achievements. As a consequence, the pressures to "win" are pervasive; no one is exempt from the pursuit of success (Merton 1968: 200; Orru 1990: 234).

Finally, in American culture, success is signified in a special way: by the accumulation of *monetary rewards*. Merton is keenly aware of the high priority awarded to money in American culture. He observes that

> in some large measure, money has been consecrated as a value in itself, over and above its expenditure for articles of consumption or its use for the enhancement of power. (1968: 190)

Merton's key point is not that Americans are uniquely materialistic; a strong interest in material well-being can be found in most societies. Rather, the distinctive feature of American culture is the preeminent role of money as the "metric" of success. As Orru puts it, "money is literally, in this context, a *currency* for measuring achievement" (1990: 235).

Merton points to an important implication of the signification of achievement with reference to monetary rewards. Monetary success is inherently open-ended. Because it is always possible in principle to have more money, "in the American Dream there is no final stopping point" (1968: 190). Cultural prescriptions thus mandate "never-ending achievement" (Passas 1990: 159). Relentless pressures to accumulate money, in turn, encourage people to disregard normative restraints when they impede the pursuit of personal goals.

In sum, dominant value patterns of American culture, specifically its achievement orientation, its competitive individualism, its universalism in goal orientations and evaluative standards—when harnessed to the preeminent goal of monetary success—give rise to a distinctive cultural ethos: the American Dream. The American Dream, in turn, encourages members of society to pursue ends, in Merton's words, "limited only by considerations of technical expediency" (1968: 189). One consequence of this open, wide-spread competitive, and anomic quest for success by any means necessary is high levels of crime. . . .

Merton's cultural critique represents only a partial explanation of the high levels of crime in the United States considered in comparative perspective. A complete explanation requires identification of the social structural underpinnings of American culture and its associated strains toward anomie. Merton's analysis stops short of an explication of the ways in which specific features of the institutional structure—beyond the class system—interrelate to generate the anomic pressures that are held to be responsible for crime (cf. Cohen 1985: 233). As a consequence, the anomie perspective is best regarded a "work in progress." In Cohen's words, Merton

> has laid the groundwork for an explanation of deviance [and crime] on the sociological level, but the task, for the most part, still lies ahead. (1985: 233)

The Institutional Dynamics of Crime

The Normal Functions of Social Institutions

Social institutions are the building blocks of whole societies. As such, they constitute the fundamental units of macro-level analysis. Institutions are "relatively stable sets of norms and values, statuses and roles, and groups and organizations" that regulate human conduct to meet the basic needs of a society (Bassis, Gelles, and Levine 1991: 142). These social needs include the need to adapt to the environment, to mobilize and deploy resources for the achievement of collective goals, and to socialize members in the society's fundamental normative patterns.

Adaptation to the environment is the primary responsibility of economic institutions, which organize the production and distribution of goods and services to satisfy the basic material requirements for human existence. The political system, or "polity," mobilizes and distributes power to attain collective goals. One collective purpose of special importance is the maintenance of public safety. Political institutions are responsible for

> protecting members of society from invasions from without, controlling crime and disorder within, and providing channels for resolving conflicts of interest. (Bassis, Gelles, and Levine 1991: 142)

The institution of the family has primary responsibility for the maintenance and replacement of members of society. These tasks involve setting the limits of legitimate sexual relations among adults; the physical care and nurturing of children; and the socialization of children into the values, goals, and beliefs of the dominant culture. In addition, a particularly important function of the family in modern societies is to provide emotional support for its members. To a significant degree, the family serves as a refuge from the tensions and stresses generated in other institutional domains. In this idea of the family as a "haven" from the rigors of the public world lies the implicit recognition of the need to counterbalance and temper the harsh, competitive conditions of public life (Lasch 1977).

The institution of education shares many of the socialization functions of the family. Like the family, schools are given responsibility for transmitting basic cultural standards to new generations. In modern industrial societies, schools are also oriented toward the specific task of preparing youth for the demands of adult occupational roles. In addition, education is intended to enhance personal adjustment, facilitate the development of individual human potential, and advance the general "knowledge base" of the culture.

These four social institutions—the economy, polity, family, and education—are the focus of our explanation of crime. They do not, of course, exhaust the institutional structure of modern societies, nor are they the only institutions with relevance to crime. However, the interconnections among these four institutions are central to an institutional analysis of crime in modern societies, in general, and of the exceptionally high levels of crime in the United States, in particular.

Social institutions are to some extent distinct with respect to the primary activities around which they are organized. At the same time, however, the functions of institutions are overlapping and interdependent. For example, the performance of the economy is dependent on the quality of the "human capital" (i.e., the motivations, knowledge, and skills) cultivated in the schools. The capacity of the schools to develop human capital is circumscribed by the individual backgrounds, what Pierre Bourdieu refers to as the "cultural capital," that students bring with them from their families (MacLeod 1987: 11–14). The effective functioning of all three of these institutions—the economy, education, and the family—presupposes an environment with at least a modicum of social order, for which the polity is largely responsible. Finally, the capacity of the polity to promote the collective good depends on the nature and quality of economic and human resources supplied by the other institutions.

The interdependence of major social institutions implies that some coordination and cooperation among institutions is required for societies to "work" at all. The requirements for the effective functioning of any given institution, however, may conflict with the requirements of another. This potential for conflict is illustrated by the particularly stark contrast between the dominant values embodied in two institutions: the economy and the family.

Economic life and family life are supposed to be governed by fundamentally different standards in modern industrial societies. Family relationships are expected to be regulated by the norm of particularism, and positions and roles in the family are allocated, in large measure, on the basis of ascribed characteristics. Each member is entitled to special considerations by virtue of his or her unique identity and position in the family. In contrast, economic relationships, such as transactions in the marketplace, are supposed to entail universalistic orientations, and economic positions are supposed to be filled according to achievement criteria. Persons who occupy the same or functionally equivalent statuses are to be treated similarly, and access to these statuses is supposed to be gained by demonstrating the capacity to successfully perform their duties and responsibilities. There is thus an inevitable tension between the kinds of normative orientations required for the effective functioning of the family and those required for the efficient operation of a market economy.

Any given society will therefore be characterized by a distinctive arrangement of social institutions that reflects a balancing of the sometimes competing claims and requisites of the different institutions, yielding a distinctive institutional balance of power. Further, the nature of the resulting configuration of institutions is itself intimately related to the larger culture. Indeed,

our basic premise about social organization is that culture and the institutional balance of power are mutually reinforcing. On the one hand, culture influences the character of institutions and their positions relative to one another. Culture is in a sense "given life" in the institutional structure of society. On the other hand, the patterns of social relationships constituting institutions, which Parsons (1964: 239) terms the "backbone" of the social system, reproduce and sustain cultural commitments. This is, ultimately, where culture "comes from."

In the macrocriminological analysis of a concrete social system, then, the task is to describe the interpenetration of cultural and institutional patterns, to trace the resulting interconnections among institutions that constitute the institutional balance of power, and finally, to show how the institutional balance of power influences levels of crime. In the following sections, we apply this kind of analysis to the relationships among culture, institutional functioning, and crime in the United States.

The American Dream and the Institutional Balance of Power

. . . The core elements of the American Dream—a strong achievement orientation, a commitment to competitive individualism, universalism, and most important, the glorification of material success—have their institutional underpinnings in the economy. The most important feature of the economy of the United States is its capitalist nature. The defining characteristics of any capitalist economy are private ownership and control of property, and free market mechanisms for the production and distribution of goods and services.

These structural arrangements are conducive to, and presuppose, certain cultural orientations. For the economy to operate efficiently, the private owners of property must be profit-oriented and eager to invest, and workers must be willing to exchange their labor for wages. The motivational mechanism underlying these conditions is the promise of financial returns. The internal logic of a capitalist economy thus presumes that an attraction to monetary rewards as a result of achievement in the marketplace is widely diffused throughout the population (cf. Passas 1990: 159).

A capitalist economy is also highly competitive for all those involved, property owners and workers alike. Firms that are unable to adapt to shifting consumer demands or to fluctuations in the business cycle are likely to fail. Workers who are unable to keep up with changing skill requirements or who are unproductive in comparison with others are likely to be fired. This intense competition discourages economic actors from being wedded to conventional ways of doing things and instead encourages them to substitute new techniques for traditional ones if they offer advantages in meeting economic goals. In short, a capitalist economy naturally cultivates a competitive, innovative spirit.

These structural and cultural conditions are common to all capitalist societies. What is distinctive about the United States, however, is the *exaggerated* emphasis on monetary success and the *unrestrained* receptivity to innovation. The goal of monetary success overwhelms other goals and becomes the principal measuring rod for achievements. The resulting proclivity and pressures to innovate resist any regulation that is not justified by purely technical considerations. The obvious question that arises is why cultural orientations that express the inherent logic of capitalism have evolved to a particularly extreme degree in American society. The answer, we submit, lies in the inability of other social institutions to tame economic imperatives. In short, the institutional balance of power is tilted toward the economy. . . .

Capitalism developed in the United States without the institutional restraints found in other societies. As a consequence, the economy assumed an unusual dominance in the institutional structure of society from the very beginning of the nation's history. This economic dominance, we

argue, has continued to the present and is manifested in three somewhat different ways: (1) in the *devaluation* of noneconomic institutional functions and roles; (2) in the *accommodation* to economic requirements by other institutions; and (3) in the *penetration* of economic norms into other institutional domains.

Consider the relative devaluation of the distinctive functions of education and of the social roles that fulfill these functions. Education is regarded largely as a means to occupational attainment, which in turn is valued primarily insofar as it promises economic rewards. The acquisition of knowledge and learning for its own sake is not highly valued. Effective performance of the roles involved with education, accordingly, do not confer particularly high status. The "good student" is not looked up to by his or her peers; the "master teacher" receives meager financial rewards and public esteem in comparison with those to be gained by success in business.

Similar processes are observed in the context of the family, although the tendency toward devaluation is perhaps not as pronounced as in other institutional arenas. There is indeed a paradox here because "family values" are typically extolled in public rhetoric. Nevertheless, the lack of appreciation for tasks such as parenting, nurturing, and providing emotional support to others is manifested in actual social relationships. It is the home owner rather than the homemaker who is widely admired and envied—and whose image is reflected in the American Dream. Indeed, perhaps the most telling evidence of the relative devaluation of family functions is the inferior status in our society of those persons most extensively involved in these activities: women.

The relative devaluation of the family in comparison with the economy is not an inevitable consequence of the emergence of a modern, industrial society, whether capitalist or socialist. Adler (1983: 131) points to nations such as Bulgaria, the (then) German Democratic Republic, Japan, Saudi Arabia, and Switzerland to illustrate the possibilities for maintaining a strong commitment to the family despite the profound social changes that accompany the transformation from agriculturally based economies to industrial economies. Each of these countries has made extensive, and sometimes costly, efforts to preserve the vitality of the family. Furthermore, these are precisely the kinds of societies that exhibit low crime rates and are not, in Adler's words, "obsessed with crime."

The distinctive function of the polity, providing for the collective good, also tends to be devalued in comparison with economic functions. The general public has little regard for politics as an intrinsically valuable activity and confers little social honor on the role of the politician. Perhaps as a result, average citizens are not expected to be actively engaged in public service, which is left to the "career" politician. The contrast with economic activity is illuminating. The citizen who refuses to vote may experience mild social disapproval; the "able-bodied" adult who refuses to work is socially degraded. Economic participation is obligatory for most adults. In contrast, even the minimal form of political participation entailed in voting (which has more in common with shopping than with work) is considered discretionary, and useful primarily to the extent that it leads to tangible economic rewards (e.g., lower taxes).

Moreover, the very purpose of government tends to be conceptualized in terms of its capacity to facilitate the individual pursuit of economic prosperity. A good illustration is the advice given to the Democratic ticket in the 1992 presidential campaign by the conservative columnist, George Will. Will chastised liberal Democrats for allegedly becoming preoccupied with issues of rights based on ethnicity and sexuality and advised the Democratic presidential candidates to remember the following point that two popular presidents—Franklin Roosevelt and Ronald Reagan—understood very well:

> Americans are happiest when pursuing happiness, happiness understood as material advancement, pursued with government's help but not as a government entitlement. (Will 1992: E5)

Will's advice to liberal Democrats is revealing, not only of the core content of the American Dream and its effect on popular views of government, but of a particular kind of collective "right" to which Americans *are* entitled: the right to consume (cf. Edsall 1992: 7). Both of the major political parties celebrate the right to acquire material possessions; they differ mainly with respect to the proper degree of governmental involvement in expanding access to the means of consumption. No matter which party is in power, the function of government, at least in the domestic sphere, remains subsidiary to individual economic considerations.

Interestingly, one distinctive function of the polity does not appear to be generally devalued, namely, crime control. There is widespread agreement among the American public that government should undertake vigorous efforts to deal with the crime problem. If anything, Americans want government to do more to control crime. Yet, this apparent exception is quite compatible with the claim of economic dominance. Americans' "obsession" with crime is rooted in fears that crime threatens, according to political analyst Thomas Edsall (1992: 9) "their security, their values, their rights, and their livelihoods and the competitive prospects of their children." In other words, because crime control bears directly on the pursuit of the American Dream, this particular function of the polity receives high priority.

A second way in which the dominance of the economy is manifested is in the *accommodations* that emerge in those situations in which institutional claims are in competition. Economic conditions and requirements typically exert a much stronger influence on the operation of other institutions than vice versa. For example, family routines are dominated by the schedules, rewards, and penalties of the labor market. Consider the resistance of employers (and their representatives in government) to proposals for maternity leaves, flexible hours, or on-the-job child care. The contrast between the United

States and another capitalist society with very low crime rates—Japan—is striking in this regard. In Japan, business enterprises are accommodated to the needs of the family, becoming in some respects a "surrogate family," with services ranging from child rearing to burial (Adler 1983: 132).

The most important way that family life is influenced by the economy, however, is through the necessity for paid employment to support a family. Joblessness makes it difficult for families to remain intact and to form in the first place. In the urban underclass, where rates of joblessness are chronically high, so too are rates of separation, divorce, single-parent households, and births to unmarried women (Wilson 1987).

Educational institutions are also more likely to accommodate to the demands of the economy than is the economy to respond to the requirements of education. The timing of schooling reflects occupational demands rather than intrinsic features of the learning process or personal interest in the pursuit of knowledge. People go to school largely to prepare for "good" jobs, and once in the labor market, there is little opportunity to pursue further education for its own sake. When workers do return to school, it is almost always to upgrade skills or credentials to keep pace with job demands, to seek higher paying jobs, or to "retool" during spells of unemployment. At the organizational level, schools are dependent on the economy for financial resources, and thus it becomes important for school officials to convince business leaders that education is suitably responsive to business needs.

The polity likewise is dependent on the economy for financial support. Governments must accordingly take care to cultivate and maintain an environment hospitable to investment. If they do not, they run the risk of being literally "downgraded" by financial markets, as happened to Detroit in 1992 when Moody's Investors Service dropped the city's credit rating to non-investment grade. Cities have little choice but to accommodate to market demands in such situations. "A city proposes, Moody's disposes. There is no appeals court or court of last ratings resort" (*New York Times*, 1992: C1). The pursuit of the collective good is thus circumscribed by economic imperatives.

A final way in which the dominance of the economy in the institutional balance of power is manifested is in the *penetration* of economic norms into other institutional areas. Schools rely on grading as a system of extrinsic rewards, like wages, to insure compliance with goals. Learning takes place within the context of individualized competition for these external rewards, and teaching inevitably tends to become oriented toward testing. Economic terminology permeates the very language of education, as in the recent emphasis in higher education on "accountability" conceptualized in terms of the "value-added" to students in the educational production process.

Within the polity, a "bottom-line" mentality develops. Effective politicians are those who deliver the goods. Moreover, the notion that the government would work better if it were run more like a business continues to be an article of faith among large segments of the American public.

The family has probably been most resistant to the intrusion of economic norms. Yet even here, pressures toward penetration are apparent. Contributions to family life tend to be measured against the all-important "breadwinner" role, which has been extended to include women who work in the paid labor force. No corresponding movement of men into the role of "homemaker" has occurred, and a declining number of women desire or can afford to occupy this role on a full-time basis. Here again, shifts in popular terminology are instructive. Husbands and wives are "partners" who "manage" the household "division of labor." We can detect no comparable shifts in kin-based terminology, or primary group norms, from the family to the workplace.

In sum, the social organization of the United States is characterized by a striking dominance of the economy in the institutional balance of power. As a result of this economic dominance, the inherent tendencies of a capitalist economy to orient the members of society toward an unrestrained pursuit of economic achievements are developed to an extreme degree. These tendencies are expressed at the cultural level in the preeminence of monetary success as the overriding goal—the American Dream—and in the relative deemphasis placed on the importance of using normative means to reach this goal—anomie. The anomic nature of the American Dream and the institutional structure of American society are thus mutually supportive and reinforcing. The key remaining question is the impact of this type of social organization on crime.

Anomie, Weak Social Controls, and Crime

The American Dream contributes to high levels of crime in two important ways, one direct and the other indirect. It has a direct effect on crime through the creation of an anomic normative order, that is, an environment in which social norms are unable to exert a strong regulatory force on the members of society. It has an indirect effect on crime by contributing to an institutional balance of power that inhibits the development of strong mechanisms of external social control. The criminogenic tendencies of the American Dream are thus due in part to the distinctive content of the cultural values and beliefs that comprise it and in part to the institutional consequences of these values and beliefs.

One criminogenic aspect of the specific content of the American Dream is the expression of the primary success goal in monetary terms. Because monetary success is inherently open-ended and elusive, the adequacy of the legitimate means for achieving this particular cultural goal is necessarily suspect. No matter how much money someone is able to make by staying within legal boundaries, illegal means will always offer further advantages in pursuit of the ultimate goal. There is thus a perpetual attractiveness associated with

illegal activity that is an inevitable corollary of the goal of monetary success.

This culturally induced pressure to "innovate" by using illegitimate means is exacerbated by the dominance of the economy in the institutional balance of power. There are, of course, important noneconomic tasks carried out in other institutional arenas, tasks associated with goals that might in fact be readily attainable within the confines of the legal order. However, as we have suggested, roles effectively performed in the capacity of being a parent or spouse, a student or scholar, an engaged citizen or public servant are simply not the primary bases upon which success and failure are defined in American society. The dominance of the economy continuously erodes the structural supports for functional alternatives to the goal of economic success.

Nor does the ethos of the American Dream contain within it strong counterbalancing injunctions against substituting more effective illegitimate means for less effective legitimate means. To the contrary, the distinctive cultural "value" accompanying the monetary success goal in the American Dream is the *devaluation* of all but the most technically efficient means.

The American Dream does not completely subsume culture. There are other elements of culture that define socially acceptable modes of behavior and that affirm the legitimacy of social norms, including legal norms. In principle, these other cultural elements could counterbalance the anomic pressures that emanate from the American Dream. However, the very same institutional dynamics that contribute to the pressures to innovate in the pursuit of economic goals also make it less likely that the anomic pressures inherent in the American Dream will in fact be counterbalanced by other social forces.

As noneconomic institutions are relatively devalued, are forced to accommodate to economic needs, and are penetrated by economic standards, they are less able to fulfill their distinctive functions effectively. These functions include socialization into acceptance of the social norms. Weak families and poor schools are handicapped in their efforts to promote allegiance to social rules, including legal prohibitions. As a result, the pressures to disregard normative constraints in the pursuit of the goal of monetary success also tend to undermine social norms more generally. In the absence of the cultivation of strong commitments to social norms, the selection of the means for realizing goals *of any type* is guided mainly by instrumental considerations.

In addition, the relative impotence of noneconomic institutions is manifested in a reduced capacity to exert external social control. The government is constrained in its capacity to provide public goods that would make crime less attractive and in its efforts to mobilize collective resources—including moral resources—to effectively deter criminal choices. Single-parent families or those in which both parents have fulltime jobs, all else equal, are less able to provide extensive supervision over children. All families must rely to some extent on other institutions, usually the schools, for assistance in social control. Yet poorly funded or crowded schools also find it difficult to exert effective supervision, especially when students see little or no connection between what is taught in the classroom and what is valued outside of it.

Finally, weak institutions invite challenge. Under conditions of extreme competitive individualism, people actively resist institutional control. They not only fall from the insecure grasp of powerless institutions, sometimes they deliberately, even proudly, push themselves away. The problem of "external" social control, then, is inseparable from the problem of the "internal" regulatory force of social norms, or anomie. Anomic societies will inevitably find it difficult and costly to exert social control over the behavior of people who feel free to use whatever means that prove most effective in reaching personal goals.

Hence the very sociocultural dynamics that make American institutions weak also enable and entitle Americans to defy institutional controls. If Americans are exceptionally resistant to social control—and therefore exceptionally vulnerable to criminal temptations—it is because they live in a society that enshrines the unfettered pursuit of individual material success above all other values. In the United States, anomie is a virtue.

Conclusion

This reformulation of Merton's classic theory of social structure and anomie is intended to challenge criminologists and policymakers alike to think about crime in America as a macro-level product of widely admired cultural and social structures with deep historical roots. Criminological theories that neglect the ironic interdependence between crime and the normal functioning of the American social system will be unable to explain the preoccupation with crime that so dramatically separates the United States from other developed societies. Significant reductions in crime will not result from reforms limited to the criminal justice system, which is itself shaped in important ways by the same cultural and social forces—the same desperate emphasis on ends over means—that produce high rates of crime. Nor will social reforms, whatever their other merits, that widen access to legitimate opportunities for persons "locked out" of the American Dream bring relief from the crimes of those who are "locked in" the American Dream, exposed to its limitless imperatives in the absence of moderating social forces. Reducing these crimes will require fundamental social transformations that few Americans desire, and a rethinking of a dream that is the envy of the world.

Discussion Questions

1. What are the core features of the American Dream? Do you agree with Rosenfeld and Messner's characterization of the American Dream?

2. Describe *how* the dominance of the economy interferes with the effective functioning of

other institutions (family, school, polity) in the United States.

3. What policy recommendations would Rosenfeld and Messner make for controlling crime? Would they recommend increasing the opportunities for monetary success, as do many strain theorists?

4. Rosenfeld and Messner argue that the American Dream and the dominance of the economy promote crime by reducing social control (see Part V). Do you think that the American Dream and the dominance of the economy also promote the types of strain described by Merton and Agnew?

16. Pressured Into Crime: General Strain Theory

Robert Agnew

According to Merton (1938) and most subsequent strain theories, crime results from the inability to achieve monetary success or other positively valued goals through legitimate channels. This goal blockage creates strain or frustration in the individual, which increases the likelihood of a criminal response. Whether individuals respond to strain with crime is said to depend on several factors, such as the level of social control and whether the individual associates with criminal others. Evidence for this version of strain theory is mixed and, partly as a consequence, strain theory no longer occupies the dominant position that it once did (see Agnew, 2000; Akers and Sellers, 2008; Burton and Cullen, 1992).

Agnew presents a new, much broader version of strain theory in the following selection—which is adapted from his recent book Pressured Into Crime: An Overview of General Strain Theory *(2006a). In the first part of the selection, Agnew defines "strains," and notes that the failure to achieve positively valued goals is only one of several types of strain. Strains also involve the loss of valued possessions and negative or aversive treatment by others. He goes on to distinguish between objective and subjective strains, as well as experienced, vicarious, and anticipated strains. He then describes the characteristics of those strains most likely to result in crime—a critical task since the research suggests that some strains lead to crime*

while others do not. The second part of the selection examines the reasons why certain strains increase the likelihood of crime. As Agnew states, strains lead to crime primarily because they increase negative emotions, such as anger and frustration, which create pressure for corrective action. But strains contribute to crime for other reasons as well. The final section describes why some people are more likely than others to cope with strains through crime.

The research on Agnew's strain theory is generally promising (for summaries, see Agnew, 2001, 2006a, b, 2009a, b). Studies suggest that most of the strains he lists increase the likelihood of crime, with certain of these strains being among the most important causes of crime. Further, these strains increase crime partly through their effect on negative emotions like anger. The research on those factors said to influence the likelihood that people will respond to strains with crime, however, has produced mixed results.

References

Agnew, Robert. 2000. "Sources of Criminality: Strain and Subcultural Theories." In Joseph F. Sheley (ed.), *Criminology: A Contemporary Handbook*, 3rd edition, pp. 349–371. Belmont, CA: Wadsworth.

——. 2001. "Building on the Foundation of General Strain Theory: Specifying the Types of Strain Most

Adapted with permission from *Pressured Into Crime: An Overview of General Strain*, copyright © 2006 by Roxbury Publishing Company.

Likely to Lead to Crime and Delinquency." *Journal of Research in Crime and Delinquency* 38: 319–361.

——. 2006a. *Pressured Into Crime: An Overview of General Strain Theory.* Los Angeles: Roxbury Publishing.

——. 2006b. "General Strain Theory: Current Status and Directions for Further Research." In Francis T. Cullen, John Paul Wright, and Kristie R. Blevins (eds.), *Taking Stock: The Status of Criminological Theory—Advances in Criminological Theory*, Volume 15, pp. 101–123. New Brunswick, NJ: Transaction.

——. 2009a. *Juvenile Delinquency: Causes and Control*, 3rd edition. New York: Oxford University Press.

——. 2009b. "General Strain Theory." In Marvin D. Krohn, Alan J. Lizotte, and G. P. Hall (eds.), *Handbook on Crime and Delinquency*, pp. 169–185. New York: Springer.

Akers, Ronald L. and Christine S. Sellers. 2008. *Criminological Theories: Introduction and Evaluation.* New York: Oxford University Press.

Burton, Velmer S., Jr. and Francis T. Cullen. 1992. "The Empirical Status of Strain Theory." *Journal of Crime and Justice* 15: 1–30.

Merton, Robert K. 1938. "Social Structure and Anomie." *American Sociological Review* 3: 672–673.

———•———

According to general Strain theory (GST), people engage in crime because they experience strains or stressors. For example, they are in desperate need of money or they believe they are being mistreated by their family members. They become upset, experiencing a range of negative emotions, including anger, frustration, and depression. And they may cope with their strains and negative emotions through crime. Crime is a way to reduce or escape from strains. For example, individuals engage in theft to obtain the money they desperately need or they run away from home to escape their abusive parents. Crime is a way for individuals to seek revenge against those who have wronged them. For example, individuals assault those who have mistreated them. And

crime is a way to alleviate the negative emotions that result from strains. For example, individuals use illegal drugs to make themselves feel better.

Not all individuals, however, respond to strains with crime. If someone steps on your foot, for example, your are probably unlikely to respond by punching the person. Some people are more likely than others to cope with strains through crime. Criminal coping is more likely when people lack the ability to cope in a legal manner. For example, crime is more likely when people do not have the verbal skills to negotiate with those who mistreat them or do not have others they can turn to for help. Criminal coping is more likely when the costs of crime are low. For example, crime is more likely when people are in environments where the likelihood of being sanctioned for crime is low. And criminal coping is more likely when people are disposed to crime. For example, assault is more likely when people believe that violence is an appropriate response to being treated in a disrespectful manner.

I briefly elaborate on these arguments below. First, I define strains and describe the types of strains most likely to lead to crime. Next, I discuss why strains increase the likelihood of crime. Finally, I examine why some people are more likely than others to respond to strains with crime.

What Are Strains?

Strains refer to events or conditions that are disliked by the individual. There are three major types of strains. Individuals may lose something they value (lose something good). Perhaps their money or property is stolen, a close friend or family member dies, or a romantic partner breaks up with them. Individuals may be treated in an aversive or negative manner by others (receive something bad). Perhaps they are sexually or physically abused by a family member, their peers insult or ridicule them, or their employer treats them in a disrespectful manner. And individuals may be unable to achieve their goals (fail to get something they want). Perhaps they have less money, status, or autonomy than they want.

Objective and subjective strains. Some events and conditions are disliked by most people or at least by most people in a given group. For example, most people dislike being physically assaulted or deprived of adequate food and shelter. And it has been argued that most males dislike having their masculine status called into question (Messerschmidt 1993). I refer to these events and conditions as objective strains, because they are generally disliked. It is possible to determine the *objective strains* for a group by interviewing a carefully selected sample of group members or people familiar with the group being examined. We can ask these people how much they (or the group members) would dislike a range of events and conditions (see Turner and Wheaton 1995).

It is important to keep in mind, however, that people sometimes differ in their subjective evaluation of the same events and conditions—even those events and conditions classified as objective strains. So a given objective strain, like a death in the family, may be strongly disliked by one person but only mildly disliked by another. This is because the subjective evaluation of objective strains is influenced by a range of factors, including peoples' personality traits, goals and values, and prior experiences. Wheaton (1990), for example, found that there was some variation in how people evaluated their divorce. Among other things, the quality of their prior marriage strongly influenced their evaluation, with people in bad marriages evaluating their divorce in positive terms. I therefore make a distinction between objective and *subjective strains*. While an objective strain refers to an event or condition that is disliked by most people or most people in a given group, a subjective strain refers to an event or condition that is disliked by the particular person or persons being examined (see Agnew 2001). As just suggested, there is only partial overlap between objective and subjective strains.

Most of the research on strain theory focuses on objective strains. Researchers ask respondents whether they have experienced events and conditions that are assumed to be disliked. For example, they ask respondents whether they have received failing grades at school. No attempt is made to measure the respondents' subjective evaluation of these events and conditions (although see Agnew and White 1992; Sharp et al. 2001). This may cause researchers to underestimate the effect of strains on crime, because objective strains are not always disliked by the individuals being examined. Some people, for example, may not be particularly bothered by the fact that they have received failing grades. It is therefore desirable for criminologists to measure both the individual's exposure to objective strains and the individual's *subjective evaluation* of these strains (e.g., ask individuals whether they have received failing grades *and*, if so, how much they dislike such grades).

Experienced, vicarious, and anticipated strains. GST focuses on the individual's personal experiences with strains; that is, did the individual personally experience disliked events or conditions. For example, was the individual physically assaulted. Personal experiences with strains should bear the strongest relationship to crime. However, it is sometimes important to consider the individual's vicarious and anticipated experiences with strains as well (see Agnew 2002; Eitle and Turner 2003).

Vicarious strains refer to the strains experienced by others around the individual, especially close others like family members and friends. For example, were any of the individual's family members or friends physically assaulted. Vicarious strains can also upset the individual and lead to criminal coping. Agnew (2002), for example, found that individuals were more likely to engage in crime if they reported that their family members and friends had been the victims of serious assaults (also see Eitle and Turner 2002; Maxwell 2001; Mullins et al. 2004). This held true even after Agnew took account of other factors, like the individual's own victimization experiences and prior criminal history. Vicarious strains may have increased the likelihood of crime for several reasons. For example, perhaps individuals were seeking revenge against those who had victimized their family and friends. Or perhaps individuals were seeking to prevent the perpetrators from causing further harm. Vicarious strains are most likely to cause crime when they are serious, involve someone that the individual cares about and has assumed responsibility for protecting, involve unjust treatment, and pose a threat to others (see Agnew 2002 for a fuller discussion).

It is also sometimes important to consider anticipated experiences with strains. *Anticipated strains* refer to the individual's expectation that his or her current strains will continue into the future or that new strains will be experienced. For example, individuals may anticipate that they will be the victims of physical assault. Like vicarious strains, anticipated strains may upset individuals and lead to criminal coping. Individuals may engage in crime to prevent anticipated strains from occurring, to seek revenge against those who might inflict such strains, or to alleviate negative emotions. To illustrate, many adolescents, particularly in high-crime communities, anticipate that they will be the victims of violence. They often (illegally) carry weapons as a result and they may even engage in violence against others in an effort to reduce the likelihood that they will be victimized. In this area, Anderson (1999) argues that the young men in very poor, high-crime communities often try to reduce the likelihood they will be victimized by adopting a tough demeanor and responding to even minor shows of disrespect with violence. Anticipated strains are most likely to result in crime when individuals believe that they have a high probability of occurring in the near future, they will be serious in nature, and they will involve unjust treatment by others (see Agnew 2002).

What Are the Characteristics of Those Types of Strains Most Likely to Cause Crime?

Not all strains result in crime. In fact, the experience of some strains may reduce the likelihood of crime. This is the case, for example, with parental discipline that is consistent and fair. Juveniles may not like such discipline, but much data suggest that it reduces the likelihood of crime (Agnew 2005). Strains are most likely to cause crime when they: 1) are seen as high in magnitude, 2) are seen as unjust, 3) are associated with low social control, and 4) create some pressure or incentive to engage in criminal coping. Strains with these characteristics are more likely to elicit strong negative emotions, reduce the ability to engage in legal coping, reduce the perceived costs of crime, and create a disposition for crime.

The strain is seen as high in magnitude. Imagine that you are chatting with a group of acquaintances and someone reacts to a remark you make by stating "you don't know what you're talking about." Now imagine the same situation, but this time someone reacts to your remark by stating "you're an asshole" and then shoving you. Both reactions are likely to upset you, but I think most people would agree that the second reaction is more likely to lead to crime. Part of the reason for this is that the second reaction is more severe than the first. Generally speaking, strains that are seen as more severe or higher in magnitude are more likely to result in crime. The severity of the strain refers to the extent to which the strain is negatively evaluated; that is, the extent to which it is disliked and viewed as having a negative impact on one's life. Among other things, severe strains are more likely to elicit strong negative emotions, which create pressure for corrective action, and they are more difficult to cope with in a legal manner (e.g., it is more difficult to legally cope with a large rather than a small need for money).

A strain is more likely to be seen as severe if: a) it is high in degree or size (e.g., a large versus a small financial loss); b) it is frequent, recent, of long duration, and expected to continue in the future; and c) it threatens the *core* goals, needs, values, activities, and/or identities of the individual (e.g., does the strain threaten a core identity, perhaps one's masculine identity, or a secondary identity, perhaps one's identity as a good chess player).

The strain is seen as unjust. Imagine you are walking down the street. Someone accidentally trips on a crack in the sidewalk, bumps into you, and knocks you to the ground. Now imagine that you are walking down the street and someone deliberately shoves you aside, knocking you to the ground. Both incidents qualify as strains; being knocked to the ground is disliked by most people. But I think most people would agree that the second incident is more likely to result in crime. Even though both incidents involve the same amount of physical harm, the behavior in the second incident is more likely to be seen as unjust. Unjust strains are more likely to lead to crime for several reasons; most notably the fact that they make individuals more angry.

A strain is more likely to be seen as unjust when it involves the voluntary and intentional violation of a relevant justice norm or rule. Most strains involve a perpetrator who does something to a victim. We are more likely to view the perpetrator's behavior as unjust if the perpetrator freely chose to treat the victim in a way that he or she knew would probably be disliked (the "voluntary and intentional" part). We are less likely to view the behavior as unjust if it is the result of such things as reasonable accident or chance. That is why we are less upset by an accidental bump than by a deliberate shove, even though both may cause the same physical harm. We are also less likely to view strains as unjust if they are the result of our own behavior (e.g., we injure ourselves while behaving in a reckless manner) or natural forces (e.g., our home suffers damage during a storm).

Unjust behavior, however, involves more than a voluntary and intentional effort to harm someone. For example, parents voluntarily and intentionally punish their children on a regular basis, but we usually do not view their behavior as unjust. In order for voluntary and intentional behaviors to be seen as unjust, they must also violate a relevant justice rule. In particular, researchers have discovered that most people employ certain rules to determine whether a particualr behavior is just or unjust (see Agnew 2001, for a fuller discussion).

For example, the voluntary and intentional infliction of strain is more likely to be seen as unjust when victims believe that the strain they have experienced is undeserved and not in the service of some greater good (e.g., God or country).

The strain is associated with low social control. Consider the following two strains. First, someone is unemployed for a long period of time. Second, a well-paid lawyer has to work long hours on a regular basis, often performing difficult and complex tasks. I think most people would agree that the first strain is more likely to result in crime. This example highlights a third factor affecting the likelihood that strains will lead to crime. Strains are more likely to lead to crime when they are associated with low social control.

There are several types of social control, with each referring to a factor or set of factors that restrains the individual from crime. There is *direct control*, which refers to the extent to which others set rules that prohibit crime, monitor the individual's behavior, and consistently sanction the individual for rule violations. There is the individual's *emotional bond or attachment to conventional others*, such as family members and teachers. There is the *individual's investment in conventional institutions*, such as school and work. It is easier to engage in crime when emotional bonds and investments are weak, since there is less to lose through crime. And there is the individual's *beliefs regarding crime*. It is easier to engage in crime when one does not believe that it is wrong to do so.

Certain strains are associated with low levels of social control. For example, this is the case with parental rejection. Children who are rejected by their parents probably have little emotional bond to them and are probably subject to little direct control by them. To give another example, those strains involving unemployment and work in the secondary labor market ("bad jobs") are associated with a low investment in conventional institutions. Strains associated with low social control are more likely to result in crime because they reduce the costs of crime, among other things.

The strain creates some pressure or incentive for criminal coping. A final factor affecting the likelihood that a strain will lead to crime is the extent to which the strain creates some incentive or pressure to engage in criminal coping. Certain strains are more easily resolved through crime and/or less easily resolved through legal channels than other strains (see Brezina 2000). As a consequence, individuals have more incentive to cope with these strains through crime. For example, that type of strain involving a desperate need for money is more easily resolved through crime than is that type involving the inability to achieve educational success. It is much easier to get money through crime than it is to get educational success. Also, certain strains are associated with exposure to others who model crime, reinforce crime, teach beliefs favorable to crime, or otherwise try to pressure or entice the individual into crime. For example, individuals who experience child abuse are exposed to criminal models—who may foster the belief that crime is an appropriate way to deal with one's problems. To give another example, many interpersonal disputes occur before an audience, with the audience members often urging or pressuring the disputants to engage in violence.

What specific strains are most likely to cause crime? Drawing on the above discussion, it is predicted that the following specific strains are most likely to cause crime:

- Parental rejection.
- Supervision/discipline that is erratic, excessive, and/or harsh.
- Child abuse and neglect.
- Negative secondary school experiences (e.g., low grades, negative relations with teachers, the experience of school as boring and a waste of time).
- Abusive peer relations (e.g., insults, threats, physical assaults).
- Work in the secondary labor market (i.e., "bad jobs" that pay little, have few benefits, little opportunity for advancement, and unpleasant working conditions).
- Chronic unemployment.

- Marital problems.
- The failure to achieve selected goals, including thrills/excitement, high levels of autonomy, masculine status, and the desire for much money in a short period of time.
- Criminal victimization.
- Residence in economically deprived communities.
- Homelessness.
- Discrimination based on characteristics such as race/ethnicity and gender.

Data support these predictions, although the effect of certain of these strains—such as abusive peer relations and discrimination—has not been well examined (see Agnew 2006).

It should also be noted that crime is especially likely when individuals experience two or more strains close together in time. Experiencing several strains at once is especially likely to generate negative emotions and tax the individual's ability to cope in a legal manner. Unfortunately, it is not uncommon for strains to occur together. One strain, such as a job loss, frequently leads to other strains—such as family conflict (see De Coster and Kort-Butler 2004; Pearlin 1989; Wethington 2000). As a consequence, researchers who test GST should employ cumulative measures, which count the number of different strains conducive to crime that are experienced.

Why Do Strains Increase the Likelihood of Crime?

Strains lead individuals to commit crimes for several reasons, the most important of which involves the effect of strains on negative emotions.

Strains Lead to Negative Emotions

Strains increase the likelihood that individuals will experience a range of negative emotions, including anger, frustration, jealousy, depression, and fear. These negative emotions increase the likelihood of crime for several reasons. Most notably, they create pressure for corrective action. Individuals feel bad and want to do something about it. As indicated above, crime is one possible response. Crime may be used to reduce or escape from strains, obtain revenge, and alleviate negative emotions (through illegal drug use). Negative emotions may also reduce the ability to cope in a legal manner, reduce the perceived costs of crime, and create a disposition for crime. For example, angry individuals have more trouble reasoning with others, are less aware of and concerned about the costs of crime, and have a desire for revenge. Most research on GST has focused on the emotion of anger, and studies suggest that anger partly explains the effect of strains on crime—particularly violent crime (Agnew 2006). Other emotions may be more relevant to other types of crime. For example, frustration may be most relevant to the explanation of property crime, while depression may help explain drug use.

Strains Lead to the Personality Traits of Negative Emotionality and Low Constraint

Individuals who possess the trait of negative emotionality are easily upset, experience intense emotions when upset, and have an aggressive interactional style. Those possessing the trait of low constrainttend to act without thinking, engage in risky behaviors, reject social norms, and show little concern for others. Not surprisingly, these traits increase the likelihood of crime.

Some studies suggest that strains may also increase crime through their effect on these traits (Agnew 2006; Agnew et al. 2002). In particular, chronic or repeated strains may reduce the ability of individuals to cope in a legal manner. As a consequence, new strains are more likely to be experienced as overwhelming and elicit strong emotional reactions. You may have experienced this phenomena yourself. When things are going well in your life, it is often easy to cope with the occasional strain. But when things are going poorly (you are experiencing a lot of strains), even a minor strain may overwhelm and upset you. Also, certain strains, like harsh and erratic parental discipline, may contribute to low constraint. Parents who employ harsh, erratic disciplinary techniques fail to teach their children to exercise self restraint. In

fact, they model low constraint. Children only learn to restrain themselves when they are consistently sanctioned for their misbehavior in an appropriate manner. Limited data provide support for these arguments (Agnew 2006; Agnew et al. 2002; Anderson 1999; Bernard 1990; Colvin 2000).

Strains May Reduce Levels of Social Control

Strains may also lead to reductions in the major types of social control. This argument has been made by most of the leading strain theorists. Many strains involve negative treatment by conventional others, like parents, spouses, teachers, and employers. Further, these strains are often chronic or occur on a repeated basis. Such strains include child abuse, harsh discipline by parents, demeaning treatment by teachers, the receipt of low grades, conflict with spouses, unemployment, and work in "bad" jobs. These strains may reduce one's emotional bond to conventional others. Child abuse, for example, is likely to reduce the child's bond to parents. These strains may also reduce one's investment in conventional activities. Chronic unemployment, for example, represents a major reduction in one's investment in conventional activities. Further, these strains may reduce levels of direct control by causing individuals to retreat from conventional others, like parents and teachers. And these effects may reduce the individual's belief that crime is wrong, since the individual's ties to those who teach this belief are weakened. Also, individuals are less likely to accept societal norms condemning crime when they fail to reap the benefits that society has to offer, like a good education, a good job, and a loving family. Individuals who are very poor, for example, are less likely to condemn criminal methods for obtaining money. Data provide some support for these arguments (e.g., Agnew 2006; Elliott et al. 1985; Paternoster and Mazerolle 1994).

Strains May Foster the Social Learning of Crime

Finally, strains may foster the social learning of crime. Most notably, strains increase the likelihood that individuals will join or form criminal groups, like delinquent peer groups and gangs. The members of such groups, in turn, model crime, reinforce crime, and teach beliefs favorable to crime. As just indicated, strains often reduce levels of social control, which increases the likelihood that individuals will come in contact with criminal groups and frees individuals to associate with such groups. Strains also increase the appeal of criminal groups. In particular, the victims of strains often view criminal groups as a solution to their strains. For example, individuals who cannot achieve status through conventional channels, like educational and occupational success, often join criminal gangs because the gang makes them feel important, respected, and/or feared (see especially Cohen 1955). Further, strains directly increase the likelihood that individuals will come to view crime as a desirable, justifiable, or at least excusable form of behavior. For example, many strains involve unjust treatment by others. Such treatment may foster the belief that crime is justified since it is being used to "right" an injustice. Studies also provide some support for these arguments (Agnew 2006; Paternoster and Mazerolle 1994).

Why Are Some People More Likely Than Others to Cope with Strains Through Crime?

Not all people cope with strains through crime. Most people, in fact, cope in a legal manner. For example, they negotiate with the people who irritate or harass them, they file complaints against the people who wrong them, or they alleviate their negative emotions by exercising or listening to music. A number of factors influence how individuals cope with the strains and negative emotions they experience. Criminal coping is most likely when:

Individuals lack the ability to cope with strains in a legal manner. Some individuals are less able to cope with strains in a legal manner than others. Their ability to cope in a legal manner is partly a function of their individual traits, like their intelligence, social and problem-solving skills, and personality traits. It is partly a function of the resources they possess, including their financial resources. And it is partly a function of their level of conventional social support. Are there conventional others, such as parents and friends, that they can turn to for aid and comfort?

The costs of criminal coping are low. Many individuals avoid criminal coping because the costs of crime are high for them. There is a good chance that they will be sanctioned by others if they engage in crime. They also have a lot to lose if they engage in crime; they might get expelled from school, lose their job, or jeopardize their relationship with people they care about. Further, engaging in crime will make them feel guilty, because they believe that crime is wrong. But for other individuals, the costs of criminal coping are low. They are in environments where the likelihood of sanction for crime is small. Perhaps they are poorly supervised by their parents, their friends do not care if they engage in crime, and neighborhood residents seldom report crimes to the police. They do not have jobs to lose or close relationships with others that might be jeopardized by crime. And they do not believe that crime is wrong. Such individuals, then, are more likely to cope with strains through crime.

Individuals are disposed to crime. Some individuals are more disposed than others to respond to strains with crime. They may possess personality traits which increase their inclination to crime, such as the traits of negative emotionality and low constraint. Also, some individuals may believe that crime is an appropriate response to certain strains, like disrespectful treatment by others. Further, some individuals may associate with criminal others, who model and reinforce crime. This too increases their disposition to respond to strains with crime.

Studies provide mixed support for these arguments. Some studies find that certain of the above factors increase the likelihood that individuals will respond to strains with crime, while other studies do not. Agnew (2006) discusses some possible reasons for these mixed findings.

Conclusion

Why do individuals engage in crime according to GST? They experience strains, become upset as a result, and may cope with their strains and negative emotions through crime. Criminal coping is especially likely if they lack the ability to cope in a legal manner, their costs of crime are low, and they are disposed to crime. Crime may allow them to reduce or escape from their strains, obtain revenge, or alleviate their negative emotions (through illegal drug use).

While GST focuses on the explanation of individual differences in offending, it can also shed light on patterns of offending over the life course, group differences in crime, and community and societal differences in crime. Such patterns and differences can be partly explained in terms of differences in the exposure to strains conducive to crime and in the possession of those factors that influence the likelihood of criminal coping. For example, gender differences in crime are partly due to the fact that males are more often exposed to strains conducive to crime and are more likely to cope with strains through crime (Broidy and Agnew 1997).

GST also provides recommendations for reducing crime. Crime can be reduced by reducing individuals' exposure to strains conducive to crime and their likelihood of responding to strains with crime. Strategies for reducing the exposure to strains include a) eliminating strains conducive to crime, b) altering strains so as to make them less conducive to crime (e.g., reducing their magnitude or perceived injustice), c) removing individuals from strains conducive to crime, d) equipping individuals with the traits and skills to avoid strains conducive to crime; and e) altering the perceptions and goals of individuals to reduce subjective strains. Strategies for reducing the likelihood that individuals will respond to strains with crime include a) improving conventional coping skills and resources, b) increasing social support, c) reducing association with delinquent peers and beliefs favorable to crime.

GST presents a rather different explanation of crime than that offered by the other leading crime theories. GST is the only theory to focus explicitly on *negative relationships with others:* relationships in which others take the individual's valued possessions, treat the individual in an aversive manner, or prevent the individual from achieving his or her goals. Further, GST is the only theory to argue that individuals are *pressured into crime* by these negative relationships and the emotions that result from them. At the same time, GST is intimately related to the other leading theories of crime. As argued earlier, strains may contribute to personality traits conducive to crime, reduce social control, and foster the social learning of crime. Further, the factors associated with all of these theories interact with one another in their effect on cirme. In particular, the effect of strains on crime is influenced or conditioned by personality traits, level of social control, and those factors that foster the social learning of crime—like association with criminal peers.

Discussion Questions

1. Give examples of the types of questions you might ask to measure the three major types of strain listed by Agnew.
2. List three strains that are relatively likely to cause crime, and three strains with a low relative likelihood of causing crime. Justify your selection of strains.
3. *Why* do strained individuals sometimes turn to crime?
4. Drawing on Agnew, describe the type of person who would be *most likely* to respond to strain with crime.
5. What policy recommendation might Agnew make for controlling crime?
6. Describe the ways in which general strain theory is related to control and social learning theories, including the ways in which variables from these theories work together to cause crime.

PART VI

Varieties of Control Theory

Sociological explanations of crime have been dominated by three main traditions: differential association/learning theory, anomie/strain theory, and control theory. Other theories have been set forth, but usually they have either integrated concepts from, or have been developed explicitly to challenge, these three dominant traditions. The enduring appeal of these traditions is in part due to the elegant way in which original statements of the theories conveyed powerful theses as to the origins of criminal conduct. Indeed, each perspective was authored by a scholar of enormous accomplishment: anomie/strain theory by Robert K. Merton; differential association theory by Edwin Sutherland; and control theory by Travis Hirschi.

Hirschi was not the first control theorist. As noted previously, Shaw and McKay (Chapter 7) tied delinquency to the attenuation of control in inner-city areas. Other theorists focused on how types of control—usually differentiating between those inside individuals (e.g., conscience) and those outside individuals (e.g., parental reactions)—were related to wayward behavior. For example, Reiss (1951) delineated "personal and social controls," and Nye (1958) emphasized controls that were "internal," "direct," and "indirect." Sykes and Matza (Chapter 17 in this part) also are seen as control theorists, because they examined how people become free to commit crime only when beliefs can be evoked to "neutralize" the restraint normative standards usually exert over them. Furthermore, Walter Reckless (1961) advanced the "containment theory" perspective

that anticipated many of the ideas that Hirschi would later formalize.

Despite these predecessors, it was Hirschi's "social bond theory," published in *Causes of Delinquency* (1969), that emerged as the preeminent statement of control theory (Chapter 18 in this part). In this work, Hirschi divided criminological theory into three main perspectives, which he identified by the terms "control theory," "strain theory," and "cultural deviance theory"—a term he used for differential association/learning approaches (see also Kornhauser, 1978). He argued that these three perspectives were incompatible, and that they should be seen as rivals to be tested empirically against one another. Thus, in *Causes of Delinquency*, Hirschi not only set forth his social bond theory but also presented data showing the merits of his perspective and the comparative weaknesses of strain and cultural deviance perspectives.

Up until this time, most theoretical statements were just that—essays proposing a plausible explanation of crime. Hirschi, however, "upped the ante" by showing that theories could be tested and by claiming that empirical evidence should be the arbiter of which perspective deserved allegiance. In particular, Hirschi revealed the utility of using survey research to test theories. In this method, respondents—usually juveniles in a high school—would be given a questionnaire that contained *both* measures of theoretical concepts and a "self-report" scale of delinquency. In this way, it would be possible to see which theory, as operationalized by the measures on the questionnaire, could explain more or less involvement in delinquency. It is noteworthy that this approach is the chief way in which criminologists test micro-level theories of crime.

We will turn shortly to Hirschi's social bond theory. As a prelude, however, we will focus on perhaps his two most important theoretical predecessors: first, techniques of neutralization theory by Gresham M. Sykes and David Matza (1957 [Chapter 17 in this part]) and, second, containment theory by Walter C. Reckless (1961).

Techniques of Neutralization

Sykes and Matza's delinquency theory represents both the embrace of and departure from Sutherland's differential association perspective (see Chapter 10 in Part IV). Sutherland had proposed that individuals enter crime because they learn definitions favorable to violation of the law. He was largely silent, however, on the content of these definitions. Building on Sutherland, Sykes and Matza provide insight on what specific definitions or beliefs might encourage offending. They delineate a core set of beliefs—which they label "techniques of neutralization"—that they argue are learned and permit law-breaking to take place. Unlike Sutherland, however, they do not see most offenders as becoming so enmeshed in a criminal value system as to reject the norms of the larger conventional society. Thus, they criticize in particular subcultural theories, such as the one proposed by Cohen (1955 [Chapter 14]), that portray youngsters as learning a value system that celebrates crime and opposes prosocial normative standards. In these subcultures, conventional society is stood on its head. "Conformity" entails following antisocial values and breaking the law without guilt or remorse.

Most youths, observe Sykes and Matza, cannot escape the powerful socializing influences of conventional society. Subcultural members are the rare exception, not the rule. Parents, teachers, ministers, and criminal justice officials provide a unified message that crime is wrong and that youngsters should obey the law. Under normal circumstances, therefore, children come to internalize and believe in the morality of the dominant normative system. Thoughts of violating normative standards evoke feelings of guilt and shame. Individuals know and respect right from wrong. As a result, they are controlled by their conventional beliefs.

But if this is so, how is it possible—as Sykes and Matza put it—that people violate laws that they believe in? Sykes and Matza's contribution is in developing a *theory of how controls are neutralized*. They argue that there are sets of beliefs that, when invoked, in effect say that it is "okay" to commit a criminal act "in this circumstance." They group these crime-justifying beliefs into five categories, which they call "techniques of neutralization."

To give but one example, many college students illegally download music and computer programs. These same students would never even think to pilfer a fellow student's books, cell phone, or purse, for this would be "stealing" and clearly morally wrong. After all, they are not "thieves." But appropriating music and software incurs little guilt or shame because it can be justified by explaining that such conduct "does not hurt anyone." This technique, which neutralizes normative controls, is what Sykes and Matza call "denial of injury." Another neutralizing justification might be that music and computer companies are monopolistic and charge excessively high prices. They are unfair and deserve to have their property taken. Sykes and Matza would term this "denial of the victim." There is, in fact, some evidence that these types of beliefs identified by Sykes and Matza do facilitate criminal involvement not only for juveniles but also for adults (Benson, 1985 [Chapter 42 in Part XIII; Maruna and Copes, 2005).

In a way, Sykes and Matza bridge differential association and control theories. Similar to the Sutherland tradition, they argue that learned beliefs or definitions lead to crime. But similar to control theory, they do not see a society wracked by culture conflict. Rather, in their theoretical world, there is a dominant normative system about which there is consensus and into which virtually everyone is socialized. Again, this means that controls are present over most of us most of the time. The theoretical task is to explain why, under certain circumstances, individuals are able to ignore the very normative standards that they typically believe and that typically control them. For Sykes and Matza, techniques of neutralization comprise the solution to this criminological puzzle.

Containment Theory

Twentieth-century sociological criminology was largely dominated by the "big three" theories: strain, differential association (also called "cultural deviance" or "social learning"), and control. As noted above, Travis Hirschi clearly demarcated these three perspectives and called for a rigorous empirical competition to see which theory would still be standing after all the data were counted.

Walter Reckless was equally perceptive about the need to "make sense" of the prevailing theoretical paradigms so as to show how his "containment theory" differed. His terminology proved to be less compelling than Hirschi's characterization of competing frameworks; still, he offered a similar understanding of alternative theories and of what was distinctive and important about his brand of control theory.

Thus, Reckless identified two categories of theories that were popular in his day: "push" theories and "pull" theories. When answering why people committed criminal acts, push theories demarcated forces that would "push" or propel individuals onto the other side of the law. Strain theories fell into this category (see Part V). Reckless also believed that Bonger's depiction of the way capitalism creates intense pressures toward crime would qualify as a push theory (see Chapter 23 in this volume). In contrast, pull theories showed how people could be lured

into crime by providing antisocial models and criminal companions. Differential association or social learning theories would fall into this rubric (see Part IV). Reckless also made room for pushes toward crime that emerge from deeply within the individual. Although not well developed, he argued that pushes would be "psychologic or organic in origin" and include

> . . . extreme restlessness and discontent, marked inner tensions, hostility, aggressiveness, aggrandizement and need for immediate gratification, extreme suggestibility, rebellion against authority, sibling rivalry, hypersensitivity, strong feelings of inadequacy and inferiority, guilt reactions, mental conflicts, anxieties, compulsions, phobias, organic impairments (brain damage, epilepsy, and so on). (Reckless, 1961: 356)

In making these observations, he recognized that individual traits could be implicated in crime causation (see Parts I, II, and XII in this volume).

Reckless believed, however, that "push" and "pull" theories were incomplete. His main criticism was that they assumed that there was an ineluctable relationship between a strong push or pull and participating in crime. To be sure, Reckless was schooled at the University of Chicago and was intellectually partial to Shaw and McKay's (Chapter 7) perspective on crime. He agreed that social disorganization was an important source of wayward conduct—a point we will return to shortly. Reckless had an insight, however, that escaped others: What about the "good boy" in the "bad areas"? In disorganized inner-city neighborhoods, many boys (and girls) did not succumb to the criminogenic pushes and pulls that surrounded them. How did they *resist* these criminal influences? What made them different from the boys (and girls) who were propelled or lured into crime? In a series of empirical studies, Reckless proposed that a "good self-concept" *insulated* these boys from the "bad neighborhoods" in which they resided (see Reckless et al., 1957; see also Scarpitti, 2002). But self-concept was only one factor that played a role in insulating against crime and in controlling wayward impulses. A more comprehensive "containment theory" was needed to capture Reckless's (1961) thoughts on this matter. Indeed, a major advantage of Reckless's theory was that its scope included internal and external sources of control. Notably, subsequent control theories would tend to emphasize the importance of one or the other of these dimensions.

Reckless grouped one important set of controls under the category of "outer containment." To a large extent, this insight arose from his witnessing the disorganization that prevailed in Chicago during his graduate school days. But Reckless had another source for his insight: anthropology (see 1961: 337–340). At one point, he had considered a scholarly career in archaeology and had traveled to the Middle East. During this venture, he was struck by how "contained" these societies were—how unlike they were from the more socially open United States—and thus how little crime was experienced (personal interview with F. Cullen, 1980). In any event, for Reckless, outer containment is substantially the opposite of social disorganization. It occurs when individuals are enmeshed in "effective family life and an effective supporting structure in the neighborhood and the larger society" (1961: 352).

Again, however, Reckless realized that outer containment was often weak or not sufficiently strong to control the strong pulls and pushes individuals might experience. In such cases, the crucial last line of defense was whether a person had developed "inner containment." Reckless (1961: 355) included a lengthy roster of components within this construct:

> ... inner containment consists of good self-control, ego strength, well developed superego (conscience), good self-concept, high resistance to diversions, high frustration tolerance, high sense of responsibility, goal orientation, ability to find substitute satisfactions, tension-reducing rationalizations, and so on.

In the end, Reckless's multidimensional concept of inner containment may have proved too detailed and too difficult to measure. Indeed, it is instructive that his own empirical research focused only on the "self-concept as an insulator." Scientific paradigms, including criminological theories, earn support not only based on their potential accuracy but also based on whether they are stated in a parsimonious way such that they can be easily understood and tested. Travis Hirschi's "social bond theory" would have these characteristics. He would clearly specify four social bonds (attachment, commitment, involvement, and belief) and then show how these bonds could be measured and tested against competing theories. Combined with its intellectual rigor, the parsimony and testability of his perspective would contribute to social bond theory playing a major role in American criminology to this day.

Social Bond Theory

Although often unstated, most theories of crime make assumptions about human nature and its potential influence on behavior. For strain and cultural deviance theories, humans are usually considered to be "blank slates" onto which society writes its script for the person's life. On occasion, scholars in these traditions will admit that humans have innate or universal drives, but they do not see these forces as inherently criminogenic. Take, for example, the ninth proposition of Sutherland's differential association theory (see Chapter 10), which states that, "while criminal behavior is an expression of general needs and values, it is not explained by those general needs and values since noncriminal behavior is an expression of the same needs and values" (Sutherland and Cressey, 1970: 76).

Once they have rejected the notion that humans are driven to break the law because of their "nature," strain and cultural deviance theorists must address the question: "Well, then, why do people commit crimes?" The theoretical challenge is to discern what social conditions *motivate* individuals to engage in illegal acts. For strain theory, the motivation is rooted in negative social relations and experiences that expose people to strain; crime is a way of relieving or otherwise responding to this strain. For cultural deviance or learning theories, the motivation is created by social relations or experiences in which individuals learn to positively value crime, at least under some circumstances. Just as youths learn to like going to baseball games, they can learn to like breaking windows, shoplifting from stores, and beating up others.

As Hirschi notes, control theorists start out with a different premise about human nature: people will "naturally" break the law. It is not necessary to show that humans have an "id," as psychoanalytic theory would suggest, or that they have unique "animal impulses" or are innately aggressive, as some biological theories contend. Rather, for control theorists, it is sufficient to observe that like other animals, humans seek gratification and that crime is often an easy means to secure such gratification (see also Gottfredson and Hirschi, 1990). People may vary in their need for gratification, but humans generally have enough desire to seek pleasure that they have ample motivation to commit crimes on a regular basis.

This assumption has important theoretical implications. If all humans have motivations for crime, then theories that set forth special explanations of criminal motivation—such as strain and cultural deviance theories—are not needed. They are explaining something that does not need explaining; they are addressing the wrong question. Thus, rather than asking, "Why do they do it?," criminologists should be asking, "Why don't they do it?," (Hirschi, 1969: 34). That is, if humans' natural pursuit of gratification makes crime attractive, what is it that stops them from acting on this impulse?

The answer, of course, is the *control* that society exerts over individuals. According to Hirschi (1969: 16), "control theories assume that delinquent acts result when an individual's bond to society is weak or broken." It follows that *variation in control*, not variation in motivation, explains why some people break the law more than others. The theoretical task thus is to uncover the nature of social control and how it constrains, people from acting out their underlying wayward urges.

In *Causes of Delinquency* (1969), Hirschi set forth what remains, even to this day, the most influential variant of control theory, which he called "social bond" theory (see the selection in Chapter 18). This perspective is distinctly sociological, because Hirschi focused not on internal controls, such as a superego or inner containment, but rather on how an individual's *bond* to *society* influences decisions to break the law. He did not deny that internal controls exist—individual conduct is affected by what people think and anticipate will happen to them—but ultimately these controls originate with and are sustained by the person's bond to society.

Hirschi's theoretical genius is seen in his willingness to move beyond the general proposition that weak controls cause crime to specifying the four major elements of the social bond: attachment, commitment, involvement, and belief. In essence, Hirschi argued that delinquency would be low among youngsters who are attached to and care about the opinions of others—especially their parents, whose commitment to school gives them a strong investment in conformity that they do not wish to risk by getting into trouble, who are involved in conventional activities that occupy their time, and who believe they should obey rules. In contrast, youths who are not close to their parents, have few prospects for a successful future, are idle after school hours, and have no allegiance to conventional morality are prime candidates for delinquency.

Self-Control Theory

Two decades after the publication of *Causes of Delinquency*, Travis Hirschi joined with Michael Gottfredson to author *A General Theory of Crime*

(1990), a volume in which he set forth the premise that a lack of "self-control" was the chief source of criminal behavior (see Chapter 19 in this part). In this book, Gottfredson and Hirschi did not explicitly try to reconcile social bond and self-control theories. It is clear, however, that Hirschi's thinking about crime had changed over time and that his latest work was a marked departure from his earlier theorizing. In particular, whereas Hirschi's social bond theory located control in a person's *relation to society*, self-control theory moved the locus of control *inside the individual*. To a large extent, Hirschi now saw crime as rooted not in social experiences but in individual differences that developed early in life and had effects across the life course (see Parts II and XII).

Gottfredson and Hirschi embraced the view that criminal behavior is gratifying; indeed, they observed that crime is an easy source of short-term pleasure because committing a crime requires few skills and opportunities to offend are readily available. Why, then, would people bypass the chance to gain easy gratification through crime? Why don't they do it? The answer to this classic control theory question, as in *Causes of Delinquency*, is that controls hold these impulses in check; but unlike before, Gottfredson and Hirschi asserted that self-control, not social bonds, is the chief source of resistance against criminal temptations.

Social bond theory was largely an explanation of *juvenile* delinquency, focusing on how adolescents attach to parents, commit to school, are involved in recreational activities, and the like. By 1990, however, research had revealed that many wayward youths do not suddenly become seriously delinquent in their teen years. Instead, they begin to manifest conduct problems in childhood—problems that evolve into delinquency (see Moffitt, 1993 [Chapter 38]; Patterson et al., 1989. This continuity or stability in misconduct suggests that the roots of crime lie not in adolescence but in the first years of life. It would follow, of course,

that criminologists should search for the causes of crime in childhood and not, as had previously been the case, in the experiences of juveniles in the teenage years.

The critical social milieu in childhood is the family, and the critical experiences children encounter are intimately shaped by their parents. What, then, distinguishes the children who can resist seeking immediate gratification from those who act on their impulses, engaging in such precursors of delinquency as stealing, bullying, and lying? For Gottfredson and Hirschi, the key differentiating factor is whether a child can exercise "self-control." They reject the idea that this self-control is caused by biological predispositions (see, however, Wright and Beaver, 2005). Instead, here they remain sociologists in attributing the inculcation of self-control to how parents raise their children. In particular, they assert that parents who monitor their children, recognize deviant behavior when it occurs, and then correct this conduct will instill self-control. Conversely, say Gottfredson and Hirschi (1990: 97), "the major 'cause' of low self-control thus appears to be ineffective child-rearing" (for an assessment of this parenting thesis, see Cullen et al., 2008).

Gottfredson and Hirschi contend that the level of self-control, once established in childhood, is an enduring propensity or individual difference that has *general* effects in a person's life. This explains why there is stability of offending across the life course. The continuing lack of self-control also explains why criminal offenders also engage in activities that are "analogous" to crime—that is, acts, such as smoking, drinking, skipping school, having unprotected sex, and driving fast, which, like crime, provide easy and immediate gratification. As Gottfredson and Hirschi note, traditional sociological theories of crime have not shown that they can account for these key empirical facts: the early emergence of conduct problems, the stability of offending, and the participation of criminals in wide-ranging forms of deviance.

Notably, since its publication in 1990, Gottfredson and Hirschi's theory has been subjected to extensive conceptual analysis and empirical investigation (see Goode, 2008). Some of the bolder claims of the theory have not been supported, such as the contention that social learning variables (e.g., antisocial values) are unrelated to crime. Even so, there is now extensive evidence linking self-control to crime and "analogous behaviors" across social groups (e.g., gender and age) and across cultures (Gottfredson, 2006; Pratt and Cullen, 2000).

Social Bonds Across the Life Course

Although they share certain features because they are both control theories, self-control theory and social bond theory are incompatible in fundamental ways (compare Hirschi and Gottfredson, 1995, with Sampson and Laub, 1995). Social bond theory asserts that experiences beyond childhood can affect a person's ties to conventional society, and thus that as bonds strengthen or weaken, people's involvement in crime can ebb and flow. In contrast, self-control theory contends that criminal propensities are established in childhood, and thus that misconduct is stable across the life course. Even more provocatively, self-control theory claims that any apparent empirical relationship between social bonds (e.g., attachment to others, commitment to schooling) and crime is spurious. Self-control would account for both the bond and the level of crime. Thus, if being in a good marriage is associated with less crime, Gottfredson and Hirschi would argue that this is because people with high levels of self-control are both more likely to have good marriages and less likely to engage in crime.

Ironically, social bond theory received its most potent shot in the arm from two former students of Gottfredson and Hirschi, Robert Sampson and John Laub (1993 [Chapter 39 in Part XII]). Sampson and Laub agree with their mentors that sociological theorists have largely neglected the "considerable evidence that antisocial behavior is relatively stable across stages of the life course" (1993: 11). But they take Gottfredson and Hirschi to task for committing what Elliott Currie (1985: 185) calls the "fallacy of intractability—the belief that because childhood problems often appear early in life they are therefore fundamentally irreversible, portents of criminality worsening into adulthood." While there is continuity in antisocial behavior, observe Sampson and Laub, there is also *change*. Some problem children grow up to be delinquents, but others do not; some delinquents become adult criminals, but others do not; some adult criminals persist in their offending, but others do not.

Individual difference theories, such as Gottfredson and Hirschi's self-control theory, are adept at explaining *continuity* in problem behavior. Once equipped with an enduring criminal propensity, people carry this trait from situation to situation and from one age to the next. These theories encounter difficulty, however, in explaining *change* in behavior. If, for example, a person has low self-control, why would he or she ever stop being criminal? Or why would a juvenile who had no record of childhood misconduct—and thus whose parents instilled self-control—start getting into trouble in the teenage years (see Moffitt, Chapter 38)?

Using a life-course perspective, Sampson and Laub suggest that people usually are on certain "trajectories" that result in continuity of behavior. Even so, people also experience "transitions," life-events that may serve as "turning points" that evoke behavioral change. Sampson and Laub propose that establishing *social bonds*, such as through schooling or marriage, is a salient reason why people are redirected away from crime and into conformity. Explaining change, in short, requires a consideration of sociological factors.

Although borrowing from Hirschi's social bond theory, Sampson and Laub do not simply rehash this perspective. First, while Hirschi focused on the juvenile years, Sampson and Laub examine the entire life course, from childhood to adulthood. Second, they develop an integrated theoretical perspective, accepting that individual differences and social bonds combine to explain the onset of and desistance from criminal behavior. Third, they argue that the key issue is not whether a social bond exists but whether the bond is of high *quality*. Quality relationships—such as a good marriage or a rewarding job—engender close attachment, growing commitment, and reciprocity. In turn, note Sampson and Laub (1993: 141), "relations characterized by an extensive set of obligations, expectations, and interdependent social networks are better able to facilitate social control."

As discussed above, Sampson and Laub merged social bond theory with the notion that crime should be studied as a developmental process that occurs across the life course. Their contribution is thus two-fold. First, they elaborate social bond theory and show its relevance not only to crime in adolescence but also to crime in adulthood. Importantly, their theory argues

that informal social controls are *age-graded*, with different types of bonds affecting individuals at different stages in life (e.g., bonds to parents in childhood, to school in adolescence, to work in adulthood). The evidence is largely consistent with their theoretical predictions (Laub et al., 2006).

Second, they furnish one of the most important *life-course theories of crime*, a model that accounts for both continuity and change across time. For this reason, although we have discussed Sampson and Laub's perspective with regard to social bond theory here, their work is relevant to Part XIII, where "Developmental Theories" are discussed. In this section, we review their most recent theoretical views (Laub and Sampson, 2003 [Chapter 39]). At that later juncture, we will also have more to say about how Sampson and Laub's ideas converge with and differ from competing life-course theories of crime, including Gottfredson and Hirschi's self-control approach.

References

Benson, Michael L. 1985. "Denying the Guilty Mind: Accounting for Involvement in a White-Collar Crime." *Criminology* 23: 583–607.

Cohen, Albert K. 1955. *Delinquent Boys: The Culture of the Gang.* New York: Free Press.

Cullen, Francis T., James D. Unnever, John Paul Wright, and Kevin M. Beaver. 2008. "Parenting and Self-Control." In Erich Goode (ed.), *Out of Control: Assessing the General Theory of Crime*, pp. 61–74. Stanford, CA: Stanford University Press.

Currie, Elliott. 1985. *Confronting Crime: An American Challenge.* New York: Pantheon.

Goode, Erich, ed. 2008. *Out of Control: Assessing the General Theory of Crime.* Stanford, CA: Stanford University Press.

Gottfredson, Michael R. 2006. "The Empirical Status of Control Theory in Criminology." In Francis T. Cullen, John Paul Wright, and Kristie R. Blevins

(eds.), *Taking Stock: The Status of Criminological Theory—Advances in Criminological Theory*, Volume 15, pp. 77–100. New Brunswick, NJ: Transaction Publishers.

Gottfredson, Michael R. and Travis Hirschi. 1990. *A General Theory of Crime.* Stanford, CA: Stanford University Press.

Hirschi, Travis. 1969. *Causes of Delinquency.* Berkeley: University of California Press.

Hirschi, Travis and Michael R. Gottfredson. 1995. "Control Theory and the Life-Course Perspective." *Studies on Crime and Crime Prevention* 4: 131–142.

Kornhauser, Ruth Rosner. 1978. *Social Sources of Delinquency: An Appraisal of Analytic Models.* Chicago: University of Chicago.

Laub, John H. and Robert J. Sampson. 2003. *Shared Beginnings, Divergent Lives: Delinquent Boys to Age 70.* Cambridge, MA: Harvard University Press.

Laub, John H., Robert J. Sampson, and Gary Sweeten. 2006. "Assessing Sampson and Laub's Life-Course

Theory of Crime." In Francis T. Cullen, John Paul Wright, and Kristie R. Blevins (eds.), *Taking Stock: The Status of Criminological Theory—Advances in Criminological Theory*, Volume 15, pp. 313–333. New Brunswick, NJ: Transaction.

Maruna, Shaad and Heath Copes. 2005. "What Have We Learned from Five Decades of Neutralization Research?" In Michael Tonry (ed.), *Crime and Justice: A Review of Research*, Volume 32, pp. 221–320. Chicago: University of Chicago Press.

Moffitt, Terrie E. 1993. "Adolescence-Limited and Life-Course-Persistent Antisocial Behavior: A Developmental Taxonomy." *Psychological Review* 100: 674–701.

Nye, F. Ivan. 1958. *Family Relationships and Delinquent Behavior*. New York: John Wiley.

Patterson, Gerald R., Barbara DeBaryshe, and Elizabeth Ramsey. 1989. "A Developmental Perspective on Antisocial Behavior." *American Psychologist* 44: 329–335.

Pratt, Travis C. and Francis T. Cullen. 2000. "The Empirical Status of Gottfredson and Hirschi's General Theory of Crime: A Meta-Analysis." *Criminology* 38: 931–964.

Reckless, Walter C. 1961. *The Crime Problem*, 3rd edition. New York: Appleton-Century-Crofts.

Reckless, Walter C., Simon Dinitz, and Ellen Murray. 1957. "The 'Good Boy' in a High Delinquency Area." *Journal of Criminal Law, Criminology, and Police Science* 48: 18–25.

Reiss, Albert J., Jr. 1951. "Delinquency as the Failure of Personal and Social Controls." *American Sociological Review* 16: 196–207.

Sampson, Robert J. and John H. Laub. 1993. *Crime in the Making: Pathways and Turning Points Through Life*. Cambridge, MA: Harvard University Press.

——. 1995. "Understanding Variability in Lives Through Time: Contributions of Life Course Criminology." *Studies on Crime and Crime Prevention* 4: 143–158.

Scarpitti, Frank R. 2002. "The Good Boy in a High-Delinquency Area—40 Years Later." In Gilbert Geis and Mary Dodge (eds.), *Lessons of Criminology*, pp. 65–94. Cincinnati: Anderson.

Sutherland, Edwin H. and Donald R. Cressey. 1970. *Principles of Criminology*, 8th edition. Philadelphia: Lippincott.

Sykes, Gresham M. and David Matza. 1957. "Techniques of Neutralization: A Theory of Delinquency." *American Sociological Review* 22: 664–673.

Wright, John Paul and Kevin M. Beaver. 2005. "Do Parents Matter in Creating Self-Control in Their Children? A Genetically Informed Test of Gottfredson and Hirschi's Theory of Low Self-Control." *Criminology* 43: 1169–1202.

17. Techniques of Neutralization

Gresham M. Sykes and David Matza

Sykes and Matza, like Sutherland, feel that criminal behavior is learned. And like Sutherland, they feel that part of that learning involves "motives, drives, rationalizations, and attitudes favorable to violation of law." They state, however, that the specific content of these rationalizations and attitudes has not received much attention. When they wrote their article in 1957, the dominant view was that delinquents held values which were the opposite of middle-class values. Delinquents, in particular, were said to generally approve of acts such as theft and fighting. This position, represented in the work of Albert Cohen (see Chapter 14 in Part V), is attacked by Sykes and Matza (also see Matza, 1964).

The first part of their article presents evidence suggesting that delinquents do not generally approve of delinquency. The second part of their article presents an alternative formulation, in which they contend that delinquents are able to engage in delinquency by employing certain "techniques of neutralization." Although delinquents believe that delinquency is generally bad, they claim that their delinquent acts are justified for any one of several reasons (e.g., the victim had it coming, they didn't really hurt anybody). These justifications are said to be used before the delinquent act and they make the delinquent act possible by neutralizing the individual's belief that it is bad.

Because Sykes and Matza believe that these justifications for crime were learned, they are sometimes defined as "learning" theorists in the Sutherland tradition (see Part IV). In a fundamental way, however, their perspective is a control theory. Thus, Sykes and Matza do not see offenders as members of delinquent subcultures immune from the larger society's normative mandates. Rather, youngsters are socialized to hold conventional or prosocial beliefs that would typically prevent them from breaking the law. It is only when these normative controls are neutralized that individuals are able to commit specific criminal acts under specific circumstances. In short, techniques of neutralization are the mechanisms that people use to escape society's controls and feel free to engage in crime.

Data provide some support for neutralization theory. Much evidence suggests that offenders commonly justify or excuse their crimes using the neutralizations described by Sykes and Matza, as well as additional neutralizations identified by others (see Maruna and Copes, 2005). This is true of rapists (Scully and Marolla, 1984), white-collar criminals (Benson, 1985 [Chapter 42]), and others. Further, studies indicate that individuals differ in the extent to which they accept the neutralizations. Those individuals who accept more neutralizations usually engage in more crime. Some argue that

Reprinted from Gresham M. Sykes and David Matza, "Techniques of Neutralization: A Theory of Delinquency" in the *American Sociological Review* 22. Copyright © 1957.

this is because offenders use neutralizations to justify or excuse their crimes after the fact, but a few studies using longitudinal data have found that individuals who accept more neutralizations engage in more subsequent crime (see Agnew, 1994). Studies also suggest that the effect of neutralizations on crime is influenced by several factors (see Agnew, 1994). Neutralizations, for example, are more likely to lead to crime among individuals who associate with delinquent peers. Such findings reflect the fact that neutralizations do not so much cause crime as make it easier for motivated individuals to engage in crime (by reducing their guilt).

The data, then, do suggest that the techniques of neutralization may well be a "crucial component" of Sutherland's "definitions favorable to violation of law." Maruna and Copes (2005) provide an excellent overview of the research on neutralization theory and provide several suggestions for further research. For example, they suggest that some neutralizations may be more likely than others to foster crime.

References

Agnew, Robert. 1994. "The Techniques of Neutralization and Violence." *Criminology* 32: 555–580.

Benson, Michael L. 1985. "Denying the Guilty Mind: Accounting for Involvement in White-Collar Crime." *Criminology* 23: 583–608.

Maruna, Shadd and Heith Copes. 2005. "What Have We Learned From Five Decades of Neutralization Research?" In Michael Tonry (ed.), *Crime and Justice: A Review of Research*, Volume 32, pp. 221–320. Chicago: University of Chicago Press.

Matza, David. 1964. *Delinquency and Drift*. New York: Wiley.

Scully, Diana, and Joseph Marolla. 1984. "Convicted Rapists' Vocabulary of Motive: Excuses and Justifications." *Social Problems* 31: 530–544.

In attempting to uncover the roots of juvenile delinquency, the social scientist has long since ceased to search for devils in the mind or stigma of the body. It is now largely agreed that delinquent behavior, like most social behavior, is learned and that it is learned in the process of social interaction.

The classic statement of this position is found in Sutherland's theory of differential association, which asserts that criminal or delinquent behavior involves the learning of (a) techniques of committing crimes and (b) motives, drives, rationalizations, and attitudes favorable to the violation of law. Unfortunately, the specific content of what is learned—as opposed to the process by which it is learned—has received relatively little attention in either theory or research. Perhaps the single strongest school of thought on the nature of this content has centered on the idea of a delinquent sub-culture. The basic characteristic of the delinquent sub-culture, it is argued, is a system of values that represents an inversion of the values held by respectable, law-abiding society. The world of the delinquent is the world of the law-abiding turned upside down and its norms constitute a countervailing force directed against the conforming social order. Cohen sees the process of developing a delinquent sub-culture as a matter of building, maintaining, and reinforcing a code for behavior which exists by opposition, which stands in point by point contradiction to dominant values, particularly those of the middle class. Cohen's portrayal of delinquency is executed with a good deal of sophistication, and he carefully avoids overly simple explanations such as those based on the principle of "follow the leader" or easy generalizations about "emotional disturbances." Furthermore, he does not accept the delinquent sub-culture as something given, but instead systematically examines the function of delinquent values as a viable solution to the lower-class, male child's problems in the area of social status. Yet in spite of its virtues, this image of juvenile delinquency as a form of behavior based on competing or countervailing values and norms appears to suffer from a number of serious defects. It is the nature of these defects and a possible alternative or modified explanation for a large portion of juvenile delinquency with which this paper is concerned.

The difficulties in viewing delinquent behavior as springing from a set of deviant values and norms—as arising, that is to say, from a situation in which the delinquent defines his delinquency as "right"—are both empirical and theoretical. In the first place, if there existed in fact a delinquent sub-culture such that the delinquent viewed his illegal behavior as morally correct, we could reasonably suppose that he would exhibit no feelings of guilt or shame at detection or confinement. Instead, the major reaction would tend in the direction of indignation or a sense of martyrdom. It is true that some delinquents do react in the latter fashion, although the sense of martyrdom often seems to be based on the fact that others "get away with it" and indignation appears to be directed against the chance events or lack of skill that led to apprehension. More important, however, is the fact that there is a good deal of evidence suggesting that many delinquents *do* experience a sense of guilt or shame, and its outward expression is not to be dismissed as a purely manipulative gesture to appease those in authority. Much of this evidence is, to be sure, of a clinical nature or in the form of impressionistic judgments of those who must deal first hand with the youthful offender. Assigning a weight to such evidence calls for caution, but it cannot be ignored if we are to avoid the gross stereotype of the juvenile delinquent as a hardened gangster in miniature.

In the second place, observers have noted that the juvenile delinquent frequently accords admiration and respect to law-abiding persons. The "really honest" is often revered, and if the delinquent is sometimes overly keen to detect hypocrisy in those who conform, unquestioned probity is likely to win his approval. A fierce attachment to a humble, pious mother or a forgiving, upright priest (the former, according to many observers, is often encountered in both juvenile delinquents and adult criminals) might be dismissed as rank sentimentality, but at least it is clear that the delinquent does not necessarily regard those who abide by the legal rules as immoral. In a similar vein, it can be noted that the juvenile delinquent may exhibit great resentment if illegal behavior is imputed to "significant others" in his immediate social environment or to heroes in the world of sport and entertainment. In other words, if the delinquent does hold to a set of values and norms that stand in complete opposition to those of respectable society, his norm-holding is of a peculiar sort. While supposedly thoroughly committed to the deviant system of the delinquent sub-culture, he would appear to recognize the moral validity of the dominant normative system in many instances.

In the third place, there is much evidence that juvenile delinquents often draw a sharp line between those who can be victimized and those who cannot. Certain social groups are not to be viewed as "fair game" in the performance of supposedly approved delinquent acts while others warrant a variety of attacks. In general, the potentiality for victimization would seem to be a function of the social distance between the juvenile delinquent and others and thus we find implicit maxims in the world of the delinquent such as "don't steal from friends" or "don't commit vandalism against a church of your own faith." This is all rather obvious, but the implications have not received sufficient attention. The fact that supposedly valued behavior tends to be directed against disvalued social groups hints that the "wrongfulness" of such delinquent behavior is more widely recognized by delinquents than the literature has indicated. When the pool of victims is limited by considerations of kindship, friendship, ethnic group, social class, age, sex, etc., we have reason to suspect that the virtue of delinquency is far from unquestioned.

In the fourth place, it is doubtful if many juvenile delinquents are totally immune from the demands for conformity made by the dominant social order. There is a strong likelihood that the family of the delinquent will agree with respectable society that delinquency is wrong, even though the family may be engaged in a variety of illegal activities. That is, the parental posture conducive to delinquency is not apt to be a positive prodding. Whatever may be the influence of parental example, what might be called the "Fagin" pattern of socialization into delinquency is probably rare. Furthermore, as Redl has indicated, the idea that certain neighborhoods are completely delinquent, offering the child a model for delinquent behavior without reservations, is simply not supported by the data.

The fact that a child is punished by parents, school officials, and agencies of the legal system for his delinquency may, as a number of observers have cynically noted, suggest to the child that he should be more careful not to get caught. There is an equal or greater probability, however, that the child will internalize the demands for conformity. This is not to say that demands for conformity cannot be counteracted. In fact, as we shall see shortly, an understanding of how internal and external demands for conformity are neutralized may be crucial for understanding delinquent behavior. But it is to say that a complete denial of the validity of demands for conformity and the substitution of a new normative system is improbable, in light of the child's or adolescent's dependency on adults and encirclement by adults inherent in his status in the social structure. No matter how deeply enmeshed in patterns of delinquency he may be and no matter how much this involvement may outweigh his associations with the law-abiding, he cannot escape the condemnation of his deviance. Somehow the demands for conformity must be met and answered; they cannot be ignored as part of an alien system of values and norms.

In short, the theoretical viewpoint that sees juvenile delinquency as a form of behavior based on the values and norms of a deviant subculture in precisely the same way as law-abiding behavior is based on the values and norms of the larger society is open to serious doubt. The fact that the world of the delinquent is embedded in the larger world of those who conform cannot be overlooked nor can the delinquent be equated with an adult thoroughly socialized into an alternative way of life. Instead, the juvenile delinquent would appear to be at least partially committed to the dominant social order in that he frequently exhibits guilt or shame when he violates its proscriptions, accords approval to certain conforming figures, and distinguishes between appropriate and inappropriate targets for his deviance. It is to an explanation for the apparent paradoxical fact of his delinquency that we now turn.

As Morris Cohen once said, one of the most fascinating problems about human behavior is why men violate the laws in which they believe. This is the problem that confronts us when we attempt to explain why delinquency occurs despite a greater or lesser commitment to the usages of conformity. A basic clue is offered by the fact that social rules or norms calling for valued behavior seldom if ever take the form of categorical imperatives. Rather, values or norms appear as *qualified* guides for action, limited in their applicability in terms of time, place, persons, and social circumstances. The moral injunction against killing, for example, does not apply to the enemy during combat in time of war, although a captured enemy comes once again under the prohibition. Similarly, the taking and distributing of scarce goods in a time of acute social need is felt by many to be right, although under other circumstances private property is held inviolable. The normative system of a society, then, is marked by what Williams has termed *flexibility*; it does not consist of a body of rules held to be binding under all conditions.

This flexibility is, in fact, an integral part of the criminal law in that measures for "defenses to crimes" are provided in pleas such as nonage, necessity, insanity, drunkenness, compulsion, self-defense, and so on. The individual can avoid moral culpability for his criminal action—and thus avoid the negative sanctions of society—if he can prove that criminal intent was lacking.

It is our argument that much delinquency is based on what is essentially an unrecognized extension of defenses to crimes, in the form of justifications for deviance that are seen as valid by the delinquent but not by the legal system or society at large.

These justifications are commonly described as rationalizations. They are viewed as following deviant behavior and as protecting the individual from self-blame and the blame of others after the act. But there is also reason to believe that they precede deviant behavior and make deviant behavior possible. It is this possibility that Sutherland mentioned only in passing and that other writers have failed to exploit from the viewpoint of sociological theory. Disapproval flowing from internalized norms and conforming others in the social environment is neutralized, turned back, or deflected in advance. Social controls that serve to check or inhibit deviant motivational patterns are rendered inoperative, and the individual is freed to engage in delinquency without serious damage to his self image. In this sense, the delinquent both has his cake and eats it too, for he remains committed to the dominant normative system and yet so qualifies its imperatives that violations are "acceptable" if not "right." Thus the delinquent represents not a radical opposition to law-abiding society but something more like an apologetic failure, often more sinned against than sinning in his own eyes. We call these justifications of deviant behavior techniques of neutralization; and we believe these techniques make up a crucial component of Sutherland's "definitions favorable to the violation of law." It is by learning these techniques that the juvenile becomes delinquent, rather than by learning moral imperatives, values or attitudes standing in direct contradiction to those of the dominant

society. In analyzing these techniques, we have found it convenient to divide them into five major types.

The Denial of Responsibility

In so far as the delinquent can define himself as lacking responsibility for his deviant actions, the disapproval of self or others is sharply reduced in effectiveness as a restraining influence. As Justice Holmes has said, even a dog distinguishes between being stumbled over and being kicked, and modern society is no less careful to draw a line between injuries that are unintentional, i.e., where responsibility is lacking, and those that are intentional. As a technique of neutralization, however, the denial of responsibility extends much further than the claim that deviant acts are an "accident" or some similar negation of personal accountability. It may also be asserted that delinquent acts are due to forces outside of the individual and beyond his control such as unloving parents, bad companions, or a slum neighborhood. In effect, the delinquent approaches a "billiard ball" conception of himself in which he sees himself as helplessly propelled into new situations. From a psychodynamic viewpoint, this orientation toward one's own actions may represent a profound alienation from self, but it is important to stress the fact that interpretations of responsibility are cultural constructs and not merely idiosyncratic beliefs. The similarity between this mode of justifying illegal behavior assumed by the delinquent and the implications of a "sociological" frame of reference or a "humane" jurisprudence is readily apparent. It is not the validity of this orientation that concerns us here, but its function of deflecting blame attached to violations of social norms and its relative independence of a particular personality structure. By learning to view himself as more acted upon than acting, the delinquent prepares the way for deviance from the dominant normative system without the necessity of a frontal assault on the norms themselves.

The Denial of Injury

A second major technique of neutralization centers on the injury or harm involved in the delinquent act. The criminal law has long made a distinction between crimes which are *mala in se* and *mala prohibita*—that is between acts that are wrong in themselves and acts that are illegal but not immoral—and the delinquent can make the same kind of distinction in evaluating the wrongfulness of his behavior. For the delinquent, however, wrongfulness may turn on the question of whether or not anyone has clearly been hurt by his deviance, and this matter is open to a variety of interpretations. Vandalism, for example, may be defined by the delinquent simply as "mischief"—after all, it may be claimed, the persons whose property has been destroyed can well afford it. Similarly, auto theft may be viewed as "borrowing," and gang fighting may be seen as a private quarrel, an agreed upon duel between two willing parties, and thus of no concern to the community at large. We are not suggesting that this technique of neutralization, labelled the denial of injury, involves an explicit dialectic, rather, we are arguing that the delinquent frequently, and in a hazy fashion, feels that his behavior does not really cause any great harm despite the fact that it runs counter to law. Just as the link between the individual and his acts may be broken by the denial of responsibility, so may the link between acts and their consequences be broken by the denial of injury. Since society sometimes agrees with the delinquent, e.g., in matters such as truancy, "pranks," and so on, it merely reaffirms the idea that the delinquent's neutralization of social controls by means of qualifying the norms is an extension of common practice rather than a gesture of complete opposition.

The Denial of Victim

Even if the delinquent accepts the responsibility for his deviant actions and is willing to admit that his deviant actions involve an injury or hurt, the moral indignation of self and others may be neutralized by an insistence that the injury is not wrong in light of the circumstances. The injury, it may be claimed, is not really an injury; rather, it is a form of rightful retaliation or punishment. By a subtle alchemy the delinquent moves himself into the position of an avenger and the victim is transformed into a wrong-doer. Assaults on homosexuals or suspected homosexuals, attacks on members of minority groups who are said to have gotten "out of place," vandalism as revenge on an unfair teacher or school official, thefts from a "crooked" store owner—all may be hurts inflicted on a transgressor, in the eyes of the delinquent. As Orwell has pointed out, the type of criminal admired by the general public has probably changed over the course of years and Raffles no longer serves as a hero; but Robin Hood, and his latter day derivatives such as the tough detective seeking justice outside the law, still capture the popular imagination, and the delinquent may view his acts as part of a similar role. To deny the existence of the victim, then, by transforming him into a person deserving injury is an extreme form of a phenomenon we have mentioned before, namely, the delinquent's recognition of appropriate and inappropriate targets for his delinquent acts. In addition, however, the existence of the victim may be denied for the delinquent, in a somewhat different sense, by the circumstances of the delinquent act itself. Insofar as the victim is physically absent, unknown, or a vague abstraction (as is often the case in delinquent acts committed against property), the awareness of the victim's existence is weakened. Internalized norms and anticipations of the reactions of others must somehow be activated, if they are to serve as guides for behavior; and it is possible that a diminished awareness of the victim plays an important part in determining whether or not this process is set in motion.

The Condemnation of the Condemners

A fourth technique of neutralization would appear to involve a condemnation of the condemners or, as McCorkle and Korn have phrased it, a rejection of the rejectors. The delinquent shifts the focus of attention from his own deviant acts to the motives and behavior of those who disapprove of his violations. His condemners, he may claim, are hypocrites, deviants in disguise, or impelled by personal spite. This orientation toward the conforming world may be of particular importance when it hardens into a bitter cynicism directed against those assigned the task of enforcing or expressing the norms of the dominant society. Police, it may be said, are corrupt, stupid, and brutal. Teachers always show favoritism and parents always "take it out" on their children. By a slight extension, the rewards of conformity—such as material success—become a matter of pull or luck, thus decreasing still further the stature of those who stand on the side of the law-abiding. The validity of this jaundiced viewpoint is not so important as its function in turning back or deflecting the negative sanctions attached to violations of the norms. The delinquent, in effect, has changed the subject of the conversation in the dialogue between his own deviant impulses and the reactions of others; and by attacking others, the wrongfulness of his own behavior is more easily repressed or lost to view.

The Appeal to Higher Loyalties

Fifth, and last, internal and external social controls may be neutralized by sacrificing the demands of the larger society for the demands of the smaller social groups to which the delinquent belongs such as the sibling pair, the gang, or the friendship clique. It is important to note that the delinquent does not necessarily repudiate the imperatives of the dominant normative system, despite his failure to follow them. Rather, the delinquent may see himself as caught up in a dilemma that must be resolved, unfortunately, at the cost of violating the law. One aspect of this situation has been studied by Stouffer and Toby in their research on the conflict between particularistic and universalistic demands, between the claims of friendship and general social obligations, and their results suggest that "it is possible to classify people according to a predisposition to select one or the other horn of a dilemma in role conflict." For our purposes, however, the most important point is that deviation from certain norms may occur not because the norms are rejected but because other norms, held to be more pressing or involving a higher loyalty, are accorded precedence. Indeed, it is the fact that both sets of norms are believed in that gives meaning to our concepts of dilemma and role conflict.

The conflict between the claims of friendship and the claims of law, or a similar dilemma, has of course long been recognized by the social scientist (and the novelist) as a common human problem. If the juvenile delinquent frequently resolves his dilemma by insisting that he must "always help a buddy" or "never squeal on a friend," even when it throws him into serious difficulties with the dominant social order, his choice remains familiar to the supposedly law-abiding. The delinquent is unusual, perhaps, in the extent to which he is able to see the fact that he acts in behalf of the smaller social groups to which he belongs as a justification for violations of society's norms, but it is a matter of degree rather than of kind.

"I didn't mean it." "I didn't really hurt anybody." "They had it coming to them." "Everybody's picking on me." "I didn't do it for myself." These slogans or their variants, we hypothesize, prepare the juvenile for delinquent acts. These "definitions of the situation" represent tangential or glancing blows at the dominant normative system rather than the creation of an opposing ideology; and they are extensions of patterns of thought prevalent in society rather than something created *de novo*.

Techniques of neutralization may not be powerful enough to fully shield the individual from the force of his own internalized values and the reactions of conforming others, for as we have pointed out, juvenile delinquents often appear to suffer from feelings of guilt and shame when called into account for their deviant behavior. And some delinquents may be so isolated from the world of conformity that techniques of neutralization need not be called into play. Nonetheless, we would argue that techniques of neutralization are critical in lessening the effectiveness of social controls and that they lie behind a large share of delinquent behavior.

Empirical research in this area is scattered and fragmentary at the present time, but the work of Redl, Cressy, and others has supplied a body of significant data that has done much to clarify the theoretical issues and enlarge the fund of supporting evidence. Two lines of investigation seem to be critical at this stage. First, there is need for more knowledge concerning the differential distribution of techniques of neutralization, as operative patterns of thought, by age, sex, social class, ethnic group, etc. On *a priori* grounds it might be assumed that these justifications for deviance will be more readily seized by segments of society for whom a discrepancy between common social ideals and social practice is most apparent. It is also possible however, that the habit of "bending" the dominant normative system—if not "breaking" it—cuts across our cruder social categories and is to be traced primarily to patterns of social interaction within the familial circle. Second, there is need for a greater understanding of the internal structure of techniques of neutralization, as a system of beliefs and attitudes, and its relationship to various types of delinquent behavior. Certain techniques of neutralization would appear to be better adapted to particular deviant acts than to others, as we have suggested, for example, in the case of offenses against property and the denial of the victim. But the issue remains far from clear and stands in need of more information.

In any case, techniques of neutralization appear to offer a promising line of research in enlarging and systematizing the theoretical grasp of juvenile delinquency. As more information is uncovered concerning techniques of neutralization, their origins, and their consequences, both juvenile delinquency in particular, and deviation from normative systems in general may be illuminated.

Discussion Questions

1. In their article, Sykes and Matza paraphrase Morris Cohen: "one of the most fascinating problems about human behavior is why men violate the laws in which they believe." What solution do Sykes and Matza offer to this problem?

2. Most students disapprove of cheating on exams, but many nevertheless cheat. List possible justifications such students might give for their cheating behavior. Which techniques of neutralizations do these justifications illustrate?

3. Sykes and Matza argue that the techniques of neutralization are learned from others. They do not, however, describe those groups or types of individuals that are most likely to employ the techniques of neutralization. What groups or categories of individuals do you think are most likely to employ the techniques of neutralization (and why)?

18. Social Bond Theory

Travis Hirschi

Although Causes of Delinquency *is a complex book filled with intricate theoretical discussions and numerous statistical analyses, Hirschi's theory has an appealing quality: It can be simply stated and thus easily understood and studied by criminologists. Indeed, his theory can be reduced to two propositions. First, delinquency and social bonds are inversely related. Second, the concept of social bonds has four elements—attachment, commitment, involvement, and belief—which independently and in combination restrain criminal conduct.*

But how exactly do these bonds exert control over youngsters? Hirschi argued that youths could be attached to peers, teachers, and other adults, although relationships with parents are most crucial. Attachment involves an emotional connection to another person. When such a relationship exists, youths will be more likely to care what that other person thinks of them. In turn, when in a situation where the opportunity for trouble presents itself, they will be restrained from delinquency if they are concerned that such action will disappoint the other person or disrupt this relationship.

The importance of attachment is that during the teenage years, youths are frequently outside their parents' watchful eyes. In such instances, parents cannot exert "direct control"—that is, personally supervise their children and punish misconduct when it occurs. They can, however, exert "indirect control" if youths take into account their parents' preferences. When attachment is strong,

observed Hirschi, "the parent is psychologically present when temptation to commit a crime appears. If, in the situation of temptation, no thought is given to parental reaction, the child is to this extent free to commit the act" (1969: 88).

Much like rational choice theory (see Part X), Hirschi suggested that there is a "rational component" to conformity, which he calls "commitment." Juveniles who are doing well in school and have bright prospects ahead are less likely to engage in acts that will jeopardize their future. Conversely, uncommitted youths—those with little or no stake in conformity—have nothing to lose and thus are freer to break the law.

Hirschi also contended that the mere involvement in conventional activities facilitates control. If idleness presents opportunities for crime, filling up a youth's day with wholesome activities—such as school and recreational pursuits—leaves little time for getting into trouble.

Finally, Hirschi (1969: 26) argued that youths who believe that they should "obey the rules of society" are less likely to violate them. The social bond of "belief" is controversial because such beliefs or "definitions" are also central to differential association theory (or what Hirschi called "cultural deviance" theory). Hirschi contended, however, that an important analytical distinction could be made: While cultural deviance theorists like Sutherland (Chapter 10) focus on beliefs that positively value crime ("definitions favorable to

Reprinted by permission of Transaction Publishers. Travis Hirschi, "Social Bond Theory" from *Causes of Delinquency*. Copyright © 1969 by Transaction Publishers.

violation of the law"), control theorists focus on beliefs that proscribe crime. "Delinquency is not caused by beliefs that require delinquency," noted Hirschi (1969: 198), "but rather made possible by the absence of (effective) beliefs that forbid delinquency."

Hirschi's social bond theory has been subjected to numerous empirical tests—perhaps more than any other theory. Although empirical confirmation of the theory varies by such factors as a study's methodology (Agnew, 1985; Costello and Vowell, 1999; Kempf, 1993; Krohn, 2000; Kubrin et al., 2009), overall there is fairly consistent support for the general thesis that weak social bonds increase the risk of being involved in criminal behavior (Akers and Sellers, 2008; Sampson and Laub, 1993). Hirschi's claim that competing perspectives—especially "cultural deviance" theories—are not empirically viable, however, is mistaken (Akers and Sellers, 2008; Krohn, 2000; Kubrin et al., 2009). A further limitation is that Hirschi's approach is largely astructural and ahistorical. Unlike Shaw and McKay (Chapter 7), he does not examine how macrosocial changes occurring in the United States affect the strength of social bonds for people located in different sectors of American society (see also Sampson and Wilson, 1995 [Chapter 8 in this volume]; Sampson and Laub, 1994).

References

Agnew, Robert. 1985. "Social Control Theory and Delinquency: A Longitudinal Test." *Criminology* 23: 47–61.

Akers, Ronald L. and Christine S. Sellers. 2008. *Criminological Theories: Introduction, Evaluation, and Application*, 5th edition. Los Angeles: Roxbury.

Costello, Barbara J. and Paul R. Vowell. 1999. "Testing Control Theory and Differential Association: A Reanalysis of the Richmond Youth Project Data." *Criminology* 37: 815–842.

Hirschi, Travis. 1969. *Causes of Delinquency*. Berkeley: University of California Press.

Kempf, Kimberly L. 1993. "The Empirical Status of Hirschi's Control Theory." In Freda Adler and William S. Laufer (eds.), *New Directions in Criminological Theory: Advances in Criminological Theory*, Volume 4, pp. 143–185. New Brunswick, NJ: Transaction.

Krohn, Marvin. 2000. "Control and Deterrence Theories of Criminality." In Joseph F. Sheley (ed.), *Criminology: A Contemporary Handbook*, 3rd edition, pp. 372–399. Belmont, CA: Wadsworth.

Kubrin, Charis E., Thomas D. Stucky, and Marvin D. Krohn. 2009. *Researching Theories of Crime and Deviance*. New York: Oxford University Press.

Sampson, Robert J. and John H. Laub. 1993. *Crime in the Making: Pathways and Turning Points Through Life*. Cambridge, MA: Harvard University Press.

——. 1994. "Urban Poverty and the Family Context of Delinquency: A New Look at Structure and Process in a Classic Study." *Child Development* 65: 523–540.

Sampson, Robert J. and William Julius Wilson. 1995. "Toward a Theory of Race, Crime, and Urban Inequality." In John Hagan and Ruth D. Peterson (eds.), *Crime and Inequality*, pp. 36–54. Stanford, CA: Stanford University Press.

Three fundamental perspectives on delinquency and deviant behavior dominate the current scene. According to *strain* or motivational theories, legitimate desires that conformity cannot satisfy force a person into deviance. According to *control* or bond theories, a person is free to commit delinquent acts because his ties to the conventional order have somehow been broken. According to *cultural deviance* theories, the deviant conforms to a set of standards not accepted by a larger or more powerful society. Although most current theories of crime and delinquency contain elements of at least two and occasionally all three of these perspectives, reconciliation of their assumptions is very difficult. If, as the control theorist assumes, the ties of many persons to the conventional order may be weak or virtually nonexistent, the strain theorist, in accounting for their deviance, builds into his explanation pressure that is unnecessary. If, on the other hand, it is reasonable to assume with the strain theorist that everyone is at some point strongly tied to *the* conventional system, then it is unreasonable to assume that many are not (control theories), or that many are tied to different "conventional" systems (cultural deviance theories) . . . .

Control theories assume that delinquent acts result when an individual's bond to society is weak or broken. Since these theories embrace two highly complex concepts, the *bond* of the individual to *society*, it is not surprising that they have at one time or another formed the basis of explanations of most forms of aberrant or unusual behavior. It is also not surprising that control theories have described the elements of the bond to society in many ways, and that they have focused on a variety of units as the point of control . . . .

Elements of the Bond

Attachment

In explaining conforming behavior, sociologists justly emphasize sensitivity to the opinion of others. Unfortunately, as suggested in the preceding chapter, they tend to suggest that man *is* sensitive to the opinion of others and thus exclude sensitivity from their explanations of deviant behavior. In explaining deviant behavior, psychologists, in contrast, emphasize insensitivity to the opinion of others. Unfortunately, they too tend to ignore variation, and, in addition, they tend to tie sensitivity inextricably to other variables, to make it part of a syndrome or "type," and thus seriously to reduce its value as an explanatory concept. The psychopath is characterized only in part by "deficient attachment to or affection for others, a failure to respond to the ordinary motivations founded in respect or regard for one's fellows"; he is also characterized by such things as "excessive aggressiveness," "lack of superego control," and "an infantile level of response." Unfortunately, too, the behavior that

psychopathy is used to explain often becomes part of the *definition* of psychopathy. As a result, in Barbara Wootton's words:

> [The psychopath] is ... *par excellence*, and without shame or qualification, the model of the circular process by which mental abnormality is inferred from anti-social behavior while anti-social behavior is explained by mental abnormality.

The problems of diagnosis, tautology, and name-calling are avoided if the dimensions of psychopathy are treated as causally and therefore problematically interrelated, rather than as logically and therefore necessarily bound to each other. In fact, it can be argued that all of the characteristics attributed to the psychopath follow from, are effects of, his lack of attachment to others. To say that to lack attachment to others is to be free from moral restraints is to use lack of attachment to explain the guiltlessness of the psychopath, the fact that he apparently has no conscience or superego. In this view, lack of attachment to others is not merely a symptom of psychopathy, it is psychopathy; lack of conscience is just another way of saying the same thing; and the violation of norms is (or may be) a consequence.

For that matter, given that man is an animal, "impulsivity" and "aggressiveness" can also be seen as natural consequences of freedom from moral restraints. However, since the view of man as endowed with natural propensities and capacities like other animals is peculiarly unpalatable to sociologists, we need not fall back on such a view to explain the amoral man's aggressiveness. The process of becoming alienated from others often involves or is based on active interpersonal conflict. Such conflict could easily supply a reservoir of *socially derived* hostility sufficient to account for the aggressiveness of those whose attachments to others have been weakened.

Durkheim said it many years ago: "We are moral beings to the extent that we are social beings." This may be interpreted to mean that we are moral beings to the extent that we have "internalized the norms" of society. But what does it mean to say that a person has internalized the norms of society? The norms of society are by definition shared by the members of society. To violate a norm is, therefore, to act contrary to the wishes and expectations of other people. If a person does not care about the wishes and expectations of other people—that is, if he is insensitive to the opinion of others—then he is to that extent not bound by the norms. He is free to deviate.

The essence of internalization of norms, conscience, or super-ego thus lies in the attachment of the individual to others. This view has several advantages over the concept of internalization. For one, explanations of deviant behavior based on attachment do not beg the question, since the extent to which a person is attached to others can be measured independently of his deviant behavior. Furthermore, change or variation in behavior is explainable in a way that it is not when notion of internalization or superego are used. For example, the divorced man is more likely after divorce to commit a number of deviant acts, such as suicide or forgery. If we explain these acts by reference to the superego (or internal control), we are forced to say that the man "lost his conscience" when he got a divorce; and, of course, if he remarries, we have to conclude that he gets his conscience back.

This dimension of the bond to conventional society is encountered in most social control-oriented research and theory. F. Ivan Nye's "internal control" and "indirect control" refer to the same element, although we avoid the problem of explaining changes over time by locating the "conscience" in the bond to others rather than making it part of the personality. Attachment to others is just one aspect of Albert J. Reiss's "personal controls"; we avoid his problems of tautological empirical *observations* by making the relationship between attachment and delinquency problematic rather than definitional. Finally, Scott Briar and Irving Piliavin's "commitment" or "stake in conformity" subsumes attachment, as their

discussion illustrates, although the terms they use are more closely associated with the next element to be discussed.

Commitment

"Of all passions, that which inclineth men least to break the laws, is fear. Nay, excepting some generous natures, it is the only thing, when there is the appearance of profit or pleasure by breaking the laws, that makes men keep them." Few would deny that men on occasion obey the rules simply from fear of the consequences. This rational component in conformity we label commitment. What does it mean to say that a person is committed to conformity? In Howard S. Becker's formulation it means the following:

> First, the individual is in a position in which his decision with regard to some particular line of action has consequences for other interests and activities not necessarily [directly] related to it. Second, he has placed himself in that position by his own prior actions. A third element is present though so obvious as not to be aware [of other interests] and must recognize that his decision in this case will have ramifications beyond it.

The idea, then, is that the person invests time, energy, himself, in a certain line of activity—say, getting an education, building up a business, acquiring a reputation for virtue. When or whenever he considers deviant behavior, he must consider the costs of this deviant behavior, the risk he runs of losing the investment he has made in conventional labor.

If attachment to others is the sociological counterpart of the superego or conscience, commitment is the counterpart of the ego or common sense. To the person committed to conventional lines of action, risking one to ten years in prison for a ten-dollar holdup is stupidity, because to the committed person the costs and risks obviously exceed ten dollars in value. (To the psychoanalyst, such an act exhibits failure to be governed by the "reality-principle.") In the sociological control theory, it can be and is generally assumed that the decision to commit a criminal act may well be rationally determined—that the actor's decision was not irrational given the risks and costs he faces. Of course, as Becker points out, if the actor is capable of in some sense calculating the costs of a line of action, he is also capable of calculational errors: ignorance and error return, in the control theory, as possible explanations of deviant behavior.

The concept of commitment assumes that the organization of society is such that the interests of most persons would be endangered if they were to engage in criminal acts. Most people, simply by the process of living in an organized society, acquire goods, reputations, prospects that they do not want to risk losing. These accumulations are society's insurance that they will abide by the rules. Many hypotheses about the antecedents of delinquent behavior are based on this premise. For example, Arthur L. Stinchcombe's hypothesis that "high school rebellion . . . occurs when future status is not clearly related to present performance" suggests that one is committed to conformity not only by what one has but also by what one hopes to obtain. Thus "ambition" and/or "aspiration" play an important role in producing conformity. The person becomes committed to a conventional line of action, and he is therefore committed to conformity.

Most lines of action in a society are of course conventional. The clearest examples are educational and occupational careers. Actions thought to jeopardize one's chances in these areas are presumably avoided. Interestingly enough, even nonconventional commitments may operate to produce conventional conformity. We are told, at least, that boys aspiring to careers in the rackets or professional thievery are judged by their "honesty" and "reliability"—traits traditionally in demand among seekers of office boys.

Involvement

Many persons undoubtedly owe a life of virtue to a lack of opportunity to do otherwise. Time and energy are inherently limited: "Not that I would not, if I could, be both handsome and fat and well dressed, and a great athlete, and make a million a year, be a wit, a bon vivant, and a lady killer, as well as a philosopher, a philanthropist, a statesman, warrior, and African explorer, as well as a 'tone-poet' and saint. But the thing is simply impossible." The things that William James here says he would like to be or do are all, I suppose, within the realm of conventionality, but if he were to include illicit actions he would still have to eliminate some of them as simply impossible.

Involvement or engrossment in conventional activities is thus often part of a control theory. The assumption, widely shared, is that a person may be simply too busy doing conventional things to find time to engage in deviant behavior. The person involved in conventional activities is tied to appointments, deadlines, working hours, plans, and the like, so the opportunity to commit deviant acts rarely arises. To the extent that he is engrossed in conventional activities, he cannot even think about deviant acts, let alone act out his inclinations.

This line of reasoning is responsible for the stress placed on recreational facilities in many programs to reduce delinquency, for much of the concern with the high school dropout, and for the idea that boys should be drafted into the Army to keep them out of trouble. So obvious and persuasive is the idea that involvement in conventional activities is a major deterrent to delinquency that it was accepted even by Sutherland:

> In the general area of juvenile delinquency it is probable that the most significant difference between juveniles who engage in delinquency and those who do not is that the latter are provided abundant opportunities of a conventional type for satisfying their recreational interests, while the former lack those opportunities or facilities.

The view that "idle hands are the devil's workshop" has received more sophisticated treatment in recent sociological writings on delinquency. David Matza and Gresham M. Sykes, for example, suggest that delinquents have the values of a leisure class, the same values ascribed by Veblen to *the* leisure class: a search for kicks, disdain of work, a desire for the big score, and acceptance of aggressive toughness as proof of masculinity. Matza and Sykes explain delinquency by reference to this system of values, but they note that adolescents at all class levels are "to some extent" members of a leisure class, that they "move in a limbo between earlier parental domination and future integration with the social structure through the bonds of work and marriage." In the end, then, the leisure of the adolescent produces a set of values, which, in turn, leads to delinquency.

Belief

Unlike the cultural deviance theory, the control theory assumes the existence of a common value system within the society or group whose norms are being violated. If the deviant is committed to a value system different from that of conventional society, there is, within the context of the theory, nothing to explain. The question is, "Why does a man violate the rules in which he believes?" It is not, "Why do men differ in their beliefs about what constitutes good and desirable conduct?" The person is assumed to have been socialized (perhaps imperfectly) into the group whose rules he is violating; deviance is not a question of one group imposing its rules on the members of another group. In other words, we not only assume the deviant *has* believed the rules, we assume he believes the rules even as he violates them.

How can a person believe it is wrong to steal at the same time he is stealing? In the strain theory, this is not a difficult problem. (In fact, as suggested in the previous chapter, the strain theory was devised specifically to deal with this question.) The motivation to deviance adduced by the strain theorist is so strong that we can well understand the deviant act even assuming the deviator believes strongly that it is wrong.

However, given the control theory's assumptions about motivation, if both the deviant and the nondeviant believe the deviant act is wrong, how do we account for the fact that one commits it and the other does not?

Control theories have taken two approaches to this problem. In one approach, beliefs are treated as mere words that mean little or nothing if the other forms of control are missing. "Semantic dementia," the dissociation between rational faculties and emotional control which is said to be characteristic of the psychopath, illustrates this way of handling the problem. In short, beliefs, at least insofar as they are expressed in words, drop out of the picture; since they do not differentiate between deviants and nondeviants, they are in the same class as "language" or any other characteristic common to all members of the group. Since they represent no real obstacle to the commission of delinquent acts, nothing need be said about how they are handled by those committing such acts. The control theories that do not mention beliefs (or values), and many do not, may be assumed to take this approach to the problem.

The second approach argues that the deviant rationalizes his behavior so that he can at once violate the rule and maintain his belief in it. Donald R. Cressey has advanced this argument with respect to embezzlement, and Sykes and Matza have advanced it with respect to delinquency. In both Cressey's and Sykes and Matza's treatments, these rationalizations (Cressey calls them "verbalizations," Sykes and Matza term them "techniques of neutralization") occur prior to the commission of the deviant act. If the neutralization is successful, the person is free to commit the act(s) in question. Both in Cressey and in Sykes and Matza, the strain that prompts the effort at neutralization also provides the motive force that results in the subsequent deviant act. Their theories are thus, in this sense, strain theories. Neutralization is difficult to handle within the context of a theory that adheres closely to control theory assumptions, because in the control theory there is no special motivational force to account for the neutralization. This difficulty is especially noticeable in Matza's later treatment of this topic, where the motivational component, the "will to delinquency" appears *after* the moral vacuum has been created by the techniques of the neutralization. The question thus becomes: Why neutralize?

In attempting to solve a strain theory problem with control theory tools, the control theorist is thus led into a trap. He cannot answer the crucial question. The concept of neutralization assumes the existence of moral obstacles to the commission of deviant acts. In order plausibly to account for a deviant act, it is necessary to generate motivation to deviance that is at least equivalent in force to the resistance provided by these moral obstacles. However, if the moral obstacles are removed, neutralization and special motivation are no longer required. We therefore follow the implicit logic of control theory and remove these moral obstacles by hypothesis. Many persons do not have an attitude of respect toward the rules of society; many persons feel no moral obligation to conform regardless of personal advantage. Insofar as the values and beliefs of these persons are consistent with their feelings, and there should be a tendency toward consistency, neutralization is unnecessary; it has already occurred.

Does this merely push the question back a step and at the same time produce conflict with the assumption of a common value system? I think not. In the first place, we do not assume, as does Cressey, that neutralization occurs in order to make a specific criminal act possible. We do not assume, as do Sykes and Matza, that neutralization occurs to make many delinquent acts possible. We do not assume, in other words, that the person constructs a system of rationalizations in order to justify commission of acts he *wants* to commit. We assume, in contrast, that the beliefs that free a man to commit deviant acts are *unmotivated* in the sense that he does not construct or adopt them in order to facilitate the attainment of illicit ends. In the second place, we do not assume, as does Matza, that "delinquents concur in the conventional assessment of delinquency." We assume, in contrast, that there is *variation* in the extent to which people believe they should obey the rules of society, and, furthermore, that the less a person believes he should obey the rules, the more likely he is to violate them.

In chronological order, then, a person's beliefs in the moral validity of norms are, for no teleological reason, weakened. The probability that he will commit delinquent acts is therefore increased. When and if he commits a delinquent act, we may justifiably use the weakness of his beliefs in explaining it, but no special motivation is required to explain either the weakness of his beliefs or, perhaps, his delinquent act.

The keystone of this argument is of course the assumption that there is variation in belief in the moral validity of social rules. This assumption is amenable to direct empirical test and can thus survive at least until its first confrontation with data. For the present, we must return to the idea of a common value system with which this section was begun.

The idea of a common (or, perhaps better, a single) value system is consistent with the fact, or presumption, of variation in the strength of moral beliefs. We have not suggested that delinquency is based on beliefs counter to conventional morality; we have not suggested that delinquents do not believe delinquent acts are wrong, but the meaning and efficacy of such beliefs are contingent upon other beliefs and, indeed, on the strength of other ties to the conventional order.

Where Is the Motivation?

The most disconcerting question the control theorist faces goes something like this: "Yes, but *why* do they do it?" In the good old days, the control theorist could simply strip away the "veneer of civilization" and expose man's "animal impulses" for all to see. These impulses appeared to him (and apparently to his audience) to provide a plausible account of the motivation to crime and delinquency. His argument was *not* that delinquents and criminals alone are animals, but that we are all animals, and thus all naturally capable of committing criminal acts. It took no great study to reveal that children, chickens, and dogs occasionally assault and steal from their fellow creatures; that children, chickens, and dogs also behave for relatively long periods in a perfectly moral manner. Of course the acts of chickens and dogs are not "assault" or "theft," and such behavior is not "moral"; it is simply the behavior of a chicken or a dog. The chicken stealing corn from his neighbor knows nothing of the moral law; he does not *want* to violate rules; he wants merely to eat corn. The dog maliciously destroying a pillow or feloniously assaulting another dog is the moral equal of the chicken. No motivation to deviance is required to explain his acts. So, too, no special motivation to crime within the human animal was required to explain his criminal acts.

Times changed. It was no longer fashionable (within sociology, at least) to refer to animal impulses. The control theorist tended more and more to deemphasize the motivational component of his theory. He might refer in the beginning to "universal human needs," or some such, but the driving force behind crime and delinquency was rarely alluded to. At the same time, his explanations of crime and delinquency left the reader uneasy. What, the reader asked, is the control theorist assuming? Albert K. Cohen and James F. Short answer the question this way:

> ... it is important to point out one important limitation of both types of theory. They [culture conflict and social disorganization theories] are both *control* theories in the sense that they explain delinquency in terms of the *absence* of effective controls. They appear, therefore, to imply a model of motivation that assumes that the impulse to delinquency is an inherent characteristic of young people and does not itself need to be explained; it is something that erupts when the lid—i.e.,

internalized cultural restraints or external authority—is off.

There are several possible and I think reasonable reactions to this criticism. One reaction is simply to acknowledge the assumption, to grant that one is assuming what control theorists have always assumed about the motivation to crime—that it is constant across persons (at least within the system in question):

> There is no reason to assume that only those who finally commit a deviant act usually have the impulse to do so. It is much more likely that most people experience deviant impulses frequently. At least in fantasy, people are much more deviant than they appear.

There is certainly nothing wrong with *making* such an assumption. We are free to assume anything we wish to assume; the truth of our theory is presumably subject to empirical test.

A second reaction, involving perhaps something of a quibble, is to defend the logic of control theory and to deny the alleged assumption. We can say the fact that control theory suggests the absence of something causes delinquency is not a proper criticism, since negative relations have as much claim to scientific acceptability as do positive relations. We can also say that the present theory does not impute an inherent impulse to *delinquency* to anyone. That, on the contrary, it denies the necessity of such an imputation:

> The desires, and other passions of man, are in themselves no sin. No more are the actions, that proceed from those passions, till they know a law that forbids them.

A third reaction is to accept the criticism as valid, to grant that a complete explanation of delinquency would provide the necessary impetus, and proceed to construct an explanation of motivation consistent with control theory. Briar and Piliavin provide situational motivation:

We assume these acts are prompted by short-term situationally induced desires experienced by all boys to obtain valued goods, to portray courage in the presence of, or be loyal to peers, to strike out at someone who is disliked, or simply to "get kicks."

. . . There are several additional accounts of "why they do it" that are to my mind persuasive and at the same time generally compatible with control theory. But while all of these accounts may be compatible with control theory, they are by no means deducible from it. Furthermore, they rarely impute built-in, unusual motivation to the delinquent: he is attempting to satisfy the same desires, he is reacting to the same pres-sures as other boys (as is clear, for example, in the previous quotation from Briar and Piliavin). In other words, if included, these accounts of motivation would serve the same function in the theory that "animal impulses" traditionally served: they might add to its persuasiveness and plausibility, but they would add little else, since they do not differentiate delinquents from nondelinquents.

In the end, then, control theory remains what it has always been: a theory in which deviation is not problematic. The question "Why do they do it?" is simply not the question the theory is designed to answer. The question is, "Why don't we do it?" There is much evidence that we would if we dared.

Discussion Questions

1. Why does Hirschi say that the key question for criminologists to answer is "Why don't they do it?" as opposed to "Why do they do it?"
2. How does control theory differ from strain theory and cultural deviance (i.e., differential association) theory?
3. What are the four elements of the social bond? How does each one help to control a youth from engaging in delinquency?
4. What factors in American society might cause social bonds to be weaker in inner-city neighborhoods?

19. A General Theory of Crime

Michael R. Gottfredson and Travis Hirschi

Traditional sociological theories placed their primary focus on the social experiences of youths outside the family. For differential association theory, for example, most attention has been given to the role of peer groups in fostering delinquency; for strain theory, the lack of opportunities in school and in the labor market is considered as the source of crime-inducing frustration. In contrast, Gottfredson and Hirschi have redirected the attention of criminologists to the family and to what parents do, or do not do, during childhood.

In his social bond theory, Hirschi emphasized the importance of "indirect control"—how close attachment to parents allows the parents to have a "psychological presence" when youths are not under their surveillance. Gottfredson and Hirschi, however, argue that "direct control" is the key to effective parenting (see Wells and Rankin, 1988). Unless parents monitor their children closely and then take steps to punish misbehavior when it occurs—that is, unless they teach children that breaking rules has consequences—self-control will not be instilled. Instead, the child "will tend to be impulsive, insensitive, physical (as opposed to mental), risk-taking, short-sighted, and nonverbal" (Gottfredson and Hirschi, 1990: 90). As they endlessly succumb to life's temporary temptations, children burdened with low self-control will constantly engage in crime and other forms of deviance. They also will lack the persistence needed to succeed in school, in the workplace, *and in social relationships. In short, they will be consigned to a wayward life replete with brushes with the law and with personal and social failure.*

We should note that Gottfredson and Hirschi differentiate between "criminality," which is the propensity to offend, and "crime," which is an actual event in which a law is broken. They recognize that a propensity cannot be acted on unless the opportunity to do so exists. As a result, they see crime as a by product of people with low self-control, who have high criminogenic propensities, coming into contact with illegal opportunities. Still, given that most offenses are easy to commit and opportunities for crime are constantly available, over time people with low self-control inevitably will become deeply involved in criminal behavior. That is, self-control, not opportunities, will be the primary determinant of people's involvement in crime across their life course.

Similar to social bond theory, the core premise of Gottfredson and Hirschi's theory is easily identified and thus amenable to testing: the lower a person's self-control, the higher his or her involvement in criminal behavior and in acts analogous to crime. Not surprisingly, therefore, there is now a growing body of research assessing self-control theory (for just a few of many possible examples, see Benson and Moore, 1992; Evans et al., 1997; Grasmick et al., 1993; Sellers, 1999). In general, there is fairly consistent support for Gottfredson and Hirschi's theoretical predictions—a fact that

Reprinted from *A General Theory of Crime* by Michael R. Gottfredson and Travis Hirschi. Copyright © 1990 by the Board of Trustees of the Leland Stanford Junior University. With the permission of Stanford University Press, www.sup.org.

ensures that their self-control theory will remain an important theoretical perspective in the time ahead (Gottfredson, 2006). The consistent support for the perspective is most apparent in Pratt and Cullen's (2000) meta-analysis of the existing empirical research. They report that across studies testing Gottfredson and Hirschi's theory, low self-control "had an effect size that exceeded .20"—a finding that would "rank self-control as one of the strongest known correlates of crime" (Pratt and Cullen, 2000: 951–952).

The limits of self-control theory, however, should also be mentioned (see Goode, 2008). Thus, in empirical tests, low self-control cannot, as Gottfredson and Hirschi predict, explain away the effects on crime of other sociological factors, especially the effects of differential association/social learning variables (see, for example, Evans et al., 1997; Pratt and Cullen, 2000; Unnever et al., 2006). Perhaps more consequential, Gottfredson and Hirschi commit what Currie (1985: 185) calls the "fallacy of autonomy—the belief that what goes on inside the family can usefully be separated from the forces that affect it from the outside: the larger social context in which families are embedded for better or for worse." Thus, despite emphasizing the salience of parenting in crime causation, Gottfredson and Hirschi remain largely silent on the social forces that are transforming the American family and challenging the ability of parents to raise their children effectively.

References

Benson, Michael L. and Elizabeth Moore. 1992. "Are White-Collar and Common Offenders the Same?" *Journal of Research in Crime and Delinquency* 29: 251–272.

Currie, Elliott. 1985. *Confronting Crime: An American Challenge*. New York: Pantheon.

Evans, T. David, Francis T. Cullen, Velmer S. Burton, Jr., R. Gregory Dunaway, and Michael L. Benson. 1997. "The Social Consequences of Self-Control: Testing the General Theory of Crime." *Criminology* 35: 475–504.

Goode, Erich, ed. 2008. *Out of Control: Assessing the General Theory of Crime*. Stanford, CA: Stanford University Press.

Gottfredson, Michael R. 2006. "The Empirical Status of Control Theory in Criminology." In Francis T. Cullen, John Paul Wright, and Kristie R. Blevins (eds.), *Taking Stock: The Status of Criminological Theory—Advances in Criminological Theory*, Volume 15, pp. 77–100. New Brunswick, NJ: Transaction.

Gottfredson, Michael R. and Travis Hirschi. 1990. *A General Theory of Crime*. Stanford, CA: Stanford University Press.

Grasmick, Harold G., Charles R. Tittle, Robert J. Bursik, Jr., and Bruce K. Arneklev. 1993. "Testing the Core Empirical Implications of Gottfredson and Hirschi's General Theory of Crime." *Journal of Research in Crime and Delinquency* 30: 5–29.

Pratt, Travis C. and Francis T. Cullen. 2000. "The Empirical Status of Gottfredson and Hirschi's General Theory of Crime: A Meta-Analysis." *Criminology* 38: 931–964.

Sellers, Christine S. 1999. "Self-Control and Intimate Violence: An Examination of the Scope and Specification of the General Theory of Crime." *Criminology* 37: 375–404.

Unnever, James D., Francis T. Cullen, and Robert Agnew. 2006. "Why Is 'Bad' Parenting Criminogenic? Implications From Rival Theories." *Youth Violence and Juvenile Justice* 4: 3–33.

Wells, L. Edward and Joseph H. Rankin. 1988. "Direct Parental Controls and Delinquency." *Criminology* 26: 263–285.

Theories of crime lead naturally to interest in the propensities of individuals commiting criminal acts. These propensities are often labeled "criminality." In pure classical theory, people committing criminal acts had no special propensities. They merely followed the universal tendency to enhance their own pleasure. If they differed from noncriminals, it was with respect to their location in or comprehension of relevant sanction systems. For example, the individual cut off from the community will suffer less than others from the ostracism that follows crime; the individual unaware of the natural or legal consequences of criminal behavior cannot be controlled by these consequences to the degree that people aware of them are controlled; the atheist will not be as concerned as the believer about penalties to be exacted in a life beyond death. Classical theories on the whole, then, are today called *control theories*, theories emphasizing the prevention of crime through consequences painful to the individual.

Although, for policy purposes, classical theorists emphasized legal consequences, the importance to them of moral sanctions is so obvious that their theories might well be called underdeveloped *social control* theories. In fact, Bentham's list of the major restraining motives—motives acting to prevent mischievous acts—begins with goodwill, love of reputation, and the desire for amity (1970: 134–36). He goes on to say that fear of detection prevents crime in large part because of detection's consequences for "reputation, and the desire for amity" (p. 138). Put another way, in Bentham's view, the restraining power of legal sanctions in large part stems from their connection to social sanctions.

If crime is evidence of the weakness of social motives, it follows that criminals are less social than noncriminals and that the extent of their asociality may be determined by the nature and number of their crimes. Calculation of the extent of an individual's mischievousness is a complex affair, but in general the more mischievous or depraved the offenses, and the greater their number, the more mischievous or depraved the offender (Bentham 1970: 134–42). (Classical theorists thus had reason to be interested in the seriousness of the offense. The relevance of seriousness to current theories of crime is not so clear.)

Because classical or control theories infer that offenders are not restrained by social motives, it is common to think of them as emphasizing an asocial human nature. Actually, such theories make people only as asocial as their acts require. Pure or consistent control theories do not add criminality (i.e., personality concepts or attributes such as "aggressiveness" or "extraversion") to individuals beyond that found in their criminal acts. As a result, control theories are suspicious of images of an antisocial, psychopathic, or career offender, or of an offender whose motives to crime are somehow larger than those given in the crimes themselves. Indeed, control theories are compatible with the view that the balance of the total control structure favors conformity, even among offenders:

> For in every man, be his disposition ever so depraved, the social motives are those which . . . regulate and determine the general tenor of his life. . . . The general and standing bias of every man's nature is, therefore, towards that side to which the force of the social motives would determine him to adhere. This being the case, the force of the social motives tends continually to put an end to that of the dissocial ones; as, in natural bodies, the force of friction tends to put an end to that which is generated by impulse. Time, then, which wears away the force of the dissocial motives, adds to that of the social. (Bentham 1970: 141)

Positivism brought with it the idea that criminals differ from noncriminals in ways more radical than this, the idea that criminals carry within themselves properties peculiarly and positively conducive to crime. [Previously], we examined the efforts of the major disciplines to identify these properties. Being friendly to both the classical and positivist traditions, we expected to end up with a list of individual properties reliably identified by competent research as useful in the description of "criminality"—such properties as aggressiveness, body build, activity level, and intelligence. We further expected that we would be able to connect these individual-level correlates of criminality directly to the classical idea of crime. As our review progressed, however, we were forced to conclude that we had overestimated the success of positivism in establishing important differences between "criminals" and "noncriminals" beyond their tendency to commit criminal acts. Stable individual differences in the tendency to commit criminal acts were clearly evident, but many or even most of the other differences between offenders and non-offenders were not as clear or pronounced as our reading of the literature had led us to expect.

If individual differences in the tendency to commit criminal acts (within an overall tendency for crime to decline with age) are at least potentially explicable within classical theory by reference to the social location of individuals and their comprehension of how the world works, the fact remains that classical theory cannot shed much light on the positivistic finding (denied by most positivistic theories...) that these differences *remain reasonably stable with change in the social location of individuals and change in their knowledge of the operation of sanction systems.* This is the problem of self-control, the differential tendency of people to avoid criminal acts whatever the circumstances in which they find themselves. Since this difference among people has attracted a variety of names, we begin by arguing the merits of the concept of self-control.

Self-Control and Alternative Concepts

Our decision to ascribe stable individual differences in criminal behavior to self-control was made only after considering several alternatives, one of which (criminality) we had used before (Hirschi and Gottfredson 1986). A major consideration was consistency between the classical conception of crime and our conception of the criminal. It seemed unwise to try to integrate a choice theory of crime with a deterministic image of the offender, especially when such integration was unnecessary. In fact, the compatibility of the

classical view of crime and the idea that people differ in self-control is, in our view, remarkable. As we have seen, classical theory is a theory of social or external control, a theory based on the idea that the costs of crime depend on the individual's current location in or bond to society. What classical theory lacks is an explicit idea of self-control, the idea that people also differ in the extent to which they are vulnerable to the temptations of the moment. Combining the two ideas thus merely recognizes the simultaneous existence of social and individual restraints on behavior.

An obvious alternative is the concept of criminality. The disadvantages of that concept, however, are numerous. First, it connotes causation or determinism, a positive tendency to crime that is contrary to the classical model and, in our view, contrary to the facts. Whereas self-control suggests that people differ in the extent to which they are restrained from criminal acts, criminality suggests that people differ in the extent to which they are compelled to crime. The concept of self-control is thus consistent with the observation that criminals do not require or need crime, and the concept of criminality is inconsistent with this observation. By the same token, the idea of low self-control is compatible with the observation that criminal acts require no special capabilities, needs, or motivation; they are, in this sense, available to everyone. In contrast, the idea of criminality as a special tendency suggests that criminal acts require special people for their performance and enjoyment. Finally, lack of restraint or low self-control allows almost any deviant, criminal, exciting, or dangerous act; in contrast, the idea of criminality covers only a narrow portion of the apparently diverse acts engaged in by people at one end of the dimension we are now discussing.

The concept of conscience comes closer than criminality to self-control, and is harder to distinguish from it. Unfortunately, that concept has connotations of compulsion (to conformity) not, strictly speaking, consistent with a choice model (or with the operation of conscience). It does not seem to cover the behaviors analogous to crime that appear to be controlled by natural sanctions rather than social or moral sanctions, and in the end it typically refers to how people feel about their acts rather than to the likelihood that they will or will not commit them. Thus accidents and employment instability are not usually seen as produced by failures of conscience, and writers in the conscience tradition do not typically make the connection between moral and prudent behavior. Finally, conscience is used primarily to summarize the results of learning via negative reinforcement, and even those favorably disposed to its use leave little more to say about it (see, e.g., Eysneck 1977; Wilson and Herrnstein 1985).

We are now in position to describe the nature of self-control, the individual characteristic relevant to the commission of criminal acts. We assume that the nature of this characteristic can be derived directly from the nature of criminal acts. We thus infer from the nature of crime what people who refrain from criminal acts are like before they reach the age at which crime becomes a logical possibility. We then work back further to the factors producing their restraint, back to the causes of self-control. In our view, lack of self-control does not require crime and can be counteracted by situational conditions or other properties of the individual. At the same time, we suggest that high self-control effectively reduces the possibility of crime—that is, those possessing it will be substantially less likely at all periods of life to engage in criminal acts.

The Elements of Self-Control

Criminal acts provide *immediate* gratification of desires. A major characteristic of people with low self-control is therefore a tendency to respond to tangible stimuli in the immediate environment, to have a concrete "here and now" orientation. People with high self-control, in contrast, tend to defer gratification.

Criminal acts provide easy or simple gratification of desires. They provide money without

work, sex without courtship, revenge without court delays. People lacking self-control also tend to lack diligence, tenacity, or persistence in a course of action.

Criminal acts are *exciting, risky, or thrilling.* They involve stealth, danger, speed, agility, deception, or power. People lacking self-control therefore tend to be adventuresome, active, and physical. Those with high levels of self-control tend to be cautious, cognitive, and verbal.

Crimes provide *few or meager long-term benefits*. They are not equivalent to a job or a career. On the contrary, crimes interfere with long-term commitments to jobs, marriages, family, or friends. People with low self-control thus tend to have unstable marriages, friendships, and job profiles. They tend to be little interested in and unprepared for long-term occupation pursuits.

Crimes require *little skill or planning*. The cognitive requirements for most crimes are minimal. It follows that people lacking self-control need not possess or value cognitive or academic skills. The manual skills required for most crimes are minimal. It follows that people lacking self-control need not possess manual skills that require training or apprenticeship.

Crimes often result in *pain or discomfort for the victim*. Property is lost, bodies are injured, privacy is violated, trust is broken. It follows that people with low self-control tend to be self-centered, indifferent, or insensitive to the suffering and needs of others. It does not follow, however, that people with low self-control are routinely unkind or antisocial. On the contrary, they may discover the immediate and easy rewards of charm and generosity.

Recall that crime involves the pursuit of immediate pleasure. It follows that people lacking self-control will also tend to pursue immediate pleasures that are *not* criminal: They will tend to smoke, drink, use drugs, gamble, have children out of wedlock, and engage in illicit sex.

Crimes require the interaction of an offender with people or their property. It does not follow that people lacking self-control will tend to be gregarious or social. However, it does follow that, other things being equal, gregarious or social people are more likely to be involved in criminal acts.

The major benefit of many crimes is not pleasure but relief from momentary irritation. The irritation caused by a crying child is often the stimulus for physical abuse. That caused by a taunting stranger in a bar is often the stimulus for aggravated assault. It follows that people with low self-control tend to have minimal tolerance for frustration and little ability to respond to conflict through verbal rather than physical means.

Crimes involve the risk of violence and physical injury, of pain and suffering on the part of the offender. It does not follow that people with low self-control will tend to be tolerant of physical pain or to be indifferent to physical discomfort. It does follow that people tolerant of physical pain or indifferent to physical discomfort will be more likely to engage in criminal acts whatever their level of self-control.

The risk of criminal penalty for any given criminal act is small, but this depends in part on the circumstances of the offense. Thus, for example, not all joyrides by teenagers are equally likely to result in arrest. A car stolen from a neighbor and returned unharmed before he notices its absence is less likely to result in official notice than is a car stolen from a shopping center parking lot and abandoned at the convenience of the offender. Drinking alcohol stolen from parents and consumed in the family garage is less likely to receive official notice than drinking in the parking lot outside a concert hall. It follows that offenses differ in their validity as measures of self-control: those offenses with large risk of public awareness are better measures than those with little risk.

In sum, people who lack self-control will tend to be impulsive, insensitive, physical (as opposed to mental), risk-taking, short sighted, and nonverbal, and they will tend therefore to engage in criminal and analogous acts. Since these traits can be identified prior to the age of responsibility for crime, since there is considerable tendency for these traits to come together in the same people, and since the traits tend to persist through life, it seems reasonable to consider them as comprising a stable construct useful in the explanation of crime.

The Many Manifestations of Low Self-Control

Our image of the "offender" suggests that crime is not an automatic or necessary consequence of low self-control. It suggests that many noncriminal acts analogous to crime (such as accidents, smoking, and alcohol use) are also manifestations of low self-control. Our image therefore implies that no specific act, type of crime, or form of deviance is uniquely required by the absence of self-control.

Because both crime and analogous behaviors stem from low self-control (that is, both are manifestations of low self-control), they will all be engaged in at a relatively high rate by people with low self-control. Within the domain of crime, then, there will be much versatility among offenders in the criminal acts in which they engage.

Research on the versatility of deviant acts supports these predictions in the strongest possible way. The variety of manifestations of low self-control is immense. In spite of years of tireless research motivated by a belief in specialization, no credible evidence of specialization has been reported. In fact, the evidence of offender versatility is overwhelming (Hirschi 1969; Hindelang 1971; Wolfgang, Figlio, and Sellin 1972; Petersilia 1980; Hindelang, Hirschi, and Weis 1981; Rojek and Erickson 1982; Klein 1984).

By versatility we mean that offenders commit a wide variety of criminal acts, with no strong inclination to pursue a specific criminal act or a pattern of criminal acts to the exclusion of others. Most theories suggest that offenders tend to specialize, whereby such terms as robber, burglar, drug dealer, rapist, and murderer have predictive or descriptive import. In fact, some theories create offender specialization as part of their explanation of crime. For example, Cloward and Ohlin (1960) create distinctive subcultures of delinquency around particular forms of criminal behavior, identifying subcultures specializing in theft, violence, or drugs. In a related way, books are written about white-collar crime as though it were a clearly distinct specialty requiring a unique explanation. Research projects are undertaken for the study of drug use, or vandalism, or teen pregnancy (as though every study of delinquency were not a study of drug use and vandalism and teenage sexual behavior). Entire schools of criminology emerge to pursue patterning, sequencing, progression, escalation, onset, persistence, and desistance in the career of offenses or offenders. These efforts survive largely because their proponents fail to consider or acknowledge the clear evidence to the contrary. Other reasons for survival of such ideas may be found in the interest of politicians and members of the law enforcement community who see policy potential in criminal careers or "career criminals" (see, e.g., Blumstein et al. 1986).

Occasional reports of specialization seem to contradict this point, as do everyday observations of repetitive misbehavior by particular offenders. Some offenders rob the same store repeatedly over a period of years, or an offender commits several rapes over a (brief) period of time. Such offenders may be called "robbers" or "rapists." However, it should be noted that such labels are retrospective rather than predictive and that they typically ignore a large amount of delinquent or criminal behavior by the same offenders that is inconsistent with their alleged specialty. Thus, for example, the "rapist" will tend also to use drugs, to commit robberies and burglaries (often in concert with the rape), and to have a record for violent offenses other than rape. There is a perhaps natural tendency on the part of observers (and in official accounts) to focus on the most serious crimes in a series of events, but this tendency should not be confused with a tendency on the part of the offender to specialize in one kind of crime.

Recall that one of the defining features of crime is that it is simple and easy. Some apparent specialization will therefore occur because obvious opportunities for an easy score will tend to repeat themselves. An offender who lives next to a shopping area that is approached by pedestrians will have repeat opportunities for purse snatching, and this may show in his arrest record. But even here the specific "criminal career" will tend to quickly run its course and to be followed by offenses whose content and character is likewise determined by coincidence and opportunity (which is the reason why some form of theft is always the best bet about what a person is likely to do next).

The evidence that offenders are likely to engage in noncriminal acts psychologically or theoretically equivalent to crime is, because of the relatively high rates of these "noncriminal" acts, even easier to document. Thieves are likely to smoke, drink, and skip school at considerably higher rates than nonthieves. Offenders are considerably more likely than nonoffenders to be involved in most types of accidents, including household fires, auto crashes, and unwanted pregnancies. They are also considerably more likely to die at an early age (see, e.g. Robins 1966; Eysenck 1977; Gottfredson 1984).

Good research on drug use and abuse routinely reveals that the correlates of delinquency and drug use are the same. As Akers (1984) has noted,

> compared to the abstaining teenager, the drinking, smoking and drug-taking teen is much more likely to be getting into fights, stealing, hurting other people, and committing other delinquencies.

Akers goes on to say, "but the variation in the order in which they take up these things leaves little basis for proposing the causation of one by the other." In our view, the relation between drug use and delinquency is not a causal question. The correlates are the same because drug use and delinquency are both manifestations of an under-lying tendency to pursue short-term, immediate pleasure. This underlying tendency (i.e., lack of self-control) has many manifestations, as listed by Harrison Gough (1948):

> unconcern over the rights and privileges of others when recognizing them would interfere with personal satisfaction in any way; impulsive behavior, or apparent incongruity between the strength of the stimulus and the magnitude of the behavioral response; inability to form deep or persistent attachments to other persons or to identify in interpersonal relationships; poor judgment and planning in attaining defined goals; apparent lack of anxiety and distress over social maladjustment and unwillingness or inability to consider maladjustment qua mal-adjustment; a tendency to project blame onto others and to take no responsibility for failures; meaningless prevarication, often about trivial matters in situations where detection is inevi-table; almost complete lack of dependability . . . and willingness to assume responsibility; and, finally, emotional poverty. [p. 362]

This combination of characteristics has been revealed in the life histories of the subjects in the famous studies by Lee Robins. Robins is one of the few researchers to focus on the varieties of deviance and the way they tend to go together in the lives of those she designates as having "anti-social personalities." In her words:

> We refer to someone who fails to maintain close personal relationships with anyone else, [who] performs poorly on the job, who is involved in illegal behaviors (whether or not apprehended), who fails to support himself and his dependents without outside aid, and who is given to sudden changes of plan and loss of temper in response to what appear to others as minor frustrations. (1978: 255)

For 30 years Robins traced 524 children referred to a guidance clinic in St. Louis, Missouri, and she compared them to a control group matched on IQ, age, sex, and area of the city. She discovered that, in comparison to the control group, those people referred at an early age were more likely to be arrested as adults (for a wide variety of offences), were less likely to get married, were more likely to be divorced, were more likely to marry a spouse with a behavior problem, were less likely to have children (but if they had children were likely to have children were more likely to have children with behavior problems), were more likely to be unemployed, had considerably more frequent job changes, were more likely to be on welfare, had fewer contacts with relatives, had fewer friends, were substantially less likely to attend church, were less likely to serve in the armed forces and more likely to be dishonorably discharged if they did serve, were more likely to exhibit physical evidence of excessive alcohol use, and were more likely to be hospitalized for psychiatric problems (1966: 42–73).

Note that these outcomes are consistent with four general elements of our notion of low self-control: basic stability of individual differences over a long period of time; great variability in the kinds of criminal acts engaged in; conceptual or causal equivalence of criminal and noncriminal acts; and inability to predict the specific forms of deviance engaged in, whether criminal or non-criminal. In our view, the idea of an antisocial personality defined by certain behavioral conse-quences is too positivistic or deterministic, sug-gesting that the offender must do certain things given his antisocial personality. Thus we would say only that the subjects in question are *more likely* to commit criminal acts (as the data indicate they are). We do not make commission of criminal acts part of the definition of the individual with low self-control.

Be this as it may, Robins's retrospective research shows that predictions derived from a concept of antisocial personality are highly con-sistent with the results of prospective longitudinal and cross-sectional research: offenders do not specialize; they tend to be involved in accidents, illness, and death at higher rates than the general population; they tend to have difficulty persisting in a job regardless of the particular characteristics of the job (no job will turn out to be a good job); they have difficulty acquiring and retaining friends; and they have difficulty meeting the demands of long-term financial commitments (such as mortgages or car payments) and the demands of parenting.

Seen in this light, the "costs" of low self-control for the individual may far exceed the costs of his criminal acts. In fact, it appears that crime is often among the least serious consequences of a lack of self-control in terms of the quality of life of those lacking it.

The Causes of Self-Control

We know better what deficiencies in self-control lead to than where they come from. One thing is, however, clear: low self-control is not produced by training, tutelage, or socialization. As a matter of fact, all of the characteristics associated with low self-control tend to show themselves in the absence of nurturance, discipline, or training. Given the classical appreciation of the causes of human behavior, the implications of this fact are straightforward: the causes of low self-control are negative rather than positive; self-control is unlikely in the absence of effort, intended or unintended, to create it. (This assumption separates the present theory from most modern theories of crime, where the offender is automatically seen as a product of possessive forces, a creature of learning, particular pressures, or specific defect. We will return to this comparison once our theory has been fully explicated.)

At this point it would be easy to construct a theory of crime causation, according to which characteristics of potential offenders lead them ineluctably to the commission of criminal acts. Our task at this point would simply be to identify the likely sources of impulsiveness, intelligence, risk-taking, and the like. But to do so would be to follow the path that has proven so unproductive in the past, the path according to which criminals commit crimes irrespective of the characteristics of the setting or situation.

We can avoid this pitfall by recalling the elements inherent in the decision to commit a criminal act. The object of the offense is clearly pleasurable, and universally so. Engaging in the act, however, entails some risk of social, legal, and/or natural sanctions. Whereas the pleasure attained by the act is direct, obvious, and immediate, the pains risked by it are not obvious, or direct, and are in any event at greater remove from it. It follows that, though there will be little variability among people in their ability to see the pleasures of crime, there will be considerable variability in their ability to calculate potential pains. But the problem goes further than this: whereas the pleasures of crime are reasonably equally distributed over the population, this is not true for the pains. Everyone appreciates money; not everyone dreads parental anger or disappointment upon learning that the money was stolen.

So, the dimensions of self-control are, in our view, factors affecting calculation of the consequences of one's acts. The impulsive or short-sighted person fails to consider the negative or painful consequences of his acts; the insensitive person has fewer negative consequences to consider; the less intelligent person also has fewer negative consequences to consider (has less to lose).

No known social group, whether criminal or noncriminal, actively or purposefully attempts to reduce the self-control of its members. Social life is not enhanced by low self-control and its consequences. On the contrary, the exhibition of these tendencies undermines harmonious group relations and the ability to achieve collective ends. These facts explicitly deny that a tendency to crime is a product of socialization, culture, or positive learning of any sort.

The traits composing low self-control are also not conducive to the achievement of long-term individual goals. On the contrary, they impede educational and occupational achievement, destroy interpersonal relations, and undermine physical health and economic well-being. Such facts explicitly deny the notion that criminality is an alternative route to the goals otherwise obtainable through legitimate avenues. It follows that people who care about the interpersonal skill, educational and occupational achievement, and physical and economic well-being of those in their care will seek to rid them of these traits.

Two general sources of variation are immediately apparent in this scheme. The first is the variation among children in the degree to which they manifest such traits to begin with. The second is the variation among caretakers in the degree to which they recognize low self-control and its consequences and the degree to which they are willing and able to correct it. Obviously, therefore, even at this threshold level the sources of low self-control are complex.

There is good evidence that some of the traits predicting subsequent involvement in crime appear as early as they can be reliably measured, including low intelligence, high activity level, physical strength, and adventuresomeness (Glueck and Glueck 1950; West and Farrington 1973). The evidence suggests that the connection between these traits and commission of criminal acts ranges from weak to moderate. Obviously, we do not suggest that people are born criminals, inherit a gene for criminality, or anything of the sort. In fact, we explicitly deny such notions . . . . What we do suggest is that individual differences may have an impact on the prospects for effective socialization (or adequate control). Effective socialization is, however, always possible whatever the configuration of individual traits.

Other traits affecting crime appear later and seem to be largely products of ineffective or incomplete socialization. For example, differences in impulsivity and insensitivity become noticeable later in childhood when they are no longer common to all children. The ability and willingness to delay immediate gratification for some larger purpose may therefore be assumed to be a consequence of training. Much parental action is in fact geared toward suppression of impulsive behavior, toward making the child consider the long-range consequences of acts. Consistent sensitivity to the needs and feelings of others may also be assumed to be a consequence of training. Indeed, much parental behavior is directed toward teaching the child about the rights and feelings of others, and of how these rights and feelings ought to constrain the child's behavior. All of these points focus our attention on child-rearing.

Child-Rearing and Self-Control: The Family

The major "cause" of low self-control thus appears to be ineffective child-rearing. Put in positive terms, several conditions appear necessary to produce a socialized child. Perhaps the place to begin looking for these conditions is the research literature on the relation between family conditions and delinquency. This research (e.g., Glueck and Glueck 1950; McCord and McCord 1959) has examined the connection between many family factors and delinquency. It reports that discipline, supervision, and affection tend to be missing in the homes of delinquents, that the behavior of the parents is often "poor" (e.g., excessive drinking and poor supervision [Glueck and Glueck 1950: 110–11]), and that the parents of delinquents are unusually likely to have criminal records themselves. Indeed, according to Michael Rutter and Henri Giller, "of the parental characteristics associated with delinquency, criminality is the most striking and most consistent" (1984: 182).

Such information undermines the many explanations of crime that ignore the family, but in this form it does not represent much of an advance over the belief of the general public (and those who deal with offenders in the criminal justice system) that "defective upbringing" or "neglect" in the home is the primary cause of crime.

To put these standard research findings in perspective, we think it necessary to define the conditions necessary for adequate child-rearing to occur. The minimum conditions seem to be these: in order to teach the child self-control, someone must (1) monitor the child's behavior; (2) recognize deviant behavior when it occurs; and (3) punish such behavior. This seems simple and obvious enough. All that is required to activate the system is affection for *or* investment in the child. The person who cares for the child will watch his behavior, see him doing things he should not do, and correct him. The result may be a child more capable of delaying gratification, more sensitive to the interests and desires of others, more independent, more willing to accept restraints on his activity, and more unlikely to use force or violence to attain his ends.

When we seek the causes of low self-control, we ask where this system can go wrong. Obviously, parents do not prefer their children to be unsocialized in the terms described. We can therefore rule out in advance the possibility of positive socialization to unsocialized behavior (as cultural or subcultural deviance theories suggest). Still, the system can go wrong at any one of four places. First, the parents may not care for the child (in which case none of the other conditions would be met); second, the parents, even if they care, may not have the time or energy to monitor the child's behavior; third, the parents, even if they care *and* monitor, may not see anything wrong with the child's behavior; finally, even if everything else is in place, the parents may not have the inclination or the means to punish the child. So, what may appear at first glance to be nonproblematic turns out to be problematic indeed. Many things can go wrong. According to much research in crime and delinquency, in the homes of problem children many things have gone wrong: "Parents of stealers do not track ([they] do not interpret stealing . . . as 'deviant'); they do not punish; and they do not care" (Patterson 1980: 88–89; see also Glueck and Glueck 1950; McCord and McCord 1959; West and Farrington 1977).

Let us apply this scheme to some of the facts about the connection between child socialization and crime, beginning with the elements of the child-rearing model.

The Attachment of the Parent to the Child

Our model states that parental concern for the welfare or behavior of the child is a necessary condition for successful child-rearing. Because it is too often assumed that all parents are alike in their love for their children, the evidence directly on this point is not as good or extensive as it could be. However, what exists is clearly consistent with the model. Glueck and Glueck (1950: 125–28) report that, compared to the fathers of delinquents, fathers of nondelinquents were twice as likely to be warmly disposed toward their sons and one-fifth as likely to be hostile toward them. In the same sample, 28 percent of the mothers of delinquents were characterized as "indifferent or hostile" toward the child as compared to 4 percent of the mothers of nondelinquents. The evidence suggests that stepparents are especially unlikely to have feelings of affection toward their stepchildren (Burgess 1980), adding in contemporary society to the likelihood that children will be "reared" by people who do not especially care for them.

Parental Supervision

The connection between social control and self-control could not be more direct than in the case of parental supervision of the child. Such supervision presumably prevents criminal or analogous acts and at the same time trains the child to avoid them on his own. Consistent with this assumption, supervision tends to be a major predictor of delinquency, however supervision or delinquency is measured (Glueck and Glueck 1950; Hirschi 1969; West and Farrington 1977; Riley and Shaw 1985).

Our general theory in principle provides a method of separating supervision as external control from supervision as internal control. For one thing, offenses differ in the degree to which they can be prevented through monitoring; children at one age are monitored much more closely than children at other ages; girls are supervised more closely than boys. In some situations, monitoring is universal or nearly constant; in other situations monitoring for some offenses is virtually absent. In the present context, however, the concern is with the connection between supervision and self-control, a connection established by the stronger tendency of those poorly supervised when young to commit crimes as adults (McCord 1979).

Recognition of Deviant Behavior

In order for supervision to have an impact on self-control, the supervisor must perceive deviant behavior when it occurs. Remarkably, not all parents are adept at recognizing lack of self-control. Some parents allow the child to do pretty much as he pleases without interference. Extensive television-viewing is one modern example, as is the failure to require completion of homework, to prohibit smoking, to curtail the use of physical force, or to see to it that the child actually attends school. (As noted, truancy among second-graders presumably reflects on the adequacy of parental awareness of the child's misbehavior.) Again, the research is not as good as it should be, but evidence of "poor conduct standards" in the homes of delinquents is common.

Punishment of Deviant Acts

Control theories explicitly acknowledge the necessity of sanctions in preventing criminal behavior. They do not suggest that the major sanctions are legal or corporal. On the contrary, as we have seen, they suggest that disapproval by people one cares about is the most powerful of sanctions. Effective punishment by the parent or major caretaker therefore usually entails nothing more than explicit disapproval of unwanted behavior. The criticism of control theories that dwells on their alleged cruelty is therefore simply misguided or ill informed (see, e.g., Currie 1985).

Not all caretakers punish effectively. In fact, some are too harsh and some are too lenient (Glueck and Glueck 1950; McCord and McCord

1959; West and Farrington 1977; see generally Loeber and Stouthamer-Loeber 1986). Given our model, however, rewarding good behavior cannot compensate for failure to correct deviant behavior. (Recall that, in our view, deviant acts carry with them their own rewards . . . .)

Given the consistency of the child-rearing model with our general theory and with the research literature, it should be possible to use it to explain other family correlates of criminal and otherwise deviant behavior.

Parental Criminality

Our theory focuses on the connection between the self-control of the parent and the subsequent self-control of the child. There is good reason to expect, and the data confirm, that people lacking self-control do not socialize their children well. According to Donald West and David Farrington, "the fact that delinquency is transmitted from one generation to the next is indisputable" (1977: 109; see also Robins 1966). Of course our theory does not allow transmission of criminality, genetic or otherwise. However, it does allow us to predict that some people are more likely than others to fail to socialize their children and that this will be a consequence of their own inadequate socialization. The extent of this connection between parent and child socialization is revealed by the fact that in the West and Farrington study fewer than 5 percent of the families accounted for almost half of the criminal convictions in the entire sample. (In our view, this finding is more important for the theory of crime, and for public policy, than the much better-known finding of Wolfgang and his colleagues [1972] that something like 6 percent of *individual* offenders account for about half of all criminal acts.) In order to achieve such concentration of crime in a small number of families, it is necessary that the parents and the brothers and sisters of offenders also be unusually likely to commit criminal acts.

Why should the children of offenders be unusually vulnerable to crime? Recall that our theory assumes that criminality is not something the parents have to work to produce; on the contrary, it assumes that criminality is something they have to work to avoid. Consistent with this view, parents with criminal records do *not* encourage crime in their children and are in fact as disapproving of it as parents with no record of criminal involvement (West and Farrington 1977). Of course, not wanting criminal behavior in one's children and being upset when it occurs do not necessarily imply that great effort has been expended to prevent it. If criminal behavior is oriented toward short-term rewards, and if child-rearing is oriented toward long-term rewards, there is little reason to expect parents themselves lacking self-control to be particularly adept at instilling self-control in their children.

Consistent with this expectation, research consistently indicates that the supervision of delinquents in families where parents have criminal records tends to be "lax," "inadequate," or "poor." Punishment in these families also tends to be easy, short-term, and insensitive—that is, yelling and screaming, slapping and hitting, with threats that are not carried out.

Such facts do not, however, completely account for the concentration of criminality among some families. A major reason for this failure is probably that the most subtle element of child-rearing is not included in the analysis. This is the element of *recognition* of deviant behavior. According to Gerald Patterson (1980), many parents do not even recognize *criminal* behavior in their children, let alone the minor forms of deviance whose punishment is necessary for effective child-rearing. For example, when children steal outside the home, some parents discount reports that they have done so on the grounds that the charges are unproved and cannot therefore be used to justify punishment. By the same token, when children are suspended for misbehavior at school, some parents side with the child and blame the episode on prejudicial mistreatment by teachers. Obviously, parents who cannot see the misbehavior of their children are in no position to correct it, even if they are inclined to do so. . . .

Discussion Questions

1. What is low self-control? What are its main elements?
2. Give examples of acts that are "analogous" to crime? Why do Gottfredson and Hirschi believe that low self-control explains both crime and these analogous acts?
3. How does Gottfredson and Hirschi's self-control theory differ from Hirschi's earlier social bond theory?
4. What is the main reason that people have low self-control? In turn, based on Gottfredson and Hirschi's theory, what would be the best way to try to reduce crime?

SECTION 3

Rethinking Criminology

PART VII

Labeling, Interaction, and Crime: Societal
Reaction and the Creation of Criminals

PART VIII

Critical Criminology: Power, Peace, and Crime

PART IX

Feminist Theories: Gender, Power, and Crime

Labeling, Interaction, and Crime: Societal Reaction and the Creation of Criminals

Nearly all criminological theories use the *offender* as the starting point of their analysis. Vigorous debates subsequently ensue over whether the key cause of crime is found inside or outside the offender, and, in either case, there is the additional debate over which specific individual difference or which social experience trumps the others as the preeminent criminogenic factor. Still, these differences aside, there is consensus that the search for crime's etiology must begin by studying the people who break the law.

The distinctiveness of the "labeling" or "societal reaction" perspective, however, lies in its rejection of using the offender as the lynchpin of criminological analysis. Labeling theory proposes that we focus our attention not on the behavior of offenders but on the *behavior of those who label, react to, and otherwise seek to control offenders*. Labeling theory argues that it is these efforts at social control that ultmately trigger the processes that trap individuals in criminal career. Labeling or societal reaction thus has ironic and unanticipated effects; it creates the very thing it is intended to stop—it produces a self-fulfilling prophecy.

Creating Criminals: Secondary Deviance

Many early criminologists recognized that placing people in prisons—or "houses of corruption" as Shaw (1966 [1930]) called them—could

deepen involvement in crime. These insights on the effects of "labeling," however, were largely voiced in passing and were not integrated into the scholar's theory of criminal behavior. Frank Tannenbaum's (1938: 19–21) discussion of the "dramatization of evil" stands out as a noteworthy exception to this tendency to treat the effects of labeling as a subsidiary concern. For this reason, the roots of labeling theory are often traced to his work.

In *Crime and the Community*, Tannenbaum endorsed the view of the Chicago school that crime was not a manifestation of individual differences but learned as part of an "educational process" in the community. Youths were surrounded by criminal influences, including gangs and older offenders. Even so, a "decisive step in the education of the criminal" is being arrested and having his or her delinquent status held up for public scrutiny—that is, having one's evil "dramatized" (1938: 71). In his most famous passage, Tannenbaum asserted that "the process of making the criminal, therefore, is a process of tagging, defining, identifying, segregating, describing, emphasizing, making conscious and self-conscious; it becomes a way of stimulating, suggesting, emphasizing, and evoking the very traits that are complained of" (p. 20).

In setting forth this thesis, Tannenbaum anticipated many of the key ideas elaborated by later labeling theorists. He noted, for example, that once arrested and labeled a criminal, a youth is forced "into companionship with other children similarly defined," the result of which is that the youth is exposed to criminal "mores" and "has a new set of experiences that lead directly to a criminal career" (p. 20). Youngsters also begin to think differently about themselves. "In this entirely new world," observed Tannenbaum, "he is made conscious of himself as a different human being than he was before his arrest. He becomes classified as a thief, perhaps, and the entire world about him has suddenly become a different place for him and will remain different for the rest of his life" (p. 19). In the end, by labeling a juvenile with the official status of a delinquent, "the person becomes the thing he is described as being" (p. 20). The best policy in dealing with juveniles is "a refusal to dramatize the evil. The less said about it the better" (p. 20).

The idea that reacting to wayward conduct only makes it worse was conceptualized even more clearly by Edwin Lemert (Chapter 20 in this part). Writing in 1951, he introduced the concepts of "primary" and "secondary" deviance (see also Lemert, 1972). For Lemert, primary deviations occur for a wide range of reasons, some individual and some situational. These deviations are seen by individuals as peripheral to their identity and to the conventional social roles they typically perform on a daily basis. The inconsistency of deviating but not seeing this conduct as a reflection on one's identity creates tension that is "rationalized or otherwise dealt with as functions of a socially accepted role" (Lemert, 1951: 75). One might drink a great deal, but still see oneself as a college student, not a "drunk."

Secondary deviance occurs when the individual no longer dissociates from their deviation. Instead, the person's "life and identity are organized around the facts of deviance" (Lemert, 1972: 63). But what causes this qualitative shift from primary to secondary deviance? Lemert argued that the key factor prompting a person's life to coalesce around deviance is the "reactions of others." Typically, a gradual process unfolds in which a cycle of deviation and negative reactions from others is repeated and amplified. Continued deviations call forth increasingly stigmatizing reactions from others. In the course of this interaction, the person eventually accepts his or her "deviant social status" and makes "efforts at adjustment based on the associated role" (1951: 77). They see themselves as deviant, and make life choices that are constrained by and reaffirm their deviant status. "When a person begins to employ his deviant behavior or a role based upon it as a means of defense, attack, or adjustment to the overt and covert problems created by the consequent societal reaction to him," stated Lemert (1951: 76), "his deviation is secondary."

Thus, Lemert and Tannenbaum both proposed that when wayward people experience stigmatizing societal reactions, their world is transformed into one in which their criminal (or deviant) status defines their social existence and self-conception. The result is a deepening, not a reduction, of their criminality. Neither Lemert's nor Tannenbaum's insights, however, gained the sustained attention of their contemporaries. It was not until the mid-1960s, with the writings of Howard Becker (1963), Kai Erikson (1966), John Kitsuse (1964), Edwin Schur (1969), and others, that an identifiable school of criminology emerged that self-consciously referred to itself as "labeling" or "societal reaction" theory. In fact, it was at this time that the earlier works of Lemert and Tannenbaum were resurrected and redefined as falling within the tradition of labeling theory.

The Rise and Fall of Labeling Theory

Extending the work of Lemert and Tannenbaum, a group of scholars in the 1960s and early 1970s argued that societal reaction, not the offender, should be the centerpiece of criminological analysis. They focused on three issues that, in one way or another, challenged the assumptions traditionally held in the discipline.

First, criminologists usually define crime as "behavior that violates a criminal law." For labeling theorists, however, this definition takes the existing laws as a given rather than treating them as a social reality that has been "constructed." A systematic analysis of "societal reactions" questions existing reality and asks why certain behaviors are labeled as crime and others are not. It also asks why definitions of these behaviors can change over time.

Take, for example, the sexual assault of women that occurs on a date. Until recently, these assaults were not seen or treated as a "rape." This label was largely reserved for those victimizations in which a woman was raped by a stranger and visibly injured in the process of resisting the assault—the signs that a "real rape" had taken place (Estrich, 1987). The lengthy struggle of women's rights groups, however, challenged what should be considered a rape. The invention and growing acceptance of the concept of "date rape" redefined sexual assaults committed in intimate relationships. Coercion, not whether the victim and offender knew one another, was trumpeted as the criterion that should distinguish when the crime of rape has been committed. A new reality thus was constructed in which the legal category of rape took on expanded meaning and encompassed a wider range of victimizations.

Second, once labels or categories of crime have been invented, not everyone who "breaks the law" is detected and designated a "criminal." Being a "criminal," therefore, does not depend only on a person's actions but on how others react to that person. Various factors—legal and extralegal—affect whether a label is attached and, as a result, the person's public reputation is qualitatively altered.

Commenting on the concept of deviance—in words that just as well could be applied to the concept of crime—Howard Becker (1963) captured the thrust of the labeling theory argument that deviance is socially constructed rather than an invariant, objective reality. He began by noting that the traditional "sociological view I have just discussed defines deviance as the infraction of some agreed-upon rule." But "such an assumption seems to me to ignore the central fact about deviance: it is created by society." More specifically, "*social groups create deviance by making the rules whose infraction constitutes deviance*, and by applying those rules to particular people and labeling them as outsiders." In Becker's view, then, "deviance is *not* a quality of the act the person commits, but rather a consequence of the application by others of rules and sanctions to the 'offender.'" Labeling or societal reaction thus creates deviants. "The deviant is one to whom the label has successfully been applied; deviant behavior is behavior that people so label" (all quotes from Becker, 1963: 8–9; emphasis in original).

While these concerns illuminated the need to study the creation and application of labels, the third focus of labeling theory was on the *consequences* of being labeled and treated as a criminal. As noted, in a rejection of offender-based explanations of crime, labeling theorists argued that reacting to people as "criminals" initiated processes that had the self-fulfilling prophecy of making the person become a criminal—someone more deeply entrenched in a criminal career. They noted that once a person bore the label of a "criminal," it became a "master status"—the most salient public feature of that person. Being a "criminal" thus serves as the focal point of virtually every interaction, a defining designation that cannot be escaped.

Drawing on the sociological theory of symbolic interactionism, labeling theorists argued that a person's identity or self-conception is shaped by the messages other people deliver as to "who the person is." Although the process is not rigidly deterministic—identities can be resisted and can be manipulated (e.g., by putting "one's best foot forward")—the constant appraisal that a person is a "criminal" eventually takes its toll. Over time, those who have been labeled come to embrace the idea that they are, in fact, "criminals." This identity in turn makes choosing crime more likely, as people act consistently with their public and now privately held identity.

Labeling not only transforms a person's identity but also his or her social relationships. Although not often phrased this way, in essence scholars saw labeling as triggering the very conditions that competing theories linked to crime. Thus, once stigmatized as a "criminal," the person loses conventional social relationships (social bond theory), is forced to associate mainly with other criminals—whether in prison or on the streets (social learning theory), and as an "ex-offender" is denied opportunities for employment (strain theory). Engulfed by these criminogenic conditions, the labeled person is constrained to pursue a life in crime.

As the 1960s progressed, labeling theory's popularity grew to the point where it rivaled, if not surpassed, that of more traditional theoretical perspectives (Cole, 1975). As Hagan (1973) notes, part of labeling theory's appeal was that it was "interesting." Criminologists are attracted to ideas, says Hagan, that reverse a "conventionally assumed causal sequence" (1973: 456), which is precisely what labeling theory attempts. Thus, common sense would dictate that arresting, trying, imprisoning, and rehabilitating offenders would make crime less likely; after all, the manifest function of processing offenders through the criminal justice system is to reduce their recidivism and to make society safer. The unique twist to labeling theory was the claim that these very efforts to prevent crime actually cause crime.

But labeling theory was appealing for another reason: the theory, if correct, contained a stinging critique of state power as exercised by the criminal justice system. Recall that during the 1960s and early 1970s, the United States was greeted with revelation after revelation of the government abusing its power—from Civil Rights demonstrators being beaten, to inmates being gunned down at Attica, to students being shot at Kent State, to Viet Nam, to Watergate, and on and on. As trust in the state plummeted—especially on university campuses—a theory that blamed the government for causing more harm than good struck a chord of truth. Labeling theory, of course, did precisely this in arguing that the criminal justice system stigmatized offenders and ultimately trapped them in a criminal career. The obvious policy implication was to reduce state intervention into the lives of offenders (Schur, 1973). Most important, juveniles were to be diverted from the system altogether, and virtually all offenders were to be kept out of prison.

The long-term viability of labeling theory as a comprehensive explanation of crime, however, was undermined by its apparent empirical weakness (see, especially, Gove, 1980; compare with Cullen and Cullen, 1978). In its most extreme and interesting form, labeling theory proposed that societal reaction, especially by the criminal justice system, was the key factor in—indeed, a necessary and sufficient condition for—offenders becoming stabilized in a criminal career. But this claim is obviously false, as early critics realized (see, e.g., Mankoff, 1971). As life-course research reveals, stability of crime and deviance often emerges early in life before formal interventions have taken place (see, e.g., Moffitt, 1993 [Chapter 38]; Sampson and Laub, 1993).

On a broader level, labeling theory wishes to pretend that being raised in criminogenic conditions for 10, 15, or 20 years is largely inconsequential. The effects of these day-in and day-out experiences—such as having a dysfunctional family life, associating with delinquent friends, and failing at school—are said to pale in comparison to the effects, albeit over a more limited time, of being arrested and perhaps jailed. This assertion is not credible and cannot be sustained empirically.

Contemporary Labeling Theories

Chastened by withering critiques of labeling theory, criminologists moved on to other theoretical frameworks. Whereas they had once embraced the theory without any evidence of its validity (Hagan, 1973), criminologists now rejected labeling theory on the grounds that the perspective "had no empirical support." More recently, however, a revisionist position has emerged which suggests that it may be premature to dismiss societal reaction as irrelevant to crime causation (Paternoster and Iovanni, 1989). Although the evidence is not consistent (Akers and Sellers, 2008), several quality longitudinal studies have shown that contact with the criminal justice system increases recidivism (Farrington, 1977; Hagan and Palloni, 1990; Palamara et al., 1986; Sampson and Laub, 1993).

Of particuar concern, over 2.3 million offenders—one in every 99.1 adults in the United States—are behind bars on any given day. For African American men ages 20 to 34, the statistics are particularly disquieting: one in nine is incarcerated (Warren, 2008). Moreover, it is estimated that over 630,000 federal and state inmates return to society annually (Travis, 2005). During the past decade, there has been a much-belated but growing recognition that successful prisoner reentry is a pressing problem (Petersilia, 2003). Imprisonment is known to disrupt family relationships and to decrease job prospects by stigmatizing people as "ex-offenders" (Pager, 2007; Pattillo et al., 2004). Programs to help those reentering the community assume productive prosocial roles are in short supply. Not surprisingly, recidivism rates among returnees are high. In fact, the existing empirical evidence suggests that placing offenders in prison does little to deter future criminality and, in fact, may be criminogenic (Nagin et al., 2009). That is, imprisonment may have labeling effects, creating rather than preventing criminal involvement (see also Cullen and Jonson, forthcoming). In this context, understanding the impact of societal reaction on individuals takes on renewed criminological significance.

Further, three theoretical developments have emerged that may help to revitalize interest in studying the effects of societal reaction: Ross Matsueda's focus on informal reactions, John Braithwaite's focus on reintegrative shaming, and Lawrence Sherman's focus on defiance.

First, within criminology, labeling theory had usually been interpreted as contending that the application of *formal* criminal sanctions was the key societal reaction that fostered career criminality. This position made sense, since criminal sanctions involved a person's official and public designation as a "criminal" and could involve a lengthy stay behind bars. Less attention was paid, however, to the potential role played by *informal* sanctions—that is, the societal reactions of parents, friends, neighbors, and the like. There is at least beginning evidence that, under some circumstances, informal societal reactions can worsen wayward conduct (see, e.g., Triplett and Jarjoura, 1994; Ward and Tittle, 1993; see also Wells and Rankin, 1988).

Ross Matsueda provides the most sophisticated theoretical statement of the potential criminogenic effects of informal labeling. Drawing on symbolic interactionism, Matsueda argues that a key proximate cause of delinquent behavior is the "reflected appraisals of others"—that is, a youth's perception that other people—especially those "significant" to the youngster (e.g., parents)— view him or her as a "delinquent." In part, this reflected appraisal is influenced by the youth's own behavior: juveniles who engage in delinquency are more likely to believe that others see them as "troublemakers." Reflected appraisals also are influenced, however, by the "actual appraisals of others." Thus, when youngsters are appraised or labeled as a delinquent (e.g., by their parents), they perceive that others see them as wayward and act upon this conception of themselves. In short, labeling creates a delinquent "self," which in turn prompts illegal conduct. It is noteworthy that Matsueda has marshaled evidence supporting this causal sequence (Bartusch and Matsueda, 1996; Matsueda, 1992; see also Heimer and Matsueda, 1994).

Second, another avenue for the revitalization of labeling theory starts with the observation that the effects of societal reaction are contingent on a range of factors. Traditional statements of labeling theory assumed that societal reaction virtually always increases crime and deviance. This thesis, however, is clearly false. Research from corrections, for example, shows that while punitive interventions have no effect or increase recidivism, rehabilitation programs reduce future criminality (Andrews and Bonta, 2003; Cullen, 2002; Cullen and Gendreau, 2000; Cullen and Jonson, forthcoming).

John Braithwaite (1989 [Chapter 21]) has developed the most noteworthy attempt to specify when societal reaction, whether formal or informal, results in more or less criminality (see also Braithwaite et al., 2006). "The first step to productive theorizing about crime is to think about the contention that labeling offenders makes things worse. The contention," observes Braithwaite (1989: 12), "is both right and wrong." When a criminal act is detected, attempts usually are made to "shame" the person, a concept used to encompass "all social processes of expressing disapproval which have the intention or effect of invoking remorse in the person being shamed and/or condemnation by others who become aware of the shaming" (p. 100). Whether such shaming "makes things worse," however, depends on the *quality* of the societal reaction.

In his central proposition, Braithwaite argues, consistent with labeling theory, that *stigmatizing* shaming increases crime. In this instance, "no effort is made to reconcile the offender with the community" (p. 101). Instead, the offender is made into an outcast and is cut off from conventional relationships. As a result, the offender joins criminal subcultures, where his or her criminality is reinforced and opportunities to commit illegal acts are plentiful.

Unlike labeling theory, however, Braithwaite recognizes that another form of societal reaction exists: *reintegrative* shaming, a process in which shaming "is followed by efforts to reintegrate the offender back into the community of law-abiding or respectable citizens through words or gestures of forgiveness or ceremonies to decertify the offender as deviant" (2002: 100–101). This type of shaming sends a message to the individual and to the larger community that the offender's behavior is wrong and should not be repeated. At the same time, the reintegrative aspect of the reaction communicates that the offender as a person is not beyond redemption. Accepting the repentant offender back into the community reinforces the offender's conventional social bonds and keeps him or her from seeking out the company of other criminals. The result is that reintegrative shaming strengthens prosocial influences in the offender's life and thus reduces recidivism.

Third, similar to Braithwaite, Lawrence Sherman (1993 [Chapter 22 in this part]) observes that, depending on the circumstances, interventions into the lives of offenders can have diverse effects. Thus, Sherman (1993: 445) contends that "legal punishment either reduces, increases, or has no effect on future crimes, depending on the type of offenders, offenses, social settings, and levels of analysis." Sherman proposes that in the face of criminal penalties, "defiance" and thus greater crime are likely to result when offenders are poorly bonded to society and define the sanctions against them as stigmatizing and unfair. In contrast, recidivism is less likely when offenders have close ties to conventional society (e.g., employed) and see the sanctions against them as deserved and fairly applied.

Sherman (2000) also understands, however, that the objective quality of the sanction is a salient consideration in whether defiant criminality is, or is not, produced by criminal justice interventions. Again, offenders may react very differently to the same sanction depending on their social bonds and sensitivity to injustice (i.e., the tendency to see attempts to control their misconduct as "disrespecting" them). Nonetheless, Sherman's theory suggests that the quality of the behavior of police, court, and correctional officials also plays a role in precipitating or depressing the likelihood of defiance. If, in interacting with offenders, these officials act with respect, with procedural fairness, and integratively, defiance is less likely to occur than if they act with disrespect, arbitrarily, and harshly. In short, defiance is the result of a complex interaction between the objective quality of the sanction being applied and how this sanction is interpreted by offenders (again, depending on their social bonds and social attitudes).

Policy Implications

The ideas of Sherman (1993, 2000) and of Braithwaite (1989) have important policy implications. Traditionally, the mantra of labeling theory was "radical non-intervention" (Schur, 1973)—to do whatever possible to limit criminal justice interventions into the lives of offenders. This perspective assumed that, due to powerful labeling effects, such legal interventions were *uniformly* harmful. Sherman and Braithwaite, however, reject this view. Although they would agree that many sanctions *as they are now being applied* are criminogenic, they believe that the potential exists to create sanctions that do more good than harm (see also Cullen, 2002; Cullen and Gendreau, 2000). The need to do so also is seemingly indisputable. Thus, with over 7 million people either incarcerated or under probation and parole supervision on any given day, talk of non-intervention is farfetched. Either those in the correctional population continue to receive traditional penalties, or an effort is made to construct more effective and humane criminal justice sanctions.

Along with a number of other scholars and activists (Braithwaite, 2002), Sherman and Braithwaite have endorsed a reform known as "restorative justice." In brief, this strategy seeks to dislodge the state from its traditional role as an adversary that exacts justice by prosecuting and inflicting pain on law-breakers. Instead, under restorative justice, the state functions as an arbiter or partner who works with the victim and the offender to reduce the harm associated with the criminal act that has been committed. This goal is achieved through a sanctioning process that "restores" victims, the community, and the offender.

A key component of this restorative strategy is a "conference" attended by the victim and offender, their family members, other community members with a stake in the proceedings, and some type of mediator. When faced with the victim, the injury caused, and the shamefulness of their conduct, offenders may be moved to apologize for the crimes they have perpetrated. In any event, the conferences reach a consensus on a plan that will enable offenders to restore the harm they have caused (e.g., by making restitution to the victim, through community service). Furthermore, these agreements reject incarceration, believing that the prison experience is stigmatizing, harm producing, and unlikely to be restorative. Rather, in exchange for working to restore their harms, offenders remain in the community where they receive support to reintegrate them into conventional social roles (e.g., help securing employment, mentoring, tutoring to achieve higher grades).

Although research on existing programs is still in its beginning stages and skeptics remain (Levrant et al., 1999), there is mounting evidence that restorative justice increases victim satisfaction and decreases recidivism (Braithwaite, 2002; McGarrell et al., 2000; Menkel-Medow, 2007). The key empirical and policy issue will be how much recidivism is reduced by restorative justice programs, especially among high-risk, serious, chronic offenders who pose the greatest threat to public safety and who typically are sentenced to lengthy prison terms. If Sherman's and Braithwaite's theories have high explanatory power, then these programs' effects could be substantial. In this case, the programs would be targeting the key underlying source of reoffending: coercive, stigmatizing criminal justice sanctions. If their theories have identified only one among many factors that cause crime, then the effects of restorative justice interventions, which do not focus on these other predictors of recidivism, are likely to be modest (Levrant et al., 1999; see, more generally, Andrews and Bonta, 2003; Cullen and Gendreau, 2000).

In closing, at this point in its development, it is unlikely that labeling theory—even in its most sophisticated forms, such as the perspectives of Matsueda, Braithwaite, and Sherman—will provide a complete explanation of criminal behavior. Frequently, it would seem, societal reaction is the result, rather than the cause, of lawbreaking. A large omission in labeling theory is that it places little focus on the early years of life during which the conduct problems that underlie much stable serious criminality first emerge.

Labeling theorists also often pay insufficient attention to how, independent of societal reaction, structural inequality and the concentration of disadvantage in inner-city communities might affect behavior. Nonetheless, scholars working in this tradition have identified a factor—stigmatizing, rejecting, nasty societal reactions—that rarely makes matters better and more often serves only to solidify an offender's commitment to a criminal career. It would be unwise, therefore, for criminologists to assume that "labeling has no effects," and more prudent for them to continue to specify the conditions under which societal reaction pushes offenders into, rather than out of, a life in crime.

References

Akers, Ronald L. and Christine S. Sellers. 2008. *Criminological Theories: Introduction, Evaluation, and Application*, 5th edition. Los Angeles: Roxbury.

Andrews, D. A. and James Bonta. 2003. *The Psychology of Criminal Conduct*, 3rd edition. Cincinnati: Anderson.

Bartusch, Dawn Jeglum and Ross L. Matsueda. 1996. "Gender, Reflected Appraisals, and Labeling: A Cross-Group Test of an Interactionist Theory of Delinquency." *Social Forces* 75: 145–177.

Becker, Howard S. 1963. *Outsiders: Studies in the Sociology of Deviance*. New York: The Free Press.

Braithwaite, John. 1989. *Crime, Shame and Reintegration*. Cambridge, UK: Cambridge University Press.

——. 2002. *Restorative Justice and Responsive Regulation*. New York: Oxford University Press.

Braithwaite, John, Eliza Ahmed, and Valerie Braithwaite. 2006. "Shame, Restorative Justice, and Crime." In Francis T. Cullen, John Paul Wright, and Kristie R. Blevins (eds.), *Taking Stock: The Status of Criminological Theory—Advances in Criminological Theory*, Volume 15, pp. 397–417. New Brunswick, NJ: Transaction.

Cole, Stephen. 1975. "The Growth of Scientific Knowledge: Theories of Deviance as a Case Study." In Lewis A. Coser (ed.), *The Idea of Social Structure: Papers in Honor of Robert K. Merton*, pp. 175–220. New York: Harcourt Brace Jovanovich.

Cullen, Francis T. 2002. "Rehabilitation and Treatment Programs." In James Q. Wilson and Joan Petersilia (eds.), *Crime: Public Policies for Crime Control*, pp. 253–289. Oakland, CA: ICS Press.

Cullen, Francis T. and John B. Cullen. 1978. "Labeling Theory and the Empty Castle Phenomenon." *Western Sociological Review* 9: 28–38.

Cullen, Francis T. and Paul Gendreau. 2000. "Assessing Correctional Rehabilitation: Policy, Practice, and Prospects." In Julie Horney (ed.), *Criminal Justice 2000: Volume 3—Policies, Processes, and Decisions of the Criminal Justice System*, pp. 109–175. Washington, DC: U.S. Department of Justice, National Institute of Justice.

Cullen, Francis T. and Cheryl Lero Jonson. Forthcoming. "Labeling Theory and Correctional Rehabilitation: Beyond Unanticipated Consequences." In David P. Farrington and Joseph Murray (eds.), *Empirical Tests of Labeling Theory: Advances in Criminological Theory*, Volume 17. New Brunswick, NJ: Transaction Publishers.

Erikson, Kai T. 1966. *Wayward Puritans: A Study in the Sociology of Deviance.* New York: John Wiley.

Estrich, Susan. 1987. *Real Rape.* Cambridge, MA: Harvard University Press.

Farrington, David P. 1977. "The Effects of Public Labeling." *British Journal of Criminology* 17: 112–125.

Gove, Walter R., ed. 1980. *The Labelling of Deviance,* 2nd edition. Beverly Hills, CA: Sage.

Hagan, John. 1973. "Labelling and Deviance: A Case Study in the 'Sociology of the Interesting.'" *Social Problems* 20: 447–458.

Hagan, John and Alberto Palloni. 1990. "The Social Reproduction of a Criminal Class in Working-Class London, Circa 1950–1980." *American Journal of Sociology* 96: 265–299.

Heimer, Karen and Ross L. Matsueda. 1994. "Role-Taking, Role Commitment, and Delinquency: A Theory of Differential Social Control." *American Sociological Review* 59: 365–390.

Kitsuse, John I. 1964. "Societal Reaction to Deviant Behavior: Problems of Theory and Method." In Howard S. Becker (ed.), *The Other Side,* pp. 87–102. New York: The Free Press.

Lemert, Edwin M. 1951. *Social Pathology: A Systematic Approach to the Theory of Sociopathic Behavior.* New York: McGraw-Hill.

——. 1972. *Human Deviance, Social Problems, and Social Control,* 2nd edition. Englewood Cliffs, NJ: Prentice-Hall.

Levrant, Sharon, Francis T. Cullen, Betsy Fulton, and John F. Wozniak. 1999. "Reconsidering Restorative Justice: The Corruption of Benevolence Revisited?" *Crime and Delinquency* 45: 3–27.

Mankoff, Milton. 1971. "Societal Reaction and Career Deviance: A Critical Analysis." *Sociological Quarterly* 12: 204–218.

Matsueda, Ross L. 1992. "Reflected Appraisals, Parental Labeling, and Delinquency: Specifying a Symbolic Interactionist Theory." *American Journal of Sociology* 6: 1577–1611.

McGarrell, Edmund F., Kathleen Olivares, Kay Crawford, and Natalie Kroovand. 2000. *Returning Justice to the Community: The Indianapolis Juvenile Restorative Justice Experiment.* Indianapolis: Hudson Institute, Crime Control Policy Center.

Menkel-Medow, Carrie. 2007. "Restorative Justice: What Is It and Does It Work?" *Annual Review of Law and Social Science* 3: 161–187.

Moffitt, Terrie E. 1993. "Adolescence-Limited and Life-Course-Persistent Antisocial Behavior: A Developmental Taxonomy." *Psychological Review* 100: 674–701.

Nagin, Daniel S., Francis T. Cullen, and Cheryl Lero Jonson. 2009. "Imprisonment and Reoffending." In Michael Tonry (ed.), *Crime and Justice: A Review of Research,* Volume 38, pp. 115–200. Chicago: University of Chicago Press.

Pager, Devah. 2007. *Marked: Race, Crime, and Finding Work in an Era of Mass Incarceration.* Chicago: University of Chicago Press.

Palamara, Frances, Francis T. Cullen, and Joanne C. Gersten. 1986. "The Effect of Police and Mental Health Intervention on Juvenile Deviance: Specifying Contingencies in the Impact of Formal Reaction." *Journal of Health and Social Behavior* 27: 90–105.

Paternoster, Raymond and LeeAnn Iovanni. 1989. "The Labeling Perspective and Delinquency: An Elaboration of the Theory and an Assessment of the Evidence." *Justice Quarterly* 6: 359–394.

Pattillo, Mary, David Weiman, and Bruce Western, eds. 2004. *Imprisoning America: The Social Effects of Mass Incarceration.* New York: Russell Sage Foundation.

Petersilia, Joan. 2003. *When Prisoners Come Home: Parole and Prisoner Reentry.* New York: Oxford University Press.

Sampson, Robert J. and John H. Laub. 1993. *Crime in the Making: Pathways and Turning Points Through Life.* Cambridge, MA: Harvard University Press.

Schur, Edwin M. 1969. "Reactions to Deviance: A Critical Assessment." *American Journal of Sociology* 75: 309–322.

——. 1973. *Radical Non-Intervention: Rethinking the Delinquency Problem.* Englewood Cliffs, NJ: Prentice-Hall.

Shaw, Clifford R. 1966 [originally published in 1930]. *The Jack-Roller: A Delinquent Boy's Own Story*. Chicago: University of Chicago Press.

Sherman, Lawrence W. 1993. "Defiance, Deterrence, and Irrelevance: A Theory of the Criminal Sanction." *Journal of Research in Crime and Delinquency* 30: 445–473.

——. 2000 (February 24). *The Defiant Imagination: Consilience and the Science of Sanctions*. The Albert M. Greefield Chair Inaugural Lecture delivered at the University of Pennsylvania, Philadelphia.

Tannenbaum, Frank. 1938. *Crime and the Community*. New York: Columbia University Press.

Travis, Jeremy. 2005. *But They All Come Back: Facing the Challenges of Prisoner Reentry*. Washington, DC: Urban Institute Press.

Triplett, Ruth A. and G. Roger Jarjoura. 1994. "Theoretical and Empirical Specification of a Model of Informal Labeling." *Journal of Quantitative Criminology* 10: 241–276.

Ward, David A. and Charles R. Tittle. 1993. "Deterrence or Labeling: The Effects of Informal Sanctions." *Deviant Behavior* 14: 43–64.

Warren, Jenifer. 2008. *One in 100: Behind Bars in America*. Washington, DC: Pew Charitable Trusts.

Wells, L. Edward and Joseph H. Rankin. 1988. "Direct Parental Controls and Delinquency." *Criminology* 26: 263–285.

20. Primary and Secondary Deviance

Edwin M. Lemert

Although Lemert's (1951) Social Pathology *was over 450 pages long, it was his short discussion of primary and secondary deviance that, ironically, proved to be the lasting contribution of this volume. Not surprisingly, then, Lemert eventually addressed these concepts in considerably more detail in a later work,* Human Deviance, Social Problems, and Social Control *(1972). In the process, Lemert both advanced and criticized labeling theory.*

Lemert realized that in cruder versions of labeling theory, people were portrayed as innocent victims who, unfairly labeled by others, are driven in a very deterministic way into a life in crime. For Lemert, however, becoming firmly rooted in crime or deviance was not a random occurrence in which the labeled person played no role. Instead, Lemert envisioned an interactionist process in which individuals deviated, were sanctioned by others, made choices that further embedded them in deviance, experienced more reactions from others, and eventually came to accept and act consistently with their public designation as a "deviant."

In Lemert's (1972: 62) framework, primary deviance "is polygenic, arising out of a variety of social, cultural, psychological, and psychological, factors." This kind of waywardness "has only marginal implications for the status and psychic structure of the person concerned" (p. 62). Deviations have more profound impacts on people's lives, however, when they inspire societal reactions. As

people are stigmatized, punished, segregated, and controlled, the "general effect is to differentiate the symbolic and interactional environment to which the person responds, so that early or adult socialization is categorically changed" (p. 63). They now come to be defined differently, which in turn affects their identity or conceptions of themselves and narrows their ability to choose conventional over wayward paths. Their "life and identity are organized around the facts of deviance," a reality that makes continued deviation likely (p. 63). Lemert calls their deviance "secondary," because this conduct is not generated by the original causes of primary deviance but rather falls into a "special class of socially defined responses which people make to problems created by the societal reaction to their deviance" (p. 63).

The distinction between primary and secondary deviance is conceptually appealing, but Lemert's assertion that they have different causes is problematic. Similar to other labeling theory arguments, a key issue is whether societal reaction is in fact required to create offenders who are deeply embedded—both psychologically and behaviorally—in a criminal lifestyle. Current criminological theory and research would suggest that stable involvement in crime is rooted more fully in individual differences and in family, school, and community life (see, e.g., Gottfredson and Hirschi, 1990 [Chapter 19]; Moffitt, 1993 [Chapter 38]; Sampson and Laub, 1993). Still, societal reaction

Reprinted from Edwin M. Lemert, "Primary and Secondary Deviance" in *Social Pathology*. Copyright © 1952 by The McGraw-Hill Companies. Reprinted by permission of The McGraw-Hill Companies.

is not inconsequential. While it may not be the main source of persistent criminality, societal reaction can reinforce a criminal lifestyle and make desistance from crime more difficult.

References

Gottfredson, Michael R. and Travis Hirschi. 1990. *A General Theory of Crime.* Stanford, CA: Stanford University Press.

Lemert, Edwin M. 1951. *Social Pathology: A Systematic Approach to the Theory of Sociopathic Behavior.* New York: McGraw-Hill.

——. 1972. *Human Deviance, Social Problems, and Social Control*, 2nd edition. Englewood Cliffs, NJ: Prentice-Hall.

Moffitt, Terrie. 1993. "Adolescence-Limited and Life-Course-Persistent Antisocial Behavior: A Developmental Taxonomy." *Psychological Review* 100: 674–701.

Sampson, Robert J. and John H. Laub. 1993. *Crime in the Making: Pathways and Turning Points Through Life.* Cambridge, MA: Harvard University Press.

Types of Deviation

There has been an embarrassingly large number of theories, often without any relationship to a general theory, advanced to account for various specific pathologies in human behavior. For certain types of pathology, such as alcoholism, crime, or stuttering, there are almost as many theories as there are writers on these subjects. This has been occasioned in no small way by the preoccupation with the origins of pathological behavior and by the fallacy of confusing *original* causes with *effective* causes. All such theories have elements of truth, and the divergent viewpoints they contain can be reconciled with the general theory here if it is granted that original causes or antecedents of deviant behaviors are many and diversified. This holds especially for the psychological process leading to similar pathological behavior, but it also holds for the situational concomitants of the intitial aberrant conduct. A person may come to use excessive alcohol not only for a wide variety of subjective reasons but also because of diversified situational influences, such as the death of a loved one, business failure, or participating in some sort of organized group activity calling for heavy drinking of liquor. Whatever the original reasons for violating the norms of the community, they are important only for certain research purposes, such as assessing the extent of the "social problem" at a given time or determining the requirements for a rational program of social control. From a narrower sociological viewpoint the deviations are not significant until they are organized subjectively and transformed into active roles and become the social criteria for assigning status. The deviant individuals must react symbolically to their own behavior aberrations and fix them in their sociopsychological patterns. The deviations remain primary deviations or symptomatic and situational as long as they are rationalized or otherwise dealt with as functions of a socially acceptable role. Under such conditions normal and pathological behaviors remain strange and somewhat tensional bedfellows in the same person. Undeniably a vast amount of such segmental and partially integrated pathological behavior exists in our society and has impressed many writers in the field of social pathology.

Just how far and for how long a person may go in dissociating his sociopathic tendencies so that they are merely troublesome adjuncts of normally conceived roles is not known. Perhaps it depends upon the number of alternative definitions of the same overt behavior that he can develop; perhaps certain physiological factors (limits) are also involved. However, if the deviant acts are repetitive and have a high visibility, and if there is a severe societal reaction, which, through a process of identification is incorporated as part of the "me" of the individual, the probability is greatly increased that the integration of existing roles will be disrupted and that reorganization based upon a new role or roles will occur. (The "me" in this context is simply the subjective aspect of the societal reaction.) Reorganization may be the adoption of another normal role in which the tendencies previously defined as "pathological" are given a more acceptable social expression. The other general possibility is the assumption of a deviant role, if such exists; or, more rarely, the person may organize an aberrant sect or group in which he creates a special role of his own. *When a person begins to employ his deviant behavior or a role based upon it as a means of defense, attack, or adjustment to the overt and covert problems created by the consequent societal reaction to him, his deviation is secondary.* Objective evidences of this change will be found in the symbolic appurtenances of the new role, in clothes, speech, posture, and mannerisms, which in some cases heighten social visibility, and which in some cases serve as symbolic cues to professionalization.

Role Conceptions of the Individual Must Be Reinforced by Reactions of Others

It is seldom that one deviant act will provoke a sufficiently strong societal reaction to bring about secondary deviation, unless in the process of introjection the individual imputes or projects meanings into the social situation which are not present. In this case anticipatory fears are involved. For example, in a culture where a child is taught sharp distinctions between "good" women and "bad" women, a single act of questionable morality might conceivably have a profound meaning for the girl so indulging. However, in the absence of reactions by the person's family, neighbors, or the larger community, reinforcing the tentative "bad-girl" self-definition, it is questionable whether a transition to secondary deviation would take place. It is also doubtful whether a temporary exposure to a severe punitive reaction by the community will lead a person to identify himself with a pathological role, unless, as we have said, the experience is highly traumatic. Most frequently there is a progressive reciprocal relationship between the deviation of the individual and the societal reaction, with a compounding of the societal reaction out of the minute accretions in the deviant behavior, until a point is reached where ingrouping and outgrouping between society and the deviant is manifest. At this point a stigmatizing of the deviant occurs in the form of name calling, labeling, or stereotyping.

The sequence of interaction leading to secondary deviation is roughly as follows: (1) primary deviation; (2) social penalties; (3) further primary deviation; (4) stronger penalties and rejections; (5) further deviation, perhaps with hostilities and resentment beginning to focus upon those doing the penalizing; (6) crisis reached in the tolerance quotient, expressed in formal action by the community stigmatizing of the deviant; (7) strengthening of the deviant conduct as a reaction to the stigmatizing and penalties; (8) ultimate acceptance of deviant social status and efforts at adjustment on the basis of the associated role.

As an illustration of this sequence the behavior of an errant schoolboy can be cited. For one reason or another, let us say excessive energy, the schoolboy engages in a classroom prank. He is penalized for it by the teacher. Later, due to clumsiness, he creates another disturbance and again he is reprimanded. Then, as sometimes happens, the boy is blamed for something he did not do. When the teacher uses the tag "bad boy" or "mischief maker" or other invidious terms, hostility and resentment are excited in the boy, and he may feel that he is blocked in playing the role expected of him. Thereafter, there may be a strong temptation to assume his role in the class as defined by the teacher, particularly when he discovers that there are rewards as well as penalties deriving from such a role. There is, of course, no implication here that such boys go on to become delinquents or criminals, for the mischief-maker role may later become integrated with or retrospectively rationalized as part of a role more acceptable to school authorities. If such a boy continues this unacceptable role and becomes delinquent, the process must be accounted for in the light of the general theory of this volume. There must be a spreading corroboration of a sociopathic self-conception and societal reinforcement at each step in the process.

The most significant personality changes are manifest when societal definitions and their subjective counterpart become generalized. When this happens, the range of major role choices becomes narrowed to one general class. This was very obvious in the case of a young girl who was the daughter of a paroled convict and who was attending a small Middle Western college. She continually argued with herself and with the author, in whom she had confided, that in reality she belonged on the "other side of the railroad tracks" and that her life could be enormously simplified by acquiescing in this verdict and living accordingly. While in her case there was a tendency to dramatize her conflicts, nevertheless there was enough societal reinforcement of her self-conception by the treatment she received in her relationship with her father and on dates with college boys to lend it a painful reality. Once these boys took her home to the shoddy dwelling in a slum area where she lived with her father, who was often in a drunken condition, they abruptly stopped seeing her again or else became sexually presumptive. . . .

Discussion Questions

1. What is the difference between primary and secondary deviance?
2. What is meant by the concept of a "societal reaction"? How do the reactions of others affect someone who is being defined as a deviant? Why does this lead, in Lemert's words, to "secondary deviance"?
3. What are the policy implications of Lemert's theory? For example, what would be the best way to respond to youths who are caught committing delinquent acts?

21. Crime, Shame, and Reintegration

John Braithwaite

Braithwaite's central thesis is that crime is higher when shaming is stigmatizing and lower when shaming is reintegrative. This thesis explains both why some societies have higher rates of crime than others and why some individuals are more likely to offend than others.

At the macro-level, Braithwaite starts with assumptions that mirror social disorganization theory: societies marked by urbanization and residential mobility are less "communitarian" and less likely to have interdependency between its citizens. When societies lack communitarianism—that is, when individuals are not "densely enmeshed in interdependencies which have the special qualities of mutuality and trust" (1989: 100)—they will engage in shaming that is stigmatizing. As large numbers of people are stigmatized, they come together to develop ongoing criminal subcultural groups that provide learning environments for crime and "illegitimate opportunities to indulge tastes." At any given time, stigmatized individuals have incentives to participate in these ongoing subcultural groups because they are excluded from conventional society. Furthermore, the process of stigmatization has a feedback effect that erodes communitarianism. The end result is a society—such as the United States—that has a high crime rate.

On the micro-level, stigmatizing shaming has its greatest negative effects on individuals with few social bonds to conventional society—especially young, unmarried, unemployed males. Lacking interdependencies that might blunt stigma and foster reintegration, these rejected individuals have their social bonds further attenuated. As controls weaken, they join criminal subcultural groups in which antisocial values are reinforced and illegitimate opportunities are made available. In short, stigmatizing shaming evokes the conditions that control theory and differential association theory link to crime. The result is the continued, if not heightened, involvement of the individual offender in criminal activities.

Unlike labeling theorists, Braithwaite does not suggest that nonintervention is the most effective criminal justice policy. In fact, shaming is necessary for social control: the offender and the larger community benefit from a public ceremony in which the criminal act—but not the criminal—is defined as immoral. This moralizing is also done informally by those in the offenders' social networks. The key issue is what follows shaming: reintegration or stigmatization. Reintegration is essential because shamed individuals are at a turning point in their lives—a time when they can reattach to conventional society or deepen their commitment to crime. When quality social relations exist, they provide the means through which offenders are given the forgiveness and support needed to become a member of the community.

Reprinted from John Braithwaite, *Crime, Shame and Reintegration*. Copyright © 1989 by Cambridge University Press. Reprinted by permission of Cambridge University Press.

Within the United States and elsewhere, "restorative justice" programs most closely mirror Braithwaite's admonition to meld shaming with reintegration (see Braithwaite, 2002). In these programs, the goal is to "restore" both the victim, who has been harmed, and the offender, who has done the harming. Victims are likely to receive both restitution and, after conveying to the offender in a face-to-face encounter the pains they have experienced, a public apology. Repentant offenders potentially are granted a measure of forgiveness by victims and are reaccepted by family and community.

Such attempts at shaming and reintegration present an appealing alternative to stigmatizing criminal justice sanctions (see Braithwaite and Mugford, 1994; Makkai and Braithwaite, 1991). Evaluations of restorative justice programs have yielded some promising results (Braithwaite, 2002; Menkel-Medow, 2007). It remains to be demonstrated, however, that these interventions have the capacity to alter the life course of persistent offenders. The critical issue, it would seem, is not the public ceremony or conference in which shaming occurs but the quality of the reintegration that follows. Unless these efforts at reintegration are prolonged and target for change the known predictors of recidivism, the reform of offenders is likely to be modest at best (see Levrant et al., 1999; more generally, see Andrews and Bonta, 2003).

References

Andrews, D. A. and James Bonta. 2003. *The Psychology of Criminal Conduct*, 3rd edition. Cincinnati: Anderson.

Braithwaite, John. 1989. *Crime, Shame and Reintegration*. Cambridge, UK: Cambridge University Press.

——. 2002. *Restorative Justice and Responsive Regulation*. New York: Oxford University Press.

Braithwaite, John and Stephen Mugford. 1994. "Conditions of Successful Reintegration Ceremonies: Dealing with Juvenile Offenders." *British Journal of Sociology* 34: 139–171.

Levrant, Sharon, Francis T. Cullen, Betsy Fulton, and John F. Wozniak. 1999. "Reconsidering Restorative Justice: The Corruption of Benevolence Revisited?" *Crime and Delinquency* 45: 3–27.

Makkai, Tony and John Braithwaite. 1994. "Reintegrative Shaming and Compliance with Regulatory Standards." *Criminology* 32: 361–386.

Menkel-Medow, Carrie. 2007. "Restorative Justice: What Is It and Does It Work?" *Annual Review of Law and Social Science* 3: 161–187.

The theory in this book suggests that the key to crime control is cultural commitments to shaming in ways that I call reintegrative. Societies with low crime rates are those that shame potently and judiciously; individuals who resort to crime are those insulated from shame over their wrongdoing. However, shame can be applied injudiciously and counterproductively; the theory seeks to specify the types of shaming which cause rather than prevent crime. . . .

The first step to productive theorizing about crime is to think about the contention that labeling offenders makes things worse. The contention is both right and wrong. The theory of reintegrative shaming is an attempt to specify when it is right and when wrong. The distinction is between shaming that leads to stigmatization—to outcasting, to confirmation of a deviant master status—versus shaming that is reintegrative, that shames while maintaining bonds of respect or love, that sharply terminates disapproval with forgiveness, instead of amplifying deviance by progressively casting the deviant out. Reintegrative shaming controls crime; stigmatization pushes offenders toward criminal subcultures. . . .

The theory of reintegrative shaming posits that the consequence of stigmatization is attraction to criminal subcultures. Subcultures supply the outcast offender with the opportunity to reject her rejectors, thereby maintaining a form of self-respect. In contrast, the consequence of reintegrative shaming is that criminal subcultures appear less attractive to the offender. Shaming is the most potent weapon of social control unless it shades into stigmatization. Formal criminal punishment is an ineffective weapon of social control party because it is a degradation ceremony with maximum prospects for stigmatization.

The nub of the theory of reintegrative shaming is therefore about the effectiveness of reintegrative shaming and the counterproductivity of stigmatization in controlling crime. In addition, the theory posits a number of conditions that make for effective shaming. Individuals are more susceptible to shaming when they are enmeshed in multiple relationships of interdependency; societies shame more effectively when they are communitarian. Variables like urbanization and residential mobility predict communitarianism, while variables like age and gender predict individual interdependency. (A schematic summary of these aspects of the theory is presented in Figure 21.1).

Some of the ways that the theory of reintegrative shaming builds on earlier theories should now be clear. Interdependency is the stuff of control theory; stigmatization comes from labeling theory; subculture formation is accounted for in opportunity theory terms; subcultural influences are naturally in the realm of subcultural theory; and the whole theory can be understood in integrative cognitive social learning theory terms such as are provided by differential association. . . .

Preventing Crime

We have seen that the micro process of shaming an individual has consequences far beyond the life of that individual. The social process of gossip links a micro incident into a macro pattern. A shaming incident reinforces cultural patterns which underwrite further cultural products like a moralistic children's story, a television program, a school teacher's homily. The latter modalities of public (societal) shaming exert pressure for further private (individual) shaming.

The reasons why reintegrative shaming works in preventing crime might be summarized as follows:

1. The deterrence literature suggests that specific deterrence associated with detection for criminal offending works primarily through fear of shame in the eyes of intimates rather than fear of formal punishment.

2. Shame not only specifically deters the shamed offender, it also generally deters many others who also wish to avoid shame and who participate in or become aware of the incident of shaming.

3. Both the specific and general deterrent effects of shame will be greater for persons who remain strongly attached in relationships of interdependency and affection because such persons will accure greater interpersonal costs from shame. This is one reason why reintegrative shaming makes for more effective social control than stigmatization.

4. A second reason for the superiority of reintegrative shaming over stigmatization is that the latter can be counterproductive by breaking attachments to those who might shame future criminality and by increasing the attractiveness of groups that provide social support for crime.

5. However, most compliance with the law is not achieved through either specific or general deterrence. Most of us comply with the law most of the time, not because we rationally weigh our fear of the consequences of detection against the benefits of the crime, but because to commit the crime is simply unthinkable to us. Shaming is the social process which leads to the cognition that a particular type of crime is unthinkable. Cultures where the social process of shaming is muted are cultures where citizens often do not internalize abhorrence for crime.

6. A third reason for the superiority of the reintegrative shaming over stigmatization is that a combination of shame at and repentance by the

offender is a more powerful affirmation of the criminal law than onesided moralizing. A shaming ceremony followed later by a forgiveness and repentance ceremony more potently builds commitment to the law than a shaming ceremony alone. Nothing has greater symbolic force in community-wide conscience-building than repentance.

7. Because shaming is a participatory form of social control, compared with formal sanctioning which is more professionalized than participatory, shaming builds consciences through citizens being instruments as well as targets of social control. Participation in expressions of abhorrence toward the criminal acts of others is part of what makes crime an abhorrent choice for ourselves to make.

8. Once consciences have been formed by cultural processes of shaming and repentance, pangs of conscience become the most effective punishment for crime because whereas conscience delivers a timely anxiety response to every involvement in crime, other negative reinforcers, including shame, are delivered unreliably or with delay.

9. Shaming is therefore both the social process which builds consciences, and the most important backstop to be used when consciences fail to deliver conformity. Formal punishment is another backstop, but a less effective one than reintegrative shaming.

10. Gossip within wider circles of acquaintances and shaming of offenders not even known to those who gossip are important for building consciences because so many crimes will not occur in the direct experiences of limited groups like families. Societal incidents of shaming remind parents and teachers of the need to moralize with their children across the whole curriculum of crimes.

11. Public shaming puts pressure on parents, teachers and others to ensure that they engage in private shaming which is sufficiently systematic, and public shaming increasingly takes over the role of private shaming once children move away from the influence of the family and school. The latter is one reason why public shaming by courts of law has a more important role to play with strictly adult offenses like crimes against the environment than with predominantly juvenile offenses like vandalism.

12. Public shaming generalizes familiar principles to unfamiliar or new contexts. It integrates new categories of wrongdoing, which may arise from technological change into pre-existing moral frameworks. Public shaming transforms the loss of life in a battle at My Lai into a "war crime" and a "massacre," and through our distant involvement in the incident of shaming, the moral category of illegal killing acquires some expanded meanings.

13. Cultures with heavy emphasis on reintegrative shaming establish a smoother transition between socialization practices in the family and socialization in the wider society. Within the family, as the child grows, social control shifts from external to internal controls; punishment-oriented cultures set this process more starkly in reverse in the public domain than do shame-oriented cultures. To the extent that crime control can be made to work by continuing to catalyze internal controls it will be more effective; this is precisely why families are more effective agents of social control than police forces.

14. Gossip and other modalities of shaming can be especially effective when the targets of shame are not directly confronted with the shame, but are directly confronted with gestures of forgiveness or reintegration. Citizens who have learnt the culture do not have to be shamed to their faces to know that they are the subject of gossip, but they may need to be directly offered gestures of acceptance before they can be confident that they are again part of the community of law abiding citizens. In other words, shaming which is excessively confrontational renders the achievement of reintegration a tall order. There is thus something to be said for hypocrisy: our friends are likely to recover from a suspicion that we have stabbed them in the back, but stabbing them in the front can be divisive!

15. The effectiveness of shaming is often enhanced by shame being directed not only at the individual offender but also at her family, or her company if she is a corporate criminal. When a collectivity as well as an individual is shamed, collectivities are put on notice as to their responsibility to exercise informal control over their members, and the moralizing impact of shaming is multiplied. For reasons which will be elaborated in the next chapter, a shamed family or company will often transmit the shame to the individual offender in a manner which is as regenerative as possible. From the standpoint of the offender, the strategy of rejecting her rejectors may resuscitate her own self-esteem, but her loved ones or colleagues will soon let her know that sinking deeper into the deviant role will only exacerbate the shame they are suffering on her behalf.

The Theory of Reintegrative Shaming

Figure 21.1 provides a schematic summary of the theory. In the first part of this chapter clear definitions are attempted for the key concepts in Figure 21.1 The cluster of six variables around interdependency at the top left of Figure 21.1 are characteristics of individuals; the three at the top right are characteristics of societies; while high levels of crime and shaming are variables which apply to both individuals and societies. The theory as summarized in Figure 21.1 thus gives an account both of why some kinds of individuals and some kinds of societies exhibit more crime.

We could get a more parsimonious theory by collapsing the similar constructs of interdependency (an individual-level variable) and communitarianism (a societal variable) into a single construct, but then we would no longer have a

Figure 21.1
Summary of the Theory of Reintegrative Shaming

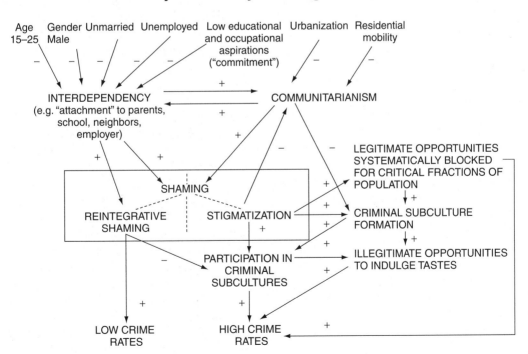

framework to predict both which individuals and which societies will have more crime. On the desirability of being able to do this I can only agree with Cressey:

> A theory explaining social behavior in general, or any specific kind of social behavior, should have two distinct but consistent aspects. First, there must be a statement that explains the statistical distribution of the behavior in time and space (epidemiology), and from which predictive statements about unknown statistical distributions can be derived. Second, there must be a statement that identifies, at least by implication, the process by which individuals come to exhibit the behavior in question, and from which can be derived predictive statements about the behavior of individuals. (Cressey, 1960:47)

Key Concepts

Interdependency is a condition of individuals. It means the extent to which individuals participate in networks wherein they are dependent on others to achieve valued ends and others are dependent on them. We could describe an individual as in a state of interdependency even if the individuals who are dependent on him are different from the individuals on whom he is dependent. Interdependency is approximately equivalent to the social bonding, attachment and commitment of control theory.

Communitarianism is a condition of societies. In communitarian societies individuals are densely enmeshed in interdependencies which have the special qualities of mutual help and trust. The interdependencies have symbolic significance in the culture of group loyalties which take precedence over individual interests. The interdependencies also have symbolic significance as attachments which invoke personal obligation to others in a community of concern, rather than simply interdependencies of convenience as between a bank and a small depositor. A communitarian culture rejects any pejorative connotation of dependency as threatening individual autonomy. Communitarian

cultures resist interpretations of dependency as weakness and emphasize the need for mutuality of obligation in interdependency (to be both dependent and dependable). The Japanese are said to be socialized not only to *amaeru* (to be succored by others) but also to *amayakasu* (to be nurturing to others) (Wagatsuma and Rosett, 1986).

Shaming means all social processes of expressing disapproval which have the intention or effect of invoking remorse in the person being shamed and/or condemnation by others who become aware of the shaming. When associated with appropriate symbols, formal punishment often shames. But societies vary enormously in the extent to which formal punishment is associated with shaming or in the extent to which the social meaning of punishment is no more than to inflict pain to tip reward-cost calculations in favor of certain outcomes. Shaming, unlike purely deterrent punishment, sets out to moralize with the offender to communicate reasons for the evil of her actions. Most shaming is neither associated with formal punishment nor perpetrated by the state, though both shaming by the state and shaming with punishment are important types of shaming. Most shaming is by individuals within interdependent communities of concern.

Reintegrative shaming is shaming which is followed by efforts to reintegrate the offender back into the community of lawabiding or respectable citizens through words or gestures of forgiveness or ceremonies to decertify the offender as deviant. Shaming and reintegration do not occur simultaneously but sequentially, with reintegration occurring before deviance becomes a master status. It is shaming which labels the act as evil while striving to preserve the identity of the offender as essentially good. It is directed at signifying evil deeds rather than evil persons in the Christian tradition of "hate the sin and love the sinner." Specific disapproval is expressed within relationships characterized by general social approval; shaming criminal behavior is complemented by ongoing social rewarding of alternative behavior patterns. Reintegrative shaming is not necessarily weak; it can be cruel, even vicious. It is not distinguished from stigmatization by its potency, but by (a) a finite rather than open-ended duration which is terminated by forgiveness; and by (b) efforts to maintain bonds of love or respect throughout the finite period of suffering shame.

Stigmatization is disintegrative shaming in which no effort is made to reconcile the offender with the community. The offender is outcast, her deviance is allowed to become a master status, degradation ceremonies are not followed by ceremonies to decertify deviance.

Criminal subcultures are sets of rationalizations and conduct norms which cluster together to support criminal behavior. The clustering is usually facilitated by subcultural groups which provide systematic social support for crime in any of a number of ways—supplying members with criminal opportunities, criminal values, attitudes which weaken conventional values of law-abidingness, or techniques of neutralizing conventional values.

Short Summary of the Theory
The following might serve as the briefest possible summary of the theory. A variety of life circumstances increase the chances that individuals will be in situations of greater interpendency, the most important being age (under 15 and over 25), being married, female, employed, and having high employment and educational aspirations. Interdependent persons are more susceptible to shaming. More importantly, societies in which individuals are subject to extensive interdependencies are more likely to be communitarian, and shaming is much more widespread and potent in communitarian societies. Urbanization and high residential mobility are societal characteristics which undermine communitarianism.

The shaming produced by interdependency and communitarianism can be either of two types—shaming that becomes stigmatization or shaming that is followed by reintegration.

The shaming engendered is more likely to become reintegrative in societies that are communitarian. In societies where shaming does become reintegrative, low crime rates are the result because disapproval is dispensed without eliciting a rejection of the disapprovers, so that the potentialities for future disapproval are not dismantled. Moreover, reintegrative shaming is superior even to stigmatization for conscience-building. . . .

Shaming that is stigmatizing, in contrast, makes criminal subcultures more attractive because these are in some sense subcultures which reject the rejectors. Thus, when shaming is allowed to become stigmatization for want of reintegrative gestures or ceremonies which decertify deviance, the deviant is both attracted to criminal subcultures and cut off from other interdependencies (with family, neighbors, church, etc.). Participation in subcultural groups supplies criminal role models, training in techniques of crime and techniques of neutralizing crime (or other forms of social support) that make choices to engage in crime more attractive. Thus, to the extent that shaming is of the stigmatizing rather than the reintegrative sort, and that criminal subcultures are widespread and accessible in the society, higher crime rates will be the result. While societies characterized by high levels of stigmatization will have higher crime rates than societies characterized by reintegrative shaming, the former will have higher or lower crime rates than societies with little shaming at all depending largely on the availability of criminal subcultures.

Yet a high level of stigmatization in the society is one of the very factors that encourages criminal subculture formation by creating populations of outcasts with no stake in conformity, no chance of self-esteem within the terms of conventional society—individuals in search of an alternative culture that allows them self-esteem. A communitarian culture, on the other hand, nurtures deviants within a network of attachments to conventional society, thus inhibiting the widespread outcasting that is the stuff of subculture formation.

For clarity of exposition the two types of shaming have been presented as a stark dichotomy. In reality, for any society some deviants are dealt with in ways that are more stigmatic while others receive more reintegrative shaming. Indeed, a single deviant will be responded to more stigmatically by some, more reintegratively by others. To the extent that the greater weight of shaming tends to stigmatization, the crime-producing processes on the right of Figure 21.1 are more likely to be triggered; to the extent that the balance of shaming tips toward reintegration, informal processes of crime control are more likely to prevail over these crime-producing processes.

The other major societal variable which fosters criminal subculture formation is systematic blockage of legitimate opportunities for critical fractions of the population. If black slum dwellers are systematically denied economic opportunities because of the stigma of their race and neighborhood, then criminal subcultures will form in these outcast neighborhoods. It can be seen that stigmatization (as opposed to social integration) as a cultural disposition may contribute to the systematic blockage of these economic opportunities; but cultural variables like stigmatization will be of rather minor importance compared with structural economic variables in determining opportunities. I have argued that the blockages in this part of the theory are not restricted to closed opportunities to climb out of poverty; systematically blocked opportunities for ever greater wealth accumulation by the most affluent of corporations often lead to corporate criminal subculture formation. . . .

Criminal subcultures are the main mechanism for constituting illegitimate opportunity structures—knowledge on how to offend, social support for offending or communication of rationalizations for offending, criminal role models, subcultural groups which assist with the avoidance of detection and which organize collective criminal enterprises. However, illegitimate opportunities are greater in some societies than others for a variety of further reasons which are not incorporated within the theory. While the effects of legitimate and illegitimate opportunities on crime are mostly mediated by participation in criminal subcultures, the blockage of legitimate opportunities combined with the availability of illegitimate opportunities can independently increase crime. Whether illegitimate opportunities to engage in crime are supplied by participation in criminal subcultures or otherwise, they must be opportunities that appeal to the tastes of tempted individuals for them to result in crime.

This summary is crudely simple because it ignores what goes on within the shaming box in Figure 21.1. That is, it ignores the treatment . . . of the social processes that combine individual acts of shaming into cultural processes of shaming which are more or less integrative: gossip, media coverage of shaming incidents, children's stories, etc. In turn, the summary has neglected how these macro processes of shaming feed back to ensure that micro practices of shaming cover the curriculum of crimes. . . .

Shunting the Colliding Locomotives of Criminological Theory

This sharp contrast with the inability of the existing dominant theories to explain much of what we know about crime is achieved, ironically, through the addition of just one element—the partitioning of shaming—as a shunt to connect these diverging theoretical tracks. Through putting the old theoretical ingredients together in a new way, we can do better at accounting for the facts than can any of these traditions separately. Moreover, we can do better compared with adding together their separate (contradictory!) elements as partial explanations within an atheoretical multi-factor model.

The top left of Figure 21.1 incorporates the key variables of control theory; the far right—opportunity theory; the middle and bottom right—subcultural theory; the bottom, particularly the bottom left—learning theory; the right side of the middle box—labeling theory. With one crucial exception (reintegrative shaming), there is therefore no originality in the elements of this theory, simply originality of synthesis.

Through the effect of interdependency in reducing crime, we can capture the explanatory successes of control theory in accounting for primary deviance. Through shunting stigmatization away from other forms of shaming (as that sort of shaming which triggers subcultural participation) we proffer a more promising approach to the explanation of secondary deviance in labeling and subcultural theory terms. We achieve a more specified theory of differential association with conventional others versus others who share a subculture. Conceived another way, it is a theory of differential shaming. Most shaming is by conventional others on the anti-criminal side of a tipping point. When stigmatization produces secondary deviance, it is because the balance of shame has tipped; for those who share the subculture there is sufficient approval for crime . . . to outweigh the shaming of conventional society.

Discussion Questions

1. What is the difference between shaming that is stigmatizing and shaming that is reintegrative?
2. In the United States, what kind of shaming is most common? Can you provide some examples?
3. Why does stigmatizing shaming cause crime? How does this relate to labeling theory?
4. If you were going to develop a reintegrative shaming program for juvenile delinquents, what would it involve?

22. Defiance Theory

Lawrence W. Sherman

For many years, both scholars and elected officials had debated both between and among themselves whether applying criminal sanctions to individuals (i.e., arresting them, sentencing them publicly in court, and supervising them in the community or behind bars) caused the offenders to "get worse" or to be "scared straight." Those in the "get worse" camp were typically called labeling theorists because, as we have seen thus far in this part of the book, they believed that stigmatizing, excluding, and harshly treating offenders only increased their likelihood of reoffending. Those in the "scared straight" camp were advocates of rational choice theory and believed that offenders would be deterred from future crime if only criminal sanctions had the correct mixture of certainty and severity of punishment (see Part X).

Lawrence Sherman, however, recognized that this debate between the labeling and deterrence theorists had grown stale. Neither side was budging from its long-standing position, and thus the result was two incompatible and, Sherman believed, limited views of what potentially happens when people are processed through the criminal justice system. Both sides, he realized, would not admit that such processing might make offenders more criminal (through labeling or a process he calls "defiance"), might deter them, or might prove irrelevant and have no effect whatsoever on recidivism. Labeling and deterrence

theorists might both be partially right and partially wrong, but each theory by itself was clearly incomplete. Given that contact with the justice system certainly had these diverse effects, Sherman reasoned that an important explanatory task was at hand: to move beyond the labeling and deterrence perspectives so as to develop a comprehensive theory of the criminal sanction, one that could account for when such sanctions created "defiance, deterrence, or irrelevance" (Sherman, 1993, 2000).

Sherman makes a beginning effort in this direction by advancing what he calls "defiance theory." He defines the concept of defiance as the "net increase in the prevalence, incidence, or seriousness of future offending against a sanctioning community caused by a proud, shameless reaction to the administration of a criminal sanction" (1993: 459). However, what would make offenders react with defiant criminality, as opposed to cooperation and future conformity, when attempts are made to control them? A number of conditions might be involved, but two broad categories can be singled out as especially significant.

First, perhaps the most critical factor is the quality of the sanctions that are administered. Sanctions can be just or unjust, and they can seek to personally stigmatize the offender or condemn only a person's wayward conduct (Braithwaite, 1989 [Chapter 21 in this part]). When police

Lawrence W. Sherman, "Defiance, Deterrence and Irrelevance: A Theory of the Criminal Sanction," *Journal of Research in Crime and Delinquency* (30) 1993, pp. 445–449, 459–461, 463–468, copyright © 1993 by Sage Publications. Reprinted by permission of Sage Publications, Inc.

officers, for example, act in a rude and discrimina-tory way, arrestees are likely to react with hostility and see their apprehension as something to be resisted. Defiance, not deterrence, is the likely result (see Paternoster et al., 1997).

Second, Sherman recognized that not all offen-ders come to the sanctioning event with the same social background; it followed that who an offender is can shape how he or she reacts to sanctions. Building on social bond theory (see Part VI), he hypothesized that those socially bonded to the con-ventional system would be most likely to be deterred, whereas those alienated from the commu-nity would be most likely to react defiantly. The troubling reality, moreover, is that those who are the most weakly socially bonded, and thus are most susceptible to perceiving actions by criminal justice personnel as unfair, are precisely the people to whom overly formal, harsh, stigmatizing sanctions are disproportionately applied (Sherman, 2000). Here, labeling theory's lesson of the self-fulfilling prophecy rings true. In these cases, the interaction of nasty sanctions and alienated, angry offenders will produce exactly the opposite outcome of what those "cracking down" on and "getting tough" with offenders hope to accomplish: high rates of defiance and reduced public safety.

References

Braithwaite, John. 1989. *Crime, Shame and Reinte-gration.* Cambridge, UK: Cambridge University Press.

Paternoster, Raymond, Robert Brame, Ronet Bachman, and Lawrence W. Sherman. 1997. "Do Fair Procedures Matter? The Effect of Procedural Justice on Spouse Assault." *Law and Society Review* 31: 163–204.

Sherman, Lawrence W. 1993. "Defiance, Deterrence, and Irrelevance: A Theory of the Criminal Sanction." *Journal of Research in Crime and Delinquency* 30: 445–473.

——. 2000 (February 24). *The Defiant Imagination: Consilience and the Science of Sanctions.* The

Albert M. Greenfield Chair Inaugural Lecture delivered at the University of Pennsylvania, Philadelphia.

———

Does punishment control crime? This ques-tion provokes fierce debates in criminology and public policy. Yet there is ample evidence that it is the wrong question. Widely varying results across a range of sanction studies suggest a far more useful question: Under what condi-tions does each type of criminal sanction reduce, increase, or have no effect on future crimes? Answering that question is central to the future of research on crime and delinquency.

That claim has no better justification than the universal presumption of criminal law that punish-ment deters (Morris 1966, p. 631). As the dosage of criminal sanctions skyrocketed in the United States over the past decade (Farrington and Langan 1992; Blumstein 1993), criminology produced increasing evidence that punishment can backfire. If our first duty is to do no harm, then criminology is morally compelled to identify the ways in which punish-ment may be causing crime and to invent alterna-tives to criminogenic practices . . . .

The absence of theoretical guidance reflects the preoccupation of modern criminology with the problem of crime causation. Yet the historic (Beccaria [1764] 1963) and conceptual core of crim-inology is the science of sanction effects, net of other causes of crime. By definition, both criminality and criminal events are responses to the formal threat of punishment attached to the legal proscription of certain behaviors. Yet the role of that threat in crime causation and prevention has received far less scientific attention than other factors.

A science of sanction effects requires explicit the-ories of those effects, not just modified theories of crime causation. Until recently, the deterrence and labeling doctrines have kept a stranglehold on the field, demanding a choice between the two (Wellford and Triplett 1992). But three new theories offer the promise of resolving that stalemate with far greater explanatory power. Most visible among criminologists is Braithwaite's (1989) theory of reintegrative shaming. Most prominent among political scientists is the procedural justice school, notably Tyler's (1990) major study of compliance. The third theory is Scheff and Retzinger's (1991) sociology of the "master emotions" of pride and shame that dominate human responses to experienced and vicarious sanctions. Each of these theories can help explain a phenomenon that Black (1983) identified in which crime is committed as an attempt at social control.

Briefly, Braithwaite (1989) argues that criminal sanctions can be delivered in either "reintegrative" or "stigmatizing" ways, the former by drawing social shame on the *act* and the latter by shaming and rejecting the *actor*. Reintegrative shaming controls crime, whereas stigmatic shaming increases it. Tyler (1990) distinguishes between sanctions citizens perceive as fair or unfair. Fair sanctions increase compliance with the law by affirming the legitimacy of law enforcement, but unfair sanctions reduce compliance by reducing legitimacy. Scheff and Retzinger (1991) argue that individuals vary in their emotional response to sanctions or shaming of any kind, depending on their social bonding to the sanctioning agent and to society in general.

This article attempts to integrate the three new theories into a "defiance" theory that accounts for some, but not all, of the facts of diverse sanction effects. . . .

Overview

Sitting in a movie theater that was showing Stanley Kubrick's *2001*, my 10-year-old son and my wife were talking. They started out in a whisper, then spoke sotto voce, then got very loud when the music was loud. Finally, another patron came over and rudely told them to "shut up." They complied. But all the way home my son protested that the chastisement was unfair. As my wife tried to justify the patron's actions by the impoliteness of their having bothered other people by loud talking, my son became more defiant. He felt so humiliated by the rudeness

of the patron's conduct that he denied the morality of the rule the patron was enforcing—arguing that people had a right to talk so that they could interpret the movie to each other. His only escape from the stigmatizing shame he had suffered was a refusal to acknowledge that shame, adopting a false pride in his own moral superiority over the disrespectful and—in his view—*unfair* patron.

Compare that episode with a recent scene from the richest county in the United States (Brown, 1993):

> A 14-year [old] freshman at McLean High School in Fairfax County [said] "I was talking to one of my friends, and [the teacher] said something like 'shut up,' and it pissed me off and I said, 'Go to hell. [Expletive] you.'" . . . "I explained why I was late [to my teacher], and she started going off on me about what I needed to do to get to school on time," said Gisela Aponte, 17, a junior at McLean. "I just freaked out and called her the B word . . . . I got Saturday detention, but I don't regret it. She deserved to be called that." . . . Some youths think they deserve as much respect as anybody else, including their elders.

In both the theater and the high school, the rule breakers were punished in a manner they defined as disrespectful. And in both cases, as Scheff and Retzinger (1991) would argue, the disrespect made them ashamed of being ashamed, infusing them with self-righteousness. In Braithwaite's (1991) commentary on Scheff and Retzinger, "Actor A gets angry at actor B for disapproving of her instead of examining the (correct or incorrect) reasons for the disapproval" (p. xi). This pattern supports Durkheim's hypothesis that "for any penalty to have an educational influence it must seem worthy of respect to the person on whom it is inflicted" (quoted in Braithwaite 1989, p. 178).

But the "unfair" sanctions had different effects on the sanctioned behavior. In the theater, my well-bonded son, under the watchful "handling" (Felson

1986) of his mother, complied with the rule despite the anger from his unacknowledged shame. In the high school, the students—perhaps poorly bonded at home and in general—defied both the rules and the sanctioners, attracting more severe sanctioning for their defiance. That sanctioning, in turn, further strengthened their denial of shame for the original rule violation and their pride in having themselves punished an unfair punishment.

These cases highlight four key concepts in the emotional response to sanctioning experiences: legitimacy, social bonds, shame, and pride. Foremost is the degree of *legitimacy* the sanctioned offender grants to the sanctioning agent's behavior, driven more by the agent's respectfulness and procedural fairness than by the substance of the morality the agent enforces (Tyler 1990). Second is the strength of the *social bond* the offender has to the sanctioning agent, the community in whose name the sanctioning agent was acting, and other close attachments (Scheff and Retzinger 1991). Third is the *shame* the offender either acknowledges or bypasses, respectively repairing or weakening social bonds to agent or community (Braithwaite 1989). Fourth is the source of *pride* the offender feels in the aftermath of the sanction: social solidarity with the relevant community or isolation from that community as an "unconquerable soul" (Henley [1875] 1954).

These concepts allow a falsifiable statement of a defiance theory of the diversity of sanctioning effects, at both individual and general levels of analysis:

1. Sanctions provoke future *defiance* of the law (persistence, more frequent or more serious violations) to the extent that offenders experience sanctioning conduct as illegitimate, that offenders have weak bonds to the sanctioning agent and community, and that offenders deny their shame and become proud of their isolation from the sanctioning community.
2. Sanctions produce future *deterrence* of lawbreaking (desistance, less frequent or less serious violations) to the extent that offenders experience sanctioning conduct as legitimate, that offenders have strong bonds to the sanctioning agent and community, and that offenders accept their shame and remain proud of solidarity with the community.
3. Sanctions become *irrelevant* to future law breaking (no effect) to the extent that the factors encouraging defiance or deterrence are fairly evenly counterbalanced . . . .

Defiance Theory

Defiance is the net increase in the prevalence, incidence, or seriousness of future offending against a sanctioning community caused by a proud, shameless reaction to the administration of a criminal sanction. Specific or individual defiance is the reaction of one person to that person's own punishment. General defiance is the reaction of a group or collectivity to the punishment of one or more of its members. Direct defiance is a crime committed against a sanctioning agent. Indirect defiance is the displaced just deserts committed against a target vicariously representing the sanctioning agents provoking the anger. Defiance is distinct from other hypothetical mechanisms by which sanctions increase crime, such as labeling (Lemert 1972), thrill seeking (Katz 1988), imitation, or brutalization (Bowers 1988). Defiance theory explains variation in criminal events, not criminality (Hirschi 1986). Defiance theory may encompass many types of crimes but may also be more powerful a predictor of predatory and competitive offenses than of mutualistic or retreatist offenses (Felson 1987).

Defiance occurs under four conditions, all of which are necessary.

1. The offender defines a criminal sanction as unfair.
2. The offender is poorly bonded to or alienated from the sanctioning agent or the community the agent represents.

3. The offender defines the sanction as stigmatizing and rejecting a person, not a lawbreaking act.
4. The offender denies or refuses to acknowledge the shame the sanction has actually caused him to suffer.

Sanctions are defined as unfair under two conditions, either of which is sufficient:

1. The sanctioning agent behaves with disrespect for the offender, or for the group to which the offender belongs, regardless of how fair the sanction is on substantive grounds.
2. The sanction is substantively arbitrary, discriminatory, excessive, undeserved, or otherwise objectively unjust.

Offenders deny shame as one of two adaptive responses to alienation, as Karl Marx put it: "impotence and indignation" (quoted in Scheff and Retzinger 1991, p. 64). The first response accepts shame and seeks escape through retreat or intoxicants, as in Anderson's (1978) "wineheads." The second denies shame and insulates against it by anger and rage in reaction to insult, as in Anderson's "hoodlums." We lack sufficient evidence or theory to specify the individual or social conditions under which alienated persons choose these alternative responses.

Defiance theory therefore predicts three reactions to punishment defined as unfair.

1. When poorly bonded offenders accept the shame an unfair stigmatizing sanction provokes, the sanction will be *irrelevant* or possibly even deterrent to future rates of offending.
2. When poorly bonded offenders deny the shame they feel and respond with rage, the unfair stigmatizing sanction will *increase* their future rates of offending. This unacknowledged shame leads to an emotion of angry pride at defying the punishment. That pride predisposes the defiant offender to repeat the sanctioned conduct,

symbolically labeling the sanctions or sanctioners, and not the offender's own acts, as truly shameful and morally deserving of punishment. In the process, the victims or targets of the sanctioned acts become vicarious substitutes for the state or its sanctioning representatives.

3. The full shame-crime sequence does not occur, however, when a well-bonded offender defines a sanction as unfair. The unfairness may weaken the deterrent effect of the sanction and make it irrelevant to future conduct. But even if the offender (like my son in the theater) denies the shame, proud defiance is unlikely because it is less valued than the pride associated with social bonds . . . .

Defining Sanctions as Unfair

Respect. The evidence suggests respect by punishers for the punished is a separate dimension from Braithwaite's (1989) distinction between reintegrative and stigmatic shaming. Rather, it is a more basic matter of treating people with human dignity. Reintegration can be done rudely, and stigma can be applied politely. As Braithwaite (1989, p. 101) points out, reintegrative shaming "can be cruel, even vicious," as long as it has a finite end point and explicit ceremonies for accepting the offender back into the community administering the punishment. It seems reasonable to posit that unfair or disrespectful sanctions that are also stigmatizing are the most likely to provoke defiance, but that still presumes the two dimensions are distinct.

Fairness and respect is also not a simple matter of whether punishment is delivered or spared, as Tyler's (1990) findings show. What is more important in Tyler's evidence is that the offender's interpretation of events gets a fair hearing and that the sanctioning decision maker considers and respects that viewpoint.

Consider this datum: in the Milwaukee domestic violence experiment, arrestees who said (in lockup) that police had not taken the time to listen to their side of the story were 36 percent more likely to be reported for assaulting the same victim over the next 6 months than those who said the police had listened to them (Bridgeforth 1990, p. 76). This fact might be a spurious result of an underlying personality type that is both more recidivistic and more likely to become defiant. But it may also reflect a history of police rudeness, or failure to listen, to that offender and members of his primary group.

It is no accident that the demographic groups with the lowest opinion of the police—minorities and young men (Wilson 1983, p. 93; Clements 1993)—are also the most subject to police-initiated encounters (Sherman 1980) that lack the legitimacy of a citizen requesting police involvement (Reiss 1971, pp. 58–59). These are also situations in which police are more likely to encounter disrespect, get injured, make arrests, and have complaints filed against them. And although mutual respect characterizes most observed police encounters, inner-city police are somewhat more likely to be uncivil than the citizens they confront (Reiss 1971, p. 144). There is much evidence that police and poor young men are caught in a shame-disrespect-anger spiral (Scheff and Retzinger 1991, p. 68). But the question for defiance theory is what effect that cycle has on the future offending of those caught up in it—on either the police (Skolnick and Fyfe 1993) or civilian side.

One answer is that the groups receiving the most disrespect from the police also have the highest participation rates in crime (Blumstein, Cohen, Roth, and Visher 1986). This fact might be dismissed as a mere artifact of measurement if arrest records were not confirmed by both self-report and victimization data. The fact is that young males, especially the poor and minorities, are much more exposed than lower crime groups to police disrespect and brutality, both vicariously and in person, *prior* to their peak years of first arrest and initial involvements in crime. This temporal order suggests a powerful role of police disrespect in sanction effects.

Substantive unfairness. Those who approach authority with defiant attitudes are often punished for their speech rather than for any substantive offense. When the criminal sanction is used in this fashion, it is substantively unjust and another potent source of defining police as illegitimate. There is no written law against "contempt of cop," of course, but it is perhaps the most consistently enforced de facto law in the country. All systematic observation studies of police decision making (Sherman 1980; Smith and Visher 1981) have found that disrespect toward police powerfully increases the odds of being arrested. The following encounter, which I observed in Minneapolis in 1981, is an extreme but hardly unprecedented example:

> The squad car drove through a 7-Eleven parking lot where one officer told a group of teenagers to leave. A few minutes later the car returned to find one long-haired young White male (who may not even have been there earlier) standing in the way of the police car as it turned in from the street. The officer, annoyed, said "I thought I told you to leave." The youth said, with asperity, "You didn't tell me nothin." The officer said "Oh yeah?" The youth said "Yeah!" The officer bolted out of the car, grabbed the youth by the hands, threw his upper body down on the hood of the car, handcuffed the youth, and locked him in the back of the car to drive him downtown. The charge was "disorderly conduct."

Once a sanction of this kind has been experienced, it is not difficult to appreciate how the offender (or his primary group) might view the police as unfair.

Other substantive sources of unfairness include the widespread nonenforcement of minor offenses (such as noise or public drinking), punctuated by arbitrary or discriminatory cases of enforcement (Reiss 1971, p. 57). "Rounding up the usual suspects" implies police laziness in looking for the truly guilty, rather than efficiency in locating the probably guilty. Courts letting suspects go on "technicalities" and juries not making the right decisions (Clements 1993) are other sources of perceived unfairness.

Remarkably, although most citizens feel unfairness is widespread, they do not feel courts or police discriminate against "people like them" (Tyler 1990, p. 50). Thus, in comparing procedural to substantive unfairness, the former seems to do far more powerful harm to legitimacy. Personal experience with unfairness, most often in the form of perceived disrespect, may be the greatest spark of defiance.

Anger and Displaced Just Deserts

Once a poorly bonded offender is punished unfairly and chooses to deny the shame of it all, he may or may not become angry at the punishers. Among the arrested suspects in the Milwaukee domestic violence experiment, 23 percent denied that it was immoral to hit your partner, but only 10 percent said the arrest had made them angry at the police (Sherman 1992, pp. 330–331). No matter what they say, we would expect almost none of them to attack the police in direct retaliation. Rather, their anger is displaced onto their present or future romantic partners or other citizens, who represent the clients police serve.

This displacement of just deserts for the wrong done to the sanctioned offender need not be a consciously articulated program. Rather, as Katz (1988) suggests, it can appear in the construction of a reputation for "badness," a "hardman" who will tolerate no disrespect and who will dominate anyone he chooses. When disrespect by another citizen is a precipitating situational cause of crime, it may actually reflect an underlying anger at the disrespect shown by police or courts in the last sanctioning encounter. Had that encounter been more respectful of the offender, perhaps the offender would be less sensitive to disrespect and less ready to punish anyone who accidentally or intentionally shows new disrespect to the offender.

Yet some defiance may be a more explicit project of displaced just deserts. Much offending occurs in cyclical but brief, multi-offense crime "sprees" or rampages, among both poor street robbers and middle-class adolescents (Katz 1988, p. 203). Such sprees might be touched off by episodes of disrespect, perhaps from authority figures other than criminal sanctioners: teachers, parents, employers.

The 1992 Rodney King verdict riot in Los Angeles illustrates this process for general defiance. The acquittal of the four accused officers symbolized the unfairness of criminal sanctions that allowed police to beat a Black man already in custody. But the riots that followed were not aimed at the police or Ventura County jurors. Rather, a major target was Korean and other Asian merchants operating in Black and Hispanic neighborhoods, 2,000 of whose businesses were destroyed (Kotkin 1993). These businesses had been repeatedly accused of disrespectful behavior toward neighborhood young people, including illegal use of deadly force against thieves (National Public Radio 1993). Those businesses thus substantively provoked the attacks on them, at least in the eyes of the attackers. But the attacks may never have occurred if the procedurally unfair beating and jury verdict had not sent the weakly bonded community into a spiral of proud defiance and rage.

Defiance theory thus calls attention to a problem that extends far beyond the criminal sanction: the conduct of everyday discourse with alienated persons who react with indignation to any hint of social disapproval. Schools, parents, employers, and fellow citizens increasingly recognize large numbers of highly "touchy," angry people ready to punish any available target for the sins of their past insulters, starting with the shame they felt as children from rejection by caretakers (Scheff and Retzinger 1991, p. 64) or historical insults to their social category. Some of them are police, some of them are criminals, and some of them merely file lawsuits . . . .

Testing Defiance Theory

The best tests of defiance theory, like all criminal sanction effects, will be randomized experiments. But that does not leave out other methods. Ethnographic work with criminals in field settings, longitudinal cohort designs, interviews with offenders immediately after arrest and on subsequent occasions, interviews with offenders' families and romantic partners, and observations of arrests and courtroom encounters can all test aspects of defiance theory. Perhaps the most important question for non-experimental methods is how offenders choose to accept or deny shame—how they choose impotence or indignation. Is that the true significance of testosterone (Booth and Osgood 1993) or body type? A strong domineering parent? A powerful social network of co-offenders, or a charismatic peer leader? These and many other questions need to be explored to further develop the causal mechanisms of defiance.

As for future experiments, randomization is only the first step. Theoretically guided measurement of causal mechanisms must also be incorporated. Observations of sanctioning experiences, for example, are needed to classify them as reintegrative or stigmatic, disrespectful or polite, consistent or arbitrary. Interviews with sanctioned and unsanctioned offenders are needed to determine their moral evaluation of the sanctioning decision and what emotional reaction they may have had. Similar detail could be sought about future crimes to capture the motivation and circumstances associated with them and test the connection (if any) to past sanctioning or more recent encounters with unfairness or disrespect.

Until recently the science of sanction effects has been short on facts and even shorter on theory. Now, it seems, the available theory has gotten ahead of the facts. The future of research in crime and delinquency will be better served if the facts and theory stay neck and neck.

Discussion Questions

1. Why is a "theory of the criminal sanction" needed? How well do criminologists explain why criminal sanctions sometimes increase, sometimes decrease, and sometimes have no effect on offender recidivism?
2. Think back to the most memorable times in your life when an authority figure—a police officer, a school principal, a teacher, a coach, or a parent—tried to sanction, punish, or reprimand you. Did you ever act or feel like acting defiantly? Alternatively, did you ever feel like you should change your behavior and act more appropriately? In these situations, what factors made the difference in how you felt and acted? How does this relate to Sherman's defiance theory?
3. Based on his defiance theory, how would Lawrence Sherman want police to act when arresting suspects? Judges when sentencing defendants? Probation and parole officers when supervising offenders in the community? Correctional officers and wardens when making and enforcing prison rules against inmates? What do you think the effects of current sanctioning practices are likely to be in these different parts of the justice system?

PART VIII

Critical Criminology: Power, Peace, and Crime

In the quarter century following World War II, notes James Patterson (1996: vii), Americans had "great expectations" about "the capacity of the United States to create a better world abroad and a happier society at home." These expectations reached a feverish pitch in the 1960s. With an economic boom under way and unprecedented support for broadening equal rights, President Lyndon Johnson called for the creation of a "great society"—a call that at the time did not seem naive. Scarcely a decade later, however, much of this optimism had turned to despair. Equal economic opportunity for all now seemed beyond reach, and racial cleavages—despite gains in formal legal rights for minorities—seemed to widen, as urban riots and white resistance to integration made clear. Viet Nam, Kent State, Attica, and Watergate—together these events and many others revealed the abuse of state power in the pursuit of questionable, if not illegal, goals. The assassinations of John and Robert Kennedy and of Martin Luther King, Jr., leaders who preached hope and peace, were perhaps the most vivid and enduring reminders that achieving true social justice remained an American dream.

What lessons were to be drawn from the failure to achieve the "great expectations" for American society? For a generation of criminologists who grew up in these tumultuous times and whose campus days were spent in protest marches, their social world had been transformed. Their utopian belief in a just society and faith in the "system" had been replaced by the sobering realization that inequality was deeply entrenched and that those in power wished to reinforce, not change, the status quo. Once all the rhetoric about America being the "land of opportunity" had been dispelled, they learned that fundamental reform would require unmasking and challenging the structures of power and the forces that undergirded them.

Equipped with this vision, criminologists in the late 1960s and early 1970s found "traditional" theories of crime—such as those covered in the previous parts of this volume—intellectually sterile, if not unthinkingly dangerous. These theories seemed blind to the central reality of American society: its pervasive economic and racial inequality. Traditional perspectives largely ignored and thus left unchallenged the powerful interests that benefited from this inequality. As a result, crime was detached from the very structural forces that sustained the mean streets of inner-city neighborhoods and, it might be added, that gave rise to rapacious corporations.

In contrast, this generation of criminologists called for a "new criminology" that would take a "critical" stance toward society and, intellectually, toward the assumptions and content of traditional criminology (Krisberg, 1975; Taylor et al., 1973). The category of "critical criminology"—sometimes also called conflict, radical, or Marxian criminology—encompasses diverse lines of inquiry (see Bohm, 1982; Milovanovic, 1982; Thomas and O'Maolchatha, 1989). At the risk of missing the richness of theorizing within this approach, however, it is possible to identify several themes that make a theoretical work distinctively "critical" in its focus.

Central Themes of Critical Criminology

First, the concepts of inequality and power are integral to any understanding of crime and its control. Building on the work of Karl Marx, critical criminologists note that capitalism enriches some and impoverishes many, thus inevitably producing a wide economic gap between the social classes. Pursuing their own interests, the affluent use their money to ensure that government policies do not threaten their position of advantage. As a result, the state—including the criminal law and the criminal justice system—operates to legitimate and protect social arrangements that benefit those profiting from capitalism.

Second, "crime" is a political, not a value-free, concept. Traditional criminology accepts that crime is behavior that violates the law. Critical criminology, however, recognizes that what is and is not outlawed reflects the power structure in society. In general, the injurious acts of the poor and powerless are defined as crime, but the injurious acts of the rich and powerful—such as corporations selling defective products or the affluent allowing disadvantaged children to go without health care—are not brought within the reach of the criminal law. Only by rejecting state definitions of crime and replacing them with a new standard—such as defining crime as the violation of human rights—can criminologists oppose, rather than reinforce, existing inequalities. "What is certain is that the legalistic definitions cannot be justified as long as they make the activity of criminologists subservient to the state," comment Schwendinger and Schwendinger (1975: 138). "In the process of redefining crime, criminologists will redefine themselves, no longer to be the defenders of order but rather the guardians of human rights."

Third, as a defender of the existing social order, the criminal justice system ultimately serves the interests of the capitalist class. The system is largely set up to process poor and minority offenders—most of whom could find no meaningful place in the labor market—while ignoring the illegalities of rich and corporate offenders. As Reiman (1984) puts it, the system is designed so that "the rich get richer and the poor get prison." In enforcing order, moreover, criminal justice officials are not beyond breaking the law themselves, such as through police brutality and receiving pay-offs in vice operations (Henderson and Simon, 1994). On a broader level, to protect its interests, the capitalist state will use its power to commit, largely with impunity, crimes against its own dissident citizens (e.g., illegal wiretapping against protesters), not to mention sponsoring covert actions to undermine other governments (Barak, 1991).

Fourth, capitalism is the root cause of criminal behavior (see Greenberg, 1993). Under capitalism, the human needs of the poor are ignored. Instead, they face demoralizing living conditions that foster crime by stunting healthy development (Currie, 1985) and/or by making crime a rational response (Gordon, 1973). More noteworthy, capitalism creates a fertile environment for crimes by corporations (Pearce, 1976). Pressures for profits, combined with lax state regulation and the infrequent application of criminal penalties, induce business enterprises to pursue profits through illegal methods. The consequences are not only huge economic losses but also violence that may well surpass that exacted by street crimes. Thus, by selling dangerously defective products, polluting the environment, and exposing workers to job hazards and toxic agents, corporations exact an enormous toll in illnesses, injuries, and deaths (see Cullen et al., 1987; Hills, 1987).

Fifth, the solution to crime is the creation of a more equitable society. Equipped with this knowledge, critical criminologists should unmask the ways in which capitalist-based exploitation creates crime and victimization. Equally important, they should not be armchair criminologists but rather should work to foster greater social justice. In particular, they should support humane policies aimed at preventing harm from occurring (see Maguire, 1988) and, more broadly, they should engage in political activity advocating a fairer distribution of wealth and power in society. For many critical criminologists, the goal of this reform effort is a socialist economy combined with a democratic political system sensitive to the needs of all citizens.

These broad principles inform much of the scholarship done under the broad name of critical criminology. Again, however, the intellectual richness of this perspective has resulted in many specific theoretical contributions—indeed, so many that it is beyond the scope of this volume to capture them all (see Greenberg, 1993; Lynch et al., 2000). Our main focus is on those works that have been particularly influential in addressing the question, why does crime occur? We should note that critical criminologists are often criticized for studying how powerful interests shape the content of law and the operation of the criminal justice system (see, e.g., Chambliss and Seidman, 1982; Quinney, 1974; Turk, 1966) instead of providing specific insights into the etiology of criminal behavior. In contrast, the strength of traditional criminology is precisely its sustained concern with explaining involvement in crime and in subjecting theories to empirical tests. Critical criminology's viability as an alternative to traditional perspectives thus depends on advancing explanations of criminality that are both theoretically persuasive and backed up by the data.

Capitalism and Crime

Most critical criminologists' thinking is influenced, at least in a general way, by the work of Karl Marx. Marx believed that in a capitalist system, the bourgeoisie—those who owned the means of production—inevitably exploited the proletariat-workers who did not own the means of production. Capitalism thus resulted in the immiseration and demoralization of the working class, a condition that would only be alleviated when workers shed their false consciousness that existing economic arrangements were legitimate, realized their joint interests, and revolted to create a socialist system.

For our purposes, it is noteworthy that Marx, despite sporadic writings on criminality and law, did not spell out systematically the connection between capitalism and crime (Greenberg, 1993; Taylor et al., 1973). It remained for Willem Bonger, a Dutch criminologist, to author in 1916 what is now considered the first classic attempt to use Marx to explain crime, *Criminality and Economic Conditions* (see Chapter 23 in this part).

Following Marx's dim view of the social consequences of capitalism, Bonger offered the central thesis that the capitalist mode of production breeds crime. Bonger believed that the key proximate cause of criminality is the mental state of egoism, whereas the social sentiment of altruism fosters prosocial conduct. Egoism is rooted in economic relations; after all, the basis of capitalism is ruthless competition and the exploitation of others in the pursuit of individual profits. The larger social good is not considered and thus altruism is not encouraged. In the proletariat, especially among those most impoverished, brutish living conditions, efforts by the bourgeoisie to incite materialistic desires, and the lack of moral training intensify egoistic impulses. Not surprisingly, criminal behavior is widespread in this class.

Anticipating the work of Edwin Sutherland on white-collar crime, Bonger also recognized that capitalism creates crime among the bourgeoisie. Crimes such as bank fraud, selling adulterated products, and large-scale swindles are at times committed by businesses that are economically imperiled. But many offenses are engaged in by those whose businesses are flourishing. These illegalities are a product of a "bourgeois environment" that inculcates, even in children, the moral principle that honesty is to be valued only so long as it does not interfere with one's advantage (Bonger, 1969 [1916]: 136). Furthermore, bourgeois crimes are made attractive because "the opportunity to commit these offenses undetected is enormous" (p. 138). This "unlimited opportunity to deceive the public" is made possible by capitalism; indeed, these "bourgeois crimes . . . can be committed only under an economic system of the kind that ours is" (p. 140). Bourgeois economic criminals, moreover, have little to fear from the criminal law. As Bonger (1969 [1916]: 142) noted, "the penalties prescribed for these crimes are relatively light as compared with those for ordinary crimes," and the "number of punishable acts is very limited as compared with those which really deserve punishment." In short, "it is these crimes which show clearly the class character of the penal law" (p. 142).

As might be anticipated, Bonger believed that under socialism—where the means of production were owned by the community—egoism would be discouraged and children would be morally educated to value altruism. Although sympathetic to his general theory, Taylor et al. (1973) take issue with Bonger's emphasis on the control of egoism as the key to reducing crime. In many ways, Bonger's theory moves away from Karl Marx and toward Emile Durkheim, the early anomie theorist who advocated the restraint of desires through moral education. This theoretical shift risks clouding Marx's fundamental focus on the misery caused by persisting inequality and on the need for working people to struggle against their exploitation. "Criminal man is consistently depicted [by Bonger] not so much as a man produced by a matrix of unequal social relationships, nor indeed as a man attempting to resolve those inequalities of wealth, power and life-chances," note Taylor et al. (1973: 235); "rather, criminal man is viewed as being in need of social control . . . . Socialism is preferable to capitalism,

most of all, because it will control the baser instincts of man."

In contrast, the centrality of the proletariat's struggle against oppression by the capitalist class is vivid in Richard Quinney's *Class, State, and Crime* (1980), an important book written a half century after Bonger's *Criminality and Economic Conditions*. "The contradictions of developing capitalism," maintained Quinney (1980: 59), "heighten the level of class struggle and thereby increase (1) the need to dominate by the capitalist class and (2) the need to accommodate and resist by the classes exploited by capitalism, particularly the working class." In an effort to secure their advantage, the capitalist class commits economic crimes, denies people basic human rights, and uses the state to protect its interests and to repress the poor. For the working class, crime is best understood as a response to their harsh, inequitable living conditions. Their illegalities "range from unconscious reactions to exploitation, to conscious acts of survival within the capitalist system, to politically conscious acts of rebellion" (p. 65).

Similar to Bonger, Quinney notes that the "only lasting solution to the crisis of capitalism is socialism" (p. 67). In the second edition of *Class, State, and Crime*, Quinney (1980) turned away from a strict Marxian theory of crime to recognize the importance of religion in human life. In his view, capitalism not only was beset by materialistic contradictions but also by a spiritual crisis—a "sacred void." Socialism thus must become spiritual, merging the secular and sacred to create a "prophetic socialist faith . . . a religious socialist culture" (p. ix). "The socialist struggle," commented Quinney, "requires a religious consciousness as much as a class consciousness . . . the religious goal transcends concrete societies. The prophetic expectation speaks finally to that which is infinite and eternal" (p. 68).

Quinney's embrace of the spiritual and its transformative powers, at the expense of the crass materialism of Marxism, is seen again in his subsequent efforts to lay the foundation for a "peacemaking criminology" (Pepinsky and

Quinney, 1991). His writings in this area helped to trigger the development of a branch of critical criminology that remains vibrant today (Fuller and Wozniak, 2006; Wozniak, 2002; Wozniak and Braswell, 2002). We will return to the peacemaking perspective at the end of this part.

Pathways to Crime

Critical criminologists such as Quinney propose that capitalism is the root cause of criminal behavior. Their analyses, however, often are couched in general terms, with bourgeois crime attributed to the need for the capitalist class to maintain its dominance and working-class crime attributed to the dehumanizing and demoralizing conditions of life under capitalism. Although useful in sensitizing scholars to processes involved in producing crime, these earlier analyses did not detail the specific factors under capitalism that foster criminal conduct. More recently, however, important efforts have been made to demarcate the specific pathways that link capitalism to crime. Elliott Currie (Chapter 24 in this part) and Mark Colvin (Chapter 25) have made significant contributions in illuminating the mechanisms through which an unequal social structure produces criminal behavior.

Like others in the critical tradition, Elliott Currie (2009 [Chapter 24]) sees capitalism as the root cause of crime—especially of the United States' high rate of serious violent crime. But he is a wise social observer, and thus he recognizes that capitalism is not unique to America but is an integral feature of the current global economy. His special insight, however, is that capitalism comes in different forms. A number of advanced industrial nations embrace a more "compassionate capitalism," in which the government takes steps to ensure that inequality does not become too widespread and that "cushions" are in place to support those who are the losers in the economic competition. In

contrast, the United States embraces a harsh brand of capitalism in which there are big winners and big losers. Compared to many advanced nations, in America the rich are richer but the poor are poorer—including poor children. Inequality (i.e., the gap between rich and poor) is thus much wider and supports for those citizens struggling to survive are less generous. The cost of enduring inequality, as a number of scholars have pointed out, is socially isolated and economically impoverished minority communities that are fertile soil for the growth of violent crime (see, e.g., Blau and Blau, 1982; Currie, 1985; Hagan, 1994; Hagan and Peterson, 1995; Peterson et al., 2006; Sampson, 1997; Short, 1997).

The culprit in this situation is the virtual omnipotence in America of what Currie calls a "market society" (see also Currie, 2009). He describes it in this way:

> By market society, I . . . mean . . . the spread of a civilization in which the pursuit of personal economic gain becomes increasingly the dominant organizing principle of social life; a social formation in which market principles, instead of being confined to some parts of the economy, and appropriately buffered and restrained by other social institutions and norms, come to suffuse the whole social fabric—and to undercut and overwhelm other principles that have historically sustained individuals, families, and communities. (1997: 151–152, emphasis in the original)

Does this description of the "institutional imbalance" between the economy and other American social institutions sound familiar? It will for those who recall Messner and Rosenfeld's (2007; see Chapter 15) extension of Merton's anomie theory. These theorists contended that the power of the "American Dream" causes economic interests to "penetrate" and weaken other institutions (e.g., the family). The resulting institutional imbalance fostered anomie and impotent informal social controls.

Currie agrees with certain points in Messner and Rosenfeld's analysis, but, as a critical criminologist, he believes that the pathways to serious crime in the United States are in a different direction. Thus, he focuses less on the breakdown of control and more on how the market economy is an amoral force that robs people of their jobs, fails to care for at-risk kids and families, and acquits the government from doing much about the human costs of inequality. He believes that this unrelenting generation of social misery and lack of support is a "toxic brew" (1997: 167). In particular, Currie identifies seven pathways through which the market economy creates high rates of serious violent crime in the United States:

> . . . the progressive destruction of livelihood; the growth of extremes of economic inequality and material deprivation; the withdrawal of public services and supports, especially for families and children; the erosion of informal and communal networks of mutual support, supervision, and care; the spread of a materialistic, neglectful, and "hard" culture; the unregulated marketing of the technology of violence; and, not least, the weakening of social and political alternatives. (1997: 154)

Mark Colvin is another critical scholar who seriously explores the complexities of crime causation. His key insight is in illuminating another pathway through which an inequitable class structure produces crime and delinquency: coercion. This idea first took form in a collaborative work with John Pauly (1983). Colvin and Pauly argue that parents' class position in the labor market shapes the methods they use to exercise control over their children. Specifically, they link the way in which parents are disciplined in the workplace to how they come to discipline their own children.

Colvin and Pauly are most concerned with those who are employed in the secondary labor market (in "dead-end jobs"), because these workers are controlled through coercive sanctions (e.g., yelling at or firing of workers).

Importing this style of control into the family, these parents tend to discipline their children coercively, attempting to enforce conformity through erratic, harsh punishment rather than through, for example, parent-child discussions aimed at developing internalized self-control. Such coercive discipline, however, proves counterproductive, alienating children and weakening bonds to parents. As problem behavior surfaces in school, the children are placed in strict or coercive class settings (e.g., special classes), further weakening their bond to society. They also are likely to associate with other alienated peers and to participate in delinquent subcultures. In short, they are on a pathway of deepening involvement in delinquency.

In *Crime and Coercion* (2000), Colvin expands on these themes, attempting to develop a more comprehensive "integrated theory of chronic criminality" (see Chapter 25, see also Colvin et al., 2002). A key premise of his perspective—again building on his work with Pauly—is that "coercive relations can appear in any number of settings, including workplaces, families, schools, among peers, and in state bureaucracies, such as welfare and criminal justice agencies" (2000: 52). Coercion—"compelling someone to act in a certain way"—not only occurs through "direct force and intimidation" but also "through the pressure of impersonal economic or social forces" (e.g., living in a community in which quality jobs have moved elsewhere) (2000: 36).

In proposing a "differential coercion theory," Colvin suggests most generally that the greater the degree of coercion, the greater the criminal involvement. More specifically, he proposes that people are most at risk for crime when they endure coercion that is harsh and erratically applied. He also details the intervening linkages, which he calls "social-psychological deficits," between the experience of coercion and crime. He argues, for example, that coercion causes criminal participation by increasing "coercive ideation," anger, feelings of humiliation, and an external locus of control and decreasing self-control, self-efficacy, and conventional social bonds (2000: 49–50). He amasses considerable evidence in favor of these premises. Recent empirical research lends further support to the core propositions of his theory (Baron, 2009; Unnever et al., 2004).

Colvin, however, is not interested in merely developing abstract theoretical principles but, similar to Elliott Currie, in placing his theory within the current American social context. In this regard, he asserts that in the United States, both interpersonal and impersonal coercion is tied to inequality. Inner-city youths thus are more likely to experience coercion in families, schools, peer groups, jobs located in the secondary labor market, and their neighborhoods. They are more often exposed to the conditions that cut off conventional life chances and ensnare them in a trajectory of chronic criminality. Also like Currie, Colvin's prescription for saving individual youths from bleak criminal futures and for reducing crime rates is clear: supportive social and criminal justice policies that reduce the multiple forms of coercion faced by our most vulnerable fellow Americans.

Peacemaking Criminology

Richard Quinney has been perhaps the most influential critical criminologist over the past three decades. In large part, Quinney's influence is due to his willingness to explore new horizons in his thinking. Unlike most criminologists, he has not staked out a theory and then defended it "to the end." Instead, his ideas have evolved, at times in ways that appear inconsistent with earlier theoretical positions. For example, in *Class, State, and Crime*, Quinney (1980) gives a classic Marxist, materialist interpretation of crime in capitalist America. By contrast, his later work on "peacemaking criminology" (presented here as Chapter 26) seems to offer a distinctly different way of understanding crime.

Paradoxically, this portrayal of his criminologies as being inconsistent with one another is both correct and incorrect. It is correct because

each step in Quinney's intellectual journey is *transformative*; that is, his ideas are not mere "add ons" to his previous thinking but emerge as qualitatively different. The portrayal of intellectual inconsistency is inaccurate because Quinney's new ideas are not a rejection of the old. Rather, the old is folded into the new as Quinney seeks to illuminate social reality in fresh ways. His theorizing is not linear but holistic (Quinney, 2002). Thus, two decades after their publication, he would not deny his materialistic insights on capitalist America because he would still view these inequitable structures as creating suffering and crime (Anderson, 2002). But in his later work, Quinney changes angles and uses the vision of peacemaking to show how individuals and social policies might create conditions in which the sources of crime will not be nourished (Wozniak et al., 2008).

Thus, writing in 1991, Quinney (Chapter 26 in this part) offered a classic statement that—along with contemporaneous writings from feminists and those with a progressive religious inspiration (Fuller, 1998; Fuller and Wozniak, 2006; Pepinsky and Quinney, 1991)—helped to initiate peacemaking criminology. Here, Quinney suggests that as individuals we are on a spiritual journey, which involves transcending one's egocentric self to understand the suffering in ourselves and in the world. Inner peace and peacemaking actions are intertwined and reinforcing. Without such peace, crime is inevitable. "Crime is suffering," Quinney reminds us, and "the ending of crime is possible only with the ending of suffering" (p. 11). But advancing peace and diminishing suffering require social justice; "this is the biblical command" (p. 11). The goal of a peacemaking criminology is thus to seek "to end suffering and thereby eliminate crime.... Without peace within us and in our actions, there can be no peace in our results. Peace is the way" (pp. 11–12).

The work of Quinney and other peacemaking criminologists is fresh, even inspiring, but is it scientific? These scholars have tended to offer a different way of thinking without providing any empirical evidence that their approach is in fact a more powerful explanation of criminal behavior than alternative theories. Recently, however, Fuller and Wozniak (2006) have derived a set of seventeen propositions that take peacemaking criminology from a perspective that sensitizes readers to different realities to one that is potentially testable just like any other theory. For example, they argue that crime and victimization will be less "when underlying social harms are more consistently addressed," and that individuals "who are responsive, mindful, and connected" will be less involved in illegal conduct (2006: 270). To the extent that scholars investigate these propositions, peacemaking criminology would earn more legitimacy among criminologists in the discipline.

Regardless, peacemaking criminology is not—and never will be—simply a dry theory; it is also a call to action. And, today, many critical scholars are embracing Quinney's prescription to make peace (Fuller, 1998; Lozoff and Braswell, 1989; Wozniak, 2002; Wozniak et al., 2008). For them, criminologists should use their knowledge and lives to create social justice. They reject, in particular, traditional "get tough" criminal justice responses to crime, which they argue attempt fruitlessly to fight violence with violence, suffering with more suffering. How many more failures will be necessary before we conclude that "wars on crime" never prove successful? Instead, they favor programs such as "restorative justice" that seek to mediate conflict, to address the real needs of victims, and to reintegrate offenders into a community that can instruct them in the ways of peace.

More generally, they assert that freeing ourselves from the burden of crime will require the ability to reject the inevitability of our current market society and related structures of inequality. The challenge is thus to *envision a new society* in which the scourges of racism, sexism, and classism are abandoned and in which the human needs of all citizens are given the highest priority. What might our society be like, they ask, if the government was less concerned with the gross national product (GNP) and with producing wealth and truly committed to seeing that every single child was born into and raised in a healthy and caring environment? This thinking is not utopian but rather a political option that must be articulated and fought for—one child at a time. Peacemaking criminology thus is not merely a theory but a way of imagining a future in which the struggle against suffering and crime is ongoing (Tifft, 2002).

References

Anderson, Kevin B. 2002. "Richard Quinney's Journey: The Marxist Dimension." *Crime and Delinquency* 48: 232–242.

Barak, Gregg, ed. 1991. *Crimes by the Capitalist State: An Introduction to State Criminality.* Albany: State University of New York Press.

Baron, Stephen W. 2009. "Differential Coercion, Street Youth, and Violent Crime." *Criminology* 47: 239–268.

Blau, Judith R. and Peter M. Blau. 1982. "The Cost of Inequality: Metropolitan Structure and Violent Crime." *American Sociological Review* 47: 114–129.

Bohm, Robert M. 1982. "Radical Criminology." *Criminology* 19: 565–589.

Bonger, Willem. 1969 [originally published in 1916]. *Criminality and Economic Conditions*, abridged edition, edited by Austin T. Turk. Bloomington: Indiana University Press.

Chambliss, William and Robert Seidman. 1982. *Law, Order, and Power*, 2nd edition. Reading, MA: Addison-Wesley.

Colvin, Mark. 2000. *Crime and Coercion: An Integrated Theory of Chronic Criminality.* New York: St. Martin's Press.

Colvin, Mark, Francis T. Cullen, and Thomas Vander Ven. 2002. "Coercion, Social Support, and

Crime: An Emerging Theoretical Consensus." *Criminology* 40: 19–42.

Colvin, Mark and John Pauly. 1983. "A Critique of Criminology: Toward an Integrated Structural-Marxist Theory of Delinquency Production." *American Journal of Sociology* 89: 513–551.

Cullen, Francis T., William J. Maakestad, and Gray Cavender. 1987. *Corporate Crime Under Attack: The Ford Pinto Case and Beyond*. Cincinnati: Anderson.

Currie, Elliott. 1985. *Confronting Crime: An American Challenge*. New York: Pantheon.

——. "Market, Crime, and Community: Toward a Mid-Range Theory of Post-Industrial Violence." *Theoretical Criminology* 1: 147–172.

——. 2009. *The Roots of Danger: Violent Crime in Global Perspective*. Upper Saddle River, NJ: Pearson Prentice Hall.

Fuller, John R. 1998. *Criminal Justice: A Peacemaking Perspective*. Boston: Allyn and Bacon.

Fuller, John R. and John F. Wozniak. 2006. "Peacemaking Criminology: Past, Present, and Future." In Francis T. Cullen, John Paul Wright, and Kristie R. Blevins (eds.), *Taking Stock: The Status of Criminological Theory—Advances in Criminological Theory*, Volume 15, pp. 251–273. New Brunswick, NJ: Transaction.

Gordon, David M. 1973. "Capitalism, Class, and Crime in America." *Crime and Delinquency* 19: 163–186.

Greenberg, David F., ed. 1993. *Crime and Capitalism: Readings in Marxist Criminology*, expanded and updated edition. Philadelphia: Temple University Press.

Hagan, John. 1994. *Crime and Disrepute*. Thousand Oaks, CA: Pine Forge Press.

Hagan, John and Ruth D. Peterson, eds. 1995. *Crime and Inequality*. Stanford, CA: Stanford University Press.

Henderson, Joel H. and David R. Simon. 1994. *Crimes of the Criminal Justice System*. Cincinnati: Anderson.

Hills, Stuart L., ed. 1987. *Corporate Violence: Injury and Death for Profit*. Totowa, NJ: Rowman and Littlefield.

Krisberg, Barry. 1975. *Crime and Privilege: Toward a New Criminology*. Englewood Cliffs, NJ: Prentice-Hall.

Lozoff, Bo and Michael Braswell. 1989. *Inner Corrections: Finding Peace and Peace Making*. Cincinnati: Anderson.

Lynch, Michael J., Raymond Michalowski, and W. Byron Groves. 2000. *A New Primer in Radical Criminology: Critical Perspectives on Crime, Power, and Identity*, 3rd edition. Monsey, NY: Criminal Justice Press.

Maguire, Brendan. 1988. "The Applied Dimension of Radical Criminology: A Survey of Prominent Radical Criminologists." *Sociological Spectrum* 8: 133–151.

Messner, Steven F. and Richard Rosenfeld. 2007. *Crime and the American Dream*, 4th edition. Belmont, CA: Wadsworth.

Milovanovic, Dragan. 1982. "Review Essay: Contemporary Directions in Critical Criminology." *Humanity and Society* 6: 303–313.

Patterson, James T. 1996. *Grand Expectations: The United States, 1945–1974*. New York: Oxford University Press.

Pearce, Frank. 1976. *Crimes of the Powerful: Marxism, Crime and Deviance*. London, UK: Pluto Press.

Pepinsky, Harold E. and Richard Quinney, eds. 1991. *Criminology as Peacemaking*. Bloomington: Indiana University Press.

Peterson, Ruth D., Lauren J. Krivo, and John Hagan, eds. 2006. *The Many Colors of Crime: Inequalities of Race, Ethnicity, and Crime in America*. New York: New York University Press.

Quinney, Richard. 1974. *Critique of Legal Order: Crime Control in Capitalist Society*. Boston: Little, Brown.

——. 1980. *Class, State, and Crime*. 2nd edition. New York: Longman.

——. 1991. "The Way of Peace: On Crime, Suffering, and Service." In Harold E. Pepinsky and Richard Quinney (eds.), *Criminology as Peacemaking*, pp. 3–13. Bloomington: University of Indiana Press.

——. 2002. "Criminologist as Witness." In Gilbert Geis and Mary Dodge (eds.), *Lessons of Criminology*, pp. 165–183. Cincinnati: Anderson.

Reiman, Jeffrey H. 1984. *The Rich Get Richer and the Poor Get Prison: Ideology, Class, and Criminal Justice*, 2nd edition. New York: John Wiley.

Sampson, Robert J. 1997. "The Embeddedness of Child and Adolescent Development: A Community-Level Perspective on Urban Violence." In Joan McCord (ed.), *Violence and Childhood in the Inner City*, pp. 31–77. Cambridge, UK: Cambridge University Press.

Schwendinger, Herman and Julia Schwendinger. 1975. "Defenders of Order or Guardians of Human Rights?" In Ian Taylor, Paul Walton, and Jock Young (eds.), *Critical Criminology*, pp. 113–146. London, UK: Routledge and Kegan Paul.

Short, James F. 1997. *Poverty, Ethnicity, and Violent Crime*. Boulder, CO: Westview.

Taylor, Ian, Paul Walton, and Jock Young. 1973. *The New Criminology: For a Social Theory of Deviance*. London, UK: Routledge and Kegan Paul.

Thomas, Jim and Aogan O'Maolchatha. 1989. "Reassessing the Critical Metaphor: An Optimistic Revisionist View." *Justice Quarterly* 6: 143–172.

Tifft, Larry L. 2002. "Crime and Peace: A Walk With Richard Quinney." *Crime and Delinquency* 48: 243–262.

Turk, Austin T. 1966. "Conflict and Criminality." *American Sociological Review* 31: 338–352.

Unnever, James, Mark Colvin, and Francis T. Cullen. 2004. "Crime and Coercion: A Test of Core Theoretical Propositions." *Journal of Research in Crime and Delinquency* 41: 244–268.

Wozniak, John F. 2002. "Toward a Theoretical Model of Peacemaking Criminology: An Essay in Honor of Richard Quinney." *Crime and Delinquency* 48: 204–231.

Wozniak, John F. and Michael Braswell, eds. 2002. "Special Issue—Criminology at the Edge: Essays in Honor of Richard Quinney." *Crime and Delinquency* 48: 199–349.

Wozniak, John F., Michael C. Braswell, Ronald E. Vogel, and Kristie R. Blevins, eds. 2008. *Transformative Justice: Critical and Peacemaking Themes Influenced by Richard Quinney*. Lanham, MD: Lexington Books.

23. Criminality and Economic Conditions

Willem Bonger

For Bonger, crime is a form of egoism—a rejection of the social instinct of altruism and of placing one's own interests above those of other people. Understanding crime, therefore, depends on answering the question, "Why does a man act egoistically?" (Bonger, 1969 [1916]: 26).

Writing in 1916, Bonger took pains to dismiss the answer of his contemporary Lombroso (see Chapter 2) and the members of his Italian or positivist school of criminology, who saw criminals' egoism as a "manifestation of atavism, that is, that some individuals present anew traits of character belonging to their very remote ancestors" (Bonger 1969 [1916]: 26). This explanation could not account, said Bonger, for evidence of altruism in earlier, supposedly less civilized times or for bourgeois crimes in the present. Referring to the lawlessness of the rich, Bonger noted that "even the Italian school is forced to admit that the stigmata found elsewhere cannot be pointed out in these individuals. Furthermore," continued Bonger, "in this case we can hardly speak of atavism. It may be that our ancestors were great offenders, but it is not probable that they ever were guilty of swindles of this kind" (p. 142).

Instead, Bonger contended that egoism was a product of the social environment and, in particular, was linked intimately to the "mode of production." In his view, capitalism breeds egoism because it is, by its very nature, an economic system in which individual self-interest is pursued regardless of its consequences on others. The bourgeoisie—those who own the means of production—thus use unscrupulous means, illegal if necessary, to protect and advance their economic advantage. In search of profits, they also exploit the proletariat, paying them as little as possible for their labor and feeling no reciprocity or sense of obligation toward them. Instead, the bourgeoisie see workers as mere instruments to serve their interests—people whose human needs and material well-being are of scant concern.

For the proletariat, capitalism causes egoism and thus crime to flourish. Their exploitive, rather than reciprocal, relationships with the bourgeoisie dull their altruistic sentiments. Brutish living conditions also serve to demoralize the proletariat, especially those in the "lower proletariat . . . who do not succeed, for any reason, in selling their labor" (p. 52). In these harsh circumstances, the moral training necessary for the development of altruism is undermined as youths are prematurely sent to work, are denied education, are raised in families and housing conditions detrimental to their healthy development, and are exposed to criminal influences on the street.

In the end, observed Bonger, "we have a right to say that the part played by economic conditions in criminality is preponderant, even decisive" (p. 197). Still, room for optimism remained. If crime "were principally the consequence of innate human qualities (atavism, for example)," as Lombroso might

Reprinted from Willem Bonger, *Criminality and Economic Conditions* (edited by Austin T. Turk). Copyright © 1969 by Indiana University Press. Reprinted by permission of Indiana University Press.

claim, "*the pessimistic conclusion that crime is a phenomenon inseparably bound up with the social life would be well founded*" (p. 197). But because "*crime is the consequence of economic and social conditions*," contended Bonger, "*we can combat it by changing those circumstances*" (p. 197). The answer is to replace capitalism by socialism, by a society in which "*the means of production are held in common*" (p. 198). According to Bonger, "*such a society will not only remove the causes which now make men egoistic, but will awaken, on the contrary, a strong feeling of altruism*" (p. 200). With the economic basis of crime thus eliminated, only crimes committed by "*pathological individuals*" would continue to exist (p. 200).

Bonger's criminology can be criticized for its rather crude economic determinism, its simple psychology of crime that tied crime only to the sentiments of egoism versus altruism, and its utopian view of socialism. Even so, Bonger's theory has value in showing that a capitalist economy has consequences, simultaneously creating demoralizing conditions that impede the healthy development of the poor and creating strong incentives for the rich to break the law.

Reference

Bonger, Willem. 1969 [originally published in 1916]. *Criminality and Economic Conditions*, abridged edition, edited by Austin T. Turk. Bloomington: Indiana University Press.

To find the causes of crime we must . . . first solve the question: "Why does an individual do acts injurious to the interests of those with whom he forms a social unit?", or in other words; "Why does a man act egoistically?"

Capitalism, Egoism, and Crime

. . . As we have seen in the preceding pages, it is certain that man is born with social instincts, which, when influenced by a favorable environment can exert a force great enough to prevent egoistic thoughts from leading to egoistic acts. And since crime constitutes a part of the egoistic acts, it is of importance, for the etiology of *crime in general*, to inquire whether the present method of production and its social consequences are an obstacle to the development of the social instincts, and in what measure. We shall try in the following pages to show the influence of the economic system and of these consequences upon the social instincts of man.

After what we have just said it is almost superfluous to remark that the egotistic tendency does not *by itself* make a man criminal. For this something else is necessary. It is possible for the environment to create a great egoist, but this does not imply that the egoist will necessarily become criminal. For example, a man who is enriched by the exploitation of children may nevertheless remain all his life an honest man from the legal point of view. He does not think of stealing, because he has a surer and more lucrative means of getting wealth, although he lacks the moral sense which would prevent him from committing a crime if the thought of it occurred to him. We shall show that, as a consequence of the present environment, man has become very egoistic and hence more *capable of crime*, than if the environment had developed the germs of altruism.

The present economic system is based upon exchange. As we saw at the end of the preceding section such a mode of production cannot fail to have an egoistic character. A society based upon exchange isolates the individuals by weakening the bond that unites them. When it is a question of exchange the two parties interested think only of their own advantage even to the detriment of the other party. In the second place the possibility of exchange arouses in a man the thought of the possibility of converting the surplus of his labor into things which increase his well-being in place of giving the benefit of it to those who are deprived of the necessaries of life. Hence the possibility of exchange gives birth to cupidity.

The exchange called simple circulation of commodities is practiced by all men as consumers, and by the workers besides as vendors of their labor power. However, the influence of this simple calculation of commodities is weak compared with that exercised by capitalistic exchange. It is only the exchange of the surplus of labor, by the producer, for other commodities, and hence is for him a secondary matter. As a result he does not exchange with a view to profit (though he tries to make as advantageous a trade as possible), but to get things which he cannot produce himself.

Capitalistic exchange, on the other hand, has another aim—that of making a profit. A merchant, for example, does not buy goods for his own use, but to sell them with advantage. He will, then, always try, on the one hand, to buy the best commodities as cheaply as possible, by depreciating them as much as he can; on the other hand, to make the purchaser pay as high a price as possible, by exaggerating the value of his wares. *By the nature of the mode of production itself* the merchant is therefore forced to make war upon two sides, must maintain his own interests against the interests of those with whom he does business. If he does not injure too greatly the interests of those from whom he buys, and those to whom he sells, it is for the simple reason that these would otherwise do business with those of his competitors who do not find their interest in fleecing their customers. Wherever competition is eliminated for whatever cause the tactics of the merchant are shown in their true light; he thinks only of his own advantage even to the detriment of those with whom he does business. "No commerce without trickery" is a proverbial expression (among consumers), and with the ancients Mercury, the god of commerce, was also the god of thieves. This is true, that the merchant and the thief are alike in taking account *exclusively* of their own interest to the detriment of those with whom they have to do. . . .

As we have seen above the merchant capitalist makes war in two directions; his interests are against those of the man who sells to him, and of the man who buys from him. This is also true of the industrial capitalist. He buys raw materials and sells what he produces. But to arrive at his product he must buy labor, and this purchase is "sui generis."

Deprived as he is of the means of production the working-man sells his labor only in order not to die of hunger. The capitalist takes advantage of this necessitous condition of the worker and exploits him. We have already indicated that capitalism has this trait in common with the earlier methods of production. Little by little one class of men has become accustomed to think that the others are destined to amass wealth for them and to be subservient to them in every way. Slavery, like the wage system, demoralizes the servant as well as the master. With the master it develops cupidity and the imperious character which sees in a fellow man only a being fit to satisfy his desires. It is true that the capitalist has not the power over the proletarian that the master has over his slave; he has neither the right of service nor the power of life and death, yet it is none the less true that he has another weapon against the proletarian, a weapon whose effect is no less terrible, namely enforeced idleness. The fact that the supply of manual labor always greatly exceeds the demand puts this weapon into the hands of every capitalist. It is not only the capitalists who carry on any business that are subjected to this influence, but also all who are salaried in their service.

Capitalism exercises in still a third manner an egoistic influence upon the capitalistic "entrepreneur." Each branch has more producers than are necessary. The interests of the capitalists are, then, opposed not only to those of the men from whom they buy or to whom they sell, but also to those of their fellow producers. It is indeed claimed that competition has the effect simply of making the product better and cheaper, but this is looking at the question from only one point of view. The fact which alone affects criminality is that competition forces the participants, under penalty of succumbing, to be as egoistic as possible. Even the producers who have the means of applying all the technical improvements to perfect their product and make it cheaper, are obliged to have recourse to gross deceits in advertising, etc., in order to injure their competitors. Rejoicing at the evil which befalls another, envy at his good fortune, these forms of egoism are the inevitable consequence of competition.

Following the same classification that we employed in the preceding chapter we come now to that part of the bourgeoisie which, without having any occupation, consumes what has been made by others. Not to feel obliged to contribute to the material well-being of humanity in proportion to one's ability must necessarily have a demoralizing influence. A parasite, one who lives without working, does not feel bound by any moral tie to his fellows, but regards them simply as things, instruments meant to serve and amuse him. Their example is a source of demoralization for those see this easy life without the power of enjoying it themselves, and awakes in them the desire to exchange their painful existence for this "dolce far niente.". . .

The Proletariat

To be thorough we begin by making mention of one of the consequences of the economic position of the proletariat, of which we have already treated briefly, namely the dependence in which persons of this class find themselves in consequence of their lacking the means of production, a state which has a prejudicial influence upon character. The oppressed resort to means by which they would otherwise scorn. As we have seen above, the basis of the social feelings is reciprocity. As soon as this is trodden under foot by the ruling class the social sentiments of the oppressed become weak towards them.

We come now . . . first to the consequences of the labor of the young. The paid labor of the young has a bad influence in several ways. First, it forces them, while they are still very young, to think only of their own interests; then, brought into contact with persons who are rough and indifferent to their well-being, they follow these only too quickly, because of their imitative tendencies, in their bad habits, grossness of speech,

etc. Finally, the paid labor of the young makes them more or less independent at an age where they have the greatest need of guidance. Even if the statistical proof of the influence of the labor of children and young people upon criminality were totally wanting, no one could deny that influence. Child labor is entirely a capitalistic phenomenon being found especially in the great manufacturing countries like England and Germany. And then one of the most salient facts of criminality is the amount of juvenile crime, which is so enormous that England, followed by other countries, has established a special system to combat this form of criminality. Certainly this increase of juvenile crime is chiefly due to the influence of bad domestic conditions (wage-labor of married women, etc.), but the labor of the young people themselves also plays its part.

It has rightly been said that work has a strong moral influence. But it is also true that immoderate labor has the contrary effect. It brutalizes a man, makes him incapable of elevated sentiments, kills as Key says (in "das Jahr-hundert des Kindes"), the man in the beast, while moderate labor ennobles the beast in the man.

The housing conditions of the proletariat have also a significance as regards criminality, and for the special group of sexual offenses their importance is very great. We shall speak of this more fully when we treat especially of these offenses, and will, for the moment, note simply their general consequences.

The disorder and squalor of the home communicate themselves to the inmates; the lack of room obliges the children to live, during a great part of the day, on the streets, with the result that they are brought into contact with all sorts of demoralizing companions. Finally, the living together of a great number of uneducated persons in one small dwelling is the cause of constant quarrels and fights. The situation of those who are merely night-lodgers is especially unfortunate, as we have already seen . . . .

As has already been said at the beginning of those observations as to the influence of the economic life upon the development of social feelings on the part of the proletariat, the egoistic side of the human character is developed by the fact that the individual is dependent, that he lives in a subordinate position, and that he feels himself poor and deprived of everything. However, in so far as the proletarian sells his labor he is guaranteed against famine, however miserable his condition, and conscious of the utility of his role in society, he feels himself, notwithstanding his poverty, a man who, except for his employer, is independent of all men. But if work is not to be found, or if the proletarian, sick and infirm, is not able to work, it goes without saying that the resulting unemployment is very demoralizing. The lack of steady work, the horrors of the penury into which he and his fall, and the long train of evils which result from both, kill the social feelings in a man, for, as we have seen above, these feelings depend upon reciprocity. Let one familiarize himself with the thought of the condition of the man who lives in the greatest poverty, *i.e.* the man who is abandoned by all, and he will understand how egoistic must be the feelings of such.

From the position in which the proletarians find themselves it follow that, towards each other, it is rather the altruistic than the egoistic feelings that develop; living less isolated than the bourgeois, they see the misfortune that strikes their neighbor, and have felt the same themselves, and above all, their economic interests are not opposed. Forced idleness—at present chronic, and acute in times of panic—modifies these conditions at times; it makes competitors of the workers, who take the bread out of each other's mouths.

The proletarian is never sure of his existence: like the sword of Damocles unemployment is constantly hanging over his head. Upon this subject Engels says:

> But far more demoralizing than poverty in its influence upon the English working man is the insecurity of his position, the necessity of living upon wages from hand to mouth, that in short which makes a proletarian of him. The smaller peasants in Germany are usually poor, and often

suffer want, but they are less at the mercy of accident, they have at least something secure. The proletarian, who has nothing but his two hands, who consumes today what he earned yesterday, who is subject to every chance, and has not the slightest guarantee for being able to earn the barest necessities of life, whom every crisis, every whim of his employer may deprive of bread, this proletarian is placed in the most revolting, inhuman position conceivable for a human being. (Engels, "Condition of the Working Class in England," p. 76)

This uncertainty of existence is one of the reasons which explain why, in relatively prosperous times the workingman often spends his wages as soon as he receives them, for he knows that the economies possible to him are so small that he could never be saved from misery in case of unemployment.

Finally we must speak of ignorance and lack of training on the part of the proletariat, as a factor of criminality . . . .

The first reason why ignorance and the lack of general culture must be ranked among the general factors of crime is this: the person who, in our present society, where the great majority of parents care very little for the education of their children, does not go to school, is deprived of the moral ideas (honesty, etc.) which are taught there, and ordinarily passes his time in idleness and vagabondage.

The second reason which makes ignorance a factor of crime, is that generally an ignorant man is, more than others, a man moved by the impulse of the moment, who allows himself to be governed by his passions, and is induced to commit acts which he would not have committed if his intellectual equipment had been different.

In the third place, it is for the following reasons that ignorance and the lack of training fall within the etiology of crime. The mind of the man whose psychic qualities, whether in the domain of the arts, or the sciences, have been developed, has become less susceptible to evil ideas. His intellectual condition constitutes thus a bridle which can restrain evil thoughts from realizing themselves; for real art and true science strengthen the social instincts . . . .

The Lower Proletariat

In the preceding pages I have already spoken of the influence exercised by bad material surroundings upon a man's character; I have pointed out the moral consequences of bad housing conditions, and also that he becomes embittered and malicious through lack of the necessaries of life. All this applies to the proletariat in general, but much more strongly still to those who do not succeed, for any reason, in selling their labor, that is the lower proletariat.

If the dwellings of the working-class are bad, those of the lower proletariat are more pitiable still. There are, through sickness or lack of work, periods of dire poverty in the life of almost every worker—for the lower proletariat these periods are without intermission. Its poverty is chronic. And when the poverty makes itself felt for a long time together, the intellectual faculties become blunted to such a point that there remains of the man only the brute, struggling for existence.

Although the material and intellectual poverty of the lower proletariat is much greater than that of the proletariat, the difference between them is only quantitative. In one connection, however, there is also a qualitative difference, a very important one, namely that the working-man is a useful being without whom society could not exist. However oppressed he may be, he is a man who has a feeling of self-respect. It is different with the member of the lower proletariat. He is not useful, but a detriment. He produces nothing, and tries to live upon what others make; he is merely tolerated. He who has lived long in poverty loses all feeling of self-respect, and lends himself to anything whatever that will suffice to prolong his existence.

In short, poverty (taken in the sense of absolute want), kills the social sentiments in man,

destroys in fact all relations between men. He who is abandoned by all can no longer have any feeling for those who have left him to his fate . . . .

Conclusions

What are the conclusions to be drawn from what has gone before? when we sum up the results that we have obtained it becomes plain that economic conditions occupy a much more important place in the etiology of crime than most authors have given them.

First we have seen that the present economic system and its consequences weaken the social feelings. The basis of the economic system of our day being exchange, the economic interests of men are necessarily found to be in opposition. This is a trait that capitalism has in common with other modes of production. But its principal characteristic is that the means of production are in the hands of a few, and most men are altogether deprived of them. Consequently, persons who do not possess the means of production are forced to sell their labor to those who do, and these, in consequence of their economic preponderance, force them to make the exchange for the mere necessaries of life, and to work as much as their strength permits.

This state of things especially stifles men's social instincts; it develops, on the part of those with power, the spirit of domination, and of insensibility to the ills of others, while it awakens jealousy and servility on the part of those who depend upon them. Further the contrary interests of those who have property, and the idle and luxurious life of some of them, also contribute to the weakening of the social instincts.

The material condition, and consequently the intellectual condition, of the proletariat are also a reason why the moral plane of that class is not so high. The work of children brings them into contact with persons to associate with whom is fatal to their morals. Long working hours and monotonous labor brutalize those who are forced into them; bad housing conditions contribute also to debase the moral sense, as do the uncertaintly of existence, and finally absolute poverty, the frequent consequence of sickness and unemployment. Ignorance and lack of training of any kind also contribute their quota. Most demoralizing of all is the status of the lower proletariat.

The economic position of woman contributes also to the weakening of the social instincts.

The present organization of the family has great importance as regards criminality. It charges the legitimate parents with the care of the education of the child; the community concerns itself with the matter very little. It follows that a great number of children are brought up by persons who are totally incapable of doing it properly. As regards the children of the proletariat, there can be no question of the education properly so-called, on account of the lack of means and the forced absence of one or both of the parents. The school tends to remedy this state of things, but the results do not go far enough. The harmful consequences of the present organization of the family make themselves felt especially in the case of the children of the lower proletariat, orphans, and illegitimate children. For these the community does but little, though their need of adequate help is the greatest.

Prostitution, alcoholism, and militarism, which result, in the last analysis, from the present social order, are phenomena that have demoralizing consequences.

As to the different kinds of crime, we have shown that the very important group of economic criminality finds its origin on the one side in the absolute poverty and the cupidity brought about by the present economic environment, and on the other in the moral abandonment and bad education of the children of the poorer classes. Then, professional criminals are principally recruited from the class of occasional criminals, who, finding themselves rejected everywhere after their liberation, fall lower and lower. The last group of economic crimes (fraudulent bankruptcy, etc.) is so

intimately connected with our present mode of production, that it would not be possible to commit it under another.

The relation between sexual crimes and economic conditions is less direct; nevertheless these also give evidence of the decisive influence of these conditions. We have called attention to the four following points.

First, there is a direct connection between the crime of adultery and the present organization of society, which requires that the legal dissolution of a marriage should be impossible or very difficult.

Second, sexual crimes upon adults are committed especially by unmarried men; and since the number of marriages depends in its turn upon the economic situation, the connection is clear; and those who commit these crimes are further almost exclusively illiterate, coarse, raised in an environment almost without sexual morality, and regard the sexual life from the wholly animal side.

Third, the causes of sexual crime upon children are partly the same as those of which we have been speaking, with the addition of prostitution.

Fourth, alcoholism greatly encourages sexual assaults.

As to the relation between crimes of vengeance and the present constitution of society, we have noted that it produces conflicts without number; statistics have shown that those who commit them are almost without exception poor and uncivilized, and that alcoholism is among the most important causes of these crimes.

Infanticide is caused in part by poverty, and in part by the opprobrium incurred by the unmarried mother (an opprobrium resulting from the social utility of marriage).

Political criminality comes solely from the economic system and its consequences.

Finally, economic and social conditions are also important factors in the etiology of degeneracy, which is in its turn a cause of crime.

Upon the basis of what has gone before, we have a right to say that the part played by economic conditions in criminality is preponderant, even decisive.

This conclusion is of the highest importance for the prevention of crime. If it were principally the consequence of innate human qualities (atavism, for example), the pessimistic conclusion that crime is a phenomenon inseparably bound up with the social life would be well founded. But the facts show that it is rather the optimistic conclusion that we must draw, that where crime is the consequence of economic and social conditions, we can combat it by changing those conditions . . . .

Discussion Questions

1. Willem Bonger and Cesare Lombroso were both writing in the same general time period. How do their theories of crime differ?
2. How does capitalism cause egoism and thus crime?

3. If Bonger were observing the United States today, what would he have to say about the nation's crime problem?
4. For Bonger, what is the solution to reducing crime?

24. Crime in a Market Society

Elliott Currie

In 1975, James Q. Wilson leveled a stinging attack on traditional sociological "thinking about crime" (see also Wilson and Herrnstein, 1985). Wilson argued that the search for "root causes" of crime was a fool's errand: these causes either did not exist or, if they did, they were beyond the control of the government. Social welfare policies would not, said Wilson, reduce crime. Instead, the solution was to use the one governmental resource that could blunt the crime rate if administered wisely: prisons. Because a relatively small group of offenders commit a disproportionately high amount of the serious crime, the key to decreasing lawlessness was to lock up the "wicked" among us. In essence, Wilson was proposing the policy of selective incapacitation.

Elliott Currie (1985, 1998) has been perhaps the most articulate progressive criminologist in responding to Wilson's reasoning—an important task given that Wilson's way of thinking would prove persuasive to conservative policymakers (see also Bennett et al., 1996). In Currie's view, the crime and policy analysis advanced by Wilson and similar conservative commentators is flawed in three important respects.

First, they have a misplaced faith in that the prisons are the solution to crime. Currie does not deny that some dangerous offenders must be incarcerated or that locking up over 2 million Americans has some effect on the crime rate. But

he points out that the six-fold increase in prison populations in the last quarter of the twentieth century did not yield a six-fold decrease in crime; in fact, crime rates rose and then fluctuated in a way that was not closely connected with rates of incarceration. In particular, Currie (1985, 1998) claims that there is little evidence that nations that imprison the highest proportion of its citizens are the safest.

Second, Currie believes that Wilson's crime analysis is flawed because his social analysis is flawed. In particular, Currie contends that conservative commentators such as Wilson fail to confront the distorting effect that America's largely unfettered capitalist system—what he calls the "market economy"—has on those people who are losing in the Social Darwinist fight to survive economically. The nation's powerful economic engine produces enormous wealth but also considerable poverty. This wide inequality creates powerful criminogenic forces, such as childhoods spent amidst the ravages of poverty, whole segments of the labor force left without the ability to secure steady employment and a meaningful livelihood, the concentration of disadvantage and associated problems in deteriorating inner cities, and so on.

The effects of these harsh and unforgiving conditions might be blunted if the government were proactive in cushioning the suffering of its people. But the

Excerpted by permission of Sage Publications, Ltd. from Elliott Currie, "Market, Crime and Community: Toward a Mid-Range Theory of Post-Industrial Violence," *Theoretical Criminology*, Vol. 1, No. 2, 1997. Copyright © 1997 by Sage Publications.

market economy has another dark side: its production of cultural values and political interests that oppose government intervention to help those in need. Thus, the market economy's emphasis on individual responsibility for failure, and its pressure on the state to reduce taxes and welfare budgets, means that social programs aimed at supporting at-risk citizens are constantly attacked as being "undeserving" and counterproductive. The result is disquieting. The combination of persisting high levels of inequality and of cutbacks in government support for the casualties of the market economy is a "toxic brew" that generates America's high rate of violent crime (see also Currie, 2009).

Third, Currie rejects Wilson's conclusion that, in essence, the government can do nothing about crime other than incarcerate more offenders. In his writings, Currie (1985, 1998) documents a variety of employment, early intervention, and criminal justice programs that have been shown to be effective and that, when taken together, could create a more "compassionate capitalism" within the United States. The nation's failure to embark vigorously on these programs reflects not the dearth of knowledge or of resources but the dominance of market society ideology and a lack of political will. The consequence of this policy approach to crime is that prisons continue to be filled to the brim but serious violence in America remains an enduring problem.

References

Bennett, William J., John J. DiIulio, Jr., and John P. Walters. 1996. *Body Count: Moral Poverty and How to Win America's War Against Crime and Drugs.* New York: Simon and Schuster.

Currie, Elliott. 1985. *Confronting Crime: An American Challenge.* New York: Pantheon.

——. 1998. *Crime and Punishment in America.* New York: Metropolitan Books.

——. 2009. *The Roots of Danger: Violent Crime in Global Perspective.* Upper Saddle River, NJ: Pearson Prentice Hall.

Willson, James Q. 1975. *Thinking About Crime.* New York: Vintage.

Wilson, James Q. and Richard J. Herrnstein. 1985. *Crime and Human Nature.* New York: Simon and Schuster.

In this paper I want to argue that it is precisely the extreme subordination of social life to the imperatives of what we rather inaccurately call the "market" that helps to explain not only the recent upsurge in volence in places like Russia and China, but also why the U.S. has long led the advanced industrial world in levels of serious violent crime—and why that unfortunate dominance continues in the face of unprecedented rates of incarceration which now surpass those of any other country in the world, advanced or otherwise, with the possible exception of —Russia (Mauer, 1995).

The Idea of Market Society

I will argue that the varying levels of serious U.S. criminal violence across the "post-industrial" societies are closely tied to the greater or lesser growth of what I call "market society." By market society I don't just mean the existence of a market *economy*—but the spread of a civilization in which the pursuit of personal economic gain becomes increasingly the dominant organizing principle of social life; a social formation in which market principles, instead of being confined to some parts of the *economy*, and appropriately buffered and restrained by other social institutions and norms, come to suffuse the whole social fabric—and to undercut and overwhelm other principles that have historically sustained individuals, families and communities.

By market society, in other words, I don't mean "market" in quite the same way that is meant when economists talk about the "free" market—the idea of an economy in which everyone gets to compete on level terrain without government interference. That is part of the *ideology* of market society, but is decreasingly its reality. We don't have that kind of market economy in the U.S., which, again, is the traditional exemplar of market society among the advanced nations: we have an economy in which increasingly those better situated are able to *insulate* themselves remarkably well from the pressure of market forces. . . . What we *do* have in the U.S., however, and to a growing degree in Britain and many other advanced industrial countries, is a society in which most areas of social life—most of the major institutions through which we grow up, earn a living, care for our bodies and minds, and put a roof over our heads—are increasingly shaped by private decisions made in the service of the accumulation of private gain. And that is what I mean by market society.

Market societies, in short, are Darwinian societies, whether or not they can be said to be "free" in any meaningful sense. They are societies which, by definition, offer few cushions against the impact of disabilities or misfortunes in the labor market and minimal public provision of social services. At best they provide basic "safety nets" for the worst victims of economic insecurity, but even those are likely to be fragile and increasingly besieged as market society advances. They are "sink or swim" societies, at least for those unable to corral enough private resources to stay afloat.

I suggest that market society, as thus defined, is a particularly fertile breeding ground for serious violent crime. . . . Our uniquely devastating experience of serious violent crime, in short, reflects the equally unique extent to which the principles of market society have driven America's social and economic development and shaped its national culture. And that not only helps us understand the state of crime—and punishment—in the U.S. itself, but offers a cautionary tale for other countries tempted to follow a similar developmental path.

. . . No one much disputes the reality of a relative absence of institutions countering the unfettered expression of the market principle in American history. In modern industrial societies those countervailing institutions have been essentially of one of two kinds; borrowing from the American economist Richard Belous (1992: 1–3), we can call them "compassionate" and "keiretsu" forms of capitalism. "Compassionate" capitalism stresses social solidarity, equity and community values; it is historically a bottom-up development rooted in traditionally strong unions, as in Scandinavia (this is similar to Will Hutton's description of the operative principles of "social market" Europe). "Keiretsu" capitalism, on the other hand, is paternalistic rather than communitarian—top-down rather than bottom-up; and has its roots in that kind of corporate paternalism rather than in a strong labor movement: Japan being the classic example. But both systems may end up in somewhat similar places when it comes to protecting ordinary people against the forces of unfettered markets. Thus taxation is relatively low in the Japanese version of "keiretsu" capitalism (or "peopleism," in Hutton's phrase); but so is inequality, and "human relations and the necessity of nurturing them are centre stage" (Hutton, 1995: 269).

Employment policy is a prime example of this rough convergence. Both Sweden, historically one of the most prominent exemplars of the compassionate model, and Japan, with a very different political history, have traditionally sought to keep workers employed even under the most adverse macroeconomic conditions. And both stand in stark contrast to the U.S. and some other exemplars of what Belous calls "contingent" capitalism, in which employers hire and fire at will and reject even the most modest government intervention in the labor market.

What makes the U.S. so distinct is that alone among post-industrial societies it has *neither* history—not the top-down but in many ways quite supportive corporatist tradition of a country like Japan, or the bottom-up, social-democratic buffers against the ravages of the market that strong labor movements and their allies successfully fought for in many European industrial countries—measures which are today, of course, under siege in many of them.

What does this have to do with violence? A great deal. This history means that the criminogenic effects of the market have traditionally been unleashed in the U.S. far more than in other advanced industrial societies. That is not to say that the U.S. is the only place they are found. Indeed part of my concern is precisely that they are becoming a familiar, even normalized part of the social landscape in many places around the world. But outside the Third World no country yet has experienced these effects in as concentrated and sustained a way as the U.S. And therein lies the core of our violence problem.

Market Society and Violent Crime

... There are at least seven of those profoundly criminogenic and closely intertwined mechanisms operating in "market society." They are not temporary aberrations, but—I would argue—intrinsic to the logic of market society itself....

1. First, *market society breeds violent crime by destroying livelihood.* It has sometimes been fashionable to argue that there are few if any connections between the labor market and crime. But the accumulating evidence strongly suggests otherwise. How individuals, families and communities fare in the labor market affects the potential for criminal violence in multiple and profound ways. On the level of individual aspirations and motivation, for example, the long-term absence of opportunities for stable and rewarding work, especially for the young, breeds alienation, undercuts the sense of having a "stake" in legitimate society, and exerts powerful pressures toward participation in illicit enterprises (Sullivan, 1985). Steady work provides one of the most important bonds that enable individuals to desist from early criminal careers (Sampson and Laub, 1993), and its absence helps explain why doing so is considerably harder for black youth in the U.S. than for their white counterparts (Elliott, 1994). Moreover, the absence of strong work opportunities undermines the effectiveness of programs to reintegrate offenders into the community, thus ensuring high rates of recidivism (Currie, 1985: Ch. 4). Long-term exclusion from stable work disrupts families and inhibits family formation in the first place (Wilson, 1987: Ch. 3), and diminishes the capacity of adults to perform credibly as role models and agents of socialization and the transmission of values to the young (Fagan et al., 1993). Less often discussed, but not less important, is the effect of *overwork* in poorly-paid jobs on the capacity of parents to provide a nurturing and competent environment for childrearing and on the capacity of communities for self-regulation and the maintenance of networks of mutual support and care. At the community level, the lack of opportunities for rewarding work breeds illicit enterprise, especially drug sales, which once established both increase the level of routine violence and weaken the community's capacity for supervision and support (Wilson, 1995). And mass exclusion from steady, well-paying work interacts with traditional gender norms to produce a broad stratum of men for whom violent means of asserting "manhood" flourish in the absence of conventional ones.

On all these counts, market society tends inherently to push the labor market in precisely the wrong directions. The fundamental problem is that in market society labor appears simply as a cost to be reduced rather than a social institution valuable in its own right—among other things, because of its capacity to promote social cohesion and personal integration. Accordingly, it is a central thrust of market society to seek to cheapen labor and/or eliminate it altogether. The result is a constant, systemic pressure toward the degradation of the labor market—through the proliferation of low-wage, high turnover jobs, endemic structural unemployment, or some combination of both. That is especially true in the context of the recurrent global overcapacity which market economies tend routinely to produce.

That combination, in fact, is what has most clearly characterized the U.S. labor market since the 1970s. The U.S. economy is often viewed as a highly successful "job machine," and its labor market policies have accordingly been widely held up as a model for the "rigid" economies of Europe to follow. But to the extent that the U.S. has indeed achieved higher job growth and lower measured unemployment than many (though not all) other advanced economies, it has been at the expense of wages and benefits—boosting the numbers of the "working poor" and creating a stratum of low-wage workers who are uniquely disadvantaged vis-à-vis their European counterparts. Thus, as of the late 1980s, as the economist Richard B. Freeman shows, men in the bottom decile of the U.S. earnings distribution earned only 38 percent of the median wage, while their counterparts in the bottom decile in Europe averaged 68 percent and in Japan 61 percent of the respective medians. The lowest-paid American workers "have lower real earnings than workers in all advanced countries for which there are comparable data"—earning less than half, for example, of what the lowest-paid German workers earn (Freeman, 1994: 12–13). That helps explain higher U.S. levels of family poverty (about which more below), and also in its own right exacerbates the criminogenic effects of overwork on families and communities. Market society can indeed, apparently, create "jobs"—lots of them. But it cannot reliably create *livelihoods*.

Moreover, the relatively low rates of official unemployment in the U.S. obscure relatively *high* levels, on average, of *non*-employment in recent years (Balls, 1994)—as measured by the proportion of working-age men who have dropped out of the labor force. . . .

Market society, moreover, tends to exacerbate the criminogenic impact of weakening labor markets through its reluctance to cushion the economic impact of joblessness or to use public resources to generate new jobs and serious training for them. The comparative figures are stunning: At the beginning of the 1990s the U.S. was spending less than half of what even the British spent, just a quarter of what the Dutch spent, and *less* than a quarter of what the Swedes

spent on labor market programs of all kinds. And a good part of what it *did* spend went for unemployment insurance. When it comes to programs to provide training and jobs outside the private labor market, these differences are much starker. Sweden spent eight times what the U.S. did, proportionately, on these "active" labor market programs (Reutersward, 1990).

2. The second—closely related—mechanism through which market society breeds violence is its *inherent tendency toward extremes of inequality and material deprivation*. The progressive elimination of good work (and the systematic resistance to an active employment policy) is part of the reason for that tendency. Another is the resistance of market societies against government intervention to offset the inadequacy of labor market incomes.

In the U.S., where "market" principles reign supreme in the absence of strong countervailing forces, income inequality has traditionally been more extreme than in other advanced societies; in the early 1980s, the share of the poorest fifth of the population in GDP was half again as high in West Germany and nearly *twice* as high in Sweden (Barr, 1992: 776). And those gaps widened substantially in the 1980s and 1990s, as the U.S. income distribution took a sharp turn toward increased inequality. . . .

The key reason for the wider spread of inequality in the U.S. is that the bottom is so far down, as recent data from the Luxembourg Income Study illustrate in sharp relief. At close to 22 percent, the child poverty rate in the U.S. towers above that of European countries—even relatively poor ones like Ireland (at about 12 percent). Child poverty rates are below 4 percent in Sweden, Belgium, Finland and Denmark; the closest competitors to the U.S. among advanced industrial nations are Canada and Australia, at roughly 14 percent (Rainwater and Smeeding, 1995, Table 2). . . .

Even more striking, from the LIS data, is the stark *inequality* in the economic condition of American children. Thus, in no European country do children in the *upper* fifth of the scale of real income match the income of comparable children in the U.S.: but only in Ireland (and Israel) are children's real incomes in the *lowest* fifth below those of the poorest American children. Poor children in the U.S., in short, are not only more numerous but also poorer than their European (or Canadian or Australian) counterparts, while the most affluent children in America are considerably *richer* than their counterparts in other advanced countries. . . .

What makes it troubling, among other things, is that both poverty and inequality are increasingly implicated in violent crime. Again, as with employment, the relationships are complex and some are indirect. Yet the evidence points strongly to a profound role for both absolute and relative deprivation. How much poverty, and how wide a spread of inequality, a society tolerates *matter* in terms of violence, and this for several related reasons.

The evidence for a strong link between income inequality and homicide in particular is long-standing, and it comes from a variety of different kinds of research carried out across a variety of different settings (cf. Blau and Blau, 1982; Currie, 1985: Ch. 5; Messner, 1989; Gartner, 1990). Notably, one recent study finds a strong and specific association between the growth of wage inequality in the U.S. since the 1970s and levels of homicide and aggravated assault (Fowles and Merva, 1996). These connections are typically drawn in terms of some conception of relative deprivation. But there is also growing evidence that poverty itself—or more precisely a syndrome of multiple deprivation (what Land et al. have usefully called "resource deprivation")—is implicated in homicide generally (Land et al., 1990; Smith and Brewer, 1992) and in family homicides in particular (Goetting, 1995).

The long-term deprivation characteristic of market society generates high levels of violent crime in part because of its impact on child development. To begin with, the link between severe economic deprivation and child abuse is one of the strongest and most recurrent in the literature on child development (Sampson, 1993). In the U.S. the risk of reported physical child abuse is seven times higher in families making below $15,000 a year than in those making more (Cappelleri et al., 1993). Poverty's strong contribution to child abuse increases the level of criminal violence both directly, by increasing violence against children, and indirectly, through the intergenerational impact of abuse on later violence (Widom, 1992). At the same time, "persistent" poverty of the kind routinely generated by market society inhibits intellectual and social development among children and predisposes them toward school failure and later economic marginality (Miller and Korenman, 1993). The more years children spend in poverty, the more their measured intellectual development falls behind, even after other factors, like family structure, are controlled (Duncan et al., 1993).

3. But the lack of public supports to ameliorate the market's impact on the well-being of families and communities involves more than just income benefits alone. The third main mechanism by which market society breeds violent crime is by *weakening other kinds of public supports* that we have good reason to believe act as strong buffers against crime.

As with the problems of inadequate livelihood and economic deprivation, the problem is that market society is *intrinsically* antagonistic to the provision of the kinds of social supports that, as Frank Cullen (1994) has detailed, may act as critical inhibitors of serious crime. Because it is a basic operating principle of market society to keep the public sector small, it forces individuals and families to rely on individual efforts to secure some of the basic of healthy human development that less Darwinian societies, even poorer ones, provide much more reliably and accessibly. Poor but relatively generous societies, accordingly, are likely to do a better job at keeping violent crime low than wealthy but mean-spirited ones.

The withdrawal of public provision has especially devastating consequences when it is combined (as it invariably is in advanced market societies) with the broad structural shifts in the labor market I have noted above. The strains between family and work offer a key example. The adoption of low-wage, high-turnover labor market strategy that is an essential feature of "contingent" capitalism tends to undercut parents' ability to nurture and supervise their children, leading, in turn, to the kinds of problems that many versions of control theory warn us about. As wage levels fall and steady full-time work is replaced by the packaging of several part time and/or temporary jobs, parents in market societies increasingly need to work excessively long hours to make ends meet—which means that their children are likely to be deprived of attention and support. Reliable and affordable child-care facilities and after-school programs could ease that strain considerably; but market societies provide them spottily and grudgingly at best.

Here too, the figures differentiating the U.S. from the "compassionate capitalist" countries are stark and consistent. Just as we are the post-industrial nation with the most meager income support for low-income families, so too we have the least developed mechanisms to mitigate the stresses between work and childrearing. Virtually every other post-industrial nation provides nearly universal care for 3- to 5-year-olds, in one way or another, and all provide some form of paid parental leave (indeed a number of *developing* countries do better in this respect) (Kamerman and Kahn, 1995). Once again, the effects on violence are multiple and complex. The tendency of market society to force parents on to their own (often slim) resources puts children at great risk of abuse and neglect; it simultaneously increases the risks of domestic violence, as the paucity of outside supports for child care combine with weak job opportunities to trap women in abusive relationships.

This pattern, moreover, applies across the board to other public institutions that could play an important role in preventing violent crime.

Widely accessible, high-quality preventive and prenatal health care, for example, might prevent some of the most basic physical and emotional traumas of childhood that we know are implicated in violent crime (Lewis et al., 1988). But the U.S. is also the only post-industrial nation without a national health system to deliver that care. (Those systems, of course, are increasingly under siege—in countries as diverse as Britain and Costa Rica as global market society advances.)

4. The withdrawal of *public* supports is compounded by the simultaneous tendency of market society to erode *informal* social supports and networks of care. This is especially a consequence of the rapid movement of capital and, accordingly, of opportunities for steady work in market society—which is characterized by the demand for "flexibility" in the workforce and by the absence of strong ties of capital to any geographic community. But what the system hails as "flexibility" from the point of view of the employer translates into rootlessness for individuals and families and atomization for communities. The result is to deplete the sources of informal support that might otherwise buffer the consequences of mass joblessness, poverty and the retreat of public social services.

If, for example, a family stressed by long working hours and unable to procure decent child care could lean on the grandparents down the street to care for the children; if they could look to uncles, cousins, and friends to help keep an eye on their teenagers when long working hours mean they can't do it themselves; then the criminogenic consequences of overemployment and poverty could arguably be mitigated. But market society systematically splits extended families and creates communities characterized by rapid geographical mobility and the consequent "thinning" of networks of close friendship and mutual care. The overall result is not unlike what social disorganization theorists have warned about since the 1920s, and recent research has repeatedly confirmed (see Sampson and Groves, 1989; Sampson, 1993; Cullen, 1994).

That "thinning" of community under the impact of market development is speeded by systematic private sector disinvestment—as the economic and social condition of the hardest-hit communities no longer suffices to justify investment in market terms—at least in the short term, which is, more and more, the operative time frame in market society. As market society progresses, in other words, we increasingly see communities with not only few *public* agencies—recreation programs, health clinics, libraries—but also few stores, restaurants or movie theatres.

The overall result is a deepening, self-fueling cycle of social impoverishment—what Jeffrey Fagan and his colleagues, in their recent multi-city study of crime, drugs and neighborhood change in the U.S., describe as a progressive "unraveling" of low-income communities. As these researchers point out, the resulting depletion of stable adult supervision and support means that youth gangs or drug dealers may become "the dominant informal control and socialization force" (Fagan et al., 1993: 4). More generally, it leaves youth more and more dependent for help, advice and role modeling on their peer groups and on an increasingly pervasive consumer culture (on which more below).

A second consequence is equally potent. As two decades of research make abundantly plain, it is precisely this sort of "social" impoverishment that is heavily implicated in severe child abuse and neglect—and which helps to explain why some low-income communities have much higher levels of child maltreatment than others (Zuravin, 1989; Garbarino and Kostelny, 1992; Sampson, 1993). It is important not to overstate this case. Even in the most "unraveled" parts of American (or Third World) cities, there remain strong families, at least some solid, longstanding communal institutions (in the U.S., notably churches); and often a handful of dedicated, if overextended, nonprofit social service agencies. But the overall drift of market society is increasingly to marginalize and, at the extreme, to overwhelm them.

5. Market society simultaneously breeds crime by *promoting a culture that exalts atomized and often brutal individual competition and consumption over the values of community, contribution and productive work.* The tendencies I have noted in the labor market, in levels of inequality, deprivation, social provision and support, are exacerbated by fundamental changes on the level of culture. Here the empirical reality is murkier and the changes harder to quantify. Yet I do not think we can adequately understand trends in crime in either the advanced or the developing world without paying these changes close attention. Market society is underpinned by a distinctive set of cultural values and norms—and as it develops, these come to push aside others which have traditionally helped communities to maintain social cohesion (and low levels of violence) in the face of economic deprivation and uncertainty.

We talk a great deal, especially in the U.S., about the links between crime and the culture of poor people. We talk hardly at all about the role of the *common* culture. There is much discussion—I think *too* much—of the culture of the underclass, but little about the culture of the *over-class* (for a fine critique of the "underclass" discussion, see Gans, 1995). That is a serious default, because we will simply not understand the character of violent crime in the contemporary world—perhaps especially youth violence—unless we view it within the context of the growth and spread of a dominant culture of exploitation, predation and indifference to human life in our time.

We can break down these developments into at least three distinct parts; first, the increasing potency and primacy of consumer values; second, and relatedly, the erosion of what I would call "craft" values; and finally the increasing institutionalization, or normalization, of a "mainstream" culture of exploitation and irresponsibility.

There is nothing new about the idea of the U.S. being an extreme example of a consumer society. What *is* new, I think, is the extent to which the other trends I have described have made young people, especially, more and more vulnerable to the appeals of a frantically consumerist culture. As we have decimated both formal and informal adult institutions of supervision, livelihood and support—and not just in poor communities—the culture's insistent proddings toward acquisition and consumption, through the advertising industry, television and the movies, are increasingly unmediated. We have some evidence for this shift that goes well beyond the anecdotal. In their recent multi-city study of drugs and crime in impoverished inner-city neighborhoods, for example, Jeffrey Fagan and his colleagues found a growing "materialism" in American inner cities—indeed, in some cities, what they describe as "hypermaterialism" (1993: 8). Nor is that phenomenon confined to drug-dealing youth gangs. Surveys have described a significant shift toward "consumption aspirations" among American adolescents generally during the 1980s; the proportion agreeing that "having lots of money" was one of their main goals in life rose from less than half in 1976 to nearly two-thirds a decade later (Crimmons et al., 1991).

A second underappreciated casualty of the spread of market culture is what I would call "craft" values—by which I mean the value of a job well done, the pleasure in productive work and creativity, the self-esteem that comes from acquiring competence and contributing your growing skills to an appreciative community. I can't measure this loss in neat numbers. But I am struck by it frequently in encounters with young people in general and delinquent youth in particular.

As market society advances, the value of work and its ability to bind individuals into a productive community life is progressively demeaned in favor of the valorization of consumption for its own sake—and of getting what you want, or getting ahead of others, by whatever means will suffice. When that cultural shift is combined with the decimation of opportunities for good work, it produces a dual assault on one of the most crucial mechanisms of social support, social control and communal engagement.

I'm suggesting, in other words, that the eclipse of stable and rewarding work in market society has, in addition to the economic and social consequences I have proposed above, a more subtle cultural one. Work stabilizes society in part through its cultural meaning—its ability to provide channels of status and esteem, and definitions of virtue and worth, that involve hierarchies of competence, diligence, and contribution. It allows for the valuing of productive means over consumerist ends, of contribution over position. One of the quieter, but I think extremely corrosive, effects of market society is to chip away at those cultural standards linking esteem to the capacity for production and contribution.

These considerations may also help explain why some poor communities manage to resist, at least for a while, the atomization and institutional disintegration that engulf others —and the accompanying levels of violence. In the U.S., that pattern is often found to be true of recent immigrant communities, as against those with a longer history of economic marginalization and longer exposure to a "hypermaterialist" dominant culture. Immigrant communities may retain strong elements of premarket values stressing family obligation and the dignity of work—values which, as a broad body of empirical research makes clear, tend to be worn down the longer immigrants reside in the U.S. and are buffeted by the onslaught of market values.

Another cultural development, equally difficult to quantify, but I think equally important in understanding the links between market society and violence, is what might be described as the spread of a culture of "normal brutality." This too, is by no means a new idea; it is prefigured in the work of a number of early criminological theorists. Around the turn of the century, for example, Enrico Ferri wrote that what he called the "law of free competition" was a "disguised form of cannibalism"—because it established, he said, the rule that "your death is my life" (1962:

84). That insight has transparent relevance for the problem of white-collar crime, but its implications are much broader. Market society promotes violent crime in part by creating something akin to a perpetual state of internal warfare in which the advancement of some is contingent on the fall of others, and in which a corresponding ethos of unconcern—of non-responsibility for others' well-being—often legitimized under the rubric of beneficent competition, pervades the common culture and the interactions of daily life.

A culture in which routinely throwing employees out of work in the name of "restructuring" is increasingly defined as thoroughly laudable business practice; where losing one's footing in the intensifying scramble for livelihood and income means more and more the possibility of falling into real social limbo; where even the most basic help for those who do "lose" is granted, if at all, grudgingly and with overt disrespect; where even the risks of disability or death from illness or accident are contingent on market income and basic health care may be withheld from those without it; where, in short, those on top continually make it clear that they have only minimal concern for the well-being of those on the bottom—is a society in which the risks of violent crime are magnified, because those on the bottom are likely to internalize and reciprocate the prevailing ethos of disregard.

The extraordinarily prescient Willem Bonger put it this way, early in the century: "He who is abandoned by all can no longer have any feeling for those who have left him to his fate" (1969: 53). We do not have much of a language for this phenomenon in contemporary criminological theory. But I don't think anyone who has spent much time with delinquent youth, repeat offenders or drug dealers in the inner cities of the advanced societies can have failed to be aware of their sense of society as a "dog-eat-dog" world. Market society's fundamental cultural attitude of nonresponsibility, in short, breeds a pervasive tendency toward "unbonding" from society of those most impacted by economic and social insecurity and impoverishment—a sense that they are not merely deprived but maltreated. What we might call a "culture of callousness," in which concern for the well-being of other people becomes steadily attenuated, is not a "subculture" confined to "lower-class" youth, but a fundamental tendency of the *dominant* culture itself which poor youth assimilate and, no doubt, magnify, but cannot be said to initiate.

6. A sixth mechanism by which market society aggravates violent crime is by deregulating the *technology of violence*. I don't think this point needs much elaboration. The level of gun involvement in violent crime—especially homicide—in the U.S. is immense, and we won't understand the American pattern of violence apart from it. That is particularly true of the sharp rise in youth homicide that scarred the country in the late 1980s and early 1990s; from 1990 through 1994, 71 percent of black and 54 percent of white juvenile homicide victims were killed by firearms (Snyder et al., 1996: 3). There is much room for debate over how *much* of the difference in rates of homicide in the U.S. versus other advanced industrial countries can be laid to the prevalence of firearms—how many gun homicides, for example, might be carried out by other means if handguns were less easily available. If we simply subtract handgun homicides from the total, for example, the U.S. rate still towers above those of most European countries and Japan. But there is no serious dispute that the virtual absence of national-level regulations on the sale and possession of firearms both distinguishes the U.S. from virtually every advanced nation and contributes substantially to the lethality of American violence (Cook et al., 1995). Nor is there dispute that the modest recent national-level legislation establishing waiting periods for gun purchases and restricting military-style assault weapons have left vast areas of the firearms market for all practical purposes untouched, notably the so-called "secondary" firearms market of informal gun shows and private sales (Cook et al., 1995: 87–90).

What is less often acknowledged is how closely this absence of public regulation of firearms meshes seamlessly with the general "market" orientation of American civilization. The unique proliferation of firearms, especially handguns, in the U.S. is often attributed to its "frontier" culture, but though there is surely some truth in that explanation, by itself it is unconvincing. Canada is also a "frontier" society, but it regulates guns far more stringently than does the U.S. and suffers only a fraction of the level of handgun violence. I think the more salient distinction involves the varying historic dominance of market culture and institutions across these two countries, which is evident across many realms of culture and social policy. It cannot be entirely coincidental that Canada has both more stringent controls over the sale of guns and (so far) a much more generous "welfare state" than the U.S., or that Canada pioneered the kind of universal medical care system which the U.S. has fiercely and effectively resisted in the name of the "free market."

7. Finally, market society breeds violent crime by *weakening or eroding alternative political values and institutions* through which those it hurts most could make sense of their situation in progressive terms and take effective collective action against it.

We don't talk about this issue much in our recent thinking about violent crime. But it has a significant, if abbreviated, history in criminology. Recall that Robert Merton's fifth "adaptation" to the condition of social "strain" was "rebellion," which

> leads men [sic] outside the environing social structure to envisage and seek to bring into being a new, that is to say, a greatly modified social structure.

Crime was only one of several possible responses to a disjunction between socially structured means and culturally prescribed ends; political action to change either or both was another. But in order to "pass into organized political action," frustration with the existing social structure had to be translated into allegiance to "new groups possessed of a new myth"—thus transforming

mere alienation into positive rebellion. That in turn required breaking the "monopoly of the imagination" imposed by what Merton called the "conservative myth"—the assertion that the deprivation and inequality were inevitable in the nature of things or the result of individual failure rather than social structural constraints (1963: 155–7).

Merton himself did not elaborate much on this point, and it has been mostly forgotten since. But the central insight is crucially important. The way in which adverse social and economic conditions affect people's propensity to crime will obviously be mediated by the cultural ideologies and communal institutions available to them to respond to that adversity. Where strong labor movements or political parties address the concerns of low-income people, or strong ethnic or communal organizations are at hand to promote the collective well-being, the frustrations of social and economic deprivation are more likely to be channeled into constructive social action. But in "market" society those institutions are weak to nonexistent; in fact, it is precisely their weakness that allows market society to flourish to begin with. And as it progresses market society tends to erode them even further—witness the rapid decline of union membership in the U.S. (and many other advanced countries) in recent years, the casualty of market-driven deindustrialization and of concerted attacks by employers in legislatures and on the shop floor.

Why is this important for understanding violent crime? Because it leaves the people most "at risk" because of deprivation and social impoverishment with little means of constructively challenging the forces that are undermining their communities, families and futures—and thereby makes it far more likely that their response will take the form of an individual lashing-out, or a gratification of individual impulse at the expense of other people in the same boat. Over time, the withering of those countervailing institutions begins to deprive them of even the language, the conceptual framework, to define their problems in collective terms and to envision a collective response.

The Future

... I have argued that market society is peculiarly conducive to violent crime, for reasons that are analytically separable but, in the real world, closely intertwined and mutually reinforcing—operating simultaneously on the levels of material well-being, social support, and cultural meaning. Thus it is not just that market society increasingly forces a harsh choice of joblessness or low-wage labor, but that in doing so it exacerbates economic inequality and plunges large segments of its population into extreme deprivation—while simultaneously both withdrawing public provision of support and chipping away relentlessly at the informal support networks that might cushion these disadvantages. All the while it is also replacing earlier communal values and norms with an increasingly strident ethos of competitive consumerism which rubs raw the frustrations that accompany the declining economic fortunes of large strata of the population, and weakening the counter-ideologies and institutions that could mobilize constructive challenges to a harsh and depriving social order. To top it off, at the extreme such a civilization laxly regulates and opportunistically promotes the marketing of the mass instruments of lethal violence. It is a potent and toxic brew. And it is, again, a mixture intrinsic to the logic of market society—a function not of its failure but of "the quality of its success," as R. H. Tawney put it in the 1920s; "its light itself a kind of darkness" (1920: 33)....

This is not the place to go into the details of what would be required to deflect this trajectory. But a few points seem clear. I have argued that market society generates several analytically separable mechanisms through which it exacerbates the problem of serious violent crime. But these are not really separable in the real world, and some of them are more central than others. In particular, it is the systematic assault on steady livelihood that is arguably the most destructive feature of the advance of market society, and the one with the most diverse and potent ramifications for families and communities; it is, therefore, also the most promising lever for change. Full employment at socially meaningful work at good wages, and with reasonable hours, at a stroke attacks many of the criminogenic features of market society—integrating individuals into a larger social purpose, stabilizing local communities, and guaranteeing sufficient income. It makes illicit markets less appealing and reduces the kinds of family stresses that put smaller children at risk of abuse and weaken the supervision of older ones.

Building that kind of strategy, in the face of the technological changes now transforming work across the globe, means moving in two directions at once (see Currie, 1995): substantially expanding employment in the public and nonprofit sectors of the economy, and developing policies for worksharing and reduction of work time. Both are worthy in themselves, but both also have enormous potential for reducing violence. If we spread work and reduce work time, we not only widen access to livelihood among people who are now cut off from the integrative and supportive effects of stable work, but we also lessen the destructive impact of *overwork*. If we invest in public-sector job creation, we provide new livelihoods for many people the private market will not employ—and we can also staff the public agencies of social support and capacity-building which market society erodes if left to its own devices: health and mental health care, public schooling, child care and skill training. An active employment policy geared to creating new jobs in the public and nonprofit sectors, in short, meshes powerfully with a commitment to the universal provision of high-quality public services; and that combination can be the core of an effective attack on the conditions that breed violent crime.

Such is the state of public discourse on these matters in most of the developed world today that calls for revitalizing an active employment strategy along these lines are sometimes dismissed as Utopian. But there is considerable evidence that it is both eminently feasible (Glyn and Rowthorn, 1994) and capable of attracting strong public support. Even in the U.S., a substantial majority, according to opinion polls, agrees that government should guarantee work for those the private economy will not or cannot hire. Criminologists need to add their voices to what should become a broad and public debate over the nature of work and of social support in the advanced societies of the 21st century. They can do so best by affirming that violence is one of the clearest costs of our increasingly heedless global assault, in the name of the market, on the preconditions of a sustaining social life.

Discussion Questions

1. What is the "market economy"? How does it produce inequality and the conditions that are conducive to high rates of violent crime in the United States?
2. Compared to other advanced industrial nations (e.g., Japan, western European countries), is the United States government more or less supportive of its citizens who are in need? Why does Currie think this is the case? What does he believe are the consequences of these government policies?
3. How is Currie's "market society" theory similar to Messner and Rosenfeld's "institutional-anomie" theory? How do the theories differ?
4. What policies would Currie's perspective on crime suggest are likely to reduce crime? What policies would Currie believe would not reduce crime?

25. Crime and Coercion

Mark Colvin

In Crime and Coercion *(2000), Mark Colvin argues that the notion that coercion causes criminal behavior is not novel but rather is found in a variety of criminological theories, including Agnew's general strain theory (Chapter 16), Cullen's social support theory (Chapter 46), and Tittle's control-balance theory (Chapter 45). Braithwaite's (Chapter 21) reintegrative shaming theory, Sherman's defiance theory (Chapter 22), and many critical theories might have been added to this roster of perspectives that, to a greater or lesser extent, would caution that coercion does not breed conformity but crime. Still, with few exceptions (Patterson et al., 1989), previous scholars have not gone beyond offering the broad insight that coercion is criminogenic to develop a systematic theory of crime and coercion. By contrast, Colvin carefully builds on previous theorizing and research to provide such a comprehensive model in his "differential coercion theory" (see also Colvin et al., 2002).*

Colvin argues that control has two fundamental dimensions, each of which can be envisioned as continuums with two qualitatively different endpoints. First, control can range from coercive to non-coercive. Second, control can range from consistent to erratic. By cross-tabulating these two dimensions into a 2 x 2 table, one can arrive at "four control types." For Colvin, the most consequential is "Type 4," which is when control is exercised coercively and erratically. Social contexts that impose coercive-erratic control generate a variety of "social-psychological deficits," including "high other-directed anger; low self-efficacy; weak, alienated social bond; coercive modeling; perceived control deficit with feelings of debasement; low self-control; [and] external locus of control" (2000: 43). These deficits in turn coalesce to create a strong predisposition for serious predatory criminal behavior. Further, when people are exposed to coercive-erratic control across time and across social contexts (i.e., family, school, workplace, community), the result is likely to be chronic or life-course-persistent offending.

It remains to be seen whether Colvin's four-fold typology of control will match the reality of wayward human behavior, which often is too complex and "messy" to fall neatly into ideal-type categories. Still, there is growing evidence that coercion is criminogenic (Colvin, 2000), and that the core propositions of his causal model have merit (Baron, 2009; Unnever et al., 2004). Furthermore, his thinking has salient policy implications. In his book, Colvin (2000: 138–175) outlines an illuminating "theory-driven response to crime." Similar to Elliott Currie (Chapter 24, 1985, 1998) and other critical theorists, he argues that the solution to crime is to create a "noncoercive society." Making strides in this direction would entail realizing the limits of punitive crime-control strategies and the wisdom of government policies that, among other things, advocated more democratic workplaces, provided

Copyright © 2000 by Mark Colvin, *Crime and Coercion: An Integrated Approach to Chronic Criminality*. Reprinted with permission of Palgrave.

broad-based economic security to all Americans, and ensured the healthy development and care of at-risk children and families.

References

Baron, Stephen W. 2009. "Differential Coercion, Street Youth, and Violent Crime." *Criminology* 47: 239–268.

Colvin, Mark. 2000. *Crime and Coercion: An Integrated Theory of Chronic Criminality.* New York: St. Martin's Press.

Colvin, Mark, Francis T. Cullen, and Thomas Vander Ven. 2002. "Coercion, Social Support, and Crime: An Emerging Theoretical Consensus." *Criminology* 40: 19–42.

Currie, Elliott. 1985. *Confronting Crime: An American Challenge.* New York: Random House.

——. 1998. *Crime and Punishment in America.* New York: Metropolitan Books.

Patterson, Gerald R., Barbara D. DeBaryshe, and Elizabeth Ramsey. 1989. "A Developmental Perspective on Antisocial Behavior." *American Psychologist* 44: 329–335.

Unnever, James, Mark Colvin, and Francis T. Cullen. 2004. "Crime and Coercion: A Test of Core Theoretical Propositions." *Journal of Research in Crime and Delinquency* 41: 244–268.

A Differential Coercion Theory of Criminality

Drawing on the insights of previous theories, we are able to discern two important dimensions of control. First is the degree of coercion, ranging from extremely high coercion to complete non-conercion. Second is the degree of consistency, ranging from highly consistent to highly erratic. With these two dimensions I construct four types of control that have profoundly different effects on criminal and non-criminal out-comes: (1) non-coercive consistent control; (2) non-coercive erratic control; (3) coercive consistent control; and (4) coercive erratic control. I label these, respectively, Type 1, Type 2, Type 3, and Type 4 control . . . .

Coercion occurs when one is compelled to act in a certain way through direct force or intimidation from others or through the pressure of impersonal economic or social forces. Interpersonal forms of coercion may or may not involve the use of violence. Coercion can involve the threat of or actual taking away of something of value, such as a person's job or other social supports. It is punitive in nature. It motivates behavior because it is physically and/or emotionally painful and because it threatens to or actually does remove both expressive and instrumental social supports. Coercion, as I am using the term, encompasses Athens's (1992) definition of coercion and includes his concept of retaliation. Retaliation, in my use of this concept, is an excessively brutal and more unrelenting form of coercion . . . .

Thus coercion can be seen as setting into motion the social-psychological dynamics that the major theories of criminality discussed earlier posit as precursors to chronic involvement in criminal behavior. Coercion creates strain in the form of anger; it contributes to weak, alienated social bonds, low self-efficacy, an external locus of control, and, if delivered on an erratic schedule, low self-control. In addition, it models behavior for the individual when that person exercises control over others. And it becomes a provocation that produces a deviant motivation. These social-psychological variables are altered depending on the degree of coercion and consistency in control relations. In the discussion below, we explore the social-psychological and behavioral outcomes produced by the four types of control.

The Varieties of Control Experiences

As discussed in the previous section, relations of control come in varying forms defined by their degree of coercion and their consistency in application. Non-coercive controls can be either consistent, firm and fair, or they are can be overly lenient, permissive, and erratic. I refer to these respectively as Type 1 and Type 2 forms of control. Coercive relations of control can be consistently punitive or erratically punitive. These are labeled Type 3 and Type 4 respectively in the following discussion. The form of control most conducive to chronic predatory criminality is Type 4, a coercive relation that is erratic and punitive. However, as discussed in this section, Type 2 control is also conducive to certain forms of criminality, as to some extent is Type 3. . . .

Each type of control has different social-psychological outcomes and thus different effects on behavior. Figure 25.1 presents the social-psychological and behavioral outcomes that emerge from each type of control. The following discussion expands upon the relationships presented in Figure 25.1. . . .

Figure 25.1
Social-Psychological and Behavioral Outcomes Predicted by Four Control Types

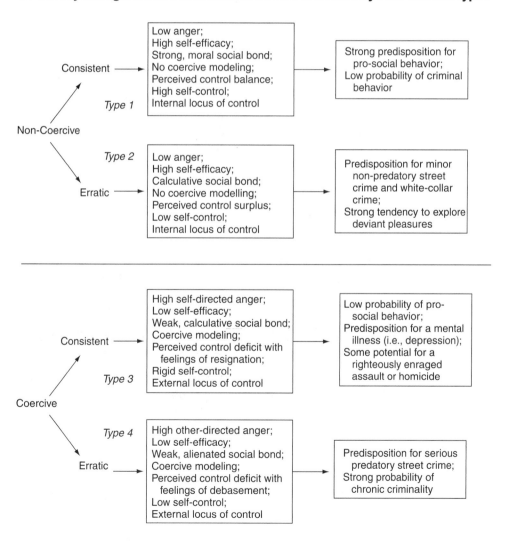

Type 1: Consistent, Non-Coercive

This is a non-coercive type of control in which strong social support of both expressive and instrumental needs are provided. It utilizes a combination of normative and remunerative control. It involves no provocation that could become the basis for recognizing a control deficit. It produces the following social-psychological outcomes:

- Low anger.
- High self-control, based on internalization of norms.
- Internal locus of control.
- High self-efficacy.
- Strong, positive, moral social bond.
- No modeling for coercive behavior.
- No perceived control deficit or control surplus (control balance).

And it produces the following behavioral outcomes:

- Generally non-criminal, non-delinquent
- Strong tendency to engage in pro-social behavior. . . .

Type 1 control is the least likely to produce a propensity for criminal or delinquent behavior and is the most likely to insulate the person from exploring the pleasures of deviance. This is not to say that a person emerging from such control relations will be completely non-deviant and law-abiding. But deviant explorations will require rationalizations that "neutralize" the guilt that would otherwise hold these individuals back from deviant activities (Sykes and Matza 1957). Some white-collar criminals (usually of a less chronic variety) and short-term exploratory offenders would fit this pattern. These offenders soon desist from deviant involvement when the rationalizations that support their behavior break down and internal moral constraints reassert themselves. Such deviant explorations may, under the right circumstances, change the type of control under which the person has operated. This change in control may move them toward one or another

of the three types discussed below. He or she may move to the lenient type if controllers ignore the deviance, or these explorations in crime may lead to one of the coercive types with subsequent impact on social-psychological and behavioral outcomes.

Type 2: Erratic, Non-Coercive

This non-coercive type of control can be described as lenient, lax, and permissive with a detached interest on the part of the controller who intervenes erratically and weakly. It provides feeble, erratic social support, which is mostly instrumental since a controller who becomes disengaged provides little expressive support. At best, inconsistent use of remunerative control is used in attempts to manipulate a subject's behavior. This control type involves no provocation that becomes the basis for recognizing a control deficit; in fact, it often involves situations in which a control surplus becomes evident as the purported controller ignores the subordinate's behavior or is manipulated to accede to the subordinate's wishes and demands. It produces the following social-psychological outcomes:

- Low anger.
- Low self-control.
- Internal locus of control.
- High self-efficacy.
- Intermediate, calculative social bond.
- No modeling for coercive behavior.
- Perception of a control surplus.

And it produces the following behavioral outcomes:

- Strong tendency to explore pleasurable deviant activities.
- Manipulation of authority figures and of rules and procedures.
- Lying.
- Strong predisposition for less predatory, minor street crime.
- Predisposition for white-collar criminality (if opportunity arises).

In this form of control, the person is usually ignored when non-compliant or is only mildly reprimanded when interventions do happen. On an erratic basis the controller may also attempt to bribe the subordinate into compliance. The person can readily predict that serious interventions will not arise from behavior, so the pursuit of pleasure or financial gain is not constrained and thus self-control is not induced. Erratic monitoring of behavior by external authorities means that the person is free to experiment and take risks. Such individuals are not driven by the compulsion of others or of events, and in fact they try to shape these to allow for greater pursuit of personal pleasure or profit. Thus they have an internal locus of control in which they direct their own pursuit toward maximization of pleasure of gain. Rules are ill defined, vague, and subject to change through persistent manipulation. Thus the person develops little in the way of appreciating limits on behavior and in this sense may exhibit distorted (even grandiose) self-efficacy (confidence) in his or her abilities to take on and overcome risks. The lenient nature of interventions (when they do occur) means that anger is not produced, although respect for authority (which presents itself as weak, detached, and apathetic) is not induced either. It is more likely that such individuals become indifferent to the demands of authority. The social bond is intermediate, based on calculation of reward through pleasure seeking. Type 2 control predisposes the person to crime and delinquency that is generally less predatory, since it is not anger-driven. With low self-control, they are highly likely to explore deviant, pleasurable experiences, such as drug use, petty theft, sexual promiscuity, drinking, and other minor delinquent acts. Their combination of low self-control, intermediate calculative social bond, and high self-efficacy allows them to calculate pleasurable outcomes without having to neutralize guilt, while feeling confident in their abilities to manipulate circumstances to reduce risks. Some may become chronically involved in these types of activities as long as pleasurable rewards outweigh

negative costs of continuing in these behaviors. When negative costs (to health, social relations, or freedom) begin to accumulate, the person is likely to desist from criminal involvement out of rational calculation that these deviant pursuits are no longer worth it. This type is congruent with the "adolescent-limited" pattern of delinquency in which juveniles engage in deviance for a period of time and then desist from deviant involvement (Moffitt 1997). Since the Type 2 pattern promotes chronic lying and manipulation, it also applies to the background of many white-collar criminals, especially to the more chronically involved ones. The patterns of control and crime emerging from Type 2 (which accounts for the majority of *offenders*) are most congruent with arguments from control theory since individuals in this pattern are acting free from external and internal constraints.

Type 3: Consistent, Coercive

Coercive control in this pattern is delivered on a consistent schedule and creates a highly punitive relationship between the controller and the subordinate. The relationship provides weak instrumental and expressive social support. In fact, to the extent that they exist at all, these social supports are constantly under threat of removal. It continually provokes recognition of a control deficit, which is obvious to the subordinate who develops a posture of resignation. The Type 3 pattern produces these social-psychological outcomes:

- High level of self-directed anger.
- Rigid self-control, based on constant fear of a painful response.
- External locus of control.
- Low self-efficacy.
- Weak, calculative social bond.
- Strong modeling for coercive behavior.
- Perception of a control deficit accompanied by resignation.

And it produces these behavioral outcomes:

- Low probability of criminal behavior.
- Low probability of pro-social behavior.

- High probability of mental health problems, such as chronic depression.
- Some potential for a righteously enraged assault or murder.

In this form of control, the person is consistently met with a punitive response when not complying with rules, which are usually highly restrictive. Behavior is rarely ignored and rewards are rarely given for compliance. This control relation produces a highly external locus of control, as the person becomes fearful, submissive, depressed, and powerless. Anger tends to be directed inward since outward expressions of anger are met immediately with punitive responses. A sense of resignation to the demands of authority leads to few displays of defiance. The consistency of coercion tends to produce someone who *rigidly* monitors his or her behavior out of fear in order to avoid negative consequences, which they learn can be avoided only by very careful monitoring of behavior and following rules to the letter. The social bond lies between intermediate and negative, based on a calculation of avoiding pain. Self-directed anger focuses the negative feelings of alienation inward rather than outward.

Type 3 control is not likely to create a predisposition for criminality because of the close monitoring of behavior by external authority. Instead of crime, this style of control is more likely to produce problems related to mental illness, such as chronic depression. Pro-social behavior, such as the pursuit of an education or any activity that involves initiative or creativity, becomes highly problematic for such a person. But this control type can *under the right circumstances* lead to an explosion of violence if inner-directed anger is suddenly transformed into outer-directed rage (Katz 1988). The coercive behavioral modeling this control type provides may help form the impetus for such a violent outburst. If the nearly constant monitoring of behavior is lifted, inner-directed anger can be redirected outward since external constraints are not replaced by internal

constraints. In fact, such a change would move the individual from a Type 3 toward a Type 4 pattern of control.

Type 4: Erratic, Coercive

This control type involves a punitive reaction to misconduct that is highly inconsistent. Social support in this control relationship is weak to non-existent. The highly erratic nature of the coercion powerfully provokes a pointed recognition of a control deficit. This control type produces the following social-psychological outcomes:

- High levels of other-directed anger and defiance.
- Low self-control.
- External locus of control.
- Low self-efficacy.
- Very weak, negative, alienated social bond.
- Strong coercive behavior modeling.
- Strong perception of control deficit accompanied by feelings of humiliation.

And it produces the following behavioral outcomes:

- Defiant and hostile acts toward authority figures.
- Coercion and intimidation of others.
- Strong predisposition for chronic involvement in predatory street crime.

In this form of control, noncompliance is, on an erratic basis, either ignored or responded to with harsh punitive measures. At times serious noncompliance is ignored and minor noncompliance is severely punished. At other times, punitive responses may occur when no misconduct has taken place at all. On occasion, coercion takes the extreme form of retaliation, in which pain is inflicted well beyond the point of submission (Athens 1992). The schedule for such punitive interventions is thus erratic and arbitrary. Coercion that is inconsistent and seems arbitrary creates a strong sense of injustice and thus generates greater anger and defiance that are directed outward (Agnew 1992).

The erratic nature of the coercion also allows the individual to periodically escape control and, on random occasions, feel a sense of autonomy. Thus the experience of coercion (when it does happen) is highly provocative since greater feelings of debasement and humiliation accompany this rude reminder of a control deficit. An external locus of control is produced in which the individual feels at the mercy of events that are beyond his or her control; the inconsistency of coercion makes negative events appear to be random occurrences not the consequence of behavior. This pattern of inconsistency also produces low self-control. Lack of self-control means that few brakes are placed on the expression of anger that is directed outward. The social bond is highly negative, based on alienation and open hostility toward authority figures. Someone experiencing this type of control develops low self-efficacy since he or she has little confidence that *in the long run* his or her behavior will make any difference in removing negative consequences that seem to arise in circumstances beyond his or her control. But in the short run, coercion against others provides a sense of power that, at least temporarily, changes the individual's position in relation to coercive control.

For individuals emerging from a Type 4 pattern of control, crime tends to be impulsive with little rational calculation of costs or benefits of behavior; such consequences cannot be predicted but are seen as matters of luck and fate. (This is a major distinction between the criminal patterns of Type 4 and Type 2 since the latter involves a higher degree of rational calculation). Only short-term advantages often in the face of immediate coercive provocation are the anticipated outcomes of criminal behavior. This type of control produces a high predisposition for chronic criminality (the "life-course persistent" offenders [Moffitt 1997]). These offenders tend to start criminal behavior at an earlier age than do other offenders. While they engage in a wide variety of criminal behaviors, this group tends to engage more than other groups in predatory street crimes, including serious violent crimes (Elliott 1994). The coercive nature of these criminal acts is modeled by the coercive controls experienced by the individual. The patterns of control and crime under Type 4 (which accounts for the majority of street *crimes*) are most congruent with the strain theory explanation offered by Agnew (1992) because the individual is acting under the pressures of extreme negative stimuli.

Coercion and Chronic Criminality

. . . I contend that coercive relations of control are conducive to chronic predatory criminality because they create a particular complex of emotions and personality traits: other-directed anger, low self-control, external locus of control, low self-efficacy, weak social bonding, coercive behavioral modeling, and perception of a control deficit that evokes debasement and humiliation. I label this complex set of emotions and traits *social-psychological deficits*. These social-psychological deficits include variables that have been related to criminal behavior and delinquency in the theories discussed earlier and in several research studies (Caspi et al., 1994; Grasmick et al., 1993; Peiser and Heaven, 1996; Shaw and Scott, 1991). But rather than viewing individuals as having hardwired personality traits (as Gottfredson and Hirschi [1990] do in their self-control theory), such traits are seen as arising out of coercive relations (initially in families [Patterson 1982]) and sustained by continuing coercive relations in a wide range of settings. The individuals who develop these social-psychological deficits have a high probability of eliciting coercive controls from authority figures and from peers. Thus there emerges a reciprocal relationship between these coercive controls and these social-psychological deficits that makes it more likely that the individual will be sustained in a path toward chronic criminality (Sampson and Laub 1993).

Together, these experiences of coercion and these social-psychological deficits contribute to the creation of *coercive ideation* in which an individual comes to view the world as an all-encompassing experience of coercion that can only be overcome through coercion. (Coercive ideation is similar to Athens's [1992] concept of *belligerency* . . . .) Following insights from Tittle's control balance theory, the individual under Type 4 control, due to its erratic application of coercion, imagines that coercive attempts to overcome such an environment can be successful (at least in the short run). In contrast, an individual under Type 3 control, with its consistent application of coercion, will find it difficult to conceive such transcendent moments of deliverance. Only in a rare circumstance can such an individual muster the rage to organize their behavior into an attack, which is often futile, on the coercive source of their continual subjugation and humiliation (Katz 1988). . . .

Coercion can be direct, arising from an actual interpersonal relationship of control, or may be indirect, arising from impersonal forces beyond the individual's control. One such impersonal force is economic. Economic conditions may compel a person to stay in a coercive relationship (at work or in a family), to leave a job he or she likes, to move to a location to which he or she does not want to go, or to take a job when he or she does not want to. Changing conditions of unemployment may, on an erratic basis, repeatedly move a person back and forth from highly coercive workplaces to the streets where little direct control exists; thus an erratic schedule of coercive control may be produced by these larger impersonal economic forces. All of these can be experienced as erratic coercion and may have the same social-psychological impact on the individual as do direct interpersonal relations that involve inconsistent coercive control.

There is a tie between interpersonal coercive relations and these impersonal forms of coercion.

A coercive interpersonal relationship may be more difficult to escape if impersonal forces do not allow access to legal escape routes. For instance, a person in a coercive relationship at work will find it difficult to escape if unemployment is high and alternative jobs are scarce. Such a situation also makes it easier to enforce a coercive control strategy at the workplace, since the threat of firing someone from the job has much greater impact if the person faces destitution as a result. Also in families, if control relations are highly coercive but the controller also holds economic power, it is much more difficult for spouses and children to escape if alternative forms of economic subsistence are truncated by larger economic conditions. These impersonal economic forces become coercive in and of themselves and they reinforce the interpersonal relations of coercion in various settings.

Coercive relations can appear in any number of settings, including workplaces, families, schools, among peers, and in state bureaucracies, such as welfare and criminal justice agencies. A person may pass through each of these settings in which various control relations are experienced. *To the extent that these settings create an accumulated experience of coercion, then greater is the likelihood that the person will experience anger, weak social bonding, an external locus of control, low self-efficacy, coercive behavior modeling, and a perception of a control deficit.* Together, these controls and social-psychological deficits contribute to the development of coercive ideation. *To the extent coercion is erratic, then the perceived control deficit will provoke feelings of debasement and humiliation, the anger will be directed outward, self-control will diminish, and coercive ideation will include the thought that a coercive environment can be overcome through coercion.* These in turn produce a stronger predisposition for chronic predatory criminality. . . .

Discussion Questions

1. What are Colvin's four types of control? Which type is most likely to produce serious offenders? Why?

2. Colvin identifies a number of "social-psychological deficits" that intervene between coercion and crime. What are these deficits? How do they relate to other theories you may have read about?

3. Based on Colvin's theory, list three factors that you believe would cause crime. Now list three factors that you think would reduce crime.

4. Have you ever been treated coercively in you life? How did you react? How might this lead you understand why coercion can backfire and cause more, rather than less, criminal behavior?

26. Peacemaking Criminology

Richard Quinney

As David Friedrichs notes (1996: 29), "the pervasiveness of violent crime must surely rank as one of the premier failures of the twentieth century." Why is this so? One popular answer is that the "war on crime" and the "war on drugs" have not been waged with sufficient vigor (Bennett et al., 1996 [Chapter 42]). This view suggests that we have been too lenient on crime. If we only would have the political will to place more offenders in prison for longer periods, we could substantially dent the crime rate and make society safer, including inner-city areas where violence is most concentrated (DiIulio, 1994).

Other commentators, however, tire of the "war" on crime and drugs mentality. This war is like Viet Nam: a conflict that cannot be won but that will needlessly consume thousands of lives and billions of dollars. The difficulty, they say, is that violence is an ineffective solution to violence; inflicting harm, even if done in the name of justice, ultimately leads to more harm. Doing violence also ignores what is the true or root cause of crime: human suffering. Making offenders suffer is like pouring salt on an open wound. Peace, not war, is the answer (Fuller, 1998; Fuller and Wozniak, 2006; Wozniak, 2002; Wozniak et al., 2008).

But what if we were to lift the blinders from our eyes and see that the way in which we are "fighting crime" simply does not work? What more evidence is needed to prove that a system whose main goal is inflicting pain on offenders is based on faulty premises? We might consider that we have conducted an experiment and this experiment has failed. Even with Viet Nam, we finally had the courage to realize that it was time to stop waging war and to pull out.

Richard Quinney encourages us to shed our preconceptions and to take a different path in our journey to help build a society in which crime might disappear. Quinney has little interest in traditional criminology and using science to understand and control crime. Rather, he bears witness to a simple truth: "crime is suffering and the ending of crime is possible only with the ending of suffering" (1991: 11). Suffering might come from the small ways in which we do violence to one another in interpersonal relationships or from the large structures at the core of society that oppress the poor and the vulnerable. The solution to such pervasive suffering is a justice that is rooted in peace. Being peacemakers depends on our understanding that we are all connected and that we have an imperative need to care for one another (see also Lozoff and Braswell, 1989). "We as human beings," reveals Quinney (1991: 11); "must be peace if we are to live in a world free of crime, in a world of peace."

Quinney's words are elegant; they move us emotionally; they ring true. The challenge, however, is that in rejecting traditional criminology with its emphasis

Excerpted with permission from Richard Quinney, "The Way of Peace: On Crime, Suffering, and Service," *Criminology as Peacemaking*, edited by Richard Quinney and Harold E. Pepinsky. Copyright © 1991. Reprinted with permission of Richard Quinney.

on testing theories, Quinney forfeits science for faith. Concepts such as "suffering" and even "peace" are ill defined, and one would not know how to empirically falsify or support the thesis that "suffering causes crime." Furthermore, the policy prescription offered by Quinney—doing and being peace—is seemingly utopian. It is difficult to see how peacemaking would handle the reality of predatory offenders and prisons filled to the brim (but see Lozoff and Braswell, 1989).

But these reservations aside, the value of Quinney's nonviolent form of criminology is precisely that it is different and thus allows us to think "outside the box." Even if we do not embrace all that he shares, "peacemaking criminology provides us with an inspiring vision, and with some initiatives which can be integrated into our response to crime" (Friedrichs, 1996: 44; see also Fuller, 1998). Once we are guided by the theme of reducing suffering through peaceful means, we have the raised consciousness to pause and think whether a current criminal justice practice—perhaps long taken for granted—truly "makes sense." We might begin to consider that, more often than not, caring and support, rather than anger and pain, may make our justice system more just, more peace giving, and more effective.

References

Bennett, William J., John J. DiIulio, Jr., and John P. Walters. 1996. *Body Count: Moral Poverty and How to Win America's War Against Crime and Drugs*. New York: Simon and Schuster.

DiIulio, John J., Jr. 1994. "The Question of Black Crime." *The Public Interest* 117 (Fall): 3–32.

Friedrichs, David O. 1996. "Peacemaking Criminology and the Punitive Conundrum: A New Foundation for Social Control in the Twenty-First Century?" In Christine T. Sistare (ed.), *Punishment: Social Control and Coercion*, pp. 27–54. New York: Peter Lang.

Fuller, John R. 1998. *Criminal Justice: A Peacemaking Perspective*. Boston: Allyn and Bacon.

Fuller, John R. and John F. Wozniak. 2006. "Peacemaking Criminology: Past, Present, and Future." In Francis T. Cullen, John Paul Wright, and Kristie R. Blevins (eds.), *Taking Stock: The Status of Criminological Theory—Advances in Criminological Theory*, Volume 15, pp. 251–273. New Brunswick, NJ: Transaction.

Lozoff, Bo and Michael Braswell. 1989. *Inner Corrections: Finding Peace and Peace Making*. Cincinnati: Anderson.

Quinney, Richard. 1991. "The Way of Peace: On Crime, Suffering, and Service." In Harold E. Pepinsky and Richard Quinney (eds.), *Criminology as Peacemaking*, pp. 3–13. Bloomington: Indiana University Press.

Wozniak, John F. 2002. "Toward a Theoretical Model of Peacemaking Criminology: An Essay in Honor of Richard Quinney." *Crime and Delinquency* 48: 204–231.

Wozniak, John F., Michael C. Braswell, Ronald E. Vogel, and Kristie R. Blevins, eds. 2008. *Transformative Justice: Critical and Peacemaking Themes Influenced by Richard Quinney*. Lanham, MD: Lexington Books.

———

Let me begin with a fundamental realization: No amount of thinking and no amount of public policy have brought us any closer to understanding and solving the problem of crime. The more we have reacted to crime, the farther we have removed ourselves from any understanding and any reduction of the problem. In recent years, we have floundered desperately in reformulating the law, punishing the offender, and quantifying our knowledge. Yet this country remains one of the most crime-ridden nations. In spite of all its wealth, economic development, and scientific advances, this country has one of the worst crime records in the world.

With such realization, we return once again—as if starting anew—to the subject of crime, a subject that remains one of our most critical indicators of the state of our personal and collective being. If what is to be said seems outrageous and heretical, it is only because it is necessarily outside the conventional wisdom both of our understanding of the problem and of our attempt to solve it. Only by entering another world—yet one that is very simple and ultimately true—can we become aware of our own condition.

A few elementary observations serve as the basis for our understanding: (1) Thought of the Western rational mode is conditional, limiting knowledge to what is already known. (2) The truth of reality is emptiness; all that is real is beyond human conception. (3) Each life is a spiritual journey into the unknown and the unknowable, beyond the egocentric self. (4) Human existence is characterized by suffering; crime is suffering; and the sources of suffering are within each of us. (5) Through love and compassion, beyond the egocentric self, we can end suffering and live in peace, personally and collectively. (6) The ending of suffering can be attained in a quieting of the mind and an opening of the heart, in being aware. (7) Crime can be ended only with the ending of suffering, only when there is peace—through the love and compassion found in awareness. (8) Understanding, service, justice: all these flow naturally from love and compassion, from mindful attention to the reality of all that is, here and now. (9) A *criminology of peacemaking*, the nonviolent criminology of compassion and service, seeks to end suffering and thereby eliminate crime. Let us elaborate on this understanding.

Awareness of Human Suffering

Suffering is the condition of our existence. In our personal lives, there are tensions and anxieties. The forms of suffering are all around us. Each day we experience the physical pains in our bodies and the psychological hurts in our hearts and minds. Our interpersonal relations often are carried out in violence of one kind or another, if only in the withholding of what might be offered. We have created societies that are filled with the sufferings of poverty, hunger, homelessness, pollution, and destruction of the environment. Globally, nations are at war and threaten not

only one another, but all of earthly life, with nuclear destruction. All these human problems, or forms of suffering, are a result of how we have lived our lives, moment by moment, day by day. The threat of nuclear war began as suffering on a very personal level and elevated gradually and systematically to the collective condition (see Walsh, 1984). The forms of suffering are symptoms of the sufferings within each of us.

If the social and global sufferings ever are to be ended, we must deal with the suffering of personal existence. What is involved, finally, is no less than the transformation of our human being. Political and economic solutions without this transformation inevitably fail. The solutions is very near to us. There is no shortcut to the ending of suffering.

Our suffering, then, and our ending of this suffering, begins in the human mind. *The Dhammapada*, the ancient text of Budhism, states: "All that we are is a result of what we have thought" (1936: 3). We act out of our thoughts and we create social worlds out of these thoughts. Being human, we have constructed webs of meaning; and with these shared meanings we have constructed our interpersonal relations, our social structure, and our societies. All is a result of what we have thought.

The reconstruction of our existence—the ending of suffering—thus begins by giving attention to the mind. It is this mind, a modern mind that is busy and scattered, that creates its own suffering. To be able to observe the mind as it is, to be able to see clearly with the mind, we begin with what must seem at first a paradox: letting go. The author of *A Gradual Awakening* observes:

> In letting go of who we imagine ourselves to be, letting go of our thinking, our attempt to control the world, we come upon our natural being which has been waiting patiently all these years for us to come home. (Levine, 1979: 39)

This open state of mind is what one Zen master calls a "beginner's mind." He (Suzuki, 1970: 21) writes:

> If your mind is empty, it is always ready for anything; it is open to everything. In the

beginner's mind there are many possibilities; in the expert's mind there are few.

We are ready to see things as they really are—beyond concepts and theories—when we have no thought of achievement, no thought of self. When our mind is open and thus compassionate toward all things, it is boundless in its understanding.

Without empty mind—without mindfulness—we are attached to our ideas, our thoughts, our mental constructions; and we take these productions to be reality itself. Many of our concepts are so deeply ingrained in our minds, in our education, and in our culture, that we forget that they completely condition our perceptions of reality (see Krishnamurti, 1975). In attachment to these mental productions, we are chained in the cave, observing merely the shadows of appearance on the wall before us. Awareness is a breaking of the chains of conditioned thought and a viewing of the reality beyond the shadows.

Without awareness, we humans are bound to the suffering caused by a grasping mind. Being attached to our thoughts, we take the thoughts to be our true selves. The mind that is attached to its own thoughts is the mind of a self-centered and possessive being. All conditioned and attached thought arises from the discursive mind of the egocentric self. That is why the sacred texts of the esoteric traditions, such as the wisdom literature of early Hinduism as found in the *Upanishads* and the *Bhagavad-Gita*, suggest that truth can be known only through union with Brahman, through that which is beyond the ego-self and its attempt at purely rational thought. In contemplation and meditation we can see the essence of all things as they rise and pass away.

The higher wisdom, the awareness of reality, can be attained only with the loss of the conditioned ego and with the realization of the transcendental Self. In other words, the essence of our existence is the interpretation of ourselves with all things. In *Samadhi*, a treatise on self development in Zen Buddhism, Mike Sayama (1986: 12) writes: "The task before us is no longer to differentiate from nature and develop the ego, but transcend the ego and realize true Self that is one with the universe." Only then can one be at home. Peace and harmony come with the awareness of the oneness of all things and the transcendence of this small self to the wholeness of reality. All of this is to be found outside of the abstracting interpretations of the rational mind.

As we mature, we move beyond the rational and linear mode of thought to a more intuitive and transcendent mode. We lose the grasping and craving self of the individualized ego and find ourselves in the realm of the universal Self. It is not natural—it is unhealthy—for the academic and the intellectual (sociologist, criminologist) to continue strictly in the rational mode of speculative and dualistic thought as he or she matures, although this is the approved and rewarded form for the modern academic. To continue solely in the rational mode of thought is retrogressive for the maturing person, and for a discipline as well.

The author of *Samadhi* concludes:

> At the most mature level of human being, a person realizes the true self which is one with the universe and experiences a meaning beyond question and articulation. Such a person transcends anxiety, is fearless and is moved by compassion. (Sayama, 1986:98)

Rather than a life primarily of acquisition and scholarly production, life now demands an inner awakening, a spiritual development. One no longer clings to rationality and the ego as the final realities; one is not trapped in the world of interpretive abstractions taking form according to attachments of an egocentric existence. Once we have mastered rationality and moved to the possibilities of perennial wisdom, we can begin to live in compassionate oneness with all that is; we can begin to understand the world by fully being aware of it.

The truth is that no amount of theorizing and rational thinking can tell us much about reality.

To enter into the essential realm requires a mind that is unattached and compassionate. In a book on perennial wisdom, Aldous Huxley (1985: x) writes:

> It is a fact, confirmed and re-confirmed during two or three thousand years of religious history, that the ultimate Reality is not clearly and immediately apprehended, except by those who have made themselves loving, pure in heart and poor in spirit.

When we allow the higher self to dwell in the depth of the particular self—when the egocentric, rational self is lost—we can attend to the unknown and unknowable mysteries of the world.

And the final expression of this realization may not be in more talk and more words, but in silence. Saint John of the Cross observed, "For whereas speaking distracts, silence and work collect thoughts and strengthen the spirit" (quoted in Huxley, 1970: 218). With the wisdom gained by awareness, there may be no further need to talk and to write discursively. One then practices what is realized—with attention and silence, in charity and humility, in the service of others.

Right Understanding

The way to awareness, and thus the ending of suffering, begins with right understanding. An understanding of the true nature of reality involves the recognition that everything is impermanent, that nothing remains the same. Within the flux of reality is the fact that every action brings a certain result. For instance,whenever our actions are motivated by greed, hatred, or delusion, the inevitable result is suffering. All of this occurs within a reality that is beyond the abstractions of a grasping and craving mind.

The true reality, beyond human conception, is what Zen Buddhism refers to as *Sunyata*: nothingness, emptiness, the void. In a recognition of the fullness of the unnameable, of emptiness, we may begin to see clearly and compassionately the concrete reality of our existence. With this understanding, as Alan Watts (1957: 125) notes, we are "at the point where there is nothing further to seek, nothing to be gained." When we are empty—within the emptiness of all—we are in the realm of ultimate reality.

Beyond Western scientism, there is liberated action freed of the separation of ourselves from the world. Watts (1957: 131) quotes a Zen line: "Only when you have no thing in your mind and no mind in things are you vacant and spiritual, empty and marvelous." This takes us beyond the products of Western thought, beyond the malaise and destruction that have resulted from being separated from the ineffable reality of our existence. By a "dropping off of body and mind," as Keiji Nishitani (1982) of the Kyoto School of Japanese Zen terms it, we allow ourselves to live in the wonder of absolute nothingness. We return to a home—we arrive at the "homeground"— where all things are in harmony with what they actually are and ought to be. It is a "coming home with empty hands," and each being has found its place among all other things. But let us beware. Even this talk takes us into the place of mental abstractions, the place where we again lose touch with reality.

It is the presumed objectivity and rationality of modern science that we hope to avoid in a new criminology. We hope to avoid the personal and social consequences of positive science because, as one humanistic philosopher (Skolimowski, 1986: 306) has noted: The mind trained in objective science

> over a number of years becomes cold, dry, uncaring, always atomized, cutting, analyzing. This kind of mind has lost the capacity for empathy, compassion, love.

Our mode of thinking affects the way we live, and in the meantime we have not gotten any closer to understanding. We seek a mind that, instead of producing conflict and violence, heals—a compassionate mind rather than an objective mind. The compassionate mind is found beyond the boundaries of Western scientific rationality.

Being on the simple path of right understanding, we create thought, words, and deeds that will end our suffering. The forest monk, Achaan Chah, writes: "Only when our words and deeds come from kindness can we quiet the mind and open the heart" (1985: 50). Our work is not only to grow in wisdom and compassion but also to help others in their suffering. This takes place not necessarily in further theoretical work, but in moment-by-moment, day-by-day, step-by-step awareness of what actually is. We are on a wandering path to emptiness, to an awareness of the fullness and wholeness of all things.

That we criminologists are to be engaged in spiritual work in order to eliminate crime may require further reflection. To be fully human presupposes the development within oneself of a quality of being that transcends material existence. It is a quality that is not acquired automatically, but one that develops slowly and needs to be tended carefully. Through inner work, we forge a link between the profane and the sacred. Indeed, all of life becomes filled with the sacred. Such a quality within each of us assures a life of growing wisdom, compassion, and service.

Nothing any longer is profane, without the transcendent dimension. The simplest actions, from eating and walking to talking and working, have a sacramental character signifying something beyond themselves. Our lives are within a realm that demands a spiritual as well as material existence. This is why the great religious traditions continue to emphasize a constant discipline of recollection, meditation, study, prayer, contemplation, and at least some measure of solitude and retirement. The Trappist monk, Thomas Merton, thus writes:

> If the salvation of society depends, in the long run, on the moral and spiritual health of individuals, the subject of contemplation becomes a vastly important one, since contemplation is one of the indications of spiritual maturity. It is closely allied to sanctity. You cannot save the world merely with a system. You cannot have peace without charity. (1979: 8)

Seeing the truth, in contemplation and meditation, sets us on a path that promotes a humane and peaceful existence. Such an existence is a reality which we can attain only in a life lived in the depth of the sacred. A life devoted to criminology cannot avoid the importance of this truth. Care has to be given to the inner life of each of us.

This life of giving attention to spiritual matters, of going beyond the self to all that is in the world, is a socially committed life. The contemplative life is not self-indulgent, for social issues cannot be faced appropriately without inner spiritual preparation (see Merton, 1962). Oppression in the world is caused by selves that are not spiritually aware, by those who live by greed, fear, egoism, and the craving for power over others. As Jacob Needleman (1980: 212–19) observes in *Lost Christianity*, the "outer" world is not out there, and the "inner" world is not solely one of personal emotions and thoughts. Both are of the same space, in interpenetration of everything. The objective is a compassionate living of each moment with all other beings—for the ending of suffering.

Compassion and Service

We are all of us interrelated—and "not just people, but animals too, and stones, clouds, trees" (Aitken, 1984: 10). Those who are enlightened in the service of others, the *Bodhisattvas* of the world, realize fully the reality of the interpenetration of all things. By experiencing the ephemeral and transparent nature of reality, by being aware of the oneness of all things, we can know the potential of peace and harmony.

Were there complete perfection and unity, there would be no suffering. Suffering has arisen out of disunity and separation from the embracing totality, and it can be ended only with the return of all sentient beings to a condition of wholeness. We have fallen from the grace of wholeness into a separation from one another and from the ground of all being, a separation that is assured by craving and grasping selves, by selves that are really an illusion. If human beings were constantly and consciously in a proper relationship with the sacred and with the natural and social environment, there would be only as much suffering as creation makes inevitable (see Huxley, 1970: 233–34). But our own created reality is one of separation, and therefore one of suffering.

Thus the healing of separation is necessary if suffering is to be ended. To begin to end suffering, we must be aware of the causes of suffering within ourselves and search for the reasons that make us suffer. The Tibetan Buddhist master, Rinpoche Kalu, says that the suffering we experience in the world "is caused by the six afflictions—ignorance, desire, pride, anger, jealousy, and greed" (Kalu, 1987: 13). The most hopeful way to attain world peace, to end global suffering, he adds, is by developing within ourselves compassion and loving-kindness toward others.

In the practice of loving-kindness, what Buddhists call *metta*, there is developed the feeling of caring and connectedness. From within, thoughts of goodwill and benevolence are extended outward, embracing all others in an increasingly wider circle. In compassion, the suffering of others is recognized out of one's own suffering, and the suffering is shared. Jack Kornfield (1985: 63) writes:

> Compassion is the tender readiness of the heart to respond to one's own or another's pain without grief or resentment or aversion. It is the wish to dissipate suffering. Compassion embraces those experiencing sorrow, and eliminates cruelty from the mind.

Looking directly at suffering, both the suffering in the world and the suffering in one's own heart and mind, we love others (as ourselves) and act in compassion to end suffering—to heal separation.

We begin our practice, then, by being aware of the ways in which suffering is manifested in each of us. "The more conscious we are in dealing with our own suffering, the more sensitive we will be in treating the pain of others" (Dass and Gorman, 1985: 86). Our responsibility is to do what we can to alleviate the concrete conditions of human suffering.

> We work to provide food for the hungry, shelter for the homeless, health care for the sick and feeble, protection for the threatened and vulnerable, schooling for the uneducated, freedom for the oppressed. (Dass and Gorman, 1985: 87)

When we acknowledge *what is* and act as witnesses in this shared reality, without attachment and judgment, we open ourselves to all suffering. Acting out of compassion without thinking of ourselves as doers, we are witnesses to what must be done. The path to the ending of suffering is through compassion rather than through the theories of science and the calculations of conditioned thought. Our sufferings are, in fact, exacerbated by science and thought. The discoveries necessary for dealing with suffering are within our being.

The truth that relieves suffering lies in the concrete moment of our awareness, an awareness that frees us from conditioned judgments, creates loving-kindness within us, and allows us to realize the absolute emptiness of all phenomena.

As long as there is suffering in this world, each of us suffers. We cannot end our suffering without ending the suffering of all others. In being witnesses to the concrete reality, and in attempting to heal the separation between ourselves and true being (the ground of all existence), we necessarily suffer with all others. But now we are fully aware of the suffering and realize how it can be eliminated. With awareness and compassion, we are ready to act.

The Way of Peace and Social Justice

From the inner understanding of our own suffering, we are prepared to act in a way of peace. As in Mahatma Gandhi's philosophy of *Satyagraha*, truth force, social action comes out of the informed heart, out of the clear and enlightened mind. The source of social action is within the human heart that has come to understand fully its own suffering and therefore the suffering of others. If human actions are not rooted in compassion, these actions will not contribute to a peaceful and compassionate world.

> If we cannot move beyond inner discord, how can we help find a way to social harmony? If we ourselves cannot know peace, *be* peaceful, how will our acts disarm hatred and violence? (Dass and Gorman, 1985: 165)

The means cannot be different from the ends; peace can come only out of peace. "There is no way to peace," said A. J. Musto. "Peace is the way."

In other words, without *inner* peace in each of us, without peace of mind and heart, there can be no *social* peace between people and no peace in societies, nations, and in the world. To be explicitly engaged in this process, of bringing about peace on all levels, of joining ends and means, is to be engaged in *peacemaking* (Musto, 1986: 8–9). In peacemaking, we attend to the ultimate purpose of our existence—to heal the separation between all things and to live harmoniously in a state of unconditional love.

The radical nature of peacemaking is clear: No less is involved than the transformation of our human being. We will indeed be engaged in action, but action will come out of our transformed being. Rather than attempting to create a good society first, and then trying to make ourselves better human beings, we have to work on the two simultaneously. The inner and the outer are the same. The human transformation in relation to action is described by Thich Nhat Hanh, the Vietnamese Buddhist peace activist, as a realization that begins in the human heart and mind:

> To realize does not only mean to act. First of all, realization connotes transforming oneself. This transformation creates a harmony between oneself and nature, between one's own joy and the joy of others. Once a person gets in touch with the source of understanding and compassion, this transformation is accomplished. When this transformation is present, all one's actions will carry the same nature and effect—protecting and building life with understanding and compassion. If one wishes to share joy and happiness with others, one should have joy and happiness within oneself. If one wishes to transmit serenity, first one should realize it oneself. Without a sane and peaceful mind, one's actions could only create more trouble and destruction in the world. (Hanh, 1985: 2; also see Hanh, 1987)

The transformation of ourselves and the world becomes our constant practice, here and now.

The practice is, in the true sense, spiritual and religious. In Buddhist terms, we become enlightened in the practice; and in Christianity, the transformation involves an inner conversion—a new age coming in both cases only when we have made ourselves ready. As a commentator (Musto, 1986: 251) on the Catholic peace tradition writes,

> Peace is not so much political revolution as personal conversion; it is not individual human ego and power at stake, but God's will to peace that only humans can accomplish on earth, as they are the recipients of God's gift and challenge to peace.

And there can be no peace without justice. This is the biblical command. A good social life—one based on equality, with the elimination of poverty, racism, sexism, and violence of all kinds—is a peaceful existence. The Old Testament Isaiah (32:7) states: "Justice will bring about peace, right will produce calm and security." Peace, the result of all the benefits of the covenant, is granted to those who fulfill the covenant by living in justice. "Peace and justice," Ronald Musto (1986: 13) observes, "are thus inextricably bound: cause and effect, journey and goal." By living the convenant—by creating justice—there is peace. The peacemakers are truly "the children of God."

All of this is to say, to us as criminologists, that crime is suffering and that the ending of crime is possible only with the ending of suffering. And the ending both of suffering and crime, which is the establishing of justice, can come only out of peace, out of a peace that is spiritually grounded in our very being. To eliminate crime—to end the construction and perpetuation of an existence that makes crime possible—requires a transformation of our human being. We as human beings must *be* peace if we are to live in a world free of crime, in a world of peace.

In recent years, we have seen several attempts at peacemaking in criminology. There have been writings and some programs employing conflict resolution, mediation, reconciliation, abolition, and humanistic action (see, for example, Abel, 1982; Currie, 1985; Pepinsky, 1988; Tifft and Sullivan, 1980; Sullivan, 1980). They offer the concrete beginnings of a *criminology of peacemaking,* a criminology that seeks to end suffering and thereby eliminate crime. It is a criminology that is based necessarily on human transformation in the achievement of peace and justice. Human transformation takes place as we change our social, economic, and political structure. And the message is clear: Without peace within us and in our actions, there can be no peace in our results. Peace is the way.

We are fully aware by now that the criminal justice system in this country is founded on violence. It is a system that assumes that violence can be overcome by violence, evil by evil. Criminal justice at home and warfare abroad are of the same principle of violence. This principle sadly dominates much of our criminology. Fortunately, more and more criminologists are realizing that

this principle is fundamentally incompatible with a faith that seeks to express itself in compassion, forgiveness, and love. When we recognize that the criminal justice system is the moral equivalent of the war machine, we realize that resistance to one goes hand-in-hand with resistance to the other.

The resistance must be in compassion and love, not in terms of the violence that is being resisted. A definition of "nonviolence" by a recent resister (Taylor, 1986: 1) is appropriate:

> Nonviolence is a method of struggling for human liberation that resists and refuses to cooperate with evil or injustice, while trying to show goodwill to all opponents encountered in the struggle, and being willing to take suffering on oneself, rather than inflicting it on others.

We are back again to the internal source of our actions: Action is the form the essence of our being takes. Thich Nhat Hanh, whose thoughts follow that same definition of nonviolence, writes:

> The chain reaction of love is the essential nature of the struggle. The usual way to generate force is to create anger, desire, and fear in people. Hatred, desire, and fear are sources of energy. But a nonviolent struggle cannot use these dangerous sources of energy, for they destroy both the people taking part in the struggle and the aim of the struggle itself. Nonviolent struggle must be nurtured by love and compassion. (Quoted in Taylor, 1986: 2)

When our hearts are filled with love and our minds with willingness to serve, we will know what has to be done and how it is to be done. Such is the basis of a *nonviolent criminology.*

We begin, then, by attending to the direction of our innermost being, the being that is the whole of reality. Out of this source, all action follows. In the words of Lao-tzu, "No action is taken, and yet nothing is left undone" (1963: 184). Everything is done out of compassion to help lessen the suffering of others.

Living in harmony with the truth, we do everything as an act of service. Criminology can be no less than this, a part of the reality of all that is—a way of peace.

Discussion Questions

1. How does peacemaking criminology differ from the other theories you have studied in this book? What makes it different?

2. Quinney proposes that suffering causes crime. Can you give three examples of how different types of suffering in our society might lead people to break the law?

3. Many theories have been subjected to empirical tests by criminologists. Is it possible to test Quinney's ideas? If so, how would you set up a study to investigate his ideas?

4. Imagine that you have been elected governor of your state. You are now in a position to establish a correctional system based on peacemaking principles. What would this system look like? How would it differ from the current correctional system?

PART IX

Feminist Theories: Gender, Power, and Crime

For much of its history, criminology as a discipline focused almost exclusively on crimes committed by men. Most empirical studies used data only on male offenders, and theories were constructed to explain why boys and men broke the law (Belknap, 1996; Leonard, 1982; Simon, 1975; Smart, 1977; Steffensmeier and Broidy, 2001). Part of the neglect of females stemmed from the disproportionate involvement of males in crime, especially serious offenses, and from the overwhelming maleness of the prison population. Women's criminality thus was seen as tangential to the crime problem—as not really worth investigating and as having no implications for the understanding of male's illegality. A more salient reason for the failure to consider gender in criminological analyses, however, was that, as was the case in other academic disciplines, criminologists were nearly all men: males were studying and writing about males.

Equally disquieting, on those infrequent occasions when female criminals received scholarly attention, the resulting analyses were decidedly sexist. Although exceptions existed (Steffensmeier and Clark, 1980), prominent scholars often viewed female criminality as a departure from "natural" female behavior—that is, maternal, passive, and gentle. What would cause such "odd," "unfemale" behavior? Female lawbreakers, it was thought, could only have contravened their feminine nature because of a pathological defect in their biological makeup or within their psyche (Klein, 1973; Smart, 1977). The traditional female role thus was seen as normal; any departure, such as crime, was seen as abnormal. In this perspective, social factors, especially gender-based inequality, were accorded little or no causal importance in the behavior of women—or, for that matter, in the behavior of men.

Starting in the 1970s and continuing to this day, such male-centered, asocial theorizing has been challenged as sexist and as theoretically impoverished. A revisionist approach, which elevated gender to the center of theoretical analysis, was fueled in important ways by the emergence of the Women's Movement and its fight for equality between the sexes. This movement had two noteworthy effects. First, as educational and occupational opportunities broadened, increasing numbers of women entered the field of criminology, bringing with them fresh insights rooted in personal histories unlike those of male criminologists. Second, the Women's Movement focused attention on the social situation of women vis-à-vis men, including such crucial issues as gender-based differences in socialization and inequalities in power. For many criminologists—especially female scholars—the idea that gender was not implicated in crime and criminal justice now seemed incongruous.

The rejection of male-centered traditional criminology has resulted in the emergence of the

320

competing paradigm of "feminist criminology." In this approach, sex is not simply another variable added to a multivariate empirical analysis (usually as a "control" variable). Rather, gender relations become central to understanding human behavior, including crime. There is a special focus on how crime is related to gender-based inequality between males and females. Finally, to a greater or lesser extent, feminist analyses—similar to critical criminology—are oriented to the production of knowledge so as to unmask and change the structural relationships in society that result in the discrimination against and the oppression of women (see Chesney-Lind, 2006; Daly and Chesney-Lind, 1988; see also Miller and Mullins, 2006; Ollenburger and Moore, 1998).

Feminist criminologists directed attention to several major questions about the causes of crime. First, how can we explain female crime? Some criminologists argue that traditional crime theories are equally applicable to males and females (e.g., Jensen and Eve, 1976; Smith and Paternoster, 1987), but feminist criminologists argue that new theories need to be developed to explain female crime or that traditional theories need to be revised in ways that accord a central role to gender. Second, how can we explain the gender gap in crime and, related to this, changes in the gender gap over time? Gender is one of the strongest correlates of crime, with rates of serious crime being many times higher among males than females (Chesney-Lind and Shelden, 2004; Steffensmeier and Allan, 2000). The size of the gender gap has decreased for certain crimes in recent decades (see Heimer, 2000), although it appears that much of this decrease may be due to changing police practices (see Chesney-Lind, 2006; Steffensmeier et al., 2005). Until the 1970s and 1980s, little effort was devoted to explaining these facts. Third, what role does gender play in the generation of male crime? While traditional theories were developed with males in mind, such theories devote little attention to the role of gender in producing male crime. Finally, how does gender "intersect" with race/ethnicity and class to affect crime (see Burgess-Proctor, 2006; Simpson and Gibbs, 2005)? Feminist criminologists have increasingly come to argue that a full understanding of crime requires that we consider gender by race/ethnicity by class groups (e.g., examine poor, white females separately from middle-class, African American females).

It is important to emphasize, however, that there is a diversity of thinking within feminist criminology, as well as a dynamism that leads to continuing theoretical developments (for an analysis of recent contributions, see Burgess-Proctor, 2006; Chesney-Lind and Shelden, 2004; Daly, 1997; Miller and Mullins, 2006, 2009). Over the past three decades, the most poignant split has been between "liberal feminists," who focus on the salience of sex-role socialization and equality of opportunities, and feminists who take a more "critical" or "radical" approach, emphasizing structural inequality in power between men and women. These latter theorists see male and female crime as fundamentally linked to patriarchy—a deeply entrenched system in which males exert dominance through their power (financial and, if necessary, physical) and through a hegemonic culture that defines male ways of doing things as "normal" and male control of women as legitimate. In general, liberal feminist views had the most powerful influence in the earlier days of feminist criminological scholarship, while more radical approaches currently direct most theory and research within the feminist paradigm.

Liberation and Crime

As the Women's Movement grew in strength and swept across the nation, it was tempting to conclude that substantial equality between men and women was within reach. Although gender socialization and inequalities ultimately would prove difficult to transform, significant social changes did occur. Almost on a daily basis, it seemed, women were breaking one social or occupational barrier after another. Witnessing these changes in progress, it became almost inevitable to ask, how will this refashioning of the experiences of women affect their criminality? For those with a sociological imagination who saw male crime as rooted in their social experiences, the answer seemed clear. If girls were raised like boys and if in their life course they had the same opportunities as boys, then it seemed logical that their behavior—including their criminal conduct—would become more like that of boys. In short, women's liberation ultimately would result in "equality on the wanted list."

These ideas informed Rita Simon's (1975) important contribution, *Women and Crime* (see also Simon, 2002). "If one assumes that the changes in women's roles, in their perceptions of self, and in their desire for expanded horizons that began in the latter part of the sixties will not be abated," observed Simon (1975: 1), "then we would expect that one of the major by-products of the women's movement will be a high proportion of women who pursue careers in crime." Simon contended that females' entry into the job market would prove particularly consequential because it would give them access to opportunities for "financial and white-collar crimes," such as "fraud, embezzlement, larceny, and forgery" (p. 2). She rejected the idea, however, that women's participation in violent crimes would increase. Arguing that women committed violent crimes largely because of the "frustration, the subservience, and the dependency that have characterized the traditional female role," Simon reasoned that occupational advancement would reduce these "feelings of being victimized and exploited" and thus would blunt "their motivation to kill" (p. 2).

This liberation thesis was stated even more boldly and eloquently by Freda Adler in her classic book, *Sisters in Crime*, which carried the revealing subtitle *The Rise of the New Female Criminal* (1975 [Chapter 27 in this part]). Adler proclaimed that women were not only committing more crimes but also were engaging in traditionally male offenses. She noted that between 1960 and 1972, female arrests increased 168 percent for burglary,

277 percent for robbery, 280 percent for embezzlement, and over 300 percent for larceny (1975: 16). She linked these dramatic shifts in female criminality to the transformation of gender roles that was then occurring in American society. "Women are no longer indentured to the kitchens, baby carriages, or bedrooms of America," observed Adler. "Allowed their freedom for the first time, women—by the tens of thousands—have chosen to desert those kitchens and plunge exuberantly into the formerly all-male quarter of the working world" (p. 12). But there was also a "shady aspect of liberation": the rise of new female criminals. "In the same way that women are demanding equal opportunity in fields of legitimate endeavor," concluded Adler, "a similar number of determined women are forcing their way into the world of major crimes" (p. 13).

The work by Adler and Simon was critically important in bringing gender into criminological discourse and in prompting sustained research on women's criminality. Still, their versions of the liberation thesis have been subjected to much critical scrutiny. Many criminologists, including later feminist scholars, have rejected this thesis (see, e.g., Belknap, 1996; Daly and Chesney-Lind, 1988; Heimer, 2000; Steffensmeier and Allan, 1996). Although several concerns have been voiced, three criticisms of the liberation thesis seem most important to review.

First, the empirical predictions of the thesis have not proven correct (see Heimer, 2000; Steffensmeier and Allan, 1996; Steffensmeier et al., 2005). While the percentage of all arrests involving females has increased a good deal since the 1960s, the largest increases involve the crimes of larceny, fraud, and forgery—which include the traditionally "female" offenses of shoplifting, passing "bad" checks, and welfare fraud. The increased involvement of females in these offenses began well before the women's movement became popular in the late 1960s. And certain data suggest that arrest statistics may exaggerate the increased involvement of females in crime. In particular, much of the increase in female arrests may be attributable to changes in police practices—with the police becoming more likely to arrest females.

Second, the liberation thesis implied (if not stated directly in places) that females' labor market participation and achievement of equality across a range of social opportunities would foster criminality. The data showed, however, that gender equality's "dark side" was not to create offenders. Instead, crime was more common among those who did *not* achieve equality—among women who were trapped in economically marginal positions (Giordano et al., 1981; Heimer, 2000; Wolfe et al., 1984). True equality, therefore, might well reduce, rather than increase, women's criminal involvement.

Third and relatedly, the focus of the liberation thesis on gender socialization and occupational opportunities did not consider the structural roots of the inequality between men and women. To be sure, as liberal feminists, scholars such as Adler and Simon were critical of the barriers that they and other women faced. More radical feminists, however, contended that the analyses of liberation theorists did not get to the core of the problem: that patriarchy—a system of men's dominance of women—underlay how women were socialized, why women experienced discrimination in the workplace, and why women were consigned—often alone and with children—to marginal economic positions. A feminist theory of crime, they claimed, thus must move beyond discussions of liberation to illuminate how power affects the crime and victimization of women.

Patriarchy and Crime

Radical feminism, which places patriarchy at the center of its analysis, has had a widespread influence on criminological scholarship (see Belknap, 1996; Burgess-Proctor, 2006; Simpson, 1989). Within criminal justice, for example, it has spawned research on gender inequities in sentencing and on how the law is used to reaffirm traditional, subordinate female roles and to control women's sexuality (e.g., the "double-standard" in the juvenile justice system of institutionalizing "promiscuous" girls but not boys) (Chesney-Lind and Shelden, 2004; Daly and Tonry, 1997). This perspective also illuminated the importance of investigating the victimization of women by men. Studies showed how male violence against women—such as nonstranger rape and the battering of intimates—was traditionally subject to virtually no sanctions by the state. Such violence was thus conceptualized as a means by which men dominate women and, in doing so, reproduce the existing patriarchal system (Daly and Chesney-Lind, 1988).

In rejecting male-centered criminology, radical feminism also argued that there would be a need to develop gender-specific theories. Because they neglected gender and ignored the role of patriarchy as the underlying social context for behavior, traditional theories were incapable of explicating the gendered experiences that were central to a full understanding of female (and male) criminality. Radical feminism helped spur a number of "qualitative" studies of female crime, wherein researchers observed and conducted intensive interviews with female offenders (e.g., Bottcher, 2001; Daly, 1992; Gilfus, 1992; Giordano et al., 2002; Miller and Mullins, 2006). Such studies shed much light on the social world of these offenders, and contributed to the development of gender-specific theories as well as to the revision of traditional theories.

Meda Chesney-Lind (1989 [Chapter 28 in this part]) provides an important example of a "feminist theory" in which considerations of patriarchy illuminate the special causes of female delinquency. She observes, for example, that "girls are frequently the recipients of violence and sexual abuse" (p. 23). Patriarchy is conducive to such abuse because females in general are objectified as "sexual property." "In a society that idealizes inequality in male/female relationships and venerates youth in women, girls are easily defined as sexually attractive by older men" (p. 24). Escape from this abuse, however, is not easy. Girls who run away often are returned to their homes by the state—a practice that ignores the girls' genuine fears of continued victimization and serves to confirm parental, patriarchal authority. The only option thus for many abused girls is to seek refuge in the "streets," where they must commit crimes to survive. But patriarchy shapes their experience and victimization here as well. "It is no accident that [these] girls . . . get involved in criminal activities that exploit their sexual object status," comments Chesney-Lind (for similar accounts and research, see Daly, 1992; Gilfus, 1992). American society has defined as desirable youthful, physically perfect women. This means that girls on the streets, who have little else of value to trade, are encouraged to use this 'resource'" (p. 24). It is noteworthy that considerations of sexual abuse, its relation to patriarchy, and its etiological role in crime have been virtually absent in the major theories of crime authored by males.

The work of Chesney-Lind illustrates what is perhaps the most prominent theme in feminist theories of crime: the idea that the oppression of women, including their criminal victimization, is a major cause of female offending (Miller and Mullins, 2006). In particular, some females engage in crime in an effort to cope with or overcome certain of the problems they face—with many of these problems stemming from the gender inequality that characterizes patriarchal society.

Gendering Traditional Theories

Along with the rise of gender-specific theories, there have also been numerous efforts to apply traditional theories to the explanation of female crime and the gender gap in crime. These efforts typically find that many of the variables that explain male crime also explain female crime. Such variables include association with delinquent peers, beliefs favorable to crime, low social and self-control, strains, the perceived costs and benefits of crime, and opportunities for crime. In fact,

reviews of the research have found that there is a great deal of overlap between the leading causes of female and male crime (Agnew, 2009; Andrews and Bonta, 1994; Hubbard and Pratt, 2002; Lanctot and Le Blanc, 2002; Steffensmeier and Broidy, 2001). (Relatedly, the conditions that predict the success in reducing crime for males are similar to those for females [Dowden and Andrews, 1999]). Further, certain of these causes go a long way toward explaining the gender gap in crime. In particular, studies suggest that most of the gender gap in crime is due to the fact that males are more likely than females to associate with delinquent peers, be low in self-control, be low in social control, and so on (e.g., Agnew, 2009; Jensen, 2003; Moffitt et al., 2001; Rowe et al., 1995; Zahn, 2009). Traditional theories, then, have much to say about the relationship between gender and crime.

At the same time, some criminologists argue that these theories are inadequate for several reasons (see Belknap and Holsinger, 2006; Chesney-Lind and Shelden, 2004; Lanctot and Le Blanc, 2002; Miller and Mullins, 2006, 2009; Steffensmeier and Broidy, 2001). While many of the same factors cause male and female crime, there is some evidence that certain factors have a larger effect on crime among males or females. For example, several studies indicate that association with delinquent peers is more likely to lead to crime among males (see Giordano, 2009; Mears et al., 1998; Piquero et al., 2005). Early puberty, however, is more likely to lead to crime among females (Fishbein et al., 2009). Traditional theories do not explain why this is the case. Also, there is evidence that certain gender-related factors neglected by traditional theories may help explain female and/or male crime. Such factors include the nature of one's gender identity, experiences with gender discrimination, differences in physical size and strength, romantic disputes and partner abuse, the timing of menstruation, and—as indicated above—sexual abuse (e.g., Belknap and Holsinger, 2006; Bottcher, 2001; Eitle, 2002; Haynie, 2003; Steffensmeier and Allan, 1996, Zahn, 2009). Finally, while traditional theories may state that males are more likely than females to possess those factors that contribute to crime, they usually do not explain why this is the case. Why, for example, are males more likely to associate with delinquent peers or be low in self-control? Given these inadequacies, many criminologists have embarked upon the task of "gendering" traditional theories; that is, devoting explicit attention to the ways in which gender might impact the causal forces identified by these theories (see Daly and Chesney-Lind, 1988; Lanctot and Le Blanc, 2002; Steffensmeier and Broidy, 2001; Zahn, 2009). In particular, how might gender affect the nature of, exposure to, and reaction to these forces? There have now been attempts to "gender" virtually all of the traditional theories described in earlier sections of this book.

There have been several recent efforts to apply biopsychological theories to the explanation of female (and male) crime and the gender gap in crime (see Fishbein et al., 2009, for an overview). The most prominent is that of Moffitt et al. (2001). They find that most of the gender difference in crime is due to the fact that females are less likely to possess the personality traits of low constraint and negative emotionality (see Chapter 5). They argue that while these traits are in part socially produced, they are also heavily influenced by biological factors—such as genetic inheritance and exposure to biological harms such as head injuries. Other biological factors have also been used to help explain sex differences in crime—although such factors are typically said to work in combination with social factors. For example, females who experience puberty at an early age are more likely to engage in delinquency, especially acts such as drinking under age, truancy, and disorderly conduct. This is partly because their early physical maturity increases the likelihood they will get involved in romantic relationships, associate with delinquent peers, and experience conflict with their parents (Fishbein et al., 2009; Haynie, 2003).

Broidy and Agnew (1997) have applied "general strain theory" to the explanation of female crime and gender differences in crime (see Agnew,

Chapter 16; Agnew, 2009). Based on a detailed review of the existing theoretical and empirical literature, they state that the gender gap in crime cannot be explained by arguing that males experience more strains than females. Males and females experience similar amounts of strains; in fact, some studies indicate that females experience more strains than males. Instead, Broidy and Agnew explain the gender gap in three ways. First, males are more likely to experience strains *conducive to crime*, such as criminal victimization. Second, males are more likely to react to strains with moral outrage, while females more often react with a combination of anger, depression, and guilt—which are less conducive to other-directed crime. Finally, males are more likely to cope with strains and negative emotions through crime. This is because they are higher in negative emotionality, lower in constraint, lower in social control, lower in social support, more likely to hold beliefs favorable to crime, and more likely to associate with delinquent peers—among other things. Broidy and Agnew explain the above differences in terms of gender differences in such things as social position and power, socialization, and identity. Broidy and Agnew also attempt to explain why some females do engage in crime. Here they argue that many females do experience strains conducive to crime, with many of these strains being linked to gender inequality and oppression. Such strains include sexual abuse, gender discrimination, and partner/dating violence.

Several theorists have applied social learning and differential association theory to the examination of gender and crime, with perhaps the most noteworthy being that of Heimer and De Coster (Chapter 29; see also Agnew, 2009; Heimer, 1996; Jensen, 2003; Mears et al. 1998; Simons et al., 2002). Heimer and De Coster (1999) embrace the central insight of social learning/differential association theory (Part IV) that "violent definitions" (i.e., beliefs approving of the use of violence) are related to violent behavior. Boys exhibit more violence because they are more likely to learn violent definitions. Their key insight is that the causal factors that produce violent definitions differ for males and females and are rooted in gender position and associated cultural meanings. For males, violent definitions are learned when parents do not directly control them and supervise the degree to which they associate with aggressive companions. For females, violence is tied more closely to the quality of interpersonal relationships and to patriarchal beliefs. Feminists often portray women as being "more concerned than males with interpersonal relationships" (pp. 284–285). Consistent with this view, females are more likely to learn violent definitions when there is a breakdown of "indirect control" or emotional bonds with the family. Furthermore, girls who embrace traditional patriarchal values are less violent because such conduct is inconsistent with the "meaning of being female" (p. 303).

Costello and Mederer (2003) apply control theory to the explanation of gender differences in crime (also see Agnew, 2009; Hagan et al., 1987, 2002; Heimer, 1996; Lanctot and Le Blanc, 2002). Being control theorists, they do not ask why men commit so much crime. Their crime requires no special explanation, since it is "natural" for people to pursue their self-interests in the most expedient manner available—including crime. Rather, they ask "Why don't women commit as much crime as men?" (Costello and Mederer, 2003: 88). They argue that the answer is that women are more controlled than men. Women are socialized to exercise more self-control and show more concern for others. Women are more closely supervised and are more likely to be sanctioned by others when they display aggressive behavior. And women are more involved in childcare and more closely tied to the household, which limits their opportunities for crime. Costello and Mederer argue that the greater control of women stems from their ability to bear and nurse children. Women's historic role as the primary caregivers of infants tied them to the home and led to the equation of femininity with self-control

and concern for others. Costello and Mederer, however, argue that this arrangement has become increasingly dysfunctional for women, and that "men must become more like women and share the constraints of caretaking" (2003: 90). This will allow women to better pursue goals that are not tied to the family and will reduce the crime of men.

Criminologists have revised still other traditional crime theories in an effort to better understand the relationship between gender and crime (Agnew, 2009). Such theories include labeling theory (see Bartusch and Matsueda, 1996; Braithwaite, 1989), deterrence and rational choice theories (Blackwell and Eschholz, 2002; Richards and Tittle, 1981; Tibbetts and Herz, 1996), and the routine activities perspective (Schwartz and Pitts, 1995). In all such cases, these theories are combined with feminist insights to better understand why females engage in crime and why males have higher rates of crime.

Masculinities and Crime: Doing Gender

In *Masculinities and Crime*, James Messerschmidt (1993 [Chapter 30]) challenges both traditional and feminist criminological theories of criminal conduct. Traditional theories may be male-centered, but they do not examine how "being male" is related to crime. Men might be strained, lack control, and differentially associate with peers, but how their gender is implicated in their behavior is not analyzed. Feminists have brought gender to the center of criminological analysis, but their vision of men tends to be stereotypical and unidimensional. In particular, when the lens of patriarchy is employed, males are conceptualized as dominant. This approach, however, ignores the considerable variations among men, especially in how they seek to affirm their masculinity.

To Messerschmidt, criminality and masculinity are intertwined. He argues that in social situations, men are constantly confronted with the task of establishing their manliness. When legitimate means of demonstrating masculinity are denied, crime becomes a resource to accomplish this task. Criminal behavior thus is best seen as a way of "doing gender."

Messerschmidt recognizes that males "do gender" largely within the confines of "hegemonic masculinity"—the prevailing idealized cultural conception which defines "masculinity" as involving the dominance of women, heterosexuality, the pursuit of sexual gratification, independence, and so on (1993: 82). Still, this general masculinity is specified by the intersection of age, class, and race. Different "masculinities"—tied to structural locations—thus emerge and have varying impacts on the rate and content of criminal behavior. For example, middle-class white boys often engage in petty delinquency to show their masculinity, but they also have access to conventional ways to "do gender," such as through success in school and, later, in the labor market. In contrast, lower-class minority boys, who face structural barriers and dismal futures, are more likely to seek to demonstrate their masculinity through repeated robberies and acts of violence. As Messerschmidt notes, the pursuit of these different masculinities both reflects and serves to reproduce the existing class, racial, and gender inequalities in society.

More recently, Messerschmidt (1999, 2004) has suggested that the role of the "body" be considered in the complex interplay between masculinity and crime. In fact, he argues for a "body friendly criminology" (1999: 200). He notes that "our bodies constrain or facilitate social action and, therefore, mediate and influence social practices." For adolescent males, for example, physical size and strength are sources of opportunity, and they structure the nature of both conformity and crime. Being large and strong allows youths to accomplish or show their masculinity by playing sports (such as football) and through heterosexual activities. It might also enable a youth, however, to gain a reputation for being an effective fighter and provide access to a gang. Alternatively, boys small in size and stature may be defined as "wimps" and be precluded from showing masculinity through sports, dating, or gang conflict. They may be pushed into a painful "subordinate masculinity," and their deviance may take a different form, such as preying on even more vulnerable youths (e.g., victimizing younger female relatives in private spaces). In any event, by introducing the concept of "the body," Messerschmidt continues his attempt to specify the conditions under which males "do gender" through crime.

Messerschmidt's focus on masculinities and on "crime as doing gender" is an important contribution that is prompting scholarly investigations (see, e.g., Gadd, 2000; Hood-Williams, 2001; Jefferson and Carlen, 1996; Miller and Mullins, 2006; Mullins, 2006). Field studies have provided some support for his argument that crime is sometimes used as a device for "accomplishing masculinity," and certain survey studies suggest that threats to one's masculine status increase the likelihood of crime (e.g., Jakupcak, 2003). His theory, however, risks *overpredicting* crime among men. By linking masculinity so closely to crime, the theory is confronted with explaining the thorny reality that most men do not commit crime most of the time (Hood-Williams, 2001). In addition, there is some controversy over how Messerschmidt's perspective might explain female crime (e.g., Heimer, 1994).

Messerschmidt (2002, 2004) argues that in certain social environments and situations, females may construct and embrace a "bad girl" femininity that involves crime. This is said to be true of many female gang members. To quote Messerschmidt (2002: 464, 470)

What is usually considered atypical behavior by girls outside the social situation of the gang is, in fact, normalized within the social context of inter-neighorhood conflict; gang-girl violence in this situation is encouraged, permitted, and privileged by both boys and girls. . . . Even though gang girls situationally engage in similar behavior as gang boys (physically violent practices), this does not . . . challenge their feminine identity. . . . In short, for many adolescent girls and young women, 'acting bad' and feminity are *not* incompatible. (our emphasis)

Miller (2002), however, argues that most gang girls embrace a masculine identity, as reflected in the title of her book about female gangs, *One of the Guys* (Miller, 2001). She explains this by stating that "it makes sense that young women would strive to adopt a gang identity as 'one of the guys,' particularly given the status and respect available within gangs to youths who exhibit characteristics typically associated with the highly valued cultural construction of gang masculinities" (Miller, 2002: 445). In any event, both Messerschmidt and Miller argue that both males *and females* sometimes use crime as a device for "accomplishing gender"—that is, for constructing and demonstrating their particular conceptions of masculinity (and perhaps femininity) in certain situations.

An Integrated Theory of Gender and Crime

In sum, a variety of theories have been used to explain female (and male) crime and the gender gap in crime. These include feminist theories, the traditional theories of crime described in previous sections of this book, and revised versions of these traditional theories. One might wonder whether it is possible to integrate certain of the theories to develop a more general theory of gender and crime. Steffensmeier and Allan (1996, 2000) have attempted such an integration, and their "gendered theory of female offending" is described in Chapter 31.

They begin by noting that traditional theories of crime help us understand female offending and the gender gap in crime, but these theories have their shortcomings. Among other things, they do not explain why the gender gap is largest for serious crimes and they shed little light on gender differences in the "context" of offending (e.g., the fact that female offending more often involves relational concerns). Steffensmeier and Allan then develop an integrated theory that draws on both traditional theories and feminist perspectives. In particular, their theory considers many of the causal factors identified in traditional theories of crime—such as level of self-control, association with criminal others, the perceived costs and benefits of crime, and routine activities. At the same time, their theory describes the many ways in which gender influences the individual's standing on these factors and sometimes the effect of these factors on crime. Further, their focus on gender leads them to identify additional factors that impact crime, such as the opportunities women have to "exploit sex as an illegal money-making service" and "the consequences of motherhood and childcare" (Steffensmeier and Allan, 1996: 474).

Their theory is designed to explain female and male offending, the gender gap in offending, and gender differences in the context of offending. While their theory may not explicity incorporate all of the factors said to affect female offending and the gender gap, their theory is the most ambitious attempt to date to fully account for the relationship between gender and crime. Additional attempts at integration are under way, with certain of these taking on one of the great challenges of crime theories—describing the ways in which gender intersects with race/ethnicity and class to affect crime. There has not been much research in this area, but the few studies that have been done suggest that gender must be considered along with class and race/ethnicity if we are to fully explain crime (e.g., Burgess-Proctor, 2006; Chesney-Lind and Shelden, 2004; Simpson and Elis, 1995; Simpson and Gibbs, 2006; Zahn, 2009).

References

Adler, Freda. 1975. *Sisters in Crime: The Rise of the New Female Criminal.* New York: McGraw-Hill.

Agnew, Robert. 2009. "The Contribution of 'Mainstream' Theories to the Explanation of Female Delinquency." In Margaret A. Zahn (ed.), *The Delinquent Girl*, pp. 7–29. Philadelphia: Temple University Press.

Andrews, D. A. and James Bonta. 1994. *The Psychology of Criminal Conduct.* Cincinnati: Anderson.

Bartusch, D. J. and Ross L. Matsueda. 1996. "Gender, Reflected Appraisals, and Labeling: A Cross-Group Test of an Interactionist Theory of Delinquency." *Social Forces* 75: 145–177.

Belknap, Joanne. 1996. *The Invisible Woman: Gender, Crime, and Justice.* Belmont, CA: Wadsworth.

Belknap, Joanne and Kristi Holsinger. 2006. "The Gendered Nature of Risk Factors for Delinquency." *Feminist Criminology* 1: 48–71.

Blackwell, Brenda Sims and Sarah Eschholz. 2002. "Sex Differences and Rational Choice: Traditional Tests and New Directions." In Alex R. Piquero and Stephen G. Tibbetts (eds.), *Rational Choice and Criminal Behavior*, pp. 109–135. New York: Routledge.

Bottcher, Jean. 2001. "Social Practices of Gender: How Gender Relates to Delinquency in the Everday Lives of High-Risk Youths." *Criminology* 39: 9–32.

Braithwaite, John. 1989. *Crime, Shame, and Re-integration.* Cambridge, UK: Cambridge University Press.

Broidy, Lisa and Robert Agnew. 1997. "Gender and Crime: A General Strain Theory Perspective." *Journal of Research in Crime and Delinquency* 34: 275–306.

Burgess-Proctor, Amanda. 2006. "Intersections of Race, Class, Gender, and Crime." *Feminist Criminology* 1: 27–47.

Chesney-Lind, Meda. 1989. "Girls' Crime and Woman's Place: Toward a Feminist Model of Female Delinquency." *Crime and Delinquency* 35: 5–29.

——. 2006. "Patriarchy, Crime, and Justice." *Feminist Criminology* 1: 6–26.

Chesney-Lind, Meda and Randall G. Shelden. 2004. *Girls, Delinquency, and Juvenile Justice*, 3rd edition. Belmont, CA: Wadsworth.

Costello, Barbara J. and Helen J. Mederer. 2003. "A Control Theory of Gender Differences in Crime and Delinquency." In Chester L. Britt and Michael R. Gottfredsaon (eds.), *Control Theories of Crime and Delinquency*, pp. 77–108. New Brunswick, NJ: Transaction.

Daly, Kathleen. 1992. "Women's Paths to Felony Court: Feminist Theories of Lawbreaking and Problems of Representation." *Southern California Review of Law and Women's Studies* 2: 11–52.

——. 1997. "Different Ways of Conceptualizing Sex/Gender in Feminist Theory and Their Implications for Criminology." *Theoretical Criminology* 1: 25–51.

Daly, Kathleen and Meda Chesney-Lind. 1988. "Feminism and Criminology." *Justice Quarterly* 5: 497–535.

Daly, Kathleen and Michael Tonry. 1997. "Gender, Race, and Sentencing." In Michael Tonry (ed.), *Crime and Justice: A Review of Research*, Volume 22, pp. 201–252. Chicago: University of Chicago Press.

Dowden, Craig and D. A. Andrews. 1999. "What Works for Female Offenders: A Meta-Analytic Review." *Crime and Delinquency* 45: 438–452.

Eitle, David J. 2002. "Exploring a Source of Deviance-Producing Strain for Females: Perceived Discrimination and General Strain Theory." *Journal of Criminal Justice* 30: 429–442.

Fishbein, Diana, Shari Miller, Donna Marie Winn, and Gayle Dakof. 2009. "Biopsychological Factors, Gender, and Delinquency." In Margaret A. Zahn (ed.), *The Delinquent Girl*, pp. 84–106. Philadelphia: Temple University Press.

Gadd, David. 2000. "Masculinities, Violence, and Defended Psychosocial Subjects." *Theoretical Criminology* 4: 429–449.

Gilfus, Mary, 1992. "From Victims to Survivors to Offenders: Women's Routes of Entry and Immersion Into Street Life." *Women & Criminal Justice* 4: 63–89.

Giordano, Peggy. 2009. "Peer Influences on Girls' Delinquency." In Margaret A. Zahn (ed.), *The Delinquent Girl*, pp. 127–145. Philadelphia: Temple University Press.

Giordano, Peggy C., Stephen A. Cernkovich, and Jennifer L. Rudolph. 2002. "Gender, Crime, and Desistance: Toward a Theory of Cognitive Transformation." *American Journal of Sociology* 107: 990–1064.

Giordano, Peggy C., Sandra Kerbel, and Sandra Dudley. 1981. "The Economics of Female Criminality: An Analysis of Police Blotters, 1890–1976." In Lee H. Bowker (ed.), *Women and Crime in America*, pp. 65–82. New York: Macmillan.

Hagan, John, Bill McCarthy, and H. Foster. 2002. "A Gendered Theory of Delinquency and Despair in the Life Course." *Acta Sociologica* 45: 37–46.

Hagan, John, John H. Simpson, and A. R. Gillis. 1987. "Class in the Household: A Power-Control Theory of Gender and Delinquency." *American Journal of Sociology* 96: 265–299.

Haynie, Dana L. 2003. "Contexts of Risk: Explaining the Link Between Girls' Pubertal Development and Their Delinquency Involvement." *Social Forces* 82: 355–397.

Heimer, Karen. 1994. "Review of *Masculinities and Crime*." *Contemporary Sociology* 23: 860–861.

——. 1996. "Gender, Interaction, and Delinquency: Testing a Theory of Differential Social Control." *Social Psychology Quarterly* 59: 39–61.

——. 2000. "Changes in the Gender Gap in Crime and Women's Economic Marginalization." In Gary LaFree (ed.), *The Nature of Crime, Continuity and Change, Criminal Justice 2000*, Volume 1, pp. 427–485. Washington, D.C.: Office of the Justice Programs, U.S. Department of Justice.

Heimer, Karen and Stacey De Coster. 1999. "The Gendering of Violent Delinquency." *Criminology* 37: 277–318.

Hood-Williams, John. 2001. "Gender, Masculinities, and Crime: From Structures to Psyches." *Theoretical Criminology* 5: 37–60.

Hubbard, Dana Jones and Travis C. Pratt. 2002. "A Meta-Analysis of the Predictors of Delinquency Among Girls." *Journal of Offender Rehabilitation* 34: 1–13.

Jakupcak, Matthew. 2003. "Masculine Gender Role Stress and Men's Fear of Emotions as Predictors of Self-Reported Aggression and Violence." *Violence and Victims* 18: 533–541.

Jefferson, Tony and Pat Carlen, eds. 1996. "Masculinities, Social Relations and Crime." *British Journal of Criminology*, Special edition, 36: 337–444.

Jensen, Gary F. 2003. "Gender Variation in Delinquency: Self-Images, Beliefs, and Peers as Mediating Mechanisms." In Ronald L. Akers and Gary F. Jensen (eds.), *Social Learning Theory and the Explanation of Crime*. New Brunswick, NJ: Transaction.

Jensen, Gary F. and Raymond Eve. 1976. "Sex Differences in Delinquency." *Criminology* 13: 427–448.

Klein, Dorie. 1973. "The Etiology of Female Crime: A Review of the Literature." *Issues in Criminology* 8: 3–30.

Lanctot, Nadine, and Marc Le Blanc. 2002. "Explaining Deviance by Adolescent Females." *Crime and Justice: A Review of Research* 29: 113–202.

Leonard, Eileen B. 1982. *Women, Crime, and Society: A Critique of Criminology Theory*. New York: Longman.

Mears, Daniel P., M. Ploeger, and Mark Warr. 1998. "Explaining the Gender Gap in Delinquency: Peer Influence and Moral Evaluations of Behavior." *Journal of Research in Crime and Delinquency* 35: 251–266.

Messerschmidt, James W. 1993. *Masculinities and Crime: Critique and Reconceptualization of Theory*. Lanham. MD: Rowman and Littlefield.

——. 1999. "Making Bodies Matter: Adolescent Masculinities, the Body, and Varieties of Violence." *Theoretical Criminology* 3: 197–220.

——. 2002. "On Gang Girls, Gender and a Structured Action Theory." *Theoretical Criminology* 6: 461–476.

——. 2004. *Flesh and Blood.* Lanham, MD: Rowman & Littlefield.

Miller, Jody. 2001. *One of the Guys: Girls, Gangs, and Gender.* New York: Oxford University Press.

——. 2002. "The Strengths and Limits of 'Doing Gender' for Understanding Street Crime." *Theoretical Criminology* 6: 433–460.

Miller, Jody and Christopher W. Mullins. 2006. "Taking Stock: The Status of Feminist Theories in Criminology." In Francis T. Cullen, John Paul Wright, and Kristie R. Blevins (eds.), *Taking Stock: The Status of Criminological Theory—Advances in Criminological Theory*, Volume 15, pp. 217–249. New Brunswick, NJ: Transaction.

——. 2009. "Feminist Theories of Girls' Delinquency." In Margaret A. Zahn (ed.), *The Delinquent Girl*, pp. 30–49. Philadelphia: Temple University Press.

Moffitt, Terrie E., Avshalom Caspi, Michael Rutter, and Phil A. Silva. 2001. *Sex Differences in Antisocial Behavior.* Cambridge, UK: Cambridge University Press.

Mullins, Christopher W. 2006. *Holding Your Square: Masculinities, Streetlife and Violence.* Portland, OR: Willan.

Ollenburger, Jane C. and Helen A. Moore. 1998. *A Sociology of Women: The Intersection of Patriarchy, Capitalism, and Colonization.* Upper Saddle River, NJ: Prentice Hall.

Piquero, N. L., A. R. Gover, J. M. MacDonald, and Alex R. Piquero. 2005. "The Influence of Delinquent Peers on Delinquency: Does Gender Matter?" *Youth & Society* 36: 251–275.

Richards, P. and Charles R. Tittle. 1981. "Gender and Percieved Chances of Arrest." *Social Forces* 59: 1182–1199.

Rowe, David C., Alexander T. Vazsonyi, and Daniel J. Flannery. 1995. "Sex Differences in Crime: Do Means and Within-Sex Variation Have Similar Causes?" *Journal of Research in Crime and Delinquency* 32: 84–100.

Schwartz, Martin D. and Victoria L. Pitts. 1995. "Exploring a Feminist Routine Activities Approach to Explaining Sexual Assault." *Justice Quarterly* 12: 9–31.

Simon, Rita James. 1975. *Women and Crime.* Lexington, MA: Lexington Books.

——. 2002. "Looking Back on 40-Plus Years as a Professional Career." In Gilbert Geis and Mary Dodge (eds.), *Lessons of Criminology*, pp. 199–218. Cincinnati: Anderson.

Simons, Ronald L., Eric Stewart, Leslie C. Gordon, Rand D. Conger, and Glen H. Elder, Jr. 2002. "A Test of Life-Course Explanations for Stability and Change in Antisocial Behavior from Adolescence to Young Adulthood." *Criminology* 40: 401–434.

Simpson, Sally S. 1989. "Feminist Theory, Crime, and Justice." *Criminology* 27: 605–631.

Simpson, Sally S. and Lori Elis. 1995. "Doing Gender: Sorting Out the Caste and Crime Conundrum." *Criminology* 33: 47–81.

Simpson, Sally S. and C. Gibbs. 2006. "Making Sense of Intersections." In Karen Heimer and Candance Krittschnitt (eds.), *New Directions in the Study of Gender, Offending, and Victimization.* New York: New York University Press.

Smart, Carol. 1977. *Women, Crime and Criminology: A Feminist Critique.* London, UK: Routledge and Kegan Paul.

Smith, Douglas A. and Raymond Paternoster. 1987. "The Gender Gap in Theories of Deviance: Issues and Evidence." *Journal of Research in Crime and Delinquency* 24: 140–172.

Steffensmeier, Darrell, and Emile Allan. 1996. "Gender and Crime: Toward a Gendered Theory of Female Offending." *Annual Review of Sociology* 22: 459–487.

——. 2000. "Looking for Patterns: Gender, Age, and Crime." In Joseph F. Sheley (ed.), *Criminology: A Contemporary Handbook*, 2nd edition, pp. 84–127. Belmont, CA: Wadsworth.

Steffensmeier, Darrell and Lisa Broidy. 2001. "Explaining Female Criminality: Historical and

Contemporary Perspectives." In Claire Renzetti and Lynne Goodstein (eds.), *Women, Crime, and Criminal Justice: Contemporary Issues.* Los Angeles: Roxbury.

Steffensmeier, Darrell and Robert E. Clark. 1980. "Sociocultural vs. Biological/Sexist Explanations of Sex Differences in Crime: A Survey of American Criminology Textbooks, 1918–1965." *American Sociologist* 15: 246–255.

Steffensmeier, Darrell, Jennifer Schwartz, Hua Zhong, and Jeff Ackerman. 2005. "An Assessment of Recent Trends in Girls' Violence Using Diverse Longitudinal Sources: Is the Gender Gap Closing?" *Criminology* 43: 355–406.

Tibbetts, Stephen G. and Denise C. Herz. 1996. "Gender Differences in Factors of Social Control and Rational Choice." *Deviant Behavior* 17: 183–208.

Wolfe, Nancy T., Francis T. Cullen, and John B. Cullen. 1984. "Describing the Female Offender: A Note on the Demographics of Arrests." *Journal of Criminal Justice* 12: 483–492.

Zahn, Margaret A., ed. 2009. *The Delinquent Girl.* Philadelphia: Temple University Press.

27. Sisters in Crime

Freda Adler

In 1938, Clifford Shaw of the Chicago school of criminology published Brothers in Crime, *a work whose title revealed his central focus on male crime. Nearly four decades later, Freda Adler (1975) signified a break with this perspective by naming her book* Sisters in Crime. *Indeed, her scholarship helped to ensure that no future generation of criminologists would ignore gender in the study of criminal behavior.*

Adler's most provocative claim was that the movement to achieve equality between the sexes would result in increasing female crime, especially in domains previously dominated by men. This liberation thesis underestimated the tenacity of existing gender roles and inequality. Gender differences in socialization and opportunities were not swept away and, in many ways, boys and girls continued to be raised in different social worlds. Accordingly, the "new female criminals" that Adler saw gathering on the horizon did not, at least in large numbers, materialize (see, however, Alarid et al., 1996).

Adler's work, however, played a major role in directing the attention of criminologists to the gender gap in crime and changes in this gap over time. Also, Adler challenged previous attempts to pathologize female offenders. Instead, she illuminated the way in which social experiences shape the life-choices, including the choice of crime, that women make. She developed the case that the major barriers to females' participation in crime are not biological but social. While later criminologists, especially radical feminists, may find the specifics of Adler's liberation thesis problematic, she still deserves much credit for ushering in a feminist paradigm that shifted attention away from the supposed abnormalities of individual female offenders and toward an appreciation of the social circumstances in which women are enmeshed.

Further, it may be premature to dismiss the possibility that long-term changes in gender roles will influence the criminal participation of women. A strong liberation thesis may be untenable, but it is not farfetched to theorize that the incremental transformation of gender roles— a transformation that affects the social experiences of women across class and racial boundaries— might be implicated in the amount and content of women's criminality. Indeed, several recent accounts relate female crime to the adoption of nontraditional gender roles and identities— although none of these accounts portray female criminals as "liberated." Rather, they argue that some females assume roles and adopt identities that allow for crime in certain situations (e.g., Messerschmidt, 2002; Miller, 2001). In terms of social change, Adler's Sisters in Crime *is still a "young" book. It will be interesting to revisit her ideas a half century from now to see if she has proven more prophetic than we now imagine.*

References

Adler, Freda. 1975. *Sisters in Crime: The Rise of the New Female Criminal.* New York: McGraw-Hill.

Excerpted with permission from Freda Adler, *Sisters in Crime.* Copyright © 1975 by Freda Adler.

Alarid, Leanne Fiftal, James W. Marquart, Velmer S. Burton, Jr., Francis T. Cullen, and Steven J. Cuvelier. 1996. "Female Crime Roles in Serious Offenses: A Study of Adult Felons." *Justice Quarterly* 13: 431–454.

Messerschmidt, James W. 2002. "On Gang Girls, Gender and a Structured Action Theory." *Theoretical Criminology* 6: 461–476.

Miller, Jody. 2001. *One of the Guys: Girls, Gangs, and Gender.* New York: Oxford University Press.

Shaw, Clifford R., with the assistance of Henry D. McKay and James F. McDonald. 1938. *Brothers in Crime.* Chicago: University of Chicago Press.

Women are no longer indentured to the kitchens, baby carriages, or bedrooms of America. The skein of myths about women is unraveling, the chains have been pried loose, and there will be no turning back to the days when women found it necessary to justify their existence by producing babies or cleaning houses. Allowed their freedom for the first time, women—by the tens of thousands—have chosen to desert those kitchens, and plunge exuberantly into the formerly all-male quarters of the working world. . . .

In the same way that women are demanding equal opportunity in fields of legitimate endeavor, a similar number of determined women are forcing their way into the world of major crimes. . . .

It is this segment of women who are pushing into—and succeeding at—crimes which were formerly committed by males only. Females like Marge are now being found not only robbing banks single-handedly, but also committing assorted armed robberies, muggings, loan-sharking operations, extortion, murders, and a wide variety of other aggressive, violence-oriented crimes which previously involved only men. . . .

By every indicator available, female criminals appear to be surpassing males in the rate of increase for almost every major crime. Although males continue to commit the greater absolute number of offenses, it is the women who are committing those same crimes at yearly rates of increase now running as high as six and seven times greater than those for males. . . .

In summary, what we have described is a gradual but accelerating social revolution in which women are closing many of the gaps, social and criminal, that have separated them from men. The closer they get, the more alike they look and act. This is not to suggest that there are no inherent differences. Differences do exist and will be elaborated later in this book, but it seems clear that those differences are not of prime importance in understanding female criminality. The simplest and most accurate way to grasp the essence of women's changing patterns is to discard dated notions of femininity. That is a role that fewer and fewer women are willing to play. In the final analysis, women criminals are human beings who have basic needs and abilities and opportunities. Over the years these needs have not changed, nor will they. But women's abilities and opportunities have multiplied, resulting in a kaleidoscope of changing patterns whose final configuration will be fateful for all of us. . . .

Social Differences

Whatever equality may have existed between Adam and Eve before the Fall, there was a clear distinction in their social roles afterward. Adam was thenceforth required to till the soil and earn his bread by the sweat of his brow; Eve was condemned to painful childbirth and total submission to her husband. In one august decree, her reproductive role and social role were established and fixed. To be a woman, then as now, meant not just to be a distinctive blend of physiological and psychological characteristics. It meant and means that one is perceived differently, treated differently, responded to differently, and the subject of different expectations. Given the varying social forces that weigh unequally on the sexes in creatures as culture-dependent as humans, it seems clear that the resulting differences in behavior owe more to wide disparities in social-role than to the narrow differences in physical and psychological makeup.

The answer to the nursery-rhyme question, "what are little girls made of?" is revealing at several different levels. The list of ingredients—"sugar and spice and everything nice"—contains both a biological theory and a social demand. We are told, first of all, that little girls are good because of their inherent structure, and secondly, that they had better be good if they hope to enjoy the status of femininity and avoid the social disapproval which accompanies deviancy. Little boys, too, are under social pressure, but of a different kind. They are made of "snakes and snails and puppy-dog tails"—a combination designed to contrast mischievously and dynamically with the inert and saccharine constitution of their female counterparts. They, too, are saddled with social and presumed biological imperatives which compress the wide-ranging human potential for variation into the narrow confines of social-role expectation. There is hardly any important individual or social area—play, personal hygiene, manners, discipline, dependency, dress, activity, career, sexual activity, aggressiveness, etc.—which has not been polarized and institutionalized as a sex-role difference. While it is true that men have tended to stigmatize women as a group, deviation from social standards is even worse—e.g., the "effeminate" man and the "masculine" woman.

Traditionally, the little girl and later the woman are confined to a low-level of noise, dirt, disorder, and physical aggression. They must be obedient, dependent, modest about their bodies, and avoid sex play as well as rough and tumble competition. But life is not all no-no's: for her pains she is allowed to turn more readily to others for gratification, to cry when hurt, to be spontaneously affectionate, and to achieve less in school and work. Whatever the natural inclination of the sexes may be, society

does not depend on spontaneous acquisition of the profile it considers desirable: besides identification with the parent of the same sex, which is probably the single most important determinant of behavior, it selects out from the random range of childhood activities those certain ones which will be accentuated or discarded. The shaping process includes toys—mechanical and problem-solving for boys, and soft and nonchallenging for girls—social structuring, individual rewards and punishments, and the satisfactions apparently inherent in conforming to role expectations. The development of aggressive and dependent traits, both of which are considered to be sex-related, is a case in point. One research study found that while aggressive boys become aggressive men and dependent girls become dependent women, the reverse was true for dependent boys and aggressive girls: as they approach maturity, they reverse themselves and also become aggressive men and dependent women, respectively. Similarly, there is a greater overlap of sex-role personality traits when the sibling in a two-child family is of the opposite sex, and this effect is greater with the younger siblings than with the older ones. Clearly, learning and social pressure are influential in effecting sex-role expectations. Extending the argument that social roles are related to biological processes only indirectly, presumably a technology which permitted father to nurture the child could result in a complete social-role reversal. In a pithy and accurate observation, Simone de Beauvoir summed up the consensus of current thinking when she said, "One is not born, but rather becomes, a woman."

In the interests of clarity, I have spoken separately of the major physical, psychological, and social characteristics which distinguish women from men, although obviously each molds the final form of the other, both clinically and theoretically. Investigations of animal behavior demonstrate, for example, that rat pups who are psychologically stimulated develop larger and presumably smarter brains than those exposed to sensory isolations; a litter born to a low-status African wild dog is less likely to survive than one born to a high-status female because the pups are less well fed and less protected by the pack; the male offspring of low-status baboon females, regardless of their innate characteristics, are less likely to become dominant than those born to high-status females because the latter spend more time in physical proximity to the inner circle of dominant males and learn dominance behavior; and the ovulatory cycle of a dove is retarded when a glass partition is placed between her and the rest of the flock, and it is stopped altogether if she is isolated in a room, unless there is a mirror. The interdependency between biological drive and learning is described in Konrad Lorenz's formulation of the concept of "instinct-training interlocking behavior:" he describes this as a blend of instinctive and learned components, with instinct guaranteeing the readiness for certain kinds of learning and behavior to occur but experience shaping its final form.

In summary, females are smaller and meeker than men, they are less stable physiologically, they produce fewer androgenic hormones, and they have been socially shaped toward passivity, dependency, and conformity. Men are bigger, stronger, more aggressive, achievement-oriented, and more willing to break rules and take risks. This profile of the "normal" male and the "normal" female is consistent with the traditional differences which, until the last few decades, have prevailed for their criminal counterparts. However, the increasing "masculinization" of female social and criminal behavior forces us to reexamine the basis for her previous feminine limitations. A common-sense approach, and one followed by even such uncommon men as Freud and Adler, would suggest that what is natural to the female could be inferred from a factual description of the way the majority of females think and feel and act. Understandably, this is what has been done, and just as understandably it has been wrong. . . .

Female Passivity: Genetic Fact or Cultural Myth?

In the past, aggression was thought to be chiefly a biologically controlled trait. As a matter of their birth and ongoing internal chemistry, males were assumed to be "naturally aggressive"—hence the explanation of their historic roles as soliders, hard-boiled businessmen, and merciless criminals. Women, on the other hand, were thought to be innately timid, passive, and conforming. Their general failure to be anything but mothers and housewives was offered as proof of their inability to be aggressive.

Of all the differences between the sexes, only four—size, strength, aggression, and dominance—have been implicated in any way with the overrepresentation of males in the criminal system.

The first two are biological givens; the other two are largely, if not entirely, socially learned. Let us examine them separately. In non-technological societies, and in earlier periods in industrial societies, physical strength was often the final arbiter of social interaction, but even so, it was not the only one. In man as well as in the apes, psychological factors including social manipulation, ruses, and group alliances were often decisive for leadership and effective action. In animals as well as men, the battle did not always go to the strong nor the race to the swift. But even if it did, this edge has been diminished by the technology of modern weapons. The deadliness of a gun is not necessarily less dangerous in the hands of a woman—although some have claimed that her lack of aggressiveness makes her a very unlikely and ineffective gunslinger. This is an interesting assumption because it is a common stereotype and is grounded in studies of male hormonal influences on lower animals, which gives it a ring of biological authenticity. There is much truth in this, but it is only a partial truth which, when stretched beyond its limits, conveys a falsehood. The truth is that in lower animals males are characteristically more aggressive, and this aggression is so directly linked to male hormones that if the male is castrated or injected with estrogen (the female hormone) he will stop fighting. Likewise, the prenatal administration of testosterone to pregnant monkeys results in pseudohermaphroditic female offspring who even three years after birth are more aggressive than normal females. However, it would be misleading to formulate the equation androgen = aggression or estrogen = nonaggression for all but the simplest and least socially developed species. Furthermore, it cannot be claimed that aggression is the exclusive prerogative of males. Mature female chimpanzees regularly drive off lower status males and any female mammal's defense of her cubs is as fierce as it is legendary.

But relevant as this is in establishing that aggression can co-exist with estrogen and can be unrelated to male hormones in mammals, the evidence for hormonal-behavioral detachment is even more compelling in subhuman primates and men. It is not possible to understand the behavior of social animals outside the context of a social situation. For example, an electric shock applied to an animal in a dominant position vis-á-vis another will result in an attack; the same stimulus applied to the same animal who is in a subdominant position vis-á-vis another will result in cringing, submissive behavior. Likewise, the response of anger vs. fear or fight vs. flight depends less on the release of specific chemicals than on whether we perceive the threatening stimulus, in relation to ourselves, to be smaller or larger. The human capacity for abstraction and symbol formulation extends the range of "size" to include factors only remotely related to actual mass, so that characteristics such as wealth, lineage, social connections, skill, and intelligence may be perceived as "big" and accorded dominance. In the evolutionary progression toward higher mammals, there is a decreasing dependency between hormones and behavior, and in humans we find an almost complete cultural "override" of innate drives and tendencies. Thus, while status and dominance appear to be constants throughout the order of social primates, culture

defines which characteristics will be labeled as dominant. Likewise, the distinctive sex-appropriate behaviors so rigidly controlled by hormones in lower animals have yielded to a rich variety of gender roles in human societies.

In *Sex and Temperament in Three Primitive Societies*, Margaret Mead described three revealing cultural variations. In one tribe, both sexes acted in the mild, parental, responsive manner we expect of women; in a second, both sexes acted in the fierce initiating fashion we expect of men; in a third, the men were chatty, wore curls, and went shopping in the manner of our stereotype of women, while the women were their unadorned, managerial, energetic partners. She concluded that sex roles were

> mere variations of human temperament, to which the members of either or both sexes may, with more or less success in the case of different individuals, be educated to approximate.

She also concluded that regardless of what social role the male plays, it is always the lead.

Regardless of what his characteristic behavior may be and even when it is imitative of "feminine behavior," it is considered high status when he adopts it. While historically and universally it is indeed a man's world, it does not follow that modern industrial man is innately more dominant than modern woman. It could be argued that the equalizing effects of a technological civilization like ours is without historical parallel and that the universal dominance of men may have resulted more from the institutionalization of man's superior strength than from any innate feminine submissiveness.

Western history is replete with examples of women who have risen above their cultural stereotype to become leaders of vigor and acclaim. Nor has their reign or tenure in office been particularly noteworthy for its tranquillity, peacefulness, or lack of aggressive adventures, all characteristics of their countrywomen in the social role of housewife. These women have, in fact, displayed a remarkable talent for ruthless and highly aggressive leadership. For instance, few world leaders have ever been so renowned for their tyrannical, belligerent rule as the English queens. One can still be stirred by the picture of Elizabeth I attired with her gold crown and shining breastplate, mounted on a white stallion, and moving like an avenging angel through her army of twenty thousand men at Tilbury...; Cleopatra of ancient Egypt, a biological woman's woman by any standards, was known for her shrewd political manipulations and insatiable appetite for military conquests; Maria Theresa was the founder of the modern Austrian state; the Russian Empress Catherine, who mothered a dozen children during her reign, still found time to annex ever-widening territories and seek new armies to defeat. In the present day, it is noteworthy that the two major countries with female rulers have both been at war within the last few years: Indira Gandhi of India and Golda Meir of Israel have shown no timidity—each, in wars across her border, has wielded political and military might as effectively as any man. Of course, such women as these who have risen to national leadership possess extraordinary characteristics which distinguish them from the mass of women—and the mass of men, for that matter. The very capacity and drive for ascension through a male world involved a selection process which would have discouraged weaker women. Notwithstanding their small numbers, the resoluteness, and fortitude of such women challenge the myth of innate female passivity. On a broader scope, and one which encompassed more ordinary women, was the female incursion into criminal areas, previously considered male, during World War II. In law-enforcing as well as law-breaking, it would appear that social position and social-role expectations are more important than sex in determining behavior.

During the early 1940s, the mobilization of males from the civil to the military sector resulted in the necessity for a large number of women to fill positions previously held by men. And fill them they did, in a way not altogether anticipated. It had been known and expected that lesser men often rise to the stature of a role thrust on them by circumstance. It should not have been surprising, therefore, that "lesser men" who happen to be women would do the same thing. What was most portentous, however, about this vocational shift was not that women could assume men's jobs, but that in doing so they could also presume to men's social roles. One need not look to psychological theories to explain the enthusiasm with which women embraced men's esteemed positions. Their own, as housewife and playmate, had been eroding for years and a desperately labor-short male establishment had further devalued it in the interests of national defense, as something akin to indolence, if not disloyalty. "Rosie the Riveter," symbol of the women working for the war, was proclaimed a heroine in song and style by a grateful country. As the residence of female status shifted from the home to the office or factory, a trip that men had made long before, the American woman accommodated so congenially to the change that few people at the time challenged her credentials to perform. However, many were concerned that she was not just commuting to her new-found roles but might settle down to stay. In unprecedented numbers women crossed the sex-role line in their jobs and in their crimes during the war years, 1940 to 1945. In that period, the crimes committed by women almost doubled in number and even began to assume the same patterns as male crime. The trend peaked in 1945 and declined rapidly after the war with the return of men to their jobs, but it could never be the same. Women were now urged to act more like women by a male establishment which wanted to return to the position it had temporarily (it hoped) vacated. But in social evolution as in biological evolution, there is no easy road back, especially since in a very profound sense the women could not go home again. Labor-saving household appliances and the denigration of the domestic work ethic they conveyed rendered her old position untenable. In addition, there was a shift in the male attitude. Men were seeing women as worthy rivals and feeling considerably less charitable and more competitive toward them. Furthermore, in a world grown too full of people, even the once sacrosanct status of motherhood was beginning to bear unhappy resemblances to overproductive pollution. With zero population as a national goal and household drudgery an accepted epithet, where was the woman to go? The road back was blocked, and while the road forward was not completely open it was now more accessible than ever before.

The pressure was all for discarding the separate-but-equal provisions of the old social contract and opting for a chance to compete in the same field and under the same conditions as men. Unfortunately, the men were not as ready for this change as the women. Psychoanalysts, long accustomed to the futile penis envy of women, were now talking about breast envy and womb envy, an example of male jealousy toward women almost unheard of in Freud's day.

While women proceeded to widen their social and criminal roles, many men, especially middle- and lower-class men, who had the least ground to yield in the status hierarchy, resisted in every way they could. . . .

Gender Equality and Crime

The old ways do indeed die hard, not only because we need our stereotypes and our subdominants, but also because cognitive systems tend to become security blankets to which we cling most tenaciously just when we are most threatened. It is perhaps for these reasons that the coming of age of the Western woman was not forecast by the behavioral scientists who should have known, but instead it caught us unawares and overtook our comfortable prejudices with a *fait accompli*. While most were predicting that it was impossible and many were arguing that it wasn't happening, it had already occurred. It is tempting to think no deeper

than an apparent fact, and it must be admitted that the "facts" of female inferiority were apparent to all who could read the figures that supported them. It did not seem productive to search out the reasons behind the figures. They were self-evident because they confirmed what we already knew about the natural superiority of men. If it were otherwise, we surely would have been told by this time. But, indeed, we were being told new "facts" in compelling ways by new figures which were challenging old theories.

In the countless indices which measure female output of degrees and income and factory production, and in the Uniform Crime Reports which tabulate her legal transgressions, these rising figures were intruding not only on our beliefs but on the mores which supported them. At first, the rising crime rates were greeted as an apparition, a mirage; at first, they were dismissed as an aberration which would correct itself by statistical adjustments; at last, they were recognized as ancient female strengths which had always been latent and were just now, at this sociotechnological juncture of history, realizing their potential. Everything we know about the history of woman and everything we see about her current behavior tells us that her past limitations as a worker and law-breaker have been largely, if not entirely, the result of her physical weakness and the cultural institutions which derived from that fact. Save only her inferiority in size and strength, her differences from men are just *that*, differences. Some confer an advantage, others a disadvantage, depending on the particular culture. In our own, given her education, aspirations (these, too, have been liberated), freedom from unwanted pregnancies, healthy assertiveness, and access to labor-saving devices, including guns, she shares the same fortunate or unfortunate criminogenic qualities as men.

I have not contended here that women are equal *to* men, simply that they are potentially the equal of men. There are many differences which we have described and no doubt more will be discovered, but all evidence points to two complementary conclusions: First, the small natural differences between the sexes have been polarized and institutionalized in special ways by different cultures to produce a gender disparity which reveals more about emotional needs of the society than about the innate possibilities of the individual. And second, when size and strength between the sexes are discounted by technology, as they have been within the ranks of men, social expectations and social roles, including the criminal roles, tend increasingly to merge.

There was a time early in the history of the physical sciences, before the concepts of mass and gravity were formulated, when the weight of an object was thought to reside within the physical boundaries of the object. Because weight is palpable and measurable, it was a conclusion which met the requirements of common sense and common experience. But the limitation of common sense is that it owes too much allegiance to the past to permit conceptual breakthroughs to the future. It is a better follower than leader. As physicists later discovered, the weight of an object is not inherent within it but rather the measure of an outside gravitational pull acting upon it. In an analogous manner, scientific thinking about human behavior has evolved in the same centrifugal direction. From the predecessors of Lombroso to the followers of Freud and into modern times, the search for the causes of female criminality have focused on her biology with scant heed to her sociology. We have only recently recognized that the clothes of social-role expectations not only make the man, they also form the woman.

Even if it is established that humans have innate biological drives, and even if it were confirmed that females have a different biogrammar (i.e., a behavioral repertoire of signals) from males, the social forces which impinge on her from without would still be decisive for her conformist as well as her deviant behavior. In the profoundest evolutionary sense, the social factors which sustain and suspend us also create our destiny, and biology must follow where society leads.

Discussion Questions

1. How do you think that the Women's Movement and the corresponding changes that were occurring in American society affected Adler's ideas on female crime as she wrote *Sisters in Crime*?
2. What is the liberation thesis? How does this relate to Adler's views about the "rise of a new female criminal"?
3. Why did Adler argue that biology is not the main cause of female behavior, including female criminality?
4. Think back to your own childhood and teenage years. How might the socialization practices that you witnessed while you were growing up be related to why the criminal behaviors of males and females differ?

28. A Feminist Theory of Female Delinquency

Meda Chesney-Lind

"There is considerable question," notes Meda Chesney-Lind (1989: 10), "as to whether existing theories that were admittedly developed to explain male delinquency can adequately explain female delinquency." But why is this necessarily the case? After all, if strain, control, or social learning are general causes of crime, might we not expect that the sources of female criminality would be the same as male criminality? In Chesney-Lind's view, however, such thinking renders gender socially irrelevant and behaviorally inconsequential. Yet gender is a master status in virtually every social interaction—a salient factor that provides meaning to and structures for behavioral options. As a result, growing up in the United States (and elsewhere), girls and boys have different experiences, they react to their experiences differently, and they are reacted to differently by those seeking to control them. Gender thus provides the ongoing, day-to-day contact through which crime is caused and accomplished.

The most defining feature of gender roles is "patriarchy." But it is precisely here that traditional theories of crime are most wanting. Because they were largely constructed to explain male criminality, the values and power relations inherent in male domination simply are never given any causal consideration. In methodological terms, one might say that traditional theories are "misspecified": they leave out a key explanatory variable—not merely women or gender, but what it means to be a female.

When patriarchy is used to inform one's criminological analysis, however, the special pathways that girls take into crime are suddenly illuminated. An important feature of the "patriarchal context" from which female delinquency flows, observes Chesney-Lind, is that girls are vulnerable to physical and sexual abuse. Faced with constant abuse, females can do little to fight back against their dominant male abusers. One option is to run away. Here, however, they face a second manifestation of patriarchy: They are defined as "runaways" and as sexually "promiscuous." According to Chesney-Lind, criminal justice agencies have traditionally sought to criminalize the behavior of these girls. They have played a role in tracking down the runaways and returning them to the very home in which the victimization had transpired.

Facing extensive physical and sexual victimization at home and with little hope of protection from the state, girls find escape in the "streets." Their quest for survival, however, leads to crimes of petty theft and panhandling. But patriarchy is reproduced on the streets as well. Their sexuality is another means of survival, and thus they risk being lured into prostitution. As Chesney-Lind (1989: 24) notes, these girls have "little else of value to trade" and thus "get involved in criminal activities that exploit their sexual object status."

The potential weakness of feminist theories is not what they include but what they exclude. Feminist

---

Meda Chesney-Lind, "Girls' Crime and Woman's Place: Toward a Feminist Model of Female Delinquency," *Crime & Delinquency* (35) 1989, pp. 10–11, 19–27, copyright © 1989 by Sage Publications. Reprinted by permission of Sage Publications, Inc.

scholars risk committing the same mistake as the criminologists they rightly criticize by simply dismissing—often on a priori, ideological grounds— theories they do not like. By calling perspectives "male-centered" and ignoring the related research studies, they are free to neglect the causal significance of conditions that have been shown empirically to affect not only boys' but also girls' delinquency. Traditional theories thus are useful in identifying factors that may, in varying degrees and in unique ways, play a role in the crime and delinquency of females (Agnew, 2009; Heimer and De Coster, 1999).

Even so, Chesney-Lind has shown the value of taking a feminist perspective to the study of delinquency. She has demarcated a pathway into crime—rooted in gender-related power inequities and the physical/sexual abuse girls endure—that would not be apparent without the lens of gender and patriarchy. Feminist theories are essential, therefore, because they force criminologists to take seriously the position that, however overlapping their experiences might be, boys and girls reside in different worlds that are circumscribed by the broader patriarchal system. Gender affects so much in our lives; the notion that crime would be the exception is, on its face, difficult to sustain.

References

Agnew, Robert. 2009. "The Contribution of 'Mainstream' Theories to the Explanation of Crime and Delinquency." In Morgoret A. Zahn (ed.), *The Delinguent Girl*, pp. 7–29. Phildelphia: Temple University Press.

Chesney-Lind, Meda. 1989. "Girls' Crime and Woman's Place: Toward a Feminist Model of Female Delinquency." *Crime and Delinquency* 35: 5–29.

Heimer, Karen and Stacy De Coster. 1999. "The Gendering of Violent Delinquency." *Criminology* 37: 277–318.

There is considerable question as to whether existing theories that were admittedly developed to explain male delinquency can adequately explain female delinquency. Clearly, these theories were much influenced by the notion that class and protest masculinity were at the core of delinquency. Will the "add women and stir approach" be sufficient? Are these really theories of delinquent behavior as some (Simons, Miller, and Aigner, 1980) have argued?

This article will suggest that they are not. The extensive focus on male delinquency and the inattention to the role played by patriarchal arrangements in the generation of adolescent delinquency and conformity has rendered the major delinquency theories fundamentally inadequate to the task of explaining female behavior. There is, in short, an urgent need to rethink current models in light of girls' situation in patriarchal society.

. . . This discussion will also establish that the proposed overhaul of delinquency theory is not, as some might think, solely an academic exercise. Specifically, it is incorrect to assume that because girls are charged with less serious offenses, they actually have few problems and are treated gently when they are drawn into the juvenile justice system. Indeed, the extensive focus on disadvantaged males in public settings has meant that girls' victimization and the relationship between that experience and girls' crime has been systematically ignored. Also missed has been the central role played by the juvenile justice system in the sexualization of girls' delinquency and the criminalization of girls' survival strategies. Finally, it will be suggested that the official actions of the juvenile justice system should be understood as major forces in girls' oppression as they have historically served to reinforce the obedience of all young women to demands of patriarchal authority no matter how abusive and arbitrary. . . .

Toward a Feminist Theory of Delinquency

To sketch out completely a feminist theory of delinquency is a task beyond the scope of this article. It may be sufficient, at this point, simply to identify a few of the most obvious problems with attempts to adapt male-oriented theory to explain female conformity and deviance. Most significant of these is the fact that all existing theories were developed with no concern about gender stratification.

Note that this is not simply an observation about the power of gender roles (though this power is undeniable). It is increasingly clear that gender stratification in patriarchal society is as powerful a system as is class. A feminist approach to delinquency means construction of explanations of female behavior that are sensitive to its patriarchal context. Feminist analysis of delinquency would also examine ways in which agencies of social control—the police, the courts, and the persons—act in ways to reinforce woman's place in male society (Harris, 1977; Chesney-Lind, 1986). Efforts to construct a feminist model of delinquency must first and foremost be sensitive to the situations of girls. Failure to consider the existing empirical evidence on girls' lives and behavior can quickly lead to stereotypical thinking and theoretical dead ends.

An example of this sort of flawed theory building was the early fascination with the notion that the women's movement was causing an increase in women's crime; a notion that is now more or less discredited (Steffensmeier, 1980; Gora, 1982). A more recent example of the same sort of thinking can be found in recent work on the "powercontrol" model of delinquency (Hagan, Simpson, and Gillis, 1987). Here, the authors speculate that girls commit less delinquency in part because their behavior is more closely controlled by the patriarchal family. The authors' promising beginning quickly gets bogged down in a very limited definition of patriarchal control (focusing on parental supervision and variations in power within the family). Ultimately, the authors' narrow formulation of patriarchal control results in their arguing that mother's work force participation (particularly in high status occupations) leads to increases in daughters' delinquency since these girls find themselves in more "egalitarian families."

This is essentially a not-too-subtle variation on the earlier "liberation" hypothesis. Now, mother's liberation causes daughter's crime. Aside from the methodological problems with the study (e.g., the authors argue that female-headed households are equivalent to upper-class "egalitarian" families where both parents work, and they measure delinquency using a six-item scale that contains no status offense items), there is a more fundamental problem with the hypothesis. There is no evidence to suggest that as women's labor force participation has increased, girls' delinquency has increased. Indeed, during the last decade when both women's labor force participation accelerated and the number of female-headed households soared, aggregate female delinquency measured both by self-report and official statistics either declined or remained stable (Ageton, 1983; Chilton and Datesman, 1987; Federal Bureau of Investigation, 1987).

By contrast, a feminist model of delinquency would focus more extensively on the few pieces of information about girls' actual lives and the role played by girls' problems, including those caused by racism and poverty, in their delinquency behavior. Fortunately, a considerable literature is now developing on girls' lives and much of it bears directly on girls' crime.

Criminalizing Girls' Survival

It has long been understood that a major reason for girls' presence in juvenile courts was the fact that their parents insisted on their arrest. In the early years, conflicts with parents were by far the most significant referral source; in Honolulu 44 percent of the girls who appeared in court in 1929 through 1930 were referred by parents.

Recent national data, while slightly less explicity, also show that girls are more likely to be referred to court by "sources other than law enforcement agencies" (which would include parents). In 1983, nearly a quarter (23 percent) of all girls but only 16 percent of boys charged with delinquent offenses were referred to court by non-law enforcement agencies. The pattern among youth referred for status offenses (for which girls are overrepresented) was even more pronounced. Well over half (56 percent) of the girls charged with these offenses and 45 percent of the boys were referred by sources other than law enforcement (Snyder and Finnegan, 1987, p. 21; see also Pope and Feyerherm, 1982).

The fact that parents are often committed to two standards of adolescent behavior is one explanation for such a disparity—and one that should not be discounted as a major source of tension even in modern families. Despite expectations to the contrary, gender-specific socialization patterns have not changed very much and this is especially true for parents' relationships with their daughters (Katz, 1979). It appears that even parents who oppose sexism in general feel "uncomfortable tampering with existing traditions" and "do not want to risk their children becoming misfits" (Katz, 1979, p. 24). Clearly, parental attempts to adhere to and enforce these traditional notions will continue to be a source of conflict between girls and their elders. Another important explanation for girls' problems with their parents, which has received attention only in more recent years, is the problem of physical and sexual abuse. Looking specifically at the problem of childhood sexual abuse, it is increasingly clear that this form of abuse is a particular problem for girls.

Girls are, for example, much more likely to be the victims of child sexual abuse than are boys. Finkelhor and Baron estimate from a review of community studies that roughly 70 percent of the victims of sexual abuse are female (Finkelhor and Baron, 1986, p. 45); they are more likely than boys to be assaulted by a family member (often a stepfather) (DeJong, Hervada, and Emmett, 1983; Russell, 1986), and, as a consequence, their abuse tends to last longer than male sexual abuse (DeJong, Hervada, and Emmett, 1983). All of these factors are associated with more severe trauma—causing dramatic short- and long-term effects in victims (Adams-Tucker, 1982). The

effects noted by researchers in this area move from the more well known "fear, anxiety, depression, anger and hostility, and inappropriate sexual behavior" (Browne and Finkelhor, 1986, p. 69) to behaviors of greater familiarity to criminologists, including running away from home, difficulties in school, truancy, and early marriage (Browne and Finkelhor, 1986).

Herman's study of incest survivors in therapy found that they were more likely to have run away from home than a matched sample of women whose fathers were "seductive" (33 percent compared to 5 percent). Another study of women patients found that 50 percent of the victims of child sexual abuse, but only 20 percent of the nonvictim group, had left home before the age of 18 (Meiselman, 1978).

Not surprisingly, then, studies of girls on the streets or in court populations are showing high rates of both physical and sexual abuse. Silbert and Pines (1981, p. 409) found, for example, that 60 percent of the street prostitutes they interviewed had been sexually abused as juveniles. Girls at an Arkansas diagnostic unit and school who had been adjudicated for either status or delinquent offenses reported similarly high levels of sexual abuse as well as high levels of physical abuse; 53 percent indicated they had been sexually abused, 25 percent recalled scars, 38 percent recalled bleeding from abuse, and 51 percent recalled bruises (Mouzakitas, 1981).

A sample survey of girls in the juvenile justice system in Wisconsin (Phelps et al., 1982) revealed that 79 percent had been subjected to physical abuse that resulted in some form of injury, and 32 percent had been sexually abused by parents or other persons who were closely connected to their families. Moreover, 50 percent had been sexually assaulted ("raped" or forced to participate in sexual acts) (Phelps et al., 1982, p. 66). Even higher figures were reported by McCormack and her associates (McCormack, Janus, and Burgess, 1986) in their study of youth in a runaway shelter in Toronto. They found that 73 percent of the females and 38 percent of the males had been sexually abused.

Finally, a study of youth charged with running away, truancy, or listed as missing persons in Arizona found that 55 percent were incest victims (Reich and Gutierres, 1979).

Many young women, then, are running away from profound sexual victimization at home, and once on the streets they are forced further into crime in order to survive. Interviews with girls who have run away from home show, very clearly, that they do not have a lot of attachment to their delinquent activities. In fact, they are angry about being labeled as delinquent, yet all engaged in illegal acts (Koroki and Chesney-Lind, 1985). The Wisconsin study found that 54 percent of the girls who ran away found it necessary to steal money, food, and clothing in order to survive. A few exchanged sexual contact for money, food, and/or shelter (Phelps et al., 1982, p. 67). In their study of runaway youth, McCormack, Janus, and Burgess (1986, pp. 392–393) found that sexually abused female runaways were significantly more likely than their nonabused counterparts to engage in delinquent or criminal activities such as substance abuse, petty theft, and prostitution. No such pattern was found among male runaways.

Research (Chesney-Lind and Rodriguez, 1983) on the backgrounds of adult women in prison underscores the important links between women's childhood victimizations and their later criminal careers. The interviews revealed that virtually all of this sample were the victims of physical and/or sexual abuse as youngsters; over 60 percent had been sexually abused and about half had been raped as young women. This situation promoted these women to run away from home (three-quarters had been arrested for status offenses) where once on the streets they began engaging in prostitution and other forms of petty property crime. They also begin what becomes a lifetime problem with drugs. As adults, the women continue in these activities since they possess truncated educational backgrounds and virtually no marketable occupational skills (see also Miller, 1986).

Confirmation of the consequences of childhood sexual and physical abuse on adult female criminal behavior has also recently come from a large quantitative study of 908 individuals with substantiated and validated histories of these victimizations. Widom (1988) found that abused or neglected females were twice as likely as a matched group of controls to have an adult record (16 percent compared to 7.5 percent). The difference was also found among men, but it was not as dramatic (42 percent compared to 33 percent). Men with abuse backgrounds were also more likely to contribute to the "cycle of violence" with more arrests for violent offenses as adult offenders than the control group. In contrast, when women with abuse backgrounds did become involved with the criminal justice system, their arrests tended to involve property and order offenses (such as disorderly conduct, curfew, and loitering violations) (Widom, 1988, p. 17).

Given this information, a brief example of how a feminist perspective on the causes of female delinquency might look seems appropriate. First, like young men, girls are frequently the recipients of violence and sexual abuse. But unlike boys, girls' victimization and their response to that victimization is specifically shaped by their status as young women. Perhaps because of the gender and sexual scripts found in patriarchal families, girls are much more likely than boys to be victims of family-related sexual abuse. Men, particularly men with traditional attitudes toward women, are likely to define their daughters or stepdaughters as their sexual property (Finkelhor, 1982). In a society that idealizes inequality in male/female relationships and venerates youth in women, girls are easily defined as sexually attractive by older men (Bell, 1984). In addition, girls' vulnerability to both physical and sexual abuse is heightened by norms that require that they stay at home where their victimizers have access to them.

Moreover, their victimizers (usually males) have the ability to invoke official agencies of social control in their efforts to keep young women at home and vulnerable. That is to say, abusers have traditionally been able to utilize the uncritical commitment of the juvenile justice system toward parental authority to force girls to obey them. Girls' complaints about abuse were, until recently, rountinely ignored. For this reason, statutes that were originally placed in law to "protect" young people have, in the case of girls' delinquency, criminalized their survival strategies. As they run away from abusive homes, parents have been able to employ agencies to enforce their return. If they persisted in their refusal to stay in that home, however intolerable, they were incarcerated.

Young women, a large number of whom are on the run from homes characterized by sexual abuse and parental neglect, are forced by the very statutes designed to protect them into the lives of escaped convicts. Unable to enroll in school or take a job to support themselves because they fear detection, young female runaways are forced into the streets. Here they engage in panhandling, petty theft, and occasional prostitution in order to survive. Young women in conflict with their parents (often for very legitimate reasons) may actually be forced by present laws into petty criminal activity, prostitution, and drug use.

In addition, the fact that young girls (but not necessarily young boys) are defined as sexually desirable and, in fact, more desirable than their olders sisters due to the double standard of aging means that their lives on the streets (and their survival strategies) take on unique shape—once again shaped by patriarchal values. It is no accident that girls on the run from abusive homes, or on the streets because of profound poverty, get involved in criminal activities that exploit their sexual object status. American society has defined as desirable youthful, physically perfect women. This means that girls on the streets, who have little else of value to trade, are encouraged to utilize this "resource" (Campagna and Poffenberger, 1988). It also means that the criminal subculture views them from this perspective (Miller, 1986).

Female Delinquency, Patriarchal Authority, and Family Courts

The early insights into male delinquency were largely gleaned by intensive field observation of delinquent boys. Very little of this sort of work has been done in the case of girls' delinquency, though it is vital to an understanding of girls' definitions of their own situations, choices, and behavior (for exceptions to this see Campbell, 1984; Peacock, 1981; Miller, 1986; Rosenberg and Zimmerman, 1977). Time must be spent listening to girls. Fuller research on the settings, such as families and schools, that girls find themselves in and the impact of variations in those settings should also be undertaken (see Figueira-McDonough, 1986). A more complete understanding of how poverty and racism shape girls' lives is also vital (see Messerschmidt, 1986; Campbell, 1984). Finally, current qualitative research on the reaction of official agencies to girls' delinquency must be conducted. This latter task, admittedly more difficult, is particularly critical to the development of delinquency theory that is as sensitive to gender as it is to race and class.

It is clear that throughout most of the court's history, virtually all female delinquency has been placed within the larger context of girls' sexual behavior. One explanation for this pattern is that familial control over girls' sexual capital has historically been central to the maintenance of patriarchy (Lerner, 1986). The fact that young women have relatively more of this capital has been one reason for the excessive concern that both families and official agencies of social control have expressed about youthful female defiance (otherwise much of the behavior of criminal justice personnel makes virtually no sense). Only if one considers the role of women's control over their sexuality at the point in their lives that their value to patriarchal society is so pronounced, does the historic pattern of jailing of huge numbers of girls guilty of minor misconduct make sense.

This framework also explains the enormous resistance that the movement to curb the juvenile justice system's authority over status offenders encountered. Supporters of this change were not really prepared for the political significance of giving youth the freedom to run. Horror stories told by the opponents of deinstitutionalization about victimized youth, youthful prostitution, and youthful involvement in pornography (Office of Juvenile Justice and Delinquency Prevention, 1985) all neglected the unpleasant reality that most of these behaviors were often in direct response to earlier victimization, frequently by parents, that officials had, for years, routinely ignored. What may be at stake in efforts to roll back deinstitutionalization efforts is not so much "protection" of youth as it is curbing the right of young women to defy patriarchy.

In sum, research in both the dynamics of girls' delinquency and offical reactions to that behavior is essential to the development of theories of delinquency that are sensitive to its patriarchal as well as class and racial context.

Discussion Questions

1. What makes Chesney-Lind's explanation of crime a "feminist" theory? How does it differ from a nonfeminist or "traditional" theory of crime? In particular, how is patriarchy central to Chesney-Lind's theory?
2. Why would Chesney-Lind criticize the work of "liberation theorists" such as Freda Adler (Chapter 27)?
3. Does Chesney-Lind believe that the causes of female crime are the same as the causes of male crime? What would she say to theorists such as Edwin Sutherland and Donald Cressey (Chapter 10) and Travis Hirschi and Michael Gottfredson (Chapters 18 and 19) who claim to have set forth "general" theories of crime that explain everyone's criminality—whether they are male or female?
4. In Chesney-Lind's theory, how does gender affect why girls turn to specific types of crime? Could nonfeminist theories explain the types of crime engaged in by girls on the street?

29. The Gendering of Violent Delinquency

Karen Heimer and Stacy De Coster

Differential association theory is one of the leading theories of crime (see Chapter 10). According to the theory, individuals learn to engage in crime from others. Most notably, they learn definitions or beliefs favorable to crime. This traditional theory has been applied to the explanation of female delinquency and the gender gap in delinquency. Typically, it is argued that males are more likely to engage in crime because they are more likely to associate with delinquent peers and learn beliefs favorable to crime (e.g., see Agnew, 2009; Giordano, 2009; Jensen, 2003; Warr, 2002). At the same time, some females do become involved with delinquent peers and learn beliefs favorable to crime. Heimer and De Coster, however, build on such accounts by combining differential association theory with "insights from feminist theories and gender studies." In doing so, they present a wonderful example of the "gendering" of a traditional crime theory.

In the selection below, Heimer and De Coster argue that males are not only more likely to be taught definitions favorable to violence, they are also more likely to learn gender definitions favorable to violence. In particular, men are more often taught to be competitive, independent, rational, and strong. Females, on the other hand, are more often taught to care for others, be passive, emotionally expressive, and weak. Further, Heimer and De Coster argue that there are gender differences in the ways that violent definitions are learned. Parents typically exercise some control over their children,

reducing their opportunities to learn violent definitions. This control can be direct, as when parents supervise their children and discipline them for misdeeds. And this control can be indirect, as when children form close emotional bonds to their parents and refrain from jeopardizing these bonds through misbehavior. Heimer and De Coster argue that indirect control is more important for girls, given that they are socialized to care about others, while direct control is more important for boys. Peers also play a key role in teaching violent definitions. Here, Heimer and De Coster argue that males are not only more likely to associate with aggressive peers, but that such peers are more likely to encourage violence in males. Finally, males are more likely to adopt violent definitions because they are more likely to have engaged in violence in the past, which leads them to rationalize or justify violent behavior.

Table 29.1 provides a good summary of the key arguments made by Heimer and De Coster. Most of these arguments were supported by their analysis of data from a nationally representative sample of adolescents (see Heimer and De Coster, 1999). As indicated in the introduction to this part, Heimer and De Coster's efforts to "gender" differential association theory have been matched by efforts to gender most of the other traditional theories of crime discussed in this book, including strain, control, labeling, and rational choice theories.

Reprinted with permission from Karen Heimer and Stacy De Coster. 1999. "The Gendering of Violent Delinquency," *Criminology*, 37, pp. 277–318.

References

Agnew, Robert. 2009. "The Contribution of 'Mainstream' Theories to the Explanation of Female Delinquency." In Margaret A. Zahn (ed.), *The Delinquent Girl*, pp. 7–29. Philadelphia: Temple University Press.

Giordano, Peggy. 2009. "Peer Influences on Girls' Delinquency." In Margaret A. Zahn (ed.), *The Delinquent Girl*, pp. 127–145. Philadelphia: Temple University Press.

Heimer, Karen and Stacy De Coster. 1999. "The Gendering of Violent Delinquency." *Criminology* 37: 277–318.

Jensen, Gary F. 2003. "Gender Variation in Delinquency: Self-Images, Beliefs, and Peers as Mediating Mechanisms." In Ronald L. Akers and Gary F. Jensen (eds.), *Social Learning Theory and the Explanation of Crime*, pp. 151–178. New Brunswick, NJ: Transaction.

Warr, Mark. 2002. *Companions in Crime*. New York: Cambridge University Press.

Youth violence is considered to be a serious contemporary problem. Yet, theoretical explanations of the causes of violent delinquency have focused on males and largely ignored females.... Better understanding youth violence, ... requires moving beyond the traditional focus on males to examine also the causes of violence among females and the sources of the gender gap in violence....

That is the task of this analysis: Specifically, we reformulate differential association theory to show how structural and cultural contexts combine to explain variation in violent delinquency within gender and variation in levels of violence across gender (i.e., the gender gap). This requires reconceptualizing differential association theory to specify how the differentiated experiences of girls and boys lead to violent offending. To date, the theory has not included explicit arguments about gender. In this work, we specify a perspective that incorporates into the differential association framework insights from feminist theories and gender studies....

Structure, Culture, and Violent Delinquency: A Differential Association Perspective

A strength of the differential association theory of crime is that it addresses the role of social structure as well as culture, at least implicitly. A core assumption of the theory is that society is characterized by normative conflict over the law, wherein some groups define crime as always wrong and others justify it under some circumstances (Sutherland 1947; Sutherland et al. 1992). According to Sutherland's principle of differential social organization, groups with high rates of crime are those whose norms, values, and practices are inconsistent with the norms expressed in the legal codes. Differential social organization thus explains variation in crime across structural groupings, such as gender, social class, race, neighborhood, and so on.

Differential social organization affects the behavior of individuals through a cultural process, differential association, in which individuals learn definitions (i.e., attitudes, rationalizations) and techniques favorable and unfavorable to law violation through interacting with significant others and reference groups. Structural positions in part determine the others with whom individuals come into contact and thus shape the content of learning. Most treatments of differential association theory therefore argue that definitions of the law mediate the influence on crime of structural factors and associations with significant others (e.g., Heimer and Matsueda 1987; Tittle et al. 1986)....

Although much of the recent research on differential association theory has focused on global indices of delinquency, Sutherland (1947) argued for the development of more precise statements of the theory to account for specific forms of offending. Classical studies of differential association, indeed, followed this course (e.g., Cressey 1953, 1954; Sutherland 1937, 1949).

Recently, Heimer (1997) has specified the differential association process leading to a specific form of offending among males—violent delinquency. She shows how one aspect of social structure, socioeconomic status (SES), shapes violent behavioral histories, parenting practices, associations with aggressive peers, the learning of violent definitions, and ultimately, violent delinquency. Specifically, she argues that boys from lower SES families have less legitimate power to deal with problems; are more receptive to alternative solutions, such as the use of physical force (see Black 1983; Cloward and Ohlin 1960; Cohen 1955); and therefore are more likely to learn definitions favorable to violence. In addition, Heimer shows that SES influences violent definitions indirectly by shaping parenting practices. Lower SES parents are less likely than higher SES parents to supervise their children closely, and consequently, these youths have more opportunities to learn violent definitions outside the family. Consistent with other work (e.g., Gecas 1979; Kohn 1977), she also finds that lower SES parents are more likely to use coercive discipline, such as commands, restrictions, threats, and physical punishment, which teaches youths that coercion and physical force are acceptable ways to solve problems. Heimer argues that youths can generalize from this to form definitions favorable to violence, thus becoming more likely to commit violent delinquency.... Finally, she maintains that youths with histories of violent delinquency are likely to continue such behavior, in part because they are more likely to seek out other aggressive youths and are more receptive to learning violent definitions.

In short, Heimer's work specifies explicit links between one structural factor, SES, and the cultural processes leading to violent delinquency among males. However, research shows that other structural factors are associated with violent delinquency, including poverty, race, and female headship (e.g., Bursik and Grasmick 1993; Peterson and Krivo 1993; Sampson 1987). Further, it is likely that gender conditions the differential association process leading to violence. The next section develops

our reformulated differential association perspective on gender and violence and then addresses the role of several structural factors.

A Theoretical Explanation of Gender and Violent Delinquency

... Feminist scholars argue that what is needed is a theory that addresses the differentiated experiences of females and males in patriarchal society (Chesney-Lind 1997; Daly and Chesney-Lind 1988; see also Campbell 1993). We attempt to move toward such a theoretical perspective by proposing an explanation of how culture and structure combine to create gendered experiences during adolescence, which in turn explain female violence as well as the gender gap in violent delinquency. More specifically, we use arguments from feminist and gender studies to specify the content of the differential association process leading to gender differences in violent delinquency and to show how this process is conditioned by the structural context. We consider two cultural outcomes—violent definitions and gender definitions—and two types of cultural processes—family controls and peer associations, as well as histories of violent behavior. One of our key arguments is that the cultural mechanisms that restrain violence by girls are more subtle and indirect than those that curb violence by boys.

The Cultural Context

Cultural definitions of violence. According to differential association theory, interactions with others and social structural context are important because they shape the learning of violent definitions, which in turn affects the likelihood that youths engage in violent delinquency. This will be the case regardless of gender, and both males and females will be more likely to behave violently when they have acquired high levels of violent definitions. The gender gap in violent delinquency, therefore, likely reflects a gender difference in levels of violent definitions—boys tend to acquire more violent definitions than girls, on average. Consistent with this, empirical research in psychology indicates that boys are more likely than girls to approve of aggression (e.g., Huesmann et al. 1992). Moreover, from a feminist perspective, greater acceptance of violent definitions among males is associated with their privileged position under patriarchy (see Campbell 1993; White and Kowalski 1994).

These empirical predictions about violent definitions can be derived from an unmodified differential association theory. They are insufficient for explaining gender differences in the process leading to violent delinquency and the gender gap in violence because they omit important aspects of the process, which we address in the following sections: First, the unmodified differential association thesis does not address potential gender differences in the ways that violent definitions are learned. Second, the unmodified theory does not address a cultural element that is important for understanding gender differences in a wide variety of behaviors—cultural definitions of gender.

Cultural definitions of gender. A key contribution of feminist and gender studies has been their focus on the powerful system of social control, patriarchy, that influences the social arrangements, cognitions, and behavior of females and males (e.g., Ferree and Hess 1987; Lorber 1994). This system of social control is effective in part because people accept and participate in reproducing definitions of the "essential natures" of the sexes as inherently different (Goffman 1977). These definitions, which we term gender definitions, tend to accentuate differences and minimize similarities between the sexes (Bem 1993; Lorber 1994). For example, research shows that in patriarchal society femininity often is equated with a high capacity for nurturance, a tendency toward passivity rather than aggressiveness, and physical and emotional weakness; by contrast, masculinity tends to be equated with competitiveness, independence, rationality, and strength (Burke 1989; Burke and Tully 1977; Jackman 1994). These gender definitions carry strong expectations for behavior in most social interactions (Goffman 1977; West and Zimmerman 1987). When people internalize these traditional gender definitions, therefore, they are motivated to act in accordance with them (see Burke 1989; Burke and Reitzes 1981). From a feminist perspective, these mechanisms constitute and important site of the reproduction of male dominance and patriarchal relations (Walby 1990).

Violent delinquency, of course, is counter to traditional definitions of femininity under patriarchy. Violence is inconsistent with nurturance, passivity, nonaggressiveness, and physical and emotional weakness. Indeed, girls' aggression is often subject to censure, in the form of either condemnation or a warning to behave "properly," which ultimately produces more feelings of guilt and anxiety about aggression among females than males (Campbell 1993). In addition, females who depart from traditional definitions of femininity by engaging in violence are labeled as more deviant than aggressive males (Schur 1984; White and Kowalski 1994). By contrast, traditional definitions of masculinity are more consistent with violent and physically aggressive behavior. Messerschmidt (1993) has argued that crime and violence, in fact, offer a way for males to claim gender when legal avenues for affirming masculinity (e.g., paid labor) are blocked (see also Campbell 1993, 58; Miller 1958).

In short, traditional gender definitions should be consequential for understanding gender differences in violent delinquency, and they should operate alongside violent definitions to motivate behavior. Quite simply, girls who accept traditional gender definitions should be relatively unlikely to engage in physical aggression and violence. For these girls, violent delinquency would be viewed as "doubly deviant," a violation of the law as well as their beliefs about femininity. Empirical research shows, consistent with this, that girls who accept traditional gender definitions are less likely than other girls to report involvement in property (Heimer 1995), violent

(Simpson and Elis 1995), and general indices of delinquency (Heimer 1996). By contrast, boys who accept traditional gender definitions may be more likely than other boys to use physical force and aggression to solve problems. Existing quantitative research does not strongly support this prediction, however (Heimer 1995, 1996; Simpson and Elis 1995)....

Direct parental controls and emotional bonding. Most feminist perspectives identify the domestic sphere as an important context in which gendered social control is produced and reproduced (see Tong 1998). In the case of violent delinquency, we argue that gendered familial control arises when parenting processes differentially influence girls' and boys' learning of violent definitions. Although studies have not examined the effects of familial controls on violent delinquency specifically, many studies have focused on familial controls and global indices of delinquency. Following this work, and Heimer's (1997) differential association explanation of male violent delinquency, we focus on three key aspects of familial controls, which we expect to influence the learning of violent definitions—supervision, discipline, and emotional bonds to family.

Some research on delinquency proposes that gendered social control arises largely because girls experience higher levels of familial controls than do boys. These studies, which pool male and female data and include sex as an exogenous variable, find that girls are supervised more closely than boys and have stronger emotional bonds to families than boys; this is said to account for part of the gender gap in common, nonviolent delinquency (Hagan et al. 1985; Jensen and Eve 1976). We argue that gender differences in levels of familial controls are important for violent delinquency primarily because they restrict opportunities to learn violent definitions more for girls than boys.

However, research that examines the effects of familial controls on global measures of delinquency for females and males separately suggests

that the mechanisms may be more complex. Beyond a gender difference in levels (i.e., means) of familial controls, research suggests that there may be a gender difference in the impact (i.e., magnitudes of effects, slopes) of these controls on delinquency (e.g., Canter 1982; Cernkovich and Giordano 1987). We argue that these differences can be seen most clearly by categorizing familial controls into two distinct types—direct parental controls, such as supervision and coercive discipline, and emotional bonding or attachment to families, which constitutes a more indirect form of control. Based on feminist arguments that females are more concerned than males with interpersonal relationships (e.g., Chodorow 1978; Gilligan 1982), some researchers suggest that emotional bonds will have a stronger impact on offending by females than by males (see Hagan et al. 1988). In addition, there is some indication in the literature that direct parental control, or supervision, has a larger inhibitory effect on delinquency among boys than girls, ironically (Heimer 1996).

Based on findings and arguments such as these, Heimer (1996) has speculated that perhaps the control mechanisms affecting delinquency are more subtle and indirect in the case of girls and more overt and direct in the case of boys. This is consistent with research that finds that mothers expect their sons, more than their daughters, to conform to external standards, hold a more punitive orientation toward raising sons than daughters, and discourage the expression of affect more in sons than in daughters (Block 1984, 87–88). We propose, therefore, that the parental control processes that shape youths' learning of violent definitions, and thereby subsequent violent delinquency, will vary across gender as follows: Girls' learning of violent definitions will be shaped primarily by the indirect control achieved through emotional bonding to families, while boys' learning of violent definitions will be shaped primarily by more direct, overt parental controls, including supervision and coercive discipline.

Associations with aggressive peers. Differential association theory also posits that associations with aggressive peers are key for learning violent definitions and thus for violent delinquency. Again, gender research suggests a modification of this thesis. Specifically, studies of gender socialization indicate that by middle childhood, male peer groups bond through transgressing rules and aggression whereas female peer groups bond through disclosing intimacies (Thorne 1993; Thorne and Luria 1986). It seems likely, therefore, that the gender gap in violent delinquency occurs in part simply because boys are more likely than girls to have aggressive friends and experience aggression in their peer groups. This is consistent with one study that finds that the gender difference in a global index of delinquency in accounted for in part by the fact that boys have more delinquent friends than girls (Morash 1986). However, most research on gender and delinquency neglects peer relationships. From a differential association perspective, a gender difference in numbers of aggressive friends should combine with gender differences in levels of exposure to parental controls to provide more opportunities for boys than girls to learn violent definitions.

Beyond a gender difference in numbers of aggressive friends, we also expect a difference in the magnitude of the effect of associating with these peers. Theoretical work on masculinity and crime suggests that male youth groups encourage aggressive posturing, which can turn into violence, as a way of displaying gender (Messerschmidt 1993; Miller 1958). This implies that even in a situation in which boys and girls have equal numbers of aggressive friends, these peers may encourage their male friends more than their female friends to form violent definitions.

Violent histories. Youths' previous experiences with violence constitute a final element of the differential association process leading to violent delinquency (Heimer 1997). First, histories of violent delinquency foster subsequent acceptance of violent definitions when youths rationalize past violent behavior. Second, violent delinquency can become rather automatic, habitual, and stable over time, so that violent histories have direct implications for future violent behavior, apart from the mechanisms discussed here. These relationships should hold across gender. But, we expect a gender difference in levels of prior violence, of course, which will combine with gender differences in levels of parental controls and aggressive peers to offer more opportunities for boys than girls to learn violent definitions.

The Link Between Structural Positions and Culture

From our perspective, social structure will condition cultural mechanisms in three general ways. First, we expect structural positions to influence violent definitions indirectly by shaping parental controls, peer associations, and violent behavioral histories. Extending Heimer's (1997) arguments beyond the focus on SES, we propose the following: Youths from structurally disadvantaged families, including lower social class, welfare, black, and female-headed families, are likely to experience lower levels of supervision and emotional bonding to families than other youths (Sampson and Laub 1993; Thomson et al. 1992) and higher levels of coercive discipline, including restrictions, threats, and physical punishment (Gecas 1979; Kohn 1977; McLeod et al. 1994). Together, these factors increase the chances that structurally disadvantaged youths learn violent definitions.... Disadvantaged youths also are more likely to form oppositional peer groups, which engage in aggressive and violent behaviors as a way of rebelling against their structural constraints (Cohen 1955; Willis 1977), thus encouraging the learning of violent definitions. In addition, if disadvantaged youths are more likely to have histories of violence, this will foster their learning of violent definitions.

Second, structural positions may influence the learning of violent definitions directly, independently of family controls, peer associations, and behavioral histories. Building on Heimer's (1997) arguments, we propose that structurally disadvantaged youths have restricted access to legitimate power and legitimate methods for dealing with problems (such as police intervention or lawsuits) and thus are receptive to alternative solutions (Cloward and Ohlin 1960; Cohen 1955). Such solutions can invoke a type of power that is independent of political and economic resources, namely, physical force (Messerschmidt 1986). So, when structurally marginalized youths are threatened, humiliated, or harmed, they are likely to perceive that they have little legitimate power with which to deal with the situation, and thus, they may be more likely to form definitions favorable to using violence and force to solve problems.

Third, we expect gender definitions, just like violent definitions, to be shaped by differential social organization. Following feminist theory and gender research, we expect gender definitions to vary with the stratification of power, as reflected by such structural positions as social class, race, and residence in a female-headed household. For example, gender roles are less rigid in middle-class than in working-class and lower-class families (Brooks-Gunn 1986; Lips 1995; Rubin 1976); higher SES families thus may be less likely to communicate traditional gender definitions to children. Race may also condition gender definitions (Baca Zinn 1990; West and Fenstermaker 1995). Specifically, African-American parents may be less likely than white parents to teach traditional gender definitions to their children (Beckett and Smith 1981; Collins, 1990). Traditional gender definitions also may be weaker in female-headed families than male-headed families because women in the former are not subject to male domination or patriarchy within the domestic sphere.

In addition to these predictions, our earlier arguments about gender differences in the cultural mechanisms leading to violent delinquency imply gender differences in the indirect influence of structural positions on violent delinquency. For example, if direct parental controls

(including supervision and coercive disciplinary strategies) are more consequential for learning violent definitions among males than females, as we have argued, the influence of structural positions on violent definitions and delinquency through these direct controls would be greater among males than among females. If indirect, emotional controls are more consequential for learning violence among females than males, structural positions will have a greater impact on females' violent delinquency through this route. Similarly, if aggressive peer groups encourage violent definitions more among boys than girls, the indirect influence of disadvantaged structural positions on learning violent definitions through peer influence may be greater among boys than girls. Finally, if accepting traditional gender definitions dissuades violent delinquency among females, yet fosters violence among males, one can expect gender differences in the indirect effects of structural positions on violence through these gender definitions.

Summary

The predictions derived from these arguments are listed in Table 1. Two of these can be derived from the classical differential association framework (Hypotheses 1 and 2). The first of these is the prototypical differential association prediction that violent delinquency results when youths learn violent definitions, regardless of gender. The second prediction is that the gender gap in violent delinquency emerges in part because boys are more likely to learn violent definitions than girls (i.e., on average, boys report higher levels of learning violent definitions than girls). However, these hypotheses are insufficient for explaining the relationship between gender and violent delinquency.

We argue that gender differences in violence emerge through a process that includes the predictions of classical differential association theory, as well as the following additional mechanisms. First, Hypothesis 3 predicts that gender differences in levels of exposure to

Table 29.1
Hypotheses

Violent Definitions
Hypotheses 1. Violent definitions will increase the likelihood of violent delinquency among both girls and boys.
Gender Differences in Levels of Cultural Factors
Hypotheses 2. Higher levels of violent definitions among boys than girls will explain part of the gender gap in violent delinquency.
Hypotheses 3. Boys will learn more violent definitions than girls in part because boys are subject to lower levels of familial control than girls, have more aggressive friends than girls, and have more experience with prior violence than girls.
Gender Differences in the Impact of Cultural Factors
Hypotheses 4. Learning traditional gender definitions will reduce the chances of violent delinquency among females and increase the chances of violent delinquency among males.
Hypotheses 5. Emotional bonds to family will have a stronger negative effect on girls' learning of violent definitions, whereas direct parental controls will have a stronger negative effect on boys' learning of violent definitions.
Hypotheses 6. Associating with aggressive peers will have a stronger positive effect on learning violent definitions among boys than girls.
Links Between Structural Positions and Cultural Factors
Hypotheses 7. Structural positions will influence violent delinquency indirectly among both females and males, by influencing familial controls, peer associations, violent definitions, and gender definitions.
Hypotheses 8. Structural positions will influence violent definitions and violent delinquency differently among females as compared to males due to gender differences in the effects of parental controls, gender definitions, and associations with aggressive peers.

cultural factors, such as direct parental controls, emotional bonds to family, aggressive peers, and violent histories, will help to explain the gender gap in violent delinquency. Second, in addition, the magnitudes of the effects of cultural factors, including gender definitions, direct parental controls, emotional bonds to family, and aggressive peers, will vary across gender (see Hypotheses 4 through 6); these differences in slopes also will contribute to the gender gap in violent delinquency. Finally, Hypothesis 7 says that structural positions will influence violence by both genders by affecting parents' direct and indirect controls, peer associations, violent behavioral histories, violent definitions, and gender definitions. Hypothesis 8 predicts gender differences in the way that structural positions shape violent delinquency through these cultural factors.

These arguments combine to suggest that violent delinquency by girls may be controlled through somewhat more subtle, covert channels than violent delinquency by boys. Emotional bonds may be more important for girls' learning about violence whereas more direct parental controls may be more important for boys' learning about violence. Girls' violence also may be curbed by inculcating traditional definitions about the meaning of femininity, whereas teaching boys traditional meanings of masculinity may encourage violence. These patterns make sense if one views traditional socialization of males as more conducive to aggressive, violent behavior, which means that controlling such behavior will require more overt and direct measures. Interestingly, Chesney-Lind and Shelden (1998: 111–112) conclude that the available research indicates that gender socialization patterns have changed relatively little since the 1970s, despite the changing roles of adult women. Our argument is that these persistent patterns of creating gender in youths may result in different pathways to restraining aggression and violence, in which females are controlled in more subtle and covert ways than are males.

Conclusions

... Overall, this work represents an important advance in the differential association tradition because it reconceptualizes the theory by incorporating theoretical arguments about gender. Specifically, we draw on feminist and gender studies to specify the role of gender definitions, as well as to develop explicit arguments about gender differences in the influence of parenting processes and peer influence. ...

The conclusion of our research is that violent delinquency is "gendered" in significant ways. Adolescent violence can be seen as a product of gendered experiences, gender socialization, and the patriarchal system in which they emerge. Thus, consistent with feminist arguments, gender differences in violence are ultimately rooted in power differences (e.g., Chesney-Lind 1997; White and Kowalski 1994). What we contribute to such feminist arguments is an explicit theoretical statement of how certain aspects of gender socialization produce gender differences in violent delinquency. Specifically, boys are more violent than girls largely because they are taught more definitions favoring such behavior; girls are less violent than boys because they are controlled through subtle mechanisms, which include learning that violence is incompatible with the meaning of gender for them and being restrained by emotional bonds to family. These findings are consistent with Block's (1984: 137–138) argument that traditional gender socialization gives boys "wings" to explore and grow as individuals, and gives girls "roots" that anchor and stabilize them; yet, wings without roots can produce undercontrolled individuals and roots without wings can create overcontrolled, "tethered" individuals. So, traditional socialization patterns contribute to high levels of male violence in our society, just as they inhibit positively valued and rewarded behavior among females, such as climbing the corporate ladder. This suggests that socializing either gender similarly to the other could have negative consequences. The best scenario may prove to be a middle ground, where both genders learn distaste for violence and learn to pursue their positive potentials.

Discussion Questions

1. How does differential association theory explain female crime and the gender gap in crime?
2. How does Heimer and De Coster's theory build on the explanation provided by differential association theory?
3. What do Heimer and De Coster mean by "gender definitions"? Describe the traditional gender definitions for males and females.
4. Heimer and De Coster state that there are "gender differences in the ways that violent definitions are learned." Describe such differences.
5. Describe the sorts of questions a researcher might ask in a survey to measure violent definitions and gender definitions.
6. Social learning theory is an elaboration of differential association theory (see Chapter 11). Using Heimer and De Coster as a model, how might one go about "gendering" social learning theory?

30. Masculinities and Crime

James W. Messerschmidt

Although sympathetic to radical feminism, James Messerschmidt observes that feminist analyses do not take seriously the study of masculinity. The tendency to attribute male behavior to patriarchy is reductionistic: it places all men in a single category—one in which "women are good, men are bad, plain and simple. And it is this essential badness that leads to patriarchy and violence against women" (1993: 43). But men are not all the same. In particular, gender intersects with race and class to create different "masculinities" or conceptions of what it means to be male. Understanding male behavior thus entails understanding the historical and structural conditions that construct the masculinities that structure male social action, including crime.

Messerschmidt makes the important insight that "crime by men is not simply an extension of the 'male sex role'" or, for that matter, of some male trait (1993: 85). In any social situation that males enter, they are faced with the ongoing task of showing that they are manly, of "accomplishing" their masculinity. Precisely what this entails differs by age-class-racial position in society. The meaning of masculinity varies by structural location, and in turn these meanings are "reproduced" or reconfirmed as men in these locations act to reaffirm their manly identities in the ways available to them.

In this framework, crime is seen as a resource for "doing gender"—that is, it is a way of showing that one is masculine. Messerschmidt argues that crime is most likely to occur when legitimate means of demonstrating masculinity are stifled. It is noteworthy that class and racial inequality restrict the conventional avenues for doing gender, such as success in school and in the labor market. In response to their emasculation and humiliation in these settings, juveniles and later adults develop "opposition masculinities," which involve the rejection of conventional ways of doing gender. Instead, criminal acts—from vandalism to violence— become vivid ways of showing their manliness. The end result, however, is that these criminal displays of masculinity only serve to restrict life chances and thus to reproduce existing structural inequalities.

Messerschmidt does not offer a class-biased theory. He recognizes that middle-class youths and adults also break the law, whether it is through juvenile mischief, displays of drunkenness, sexual harassment in the work-place, or white-collar crime. Still, in most ways, he sees more affluent white males as having access to and using "accommodating masculinities" that allow them to do gender in ways that accrue advantage and reinforce their gender, class, and racial dominance.

Finally, Messerschmidt recognizes that, in one way or another, all males act to do gender within the confines of the dominant conception of masculinity

Reprinted from James W. Messerschmidt, "Masculinities and Crime" in *Masculinities and Crime: Critique and Reconceptualization.* Copyright © 1993 by Rowman & Littlefield Publishers; reprinted by permission.

which teaches that heterosexual men are superior to women. Messerschmidt calls this "hegemonic masculinity," which is "defined through work in the paid-labor market, the subordination of women, heterosexism, and the driven uncontrollable sexuality of men" (1993: 82). "Refined further," he observes, "hegemonic masculinity emphasizes practices toward authority, control, competitive individualism, independence, aggressiveness, and the capacity for violence" (p. 82). As men do masculinity within these cultural scripts, they also reinforce their dominance over females in society.

Messerschmidt's theory can be questioned on a number of grounds: Females are omitted from the analysis; his menu listing the ways in which men can demonstrate masculinity seems narrow, ignoring, for example, being a good father, participating in voluntary organizations, talking about sports, and so on; conformity among disadvantaged groups is not easily explained; and his motivational theory—the need to do masculinity—may over-explain many criminal acts that are committed simply because they are fun or gratifying (cf. Gottfredson and Hirschi, Chapter 19). Still, for any male who has given a "high five" after scoring a basket, who has grunted with one's fellows, who has exchanged sexist jokes with "the guys," or who has performed risky acts to show he is not "chicken," the idea that masculinity is intimately involved in male behavior—including crime—has enormous intuitive appeal.

Reference

Messerschmidt, James W. 1993. *Masculinities and Crime: Critique and Reconceptualization of Theory.* Lanham, MD: Rowman and Littlefield.

Criminological theory—although traditionally written by men and primarily about boys and men—has been alarmingly gender-blind. That is, gendered men and boys have never been the object of the criminological enterprise. Feminism has challenged the overall "malestream" nature of criminology by highlighting the repeated omission and/or misrepresentation of women in criminological enquiry. The result of this critique is twofold: (1) it has increased attention to women in criminological theory and research but (2) when criminology addresses gender it speaks exclusively of women, with little or no attention directed to the impact of gender on men. Although some consideration has focused on masculinity and crime, this relationship has been examined through an essentialist, antiquated, and fallacious sex-role theory.

[I previously] demonstrated that radical feminism is not a viable alternative theory. A feminism that insists upon alleged natural differences between women and men, and goes on to explain crime committed by men in terms of that essentialism, not only homogenizes men (as does sex-role theory) but also proves itself inadequate to explaining crime committed by men. Although radical feminism is applauded for moving sexuality and gender power to the forefront of feminist thought, we are compelled to reject all forms of essentialism and reductionism....

To structure a comprehensive feminist theory of gendered crime, we must bring men into the framework. However, we should do this not by treating men as the normal subjects, but by articulating the gendered content of men's behavior and of crime. This approach requires a different theoretical lens—one that focuses on a sociology of masculinity—to comprehend why men are involved disproportionately in crime and why they commit different types of crime. In what follows, I build on the critique... by employing the insights of Giddens (1976, 1981), Connell (1987), West and Zimmerman (1987), Festermaker, West, and Zimmerman (1991), Goffman (1979), and others to present new theoretical tools for comprehending crime committed by men.

At least two significant theoretical undertakings are suggested from the criticisms outlined [previously]. First, it is essential to make the relevant theoretical links among class, gender, and race without surrendering to some type of separate systems approach (e.g., capitalism plus patriarchy). Second, it is critical to construct a theory of crime that recognizes that illegal behavior, like legal behavior, personifies synchronously both social practice and social structure. Indeed, social structures do not exist autonomously from humans; rather, they arise and endure through social practice. Social structures originate, are reproduced, and change through social practice. In short, we can only speak of *structured action*: social structures can be understood only as constituting practice; social structures, in turn, permit and preclude social action. . . .

To understand why men engage in more and different types of crimes than women and in differing amounts and forms among themselves, we need an adequate account of social action. We can begin by recognizing that in society all individuals engage in purposive behavior and monitor their own action reflexively. That is, we comprehend our actions and we modify them according to (among other things) our interpretation of other people's responses. Social action is creative, inventive, and novel, but it never occurs separately from, or external to, social structures. Social structures are constituted by social action and, in turn, provide resources and power from which individuals construct "strategies of action" (Swidler, 1986: 227). Social structures organize the way individuals think about their circumstances and generate methods for dealing with them.

Gendered Social Action and Crime

. . . Masculinity is accomplished, it is not something done to men or something settled beforehand. And masculinity is never static, never a finished product. Rather, men construct masculinities in specific social situations (although not in circumstances of their own choosing); in so doing, men reproduce (and sometimes change) social structures. As Giddens (1976: 138) forcefully argues,

every act which contributes to the reproduction of a structure is also an act of production, a novel enterprise, and as such may initiate change by altering that structure at the same time as it reproduces it.

. . . Hegemonic masculinity is the idealized form of masculinity in a given historical setting. It is culturally honored, glorified, and extolled, and this "exaltation stabilizes a structure of dominance and oppression in the gender order as a whole" (Connell, 1990: 94). In contemporary Western industrialized societies, hegemonic masculinity is defined through work in the paid-labor market, the subordination of women, heterosexism, and the driven and uncontrollable sexuality of men. Refined still further, hegemonic masculinity emphasizes practices toward authority, control, competitive individualism, independence, aggressiveness, and the capacity for violence (Connell, 1990, 1992; Segal, 1990). Because "most men benefit from the subordination of women, and hegemonic masculinity is the cultural expression of this ascendancy," most men engage in practices that attempt to sustain hegemonic masculinity (Connell, 1987: 185). Indeed, most men help maintain hegemonic masculinity (and consequently the subordination of women) by means of the practices that reflect their particular positions in society. . . .

When men enter a setting, they undertake social practices that demonstrate they are "manly." The only way others can judge their "essential nature" as men is through their behavior and appearance. Thus, men use the resources at their disposal to to communicate gender to others. For many men, crime may serve as a suitable *resource* for "doing gender"—for separating them from all that is feminine. Because types of criminality are possible only when particular social conditions present themselves, when other masculine resources are unavailable, particular types of crime can provide an alternative resource for accomplishing gender and, therefore, affirming a particular type of masculinity. For, although men are always doing masculinity, the significance of gender accomplishment is socially situated and, thus, an intermittent matter. That is, certain occasions present themselves as more intimidating for showing and affirming masculinity. As Coleman (1990: 196) states, "Such an occasion is where a man's 'masculinity' risks being called into question." The taken-for-granted "essential nature" of a man or boy can be questioned, undermined, and threatened in certain contexts, those situations where he lacks resources for masculine accomplishment.

In such predicaments, sex category is particularly salient; it is, as David Morgan (1992: 47) puts it, "more or less explicitly put on the line," and doing masculinity necessitates extra effort, generating a distinct type of masculinity. Under such conditions, performance as a member of one's sex category is subjected to extra evaluation and crime is more likely to result. Crime, therefore, may be invoked as a practice through which masculinities (and men and women) are differentiated from one another. Moreover, crime is a resource that may be summoned when men lack other resources to accomplish gender. . . .

Crime by men is not simply an extension of the "male sex role." Rather, crime by men is a form of social practice invoked as a resource, when other resources are unavailable, for accomplishing masculinity. By analyzing masculinities, then, we can begin to understand the socially constructed differences among men and thus explain why men engage in different forms of crime. . . .

Social Structures, Masculinities, and Crime in Youth Groups

I explore the way social action is linked to structured possibilities/constraints, identifying in particular how the class, race, and gendered relations in society constrain and enable the social activity of young men in the school and the youth group, and how this structured action relates to youth crime.

"Boys will be boys" differently, depending upon their position in social structures and, therefore,

upon their access to power and resources. Social structures situate young men in a common relation to other young men and in such a way that they share structural space. Collectively, young men experience their daily world from a particular position in society and differentially construct the cultural ideals of hegemonic masculinity. Thus, within the school and youth group there are patterned ways in which masculinity is represented and which depend upon structures of labor and power in class and race relations. Young men situationally accomplish public forms of masculinity in response to their socially structured circumstances; indeed, varieties of youth crime serve as a suitable resource for doing masculinity when other resources are unavailable. These forms of youth crime, as with other resources, are determined by social structures. . . .

In what follows, I attempt to identify certain of the chief class and race junctures in the social construction of youthful public masculinities and crimes—in particular, the important relationship between youth crime and school. The focus is on how some young men come to define their masculinity against the school and, in the process, choose forms of youth crime as resources for accomplishing gender and for constructing what I call *opposition masculinities*. I begin with white, middle-class boys.

White, Middle-Class Boys

Given the success of the middle-class Saints and Socs in school [two youth groups studied by other researchers], it is this very success that provides a particular resource for constructing a specific form of masculinity. In this type of masculinity, the penchant for a career is fundamental: a "calculative attitude is taken towards one's own life" and the crucial themes are "rationality and responsibility rather than pride and aggressiveness" (Connell, 1989: 296–297). Throughout their childhood development, white, middle-class boys are geared toward the ambiance and civility of the school. Within the school environment, for these boys, masculinity is normally accomplished through participation in sports and academic success. This participation in (or at least avid support for) sport creates an environment for the construction of a masculinity that celebrates toughness and endurance, incessantly advocates competiveness and shame of losing, and "connects a sense of maleness with a taste for violence and confrontation" (Kessler, Ashenden, Connell, Dowsett, 1985: 39). Yet, in addition to creating this specific type of masculinity, sport is so revered and glorified within the school that it subordinates other types of masculinity, such as the sort constructed by the "brains" who participate in nonviolent games like debate (p. 39).

Over and above sport, white, middle-class masculinity in the school is typically achieved through a reasonable level of academic success. As Tolson (1977: 34–36) argues, the middle-class family supports this trajectory: "books in the home and parental help with homework provide a continuous emotional context for academic achievement"; moreover, middle-class families also tend to emphasize the importance of obtaining the appropriate qualifications for "respectable careers" that guarantee the "security" of a "profession." As Heward (1988: 8) experienced in an English boarding school, white, middle-class parents

> planned their sons' futures carefully and then pursued their plans very actively, with the aim of placing them in suitable occupations and careers.

For the white middle class, then, manliness is about having a secure income from a "respectable" professional occupation. Thus, there is an important link between school and family in middle-class life, and both transmit class-specific notions of hegemonic masculinity to white, middle-class boys—a particular type of work in the paid-labor market, competitiveness, personal ambition and achievement, and responsibility.

Accommodating and Opposition Masculinities

Nonetheless, hegemonic masculinity also involves practices characterizing dominance, control, and independence.... Such masculine ideals are, however, the very qualities that schooling discourages. Although white, middle-class youth generally exercise greater authority and control in school than do youth from other class and race backgrounds, research on secondary schooling reveals that adaptation to the social order of the school requires that all students, regardless of their class and race, submit to rock-hard authority relations in which students are actually penalized for creativity, autonomy, and independence (Bowles and Gintis, 1976; Greenberg, 1977; Messerschmidt, 1979). In other words, white, middle-class boys, like other boys, experience a school life that is circumscribed by institutionalized authoritarian routine.

In spite of this constraint, within the school most white, middle-class boys conform, since proper credentials are necessary to attaining careers. As Greenberg (1977: 201) notes, students

> who believe that their future chances depend on school success are likely to conform if they resent the school's attempt to regulate their lives.

Within the social setting of the school, then, white, middle-class boys accomplish gender by conforming to school rules and regulations and by dominating student organizations, reflecting a wholehearted obligation to the school and its overall enterprise. White, middle-class boys "accept" school values and therefore the school exercises a prominent and influential restraint on these youth, at least within its own boundaries (Tolson, 1977: 39).

Because masculinity is a behavioral response to the particular conditions and situations in which we participate, white, middle-class boys thus do masculinity within the school in a specific way that reflects their position in the class and race divisions of labor and power. Their white, middle-class position both constrains and enables certain forms of gendered social action, and these boys monitor their action in accord with those constraints and opportunities, thus reproducing simultaneously class, race, and gender relations. Moreover, this particular masculinity is sustained as a type of collective product in a particular social setting—white middle-class schools.

However, because the school is "emasculating" in the fashion discussed earlier, white, middle-class boys who join a youth group act outside the school in ways that help restore those hegemonic masculine ideals discouraged in school. In this process of "doing gender," these boys simultaneously construct age-specific forms of criminality. Youth crime, within the social context of the youth group outside the school, serves as a resource for masculine realization and facilitates (as do such other practices as school athletics) "dominance bonding" among privileged young men (Messner, 1989: 79).

Successful "pranks," "mischief," vandalism, minor thefts, and drinking outside the school validate a boy's "essential nature." Such behaviors reflect an age-specific attempt to reestablish a public masculine identity somewhat diminished in the school, behaviors that are purposely chosen and manipulated for their ability to impress other boys. Moreover, outside the confines of the school, white, middle-class boys' masculinity is still held accountable, not to school officials, but to other white, middle-class boys. These behavioral forms help a white, middle-class boy to carve out a valued masculine identity by exhibiting those hegemonic masculine ideals the school denies—independence, dominance, daring, and control—to resolve the problem of accountability outside the school, and to establish for himself and others his "essential nature" as a "male." Indeed, most accounts of these forms of youth crime miss the significance of gender: it is young men who are overwhelmingly the perpetrators of these acts (Chesney-Lind and Shelden, 1992: 7–18). Accomplishing gender by engaging in vandalism, "pranks," and "mischief" (as an age-specific resource) incontrovertibly provides a public masculine resolution to the spectacle of self-discipline and emotional restraint in the school.

Thus we see that white, middle-class, youth masculinity is accomplished differently in separate and dissimilar social situations. For white, middle-class boys, the problem is to produce configurations of masculine behavior that can be seen by others as normative. Yet, as the social setting changes, from inside the school to outside in the youth group, so does the conceptualization of what is normative masculine behavior.

Through class appeal for educational credentials, white, middle-class boys are drawn into different masculine construction within the school: they develop an *accommodating masculinity*—a controlled, cooperative, rational gender strategy of action for institutional success. The white, middle-class boy's agenda within the school, then, is simply to become the accomplice to the institutional order, thereby reaping the privileges it offers—access to higher education and a professional career (Connell, 1989: 295–297). In other words, as white, middle-class boys accomplish gender in the school setting, they simultaneously reproduce class and race relations through the same ongoing practices.

Being a man is about developing the essential credentials to obtain a suitable middle-class occupation. However, because the school both creates and undermines hegemonic masculinity, within the company of peers outside the school some white, middle-class boys draw primarily on non-violent forms of youth crime, thus constructing an *opposition masculinity*—a masculinity based on the very hegemonic masculine ideals the school discourages. In short, white, middle-class boys are forming different types of masculinity that can be assessed and approved in both social settings (inside and outside school) as normal and natural. Through this specific type of youth crime in the peer group, middle-class masculinities are differentiated from one another.

The case of white, middle-class youth demonstrates how we maintain different gendered identities that may be emphasized or avoided, depending upon the social setting. White, middle-class boys construct their gendered actions in relation to how such actions might be interpreted by others (that is, their accountability) in the particular social context in which they occur. White, middle-class boys are doing masculinity differently because the setting and the available resources change.

School Success, Masculinity, and Youth Crime

Social control theorists argue that youth who develop close bonds to the school are the least likely to engage in youth crime (Hirschi, 1969; Wiatrowski, Griswold, and Roberts, 1981). Yet the considerable amount of youth crime committed by the Saints and the Socs (who were the school "wheels" and high academic achievers) outside the school justifies reasonable concern regarding this argument. Nevertheless, middle-class schools, like schools in other social settings, develop a status system based on academic success. Research has consistently shown that students who fail academically (for whatever reason) and/or who occupy the lowest status positions in school, exhibit the highest rates of youth crime. (See Messerschmidt, 1979 for a review of this research.) Consequently, for white, middle-class boys who are not successful at schoolwork and who do not participate in school sports or extracurricular activities, the school is a frustrating masculine experience as a result of which they are likely to search out other masculine-validating resources.

This view was demonstrated in one study of an upper-middle-class, white neighborhood, described by the authors as an "environmental paradise" that "harbors mansions and millionaires as well as deer and raccoons" (Muchlbauer and Dodder, 1983: 35). The particular neighborhood youth group which called itself "the losers," was composed primarily of boys who did not do well in school and who demonstrated little athletic interest or ability. "The losers" spent considerable time "hanging out" together at the town square, but were not at all fond of interpersonal violence and controlling turf. Rather, they engaged chiefly in acts of vandalism—such as breaking streetlamps, making graffiti, destroying traffic signs, and doing donuts on the lawns of the more affluent members of the community—as well as organizing drinking parties at public beaches and parks. Indeed, the only serious violence committed by "the losers" was the firebombing of the personal automobiles of two representatives of "emasculating" authority: the chief of police and the vice-principal of the school. Thus, the specific types of youth crime engaged in by "the losers" served as a resource for masculine construction when other types of class-specific resources were unappealing and/or unattractive (e.g., academic success).

Although this opposition masculinity outside the school is clearly not the only version of white, middle-class youth masculinity, nor perhaps the most common version, it differs considerably from that of white, working-class youth, especially because of its reduced emphasis on the public display of interpersonal aggression/violence. It follows that we must consider more closely how this type of youthful, white, middle-class, masculine construction and its attendant youth crime differs from that of youthful, white, working-class men.

White, Working-Class Boys

As exemplified by the Roughnecks and the Eses [youth groups studied by other researchers], white, working-class boys engage in such acts as vandalism, truancy, and drinking because, as demonstrated more precisely below, they also experience school authority as an "emasculating" power. Not surprisingly, many of these boys also turn to this age-specific resource for "doing gender" outside the school. And yet, they define their masculinity against the school in a different way than do white middle-class boys, a way that nevertheless leads to an in-school opposition masculinity as well.

'The Lads' and the 'Ear'oles'

Paul Willis's (1977) classic study *Learning to Labour* demonstrates how a group of white, working-class British boys ("the lads") reject both schoolwork and the "ear'oles" (earholes, or other young men who conform to the school rules) because "the lads" perceive office jobs and "bookwork" as "sissy stuff." The lads come to school armed with traditional notions of white, working-class masculinity: the idea that "real men" choose manual, not mental labor. Because of this particular gendered strategy, schooling is deemed irrelevant to their working-class future and "emasculating" to their conception of masculinity. In other words, schooling is unmanly in a different and broader way for these boys than for the white, middle-class boys discussed above. Accordingly, the lads evolve into an unstructured, counterschool group that carves out a specific masculine space within the school, its overwhelming rules, and unnerving authority.

In resisting the school, the lads construct behavior patterns that set them apart from both the ear'oles and also the school. Because the ear'oles are enthusiastic about schooling and support its rules, they are a major conformist target for the lads. One such practice for opposing the school and the ear'oles is "having a laff," that is, devising techniques to circumvent the controlled environment of the school. . . .

Another activity that distinguished the lads from the ear'oles is fighting. The lads exhibited "a positive joy in fighting, in causing fights through intimidation, in talking about fighting and about the tactics of the whole fight situation" (p. 34). Constructing masculinity around physical aggression, the lads—eschewing academic achievement—draw on an available resource that allows them to distance and differentiate themselves from the nonviolent ear'oles. As Willis (p. 34) points out,

Violence and the judgement of violence is the most basic axis of the 'lads' ascendance over the conformists, almost in the way that knowledge is for teachers.

The lads reject and feel superior to the ear'oles; moreover, they construct such practices as having a laff and fighting to demonstrate their perceived masculine eminence.

In this way, then, the lads accomplish gender in a specific relational way by opposing both the school and its conformists. Whereas white, middle-class boys are more likely to oppose school outside its boundaries but conform within school, the social setting for the lads is different. *They are the opposition both inside and outside the school.* Understandably, there is no accommodating masculinity here. Because schooling is conceived as unnecessary to their future while simultaneously encompassing effeminate endeavors, the lads earn symbolic space from the school by engaging in different forms of "pranks" and "mischief" within the school itself. Such behaviors help transcend the "sissyish" quality of the school day while simultaneously distancing the lads from the conformists.

But the lads also draw on forms of physical intimidation and violence to differentiate themselves from the ear'oles and the girls. For the lads, the fight "is the moment when you are fully tested"; it is "disastrous for your informal standing and masculine reputation if you refuse to fight or perform very amateurishly" (p. 35). In fact, physical aggressiveness seems to be an institutionalized feature of the lads' group. As Willis (p. 36) notes,

the physicality of all interactions, the mock pushing and fighting, the showing off in front of girls, the demonstrations of superiority and put-downs of the conformists, all borrow from the grammar of the real fight situation.

These activities provide the fodder with which to accomplish their gender and to establish (for the lads) their "essential male nature." They are designed with an eye to gender accountability and resultingly construct inequality among boys by attempting to place the ear'oles masculinity beneath their own within the public context of the school. The lads are constructing an opposition masculinity as a collective practice; notwithstanding, this specific type is significantly different from the white, middle-class in school accommodating masculinity and gains meaning in relation to the masculinity of the ear'oles.

Outside the School

It is not only conformists to the school whom white, working-class youth, like the lads, attempt to subordinate in the process of doing gender. In Western industrialized societies, what have become known as hate crimes—racist and anti-gay violence—are disproportionately committed by groups of white, working-class boys, crimes that can also be understood in the way discussed above (Beirne and Messerschmidt, 1991: 562–563; Comstock, 1991: 72–92).

For some white, working-class boys, their public masculinity is constructed through hostility to, and rejection of, all aspects of groups that may be considered inferior in a racist and heterosexist society. For example, the ear'oles are considered inferior and subordinate to the lads because of their conformity to, and seeming enjoyment of, effeminate schooling projects. But other groups outside the school are also viewed as inferior by many white, working-class boys. Willis (1977: 48) found that different skin color was enough for the lads to justify an attack on, or intimidation of, racial minorities. Indeed, the meaning of being a "white man" has always hinged on the existence of for example, a subordinated "black man." Thus, a specific *racial gender* is constructed through the identical practice of racist violence; a social practice that bolsters, within the specific setting of white, working-class youth groups, one's masculine "whiteness" and, therefore, constitutes race and gender simultaneously. White, working-class, youthful masculinity acquires meaning in this particular context through racist violence.

Moreover, for some white, working-class youth, homosexuality is simply unnatural and effeminate sex, and many turn this ideology into physical violence. As one white, working-class youth put it, "My friends and I go 'fag-hunting' around the neighborhood. They should all be killed" (Weissman, 1992: 173). Gay bashing serves as a resource for constructing masculinity in a specific way: physical violence against gay men in front of other young, white, working-class men reaffirms one's commitment to what is for them natural and masculine sex—heterosexuality. In other words, the victim of gay bashing serves, "both physically and symbolically, as a vehicle for the sexual status needs of the offenders in the course of recreational violence" (Harry, 1992: 15). Accordingly, gender is accomplished and normative heterosexuality is reproduced.

White, working-class boys such as the lads construct public masculinities outside the school in other ways as well. As with the Roughnecks and the Eses, the lads also occasionally participate in various forms of theft. Because they want to take part in the youth culture (go to pubs, wear the "right" clothes, date, and so on) shortage of cash becomes "the single biggest pressure, perhaps at any rate after school, in their lives" (Willis, 1977: 39). Through contacts with family and friends, many of the lads acquired part-time, after-school, and summer jobs; in fact, Willis found that it is not uncommon for these youths to work over ten hours a week during the school year. Consequently, "this ability to 'make out' in the 'real world' . . . and to deal with adults nearly on their own terms" is seen by the lads as evidence of their "essential nature" as "males"—a practice that reproduces this specific type of white, working-class masculinity (p. 39). In addition, because of their access to paid employment, the lads' involvement in theft is irregular rather than systematic, providing a little extra pocket money when needed. . . .

In this specific context, then, intermittent theft is a resource that helps construct an "out-of-school," autonomous, independent, and daring opposition masculinity. And with part-time work available as a masculine resource, outside the school these white, working-class youths only sporadically turn to theft as a resource to accomplish gender. Thus, theft not only provides these youth with a resource for doing masculinity in the specific social setting of the group, it also helps construct a gendered line of action in which future gender accountability may be at risk. That is, it contributes to the wherewithal for adequate masculine participation in the youth culture.

Yet while the part-time workplace and youth group are initially seen as superior to the school—a milieu where masculinity as they know it is accepted—these working-class boys eventually find themselves locked into dead-end jobs, making less money than those who did not participate in the group and who conformed to the school. In this way, Willis's books show how white "working-class kids get working-class jobs." The initial context, and ultimate result, of the lads' opposition masculinity in the school was an orientation toward manual labor. Through their specific construction of masculinity, the lads themselves (and, similarly, the Hamilton Park boys) thus reproduced class, race, and gender relations as the structures constituted in those relations constrain and enable their collective social action.

Lower-Working-Class, Racial-Minority Boys

Consider now how this white, working-class opposition masculinity (and the white, middle-class masculinity discussed earlier) differs from youth masculinity of lower-working-class racial minorities who engage in youth crime. Because these youth have no access to paid labor (as have the lads and Hamilton Park boys) and their parents are unable to subsidize their youth culture needs (as are the parents of white, middle-class boys), the youth gang in lower-working-class, racial-minority communities takes on a new and significant meaning inasmuch as it is here where

resources are available with which to sustain a masculine identity. For many of these youths (although far from all), life is neither the workplace nor the school; it is the street. . . .

For many lower-working-class, racial-minority boys, the street group has become both a collective solution to their prohibitions and a life-style that sometimes takes the form of street crime. For these youths, then, street crime becomes a "field of possibilities" for transcending class and race domination and an important resource for accomplishing gender.

Opposition in School

Most white, middle-class boys envision a future in mental labor and members of the white, working-class (such as Willis's lads and Sullivan's Hamilton Park youths) realistically anticipate manual-labor positions. Consequently, these youths have resources (and a future) for masculine construction that are unavailable to lower-working-class, racial-minority boys. For marginalized, racial-minority boys, no such occupational future can be realistically anticipated and, accordingly, hegemonic masculinity is severely threatened. Under such conditions, life inside school takes on a significantly different meaning. . . .

Because the school is seen simply as another institutional impediment to a future in hegemonic masculine ways and because they lack the resources of white, middle-class and working-class boys, these young men are more likely to turn to those hegemonic masculine ideals that remain available, such as physical violence.

Physical violence within the school is a resource employed for masculine construction. In situations where class and race structural disadvantage are severe, one's taken-for-granted "essential nature" is more likely to be undermined and threatened; therefore, gender is held more accountable. In short, at the level of personal practice, this translates into a display of physical violence as a specific type of in-school, opposition masculinity. . . .

Thus, for lower-working-class, racial-minority boys in the process of opposing the school, doing masculinity necessitates extra effort; consequently, they are more likely than other boys to accomplish gender within the school by constructing a physically violent opposition masculinity. And in doing so, they turn to available hegemonic masculine ideals with which to construct such masculinity. This physical violence in the school is one practice that differentiates lower-working-class opposition masculinity from the other types discussed earlier.

Opposition Outside School

In addition to opposition within the school, because the school has less significance to these youths than to young men in other social classes, the street group also takes on a distinct and significant meaning in which opposition masculinity outside the school is likewise quite different from that of other youths. Marginalized, racial-minority boys are disproportionately involved in such serious property crimes as robbery and in such publicly displayed forms of group violence as "turf wars" (Steffensmeier and Allen, 1981; Elliott and Huizinga, 1983; Tracy, Wolfgang, and Figlio, 1991). The roots of this violent street crime are found in the disconcerting nature of the school and in the social conditions of poverty, racism, negated future, and power accorded men. Because of these social conditions and their attendant possibilities/constraints, young ghetto men are the most likely to commit certain types of street crime and thus to construct a different type of opposition masculinity outside the school. . . .

Sullivan and others (Zimring and Zuehl, 1986: Conklin, 1972) have reported that most robberies are committed by a group of young street men. Within this collective setting, robbery is a means of getting money when other resources are unavailable, and is particularly attractive for young boys on the street. Robbery provides a public ceremony of domination and humiliation of others. Because young street boys are denied access to the labor market and are relegated to a social situation (the

street group) where gender accountability is augmented, they are more often involved in crimes that entail actual or possible confrontation with others. As such, robbery provides an available resource with which to accomplish gender and, therefore, to construct a specific type of public masculinity—what Katz (1988: 225–236) terms "hardmen," or men who court danger and who, through force of will, subject others to it.

"Doing stickup" is doing masculinity by manufacturing "*an angle of moral superiority* over the intended victim" and, thereby, succeeding "in making a fool of his victim" (pp. 169, 174). . . .

The robbery setting provides the ideal opportunity to construct an "essential" toughness and "maleness"; it provides a means with which to construct that certain type of masculinity—hardman. Within the social context that ghetto and barrio boys find themselves, then, robbery is a rational practice for "doing gender" and for getting money. . . .

Marginalized, racial minority boys—as with white, middle- and working-class boys—produce specific configurations of behavior that can be seen by others within the same immediate social situation as "essentially male." As we have seen, these different masculinities emerge from practices that encompass different resources and that are simultaneously based on different collective trajectories. In this way, then, class and race relations structure the age-specific form of resources used to construct specific opposition masculinities. Young, middle-class, working-class, and lower-working-class men produce unique types of masculinity (situationally accomplished by drawing on different forms of youth crime) by acknowledging an already determined future and inhabiting distinct locations within the social structural divisions of labor and power. Collectively, young men experience their everyday world from a specific position in society and so they construct differently the cultural ideals of hegemonic masculinity.

Opposition masculinities, then, are based on a specific relation to school generated by the interaction of school authority with class, race, and gender dynamics. For white, middle-class boys, a nonviolent opposition masculinity occurs primarily outside school; for white, working-class and lower-working-class, racial-minority boys, specific types of opposition masculinities prevail both inside and outside school. Yet for each group of boys, a sense of masculinity is shaped by their specific relation to the school and by their specific position in the divisions of labor and power. . . .

Discussion Questions

1. How does the concept of "masculinities" help to revise views of men held by both feminists and traditional criminologists?
2. Why do youths in different class-race locations in society engage in different amounts and types of crime?

3. Why is crime a matter of "doing gender"? Are there other ways to "do gender"?
4. Think back to your days in high school. Can you give any examples of how masculinity was involved in some delinquent act that you witnessed?

31. Toward a Gendered Theory of Female Offending

Darrell J. Steffensmeier and Emilie Allan

Steffensmeier and Allan present a general or integrated theory of gender and crime, with this theory explaining female (and male) crime, the gender gap in crime, and the context of female (and male) crime. Steffensmeier and Allan draw on several traditional crime theories in constructing their theory, including social learning, control, rational choice, and routine activities theories. They also draw on feminist theories and research, and spend much time discussing the ways in which gender influences the level of the causal forces identified by traditional theories—as well as pointing to certain causal factors neglected by these theories. The key elements of their theory are illustrated in Figure 31.1. The theory begins by pointing to the importance of the "organization of gender" and sex differences in biological factors.

The organization of gender refers to gender differences in norms, moral development, and social control. With respect to norms, females are supposed to care for others, especially family members; be subservient to the key males in their lives; act in a weak, submissive manner; and attend to their physical appearance, while protecting their "sexual virtue." With respect to moral development, females are socialized to care for others and be concerned about the maintenance of relationships, while men are socialized to be more independent and

competitive. And with respect to social control, female behavior is more closely monitored and female misbehavior is more likely to be sanctioned. As indicated below, these differences strongly influence gender differences in the motivation for and constraints against crime.

There are two major sets of sex differences in biological factors. The first involves differences in physical strength, which help account for the much lower rates of violence and certain other types of serious crime by females. The second involves reproductive-sexual differences, along with norms regarding appropriate sexual behavior for males and females. Such differences provide females with greater opportunities for prostitution and reduce their need to commit serious property crimes. These sexual and strength differences also increase the likelihood that females will align themselves with males for protection.

The above two sets of factors restrict female opportunities for crime. Females are more often confined to the home and involved in the care of others. Related to this, females are less often involved with delinquent others or engaged in unstructured, unsupervised activities with peers. The above factors also reduce the motivation for crime among females by "contributing to gender differences in tastes for risk, likelihood of shame and embarrassment, self-control, and assessment of

Reprinted with permission from Darrell Steffensmeier and Emilie Allan. 1996. "Gender and Crime: Toward a Gendered Theory of Female Offending," *Annual Review of Sociology* 22, pp. 459–487.

costs versus rewards of crime" (Steffensmeier and Allan, 1996: 478). Also, as indicated in Figure 31.1, opportunities and motivation influence one another: "being able tends to make one more willing, just as being willing increases the prospects for being able" (Steffensmeier and Allan, 1996: 478).

Finally, gender organization, sex differences in biological factors, and motivations influence the "context of offending," including the circumstances and the nature of the criminal act (e.g., the setting, victim, extent of injury, purpose of the offense). So, for example, females who commit violent crimes are more likely than males to target people they know, are less likely to use weapons, and are less likely to seriously injure their victims.

Steffensmeier and Allan's theory has not received a formal test, but it is compatible with much of the research on gender and crime and it represents perhaps the most ambitious effort to integrate both traditional and feminist theories on gender and crime.

Reference

Steffensmeier, Darrell and Emilie Allan. 1996. "Gender and Crime: Toward a Gendered Theory of Female Offending." *Annual Review of Sociology* 22: 459–487.

Shortcomings of Traditional Theories

Traditional theories are helpful in explaining overall patterns of female and male offending, and they shed some light on why female levels of offending are lower than for males. These approaches are less enlightening when seeking answers for a variety of both subtle and profound differences in female and male offending patterns.

For example: Why are serious crimes against property and against persons so much less a feature of female offending? Male criminal participation in serious crime greatly exceeds female involvement, regardless of data source, crime type, level of involvement, or measure of participation (Kruttschnitt 1994; Steffensmeier 1983; Steffensmeier and Allan 1995). Women are far less likely to be involved in serious offenses, and the monetary value of female thefts, property damage, drugs, injuries, is typically smaller than that for similar offenses committed by men.

Why are female offenders less likely to participate in or lead criminal groups? Females are also more likely than males to be solo perpetrators, or to be part of small, relatively nonpermanent crime groups. When female offenders are involved with others, particularly in more lucrative thefts or other criminal enterprises, they typically act as accomplices to males who both organize and lead the execution of the crime (see Steffensmeier 1983, for a review). Perhaps the most significant gender difference is the overwhelming dominance of males in more organized and highly lucrative crimes, whether based in the underworld or the "upperworld" (Steffensmeier 1983; Daly 1989; Commonwealth of Pennsylvania 1991). . . .

Why does female offending often involve relational concerns? Situational pressures such as threatened loss of valued relationships may play a greater role in female offending. Although the saying, "She did it all for love" is sometimes overplayed in reference to female criminality, the role of men in initiating women into crime—especially serious crime—is a consistent finding across research (Gilfus 1992; Miller 1986; Pettiway 1987; Steffensmeier 1983; Steffensmeier and Terry 1986). Such findings also suggest that women are not uniformly less amenable to risk, but rather that their risk-taking is less violative of the law and more protective of relationships and emotional commitments. . . .

Toward a Gendered Theory

No satisfactorily unified theoretical framework has yet been developed for explaining female criminality and gender differences in crime. Criminologists disagree as to whether gender-neutral (i.e., traditional theories derived from male samples) or gender-specific theories (i.e., recent approaches derived from female samples and positing unique causal paths for female as compared to male criminality) are better suited to these tasks. We take the position that the traditional gender-neutral theories provide reasonable explanations of less serious forms of female and male criminality, and for gender differences in such crime categories. Their principal shortcoming is that they are not very informative about the specific ways in which differences in the lives of men and women contribute to gender differences in type, frequency, and context of criminal behavior. Gender-specific theories are likely to be even less adequate if they require separate explanations for female crime and male crime.

Here we build on a framework for a "gendered" approach begun elsewhere (Steffensmeier and Allan 1995). This approach is compatible with the traditional, gender-neutral theories. The broad social forces suggested by traditional theories exert general causal influences on both male and female crime. But it is gender that mediates the manner in which those forces play out into sex differences in types, frequency, and contexts of crime involvements.

Key Elements of a Gendered Approach

A gendered approach should include at least four key elements. First, the perspective should help explain not only female criminality but male criminality as well, by revealing how the organization of gender deters or shapes delinquency by females but encourages it by males. We use the term "organization of gender" to refer broadly to things gendered—norms, identities, arrangements, institutions, and relations by which human sexual dichotomy is transformed into something physically and socially different.

Second, a gendered perspective should account not only for gender differences in type and frequency of crime, but also for differences in the context of offending. Even when men and women commit the same statutory offense, the "gestalt" of their offending is frequently quite

different. Because the gender differences in context are small for trivial or mild forms of lawbreaking, but large for violent and other serious forms of crime, contextual analysis can shed light on the gender differences for serious offenses—hitherto the most difficult to explain.

Third, compared to theories based on male crime, we need to consider several key ways in which women's routes to crime (especially serious crime) may differ from those of men. Building on the work of Daly (1994) and Steffensmeier (1983, 1993), such differences include: (a) the more blurred boundaries between victim and victimization in women's than men's case histories; (b) women's exclusion from most lucrative crime opportunities; (c) women's ability to exploit sex as an illegal money-making service; (d) consequences (real or anticipated) of motherhood and child care; (e) the centrality of greater relational concerns among women, and the manner in which these both shape and allow women to be pulled into criminal involvements by men in their lives; (f) the greater need of street women for protection from predatory or exploitative males.

Fourth, the perspective should explore the extent to which gender differences in crime derive not only from complex social, historical, and cultural factors, but from biological and reproductive differences as well (Kruttschnitt 1995, Udry 1995).

Figure 31.1 summarizes a gendered paradigm of offending that takes into account the four criteria enunciated above. We sketch here key features of this paradigm that affect men and women differently in terms of willingness and ability to commit crime.

The Organization of Gender

The organization of gender together with sex differences in physical-sexual characteristics contributes to male and female differences in several types of relatively enduring characteristics that increase the probability of prosocial and altruistic response on the part of females but antisocial and predatory response on the part of males.

Figure 31.1
Gendered Model of Female Offending and Gender Differences in Crime
(broken line indicates weak effect; solid line signifies strong effect)

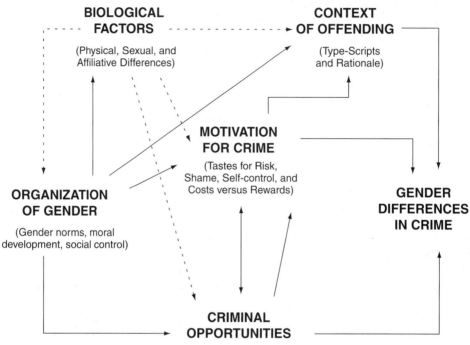

In the discussion that follows we elaborate briefly on five areas of life that inhibit female crime but encourage male crime: gender norms, moral development and affiliative concerns, social control, physical strength and aggression, and sexuality. Gender differences in these areas condition gender differences in patterns of motivation and access to criminal opportunities, as well as gender differences in the type, frequency, and context of offending. These areas are not discrete, but rather they overlap and mutually reinforce one another.

Gender norms. The greater taboos against female crime stem largely from two powerful focal concerns ascribed to women: (i) nurturant role obligations and (ii) female beauty and sexual virtue. In varied settings or situations, these concerns shape the constraints and opportunities of girls' and women's illicit activities.

Women are rewarded for their ability to establish and maintain relationships and to accept family obligations, and their identity tends to be derived from key males in their lives (e.g., father, husband). Derivative identity constrains deviance on the part of women involved with conventional males but encourages the criminal involvements of those who become accomplices of husbands or boyfriends. Greater child-rearing responsibilities further constrain female criminality.

Femininity stereotypes (e.g., weakness, submission, domestication, nurturance, and "ladylike" behavior) are basically incompatible with qualities valued in the criminal underworld (Steffensmeier 1986). The cleavage between what is considered feminine and what is criminal is sharp, while the dividing line between what is considered masculine and what is criminal is often thin. Crime is almost always stigmatizing for females, and its potential cost to life chances is much greater than for males.

Expectations regarding sexuality and physical appearance reinforce greater female dependency as well as greater surveillance by parents and husbands. These expectations also shape the deviant roles available to women (e.g., sexual media or service roles). Moreover, fear of sexual victimization diverts women from crime-likely locations (bars, nighttime streets) and reduces their opportunities to commit crimes (McCarthy and Hagan 1992; Steffensmeier 1983).

Moral development and amenability to affiliation. Gender differences in moral development (Gilligan 1982) and an apparent greater inherent readiness of women to learn parenting and nurturing (Beutel and Marini 1995; Brody 1985; Rossi 1984) predispose women toward an "ethic of care" that restrains women from violence and other criminal behavior injurious to others. Women are socialized not only to be more responsive to the needs of others but also to fear the threat of separation from loved ones. Such complex concerns inhibit women from undertaking criminal activities that might cause hurt to others and shape the "gestalt" of their criminality when they do offend.

In contrast, men who are conditioned toward status-seeking, yet marginalized from the world of work, may develop an amoral world view in which the "takers" gain superior status at the expense of the "givers." Such a moral stance obviously increases the likelihood of aggressive criminal behavior on the part of those who become "convinced that people are at each other's throats increasingly in a game of life that has no moral rules" (Messerschmidt 1986: 66).

Social control. Social control powerfully shapes women's relative willingness and ability to commit crime. Female misbehavior is more stringently monitored and corrected through negative stereotypes and sanctions (Simmons and Blyth 1987). The greater supervision and control reduces female risk-taking and increases attachment to parents, teachers, and conventional friends, which in turn reduces influence by delinquent peers (Giordano et al. 1986). Encapsulation within the family and the production of "moral culture" restricts the freedom even of adult women to explore the temptations of the world (Collins 1992).

Physical strength and aggression. The demands of the crime environment for physical power and violence help account for the less serious nature and less frequent incidence of crimes by women compared to those by men. Women may lack the power, or may be perceived by themselves or by others as lacking the violent potential, for successful completion of certain types of crime or for protection of a major "score." Hustling small amounts of money or property protects female criminals against predators who might be attracted by larger amounts. Real or perceived vulnerability can also help account for female restriction to solo roles, or to roles as subordinate partners or accomplices in crime groups. This can be seen in a variety of female offense patterns, including the exigencies of the dependent prostitute–pimp relationship (James 1977). Together, physical prowess and muscle are useful for committing crimes, for protection, for enforcing contracts, and for recruiting and managing reliable associates.

Sexuality. Reproductive-sexual differences (especially when combined with sexual taboos and titillations of the society as a whole) contribute to the far greater sexual deviance and infidelity among males. Women, on the other hand, have expanded opportunities for financial gain through prostitution and related illicit sexual roles. The possibilities in this arena reduce the need to commit the serious property crimes that so disproportionately involve males.

Although female offenders may use their sexuality to gain entry into male criminal organizations, such exploitation of male stereotypes is likely to limit their criminal opportunities within the group to roles organized around female attributes. The sexual dimension may also heighten the potential for sexual tension which can be resolved only if the female aligns herself with one man sexually, becoming "his woman."

Even prostitution—often considered a female crime—is essentially a male-dominated or -controlled criminal enterprise. Police, pimps, businessmen who employ prostitutes, and clients—virtually all of whom are male—control, in various ways, the conditions under which the prostitute works.

Access to Criminal Opportunity

The factors above—gender norms, social control, and the like—restrict female access to criminal opportunity, which in turn both limits and shapes female participation in crime. Women are also less likely than men to have access to crime opportunities as a spin-off of legitimate roles and routine activities. Women are less likely to hold jobs as truck driver, dockworker, or carpenter that would provide opportunities for theft, drug dealing, fencing, and other illegitimate activities. In contrast, women have considerable opportunity for commission, and thus for surveillance and arrest for petty forms of fraud and embezzlement.

Females are most restricted in terms of access to underworld crimes that are organized and lucrative. Institutional sexism in the underworld severely limits female involvement in crime groups, ranging from syndicates to loosely structured groups (Steffensmeier 1983; Commonwealth of Pennsylvania 1991). As in the upperworld, females in the underworld are disadvantaged in terms of selection and recruitment, in the range of career paths and access to them, and in opportunities for tutelage, skill development, and rewards.

Motivation

Gender norms, social control, lack of physical strength, and moral and relational concerns also limit female willingness to participate in crime at the subjective level—by contributing to gender differences in tastes for risk, likelihood of shame or embarrassment, self-control, and assessment of costs versus rewards of crime. Motivation is distinct from opportunity, but the two often intertwine, as when opportunity enhances temptation. As in legitimate enterprise, being able tends to make one more willing, just as being willing increases the prospects for being able. Like male offenders, female offenders gravitate to those activities that are easily available, are within their skills, provide a satisfactory return, and carry the fewest risks.

Criminal motivations and involvements are also shaped by gender differences in risk preferences and in styles of risk-taking (Hagan 1989; Steffensmeier 1980; Steffensmeier and Allan 1995). For example, women take greater risks to sustain valued relationships, whereas males take greater risks for reasons of status or competitive advantage. Criminal motivation is suppressed by the female ability to foresee threats to life chances and by the relative unavailability of type scripts that could channel females in unapproved behaviors.

Context of Offending

Many of the most profound differences between the offenses committed by men and women involve the context of offending, a point neglected by quantitative studies based on aggregate and survey data. "Context" refers to the characteristics of a particular offense, including both the circumstances and the nature of the act (Triplett and Myers 1995). Contextual characteristics include, for example, the setting, whether the offense was committed with others, the offender's role in initiating and committing the offense, the type of victim, the victim–offender relationship, whether a weapon was used, the extent of injury, the value or type of property destroyed or stolen, and the purpose of the offense. Even when males and females participate in the same types of crimes, the "gestalt" of their actions may differ markedly (Daly 1994; Steffensmeier 1983, 1993). Moreover, the more serious the offense, the greater the contextual differences by gender.

A powerful example of the importance of contextual considerations is found in the case of spousal murders, for which the female share of offending is quite high—at least one third, and perhaps as much as one half. Starting with Wolfgang's classic study of homicide, a number of writers propose that husbands and wives have equal potential for violence (Steinmetz and Lucca 1988; Straus and Gelles 1990). However, Dobash et al. (1992) point out that the context of spousal violence is dramatically different for men and women. Compared to men, women are far more likely to kill only after a prolonged period of abuse, when they are in fear for their lives and have exhausted all alternatives. A number of patterns of wife-killing by husbands are rarely if ever found when wives kill husbands: murder-suicides, family massacres, stalking, and murder in response to spouse infidelity.

In common delinquency, female prevalence approaches that of males in simple forms of delinquency like hitting others or stealing from stores or schools, but girls are far less likely to use a weapon or to intend serious injury to their victims (Kruttschnitt 1994), to steal things they cannot use (Cohen 1966), and to steal from building sites or break into buildings (Mawby 1980).

Similarly, when females commit traditional male crimes like burglary, they are less likely to be solitary (Decker et al. 1993), more likely to serve as an accomplice (e.g., drop-off driver), and less likely to receive an equal share of proceeds (Steffensmeier and Terry 1986). Also, female burglaries involve less planning and are more spontaneous, and they are more likely to occur in daytime in residences where no one is at home and with which they have prior familiarity as an acquaintance, maid, or the like (Steffensmeier 1986, 1993).

Application of Gendered Perspective to Patterns of Female Crime

The utility of a gendered perspective can be seen in its ability to explain both female and male patterns of criminal involvement as well as gender differences in crime. The perspective predicts, and finds, that female participation is highest for those crimes most consistent with traditional norms and for which females have the most opportunity, and lowest for those crimes that diverge the most from traditional gender norms and for which females have little opportunity. Let us briefly review some examples of property, violent, and public order offending patterns that can be better understood from a gendered perspective.

In the area of property crimes we have already noted that the percentage of female arrests is highest for the minor offenses like small thefts, shoplifting and passing bad checks—offenses compatible with traditional female roles in making family purchases. The high share of arrests for embezzlement reflects female employment segregation: women constitute about 90 percent of lower level bookkeepers and bank tellers (those most likely to be arrested for embezzlement), but slightly less than half of all accountants or auditors. Further, women tend to embezzle to protect their families or valued relationships, while men tend to embezzle to protect their status (Zeitz 1981).

Despite Simon's (1975) claim that female involvement in white collar crime was on the increase, in fact it is almost nonexistent in more serious occupational and/or business crimes, like insider trading, price-fixing, restraint of trade, toxic waste dumping, fraudulent product commerce, bribery, and official corruption, as well as large-scale governmental crimes (for example, the Iran-Contra affair and the Greylord scandal). Even when similar on-the-job opportunities for theft exist, women are still less likely to commit crime (Steffensmeier 1980).

The lowest percentage of female involvement is found for serious property crimes whether committed on the "street" such as burglary and robbery or in the "suite" such as insider trading or price-fixing (Steffensmeier and Allan 1995). These sorts of offenses are very much at odds with traditional feminine stereotypes, and ones to which women have very limited access. When women act as solo perpetrators, the typical robbery is a "wallet-sized" theft by a prostitute or addict (James 1977; see also Covington 1985; Pettiway 1987). However, females frequently become involved in such crimes as accomplices to males, particularly in roles that at once exploit women's sexuality and reinforce their traditional subordination to men (American Correctional Association 1983; Miller 1986; Steffensmeier and Terry 1986).

Female violence, although apparently at odds with female gender norms of gentleness and passivity, is also closely tied to the organization of gender. Unlike males, females rarely kill or assault strangers or acquaintances; instead, the female's victim tends to be a male intimate or a child, the offense generally takes place within the home, the victim is frequently drunk, and self-defense or extreme depression is often a motive (Dobash et al. 1992). For women to kill, they generally must see their situation as life-threatening, as affecting the physical or emotional well-being of themselves or their children.

The linkage between female crime and the gendered paradigm of Figure 31.1 is perhaps most evident in the case of certain public order offenses with a high percentage of female involvement, particularly the sex-related categories of prostitution and juvenile runaways—the only offense categories where female arrest rates exceed those of males. The high percentage of female arrests in these two categories reflects both gender differences in marketability of sexual services and the continuing patriarchal sexual double standard. Although customers must obviously outnumber prostitutes, they are less likely to be sanctioned. Similarly, although self-report studies show male rates of runaways to be as high as female rates, suspicion of sexual involvement makes female runaways more likely to be arrested (Chesney-Lind and Shelden 1992).

Female substance abuse (as with other patterns of female crime) often stems from relational concerns or involvements, beginning in the context of teenage dating or following introduction to drugs by husbands or boyfriends (Inciardi et al. 1993; Pettiway 1987). Women tend to be less involved in heavy drinking or hard drug use—those drugs most intimately tied to drug subcultures and the underworld more generally (Department of Health and Human Services 1984). Female addicts are less likely to have other criminal involvements prior to addiction, so the amplification of income-oriented crime is greater for female drug users. Female addict crimes are mainly prostitution, reselling narcotics or assisting male drug dealers, and property crimes such as shoplifting, forgery, and burglary (Anglin and Hser 1987).

Advantages of Paradigm

A gendered approach helps to clarify the gendered nature of both female and male offending patterns. For women, "doing gender" preempts criminal involvement or directs it into scripted paths. For example, prostitution draws on and affirms femininity, while violence draws on and affirms masculinity. . . .

Discussion Questions

1. Steffensmeier and Allan state that traditional theories can help explain female offending and the gender gap in crime, but there are some questions about gender and crime they have trouble explaining. What are these questions?

2. Briefly describe Steffensmeier and Allan's gendered theory. In particular, list and briefly discuss the major factors in their theory and how they are related to one another. List two specific factors in Steffensmeier and Allan's theory that are not considered by traditional crime theories.

3. Steffensmeier and Allan list "five areas of life that inhibit female crime but encourage male crime." What are these five areas?

4. What do Steffensmeier and Allan mean by gender differences "in the context of offending"? Describe a contextual difference in male versus female offending, and indicate how the gendered theory explains this difference.

5. What traditional theories of crime do Steffensmeier and Allan draw on in their gendered theory? Do they overlook any traditional theories?

SECTION 4

Choice, Opportunity, and Crime

PART X
Reviving Classical Theory: Deterrence and Rational Choice
Theories

PART XI
Environmental Criminology

PART X

Reviving Classical Theory: Deterrence and Rational Choice Theories

Most of the theories presented in the previous chapters focus on the factors that constrain individuals to engage in crime—factors like individual traits, disorganized communities, association with delinquent peers, and strains. The impression one gets from reading these chapters is that crime is largely the result of forces beyond an individual's control. Individuals do not choose to engage in crime, but rather their criminal behavior is determined by a variety of individual and social factors. This "deterministic" view of crime has dominated crime theory since the late 1800s. It stands in contrast to "classical theory," which dominated crime theory during the late 1700s and much of the 1800s.

According to classical theory, individuals choose to engage in crime based on a rational consideration of the costs and benefits associated with crime (see Part I for an overview). That is, individuals engage in crime when they believe that crime maximizes their net benefits (i.e., their benefits minus costs). This fundamental idea has been revived and extended in the work of several economists and criminologists, and it now once again occupies a central place in crime theory.

Deterrence Theory

Deterrence theory most fully reflects the ideas of classical theory. Deterrence theorists argue that people are rational and pursue their own interests, attempting to maximize their pleasure and minimize their pain. They choose to engage in crime if they believe it is to their advantage. The best way to prevent crime, therefore, is through punishments that are swift, certain, and appropriately severe. Deterrence theorists, like classical theorists, focus primarily on the impact of official punishments on crime. Deterrence occurs when "someone refrains from committing a crime because he or she fears the certainty, swiftness, and/or severity of formal legal punishment" (Paternoster and Bachman, 2001: 14). Note that these ideas are almost identical to those advanced by Beccaria (see Chapter 1), the first and most prominent of the classical theorists.

Deterrence theory became popular in the 1970s, stimulated in part by the work of certain economists, including Gary Becker (1968). And the theory has had an enormous impact on contemporary crime control policies. In particular, the criminal justice system in the United States has largely abandoned rehabilitation as its main crime control strategy and is instead trying to control crime by increasing the certainty and especially the severity of punishment (see Part XV in this volume; Cullen et al., 2002). For example, many states have passed "three strikes and you're out" laws, which typically impose life sentences on individuals on their third conviction for certain crimes. Most states have also made it easier to try certain serious juvenile offenders in adult court, where the penalties are generally more severe than those in juvenile court. This shift in focus is reflected in the fact that the rate of imprisonment in the United States has increased about fivefold since the early 1970s, with the United States now having the highest rate of imprisonment in the world.

Specific Deterrence

Deterrence theory makes a distinction between two types of deterrence: specific and general. Specific deterrence refers to the idea that punishment reduces the crime *of those specific people who are punished*. So, punishing someone for a crime should reduce the likelihood of further crime by that person.

Is there any evidence for specific deterence? A number of studies have tried to determine whether increasing the *severity* of punishment reduces crime. Most data suggest that more severe punishments are no more effective at reducing crime than less severe punishments. In fact, some studies suggest that more severe punishments may increase the likelihood of subsequent crime. So administering more severe punishments to people does not appear to reduce their subsequent crime (Agnew, 2009; Cullen et al., 1996; Kovandzic et al., 2004; Sherman et al., 1998).

A few studies have tried to determine whether the swiftness or *celerity* of punishment affects crime. Psychological studies on animals suggest that swift punishments are more effective at suppressing behavior than delayed punishments. The few studies on humans, however, suggest that swift punishments do not reduce subsequent offending more than delayed punishments, perhaps because humans "have a far greater congnitive capacity than do animals for connecting acts with temporally remote consequences" (Nagin and Pogarsky, 2001: 867).

And a few studies have tried to determine whether people *punished* by the justice system are less likely to engage in crime than comparable people who are *not punished*. These studies typically compare arrested or convicted people to comparable people who have not been arrested or convicted. The two groups are usually comparable in terms of the offenses they have committed and such socio-demographic characteristics as age, sex, race, and class; although they may differ in other ways that are not considered. The results of these studies are mixed, but they tend to suggest that the arrested/convicted people do *not* have lower rates of subsequent crime. Some studies, in fact, find that the arrested people have *higher* rates of subsequent crime (e.g., Huizinga et al., 2003; see Agnew, 2009; Bernburg et al., 2006; Pogarsky and Piquero, 2003, for reviews). So, overall, we may tentatively conclude that punishing people does not reduce their subsequent crime.

There are several possible reasons that punishing people may not deter them from committing further crime (see Agnew, 2009; Tonry, 2008). First, many offenders may not be that rational. As indicated in Part II, offenders are often impulsive and high in negative emotionality. And as indicated in Parts III through IX, many offenders are often pressured into crime, perhaps by the strains they experience or their association with delinquent peers. As a consequence, many offenders may not be deterred by the threat of further punishment. Second, punishment may sometimes increase strains, reduce social control, and increase the social learning of crime (see Part VII on labeling theory for a fuller discussion). For example, individuals with criminal records may have more trouble finding legitimate work, thus increasing their strain and reducing their social control. Third, the justice system does not punish in an effective way. In particular, the likelihood of punishment is very low, which may undermine the deterrent effect of punishment, since it must be certain if it is to be effective. In this area, some studies suggest that punished individuals do *not* increase their estimates of the certainty of punishment and may even lower them (see Pogarsky et al., 2004; Pogarsky et al., 2005; Pogarsky and Piquero, 2003).

Some criminologists, however, argue that the effect of punishment on crime depends on the nature of the punishment and who is punished. So, although punished offenders *as a whole* may not reduce their subsequent crime, it may be that *some* punished offenders reduce their crime and other punished offenders increase their crime. Deterrence researchers are now conducting much research in this area. Certain of this research focuses on the nature of punishments. Most notably, Braithwaite (Chapter 21) argues that some punishments are administered in ways that isolate or alienate offenders from society. In particular, punished individuals are labeled as bad or evil people, rejected by conventional others, and often treated in a harsh manner. Not surprisingly, these punishments are said to increase the likelihood of further crime. In other cases, punishments are followed by an effort to forgive the offender and reintegrate him or her back into conventional society. Some evidence suggests that these punishments are more likely to reduce at least certain types of crime (Bonta et al., 2006; Braithwaite, 1989, 2002; Braithwaite et al., 2006; McGarrell and Hipple, 2007; Sherman, 1993). Sherman (Chapter 22) makes a similar argument, and states that the effect of punishments on subsequent crime depends on the extent to which the punishments are administered in a fair and respectful manner. Studies also provide some support for this argument (Fagan and Piquero, 2007; Paternoster et al., 1997; Sherman, 1993; Sherman et al., 1992; also see Piquero et al., 2004).

Other research focuses on the characteristics of the people who are punished. Some criminologists argue that punishments are most likely to reduce crime among those who are strongly committed to conformity, especially those who are high in self-control and strongly bonded to conventional society. Individuals who are high in self-control care about and give much thought to the consequences of their behavior, so punishments should be more likely to deter them (see Chapter 19). Individuals with strong bonds have good jobs, close ties to family members, and believe that crime is wrong (see Chapter 18). Punishments should be more likely to deter them since they have much to lose if they engage in further crime. In this area, punishments are said to be especially likely to have a deterrent effect on white-collar criminals—who tend to be higher in self-control and to have more to lose through crime (Pratt et al., 2006; although see Weisburd et al., 1995).

Other criminologists, however, disagree with these arguments. They claim that individuals who are strongly committed to conformity are likely to refrain from crime regardless of whether they are punished. Punishment, then, should have little effect on their future offending. Instead, punishments should be most likely to reduce crime among those who are strongly disposed to crime, including those who are low in self-control and have weak bonds to conventional society. It is said that punishment is the only thing holding these individuals back from crime.

Finally, some criminologists propose a compromise, claiming that punishments are most likely to reduce crime among those who are neither strongly committed to crime or conformity. Although such individuals have *some* inclination to engage in crime, they are not so strongly committed to crime that they are unresponsive to punishments. Studies have produced some support for each of the above arguments (e.g., Bachman et al., 1992; Foglia, 1997; Nagin, 1998; Pogarsky, 2002, 2007; Sherman, 1993; Wikstrom, 2008; Wooldredge and Thistlethwaite, 2002; Wright et al., 2004). The most recent and perhaps best studies, however, suggest that punishments are most likely to deter crime among those who are strongly disposed to crime (Pogarsky, 2007; Tittle and Botchkovar, 2005; Wright et al., 2004).

For now, we can draw the following tentative conclusion: *Overall*, when the justice system punishes someone or punishes them more severely, that does not reduce their subsequent crime. It is probably the case, however, that *some* people reduce their crime in response to punishment and *some* people increase their crime in response to punishment. Current research is now examining those factors that influence the effect of punishment. Such research is, of course, very important, since it may help us design punishments that are effective in controlling crime.

General Deterrence

Studies on specific deterrence ask whether punishment deters crime among *those who are punished*. Studies on general deterrence ask whether punishment deters crime among people *in the general population*. In particular, it has been argued that punishment may deter crime among those who are not punished. For example, suppose several people are caught for shoplifting and are punished. Their punishment may deter *others* from shoplifting—even though these others were not punished. These others may come to feel that they too might be caught and punished if they shoplift.

Numerous studies have tried to determine whether there is a general deterrent effect—that is, whether increasing the certainty and severity of punishment reduces crime in the general population. Some studies compare areas that differ in terms of the certainty or severity of punishment. Usually states are compared; but sometimes cities or counties are compared. Certainty of punishment is usually measured in terms of the average number of arrests per officer or the arrest rate (the proportion of offenses known to the police that result in arrest). Severity is often measured in terms of the average length of prison sentence served for various crimes. These studies try to determine whether areas with a higher certainty and severity of punishment have lower crime rates. Other studies have examined whether the certainty and severity of punishment at one point in time affects crime rates at a *subsequent* point in time. For example, they may examine whether areas with a relatively high certainty and severity of punishment are more likely to experience a reduction in crime than other areas. Or they may examine the effect of policies designed to increase the certainty and severity of punishment. For example, several studies have examined the

effectiveness of policies designed to crack down on drunk driving and drug sales. Other studies have examined the effect of hiring additional police or placing more police in high crime areas or "hot spots" for crime (e.g., Braga et al., 2008; Cohen et al., 2003; Levitt, 2002; Sherman and Weisburd, 1995).

These studies have been criticized, however. Criminologists argue that they assume that people are aware of the certainty and severity of punishment in the area where they live. But data suggest that this assumption is often wrong. Many people have little idea of the true certainty and severity of punishment (see Kleck et al., 2005). In particular, people who are law-abiding often greatly overestimate the certainty and severity of punishment (Nagin, 1998). Given this fact, some criminologists argue that the best way to determine whether people are deterred by the threat of punishment is to ask them to estimate the certainty and severity of punishment—in particular, to estimate the likelihood that they will be punished if they commit a particular offense and what their punishment will be. If people are deterred by the threat of punishment, their estimate of the certainty and severity of punishment should have an effect on their level of crime. In particular, people who state that they will be caught and severely punished if they engage in crime should be less likely to engage in crime.

In sum, a range of studies have attempted to determine whether the certainty and severity of punishment are related to crime in the general population. The results of these studies do not always agree with one another, but if we look at the more recent and best research there are a few tentative conclusions we can draw (see Agnew, 2009; Levitt, 2002; Matsueda et al., 2006; Nagin, 1998; Paternoster and Bachman, 2001; Pratt et al., 2006; Tonry, 2008; Wikstrom, 2008 for overviews). Most notably, increasing the *certainty* of punishment may reduce crime by a moderate amount in some circumstances. The certainty of punishment, however, is only one of many factors influencing the level of crime. It is less important than other factors, such as the individual's beliefs regarding crime and the threat of informal punishment from family members and others. The severity of punishment is less important than the certainty of punishment, with most studies suggesting that changes in the severity of punishment have little or no effect on crime (although see Pogarsky, 2002, 2007).

As indicated, the certainty of punishment reduces crime in *some* circumstances. Limited research suggests that the effect of punishment is short-lived and is confined to the specific area in which the punishment is administered. So, punishments administered a year ago have little or no effect on current levels of crime (likewise, the individual's perception of the certainty of punishment a year ago often has little effect on their current crime). And punishments administered outside of one's community appear to have little deterrent effect. This makes sense: People are most responsive to recent punishments administered in their communities. And it jibes with recent research indicating that perceptions of the certainty of punishment are partly based on the experiences of people in one's immediate environment, such as family members, friends, neighbors, and coworkers. Further, some data suggest that punishments must be reasonably certain if offenders are to be deterred. A few studies estimate that the probability of punishment needs to be 20 percent or more if offenders are to be deterred—although more research is needed in this area (see Agnew, 2009).

Also, there is some evidence that the threat of punishment is more likely to deter some people than others. The arguments made in this area are similar to those made with respect to specific deterrence. And while studies have produced contradictory results, they tend to suggest that the threat of punishment is most likely to deter those who are strongly committed to crime—such as those who are low in self-control and do not believe that crime is wrong (see the above cited references).

In sum, general deterrence may work with certain people in some circumstances. In this area, several programs have been successful in deterring crime among people disposed to crime, such as gang members, probationers, and those who congregate in high-crime locations or "hot spots" (Braga et al., 2008; McGarrell et al., 2006; Weisburd et al., 2008). These programs have certain important features. They clearly communicate to such people that the certainty (and often severity) of punishment has increased. This communication may be direct, as when the police meet with gang members and tell them that they are being closely watched and will be sanctioned if they offend. It may also be indirect, as when the police dramatically increase the extent to which they patrol crime "hot spots." Such communication is critical, since increasing the certainty of punishment will not deter offending unless individuals are aware of the increase (see Kleck et al., 2005). These programs also closely monitor the offending behavior of those in the target group and consistently sanction infractions. Such sanctions are sometimes publicized to reinforce the message that the certainty of punishment has increased. Such programs, of course, are possible only when the police can identify, communicate with, and effectively monitor individuals who are disposed to crime.

Stafford and Warr's Reconceptualization of Deterrence Theory

A recent paper by Stafford and Warr has caused many deterrence theorists to rethink the sharp distinction between specific and general deterrence. Stafford and Warr begin their paper, reprinted in Chapter 32, by stating that deterrence researchers usually focus on either specific deterrence *or* general deterrence. If they focus on specific deterrence, they examine the impact of "an offender's direct experience with suffering a punishment" (Stafford and Warr, 1993; 126). If they focus on general deterrence, they examine the effect of *indirect experiences* with punishment (i.e., one's knowledge of the punishment of others). Further, such researchers show little concern with experiences of punishment *avoidance*. In particular, they do not ask whether individuals have committed crimes for which they have not been punished or whether they are aware of others who have committed crimes for which they have not been punished.

Stafford and Warr argue these are serious shortcomings. If we want to determine whether punishment deters crime, we need to recognize that "most people are likely to have a mixture of indirect and direct experience with punishment and punishment avoidance" (1993: 126). In particular, studies on deterrence need to examine whether individuals: (1) have been punished for any crimes they have committed (direct experiences with punishment), (2) are aware of others who have been punished for their crimes (indirect experiences with punishment), (3) have avoided punishment for crimes they have committed (direct experiences with punishment avoidance), and (4) are aware of others who have avoided punishment for their crimes (indirect experiences with punishment avoidance). Estimates of the certainty and severity of punishment should be affected by all of these factors.

Studies on deterrence fail to consider all of these factors. Studies on specific deterrence, for example, usually just examine whether individuals have direct experiences with punishment. They seldom inquire about direct experiences with punishment avoidance or indirect experiences with punishment and punishment avoidance. Studies on general deterrence just focus on indirect experiences with punishment. So, Stafford and Warr make a fundamental contribution to the deterrence literature, pointing out that the same people may have both direct and indirect experiences with punishment and that it is also important to consider punishment avoidance when testing deterrence theory.

Their reconceptualization of deterrence theory has not been extensively tested, primarily because the data necessary to fully test the theory are not available. Nevertheless, preliminary tests of the theory have been generally supportive, indicating that both direct and indirect experiences with punishment and punishment avoidance influence the perceived certainty of punishment and levels of offending. However, these effects are not always in the direction that Stafford and Warr predict. Most notably, some data suggest that—contrary to deterrence theory—direct experiences with punishment often decrease the perceived certainty of punishment and the increase the likelihood of subsequent offending (Paternoster and Piquero, 1995; Piquero and Paternoster, 1998; Piquero and Pogarsky, 2002; Pogarsky and Piquero, 2003; Pogarsky et al., 2004; Pogarsky et al., 2005; Sitren and Applegate, 2007). This issue is discussed further in Part VII on labeling theory.

Nevertheless, Stafford and Warr have caused researchers to rethink the sharp distinction between specific and general deterrence. Also, they have helped focus attention on an important but neglected issue regarding deterrence. Researchers have established that the perceived certainty of punishment affects the likelihood of crime, but they have not devoted much attention to those factors that influence perceptions of certainty (see Kleck et al., 2005; Nagin, 1998). This is a major shortcoming, because such research might help policymakers design programs that will increase the perceived certainty of punishment (and thereby reduce offending). Stafford and Warr, as indicated, argue that perceptions of certainly are a function of the individual's direct and indirect experiences with punishment and punishment avoidance. Researchers, however, are also discovering that a range of other factors affect perceptions of certainty. For example, perceptions of certainty are lower among those who are low in self-control, hold beliefs favorable to crime, associate with delinquent peers, and are male (e.g., Piquero and Pogarsky, 2002; Pogarsky et al., 2004; Pogarsky et al., 2005).

It should be noted that much of the recent research on deterrence involves the integration of deterrence theory with other theories of crime, such as control and learning theories. These other theories help deterrence theorists better specify those factors that influence perceptions of the certainty of punishment and that influence the effect of such perceptions on crime.

Rational Choice Theory

Like classical and deterrence theories, rational choice theory assumes that offenders are rational people who seek to maximize their pleasure and minimize their pain (see the excellent overviews in Matsueda et al., 2006; McCarthy, 2002; Piquero and Tibbetts, 2002). In fact, the leading proponents of rational choice theory, Ronald V. Clarke and Derek B. Cornish, state that rational choice theory's

> focus on offenders as rational decision makers calculating where their self-interest lies, and pursuing it, puts it squarely in the classical tradition as developed by Beccaria in the eighteenth century. (2001: 24)

Clarke and Cornish developed their version of rational choice theory in the mid-1980s (Clarke and Cornish, 1985; Cornish and Clarke, 1986), and it has come to have a major impact on our efforts to understand and control crime. Although their theory shares much in common with classical and deterrence theories, it builds on these theories in several important ways.

Clarke and Cornish take care to state that they do *not* assume that people are perfectly rational, carefully calculating and weighing the expected benefits and costs of potential crimes. Rather, they assume that

> offenders seek to benefit themselves by their criminal behavior; that this involves the making of decisions and of choices, however rudimentary on occasion these processes might

be; and that these processes exhibit a measure of rationality, albeit constrained by limits of time and ability and the availability of relevant information. (Cornish and Clarke, 1986: 1)

This "limited" or "bounded" rationality, then, involves some consideration of costs and benefits, although such consideration may be hurried and based on incomplete or inaccurate information.

Further, Clarke and Cornish define the costs of crime quite broadly. These costs include both formal and informal sanctions (e.g., the disapproval of parents), and "moral costs" —such as the guilt and shame one may experience from breaking the law. Classical and deterrence theories, by contrast, assume that the costs of crime are largely a function of formal sanctions. Rational choice theorists also recognize that people differ in their estimation of the benefits of crime—with some seeing the benefits as quite high. Such benefits include a range of things, such as money, status, and thrills/excitment. Classical and deterrence theories devote little attention to benefits of crime, often because they assume that the benefits are similar for most people.

Finally, rational choice theorists recognize that a range of factors influence individuals' estimates of the costs and benefits of crime. Rational choice theorists draw heavily on existing theories of crime when identifying such factors (see Figure 33.1 in Chapter 33 by Cornish and Clarke). And studies have confirmed that the estimated costs and benefits of crime are influenced by such factors as the individual's level of self-control, moral beliefs, strains, emotional state, and association with delinquent peers (e.g., Bouffard, 2002; Carmichael and Piquero, 2004; Exum, 2002; Fagan and Piquero, 2007; Matsueda et al., 2006; McCarthy, 1995; Piquero and Paternoster, 1998). For example, Nagin and Paternoster (1993) found that individuals who are low in self-control are more likely to estimate the costs of crime as low and the benefits as high (also see Piquero and Tibetts, 1996).

Rational choice theory, then, is much broader than classical and deterrence theory. Rational choice theory recognizes that individuals are not fully rational—although states that individuals do take some account of the costs and benefits of crime; it defines these costs and benefits quite broadly; and it recognizes that a range of factors influence individuals' estimates of these costs and benefits.

Several scholars, however, have challenged rational choice theory. They claim that some data suggest that offenders often commit crimes with little planning and little consideration for costs and benefits (see Birkbeck and LaFree, 1993; Carmichael and Piquero, 2004; Clarke and Cornish, 2001; Clarke and Felson, 1993; Cornish and Clarke, 1986; Exum, 2002; Meier and Miethe, 1993; Newman et al., 1997; Pogarsky, 2002; Tittle, 1995; Tunnel, 2002). Rather, they act impulsively, they act under the influence of alcohol and drugs, or they act under pressure from others. Further, their criminal acts do not appear to be in their self-interest. Rational choice theorists respond by arguing that they use a very broad definition of rationality and that with careful examination, crimes that seem impulsive or coerced often reveal some consideration for costs and benefits. And crimes that seem to work against the self-interest of the offender often carry benefits, although such benefits may be intangible, such as status or thrills and excitement.

The data provide some support for rational choice theory. A number of studies have examined whether people's estimates of the costs and benefits of crime influence their levels of offending (or their intentions to offend). Such studies have examined both the formal and informal costs of crime. In particular, they have examined the perceived likelihood that crime will result in official sanction, condemnation by family and friends, feelings of guilt and shame, physical harm, and economic problems. And such studies have examined a range of benefits, including the perceived likelihood that crime will result in monetary benefits, thrills/excitement, and status.

Most studies find that crime is more likely when its costs are seen as low and its benefits as high (e.g., Bachman et al. 1992; Fagan and Piquero, 2007; Matsueda et al., 2006; McCarthy, 1995, 2002; McCarthy and Hagan, 2005; Nagin and Paternoster, 1993; Pratt et al., 2006; Paternoster and Bachman, 2001; Piquero and Tibbetts, 2002; Tittle and Botchkovar, 2005; Ward et al., 2006). However, there is some evidence that individuals are less likely to be influenced by the perceived costs and benefits of crime when they are intoxicated or angry (Assaad and Exum, 2002; Carmichael and Piquero, 2004; Exum, 2002). Also, crime is not simply a function of its perceived costs and benefits. Other factors, such as level of selfcontrol, have a substantial impact on crime—even after we take account of the perceived costs and benefits of crime (e.g., Bachman et al., 1992; Nagin and Paternoster, 1993; Piquero and Paternoster, 1998; Piquero and Tibbetts, 1996).

The rational choice perspective appears to be rather different from the theories we have examined so far. These theories focus on the factors that constrain individuals to engage in crime, while the rational choice perspective argues that individuals frequently choose to engage in crime based on a consideration of costs and benefits. Certain theorists, however, have argued that the rational choice perspective is not really that different from existing crime theories (e.g., Akers, 1990). While rational choice theorists focus on choice, they devote much attention to the factors that constrain choice. These factors include variables from the leading crime theories, such as individual traits, attitudes toward crime, and the extent to which individuals have been reinforced and punished for crime (see the selection by Cornish and Clarke in Chapter 33). Further, the leading crime theories do not deny that individuals choose to engage in crime. They simply focus on those factors that constrain individual choice. These factors typically have to do with the benefits and costs of crime. This is most obviously the case with respect to social learning theory (see the Akers selection in Chapter 11), which explicitly focuses on the expected reinforcements (benefits) and punishments (costs) associated with crime. Akers (1990), in fact, has argued that rational choice theory is easily subsumed by his social learning theory.

Rational choice theory, then, is not as different from the leading crime theories as it might first appear. The theory, in fact, may be viewed as a form of integrated theory because it draws on the leading crime theories in order to more fully specify the costs and benefits associated with crime (see Figure 33.1 in the Cornish and Clarke selection). At the same time, rational choice theory has advanced our understanding of crime in several important ways.

Rational choice theorists argue that a complete explanation of crime must distinguish between "criminal involvement" and "criminal events." Criminal involvement deals with the decision to become involved in crime (as well as to continue in crime and to desist from crime). Criminal events deal with the decision to commit specific criminal acts. Most crime theories focus on the decision to become involved in crime but do not deal with the factors influencing the decision to commit a particular crime. These factors often have to do with the immediate circumstances and situation of the individual. Rational choice theory has directed much attention to these circumstances and situations and has thereby supplemented the approach of the leading crime theories. Much of the research stimulated by rational choice theory, in fact, focuses on the factors that offenders consider when they are thinking about committing a particular crime.

Rational choice theorists also argue that it is necessary to adopt a "crime-specific focus" when examining crime. That is, we should focus on particular types of crime, such as residential burglaries committed in middle-class suburbs, rather than examining all crimes together. This is because the costs and benefits associated with different types of crime may differ, particularly at the situational level. So, while the rational choice perspective may not be that different from the leading crime theories, it has moved us beyond these theories in important ways (see Clarke and Cornish, 2001; Cornish, 1993).

Rational choice theory has inspired a fair amount of research on the situational determinants of specific crimes, much of which is compatible with the broad view of rationality described above (see Clarke and Cornish, 2001; Nagin and Paternoster, 1993; Newman et al., 1997; Piquero and Tibbetts, 2002; Tunnel, 1992). Burglars, for example, often target unoccupied homes that can be easily entered with little risk of being seen by others. And rational choice theory has stimulated the development of a number of situationally based crime prevention efforts that attempt to reduce the perceived benefits and increase the perceived costs of crime. Examples include steering locks on cars, removable car radios, and the use of cameras to detect people who do not stop at red traffic signals (see Chapter 35 in this volume; Clarke, 1997; Clarke and Cornish, 2001; Clarke and Eck, 2005; Eck, 2002; Felson, 1998; Newman et al., 1997; Sherman et al., 1998). Many such efforts appear to be quite successful.

References

Agnew, Robert. 2009. *Juvenile Delinquency: Causes and Control.* New York: Oxford University Press.

Akers, Ronald. 1990. "Rational Choice, Deterrence, and Social Learning in Criminology: The Path Not Taken." *Journal of Criminal Law and Criminology* 81: 653–676.

Assaad, Jean-Marc and M. Lyn Exum. 2002. "Understanding Intoxicated Violence from a Rational Choice Perspective." In Alex R. Piquero and Stephen G. Tibbetts (eds.), *Rational Choice and Criminal Behavior*, pp. 65–85. New York: Routledge.

Bachman, Ronet, Raymond Paternoster, and Sally Ward. 1992. "The Rationality of Sexual Offending: Testing a Deterrence/Rational Choice Conception of Sexual Assault." *Law & Society Review* 26: 343–372.

Becker, Gary S. 1968. "Crime and Punishment: An Economic Approach." *Journal of Political Economy* 76: 169–217.

Bernburg, Jon Gunnar, Marvin D. Krohn, and Craig J. Rivera. 2006. "Official Labeling, Criminal Embeddeness, and Subsequent Delinquency." *Journal of Research in Crime and Delinquency* 43: 67–88.

Birkbeck, Christopher and Gary LaFree. 1993. "The Situational Analysis of Crime and Deviance." *Annual Review of Sociology* 19: 113–137.

Bonta, James, Rebecca Jesseman, Tanya Rugge, and Robert Cormier. 2006. "Restorative Justive and Recidivism." In D. Sullivan and L. Tifft (eds.), *Handbook of Restorative Justive*, pp. 108–120. New York: Routledge.

Bouffard, Jeffrey A. 2002. "The Influence of Emotion on Rational Decision Making in Sexual Aggression." *Journal of Criminal Justice* 30: 121–134.

Braga, Anthony A., Glenn L. Pierce, Jack McDevitt, Brenda J. Bond, and Shea Cronin. 2008. "The Strategic Prevention of Gun Violence Among Gang-Involved Offenders." *Justice Quarterly* 25: 132–162.

Braithwaite, John. 1989. *Crime, Shame and Reintegration*. Cambridge, England: Cambridge University Press.

——. 2002. *Restorative Justice and Responsive Regulation*. Oxford: Oxford University Press.

Braithwaite, John, Eliza Ahmed, and Valerie Braithwaite. 2006. "Shame, Restorative Justice, and Crime." In Francis T. Cullen, John Paul Wright, and Kristie R. Blevins (eds.), *Taking Stock: The Status of Criminological Theory—Advances in Criminological Theory*, Volume 15, pp. 397–417. New Brunswick, NJ: Transaction.

Carmichael, Stephanie and Alex R. Piquero. 2004. "Sanctions, Perceived Anger, and Criminal Offending." *Journal of Quantitative Criminology* 20: 371–393.

Clarke, Ronald V. 1997. *Situational Crime Prevention: Successful Case Studies*. Albany, NY: Harrow and Heston.

Clarke, Ronald V. and Derek B. Cornish. 1985. "Modeling Offenders' Decisions: A Framework for Research and Policy." In Michael Tonry and Norval Morris (eds.), *Crime and Justice: An Annual Review of Research*, Volume 6, pp. 147–185. Chicago: University of Chicago Press.

——. 2001. "Rational Choice." In Raymond Paternoster and Ronet Bachman (eds.), *Explaining Criminals and Crime*, pp. 23–42. Los Angeles: Roxbury Publishing.

Clarke, Ronald V. and John E. Eck. 2005. *Crime Analysis for Problem Solvers*. Washington, DC: Office of Community Policing Services, U.S. Department of Justice.

Clarke, Ronald V. and Marcus Felson, eds. 1993. *Advances in Criminological Theory, Volume 5: Routine Activity and Rational Choice*. New Brunswick, NJ: Transaction.

Cohen, Jacqueline, Wilpen Goor, and Piyusha Singh. 2003. "Estimating Intervention Effects in Varying Risk Settings: Do Police Raids Reduce Illegal Drug Dealing at Nuisance Bars?" *Criminology* 41: 257–292.

Cornish, Derek. 1993. "Theories of Action in Criminology: Learning Theory and Rational Choice Approaches." In Ronald V. Clarke and Marcus Felson (eds.), *Advances in Criminological Theory, Volume 5: Routine Activity and Rational Choice*, pp. 351–382. New Brunswick, NJ: Transaction.

Cornish, Derek B. and Ronald V. Clarke. 1986. *The Reasoning Criminal*. New York: Springer-Verlag.

Cullen, Francis T., Travis C. Pratt, Sharon Levrant Miceli, and Melissa M. Moon. 2002. "Dangerous Liaison? Rational Choice Theory as the Basis for Correctional Intervention." In Alex R. Piquero and Stephen G. Tibbetts (eds.), *Rational Choice and Criminal Behavior*, pp. 279–296. New York: Routledge.

Cullen, Francis T. John Paul Wright, and Brandon Applegate. 1996. "Control in the Community: The Limits of Reform." In Alan T. Harland (ed.), *Choosing Correctional Options That Work*, pp. 69–116. Thousand Oaks, CA: Sage.

Eck, John E. 2002. "Preventing Crime at Places." In Lawrence W. Sherman, David P. Farrington, Brandon C. Welsh, and Doris Layton MacKenzie (eds.), *Evidence-Based Crime Prevention*, pp. 241–294. London: Routledge.

Exum, M. Lyn. 2002. "The Application and Robustness of the Rational Choice Perspective in the Study of Intoxicated and Angry Intentions to Aggress." *Criminology* 40: 933–966.

Fagan, Jeffrey and Alex R. Piquero. 2007. "Rational Choice and Developmental Influences on Recidivism Among Adolescent Felony Offenders." *Journal of Empirical Legal Studies* 4: 715–748.

Felson, Marcus. 2002. *Crime and Everyday Life*, 3rd edition. Thousand Oaks, CA: Pine Forge Press.

Foglia, Wanda D. 1997. "Perceptual Deterrence and the Mediating Effect of Internalized Norms Among Inner-City Teenagers." *Journal of Research in Crime and Delinquency* 34: 414–442.

Huizinga, David, Anne Wylie Weiher, Rachele Espiritu, and Finn Esbensen. 2003. "Delinquency and Crime: Some Highlights From the Denver Youth Survey." In Terence P. Thornberry and Marvin Krohn (eds.), *Taking Stock of Delinquency*, pp. 47–91. New York: Kluwer Academic.

Kleck, Gary, Brion Sever, Spencer Li, and Marc Gertz. 2005. "The Missing Link in General Deterence Research." *Criminology* 43: 623–660.

Kovandzic, Tomislav V., John J. Sloan III, and Lynne M. Vieraitis. 2004. "'Striking Out' as Crime Reduction Policy: The Impact of 'Three Strikes' Law on Crime Rates in U.S. Cities." *Justice Quarterly* 21: 207–239.

Levitt, Steven D. 2002. "Deterrence." In James Q. Wilson and Joan Petersilia (eds.), *Crime*, pp. 435–450. Oakland, CA: ICS Press.

Matsueda, Ross L., Derek A. Keager, and David Huizinga. 2006. "Deterring Delinquents: A Rational Choice Model of Theft and Violence." *American Sociological Review* 71: 95–122.

McCarthy, Bill. 1995. "Not Just 'for the Thrill of It': An Instrumentalist Elaboration of Katz's Explanation of Sneaky Thrill Property Crime." *Criminology* 33: 519–538.

——. 2002. "New Economics of Sociological Criminology." *Annual Review of Sociology* 28: 417–442.

McCarthy, Bill and John Hagan. 2005. "Danger and the Decision to Offend." *Social Forces* 83: 1065–1096.

McGarrell, Edmund F. Steven Chermak, Jeremy M. Wilson, and Nicholas Corsaro. 2006. "Reducing Homicide Through a 'Lever-Pulling' Strategy." *Justice Quarterly* 23: 214–231.

McGarell, Edmund F. and Nataliev Kroovand Hipple. 2007. "Family Group Conferencing and Re-Offending Among First-Time Juvenile Offenders." *Justice Quarterly* 24: 221–246.

Meier, Robert F. and Terance D. Miethe. 1993. "Understanding Theories of Criminal Victimization." In Michael Tonry (ed.), *Crime and Justice*, Volume 17, pp. 459–499. Chicago: University of Chicago Press.

Nagin, Daniel S. 1998. "General Deterrence: A Review of the Empirical Evidence." In Michael Tonry (ed.), *Crime and Justice: A Review of Research*, Volume 23, pp. 1–42. Chicago: University of Chicago Press.

Nagin, Daniel S. and Raymond Paternoster. 1994. "Personal Capital and Social Control: The Deterrence Implications of a Theory of Individual Differences in Criminal Offending." *Criminology* 32: 581–606.

Nagin, Daniel S. and Greg Pogarsky. 2001. "Integrating Celerity, Impulsivity, and Extralegal Sanction Threats Into a Model of General Deterrence: Theory and Evidence." *Criminology* 39: 865–892.

Newman, Graeme, Ronald V. Clarke, and S. Giora Shoman, eds. 1997. *Rational Choice and*

Situational Crime Prevention. Aldershot, England: Ashgate.

Osgood, D. Wayne, Janet K. Wilson, Patrick O'Malley, Jerald G. Bachman, and Lloyd D. Johnson. 1996. "Routine Activities and Individual Deviant Behavior." *American Sociological Review* 61: 635–655.

Paternoster, Raymond and Ronet Bachman, eds. 2001. "Classical and Neuve Classical Schools of Criminology: Deterrence, Rational Choice, and Situational Theories of Crime." In *Explaining Criminals and Crime*, pp. 11–22. Los Angeles: Roxbury Publishing.

Paternoster, Raymond, Robert Brame, Ronet Bachman, and Lawrence W. Sherman. 1997. "Do Fair Procedures Matter? The Effect of Procedural Justice on Spouse Assault." *Law and Society Review* 31: 163–204.

Paternoster, Raymond and Alex Piquero. 1995. "Reconceptualizing Deterrence: An Empirical Test of Personal and Vicarious Experiences." *Journal of Research in Crime and Delinquency* 32: 251–286.

Piquero, Alex R., Zenta Gomez-Smith, and Lynn Langton. 2004. "Discerning Unfairness Where Others May Not: Low Self-Control and Unfair Sanction Perceptions." *Criminology* 42: 699–734.

Piquero, Alex and Raymond Paternoster. 1998. "An Application of Stafford and Warr's Reconceptualization of Deterrence to Drinking and Driving." *Journal of Research in Crime and Delinquency* 35: 3–39.

Piquero, Alex R. and Greg Pogarsky. 2002. "Beyond Stafford and Warr's Reconceptualization of Deterrence: Personal and Vicarious Experiences, Impulsivity, and Offending Behavior." *Journal of Research in Crime and Delinquency* 39: 153–186.

Piquero, Alex and Stephen Tibbetts. 1996. "Specifying the Direct and Indirect Effects of Low Self-Control and Situational Factors in Offenders' Decision Making: Toward a More Complete Model of Rational Offending." *Justice Quarterly* 13: 481–510.

——. 2002. *Rational Choice and Criminal Behavior*. New York: Routledge.

——. 2002. "Identifying 'Deterrable' Offenders: Implications for Research on Deterrence." *Justice Quarterly* 19: 431–452.

Pogarsky, Greg. 2007. "Deterrence and Individual Differences Among Convicted Offenders." *Journal of Quantitative Criminology* 23: 59–74.

Pogarsky, Greg, KiDeuck Kim, and Ray Paternoster. 2005. "Perceptual Change in the National Youth Survey: Lessons for Deterrence Theory and Offender Decision-Making." *Justice Quarterly* 22: 1–29.

Pogarsky, Greg and Alex R. Piquero. 2003. "Can Punishment Encourage Offending? Investigating the 'Resetting' Effect." *Journal of Research in Crime and Delinquency* 40: 95–120.

Pogarsky, Greg, Alex R. Piquero, and Ray Paternoster. 2004. "Modeling Change in Perceptions About Sanction Threats: The Neglected Linkage in Deterrence Theory." *Journal of Quantitative Criminology* 20: 343–369.

Pratt, Travis C., Francis T. Cullen, Kristie R. Blevins, Leah E. Daigle, and Tamara D. Madensen. 2006. "The Empirical Status of Deterrence Theory: A Meta-Analysis." In Francis T. Cullen, John Paul Wright, and Kristie R. Blevins (eds.), *Taking Stock: The Status of Criminological Theory—Advances in Criminological Theory*, Volume 15. New Brunswick, NJ: Transaction.

Sherman, Larry W. 1993. "Defiance, Deterrence, and Irrelevance: A Theory of the Criminal Sanction." *Journal of Research in Crime and Delinquency* 30: 445–473.

Sherman, Lawrence W., Denise Gottfredson, Doris MacKenzie, John Eck, Peter Reuter, and Shawn Bushway. 1998. *Preventing Crime: What Works, What Doesn't, What's Promising*. Available at <www.preventingcrime.org>.

Sherman, Lawrence W., Douglas A. Smith, Janell D. Schmidt, and Dennis Rogan. 1992. "Crime, Punishment, and Stake in Conformity: Legal and Informal Control of Domestic Violence." *American Sociological Review* 57: 680–690.

Sherman, Lawrence W. and David Weisburd. 1995. "General Deterrent Effects of Police Patrol in

Crime 'Hot Spots': A Randomized, Controlled Trial." *Justice Quarterly* 12: 625–648.

Sitren, Alicia H. and Brandon K. Applegate. 2007. "Testing the Deterrent Effects of Personal and Vicarious Experience with Punishment and Punishment Avoidance." *Deviant Behavior* 28: 29–55.

Stafford, Mark C. and Mark Warr. 1993. "A Reconceptualization of General and Specific Deterrence." *Journal of Research in Crime and Delinquency* 30: 123–135.

Tittle, Charles R. 1995. *Control Balance: Toward a General Theory of Deviance.* Boulder, CO: Westview.

Tittle, Charles R. and Ekaterina V. Botchkovar. 2005. "Self-Control, Criminal Motivation and Deterrence: An Investigation Using Russian Respondents." *Criminology* 43: 307–354.

Tonry, Michael. 2008. "Learning from the Limitations of Deterrence Research." *Crime & Justice* 37: 279–308.

Tunnel, Kenneth D. 1992. *Choosing Crime.* Chicago: Nelson-Hall.

——. 2002. "The Impulsiveness and Routinization of Decision-Making." In Alex R. Piquero and Stephen G. Tibbetts (eds.), *Rational Choice and Criminal Behavior,* pp. 265–278. New York: Routledge.

Ward, David A., Mark C. Stafford, and Louis N. Gray. 2006. "Rational Choice, Deterrence, and Theoretical Integration." *Journal of Applied Social Psychology* 36: 571–585.

Weisburd, David, Elin Waring, and Ellen Chayet. 1995. "Specific Deterrence in a Sample of Offenders Convicted of White-Collar Crimes." *Criminology* 33: 587–607.

Weisburd, David, Tomer Einat, and Matt Kowalski. 2008. "The Miracle of the Cells: An Experimental Study of Interventions to Increase Payment of Court-Ordered Financial Obligations." *Criminology & Public Policy* 7: 9–36.

Wikstrom, Per-Olof H. 2008. "Deterrence and Deterrence Experiences: Preventing Crime Through the Threat of Punishment." In Shlomo, Giora Shoham, Ori Beck, and Martin Kett (eds.), *International Handbook of Penology and Criminal Justice,* pp. 345–378. Boca Raton, FL: CRC Press.

Wooldredge, John and Amy Thistlethwaite. 2002. "Reconsidering Domestic Violence Recidivism: Conditioned Effects of Legal Controls by Individual and Aggregate Levels of Stake in Conformity." *Journal of Quantitative Criminology* 18: 45–70.

Wright, Bradley R. E., Avshalom Caspi, Terrie E. Moffitt and Ray Paternoster. 2004. "Does the Perceived Risk of Punishment Deter Criminally Prone Individuals? Rational Choice, Self-Control, and Crime." *Journal of Research in Crime and Delinquency* 41: 180–213.

32. Reconceptualizing Deterrence Theory

Mark C. Stafford and Mark Warr

Most deterrence theorists make a sharp distinction between specific and general deterrence. Specific deterrence means that punishing offenders for their crimes deters those specific offenders from further crime. General deterrence means that punishing some offenders deters people in the general population from crime, including those who were not punished. Specific and general deterrence are said to refer to distinct populations: punished offenders in the first case and the general public in the second. Specific deterrence deals with direct experiences with punishment, while general deterrence deals with indirect experiences with punishment (knowledge of the punishments received by others).

Stafford and Warr question this sharp distinction. They argue that the same people are often subject to both specific and general deterrence. In particular, individuals often have both direct and indirect experiences with punishment (e.g., knowledge of friends and neighbors who have been punished). Also, Stafford and Warr argue that deterrence theorists need to consider experiences with punishment avoidance. That is, have individuals been able to avoid punishment for any of their crimes or are they aware of others who have avoided punishment for their crimes? The authors argue that crime is a function of both direct and indirect experiences with punishment and punishment avoidance, and that researchers who consider all four of these factors should find more

support for deterrence theory. Most researchers, however, consider only direct experiences with punishment (if they are examining specific deterrence) or indirect experiences with punishment (if they are examining general deterrence).

As indicated in the Introduction to Part X, preliminary data provide some support for Stafford and Warr's reconceptualization of deterrence theory. Both direct and indirect experiences with punishment and punishment avoidance affect perceptions of the certainty of punishment (and thereby crime). However, certain studies suggest that—contrary to Statfford and Warr's theory—direct experiences with punishment reduce perceptions of certainty and increase the likelihood of further crime (see Piquero and Pogarsky, 2002).

Reference

Piquero, Alex R. and Greg Pogarsky. 2002. "Beyond Stafford and Warr's Reconceptualization of Deterrence: Personal and Vicarious Experiences, Impulsivity, and Offending Behavior." *Journal of Research in Crime and Delinquency* 39: 153–186.

T he conception of deterrence that guides... research has remained largely unchanged. A key element of that conception is the distinction between general and specific deterrence. Virtually

Mark C. Stafford and Mark Warr, "A Reconceptualization of General and Specific Deterrence," *Journal of Research in Crime and Delinquency* (30)2, pp. 123–128, 133–135, copyright © 1993 by Sage Publications. Reprinted by permission of Sage Publications, Inc.

all definitions of those phenomena point in one way or another to this distinction: Whereas general deterrence refers to the effects of legal punishment on the general public (i.e., potential offenders), specific deterrence pertains to the effects of legal punishment on those who have suffered it (i.e., punished offenders; for a review, see Gibbs 1975, pp. 32–39). For example, Nagin (1978) defines general deterrence as the

> imposition of sanctions on one person [in order to] demonstrate to the rest of the public the expected costs of a criminal act, and thereby discourage criminal behavior in the general population. (p. 96)

In contrast, Andenaes (1968) states that if persons are "deterred by the actual experience of punishment, we speak of *special* [specific] *deterrence*" (p. 78).

Both definitions recognize the importance of some kind of experience with legal punishment in deterring persons from committing crimes. But for members of the general public (general deterrence) it is indirect experience with punishment (observing or otherwise having knowledge of the punishment of others) that deters, whereas for punished offenders (specific deterrence) it is direct (personal) experience (Meier and Johnson 1977, pp. 294–95).

This conception of general and specific deterrence is widely recognized and accepted by criminologists, but it has serious shortcomings. Put briefly, we will argue that the conventional distinction between general and specific deterrence rests on faulty logic and that it has done little to clarify the deterrence process. After presenting these arguments, we propose a reconceptualization of general and specific deterrence, and apply it to some current controversies in the deterrence literature.

Distinguishing General and Specific Deterrence

Deterrence studies are classified commonly as bearing on one type of deterrence or the other, with most purportedly involving general rather than specific deterrence (see reviews by Gibbs 1975, chap. 5; Tittle 1980, chap. 1; Zimring and Hawkins 1973, chap. 4). However, the rationale for such classification is not entirely clear.

Consider a hypothetical study of what is likely to be regarded as general deterrence. In such a case, investigators might focus on persons who have never suffered any legal punishment for any crime, on the grounds that such persons have knowledge of punishment, if at all, only indirectly from the experiences of others (Gibbs 1975, pp. 34, 37). However, there are two kinds of people who have never suffered a legal punishment: (a) those who have never committed any crime (ignoring the possibility that innocent persons can be punished) and (b) those who have committed crimes but have avoided punishment. Only the first kind of person can be said to have no direct experience with legal punishment. Although the second kind of person has not suffered a legal punishment, he or she has by definition acquired experience with *avoiding punishment*, and that experience is likely to affect the chances of committing crimes again. In particular, experience with avoiding punishment is likely to affect perceptions of the certainty and severity of punishment, the two principal variables in recent deterrence studies. Of these two variables, perceptions of certainty should be affected more strongly by punishment avoidance, because getting away with a crime provides little information about the legal consequences of being caught (Paternoster 1987, p. 189; Paternoster, Saltzman, Waldo, and Chiricos 1983a, p. 281, 1983b, p. 458).

Like the concept of deterrence, which involves the omission of legally proscribed acts (Gibbs 1975, p. 3; Meier and Johnson 1977), the notion of punishment avoidance may be somewhat difficult to imagine because it refers to events that did *not* happen. However, unlike deterrence, punishment avoidance is also contingent on events that did occur, that is, the commission of crimes. Hence, in contrast to deterrence, punishment avoidance is not inherently unobservable. For example, everyone who drives in urban

America has observed another person driving in a reckless manner with no legal punishment, or has witnessed such criminal events as driving while intoxicated that did not even come to the attention of the police.

To some, the concept of punishment avoidance may appear to add little to deterrence theory, because punishment avoidance is simply the opposite of punishment itself. The distinction may be logically banal, but it is potentially critical for empirical reasons. To illustrate, it is possible that punishment avoidance does more to encourage crime than punishment does to discourage it. Offenders whose experience is limited largely to avoiding punishment may come to believe that they are immune from punishment, even in the face of occasional evidence to the contrary. Perhaps the greatest value of the concept is that it underscores the fundamental principle that no criminal act is without consequences. In the wake of a crime, offenders always will experience punishment or punishment avoidance, and it is dubious to argue that only the former impacts subsequent behavior.

The immediate point is that what usually is taken to be general deterrence is not limited necessarily to persons who have no direct experience with legal punishment. The point is crucial because, if self-report data are to be believed, there are few persons (at-least among young males) who have never avoided punishment, especially for minor offenses (for a review, see Empey and Stafford 1991, chap. 6). Consequently, the conventional distinction between general and specific deterrence rests more on the *nature* of prior direct experience with legal punishment than on the mere presence of such experience.

Direct and Indirect Experience with Punishment

Now consider a related problem with specific deterrence. Studies of specific deterrence typically focus on punished offenders (or comparisons of punished and unpunished offenders) and examine the frequency of post-punishment offending for evidence of deterrence (e.g., Murray and Cox 1979; Schneider and Ervin 1990; Smith and Gartin 1989). There is nothing intrinsically wrong with this procedure, but investigators commonly assume that an offender's direct experience with suffering a punishment is the only operative variable when it comes to predicting future behavior. In addition to ignoring the offender's experience with avoiding punishment, such an assumption overlooks the possibility that one can suffer a legal punishment and at the same time have knowledge of punishment from the experiences of others (i.e., have indirect experience with punishment).

Suppose that an individual is caught and fined after shoplifting and that this is his or her first offense of any type. The direct experience of being fined is likely to be salient, but surely its deterrent efficacy will depend on whether the individual believes or knows that other persons (particularly others like him or her) have a similar certainty and severity of punishment, or whether he or she believes that in this particular instance the punishment was ill-fated and others would have gotten away with the crime, or that they would have received a less (or more) severe punishment (Ward, Menke, Gray, and Stafford 1986, pp. 502–3).

The point to be emphasized is that in most populations—whether members of the general public or punished offenders—people are likely to have a *mixture* of indirect and direct experience with punishment and punishment avoidance. That point is not lost on all deterrence researchers. For example, Lempert (1982, p. 532), in a study of enforcement of child-support orders, observes that men who have been jailed for nonpayment often meet or hear of others who are in jail for the same offense. Hence, these men gain both direct and indirect experience with legal punishment (p. 549). However, by adopting the conventional distinction between general and specific deterrence, investigators perpetuate the notion that the two forms of deterrence occur among distinct populations.

The problem with such a notion becomes clearer when one considers that offenders often commit more than one type of crime, and that they may or may not suffer a legal punishment for each type. Consider a person who is caught and punished after committing his or her first burglary, but who has also committed other crimes (e.g., drug use, robbery, auto theft) and avoided punishment in each case. To claim that the direct experience of being punished for the burglary is the only relevant consideration in predicting the offender's future behavior is to ignore what has been said about the potential effects of punishment avoidance, not to mention the potential effects of indirect experience with punishment. Putting it more carefully, there are four relevant considerations in the example at hand: (a) the direct experience with suffering the punishment for the burglary, (b) the direct experience with punishment avoidance for the other crimes, (c) indirect experience with punishment and punishment avoidance for the burglary, and (d) indirect experience with punishment and punishment avoidance for the other crimes.

One possibility is that the direct experience with punishment for the burglary could reduce the offender's likelihood of repeating the other crimes (e.g., by increasing the perceived certainty of punishment for these offenses). However, it could also work in the reverse—the direct experience of getting away with the other crimes could increase the chances of committing further burglaries. And when one considers *indirect* experience with punishment and punishment avoidance for all of the offenses, there are still other possibilities. For example, the arrest of fellow offenders for the same crime(s) might lead to the conclusion that the odds of arrest have increased substantially.

An underlying assumption in all such possibilities is that people may estimate the certainty and severity of punishment for a particular type of crime by reference to crimes in general or at least similar types of offenses (e.g., all property crimes) rather than from information that is "crime-specific" (Gibbs 1975, p. 35; Erickson and Gibbs 1975; Paternoster 1986). If so, it almost certainly

will be true that a mixture of indirect and direct experiences with legal punishment and punishment avoidance will be relevant for most persons. Even if people estimate certainty and severity entirely from crime-specific information, a mixture of punishment experiences is likely to be relevant, and research is needed on such questions as whether direct experience with punishment and punishment avoidance affects the deterrent efficacy of indirect experience (Zimring and Hawkins 1973, pp. 224–29).

A Reconceptualization

The conceptual problems outlined above stem, we believe, from the manner in which general and specific deterrence commonly are defined. That is, the practice of distinguishing general and specific deterrence by reference to distinct populations (either the general public or punished offenders) tends to obfuscate critical issues. Instead, we propose that the distinction between the two types of deterrence be limited to contrasting kinds of experience with legal punishment. If deterrence is defined as the omission or curtailment of a criminal act out of fear of legal punishment (Gibbs 1975, p. 39), then general deterrence refers to the deterrent effect of *indirect experience with punishment and punishment avoidance* and specific deterrence refers to the deterrent effect of *direct experience with punishment and punishment avoidance*.

The proposed reconceptualization has several advantages over that currently in use. First, it recognizes the possibility that *both* general and specific deterrence can operate for any given person or in any population. Second, it treats punishment avoidance as analytically distinct from the experience of suffering a punishment.

A third advantage of the proposed reconceptualization of general and specific deterrence is its compatibility with contemporary learning theory, particularly the distinction between observational/vicarious learning and experiential learning (for discussions of the connection between deterrence concepts/principles and learning theory, see Akers 1990; Cavender 1979; Moffitt 1983). Bandura (1977), for example, argues that experiential learning

> results from the positive and negative effects that actions produce. When people deal with everyday events, some of their responses prove successful, while others have no effect or result in punishing outcomes. Through this process of differential reinforcement, successful forms of behavior are eventually selected and ineffectual ones are discarded. (p. 17)

As for observational or vicarious learning, Bandura (1977) notes that

> people can profit from the successes and mistakes of others as well as from their own experiences. In everyday situations numerous opportunities exist to observe the actions of others and the occasions on which they are rewarded, ignored, or punished.... Observed outcomes can alter behavior in their own right in much the same way as directly experienced consequences. (p. 117)

Just as recent versions of learning theory suggest that any behavior is likely to be a consequence of both observational/vicarious learning and experiential learning (e.g., Akers, Krohn, Lanza-Kaduce, and Radosevich 1979, p. 638; Bandura 1977, chap. 2), the basic premise of the proposed reconceptualization is that the rate of crime in virtually any population will be a function of both general and specific deterrence. This is not to say that the two types of deterrence will be equally important from one population to the next (Gray, Ward, Stafford, and Menke 1985, pp. 83–84). Among persons with limited direct experience with punishment and/or punishment avoidance, the rate of crime is more likely to be a function of general deterrence (indirect experience with punishment and punishment avoidance). Indeed, in the special case of persons who have no direct experience with punishment or

punishment avoidance—those who have never committed any crimes at all—the only possibly relevant consideration is general deterrence. However, among persons who have been punished many times and/or have avoided punishment repeatedly (i.e., habitual offenders), their criminal behavior should be largely a function of specific deterrence (direct experience with punishment and punishment avoidance). The implication is that individuals can be viewed as falling along a continuum characterized by general deterrence at one extreme and specific deterrence at the other....

Conclusions

While no conception is right or wrong, some are more useful than others. For more than two decades, deterrence researchers have complained that there is no systematic theory of deterrence (e.g., Gibbs 1968, p. 530, 1975, p. 2; Tittle 1985, pp. 285–87; Zintring 1978, p. 172), which is a tacit admission that conventional conceptions of general and specific deterrence have provided little or no impetus to such theorizing. As Zimring and Hawkins (1973) observe, most researchers "who ... draw this distinction [between general and specific deterrence] make no further use of it" (p. 73).

The proposed reconceptualization suggests that it is unnecessary to formulate separate theories of general and specific deterrence. Rather, a single theory is possible that centers on indirect experience with legal punishment and punishment avoidance and direct experience with legal punishment and punishment avoidance. Recognizing that people may think of punishment for crimes in general rather than in crime-specific terms, such a theory would need to consider indirect and direct experience with punishment and punishment avoidance for crimes other than those that individuals actually have committed.

Unfortunately, if the proposed reconceptualization is accepted, tests of the deterrence doctrine necessarily will become more complex.

For example, tests based on survey data would need to include, at a minimum, measures of (a) person's perceptions of their own certainty and severity of legal punishment for crimes, (b) person's perceptions of the certainty and severity of legal punishment for others (presumably those within their immediate social network), (c) self-reported criminal behavior, including self-reports of direct experience with punishment and punishment avoidance, and (d) estimates of peers's criminal behavior, including their experiences with punishment and punishment avoidance.

Of course, there are alternatives to a survey methodology, such as an experimental design. Indeed, an experimental design might facilitate an assessment of the separate effects of indirect and direct experience with legal punishment and punishment avoidance on crime (see, e.g., Sherman and Berk 1984). However, only a very complex experimental design can facilitate an examination of the *relative* effects of indirect and direct experience with punishment and punishment avoidance, which may be the more important issue as far as a theory of deterrence is concerned.

Discussion Questions

1. Describe the difference between specific and general deterrence. Give an example of a situation where there is a specific deterrent effect but no general deterrent effect.
2. Why is it important to consider experiences with punishment avoidance?
3. Suppose you want to determine whether sanctions at your school deter cheating. Drawing on Stafford and Warr, describe the types of questions you would need to ask in a survey to properly test deterrence theory.
4. Assuming that Stafford and Warr are correct in their reconceptualization of deterrence theory, what policies would you recommend for reducing cheating at your school? (Be creative, do not simply say that more cheaters should be punished.)
5. Stafford and Warr discuss direct and indirect experiences with punishment and punishment avoidance. Do you think any of these four factors has a larger effect on crime than the others? What conditions might influence the relative importance of these factors?

33. Crime as a Rational Choice

Derek B. Cornish and Ronald V. Clarke

The rational choice perspective draws heavily on classical theory and economic theories of crime, and argues that "crimes are broadly the result of rational choices based on analyses of anticipated costs and benefits" (Cornish and Clarke, 1986: vi). Individuals, then, choose to engage in crime in an effort to maximize their benefits and minimize their costs. This choice process occurs in two major stages.

First, individuals decide whether they are willing to become involved in crime to satisfy their needs (the "initial involvement model"). Individuals may consider a range of different ways of satisfying their needs—some criminal and some not. Whether they decide to engage in crime is heavily influenced by their previous learning and experience, including their moral code, view of themselves, personal and vicarious experiences of crime, and the degree to which they can plan and exercise foresight (Clarke and Cornish, 1985: 166). Their previous learning and experience, in turn, are heavily influenced by a range of background factors, including individual traits, their upbringing, and their social and demographic characteristics (e.g., sex, class). Most of the factors said to influence this decision to become involved in crime are drawn from the leading crime theories, discussed in previous sections.

Second, once individuals decide they are ready to engage in crime, they must decide to commit a particular offense (the "criminal event model"). This decision is heavily influenced by the immediate situation of the individual. The individual may have a desperate need for money or may be out with friends who suggest engaging in crime. The individual then selects a target for the offense (e.g., a home to burglarize) based on a consideration of costs and benefits (e.g., is the home occupied, is it easily accessible, is there reason to believe that it contains valuable items). The factors that individuals consider may differ dramatically from one type of crime to another, which is why rational choice theorists argue that "crime-specific" models must be employed. That is, different models of decision making are necessary for different types of crime. The leading crime theories have paid little attention to those factors that influence the decision to commit a particular criminal offense, and one of the leading contributions of rational choice theory has been to focus attention on this area. Research in this area has also contributed to the development of crime control strategies (see Chapter 35 in this volume; Clarke, 1992; Eck, 2002).

References

Clarke, Ronald V. 1992. *Situational Crime Prevention.* New York: Harrow and Heston.

Clarke, Ronald V. and Derek B. Cornish. 1985. "Modeling Offenders' Decisions: A Framework for Research and Policy." In Michael Tonry and Norval Morris (eds.), *Crime and Justice: An Annual Review of Research*, Volume 6,

Reprinted from Derek. B. Cornish and Ronald V. Clarke, "Crime as a Rational Choice" in *The Reasoning Criminal.* Copyright © 1986 by Springer-Verlag. Reprinted by permission of Springer-Verlag.

pp. 147–185. Chicago: University of Chicago Press.

Cornish, Derek B. and Ronald V. Clarke. 1986. *The Reasoning Criminal.* New York: Springer-Verlag.

Eck, John E. 2002. "Preventing Crime at Places." In Lawrence W. Sherman, David P. Farrington, Brandon C. Welsh, and Doris Layton MacKenzie (eds.), *Evidence-Based Crime Prevention,* pp. 241–294. London: Routledge.

———————

The synthesis we had suggested—a rational choice perspective on criminal behavior—was intended to locate criminological findings within a framework particularly suitable for thinking about policy-relevant research. Its starting point was an assumption that offenders seek to benefit themselves by their criminal behavior; that this involves the making of decisions and of choices, however rudimentary on occasion these processes might be; and that these processes exhibit a measure of rationality, albeit constrained by limits of time and ability and the availability of relevant information. It was recognized that this conception of crime seemed to fit some forms of offending better than others. However, even in the case of offenses that seemed to be pathologically motivated or impulsively executed, it was felt that rational components were also often present and that the identification and description of these might have lessons for crime-control policy.

Second, a crime-specific focus was adopted, not only because different crimes may meet different needs, but also because the situational context of decision making and the information being handled will vary greatly among offenses. To ignore these differences might well be to reduce significantly one's ability to identify fruitful points for intervention (similar arguments have been applied to other forms of "deviant" behavior, such as gambling: cf. Cornish, 1978). A crime-specific focus is likely to involve rather finer distinctions than those commonly made in criminology. For example, it may not be sufficient to divide burglary simply into its residential and commercial forms. It may also be necessary to distinguish between burglaries committed in middle-class suburbs, in public housing, and in wealthy residential enclaves. Empirical studies suggest that the kinds of individuals involved in these different forms of residential burglary, their motivations, and their methods all vary considerably (cf. Clarke and Hope, 1984, for a review). Similar cases could be made for distinguishing between different forms of robbery, rape, shoplifting, and car theft to take some obvious cases. (In lay thinking, of course, such distinctions are also often made, as between mugging and other forms of robbery, for example.) A corollary of this requirement is that the explanatory focus of the theory is on crimes, rather than on offenders. Such a focus, we believe, provides a counterweight to theoretical and policy preoccupations with the offender.

Third, it was argued that a decision-making approach to crime requires that a fundamental distinction be made between criminal involvement and criminal events. Criminal involvement refers to the processes through which individuals choose to become initially involved in particular forms of crime, to continue, and to desist. The decision processes in these different stages of involvement will be influenced in each case by a different set of factors and will need to be separately modeled. In the same way, the decision processes involved in the commission of a specific crime (i.e., the criminal event) will utilize their own special categories of information. Involvement decisions are characteristically multistage, extend over substantial periods of time, and will draw upon a large range of information, not all of which will be directly related to the crimes themselves. Event decisions, on the other hand, are frequently shorter processes, utilizing more circumscribed information largely relating to immediate circumstances and situations.

The above points can be illustrated by consideration of some flow diagrams that the editors previously developed (Clarke and Cornish, 1985) to model one specific form of crime, namely, burglary in a middle-class residential suburb. Figure 33.1, which represents the processes of initial involvement in this form of crime, has two decision points. The first (Box 7) is the individual's recognition of his or her "readiness" to commit the specific offense in order to satisfy certain needs for money, goods, or excitement. The preceding boxes indicate

Figure 33.1
Initial Involvement Model (example: burglary in a middle-class suburb)

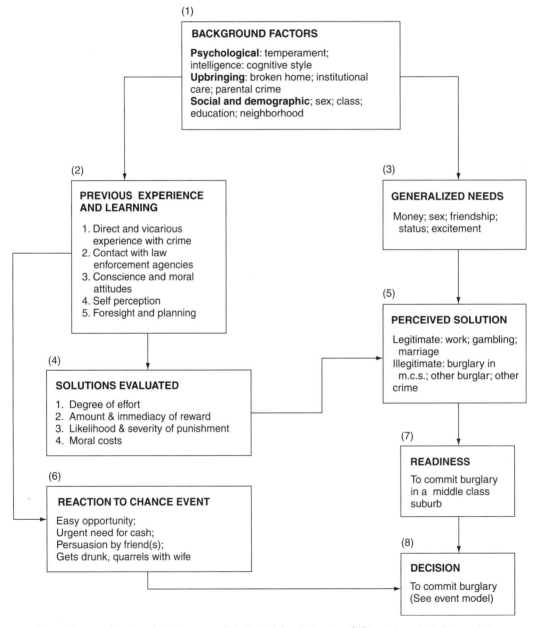

Source: *Crime and Justice*, vol. 6. M. Tonry and N. Norris (eds.), University of Chicago Press, 1985. By permission.

Figure 33.2
Event Model (example: burglary in a middle-class suburb)

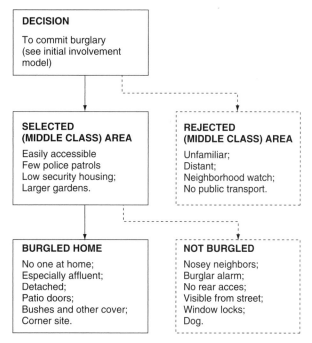

Source: *Crime and Justice*, vol. 6. M. Tonry and N. Norris (eds.), University of Chicago Press, 1985. By permission.

Figure 33.3
Continuing Involvement Model (example: burglary in a middle-class suburb)

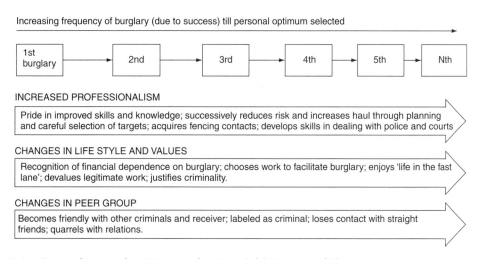

Source: *Crime and Justice*, vol. 6. M. Tonry and N. Norris (eds.), University of Chicago Press, 1985. By permission.

the wide range of factors that bring the individual to this condition. Box 1, in particular, encompasses the various historical (and contemporaneous) background factors with which traditional criminology has been preoccupied; these have been seen to determine the values, attitudes, and personality traits that dispose the individual to crime. In a rational choice context, however, these factors are reinterpreted as influencing the decisions and judgments that lead to involvement. The second decision (Box 8) actually to commit this form of burglary is the outcome of some chance event, such as an urgent need for cash, which demands action.

Figure 33.2, which is much simpler, depicts the further sequence of decision making that leads to the burglar selecting a particular house. The range of variables influencing this decision sequence is much narrower and reflects the influence of situational factors related to opportunity, effort, and proximal risks. In most cases this decision sequence takes place quite quickly. Figure 33.3 sketches the classes of variables, relating to changes in the individual's degree of professionalism, peer group, life-style, and values, that influence the constantly reevaluated decision to continue with this form of burglary.

Figure 33.4 illustrates, with hypothetical data, similar reevaluations that may lead to desistance.

Figure 33.4
Desistance Model (example: burglary in a middle-class suburb)

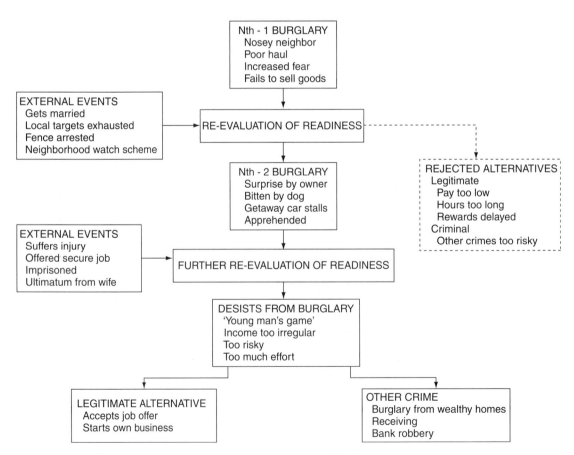

Source: *Crime and Justice*, vol. 6. M. Tonry and N. Norris (eds.), University of Chicago Press, 1985. By permission.

In this case, two classes of variables are seen to have a cumulative effect: life-events (such as marriage), and those more directly related to the criminal events themselves.

These, then, are the main features of the framework that was developed out of our review of recent work in a variety of disciplines that have an interest in crime. It differs from most existing formal theories of criminal behavior, however, in a number of respects. It is true that, like many other criminological theories, the rational choice perspective is intended to provide a framework for understanding all forms of crime. Unlike other approaches, however, which attempt to impose a conceptual unity upon divergent criminal behaviors (by subsuming them under more general concepts such as delinquency, deviance, rule breaking, short-run hedonism, criminality, etc.), our rational choice formulation sees these differences as crucial to the tasks of explanation and control. Unlike existing theories, which tend to concentrate on factors disposing individuals to criminal behavior (the initial involvement model), the rational choice approach, in addition, emphasizes subsequent decisions in the offender's career. Again, whereas most existing theories tend to accord little influence to situational variables, the rational choice approach explicitly recognizes their importance in relation to the criminal event and, furthermore, incorporates similar influences on decisions relating to involvement in crime. In consequence, this perspective also recognizes, as do economic and behaviorist theories, the importance of incentives—that is, of rewards and punishments—and hence the role of learning in the criminal career. Finally, the leitmotif encapsulated in the notion of a "reasoning" offender implies the essentially nonpathological and commonplace nature of much criminal activity. . . .

Discussion Questions

1. Does the rational choice perspective assume that offenders carefully plan all crimes?
2. Cornish and Clarke argue that we must employ a "crime-specific focus" when attempting to describe the costs and benefits offenders consider in planning their crimes. Pick two different crimes and describe how the benefits and costs that offenders may consider might differ for these crimes.
3. In discussing "criminal involvement," Cornish and Clarke distinguish between the decisions to become involved in crime, continue in crime, and desist from crime. They state that each of these decisions is influenced by different sets of factors. Describe the factors that might be relevant for each of these decisions.
4. Akers (1990) has argued that rational choice theory can be subsumed under his social learning theory (see Chapter 11 in Part IV). Do you agree?

PART XI

Environmental Criminology

Traditionally, theories of crime have focused on offenders and, in particular, on why some people are motivated to break the law. In contrast, environmental criminology is concerned not with criminals but with crime (Bottoms, 1994; Pease, 1994). Of course, for a crime to occur, there must be a criminal—that is, someone ready to offend. But there must also be another ingredient present for a criminal act to be completed: The person must also have the *opportunity to commit the crime* (see also Cloward, 1959; Cullen, 1984).

This simple observation—that is, that crime occurs only when an offender and the opportunity to offend are both present—has profound implications. Most traditional theories operate on the assumption that explaining opportunity is of secondary importance—that offenders are sufficiently motivated to find ways to break the law. Environmental criminology, however, shows that as an integral ingredient in crime, the presence or absence of opportunity shapes when and where crime events take place. The distribution of crime is thus influenced by the distribution of criminal opportunities (Cloward, 1959; Cloward and Ohlin, 1960).

Furthermore, this perspective opens up fresh ideas about *crime prevention*. Because crime is attributable to two elements—offenders and opportunities—it becomes possible to stop a crime from happening by removing either one of these two essential ingredients. Environmental criminologists suggest that manipulating opportunities is far easier than trying to make people less criminally motivated and thus is a more promising strategy for crime prevention (Clarke, 1980 [Chapter 35 in this part]). Thus, in their view, installing sturdy locks and an alarm system on one's house is a surer way to stop a burglary than trying to figure out how to turn a burglar into an upstanding citizen.

The term "environmental criminology" is really a catch-all term that encompasses a variety of different scholarly contributions (Brantingham and Brantingham, 1991). These works, however, share a common focus on two issues: (1) explaining crime events and (2) exploring the causal role of opportunity. The term "environmental" is often used as the organizing umbrella, because scholars investigate how features of the physical and social environment influence the availability of criminal opportunities and, in turn, the occurrence of crime. We should note that this approach to understanding crime could also be called "opportunity theory" (Wilcox et al., 2003).

Routine Activity Theory

As discussed in Part X, rational choice theory argues that individuals choose to engage in crime. But as Felson (1986: 119) has stated, "People make choices, but they cannot choose the choices available to them." Some people are more likely than others to confront situations where the benefits of crime are high and the costs are low. The routine activity approach deals with the factors that influence the range of choices available to individuals.

According to this theoretical perspective, three elements are necessary for a crime to occur: *Motivated offenders* must come in contact with *suitable targets* in the absence of *capable guardians*. The last two elements—suitable targets and guardianship—are best seen as the core dimensions of criminal opportunity. They must co-occur for the opportunity for crime to be present (Cohen and Felson, 1979 [Chapter 34 in this part]; Clarke and Felson, 1993).

The routine activity approach takes the supply of motivated offenders as given. Instead, the perspective explains variations in crime by variations in the supply of suitable targets (e.g., expensive, lightweight merchandise) and capable guardians (e.g., neighbors, property owners, police). Suitable targets have to do with the benefits of crime, while capable guardians have to do with the costs. According to the theory, the supply of suitable targets and the presence of capable guardians are a function of our everyday or "routine activities" (our family, work, leisure, consumption, and other activities). As a result, crime might rise in society not because of the emergence of pathological social conditions but simply because of changes in the normal ways people live.

For example, Cohen and Felson (1979) point to a major change in routine activities in the post-World War II United States: People are more likely to spend time away from home (e.g., women working). As a result, motivated offenders are more likely to encounter suitable targets in the absence of capable guardians. Thus, homes are left unprotected during the day and frequently at night, which creates opportunities for burglary. Meanwhile, individuals are more often in public locations—often alone on the streets at night—where they may fall prey to motivated offenders. Cohen and Felson discuss additional changes in routine activities during this time period, and such changes are used to explain increases in the crime rate through their effect on suitable targets and capable guardians (see also Clarke and Felson, 1993; Felson, 1995). Still, as Tittle (1995) points out, one challenge for the theory is to better specify which of our many routine activites are most relevant to the explanation of crime.

In this regard, Osgood et al. (1996) demonstrate that young adults who engage in a lot of "unstructured socializing with peers in the absence of authority figures" are more likely to engage in crime. Part of the reason for this is that they are more likely to encounter attractive opportunities for crime: Their peers provide materials (e.g., drugs, alcohol) and rewards for crime, and there are no authority figures to sanction crime.

Notably, at the same time that Cohen and Felson (1979) were formulating their theory, another group of scholars developed a very similar perspective called "lifestyle theory" (Hindelang et al., 1978). Based on victimization surveys, they noticed that certain people—such as young males—were more likely to be criminally victimized. They theorized that some groups in society tended to pursue lifestyles—or what Cohen and Felson would call "routine activities" that increased their exposure to the risk of victimization (Garofalo, 1987). Thus, as with Cohen and Felson's approach, lifestyle theory suggested that crime acts were a function not simply of offenders but also of the routines that people followed on a daily basis.

Routine activity theory was originally applied to "direct-contact predatory offenses, when at least one person directly took or damaged the person or property of another" (Felson, 2001: 43), but it has since been extended to apply to a broad range of crimes (Felson, 1995, 2001; Forde and Kennedy, 1999). Overall, the data are generally supportive of routine activity theory, as evidenced in the selection by Cohen and Felson in Chapter 34 (see also Felson, 2002). There are some problems with measuring key concepts, and not all tests are equally supportive (for overviews, see Akers and Sellers, 2008; Birkbeck and LaFree, 1993; Garofalo, 1987; Meier and Miethe, 1993; Tittle, 1995). Nonetheless, routine activity theory remains one of the most widely known and influential perspectives in contemporary criminology.

Offender Search Theory

Just because environmental criminologists are not concerned with explaining criminal dispositions or motivations does not mean that they are uninterested in offenders. But whereas traditional theorists explore how people acquire the general predisposition to break the law, the environmentalists focus on how people actually commit crimes. Their theoretical concern is thus not with how individuals develop into criminals but with the situations that allow those predisposed to crime to realize their criminal potential. That is, how do potential offenders find opportunities to offend? How do they find attractive targets that lack capable guardianship?

One influential approach to answering this question is "offender search theory" (Brantingham and Brantingham, 1993; for a summary, see Cullen et al., 2002: 32). This perspective starts with the insight that offenders, who spend most of their time not committing crimes, have routine activities just like everyone else. In the course of these activities, offenders travel between "nodes," such as home, school, work, shopping outlets, and places of leisure and entertainment (e.g., bars). In so doing, they develop "cognitive maps" or images of their environment (Taylor and Gottfredson, 1986). These maps give offenders an awareness of their environment and of where potential targets for crime might be found.

Think for a moment about selecting a restaurant for a meal in the next hour. What options first come to mind? Most often, the roster of eateries will be clustered in geographic areas that are familiar to you—that are well within the cognitive map of your local environment and along the transportation routes between the nodes where you spend the most time. On a special occasion, you might choose a restaurant that involves a fair amount of travel into an area that might require directions to find. However, most often, people eat in places that are familiar and easily accessed.

Offenders tend to search for crime targets in a similar way. "Research generally finds that crime is highly patterned by daily behavior," observe Brantingham and Brantingham (1993: 10). "Crimes tend to occur in known places or near limited travel knowledge space." Although more lucrative targets might exist elsewhere—in more affluent neighborhoods, for example—offenders thus tend to limit their "search area" for victimization targets near their nodes and travel routines. Brantingham and Brantingham (1993: 11) call this the offenders' "awareness space."

Routines thus structure crime in two ways. First, as offenders travel, opportunities for crime will simply present themselves—for example, a purse left unguarded or a car left unlocked. Second, as just intimated, when actively searching for a crime target, offenders wish to reduce effort and risk of detection. Within their "awareness space," they do not have to travel long distances to know where a potential target might exist. Further, the transaction of the crime itself becomes more predictable. They are better able to know where police patrol, when homes are left unguarded, and how to escape the crime scene quickly and with few impediments.

This focus on the causal significance of "routines" is important for another theoretical reason: It deemphasizes the pathological nature of crime and instead shows how crime is embedded in the normal aspects of everyday life. This is not to say that people do not differ in their traits or experiences that create criminal motivations. Even so, when and where crime occurs is often regulated by more mundane features of people's lives—including the routine activities of potential offenders and their potential victims.

Situational Crime Prevention Theory

The chief proposition of environmental criminology is that the nature of criminal opportunities influences the amount, nature, and location of crime. Importantly, as Pease (1994: 660) notes, "all theories of crime are also theories of crime prevention." Because theories identify the sources of crime, they tell us what conditions must be altered to eliminate such conduct. In this regard, environmental scholars argue that their "opportunity theory" suggests a very direct way to reduce crime: focus on taking away the opportunity needed to commit an offense.

Ronald Clarke (Chapter 35 in this part) is one of the most influential proponents of this idea, which he captured with the term of "situational crime prevention." In his perspective, Clarke argues that criminologists have focused too much attention on the origins of "criminal dispositions." This limited interest, he claims, is problematic because it ignores the role of opportunity in both causing and preventing crime.

In his view, more traditional theories—even if they are correct in identifying why criminal dispositions or motivations arise—provide few clues as to how to prevent crime effectively. Clarke argues that once acquired by offenders, these dispositions are hard to change through rehabilitation. Further, trying to eliminate the "root causes" of these dispositions—societal conditions such as economic inequality, community disorganization, or ineffective parenting—is difficult (see also Wilson, 1975). By contrast, Clarke contends that opportunities, which occur at the very point at which a crime would be take place, are more open to being manipulated. In other words, the focus is not crime-generating conditions that occured in the past (e.g., earlier in on offender's life) but on the present situation in which the crime transpires. This is why the perspective is called "situational crime prevention."

As a proponent of rational choice theory (Chapter 33 in Part X), Clarke believes that situational prevention strategies should focus on making the choice of crime less attractive. Unlike many deterrence theorists, however, Clarke pays relatively little attention to the role of the criminal justice system. Police typically arrive at the scene of the crime after an offender has departed, and criminal penalties are applied, if at all, in the distant future. Instead, Clarke concentrates his attention on features of the situational environment that might be changed to decrease the likely payoff from a potential crime.

Clarke (Chapter 35, see also Clarke, 1992: 13) thus focuses on strategies that might increase the effort it takes to commit a crime. Measures might include, for example, placing bars on a store window, requiring that people punch in a personal identification number for a door to open, or fencing in a yard. Clarke also favors strategies that increase the risks for offenders being detected. These measures might include installing security cameras, burglar alarms, and outside lighting or perhaps placing security tags on store merchandise and using a detector at the store's exit (Clarke, 1997).

The priority given to situations also led these scholars to explore whether crime was concentrated in certain locations. Recall that in the 1930s Shaw and McKay (Chapter 7 in Part III) had demonstrated that crime was higher in some neighborhoods than in others. But the environmental criminologists are concerned with even more specific locations. Thus, within even high-crime areas, some *places* are crime-free whereas others suffer repeated victimizations. Lawrence Sherman and his colleagues (1989) termed these places "hot spots" for crime, a now-classic concept that has received much attention (see also Eck and Weisburd, 1995; Farrell and Pease, 2001).

The interest in places has prompted scholars to explore ways in which locations troubled with crime can be made less vulnerable to offenders. Methods have included making the immediate environment less attractive to offenders (e.g., closing off streets so as to limit escape routes), making the place physically more defensible (e.g., adding locks or alarms), and enlisting people to provide surveillance. In this last category, the guardianship is provided by "place managers" whose job it is to "discourage crime" (Cullen et al., 2002; Eck, 2002; Felson, 1995). These managers might include security guards, but others might be recruited to keep an eye out for crime, such as bartenders, parking lot attendants, doormen, store clerks, and neighbors.

Again, the value of environmental criminology is that it offers a fresh perspective that demarcates the role of opportunity in causing crime and the role of closing off opportunity in reducing crime. The focus, as it has been since the early classic works in this theory, is on places or situations, not people, and on making these spaces "defensible" through shrewd "environmental design" (see, e.g., Newman, 1973). It suggests that crime can be explained and controlled without much interest in the motivations of offenders.

This perspective, however, might err in ignoring the possibility that, as it is said, "opportunity may make the offender." As Wortley (2002) points out, the nature of a situation or place can induce a person, otherwise not strongly motivated to offend, to break the law. Criminologists have previously termed these "situational motivations" (Briar and Piliavin, 1965), whereas Wortley calls them "precipitators." For example, an open window can prompt a burglary, an unattended camera a theft. Other situational precipitators are more social, such as the presence of friends urging vandalism or frustrations that cause an emotional response. Wortley's perspective is more inclusive than existing opportunity theories and urges scholars to examine the variety of ways in which situations might be involved not only in permitting but also in inducing criminal acts. Whether this approach will shape research on environmental criminology remains to be seen (for a discussion and critique, see Cornish and Clarke, 2003).

Fixing Broken Windows

In general, environmental criminologists do not see the criminal justice system as a central weapon in the fight on crime. Again, as noted, this is because the system's response to crime is reactive—it occurs after the crime has taken place. Once a crime occurs, the goal becomes to catch and then sanction those who have broken the law. Most often, offenders do their best to avoid detection, which leaves them free to victimize again. By contrast, environmental criminologists

are oriented toward *prevention*—toward arranging the physical and social environment so that a criminal event is discouraged if not made impossible. In these instances, the criminal justice system is unnecessary because the criminal act has been diverted. These scholars thus believe that communities would be safer if more thought and resources were devoted to reducing criminal opportunities as opposed to the often fruitless attempt to catch offenders after they have broken the law fled the scene of the crime.

James Q. Wilson, however, has argued that policing can be *proactive* and can do much to prevent crime in inner-city areas. Wilson has long rejected the view that poverty or social misery is at the core of crime, and, even if it were, he doubts that there is much that the government can do to eliminate such "root causes." By contrast, he is confident that if deployed strategically, police can be an integral ingredient in creating conditions that increase informal social controls, reduce opportunities for crime, and make urban neighborhoods safer.

Wilson's views have long been controversial and have often caused him to be labeled a "conservative criminologist." Below, we first review his reasons for rejecting the prevailing criminological belief—a politically progressive or liberal belief—that crime has "root causes" and that efforts should be made to change these inequitable conditions. We then proceed to consider Wilson's "broken windows" theory in which he and George Kelling articulate a vision for how police can help to transform inner-city environments into safe havens.

Rejecting Root Causes

In 1975, James Q. Wilson published *Thinking About Crime.* This volume assumed enormous importance because it outlined a fundamental critique of traditional "liberal" sociological approaches to criminal behavior. In controlling crime, Wilson argued for a paradigm shift—a whole new way of thinking that, though less grand, might well increase public safety. This alternative perspective was seen as "conservative" because it challenged the impact of social welfare responses to crime—such as programs to reduce poverty and rehabilitation for offenders—and instead argued in favor of increasing punishments.

Wilson's paradigm set forth *three* interrelated arguments that are found in whole or in part in most conservative theories of, and commentaries on, crime. First, he questioned the liberal sociological wisdom that poverty and racism are at the root of America's crime problem. Structural inequalities might be unfortunate and in need of correction, said Wilson, but they are not fundamental or "root causes" of crime. After all, crime seemed to be lower in the Great Depression when poverty and racism were widespread and to rise in the United States precisely when affluence and civil rights were expanding (see also DiIulio, 1994, 1994–1995; for an alternative view, see Currie, 1985, 1998). Striving for a more equal society would thus have little impact on crime rates.

Second, beyond structural inequality, Wilson admitted that sociologists might well have identified a set of conditions that lead to crime, in particular the antisocial attitudes that are "shaped and supported by intimate groups—the family and close friends" (Wilson, 1975: 53). The problem with these theories, argued Wilson, is that "none could supply a plausible basis for the advocacy of public policy" because they direct "attention toward conditions that cannot be easily and deliberately altered" (p. 53). For example, "if a child is delinquent because his family made him so," it is not clear what might be done (compare with Henggeler, 1999):

> No one knows how a government might restore affection, stability, and fair discipline to a family that rejects these characteristics; still less can one imagine how even a family once restored could affect a child who has passed the formative years and in any event has developed an aversion to one or both of his parents. (Wilson, 1975: 54)

In short, nearly all factors identified by traditional theories either are unimportant (structural inequality) or, even if important, are beyond change (quality of parenting). One might draw the conclusion that if crime's root causes are beyond intervention—if they cannot be fixed—then the United States would simply be "stuck" with its current levels of crime. But Wilson argued that this was an erroneous view, part of what he called the "causal fallacy"—the assumption "that no problem is adequately addressed unless its causes are eliminated" (p. 56).

As an alternative, Wilson (1975: 59) offered what he called a "policy analysis" perspective. This approach was not utopian but realistic. It starts out not by diagnosing the cause of a problem but rather by asking "what is the condition one wants to bring into being . . . and what policy tools does a government (in our case, a democratic and libertarian government) possess that might, when applied, produce at reasonable cost a desired alteration in the present condition or progress toward the desired condition?" (p. 59).

In trumpeting "policy analysis," Wilson was showing his stripes as a political scientist. Sociologists might identify grand causes of crime, but the political realities were that these conditions (such as poverty) were not going to be changed in the near future. By contrast, political science would encourage a close inspection of what resources were in fact available that could be directed to try to limit a social problem. Unlike sociology, political science operated in the realm of the possible, not in the realm of the impossible.

The problem, however, is where Wilson next turned. He concluded that social welfare programs—such as improving education or creating jobs or rehabilitating offenders—are "very difficult, quite costly, hard to manage organizationally, and liable to produce many unanticipated side effects" (p. 60). Of course, these are the very kinds of interventions that sociological criminologists were proposing. But if not social reform, then what? Here is where Wilson offered his most controversial suggestion—a view that defined him as a conservative criminologist.

Thus, the third principle he advanced was that the "instruments" most available to the government to use to reduce crime—the desired policy outcome—were the *punishments that the criminal justice system could inflict on offenders.* Even if offenders engage in crime for a host of sociological and psychological reasons, these are not the concern of the policy analyst. Instead, according to Wilson (1975: 62):

> the policy analyst is led to assume that the criminal acts *as if* crime were the product of a free choice among competing opportunities and constraints. The radical individualism of Bentham and Beccaria may be scientifically questionable but prudentially necessary. (Emphasis in the original.)

Lurking in Wilson's logic is that many people, even if driven to crime by complex reasons, are at least partially "rational." If so, then they would—as economists or rational choice theorists contend—respond to disincentives to commit crime. As crime becomes more costly, people are less likely to commit it. This new reluctance to break the law might not be all-powerful, but it might cause some offenders to reduce their criminality and others on the margins of crime to give up offending completely. Accordingly, while crime would not disappear, it might—as the policy analyst would predict—be meaningfully reduced.

The key issue is how to increase the costs of crime. The vast majority of criminologists were anti-imprisonment, arguing that these institutions were inhumane and crime-generating. But Wilson rejected this mainstream view. Again, from his policy analysis perspective, prisons were one of the few instruments available to the government to influence the payoff from crime. By pulling this lever, so to speak, the state could impose more costs on offenders and achieve a measure of deterrence. But his faith in prisons did not stop there. What about those who failed

to be deterred—high-rate chronic offenders? For these career criminals, Wilson favored their incapacitation." As Wilson (1975: 235) famously argued, "Wicked people exist. Nothing avails except to set them apart from innocent people."

Beyond his advocacy of imprisonment, Wilson also believed that police officers could be deployed more effectively. He rejected the idea that all police practices were inherently ineffective—that "nothing works" in law enforcement to reduce crime. Instead, similar to prisons, he viewed the police as one of the few instruments that the government had at its disposal to fight crime. Indeed, if police were used correctly, he believed that they were an important resource in the effort to reverse the fortunes of neighborhoods that had spiraled into crime and decline.

The Theory

In their now-famous essay, "Broken Windows: The Police and Neighborhood Safety" (Chapter 36 in this part), James Q. Wilson and George L. Kelling (1982) set forth a community informal social control theory of crime. At first glance, this description might lead to the question of why this selection is not placed in Part III on the Chicago School where similar models are discussed. However, although there is conceptual overlap, Wilson and Kelling's framework differs in three significant ways that, when taken together, make it a conservative theory of crime.

First, although focusing mainly on poor, inner-city areas, Wilson and Kelling do not discuss the potential impact on crime of inequality, racial segregation, changes in the economic structure (e.g., loss of manufacturing jobs), and the structural factors that foster social disorganization (see Part III). In short, they are not interested in the "root causes" of community-based crime. Second, for these authors, crime in a community is not due to local criminogenic social conditions but rather to the presence of, and failure to control, "disreputable" and, ultimately, "wicked" people. And third, the solution to crime is not social reform of impoverished communities but rather the use of the criminal justice system—in this case, the police—to exert more control over individuals who otherwise would choose to do bothersome and bad things.

Wilson and Kelling (1982: 31–32) are interested in why stable and safe neighborhoods "can change, in a few years or even a few months, into an inhospitable and frightening jungle" where crime is widespread. Their theory's central premise is that *unchecked social disorder or public incivility is the cause of serious crime.* Thus, they contend that "at the community level, disorder and crime are usually inextricably linked, in a kind of developmental sequence" (1982: 31). This sequence involves three stages.

First, the spiral of decline begins when "disorderly people" are allowed to take over public spaces (p. 30). Wilson and Kelling (1982: 30) note that these individuals are "not violent people, nor, necessarily, criminals, but disreputable or obstreperous or unpredictable people; panhandlers, drunks, addicts, rowdy teenagers, prostitutes, loiterers, the mentally disturbed." Although the risk of criminal victimization is not high, residents no longer feel comfortable simply strolling down the street. They are at risk of being hassled for money or by cat calls, of having to cross the street to avoid these disreputable people, and of seeing the signs of incivility—litter, broken bottles, graffiti, loud music.

Second, in response to this growing social and physical disorder, decent people become fearful and change their behavior accordingly—first by retreating to the safety of their residences and then, if able, by moving out of the neighborhood. This withdrawal from public spaces, however, leads to the "breakdown of community controls" (p. 31). Whereas once the neighborhood was filled with families who cared "for their homes, mind[ed] each other's children, and confidently frown[ed] on unwanted intruders," now wayward behavior is left "untended" (p. 31):

A piece of property is abandoned, weeds grow up, a window is smashed. Adults stop scolding rowdy children; the children, emboldened, become more rowdy. Families move out, unattached adults move in. Teenagers gather in front of the corner store. The merchant asks them to move; they refuse. Fights occur. Litter accumulates. People start drinking in front of the grocery; in time, an inebriate slumps to the sidewalk and is allowed to sleep it off. Pedestrians are approached by panhandlers. (Wilson and Kelling, 1982: 32)

Third, this escalating disorder sends the message that "no one cares" about how people behave in the community (p. 31). At this point, contend Wilson and Kelling, the "area is vulnerable to criminal invasion" (p. 32). After all, to the extent that offenders are rational, they will migrate to those neighborhoods where they can engage in crime virtually with impunity—with little fear of being reported to law enforcement by residents or of being detected by police who arrive long after offenders have fled the scene of their crime.

The genius of Wilson and Kelling was in capturing the core of their theory with the "broken windows" metaphor—a comparison that resonated with diverse audiences. Communities, they claimed, were like houses:

Social psychologists and police officers tend to agree that if a window in a building is broken and is left unrepaired, all the rest of the windows will soon be broken . . . one unrepaired broken window is a signal that no one cares, and so breaking more windows costs nothing. (Wilson and Kelling, 1982: 31; emphasis in the original)

In a similar way, disorderly conduct was an "unrepaired window." If left unfixed, the message was sent that the community was a "house" where more disorderly conduct—the breaking of more windows—would be tolerated. Eventually, so many windows would be broken—serious crime would be so rampant—that the house or community would become unlivable.

The "broken windows" metaphor not only conveyed a theory of crime but also an obvious solution to lawlessness in urban neighborhoods: *fix the broken windows*. This job might involve residents, but the repairs would mainly have to be done by police officers. They would have to take steps to maintain order.

For Wilson and Kelling, the key insight was that order maintenance involved not simply fighting crime but rather focusing on the disorder that first undermined community social controls and subsequently allowed the invasion of serious criminals. Recall that disorder was not caused by hardened criminals but by "disreputable" people. As a result, the police would now exert control over "panhandlers, drunks, addicts, rowdy teenagers, prostitutes, loiterers, the mentally retarded" (p. 30). Sometimes called "zero-tolerance" or "quality-of-life" policing (Eck and Maguire, 2000: 224; Harcourt, 2001: 1), officers would now walk the streets and religiously confront or arrest people who flouted their "obligations of civility" by congregating on corners and blocking sidewalks, sleeping in doorways, urinating in public, openly drinking alcohol, jaywalking, or otherwise disturbing the peace.

Formal control by police that fixed the "broken window" of disorder was theorized to bolster informal community controls. This zero-tolerance strategy was meant to inform offenders and residents that someone now did care about the neighborhood and that breaking windows would be punished. This message was intended to make the community inhospitable to serious criminals and to embolden residents to reassert informal controls over public spaces. Notably, "broken windows" policing became a major reform within law enforcement (Harcourt, 2001; Kelling and Coles, 1996).

The viability of the "broken windows" theory of crime hinges in large part on whether, as Wilson and Kelling predict, disorder is in fact the main cause of serious crime. Although there is some evidence of a connection (Kelling and Coles, 1996; Skogan, 1990), the relationship is likely limited in size, indirect through other processes, and conditioned by a range of factors (e.g., economic status of the community) (Harcourt, 2001; Taylor, 2001). It also is not clear whether the theory has the causal order correct, since it ignores the likely possibility that serious crime is what produces disorder and not vice versa. Finally, there is research that suggests that the link between disorder and crime is spurious: that both are caused by the underlying social conditions of the neighborhood, such as a lack of collective efficacy (Sampson and Raudenbush, 1999).

But isn't there convincing evidence that broken windows policing has resulted in miraculous reductions in crime in many communities? Didn't New York City's rate of homicide and violent crime plummet precipitously following the implementation of this model of law enforcement? If so, then the "evidence" from these natural experiments—the fact that serious crime was reduced after disorder was targeted for police intervention—would suggest that the broken windows theory of crime has merit (Kelling and Coles, 1996).

Unfortunately, reality appears to paint a more complicated picture. There is evidence, for example, that crime rates began to fall in New York City prior to the police reform movement, and that cities that did not use the broken windows approach experienced comparable declines in their lawlessness (Eck and Maguire, 2000; Harcourt, 2001). Further, the reduction of New York's crime was likely influenced by a range of factors, including economic prosperity, changes in the drug market away from "crack" cocaine and the violence it induced, and the use of a variety of police tactics that included but were not limited to "quality-of-life" enforcement aimed at order maintenance (Harcourt, 2001).

References

Akers, Ronald L. and Christine S. Sellers. 2008. *Criminological Theories: Introduction, Evaluation, and Application*. 5th edition. Los Angeles: Roxbury Publishing.

Birkbeck, Christopher and Gary LaFree. 1993. "The Situational Analysis of Crime and Deviance." *Annual Review of Sociology* 19: 113–137.

Bottoms, Anthony E. 1994. "Environmental Criminology." In Mike Maguire, Rod Morgan, and Robert Reiner (eds.), *The Oxford Handbook of Criminology*, pp. 585–656. Oxford, UK: Clarendon Press.

Brantingham, Paul J. and Patricia L. Brantingham, eds. 1991. *Environmental Criminology*, Reissued edition. Prospect Heights, IL: Waveland Press.

——. 1993. "Nodes, Paths, Edges: Considerations on the Complexity of Crime and the Physical Environment." *Environmental Psychology* 13: 3–28.

Briar, Scott and Irving Piliavin. 1965. "Delinquency, Situational Inducements, and Commitment to Conformity." *Social Problems* 13: 35–45.

Clarke, Ronald V. 1980. "'Situational' Crime Prevention: Theory and Practice." *British Journal of Criminology* 20: 136–147.

——, ed. 1992. "Introduction." In Ronald V. Clarke (ed.), *Situational Crime Prevention: Successful Case Studies*, pp. 3–36. New York: Harrow and Heston.

——, ed. 1997. *Situational Crime Prevention: Successful Case Studies*. Albany, NY: Harrow and Heston.

Clarke, Ronald V. and Marcus Felson, eds. 1993. *Advances in Criminological Theory, Volume 5: Routine Activity and Rational Choice*. New Brunswick, NJ: Transaction.

Cloward, Richard A. 1959. "Illegitimate Means, Anomie, and Deviant Behavior." *American Sociological Review* 24: 164–176.

Cloward, Richard A. and Lloyd E. Ohlin. 1960. *Delinquency and Opportunity: A Theory of Delinquent Gangs*. New York: The Free Press.

Cohen, Lawrence E. and Marcus Felson. 1979. "Social Change and Crime Rate Trends: A Routine Activity Approach." *American Sociological Review* 44: 588–607.

Cornish, Derek B. and Ronald V. Clarke. 2003. "Opportunities, Precipitators, and Criminal Decisions: A Reply to Wortley's Critique of Situational Crime Prevention." In Martha J. Smith and Derek B. Cornish (eds.), *Theory for Practice in Situational Crime Prevention—Crime Prevention Studies*, Volume 16, pp. 41–96. Monsey, NY: Criminal Justice Press.

Cullen, Francis T. 1984. *Rethinking Crime and Deviance Theory: The Emergence of a Structuring Tradition*. Totowa, NJ: Rowman and Allanheld.

Cullen, Francis T., John E. Eck, and Christopher T. Lowenkamp. 2002. "Environmental Corrections: A New Paradigm for Effective Probation and Parole Supervision." *Federal Probation* 66 (September): 28–37.

Currie, Elliot. 1985. *Confronting Crime: An American Challenge*. New York: Pantheon Books.

——. 1998. *Crime and Punishment in America*. New York: Metropolitan Books.

DiIulio, John J., Jr. 1994. "The Question of Black Crime." *Public Interest* 117 (Fall): 3–32.

——. 1994–1995. "Comment on Douglas S. Massey's *Getting Away With Murder: Segregation and Violent Crime in Urban America*." *University of Pennsylvania Law Review* 143: 1275–1284.

Eck, John E. 2002. "Preventing Crime at Places." In Lawrence W. Sherman, David P. Farrington, and Brandon K. Welsh (eds.), *Evidence-Based Crime Prevention*, pp. 241–294. New York: Routledge.

Eck, John E. and Edward R. Maguire. 2000. "Have Changes in Policing Reduced Violent Crime? An Assessment of the Evidence." In Alfred Blumstein and Joel Wallman (eds.), *The Crime Drop in America*, pp. 207–265. Cambridge, UK: Cambridge University Press

Eck, John E. and David Weisburd, eds. 1995. *Crime and Place: Crime Prevention Studies*, Volume 4. Monsey, NY: Criminal Justice Press.

Farrell, Graham and Ken Pease, eds. 2001. *Repeat Victimization: Crime Prevention Studies*, Volume 12. Monsey, NY: Criminal Justice Press.

Felson, Marcus. 1986. "Linking Criminal Choices, Routine Activities, Informal Control, and

Criminal Outcomes." In Derek B. Cornish and Ronald V. Clarke (eds.), *The Reasoning Criminal*, pp. 119–128. New York: Springer-Verlag.

——. 1995. "Those Who Discourage Crime." In John E. Eck and David Weisburd (eds.), *Crime and Place: Crime Prevention Studies*, Volume 4, pp. 53–66. Monsey, NY: Criminal Justice Press.

——. 2001. "The Routine Activity Approach." In Raymond Paternoster and Ronet Bachman (eds.), *Explaining Criminals and Crime*, pp. 43–46. Los Angeles: Roxbury Publishing.

——. 2002. *Crime and Everyday Life,* 3rd edition. Thousand Oaks, CA: Pine Forge Press.

Forde, David and Leslie Kennedy. 1999. *When Push Comes to Shove: A Routine Conflict Approach to Violence*. Albany: State University of New York Press.

Garofalo, James. 1987. "Reassessing the Life-style Model of Criminal Victimization." In Michael R. Gottfredson and Travis Hirschi (eds.), *Positive Criminology*, pp. 23–42. Newbury Park, CA: Sage.

Harcourt, Bernard E. 2001. *Illusion of Order: The False Promise of Broken Windows Policing*. Cambridge, MA: Harvard University Press.

Henggeler, Scott W. 1999. "Multisystemic Therapy: An Overview of Clinical Procedures, Outcomes, and Policy Implications." *Child Psychology and Psychiatry Review* 4: 2–10.

Hindelang, Michael J., Michael R. Gottfredson, and James Garofalo. 1978. *Victims of Personal Crime: An Empirical Foundation for a Theory of Personal Victimization*. Cambridge, MA: Ballinger.

Kelling, George L. and Catherine M. Coles. 1996. *Fixing Broken Windows: Restoring Order and Reducing Crime in Our Communities*. New York: Simon & Schuster.

Meier, Robert F. and Terance D. Miethe. 1993. "Understanding Theories of Criminal Victimization." In Michael Tonry (ed.), *Crime and Justice*, Volume 17, pp. 459–499. Chicago: University of Chicago Press.

Newman, Oscar. 1973. *Defensible Space: Crime Prevention Through Environmental Design*. New York: Macmillan.

Osgood, D. Wayne, Janet K. Wilson, Patrick O'Malley, Jerald G. Bachman, and Lloyd D. Johnson. 1996. "Routine Activities and Individual Deviant Behavior." *American Sociological Review* 61: 635–655.

Pease, Ken. 1994. "Crime Prevention." In Mike Maguire, Rod Morgan, and Robert Reiner (eds.), *The Oxford Handbook of Criminology*, pp. 659–703. Oxford, UK: Clarendon Press.

Sampson, Robert J. and Stephen W. Raudenbush. 1999. "Systematic Social Observation of Public Spaces: A New Look at Disorder in Urban Neighborhoods." *American Journal of Sociology* 3: 603–651.

Sherman, Lawrence W., Patrick R. Gartin, and Michael E. Buerger. 1989. "Hot Spots of Predatory Crime: Routine Activities and the Criminology of Place." *Criminology* 27: 27–55.

Skogan, Wesley G. 1990. *Disorder and Decline: Crime and the Spiral of Decay in American Neighborhoods*. Berkeley: University of California Press.

Taylor, Ralph B. 2001. *Breaking Away From Broken Windows: Baltimore Neighborhoods and the Nationwide Fight Against Crime, Grime, Fear, and Decline*. Boulder, CO: Westview Press.

Taylor, Ralph B. and Stephen Gottfredson. 1986. "Environmental Design, Crime, and Prevention: An Examination of Community Dynamics." In Albert J. Reis, Jr., and Michael Tonry (eds.), *Communities and Crime—Crime and Justice: A Review of Research*, Volume 8, pp. 387–416. Chicago: University of Chicago Press.

Tittle, Charles R. 1995. *Control Balance: Toward a General Theory of Deviance*. Boulder, CO: Westview.

Wilcox, Pamela, Kenneth C. Land, and Scott A. Hunt. 2003. *Criminal Circumstance: A Dynamic Multicontextual Criminal Opportunity Theory*. New York: Aldine de Gruyter.

Wilson, James Q. 1975. *Thinking About Crime*. New York: Vintage Books.

Wilson, James Q. and George L. Kelling. 1982. "Broken Windows: The Police and Neighborhood Safety." *Atlantic Monthly* (March): 29–38.

Wortley, Robert. 2002. *Situational Prison Control: Crime Prevention in Correctional Institutions*. Cambridge, UK: Cambridge University Press.

34. Routine Activity Theory

Lawrence E. Cohen and Marcus Felson

The routine activity approach is based on two rather simple ideas. First, it argues that in order for a crime to occur, motivated offenders must converge with suitable targets in the absence of capable guardians. Second, it argues that the probability of this situation occurring is influenced by our "routine activities"—including our work, family, leisure, and consumption activities. So, for example, if we spend more time in public places—such as in bars and on the street—we increase the likelihood that we will come into contact with motivated offenders in the absence of capable guardians. As a consequence, we are more likely to be victimized.

In this selection, Cohen and Felson demonstrate that these simple ideas can be used to help explain the increase in crime experienced in the United States after World War II. They show much creativity in applying these ideas, and they make a powerful case for the routine activity approach. This approach has also been used to explain geographic differences in crime rates, differences in the amount of crime experienced by sociodemographic groups (e.g., why young African American males have a high rate of crime victimization), and individual differences in crime. As was indicated in the introduction to this section, the data are generally supportive of the theory, although not all studies support the theory (see Akers and Sellers, 2008; Birkbeck and LaFree, 1993; Felson, 1998,

2001; Fisher et al., 2002; Meier and Miethe, 1993; Miethe and Meier, 1994; Tittle, 1995).

The routine activity approach is valuable because it complements traditional crime theories in a fundamental way. These theories typically focus on the factors that motivate or dispose individuals to engage in crime; that is, they try to identify what factors produce motivated offenders. In contrast, the routine activity approach usually takes the supply of motivated offenders for granted. Instead, the theory focuses on the opportunities for crime on the premise that even when a motivated offender is present, no crime can occur if no opportunity is available. Notably, Cohen and Felson's routine activity theory identifies two important dimensions of opportunity: an attractive target and the absence of capable guardianship.

The assumption that motivated offenders can be largely assumed to exist is one criticism of routine activity theory. Recognizing this limitation, Miethe and Meier (1994) developed an integrated theory that attempts to explain both offender motivation and the opportunities for crime. Other scholars have tried to extend the theory by focusing on how opportunity is linked to the social contexts in which a criminal act takes place, such as whether a neighborhood is disorganized (Wilcox et al., 2003). It is clear that routine activity theory remains an important

Reprinted from Lawrence E. Cohen and Marcus Felson, "Social Change and Crime Rate Trends: A Routine Activity Approach" in *American Sociological Review*, Vol. 44, 588–608. Copyright © 1979 by the American Sociological Association. Reprinted by permission of the American Sociological Association.

perspective that continues to generate both theoretical elaboration and empirical studies.

References

Akers, Ronald L. and Christine S. Sellers. 2008. *Criminological Theories: Introduction, Evaluation, and Application*, 5th edition. Los Angeles: Roxbury Publishing.

Birkbeck, Christopher and Gary LaFree. 1993. "The Situational Analysis of Crime and Deviance." *Annual Review of Sociology* 19: 113–137.

Felson, Marcus. 1998. *Crime and Everyday Life.* Thousand Oaks, CA: Pine Forge Press.

——. 2001. "The Routine Activity Approach." In Raymond Paternoster and Ronet Bachman (eds.), *Explaining Criminals and Crime*, pp. 43–46. Los Angeles: Roxbury Publishing.

Fisher, Bonnie S., Francis T. Cullen, and Michael G. Turner. 2002. "Being Pursued: Stalking Victimization in a National Study of College Women." *Criminology and Public Policy* 1: 257–308.

Meier, Robert F. and Terance D. Miethe. 1993. "Understanding Theories of Criminal Victimization." In Michael Tonry (ed.), *Crime and Justice: A Review of Research*, Volume 17, pp. 459–499. Chicago: University of Chicago Press.

Miethe, Terance D. and Robert F. Meier. 1994. *Crime and Its Social Context: Toward an Integrated Theory of Offenders, Victims, and Situations.* Albany: State University of New York Press.

Tittle, Charles R. 1995. *Control Balance: Toward a General Theory of Deviance.* Boulder, CO: Westview Press.

Wilcox, Pamela, Kenneth C. Land, and Scott A. Hunt. 2003. *Criminal Circumstance: A Dynamic Multicontextual Criminal Opportunity Theory.* New York: Aldine de Gruyter.

We argue that structural changes in routine activity patterns can influence crime rates by affecting the convergence in space and time of the three minimal elements of direct-contact predatory violations: (1) motivated offenders, (2) suitable targets, and (3) the absence of capable guardians against a violation. We further argue that the lack of any one of these elements is sufficient to prevent the successful completion of a direct-contact predatory crime, and that the convergence in time and space of suitable targets and the absence of capable guardians may even lead to large increases in crime rates without necessarily requiring any increase in the structural conditions that motivate individuals to engage in crime. That is, if the proportion of motivated offenders or even suitable targets were to remain stable in a community, changes in routine activities could nonetheless alter the likelihood of their convergence in space and time, thereby creating more opportunities for crimes to occur. Control therefore becomes critical. If controls through routine activities were to decrease, illegal predatory activities could then be likely to increase. . . .

Unlike many criminological inquiries, we do not examine why individuals or groups are inclined criminally, but rather we take criminal inclination as given and examine the manner in which the spatiotemporal organization of social activities helps people to translate their criminal inclinations into action. Criminal violations are treated here as routine activities which share many attributes of, and are interdependent with, other routine activities. . . .

The Minimal Elements of Direct-Contact Predatory Violations

As we previously stated, despite their great diversity, direct-contact predatory violations share some important requirements which facilitate analysis of their structure. Each successfully completed violation minimally requires an *offender* with both criminal inclinations and the ability to carry out those inclinations, a person or object providing a *suitable target* for the offender, and *absence of guardians* capable of preventing violations. We emphasize that the lack of any one of these elements normally is sufficient to prevent such violations from occurring. Though guardianship is implicit in everyday life, it usually is marked by the absence of violations, hence it is easy to overlook. While police action is analyzed widely, guardianship by ordinary citizens of one another and property as they go about routine activities may be one of the most neglected elements in sociological research on crime, especially since it links seemingly unrelated social roles and relationships to the occurrence or absence of illegal acts.

The conjunction of these minimal elements can be used to assess how social structure may affect the tempo of each type of violation. That is, the probability that a violation will occur at any specific time and place might be taken as a function of the convergence of likely offenders and suitable targets in the absence of capable guardians. Through consideration of how trends and fluctuations in social conditions affect the frequency of this convergence of criminogenic circumstances, an explanation of temporal trends in crime rates can be constructed....

The Ecological Nature of Illegal Acts

Since illegal activities must feed upon other activities, the spatial and temporal structure of routine legal activities should play an important role in determining the location, type and quantity of illegal acts occurring in a given community or society. Moreover, one can analyze how the structure of community organization as well as the level of technology in a society provide the circumstances under which crime can thrive. For example, technology and organization affect the capacity of persons with criminal inclinations to overcome their targets, as well as affecting the ability of guardians to contend with potential offenders by using whatever protective tools, weapons and skills they have at their disposal. Many technological advances designed for legitimate purposes—including the automobile, small power tools, hunting weapons, highways, telephones, etc.—may enable offenders to carry out

their own work more effectively or may assist people in protecting their own or someone else's person or property.

Not only do routine legitimate activities often provide the wherewithal to commit offenses or to guard against others who do so, but they also provide offenders with suitable targets. Target suitability is likely to reflect such things as value (i.e., the material or symbolic desirability of a personal or property target for offenders), physical visibility, access, and the inertia of a target against illegal treatment by offenders (including the weight, size, and attached or locked features of property inhibiting its illegal removal and the physical capacity of personal victims to resist attackers with or without weapons). Routine production activities probably affect the suitability of consumer goods for illegal removal by determining their value and weight. Daily activities may affect the location of property and personal targets in visible and accessible places at particular times. These activities also may cause people to have on hand objects that can be used as weapons for criminal acts or self-protection or to be preoccupied with tasks which reduce their capacity to discourage or resist offenders.

While little is known about conditions that affect the convergence of potential offenders, targets and guardians, this is a potentially rich source of propositions about crime rates. For example, daily work activities separate many people from those they trust and the property they value. Routine activities also bring together at various times of day or night persons of different background, sometimes in the presence of facilities, tools or weapons which influence the commission or avoidance of illegal acts. Hence, the timing of work, schooling and leisure may be of central importance for explaining crime rates....

Microlevel Assumptions of the Routine Activity Approach

The theoretical approach taken here specifies that crime rate trends in the post-World War II United States are related to patterns of what we have called routine activities. We define these as any recurrent and prevalent activities which provide for basic population and individual needs, whatever their biological or cultural origins. Thus routine activities would include formalized work, as well as the provision of standard food, shelter, sexual outlet, leisure, social interaction, learning and childrearing. These activities may go well beyond the minimal levels needed to prevent a population's extinction, so long as their prevalence and recurrence makes them a part of everyday life.

Routine activities may occur (1) at home, (2) in jobs away from home, and (3) in other activities away from home. The latter may involve primarily household members or others. We shall argue that, since World War II, the United States has experienced a major shift of routine activities away from the first category into the remaining ones, especially those nonhousehold activities involving nonhousehold members. In particular, we shall argue that this shift in the structure of routine activities increases the probability that motivated offenders will converge in space and time with suitable targets in the absence of capable guardians, hence contributing to significant increases in the points in the direct-contact predatory crime rates over these years.

If the routine activity approach is valid, then we should expect to find evidence for a number of empirical relationships regarding the nature and distribution of predatory violations. For example, we would expect routine activities performed within or near the home and among family or other primary groups to entail lower risk of criminal victimization because they enhance guardianship capabilities. We should also expect that routine daily activities affect the location of property and personal targets in visible and accessible places at particular times, thereby influencing their risk of victimization. Furthermore, by determining their size and weight and in some cases their value, routine production activities should affect the suitability of consumer goods for illegal removal. Finally, if the routine activity approach

is useful for explaining the paradox presented earlier, we should find that the circulation of people and property, the size and weight of consumer items etc., will parallel changes in crime rate trends for the post-World War II United States.

The veracity of the routine activity approach can be assessed by analyses of both microlevel and macrolevel interdependencies of human activities. While consistency at the former level may appear noncontroversial, or even obvious, one nonetheless needs to show that the approach does not contradict existing data before proceeding to investigate the latter level.

Empirical Assessment

Circumstances and Location of Offenses

The routine activity approach specifies that household and family activities entail lower risk of criminal victimization than nonhousehold-nonfamily activities, despite the problems in measuring the former.

National estimates from large-scale government victimization surveys in 1973 and 1974 support this generalization (see methodological information in Hindelang et al., 1976: Appendix 6). Table 34.1 presents several incident-victimization rates per 100,000 population ages 12 and older. Clearly, the rates in Panels A and B are far lower at or near home than elsewhere and far lower among relatives than others. The data indicate that risk of victimization varies directly with social distance between offender and victim. Panel C of this table indicates, furthermore, that risk of lone victimization far exceeds the risk of victimization for groups. These relationships are strengthened by considering time budget evidence that, on the average, Americans spend 16.26 hours per day at home, 1.38 hours on streets, in parks, etc., and 6.36 hours in other places (Szalai, 1972:795). Panel D of Table 34.1 presents our estimates of victimization per billion person-hours spent in such locations. For example, personal larceny rates (with contact) are 350 times higher at the hands of

Table 34.1
Incident-Specific Risk Rates for Rape, Robbery, Assault and Personal Larceny with Contact,
United States, 1974

		Rape	Robbery	Assault	Personal Larceny with Contact	Total
A.* PLACE OF RESIDENCE	In or near home	63	129	572	75	839
	Elsewhere	119	584	1,897	1,010	3,610
B.* VICTIM–OFFENDER RELATIONSHIP	(Lone Offender)					
	Relative	7	13	158	5	183
	Well Known	23	30	333	30	416
	Casual Acquaintance	11	26	308	25	370
	Don't Know/Sight Only	106	227	888	616	1,837
	(Multiple Offender)					
	Any Known	10***	68	252	43	373
	All Strangers	25***	349	530	366	1,270
C.* NUMBER OF VICTIMS	One	179	647	2,116	1,062	4,004
	Two	3	47	257	19	326
	Three	0	13	53	3	9
	Four Plus	0	6	43	1	50
D.** LOCATION AND RELATIONSHIP (sole offender only)	Home, Stranger	61	147	345	103	654
	Home, Nonstranger	45	74	620	22	761
	Street, Stranger	1,370	7,743	15,684	7,802	32,460
	Street, Nonstranger	179	735	5,777	496	7,167
	Elsewhere, Stranger	129	513	1,934	2,455	4,988
	Elsewhere, Nonstranger	47	155	1,544	99	1,874

* Calculated from Handelang et al., 1977: Tables 3.16, 3.18, 3.27, 3.28. Rates are per 100,000 persons ages 12 and over.

** See fn. 6 for source. Rates are per billion person-hours in stated locations.

*** Based on white data only due to lack of suitable sample size for nonwhites as victims of rape with multiple offenders.

strangers in streets than at the hands of nonstrangers at home. Separate computations from 1973 victimization data (USDJ, 1976: Table 48) indicate that there were two motor vehicle thefts per million vehicle-hours parked at or near home, 55 per million vehicle-hours in streets, parks, playgrounds, school grounds or parking lots, and 12 per million vehicle-hours elsewhere. While the direction of these relationships is not surprising, their magnitudes should be noted. It appears that risk of criminal victimization varies dramatically among the circumstances and locations in which people place themselves and their property.

Target Suitability

Another assumption of the routine activity approach is that target suitability influences the occurrence of direct-contact predatory violations. Though we lack data to disaggregate all major components of target suitability (i.e., value, visibility, accessibility and inertia), together they imply that expensive and movable durables, such as vehicles and electronic appliances, have the highest risk of illegal removal.

As a specific case in point, we compared the 1975 composition of stolen property reported in the Uniform Crime Report (FBI, 1976: Tables 26–7) with national data on personal consumer expenditures for goods (CEA, 1976: Tables 13–16) and to appliance industry estimates of the value of shipments the same year (*Merchandising Week*, 1976). We calculated that $26.44 in motor vehicles and parts were stolen for each $100 of these goods consumed in 1975, while $6.81 worth of electronic appliances were stolen per $100 consumed. Though these estimates are subject to error in citizen and police estimation, what is important here is their size relative to other rates. For example, only 8¢ worth of nondurables and 12¢ worth of furniture and nonelectronic household durables were stolen per $100 of each category consumed, the motor vehicle risk being, respectively, 330 and 220 times as great. Though we lack data on the "stocks" of goods subject to risk, these "flow" data clearly support our assumption that

vehicles and electronic appliances are greatly over-represented in thefts.

The 1976 Buying Guide issue of *Consumer Reports* (1975) indicates why electronic appliances are an excellent retail value for a thief. For example, a Panasonic car tape player is worth $30 per lb., and a Phillips phonograph cartridge is valued at over $5,000 per lb., while large appliances such as refrigerators and washing machines are only worth $1 to $3 per lb. Not surprisingly, burglary data for the District of Columbia in 1969 (Scarr, 1972: Table 9) indicate that home entertainment items alone constituted nearly four times as many stolen items as clothing, food, drugs, liquor, and tobacco combined and nearly eight times as many stolen items as office supplies and equipment. In addition, 69 percent of national thefts classified in 1975 (FBI, 1976: Tables 1, 26) involve automobiles, their parts or accessories, and thefts from automobiles or thefts of bicycles. Yet radio and television sets plus electronic components and accessories totaled only 0.10 percent of the total truckload tonnage terminated in 1973 by intercity motor carriers, while passenger cars, motor vehicle parts and accessories, motorcycles, bicycles, and their parts, totaled only 5.5 percent of the 410 million truckload tons terminated (ICC, 1974). Clearly, portable and movable durables are reported stolen in great disproportion to their share of the value and weight of goods circulating in the United States.

Family Activities and Crime Rates

One would expect that persons living in single-adult households and those employed outside the home are less obligated to confine their time to family activities within households. From a routine activity perspective, these persons and their households should have higher rates of predatory criminal victimization. We also expect that adolescents and young adults who are perhaps more likely to engage in peer group activities rather than family activities will have higher rates of criminal victimization. Finally, married persons should have lower rates than others. . . . We note that victimization rates appear to be related inversely to age and are lower for persons in "less active" statuses (e.g., keeping house, unable to work, retired) and persons in intact marriages. A notable exception is ... where persons unable to work appear more likely to be victimized by rape, robbery and personal larceny with contact than are other "inactive persons." Unemployed persons also have unusually high rates of victimization. However, these rates are consistent with the routine activity approach offered here: the high rates of victimization suffered by the unemployed may reflect their residential proximity to high concentrations of potential offenders as well as their age and racial composition, while handicapped persons have high risk of personal victimization because they are less able to resist motivated offenders. Nonetheless, persons who keep house have noticeably lower rates of victimization than those who are employed, unemployed, in school or in the armed forces....

Burglary and robbery victimization rates are about twice as high for persons living in single-adult households as for other persons in each age group examined. Other victimization data (USDJ, 1976: Table 21) indicate that, while household victimization rates tend to vary directly with household size, larger households have lower rates per person. For example, the total household victimization rates (including burglary, household larceny, and motor vehicle theft) per 1,000 households were 168 for single-person households and 326 for households containing six or more persons. Hence, six people distributed over six single-person households experience an average of 1,008 household victimizations, more than three times as many as one six-person household. Moreover, age of household head has a strong relationship to a household's victimization rate for these crimes. For households headed by persons under 20, the motor vehicle theft rate is nine times as high, and the burglary and household larceny rates four times as high as those for households headed by persons 65 and over (USDJ, 1976: Table 9).

While the data presented in this section were not collected originally for the purpose of testing the routine activity approach, our efforts to rework them for these purposes have proven fruitful. The routine activity approach is consistent with the data examined and, in addition, helps to accommodate within a rather simple and coherent analytical framework certain findings which, though not necessarily new, might otherwise be attributed only "descriptive" significance. In the next section, we examine macrosocial trends as they relate to trends in crime rates.

Changing Trends in Routine Activity Structure and Parallel Trends in Crime Rates

The main thesis presented here is that the dramatic increase in the reported crime rates in the U.S. since 1960 is linked to changes in the routine activity structure of American society and to a corresponding increase in target suitability and decrease in guardian presence. If such a thesis has validity, then we should be able to identify these social trends and show how they relate to predatory criminal victimization rates.

Trends in Human Activity Patterns

The decade 1960–1970 experienced noteworthy trends in the activities of the American population. For example, the percent of the population consisting of female college students increased 118 percent (USBC, 1975: Table 225). Married female labor force participant rates increased 31 percent (USBC, 1975: Table 563), while the percent of the population living as primary individuals increased by 34 percent (USBC, 1975: Table 51; see also Kobrin, 1976). We gain some further insight into changing routine activity patterns by comparing hourly data for 1960 and 1971 on households *unattended* by persons ages 14 or over when U.S. census interviewers first called.... These data suggest that the proportion of households unattended at 8 A.M. increased by almost half between 1960 and 1971. One also finds increases in rates of out-of-town travel, which provides greater opportunity for both daytime and nighttime burglary of residences. Between 1960 and 1970, there was a 72 percent increase in state and national park visits per capita (USBC, 1975), an 144 percent increase in the percent of plant workers eligible for three weeks vacation (BLS, 1975: Table 116), and an 184 percent increase in overseas travellers per 100,000 population (USBC, 1975: Table 366). The National Travel Survey, conducted as part of the U.S. Census Bureau's Census of Transportation, confirms the general trends, tallying an 81 percent increase in the number of vacations taken by Americans from 1967 to 1972, a five-year period (USBC, 1973a: Introduction).

The dispersion of activities away from households appears to be a major recent social change. Although this decade also experienced an important 31 percent increase in the percent of the population ages 15–24, age structure change was only one of many social trends occurring during the period, especially trends in the circulation of people and property in American society.

The importance of the changing activity structure is underscored by taking a brief look at demographic changes between the years 1970 and 1975, a period of continuing crime rate increments. Most of the recent changes in age structure relevant to crime rates already had occurred by 1970; indeed, the proportion of the population ages 15–24 increased by only 6 percent between 1970 and 1975, compared with a 15 percent increase during the five years 1965 to 1970. On the other hand, major changes in the structure of routine activities continued during these years. For example, in only five years, the estimated proportion of the population consisting of husband-present, married women in the labor force households increased by 11 percent, while the estimated number of non-husband-wife households per 100,000 population increased from 9,150 to 11,420, a 25 percent increase (USBC, 1976: Tables 50, 276; USBC, 1970–1975). At the same time, the percent of

population enrolled in higher education increased 16 percent between 1970 and 1975.

Related Property Trends and Their Relation to Human Activity Patterns

Many of the activity trends mentioned above normally involve significant investments in durable goods. For example, the dispersion of population across relatively more households (especially non-husband-wife households) enlarges the market for durable goods such as television sets and automobiles. Women participating in the labor force and both men and women enrolled in college provide a market for automobiles. Both work and travel often involve the purchase of major movable or portable durables and their use away from home.

Considerable data are available which indicate that sales of consumer goods changed dramatically between 1960 and 1970 (as did their size and weight), hence providing more suitable property available for theft. For example, during this decade, constant-dollar personal consumer expenditures in the United States for motor vehicles and parts increased by 71 percent, while constant-dollar expenditures for other durables increased by 105 percent (calculated from CEA, 1976: Table B-16). In addition, electronic household appliances and small household shipments increased from 56.2 to 119.7 million units (*Electrical Merchandising Week,* 1964; *Merchandising Week,* 1973). During the same decade, appliance imports increased in value by 681 percent (USBC, 1975: Table 1368).

This same period appears to have spawned a revolution in small durable product design which further feeds the opportunity for crime to occur. Relevant data from the 1960 and 1970 Sears catalogs on the weight of many consumer durable goods were examined. Sears is the nation's largest retailer and its policy of purchasing and relabeling standard manufactured goods makes its catalogs a good source of data on widely merchandised consumer goods. The lightest television listed for sale in 1960 weighed 38 lbs., compared with 15 lbs. for 1970. Thus, the lightest televisions were 2½ times as heavy in 1960 as 1970. Similar trends are observed for dozens of other goods listed in the Sears catalog. Data from *Consumer Reports Buying Guide*, published in December of 1959 and 1969, show similar changes for radios, record players, slide projectors, tape recorders, televisions, toasters and many other goods. Hence, major declines in weight between 1960 and 1970 were quite significant for these and other goods, which suggests that the consumer goods market may be producing many more targets suitable for theft. In general, one finds rapid growth in property suitable for illegal removal and in household and individual exposure to attack during the years 1960–1975.

Related Trends in Business Establishments

Of course, as households and individuals increased their ownership of small durables, businesses also increased the value of the merchandise which they transport and sell as well as the money involved in these transactions. Yet the Census of Business conducted in 1958, 1963, 1967, and 1972 indicate that the number of wholesale, retail, service, and public warehouse establishments (including establishments owned by large organizations) was a nearly constant ratio of one for every 16 persons in the United States. Since more goods and money were distributed over a relatively fixed number of business establishments, the tempo of business activity per establishment apparently was increasing. At the same time, the percent of the population employed as sales clerks or salesmen in retail trade declined from 1.48 percent to 1.27 percent between 1960 and 1970, a 14.7 percent decline (USBC, 1975: Table 589).

Though both business and personal property increased, the changing pace of activities appears to have exposed the latter to greater relative risk of attack, whether at home or elsewhere, due to the dispersion of goods among many more households, while concentrating goods in business establishments. However, merchandise in retail establishments with heavy volume and few employees to guard it probably is exposed to major increments in risk of illegal removal than is most other business property.

Composition of Crime Trends

If these changes in the circulation of people and property are in fact related to crime trends, the *composition* of the latter should reflect this. We expect relatively greater increases in personal and household victimization as compared with most business victimizations, while shoplifting should increase more rapidly than other types of thefts from businesses. We expect personal offenses at the hands of strangers to manifest greater increases than such offenses at the hands of nonstrangers. Finally, residential burglary rates should increase more in daytime than nighttime.

The available time series on the composition of offenses confirm these expectations. For example, Table 39.1 shows that commercial burglaries declined from 60 percent to 36 percent of the total, while daytime residential burglaries increased from 16 percent to 33 percent. Unlike the other crimes against business, shoplifting increased its share. Though we lack trend data on the circumstances of other violent offenses, murder data confirm our expectations. Between 1963 and 1975, felon-type murders increased from 17 percent to 32 percent of the total. Compared with a 47 percent increase in the rate of relative killings in this period, we calculated a 294 percent increase in the murder rate at the hands of known or suspected felon types.

Thus the trends in the composition of recorded crime rates appear to be highly consistent with the activity structure trends noted earlier. In the next section we apply the routine activity approach in order to model crime rate trends and social change in the post-World War II United States.

The Relationship of the Household Activity Ratio to Five Annual Official Index Crime Rates in the United States, 1947–1974

In this section, we test the hypothesis that aggregate official crime rate trends in the United States vary directly over time with the dispersion of activities away from family and household. The limitations of annual time series data do not allow construction of direct measures of changes in hourly activity patterns, or quantities, qualities and movements of exact stocks of household durable goods, but the Current Population Survey does provide related time series on labor force and household structure. From these data, we calculate annually (beginning in 1947) a household activity ratio by adding the number of married, husband-present female labor force participants (source: BLS, 1975: Table 5) to the number of non-husband-wife households (source: USBC, 1947–1976), dividing this sum by the total number of households in the U.S. (source: USBC, 1947–1976). This calculation provides an estimate of the proportion of American households in year t expected to be most highly exposed to risk of personal and property victimization due to the dispersion of their activities away from family and household and/or their likelihood of owning extra sets of durables subject to high risk of attack. Hence, the household activity ratio should vary directly with official index crime rates.

Our empirical goal in this section is to test this relationship, with controls for those variables which other researches have linked empirically to crime rate trends in the United States. Since various researches have found such trends to increase with the proportion of the population in teen and young adult years (Fox, 1976; Land and Felson, 1976; Sagi and Wellford, 1968; Weliford, 1973), we include the population ages 15–24 per 100,000 resident population in year t as our first control variable (source: USBC, various years). Others (e.g., Brenner, 1976a; 1976b) have found unemployment rates to vary directly with official crime rates over time, although this relationship elsewhere has been shown to be empirically questionable (see Mansfield et al., 1974: 463; Cohen and Felson, 1979). Thus, as our second control variable, we take the standard annual unemployment rate (per 100 persons ages 16 and over) as a measure of the business cycle (source: BLS, 1975).

Four of the five crime rates that we utilize here (forcible rape, aggravated assault, robbery and burglary) are taken from FBI estimates of offenses per 100,000 U.S. population (as revised and reported in OMB, 1973).... For our homicide indicator we employ the homicide mortality rate taken from the vital statistics data collected by the Bureau of the Census (various years)....

Findings

Our time-series analysis for the years 1947–1974 consistently revealed positive and statistically significant relationships between the household activity ratio and each official crime rate change....

Discussion

In our judgment many conventional theories of crime (the adequacy of which usually is evaluated by cross-sectional data, or no data at all) have difficulty accounting for the annual changes in crime rate trends in the post-World War II United States. These theories may prove useful in explaining crime trends during other periods, within specific communities, or in particular subgroups of the population. Longitudinal aggregate data for the United States, however, indicate that the trends for many of the presumed causal variables in these theoretical structures are in a direction opposite to those hypothesized to be the causes of crime. For example, during the decade 1960–1970, the percent of the population below the low-income level declined 44 percent and the unemployment rate declined 186 percent. Central city population as a share of the whole population declined slightly, while the percent of foreign stock declined 0.1 percent, etc. (see USBC, 1975: 654, 19, 39).

On the other hand, the convergence in time and space of three elements (motivated offenders, suitable targets, and the absence of capable guardians) appears useful for understanding crime rate trends. The lack of any of these elements is sufficient to prevent the occurrence of a successful direct-contact predatory crime. The convergence in time and space of suitable targets and the absence of capable guardians can lead to large increases in crime rates without any increase or change in the structural conditions that motivate individuals to engage in crime. Presumably, had the social indicators of the variables hypothesized to be the causes of crime in conventional theories changed in the direction of favoring increased crime in the post-World War II United States, the increases in crime rates likely would have been even more staggering than those which were observed. In any event, it is our belief that criminologists have underemphasized the importance of the convergence of suitable targets and the absence of capable guardians in explaining recent increases in the crime rate. Furthermore, the effects of the convergence in time and space of these elements may be multiplicative rather than additive. That is, their convergence by a fixed percentage may produce increases in crime rates far greater than that fixed percentage, demonstrating how some relatively modest social trends can contribute to some relatively large changes in crime rate trends. . . .

Without denying the importance of factors motivating offenders to engage in crime, we have focused specific attention upon violations themselves and the prerequisites for their occurrence. However, the routine activity approach might in the future be applied to the analysis of offenders and their inclinations as well. For example, the structure of primary group activity may affect the likelihood that cultural transmission or social control of criminal inclinations will occur, while the structure of the community may affect the tempo of criminogenic peer group activity. We also may expect that circumstances favorable for carrying out violations contribute to criminal inclinations in the long run by rewarding these inclinations.

We further suggest that the routine activity framework may prove useful in explaining why the criminal justice system, the community and the family have appeared so ineffective in exerting social control since 1960. Substantial increases in the opportunity to carry out predatory violations may have undermined society's mechanisms for social control. For example, it may be difficult for institutions seeking to increase the certainty, celerity and severity of punishment to compete with structural changes resulting in vast increases in the certainty, celerity and value of rewards to be gained from illegal predatory acts.

It is ironic that the very factors which increase the opportunity to enjoy the benefits of life also may increase the opportunity for predatory violations. For example, automobiles provide freedom of movement to offenders as well as average citizens and offer vulnerable targets for theft. College enrollment, female labor force participation, urbanization, suburbanization, vacations, and new electronic durables provide various opportunities to escape the confines of the household while they increase the risk of predatory victimization. Indeed, the opportunity for predatory crime appears to be enmeshed in the opportunity structure for legitimate activities to such an extent that it might be very difficult to root out substantial amounts of crime without modifying much of our way of life. Rather than assuming that predatory crime is simply an indicator of social breakdown, one might take it as a by product of freedom and prosperity as they manifest themselves in the routine activities of everyday life.

Discussion Questions

1. According to the routine activity approach, it is possible to experience large increases in the crime rate *without* any increase in the supply of motivated offenders. How can this be?
2. What do Cohen and Felson mean by "suitable targets" and "the absence of capable guardians"?

Describe how targets and guardianship have changed in the United States since World War II.
3. Describe the "routine activities" in which you engage. How might these activities increase or decrease your chance of criminal victimization?
4. Young people and males have higher rates of criminal victimization. How might the routine activities approach explain this?

35. Situational Crime Prevention

Ronald V. Clarke

This essay by Ronald Clarke (1980) is one of the early—and now classic—statements of "environmental criminology." Clarke stakes out the theoretical turf for an environmental perspective by illuminating both the limitations of traditional criminology and the promise of a novel vision of crime and its prevention.

Although there are diverse traditional theories—biological, psychological, sociological—Clarke argues that they share a common focus on uncovering what creates a "disposition" or motivation in individuals to want to break the law. People with this criminal disposition presumably carry it around with them across space and across time. This disposition explains why they offend at any given moment and, ultimately, why they have careers in crime.

The dispositional perspective also suggests a specific approach to crime prevention: To reduce offending, the challenge is how to eliminate a person's criminal predisposition. Doing so might involve rehabilitating an offender or, even better, attacking root causes of crime such as poor parenting practices or disorganized neighborhood conditions.

Clarke's criticism is two-fold. First, although not denying that people differ in their dispositions to offend, he notes that an actual criminal act depends on situational factors. Traditional theories, however, limit their attention to more distant factors involved in the creation of a criminal disposition (e.g., traits that are inherited; family life growing up). But people disposed to offend still must decide

whether to break the law in any given situation, and the nature of the situation can affect their choices (see Cornish and Clarke, Chapter 33 in Part X). Thus, even for a person predisposed to break the law, the presence of a police officer might make robbing a bank unattractive, whereas the presence of an alarm system might dissuade the offender from burglarizing a house.

One rebuttal to Clarke's view is that criminals' disposition to offend is so strong that, if their crime is foiled in one situation, they will simply move on and find another target to victimize. This process is called "displacement." However, research indicates that while it occurs, displacement is almost never total (Pease, 1994). When their crimes are thwarted, some offenders might search out other targets, but others just give up and do not break the law on this occasion.

This insight leads to Clarke's second criticism: Dispositional theories provide few practical tips on how to reduce crime. In his view, criminal dispositions are daunting to change because it is difficult to rehabilitate offenders (but see Cullen, 2002) or to eliminate the distant or "root causes" of these dispositions (see also Wilson, 1975). By contrast, the components of situations are easier to manipulate. The key in doing this situational intervention effectively is to make the choice of crime more difficult or less appealing.

Although Clarke's (1992; Cornish and Clarke, 2003) thinking would evolve, in this essay he

Reprinted with permission from Ronald V. Clarke. 1980. "'Situational' Crime Prevention: Theory and Practice," *British Journal of Criminology* 20 (April, 1980), pp. 136–147.

identified two general categories of situational factors that could be manipulated to prevent crime. First, it is possible to reduce "physical opportunities" needed to commit crime. This might involve using stronger material for coin boxes in public telephones or putting steering column locks on automobiles. Second, for those disposed to offend, it is possible to increase the "risks of being caught." Clarke admits the limits of trying to increase the deterrence achieved by police, but suggests that many other members of the public might provide a presence that would dissuade criminals from offending in a particular situation (e.g., the use of doormen or parking lot attendants).

Clarke's perspective can be criticized for downplaying the need to explain why some people arrive at situations ready to offend whereas others do not. Still, his situational or environmental focus is necessary for a more complete understanding of why crime occurs on some occasions and in some places—and not others. Further, his perspective has contributed to an emerging body of experiments showing that situational crime prevention can make society safer from crime (Clarke, 1992). Few other criminological theories can make this claim.

References

Clarke, Ronald V. 1980. "'Situational' Crime Prevention: Theory and Practice." *British Journal of Criminology* 20: 136–147.

——, ed. 1992. *Situational Crime Prevention: Successful Case Studies.* New York: Harrow and Heston.

Cornish, Derek B. and Ronald V. Clarke. 2003. "Opportunities, Precipitators, and Criminal Decisions: A Reply to Whortley's Critique of Situational Crime Prevention." *Crime Prevention Studies* 16: 41–96.

Cullen, Francis T. 2002. "Rehabilitation and Treatment Programs." In James Q. Wilson and Joan Petersilia (eds.), *Crime: Public Policies for Crime Control*, 2nd edition, pp. 253–289. Oakland, CA: ICS Press.

Pease, Ken. 1994. "Crime Prevention." In Mike Maguire, Rod Morgan, and Robert Reiner (eds.), *The Oxford Handbook of Criminology*, pp. 659–703. Oxford, UK: Clarendon Press.

Wilson, James Q. 1975. *Thinking About Crime.* New York: Vintage Books.

———

Conventional wisdom holds that crime prevention needs to be based on a thorough understanding of the causes of crime. Though it may be conceded that preventive measures (such as humps in the road to stop speeding) can sometimes be found without invoking sophisticated causal theory, "physical" measures which reduce opportunities for crime are often thought to be of limited value. They are said merely to suppress the impulse to offend which will then manifest itself on some other occasion and perhaps in even more harmful form. Much more effective are seen to be "social" measures (such as the revitalisation of communities, the creation of job opportunities for unemployed youth, and the provision of sports and leisure facilities), since these attempt to remove the root motivational causes of offending. These ideas about prevention are not necessarily shared by the man-in-the-street or even by policemen and magistrates, but they have prevailed among academics, administrators and others who contribute to the formulation of criminal policy. They are also consistent with a preoccupation of criminological theory with criminal "dispositions" (cf. Ohlin, 1970; Gibbons, 1971; Jeffery, 1971) and the purpose of this paper is to argue that an alternative theoretical emphasis on choices and decisions made by the offender leads to a broader and perhaps more realistic approach to crime prevention.

'Dispositional' Theories and Their Preventive Implications

. . . [C]riminological theories have been little concerned with the situational determinants of crime. Instead, the main object of these theories (whether biological, psychological, or sociological in orientation) has been to show how some people are born with, or come to acquire,

a "disposition" to behave in a consistently criminal manner. . . .

[T]he dispositional bias remains and renders
criminological theory unproductive in terms of
the preventive measures which it generates.
People are led to propose methods of preventive
intervention precisely where it is most difficult to
achieve any effects, i.e. in relation to the psychological events or the social and economic conditions
that are supposed to generate criminal dispositions. As James Q. Wilson (1975) has argued,
there seem to be no acceptable ways of modifying
temperament and other biological variables, and it
is difficult to know what can be done to make
parents more inclined to love their children or
exercise consistent discipline. Eradicating poverty
may be no real solution either, in that crime rates
have continued to rise since the war despite great
improvements in economic conditions. And even
if it were possible to provide people with the kinds
of jobs and leisure facilities they might want, there
is still no guarantee that crime would drop; few
crimes require much time or effort, and work and
leisure in themselves provide a whole range of
criminal opportunities. As for violent crime, there
would have to be a much clearer link between this
and media portrayals of violence before those who
cater to popular taste would be persuaded to
change their material. Finally, given public attitudes to offending which, judging by some opinion
surveys, can be quite punitive, there may not be a
great deal of additional scope for policies of diversion and decriminalisation which are favoured by
those who fear the consequences of "labelling."

These difficulties are primarily practical, but
they also reflect the uncertainties and inconsis-
tencies of treating distant psychological events
and social processes as the "causes" of crime. . . .

Crime as the Outcome of Choice

Some of the above theoretical difficulties could be
avoided by conceiving of crime not in dispositional terms, but as being the outcome of

immediate choices and decisions made by the
offender. This would also have the effect of
throwing a different light on preventive options.

. . .[C]ommonsense as well as the evidence of
ethnographic studies of delinquency (e.g. Parker,
1974) strongly suggest that people are usually
aware of consciously choosing to commit
offences. This does not mean that they are fully
aware of all the reasons for their behaviour nor
that their own account would necessarily satisfy a
criminologically sophisticated observer, who
might require information at least about (i) the
offender's motives; (ii) his mood; (iii) his moral
judgments concerning the act in question and the
"techniques of moral neutralisation" open to him
(cf. Matza, 1963); (iv) the extent of his criminal
knowledge and his perception of criminal opportunities; (v) his assessment of the risks of being
caught as well as the likely consequences; and
finally, as well as of a different order, (vi) whether
he has been drinking. These separate components
of subjective state and thought processes which
play a part in the decision to commit a crime will
be influenced by immediate situational variables
and by highly specific features of the individual's
history and present life circumstances in ways
that are so varied and countervailing as to
render unproductive the notion of a generalised
behavioural disposition to offend. Moreover, as
will be argued below, the specificity of the influences upon different criminal behaviours gives
much less credence to the "displacement"
hypothesis; the idea that reducing opportunities
merely results in crime being displaced to some
other time or place has been the major argument
against situational crime prevention.

In so far as an individual's social and physical
environments remain relatively constant and his
decisions are much influenced by past experience,
this scheme gives ample scope to account not only
for occasional offending but also for recidivism;
people acquire a repertoire of different responses
to meet particular situations and if the circumstances are right they are likely to repeat those

responses that have previously been rewarding. . . . There are three features, however, which are particularly worth drawing out for the sake of the ensuing discussion about crime prevention: first, explanation is focused more directly on the criminal event; second, the need to develop explanations for separate categories of crime is made explicit; and, third, the individual's current circumstances and the immediate features of the setting are given considerably more explanatory significance than in "dispositional" theories.

Preventive Implications of a 'Choice' Model

In fact, just as an understanding of past influences on behaviour may have little preventive pay-off, so too there may be limited benefits in according greater explanatory importance to the individual's current life circumstances. For example, the instrumental attractions of delinquency may always be greater for certain groups of individuals such as young males living in inner city areas. And nothing can be done about a vast range of misfortunes which continually befall people and which may raise the probability of their behaving criminally while depressed or angry.

Some practicable options for prevention do arise, however, from the greater emphasis upon situational features, especially from the direct and immediate relationship between these and criminal behaviour. By studying the spatial and temporal distribution of specific offences and relating these to measurable aspects of the situation, criminologists have recently begun to concern themselves much more closely with the possibilities of manipulating criminogenic situations in the interests of prevention. . . .

The suggestions for prevention arising out of the "situational" research that has been done can be conveniently divided into measures which (i) reduce the physical opportunities for offending or (ii) increase the chances of an offender being caught.

These categories are discussed separately below though there is some overlap between them; for example, better locks which take longer to overcome also increase the risks of being caught . . .

Reducing Physical Opportunities for Crime and the Problem of Displacement

Variations in physical opportunities for crime have sometimes been invoked to explain differences in crime rates within particular cities (e.g. Boggs, 1965; Baldwin and Bottoms, 1975) or temporal variations in crime; for example, Wilkins (1964) and Gould and his associates (Gould, 1969; Mansfield et al., 1974) have related levels of car theft to variations in the number of vehicles on the road. But these studies have not generally provided practicable preventive ideas—for example, the number of cars on the road cannot be reduced simply to prevent their theft—and it is only recently that there has been a concerted effort on the part of criminologists to find viable ways of blocking the opportunities for particular crimes.

The potential for controlling behaviour by manipulating opportunities is illustrated vividly by a study of suicide in Birmingham (Hassal and Trethowan, 1972). This showed that a marked drop in the rates of suicide between 1962 and 1970 was the result of a reduction in the poisonous content of the gas supplied to householders for cooking and heating, so that it became much more difficult for people to kill themselves by turning on the gas taps. Like many kinds of crime, suicide is generally regarded as being dictated by strong internal motivation and the fact that its incidence was greatly reduced by a simple (though unintentional) reduction in the opportunities to commit it suggests that it may be possible to achieve similar reductions in crime by "physical" means. Though suicide by other methods did not increase in Birmingham, the study also leads to direct consideration of the fundamental theoretical problem of "displacement" which, as Reppetto (1976) has pointed out, can occur in four different ways: time, place, method, and type of offence. In other words, does reducing opportunities or increasing the risks result merely in the offender choosing his moment more carefully or in seeking some other, perhaps more harmful method of gaining his ends? Or, alternatively, will he shift his attention to a similar but unprotected target, for example, another house, car or shop? Or, finally, will he turn instead to some other form of crime?

For those who see crime as the outcome of criminal disposition, the answers to these questions would tend to be in the affirmative ("bad will out") but under the alternative view of crime represented above matters are less straightforward. Answers would depend on the nature of the crime, the offender's strength of motivation, knowledge of alternatives, willingness to entertain them, and so forth. In the case of opportunistic crimes (i.e. ones apparently elicited by their very ease of accomplishment such as some forms of shoplifting or vandalism) it would seem that the probability of offending could be reduced markedly by making it more difficult to act. For crimes such as bank robbery, however, which often seem to be the province of those who make a living from crime, reducing opportunities may be less effective. (This may be less true of increasing the risks of being caught except that for many offences the risks may be so low at present that any increase would have to be very marked.) Providing effective protection for a particular bank would almost certainly displace the attention of potential robbers to others, and if all banks were given increased protection many robbers would no doubt consider alternative means of gaining their ends. It is by no means implausible, however, that others—for example, those who do not have the ability to develop more sophisticated methods or who may not be willing to use more violence—may accept their reduced circumstances and may even take legitimate employment.

It is the bulk of offences, however, which are neither "opportunistic" nor "professional" that pose the greatest theoretical dilemmas. These offences include many burglaries and instances of auto-crime where the offender, who may merely supplement his normal income through the proceeds of crime, has gone out with the deliberate intention of committing the offence and has sought out the opportunity to do so. The difficulty posed for measures which reduce opportunity is one of the vast number of potential targets combined with the generally low overall level of security. Within easy reach of every house with a burglar alarm, or car with an anti-theft device, are many others without such protection.

In some cases, however, it may be possible to protect a whole class of property, as the Post Office did when they virtually eliminated theft from telephone kiosks by replacing the vulnerable aluminum coinboxes with much stronger steel ones (cf. Mayhew et al., 1976). A further example is provided by the recent law in this country which requires all motor-cyclists to wear crash helmets. This measure was introduced to save lives, but it has also had the unintended effect of reducing thefts of motor-cycles (Mayhew et al., 1976). This is because people are unlikely to take someone else's motorbike on the spur of the moment unless they happen to have a crash helmet with them—otherwise they could easily be spotted by the police. But perhaps the best example comes from West Germany where, in 1963, steering column locks were made compulsory on *all* cars, old and new, with a consequent reduction of more than 60 per cent in levels of taking and driving away (Mayhew et al., 1976). (When steering column locks were introduced in this country in 1971 it was only to new cars and, although these are now at much less risk of being taken, overall levels of car-taking have not yet diminished because the risk to older cars had increased as a result of displacement).

Instances where criminal opportunities can be reduced for a whole class of property are comparatively few, but this need not always be a fatal difficulty. There must be geographical and temporal limits to displacement so that a town or city may be able to protect itself from some crime without displacing it elsewhere. The less determined the offender, the easier this will be; a simple example is provided by Decker's (1972) evidence that the use of "slugs" in parking-meters in a New York district was greatly reduced by replacing the meters with ones which incorporated a slug-rejector device and in which the last coin inserted was visible in a plastic window. For most drivers there would be little advantage in parking their cars in some other district just because they could continue to use slugs there.

The question of whether, when stopped from committing a particular offence, people would turn instead to some other quite different form of crime is much more difficult to settle empirically, but many of the same points about motivation, knowledge of alternatives and so forth still apply. Commonsense also suggests, for example, that few of those Germans prevented by steering column locks from taking cars to get home at night are likely to have turned instead to hijacking taxis or to mugging passers-by for the money to get home. More likely, they may have decided that next time they would make sure of catching the last bus home or that it was time to save up for their own car.

Increasing the Risks of Being Caught

In practice, increasing the chances of being caught usually means attempting to raise the chances of an offender being seen by someone who is likely to take action. The police are the most obvious group likely to intervene effectively, but studies of the effectiveness of this aspect of their deterrent role are not especially encouraging (Kelling et al., 1974; Manning, 1977; Clarke and Hough, 1980). The reason seems to be that, when set against the vast number of opportunities for

offending represented by the activities of a huge population of citizens for the 24 hours of the day, crime is a relatively rare event. The police cannot be everywhere at once and, moreover, much crime takes place in private. Nor is much to be expected from the general public (Mayhew et al., 1979). People in their daily round rarely see crime in progress; if they do they are likely to place some innocent interpretation on what they see; they may be afraid to intervene or they may feel the victims would resent interference; and they may encounter practical difficulties in summoning the police or other help in time. They are much more likely to take effective action to protect their own homes or immediate neighbourhood, but they are often away from these for substantial periods of the day and, moreover, the risks of crime in residential settings, at least in many areas of this country, are not so great as to encourage much vigilance. For instance, assuming that about 50 percent of burglaries are reported to the police (cf. Home Office, 1979), a house in this country will on average be burgled once every 30 years. Even so, there is evidence (Department of the Environment, 1977; Wilson, 1978) that "defensible space" designs on housing estates confer some protection from vandalism, if not as much as might have been expected from the results of Newman's (1973) research into crime on public housing projects in the United States (cf. Clarke, 1979; Mayhew, 1979).

A recent Home Office Research report (Mayhew et al., 1979) has argued, however, that there is probably a good deal of unrealised potential for making more deliberate use of the surveillance role of employees who come into regular and frequent contact with the public in a semi-official capacity. Research in the United States (Newman, 1973; Reppetto, 1974) and Canada (Waller and Okhiro, 1978) has shown that apartment blocks with doormen are less vulnerable to burglary, while research in this country has shown that vandalism is much less of a problem on buses with conductors (Mayhew et al., 1976) and on estates with resident caretakers (Department of the Environment, 1977). There is also evidence (in Post Office records) that public telephones in places such as pubs or launderettes, which are given some supervision by staff, suffer almost no vandalism in comparison with those in kiosks; that car parks with attendants in control have lower rates of auto-crime (*Sunday Times*, April 9, 1978); that football hooliganism on trains has been reduced by a variety of measures including permission for club stewards to travel free of charge; and that shoplifting is discouraged by the presence of assistants who are there to serve the customers (Walsh, 1978). Not everybody employed in a service capacity would be suited or willing to take on additional security duties, but much of their deterrent role may result simply from their being around. Employing more of them, for greater parts of the day, may therefore be all that is needed in most cases. In other cases, it may be necessary to employ people more suited to a surveillance role, train them better to carry it out, or even provide them with surveillance aids. Providing the staff at four London Underground stations with closed circuit television has been shown in a recent Home Office Research Unit study (Mayhew et al., 1979) to have substantially reduced theft and robbery offences at those stations.

Some Objections

Apart from the theoretical and practical difficulties of the approach advocated in this paper, it is in apparent conflict with the "nothing works" school of criminological thought as given recent expression by Wolfgang (1977): ". . . the weight of empirical evidence indicates that no current preventative, deterrent, or rehabilitative intervention scheme has the desired effect of reducing crime." But perhaps a panacea is being sought when all it may be possible to achieve is a reduction in particular forms of crime as a result of specific and sometimes localised measures. Examples of such reductions are given above and, while most of these relate to rather commonplace offences of

theft and vandalism, there is no reason why similar measures cannot be successfully applied to other quite different forms of crime. It has been argued by many people (Rhodes, 1977, provides a recent example) that reducing the availability of hand-guns through gun-control legislation would reduce crimes of violence in the United States and elsewhere. Speeding and drunken driving could probably be reduced by fitting motor vehicles with devices which are now at an experimental stage (Ekblom, 1979). And there is no doubt (Wilkinson, 1977) that the rigorous passenger and baggage screening measures introduced at airports, particularly in the United States, have greatly reduced the incidence of airline hijackings. There are many crimes, however, when the offender is either so determined or so emotionally aroused that they seem to be beyond the scope of this approach. A further constraint will be costs: many shops, for example, which could reduce shoplifting by giving up self-service methods and employing more assistants or even store detectives, have calculated that this would not be worth the expense either in direct costs or in a reduction of turnover. Morally dubious as this policy might at first sight appear, these shops may simply have learned a lesson of more general application, i.e. a certain level of crime may be the inevitable consequence of practices and institutions which we cherish or find convenient and the "cost" of reducing crime below this level may be unacceptable.

The gradualist approach to crime prevention advocated here might also attract criticism from some social reformers, as well as some deviancy theorists, for being unduly conservative. The former group, imbued with dispositional theory, would see the only effective way of dealing with crime as being to attack its roots through the reduction of inequalities of wealth, class and education—a solution which, as indicated above, has numerous practical and theoretical difficulties. The latter group would criticise the approach, not for its lack of effectiveness but—on the grounds that there is insufficient consensus in society about what behaviour should be treated as crime—for helping to preserve an undesirable status quo. Incremental change, however, may be the most realistic way of achieving consensus as well as a more equitable society. Most criminologists would probably also agree that it would be better for the burden of crime reduction to be gradually shifted away from the criminal justice system, which may be inherently selective and punitive in its operation, to preventive measures whose social costs may be more equitably distributed among all members of society. The danger to be guarded against would be that the attention of offenders might be displaced away from those who can afford to purchase protection to those who cannot. This probably happens already to some extent and perhaps the best way of dealing with the problem would be through codes of security which would be binding on car manufacturers, builders, local transport operators and so forth. Another danger is that those who have purchased protection might become less willing to see additional public expenditure on the law enforcement and criminal justice services—and this is a problem that might only be dealt with through political leadership and public education.

Many members of the general public might also find it objectionable that crime was being stopped, not by punishing wrong-doers, but by inconveniencing the law-abiding. The fact that opportunity-reducing and risk-increasing measures are too readily identified with their more unattractive aspects (barbed wire, heavy padlocks, guard-dogs and private security forces) adds fuel to the fire. And in some of their more sophisticated forms (closed circuit television surveillance and electronic intruder alarms) they provoke fears, on the one hand, of "big brother" forms of state control and, on the other, of a "fortress society" in which citizens in perpetual fear of their fellows scuttle from one fortified environment to another.

Expressing these anxieties has a value in checking potential abuses of power, and questioning the means of dealing with crime can also help to keep the problem of crime in perspective. But it should also be said that the kind of measures discussed above need not always be obtrusive (except where it is important to maximise their deterrent effects) and need not in any material way infringe individual liberties or the quality of life. Steel cash compartments in telephone kiosks are indistinguishable from aluminum ones, and vandal-resistant polycarbonate looks just like glass. Steering column locks are automatically brought into operation on removing the ignition key, and many people are quite unaware that their cars are fitted with them. "Defensible space" designs in housing estates have the additional advantage of promoting feelings of neighbourliness and safety, though perhaps too little attention has been paid to some of their less desirable effects such as possible encroachments on privacy as a result of overlooking. And having more bus conductors, housing estate caretakers, swimming bath attendants and shop assistants means that people benefit from improved services—even if they have to pay for them either directly or through the rates. . . .

Summary

It is argued that the "dispositional" bias of most current criminological theory has resulted in "social" crime prevention measures being given undue prominence and "situational" measures being devalued. An alternative theoretical emphasis on decisions and choices made by the offender (which in turns allows more weight to the circumstances of offending) results in more support for a situational approach to prevention. Examples of the effectiveness of such an approach are provided and some of the criticisms that have been made of it on social and ethical grounds are discussed.

Discussion Questions

1. What is a "dispositional" theory? Why would the conditions identified by dispositional theories as causing crime be difficult to change?

2. How does a "dispositional" theory differ from a "situational" or environmental criminology theory?

3. What is "displacement"? Why is displacement a concern for those, like Ronald Clarke, who favor a situational approach to crime prevention?

4. Think about where you live, work, or attend college. Can you identify any changes that might be made to your immediate environment that would make it less vulnerable to being victimized by an offender?

36. Broken Windows

James Q. Wilson and George L. Kelling

*There is a long tradition within criminology—
extending to the Chicago School and the work of
Shaw and McKay—of attributing high rates of
crime in inner-city areas to a breakdown in community control (see Part III). In setting forth their
"broken windows" theory, James Q. Wilson and
George L. Kelling embrace this thesis but then
proceed to offer an alternative vision for why
informal controls in impoverished areas become
ineffective (see also Kelling and Coles, 1996).*

*Sociological perspectives see community social
control as an intervening condition between structural conditions on one side of the causal model
and crime on the other side (structural conditions
→ breakdown of control → high crimes rates).
Such structural conditions might include the concentration of disadvantage, heterogeneity, racial
segregation, family disruption, residential mobility, and/or the loss of industry and jobs. By contrast, Wilson and Kelling remain silent on the
importance of these factors and thus implicitly
suggest that they do not determine which communities have high rates of crime.*

*Indeed, Wilson and Kelling imply that struc-
tural "root causes" do not distinguish safe from
unsafe neighborhoods. For them, communities are
not static entities whose decline into a crime-
ridden state is compelled by the weight of structural risk factors. Rather, communities are
dynamic and amenable to change. Their fate is
not foreordained but varies by whether steps are*

*taken to ensure that the small problem of minor
misconduct does not escalate into the large problem of serious crime.*

*Communities thus are like houses that experi-
ence a broken window. Consider one house in
which a window is smashed, but the owner hurries
out to the hardware store and immediately
replaces the shattered pane of glass. The house's
problem has been fixed, and the message has been
sent that the resident is present, takes care of the
property, and might be watching for the next
vandal. But then consider a second house in
which the smashed window is left untended.
After a while, the sight of the broken window
sends a different message—this time that nobody
cares the upkeep of the house. A rock is
tossed through another window. And if this pane
of glass is not replaced, pretty soon the house's
windows become a target for many rocks thrown
by many people.*

*Wilson and Kelling use this "broken windows"
metaphor to outline the process by which neighborhoods spiral into decline. Many inner-city
communities are likely to be locations that attract
"disreputable" people—rowdy teenagers who congregate on corners and deface buildings with graffiti, panhandlers and prostitutes who approach
passersby, the mentally ill who wander the streets
and talk to themselves, and those with chronic
substance abuse problems who sleep in doorways
and urinate in alleys. If the behavior of these*

Copyright © 1982 by James Q. Wilson and George L. Kelling, "Broken Windows," *The Atlantic Monthly*, 249(3), pp. 29–38.
Reprinted with permission.

disreputable people is allowed to get bothersome—if they are allowed to "take over" public spaces—the neighborhood will descend into a state of disorder.

Disorder is a problem because, like a broken window, it conveys the message that nobody is "home" who cares enough to maintain order. When this occurs, respectable people become fearful to venture into public; they retreat into their residences or move to other communities. Informal social controls thus weaken. Meanwhile more hardened offenders "invade" the area because they realize that this is a place where serious crime elicits little threat of punishment; they will be free, in short, to break as many windows as they wish.

Thus, the causal model suggested by Wilson and Kelling is as follows: disorder → breakdown of control → high crime rates. This model is important because, unlike many criminological theories, it contains a clear blueprint for making communities safer: restore order. This prescription, however, leads to the more exacting question of who is going to curtail disorder. That is, who is going to fix the broken windows?

Wilson and Kelling propose that the police should be the key agents in reestablishing control. To accomplish this task, officers must spend less time racing to crime scenes in vehicles with lights flashing and sirens blaring. Instead, officers need to return to a style of enforcement used by their predecessors, in which they walk the beat in neighborhoods, come to know the residents, and personally take steps to maintain order. Disreputable people are not to be ignored. Instead, officers would encourage them to "move on" and, when possible, arrest them for minor infractions of the law. The officers' zero tolerance for distruptive conduct would make public spaces orderly and give respectable citizens the confidence once again to take to the streets.

"Broken windows" or "zero-tolerance" policing is controversial on three counts. First, it is not clear that it is effective in reducing serious crime (compare Kelling and Coles, 1996, with Harcourt, 2001). Second, this approach divides the world into "disreputable" and "respectable" people. It then assumes that it is acceptable to aggressively police this category of bothersome individuals, regardless of the circumstances and personal vulnerabilities that may have led them to become "disreputable" (Harcourt, 2001). Third, by trumpeting the preventative powers of policing, commentators are largely free to ignore the role inequitable structural conditions play in creating and nourishing community decline and crime (Taylor, 2001).

References

Harcourt, Bernard E. 2001. *Illusion of Order: The False Promise of Broken Windows Policing.* Cambridge, MA: Harvard University Press.

Kelling, George L. and Catherine M. Coles. 1996. *Fixing Broken Windows: Restoring Order and Reducing Crime in Our Communities.* New York: Simon & Schuster.

Taylor, Ralph B. 2001. *Breaking Away From Broken Windows: Baltimore Neighborhoods and the Nationwide Fight Against Crime, Grime, Fear, and Decline.* Boulder, CO: Westview Press.

In the mid-1970s, the state of New Jersey announced a "Safe and Clean Neighborhoods Program," designed to improve the quality of community life in twenty-eight cities. As part of that program, the state provided money to help cities take police officers out of their patrol cars and assign them to walking beats. The governor and other state officials were enthusiastic about using foot patrol as a way of cutting crime, but many police chiefs were skeptical. Foot patrol, in their eyes, had been pretty much discredited. It reduced the mobility of the police, who thus had difficulty responding to citizen calls for service, and it weakened headquarters control over patrol officers.

Many police officers also disliked foot patrol, but for different reasons: it was hard work, it kept them outside on cold, rainy nights, and it reduced their chances for making a "good pinch." In some departments, assigning officers to foot patrol had been used as a form of punishment. And academic experts on policing doubted that foot patrol would have any impact on crime rates; it was, in the opinion of most, little more than a sop to public opinion. But since the state was paying for it, the local authorities were willing to go along.

Five years after the program started, the Police Foundation, in Washington, D.C., published an evaluation of the foot-patrol project. Based on its analysis of a carefully controlled experiment carried out chiefly in Newark, the foundation concluded, to the surprise of hardly anyone, that foot patrol had not reduced crime rates. But residents of the foot-patrolled neighborhoods seemed to feel more secure than persons in other areas, tended to believe that crime had been reduced, and seemed to take fewer steps to protect themselves from crime (staying at home with the doors locked, for example). Moreover, citizens in the foot-patrol areas had a more favorable opinion of the police than did those living elsewhere. And officers walking beats had higher morale, greater job satisfaction, and a more favorable attitude toward citizens in their neighborhoods than did officers assigned to patrol cars.

These findings may be taken as evidence that the skeptics were right—foot patrol has no effect on crime; it merely fools the citizens into thinking that they are safer. But in our view, and in the view of the authors of the Police Foundation study (of whom Kelling was one), the citizens of Newark were not fooled at all. They knew what the foot-patrol officers were doing, they knew it was different from what motorized officers do, and they knew that having officers walk beats did in fact make their neighborhoods safer.

But how can a neighborhood be "safer" when the crime rate has not gone down—in fact, may have gone up? Finding the answer requires first that we understand what most often frightens people in public places. Many citizens, of course, are primarily frightened by crime, especially crime involving a sudden, violent attack by a stranger. This risk is very real, in Newark as in many large cities. But we tend to overlook or forget another source of fear—the fear of being bothered by disorderly people. Not violent people, nor, necessarily, criminals, but disreputable or obstreperous or unpredictable people: panhandlers, drunks, addicts, rowdy teenagers, prostitutes, loiterers, the mentally disturbed.

What foot-patrol officers did was to elevate, to the extent they could, the level of public order in these neighborhoods. Though the neighborhoods were predominantly black and the foot patrolmen were mostly white, this "order-maintenance" function of the police was performed to the general satisfaction of both parties.

One of us (Kelling) spent many hours walking with Newark foot-patrol officers to see how they defined "order" and what they did to maintain it. One beat was typical: a busy but dilapidated area in the heart of Newark, with many abandoned buildings, marginal shops (several of which prominently displayed knives and straight-edged razors in their windows), one large department store, and, most important, a train station and several major bus stops. Though the area was run-down, its streets were filled with people, because it was a major transportation center. The good order of this area was important not only to those who lived and worked there but also to many others, who had to move through it on their way home, to supermarkets, or to factories.

The people on the street were primarily black; the officer who walked the street was white. The people were made up of "regulars" and "strangers." Regulars included both "decent folk" and some drunks and derelicts who were always there but who "knew their place." Strangers were, well, strangers, and viewed suspiciously, sometimes apprehensively. The officer—call him Kelly— knew who the regulars were, and they knew him. As he saw his job, he was to keep an eye on strangers, and make certain that the disreputable regulars observed some informal but widely understood rules. Drunks and addicts could sit on the stoops, but could not lie down. People could drink on side streets, but not at the main intersection. Bottles had to be in paper bags. Talking to, bothering, or begging from people waiting at the bus stop was strictly forbidden. If a dispute erupted between a businessman and a customer, the businessman was assumed to be right, especially if the customer was a stranger. If a stranger loitered, Kelly would ask him if he had any means of support and what his business was; if he gave unsatisfactory answers, he was sent on his way. Persons who broke the informal rules, especially those who bothered people waiting at bus stops, were arrested for vagrancy. Noisy teenagers were told to keep quiet.

These rules were defined and enforced in collaboration with the "regulars" on the street. Another neighborhood might have different rules, but these, everybody understood, were the rules for this neighborhood. If someone violated them, the regulars not only turned to Kelly for help but also ridiculed the violator. Sometimes what Kelly did could be described as "enforcing the law," but just as often it involved taking informal or extralegal steps to help protect what the neighborhood had decided was the appropriate level of public order. Some of the things he did probably would not withstand a legal challenge.

A determined skeptic might acknowledge that a skilled foot-patrol officer can maintain order but still insist that this sort of "order" has little to do with the real sources of community fear—that is, with violent crime. To a degree, that is true. But two things must be borne in mind. First, outside observers should not assume that they know how much of the anxiety now endemic in many big-city neighborhoods stems from a fear of "real" crime and how much from a sense that the street is disorderly, a source of distasteful, worrisome encounters. The people of Newark, to judge from their behavior and their remarks to interviewers, apparently assign a high value to public order, and feel relieved and reasured when the police help them maintain that order.

Second, at the community level, disorder and crime are usually inextricably linked, in a kind of developmental sequence. Social psychologists and police officers tend to agree that if a window in a building is broken *and is left unrepaired,* all the rest of the windows will soon be broken. This is as true in nice neighborhoods as in run-down ones. Window-breaking does not necessarily occur on a large scale because some areas are inhabited by determined window-breakers whereas others are populated by window-lovers; rather, one unrepaired broken window is a signal that no one cares, and so breaking more windows costs nothing. (It has always been fun.)

Philip Zimbaldo, a Stanford psychologist, reported in 1969 on some experiments testing the broken-window theory. He arranged to have an automobile without license plates parked with its hood up on a street in the Bronx and a comparable automobile on a street in Palo Alto, California. The car in the Bronx was attacked by "vandals" within ten minutes of its "abandonment." The first to arrive were a family—father, mother, and young son—who removed the radiator and battery. Within twenty-four hours, virtually everything of value had been removed. Then random destruction began—windows were smashed, parts torn off, upholstery ripped. Children began to use the car as a playground. Most of the adult "vandals" were well-dressed, apparently clean-cut whites. The car in Palo Alto sat untouched for more than a week. Then Zimbardo smashed part of it with a sledge-hammer. Soon, passersby were joining in. Within a few hours, the car had been turned upside down and utterly destroyed. Again, the "vandals" appeared to be primarily respectable whites.

Untended property becomes fair game for people out for fun or plunder, and even for people who ordinarily would not dream of doing such things and who probably consider themselves law-abiding. Because of the nature of community life in the Bronx—its anonymity, the frequency with which cars are abandoned and things are stolen or broken, the past experience of "no one caring"—vandalism begins much more quickly than it does in staid Palo Alto, where people have come to believe that private possessions are cared for, and that mischievous behavior is costly. But vandalism can occur anywhere once communal barriers—the sense of mutual regard and the obligations of civility—are lowered by actions that seem to signal that "no one cares."

We suggest that "untended" behavior also leads to the breakdown of community controls. A stable neighborhood of families who care for their homes, mind each other's children, and confidently frown on unwanted intruders can change, in a few years or even a few months, to an inhospitable and frightening jungle. A piece of property is abandoned, weeds grow up, a window is smashed. Adults stop scolding rowdy children; the children, emboldened, become more rowdy. Families move out, unattached adults move in. Teenagers gather in front of the corner store. The merchant asks them to move; they refuse. Fights occur. Litter accumulates. People start drinking in front of the grocery; in time, and inebriate slumps to the sidewalk and is allowed to sleep it off. Pedestrians are approached by panhandlers.

At this point it is not inevitable that serious crime will flourish or violent attacks on strangers will occur. But many residents will think that crime, especially violent crime, is on the rise, and they will modify their behavior accordingly. They will use the streets less often, and when on the streets will stay apart from their fellows, moving with averted eyes, silent lips, and hurried steps. "Don't get involved." For some residents, this growing atomization will matter little, because the neighborhood is not their "home" but "the place where they live." Their interests are elsewhere; they are cosmopolitans. But it will matter greatly to other people, whose lives derive meaning and satisfaction from local attachments rather than worldly involvement; for them, the neighborhood will cease to exist except for a few reliable friends whom they arrange to meet.

Such an area is vulnerable to criminal invasion. Though it is not inevitable, it is more likely that

here, rather than in places where people are confident they can regulate public behavior by informal controls, drugs will change hands, prostitutes will solicit, and cars will be stripped. That the drunks will be robbed by boys who do it as a lark, and the prostitutes' customers will be robbed by men who do it purposefully and perhaps violently. That muggings will occur.

Among those who often find it difficult to move away from this are the elderly. Surveys of citizens suggest that the elderly are much less likely to be the victims of crime than younger persons, and some have inferred from this that the well-known fear of crime voiced by the elderly is an exaggeration: perhaps we ought not to design special programs to protect older persons; perhaps we should even try to talk them out of their mistaken fears. This argument misses the point. The prospect of a confrontation with an obstreperous teenager or a drunken panhandler can be as fear-inducing for defenseless persons as the prospect of meeting an actual robber; indeed, to a defenseless person, the two kinds of confrontation are often indistinguishable. Moreover, the lower rate at which the elderly are victimized is a measure of the steps they have already taken—chiefly, staying behind locked doors—to minimize the risks they face. Young men are more frequently attacked than older women, not because they are easier or more lucrative targets but because they are on the streets more.

Nor is the connection between disorderliness and fear made only by the elderly. Susan Estrich, of the Harvard Law School, has recently gathered together a number of surveys on the sources of public fear. One, done in Portland, Oregon, indicated that three fourths of the adults interviewed cross to the other side of a street when they see a gang of teenagers; another survey, in Baltimore, discovered that nearly half would cross the street to avoid even a single strange youth. When an interviewer asked people in a housing project where the most dangerous spot was, they mentioned a place where young persons gathered to drink and play music, despite the fact that not a single crime had occurred there. In Boston public housing projects, the greatest fear was expressed by persons living in the buildings where disorderliness and incivility, not crime, were the greatest. Knowing this helps one understand the significance of such otherwise harmless displays as subway graffiti. As Nathan Glazer has written, the proliferation of graffiti, even when not obscene, confronts the subway rider with the "inescapable knowledge that the environment he must endure for an hour or more a day is uncontrolled and uncontrollable, and that anyone can invade it to do whatever damage and mischief the mind suggests."

In response to fear, people avoid one another, weakening controls. Sometimes they call the police. Patrol cars arrive, an occasional arrest occurs, but crime continues and disorder is not abated. Citizens complain to the police chief, but he explains that his department is low on personnel and that the courts do not punish petty or first-time offenders. To the residents, the police who arrive in squad cars are either ineffective or uncaring; to the police, the residents are animals who deserve each other. The citizens may soon stop calling the police, because "they can't do anything."

The process we call urban decay has occurred for centuries in every city. But what is happening today is different in at least two important respects. First, in the period before, say, World War II, city dwellers—because of money costs, transportation difficulties, familial and church connections—could rarely move away from neighborhood problems. When movement did occur, it tended to be along public-transit routes. Now mobility has become exceptionally easy for all but the poorest or those who are blocked by racial prejudice. Earlier crime waves had a kind of built-in self-correcting mechanism: the determination of a neighborhood or community to reassert control over its turf. Areas in Chicago, New York, and Boston would experience crime and gang wars, and then normalcy would return, as the families for whom no alternative residences were possible reclaimed their authority over the streets.

Second, the police in this earlier period assisted in that reassertion of authority by acting, sometimes violently, on behalf of the community. Young toughs were roughed up, people were arrested "on suspicion" or for vagrancy, and prostitutes and petty thieves were routed. "Rights" were something enjoyed by decent folk, and perhaps also by the serious professional criminal, who avoided violence and could afford a lawyer.

This pattern of policing was not an aberration or the result of occasional excess. From the earliest days of the nation, the police function was seen primarily as that of a night watchman: to maintain order against the chief threats to order—fire, wild animals, and disreputable behavior. Solving crimes was viewed not as a police responsibility but as a private one. In the March, 1969, *Atlantic*, one of us (Wilson) wrote a brief account of how the police role had slowly changed from maintaining order to fighting crimes. The change began with the creation of private detectives (often ex-criminals), who worked on a contingency-fee basis for individuals who had suffered losses. In time, the detectives were absorbed into municipal police agencies and paid a regular salary; simultaneously, the responsibility for prosecuting thieves was shifted from the aggrieved private citizen to the professional prosecutor. This process was not complete in most places until the twentieth century.

In the 1960s, when urban riots were a major problem, social scientists began to explore carefully the order-maintenance function of the police, and to suggest ways of improving it—not to make streets safer (its original function) but to reduce the incidence of mass violence. Order-maintenance became, to a degree, coterminous with "community relations." But, as the crime wave that began in the early 1960s continued without abatement throughout the decade and into the 1970s, attention shifted to the role of the police as crime-fighters. Studies of police behavior ceased, by and large, to be accounts of the order-maintenance function and became, instead, efforts to propose and test ways whereby the police could solve more crimes, make more arrests, and gather better evidence. If these things could be done, social scientists assumed, citizens would be less fearful.

A great deal was accomplished during this transition, as both police chiefs and outside experts emphasized the crime-fighting function in their plans, in the allocation of resources, and in deployment of personnel. The police may well have become better crime-fighters as a result. And doubtless they remained aware of their responsibility for order. But the link between order-maintenance and crime-prevention, so obvious to earlier generations, was forgotten.

That link is similar to the process whereby one broken window becomes many. The citizen who fears the ill-smelling drunk, the rowdy teenager, or the importuning beggar is not merely expressing his distaste for unseemly behavior; he is also giving voice to a bit of folk wisdom that happens to be a correct generalization—namely, that serious street crime flourishes in areas in which disorderly behavior goes unchecked. The unchecked panhandler is, in effect, the first broken window. Muggers and robbers, whether opportunistic or professional, believe they reduce their chances of being caught or even identified if they operate on streets where potential victims are already intimidated by prevailing conditions. If the neighborhood cannot keep a bothersome panhandler from annoying passersby, the thief may reason, it is even less likely to call the police to identify a potential mugger or to interfere if the mugging actually takes place.

Some police administrators concede that this process occurs, but argue that motorized-patrol officers can deal with it as effectively as foot-patrol officers. We are not so sure. In theory, an officer in a squad car can observe as much as an officer on foot; in theory, the former can talk to as many people as the latter. But the reality of police-citizen encounters is powerfully altered by the automobile. An officer on foot cannot separate himself from the street people; if he is approached, only his uniform and his personality can help him manage whatever is about to happen. And he can never be certain what that will be—a request for directions, a plea for help, an angry denunciation, a teasing remark, a confused babble, a threatening gesture.

In a car, an officer is more likely to deal with street people by rolling down the window and looking at them. The door and the window exclude the approaching citizen; they are a barrier. Some officers take advantage of this barrier, perhaps unconsciously, by acting differently if in the car than they would on foot. We have seen this countless times. The police car pulls up to a corner where teenagers are gathered. The window is rolled down. The officer stares at the youths. They stare back. The officer says to one, "C'mere." He saunters over, conveying to his friends by his elaborately casual style the idea that he is not intimidated by authority. "What's your name?" "Chuck." "Chuck who?" "Chuck Jones." "What'ya doing, Chuck?" "Nothin'." "Got a P. O. [parole officer]?" "Nah." "Sure?" "Yeah." "Stay out of trouble, Chuckie." Meanwhile, the other boys laugh and exchange comments among themselves, probably at the officer's expense. The officer stares harder. He cannot be certain what is being said, nor can he join in and, by displaying his own skill at street banter, prove that he cannot be "put down." In the process, the officer has learned almost nothing, and the boys have decided the officer is an alien force who can safely be disregarded, even mocked.

Our experience is that most citizens like to talk to a police officer. Such exchanges give them a sense of importance, provide them with the basis for gossip, and allow them to explain to the authorities what is worrying them (whereby they gain a modest but significant sense of having "done something" about the problem). You approach a person on foot more easily, and talk to him more readily, than you do a person in a car. Moreover, you can more easily retain some anonymity if you draw an officer aside for a private chat. Suppose you want to pass on a tip about who is stealing handbags, or who offered to sell you a stolen TV. In the inner city, the culprit, in all likelihood, lives nearby. To walk up to a marked patrol car and lean in the window is to convey a visible signal that you are a "fink."

The essence of the police role in maintaining order is to reinforce the informal control mechanisms of the community itself. The police cannot, without committing extraordinary resources, provide a substitute for that informal control. On the other hand, to reinforce those natural forces the police must accommodate them. And therein lies the problem.

Should police activity on the street be shaped, in important ways, by the standards of the neighborhood rather than by the rules of the state? Over the past two decades, the shift of police from order-maintenance to law-enforcement has brought them increasingly under the influence of legal restrictions, provoked by media complaints and enforced by court decisions and departmental orders. As a consequence, the order-maintenance functions of the police are now governed by rules developed to control police relations with suspected criminals. This is, we think, an entirely new development. For centuries, the role of the police as watchmen was judged primarily not in terms of its compliance with appropriate procedures but rather in terms of its attaining a desired objective. The objective was order, an inherently ambiguous term but a condition that people in a given community recognized when they saw it. The means were the same as those the community itself would employ, if its members were sufficiently determined, courageous, and authoritative. Detecting and apprehending criminals, by contrast, was a means to an end, not an end in itself; a judicial determination of guilt or innocence was the hoped-for result of the law-enforcement mode. From the first, the police were expected to follow rules defining that process, though states differed in how stringent the rules should be. The criminal-apprehension process was always understood to involve individual rights, the violation of which was unacceptable because it meant that the violating officer would be acting as a judge and jury—and that was not his job. Guilt or innocence was to be determined by universal standards under special procedures.

Ordinarily, no judge or jury ever sees the persons caught up in a dispute over the appropriate level of neighborhood order. That is true not only because most cases are handled informally on the street but also because no universal standards are available to settle arguments over disorder, and thus a judge may not be any wiser or more effective than a police officer. Until quite recently in many states, and even today in some places, the police make arrests on such charges as "suspicious person" or "vagrancy" or "public drunkenness"—charges with scarcely any legal meaning. These charges exist not because society wants judges to punish vagrants or drunks but because it wants an officer to have the legal tools to remove undersirable persons from a neighborhood when informal efforts to preserve order in the streets have failed.

Once we begin to think of all aspects of police work as involving the application of universal rules under special procedures, we inevitably ask what constitutes an "undesirable person" and why we should "criminalize" vagrancy or drunkenness. A strong and commendable desire to see that people are treated fairly makes us worry about allowing the police to rout persons who are undesirable by some vague or parochial standard. A growing and not-so-commendable utilitarianism leads us to doubt that any behavior that does not "hurt" another person should be made illegal. And thus many of us who watch over the police are reluctant to allow them to perform, in the only way they can, a function that every neighborhood desperately wants them to perform.

This wish to "decriminalize" disreputable behavior that "harms no one"—and thus remove the ultimate sanction the police can employ to maintain neighborhood order—is, we think, a mistake. Arresting a single drunk or a single vagrant who has harmed no identifiable person seems unjust, and in a sense it is. But failing to do anything about a score of drunks or a hundred vagrants may destroy an entire community. A particular rule that seems to make sense in the individual case makes no sense when it is made a universal rule and applied to all cases. It makes no sense because it fails to take into account the connection between one broken window left untended and a thousand broken windows. Of course, agencies other than the police could attend to the problems posed by drunks or the mentally ill, but in most communities—especially where the "deinstitutionalization" movement has been strong—they do not.

The concern about equity is more serious. We might agree that certain behavior makes one person more undesirable than another, but how do we ensure that age or skin color or national origin or harmless mannerisms will not also become the basis for distinguishing the undesirable from the desirable? How do we ensure, in short, that the police do not become the agents of neighborhood bigotry?

We can offer no wholly satisfactory answer to this important question. We are not confident that there is a satisfactory answer, except to hope that by their selection, training, and supervision, the police will be inculcated with a clear sense of the outer limit of their discretionary authority. That limit, roughly, is this—the police exist to help regulate behavior, not to maintain the racial or ethnic purity of a neighborhood.

Consider the case of the Robert Taylor Homes in Chicago, one of the largest public housing projects in the country. It is home for nearly 20,000 people, all black, and extends over ninety-two acres along South State Street. It was named after a distinguished black who had been, during the 1940s, chairman of the Chicago Housing Authority. Not long after it opened, in 1962, relations between project residents and the police deteriorated badly. The citizens felt that the police were insensitive or brutal; the police, in turn, complained of unprovoked attacks on them. Some Chicago officers tell of times when they were afraid to enter the Homes. Crime rates soared.

Today, the atmosphere has changed. Police-citizen relations have improved—apparently, both sides learned something from the earlier experience. Recently, a boy stole a purse and ran off. Several young persons who saw the theft voluntarily passed along to the police information on the identity and residence of the thief, and they did this publicly, with friends and neighbors looking on. But problems persist, chief among them the presence of youth gangs that terrorize residents and recruit members in the project. The people expect the police to "do something" about this, and the police are determined to do just that.

But do what? Though the police can obviously make arrests whenever a gang member breaks the law, a gang can form, recruit, and congregate without breaking the law. And only a tiny fraction of gang-related crimes can be solved by an arrest; thus, if an arrest is the only recourse for the police, the residents' fears will go unassuaged. The police will soon feel helpless, and the residents will again believe that the police "do nothing." What the police in fact do is to chase known gang members out of the project. In the words of one officer, "We kick ass." Project residents both know and approve of this. The tacit police-citizen alliance in the project is reinforced by the police view that the cops and the gangs are the two rival sources of power in the area, and that the gangs are not going to win.

None of this is easily reconciled with any conception of due process or fair treatment. Since both residents and gang members are black, race is not a factor. But it could be. Suppose a white project confronted a black gang, or vice versa. We would be apprehensive about the police taking sides. But the substantive problem remains the same: how can the police strengthen the informal social-control mechanisms of natural communities in order to minimize fear in public places? Law enforcement, per se, is no answer. A gang can weaken or destroy a community by standing about in a menacing fashion and speaking rudely to passersby without breaking the law.

We have difficulty thinking about such matters, not simply because the ethical and legal issues are so complex but because we have become accustomed to thinking of the law in essentially individualistic terms. The law defines *my* rights, punishes *his* behavior, and is applied by *that* officer because of *this* harm. We assume, in thinking this way, that what is good for the individual will be good for the community, and what doesn't matter when it happens to one person won't matter if it happens to many. Ordinarily, those are plausible assumptions. But in cases where behavior that is tolerable to one person is intolerable to many others, the reactions of the others—fear, withdrawal, flight—may ultimately make matters worse for everyone, including the individual who first professed his indifference.

It may be their greater sensitivity to communal as opposed to individual needs that helps explain why the residents of small communities are more satisfied with their police than are the residents of similar neighborhoods in big cities. Elinor Ostrom and her co-workers at Indiana University compared the perception of police services in two poor, all-black Illinois towns—Phoenix and East Chicago Heights—with those of three comparable all-black neighborhoods in Chicago. The level of criminal victimization and the quality of police-community relations appeared to be about the same in the towns and the Chicago neighborhoods. But the citizens living in their own villages were much more likely than those living in the Chicago neighborhoods to say that they do not stay at home for fear of crime, to agree that the local police have "the right to take any action necessary" to deal with problems, and to agree that the police "look out for the needs of the average citizen." It is possible that the residents and the police of the small towns saw themselves as engaged in a collaborative effort to maintain a certain standard of communal life, whereas those of the big city felt themselves to be simply requesting and supplying particular services on an individual basis.

If this is true, how should a wise police chief deploy his meager forces? The first answer is that nobody knows for certain, and the most prudent course of action would be to try further variations on the Newark experiment, to see more precisely what works in what kinds of neighborhoods. The second answer is also a hedge—many aspects of order-maintenance in neighborhoods can probably best be handled in ways that involve the police minimally, if at all. A busy, bustling shopping center and a quiet, well-tended suburb may need almost no visible police presence. In both cases, the ratio of respectable to disreputable people is ordinarily so high as to make informal social control effective.

Even in areas that are in jeopardy from disorderly elements, citizen action without substantial police involvement may be sufficient. Meetings between teenagers who like to hang out on a particular corner and adults who want to use that corner might well lead to an amicable agreement on a set of rules about how many people can be allowed to congregate, where, and when.

Where no understanding is possible—or if possible, not observed—citizen patrols may be a sufficient response. There are two traditions of communal involvement in maintaining order. One, that of the "community watchmen," is as old as the first settlement of the New World. Until well into the nineteenth century, volunteer watchmen, not policemen, patrolled their communities to keep order. They did so, by and large, without taking the law into their own hands—without, that is, punishing persons or using force. Their presence deterred disorder or alerted the community to disorder that could not be deterred. There are hundreds of such efforts today in communities all across the nation. Perhaps the best known is that of the Guardian Angels, a group of unarmed young persons in distinctive berets and T-shirts, who first came to public attention when they began patrolling the New York City subways but who claim now to have chapters in more than thirty American cities. Unfortunately, we have little information about the effect of these groups on crime. It is possible, however, that whatever their effect on crime, citizens find their presence reassuring, and that they thus contribute to maintaining a sense of order and civility.

The second tradition is that of the "vigilante." Rarely a feature of the settled communities of the East, it was primarily to be found in those frontier towns that grew up in advance of the reach of government. More than 350 vigilante groups are known to have existed; their distinctive feature was that their members did take the law into their own hands, by acting as judge, jury, and often executioner as well as policeman. Today, the vigilante movement is conspicuous by its rarity, despite the great fear expressed by citizens that the older cities are becoming "urban frontiers." But some community-watchmen groups have skirted the line, and others may cross it in the future. An ambiguous case, reported in the *Wall Street Journal*, involved a citizens' patrol in the Silver Lake area of Belleville, New Jersey. A leader told the reporter, "We look for outsiders." If a few teenagers from outside the neighborhood enter it, "we ask them their business," he said. "If they say they're going down the street to see Mrs. Jones, fine, we let them pass. But then we follow them down the block to make sure they're really going to see Mrs. Jones."

Though citizens can do a great deal, the police are plainly the key to order-maintenance. For one thing, many communities, such as the Robert Taylor Homes, cannot do the job by themselves. For another, no citizen in a neighborhood, even an organized one, is likely to feel the sense of responsibility that wearing a badge confers. Psychologists have done many studies on why people fail to go to the aid of persons being attacked or seeking help, and they have learned that the cause is not "apathy" or "selfishness" but the absence of some plausible grounds for feeling that one must personally accept responsibility. Ironically, avoiding responsibility is easier when a lot of people are standing about. On streets and in public places, where order is so important, many people are likely to be "around," a fact that reduces the chance of any one person acting as the agent of the community. The police officer's uniform singles him out as a person who must accept responsibility if asked.

In addition, officers, more easily than their fellow citizens, can be expected to distinguish between what is necessary to protect the safety of the street and what merely protects its ethnic purity.

But the police forces of America are losing, not gaining, members. Some cities have suffered substantial cuts in the number of officers available for duty. These cuts are not likely to be reversed in the near future. Therefore, each department must assign its existing officers with great care. Some neighborhoods are so demoralized and crime-ridden as to make foot patrol useless; the best the police can do with limited resources is respond to the enormous number of calls for service. Other neighborhoods are so stable and serene as to make foot patrol unnecessary. The key is to identify neighborhoods at the tipping point—where the public order is deteriorating but not unreclaimable, where the streets are used frequently but by apprehensive people, where a window is likely to be broken at any time, and must quickly be fixed if all are not to be shattered.

Most police departments do not have ways of systematically identifying such areas and assigning officers to them. Officers are assigned on the basis of crime rates (meaning that marginally threatened areas are often stripped so that police can investigate crimes in areas where the situation is hopeless) or on the basis of calls for service (despite the fact that most citizens do not call the police when they are merely frightened or annoyed). To allocate patrol wisely, the department must look at the neighborhoods and decide, from first-hand evidence, where an additional officer will make the greatest difference in promoting a sense of safety.

One way to stretch limited police resources is being tried in some public-housing projects. Tenant organizations hire off-duty police officers for patrol work in their buildings. The costs are not high (at least not per resident), the officer likes the additional income, and the residents feel safer. Such arrangements are probably more successful than hiring private watchmen, and the

Newark experiment helps us understand why. A private security guard may deter crime or misconduct by his presence, and he may go to the aid of persons needing help, but he may well not intervene—that is, control or drive away—someone challenging community standards. Being a sworn officer—a "real cop"—seems to give one the confidence, the sense of duty, and the aura of authority necessary to perform this difficult task.

Patrol officers might be encouraged to go to and from duty stations on public transportation and, while on the bus or subway car, enforce rules about smoking, drinking, disorderly conduct, and the like. The enforcement need involve nothing more than ejecting the offender (the offense, after all, is not one with which a booking officer or a judge wishes to be bothered). Perhaps the random but relentless maintenance of standards on buses would lead to conditions on buses that approximate the level of civility we now take for granted on airplanes.

But the most important requirement is to think that to maintain order in precarious situations is a vital job. The police know this is one of their functions, and they also believe, correctly, that it cannot be done to the exclusion of criminal investigation and responding to calls. We may have encouraged them to suppose, however, on the basis of our oft-repeated concerns about serious, violent crime, that they will be judged exclusively on their capacity as crime-fighters. To the extent that this is the case, police administrators will continue to concentrate police personnel in the highest-crime areas (though not necessarily in the areas most vulnerable to criminal invasion), emphasize their training in the law and criminal apprehension (and not their training in managing street life), and join too quickly in campaigns to decriminalize "harmless" behavior (though public drunkenness, street prostitution, and pornographic displays can destroy a community more quickly than any team of professional burglars).

Above all, we must return to our long-abandoned view that the police ought to protect communities as well as individuals. Our crime statistics and victimization surveys measure individual losses, but they do not measure communal losses. Just as physicians now recognize the importance of fostering health rather than simply treating illness, so the police—and the rest of us—ought to recognize the importance of maintaining, intact, communities without broken windows.

Discussion Questions

1. Describe a community that is orderly. How does it differ from a community that is disorderly? What are the social and physical characteristics that would prompt you to define a neighborhood as disorderly?
2. According to Wilson and Kelling, how is disorder related to serious crime? How is this relationship captured by the "broken windows" metaphor that they use?
3. How does Wilson and Kelling's "broken windows" theory of crime compare with the community-based theories in Part III of this book (recall the Chicago School)? If you were to diagram the theories, how would their causal models differ? In turn, how might their policy recommendations differ?
4. What is "broken windows policing"? Is the emphasis on crime fighting or is it on order maintenance? Why? Even if this approach is effective, do you think it is fair to concentrate police attention—including arrests for minor infractions—on the different types of people that would be considered "disreputable" and disorderly?
5. Do you think that Wilson and Kelling's use of the phrase "broken windows" contributed to the popularity of their theory?

SECTION 5

Key Developments in Criminology

PART XII
Developmental Theories: Crime and the Life Course

PART XIII
Theories of White-Collar Crime

PART XIV
Pulling It All Together: Integrated Theories of Crime

PART XV
Putting Theory to Work: Guiding Crime Control Policy

PART XII

Developmental Theories: Crime and the Life Course

Psychologists have long understood that human personality and behavioral patterns emerge through a developmental process that unfolds from birth onward. They study infants and their interaction with mothers; they have specialized courses in "child psychology" and "adolescent psychology." They take for granted that what occurs early in life may shape—sometimes profoundly—what occurs later in life.

Until relatively recently—the last decade or so—most criminologists systematically ignored these fundamental insights of psychology (for exceptions, see scholars in Part II). Equipped with a thoroughly sociological worldview, they had little interest in tracing how individuals *develop* over time. Instead, they were concerned with what happens when individuals are placed in a particular *social context*. This distinction is somewhat subtle, but it is important. A developmental perspective focuses on the individual and how the person's life unfolds as he or she traverses through different contexts. A traditional criminological perspective is more interested in which contexts—or features of the context—are crime-inducing. Another way of phrasing this issue is that a developmental perspective is *dynamic,* studying whether an individual's behavior remains stable or changes over time. A traditional criminological perspective often is *static,* assuming that contexts have stable and enduring effects on the people caught in them.

This characterization might be a bit of an overstatement, for there are always exceptions to the rule. Even so, most criminological theories have paid, at best, only a vague and implicit attention to what goes on during childhood. Let us take, for example, Hirschi's (1969 [Chapter 19 in this volume]) social bond theory in which he argues that attachment to parents is a significant indirect social control. Psychologists have published volumes of studies on the concept of attachment and on what attachment between infants and parents involves (see, e.g., Bowlby, 1969). In contrast, in Hirschi's theory, there is only the vague sense that attachment to parents must have evolved sometime in childhood. But this process is not investigated or *given any theoretical weight;* that is, it is not an object of study and its implications for understanding the origins and effects of the social bond are left unexplored.

Or to take but one other example, let us consider social disorganization theory (see Part III in this volume). The theory logically suggests that the effects of social disorganization are restricted to the present moment. We would anticipate that growing up in a disorganized neighborhood—spending years in a "delinquency area," to use Shaw and McKay's term—would have some criminogenic effect above and beyond simply being in such a community at the current time. If this were the case, we might expect that theorists would investigate how the length of residing in a troubled area affects youths; or they might explore the effects of disorganization on children versus, say, adolescents. But, at least traditionally, questions of this nature escaped systematic study by social disorganization theorists (for an exception, see Sampson, 1997).

The downplaying of childhood was probably not a conscious conclusion that the early years in life were uninvolved in crime; after all, who would really say that what goes on in childhood is unimportant? Rather, it reflected the intellectual evolution of criminology in directions that simply placed childhood "on the back burner"—just far enough out of mind that the implications of taking childhood seriously did not have to be entertained. Two factors contributed to this neglect of the early years of life and, in turn, of considering crime as a developmental process.

First, research studies reveal that participation in crime peaks during the teenage years. Crime is highest around age 17 or 18, with violent crime reaching its apex a bit later (Agnew, 2001; Caspi and Moffitt, 1995; Federal Bureau of Investigation, 2004). As Caspi and Moffitt (1995: 493) note, "the majority of criminal offenders are teenagers; by the early 20s, the number of active offenders decreases by over 50 percent; by age 28, almost 85 percent of former delinquents desist from offending." Given these empirical realities, the relevance of childhood experiences was not readily apparent. Rather, it "made sense" to ask what was special about the *juvenile* years—peer relationships, school experiences, frustration in the job market, labeling by police, threats to masculinity, and so on—that suddenly compels large numbers of American youths to break the law, with some doing so at a high rate. This search for the criminogenic conditions that are integral to the teenage years is why a large proportion of crime theories were actually put forth as theories of "delinquency."

Second, the focus on juveniles not only seemed reasonable—given their high involvement in crime—but also *practical*. Studying crime and testing criminological theories is often a daunting task. But teenagers are an ideal population to investigate. Thus, in any community, most of them congregate daily in one place: the schools. Researchers found it convenient to arrive at a high school and, over a day or two, distribute questionnaires for students to complete. These survey instruments would contain both questions measuring different theories and questions measuring involvement in crime (called a "self-report delinquency scale"). Relying on students had one other advantage: They were used to filling out pencil and paper "tests," which questionnaires approximated. Not surprisingly, literally hundreds of these studies were conducted, and they largely form the basis for current assessments of whether or not given theories are empirically supported.

It is important to note that the vast majority of these surveys were *cross-sectional* in design; that is, they did not follow youngsters over time (a *longitudinal* study) but rather studied them by taking a "slice" or "cross section" of their lives at one time and place. Again, cross-sectional studies are time and cost effective. Tracing what happens in an individual's life over several years is difficult and requires an ongoing team of researchers. Studying the goings on in someone's life from *childhood* into later years is extremely challenging. The point is that surveying juveniles cross-sectionally was practical and within reach of many scholars. But by choosing this approach, it was not possible to consider the role of childhood and human development in crime; such questions fell outside the dominant research design employed by criminologists.

Gradually, however, findings from the limited number of longitudinal studies gained notice (see, e.g., Farrington 1995, 2003; Farrington and Loeber, 1999; Loeber et al., 2003; Robins and Wish, 1977). Most notably, spurred by the work of Sampson and Laub (1993; see also Laub and Sampson, 1991), scholars paid renewed attention to the research of Sheldon and Eleanor Glueck (1950 [Chapter 37 in this part]). Sheldon Glueck was a professor in the law school at Harvard University; reflecting the gender bias of the times, his wife, Eleanor, was consigned to a soft-money research assistant position. Their most famous investigation involved a longitudinal study of 500 delinquents and a matched sample of 500 nondelinquent boys. Both groups consisted of white males ages 10 to 17. The delinquent boys were selected from two juvenile reformatories in Massachusetts, whereas the nondelinquents were from Boston public schools. The study, which spanned 1949 to 1963, included follow-up of the sample at age 25 and at age 32 (Laub and Sampson, 1991; Sampson and Laub, 1993).

Although the Gluecks' research received much attention when published, it also was attacked by Edwin Sutherland for not testing any theory about crime and for downplaying sociological factors. Sociologists in general came to reject the Gluecks' work, stereotyping it as methodologically flawed and as portraying offenders as biologically deficient. In the ensuing years, their writings were infrequently read (Laub and Sampson, 1991). This neglect was unfortunate, because the Gluecks' detailed study provided insights that would come to occupy a central place within criminology in the 1990s and beyond (Laub and Sampson, 1991). For our purposes, three contributions are most significant.

First, the Gluecks showed the importance of discovering empirically how delinquents and nondelinquents differ from one another. They embraced an "eclectic" or "multifactor" approach in which conclusions about the causes of crime were not driven by any single theory but by the data. This was a prelude to today's scholars' search for "risk factors" that place youngsters in jeopardy of offending (see, e.g., Loeber and Farrington, 1998). Second, they established that early antisocial conduct was tied to later criminal behavior. That is, there is a good deal of stability in waywardness from youth into early adulthood. Criminal involvement thus is developmental; what happens at one stage in life influences what happens at the next stage in life. Third, they demonstrated that antisocial youths not only are shaped by their circumstances (e.g.,

quality of family) but also impact their social world. Delinquent youngsters, for example, dislike and misbehave at school, and they choose friends who are similarly delinquent. As such, they are architects of their future, making decisions that potentially impoverish their lives. The role of offenders in knifing off prosocial opportunities is an insight that would reappear in later developmental theories.

Contemporary criminologists' consciousness about these and similar findings were especially raised by the writings of a limited group of controversial but prominent scholars (Gottfredson and Hirschi, 1990; Wilson and Herrnstein, 1985). Their central observation was that relatively few youths suddenly become serious, chronic offenders during the juvenile years. Although what we call "crime" may first emerge during adolescence, a range of "conduct problems"—precursors to crime, such as bullying, lying, stealing—arise during childhood. In short, childhood antisocial behavior is perhaps the strongest predictor of involvement in serious juvenile offending.

The theoretical implications of this insight are profound. First, it suggests that the central causes of crime likely lie in childhood and thus that theories need to take this fact into account. Second, theories that have focused exclusively on "what happens" in the teenage years and beyond are incomplete, if not fully incorrect. In short, most existing theories of crime are wrong because they attribute crime to conditions (e.g., dropping out of school, unemployment) that occur long after individuals start a trajectory into crime during childhood. Third, the link between childhood and later deviance—although not ironclad—is sufficiently strong to show that involvement in crime is a dynamic, developmental process. Accordingly, criminological theory should become largely a branch of "developmental criminology" (see, more generally, Le Blanc and Loeber, 1998; Loeber and Le Blanc, 1990; Loeber and Stouthamer-Loeber, 1996). Other scholars, making the same point, preferred to label this new paradigm—this fresh way of thinking about and researching crime—"life-course criminology" (Benson, 2002; Sampson and Laub, 1990, 1992, 1993, 1995; see also Farrington, 2005).

To date, the most sophisticated scholarship within developmental criminology has been empirical and descriptive, as researchers have used longitudinal designs to document the factors that place individuals at risk for crime at different points in the life course. Unfortunately, developmental *theories* of crime—attempts to explain why people develop into and out of crime—have lagged behind. Still, important conceptual frameworks have been advanced. We believe that it is useful to separate these initial theories into three categories: (1) theories of continuity; (2) theories of continuity *or* change; and (3) theories of continuity *and* change.

Continuity

A developmental pattern over the life course can be marked by *continuity*—the behavior is stable and continuous—or marked by *change*—behavior on one pathway departs and heads in an alternative direction. As noted, life-course theories differ in whether they predict that the dominant pattern in the development of criminal conduct is continuity or change. As a group, these authors tend to agree that childhood is a time during which a criminal trajectory—especially for the most serious, chronic offenders—starts. They use the term "onset" to describe this initial entry into crime. They also tend to agree that some individual differences in the propensity for crime are established. They use the term "heterogeneity" (as opposed to "homogeneity") to describe how people vary in their orientation toward criminal conduct. But despite these points of agreement, theorists begin to part company when deciding the importance of the role played in crime causation by the criminal propensities that emerge in childhood.

For example, are criminal propensities developed in childhood carried by a person throughout life? If some people enter a life course of crime

in their early years, are there others who start offending later in life—such as during adolescence? If so, do these early and late starters into crime differ from one another? Furthermore, among those who show signs of criminal propensity during childhood, are there some who continue into serious delinquency and others who do not? How might we explain how youngsters—or adults—escape the life of crime that seemingly lay ahead for them? It is challenging questions such as these that developmental theories of crime seek to answer.

Individual trait perspectives (see Part II) tend to be *continuity* theories. Typically, the reasoning is that once a trait emerges or becomes part of someone's personality, this trait is difficult to "get rid of." A person thus carries the criminogenic trait across time and, within any one time, across social contexts. Because the trait is enduring, involvement in crime also tends to be enduring. In short, the trait produces continuity in criminal behavior.

Within criminology, sociological perspectives tend to be implicitly continuity theories. We say "implicitly," because the issue of continuity is not directly addressed and thus the theory's stance on the issue must be inferred from its logic. In any event, most sociological theories imply that once people become criminal—whether due to strain, a broken social bond, or perhaps differential association—they will tend to stay criminal. They rarely address the issue of "desistance" or the process whereby people stop committing crimes.

Of course, sociological theories could be used—and in a limited number of cases have been used—to explain why people stop committing crimes (see, e.g., Agnew, 1997; Sampson and Laub, 1993; Thornberry, 1987 [Chapter 44 in this volume]; Warr, 1998). Indeed, these theories are more amenable to explaining change than are trait theories: If social situations change (e.g., strain is eliminated, bonds are established), then it would seem logical that crime will decrease or stop. To explain desistance, individual trait theorists would have to explain how the crime-inducing trait somehow vanished—a more difficult task than explaining a change in social conditions external to the individual.

In this context, within the existing developmental models, the most important continuity perspective is Gottfredson and Hirschi's (1990) *self-control theory*, which they published in their now classic *A General Theory of Crime* (see also Gottfredson, 2006; Hirschi and Gottfredson, 1995). We are reviewing their thinking here because of its relevance to life-course criminology. Gottfredson and Hirschi's theory, however, was previously studied in Part VI, where "varieties of control theory" were presented (for a review of this work, see the introductions to Part VI and Chapter 19). It might be advantageous for readers to revisit these earlier materials.

As may be recalled, Gottfredson and Hirschi suggest that an enduring propensity to commit crime, which they call "low self-control," emerges in childhood (by about age 8). They link the failure to develop internal controls to the failure of parents to supervise their children, to recognize behavior that is deviant, and then to punish and correct such conduct when it occurs. Individuals with low self-control "will tend to be impulsive, insensitive, physical (as opposed to mental), risk-taking, short-sighted, [and] nonverbal" (1990: 90). Further, "since there is considerable tendency for these traits to come together in the same people, and since the traits tend to persist through life, it seems reasonable to consider them as comprising a stable construct useful in the explanation of crime" (pp. 90–91). It also is relevant that Gottfredson and Hirschi believe that, once established, low self-control is highly resistant to being altered—even if individuals experience fortuitous changes in their life circumstances (e.g., acquire a good job) or the planned interventions of the criminal justice system (e.g., rehabilitation programs).

Thus, according to Gottfredson and Hirschi, individuals with low self-control carry this bundle of traits with them wherever they go and for however long they are on this earth. In childhood, they bully, lie, and steal; as teenagers and adults, they avail themselves of the opportunity to become involved in a range of delinquencies and crimes. Low self-control—their tendency to seek immediate gratification, to take risks, to be unmindful of future consequences—infects virtually every aspect of their lives. They not only break the law but also are more likely to create public disorder, to drink and take drugs, to drive under the influence of intoxicants and get in accidents, and to become ill and die young. They are poor at forming and sustaining quality friendships and marital relationships, father or mother children out of wedlock, suffer more divorces, drop out of school more often, and have difficulty finding and keeping employment. Those with low self-control are, in short, architects of a life that is replete with crime, deviance, and social failure.

Four final observations are required. First, it should be clear why Gottfredson and Hirschi's perspective is a *continuity theory*. Individuals, it is said, can never escape their low self-control. People do not change, and if they do, it is merely because opportunities to express their low self-control have been limited. As a result, they tend to be involved in crime and/or other manifestations of social failure throughout their lives. Stability of antisocial conduct—not change from antisocial to prosocial conduct—is thus a core premise of self-control theory.

Second, Gottfredson and Hirschi's model begins as a sociological theory but ends as an individual differences theory. Low self-control is not due to biological deficiencies or to psychological dysfunction. Rather, it is produced by differential social experience: Good parental monitoring instills self-control, whereas poor parental monitoring does not. But once implanted, these differences in self-control among individuals are virtually intractable and set for life. Self-control thus differentiates who people are—their core individual traits—and, in turn, differentiates the life course that these people will experience.

Third, self-control theory is a rejection of the fundamental premise of Hirschi's social bond theory (Evans et al., 1997; Taylor, 2001). Previously, Hirschi proposed that weak social bonds caused criminal involvement. Now, Hirschi and Gottfredson (1995) maintain that *both* weak social bonds *and* crime are caused by the underlying trait of low self-control (i.e., people lacking in self-control not only commit crimes but also fail at school, jobs, social relationships). In methodological terms, the relationship between social bonds and crime is held to be spurious (Evans et al., 1997; Wright et al., 1999).

Fourth, Gottfredson and Hirschi do not deny that, overall, crime increases in the teenage years and declines as people grow older; in fact, they assert that this age-crime curve is "invariant" across societies. This rise and fall in crime rates would seem to contradict their theory; after all, it means that some people must be entering and leaving crime. Gottfredson and Hirschi do admit that why the age-crime curve exists is a social science mystery that has not yet been adequately solved by any criminological theory—including theirs. Regardless, they answer their critics in this way: At any given point in the life course, individuals low in self-control will have higher criminal involvement—and other manifestations of social failure—than individuals higher in self-control. Thus, although "crime everywhere declines with age . . . differences in 'crime' tendency across individuals remains relatively stable over the life course" (Gottfredson and Hirschi, 1990: 144).

Continuity or Change

Terrie Moffitt (1993 [Chapter 38 in this volume]) approaches the age-crime curve in a very different way (see also Caspi and Moffitt, 1995). She suggests that the jump in crime during the teenage years conceals two groups that take very different developmental pathways into crime. One group, which she calls *life-course-persistent* offenders (LCPs), start antisocial acts early and continue their waywardness into and beyond

adolescence. The second group, which she calls *adolescence-limited* offenders (ALs), start and finish their criminality during the teenage years. The age-crime curve is high during adolescence because of the high offending of the LCPs and the temporary offending of the ALs. Theoretically, the task is to explain why one group, the LCPs, manifest continuity in offending, while the other group, the ALs, manifest discontinuity or change in offending. Because youngsters tend to take one pathway or the other, her theory is a theory of continuity *or* change.

Life-course-persistent offenders make up only a small percentage—perhaps about 5 percent—of the population. According to Moffitt (1993), "continuity is the hallmark" of this group (p. 679), with their antisocial behavior "stable from preschool to adulthood" (p. 680). Thus, at age 4, they bite and hit others; at age 10, they skip school and steal from stores; at age 16, they sell drugs and steal vehicles; at age 20, they rape and rob; and at age 30, they engage in fraud and child abuse (p. 679). In her view, "the underlying disposition remains the same, but its expression changes form as new social opportunities arise at different points in development" (p. 679). Of course, this leads to the question: What creates this "underlying disposition" that is powerful enough to create persistent offending across the life course?

Whereas Gottfredson and Hirschi link criminal propensity to inadequate parenting, Moffitt outlines a more complicated developmental process in which individual traits interact with the social environment to entrench youngsters in persistent antisociality. The development into life-course-persistent offending starts with "neuropsychological deficits." Essentially, when normal brain development is disrupted—such as through exposure to drugs and poor nutrition in the prenatal period or through injury and exposure to toxins (e.g., lead) during childhood—psychological deficits are produced. These typically include "high activity level, irritability, poor self-control, and low cognitive ability" (p. 683).

These traits or individual differences are linked directly to misconduct and social failure throughout life. Again, this view is similar to Gottfredson and Hirschi's theory of low self-control. But Moffitt argues that these deficits also lock individuals into crime by the way in which they interact with the social environment to create disadvantages that "ensnare" people in an antisocial life. In childhood, for example, people with neuropsychological deficits often evoke harsh and erratic parenting, which in turn exacerbates their antisocial orientation. They are more likely to fail at school or to become pregnant as teens—choices that restrict their ability to enter conventional social roles that might extricate them from crime. Or they may lose jobs or end up in prison, experiences that make exiting from their developmental pattern difficult. In short, individual deficits or traits produce stability in offending in two interrelated ways: first, by their constant or "contemporary" effects (i.e., always being "in" the individual); and second, by the way they foster "cumulative continuity"—a mounting array of lost opportunities, failures, and poor choices that "prune away the options for change" (p. 684).

"Adolescence-limited" offenders, as their label implies, restrict their criminality largely to the teenage years. Moffitt contends that as youths enter adolescence, their chief developmental challenge is to overcome the "maturity gap" created by the mismatch between their adult biological development and modern society's expectation that they refrain from adult behaviors for several years (e.g., sexual activity, smoking, consuming goods). This gap between biological and social maturity is a source of dissatisfaction and motivation for delinquency. The motivation is translated into behavior through "social mimicry"—a process whereby youngsters model the delinquency conduct of other adolescents, usually LCPs in their own age cohort or older youths. Delinquency also occurs because it is self-reinforcing in that it shows, symbolically, autonomy from adults and maturity. Thus,

"every curfew broken, car stolen, joint smoked, and baby conceived is a statement of independence" (Caspi and Moffitt, 1995: 500).

Adulthood, however, brings desistance from crime. As the maturity gap closes, adult conventional roles become available (e.g., jobs, marriage), and the consequences for misconduct escalate, there is a corresponding decrease in the appeal of, and reinforcements for, delinquency. Misfortune during the teenage years—such as drug abuse, incarceration, or prematurely becoming a parent—traps a few ALs in crime well into the adult years. But unlike the LCPs, most of the ALs are able to take advantage of conventional opportunities to change and move on with their lives. Their antisocial conduct is thus characterized by discontinuity, not continuity, and is limited to their adolescent years.

Moffitt's two-group taxonomy—ALs and LCPs—has come under scrutiny, with some scholars questioning whether such groups exist and others arguing that there may be more than just two groups (see, e.g., Blokland et al., 2005; Laub and Sampson, 2003; Sampson and Laub, 2005). Moffitt (2006) has reviewed much of this evidence (see also Moffit et al., 2001; Piquero and Moffitt, 2005). Although not denying the existence of other offender groups that may have distinct developmental pathways, she argues that a large proportion of offending can be explained by her theory. In particular, Moffitt (2006: 301–302) concludes that after a decade of research, "what can be stated with some certainty is that the hypothesized life-course persistent antisocial individual exists, at least during the first three decades of life."

Continuity and Change

In 1985, while researching the archives of Sheldon and Eleanor Glueck (Chapter 37), John Laub was startled to discover that the longitudinal data collected by the Gluecks were gathering dust in the subbasement of the Harvard Law School Library. Stored in tens of boxes, this information was an untapped source of detailed information on Boston-area youngsters. Recall that the Gluecks had collected detailed information on 500 delinquent boys and a matched sample of 500 nondelinquent boys. These youths, born in the Great Depression, were between the ages of 10 and 17. The Gluecks then conducted follow-ups with them at age 25 and at age 32 (Sampson and Laub, 1993).

Along with his collaborator Robert Sampson, Laub quickly realized the rich criminological treasure that lay before him: He had rediscovered one of the great longitudinal data sets ever collected. But the information was in raw form and reconstructing the files for use required years of painstaking work. Later, Laub and Sampson (2003) would add new information to the original data set. They would follow up the 500 delinquents in the sample until age 70 and conduct intensive interviews with 52 of them.

Based on the original and newly collected data, the theorists published two classic books. In the first, they presented their age-graded theory of informal social control (Sampson and Laub, 1993). In the second, they presented a revised theory. This newer volume was consistent with their earlier thinking but, based on a longer view of adulthood (to age 70), introduced a more elaborate theoretical model (Laub and Sampson, 2003 [Chapter 39 in this part]). In both works, the authors emphasized the importance of a life-course perspective that explained both continuity and change in behavior.

In their first book, *Crime in the Making*, Robert Sampson and John Laub (1993) set forth an important paradigm for understanding the development of crime (see the discussion of their work in the introduction to Part VI). Notably, they subtitled their book *Pathways and Turning Points Through Life*. By "pathways," they were alluding to the fact that people can be caught in life trajectories that form a continuous line over a substantial time period. With regard to crime, they noted that the trajectory may extend to childhood, and that there is "considerable

evidence that antisocial behavior is relatively stable across stages of the life course" (p. 11). By "turning points," they were raising the possibility that entering a criminal trajectory is not a life sentence. Research shows that many offenders experience points at which they change and turn away from crime. In short, offending is characterized by both continuity *and* change. For Sampson and Laub and other scholars, the theoretical task was thus to explain what creates continuity along criminal pathways and what creates change at key turning points in life.

Sampson and Laub (1993) hypothesized that a complex set of factors combine to entrench a child on an antisocial pathway (see also Sampson and Laub, 1994). They recognized that some of these conditions are the kinds of individual differences that psychologists emphasize, such as a difficult temperament and early conduct problems. Other factors, however, are rooted in the disadvantaged and unstable social context into which a child is born. These individual and social structural conditions coalesce to foster a family life that is marked by ineffective and rejecting parenting, to decrease the chances that children will succeed at and be committed to school, and to cause children to seek out and be exposed to delinquent peers and siblings. For youths with these individual traits and social experiences, delinquent behavior is the likely result. In turn, delinquency weakens social bonds, which makes future delinquency and then adult crime more likely. Incarceration also might occur, which increases criminality because it, too, diminishes the strength of ties to conventional society.

This interactive process—one in which social bonds weakened by crime in turn lead to more crime that further weakens bonds, and so on—creates the kind of "cumulative continuity" described by Moffitt (1993). As time goes on and chances to establish social bonds—at school, at work, within the family, with a marriage—are "knifed off," a criminal life-course becomes probable. Even so, Sampson and Laub did not believe that people are consigned to be life-course-persistent offenders. Change, not just continuity, is possible.

In turning away from crime, the key agent of change is establishing conventional social bonds. Here, Sampson and Laub, once students of Travis Hirschi in graduate school, essentially apply Hirschi's social bond theory to their life-course perspective. As a general principle, the presence or absence of social ties determines whether people offend. By implication, if offenders are able to secure social bonds, they will experience renewed social control that has the potential to change their behavior. Social bonds can arise during childhood (e.g., attachment to parents), in adolescence (e.g., ties to school), and in adulthood (e.g., marriage). Importantly, Sampson and Laub note that change is induced when offenders acquire *quality* social bonds—such as a "good" marriage or a "good" job.

Ironically, Sampson and Laub's use of social bond theory placed them in opposition to the theoretical position that Hirschi had later taken with Michael Gottfredson. Recall that Gottfredson and Hirschi (1990 [Chapter 19]) believed that social bonds have no causal impact on crime. Any relationship between bonds and crime was seen to be spurious—a correlation that exists because low self-control produces both weak bonds and criminal involvement (see also Hirschi and Gottfredson, 1995). In contrast, although not disputing that individual differences such as self-control are important, Sampson and Laub (1993, 1995) asserted that social bonds—fresh ties to conventional society—might allow people to overcome their criminal propensities and divert them from crime. Although not plentiful, research suggests that Sampson and Laub's version is more correct, with both low self-control *and* social bonds implicated in crime across the life-course (Evans et al., 1997; Wright et al., 1999; see also Laub et al., 2006; Sampson and Laub, 1990, 1993; however, see Hirschi and Gottfredson, 2000).

Again, Gottfredson and Hirschi argue that the trait of low self-control creates continuity of offending across time. Moffitt proposes that some offenders—the LCPs—also show remarkable continuity in antisocial conduct from childhood onward. But she suggests that another group—the ALs—are marked by change: into offending in adolescence and then out of offending in adulthood. By contrast, Sampson and Laub contend that *the same individual* can experience both continuity and change in offending.

This focus on change is even more pronounced in Laub and Sampson's (2003 [Chapter 39 in this part]) revised theory (see also Laub et al., 2006; Sampson and Laub, 2005). As noted, this work was based on a follow-up of the original Glueck sample until age 70. Previous longitudinal projects traced offenders into their 30s and perhaps into middle age. But Laub and Sampson pursued a true *life-course* study! Notably, from this vantage point, their analysis showed that virtually all offenders desisted from crime. For even the most persistent criminals, it appears that change is inevitable.

In their revised theory, Laub and Sampson retain the core thesis that structural turning points—marriage, employment, military service—are potential sources of informal social control that foster desistance from crime. But they broaden this perspective to argue that such structural positions involve multiple processes:

> Each of these creates new situations that (1) knife off the past from the present; (2) provide not only supervision and monitoring but opportunities for social support and growth; (3) bring change and structure routine activities; and (4) provide an opportunity for identity transformation. (Laub and Sampson, 2003: 148–149)

Let us take marriage as an example. Once married, an offender's life is potentially transformed. The spouse provides emotional support to help with stresses and rough times. She (or "he" in other samples) also curtails her husband's comings and goings. She makes sure he goes to work and arrives home for dinner. These prosocial routine activities give him little chance to be in situations where trouble arises (e.g., in a bar getting drunk, on the street at night). His affiliations with former "bad friends" are stopped (see also Warr, 1998, 2002), especially if his wife and he move to a "better" neighborhood. When children are born, the now ex-offender might have a new "script" or "identity" as a "provider" and "good father." Crime thus becomes an increasingly distant pastime as the *process of desistance* runs its course.

At times, desistance thus happens virtually "by default." There is no conscious decision to stop being a criminal. In Laub and Sampson's (2003: 147) sample, many "men made a commitment to go straight without even realizing it. Before they knew it, they has invested so much in a marriage or a job that they did not want to risk losing their investment." But in an important—and theoretically controversial—assertion, Laub and Sampson also suggest that the decision to desist (or, for that matter, to persist in crime) also involves *human agency.*

"Human agency" is a somewhat vague concept, but its core idea is that people are not unthinking billiard balls who are bounced in and out of crime by the deterministic forces around them. Instead, we all have a subjective reality that affects our choices. To be sure, circumstances bound and shape what we do, for we can only choose from the options available to us. For many inner-city youngsters, the choice is not between going to Harvard or joining a gang but perhaps between working in a minimum-wage job or stealing and partying on the streets. Even so, in situations where a turning point is possible, offenders can act to move out of crime or to stay in crime. For example, when a good marital relationship is possible, a person can prove unfaithful, disdain his wife's wishes by getting drunk with his buddies, neglect his children, and walk off his job in defiance of a boss he dislikes. Or he can resist these temptations and build a marriage that persists and makes crime less meaningful.

The theoretical idea of "human agency" is noteworthy for two other reasons. First, it is a way of "bringing motivation back in" to control theory.

Recall that control theorists such as Hirschi (1969 [Chapter 18]) take the motivation or predisposition to offend for granted; humans by their nature are gratification seekers and must be restrained from pursuing their self-interest through crime. Laub and Sampson (2003 [Chapter 39]), however, assert that humans act in part because of what they "will" themselves to do. They can decide to act differently—or not. Human agency thus is a conduit for the motivation to change.

Importantly, unlike with many alternative theories, Laub and Sampson do not see motivation as an enduring trait or orientation. And unlike with rational choice theories, they do not see motivation as a cold calculation of costs and benefits. Rather, motivation is situational and emerges from the person-environment interaction. For example, if a male offender falls into a close relationship with a woman, he may be inspired to "go straight." If this relationship had not occurred, the motivation to desist may not have arisen. Conversely, meeting a potential partner is no guarantee that conformity will follow. The offender still has to exercise agency; he still has to develop the will to change.

Second, the idea that change in a criminal life course is contingent on situated choices and human agency challenges more neatly packaged developmental theories—most notably Moffitt's theory of ALs and LCPs. The very idea that crime is "developmental" presupposes that offenders enter into and out of crime in a *predictable sequence of steps.* Their lives are held to unfold in defined stages.

By contrast, Laub and Sampson (2003) believe that adult development is, to an important degree, *unpredictable.* Thus, it is impossible to predict from childhood factors how long "life-course-persistent offenders" will in fact persist in their criminality in adulthood. All offenders eventually give up crime—age, or death, seems to have that effect. But at what precise point people desist is a matter of good fortune (e.g., getting a good job), situational dynamics, and human agency. Thus, while desistance is a process with definable patterns, it has an emergent, contingent quality that is not captured by the notion of universal developmental sequences. Put another way, lives do not "unfold" but rather are shaped and chosen, often in idiosyncratic ways.

Understanding Change

In developing their concept of "human agency," Laub and Sampson (2003) have revealed the importance of understanding not only why people enter crime ("onset") and stay in crime ("persistence") but also why they leave crime ("desistance"). Scholars have now begun to explore in detail the desistance process (see, e.g., Maruna, 2001). In this regard, important insights on why individuals embedded in a criminal trajectory change and stop offending have been developed by Peggy Giordano, Stephen Cernkovich, and Jennifer Rudolph (2002).

Giordano et al. agree with Sampson and Laub's (1993) initial theory that acquiring social bonds, such as a marriage or a job, facilitates desistance. But they also concur with their revised theory, discussed just above, that human agency is involved in this process. Social bonds are not simply magically developed or unwillingly imposed. Career criminals must take advantage of opportunities for desistance. A quality relationship or a decent job can be lost if an offender chooses not to return home at night or to show up for work. In essence, then, offenders must exercise human agency by choosing to change.

However, for Giordano et al., such human agency can be unpacked into four "cognitive shifts." In their perspective, offenders encounter potential social bonds, which they call "hooks for change." These might include a budding intimate relationship or an offer of employment. But these opportunities may be forfeited unless an offender experiences a fundamental "cognitive transformation." This transformation, again, occurs through four steps.

First, the offender must possess a general openness to change. Second, the person must look favorably upon a specific hook for change and see embracing this hook (e.g., a new relationship) as being "fundamentally incompatible with continued deviation" (Giordano et al., 2002: 1001). Third, the offender must begin to fashion a new conventional identity, what Giordano and colleagues call a "replacement self" (p. 1001). Fourth, the individual must come to see continued wayward conduct negatively. Thus, a "deviant behavior or lifestyle" is no longer viewed as "positive, viable, or even personally relevant" (p. 1002). In this way, the motivation to deviate vanishes as the offender is cognitively transformed into a conventional member of society.

In short, desistance is a dynamic, interactive process that involves both opportunities or hooks for change and active efforts by offenders to interpret their world and themselves differently. The value of Giordano et al.'s framework is that it moves us beyond the broad view that offenders exercise human agency to an understanding of what such agency might entail. For them, human agency is not simply will power but ways of thinking—cognitive shifts—that motivate offenders to act differently. Further investigations into the nature and effects of the cognitive-transformation process promise to enrich our understanding of how, after a lengthy criminal career, offenders change and desist from a life in crime.

The Future of Developmental Criminology

Developmental theories are now center stage in criminology. Even if one takes issue with the main theories that have been set forth, the fundamental point underlying these perspectives is indisputable: Crime is a dynamic process that potentially begins in childhood and occurs across the life course. Accordingly, the challenge for all theoretical criminology is to explain continuity and/or change in criminal involvement. For many years, however, traditional theories remained largely silent on these key issues. This does not mean that traditional perspectives have no value. But it does mean that their credibility will be judged, in large part, by how well they are able to address the key life-course issues of continuity and change in offending. Sampson and Laub provide an example of how this might be accomplished when they use social bond theory to illuminate why offenders become entrenched in and escape from a criminal trajectory. In any event, for the next decade and beyond, the developmental or life-course perspective almost certainly will be the dominant theoretical and research paradigm in the field of criminology.

References

Agnew, Robert. 1997. "Stability and Change in Crime Over the Life Course: A Strain Theory Explanation." In Terence P. Thornberry (ed.), *Developmental Theories of Crime and Delinquency: Advances in Criminological Theory*, Volume 7, pp. 101–132. New Brunswick, NJ: Transaction.

——. 2001. *Juvenile Delinquency: Causes and Control.* Los Angeles: Roxbury Publishing.

Benson, Michael L. 2002. *Crime and the Life Course: An Introduction.* Los Angeles: Roxbury Publishing.

Blokland, Arjan A. J., Daniel S. Nagin, and Paul Nieuwbeerta. 2005. "Life Span Offending Trajectories of a Dutch Conviction Cohort." *Criminology* 43: 919–954.

Bowlby, John. 1969. *Attachment and Loss: Volume I, Attachment.* New York: Basic.

Caspi, Avshalom and Terrie E. Moffitt. 1995. "The Continuity of Maladaptive Behavior: From Description to Understanding in the Study of Antisocial Behavior." In Dante Cicchetti and Donald J. Cohen (eds.), *Manual of Developmental Psychology*, pp. 472–511. New York: John Wiley.

Evans, T. David, Francis T. Cullen, Velmer S. Burton, Jr., R. Gregory Dunaway, and Michael L. Benson. 1997. "The Social Consequences of Self-Control: Testing the General Theory of Crime." *Criminology* 35: 475–500.

Farrington, David P. 1995. "The Development of Offending and Antisocial Behavior From Childhood: Key Findings From the Cambridge Study in Delinquent Development." *Journal of Child Psychology and Psychiatry* 36: 929–964.

——. 2003. "Key Results From the First Forty Years of the Cambridge Study in Delinquent Development." In Terence P. Thornberry and Marvin D. Krohn (eds.), *Taking Stock of Delinquency: An Overview of Findings From Contemporary Longitudinal Studies*, pp. 137–183. New York: Kluwer/Plenum.

——, ed. 2005. *Integrated Development and Life-Course Theories of Offending: Advances in Criminological Theory*, Volume 14. New Brunswick, NJ: Transaction.

Farrington, David P. and Rolf Loeber. 1999. "Transatlantic Replicability of Risk Factors in the Development of Delinquency." In Patricia Cohen, Cheryl Slomkowski, and Lee N. Robins (eds.), *Historical and Geographical Influences on Psychopathology*, pp. 299–329. Mahway, NJ: Lawrence Erlbaum.

Federal Bureau of Investigation. 2004. *Crime in the United States 2003: Uniform Crime Reports.* Washington, DC: U.S. Government Printing Office.

Giordano, Peggy C., Stephen A. Cernkovich, and Jennifer L. Rudolph. 2002. "Gender, Crime, and Desistance: Toward a Theory of Cognitive Transformation." *American Journal of Sociology* 107: 990–1064.

Glueck, Sheldon and Eleanor Glueck. 1950. *Unraveling Juvenile Delinquency.* New York: Commonwealth Fund.

Gottfredson, Michael R. 2006. "The Empirical Status of Control Theory in Criminology." In Francis T. Cullen, John Paul Wright, and Kristie R. Blevins (eds.), *Taking Stock: The Status of Criminological Theory—Advances in Criminological Theory*, Volume 15, pp. 77–100. New Brunswick, NJ: Transaction.

Gottfredson, Michael R. and Travis Hirschi. 1990. *A General Theory of Crime*. Stanford, CA: Stanford University Press.

Hirschi, Travis. 1969. *Causes of Delinquency*. Berkeley, CA: University of California Press.

Hirschi, Travis and Michael R. Gottfredson. 1995. "Control Theory and the Life-Course Perspective." *Studies on Crime and Crime Prevention* 4: 131–142.

——. 2000. "In Defense of Self-Control." *Theoretical Criminology* 4: 55–69.

Laub, John H. and Robert J. Sampson. 1991. "The Sutherland-Glueck Debate: On the Sociology of Criminological Knowledge." *American Journal of Sociology* 96: 1402–1440.

——. 2003. *Shared Beginnings, Divergent Lives: Delinquent Boys to Age 70*. Cambridge, MA: Harvard University Press.

Laub, John H., Robert J. Sampson, and Gary Sweeten. 2006. "Assessing Sampson and Laub's Life-Course Theory of Crime." In Francis T. Cullen, John Paul Wright, and Kristie R. Blevins (eds.), *Taking Stock: The Status of Criminological Theory—Advances in Criminological Theory*, Volume 15, pp. 313–333. New Brunswick, NJ: Transaction.

Le Blanc, Marc and Rolf Loeber. 1998. "Developmental Criminology Updated." In Michael Tonry (ed.), *Crime and Justice: A Review of Research*, Volume 23, pp. 115–198. Chicago: University of Chicago Press.

Loeber, Rolf and David P. Farrington, eds. 1998. *Serious and Violent Juvenile Offenders: Risk Factors and Successful Interventions*. Thousand Oaks, CA: Sage.

Loeber, Rolf, David P. Farrington, Magda Stouthamer-Loeber, Terrie E. Moffitt, Avshalom Caspi, Helene Raskin White, Evelyn H. Wei, and Jennifer M. Beyers. 2003. "The Development of Male Offending: Key Findings From 14 Years of the Pittsburgh Youth Study." In Terence Thornberry and Marvin D. Krohn (eds.), *Taking Stock of Delinquency: An Overview of the Findings From Contemporary Longitudinal Studies*, pp. 93–136. New York: Kluwer Academic/Plenum.

Loeber, Rolf and Marc Le Blanc. 1990. "Toward a Developmental Criminology." In Michael Tonry and Norval Morris (eds.), *Crime and Justice: A Review of Research*, Volume 12, pp. 375–473. Chicago: University of Chicago Press.

Loeber, Rolf and Magda Stouthamer-Loeber. 1996. "The Development of Offending." *Criminal Justice and Behavior* 23: 12–24.

Maruna, Shadd. 2001. *Making Good: How Ex-Convicts Reform and Rebuild Their Lives*. Washington, DC: American Psychological Association.

Moffitt, Terrie. 1993. "Adolescence-Limited and Life-Course-Persistent Antisocial Behavior: A Developmental Taxonomy." *Psychological Review* 100: 674–701.

——. 2006. "A Review of Research on the Taxonomy of Life-Course Persistent Versus Adolescence-Limited Antisocial Behavior." In Francis T. Cullen, John Paul Wright, and Kristie R. Blevins (eds.), *Taking Stock: The Status of Criminological Theory—Advances in Criminological Theory*, Volume 15, pp. 277–311. New Brunswick, NJ: Transaction.

Moffitt, Terrie E., Avshalom Caspi, Michael Rutter, and Phil A. Silva. 2001. *Sex Differences in Antisocial Behavior: Conduct Disorder, Delinquency, and Violence in the Dunedin Longitudinal Study*. Cambridge, UK: Cambridge University Press.

Piquero, Alex R. and Terrie E. Moffitt. 2005. "Explaining the Facts of Crime: How the Developmental Taxonomy Replies to Farrington's Invitation." In David P. Farrington (ed.), *Integrated Developmental and Life-Course Theories of Offending: Advances in Criminological Theory*, Volume 14, pp. 51–72. New Brunswick, NJ: Transaction.

Robins, Lee N. and Eric Wish. 1977. "Childhood Deviance as a Developmental Process: A Study of 223 Urban Black Men From Birth to 18." *Social Forces* 56: 448–473.

Sampson, Robert J. 1997. "The Embeddedness of Child and Adolescent Development: A Community-Level Perspective on Urban Violence." In Joan McCord (ed.), *Violence and Childhood in the Inner City*, pp. 31–77. Cambridge, UK: Cambridge University Press.

Sampson, Robert J. and John H. Laub. 1990. "Crime and Deviance Over the Life Course: The Salience of Adult Social Bonds." *American Sociological Review* 44: 609–627.

——. 1992. "Crime and Deviance Over the Life Course." *Annual Review of Sociology* 18: 63–84.

——. 1993. *Crime in the Making: Pathways and Turning Points Through Life.* Cambridge, MA: Harvard University Press.

——. 1994. "Urban Poverty and the Family Context of Delinquency: A New Look at Structure and Process in a Classic Study." *Child Development* 65: 523–540.

——.1995. "Understanding Variability in Lives Through Time: Contributions of Life-Course Criminology." *Studies on Crime and Crime Prevention* 4: 143–158.

——. 2005. "A Life-Course View of the Development of Crime." *Annals of the American Academy of Political and Social Science* 602: 12–45.

Taylor, Claire. 2001. "The Relationship Between Social and Self-Control: Tracing Hirschi's Criminological Career." *Theoretical Criminology* 5: 369–388.

Thornberry, Terence P. 1987. "Toward an Interactional Theory of Delinquency." *Criminology* 25: 863–891.

Warr, Mark. 1998. "Life-Course Transitions and Desistance From Crime." *Criminology* 36: 183–216.

——. 2002. *Companions in Crime: The Social Aspects of Criminal Conduct.* Cambridge, UK: Cambridge University Press.

Wilson, James Q. and Richard J. Herrnstein. 1985. *Crime and Human Nature.* New York: Simon & Schuster.

Wright, Bradley R. Entner, Avshalom Caspi, Terrie E. Moffitt, and Phil A. Silva. 1999. "Low Self-Control, Social Bonds, and Crime: Social Causation, Social Selection, or Both?" *Criminology* 37: 479–514.

37. Unraveling Juvenile Delinquency

Sheldon Glueck and Eleanor Glueck

The Gluecks begin their 1950 book Unraveling Juvenile Delinquency *by arguing that no one theoretical approach or disciplinary perspective is sufficient for studying the causes of delinquency. A full explanation of delinquency requires that factors from all disciplines be considered, including biological, psychological, and sociological factors. This "multi-factor" approach guided their analysis in* Unraveling Juvenile Delinquency *and is one of the distinguishing features of their work. In particular, their list of causal factors includes variables from all domains—ranging from physique to temperamental traits to family factors. The reader may wonder, then, why their article is included in the section on individual traits and crime.*

Part of the response is that their study was published at a time when sociological theories were coming to dominate the discipline of criminology (see Laub and Sampson, 1991). Although the Gluecks' study focuses on factors from all domains, it assigns special importance to biological and psychological factors; the study stood out for this reason. With the exception of the family, the importance of social factors is discounted or not considered. For example, they argue that while delinquency is associated with school factors (e.g., low achievement, dislike of school) and association with delinquent peers, such factors do not have a causal effect on delinquency. Rather, they are simply another reflection of the individual traits and early family problems that cause delinquency.

The selection that follows summarizes the major findings from a study that the Gluecks began in 1939. The Gluecks compared 500 institutionalized delinquent boys in Massachusetts to a matched sample of 500 nondelinquent boys from the Boston area. The delinquents and nondelinquents were matched by age, race/ethnicity, neighborhood characteristics, and intelligence (the matching procedure helped ensure that the two groups were similar on these traits). The Gluecks then collected a wide range of data on these boys from several sources, and Unraveling Juvenile Delinquency *describes the results of their comparisons. They conclude that delinquency results from the interplay between somatic (physique), temperamental, intellectual, and sociocultural (especially family) forces. They do not describe the interactions between these factors in any detail, however.*

Their study has been critiqued on a number of points, and Sampson and Laub (1993) recently reanalyzed the Gluecks' data, partly in an effort to overcome many of these criticisms. Nevertheless, many of their findings have stood the test of time. Other findings, however, have been challenged. Certain data suggest that school factors and association with delinquent peers do have some causal impact on delinquency (see Agnew, 2005; Vold et al., 2002; also see Wilson and Herrnstein, 1985).

Reprinted from Sheldon and Eleanor Glueck, *Unraveling Juvenile Delinquency.* Copyright © 1950 by Commonwealth Fund. Reprinted by permission of the Commonwealth Fund.

References

Agnew, Robert. 2009. *Juvenile Delinquency: Causes and Control*, 3rd edition. Los Angeles: Roxbury.

Glueck, Sheldon and Eleanor Glueck. 1950. *Unraveling Juvenile Delinquency*. New York: The Commonwealth Fund.

Laub, John H. and Robert J. Sampson. 1991. "The Sutherland-Glueck Debate: On the Sociology of Criminological Knowledge." *American Journal of Sociology* 96: 1402–1440.

Sampson, Robert J. and John H. Laub. 1993. *Crime in the Making*. Cambridge, MA: Harvard University Press.

Vold, George B., Thomas J. Bernard, and Jeffrey B. Snipes. 2002. *Theoretical Criminology*. New York: Oxford University Press.

Wilson, James Q. and Richard J. Herrnstein. 1985. *Crime and Human Nature*. New York: Touchstone.

By and large, examination of existing researches in juvenile delinquency discloses a tendency to emphasize a particular approach or explanation. Proponents of various theories of causation still too often insist that the truth is to be found only in their own special fields of study, and that, *ex hypothesi*, researches made by those working in other disciplines can contribute very little to the understanding and management of the crime problem. Like the blind men and the elephant of the fable, each builds the entire subject in the image of that piece of it which he happens to have touched.

Yet it stands to reason that since so little is as yet known about the intricacies of normal human behavior, it is the better part of wisdom not to be overawed by any branch of science or methodology to the neglect of other promising leads in the study of aberrant behavior. When, therefore, research into the causes of delinquency emphasizes the sociologic, or ecologic, or cultural, or psychiatric, or psychoanalytic, or anthropologic approach, relegating the others to a remote position, if not totally ignoring them, we must immediately be on guard. The problems of human motivation and behavior involve the study of man as well as society, of nature as well as nurture, of segments or mechanisms of human nature as well as the total personality, of patterns of intimate social activity as well as larger areas of social process or masses of culture. They involve, therefore, the participation of several disciplines. Without recognition of such factors, bias must weaken the validity of both method and interpretation.

For example, a weakness or an incompleteness of much sociologic reasoning on the causal process in crime is the assumption that the mass social stimulus to behavior, as reflected in the particular culture of a region, is alone, or primarily, the significant causal force. This presupposition ignores two undeniable facts: first, that in every society—whether largely rural or largely urban, whether agricultural or industrial, whether composed essentially of one ethnic group or of many or of a consistent culture or several clashing ones, whether existing at one historic period or another—there have been individuals who would not or could not conform to the taboos and laws prohibiting particular forms of behavior; second, and relatedly, that differences exist in the responses of various individuals or classes of persons to many of the elements in the culture-complex of a region.

As an illustration of the mass-culture approach to crime causation we may cite the studies of human ecology, the relation of neighborhood to human behavior, especially to delinquency. The numerous area-studies have revealed certain crude correlations between the gross physical make-up and composite culture of different zones of a city, on the one hand, and the incidence of delinquency and other aspects of social pathology, on the other. The most frequently quoted finding of these sociologic contributions is that there is a typical patterning of delinquency rates in different urban regions, the general trend of variation being from the highest rate in core-areas around central parts of cities and business districts to a lesser and lesser incidence in zones farther removed from the central section. The area of highest incidence of delinquency is also one of deterioration, in the sense that from a physical standpoint it is likely to be adjacent to industry and commerce and to be a neighborhood of dilapidated houses, dirty alleys, low rents, much poverty and dependency, and inadequate recreational facilities. From a cultural standpoint it is a place where the neighborhood has ceased to be an integrated and integrative agency of sentiments, values, behavior standards, and social control; has drawn in peoples of differing and more or less conflicting mores, morals, and standards of behavior; has to some extent developed a tradition of delinquency; and has largely failed to furnish unifying and edifying substitutes for the crumbling traditional patterns of behavior and authority.

This kind of approach to the problem of delinquency, although of much aid in studying the phenomenon in the mass, is of relatively little help in exploring the mechanisms of causation. These mechanisms are operative, not in the external area or culture, but in the mental life of the individual, and in detail as well as en masse. The area-studies establish that a region of economic and cultural disorganization tends to have a criminogenic effect on people residing therein; but the studies fail to emphasize that this influence affects only a selected group comprising a relatively small proportion of all residents. They do not reveal why the deleterious influences of even the most extreme delinquency area fail to turn the great majority of its boys into persistent delinquents. They do not disclose whether the children who do not succumb to the evil and disruptive neighborhood influence differ from those who become delinquents and if so, in what respects. Until they take this factor into account, they cannot penetratingly describe even the culture of the delinquency area. For to say that certain bacteria have a fatal effect on some individuals but no such effect on the majority without describing the differently reacting persons or explaining the differential

influences, is to describe that infective agent inadequately.

The true significance of the factors dealt with by the area sociologist can be determined only through close study of the points of impact of social forces upon individuals and classes of varying biologic make-up and childhood conditioning. The varieties of the physical, mental, and social history of different persons must determine, in large measure, the way in which they will be influenced by social disorganization, culture conflict, and the growing-pains of the city. To overemphasize the neighborhood matrix as a coherent whole and underemphasize or virtually ignore the biologic make-up and developmental history of the different human beings who themselves contribute to the modification of that matrix is to overlook many of the factors that account for variations in the effect of the culture on the human beings and thereby to distort reality with reference not only to the casual problem but even to the nature of the culture in question.

After presenting a great many studies showing the regional distribution of delinquency and stressing the influence of the disintegrating culture of the delinquency area on the behavior of its inhabitants, the ecologic sociologists are compelled to resort to psychologic insights when they come to grapple realistically with causal influences in the individual case. For example, Shaw's work, *The Natural History of a Delinquent Career*, begins with the familiar sociologic analysis of "A Delinquency Area." But it ends, significantly, with an analysis by a prominent ecologic sociologist employing such specific and individualized psychologic-psychiatric concepts as the precocious personality, the inferiority complex, and the difficult personality problem. The conclusion implied is that the delinquency area is after all not the major villain to be unmasked and coped with, but rather that the

> personality type, as revealed in his [the individual boy's] autobiography, would require, if reformation is to be achieved, individualized treatment by a skilled and sympathetic person.

The same enthusiastic emphasis on a single approach to crime causation—this time involving the economic factor of poverty—is to be found in many European studies of crime and it has proved equally sterile and distorted without psychologic adjuncts. Since poverty operates differently on various types of persons, it should have been obvious that something more than the sociologic-economic datum of poverty (or unemployment, or the fluctuations in the price of some standard commodity, or the vicissitudes of the business cycle) had to be examined before the role of poverty in the genesis of delinquency or crime could be understood.

Unilateral study of the causes of delinquency and criminalism is not confined to some sociologists and economists. Such an approach has also existed on the part of proponents of various biologic theories. Lombroso's belated recognition of the operation of sociologic factors was submerged in his persistent enthusiasm for the theory that crime is often the natural activity of persons destined from birth, by virtue of atavism (hereditary reversion or throwback to some remote ancestry), to become criminal. More recently, some enthusiastic endocrinologists have also made claims for the exclusiveness or primacy of glandular dysfunction as the causal agency in delinquency, without recognizing that any unilateral approach is a distortion of reality. Psychoanalytic explanations of delinquency are also inclined to an overemphasis of a single point of view; but the general acceptance of the role of early environmental conditioning upon the development of personality and character tends to make psychoanalysts recognize the importance of both biologic and cultural forces and of the interchanging influences of endowment and nurture in the genesis of maladapted behavior.

Other illustrations could be given of the tendency toward one-sided study of the causes of delinquency which springs from specialization in some particular science or method. But enough has been said to indicate that this is a pitfall which we have made every effort to avoid in the planning and execution of a research designed to throw light on the complexities of the causal process in delinquency.

Need for Eclectic Approach to Study of Crime Causation

At the present stage of knowledge an eclectic approach to the study of the causal process in human motivation and behavior is obviously necessary. It is clear that such an inquiry should be designed to reveal meaningful integrations of diverse data from several levels of inquiry. There is need for a systematic approach that will not ignore any promising leads to crime causation, covering as many fields and utilizing as many of the most reliable and relevant techniques of investigation and measurement as are necessary for a fair sampling of the various aspects of a complex biosocial problem. Ideally, the focus in such a study should be upon the selectivity that occurs when environment and organism interact. The searchlight should be played upon the point of contact between specific social and biologic processes as they coalesce, accommodate, or conflict in individuals. . . .

Dynamic Pattern of Delinquency

In the foregoing chapters we have unraveled and laid out the separate strands of the tangled skein of causation. Here we shall see if we can reweave them into a meaningful pattern without leaving too many loose ends. If we are to isolate the probable causal factors, we must focus attention on the ones that differentiate the delinquents and nondelinquents and that were operative before delinquency became evident. Factors that come into play after persistent antisocial behavior is established can hardly be regarded as relevant to the original etiology of maladaptation, except as they may reflect deep-rooted forces which do not make themselves felt in a tendency to dissocial behavior until puberty or adolescence is reached. . . .

Factors with Probable Causal Significance

We are now ready to focus attention on those factors that may have causal significance. It should be emphasized that in examining the tapestry of delinquency it is difficult to differentiate the warp of hereditary (genetic) factors from the woof of conditioned (environmental, cultural) factors. It is as yet too early to arrive at unassailable conclusions regarding the relative degrees of participation of biological and social factors in human behavior in general; and criminology, being a dependent discipline, must await the evidence of other sciences.

It is well nigh impossible to differentiate with assurance the completely innate from the completely acquired in the etiology of antisocial behavior. Birth injuries or anomalies of embryologic development may be confused with inherited conditions. Social inheritance may be mistaken for biologic. Certain inherited physical or mental traits may be confused with a "criminal instinct." The mechanisms of human heredity are as yet far from clear, especially where mental abnormalities are involved.

Nevertheless, our data do permit a rough division. There are, on the one hand, factors that are closer to the genetic than to the environmental end of the biosocial scale, and, on the other, those that are closer to the "conditioned," cultural end of the scale.

Physique

The data closest to the genetic are those dealing with the bodily morphology—the physique—of the two groups of boys under study. The most striking finding in the anthropologic analysis is the very high incidence of mesomorphic (muscular, solid) dominance in the body structure of the delinquents. Among the non-delinquents, on the other hand, there is a considerable incidence of ectomorphic (linear, thin) dominance. This basic difference in bodily morphology (the more subtle ones we are not at present bringing into the discussion) may reasonably be regarded as fundamentally related to differences in natural energy-tendencies. . . . *Thus, the delinquents, as a group, tend toward the outline of a solid, closely-knit, muscular type, one in which there is a relative predominance of muscle, bone, and connective tissue.* There may be contradictory, dysplastic components in individual instances, but the general tendency is mesomorphic. To the outlines of this solidly-structured, muscular, anatomical pattern derived by anthropologic analysis should now be added the evidence obtained from other sources, independently arrived at by other means. For example, a much higher proportion of the delinquents than of the non-delinquents are reported to have been extremely restless as young children in terms of energy output, and a considerably higher proportion of them were persistent enuretics. The health examination disclosed, by way of contrast, that neurologic handicaps and dermographia are less prevalent among the delinquents than among the control group.

Temperamental Traits and Emotional Dynamics

No direct statistical linkage between physique types and psychologic factors has been attempted here. It may be that when somatotypes are interrelated with temperament-types and character-types, meaningful associations will emerge. In the meantime, a general review of the traits of temperament and the emotional dynamics of the two groups permits us to make a rough association between the two orders of data. Let us consider, first, the dynamics of personality as disclosed by the Rorschach Test, which projects essentially subconscious materials. Such dynamics involve both the impulsive tendencies and desires and the inhibiting apparatus. The delinquents have been found to be considerably more extroversive in their trends of action, more vivacious, more emotionally labile or impulsive (as opposed to stability of emotional expression), more destructive and sadistic, more aggressive and adventurous. Accompanying these more excessive dynamic emotional tendencies is the lesser self-control of the delinquents. Reviewing next what may be called emotional attitudes in contrast to dynamisms, it will be recalled that the delinquents have been found by the Rorschach Test to be more hostile, defiant, resentful, and suspicious than the non-delinquents. The delinquent group, further, contains a higher proportion of socially assertive boys; of boys who have a feeling of not being recognized or appreciated; and of boys characterized by oral trends (unconsciously motivated by a desire to be looked after without effort) and by narcissistic trends (reflecting a strong need for status, power, and superiority). They are also less conventional (as disclosed by both the Rorschach Test and the psychiatric interview), less cooperative, less inclined to meet the expectations of others, less dependent upon others, and far less submissive to authority or more ambivalent to it. To these traits can now be added others obtained through the psychiatric interview, which tend to support some of the findings from the deeper layers tapped by the Rorschach Test: The delinquents, as a group, are more stubborn and egocentric, less critical of themselves, and more sensual than the non-delinquents. They are far less conscientious, less practical and realistic, less aesthetic, and less "adequate." The psychiatric examination has also revealed that twice as many delinquents as non-delinquents evidence conflicts resulting from all sorts of environmental stresses.... In respect to feelings of physical or mental inferiority (largely the latter), in sexual identification, in the relationship between boy and father and between boy and mother, and in stress growing out of companionship, a consistently greater proportion of conflicts was found among the delinquents than among the non-delinquents.

It is, however, in the manner in which they typically resolve such conflicts that the distinction between the two groups under comparison weaves most meaningfully into the general pattern. More than twice as many delinquents tend to resolve mental conflicts by extroversion of action and/or feeling (largely the former); while, by way of contrast, eight times as many non-delinquents as delinquents tend to resolve their conflicts by introversion....

On the whole, the delinquents are more extroverted, vivacious, impulsive, and less self-controlled than the non-delinquents. They are more hostile, resentful, defiant, suspicious, and destructive. They are less fearful of failure or defeat than the non-delinquents. They are less concerned about meeting conventional expectations, and are more ambivalent toward or far less submissive to authority. They are, as a group, more socially assertive. To a greater extent than the control group, they express feelings of not being recognized or appreciated.

Intellectual Traits

The instruments of adaptive behavior are not only physiologic and affective but also intellectual. The findings in this area must therefore be woven into the total dynamic pattern. General intelligence in the two groups under comparison is of course similar, by virtue of the manner in which the boys were originally selected and matched. Still, certain differences in the constituents of intelligence have been found which, though separately not large, show quite a definite trend. First, the delinquents, as a group, are distinguished from the non-delinquents in having a lesser capacity to approach problems methodically. Such a trait possibly bears on the capacity to reflect on contemplated behavior and to assess its consequences. The delinquents have less verbal intelligence, scoring lower than the control group on the Vocabulary, Information, Comprehension, and Digit Symbol subtests of the Wechsler-Bellevue Scale. On the other hand, they attained a somewhat higher score on two out of five of the performance subtests, namely, Block Design and Object Assembly.... These findings seem to indicate that the delinquent group is made up of a somewhat greater variety of intelligence than the non-delinquent, despite the fact that the two groups were originally matched by intelligence quotient.

Greater variability is also evident among the delinquents as individuals in their responses to the verbal series of intelligence tests and their scores on the achievement tests in reading and arithmetic. This greater scatter may reflect greater emotional disharmony, which, in turn, affects intellectual tasks. *The delinquents tend to express themselves intellectually in a direct, immediate, and concrete manner rather than through the use of intermediate symbols or abstractions. There seems also to be a somewhat greater emotional disharmony connected with their performance of intellectual tasks.*

Behavior Reflecting Significant Traits

Certain forms of behavior, in and out of school, are in a sense not fundamentally etiologic. But since they reflect, at least partially, temperamental tendencies and character traits that have their roots in early childhood, they may be included in the general pattern. These forms of behavior are school attainment, school misbehavior, general misbehavior tendencies, use of leisure, and type of companions.

School Attainment
Although school attainment itself cannot be regarded as a causal factor, it nevertheless may reflect either temperamental and intellectual differences or variations in early environment and training. The school accomplishment of the delinquents was definitely inferior to that of the control group. (The reader is reminded that the boys were matched by age, and that they were of like age upon school entrance). . . . The poorer school achievement of the delinquent boys is reflected in their attitude toward schooling. Far more of them than of the non-delinquents markedly disliked school, and far fewer expressed any desire for education beyond grade school. To a much greater extent than the non-delinquents, they revealed themselves as misfits in the school situation. As a group, they were less interested in academic tasks, less attentive in class, more often

tardy, less reliable, more careless in their work, lazier, more restless, less truthful, and they sought harder to attract attention to themselves. *Here again, we have strands of the delinquent pattern, namely, evidences of restless energy with accompanying difficulties in social adaptation and conformity to a regime of rules and discipline involving distasteful intellectual tasks.*

School Misbehavior
Probably bound up with somatic and temperamental traits, as well as with their home background, are the manifestations of maladaptive behavior displayed by the delinquents in school in marked excel over the non-delinquents. (School misbehavior characterized almost all the delinquents, compared with less than a fifth of the control group.) The average age of the delinquents at first school misbehavior was nine and a half—fully three years younger than the mean age of the small number of non-delinquents when they showed the first evidences of any maladaptive behavior in school. At the time the delinquents were, on the average, in the fourth grade, and the non-delinquents in the seventh.

As to the nature of their misconduct, there is manifest, first, a very marked attempt on the part of the delinquents to escape from the burdensome restraints of the school regime by persistent truancy. Other kinds of school misconduct in which the delinquents greatly exceeded the non-delinquents (disobedience, disorderliness, stubbornness, sullenness, impertinence, defiance, and impudence) are to be expected in the light of the predominance of traits already noted. Although still other types of misconduct (quarrelsomeness, cruelty, domineering attitude, and destruction of school materials) involve relatively small numbers of boys, the delinquents considerably exceeded the non-delinquents in all of them. *Some manifestations of school misconduct may, of course, be essentially reactive; others seem to reflect root traits and fundamental drives. They all fit consistently, however, into the temperamental segment of the general pattern that has been inductively achieved.*

General Misbehavior Tendencies

As for the misbehavior tendencies of the two sets of boys outside of school, the delinquents, far more than the control group, were in the habit of stealing rides or hopping trucks, committing acts of destructive mischief, setting fires, sneaking into theatres without paying, running away from home, bunking out, and keeping late hours. In marked excel over the non-delinquents, they also gambled and begged, and a far greater proportion of them began to smoke or drink at a very early age. *In their general misbehavior tendencies, there is further evidence of a driving, uninhibited energy and thirst for adventure on the part of the delinquents.*

Leisure Time and Companions

Passing in review the findings regarding the leisure-time activities of the boys, we again see marked differences, which take their place significantly in the general pattern. Less than half as many of the delinquents as of the non-delinquents spent some of their leisure time at home. This may have resulted from the fact that far fewer of the delinquents' families indulged in family group recreations and also from the reluctance of the parents to entertain the boys' friends at home. The delinquents, far more than the non-delinquents, preferred to play in distant neighborhoods and to hang around street corners, vacant lots, waterfronts, railroad yards, and poolrooms. They expressed a much greater preference for adventurous activities. Perhaps that is why they gravitated toward the more exciting street trades in seeking after-school jobs. Apart from concrete outlets for restless energy, many more of them sought vicarious adventure through the movies.

As might be expected from the foregoing, the delinquents were less inclined to supervised recreational activities than the non-delinquents, and were also far less willing to spend any of their leisure hours in the circumscribed areas of playgrounds. This dislike of controlled environments may also be partially reflected in the far higher proportion of them who were neglectful of their church duties. In their choice of companions, also, they differed greatly from the control group. Almost all of them, in contrast to very few of the non-delinquents, preferred to chum with other delinquents. More than half of them, compared with less than one percent of the non-delinquents, were members of gangs. In far higher measure than the control group, their companions were older boys—possibly indicating a search for temperamentally congenial "ego-ideals."

In their recreational activities and companionship, the delinquents further evidence a craving for adventure and for opportunities to express aggressive energy-output, with the added need of supportive companionship in such activities. Thus far it seems clear that the physical, temperamental, intellectual, and behavioral segments of the inquiry tend to interweave into a meaningful pattern: The delinquents, far more than the non-delinquents, are of the essentially mesomorphic, energetic type, with tendencies to restless and uninhibited expression of instinctual-affective energy and to direct and concrete, rather than symbolic and abstract, intellectual expression. It is evidently difficult for them to develop the high degree of flexibility of adaptation, self-management, self-control, and sublimation of primitive tendencies and self-centered desires demanded by the complex and confused culture of the times. Nevertheless, there are some delinquents who do not fit into this pattern, either on a somatic or a temperamental level; and there are some non-delinquents who do.

Socio-Cultural Factors

An examination of socio-cultural factors should shed some light on the reasons for these difficulties of adaptation. Character is the result of training as well as of natural equipment. Mechanisms of sublimation and of constructive or harmless energy-canalization, as well as "knowledge of right and wrong," are part of the apparatus of character expression. However, a boy does not express himself in a vacuum, but in a cultural milieu ranging from the intimate, emotion-laden atmosphere of the home to that of the school, the neighborhood, and general society. Primitive tendencies are morally and legally neutral. It is the existence of laws and taboos that qualifies their expression in certain ways as delinquent, or criminal, or otherwise dissocial or anti-social from the point of view of the particular society and culture in question. Adaptation to the demands and prohibitions of any specific social organization requires certain physical, temperamental, and intellectual capacities dependent upon the values protected by that society through law and custom and characteristics of the cultural matrix.

Modern culture, especially in crowded urban centers, is highly complex, and it is ill-defined because of conflicting values. The demands upon the growing human organism by every vehicle of today's culture are numerous, often subtle, and sometimes inconsistent. This is true of the home, the school, the neighborhood, and the general, all-pervasive culture of the times. Against insistence that he be honest, nonaggressive, self-controlled, and the like, the child soon finds vivid contradicting attitudes, values, and behavior all about him in an environment that in large measure rewards selfishness, aggression, a predatory attitude, and success by any means. Thus, the demands made upon the growing child at every level at which he is called upon to adapt his natural inclinations to the taboos, laws, and other prohibitions are neither simple nor well defined. They require a great deal of adaptive power, self-control, and self-management, the ability to choose among alternative values and to postpone immediate satisfactions for future ones—all this in a cultural milieu in which fixed points are increasingly difficult to discern and to hold to. This means that during the earliest years, when the difficult task of internalization of ideals and symbols of authority is in process, desirable attitudes and behavior

standards are not clearly enough defined, or are inconsistent, leaving a confused residue in the delicate structure of personality and character.

While responses to the complex modern culture differ with the varying constitution and temperament of each person subjected to it, the basic desires of the growing child, especially as he emerges into adolescence, are similar and imperative. Clinical experience has shown that among these are the striving for happiness and for expression of a desire for freedom from restraint; the thirst for new experience and for the satisfaction of curiosity; the need for an assured feeling of security and affectional warmth from parents, other adults whom the child admires, and companions; the desire to achieve a feeling of success and status.

How did the home conditions of the delinquents and non-delinquents in this study tend to facilitate or hamper the process of internalization of authority, the taming and sublimation of primitive impulses, and the definition of standards of good and bad? To answer this significant question requires, first, a review of the findings concerning the background of the parents of the boys; for the parents are not only the products of the biologic and cultural systems in which they were born and reared, but also the transmitters of that biosocial heritage to their children. We found that while the divergencies between the delinquents and non-delinquents were sometimes not as marked as those found in other aspects of the research, *the biosocial legacy of the parents of the delinquents was consistently poorer than that of the non-delinquents.* There was a greater incidence of emotional disturbances, mental retardation, alcoholism, and criminalism among the families of the mothers of the delinquents. These differences existed despite the fact that the economic condition of the homes in which the mothers of the delinquent boys had been reared was not very different from that of the homes in which the mothers of the non-delinquents grew up. In the families of the fathers of the delinquents, also, there was more emotional disturbance and criminalism than among the families of the fathers of the non-delinquents.

Thus, to the extent that the parents of the boys communicated the standards and ideals of their own rearing to that of their children, it is evident that the social—and perhaps, partially also, bio-logic—legacy of the delinquents was worse than that of the non-delinquents.

As for the parents themselves, their biosocial handicaps should be considered as at least partly influencing their capacity to rear their children properly. A higher proportion of the parents of the delinquents suffered from serious physical ailments, were mentally retarded, emotionally disturbed, alcoholic, and—most significant— many more of them had a history of delinquency.

The generally poorer hygienic and moral climate in which the delinquents were reared is further emphasized in the greater burden among their brothers and sisters of serious physical ailments, mental retardation, emotional disturbances, excessive drinking, and delinquency.

These are not the only ways in which the familial background of the delinquents was less adequate than that of the non-delinquents. There are other aspects of family life in which the delinquents were more deprived, often markedly so. For example: A somewhat higher proportion of their parents than of the parents of the non-delinquents came to the responsibilities of marriage with no more than grade-school education. A far higher proportion of the marriages proved to be unhappy. (More of the homes of the delinquents were broken by desertion, separation, divorce, or death of one or both parents, many of the breaches occurring during the early childhood of the boys. Because of this, many more delinquents than non-delinquents have had substitute parents, and more of them were shifted about from one household to another during their formative years. Further, there has been less of an effort among the families of the delinquent group to set up decent standards of conduct—less ambition, less self-respect, and less planning for the future.

As for the economic status of the two groups of families, a finding has emerged which is particularly significant in view of the fact that the boys were matched at the outset on the basis of residence in underprivileged areas, namely, that sporadic or chronic dependency has been markedly more prevalent among the families of the delinquents. This is attributable, at least in part, to the far poorer work habits of the fathers, and in part also to less planful management of the family income.

These differences between the families of the delinquents and the families of the non-delinquents do not so much pertain to the obvious issue of the relationship of dependence or poverty to crime (the vast majority of both groups of families are of the underprivileged class); they are important, rather, as reflecting the differences in the quality of the adults in the families and therefore the variance in influence on the children.

The greater inadequacy of the parents of the delinquents is also reflected in the extremes of laxity and harshness with which they attempted to meet the disciplinary problems of their children and in the greater carelessness of their supervision of the children, amounting often to outright neglect.

It is, however, within the family emotional setting—the family drama—that the most deep-rooted and persistent character and personality traits and distortions of the growing child are developed.

We may at once dispose of the claim often made that being the only or the firstborn, or the youngest child has special implications for delinquency. The fact is that, in our study, a *lower* proportion of the delinquents than of the non-delinquents were so placed in order of birth.

In interpersonal family relationships, however, we found an exceedingly marked difference between the two groups under comparison. A much higher proportion of the families of the delinquents were disorganized (not cohesive). Family disorganization, with its attendant lack of warmth and of respect for the integrity of each member, can have serious consequences for the growing child. It may prevent the development of both an adequate sense of responsibility and an effective mechanism for the inhibition of conduct that might disgrace the family name. Since the family is the first and foremost vehicle for the transmission of the values of a culture to the young child, non-cohesiveness of the family may leave him without ethical moorings or convey to him a confused and inconsistent cultural pattern.

Apart from the lesser cohesiveness of the families in which the delinquents grew up, many more of their fathers, mothers, brothers, and sisters have been indifferent or frankly hostile to the boys. A far *lower* proportion of the delinquents than of the non-delinquents have been affectionately attached to their parents; and considerably more of them have felt that their parents have not been concerned about their welfare. Finally, twice as many of the delinquents do not look upon their fathers as acceptable symbols for emulation.

These far-spread and marked differences cannot be attributable only to cultural inequalities in the two groups. Culture does not originate or operate in a vacuum. It is made, modified, and transmitted by human beings. The greater criminalism of the antecedents of the delinquent group, for example, cannot be attributed to a cultural tradition of lawlessness in these families, but must have sprung from individuals whose physical and psychologic equipment inclined them to select the antisocial culture as opposed to the conventional, or who found the former more congenial to their biologic tendencies.

In the light of the obvious inferiority of the families of the delinquents as sources of sound personality development and character formation, it is not surprising that these boys were never adequately socialized, and that they developed persistent antisocial tendencies, even apart from the fundamental somatic and temperamental differentiations between them and the non-delinquents.

Without attempting a psychoanalytic discussion of interpersonal emotional dynamics, we may point out that the development of a mentally hygienic and properly oriented superego (conscience) must have been greatly hampered by the kind of parental ideals, attitudes, temperaments, and behavior found to play such a major role on the family stage of the delinquents.

The Causal Complex

It will be observed that in drawing together the more significant threads of each area explored, we have not resorted to a theoretical explanation from the standpoint, exclusively, of any one discipline. It has seemed to us, at least at the present stage of our reflections upon the materials, that it is premature and misleading to give exclusive or even primary significance to any one of the avenues of interpretation. On the contrary, the evidence seems to point to the participation of forces from several areas and levels in channeling the persistent tendency to socially unacceptable behavior. The foregoing summation of the major resemblances and dissimilarities between the two groups included in the present inquiry indicates that the separate findings, independently gathered, integrate into a dynamic pattern which is neither exclusively biologic nor exclusively socio-cultural, but which derives from an interplay of somatic, temperamental, intellectual, and socio-cultural forces.

We are impelled to such a multidimensional interpretation because, without it, serious gaps appear. If we resort to an explanation exclusively in terms of somatic constitution, we leave unexplained why most persons of mesomorphic tendency do *not* commit crimes; and we further leave unexplained how bodily structure affects behavior. If we limit ourselves to a socio-cultural explanation, we cannot ignore the fact that socio-cultural forces are selective; even in underprivileged areas most boys do *not* become delinquent and many boys from such areas do not develop into persistent offenders.

And, finally, if we limit our explanation to psychoanalytic theory, we fail to account for the fact that the great majority of non-delinquents, as well as of delinquents, show traits usually deemed unfavorable to sound character development, such as vague feelings of insecurity and feelings of not being wanted; the fact that many boys who live under conditions in which there is a dearth of parental warmth and understanding nevertheless remain non-delinquent; and the fact that some boys, under conditions unfavorable to the development of a wholesome superego, do not become delinquents, but do become neurotics.

If, however, we take into account the dynamic interplay of these various levels and channels of influence, a tentative causal formula or law emerges, which tends to accommodate these puzzling divergencies so far as the great mass of delinquents is concerned:

The delinquents as a group are distinguishable from the non-delinquents: (1) physically, *in being essentially mesomorphic in constitution (solid, closely knit, muscular);* (2) temperamentally, *in being restlessly energetic, impulsive, extroverted, aggressive, destructive (often sadistic)—traits which may be related more or less to the erratic growth pattern and its physiologic correlates or consequences;* (3) in attitude, *by being hostile, defiant, resentful, suspicious, stubborn, socially assertive, adventurous, unconventional, non-submissive to authority;* (4) psychologically, *in tending to direct and concrete, rather than symbolic, intellectual expression, and in being less methodical in their approach in problems;* (5) socio-culturally, *in having been reared to a far greater extent than the control group in homes of little understanding, affection, stability, or moral fibre by parents usually unfit to be effective guides and protectors, or, according to psychoanalytic theory, desirable sources for emulation and the construction of a consistent, well-balanced, and socially normal superego during the early stages of character development.* While in individual cases the stresses contributed by any one of the above pressure-areas of dissocial-behavior tendency may adequately account for persistence in delinquency, in general the high probability of delinquency is dependent upon the interplay of the conditions and forces from all these areas.

In the exciting, stimulating, but little-controlled and culturally inconsistent environment of the underprivileged area, such boys readily give expression to their untamed impulses and their self-centered desires by means of various forms of delinquent behavior. Their tendencies toward uninhibited energy-expression are deeply anchored in soma and psyche and in the malformations of character during the first few years of life. . . .

Discussion Questions

1. Many of the theories described in this reader argue that crime and delinquency are caused by the social environment—by one's family and friends, social class position, neighborhood characteristics, etc. Being as specific as you can in your response, why would the Gluecks criticize such approaches?

2. Drawing on the Gluecks, describe the individual traits and social environment that characterized the delinquents in their sample.

3. Even though delinquents are more likely than nondelinquents to do poorly at school and experience other school problems, the Gluecks argue that school factors do not cause delinquency. Why do they make this argument?

38. Pathways in the Life Course to Crime

Terrie E. Moffitt

Moffitt begins her article by arguing that there are two major types of antisocial persons: a small group of persons who engage in antisocial behavior at a high rate over much of their life ("life-course-persistent" offenders), and a much larger group of those who limit their antisocial behavior to the adolescent years ("adolescence-limited" offenders). She then develops a theory of antisocial behavior for each group. The theory designed to explain life-course-persistent antisocial behavior is most relevant to this section. It represents one of the best attempts to integrate biological, psychological, and sociological variables in the recent literature.

At the heart of the theory is the assertion that persistent antisocial behavior is a product of the interaction between individual traits and the social environment. Moffitt begins by describing certain traits that predispose one to antisocial behavior, and she argues that such traits are a function of biological factors and the early family environment. She then describes the various ways in which individual traits and the social environment mutually influence one another. In certain cases, an escalating process occurs: negative environments exacerbate negative traits and negative traits increase the likelihood of exposure to negative environments. By late adolescence, those traits conducive to antisocial behavior may be so

entrenched that changing the person's behavior becomes extremely difficult. A pattern of persistent antisocial behavior has been established. Adolescence-limited antisocial behavior, however, is not fueled by individual traits and, for reasons indicated in the selection, such behavior is abandoned in early adulthood.

Moffitt's theory is distinguished by its description of the various ways in which individual traits and the social environment may interact with one another to produce persistent antisocial behavior. It is also one of a group of theories that attempts to explain patterns in antisocial behavior over the life course. As Moffitt points out, most traditional crime theories focus on the explanation of adolescent crime; they do not attempt to explain patterns of offending over time.

Moffitt's theory is compatible with much data on antisocial behavior, and key portions of her theory have received qualified empirical support (see Bartusch et al., 1997; Moffitt, 1997, 2006; Moffitt et al., 2001; Nagin et al., 1995; Piquero and Moffitt, 2005; Tibbetts and Piquero, 1999). Still, it remains to be seen if offenders fall into two neatly packaged groups of offenders. Some studies suggest that there might be more than two categories of criminals (D'Unger et al., 1998; Loeber and Stouthamer-Loeber, 1998), while scholars such as Hirschi and Gottfredson (2000) continue to maintain that offenders differ not qualitatively

Reprinted from Terrie E. Moffitt, "Adolescence-Limited and Life-Course-Persistent Antisocial Behavior: A Developmental Taxonomy" in *Psychological Review* 100. Copyright © 1993 by American Psychological Association. Adapted with permission.

but only in the degree to which they exhibit criminal propensities.

References

Bartusch, Dawn R. Jeglum, Donald R. Lynam, Terrie E. Moffitt, and Phil A. Silva. 1997. "Is Age Important? Testing a General Versus a Developmental Theory of Antisocial Behavior". *Criminology* 35: 13–48.

D'Unger, Amy V., Kenneth C. Land, Patricia L. McCall, and Daniel S. Nagin. 1998. "How Many Latent Classes of Delinquent/Criminal Careers? Results From Mixed Poisson Regression Analyses." *American Journal of Sociology* 103: 1593–1630.

Hirschi, Travis and Michael R. Gottfredson. 2000. "In Defense of Self-Control." *Theoretical Criminology* 4: 55–69.

Loeber, Rolf and Magda Stouthamer-Loeber. 1998. "Development of Juvenile Aggression and Violence: Some Misconceptions and Controversies." *American Psychologist* 53: 242–259.

Moffitt, Terrie E. 1993. "Adolescence-Limited and Life-Course-Persistent Antisocial Behavior: A Developmental Taxonomy." *Psychological Review* 100: 674–701.

——. 1997. "Adolescence-Limited and Life-Course-Persistent Offending: A Complementary Pair of Developmental Theories." In Terence P. Thornberry (ed.), *Developmental Theories of Crime and Delinquency, Advances in Criminological Theory*, Volume 7, pp. 11–54. New Brunswick, NJ: Transaction.

——. 2006. "A Review of Research on the Taxonomy of Life-Course Persistent Versus Adolescence-Limited Antisocial Behavior." In Francis T. Cullen, John Paul Wright, and Kristie R. Blevins (eds.), *Taking Stock: The Status of Criminological Theory—Advances in Criminological Theory*, Volume 15, pp. 277–311. New Brunswick, NJ: Transaction.

Moffitt, Terrie E., Avshalom Caspi, Michael Rutter, and Phil A. Silva. 2001. *Sex Differences in Antisocial Behavior: Conduct Disorder, Delinquency, and Violence in the Dunedin Longitudinal Study*. Cambridge, UK: Cambridge University Press.

Nagin, Daniel S., David P. Farrington, and Terrie E. Moffitt. 1995. "Life-Course Trajectories of Different Types of Offenders." *Criminology* 33: 111–139.

Piquero, Alex R. and Terrie E. Moffitt. 2005. "Explaining the Facts of Crime: How the Developmental Taxonomy Replies to Farrington's Invitation." In David P. Farrington (ed.), *Integrated Developmental and Life-Course Theories of Offending: Advances in Criminological Theory*, Volume 14, pp. 51–72. New Brunswick, NJ: Transaction.

Tibbetts, Stephen G. and Alex R. Piquero. 1999. "The Influence of Gender, Low Birth Weight, and Disadvantaged Environment in Predicting Early Onset of Offending: A Test of Moffitt's Interactional Hypthesis." *Criminology* 37: 843–877.

———————————————

There are marked individual differences in the stability of antisocial behavior. Many people behave antisocially, but their antisocial behavior is temporary and situational. In contrast, the antisocial behavior of some people is very stable and persistent. Temporary, situational antisocial behavior is quite common in the population, especially among adolescents. Persistent, stable antisocial behavior is found among a relatively small number of males whose behavior problems are also quite extreme. The central tenet of this article is that temporary versus persistent antisocial persons constitute two qualitatively distinct types of persons. In particular, I suggest that juvenile delinquency conceals two qualitatively distinct categories of individuals, each in need of its own distinct theoretical explanation....

For delinquents whose criminal activity is confined to the adolescent years, the causal factors may be proximal, specific to the period of adolescent development, and theory must account for the discontinuity in their lives. In contrast, for persons whose adolescent delinquency is merely one inflection in a continuous lifelong antisocial

Figure 38.1
Hypothetical Illustration of the Changing Prevalence of Participation in Antisocial Behavior Across the Life Course (The solid line represents the known curve of crime over age. The arrows represent the duration of participation in antisocial behavior by individuals)

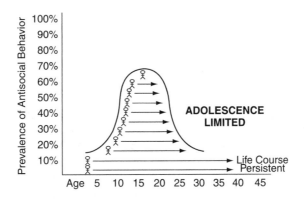

course, a theory of antisocial behavior must locate its causal factors early in their childhoods and must explain the continuity in their troubled lives....

Figure 38.1 depicts the typological thesis to be argued here. A small group of persons is shown engaging in antisocial behavior of one sort or another at every stage of life. I have labeled these persons *life-course-persistent* to reflect the continuous course of their antisocial behavior. A larger group of persons fills out the age-crime curve with crime careers of shorter duration. I have labeled these persons *adolescence-limited* to reflect their more temporary involvement in antisocial behavior. Thus, timing and duration of the course of antisocial involvement are the defining features in the natural histories of the two proposed types of offenders....

Life-Course-Persistent Antisocial Behavior

Continuity of Antisocial Behavior Defined

As implied by the label, continuity is the hallmark of the small group of life-course persistent antisocial persons. Across the life course, these individuals exhibit changing manifestations of antisocial behavior: biting and hitting at age 4, shoplifting and truancy at age 10, selling drugs and stealing cars at age 16, robbery and rape at age 22, and fraud and child abuse at age 30; the underlying disposition remains the same, but its expression changes form as new social opportunities arise at different points in development. This pattern of continuity across age is matched also by cross-situational consistency: life-course-persistent antisocial persons lie at home, steal from shops, cheat at school, fight in bars, and embezzle at work (Farrington, 1991; Loeber, 1982; Loeber and Baicker-McKee, 1989; Robins, 1966, 1978; White et al., 1990)....

Beginnings: Neuropsychological Risk for Difficult Temperament and Behavioral Problems

If some individuals' antisocial behavior is stable from preschool to adulthood as the data imply, then investigators are compelled to look for its roots early in life, in factors that are present before or soon after birth. It is possible that the etiological chain begins with some factor capable of producing individual differences in the neuropsychological functions of the infant nervous system. Factors that influence infant neural development are myriad, and many of them have been empirically linked to antisocial outcomes.

One possible source of neuropsychological variation that is linked to problem behavior is disruption in the ontogenesis of the fetal brain. Minor physical anomalies, which are thought to be observable markers for hidden anomalies in neural development, have been found at elevated rates among violent offenders and subjects with antisocial personality traits (Fogel, Mednick, and Michelson, 1985; E. Kandel, Brennan, and Mednick, 1989; Paulhus and Martin 1986). Neural development may be disrupted by maternal drug abuse, poor prenatal nutrition, or pre or postnatal exposure to toxic agents (Needleman and Beringer, 1981; Rodning, Beckwith, and Howard, 1989; Stewart, 1983). Even brain insult suffered because of complications during delivery has been empirically linked to later violence and antisocial behavior in carefully designed longitudinal studies (E. Kandel and Mednick, 1991; Szatmari, Reitsma-Street, and Offord, 1986). In addition, some individual differences in neuropsychological health are heritable in origin (Borecki and Ashton, 1984; Martin, Jardine, and Eaves, 1984; Plomin, Nitz, and Rowe, 1990; Tambs, Sundet, and Magnus, 1984; Vandenberg, 1969). Just as parents and children share facial resemblances, they share some structural and functional similarties within their nervous systems. After birth, neural development may be disrupted by neonatal deprivation of nutrition, stimulation, and even affection (Cravioto and Arrieta, 1983; Kraemer, 1988; Meany, Aitken, van Berkel, Bhatnagar, and Sapolsky, 1988). Some studies have pointed to child abuse and neglect as possible sources of brain injury in the histories of delinquents with neuropsychological impairment (Lewis, Shanok, Pincus, and Glaser, 1979; Milner and McCanne, 1991; Tarter, Hegedus, Winsten, and Alterman, 1984).

There is good evidence that children who ultimately become persistently antisocial do suffer from deficits in neuropsychological abilities. I have elsewhere reviewed the available empirical and theoretical literatures: the link between neuropsychological impairment and antisocial outcomes is one of the most robust effects in the study of antisocial behavior (Moffitt, 1990b; Moffitt and Henry, 1991; see also Hirschi and Hindelang, 1977). Two sorts of neuropsychological deficits are empirically associated with antisocial behavior: verbal and "executive" functions. The verbal deficits of antisocial children are pervasive, affecting receptive listening and reading, problem solving, expressive speech and writing, and memory. In addition, executive deficits produce what is sometimes referred to as a compartmental learning disability (Price, Daffner, Stowe, and Mesulam, 1990), including symptoms such as inattention and impulsivity. These cognitive deficits and antisocial behavior share variance that is independent of social class, race, test motivation, and academic attainment (Lynam, Moffitt, and Stouthamer-Loeber, 1993; Moffitt, 1990b). In addition, the relation is not an artifact of slow witted delinquents' greater susceptibility to detection by police; undetected delinquents have weak cognitive skills too (Moffitt and Silva, 1988a).

The evidence is strong that neuropsychological deficits are linked to the kind of antisocial behavior that begins in childhood and is sustained for lengthy periods. In a series of articles (Moffitt, 1990a; Moffitt and Henry, 1989; Moffitt and Silva, 1988b), I have shown that poor verbal and executive functions are associated with antisocial behavior, if it is extreme and persistent. In these studies, adolescent New Zealand boys who exhibited symptoms of both conduct disorder and attention-deficit disorder with hyperactivity (ADDH) scored very poorly on neuropsychological tests of verbal and executive functions and had histories of extreme antisocial behavior that persisted from age 3 to age 15. Apparently, their neuropsychological deficits were as long standing as their antisocial behavior; at ages 3 and 5 these boys had scored more than a standard deviation below the age norm for boys on the Baviev and McCarthy tests of motor coordination and on the Stanford-Binet test of cognitive performance. Contrast groups of boys with single diagnoses of either conduct disorder or ADDH did not have neuropsychological deficits or cognitive-motor delays, but neither were their behavior problems stable over time.

In a study designed to improve on measurement of executive functions (White, Moffitt, Caspi, Jeglum, Needles, and Stouthamer-Loeber, in press), we gathered data on self-control and impulsivity for 430 Pittsburgh youths. Twelve measures were taken from multiple sources (mother, teacher, self, and observer) by using multiple methods (rating scales, performance tests, computer games, Q sorts, and videotaped observations). A linear composite of the impulsivity measures was strongly related to the 3-year longevity of antisocial behavior, even after controlling for IQ, race, and social class. Boys who were very delinquent from ages 10 to 13 scored significantly higher on impulsivity than both their nondelinquent and temporarily delinquent agemates. Taken together, the New Zealand and Pittsburgh longitudinal studies suggest that neuropsychological dysfunctions that manifest themselves as poor scores on tests of language and self-control—and as the inattentive, overactive, and impulsive symptoms of ADDH—are linked with the early childhood emergence of aggressive antisocial behavior and with its subsequent persistence.

Neuropsychological variation and the 'difficult' infant. Before describing how neuropsychological variation might constitute risk for antisocial behavior, it is useful to define what is meant here by neuropsychological. By combining neuro with psychological, I refer broadly to the extent to which anatomical structures and physiological processes within the nervous system influence phychological characteristics such as temperament, behavioral development, cognitive abilities, or all three. For example, individual variation in brain function may engender differences between children in activity level, emotional reactivity, or self-regulation (temperament); speech, motor coordination, or impulse control (behavioral development); and attention, language, learning, memory, or reasoning (cognitive abilities).

Children with neurological difficulties severe enough to constitute autism, severe physical handicap, or profound mental retardation are usually identified and specially treated by parents and professionals. However, other infants have subclinical levels of problems that affect the difficulty of rearing them, variously referred to as difficult temperament, language or motor delays, or mild cognitive deficits. Compromised neuropsychological functions are associated with a variety of consequences for infants' cognitive and motor development as well as for their personality development (Rothbart and Derryberry, 1981). Toddlers with subtle neuropsychological deficits may be clumsy and awkward, overactive, inattentive, irritable, impulsive, hard to keep on schedule, delayed in reaching developmental milestones, poor at verbal comprehension, deficient at expressing themselves, or slow at learning new things (Rutter, 1977, 1983; Thomas and Chess, 1977; Wender, 1971).

Hertzig (1983) has described an empirical test of the proposed relationship between neurological damage and difficult behavior in infancy. She studied a sample of 66 low-birth-weight infants from intact middle-class families. Symptoms of brain dysfunction detected during neurological examinations were significantly related to an index of difficult temperament taken at ages 1, 2, and 3 (Thomas and Chess, 1977; the index comprised rhythmicity, adaptability, approach-withdrawal, intensity, and mood). The parents of the children with neurological impairment and difficult temperament more often sought help from child psychiatrists as their children grew up, and the most frequent presenting complaints were immaturity, overactivity, temper tantrums, poor attention, and poor school performance. Each of these childhood problems has been linked by research to later antisocial outcomes (cf. Moffitt, 1990a, 1990b). Importantly, the impairments of the children with neural damage were not massive; their mean IQ score was 96 (only 4 points below the population mean). Hertzig's study showed that even subtle neurological deficits can influence an infant's temperament and behavior, the difficulty of rearing the infant, and behavioral problems in later childhood.

Child-environment covariation in nature: A source of interactional continuity. Up to this point, I have emphasized in this article the characteristics of the developing child as if environments were held constant. Unfortunately, children with cognitive and temperamental disadvantages are not generally born into supportive environments, nor do they even get a fair chance of being randomly assigned to good or bad environments. Unlike the aforementioned infants in Hertzig's (1983) study of temperament and neurological symptoms, most low-birthweight infants are not born into intact, middle-class families. Vulnerable infants are disproportionately found in environments that will not be ameliorative because many sources of neural maldevelopment co-occur with family disadvantage or deviance.

Indeed, because some characteristics of parents and children tend to be correlated, parents of children who are at risk for antisocial behavior often inadvertently provide their children with criminogenic environments (Sameroff and Chandler, 1975). The intergenerational transmission of severe antisocial behavior has been carefully documented in a study of three generations (Huesmann et al., 1984). In that study of 600 subjects, the stability of individuals' aggressive behavior from age 8 to age 30 was exceeded by the stability of aggression across the generations: from grandparent to parent to child. Thus, with regard to risk for antisocial behavior, nature does not follow a 2×2 design with equal cell sizes.

Parents and children resemble each other on temperament and personality. Thus, parents of children who are difficult to manage often lack the necessary psychological and physical resources to cope constructively with a difficult child (Scarr and McCartney, 1983; Snyder and Patterson, 1987). For example, temperamental traits such as activity level and irritability are known to be partly heritable (Plomin, Chipuer, and Loehlin, 1990). This suggests that children whose hyperactivity and angry outbursts might be curbed by firm discipline will tend to have parents who are inconsistent disciplinarians; the parents tend to be impatient and irritable too. The converse is also true: Empirical evidence has been found for a relationship between variations in parents' warmth and infants' easiness (Plomin, Chipuer, and Loehlin, 1990).

Parents and children also resemble each other on cognitive ability. The known heritability of measured intelligence (Loehlin, 1989; Plomin, 1990) implies that children who are most in need of remedial cognitive stimulation will have parents who may be least able to provide it. Moreover, parents' cognitive abilities set limits on their own educational and occupational attainment (Barrett and Depinet, 1991). As one consequence, families whose members have below-average cognitive capacities will often be least able financially to obtain professional interventions or optimal remedial schooling for their at-risk children.

Even the social and structural aspects of the environment may be stacked against children who enter the world at risk. Plomin and Bergeman (1990) have shown that there are genetic components to measures that are commonly used by developmental psychologists to assess socialization environments. For example, the Home Observation for Measurement of the Environment scale, the Moos Family Environment scales, and the Holmes and Rahe scales of stressful life events all revealed the influence of heritable factors when they were examined with behavior genetic research designs (Plomin and Bergeman, 1990). Vulnerable children are often subject to adverse homes and neighborhoods because their parents are vulnerable to problems too (cf. Lahey et al., 1990).

Importantly, although examples from behavior genetics research have been cited in the previous three paragraphs, the perverse compounding of children's vulnerabilities with their families' imperfections does not require that the child's neuropsychological risk arise from any genetic disposition. In fact, for my purposes, it is immaterial whether parent-child similarities arise from shared genes or shared homes. A home environment wherein prenatal care is haphazard, drugs are used during pregnancy, and infants' nutritional needs are neglected is a setting where sources of children's neuropsychological dysfunction that are clearly environmental coexist with a criminogenic social environment.

Problem child–problem parent interactions and the emergence of antisocial behaviors. I believe that the juxtaposition of a vulnerable and difficult infant with an adverse rearing context initiates risk for the life-course-persistent pattern of antisocial behavior. The ensuing process is a transactional one in which the challenge of coping with a difficult child evokes a chain of failed parent-child encounters (Sameroff and Chandler, 1975). The assertion that children exert important effects on their social environments is useful in understanding this hypothetical process (Bell and Chapman, 1986). It is now widely acknowledged that personality and behavior are shaped in large measure by interactions between the person and the environment (cf. Buss, 1987; Plomin, DeFries, and Loehlin, 1977; Scarr and McCartney, 1983). One form of interaction may play a particularly important role both in promoting an antisocial style and in maintaining its continuity across the life course: *Evocative* interaction occurs when a child's behavior evokes distinctive responses from others (Caspi et al., 1987).

Children with neuropsychological problems evoke a challenge to even the most resourceful, loving, and patient families. For example, Tinsley and Parke (1983) have reviewed literature showing that low-birth-weight, premature infants negatively influence the behavior of their caretakers; they arrive before parents are prepared, their crying patterns are rated as more disturbing and irritating, and parents report that they are less satisfying to feed, less pleasant to hold, and more demanding to care for than healthy babies. Many parents of preterm infants hold unrealistic expectations about their children's attainment of developmental milestones, and these may contribute to later dysfunctional parent-child relationships (Tinsley and Parke, 1983). More disturbing, an infant's neurological health status has been shown to be related to risk for maltreatment and neglect (Friedrich and Boriskin, 1976; Frodi et al., 1978; Hunter, Kilstrom, Kraybill, and Loda, 1978; Milowe and Lowrie, 1964; Sandgrund, Gaines, and Green, 1974).

Numerous studies have shown that a toddler's problem behaviors may affect the parents' disciplinary strategies as well as subsequent interactions with adults and peers (Bell and Chapman, 1986; Chess and Thomas, 1987). For example, children characterized by a difficult temperament in infancy are more likely to resist their mothers' efforts to control them in early childhood (Lee and Bates, 1985). Similarly, mothers of difficult boys experience more problems in their efforts to socialize their children. Maccoby and Jacklin (1983) showed that over time these mothers reduce their efforts to actively guide and direct their children's behavior and become increasingly less involved in the teaching process. In a study of unrelated mothers and children, K. E. Anderson, Lytton, and Romney (1986) observed conduct-disordered and nonproblem boys interacting with mothers of conduct-disordered and nonproblem sons in unrelated pairs. The conduct-disordered boys evoked more negative reactions from both types of mothers than did normal boys, but the two types of mothers did not differ from each other in their negative reactions. It may well be that early behavioral difficulties contribute to the development of persistent antisocial behavior by evoking responses from the interpersonal social environment, responses that exacerbate the child's tendencies (Goldsmith, Bradshaw, and Rieser-Danner, 1986; Lytton, 1990). "The child acts; the environment reacts; and the child reacts back in mutually interlocking evocative interaction" (Caspi et al., 1987, p. 308).

Such a sequence of interactions would be most likely to produce lasting antisocial behavior problems if caretaker reactions were more likely to exacerbate than to ameliorate children's problem behavior. To my knowledge, students of child effects have not yet tested for interactions between child behavior and parental deviance or poor parenting, perhaps because very disadvantaged families are seldom studied with such designs. Nonetheless, some data suggest that children's predispositions toward antisocial behavior may be exacerbated under deviant rearing conditions. In the New Zealand longitudinal study, there was a significant interaction effect between children's neuropsychological deficit and family adversity on one type of delinquent act: aggressive confrontation with a victim or adversary. Among the 536 boys in the sample, the 75 boys who had both low neuropsychological test scores and adverse home environments earned a mean aggression score more than four times greater than that of boys with either neuropsychological problems or adverse homes (Moffitt, 1990b). The index of family adversity included parental characteristics such as poor mental health and low intelligence as well as socioeconomic status. Behavior-genetic adoption studies of antisocial behavior often report a similar pattern of findings, wherein the highest rates of criminal outcomes are found for adoptees whose foster parents, as well as their biological parents, were deviant (e.g. Mednick, Gabrielli, and Hutchings, 1984). Thus, children's predispositions may evoke exacerbating responses from the environment and may also render them more vulnerable to criminogenic environments.

If the child who "steps off on the wrong foot" remains on an ill-starred path, subsequent stepping-stone experiences may culminate in life-course-persistent antisocial behavior. For life-course-persistent antisocial individuals, deviant behavior patterns later in life may thus reflect early individual differences that are perpetuated or exacerbated by interactions with the social environment: first at home, and later at school. Quay (1987) summarized this as

this youth is likely to be at odds with everyone in the environment, and most particularly with those who must interact with him on a daily basis to raise, educate, or otherwise control him.... This pattern is the most troublesome to society, seems least amenable to change, and has most pessimistic prognosis for adult adjustment. (p. 121)

However, inauspicious beginnings do not complete the story. In the New Zealand study, for example, a combination of preschool measures of antisocial behavior and cognitive ability was able to predict 70 percent of the cases of conduct disorder at age 11 but at the cost of a high false-positive rate (White et al., 1990). The next section explores the specific interactional processes that nourish and augment the life-course-persistent antisocial style beyond childhood.

Maintenance and Elaboration Over the Life Course: Cumulative Continuity, Contemporary Continuity, and Narrowing Options for Change

In the previous section, the concept of evocative person-environment interaction was called on to describe how children's difficult behaviors might affect encounters with their parents. Two additional types of interaction may help to explain how the life-course-persistent individual's problem behavior, once initiated, might promote its own continuity and pervasiveness. *Reactive* interaction occurs when different youngsters exposed to the same environment experience it, interpret it, and react to it in accordance with their particular style. For example, in interpersonal situations where cues are ambiguous, aggressive children are likely to mistakenly attribute harmful intent to others and then act accordingly (Dodge and Frame, 1982). *Proactive* interaction occurs when people select or create environments that support their styles. For example, antisocial individuals appear to be likely to affiliate selectively with antisocial others, even when selecting a mate. Some evidence points to nonrandom mating along personality traits related to antisocial behavior (Buss, 1984), and there are significant spouse correlations on conviction for crimes (e.g., Baker, Mack, Moffitt, and Mednick, 1989).

The three types of person-environment interactions can produce two kinds of consequences in the life course: *cumulative consequences* and *contemporary consequences* (Caspi and Bem, 1990). Early individual differences may set in motion a downhill snowball of cumulative continuities. In addition, individual differences may themselves persist from infancy to adulthood, continuing to influence adolescent and adult behavior in a proximal contemporary fashion. Contemporary continuity arises if the life-course-persistent person continues to carry into adulthood the same underlying constellation of traits that got him into trouble as a child, such as high activity level, irritability, poor self-control, and low cognitive ability.

The roles of cumulative and contemporary continuities in antisocial behavior have been explored by Caspi, Bem, and Elder (1989; Caspi et al., 1987), using data from the longitudinal Berkeley Guidance Study. They identified men who had a history of temper tantrums during late childhood (when tantrums are not developmentally normative). Then they traced the continuities and consequences of this personality style across the subsequent 30 years of the subjects' lives and into multiple diverse life domains: education, employment, and marriage. A major finding was that hot-tempered boys who came from middle-class homes suffered a progressive deterioration of socioeconomic status as they moved through the life course. By age 40, their occupational status was indistinguishable from that of men born into the working class. A majority of them held jobs of lower occupational status than those held by their fathers at a comparable age. Did these men fail occupationally because their earlier ill-temperedness started them down a particular path (cumulative consequences) or because their current ill-temperedness handicapped them in the world of work (contemporary consequences)?

Cumulative consequences were implied by the effect of childhood temper on occupational status at midlife: Tantrums predicted lower educational attainment, and educational attainment, in turn, predicted lower occupational status. Contemporary consequences were implied by the strong direct link between ill-temperedness and occupational stability. Men with childhood tantrums continued to be hot-tempered in adulthood, where it got them into trouble in the world of work. They had more erratic work lives, changing jobs more frequently and experiencing more unemployment between ages 18 and 40. Ill-temperedness also had a contemporary effect on marital stability. Almost half (46 percent) of the men with histories of childhood tantrums had divorced by age 40 compared with only 22 percent of other men.

Elsewhere, I describe in detail some of the patterns of interaction between persons and their social environments that may promote antisocial continuity across time and across life domains (Caspi and Moffitt, in press-b). Two sources of continuity deserve emphasis here because they narrow the options for change. These processes are (a) failing to learn conventional prosocial alternatives to antisocial behavior and (b) becoming ensnared in a deviant life-style by crime's consequences. These concepts have special implications for the questions of why life-course-persistent individuals fail to desist from delinquency as young adults and why they are so impervious to intervention.

A restricted behavioral repertoire. This theory of life-course-persistent antisocial behavior asserts that the causal sequence begins very early and the formative years are dominated by chains of cumulative and contemporary continuity. As a consequence, little opportunity is afforded for the life-course-persistent antisocial individual to learn a behavioral repertoire of prosocial alternatives. Thus, one overlooked and pernicious source of continuity in antisocial behavior is simply a lack of recourse to any other options. In keeping with this prediction, Vitaro, Gagnon, and Tremblay (1990) have shown that aggressive children whose behavioral repertoires consist almost solely of antisocial behaviors are less likely to change over years than are aggressive children whose repertoires comprise some prosocial behaviors as well.

Life-course-persistent persons miss out on opportunities to acquire and practice prosocial alternatives at each stage of development. Children with poor self-control and aggressive behavior are often rejected by peers and adults (Coie, Belding, and Underwood, 1988; Dodge, Coie, and Brakke, 1982; Vitaro et al., 1990). In turn, children who have learned to expect rejection are likely in later settings to withdraw or strike out preemptively, precluding opportunities to affiliate with prosocial peers (Dodge and Frame, 1982; Dodge and Newman, 1981; LaFrenier and Sroufe, 1985; Nasby, Hayden, and DePaulo, 1980). Such children are robbed of chances to practice conventional social skills. Alternatively, consider this sequence of narrowing options: Behavior problems at school and failure to attain basic math and reading skills place a limit on the variety of job skills that can be acquired and thereby cut off options to pursue legitimate employment as an alternative to the underground economy (Farrington, Gallagher, Morley, Ledger, and West, 1986; Maughan, Gray, and Rutter, 1985; Moffitt, 1990a). Simply put, if social and academic skills are not mastered in childhood, it is very difficult to later recover lost opportunities.

Becoming ensnared by consequences of antisocial behavior. Personal characteristics such as poor self-control, impulsivity, and inability to delay gratification increase the risk that antisocial youngsters will make irrevocable decisions that close the doors of opportunity. Teenaged parenthood, addiction to drugs or alcohol, school dropout, disabling or disfiguring injuries, patchy work histories, and time spent incarcerated are *snares* that diminish the probabilities of later success by eliminating opportunities for breaking the chain of cumulative continuity (Cairns and Cairns, 1991; J. Q. Wilson and Herrnstein, 1985). Similarly, labels accrued early in life can foreclose

later opportunities; an early arrest record or a "bad" reputation may rule out lucrative jobs, higher education, or an advantageous marriage (Farrington, 1977; Klein, 1986; West, 1982). In short, the behavior of life-course-persistent antisocial persons is increasingly maintained and supported by narrowing options for conventional behavior.

Interventions with life-course-persistent persons have met with dismal results (Lipton, Martinson, and Wilks, 1975; Palmer, 1984; Sechrest, White, and Brown, 1979). This is not surprising, considering that most interventions are begun relatively late in the chain of cumulative continuity. The forces of continuity are formidable foes (Caspi and Moffitt, in press-a). After a protracted deficient learning history, and after options for change have been eliminated, efforts to suppress antisocial behavior will not automatically bring prosocial behavior to the surface in its place. Now-classic research on learning shows conclusively that efforts to extinguish undesirable behavior will fail unless alternative behaviors are available that will attract reinforcement (Azrin and Holz, 1966). My analysis of increasingly restricted behavioral options suggests the hypothesis that opportunities for change will often be actively transformed by life-course-persistents into opportunities for continuity: Residential treatment programs provide a chance to learn from criminal peers, a new job furnishes the chance to steal, and new romance provides a partner for abuse. This analysis of life-course-persistent antisocial behavior anticipates disappointing outcomes when such antisocial persons are thrust into new situations that purportedly offer the chance "to turn over a new leaf."

The Reason for Persistence: Traits, Environments, and Developmental Processes

According to some accounts of behavioral continuity, an ever present underlying trait generates antisocial outcomes at every point in the life span (e.g., Gottfredson and Hirschi, 1990). By other accounts, antisocial behavior is sustained by environmental barriers to change (e.g., Bandura, 1979, pp. 217–224). In this theory of life-course-persistent antisocial behavior, neither traits nor environments account for continuity.

True, the theory begins with a trait: variation between individuals in neuropsychological health. The trait is truly underlying in that it seldom comes to anyone's attention unless an infant is challenged by formal examinations; it is manifested behaviorally as variability in infant temperament, developmental milestones, and cognitive abilities.

Next, the theory brings environments into play. Parents and other people respond to children's difficult temperaments and developmental deficits. In nurturing environments, toddlers' problems are often corrected. However, in disadvantaged homes, schools, and neighborhoods, the responses are more likely to exacerbate than amend. Under such detrimental circumstances, difficult behavior is gradually elaborated into conduct problems and a dearth of prosocial skills. Thus, over the years, an antisocial personality is slowly and insidiously constructed. Likewise, deficits in language and reasoning are incrementally elaborated into academic failure and a dearth of job skills. Over time, accumulating consequences of the youngster's personality problems and academic problems prune away the options for change.

This theory of life-course-persistent antisocial behavior emphasizes the constant process of reciprocal interaction between personal traits and environmental reactions to them. The original attribute is thus elaborated on during development, to become a syndrome that remains conceptually consistent, but that gains new behavioral components (Caspi and Bem, 1990). Through that process, relatively subtle childhood variations in neuropsychological health can be transformed into an antisocial style that pervades all domains of adolescent and adult behavior. It is this infiltration of the antisocial disposition into the multiple domains of a life that diminishes the likelihood of change.

When in the life course does the potential for change dwindle to nil? How many person-environment interactions must accumulate before the life-course-persistent pattern becomes set? I have argued that a person-environment interaction process is needed to predict emerging antisocial behavior, but after some age will the "person" main effect predict adult outcomes alone? An answer to these questions is critical for prevention efforts. The well-documented resistance of antisocial personality disorder to treatments of all kinds seems to suggest that the life-course-persistent style is fixed sometime before age 18 (Suedfeld and Landon, 1978). Studies of crime careers reveal that it is very unusual for males to first initiate crime after adolescence, suggesting that if an adult is going to be antisocial, the pattern must be established by late adolescence (Elliott, Huizinga, and Menard, 1989).[1] At the same time, efforts to predict antisocial outcomes from childhood conduct problems yield many errors (e.g., White et al., 1990). These errors seem to suggest that antisocial styles become set sometime after childhood . . . .

Adolescence-Limited Antisocial Behavior

Discontinuity: The Most Common Course of Antisocial Behavior

As implied by the proffered label, discontinuity is the hallmark of teenaged delinquents who have no notable history of antisocial behavior in childhood and little future for such behavior in adulthood. However, the brief tenure of their delinquency should not obscure their prevalence in the population or the gravity of their crimes. In contrast with the rare life-course-persistent type, adolescence-limited delinquency is ubiquitous. Several studies have shown that about one third of males are arrested during their lifetime for a serious criminal offense, whereas fully four fifths of males have police contact for some minor infringement (Farrington, Ohlin, and Wilson, 1986). Most of these police contacts are made during the adolescent years. Indeed, numerous rigorous self-report studies have now documented that it is statistically aberrant to refrain from crime during adolescence (Elliott et al., 1983; Hirschi, 1969; Moffitt and Silva, 1988c).

Compared with the life-course-persistent type, adolescence-limited delinquents show relatively little continuity in their antisocial behavior. Across age, change in delinquent involvement is often abrupt, especially during the periods of onset and desistance. For example, in my aforementioned longitudinal study of a representative sample of boys, 12 percent of the youngsters were classified as new delinquents at age 13; they had no prior history of antisocial behavior from age 5 to age 11. Between age 11 and age 13, they changed from below the sample average to 1.5 standard deviations above average on self-reported delinquency (Moffitt, 1990a). By age 15, another 20 percent of this sample of boys had joined the newcomers to delinquency despite having no prior history of antisocial behavior (Moffitt, 1991). Barely into mid-adolescence, the prevalence rate of markedly antisocial boys had swollen from 5 percent at age 11 to 32 percent at age 15. When interviewed at age 18, only 7 percent of the boys denied all delinquent activities. By their mid-20s, at least three fourths of these new offenders are expected to cease all offending (Farrington, 1986).

Adolescence-limited delinquents may also have sporadic, crime-free periods in the midst of their brief crime "careers." Also, in contrast with the life-course-persistent type, they lack consistency in their antisocial behavior across situations. For example, they may shoplift in stores and use drugs with friends but continue to obey the rules at school. Because of the chimeric nature of their delinquency, different reporters (such as self, parent, and teacher) are less likely to agree about their behavior problems when asked to complete rating scales or clinical interviews (Loeber, Green, Lahey, and Stouthamer-Loeber, 1990; Loeber and Schmaling, 1985).

These observations about temporal instability and cross-situational *in*consistency are more than merely descriptive. They have implications for a theory of the etiology of adolescence-limited delinquency. Indeed, the flexibility of most delinquents' behavior suggests that their engagement in deviant life-styles may be under the control of reinforcement and punishment contingencies.

Unlike their life-course-persistent peers, whose behavior was described as inflexible and refractory to changing circumstances, adolescence-limited delinquents are likely to engage in antisocial behavior in situations where such responses seem profitable to them, but they are also able to abandon antisocial behavior when prosocial styles are more rewarding. They maintain control over their antisocial responses and use antisocial behavior only in situations where it may serve an instrumental function. Thus, principles of learning theory will be important for this theory of the cause of adolescence-limited delinquency.

A theory of adolescence-limited delinquency must account for several empirical observations: modal onset in early adolescence, recovery by young adulthood, widespread prevalence, and lack of continuity. Why do youngsters with no history of behavior problems in childhood suddenly become antisocial in adolescence? Why do they develop antisocial problems rather than other difficulties? Why is delinquency so common among teens? How are they able to spontaneously recover from an antisocial life-style within a few short years?

Just as the childhood onset of life-course-persistent persons compelled me to look for causal factors early in their lives, the coincidence of puberty with the rise in the prevalence of delinquent behavior compels me to look for clues in adolescent development. Critical features of this developmental period are variability in biological age, the increasing importance of peer relationships, and the budding of teenagers' self-conscious values, attitudes, and aspirations. These developmental tasks form the building blocks for a theory of adolescence-limited delinquency.

Beginnings: Motivation, Mimicry, and Reinforcement

Why do adolescence-limited delinquents begin delinquency? The answer advanced here is that their delinquency is "social mimicry" of the antisocial style of life-course-persistent youths. The concept of social mimicry is borrowed from ethology. Social mimicry occurs when two animal species share a single niche and one of the species has cornered the market on a resource that is needed to promote fitness (Moynihan, 1968). In such circumstances, the "mimic" species adopts the social behavior of the more successful species to obtain access to the valuable resource. For example, cowbird chicks, who are left by their mothers to be reared in the nests of unsuspecting parent birds, learn to behave like the parent birds' own true chicks and thus stimulate the parents to drop food their way. Social mimicry may also allow some species to safely pass among a more successful group and thus share access to desired resources. For example, some monkey species have learned to mimic bird calls. One such species of monkeys, rufous-naped tamarins, is able to share the delights of ripe fruit after a tree has been located by tyrant flycatchers, whose superior avian capacities in flight and distance vision better equip them to discover bearing trees. Similarly, zebras are sensitive to the social signals of impalas and gazelles and thus benefit from the latter species' superior sensitivity to approaching predators (E. O. Wilson, 1975).

If social mimicry is to explain why adolescence-limited delinquents begin to mimic the antisocial behavior of their life-course-persistent peers, then, logically, delinquency must be a social behavior that allows access to some desirable resource. I suggest that the resource is mature status, with its consequent power and privilege.

Before modernization, biological maturity came at a later age, social adult status arrived at an earlier age, and rites of passage more clearly delineated the point at which youths assumed new roles and responsibilities. In the past century, improved nutrition and health care have decreased the age of biological maturity at the rate of three tenths of a year per decade (Tanner, 1978; Wyshak and Frisch, 1982). Simultaneously, modernization of work has delayed the age of labor-force participation to ever later points in development (Empey, 1978; Horan and Hargis, 1991; Panel on Youth of the President's Science Advisory Commitee, 1974). Thus, secular changes in health and work have lengthened the duration of adolescence. The ensuing gap leaves modern teenagers in a 5- to 10-year role vacuum (Erikson, 1960). They are biologically capable and compelled to be sexual beings, yet they are asked to delay most of the positive aspects of adult life (see Buchanan, Eccles, and Becker, 1992, for a review of studies of the compelling influence of pubertal hormones on teens' behavior and personality). In most American states, teens are not allowed to work or get a driver's license before age 16, marry or vote before age 18, or buy alcohol before age 21, and they are admonished to delay having children and establishing their own private dwellings until their education is completed at age 22, sometimes more than 10 years after they attain sexual maturity. They remain financially and socially dependent on their families of origin and are allowed few decisions of any real import. Yet they want desperately to establish intimate bonds with the opposite sex, to accrue material belongings, to make their own decisions, and to be regarded as consequential by adults (Csikszentmihalyi and Larson, 1984). Contemporary adolescents are thus trapped in a *maturity gap*, chronological hostages of a time warp between biological age and social age.

This emergent phenomenology begins to color the world for most teens in the first years of adolescence. Steinberg has shown that, between ages 10 and 15, a dramatic shift in youngsters' self-perceptions of autonomy and self-reliance takes place. Moreover, the timing of the shift for individuals is connected with their pubertal maturation (Steinberg, 1987; Steinberg and Silverberg, 1986; Udry, 1988). At the time of biological maturity, salient pubertal changes make the remoteness of ascribed social maturity painfully apparent to teens. This new awareness coincides with their promotion into a high school society that is numerically dominated by older youth. Thus, just as teens begin to feel the discomfort of the maturity gap, they enter a social reference group that has endured the gap for 3 to 4 years and has already perfected some delinquent ways of coping with it. Indeed, several researchers have noted that this life course transition into high school society may place teens at risk for antisocial behavior. In particular, exposure to peer models, when coupled with puberty, is an important determinant of adolescence-onset cases of delinquency (Caspi, Lynam, Moffitt, and Silva, 1993; Magnusson, 1988; Simmons and Blyth, 1987).

Life-course-persistent youngsters are the vanguard of this transition. Healthy adolescents are capable of noticing that the few life-course-persistent youths in their midst do not seem to suffer much from the maturity gap. (At a prevalence rate of about 5 percent, one or two such experienced delinquents in every classroom might be expected.) Already adept at deviance, life-course-persistent youths are able to obtain possessions by theft or vice that are otherwise inaccessible to teens who have no independent incomes (e.g., cars, clothes, drugs, or entry into adults-only leisure settings). Life-course-persistent boys are more sexually experienced and have already initiated relationships with the opposite sex. Life-course-persistent boys appear relatively free of their families of origin; they seem to go their own way, making their own rules. As evidence that they make their own decisions, they take risks and do dangerous things that parents could not possibly endorse. As evidence that they have social consequence in the adult world, they have personal attorneys, social workers, and probation officers; they operate small businesses in the underground economy; and they have fathered children (Weiher, Huizinga, Lizotte, and Van Kammen, 1991). Viewed from within

contemporary adolescent culture, the antisocial precocity of life-course-persistent youths becomes a coveted social asset (cf. Finnegan, 1990a, 1990b; Jessor and Jessor, 1977; Silbereisen and Noack, 1988). Like the aforementioned bird calls that were mimicked by hungry tamarin monkeys, antisocial behavior becomes a valuable technique that is demonstrated by life-course-persistents and imitated carefully by adolescence-limiteds. The effect of peer delinquency on the onset of delinquency is among the most robust facts in criminology research (Elliott and Menard, in press; Jessor and Jessor, 1977; Reiss, 1986; Sarnecki, 1986). However, is there evidence consistent with a social mimicry interpretation? I describe the evidence in the next section.

Social mimicry and the relationships between life-course-persistent and adolescence-limited delinquents. One hypothesized by-product of the maturity gap is a shift during early adolescence by persistent antisocial youth from peripheral to more influential positions in the peer social structure. This shift should occur as aspects of the antisocial style become more interesting to other teens. In terms of its epidemiology, delinquent participation shifts from being primarily an individual psychopathology in childhood to a normative group social behavior during adolescence and then back to psychopathology in adulthood. Consider that the behavior problems of the few pioneering antisocial children in an age cohort must develop on an individual basis; such early childhood pioneers lack the influence of delinquent peers (excepting family members). However, near adolescence, a few boys join the life-course-persistent ones, then a few more, until a critical mass is reached when almost all adolescents are involved in some delinquency with age peers. Elliott and Menard (in press) have analyzed change in peer group membership from age 11 to age 24 in a national probability sample. Their data show a gradual population drift from membership in nondelinquent peer groups to membership in delinquent peer groups up to age 17; the trend reverses thereafter.

For example, 78 percent of 11-year-olds reported no or minimal delinquency among their friends. In contrast, 66 percent of 17-year-olds reported substantial delinquency on the part of the friends in their group.

The word *friends* in the previous sentence seems to imply a personal relationship between life-course-persistents and adolescence-limiteds that is implausible. Much evidence suggests that, before adolescence, life-course-persistent antisocial children are ignored and rejected by other children because of their unpredictable, aggressive behavior (Coie et al., 1988; Dodge et al., 1982). After adolescence has passed, life-course-persistent adults are often described as lacking the capacity for loyalty or friendship (Cleckley, 1976; Robins, 1985). At first, these observations may seem contrary to my assertion that life-course-persistents assume social influence over youths who admire and emulate their style during adolescence. However, it is important to recall that social mimicry required no exchange of affection between the successful birds and their monkey mimics. In this theory, adolescents who wish to prove their maturity need only notice that the style of life-course-persistents resembles adulthood more than it resembles childhood. Then they need only observe antisocial behavior closely enough and long enough to imitate it successfully. What is contended is that adolescence-limited youths as models, and life-course-persistent teens should regard themselves as magnets for other teens. Neither perception need involve reciprocal liking between individuals.

A modeling role would imply that measures of exposure to delinquent peers (e.g., knowledge of their delinquent behavior or time spent in proximity to them) should be better predictors of self-delinquency than measures of relationship quality (e.g., shared attitudes or attachment to delinquent peers). Few studies have parsed peer-delinquency effects into separate components, but two findings consistent with this prediction have been reported from the National Youth Survey, a representative sample of more than 500 teens. Agnew (1991) examined relationship characteristics in interaction with levels of peer delinquency. He argued that attachment to peers should encourage deviance if peers are delinquent but discourage it if they are not. Agnew's results showed that such interaction terms were good predictors. However, the results also showed that time spent with delinquent peers was a stronger unique predictor of self-delinquency than the interaction between peer attachment and peer crime. Warr and Stafford (1991) found that the knowledge of friends' delinquent behavior was 2.5 to 5 times more important for self-delinquency than friends' attitudes about delinquency. (This pattern has been replicated in another sample by Nagin and Paternoster, 1991.) Moreover, the effect of peer delinquency was direct; it was not mediated by influencing the respondents' attitudes to be more like those of deviant peers. These findings are not consistent with the notion that teens take up delinquency after pro-delinquency attitudes are transferred in the context of intimate social relations. Rather, Warr and Stafford concluded that the data on peer effects are best interpreted in terms of imitation or vicarious reinforcement.

A magnet role would imply that children who were rejected and ignored by others should experience newfound "popularity" as teens, relative to their former rejected status. That is, life-course-persistent youth should encounter more contacts with peers during adolescence when other adolescents draw near so as to imitate their life-style. Some research is consistent with this interpretation. For example, in a study of 450 students in middle school, aggressive youths who were rejected by their peers reported that they did not feel lonely, whereas submissive rejected youths did feel lonely (Parkhurst and Asher, 1992). Similarly, aggressive seventh-graders in the Carolina Longitudinal Study were rated as popular as often as nonaggressive youths by both teachers and themselves and were as likely as other youths to be nuclear members of peer groups (Cairns, Cairns, Neckerman, Gest, and Gariepy, 1988). In their review of peer-relationship studies, Coie, Dodge, and Kupersmidt (1990) noted that the relationship between overt aggression and peer rejection is weaker or absent in adolescent samples compared with child samples. Findings such as these suggest that aggressive teens experience regular contacts with peers, however short-lived. Similarly, in the Oregon Youth Study, rejection by peers at age 10 was prognostic of greater involvement with delinquent peers 2 years later (Dishion, Patterson, Stoolmiller, and Skinner, 1991). Although the Oregon researchers interpreted their results as suggesting that aggressive children seek delinquent friends, their data are equally consistent with my interpretation that aggressive youths begin to serve as a magnet for novice delinquents during early adolescence. Definitive sociometric research must follow up aggressive-rejected children to test whether they develop networks in adolescence that include late-onset delinquents of the adolescence-limited type.

Researchers from the Carolina Longitudinal Study have carefully documented that boys with an aggressive history do participate in peer networks in adolescence but that the networks are not very stable (Cairns et al., 1988). Consistent with a social mimicry hypothesis, delinquent groups have frequent membership turnover. In addition, the interchanges between network members are characterized by much reciprocal antisocial behavior (Cairns et al., 1988). Reiss and Farrington (1991) have shown that the most experienced high-rate young offenders tend to recruit different co-offenders for each offense.

Life-course-persistents serve as core members of revolving networks, by virtue of being role models or trainers for new recruits (Reiss, 1986). They exploit peers as drug customers, as fences, as lookouts, or as sexual partners. Such interactions among life-course-persistent and adolescence-limited delinquents may represent a symbiosis of mutual exploitation. Alternatively, life-course-persistent offenders need not even be aware of all of the adolescence-limited youngsters who imitate their style. Unlike adolescence-limited offenders, who appear to need peer support for crime, life-course-persistent offenders are willing to offend alone (Knight and West, 1975). The point is that the phenomena of "delinquent peer networks" and "co-offending" during the adolescent period do not necessarily connote supportive friendships that are based on intimacy, trust, and loyalty, as is sometimes assumed. Social mimicry of delinquency can take place if experienced offenders actively educate new recruits. However, it can also take place if motivated learners merely observe antisocial models from afar.

Reinforcement of delinquency by its 'negative' consequences. For teens who become adolescence-limited delinquents, antisocial behavior is an effective means of knifing-off childhood apron strings and of proving that they can act independently to conquer new challenges (Erikson, 1960). Hypothetical reinforcers for delinquency include damaging the quality of intimacy and communication with parents, provoking responses from adults in positions of authority, finding ways to look older (such as by smoking cigarettes, being tattooed, playing the big spender with ill-gotten gains), and tempting fate (risking pregnancy, driving while intoxicated, or shoplifting under the noses of clerks). None of these putative reinforcers may seem very pleasurable to the middle-aged academic, but each of the aforementioned consequences is a precious resource to the teenager and can serve to reinforce delinquency. Bloch and Niederhoffer (1958) have offered an anthropological perspective:

> It is almost as if the contemporary young person, in the absence of puberty rituals and ordeals, is moved to exclaim: If you don't care to test us, then we will test ourselves! (p. 28)

I suggest that every curfew violated, car stolen, drug taken, and baby conceived is a statement of personal independence and thus a reinforcer for delinquent involvement. Ethnographic interviews with delinquents reveal that proving maturity and autonomy are strong personal motives for offending (e.g., Goldstein, 1990). Such hypothetical reinforcing properties have not been systematically tested for most types of delinquent acts. However, epidemiological studies have confirmed that adolescent initiation of tobacco, alcohol, and drug abuse are reinforced because they symbolize independence and maturity to youth (D. Kandel, 1980; Mausner and Platt, 1971).

In summary, in this narrative account of the etiology of adolescent-onset delinquency I have emphasized three conditions: motivation, mimicry, and reinforcement. I have suggested that a secular change in the duration of adolescence has generated an age-dependent motivational state. In addition, life-course-persistent antisocial models must be available so that their delinquent behaviors can be imitated. Finally, adolescents' fledgling attempts to mimic antisocial styles will continue if they are socially reinforced by the "negative consequences" of crime.

Why Doesn't Every Teenager Become Delinquent?

The proffered theory of adolescence-limited delinquency regards this sort of delinquency as an adaptive response to contextual circumstances. As a consequence, the theory seems to predict that every teen will engage in delinquency. Data from epidemiological studies using the self-report method suggest that almost all adolescents do commit some illegal acts (Elliott et al., 1983). In addition, even studies using official records of arrest by police find surprisingly high prevalence rates (for a review see Farrington, Ohlin, and Wilson, 1986). Nevertheless, some youths commit less delinquency than others, and a small minority abstains completely. Unfortunately, almost no research sheds light on the characteristics of teens who abstain from antisocial behavior altogether. Speculations are thus ill-informed by empirical observations. However, some predictions may be derived from the present theory of adolescence-

limited delinquency. The predictions center on two theoretical prerequisites for adolescent-onset delinquency: the motivating maturity gap and antisocial role models. Some youths may skip the maturity gap because of late puberty or early initiation into adult roles. Others may find few opportunities for mimicking life-course-persistent delinquent models.

Some youths who refrain from antisocial behavior may, for some reason, not sense the maturity gap and therefore lack the hypothesized motivation for experimenting with crime. Perhaps such teens experience very late puberty so that the gap between biological and social adulthood is not signaled to them early in adolescence. For example, Caspi and Moffitt (1991) have shown that girls who do not menstruate by age 15 tend not to become involved in delinquency; in fact they evidence fewer than normal behavior problems as teens. Perhaps other abstainers belong to cultural or religious subgroups in which adolescents are given legitimate access to adult privileges and accountability. In his vivid ethnographic account of "old heads" and teenaged boys in a poor black neighborhood, Anderson (1990) described how mature community leaders drew certain boys into their own work and social lives, deliberately and publicly initiating the boys into manhood (and preventing delinquent involvement).

Some nondelinquent teens may lack structural opportunities for modeling antisocial peers. Adolescent crime rates are generally lower in rural areas than in inner-city areas (Skogan, 1979, 1990). Teens in urban areas are surrounded by a greater density of age peers (and have readier unsupervised access to them through public transportation and meeting venues such as parks and shopping malls) than are teens in relatively isolated rural areas. For instance, Sampson and Groves (1989) determined that the strongest community-level correlate of local rates of robbery and violence was the presence of "unsupervised groups of teenagers hanging out and making a nuisance" (p. 789). In that study, more traditional community correlates of crime, such as socioeconomic status, residential mobility, and ethnicity, were mediated by the teenaged social scene. School structures may also constrain or facilitate access to life-course-persistent models. Caspi et al. (1993) found that early puberty was associated with delinquency in girls but only if they had access to boys through attending coed high schools. Girls who were enrolled in girls' schools did not engage in delinquency. In that study, the difference in delinquent involvement between coed and single-sex school settings could not be explained by any personal or family characteristics that may have influenced how the girls came to be enrolled in their schools; access to delinquent role models was clearly the best explanation for the girls' behavior problems.

Youths may also be excluded from opportunities to mimic antisocial peers because of some personal characteristics that make them unattractive to other teens or that leave them reluctant to seek entry to newly popular delinquent groups. Shedler and Block (1990) found such an effect on the use of illegal drugs. They compared the personality styles of three adolescent groups: teens who abstained from trying any drug, teens who experimented with drugs, and teens who were frequent heavy drug users. Adolescents who experimented were the best adjusted teens in the sample. As expected, frequent users were troubled teens, who were alienated and antisocial. However, the abstainers were also problem teens: They were "relatively tense, overcontrolled, emotionally constricted . . . somewhat socially isolated and lacking in interpersonal skills" (p. 618). This personality style was not a consequence of failing to try drugs. Rather, it was an enduring personality configuration. At age 7, these abstainers had been prospectively described by raters as

> overcontrolled, timid, fearful and morose . . . they were not warm and responsive, not curious and open to new experience, not active, not vital, and not cheerful. (pp. 619–620)

Similarly, Farrington and West (1990) reported that boys from criminogenic circumstances who did not become delinquent seemed nervous and withdrawn and had few or no friends. These provocative findings remind us that deviance is defined in relationship to its normative context. During adolescence, when delinquent behavior becomes the norm, nondelinquents warrant our scientific scrutiny.

In summary, this theory of adolescence-limited delinquency suggests that adolescents who commit no antisocial behavior at all have either (a) delayed puberty, (b) access to roles that are respected by adults, (c) environments that limit opportunities for learning about delinquency, (d) personal characteristics that exclude them from antisocial peer networks, or (e) all four. Research is needed to determine whether or not abstaining from delinquency is necessarily a sign of good adolescent adjustment. . . .

Desistance From Crime: Adolescence-Limiteds Are Responsive to Shifting Reinforcement Contingencies

By definition, adolescence-limited delinquents generally do not maintain their delinquent behavior into adulthood. The account of life-course-persistent persons I made earlier in this article required an analysis of maintenance factors. In contrast, this account of adolescence-limited delinquents demands an analysis of desistance: Why do adolescence-limited delinquents desist from delinquency? This theory's answer: Healthy youths respond adaptively to changing contingencies. If motivational and learning mechanisms initiate and maintain their delinquency, then, likewise, changing contingencies can extinguish it . . . .

With the inevitable progression of chronological age, more legitimate and tangible adult roles become available to teens. Adolescence-limited delinquents gradually experience a loss of motivation for delinquency as they exit the maturity gap. Moreover, when aging delinquents attain some of the privileges they coveted as teens, the consequences of illegal behavior shift from rewarding to punishing, *in their perception*. An adult arrest record will limit their job opportunities, drug abuse keeps them from getting to work on time, drunk driving is costly, and bar fights lead to accusations of unfit parenthood. Adolescence-limited delinquents have something to lose by persisting in their antisocial behavior beyond the teen years.

There is some evidence that many young adult offenders weigh the relative rewards from illegal and conventional activities when they contemplate future offending. In a study of three samples, the effect of age on criminal participation was mediated by young men's expectations about whether illegal earnings would exceed earnings from a straight job (Piliavin, Thornton, Gartner, and Matsueda, 1986). Important for this theory, research shows that "commitment costs" are among the factors weighed by young adults when they decide to discontinue offending. In the criminological subfield of perceptual deterrence research, commitment costs are defined as a person's judgment that past accomplishments will be jeopardized or that future goals will be foreclosed (Williams and Hawkins, 1986). Criminal behavior incurs commitment costs if it risks informal sanctions (disapproval by family, community, or employer) as well as formal sanctions (arrest or conviction penalty). Given that very few delinquent acts culminate in formal sanctions, perceptual deterrence theories consider informal sanctions as keys to deterrence. Paternoster and colleagues have tested the proposed effects of commitment costs and informal sanctions in a follow-up study of 300 young adults. They found that criminal offending 1 year later was best predicted by prospective indexes of commitment costs ($r = -.23$) and informal sanctions ($r = -.40$). Those variables outdid gender, perceived risk of arrest, grade point average, and peer attachment (Paternoster, Saltzman, Waldo, and Chiricos, 1983).

Options for change. Consistent with this motivational analysis, the antisocial behavior of many delinquent teens has been found to decline after they leave high school (Elliott and Voss, 1974), join the army (Eider, 1986; Mattick, 1960), marry

a prosocial spouse (Sampson and Laub, 1990), move away from the old neighborhood (West, 1982), or get a full-time job (Sampson and Laub, 1990). As these citations show, links between the assumption of adult roles and criminal desistance have been observed before. The issue left unaddressed by theory is why are some delinquents able to desist when others are not? What enables adolescence-limited delinquents to make these (often abrupt) transitions away from crime? Why do adolescence-limited delinquents come to realize that they have something to lose, whereas life-course-persistent delinquents remain undeterred? Here, two positions are advanced: Unlike their life-course-persistent counterparts, adolescence-limited delinquents are relatively exempt from the forces of (a) cumulative and (b) contemporary continuity.

First, without a lifelong history of antisocial behavior, the forces of cumulative continuity have had fewer years in which to gather the momentum of a downhill snowball. Before taking up delinquency, adolescence-limited offenders had ample years to develop an accomplished repertoire of prosocial behaviors and basic academic skills. These social skills and academic achievements make them eligible for postsecondary education, good marriages, and desirable jobs.

The availability of alternatives to crime may explain why some adolescence-limited delinquents desist later than others. (As shown in Figure 38.1, the desistance portion of the age-crime curve slopes more gradually than the abrupt criminal initiation portion.) Although the forces of cumulative continuity build up less momentum over the course of their relatively short crime careers, many adolescence-limited youths will fall prey to many of the same snares that maintain continuity among life-course-persistent persons. Those whose teen forays into delinquency inadvertently attracted damaging consequences may have more difficulty desisting. A drug habit, an incarceration, interrupted education, or a teen pregnancy are snares that require extra effort and time from which to escape. Thus, this theory predicts that variability in age at desistance from crime should be accounted for by the cumulative number and type of ensnaring life events that entangle persons in a deviant life-style.

Second, in stark contrast with the earlier account of life-course-persistent offenders, personality disorder and cognitive deficits play no part in the delinquency of adolescence-limited offenders. As a result, they are exempt from the sources of contemporary continuity that plague their life-course-persistent counterparts. In general, these young adults have adequate social skills, they have a record of average or better academic achievement, their mental health is sturdy, they still possess the capacity to forge close attachment relationships, and then, retain the good intelligence they had when they entered adolescence. One study of girls who grew up in institutional care has illustrated that individual differences influence which adolescents are able to

attain prosocial outcomes in young adulthood (Quinton and Rutter, 1988). In that study, some girls reared in institutions were able to escape adversity for advantage through marriage to a supportive husband, but a constellation of individual psychological attributes determined which girls were able to marry well.

At the crossroads of young adulthood, adolescence-limited and life-course-persistent delinquents go different ways. This happens because the developmental histories and personal traits of adolescence-limiteds allow them the option of exploring new life pathways. The histories and traits of life-course-persistents have foreclosed their options, entrenching them in the antisocial path. To test this hypothesis, research must examine conditional effects of individual histories on opportunities for desistance from crime . . . .

Note

1. Between 9 percent and 22 percent of males not arrested as juveniles are arrested as adults, suggesting that adult-onset offenders constitute between 5 percent and 15 percent of all males (for a review see Farrington, Ohlin, and Wilson, 1986). However, estimates that are based on such official data are too high because most offenders engage in crime for some time before they are first arrested. Longitudinal studies of self-report delinquency show that only 1 percent to 4 percent of males commit their first criminal offense after age 17 (Elliott, Huizinga, and Menard, 1989). Adult-onset crime is not only very unusual, but it tends to be low rate, nonviolent (Blumstein and Cohen, 1987), and generally not accompanied by the many complications that attend a persistent and pervasive antisocial lifestyle. (Farrington, Loeber, Elliott, et al., 1990)

Discussion Questions

1. Describe the different ways in which individual traits and environmental factors interact with (or influence) one another to produce persistent antisocial behavior.
2. What types of individual traits foster antisocial behavior, according to Moffitt? *Why* do these traits increase the likelihood of antisocial behavior?
3. Describe Moffitt's theory of adolescence-limited antisocial behavior. Why is it that individuals in the "adolescence-limited" group are able to desist from crime in early adulthood while individuals in the "life-course-persistent" group are not?
4. Why does Moffitt state that adolescence-limited antisocial behavior is *not pathological* while life-course-persistent antisocial behavior is *pathological?*

39. A Theory of Persistent Offending and Desistance from Crime

John H. Laub and Robert J. Sampson

Consider a male college student who has an unhealthy lifestyle. He smokes, binge drinks with friends several nights a week, stays out late in bars whenever possible, never exercises, and "blows off" classes regularly. On campus one day, he meets a coed who is attractive, humorous, and seems to understand him. They start to date and "hang out" together.

Although his new girlfriend likes to "party" once in a while, she is also serious about school and urges him to take classes with her. Being with her during weekdays also means going with her to the library most evenings. Avid about fitness, she brings him to the health club on campus and encourages him to start a running program. As time passes, his days are filled with a new routine: going to classes, going to the library, going to the health club, going to dinner with his girlfriend. He starts to lose touch with his former drinking buddies. Her friends, in fact, become his friends. He sometimes misses the old days of partying and promiscuity, but his new life has special rewards that he would be foolish to squander through some irresponsible conduct. He is, as they say, a "changed man."

This fictitious scenario is a way of understanding how, according to Laub and Sampson (2003), persistent offenders come to change their life course and desist from crime (see also Laub

et al., 2006; Sampson and Laub, 2005). There are four features to this change process. First, the offender experiences a structural turning point. This might be a new relationship (or marriage), a good job, or perhaps military service. Second, as a result of this turning point, the offender is subjected to increased informal social control; he or she is monitored and sanctioned for deviant conduct. These relationships also offer support, which can lessen crime directly and indirectly by increasing the bond of attachment. Third, the routine activities of the offender are transformed from unstructured and oriented toward deviant locations (e.g., bars) to being structured and filled with prosocial responsibilities. In effect, the offender is cut off from deviant influences, especially antisocial peers. Fourth, almost "by default" there is a commitment to a new life. So much is invested in the new relationships and lifestyle that sacrificing everything for a criminal adventure would be too costly. To use Hirschi's (Chapter 18) terms, the bond of commitment has grown strong and insulates against further offending.

Laub and Sampson, however, do not see this process of change and desistance as inevitable. Along the way, offenders—as with our college student described above—exercise human agency. There is a subjective dimension to our

Reprinted with permission from John H. Laub and Robert J. Sampson. 2003. *Shared Beginnings, Divergent Lives: Delinquent Boys to Age 70*. Cambridge, MA: Harvard University Press.

lives. We are affected by our circumstances, including newly formed intimate relationships, enjoyable jobs, and a call to serve our country. But we also are willful creatures and thus make choices—exercise "agency"—within these circumstances. That is, choices are "situated," but they are choices nonetheless.

Our college student might have decided to "blow off" a date with his new girlfriend—thus ending their relationship—in favor of a night of drinking with his friends. He might have decided that his increasingly conventional lifestyle was too boring. And he might have defined his girlfriend's monitoring as incessant nagging and defiantly told her to mind her own business. In short, structural turning points might provide the opportunity to enter the change process, but they do not enforce conformity in some deterministic way. In the end, wayward college students—and offenders—play an active role in making their futures.

This view has large implications for life-course theories. In particular, it suggests that, at least in adulthood, there is no clearly predictable developmental sequence as theorists like Moffitt (1993 [Chapter 38]) would propose. Offenders do not belong to groups in which everyone's life in crime unfolds in the same way. Rather, Laub and Sampson propose that both persistence (or continuity) and change are affected by fortuitous events (e.g., meeting the right marital partner, getting a good job) and by human agency—the will people exercise and the choices they make.

Note that fortuitous events and human agency are, by their nature, rather unpredictable. They can happen by chance or arise because situations change. This means that an offender's destiny is not determined in childhood or adolescence. What occurs in adulthood also matters. Life does not simply unfold but rather is constructed as situations and offenders' reactions to them emerge at unexpected times and in indeterminate ways.

References

Laub, John H. and Robert J. Sampson. 2003. *Shared Beginnings, Divergent Lives: Delinquent Boys to Age 70.* Cambridge, MA: Harvard University Press.

Laub, John H., Robert J. Sampson, and Gary Sweeten. 2006. "Assessing Sampson and Laub's Life-Course Theory of Crime." In Francis T. Cullen, John Paul Wright, and Kristie R. Blevins (eds.), *Taking Stock: The Status of Criminological Theory—Advances in Criminological Theory*, Volume 15, pp. 313–333. New Brunswick, NJ: Transaction.

Moffitt, Terrie E. 1993. "Adolescence-Limited and Life-Course-Persistent Antisocial Behavior: A Developmental Taxonomy." *Psychological Review* 100: 674–701.

Sampson, Robert J. and John H. Laub. 2005. "A Life-Course View of the Development of Crime." *Annals of the American Academy of Political and Social Science* 602: 12–45.

We seek a theory of social control that will identify sources of persistence in and desistance from crime. What sustains persistent offending? What keeps some offenders from moving to more conventional pathways? In a similar vein, how do offenders go straight? How do offenders shift from crime and deviance to more conventional pathways? How do ex-offenders maintain conformity to the law? The central question we seek to answer is: what are the mechanisms underlying the processes of persistent offending and desistance from crime?

One of our theoretical goals is to expand the understanding of informal and formal social control across the life course. In the follow-up, we focused our attention on work, family, the military, community organizations, and neighborhood hangouts (for example, taverns) as well as on formal social control institutions like the police, prison, and parole. Thus we propose to examine a wide array of institutions that we believe influence both formal and informal social control. At the same time, we explicitly recognize that these institutions are embedded in a specific local culture (place) as well as a specific historical context (time)....

We also believe that human agency (or personal choice) and situational context, especially routine activities, are vitally important for understanding patterns of stability and change in criminal behavior over the life course. Individuals make choices and are active participants in the construction of their lives. For example,... calculated and articulated resistance to authority is a recurrent theme in the lives of persistent offenders. At times crime is attractive because it is exciting and seductive (see Katz 1988). In crucial ways, then, crime is more than a weakening of social bonds—human agency must be recognized as an important element of understanding crime and deviance over the life course.

Situational contingencies and routine activities may also lure individuals toward or away from crime, and these contingencies and activities need to be systematically incorporated into our understanding of criminal trajectories over the life course. For example, we found persistent offenders to have rather chaotic and unstructured lives across multiple dimensions (such as living arrangements, work, and family). Routine activities for these men were loaded with opportunities for crime and extensive associations with like-minded offenders. Thus situational variation, especially in lifestyle activities, needs to be taken into account when explaining continuity and change in criminal behavior over the life course....

Desistance by Default

The process of desistance is complex and occurs for all types of offenders (for example, serious and nonserious, violent and nonviolent) at different ages over the life course. Although there are multiple pathways to desistance, our data indicate that desistance is facilitated by self-described "turning points"—changes in situational and structural life circumstances like a good marriage or a stable job—in combination with individual actions (that is, personal agency). Although age is clearly important in understanding desistance, a focus on age and age alone obfuscates understanding the life course of crime. From our perspective, desistance is best viewed as a process realized over time, not a single event.

Our stance on the desistance process contrasts with emerging theories of desistance that emphasize cognitive transformations or identity shifts as necessary for desistance to occur (see Giordano, Cernkovich, and Rudolph 2002; Maruna 2001). We believe that most offenders desist in response to structural turning points that serve as the catalyst for long-term behavioral change. The image of "desistance by default" best fits the desistance process we found in our data. Desistance for our subjects was not necessarily a conscious or deliberate process, but rather the consequence of what Howard Becker calls "side bets" (1960, 38). Many men made a commitment to go straight without even realizing it. Before they knew it, they had invested so much in a marriage or a job that they did not want to risk losing their investment (H. Becker 1960, 1964; see also Matsueda and Heimer 1997, 171). In other words, "habits provide an anchor by strengthening the forces making for persistence in behavior" (G. Becker and Murphy 2000, 152). We agree that the offenders' own perspectives and words need to be brought into the understanding of desistance, and we believe we have done so. However, offenders can and do desist without a conscious decision to "make good" (compare Maruna 2001), and offenders can and do desist without a "cognitive transformation" (compare Giordano, Cernkovich, and Rudolph 2002).

Some of the men we studied, of course, did want to make good, and they in fact desisted from crime. Consider, for example, Richard and his wife, who have taken in foster children who were wards of the state for many years. Our main point is that many of the desisters did not seek to make good—they simply desisted with little if any cognitive reflection on the matter. "Redemption scripts" (Maruna 2001) were also noticeably absent in most of the life-history narratives. The majority of men we interviewed desisted from crime largely because they were able to capitalize on key structural and situational circumstances. They often selected these structural and situational circumstances (for example, they decided to get married, get that job, hang out with those friends), but these institutions and relationships in turn influenced the men as well (see also G. Becker and Murphy 2000). Thus the developmental phase of cognitive transformation or making good is not a necessary pathway to desistance.

(De)Connectivity and Marginality

Men who desisted from crime were embedded in structured routines, socially bonded to wives, children, and significant others, drew on resources and social support from their relationships, and were virtually and directly supervised and monitored. In other words, structures, situations, and persons offered nurturing and informal social control that facilitated the process of desistance from crime. Even the most hardened offender is not a persistent offender in the true sense of the term and, as we have observed in our long-term follow-up study, virtually all offenders eventually desist albeit at different rates and ages.

The key question is, What is it about "persistent" offenders that distinguishes them from other offenders? In our view, more than being identified by a single trait like poor verbal intelligence or low self-control or even a series of static traits, the persistent offender, to the extent the term has meaning, seems devoid of linking structures at each phase of the life course, especially involving relationships that can provide nurturing, social support, and informal social control. Generally, the persistent offenders we interviewed experienced residential instability, marital instability, job instability, failure in school and the military, and relatively long periods of incarceration. Except when in prison or jail, they were "social nomads," to use Foucault's term (1995 [1975]). In contrast to the men who

desisted from crime, the life of the persistent offender was marked by marginality and a lack of structure that led to even more situations conducive to crime. For those without permanent addresses, steady jobs, spouses, children, and other rooted forms of life, crime and deviance is an unsurprising result—even for those possessing so-called prosocial traits. As a consequence of chaotic and unstructured routines, one has increased contact with those individuals who are similarly situated—in this case, similarly unattached and free from nurturing, social capital or support, and informal social control. Thus while group offending may well decline with age (Warr 2002, 130), we find in our narrative data that the influence of deviant peers and criminal networks is particularly salient in the lives of persistent offenders.

Will: The Power of Human Agency

For a number of our formerly delinquent men, personal agency looms large in the processes of persistence and desistance from crime. Our narratives showed that some men who persisted in crime consciously chose to continue involvement in crime and did not apologize or make excuses for their criminal behavior (see also Katz 1988). Many men who desisted from crime similarly displayed a variety of voluntaristic actions that facilitated the process of desistance. In our life-history narratives, one thus sees strong evidence for both will/human agency and "commitment by default" (H. Becker 1960), often in the same man's life. In other words, there is no escaping the tension surrounding conscious action and unconscious action generated by default . . . .

In our view, both objective and subjective factors are implicated in the processes by which some offenders commit crime at a higher rate and for a longer period of time than other offenders (see also Giordano, Cernkovich, and Rudolph 2002; Maruna 2001; Shover 1996). The linked ideas of "contingencies" and "intercontingencies" are useful in this discussion (see H. Becker 1998, 28–35). Events and their resulting actions are contingent upon other events and their accompanying actions. Intercontingencies are events and actions that are dependent upon events and actions by other people. Thus a quality marriage may be a turning point for some men because of the event itself, their subjective state, and the behavior of others around them as well as the subsequent events that result because of the fact that they are now married.

Perhaps the concept that best captures this theoretical idea is "situated choice." Our interest is the interaction between life-course transitions, macro-level events, situational context, and individual will. Moreover, we recognize that both the social environment and the individual are influenced by the interaction of structure and choice. This view of individual choice extends well beyond selection effects—structures are determined by individual choices, and in turn structures constrain, modify, and limit individual choices. In other words, choices are always embedded in social structures. Following Gary Becker and Kevin Murphy (2000), we believe that the interaction of choice and structure produces behavior that cannot be predicted from a focus on one or the other. From our perspective, it is particularly important to reconcile the idea of choice or will with a structuralist notion of turning points (Abbott 1997, 96–97). Indeed, as Abbott has written, "A major turning point has the potential to open a system the way a key has the potential to open a lock . . . action is necessary to complete the turning" (1997, 102). In this instance, action is both thought and behavior, and thus individual action needs to align with the social structure in order to produce behavioral change and to maintain change (or stability?) over the life course. As noted above, this process of change reflects the continuous interplay between purposeful action and default "side bets" (H. Becker 1960) that accumulate over time . . . .

Implications for Developmental Criminology

If one defines development as life-history change, then developmental criminology should focus on changes in the development of crime and antisocial behavior over time. Relying on what Michael Tonry and David Farrington (1995) refer to as the central insight from Shakespeare—that the child is father to the man (see Caspi 2000)—researchers have addressed how developmental processes are linked to the onset, continuation, and cessation of criminal and antisocial behavior. Much has been learned and developmental criminology is now ascendant. One of the most popular and compelling theories of crime in the developmental camp is Terrie Moffitt's dual taxonomy theory of offending.

In our view, the character of "development" in developmental criminology is a key theoretical issue. Lewontin has stated that "the term *development* is a metaphor that carries with it a prior commitment to the nature of the process" (2000, 5). Using the analogy of a photographic image, Lewontin argues that the way the term "development" is used is a process that makes the latent image apparent. This seems to be what developmental criminological theory is all about. For example, in Moffitt's theory of crime, the environment offers a "set of enabling conditions" that allow individual traits to express themselves. Although reciprocal interactions with the environment are allowed, life-course-persistent offenders and adolescence-limited offenders follow a preprogrammed line of development—an unwinding, an unfolding, or an unrolling of what is fundamentally "already there." The view of development as a predetermined unfolding is linked to a typological understanding of the world—different internal programs will have different outcomes for individuals of a different type. Lewontin writes, "If the development of an individual is the unfolding of a genetic program immanent in the fertilized egg, then variations in the outcome of development must be consequences of variations in that program" (2000, 17).

Debates about development in the social sciences are not new (see, for example, the exchange between Dannefer (1984) and Baltes and Nesselroade (1984)). As noted, some developmentalists recognize social interactions, but in the end they embrace a between-individual focus that emphasizes the primacy of early childhood attributes that are presumed to be stable. We view the life course as something altogether different. Furthermore, we see development as it is typically defined and emphasized in the literature as not necessarily pertinent to the study of situated human behavior. In our theory of crime, development is better conceived as the constant interaction between individuals and their environment, coupled with the factor of chance or "random developmental noise" (Lewontin 2000, 35–36). Recognizing developmental noise implies that "the organism is determined neither by its genes nor by its environment nor even by interaction between them, but bears a significant mark of random processes" (2000, 38).

From this view it makes sense that we uncovered enormous heterogeneity in criminal offending over the life course. Some offenders start early and stop; others start early and continue for long periods of time. A sizable portion of the offending population displays a zigzag pattern of offending over long time periods. Most important, long-term patterns of offending cannot be explained by individual differences (for example, low verbal IQ), childhood characteristics (for example, early onset of misbehavior), or adolescent characteristics (for example, chronic juvenile offending). In our conception of development, then, the sum of the parts includes individual differences, environmental differences, social interactions, and random, chance events. All of this leads to considerable "noisy, unpredictable development." Coupled with the analyses presented throughout this book, this description captures well the life-course reality of much crime . . . .

Conclusion

Whereas in *Crime in the Making* we saw informal social control as the primary explanation of crime and desistance over the life course, here we offer a more nuanced perspective. As David Matza said almost forty years ago, the missing element in traditional social control theory is human agency (1964, 183); motivation has always been its weakest link. Moreover, as we argued in the past, traditional social control theory suffers from other problems: it is narrowly portrayed as a static, cross-sectional theory that ignores the dynamic, longitudinal aspects of informal social control and support; the theory neglects the role of social structure in the social bonding process; and the theory fails to appreciate the feedback effects of crime and incarceration on social bonds as an important part of the causal story. And though beyond the scope of this book, traditional social control cannot easily explain (or possibly even comprehend) crime that results when individuals are socially bonded and tightly connected to strong subcultures or higher-echelon segments of society. Events such as the Enron and WorldCom scandals, alleged insider trading by Martha Stewart, terrorism here and abroad, and sex abuse by priests in the Catholic Church should cause even the most ardent supporter of traditional social control theory some discomfort and consternation.

Although we do not abandon control theory, we see other concepts as equally relevant for understanding persistent offending and desistance from crime over the life course. [T]hese concepts include personal agency and situated choice, routine activities, aging, macro-level historical events, and local culture and community context. We have thereby offered an expanded vision of our age-graded theory of informal social control presented in *Crime in the Making* and our other writings over the last decade . . . . Integrative and emergent findings pushed us to expand our theory of informal social control to include, among others, the idea of situated choice as central to an understanding of crime from childhood through old age. As the Glueck men near the end of their lives, the complexities and possibilities of such choices become ever more apparent and, inevitably, ever more consequential.

Discussion Questions

1. Describe the process by which persistent offenders desist from crime. What is "desistance by default"?

2. Why would Laub and Sampson argue that most criminological theories are overly deterministic? How does their construct of "human agency" try to fix this deficiency?

3. Why would Laub and Sampson reject the idea that crime is a development process that unfolds across the entire life course? Would they support or oppose Moffitt's theory?

4. Based on their theory of self-control, how might Gottfredson and Hirschi criticize Laub and Sampson's perspective and, in particular, their view of human agency?

40. Cognitive Transformation and Desistance from Crime

Peggy C. Giordano, Stephen A. Cernkovich, and Jennifer L. Rudolph

Most theories of crime are explanations of the onset and persistence of offending. That is, they try to explain why some individuals but not others engage in crime. Developmental theories, however, take a broader view, following offenders across the life course. As is now well established, virtually all career criminals eventually desist from lawbreaking. But why is this so? In part, it seems that quitting crime, much like giving up contact sports, is part of the aging process. Still, as Laub and Sampson (2003 [Chapter 39]) have shown, individual offenders desist at varying points in adulthood that are not easily predicted in advance. Desistance cannot be assumed; when and why it occurs must be explained.

Giordano, Cernkovich, and Rudolph's (2002) special contribution is to take seriously the process of desistance. Their theoretical framework involves two interrelated components. First, in order to desist from crime, offenders must have opportunities to develop conventional ties to society. This might involve a prosocial intimate relationship or a decent job. Giordano and colleagues refer to these as "hooks for change."

Second, ties to society—social bonds, as they are commonly called—do not develop automatically. Bonds are a two-way street; they involve a reciprocal relationship between the offender and someone in his or her environment. "Hooks" thus present the chance to leave crime and join conventional society.

They will be meaningless, however, if they are squandered. In fact, offenders typically have unstable personal relationships and job histories. They are often the architects of the misery in their lives.

Thus, Giordano et al. argue that desistance requires another component: cognitive transformation. In essence, this means that offenders are open to change and see a given "hook" as offering an attractive alternative to their current life on the street. Offenders also must create a new, prosocial identity; no longer can they see themselves as a "criminal." Finally, they must define crime and its accompanying lifestyle as undesirable and as inconsistent with who they now are. When these cognitive shifts occur, offenders are ready to take advantage of hooks for change and to desist from their criminal career.

Similar to Laub and Sampson (2003), Giordano et al. propose that desistance involves human agency. Offenders are not simply moved into and out of crime by the forces within and around them. To be sure, opportunities for change are important. But they recognize as well that such opportunities must be seized. In this regard, Giordano et al. alert us to the cognitive shifts that must transpire for human agency to be directed in a conventional direction.

Finally, it is relevant that their analysis is consistent with research on correctional rehabilitation. Studies suggest that "cognitive-behavioral" programs are effective in reducing recidivism (MacKenzie, 2006). Further, in concluding her What Works in

© 2002 by the University of Chicago. All rights reserved.

Corrections, *MacKenzie (2006: 337) has recently proposed a "cognitive transformation theory," arguing that "individual-level change must precede changes in ties or bonds to social institutions." Echoing the views of Giordano et al., she notes that while opportunities to form bonds are essential, they will not produce behavior change in and of themselves. Rather, the research reveals that for offender reform and desistance to take place, another precondition must be present: "a cognitive transformation must occur within the individual" (2006: 337; see also Maruna, 2001).*

References

Giordano, Peggy C., Stephen A. Cernkovich, and Jennifer L. Rudolph. 2002. "Gender, Crime, and Desistance: Toward a Theory of Cognitive Transformation." *American Journal of Sociology* 107: 990–1064.

Laub, John H. and Robert J. Sampson. 2003. *Shared Beginnings, Divergent Lives: Delinquent Boys to Age 70.* Cambridge, MA: Harvard University Press.

MacKenzie, Doris Layton. 2006. *What Works in Corrections? Reducing the Criminal Activities of Offenders and Delinquents.* New York: Cambridge University Press.

Maruna, Shadd. 2001. *Making Good: How Ex-Convicts Reform and Rebuild Their Lives.* Washington, DC: American Psychological Association.

In a series of recent analyses, Robert Sampson and John Laub highlight the importance of marital attachment and job stability as key factors associated with desistance from crime (Laub, Nagin, and Sampson 1998; Laub and Sampson 1993; Sampson and Laub 1993). While the delinquents they studied were more likely than others to continue to offend as adults, there was considerable variability in the success of their adult transitions and in the timing of movement away from a criminal lifestyle. Sampson and Laub develop a social control explanation that emphasizes the gradual buildup of investments that tend to accrue in the presence of strong bonds of attachment ("the good marriage effect") and steady employment. This focus on variability and on the impact of adult social bonds also adds to the broader intellectual tradition that emphasizes the ways in which socialization and development continue across the full range of the individual life course (Claussen 1993; Elder 1998; Josselson 1996; Shanahan 2000) . . . . These narratives . . . are useful not only as an aid in interpreting the quantitative findings, but they also provide a close-in perspective on mechanisms through which actors indicate that changes in life direction have been accomplished. It is primarily through our analyses of these narratives that we developed a somewhat different perspective on desistance. Our provisional theory centers on the *cognitive shifts* that frequently occure as an integral part of the desistance process. For purposes of exposition, we contrast this "theory of cognitive transformation" with the social control framework Sampson and Laub and other scholars have emphasized. While our ideas are not fundamentally incompatible with a social control approach, we cover somewhat different conceptual terrain.

Social control theory emphasizes the ways in which a close marital bond or stable job gradually exerts a constraining influence on behavior as—over a period of time—actors build up higher levels of commitment (capital) via the traditional institutional frameworks of family and work. Social control is thus essentially a theory of constraint that is focused on the long haul.

In our view, this provides an important but incomplete accounting of change processes, because the perspective tends to bracket off the "up front" work accomplished by actors themselves—as they make initial moves toward, help to craft, and work to sustain a different way of life. We wish to emphasize the actor's own role in creatively and selectively appropriating elements in the environment (we will refer to these elements as "hooks for change"), including, but not limited to, such positive influences as a spouse. We argue that these elements will serve well as catalysts for lasting change when they energize rather fundamental shifts in identity and changes in the meaning and desirability of deviant/criminal behavior itself. The latter notion contrasts with a basic assumption of control theory—that an individual's motivation or proclivity to deviate can be considered a constant, while it is the degree of external and internal control that varies considerably (e.g., across individuals or across the period encompassed by an individual life course).

In emphasizing cognitive and identity transformations and the actor's own role in the transformation process, our perspective seems most compatible with the basic tenets of symbolic interaction. This more "agentic" view of desistance balances some of the exteriority and constraint assumptions implicit in a control approach. It is useful for (1) highlighting the important period when actors make initial attempts to veer off a deviant pathway (when, almost by definition, various forms of capital have not had much chance to accumulate); (2) accommodating the observation that quite a few individuals exposed to prosocial experiences like those associated with marriage or job opportunities fail to take advantage of them (they persist in offending anyway); and (3) focusing on cognitive changes, rather than a small set of predictors. This provides a measure of conceptual flexibility. That is, it takes into consideration individuals who manage to change their life direction, even in the absence of traditional frameworks of support and resources like those provided by a spouse or good job . . . .

Toward a Theory of Cognitive Transformation

Chronic offenders who eventually desist from criminal involvement have by definition moved away from the familiar world their past behaviors represent. At a minimum, it is reasonable to assume that such actors will have a heightened awareness of having done so. . . . However, we posit an even more essential link between cognitive

and behavioral changes in our suggestion that "cognitive shifts" can be considered fundamental to the transformation process . . . .

The environment can thus provide a kind of scaffolding that makes possible the construction of significant life changes. Nonetheless, individuals themselves must attend to these new possibilities, discard old habits, and begin the process of crafting a different way of life. At the point of change, this new lifestyle will necessarily be "at a distance" or a "faint" possibility. Therefore, the individual's subjective stance is especially important during the early stages of the change process. At a basic level, one must resonate with, move toward, or select the various catalysts for change.

We might refer to potentially prosocial features of the environment as catalysts, change agents, causes, or even turning points (Laub and Sampson 2001; Maruna 2001), but we prefer to call them "hooks for change" for two reasons. First, consistent with Mead's notion of opening the door to certain stimuli and closing it to others, we wish to emphasize the actor's own role in latching onto opportunities presented by the broader environment. Second, we recognize that actors' accounts within a narrative or life history will not access the full array of influences that literally produced successful changes. Instead, like novels, situation comedies, or grant proposals, narratives (here, narratives of change) have hooks—shorthand ways to describe what seems essential from the communicator's point of view. This linguistic selection process reflects (albeit imperfectly) and enlivens a set of cognitive representations. Linguistic and cognitive hooks are important to consider, for as Mead (1964) suggested, together they can serve as an organizing process that actually helps to push along the changes.

Types of Cognitive Transformations

Conceptually, we distinguish four types of intimately related cognitive transformations. The first, and arguably the most fundamental, is a shift in the actor's basic openness to change. The importance of this readiness for change has been discussed extensively in various treatment literatures, especially those dealing with addictions (see, e.g., Boyle, Polinsky, and Hser 2000; De Leon et al. 1994; Miller 1985). Here we will simply note that this idea of a general cognitive openness needs to be distinguished conceptually from a related kind. The second type of cognitive shift relates more directly to one's exposure to a particular hook or set of hooks for change (e.g., an increased recognition of the desirability of changing is conceptually distinct from an increased receptivity to the prospect of marriage). This type of cognitive transformation is central to our conceptual emphasis because it focuses direct attention on the reciprocal relationship between actor and environment. That is, while a general openness to change seems necessary, by itself it is often insufficient. A fundamental premise is that both exposure to a hook and one's attitude toward it are important elements of successful change. In addition to externally manipulated shifts (e.g., actor is offered a job), then, we must consider that what changes may primarily involve either the hook's perceived availability and its meaning, salience, or importance for the individual. The latter types of shifts are not, however, simply the result of individualistic mental processes. Instead, the hook for change can play an important role in fostering these very transformations. Eventually, as we discuss in more detail below, successful hooks will need to influence the actor to make a particular sort of cognitive connection, consistent with the idea of reflexivity described above. The actor must not only regard the new environmental situation as a positive development (e.g., experience high attachment to a spouse), but must also define the new state of affairs as fundamentally incompatible with continued deviation. We consider this more problematic (that is to say, subject to variability) than do control theorists, who have traditionally argued that prosocial actions flow naturally from strong attachments (Hirschi 1969).

An especially important feature of human consciousness explored by Mead (1964) is the ability to focus reflectively on the self. Thus, a third type of cognitive transformation occurs when actors are able to envision and begin to fashion an appealing and conventional "replacement self" that can supplant the marginal one that must be left behind. This can obviously facilitate the connecting tasks outlined above (to the degree that it becomes inappropriate for "someone like me" to do "something like that"), but the new identity can be considered a broader, more all-encompassing personal construct. If, as Mead suggested, cognitions serve as an organizing process, then identity provides a higher level of organization and coherence to one's cognitions. This involves more than a mental tidying up, because the new or refashioned identity can act as a cognitive filter for decision making. This filtering process is particularly critical as one moves into the future and inevitably encounters novel situations (Matsueda and Heimer 1997).

Unlike adults who have built up a relatively successful life course, chronic offenders can ill afford to draw on prior experiences and habits as they attempt to forge ahead. Hooks for change can provide an important opening in the direction of a new identity and concrete reinforcement during all phases of the transformation process. In some instances, the presence of the environmental stimulus is integral to the development of the replacement self (e.g., one's identity as a traditional wife requires a husband—ideally a correspondingly respectable one). A key point here is that the identity transformation potential presented by the various hooks for change needs to be distinguished conceptually from its qualities of control. While in practice these processes often coalesce, in the long run a solid replacement self may prove the stronger ally of sustained behavior change (e.g., as the actor encounters new situations outside of the spouse's purview, divorces a focal spouse, or experiences the loss of a particular job).

The fourth type of cognitive change (the capstone) involves a transformation in the way the actor views the deviant behavior or lifestyle itself. We assume that criminal/antisocial behaviors, like conforming actions, are imbued with meaning and significance (e.g., "aggression works" [Cairns 1979], stealing offers "sneaky thrills" [Katz 1988], and drugs and alcohol can be even more relentlessly seductive). Thus, the desistance process can be seen as relatively complete when the actor no longer sees these same behaviors as positive, viable, or even personally relevant. As stated earlier, this differs from a control position, where motivation to deviate is viewed as a relative constant, while it is the degree of control that is conceptualized as varying significantly.

Our fundamental premise is that the various cognitive transformations not only relate to one another (an ideal typical sequence: and overall "readiness" influences receptivity to one or more hooks for change, hooks influence the shift in identity, and identity changes gradually decrease the desirability and salience of the deviant behavior), but they also inspire and direct behavior. Actions that flow from these cognitive shifts, and that cannot be explained solely with reference to predictor effects (e.g., where the spouse forces the actor to discard bad companions), we consider agentic moves. Both cognitive shifts and the agentic moves that connect to them will be associated with sustained behavioral change . . . .

Conclusions

Although our theory of cognitive transformation is admittedly quite provisional, we believe our focus adds to an understanding of desistance mechanisms. Individuals vary in what they bring to the change process, including differences in preferences and levels of motivation. The idea that there is a dynamic interplay between the individual and catalysts for change helps explain why some individuals exposed to a given catalyst (or an entire arsenal of catalysts) fail to hook onto them, others find success at time Y when they have failed miserably at time X, and still others manage successful changes using very limited resources.

In addition, the hooks themselves can be seen to vary in their transformative potential. These variations also link to cognitive processes. Successful hooks tend to provide the actor with a detailed plan of action or a fairly elaborate *cognitive blueprint* for proceeding as a changed individual. It is also beneficial if hooks contain a *projective* element directing the actor's attention toward present and future concerns. Related to this, hooks that are associated with *positive themes* and link in straightforward ways to prosocial normative repertoires will fare better. More useful hooks for change will not only provide the actor with new definitions and replacement behaviors, but will offer at least the broad outlines of a satisfying, conventional *replacement self*—one that is seen as fundamentally incompatible with continued deviation. Finally, hooks for change will be more successful when they provide a *gateway to conforming others* who can reinforce the actor's initial forays into more prosocial territory. This notion is entirely consistent with the traditional sociological emphasis on the influential role of the social network. But here we have showcased the volitional or agentic aspects of movement toward these potentially helpful affiliations. Particularly as we focus on adult friendships and romantic liaisons, the individual has an important role in selecting others who have the potential to be good influences, while "knifing off" undesirable companions (Emirbayer and Goodwin 1994).

As we stated at the outset, the perspective we outlined is generally compatible with Sampson and Laub's (1993) theory of informal control, and the two perspectives can profitably be integrated. . . .

It may be even more useful to combine some of the ideas we developed here with Sampson and Laub's focus on an investment buildup. We agree completely with the key premise that highly invested actors will develop a strong stake in conformity and will not wish to jeopardize what they have accumulated by reverting to criminal activity. Across a variety of time periods and different sample groups, it is likely that a good marriage relationship combined with a stable job will continue to form the most solid basis around which to build a more prosocial way of life. However, we have emphasized here that individuals need a minimum level of resources to draw on in order to begin such a transformation process. Individual and cultural preferences, constraints, and opportunities will figure into the kind of strategies adapted (that is, some offenders may have to work with only parts of the respectability package or rely on different hooks for change entirely). Actors themselves must recognize the need to start "saving" and develop a high level of commitment to the plan. They may also call on help from others—ideally, professionals or others in the network who have a stronger portfolio of prosocial behavior. These others can provide structure and guidance all along the way. Over time, actors will not only

have built up a meaningful level of savings, but will actually come to enjoy the investing process. In turn, they will refrain from criminal or deviant behavior, not just because they have much to lose, but also because they have begun to look back with increasing disdain on their former spendthrift ways. These individually and socially structured differences in motivation and preference, the processes of interaction and communication that solidify them, and the gradual redefinitions that result are arguably as important as the "stake" itself. Indeed, they help us to understand how and why the buildup occurs. However, we also recognize that the product of all these dynamic processes is enhanced *internalized control,* perhaps the most important type of cognitive transformation.

Discussion Questions

1. What is "desistance"? Why might the causes for entering crime differ from the causes for leaving crime? How might this have to do with the age at which a person starts and ends a criminal career?
2. What is a "hook for change"? How might it occur in a person's social environment?

How might a correctional program be a "hook"?
3. Why is a "cognitive transformation" important for desistance to occur? How does this concept compare with Laub and Sampson's idea of "human agency"?
4. What are the four stages or components of the cognitive transformation that offenders must make in order to change and desist from crime?

PART XIII

Theories of White-Collar Crime

Every few years, it seems as though there is a new scandal in the business world. Most recently, it was the Ponzi scheme of Bernard Madoff, alleged to have cost unsuspecting investors $65 billion. Early in the first decade of the 2000s, Enron was the scandal of the day, although it had competition from frauds perpetrated at such companies as WorldCom, Adelphia, and Tyco. Before that, there were massive criminal enterprises in the savings and loan industry and, before that, insider trading on Wall Street, with Michael Milkin of Drexel Burnham Lambert being the most prominent figure convicted. The executives in these cases received lengthy prison terms, extending tens of years and effectively consigning some to spending the remainder of their lives behind bars. The public showed little sympathy for these offenders, jeering at them in person and cheering their harsh penalties. Once-respected community members, now they were seen as "bad guys"—as white-collar super-predators who should receive no mercy for exploiting the trust that innocent shareholders and customers had placed in them (Cullen et al., 2009).

For those coming of adult age in the past decade or two, the willingness of judges to impose harsh sanctions on white-collar offenders might not be surprising. After all, does not "everyone" know what white-collar crime is—at least in a general way—and does not "everyone" believe that criminals, whether rich or poor, should be treated equally? But these sentiments did not always exist. When Edwin H. Sutherland first published his essay on "white-collar crimina-

lity" in 1940 (Chapter 41 in this part), the scholarly community was stunned by his claims that "respectable" executives, physicians, and politicians—among others wearing "white-collars"—frequently violated the public's trust and committed frauds costing millions of dollars. At the time, the concept of white-collar crime did not exist in the lexicon of the United States or of other nations. It was as though Sutherland had flicked a criminological light switch, illuminating a realm of criminality that heretofore had existed but remained unseen (Geis and Goff, 1983).

Sutherland's work, however, did not immediately precipitate widespread condemnation of offenders in white collars. Books today sport accusatory titles such as *The Predator's Ball* and *Infectious Greed* (Cullen et al., 2009). But in 1962, a volume on a major corporate price-fixing scheme carried the kinder title of *The Gentlemen Conspirators*. In 1968, the President's Commission on Law Enforcement and Administration of Justice echoed this view, concluding that the "public tends to be indifferent to business crime or even to sympathize with the offenders who have been caught" (1968: 158). Similarly, in his classic *Thinking About Crime*, James Q. Wilson (1975: xx) argued that he would not focus on white-collar crime because of his "conviction, which I believe is the conviction of most citizens, that predatory street crime is a far more serious matter than consumer fraud [and] antitrust violations."

Not long thereafter, however, a number of factors coalesced to increase concern about white-collar offending. First, the turbulence of the 1960s and early 1970s—including the Viet Nam War, Watergate, and student protesters shot down at Kent State University—caused the public to mistrust those in power, including government and corporate officials. Between 1966 and 1971, for example, confidence in "major companies" dropped from 55 percent to just 26 percent (Lipset and Schneider, 1983). Second, the civil rights movement increased the salience of equality before the law, making it more difficult to ignore the crimes of the rich and powerful. Third, the consumer and environmental movements disclosed how corporations were defrauding customers and wantonly polluting rivers, the soil, and the air. Fourth, television shows, such as the highly rated *60 Minutes,* regularly publicized how those in positions of power abused the trust placed in them. These investigative reports often juxtaposed victims—whose lives were ruined financially through sneaky frauds or physically by exposure to toxic chemicals like asbestos—with smug, prevaricating executives who, in the face of incontrovertible evidence, tried to deny any corporate wrongdoing. And fifth, celebrated prosecutions of white-collar offenders were greeted with praise, not indifference, by the public. Prosecutors learned that it was in their self-interest to "go after" corrupt practices in high places in American society because these criminal cases could bring them acclaim and votes (Benson and Cullen, 1998; Cullen et al., 2006; Cullen et al., 2009). In a dialectical way, these prosecutions reflected and deepened public resentment toward white-collar illegality.

A generation of scholars grew up in and was schooled during this time period. Their parents had first weathered the Great Depression and World War II but then had enjoyed the prosperity and optimism of the 1950s. But this newer generation of the 1960s was enmeshed in a far different social environment. They had witnessed the assassination of leaders who spoke of hope and justice—the Kennedy brothers and

Martin Luther King; they had heard promises of a great society where poverty and injustice would be eliminated go sadly unrealized; and they had seen people in power lie to them and abuse their trust. In short, this generation was prepared to question those in authority and traditional understandings about the world—including the notion that criminals were found only in the lower echelons of society.

Thus, in this context, criminological attention to white-collar crime increased dramatically. It was easy to believe that power and privilege nurtured not morality but a sense of entitlement and impunity from consequences. Many younger scholars—being angry at the rich and powerful who sat atop an inequitable society and aching for greater social justice—rediscovered Sutherland's work on white-collar crime and embraced the study of lawlessness in the upperworld. To be sure, most criminologists continued to spend their time investigating traditional street crime. Even so, the analysis of white-collar crime emerged from obscurity to become a recognized specialization within the field of criminology (Cullen and Benson, 1993; Shover and Cullen, 2008).

As might be anticipated, this scholarly attention has produced important insights on the origins of white-collar crime. We review these different theoretical approaches below. First, however, we will focus on two important issues: what white-collar crime is and why studying it is important.

The Concept of White-Collar Crime

Sutherland had worked for over a decade collecting relevant materials before he was ready to set forth the concept of white-collar crime (Geis and Goff, 1983). He presented his essay, "White-Collar Criminality," to a combined meeting of economists and sociologists on December 27, 1939; the work would be published shortly thereafter in a sociology journal (see Chapter 41). Sutherland was not the first to call attention to crime in the business world. In 1907, for example, sociologist E. A. Ross published *Sin and Society: An Analysis of Latter-Day Iniquity.* In this slim volume, he showed how recent changes in the economy had created fresh opportunities for large industrial corporations to victimize citizens. Ross described these executives as "criminaloids," and he called for them to be held accountable for their companies' misdeeds and to be placed in prison. Despite the power of Ross's insights and rhetoric, he did not fundamentally reshape criminology. Rather, this accomplishment fell to Sutherland and the address he delivered shortly after Christmas in 1939. This day would establish him as the revered "father of white-collar crime."

As he rose to the podium, Sutherland understood that he would be challenging the powerful conventional wisdom that crime was a lower-class phenomenon. Scholars commonly linked criminality to poverty. After all, were not jails filled with the poor? The real debate was whether poverty was a social experience that created criminal motivations or was merely a reflection of bad traits, such as feeblemindedness and psychopathology, that also caused crime. Sutherland (1940: 1) was prepared, however, to speak of "crime in relation to business."

It is not always clear why a scholar—in this case, Sutherland—would see the world differently than most of his peers. Sutherland (1940: 1) claimed that he was no "muckraker" and that he was disinterested in "reforming anything but criminology." His intent, he said, was scientific—to suggest that theories that explain only lower-class crime are inadequate because they cannot explain business crime. Gilbert Geis and Colin Goff (1983), biographers of Sutherland, find his portrayal of his motives misleading. They are persuaded that Sutherland had a hidden, reformist agenda that sprang from his outrage over the swindles perpetrated by business executives and professionals. They trace this reformist impulse to "the Midwestern soil of Sutherland's early home life" (1983: xx).

Born in 1883, Sutherland spent most of his youth in Grand Island, Nebraska, where his father, a Baptist minister, was president of the local college. Sutherland would not remain a devout Christian, but the lessons he learned were not forfeited as he grew into adulthood. "Most prominently," observe Geis and Goff (1983: xviii), "there is a religious commitment that, at its best, demands that the ethics of Christianity be maintained in human and business relationships." They continue in noting that "at times, the tone of Sutherland's work on white-collar crime is reminiscent of the preaching of outraged biblical prophets" (1983: xviii; see also Gaylord and Galliher, 1988).

Sutherland's insights on crime in the business world might have slipped into scholarly oblivion, however, if he had not encapsulated them within the concept of white-collar crime. As Geis and Goff (1983: xiii) highlight, Sutherland added this term "to the American vocabulary." His construct was memorable precisely because the phrase "white-collar" conjures up an image of a certain kind of worker. In Sutherland's day, this was a person in the managerial or professional class. There simply was no ambiguity as to who Sutherland was indicting: respected members of the community who used their trusted occupational positions to exploit the public.

The difficulty, however, was that Sutherland's actual definition of white-collar crime was criminologically ambiguous. In his 1949 book, *White Collar Crime,* later republished with the subtitle *The Uncut Version,* Sutherland (1983: 7) defined white-collar crime "approximately as a crime committed by a person of respectability and high social status in the course of his occupation." Somewhat puzzlingly, he preceded this definition with the caution that this "concept is not intended to be definitive, but merely to call attention to crimes which are not ordinarily included within the scope of criminology" (1983: 7). Sutherland thus sensitized scholars to a new domain of crime but did not clearly demarcate its boundaries.

Indeed, criminologists are still debating what conduct should fall under the concept of "white-collar crime." Most crimes are defined by the behavior in question and not by the status of the offender. Thus, a street robbery by someone who is an executive and by an unemployed youth is a robbery in both cases. Sutherland, however, offered two distinct criteria. First, the crime had to be committed "in the course of his [or her] occupation." Second, it had to be undertaken by a "person of respectability and high social status." This latter standard creates much of the difficulty. How much respectability and how much social status must a person possess to qualify as a "white-collar" criminal? Let's assume that a lowly bank teller embezzles several hundred dollars, whereas a bank president embezzles several million dollars. One might argue that an embezzlement is an embezzlement—regardless of the person's social status. Still, calling both embezzlements white-collar crime seems to violate the spirit of Sutherland's original conceptualization. He wished us to focus on the crimes of the rich and powerful.

These conceptual issues are not merely esoteric ruminations, because they have profound theoretical implications. Employees at the bottom rungs of a company might have traits and social experiences more similar to those from the lower classes. Theories designed mainly to explain street crime by members of the lower class thus might also be able to explain these employees' wayward actions. By contrast, those who have risen to the very top of a company may have exceptional traits (intelligence) and experiences (Ivy League educations) that make them more unlike others in society. Explaining their behavior with traditional theories thus might be far more difficult. Further, when scholars test theories, they have to decide whom to "count" as a white-collar offender in their sample. The definition used to include or exclude offenders from the analysis can greatly influence the results that are reported.

A related conceptual issue is what counts as "crime." Some of Sutherland's contemporaries argued that the safest course was to count only those acts that had been determined by a court to have been criminal (i.e., that rely on convictions) (see Tappan, 1947). Sutherland rejected this idea because he realized that many of the harms perpetrated by companies were not treated as crimes. These companies could escape criminal prosecution because they possessed the power to shape what laws passed and how existing statutes were enforced. Calculating the number of their convictions thus would yield a misleading enumeration of how many white-collar crimes actually were committed. In essence, they were able to engage in criminal conduct with virtual impunity. Instead, Sutherland (1940: 6) argued that "convictability" should be central to the decision on what counts as a white-collar crime. Here, he suggested that the key issue is whether a white-collar offense could potentially be prosecuted under the criminal law. If so, then it should be viewed by criminologists as a crime.

Sutherland cemented his status as the father of this area of study with the publication in 1949 of *White Collar Crime.* This volume presented the results of Sutherland's analysis of the legal violations of the 70 largest industrial and commercial corporations over the course of their lifetime, which averaged about 45 years. He discovered that every company had at least one adverse legal decision and that they averaged 14 violations. Fully 98 percent had two or more transgressions, leading Sutherland to conclude that most corporations were "recidivists."

One objection to his findings was that in calculating the number of violations, he counted not only criminal convictions but also decisions against companies in civil courts and by regulatory agencies. Sutherland defended this methodological choice by noting that the vast majority of the behaviors sanctioned civilly and by agencies would have been criminal if prosecuted. This is his convictability standard mentioned previously. He also asserted that he was measuring only wayward conduct for which corporations had been detected, a fraction of the illegalities that they undoubtedly had committed since most offenses were concealed and thus never uncovered. Still, even when he limited his study to adverse criminal decisions, he found that 60 percent of the corporations had been "convicted in criminal courts" and had "an average of approximately four convictions each" (1983: 23). He then poignantly captured the core message these statistics communicated. "In many states," Sutherland (1983: 23) observed, "persons with four convictions are defined by statute to be 'habitual offenders.'"

Sutherland's *White Collar Crime* thus succeeded in presenting hard data revealing that nearly all major companies broke the law and might well be considered career criminals. He presented these findings as though he were merely being a good scientist, but his stigmatizing corporations as "recidivists" and "habitual offenders" was strategically important in serving his reformist impulses. It was Sutherland's efforts to pierce the veil of respectability behind which large and powerful business broke the law with impunity and to show the moral equivalency between corporate criminals and street criminals. In a scholarly but subversive way, he thus deconstructed the traditional beliefs that crime was the exclusive province of the poor and that high social status was a sign of moral superiority.

Finally, *White Collar Crime* was not really a study of all types of white-collar offenses. Rather, as stated, Sutherland restricted his empirical analysis to crimes by corporations. This was courageous because it meant that he was "taking on" America's most powerful bastion—a reality Sutherland confronted when the publisher of his 1949 book made him delete all companies' names so as to avoid potential lawsuits for libel (the names were restored in the 1983 "uncut version") (see Geis and Goff, 1983). His focus also was substantively important, because it sensitized subsequent generations of scholars about the prevalence of crimes by corporations and about the importance of studying lawlessness by society's most influential actors (see, in particular, Clinard and Yeager, 1980).

Why Studying White-Collar Crime Is Important

In his 1940 essay (Chapter 41), Sutherland also identified why it is important to study white-collar crime. First, he juxtaposed the public's ignorance about these offenses to the costs that upperworld criminality exacted. Based on the materials he had collected, he disclosed that a single scandal could cost millions of dollars. More instructive, he showed that the "financial cost of white-collar crime is probably several times as great as the financial cost of all the crimes which are customarily regarded as the 'crime problem'" (1940: 4–5). This claim is crucial because it shows why a limited view of the "crime problem" exposes the public to illegal exploitation that is largely hidden from view. It is Sutherland's way, in short, of arguing that white-collar crimes are not minor indiscretions but avenues through which innocent citizens are victimized.

Further, he pointed out that white-collar crime has what is now known as "social costs." Bad as the economic costs are, said Sutherland, their more worrisome effect is that they "lower morale" and produce "social disorganization on a large scale" (1940: 5). Why is this? He argued that a special quality of upperworld offenses is that they "violate trust and therefore create distrust"—all of which "damages social relations" (1940: 5). Take again the case of Bernard Madoff, who directed his now-infamous Ponzi scheme. This criminal enterprise continued for years because so many investors trusted Madoff. When the enterprise fell apart, many lost millions; some lost their life savings. But beyond the immediate victims of his fraud, the scandal may have far-reaching effects to the extent that it erodes the general public's confidence in financial institutions. Many Americans may well ask: Whom is it now safe to trust with my money? Is everyone on Wall Street a crook?

A common rejoinder to Sutherland's observations is that even if white-collar crimes exact a huge financial toll and perhaps lower confidence in central institutions, at least these offenses do not take lives or hurt people. After all, are not Americans more concerned about street crimes because they involve shootings, rapes, and muggings? Contemporary scholars have addressed this issue, showing that the "physical costs" of unlawful white-collar practices—people killed, injured, and made ill—dwarf those of traditional street crimes (Cullen et al., 2006).

The reason for this is that corporations touch Americans every day and in many ways. Most often, their influence is positive and integral to our way of life, providing us with employment and the products we consume. The difficulty, however, is when companies' amorality causes them to pursue profits with little consideration of the health and safety of others. When safety regulations are violated, for example, workers can be injured or die, such as when coal mines collapse. Less obvious but more pernicious are the toxins employees are illegally exposed to in the workplace (e.g., asbestos), which cause them to become chronically or terminally ill (see, e.g., Brodeur, 1985). Consumers have been sold not only falsely advertised goods but also products that endanger their lives, including, for example, defective pharmaceuticals and defective automobiles (Braithwaite, 1984; Cullen et al., 2006). And residents of communities have developed illnesses and experienced slow, painful deaths from toxic agents and pollutants unlawfully buried, dumped into rivers, or released into the air (Cullen et al., 2006).

In short, the inordinate costs of upperworld illegalities comprise a compelling reason for why this side of the crime problem warrants close attention. Sutherland, however, also voiced a more esoteric reason for studying white-collar criminality: it called into question virtually all theories of crime. Sutherland believed that for criminology to be truly scientific, scholars had to develop "general" theories—that is, theoretical models capable of explaining all varieties of illegal conduct. As noted previously, the prevailing

theories of his day were constructed only to account for traditional street crimes, such as theft, robbery, or assault. This created a special problem because of the view at this time that street offenses were concentrated in the lower class. This meant that the extant paradigms linked crime in some way to poverty. Once white-collar crimes were brought within criminology, the limits of these theories were apparent; they were not general explanations. As Sutherland (1940: 10) proposed, "the generalization that criminality is closely associated with poverty obviously does not apply to white-collar criminals. With a small number of exceptions, they are not in poverty, were not reared in slums or badly deteriorated families, and are not feebleminded or psychopathic."

Even today, a way of challenging frameworks claiming to be general theories, especially those linking wayward conduct to some personal failing (e.g., low self-control, low I.Q.), is to point out their inability to account for crimes by the rich and powerful (Friedrichs and Schwartz, 2008). One solution to this problem is to conclude that theories of white-collar offenders as opposed to street offenders (e.g., life-course-persistent criminals) are not explained by the same factors. In this view, theories should be specific to certain populations and behaviors rather than general. As Friedrichs and Schwartz (2008: 147–148) note, "it is difficult to imagine that the criminal motivations and crime patterns of inner-city teenage males are not fundamentally different from the criminal motivations and crime patterns of upper-class middle-aged corporate executives."

The other solution is to develop general theories that use the same core variables to explain all types of crime but to argue that the content of those variables differs across offense types (Agnew et al., 2009). We will revisit Sutherland's explanation of white-collar crime shortly. But for now we can point out that he used this second strategy to argue for the generality of his theory of differential association. In brief, he proposed that learning definitions favorable to violating the law occurred in both inner-city neighborhoods and in corporate organizations. The content of those definitions might differ—in the city streets one might be praised for stealing with a gun while in company suites one might be praised for stealing with a computer—but the process of differential association was the same.

In any event, once white-collar criminality is recognized, the theoretical chore for scholars becomes more complex. It is not enough to attribute crime to individual and social pathologies when these traits do not mark "respectable" executives, professionals, and politicians who wear white-collars but nonetheless offend habitually. Sutherland's (1940) early essay thus identified why white-collar crime is theoretically important.

Theories of White-Collar Crime

White-collar crime is a conceptual umbrella that covers explanations of diverse types of behaviors, including crimes by corporations, by individuals against corporations, by doctors and lawyers, by priests and professors, and by politicians and governments. Some illegalities clearly are intended to do harm (e.g., defrauding investors), while in others the criminal intent is fuzzy and involves negligence or recklessness (e.g., marketing a product that might be defective). Understandably, then, explanations of these often-dissimilar offenses tend to differ in the specific mix of causal factors that they emphasize. Still, it appears that most theories of white-collar crime tend to incorporate one or more of four central factors: exposure to a criminal culture, life in a competitive financial system, unique illegitimate opportunities produced by a legitimate work setting, and the decision to break the law by respectable people. We consider these criminogenic factors below.

Exposure to a Criminal Culture

In his differential association theory, Sutherland proposed that individuals offend because they are exposed to definitions favorable to crime and to the techniques needed to commit any given

criminal act (e.g., to pull off a "con job") (see Sutherland, 1937; Sutherland and Cressey, Chapter 10). In short, crime is learned, largely by interacting with others who are already involved in criminal pursuits.

As a member of the Chicago School of criminology (Part III), Sutherland was comfortable applying his theory to the explanation of crime in disorganized inner-city areas. He largely embraced the views of Shaw and McKay (Chapter 7) and others that criminal traditions were transmitted through criminal networks, gangs, and family members (e.g., older to younger siblings). Socially disorganized neighborhoods experienced culture conflict and were not organized against crime. Youngsters raised in these areas thus were likely to come into contact with definitions favorable to the violation of the law. Sutherland thus systematized the views of the Chicago School into a set of principles that comprised a coherent theory of crime.

Sutherland's (1940 [Chapter 41]) stunning departure was in proposing that many sectors in the "legitimate" world of work also were socially disorganized and thus more organized for crime than against it. Theoretically, he was making the bold claim—as noted above—that he had developed a general theory capable of explaining all varieties of crime. But more provocatively, he was also suggesting that criminal conduct existed in the higher reaches of society and that it was comparable—at least in its causes—with the wayward behavior of disreputable offenders at the bottom rungs of the social order. Respectability thus was a thin veil that, when pierced, revealed that crooks were found all across the class structure.

In *White Collar Crime*, Sutherland described how criminal cultures flourished in many white-collar sectors. As newcomers arrived for work, they soon learned that certain unethical and illegal business practices were normative. Efforts were made to teach these rookies criminal values and skills, whether that might be how to fix prices or how to mislead customers into purchasing unwanted or defective products. Newcomers' resistance to breaking the law was treated as a sign that the worker was not a "team player" and was grounds for shaming and denying advancement in the company. Engaging in shady dealings that increased profits was rewarded with praise and upward mobility. In short, many companies were organized for crime and provided strong differential association that favored legal violations. As Sutherland (1983: 245) observed:

> White collar criminals... are seldom recruited from juvenile delinquents. As part of the process of learning practical business, a young man with idealism and thoughtfulness for others is inducted into white collar crime. In many cases, he is ordered by managers to do things which he regards as unethical or illegal, while in other cases he learns from those who have the same rank as his own how they make a success. He learns specific techniques of violating the law, together with definitions of situations in which those techniques may be used. Also, he develops a general ideology...[that] is transmitted as a generalization by phrases such as "We are not in business for our health," "Business is business," and "No business was ever built on the beatitudes." These generalizations... assist the neophyte in business to accept the illegal practices and provide rationalizations for them.

More contemporary scholars have built on this insight from Sutherland by noting that companies differ in their ethical climates or organizational cultures, which are often shaped by the orientations of upper-level corporate managers (Clinard, 1983; Clinard and Yeager, 1980). Variations in illegalities thus are linked to the degree to which corporate cultures support criminal practices. This theory thus suggests that white-collar crime is not the result of a "few bad apples" but of a "rotten barrel."

Scholars have also endeavored to identify corporate cultures that, though not explicitly criminal, encourage decisions that can result in reckless acts that can jeopardize the health and safety of workers and consumers. Consider, for example, the tragic explosion of the space shuttle *Challenger* in which seven astronauts, and teacher Christa McCauliffe, perished. The decision to launch *Challenger* was made despite low temperatures (36 degrees) on January 28, 1986, and the knowledge that crucial O-ring seals on the solid rocket booster could crack and have a fatal malfunction in cold weather (Vaughan, 1996). Or consider the decision by Ford Motor Company to market its Pinto. The Pinto's gas tank was placed six inches from the rear bumper. In a rear-end collision at as low as 30 mph, the bumper would push the gas tank forward into bolts that could pierce the tank and cause the vehicle to explode into flames (Cullen et al., 2006). What would cause managers at NASA to launch the *Challenger* and Ford to market the Pinto?

One answer is that they were "amoral calculators" that simply were willing to risk human lives in the name of profit. NASA officials were facing shrinking budgets and the need to make the space shuttle program economical; Ford officials were facing competition from Japanese subcompacts and were rushing to market the Pinto. Diane Vaughan (1992, 1996) has provided a more nuanced understanding of the *Challenger* launch, which also is relevant to cases, such as the Pinto, that involve the marketing of defective products. She illuminates how, within work groups in organizations who are under pressure to produce results, cultural values can arise that result in the "normalization of deviance." When dangerous risks arise, there is a tendency for the group to define these as technical issues that can be either safely ignored or solved. As risks mount, the work group progressively defines them as acceptable and opposes alternative interpretations. From the outside, it might seem "obvious" that launching a space shuttle in cold weather is an unnecessary chance to take and that placing a gas tank next to a bumper where it is easily ruptured is a criminally reckless act (Cullen et al., 2006). But inside the organizations, norms arise to minimize or "normalize" the risk (e.g., "Shuttles have flown safely in temperatures almost this cold before"; "Overall, the Pinto is safer than other small cars").

Vaughan's point is that organizational cultures often are complex and lead to deviant, if not criminal, conduct in subtle ways. The "normalization of deviance" is one way that work groups remain collectively blind to how their decisions expose others to potentially deadly hazards. Risky decisions thus are not simply a matter of individual rational choices but are shaped by worldviews that emerge in the context of a government agency or corporation. Culture is not static but dynamic. Workers "make culture" but, ironically, are then constrained by the very culture they have produced—at times in ways they would never have intended.

Competitive Financial World

Sutherland asserted that the defining feature of white-collar crime is that it is committed by people who are working in high-status positions. Accordingly, these offenders are not disadvantaged but are in an occupational environment where money is present, if not preeminent. Some scholars have proposed that, with regard to white-collar crime, money is the root of all evil. What is less clear, however, is why this is the case.

One thesis is that people commit crimes to solve financial woes—whether as individuals or as organizations. Cressey (1953) was an early advocate of this view, suggesting that embezzlement is a response to a "non-shareable problem," such as worries over unpaid gambling debts or excessive family expenses. Cressey also noted, however, that exbezzlement is a solution to financial difficulties only when a person is in a position of trust and can rationalize feelings of guilt. Still, not all embezzlers or white-collar criminals are motivated by deprivation (Agnew et al., 2009; Dodge, 2009). Others steal, for example, to enjoy lavish lifestyles.

On a broader level, scholars argue that white-collar crime is nurtured by a competitive financial world in which the press for profits is ever-present. More radical theorists suggest that capitalism fosters a competitive, laissez-faire ideology

in which the maximization of profits supersedes concerns for the well-being of workers, customers, or the community. Corporations thus seek to use any means necessary to make money. This might involve committing antitrust violations, exposing workers to dangerous toxins and hiding the medical consequences from them (e.g., asbestos), or dumping hazardous products banned in the United States into overseas markets. Benson and Simpson (2009: 82–83) note a minor but instructive example of amoral conduct: "The Campbell's Soup Company promoted its 'chunky style' soup by putting marbles in the bottom of the bowl so that the soup would appear absolutely filled with meat and vegetables—in other words, 'chunkier.'"

In a similar vein, Merton's (1938 [see Chapter 13]) anomie theory would be relevant. Merton argued that the emphasis on the American Dream, embodied in material success, was a core American value. In this context, the excessive emphasis on financial achievement in companies could weaken moral norms and cause them to lose their regulatory influence. In short, these conditions would generate "anomie," which in turn would produce high rates of deviant practices.

Opportunities to Offend

The world of work is filled not only with legitimate opportunity for success but also, ironically, with illegitimate opportunities to offend (Benson and Simpson, 2009). In many ways, we see employment as insulating individuals from a life in crime. But as Sutherland understood, the workplace is replete with enticing criminal opportunities. Shover and Hochstetler (2006 [Chapter 43 in this Part]) use the concept of "lure" to describe the presence of attractive targets for offending in white-collar settings.

Scholars have long noted that the key ingredient of these illegitimate opportunities is that business and professional work necessarily involves trust and, most often, minimal oversight. In fact, Friedrichs (2004) called his comprehensive book on white-collar crime *Trusted Criminals*. The stubborn reality is that our economic system cannot function without our willingness to trust others. In our daily lives, we assume that we can trust that financial advisors are investing and not pilfering our money, that companies' products perform as advertised and are not defective, that bids on government projects (e.g., road construction) are competitive and not rigged, and that doctors undertake medical procedures (e.g., tests or surgeries) that are warranted and not just to secure higher fees. Most often, these assumptions are correct, but this is not always the case. At times, our trust proves misplaced, and white-collar crimes transpire.

As Benson and Simpson (2009) point out, many street crimes involve gaining access to a place unlawfully (e.g., when burglarizing a house), coming into personal contact with a victim (e.g., during a robbery), and engaging in conduct that is widely seen as disreputable. By contrast, working in an occupation or for an organization creates opportunities for criminal behavior of a different nature. Three properties, they claim, characterize many white-collar offenses: "(1) the offender has *legitimate access* to the location in which the crime is committed, (2) the offender is *spatially separated* from the victim, and (3) the offender's actions have a *superficial appearance of legitimacy*" (Benson and Simpson, 2009: 80, emphasis in the original). These conditions thus provide ample opportunities to deceive others and to conceal conspiracies to offend. Consider, for example, those who perpetrate financial frauds (e.g., Enron), such as falsely reporting a company's profitability so as to keep stock prices high and induce investment. They travel to their office each day, never see the shareholders they dupe, and appear to be paragons of virtue in their office communities. Who would expect that these respectable executives, behind the closed doors of their corporate suites, are engaged in an active conspiracy to deceive and defraud others of massive amounts of money?

As Shover and Hochstetler (2006: 29, Chapter 43) point out, "lure" or the chance to offend is not a full-fledged criminal opportunity unless "credible oversight" is lacking. We devote an immense amount of resources to policing and to preventing street crimes. However, the regulatory and criminal justice systems often provide oversight of the powerful lures in white-collar settings that is absent or ineffective. In fact, Michalowski and Kramer (2006) use the concept of "state-corporate crime" to describe offenses that occur because either the state permitted or even facilitated them.

For example, in 1991, 24 workers at the Imperial Food Products, Inc.—a chicken-processing plant in Hamlet, North Carolina—perished in a fire. The company's owner served over four years in prison on criminal charges, blamed for the deaths because a fire-exit door had been chained shut so as to prevent employees from pilfering chicken parts. Although the owner's culpability was clear, this incident might be considered a state-corporate crime because of the government's negligence in permitting unsafe work conditions (Aulette and Michalowski, 1993). Thus, the state's Occupational Safety and Health Administration had not inspected the building in eleven years. The agency had permitted workers to enter a plant that was 100 years old, had no sprinklers, and had inadequate means of escape. This reluctance to regulate was part of an attempt by the government to make North Carolina "friendly" to business by minimizing adherence to "costly" worker safety standards. Arguably, this meant that government officials placed corporate economic interests above the health interests of workers. Without this state-corporate cooperation, the opportunity for the lethal crime at the Imperial Food Products plant would not have existed.

Decision-Making by Respectable Offenders

In using the concept of white-collar crime, Sutherland raised the conundrum of how it is that respectable members of the community engage in disreputable acts. One solution to this problem is to dispute that these offenders were ever respectable. It may be that they share traits with street offenders that make them predisposed to criminal conduct (e.g., low self-control or anti-social personality) (Gottfredson and Hirschi, 1990; see also Croall, 2001). The other solution is to argue that white-collar offenders must somehow deal with their cognitive dissonance of being "a good person doing a bad thing."

Scholars argue that white-collar offenders resolve this dissonance through the use of "techniques of neutralization." As might be recalled from Chapter 17 in Part VI, Sykes and Matza (1957) proposed that for crime to occur, people had to invoke beliefs that would neutralize normative controls. These "techniques" explained why breaking the law in a particular situation was permissible. Upperworld criminals often mobilize such justifications so as to permit their illegal acts to proceed. For example, embezzlers will argue that "I was just borrowing the money and was going to pay it back." Or a price-fixer will say that "I was just doing what everyone did in my business." Or perhaps a doctor committing Medicaid fraud will explain that "I billed the government for services I did not perform because this program underpays me for the quality medical procedures I give my patients."

In Chapter 42 in this section, Michael Benson (1985) describes this process as "denying the guilty mind." He adopts the concept of "accounts" for the justifications that white-collar offenders use that permit them to neutralize feelings of guilt before and then following their criminal activities. Their goal is to break the law but nonetheless to deny that they are a "true criminal." In particular, accounts explain why a crime is not really serious and why the offender is not really blameworthy. Further, Benson observes that accounts are not merely invented by offenders but are tied to their social situation. Thus, in a capitalist system, employees are likely to explain their criminality by arguing that their illegal practices were necessary to make profits for shareholders and to keep the firm afloat. Or when working in a large corporation, they may excuse their participation in a fraudulent scheme by asserting that they "were just following orders."

Neal Shover and Andrew Hochstetler (2006 [Chapter 43]) argue that white-collar crime is "chosen." They also assert that this choice is rational to the extent that offenders judge that the benefits of their white-collar offense will outweigh the potential costs. But like Benson, they propose that this "rational choice" must be placed within a broader social context. In offering an integrated theory, they thus start by noting that white-collar settings are filled with "lure"—that is, with temptations to pilfer money or to make profits in illegal ways. As discussed above, this lure is transformed into a criminal opportunity when oversight is lacking. Due to weak informal and formal controls, this is often the case. Still, when two workers see a criminal opportunity, one but not the other might see choosing white-collar crime as rational. Why is this? Individuals respond differently to opportunities depending on their internal self-restraints and on their criminal predispositions. In short, the choice to offend is a by-product of how much lure exists, how much oversight and risk of sanctioning are present, and how much the individual can resist temptations or is motivated to offend.

Conclusion

By introducing the concept of white-collar crime, Sutherland should be credited with enriching the criminological enterprise. His work, and the research it inspired, illuminated that respectable members of society could engage in crimes that exact huge costs on workers, consumers, and the public. It became apparent how occupations and organizations provide many opportunities to offend, often under the mask of legitimacy. This scholarship also challenged theorists to explain a domain of crime that had been ignored. In response, efforts were made to identify specific causes of upperworld waywardness and to make efforts to construct integrated models of white-collar crime (see, e.g., Coleman, 1987). This explanatory task, however, was particularly daunting for approaches claiming to be "general theories" of crime, especially if they linked offending to personal of social pathologies. In the end, the study of white-collar criminality forces theorists to forfeit simplistic ideas as to who criminals are and why they might offend. It compels a deeper understanding of the diverse nature of crime and how it can emerge not only in city streets but also in corporate suites.

References

Agnew, Robert, Nicole Leeper Piquero, and Francis T. Cullen. 2009. "General Strain Theory and White-Collar Crime." In Sally Simpson and David Weisburd (eds.), *The Criminology of White-Collar Crime*, pp. 35–60. New York: Elsevier/JAI Press.

Aulette, Judy R. and Raymond Michalowski. 1993. "Fire in the Hamlet: A Case Study of a State-Corporate Crime." In Kenneth D. Tunnell (ed.), *Political Crime in Contemporary America: A Critical Approach*, pp. 171–206. New York: Garland.

Benson, Michael L. 1985. "Denying the Guilty Mind: Accounting for Involvement in a White-Collar Crime." *Criminology* 23: 583–607.

Benson, Michael L. and Francis T. Cullen. 1998. *Combating Corporate Crime: Local Prosecutors at Work*. Boston: Northeastern University Press.

Benson, Michael L. and Sally S. Simpson. 2009. *White-Collar Crime: An Opportunity Perspective*. New York: Routledge.

Braithwaite, John. 1984. *Corporate Crime in the Pharmaceutical Industry*. London: Routledge and Kegan Paul.

Brodeur, Paul. 1985. *Outrageous Misconduct: The Asbestos Industry on Trial*. New York: Pantheon Books.

Clinard, Marshall B. 1983. *Corporate Ethics and Crime: The Role of Middle Management*. Beverly Hills, CA: Sage.

Clinard, Marshall B. and Peter C. Yeager. 1980. *Corporate Crime*. New York: Free Press.

Coleman, James William. 1987. "Toward an Integrated Theory of White-Collar Crime." *American Journal of Sociology* 2: 406–439.

Cressey, Donald R. 1953. *Other People's Money: A Study in the Social Psychology of Embezzlement*. New York: Free Press.

Croall, Hazel. 2001. *Understanding White Collar Crime*. Buckingham, UK: Open University Press.

Cullen, Francis T. and Michael L. Benson. 1993. "White-Collar Crime: Holding a Mirror to the Core." *Journal of Criminal Justice Education* 4: 325–347.

Cullen, Francis T., Gray Cavender, William J. Maakestad, and Michael Benson. 2006. *Corporate Crime Under Attack: The Fight to Criminalize Business Violence*, 2nd edition. Cincinnati, OH: Anderson/LexisNexis.

Cullen, Francis T., Jennifer L. Hartman, and Cheryl Lero Jonson. 2009. "Bad Guys: Why the Public Supports Punishing White-Collar Offenders." *Crime, Law, and Social Change* 51: 31–44.

Dodge, Mary. 2009. *Women and White-Collar Crime*. Upper Saddle River, NJ: Pearson.

Friedrichs, David O. 2004. *Trusted Criminals: White-Collar Crime in Contemporary Society*. Belmont, CA: Wadsworth.

Friedrichs, David O. and Martin D. Schwartz. 2008. "Low Self-Control and High Organizational Control: The Paradoxes of White-Collar Crime." In Erich Goode (ed.), *Out of Control: Assessing the General Theory of Crime*, pp. 145–159. Stanford, CA: Stanford University Press.

Gaylord, Mark S. and John F. Galliher. 1988. *The Criminology of Edwin Sutherland*. New Brunswick, NJ: Transaction.

Geis, Gilbert and Colin Goff. 1983. "Introduction." In Edwin H. Sutherland (ed.), *White Collar Crime: The Uncut Version*, pp. ix–xxxiii. New Haven, CT: Yale University Press.

Gottfredson, Michael R. and Travis Hirschi. 1990. *A General Theory of Crime.* Stanford, CA: Stanford University Press.

Lipset, Seymour M. and William Schneider. 1983. *The Confidence Gap: Business, Labor, and Government in the Public Mind.* New York: Free Press.

Merton, Robert K. 1938. "Social Structure and Anomie." *American Sociological Review* 3: 672–682.

Michalowski, Raymond J. and Ronald C. Kramer, eds. 2006. *State-Corporate Crime: Wrongdoing at the Intersection of Business and Government.* New Brunswick, NJ: Rutgers University Press.

President's Commission on Law Enforcement and Administration of Justice. 1968. *Challenge of Crime in a Free Society.* New York: Avon.

Ross, E. A. 1907. *Sin and Society: An Analysis of Latter-Day Iniquity.* New York: Harper and Row.

Shover, Neal and Francis T. Cullen. 2008. "Studying and Teaching White-Collar Crime: Populist and Patrician Perspectives." *Journal of Criminal Justice Education* 19: 155–174.

Shover, Neal and Andy Hochstetler. 2006. *Choosing White-Collar Crime.* New York: Cambridge University Press.

Sutherland, Edwin H. 1937. *The Professional Thief: By a Professional Thief.* Chicago: University of Chicago Press.

——. 1940. "White Collar Criminality." *American Sociological Review* 5: 1–12.

——. 1983 [originally published in 1949]. *White Collar Crime: The Uncut Version.* New Haven, CT: Yale University Press.

Sykes, Gresham M. and David Matza. 1957. "Techniques of Neutralization: A Theory of Delinquency." *American Sociological Review* 22: 664–673.

Tappan, Paul. 1947. "Who Is the Criminal?" *American Sociological Review* 12: 96–102.

Vaughan, Diane. 1992. "The Macro-Micro Connection in White-Collar Crime Theory." In Kip Schlegel and David Weisburd (eds.), *White-Collar Crime Reconsidered*, pp. 124–145. Boston: Northeastern University Press.

——. 1996. *The Challenger Launch Decision: Risky Technology, Culture, and Deviance at NASA.* Chicago: University of Chicago Press.

Wilson, James Q. 1975. *Thinking About Crime.* New York: Vintage.

41. White-Collar Criminality

Edwin H. Sutherland

On December 27, 1939, Edwin H. Sutherland ascended the podium to address the joint meeting of the American Economic Society and the American Sociological Society. His remarks were published shortly thereafter in February 1940 in the American Sociological Review; *this article is reprinted here. Then on the faculty of Indiana University, Sutherland was granted this honor because he was president of the ASS—an acronym that eventually led to the organization's name change to the American Sociological Association (Geis and Goff, 1983)!*

His topic for this mixed audience seemed quite appropriate: crime in the business world. He started by noting that economists know much about business but not about crime, whereas sociologists "are well acquainted with crime but not accustomed to consider it as expressed in business" (1940: 1). Sutherland had been collecting relevant materials since 1928 but had not presented them in a systematic fashion. On this occasion, however, he transformed the face of criminology by proposing to talk about "white-collar criminality." For this reason, he will always be known as the "father of white-collar crime."

The term "white-collar" was a brilliant choice because it immediately conjured up an image of people in managerial and executive positions— "respectable or at least respectable business and professional men," to use Sutherland's (1940: 1) words. This imagery was powerful precisely because it contradicted the prevailing view that criminals

came from the lower class and often were fully unemployed. To suggest that upstanding white-collar workers were comparable with lower-class thugs was a poignant, if not radical, suggestion.

To avoid criticism, Sutherland asserted that his intentions were purely scientific. His comparison of white-collar and lower-class offenders that evening, he said, was merely to raise issues pertinent to "developing theories of criminal behavior, not for the purpose of muckraking or of reforming anything except criminology" (1940: 1). Geis and Goff (1983) find Sutherland's remarks to be disingenuous. In their view, Sutherland claimed the veneer of value-free science to mask his underlying outrage over the immoral practices that went unchecked in the domains of business, the professions, and politics.

Sutherland made three important contributions in his presentation and subsequent published essay. First, he not only introduced the construct of white-collar crime but also noted what kinds of actions fell under this conceptual umbrella. Most notably, he observed that "crime" could not be limited to those actions that resulted in an arrest by a police officer and/or a conviction by a criminal court. This was because most of the illegal actions by business executives, doctors, and politicians, for example, never came to the attention of the criminal law. These white-collar citizens engaged in scandals and swindles with impunity because they had the power to shape the passage and enforcement of criminal statutes. Thus,

Edwin H. Sutherland, 1940. "White-Collar Criminality." *American Sociological Review* 5 (February), pp. 1–12.

according to Sutherland, the key issue in defining white-collar crime was "convictability"—whether schemes could be prosecuted under the criminal law even if they never were.

Second, Sutherland put to rest any notion that the crimes by respectable members of society did little damage. A single white-collar criminal enterprise could illegally appropriate thousands if not millions of dollars. In fact, Sutherland (1940: 4–5) observed, the "financial cost of white-collar crime is probably several times as great as the financial cost of all the crimes which are customarily regarded as the 'crime problem.'" Even more pernicious, however, is the impact of these offenses on the social fabric. When respectable people violate the trust inherent in their occupational position—for example, when bank presidents embezzle other people's money or executives' false product advertisements defraud their customers—they "damage the social relations" and "create distrust, which lowers social morale and produces social disorganization on a large scale" (1940: 5).

Third, Sutherland challenged the validity of existing criminological theories that inevitably explained crime by some characteristic supposedly linked to the lower class, whether that might be living in poverty or in a disorganized neighborhood or traits such as feeblemindedness or psychopathology. Obviously, members of the white-collar class were not marked by such social or personal disadvantage, and thus the source of their criminality must lie elsewhere. As a result, the reigning paradigms were flawed; they were not general theories capable of explaining involvement in all types of crime.

By contrast, this presented Sutherland with an opportunity to trumpet his own theory of differential association, which was presented earlier in this book (see Chapter 10). It was a general, not a class-biased explanation. Thus, Sutherland claimed that just as juveniles might learn definitions favorable to violation of the law from gang members in their neighborhoods, so too were executives taught by co-workers that fraudulent

schemes were just a smart way of doing business. The white-collar world also was "disorganized" in the sense that, similar to an inner-city slum, it was more organized to support criminal conduct than it was to combat it. In short, the concepts of differential association and social disorganization were able to explain the crimes of the rich and poor, and therefore they comprised a general theory of crime.

Nearly a decade after his initial essay, Sutherland (1949 [1983]) published his classic book, White Collar Crime. *This work documented the extent of criminal activity in corporate America and also expanded his theory of white-collar crime. This was his last major contribution. Sutherland's life was cut short on October 11, 1950, when he died after suffering a stroke and hitting his head on a concrete pathway on the campus of Indiana University (Geis and Goff, 1983). The study of white-collar crime would receive some attention in the years to follow, but it did not re-emerge as a major topic in criminology until the 1970s and 1980s. At that time, a generation of scholars raised and radicalized in the tumultuous 1960s was anxious to illuminate how power often allowed those populating white-collar positions to break the law with impunity (Cullen et al., 2006).*

References

Cullen, Francis T., Gray Cavender, William J. Maakestad, and Michael Benson. 2006. *Corporate Crime Under Attack: The Fight to Criminalize Business Violence*, 2nd edition. Cincinnati, OH: Anderson/LexisNexis.

Geis, Gilbert and Colin Goff. 1983. "Introduction." In Edwin H. Sutherland, *White Collar Crime: The Uncut Version*, pp. ix–xxxiii. New Haven, CT: Yale University Press.

Sutherland, Edwin H. 1940. "White Collar Criminality." *American Sociological Review* 5: 1–12.

——. 1983 [originally published in 1949]. *White Collar Crime: The Uncut Version*. New Haven, CT: Yale University Press.

THIS PAPER is concerned with crime in relation to business. The economists are well acquainted with business methods but not accustomed to consider them from the point of view of crime; many sociologists are well acquainted with crime but not accustomed to consider it as expressed in business. This paper is an attempt to integrate these two bodies of knowledge. More accurately stated, it is a comparision of crime in the upper or white-collar class, composed of respectable or at least respected business and professional men, and crime in the lower class, composed of persons of low socioeconomic status. This comparison is made for the purpose of developing the theories of criminal behavior, not for the purpose of muckraking or of reforming anything except criminology.

The criminal statistics show unequivocally that crime, *as popularly conceived and officially measured*, has a high incidence in the lower class and a low incidence in the upper class; less than two percent of the persons committed to prisions in a year belong to the upper class. These statistics refer to criminals handled by the police, the criminal and juvenile courts, and the prisons, and to such crimes as murder, assault, burglary, robbery, larceny, sex offenses, and drunkenness, but exclude traffic violations.

The criminologists have used the case histories and criminal statistics derived from these agencies of criminal justice as their principal data. From them, they have derived general theories of criminal behavior. These theories are that, since crime is concentrated in the lower class, it is caused by poverty or by personal and social characteristics believed to be associated statistically with poverty, including feeblemindedness, psychopathic deviations, slum neighborhoods, and "deteriorated" families. This statement, of course, does not do justice to the qualifications and variations in the conventional theories of criminal behavior, but it presents correctly their central tendency.

The thesis of this paper is that the conception and explanations of crime which have just been described are misleading and incorrect, that crime is in fact not closely correlated with poverty or with the psychopathic and sociopathic conditions associated with poverty, and that an adequate explanation of criminal behavior must proceed along quite different lines. The conventional explanations are invalid principally because they are derived from biased samples. The samples are biased in that they have not included vast areas of criminal behavior of persons not in the lower class. One of these neglected areas is the criminal behavior of business and professional men, which will be analyzed in this paper.

The "robber barons" of the last half of the nineteenth century were white-collar criminals, as practically everyone now agrees. Their attitudes are illustrated by these statements: Colonel Vanderbilt asked, "You don't suppose you can run a railroad in accordance with the statutes, do you?" A. B. Stickney, a railroad president, said to sixteen other railroad presidents in the home of J. P. Morgan in 1890, "I have the utmost respect for you gentleman, individually, but as railroad presidents I wouldn't trust you with my watch out of my sight." Charles Francis Adams said, "The difficulty in railroad management . . . lies in the covetousness, want of good faith, and low moral tone of railway managers, in the complete absence of any high standard of commercial honesty."

The present-day white-collar criminals, who are more suave and deceptive than the "robber barons," are represented by Krueger, Stavisky, Whitney, Mitchell, Foshay, Insull, the Van Sweringens, Musica-Coster, Fall, Sinclair, and many other merchant princes and captains of finance and industry, and by a host of lesser followers. Their criminality has been demonstrated again and again in the investigations of land offices, railways, insurance, munitions, banking, public utilities, stock exchanges, the oil industry, real estate, reorganization committees, receiverships, bankruptcies, and politics. Individual cases of such criminality are reported frequently, and in many periods more important crime news may be found on the financial pages of newspapers than on the front pages. White-collar criminality is found in every occupation, as can be discovered readily in casual conversation with a representative of an occupation by asking him, "What crooked practices are found in your occupation?"

White-collar criminality in business is expressed most frequently in the form of misrepresentation in financial statements of corporations, manipulation in the stock exchange, commercial bribery, bribery of public officials directly or indirectly in order to secure favorable contracts and legislation, misrepresentation in advertising and salesmanship, embezzlement and misapplication of funds, short weights and measures and misgrading of commodities, tax frauds, misapplication of funds in receiverships and bankruptcies. These are what Al Capone called "the legitimate rackets." These and many others are found in abundance in the business world.

In the medical profession, which is here used as an example because it is probably less criminalistic than some other professions, are found illegal sale of alcohol and narcotics, abortion, illegal services to underworld criminals, fraudulent reports and testimony in accident cases, extreme cases of unnecessary treatment, fake specialists, restriction of competition, and fee-splitting. Fee-splitting is a violation of a specific law in many states and a violation of the conditions of admission to the practice of medicine in all. The physician who participates in fee-splitting tends to send his patients to the surgeon who will give him the largest fee rather than to the surgeon who will do the best work. It has been reported that two thirds of the surgeons in New York City split fees, and that more than one half of the physicians in a central western city who answered a questionnaire on this point favored fee-splitting.

These varied types of white-collar crimes in business and the professions consist principally of violation of delegated or implied trust, and many of them can be reduced to two categories: misrepresentation of asset values and duplicity in the manipulation of power. The first is approximately the same as fraud or swindling; the second

is similar to the double-cross. The latter is illustrated by the corporation director who, acting on inside information, purchases land which the corporation will need and sells it at a fantastic profit to his corporation. The principle of this duplicity is that the offender holds two antagonistic positions, one of which is a position of trust, which is violated, generally by misapplication of funds, in the interest of the other position. A football coach, permitted to referee a game in which his own team was playing, would illustrate this antagonism of positions. Such situations cannot be completely avoided in a complicated business structure, but many concerns make a practice of assuming such antagonistic functions and regularly violating the trust thus delegated to them. When compelled by law to make a separation of their functions, they make a nominal separation and continue by subterfuge to maintain the two positions.

An accurate statistical comparison of the crimes of the two classes is not available. The most extensive evidence regarding the nature and prevalence of white-collar criminality is found in the reports of the larger investigations to which reference was made. Because of its scattered character, that evidence is assumed rather than summarized here. A few statements will be presented, as illustrations rather than as proof of the prevalence of this criminality.

The Federal Trade Commission in 1920 reported that commercial bribery was a prevalent and common practice in many industries. In certain chain stores, the net shortage in weights was sufficient to pay 3.4 percent on the investment in those commodities. Of the cans of ether sold to the Army in 1923–1925, 70 percent were rejected because of impurities. In Indiana, during the summer of 1934, 40 percent of the ice cream samples tested in a routine manner by the Division of Public Health were in violation of law. The Comptroller of the Currency in 1908 reported that violations of law were found in 75 percent of the banks examined in a three months' period. Lie detector tests of all employees in several Chicago banks, supported in almost all cases by confessions, showed that

20 percent of them had stolen bank property. A public accountant estimated, in the period prior to the Securities and Exchange Commission, that 80 percent of the financial statements of corporations were misleading. James M. Beck said, "Diogenes would have been hard put to it to find an honest man in the Wall Street which I knew as a corporation lawyer" (in 1916).

White-collar criminality in politics, which is generally recognized as fairly prevalent, has been used by some as a rough gauge by which to measure white-collar criminality in business. James A. Farley said, "The standards of conduct are as high among officeholders and politicians as they are in commercial life," and Cermak, while mayor of Chicago, said, "There is less graft in politics than in business." John Flynn wrote, "The average politician is the merest amateur in the gentle art of graft, compared with his brother in the field of business." And Walter Lippmann wrote, "Poor as they are, the standards of public life are so much more social than those of business that financiers who enter politics regard themselves as philanthropists."

These statements obviously do not give a precise measurement of the relative criminality of the white-collar class, but they are adequate evidence that crime is not so highly concentrated in the lower class as the usual statistics indicate. Also, these statements obviously do not mean that every business and professional man is a criminal, just as the usual theories do not mean that every man in the lower class is a criminal. On the other hand, the preceding statements refer in many cases to the leading corporations in America and are not restricted to the disreputable business and professional men who are called quacks, ambulance chasers, bucket-shop operators, dead-beats, and fly-by-night swindlers.

The financial cost of white-collar crime is probably several times as great as the financial cost of all the crimes which are customarily regarded as the "crime problem." An officer of a chain grocery store in one year embezzled $600,000, which was six times as much as the annual losses from five hundred burglaries and robberies of the stores in that chain. Public enemies numbered one to six secured $130,000 by burglary and robbery in 1938, while the sum stolen by Krueger is estimated at $250,000,000, or nearly two thousand times as much. *The New York Times* in 1931 reported four cases of embezzlement in the United States with a loss of more than a million dollar each and a combined loss of nine million dollars. Although a million-dollar burglar or robber is practically unheard of, these million-dollar embezzlers are small-fry among white-collar criminals. The estimated loss to investors in one investment trust from 1929 to 1935 was $580,000,000, due primarily to the fact that 75 percent of the values in the portfolio were in securities of affiliated companies, although it advertised the importance of diversification in investments and its expert services in selecting safe securities. In Chicago, the claim was made six years ago that householders had lost $54,000,000 in two years during the administration of a city sealer who granted immunity from inspection to stores which provided Christmas baskets for his constituents.

The financial loss from white-collar crime, great as it is, is less important than the damage to social relations. White-collar crimes violate trust and therefore create distrust, which lowers social morale and produces social disorganization on a large scale. Other crimes produce relatively little effect on social institutions or social organization.

White-collar crime is real crime. It is not ordinarily called crime, and calling it by this name does not make it worse, just as refraining from calling it crime does not make it better than it otherwise would be. It is called crime here in order to bring it within the scope of criminology, which is justified because it is in violation of the criminal law. The crucial question in this analysis is the criterion of violation of the criminal law. The crucial question in this analysis is the criterion of violation of the criminal law. Conviction in the criminal court, which is sometimes suggested as the criterion, is not adequate because a large proportion of those who commit crimes are not convicted in criminal courts. This criterion, therefore, needs to be supplemented. When it is supplemented, the criterion of the crimes of one class must be kept consistent in general terms with the criterion of the crimes of the other class. The definition should not be the spirit of the law for white-collar crimes and the letter of the law for other crimes, or in other respects be more liberal for one class than for the other. Since this discussion is concerned with the conventional theories of the criminologists, the criterion of white-collar crime must be justified in terms of the procedures of those criminologists in dealing with other crimes. The criterion of white-collar crimes, as here proposed, supplements convictions in the criminal courts in four respects, in each of which the extension is justified because the criminologists who present the conventional theories of criminal behavior make the same extension in principle.

First, other agencies than the criminal court must be included, for the criminal court is not the only agency which makes official decisions regarding violations of the criminal law. The juvenile court, dealing largely with offenses of the children of the poor, in many states is not under the criminal jurisdiction. The criminologists have made much use of case histories and statistics of juvenile delinquents in constructing their theories of criminal behavior. This justifies the inclusion of agencies other than the criminal court which deal with white-collar offenses. The most important of these agencies are the administrative boards, bureaus, or commissions, and much of their work, although certainly not all, consists of cases which are in violation of the criminal law. The Federal Trade Commission recently ordered several automobile companies to stop advertising their interest rate on installment purchases as 6 percent, since it was actually 11½ percent. Also it filed complaint against *Good Housekeeping*, one of the Hearst publications, charging that its seals led the public to believe that all products bearing those seals had been

tested in their laboratories, which was contrary to fact. Each of these involves a charge of dishonesty, which might have been tried in a criminal court as fraud. A large proportion of the cases before these boards should be included in the data of the criminologists. Failure to do so is a principal reason for the bias in their samples and the errors in their generalizations.

Second, for both classes, behavior which would have a reasonable expectancy of conviction if tried in a criminal court or substitute agency should be defined as criminal. In this respect, convictability rather than actual conviction should be the criterion of criminality. The criminologists would not hesitate to accept as data a verified case history of a person who was a criminal but had never been convicted. Similarly, it is justifiable to include white-collar criminals who have not been convicted, provided reliable evidence is available. Evidence regarding such cases appears in many civil suits, such as stockholders' suits and patent-infringement suits. These cases might have been referred to the criminal court but they were referred to the civil court because the injured party was more interested in securing damages than in seeing punishment inflicted. This also happens in embezzlement cases, regarding which surety companies have much evidence. In a short consecutive series of embezzlements known to a surety company, 90 percent were not prosecuted because prosecution would interfere with restitution or salvage. The evidence in cases of embezzlement is generally conclusive, and would probably have been sufficient to justify conviction in all of the cases in this series.

Third, behavior should be defined as criminal if conviction is avoided merely because of pressure which is brought to bear on the court or substitute agency. Gangsters and racketeers have been relatively immune in many cities because of their pressure on prospective witnesses and public officials, and professional thieves, such as pickpockets and confidence men who do not use strong-arm methods, are even more frequently immune. The conventional criminologists do not hesitate to include the life histories of such criminals as data, because they understand the generic relation of the pressures to the failure to convict. Similarly, white-collar criminals are relatively immune because of the class bias of the courts and the power of their class to influence the implementation and administration of the law. This class bias affects not merely present-day courts but to a much greater degree affected the earlier courts which established the precedents and rules of procedure of the present-day courts. Consequently, it is justifiable to interpret the actual or potential failures of conviction in the light of known facts regarding the pressures brought to bear on the agencies which deal with offenders.

Fourth, persons who are accessory to a crime should be included among white-collar criminals as they are among other criminals. When the Federal Bureau of Investigation deals with a case of kidnapping, it is not content with catching the offenders who carried away the victim; they may catch and the court may convict twenty-five other persons who assisted by secreting the victim, negotiating the ransom, or putting the ransom money into circulation. On the other hand, the prosecution of white-collar criminals frequently stops with one offender. Political graft almost always involves collusion between politicians and business men but prosecutions are generally limited to the politicians. Judge Manton was found guilty of accepting $664,000 in bribes, but the six or eight important commercial concerns that paid the bribes have not been prosecuted. Pendergast, the late boss of Kansas City, was convicted for failure to report as a part of his income $315,000 received in bribes from insurance companies but the insurance companies which paid the bribes have not been prosecuted. In an investigation of an embezzlement by the president of a bank, at least a dozen other violations of law which were related to this embezzlement and involved most of the other officers of the bank and the officers of the clearing house, were discovered but none of the others was prosecuted.

This analysis of the criterion of white-collar criminality results in the conclusion that a description of white-collar criminality in general terms will be also a description of the criminality of the lower class. The respects in which the crimes of the two classes differ are the incidentals rather than the essentials of criminality. They differ principally in the implementation of the criminal laws which apply to them. The crimes of the lower class are handled by policemen, prosecutors, and judges, with penal sanctions in the form of fines, imprisonment, and death. The crimes of the upper class either result in no official action at all, or result in suits for damages in civil courts, or are handled by inspectors, and by administrative boards or commissions, with penal sanctions in the form of warnings, orders to cease and desist, occasionally the loss of a license, and only in extreme cases by fines or prison sentences. Thus, the white-collar criminals are segregated administratively from other criminals, and largely as a consequence of this are not regarded as real criminals by themselves, the general public, or the criminologists.

This difference in the implementation of the criminal law is due principally to the difference in the social position of the two types of offenders. Judge Woodward, when imposing sentence upon the officials of the H.O. Stone and Company, bankrupt real estate firm in Chicago, who had been convicted in 1933 of the use of the mails to defraud, said to them, "You are men of affairs, of experience, of refinement and culture, of excellent reputation and standing in the business and social world." That statement might be used as a general characterization of white-collar criminals for they are oriented basically to legitimate and respectable careers. Because of their social status they have a loud voice in determining what goes into the statutes and how the criminal law as it affects themselves is implemented and administered. This may be illustrated from the Pure Food and Drug Law. Between 1879 and 1906, 140 pure food and drug bills were presented in Congress and all failed because of the importance of the persons who would be affected. It took a highly dramatic performance by Dr. Wiley in 1906 to induce Congress to enact the law. That law, however, did not create a new crime, just as the federal Lindbergh kidnapping law did not create a new crime; it merely provided a more efficient implementation of a principle which had been formulated previously in state laws. When an amendment to this law, which would bring within the scope of its agents fraudulent statements made over the radio or in the press, was presented to Congress, the publishers and advertisers organized support and sent a lobby to Washington which successfully fought the amendment principally under the slogans of "freedom of the press" and "dangers of bureaucracy." This proposed amendment, also, would not have created a new crime, for the state laws already prohibited fraudulent statements over the radio or in the press; it would have implemented the law so it could have been enforced. Finally, the Administration has not been able to enforce the law as it has desired because of the pressures by the offenders against the law, sometimes brought to bear through the head of the Department of Agriculture, sometimes through congressmen who threaten cuts in the appropriation, and sometimes by others. The statement of Daniel Drew, a pious old fraud, describes the criminal law with some accuracy, "Law is like a cobweb; it's made for flies and the smaller kinds of insects, so to speak, but lets the big bumblebees break through. When technicalities of the law stood in my way, I have always been able to brush them aside easy as anything."

The preceding analysis should be regarded neither as an assertion that all efforts to influence legislation and its administration are reprehensible nor as a particularistic interpretation of the criminal law. It means only that the upper class has greater influence in moulding the criminal law and its administration to its own interests than does the lower class. The privileged position of white-collar criminals before the law results to a slight extent from bribery and political pressures, principally from the respect in which they are held and

without special effort on their part. The most powerful group in medieval society secured relative immunity by "benefit of clergy," and now our most powerful groups secure relative immunity by "benefit of business or profession."

In contrast with the power of the white-collar criminals is the weakness of their victims. Consumers, investors, and stockholders are unorganized, lack technical knowledge, and cannot protect themselves. Daniel Drew, after taking a large sum of money by sharp practice from Vanderbilt in the Erie deal, concluded that it was a mistake to take money from a powerful man on the same level as himself and declared that in the future he would confine his efforts to outsiders, scattered all over the country, who wouldn't be able to organize and fight back. White-collar criminality flourishes at points where powerful business and professional men come in contact with persons who are weak. In this respect, it is similar to stealing candy from a baby. Many of the crimes of the lower class, on the other hand, are committed against persons of wealth and power in the form of burglary and robbery. Because of this difference in the comparative power of the victims, the white-collar criminals enjoy relative immunity.

Embezzlement is an interesting exception to white-collar criminality in this respect. Embezzlement is usually theft from an employer by an employee, and the employee is less capable of manipulating social and legal forces in his own interest than is the employer. As might have been expected, the laws regarding embezzlement were formulated long before laws for the protection of investors and consumers.

The theory that criminal behavior in general is due either to poverty or to the psychopathic and sociopathic conditions associated with poverty can now be shown to be invalid for three reasons. First, the generalization is based on a biased sample which omits almost entirely the behavior of white-collar criminals. The criminologists have restricted their data, for reasons of convenience and ignorance rather than of principle, largely to cases dealt with in criminal courts and juvenile courts, and these agencies are used principally for criminals from the lower economic strata. Consequently, their data are grossly biased from the point of view of the economic status of criminals and their generalization that criminality is closely associated with poverty is not justified.

Second, the generalization that criminality is closely associated with poverty obviously does not apply to white-collar criminals. With a small number of exceptions, they are not in poverty, were not reared in slums or badly deteriorated families, and are not feebleminded or psychopathic. They were seldom problem children in their earlier years and did not appear in juvenile courts or child guidance clinics. The proposition, derived from the data used by the conventional criminologists, that "the criminal of today was the problem child of yesterday" is seldom true of white-collar criminals. The idea that the causes of criminality are to be found almost exclusively in childhood similarly is fallacious. Even if poverty is extended to include the economic stresses which afflict business in a period of depression, it is not closely correlated with white-collar criminality. Probably at no time within fifty years have white-collar crimes in the field of investments and of corporate management been so extensive as during the boom period of the twenties.

Third, the conventional theories do not even explain lower class criminality. The sociopathic and psychopathic factors which have been emphasized doubtless have something to do with crime causation, but these factors have not been related to a general process which is found both in white-collar criminality and lower class criminality and therefore they do not explain the criminality of either class. They may explain the manner or method of crime—why lower class criminals commit burglary or robbery rather than false pretenses.

In view of these defects in the conventional theories, an hypothesis that will explain both white-collar criminality and lower class criminality is needed. For reasons of economy, simplicity, and logic, the hypothesis should apply to both classes, for this will make possible the analysis of causal factors freed from the encumbrances of the administrative devices which have led criminologists astray. Shaw and McKay and others, working exclusively in the field of lower class crime, have found the conventional theories inadequate to account for variations within the data of lower class crime and from that point of view have been working toward an explanation of crime in terms of a more general social process. Such efforts will be greatly aided by the procedure which has been described.

The hypothesis which is here suggested as a substitute for the conventional theories is that white-collar criminality, just as other systematic criminality, is learned; that it is learned in direct or indirect association with those who already practice the behavior; and that those who learn this criminal behavior are segregated from frequent and intimate contacts with law-abiding behavior. Whether a person becomes a criminal or not is determined largely by the comparative frequency and intimacy of his contacts with the two types of behavior. This may be called the process of differential association. It is a genetic explanation both of white-collar criminality and lower class criminality. Those who become white-collar criminals generally start their careers in good neighborhoods and good homes, graduate from colleges with some idealism, and with little selection on their part, get into particular business situations in which criminality is practically a folkway and are induced into that system of behavior just as into any other folkway. The lower class criminals generally start their careers in deteriorated neighborhoods and families, find delinquents at hand from whom they acquire the attitudes toward, and techniques of, crime through association with delinquents and in partial segregation from law-abiding people. The essentials of the process are the same for the two classes of criminals. This is not entirely a process of assimilation, for inventions are frequently made, perhaps more frequently in white-collar crime than in lower class crime. The inventive geniuses for the lower class criminals are generally professional criminals, while the inventive geniuses for many kinds of white-collar crime are generally lawyers.

A second general process is social disorganization in the community. Differential association culminates in crime because the community is not organized solidly against that behavior. The law is pressing in one direction, and other forces are pressing in the opposite direction. In business, the "rules of the game" conflict with the legal rules. A business man who wants to obey the law is driven by his competitors to adopt their methods. This is well illustrated by the persistence of commercial bribery in spite of the strenuous efforts of business organizations to eliminate it. Groups and individuals are individuated; they are more concerned with their specialized group or individual interests than with the larger welfare. Consequently, it is not possible for the community to present a solid front in opposition to crime. The Better Business Bureaus and Crime Commissions, composed of business and professional men, attack burglary, robbery, and cheap swindles, but overlook the crimes of their own members. The forces which impinge on the lower class are similarly in conflict. Social disorganization affects the two classes in similar ways.

I have presented a brief and general description of white-collar criminality on a framework of argument regarding theories of criminal behavior. That arguments, stripped of the description, may be stated in the following propositions:

1. White-collar criminality is real criminality, being in all cases in violation of the criminal law.
2. White-collar criminality differs from lower class criminality principally in an implementation of the criminal law which segregates white-collar criminals administratively from other criminals.
3. The theories of the criminologists that crime is due to poverty or to psychopathic and sociopathic conditions statistically associated with poverty are invalid because, first, they are derived from samples which are grossly biased with respect to socioeconomic status; second, they do not apply to the white-collar criminals; and third, they do not even explain the criminality of the lower class, since the factors are not related to a general process characteristic of all criminality.
4. A theory of criminal behavior which will explain both white-collar criminality and lower class criminality is needed.
5. An hypothesis of this nature is suggested in terms of differential association and social disorganization.

Discussion Questions

1. Why is Sutherland called the "father of white-collar crime"?
2. What is white-collar crime? How does it differ from street crime?
3. What is a "general theory" of crime? Why did Sutherland believe that his theory of differential association explained both white-collar and traditional street crimes?
4. Do you think that it might be possible to have separate theories for, say, robbery and for price-fixing? Do you think that all theories of crime should be general or that specialized theories might be required to explain different types of crime?
5. Why might white-collar crimes be more harmful to society than street crime?

42. Denying the Guilty Mind

Michael L. Benson

Michael Benson (1985) suggests that individuals' "subjective experience" shapes why they might commit a crime and how they cope with their detection for a legal transgression. His specific interest is in the "guilty mind"—the need to deny criminal intent—and its integral role in the process of white-collar offending. His insights are drawn primarily from interviews he conducted with thirty people convicted of white-collar illegalities.

White-collar offenders typically do not have an arrest record and thus do not embrace a self-concept as a "criminal." As a result, when they break the law, they experience a cognitive dissonance caused by the gap between their identity as a respectable person and the reality of their criminal involvement. Benson suggests that they cope with this subjective experience by "denying the guilty mind." That is, they offer "accounts" or justifications for why their behavior does not define them as an offender and, in particular, as the moral equivalent of a traditional street criminal. For example, having embarked on a white-collar offense, they might offer the account that their illegal actions were undertaken "for the good of the corporation" and did "not really hurt anyone."

These accounts come in two varieties. One type, akin to Sykes and Matza's "techniques of neutralization" (see Chapter 17), occurs prior to a criminal act or during an ongoing criminal enterprise that might last months or years (e.g., price-fixing or Ponzi scheme).

These accounts relieve white-collar offenders of feelings of guilt and thus allow the conduct to continue. A second type, akin to the psychological construct of "rationalization," occurs after the act, especially when a conviction is forthcoming. These accounts allow offenders to cope with the stigma of being publicly defined as a criminal. Again, this is accomplished by furnishing offenders with an explanation or excuse for their conduct that allows them to announce to others that they did not formulate a guilty mind or intent and thus were not really a criminal.

Importantly, white-collar offenders do not simply invent accounts from whole cloth. Rather, the social-psychological mechanisms available to deny their guilty minds flow from their structural locations. "Corporate capitalism," notes Benson (1985: 588), "creates opportunities for particular forms of crime and at the same time creates, or makes plausible, certain types of justifications and mitigations for engaging in crime." For example, decisions in corporations, such as whether to market a defective product, are often diffused—that is, made by executives spread across different units and several levels of the company bureaucracy. Even if an executive knows that a defective product is being marketed, the person can use his or her location in this bureaucracy to avoid any responsibility for selling the faulty, if not dangerous, item to unsuspecting consumers. Thus, even though participating in the decision to manufacture the product, the executive can deny criminal intent by

Michael L. Benson. 1985. "Denying the Guilty Mind: Accounting for Involvement in White-Collar Crime." *Criminology* 23 (November), pp. 583-607.

invoking the account that "it was not really my decision" or that "I was only following orders."

The accounts offenders use also are shaped by the specific criminal enterprises in which they are engaged. For example, those violating antitrust laws often commit their crimes on behalf of the corporation. Although they realize that fixing prices or rigging bids is against antitrust laws, they can neutralize the subjective experience of guilt by saying that "everyone does it" in their industrial sector and that their company would go bankrupt, and good people would lose their jobs, if they tried to obey laws that competing companies ignore. When arrested, they deny blame by saying that they were unfairly selected by politically motivated prosecutors. This is the sense of injustice that occurs when "everyone is speeding" on the highway and you are the only one "pulled over" and given a ticket by the police. Of course, the fact that antitrust violations defraud consumers of millions of dollars is not considered in their moral interpretation.

Embezzlers, to give another example, face a trickier task in denying their guilt. After all, they have been, so to speak, caught with their hand in the till. They are not helping their corporation but stealing from it. The challenge is to deny that they are, in essence, a true criminal. Thus, these accounts might point out that they had an impeccably honest past and were driven to embezzle by unusual financial woes. Offenders might explain that they did not plunder the company's treasury but "only took what they needed" or that they "intended to put the money back" (see also Cressey, 1953).

More broadly, Benson notes that to deny the guilty mind effectively—to have those close to them and in their community not see them as a criminal—white-collar offenders have to invoke accounts that target two considerations. First, they must minimize the seriousness of their criminal act. Again, this might be accomplished by explaining that no individual suffered any real harm or that the practice was a selfless act needed to keep their company afloat in difficult economic times. Second, they must convince

others that their blameworthiness was slight, if not non-existent. This might be accomplished by saying that the standards regulating tax submissions or regulating business practices were too complex to understand and follow. Or it might be possible to assert that the criminal act was an inexplicable lapse in judgment made under duress and by someone known by all to be a "good person."

In short, Benson sensitizes us to the reality that the decision to offend flows from a complex subjective reality that is shaped intimately by white-collar criminals' location in their life course (adults employed), in a particular society (capitalist America), and in a specific occupation (corporate employee). His analysis moves us away from the simplistic view that engaging in white-collar crime is just like any other business decision: a cold calculation of costs and benefits. By contrast, he teaches us that the social psychology of offending is complex and involves accessing available cultural accounts that allow individuals to justify breaking the law and, subsequently, to attempt to cope with the stigma of a conviction. Accordingly, he enriches our understanding of the conundrum that Edwin Sutherland first identified: how those in respectable social positions, presumably socialized to be burdened with a guilty mind when they contemplate doing wrong, can nonetheless engage in highly disreputable criminal acts.

References

Benson, Michael L. 1985. "Denying the Guilty Mind: Accounting for Involvement in a White-Collar Crime." *Criminology* 23: 583–607.

Cressey, Donald R. 1953. *Other People's Money: A Study in the Social Psychology of Embezzlement.* New York: Free Press.

The subjective experiences of those who pass through the criminal justice system have seldom been given explicit attention by the criminologist. In particular, little attention has been paid to the offender's account of involvement in the offense. In the case of white-collar criminals, the failure to analyze the offender's explanation for involvement in the offense is especially noteworthy. Although white-collar offenders are assumed to suffer subjectively as a result of the public humiliation of adjudication as criminals, they are also assumed, paradoxically, to be able to maintain a noncriminal self-concept and to successfully deny the criminality of their actions (Conklin, 1977).

The present study treats the accounts given by a sample of convicted white-collar offenders, focusing specifically on the techniques they use to deny their own criminality. The emphasis is on general patterns and regularities in the data. The central research question is: How do convicted white-collar offenders account for their adjudication as criminals? While researchers have frequently expressed outrage at the denial of criminality that is thought to be typical of white-collar criminals, few attempts have been made to understand how this process occurs or to relate it to general deviance theory....

Corporate capitalism creates opportunities for particular forms of crime and at the same time creates, or makes plausible, certain types of justifications and mitigations for engaging in crime. The diffusion of responsibility in corporations, for example, makes it plausible for an actor to either deny responsibility altogether or to partially excuse actions by claiming to have been working at the request of superiors. The widespread acceptance of such concepts as profit, growth, and free enterprise makes it plausible for an actor to argue that governmental regulations run counter to more basic societal values and goals. Criminal behavior can then be characterized as being in line with other higher laws of free enterprise (Denzin, 1977: 919). More generally, the idea, which seems to be at the core of capitalist economies, that society benefits most through the individual competitive strivings of its members, as opposed to the opposite notion that society benefits most through the submerging of individual goals in favor of group needs, would

seem to provide a moral environment which facilitates the rationalization of criminal behavior. The idea of "just trying to get ahead" becomes an understandable and perhaps acceptable motive even when it occasionally leads to behavior that violates the law. A similar defense (or motive) would not seem to be possible in societies that do not promote individual material success as a desirable goal.

The study of accounts, therefore, can reveal how history and social structure make possible certain characterizations of events. This creates a moral environment conducive to crime in two ways. Convicted offenders can rationalize their behavior to themselves prior to engaging in crimes. After the discovery of an offender's involvement in criminal activity, he may be able to avoid the stigma of being labeled a criminal through the use of proper accounting practices....

Denying the Guilty Mind

The most consistent and recurrent pattern in the interviews, though not present in all of them, was denial of criminal intent, as opposed to the outright denial of any criminal behavior whatsoever. Most offenders acknowledged that their behavior probably could be constructed as falling within the conduct proscribed by statute, but they uniformly denied that their actions were motivated by a guilty mind....

Although the offenders displayed a variety of different emotions with respect to their experiences, they were nearly unanimous in denying basic criminality. To see how white-collar offenders justify and excuse their crimes, we turn to their accounts. The small number of cases rules out the use of any elaborate classification techniques. Nonetheless, it is useful to group offenders by offense when presenting their interpretations.

Antitrust Violators
Four of the offenders had been convicted of antitrust violations, all in the same case involving the building and contracting industry. Four major

themes characterized their accounts. First, antitrust offenders focused on the everyday character and historical continuity of their offenses.

> It was a way of doing business before we even got into the business. So it was like why do you brush your teeth in the morning or something.... It was part of the everyday.... It was a method of survival.

The offenders argued that they were merely following established and necessary industry practices. These practices were presented as being necessary for the well-being of the industry as a whole, not to mention their own companies. Further, they argued that cooperation among competitors was either allowed or actively promoted by the government in other industries and professions.

The second theme emphasized by the offenders was the characterization of their actions as blameless. They admitted talking to competitors and admitted submitting intentionally noncompetitive bids. However, they presented these practices as being done not for the purpose of rigging prices nor to make exorbitant profits. Rather, the everyday practices of the industry required them to occasionally submit bids on projects they really did not want to have. To avoid the effort and expense of preparing full-fledged bids, they would call a competitor to get a price to use. Such a situation might arise, for example, when a company already had enough work for the time being, but was asked by a valued customer to submit a bid anyway.

> All you want to do is show a bid, so that in some cases it was for as small a reason as getting your deposit back on the plans and specs. So you just simply have no interest in getting the job and just call to see if you can find someone to give you a price to use, so that you didn't have to go through the expense of an entire bid preparation. Now that is looked on very unfavorably, and it is a technical violation, but it was strictly an opportunity to

keep your name in front of a desired customer. Or you may find yourself in a situation where somebody is doing work for a customer, has done work for many, many years and is totally acceptable, totally fair. There is no problem. But suddenly they (the customer) get an idea that they ought to have a few tentative figures, and you're called in, and you are in a moral dilemma. There's really no reason for you to attempt to compete in that circumstance. And so there was a way to back out.

Managed in this way, an action that appears on the surface to be a straightforward and conscious violation of antitrust regulations becomes merely a harmless business practice that happens to be a "technical violation." The offender can then refer to his personal history to verify his claim that, despite technical violations, he is in reality a law-abiding person. In the words of one offender, "Having been in the business for 33 years, you don't just automatically become a criminal overnight."

Third, offenders were very critical of the motives and tactics of prosecutors. Prosecutors were accused of being motivated solely by the opportunity for personal advancement presented by winning a big case. Further, they were accused of employing prosecution selectively and using tactics that allowed the most culpable offenders to go free. The Department of Justice was painted as using antitrust prosecutions for political purposes.

The fourth theme emphasized by the antitrust offenders involved a comparison between their crimes and the crimes of street criminals. Antitrust offenses differ in their mechanics from street crimes in that they are not committed in one place and at one time. Rather, they are spatially and temporally diffuse and are intermingled with legitimate behavior. In addition, the victims of antitrust offenses tend not to be identifiable individuals, as is the case with most street crimes. These characteristics are used by antitrust violators to contrast their own behavior with that of common stereotypes of criminality. Real crimes are pictured as discrete events that have beginnings and ends and involve individuals who directly and purposely victimize someone else in a particular place and at a particular time.

> It certainly wasn't a premediated type of thing in our cases as far as I can see....To me it's different than—and I sitting down and we plan, well, we're going to rob this bank tomorrow and premeditatedly go in there.... That wasn't the case at all....It wasn't like sitting down and planning I'm going to rob this bank type of thing....It was just a common everyday way of doing business and surviving.

A consistent thread running through all of the interviews was the necessity for antitrust-like practices, given the realities of the business world. Offenders seemed to define the situation in such a manner that two sets of rules could be seen to apply. On the one hand, there are the legislatively determined rules—laws—which govern how one is to conduct one's business affairs. On the other hand, there is a higher set of rules based on the concepts of profit and survival, which are taken to define what it means to be in business in a capitalistic society. These rules do not just regulate behavior; rather, they constitute or create the behavior in question. If one is not trying to make a profit or trying to keep one's business going, then one is not really "in business." Following Searle (1969: 33–41), the former type of rule can be called a regulative rule and the latter type a constitutive rule. In certain situations, one may have to violate a regulative rule in order to conform to the more basic constitutive rule of the activity in which one is engaged.

This point can best be illustrated through the use of an analogy involving competitive games. Trying to win is a constitutive rule of competitive games in the sense that if one is not trying to win, one is not really playing the game. In competitive games, situations may arise where a player deliberately breaks the rules even though he knows or expects he will be caught. In the game of basketball, for example, a player may deliberately foul an opponent to prevent him from making a sure basket. In this instance, one would understand that the fouler was trying to win by gambling that the opponent would not make the free throws. The player violates the rule against fouling in order to follow the higher rule of trying to win.

Trying to make a profit or survive in business can be thought of as a constitutive rule of capitalist economies. The laws that govern *how* one is allowed to make a profit are regulative rules, which can understandably be subordinated to the rules of trying to survive and profit. From the offender's point of view, he is doing what businessmen in our society are supposed to do—that is, stay in business and make a profit. Thus, an individual who violates society's laws or regulations in certain situations may actually conceive of himself as thereby acting more in accord with the central ethos of his society than if he had been a strict observer of its law. One might suggest, following Denzin (1977), that for businessmen in the building and contracting industry, an informal structure exists below the articulated legal structure, one which frequently supersedes the legal structure. The informal structure may define as moral and "legal" certain actions that the formal legal structure defines as immoral and "illegal."

Tax Violators

Six of the offenders interviewed were convicted of income tax violations. Like antitrust violators, tax violators can rely upon the complexity of the tax laws and an historical tradition in which cheating on taxes is not really criminal. Tax offenders would claim that everybody cheats somehow on their taxes and present themselves as victims of an unlucky break, because they got caught.

> Everybody cheats on their income tax, 95 percent of the people. Even if it's for ten dollars it's the same principle. I didn't cheat. I just didn't know how to report it.

The widespread belief that cheating on taxes is endemic helps to lend credence to the offender's claim to have been singled out and to be no more guilty than most people.

Tax offenders were more likely to have acted as individuals rather than as part of a group and, as a result, were more prone to account for their offenses by referring to them as either mistakes or the product of special circumstances. Violations were presented as simple errors which resulted from ignorance and poor record-keeping. Deliberate intention to steal from the government for personal benefit was denied.

> I didn't take the money. I have no bank account to show for all this money, where all this money is at that I was supposed to have. They never found the money, ever. There is no Swiss bank account, believe me.
>
> My records were strictly one big mess. That's all it was. If only I had an accountant, this wouldn't even of happened. No way in God's creation would this ever have happened.

Other offenders would justify their actions by admitting that they were wrong while painting their motives as altruistic rather than criminal. Criminality was denied because they did not set out to deliberately cheat the government for their own personal gain. Like the antitrust offenders discussed above, one tax violator distinguished between his own crime and the crimes of real criminals.

> I'm not a criminal. That is, I'm not a criminal from the standpoint of taking a gun and doing this and that. I'm a criminal from the standpoint of making a mistake, a serious mistake.... The thing that really got me involved in it is my feeling for the employees here, certain employees that are my right hand. In order to save them a certain amount of taxes and things like that, I'd extend money to them in cash, and the money came from these sources that I took it from. You know, cash sales and things of that nature, but practically all of it was turned over to the employees, because of my feeling for them.

All of the tax violators pointed out that they had no intention of deliberately victimizing the government. None of them denied the legitimacy of the tax laws, nor did they claim that they cheated because the government is not representative of the people (Conklin, 1977: 99). Rather, as a result of ignorance or for altruistic reasons, they made decisions which turned out to be criminal when viewed from the perspective of the law. While they acknowledged the technical criminality of their actions, they tried to show that what they did was not criminally motivated.

Violations of Financial Trust

Four offenders were involved in violations of financial trust. Three were bank officers who embezzled or misapplied funds, and the fourth was a union official who embezzled from a union pension fund. Perhaps because embezzlement is one crime in this sample that can be considered *mala in se*, these offenders were much more forthright about their crimes. Like the other offenders, the embezzlers would not go so far as to say "I am a criminal," but they did say "What I did was wrong, was criminal, and I knew it was." Thus, the embezzlers were unusual in that they explicitly admitted responsibility for their crimes. Two of the offenders clearly fit Cressey's scheme as persons with financial problems who used their positions to convert other people's money to their own use.

Unlike tax evasion, which can be excused by reference to the complex nature of tax regulations or antitrust violations, which can be justified as for the good of the organization as a whole, embezzlement requires deliberate action on the part of the offender and is almost inevitably committed for personal reasons. The crime of embezzlement, therefore, cannot be accounted for by using the same techniques that tax violators or antitrust violators do. The act itself can only be explained by showing that one was under extraordinary circumstances which explain one's uncharacteristic behavior. Three of the offenders referred explicitly to extraordinary circumstances and presented the offense as an aberration in their life history. For example, one offender described his situation in this manner:

> As a kid, I never even—you know kids will sometimes shoplift from the dime store—I never even did that. I had never stolen a thing in my life and that was what was so unbelievable about the whole thing, but there were some psychological and personal questions that I wasn't dealing with very well. I wasn't terribly happily married. I was married to a very strong-willed woman and it just wasn't working out.

The offender in this instance goes on to explain how, in an effort to impress his wife, he lived beyond his means and fell into debt.

A structural characteristic of embezzlement also helps the offender demonstrate his essential lack of criminality. Embezzlement is integrated into ordinary occupational routines. The illegal action does not stand out clearly against the surrounding set of legal actions. Rather, there is a high degree of surface correspondence between legal and illegal behavior. To maintain this correspondence, the offender must exercise some restraint when committing his crime. The embezzler must be discrete in his stealing; he cannot take all of the money available to him without at the same time revealing the crime. Once exposed, the offender can point to this restraint on his part as evidence that he is not really a criminal. That is, he can compare what happened with what could have happened in order to show how much more serious the offense could have been if he was really a criminal at heart.

> What I could have done if I had truly had a devious criminal mind and perhaps if I had been a little smarter—and I am not saying that with any degree of pride or any degree of modesty whatever, [as] it's being smarter in a bad, an evil way—I could have pulled this off on a grander scale and I might still be doing it.

Even though the offender is forthright about admitting his guilt, he makes a distinction between himself and someone with a truly "devious criminal mind."

Contrary to Cressey's (1953: 57–66) findings, none of the embezzlers claimed that their offenses were justified because they were underpaid or badly treated by their employers. Rather, attention was focused on the unusual circumstances surrounding the offense and its atypical character when compared to the rest of the offender's life. This strategy is for the most part determined by the mechanics and organizational format of the offense itself. Embezzlement occurs within the organization but not for the organization. It cannot be committed accidentally or out of ignorance. It can be accounted for only by showing that the actor "was not himself" at the time of the offense or was under such extraordinary circumstances that embezzlement was an understandable response to an unfortunate situation. . . .

Summary and Implications

This study of convicted white-collar offenders has examined their accounts of their crimes. In particular, attention was given to the techniques used by offenders to deny their criminality and to maintain a legitimate persona. Accounts appear to be structured by the nature of the offense, its organizational format and history, and by the requirement that they undermine the conditions of successful degradation ceremonies. The most consistent and strongly emphasized theme manifested in the interviews was the denial of criminal intent.

In effect, offenders attempt to adjust the normative lens through which their offenses are viewed by society. Societal reaction to crimes and criminals varies according to many factors. Although there is no clear-cut consensus on the number and relative importance of factors, it can be assumed that two elements of significance are (1) the seriousness of the offense, and (2) the blameworthiness of the offender. Any offender interested in avoiding being labeled a criminal must be able to minimize the blameworthiness and seriousness of his actions to a degree such that the label "criminal" will be regarded as inappropriate.

It can be suggested that the presentability of an offense may play an important role in an offender's decision to commit that offense. That is, for individuals interested in maintaining a noncriminal identity, offenses that appear, or can be made to appear, less serious and less blameworthy will be more attractive than those that cannot be so presented. White-collar crimes are often structured or organizationally situated such that they are more malleable in this regard than traditional crimes. . . .

Seriousness

The partial legitimacy of the outcomes of some white-collar crimes seems to play an important role in the offender's minimization of seriousness. Some antitrust offenses, tax violations, and false statements made to lending institutions have as their outcomes more than just illegal gain for the perpetrators. They may also shore up a failing business or provide stability in employment. While defrauding the Medicaid system, a doctor or dentist may also be providing at least some much-needed services for the poor. The harm experienced by the victim or victims is balanced against the benefits derived by other uninvolved parties, such as employees and family. The congruence of legitimacy and illegitimacy that characterizes the commission of white-collar and corporate crimes (Clinard and Quinney, 1973) may be reproduced in the final products of those crimes and in the justifications presented by offenders.

A belief in widespread illegality was frequently expressed in the interviews. It seemed to be assumed that everybody is unscrupulous in one way or another. This fosters a callousness of attitude with regard to criminal behavior (Denzin, 1977). Criminal behavior is seen as acceptable and necessary for survival in the business world. This belief leads to the view that certain types of law violations, since they are normal, are not really serious crimes, which provides a blanket excuse for illegal behavior.

The belief in widespread illegality extends beyond the legitimate business world to society at large, which offenders seem to assume is at the mercy of rampant and unpunished street criminality. The lack of identifiable individual victims has been suggested as one of the reasons for the lack of societal concern with white-collar criminality. This characteristic of white-collar offenses may also be used by offenders before they commit their crimes. That is, the lack of individual victims may help the offender in using the familiar neutralization techniques of denying the victim and the harm.

Blameworthiness

The complexity of the laws and regulations governing the business world seems to facilitate relieving the offender's sense of blameworthiness. Crimes committed out of ignorance or inattention to detail are less offensive to the social conscience than those deliberately committed. Unlike the common street crimes, it is possible to accidentally violate laws that govern the conduct of businesses, professions, and industries. This means that the motives underlying conduct cannot automatically be inferred from the conduct itself. An offense that would be considered blameworthy if committed knowingly may be excusable, or at least understandable, if committed out of ignorance. Complexity gives rise to an ambiguity in the connection between the act and its motive. This may allow offenders to persuade themselves and others that the motive was not really criminal, so therefore the act was not really a crime.

Such a process may even work in advance of the crime when offenders maintain a concerted ignorance of the law or of the activities of subordinates. Katz (1979a) has argued that individuals involved in organizational crimes are frequently aware that there is a chance that the crime will eventually come to light. Yet, even though discovery is a possibility, offenders may nonetheless choose to participate provided that they can construct anticipatory defenses that will allow them to eventually deny blameworthiness. Many features of corporate organization facilitate the building of these "metaphysical escapes" (Katz, 1979a). In other words, offenders may purposely attempt to structure crimes so that the connection between act and motive remains ambiguous and deniable.

Individuals who commit crimes outside an organizational context or who act against organizations (embezzlers) may attempt to reduce their blameworthiness by setting the crime within the context of an otherwise impeccable life. If a crime can be shown to be an aberration, then its importance as an indicator of the offender's true character is dramatically reduced. His or her personality can be shown to have both good and bad points with the good outnumbering the bad. The obvious inconsistency of the offender's conviction vis-à-vis the rest of his life may be handled by family, friends, and perhaps society at large by denying the implications of the offender's actions

in order to maintain a consistent and favorable attitude toward him (Geis, 1982: 97).

As with the use of concerted ignorance, the process of setting the crime within a context of impeccability may be used by offenders prior to the illegal act as a neutralization technique. A lifetime of socially acceptable and desirable behavior in one arena is used to excuse an occasional indiscretion in another.

What needs to be determined is how effective these strategies are in helping the offender avoid stigmatization as a criminal—that is, avoid being thought of and treated like a criminal by others. If certain classes of offenders can commit crimes, be convicted, and yet still, through the use of appropriate accounting strategies, avoid being labeled as criminals, then one of the primary functions of the criminal law and the criminal justice system—the symbolic separation of the offender from the community—is negated. A moral environment is thereby perpetuated in which the symbolic consequences of criminal behavior for some offenders can largely be ignored.

Discussion Questions

1. Why is "denying the guilty mind" so important to white-collar offenders? Why do they not just accept that they are "criminals" and then break the law without any guilt?
2. Why do different kinds of white-collar offenders have to use different kinds of accounts to justify their criminal behavior? For example, how might the account or justification used by someone engaging in price-fixing differ from that of someone engaging in embezzlement?
3. If you were Bernard Madoff and you were now sitting in prison convicted of a $65 million Ponzi scheme, how might you deny your guilty mind?

4. On college campuses, students commit wayward acts that, though not officially white-collar offenses, are not traditional street crimes either. This might involve using pirated computer software or illegally downloading music. What accounts might college students use that allow them to deny their guilty mind and then go ahead and commit these acts?
5. Benson argues that accounts that are used to deny the guilty mind are shaped by where a person is in society. How might the accounts of white-collar executives employed in corporations differ from those used by street offenders residing in a disadvantaged urban neighborhood?

43. Choosing White-Collar Crime

Neal Shover and Andy Hochstetler

In Choosing White-Collar Crime, *Neal Shover and Andy Hochstetler (2006) make the simple but important observation that participation in white-collar crime is chosen. This choice is "reasoned" in that offenders judge that the benefits outweigh the likely costs of their action. To this extent, Shover and Hochstetler agree with scholars who propose that crime is a "rational choice" (see, e.g., Cornish and Clarke in Chapter 33). At the same time, they avoid the trap of reductionism—of seeing the theorist's job as simply hypothesizing that offenders, like people in general, make choices that serve their self-interests. Rather, a complete explanation of a criminal choice—whether by a white-collar or street offender—must place that decision within a broader set of circumstances and personal attributes.*

In some ways, Shover and Hochstetler's framework overlaps with routine activity theory (see Cohen and Felson, Chapter 34). They begin their explanation with the fascinating construct of "lure," which they say "is arrangements or situations that turn heads. Like tinsel to a child, it draws attention" (2006: 27). They continue to say that "lure is not criminal opportunity, but in the absence of credible oversight it is" (p. 28). In the language of routine activity theory, lure is thus roughly equivalent to "target attractiveness." It becomes a full-fledged criminal opportunity when it is combined with a lack of "capable guardianship." Thus, illegal immigrants who will work below minimum wage in sweat-shop conditions are lure to a company manager trying to maximize profits. It is a criminal

opportunity when there is virtually no possibility that hiring these employees will ever be detected or bring any legal consequences.

Unlike routine activity theory, however, Shover and Hochstetler do not lump all offenders into the undifferentiated category of "motivated offenders." Rather, they are careful to note that "lure does not evoke a uniform response either from individuals or organizations. Most remain blithely unaware of it" (p. 28). Other people, however, perceive lure or even seek it out. In short, offenders, including organizations, are not homogeneous but heterogeneous; they vary in their criminal propensity. That is, they differ in their inability to resist illegal temptations or in their active propensity to take advantage of criminal opportunities that present themselves.

Shover and Hochstetler do not deny that features of lower-class urban life might be criminogenic (e.g., family conflict, deprivation). But they make an important insight in suggesting that middle-class family and community life might also be a "generative world"—that is, a place that generates orientations conducive to crime. Growing up, middle-class youths are taught to exert social power in relationships, to take risks, and to be competitive. They might learn from their social advantage to be arrogant and uncaring toward others or to internalize a sense of entitlement. They also might develop linguistic skills that allow them to neutralize constraints and to deny their guilty mind when it tries to surface (see

Neal Shover and Andy Hochstetler. 2006. *Choosing White-Collar Crime*. New York: Cambridge University Press.

Benson, Chapter 42). *In organizational settings, these orientations and cultural capital might facilitate not only their advance up the corporate ladder but also their criminality. (The construct of the generative world is only touched in the forthcoming excerpt, but see Chapter 3 in* Choosing White-Collar Crime *for a more in-depth discussion.)*

Thus, think of an executive whose middle-class background has prepared him or her to wield power and take risks to out-compete other companies, to be insensitive to the harm that possible victims might endure, and to use well-developed linguistic skills to neutralize any feelings of guilt that might arise. Might this executive be lured by the promise of profits to defraud investors by exaggerating the true financial well-being of the company, to fix prices, or to market a product that has defects? And might the executive be even more likely to engage in such illegal conduct if surrounded in a corporation by like-minded co-workers also drawn from privileged backgrounds?

Other factors also play a role in whether individuals seek out or fall prey to lure. As control theorists have pointed out (see Part VI), people differ in the capacity for self-restraint. It is possible that permissive parental child-rearing, which can take place in privileged families, might produce offspring who grow up to have weak internal moral and psychological controls. The organizational context, however, also may vary in whether it encourages self-restraint or, alternatively, promotes risk-taking and bending the rules.

White-collar workers confront as well differences in external social controls, in particular the threat that the state will sanction them for illegal behavior. Similar to street offenders, it appears that upperworld lawbreakers pay more attention to the profits from their schemes than to the risk of being detected and punished. In part, this is because the benefits of white-collar crime are often easily seen and large. But it is also because state oversight in the corporate and professional world has traditionally been limited, if not absent. As a result, committing a white-collar crime is often an eminently rational choice: high and certain benefits as compared with low and uncertain costs.

Shover and Hochstetler note, however, that more enforcement efforts—those that involve using criminal prosecutions and advertising convictions—might well diminish upperworld waywardness (see also Benson and Cullen, 1998; Cullen et al., 2006). These efforts at deterrence should have meaningful effects for two reasons. First, they would raise costs where, at present, the threat of punishment is weak. And second, unlike many street offenders who are impoverished, white-collar offenders have social bonds—families, jobs, community ties—that they would not wish to jeopardize by being sent to prison (see Sherman, Chapter 22).

In many ways, Shover and Hochstetler see all crime—whether by those on city streets or in corporate suites—as a choice that is shaped by lure, predispositions generated both in childhood and in adulthood, self-restraint, and oversight by guardians, including the criminal justice systems. The processes by which traditional and white-collar crimes are produced are thus similar. What differs is the social context from which each type of offender is drawn and the content of what they experience.

Further, Shover and Hochstetler embrace a rational choice perspective but in a nuanced fashion. For them, a choice is "rational" in the sense that at the point at which an offense is committed, the individual senses that the benefits of the criminal act are worth the risk of punishment. But as Shover and Hochstetler also inform us, two individuals standing before the same criminal opportunity—such as the chance to embezzle company funds—will not see the choice to be made as equally rational. For the embezzler, the lure of siphoning off thousands of dollars with little chance of detection is too good to pass up. For the non-embezzler, this lure might never come to mind, or, even if the thought of stealing enters into consciousness, it would be readily dismissed as immoral and as risking everything the person had spent his or her life building. In a sense, the key explanatory task, which Shover and

Hochstetler take on, is in accounting for why the lure of crime is a rational choice for one person (or organization) but not for another.

References

Benson, Michael L. and Francis T. Cullen. 1998. *Combating Corporate Crime: Local Prosecutors at Work*. Boston: Northeastern University Press.

Cullen, Francis T., Gray Cavender, William J. Maakestad, and Michael Benson. 2006. *Corporate Crime Under Attack: The Fight to Criminalize Business Violence*, 2nd edition. Cincinnati, OH: Anderson/LexisNexis.

Shover, Neal and Andy Hochstetler. 2006. *Choosing White-Collar Crime*. New York: Cambridge University Press.

Lure

Lure is arrangements or situations that turn heads. Like tinsel to a child, it draws attention. Lure is a purse left unattended where there is heavy pedestrian traffic. It is cost-plus contracts between government and business firms. And lure is officers and representatives of Fortune 500 corporations doing business with officials of fledgling nations eager for investment and economic development. Lure need not be economic, however. It is also access to dependent and vulnerable populations, whether these be children, prisoners, the sick, the aged or economically marginal workers. Recall the Imperial Food Products fire. Because North Carolina is a right-to-work state, a high proportion of its workforce are not union members. Imperial's employees had little bargaining power with the company, and this probably contributed to the plant's unsafe working conditions. In the contemporary economy, a telling example of lure in human form is the availability of a ready supply of non-English-speaking illegal residents. In 2003, two plant managers of Tyson Foods, the world's largest processor of chicken, pleaded guilty to conspiracy to smuggle undocumented workers into the United States. The workers, who were paid $7.15 per hour, were employed at a Tyson processing plant in Shelbyville, Tennessee (*National Law Journal*, 2004).

Lure is not criminal opportunity, but in the absence of credible oversight it is. Lure does not evoke a uniform response either from individuals or organizations. Many remain blithely unaware of it – they simply do not see what is apparent to others–and most who do take notice of lure react with seeming indifference. Grandmothers come to mind. We know, however, that some who chance upon and take notice of lure turn their attention immediately to whether or not there is credible oversight. Lure makes the tempted and criminally predisposed sensitive to whether or not their actions are being monitored and how oversight might be defeated. Part of the attraction of many types of lure is the apparent ease of exploitation. In the postmillennia world this may require "not much more than the ability to read, write, and fill out forms, along with some minimum level of presentation of a respectable self" (Weisburd et al., 1991:182–83). Provision of health care services is an example. The treatment and services medical patients receive are converted by physicians and their assistants into billable hours reported on standardized forms submitted for reimbursement. Medicaid investigators regularly discover fraudulent claims; some psychiatrists bill for time spent having sex with patients (Jesilow, Pontell, and Geis, 1993). Offenders may have plans for dealing with unanticipated contingencies, but generally these are not complex. They recognize that in the unlikely event that officials put investigators on the trail, it is not difficult to stay ahead of or elude them entirely. . . .

The Predisposed and Tempted

Criminal opportunities are arrangements or situations that offer potential for criminal reward with little apparent risk of detection or penalty

(Coleman, 1987). Opportunity is in the eye of the beholder, but there is an objective and common-sense aspect to many criminal opportunities. This is why a high proportion of adults see and recognize it in similar circumstances. It is the reason we are cautioned, and we recognize wisdom in the admonition not to leave our automobile keys in the ignition switch or leave attractively wrapped gifts in plain sight while away from our cars. Regardless of how legitimate and convincing telephone callers may seem, the prudent do not give their checking account number to strangers. Widely shared understandings about situations where one is vulnerable are the reason secretaries who are harassed sexually by day do not work overtime. Criminal opportunities are found throughout the diverse spheres and routines of everyday life, but they cluster in the workplace.

The availability of lure is a key determinant of the supply of opportunities for white-collar crime, but for a high rate of crime to occur opportunities must be coupled with an ample supply of individuals and organizations who are aware of their existence and prepared to exploit them. The sources and precise nature of what distinguishes the criminally predisposed is varied, and it differs for individuals and organizations. Organizations that are *predisposed* to exploit lure are distinguished by structural, cultural, or procedural characteristics that increase the odds that their personnel will recognize and exploit lure. Tempted individuals possess qualities or experiences that make them more likely than peers who lack these distinctions to weigh exploitation of lure. Research into the lives of street criminals has shown that some go about their daily activities alert to and searching for criminal opportunities while others pay little attention to these unless they encounter something that piques their interest (Shover, 1996). The same is true of white-collar criminals (Weisburd et al., 2001).

The supply of predisposed organizations and tempted individuals varies temporally and spatially even as the pool from which it winnows

grows larger.... There appears to be no shortage of potential recruits to white-collar crime. The backgrounds and characteristics of those who step forward to take their place in the ranks differ conspicuously from what is typical of street criminals. Indisputably, they are more advantaged by material circumstances and respectability....

The backgrounds of white-collar criminals are tilted conspicuously toward the middle and upper classes. Children of these worlds have little material need, yet many appear as ready recruits to white-collar crime. Products of privilege and location in the class structure where personal respect is granted routinely and rarely disputed openly, they also exploit positions of organizational power. The ease with which the products of privilege turn to crime suggests there may be qualities and pathologies in their *generative worlds* that are functional equivalents of family conflict and deprivation that figure prominently in the early lives of street criminals. Whether at home, at school, or engaged in leisure activities, social and cultural conditions of middle-class life appear to generate ample and probably increasing numbers of individuals prepared to commit white-collar crime. Hagan (1992) notes that both social power and risk taking characteristic of privileged classes may contribute to crime and delinquency in children from these worlds. Others point out as well that social class "alters a variety of life contexts and chances" from differences in economic opportunities to culture, and this can increase delinquency by privileged youth (Wright et al., 1999:178). The sources of variation in the supply of predisposed organizations probably is explained by factors that overlap only in part with these....

Self-Restraint and Oversight

Lure becomes criminal opportunity in the absence of credible oversight. When the criminally predisposed and the momentarily tempted sense attentiveness by others, they move on. In this chapter we suggest that the changes described in chapter 2 coupled with the presence of a large population of the tempted and predisposed produced in the generative worlds sketched in chapter 3 give reason to believe that white-collar crime has increased substantially. It is impossible to estimate the magnitude and parameters of the increase, but the logic of rational-choice theory gives reason to believe it may be substantial.

Self-restraint is the first line of defense against criminal decision making by any who are attracted by lure. This is the willingness of individuals and groups to be constrained in their consideration of options not by fear of legal penalties but instead by potential self-reproach borne of a guilty conscience or concern for the opinions of others. Commitment to norms of morality and ethics, self-respect, and determination not to let down those who look to them for exemplary conduct and community standing are among the most important reasons many obey the law (Paternoster and Simpson, 1993). Lure is seen more quickly as criminal opportunity where decision makers are indifferent to the tug of conscience, reputation, or concern for family and peers. Crime-as-choice theory leads to expectation that fear of adverse publicity restrains the behavior of potential white-collar offenders. There is no doubt, for example, that owners and managers of many organizations value their good reputation and emphasize to employees the importance of operating ethically and in compliance with law. The large sums of money invested by some companies in advertising and charitable contributions leaves little doubt that for some an upstanding reputation whether earned or manufactured is a valued asset.

Few doubt as well that weak self-control is linked not only to criminal participation but to a variety of risky and deviant behaviors. Renewed interest in self-restraint in recent years was spurred by a bevy of analytically hard-nosed commentators who charge increasing failure by parents, schools, and churches to provide young people with adequate moral education. Moral education equips individuals to assess options constrained by altruism and the recognized importance of deferred gratification (Dilulio, 1991; Gottfredson and Hirschi, 1990; Wilson, 1975). It insulates individuals from concern with if not recognition of lure.

The worlds that generate white-collar offenders and the settings where they make criminal decisions are nested in larger moral contexts, and these are significant as sources of self-restraint or as crime facilitators (Vaughan, 1992). Criminal decisions are more likely in permissive cultures where infraction generally meets with indifference or indulgence from superiors and others.

State Oversight

Self-restraint and private oversight, the first lines of defense against unethical and criminal decisions, are imperfect, and this is one reason why the state and its oversight apparatus are on standby. If offenders weigh the costs and benefits of crime with any care, they likely will take account of the odds of being caught and possible sanctions. As compared with the perceived risk of committing street crimes, white-collar crime generally is seen as safer. This probably comes from recognition that many white-collar crimes occur far from the watchful eye of authorities, and, absent extraordinary and therefore unlikely investigation, offenders can operate with impunity. In the 2000 National Public Survey on White Collar Crime, a national sample of adults in the U.S. were asked to estimate the odds of being caught and punished for the crimes of robbery and fraud. Not surprising, they see fraud as much safer (Rebovich and Layne, 2000:18).

State oversight can take the form of direct observation by human beings or impersonal monitoring via periodic audits, television cameras, or computer programs. The fact that an avoidable harm or form of predation may threaten or injure others does not ensure it will be the focus of oversight, however. The state can turn a blind eye toward predatory or injurious behaviors, or it can choose to make them the focus of attention. It can take the lead identifying and crafting oversight, or it can wait until compelled to do so through action by citizens and organized groups. Stalking and environmental degradation are examples of harmful conduct for which the state provided little oversight until recent decades. . . .

Threat and Choice

Both street criminals and white-collar criminals calculate before committing crime; both choose to break the law. Investigators of white-collar crime generally have ignored research on decision making by other types of offenders and the similarites to decision making by white-collar offenders. Evidence is not compelling or voluminous, but it suggests for example, that street offenders and white-collar offenders weigh the potential payoffs from crime more heavily than the estimated risk (Shover and Honaker, 1992; Simpson and Koper, 1992). They focus on immediate reward and shortcuts to goals and may fail to see moral implications that affect others (Gottfredson and Hirschi, 1990; Simpson and Piquerro, 2001b). Individual propensity shapes what they weigh and choose (Tibbets and Gibson, 2002:18). Many operate in environments where they "carry on as if nothing were wrong when they continually face evidence that something [is] wrong" (Vaughan, 1998:32). In the presence of like-mineded companions, they can put out of mind how the larger public would judge their action and thereby blunt the deterrent effect of legal threats. In their efforts to cope with immediate crisis and daily hassles, these become remote and ill-considered contingencies (Vandivier, 2001; Warr, 2002). Rational-choice theory accommodates this contextual and individual variation. Weisburd and associates (2001:150) remark that:

> one implication of our emphasis on crisis and opportunity is that crimes committed by

people in our sample often involve decision-making processes that are, within their context and in the understanding of the offender, reasoned. In this sense, the offenders we study appear to follow a rational model of offending.

White-collar crime is committed because some people estimate the payoff as greater than the risks or consequences of being caught. Seen in this way, it is sound crime-control policy to escalate the perceived risks of it while increasing legitimate opportunities and perceived payoff from noncriminal conduct. The key lies in using public policy to constrain individual decision making so that those who consider crime do not find it to be a profitable option. Cost-efficient ways that the state could improve reward for noncriminal conduct among those who might otherwise consider white-collar crime are difficult to imagine. It is unfathomable to think that reward and additional largesse could increase compliance by upperworld offenders. Citizens would not be pleased with the tax burden for this purpose at any rate. The natural consequences of much white-collar offending are mild by comparison to other criminal acts and its inherent dangers do not elicit panic, nausea or other unpleasant sensations. For these reasons, the criminal law may hold the greatest promise for intruding on decision making and introducing corrective thoughts into the calculus of organizational and individual offenders.

A prominent research design for investigating deterrence of white-collar crime is to examine the subsequent, short-term effect of increased sanctions or criminal prosecutions on a specific type of offending. Block, Nold, and Sidak (1981) investigated antitrust laws and bread pricing by bakeries. When firms were charged with price fixing and faced with the possibility of civil suits, the price of their bread fell. Since then, many places or industries where the state increased enforcement have been investigated; the change in behavior of the sanctioned companies or of all firms of the sanctioned type is measured in these quasi-experiments. For example, inspections and penalties for workplace safety violations reduce injuries in sanctioned firms (Mendelhoff and Gray, 2005). The jury is still out on whether the accumulated findings provide support for deterrence (Simpson, 2002). Independent and dependent variables are very different from study to study. Various controls are utilized and findings are mixed. The state's general capacity to influence both street crime and white-collar crime is difficult to demonstrate empirically using short-term correlations between specific enforcement and crime.

Nevertheless, variation in threatened aversive consequences is a fundamental explanatory variable in the theory of crime as choice (Shover and Bryant, 1993; Cohen and Simpson, 1997). Given the proven capacity for rational responses to markets, it is not a large leap to the conclusion that threatened and actual consequences can reduce rates of some types of crime. The threat of arrest for domestic violence is more effective for men with jobs than for the unemployed (Berk et al., 1992; Pate and Hamilton, 1992). White-collar offenders also should be more responsive to changes in punishment than street offenders. They may be more aware of the level of intolerance expressed in the message of changing enforcement and it may mean more to them. Should the state decide to send a message into the boardrooms and cubicles of formal organizations that it is serious about a particular crime, or crime generally, the stretch is shorter than it is to the backseat of a car occupied by impoverished and drug addicted youth. A harshly worded letter to executives can get attention and a series of arrests and jail sentences clarifies the point. Street offenders receive no trade newsletters and when one of theirs has been imprisoned it is not relevant or shocking. Some in their ranks may pay heed, however, when they read one of the billboards that says, "you + illegal gun = federal prison," or "a gun crime gets you five" that appear in many U.S. cities today. The message gets across more clearly when all know from local gossip and

nightly news that it is true. Such a serious reminder well-placed can turn conversations and throw cold water on criminal plans. Those drafting ethical guidelines and administering educational programs in corporations could take a lesson.

Research on target hardening and situational crime prevention shows that few street offenders will choose to offend when the odds of being caught near certainty, where success requires creativity or significant effort, and where returns will be insignificant. Accounting firms that inflate earnings estimates to meet quarterly objectives, grocery clerks who ring employee discounts for friends, and street-corner drug dealers share a potential for significant painful consequences and are alike in this: many either ignore or view as unlikely these contingencies. Few clear-headed offenders with anything appreciable to lose would commit crime if they thought criminal prosecution or long-term imprisonment were likely consequences. Most are aware that their acts have the potential for criminal penalties if things go badly, but that is not the outcome they expect. They hope to avoid penalties by hiding their intent and responsibility. Like street offenders, most white-collar offenders do not pin their hopes on the number of months prescribed by the sentencing tables for convicted felons but on avoiding entirely this penalty. Both groups look at the risks of detection optimistically. Yet, the lives and generative worlds of street offender are different in many respects.

Street offenders continue in crime because they avoid honest evaluation of dismal prospects or reach a point where they do not care. White-collar offenders' positive thinking can result from the calculation that punishing their acts is a low priority for the state. Confidence among white-collar offenders can be the result of accurate evaluation as well as predisposition with roots in their backgrounds. The paucity of research on white-collar criminal decision making limits what can be concluded about the generality of the decision-making process. Such differences as there are, however, are explicable in the logic of rational-choice theory. These provide little justification for assuming that deterrent measures or crime-control strategies now aimed at other crime would be less effective in white-collar worlds.

Discussion Questions

1. What is meant by the concept of "lure"? How might it overlap with the concept of "target attractiveness" from Cohen and Felson's routine activity theory (see Chapter 34)? Now, think about your own environment in college. Are there any "lures" for crime?

2. On occasion, college professors commit white-collar crimes. One of these is in their research when, on a federally funded project, they falsify their findings so as to show that their ideas are correct or that they have made a new discovery. How would Shover and Hochstetler explain professors engaging in such fraudulent research?

3. Shover and Hochstetler suggest that growing up in a middle-class household is a "generative world" for white-collar crime. If you grew up in a more advantaged family, are there any experiences you can point to that might predispose those from more affluent communities to commit white-collar offenses when they enter the workforce?

4. Why might "getting tough" with white-collar offenders be more likely to have a deterrent effect than "getting tough" on street offenders?

5. Do you think that "general" theories of crime can help to explain white-collar crime? What about Ronald Akers's social learning theory (see Chapter 11)? What about Robert Agnew's general strain theory (see Chapter 16)? What about Gottfredson and Hirschi's self-control theory? Do you think white-collar offenders have more or less self-control?

PART XIV

Pulling It All Together: Integrated Theories of Crime

We have examined several major theories of crime up to this point, including biological, psychological, and sociological theories. Most of these theories were at the "micro" level, attempting to explain the criminal behavior of individuals; some were at the "macro" level, attempting to explain crime rates in social groups. Included in our examination were the three major theories in contemporary criminology: learning, strain/anomie, and control theories. We typically concluded our review of each theory by stating that it had *some* empirical support. In particular, certain of the variables identified by the theory were able to explain *some* of the variation in crime. Given this conclusion, it is natural to ask about the possibility of integrating these theories so that we might explain more of the variation in crime. It is to this topic that we now turn: integrated theories of crime.

The most comprehensive discussion of integrated theories is provided in an edited volume by Messner et al. (1989). Messner et al. begin their volume by stating that "to integrate theories is to formulate relationships among them" (1989: 1). Integrated theories, then, do more than simply list variables from different theories. They attempt to describe the relationships among these variables. Several strategies for integration have been described (Akers and Sellers, 2008; Barak, 1998; Bernard and Snipes, 1996; Einstadter and Henry, 2006; Farrington, 2005; Hirschi, 1979;

Messner et al., 1989; Miethe and Meier, 1994; Robinson, 2004; Tittle, 1995). The most commonly used is the "end-to-end" strategy, in which theorists describe the temporal ordering between variables, "so that the dependent variables of some theories constitute the independent variables of others." A theorist, for example, might argue that high levels of strain lead individuals to form or join delinquent subcultures, which in turn leads to crime.

Integrated theories actually have a long history in criminology. Lombroso, for example, proposed what is essentially an integrated theory of crime in his later work, arguing that a full explanation of crime requires that we take account of biological, psychological, social, and other variables (e.g., the climate). Several integrated theories have already been presented in this volume. Recent work in biology and psychology tends to integrate theories across different disciplines ("interdisciplinary integration"), combining variables from biological, psychological, and sociological theories. These theories typically argue that the social environment and biological factors of both a genetic and non-genetic nature affect the development of individual traits conducive to crime, such as impulsivity and irritability. Such traits, in turn, influence the social environment (e.g., irritable individuals are more likely to provoke negative responses from others and sort themselves into negative environments, such as delinquent peer groups). Further, traits and the social environment interact in their effect on crime, such that crime is most likely when individuals with traits such as irritability and impulsivity are in environments conducive to crime. Moffitt's theory of life-course-persistent and adolescence-limited offending, reprinted in Chapter 38, is perhaps the leading biosocial theory of crime today (also see Chapter 6; Brennan and Raine, 1997; Farrington, 2005; Robinson, 2004).

We have also had several examples of integrated theory within the discipline of sociology. Shaw and McKay's theory, described in Chapter 7, combines elements from strain, learning, and control theories. Cohen's theory (Chapter 14) is a deliberate effort to combine strain and differential association/cultural deviance theories. Cohen, in particular, uses strain theory to help explain the origin of deviant subcultures. He then argues that deviant subcultures condition the impact of strain on crime. That is, strained individuals are more likely to engage in crime if they form or join a deviant subculture such as a delinquent gang (see Cloward and Ohlin, 1960, for a similar set of arguments). Elliott and colleagues (1979, 1985, 1989) present an end-to-end integration of the three leading sociological theories of crime: strain, social control, and differential association/social learning theory. Two major pathways to delinquency are described: (1) low social control increases the likelihood of association with delinquent peers, which increases the likelihood of delinquency; and (2) individuals high in social control experience strain, which reduces their level of control, which in turn increases their likelihood of association with delinquent peers and thereby delinquency.

Many additional examples of integrated theory can be given (e.g., Bernard, 1990; Bernard et al., 2009; Braithwaite in Chapter 21; Catalano and Hawkins, 1996; Colvin in Chapter 25; Gold, 1963, Hagan et al., 1987; Johnson, 1979; Miethe and Meier, 1994; Pearson and Weiner, 1985; Vila, 1994; Wilcox et al., 2003). Most integrations are at the micro level: Theorists integrate two or more

theories that seek to explain individual deviance. A few theorists, however, have attempted to integrate macro-level theories (see Colvin, Chapter 25; Messner et al., 1989). Macro-level theories attempt to explain crime rates in groups, most commonly in terms of the cultural and structural properties of these groups. Messner and Rosenfeld's institutional-anomie theory (Chapter 15) can be viewed as an integrated macro theory: They integrate Merton's macro-level emphasis on the cultural system (the cultural system emphasizes the unrestrained pursuit of money by everyone) with structural arguments that are compatible with social disorganization theory (the dominance of the economy weakens the ability of other institutions to effectively socialize people and sanction deviance). There have also been some attempts to integrate macro-level and micro-level theories (see Akers, 1998; Messner et al., 1989). Theorists describe the ways in which macro-level variables ultimately influence the criminal behavior of individuals. In doing so, they better describe how such variables affect crime rates, for crime rates are based on individual criminal behavior.

In sum, there have been efforts at theoretical integration throughout the history of criminology—with such efforts becoming especially common in recent years. It is important to note, however, that not everyone agrees that integration is a good strategy. The most common objection is that the theories being integrated are often based on opposing assumptions (because theories were often developed in opposition to one another; see Hirschi, 1989). Therefore, integration is impossible without fundamentally altering the theories that are being combined.

For example, strain theory assumes that the motivation to crime (the frustration and anger that individuals experience) is variable. Such variation explains the variation in crime. Many control theories, however, assume that the motivation to crime is largely constant. That is, everyone experiences more or less the same amount of motivation for crime (greed, anger, etc.). Variation in crime is explained by variation in social restraints or controls. People high in social control do not act on their motivations for crime, while people low in social control often do. Given these opposing assumptions, how does one integrate strain and control theory in a way that preserves the integrity of both? Likewise, differential association theory assumes that our society is characterized by cultural conflict, with some individuals being exposed to definitions that are conducive to crime. Social control theory, however, assumes that our society is largely conventional. It denies that people engage in crime because of procriminal definitions. At most, ineffective socialization results in amoral individuals: those who believe that crime is neither good nor bad. Once more, theoretical integration seems impossible without substantially altering at least one of the theories involved. Given this situation, theorists such as Hirschi (1979, 1989) have questioned the strategy of integration and have instead suggested that we focus on the development of individual theories. Hirschi contends that the potential of most crime theories is far from tapped (see Bernard and Snipes, 1996; Elliott et al., 1979, 1985; and Messner et al., 1989 for excellent discussions of these issues, including critiques of Hirschi's argument).

The chapters in this section present four of the leading integrated theories in criminology. Most focus on the explanation of individual levels of offending and draw on the leading sociological theories of crime. The first selection, Thornberry's (1987 [Chapter 44]) interactional theory of delinquency, combines control and learning theories. The theory consists largely of an end-to-end integration of micro-level variables, although Thornberry does describe how certain macro-level variables may affect the micro-level variables in his theory. Thornberry's theory also devotes much attention to developmental processes and reciprocal effects. He describes how the variables in his theory change in importance over the life course, and he uses his theory to explain career patterns in crime (e.g., why some people desist from crime at adulthood and

others do not). Further, he recognizes that the causal ordering between the variables in his theory is more complex than is commonly portrayed. Most theorists simply argue that one variable, such as family attachment, causes another, such as school commitment. Thornberry, however, argues that most variables have reciprocal causal effects on one another (e.g., family attachment has a causal effect on school commitment and school commitment has a causal effect on family attachment). Delinquency itself is involved in this pattern of reciprocal causation. Tentative data provide some support for key parts of Thornberry's interactional theory, suggesting that certain variables do have reciprocal causal effects on one another and that the importance of certain variables changes over time—although more research is needed in these areas (see Kubrin et al., 2009; Thornberry, 1996; Thornberry et al., 1998; Thornberry et al., 2003 for reviews).

It should be noted that Thornberry and Krohn (2005) have recently expanded interactional theory. They now consider a broader range of age periods, including the preschool and childhood years. And they now discuss the role of biological factors and individual traits in the development of delinquency. In particular, they note that a small percentage of individuals begin engaging in delinquency during the preschool years, with many of these individuals becoming high-rate offenders over much of their lives. Their offending is said to be partly due to individual traits such as negative emotionality and impulsivity. These traits, in turn, are a function of both biological factors and the social environment. Their offending is also a function of a range of parenting problems, many of which result from the stresses of chronic poverty and residence in deprived communities. Individuals who start offending during the adolescent years, however, are less likely to possess traits conducive to crime or come from extremely deprived environments. Rather, their offending is best explained in terms of the social changes associated with adolescence. Adolescents experience an increased need for autonomy, which often leads to conflicts with and alienation from parents and teachers, as well as increased association with peers. These changes set in motion the causal processes described by Thornberry in Chapter 44.

While Thornberry uses the "end-to-end" strategy of integration (or a variation of it that recognizes reciprocal effects), others have employed alternative strategies. One such strategy is exemplified by Akers (1985, 1989, 1998; Akers and Sellers, 2008). He notes that his social learning theory is more general than other micro-level theories in sociology. He then argues that the concepts from these theories can be rephrased using the language of social learning theory ("conceptual integration"). Hirschi's bond of commitment, for example, essentially refers to "negative punishment" (we refrain from doing something because we fear that we will lose our current rewards). Further, social learning theory can be used to make predictions about the relationships between these concepts and their effect on deviance. Akers does acknowledge that, in certain cases, these predictions differ from those of the original theories. Control and social learning theories, for example, make different predictions about the effect of attachment on crime (control theorists argue that attachments to all others reduce crime, while learning theorists argue that only attachments to conventional others reduce crime). Such differences can and have been empirically examined (e.g., Conger, 1976). Akers, then, argues that several micro-level theories can be subsumed (with some modification) under his more general social learning theory (also see Pearson and Weiner, 1985). (He also argues that social learning theory can be the vehicle for integrating macro- and micro-level theories, since it can explain the mechanisms by which macro-level variables ultimately affect the individual [Akers, 1998; Chapter 11].)

Another strategy for integration is illustrated by the Cullen and Tittle selections (as well as the Braithwaite selection in Chapter 21 and the Colvin selection in Chapter 25). Cullen (1994 [Chapter 46]) does not present an end-to-end integration of variables, nor does he attempt to subsume several theories under a more general theory. Rather, Cullen points to a central causal process—the extent to which social support is provided to individuals—that affects crime for reasons related to strain, social control, and social learning theories. The concept of social support is explicitly and implicitly discussed in a number of crime theories. Cullen draws on these theories and the literature on social support in developing his theory. According to Cullen, social support has a direct causal effect on crime; it has a causal effect on other variables that influence crime, such as social control; and it conditions the effect of other variables on crime (e.g., strain is most likely to lead to crime when social support is low). Cullen, then, achieves integration by highlighting and elaborating on a common theme in several crime theories. (We should note that Cullen and Colvin recently proposed that their respective theories be combined into a still more general theory of crime, one that takes account of both the individual's level of social support and the coercion to which they are subject [Colvin et al., 2002].)

Cullen's theory is compatible with much existing data and has received tentative support in preliminary empirical tests (e.g., Crean, 2004; Pratt and Cullen, 2005; Pratt and Godsey, 2003; Ren et al., 2008; Scarpa and Haden, 2006; Wright and Cullen, 2001; Wright et al., 2000). At the macro-level, studies suggest that crime rates are lower in countries and communities that provide more social support. Such support includes welfare assistance, unemployment insurance, high levels of state spending on health care and education, and private charitable contributions. This support directly reduces crime rates and also reduces the effects of economic deprivation and inequality on crime rates. At the individual level, studies suggest that people who receive social support from conventional others, such as parents, are lower in crime. Also, some data support certain of the other propositions of Cullen's theory. For example,

Robbers (2004) found that conventional social support sometimes reduces the effect of strains on crime.

Tittle (1995 [Chapter 45]) points to another central causal process, the amount of "control imbalance" experienced by the individual, and argues that control imbalance affects crime for reasons related to several theories, particularly strain, control, and deterrence/rational choice theories. A control imbalance occurs when individuals are subject to more or less control than they exercise over others. Individuals who experience "control deficits" (are subject to more control than they can exercise) may engage in deviance to reduce such deficits, while those who experience "control surpluses" (are subject to less control than they exercise) may engage in deviance to assert or extend their control. A variety of individual factors (e.g., intelligence, interpersonal skills) and social factors (e.g., gender, age, class, the groups one belongs to) influence the degree of control deficit or surplus one experiences.

Whether individuals experiencing control imbalances engage in deviance depends on several factors. Do other factors, such as a strong desire for autonomy and the blockage of important goals, increase their predisposition to deviance? Do they experience situational provocations that remind them of their control imbalance, with such provocations involving treatment that they find debasing or humiliating (e.g., verbal and physical abuse)? Is there an opportunity to engage in deviance (e.g., a person must be available to assault, property must be available to vandalize)? Do the benefits of deviance outweigh the costs? And are a variety of other factors conducive to deviance—for example, do the person's moral beliefs allow him or her to engage in deviance? The central variable in the theory, however, is control imbalance—which exerts a large effect on the predisposition for deviance and the constraints against (or costs of) deviance.

Tittle (1995) notes that his theory can explain many of the known facts about crime, such as the relationship between sex, age, race, and marital status and certain types of deviance. This does not, of course, mean that the theory is correct. Other explanations for these facts can also be advanced. Several studies have examined Tittle's theory, and there is good evidence that control imbalances increase the likelihood of crime and deviance (e.g., Baron and Forde, 2007; Curry and Piquero, 2003; Piquero and Hickman, 1999; Piquero and Piquero, 2006). Research on whether control imbalances are more likely to affect crime and deviance under the conditions described by Tittle has produced mixed results. For example, certain research finds that control imbalances have a larger effect on crime/deviance when self-control is low, while other research does not find this (Baron and Forde, 2007; Curry and Piquero, 2003; see also Tittle, 2004).

The final integrated theory in this section is Agnew's general theory of crime and delinquency. Unlike Tittle and Cullen, this theory does *not* focus on a central causal variable such as control imbalance or social support. And unlike Thornberry, it does not attempt to describe how concepts from the leading crime theories are related to one another. Rather, Agnew's general theory employs what Bernard and Snipes call a "variable-centered" approach to integration. According to Bernard and Snipes (1996: 322):

> There has been too much emphasis in the integration debate on theories themselves and not enough emphasis on the observable variables and the observable relations among them.

Agnew's theory attempts to describe those variables that have relatively large, direct effects on crime. There are a good number of such variables, but Agnew groups them into five clusters: (1) the personality traits of low constraint and negative emotionality; (2) poor parenting practices and no/bad marriages; (3) negative school experiences and limited education; (4) peer delinquency; and (5) unemployment and work in "bad" jobs. The variables in each cluster are said to affect crime for reasons related to all of the leading crime theories. Poor parenting practices, for example, are said to reduce control, increase strain, and foster the social learning of crime. Agnew then describes how these clusters are related to one another and how they work together to affect crime. In doing so, he draws heavily on previous integrated theories, particularly Thornberry's theory. Among other things, Agnew argues that the clusters are reciprocally related to one another (poor parenting causes peer delinquency, and peer delinquency causes poor parenting), that the clusters interact in affecting crime and one another (e.g., poor parenting is more likely to lead to crime among those high in peer delinquency), and that prior crime leads to subsequent crime under certain conditions. While Agnew's general theory has not yet been tested, much data is compatible with it (see Agnew, 2005, 2009).

The four selections in this section, then, present varied approaches to constructing an integrated theory of crime. Some try to describe the relationships among various theories of crime, such as control, social learning, and strain theories. Some try to draw on these theories and related research to identify a central causal variable that impacts crime. And some try to identify and describe the relationships between those "concrete" or "observable" variables that cause crime. While all of these integrated theories are popular, none of them is generally viewed as the definitive explanation of crime. Rather, the search for a general theory of crime continues. You will notice, however, that integrated theories are becoming increasingly sophisticated over time.

Most integrated theories still focus on the explanation of individual-level offending. Such theories, however, are starting to consider a broader range of causes, including biological, psychological, and "macro-level" factors (group, community, and societal characteristics). Most theories argue that a complete explanation of crime requires a consideration of both "background" factors, such as level of self-control, and situational factors, like exposure to provocations or attractive targets for crime. Most theories now argue that the casual factors they examine are often reciprocally related to one another and to crime. Many theories argue that the impact of causal factors on crime often varies over the life course (e.g., parenting practices have a larger effect on crime in early adolescence versus early adulthood). Many theories recognize that the causal factors they identify interact with one another in their effect on crime (the effect of one factor on crime, like poor parenting, depends on the level of other factors, such as association with delinquent peers). And many theories argue that explanations of crime may vary somewhat according to type of offender (e.g., male versus female, adolescence-limited versus life-course-persistent) and type of crime (see Chapter 33 by Cornish and Clarke). So while we have not yet developed the definitive general theory of crime, there seems little doubt that our explanations are becoming more complete. At the same time, it is also quite certain that many criminologists will heed Hirschi's advice and work on the refinement of individual theories. Such work, of course, will ultimately contribute to theoretical integration since the strength of an integrated theory reflects the strength of its component parts.

References

Agnew, Robert. 2005. *Why Do Criminals Offend? A General Theory of Crime and Delinquency*. New York: Oxford University Press.

Agnew, Robert. 2009. *Juvenile Delinquency: Causes and Control*, 3rd edition. New York: Oxford University Press.

Akers, Ronald L. 1985. *Deviant Behavior: A Social Learning Approach*. Belmont, CA: Wadsworth.

——. 1989. "A Social Behaviorist's Perspective on Integration of Theories of Crime and Deviance." In Steven F. Messner, Marvin D. Krohn, and Allen E. Liska (eds.), *Theoretical Integration in the Study of Deviance and Crime: Problems and Prospects*, pp. 23–36. Albany: State University of New York Press.

——. 1998. *Social Learning Theory and Social Structure: A General Theory of Crime and Deviance*. Boston: Northeastern University Press.

Akers, Ronald L. and Christine S. Sellers. 2008. *Criminological Theories: Introduction, Evaluation, and Application*, 5th edition. New York: Oxford University Press.

Barak, Gregg. 1998. *Integrating Criminologies*. Boston: Allyn and Bacon.

Baron, Stephen W. and David R. Forde. 2007. "Street Youth Crime: A Test of Control Balance Theory." *Justice Quarterly* 24: 335–355.

Bernard, Thomas J. 1990. "Angry Aggression Among the 'Truly Disadvantaged.'" *Criminology* 28: 73–96.

Bernard, Thomas J. and Jeffrey B. Snipes. 1996. "Theoretical Integration in Criminology." In Michael Tonry (ed.), *Crime and Justice*, Volume 20, pp. 301–348. Chicago: University of Chicago Press.

Bernard, Thomas J., Jeffrey B. Snipes, and Alexander L. Gerould. 2009. *Vold's Theoretical Criminology*. New York: Oxford University Press.

Brennan, Patricia A. and Adrian Raine. 1997. "Biosocial Bases of Antisocial Behavior: Psychophysiological, Neurological and Cognitive Factors." *Clinical Psychology Review* 17: 589–604.

Catalano, Richard F. and J. David Hawkins. 1996. "The Social Development Model: A Theory of Antisocial Behavior." In J. David Hawkins (ed.), *Delinquency and Crime: Current Theories*, pp. 149–197. Cambridge, UK: Cambridge University Press.

Cloward, Richard A. and Lloyd Ohlin. 1960. *Delinquency and Opportunity*. New York: Free Press.

Colvin, Mark, Francis T. Cullen, and Thomas Vander Ven. 2002. "Coercion, Social Support, and Crime: An Emerging Theoretical Consensus." *Criminology* 40: 19–42.

Conger, Rand D. 1976. "Social Control and Social Learning Models of Delinquent Behavior: A Synthesis." *Criminology* 14: 17–40.

Crean, Hugh F. 2004. "Social Support, Conflict, Major Life Stressors, and Adaptive Coping Strategies in Latino Middle School Students: An Integrative Model." *Journal of Adolescent Research* 19: 657–676.

Cullen, Francis T. 1984. *Rethinking Crime and Deviance Theory*. Totowa, NJ: Rowman and Allanheld.

Curry, Theodore R. and Alex R. Piquero. 2003. "Control Ratios and Defiant Acts of Deviance: Assessing Additive and Conditional Effects With Constraints and Impulsivity." *Sociological Perspectives* 46: 397–415.

Einstadter, Werner J. and Stuart Henry. 2006. *Criminological Theory*. Lanham, MD: Rowman and Littlefield.

Elliott, Delbert S., Suzanne S. Ageton, and Rachelle J. Canter. 1979. "An Integrated Theoretical Perspective on Delinquent Behavior." *Journal of Research in Crime and Delinquency* 16: 3–27.

Elliott, Delbert S., David Huizinga, and Suzanne S. Ageton. 1985. *Explaining Delinquency and Drug Use*. Beverly Hills, CA: Sage.

Elliott, Delbert S., David Huizinga, and Scott Menard. 1989. *Multiple Problem Youth: Delinquency, Substance Use, and Mental Health Problems*. New York: Springer-Verlag.

Farrington, David. 2005. "The Integrated Cognitive Antisocial Potential (ICAP) Theory." In David P. Farrington (ed.), *Integrated Developmental and Life-Course Theories of Offending, Advances in Criminological Theory*, Volume 14, pp. 73–92. New Brunswick, NJ: Transaction.

Gold, Martin. 1963. *Status Forces in Delinquent Boys*. Ann Arbor: Institute for Social Research, University of Michigan.

Hagan, John, John H. Simpson, and A. R. Gillis. 1987. "Class in the Household: A Power-Control Theory of Gender and Delinquency." *American Journal of Sociology* 96: 265–299.

Hirschi, Travis. 1979. "Separate and Unequal Is Better." *Journal of Research in Crime and Delinquency* 16: 34–38.

——. 1989. "Exploring Alternatives to Integrated Theory." In Steven F. Messner, Marvin D. Krohn, and Allen E. Liska (eds.), *Theoretical Integration in the Study of Deviance and Crime:*

Problems and Prospects, pp. 37–49. Albany: State University of New York Press.

Johnson, Richard E. 1979. *Juvenile Delinquency and Its Origins*. Cambridge, UK: Cambridge University Press.

Kubrin, Charis E., Thomas D. Stucky, and Marvin D. Krohn. 2009. *Researching Theories of Crime and Deviance*. New York: Oxford University Press.

Messner, Steven F., Marvin D. Krohn, and Allen E. Liska, eds. 1989. *Theoretical Integration in the Study of Deviance and Crime: Problems and Prospects*. Albany: State University of New York Press.

Miethe, Terance D. and Robert F. Meier. 1994. *Crime and Its Social Context*. Albany: State University of New York Press.

Pearson, Frank S. and Neil Alan Weiner. 1985. "Toward an Integration of Criminological Theories." *Journal of Criminal Law and Criminology* 76: 116–150.

Piquero, Alex R. and Matthew Hickman. 1999. "An Empirical Test of Tittle's Control Balance Theory." *Criminology* 37: 319–342.

Piquero, Nicole Leeper and Alex R. Piquero. 2006. "Control Balance and Exploitative Corporate Crime." *Criminology* 44: 397–430.

Pratt, Travis C. and Francis T. Cullen. 2005. "Assessing Macro-Level Predictors and Theories of Crime: A Meta-Analysis." In Michael Tonry (ed.), *Crime and Justice: A Review of Research*, Volume 32, pp. 373–450. Chicago: University of Chicago Press.

Pratt, Travis C. and Timothy W. Godsey. 2003. "Social Support, Inequality, and Homicide: A Cross-National Test of an Integrated Theoretical Model." *Criminology* 41: 611–644.

Ren, Ling, Johong Zhao, and Nicholas P. Lovrich. 2008. "Liberal Versus Conservative Public Policies on Crime: What Was the Comparative Track Record During the 1990s?" *Journal of Criminal Justice* 36: 316–325.

Robbers, Monica L. P. 2004. "Revisiting the Moderating Effect of Social Support on Strain: A Gendered Test." *Sociological Inquiry* 74: 545–569.

Robinson, Matthew B. 2004. *Why Crime? An Integrated Systems Theory of Antisocial*

Behavior. Upper Saddle River, NJ: Pearson Prentice Hall.

Scarpa, Angela and Sara C. Haden. 2006. "Community Violence Victimization and Aggressive Behavior: The Moderating Effects of Coping and Social Support." *Aggressive Behavior* 32: 502–515.

Thornberry, Terence P. 1987. "Toward an Interactional Theory of Delinquency." *Criminology* 25: 863–891.

——. 1996. "Empirical Support for Interactional Theory: A Review of the Literature." In J. David Hawkins (ed.), *Delinquency and Crime: Current Theories*, pp. 198–235. Cambridge, UK: Cambridge University Press.

Thornberry, Terence P. and Marvin D. Krohn. 2005. "Applying Interactional Theory to the Explanation of Continuity and Change in Antisocial Behavior." In David P. Farrington (ed.), *Integrated Developmental and Life-Course Theories of Offending*, pp. 183–210. New Brunswick, NJ: Transaction.

Thornberry, Terence P., Marvin D. Krohn, Alan J. Lizotte, Carolyn A. Smith, and Pamela K. Porter. 1998. "Taking Stock: An Overview of Findings From the Rochester Youth Development Survey." Paper presented at the annual meeting of the American Society of Criminology, Washington, D.C.

Thornberry, Terence P., Alan J. Lizotte, Marvin D. Krohn, Carolyn A. Smith, and Pamela K. Porter. 2003. "Causes and Consequences: Findings From the Rochester Youth Development Survey." In Terence P. Thornberry and Marvin D. Krohn (eds.), *Taking Stock of Delinquency*, pp. 11–46. New York: Kluwer Academic/Plenum.

Tittle, Charles R. 1995. *Control Balance: Toward a General Theory of Deviance*. Boulder, CO: Westview.

——. 2004. "Refining Control Balance Theory." *Theoretical Criminology* 8: 395–428.

Vila, Bryan. 1994. "A General Paradigm for Understanding Criminal Behavior: Extending Evolutionary Ecological Theory." *Criminology* 32: 311–359.

Wilcox, Pamela, Kenneth C. Land, and Scott A. Hunt. 2003. *Criminal Circumstance: A Dynamic,*

Multi-Contextual Criminal Opportunity Theory. New York: Aldine de Gruyter.

Wright, John Paul. 1995. "Parental Support and Juvenile Delinquency: A Test of Social Support Theory." Unpublished Ph.D. dissertation, University of Cincinnati.

Wright, John Paul and Francis T. Cullen. 2001. "Parental Efficacy and Delinquent Behavior: Do Control and Support Matter?" *Criminology* 39: 677–706.

Wright, John Paul, Francis T. Cullen, and John D. Wooldredge. 2000. "Parental Support and Juvenile Delinquency." In Greer Litton Fox and Michael L. Benson (eds.), *Families, Crime, and Criminal Justice*, pp. 139–161. New York: JAI.

44. Toward an Interactional Theory of Delinquency

Terence P. Thornberry

Thornberry's interactional theory of delinquency draws on Hirschi's control theory (see Chapter 18) and differential association/social learning theory (see Chapters 10 and 11). Weak social bonds, association with delinquent peers, and delinquent values all contribute to delinquent behavior. Further, Thornberry argues that there is good reason to believe that many of the variables in his model have reciprocal effects on one another. So, while one might argue that association with delinquent peers increases the likelihood of delinquency, it is also reasonable to argue that delinquency increases the likelihood of association with delinquent peers. Such reciprocal effects are quite important, for they suggest that many youths get involved in an "amplifying causal structure" that leads to greater and greater involvement in delinquency. Thornberry also argues that the causes of delinquency change over the life course of the individual. For example, the importance of parental attachment diminishes as the adolescent ages, while new variables—like commitment to conventional activities (job, college, military)—enter the model. Most models of delinquency focus on mid-adolescence and do not consider such developmental trends. The consideration of such trends allows Thornberry to better explain patterns in delinquency over the life course—like the fact that most offenders desist from delinquency in late

adolescence. While Thornberry's integrated theory is phrased primarily at the micro-level, he does discuss the role of structural variables like social class and gender. He argues that such variables are important because they affect one's initial level of social control and exposure to delinquent peers, values, and behaviors.

Only a few studies have examined reciprocal relationships and developmental patterns of the type described by Thornberry (see Kubrin et al., 2009; Thornberry, 1996; Thornberry et al., 1998; Thornberry et al., 2003, for summaries). These studies find support for some of the reciprocal relationships in Thornberry's model, particularly reciprocal relationships between the learning variables (delinquent values and peers) and delinquency. These studies also suggest that certain of the causes of delinquency may vary in importance over the life course, although it is too early to draw any firm conclusions in this area. In sum, the core arguments of Thornberry's theory have some support and the data certainly suggest that theories of crime need to consider both reciprocal effects and developmental issues. At the same time, it should be noted that Thornberry and Krohn (2005) recently suggested a revision in their integrated theory, with their revision looking at additional stages of the life course and incorporating biological variables and individual traits.

Reprinted from Terence P. Thornberry, "Toward an Interactional Theory of Delinquency" in *Criminology* 25. Copyright © 1987 by the American Society of Criminology. Reprinted by permission of the American Society of Criminology.

References

Kubrin, Charis E., Thomas D. Stucky, and Marvin D. Krohn. 2009. *Researching Theories of Crime and Deviance*. New York: Oxford University Press.

Thornberry, Terence P. 1996. "Empirical Support for Interactional Theory." In J. David Hawkins (ed.), *Delinquency and Crime: Current Theories*, pp. 198–235. Cambridge, UK: Cambridge University Press.

Thornberry, Terence P. and Marvin D. Krohn. 2005. "Applying Interactional Theory to the Explanation of Continuity and Change in Antisocial Behavior." In David P. Farrington (ed.), *Integrated Developmental and Life-Course Theories of Offending*, pp. 183–210. New Brunswick, NJ: Transaction.

Thornberry, Terence P., Marvin D. Krohn, Alan J. Lizotte, Carolyn A. Smith, and Pamela K. Porter. 1998. "Taking Stock: An Overview of Findings From the Rochester Youth Development Survey." Paper presented at the annual meeting of the American Society of Criminology, Washington, D.C.

Thornberry, Terence P., Alan J. Lizotte, Marvin D. Krohn, Carolyn A. Smith, and Pamela K. Porter. 2003. "Causes and Consequences of Delinquency." In Terence P. Thornberry and Marvin D. Krohn (eds.), *Taking Stock of Delinquency*, pp. 11–46. New York: Kluwer Academic.

A variety of sociological theories have been developed to explain the onset and maintenance of delinquent behavior. Currently, three are of primary importance: social control theory (Hirschi, 1969), social learning theory (Akers, 1977), and integrated models that combine them into a broader body of explanatory principles (Elliott, Ageton, and Canter, 1979; Elliott, Huizinga, and Ageton, 1985).

Control theory argues that delinquency emerges whenever the social and cultural constraints over human conduct are substantially attenuated. As Hirschi states in his classic presentation (1969), control theory assumes that we would all be deviant if only we dared. Learning theory, on the other hand, posits that there is no natural impulse toward delinquency. Indeed, delinquent behavior must be learned through the same processes and mechanisms as conforming behavior. Because of these different starting points, control and learning models give causal priority to somewhat different concepts, and integrated models capitalize on these complementary approaches. Muting the assumptive differences, integrated theories meld together propositions from these (and sometimes other theories—for example, strain) to explain delinquent behavior.

Although these approaches have substantially informed our understanding of the causes of delinquency, they and other contemporary theories suffer from three fundamental limitations. First, they rely on unidirectional rather than reciprocal causal structures. By and large, current theories ignore reciprocal effects in which delinquent behavior is viewed as part of a more general social nexus, affected by, but also affecting, other social factors. Second, current theories tend to be nondevelopmental, specifying causal models for only a narrow age range, usually midadolescence. As a result, they fail to capitalize on developmental patterns to explain the initiation, maintenance, and desistance of delinquency. Finally, contemporary theories tend to assume uniform causal effects throughout the social structure. By ignoring the person's structural position, they fail to provide an understanding of the sources of initial variation in both delinquency and its presumed causes. In combination, these three limitations have led to theories that are narrowly conceived and which provide incomplete and, at times, misleading models of the causes of delinquency.

The present article develops an interactional theory of delinquency that addresses and attempts to respond to each of these limitations. The model proposed here pays particular attention to the first issue, recursive versus reciprocal causal structures, since the development of dynamic models is seen as essential to represent accurately the interactional settings in which delinquency develops.

Origins and Assumptions

The basic premise of the model proposed here is that human behavior occurs in social interaction and can therefore best be explained by models that focus on interactive processes. Rather than viewing adolescents as propelled along a unidirectional pathway to one or another outcome—that is, delinquency or conformity—it argues that adolescents interact with other people and institutions and that behavioral outcomes are formed by that interactive process. For example, the delinquent behavior of an adolescent is formed in part by how he and his parents *interact* over time, not simply by the child's perceived, and presumably invariant, *level* of attachment to parents. Moreover, since it is an interactive system, the behaviors of others—for example, parents and school officials—are influenced both by each other and by the adolescent, including his or her delinquent behavior. If this view is correct, then interactional effects have to be modeled explicitly if we are to understand the social and psychological processes involved with initiation into delinquency, the maintenance of such behavior, and its eventual reduction.

Interactional theory develops from the same intellectual tradition as the theories mentioned above, especially the Durkheimian tradition of social control. It asserts that the fundamental cause of delinquency lies in the weakening of social constraints over the conduct of the individual. Unlike classical control theory, however, it does not assume that the attenuation of controls leads directly to delinquency. The weakening of controls simply allows for a much wider array of behavior, including continued conventional action, failure as indicated by school dropout and sporadic employment histories, alcoholism, mental illness, delinquent and criminal careers, or some combination of these outcomes. For the freedom resulting from weakened bonds to be channeled into delinquency, especially serious prolonged delinquency, requires an interactive setting in which

delinquency is learned, performed, and reinforced. This view is similar to Cullen's structuring perspective which draws attention to the indeterminancy of deviant behavior.

> It can thus be argued that there is an *indeterminate* and not a determinate or etiologically specific relationship between motivational variables on the one hand and any particular form of deviant behavior on the other hand. (Cullen, 1984: 5)

Although heavily influenced by control and learning theories, and to a lesser extent by strain and culture conflict theories, this is not an effort at theoretical integration as that term is usually used (Elliott, 1985). Rather, this paper is guided by what we have elsewhere called theoretical elaboration (Thornberry, 1987). In this instance, a basic control theory is extended, or elaborated upon, using available theoretical perspectives and empirical findings to provide a more accurate model of the causes of delinquency. In the process of elaboration, there is no requirement to resolve disputes among other theories—for example, their different assumptions about the origins of deviance (Thornberry, 1987: 15–18); all that is required is that the propositions of the model developed here be consistent with one another and with the assumptions about deviance stated above.

Organization

The presentation of the interactional model begins by identifying the central concepts to be included in the model. Next, the underlying theoretical structure of the proposed model is examined and the rationale for moving from unidirectional to reciprocal causal models is developed. The reciprocal model is then extended to include a developmental perspective, examining the theoretical saliency of different variables at different developmental stages. Finally, the influence of the person's position in the social structure is explored. Although in some senses the last issue is logically prior to the others, since it is concerned with sources of initial variation in the causal variables, it is discussed last so that the reciprocal relationships among the concepts—the heart of an interactional perspective—can be more fully developed.

Theoretical Concepts

Given these basic premises, an interactional model must respond to two overriding issues. First, how are traditional social constraints over behavior weakened and, second, once weakened, how is the resulting freedom channeled into delinquent patterns? To address these issues, the present article presents an initial version of an interactional model, focusing on the interrelationships among six concepts: attachment to parents, commitment to school, belief in conventional values, associations with delinquent peers, adopting delinquent values, and engaging in delinquent behavior. These concepts form the core of the theoretical model since they are central to social psychological theories of delinquent behavior. These concepts form the core of the theoretical model since they are central to social psychological theories of delinquency and since they have been shown in numerous studies to be strongly related to subsequent delinquent behavior (see Elliott et al., 1985, chs. 1–3, for an excellent review of this literature).

The first three derive from Hirschi's version of control theory (1969) and represent the primary mechanisms by which adolescents are bonded to conventional middle-class society. When those elements of the bond are weakened, behavioral freedom increases considerably. For that freedom to lead to delinquent behavior, however, interactive settings that reinforce delinquency are required. In the model, those settings are represented by two concepts: associations with delinquent peers and the formation of delinquent values which derive primarily from social learning theory.

For the purpose of explicating the overall theoretical perspective, each of these concepts is defined quite broadly. Attachment to parents includes the affective relationship between parent and child, communication patterns, parenting skills such as monitoring and discipline, parent-child conflict, and the like. Commitment to school refers to the stake in conformity the adolescent has developed and includes such factors as success in school, perceived importance of education, attachment to teachers, and involvement in school activities. Belief in conventional values represents the granting of legitimacy to such middle-class values as education, personal industry, financial success, deferral of gratification, and the like.

Three delinquency variables are included in the model. Association with delinquent peers includes the level of attachment to peers, the delinquent behavior and values of peers, and their reinforcing reactions to the adolescent's own delinquent or conforming behavior. It is a continuous measure that can vary from groups that are heavily delinquent to those that are almost entirely nondelinquent. Delinquent values refer to the granting of legitimacy to delinquent activities as acceptable modes of behavior as well as a general willingness to violate the law to achieve other ends.

Delinquent behavior, the primary outcome variable, refers to acts that place the youth at risk for adjudication; it ranges from status offenses to serious violent activities. Since the present model is an interactional one, interested not only in explaining delinquency but in explaining the effects of delinquency on other variables, particular attention is paid to prolonged involvement in serious delinquency. . . .

Model Specification

A causal model allowing for reciprocal relationships among the six concepts of interest—attachment to parents, commitment to school, belief in conventional values, association with delinquent peers, delinquent values, and delinquent behavior—is presented in Figure 44.1. This model refers to the period of early adolescence, from about ages 11 to 13, when delinquent careers are beginning, but prior to the period at which delinquency reachers its apex in terms of seriousness and frequency. In the following sections the model is extended to later ages.

The specification of causal effects begins by examining the three concepts that form the heart of social learning theories of delinquency—delinquent peers, delinquent values, and delinquent behavior. For now we focus on the reciprocal nature of the relationships, ignoring until later variations in the strength of the relationships.

Traditional social learning theory specifies a causal order among these variables in which delinquent associations affect delinquent values and, in turn, both produce delinquent behavior (Akers, Krohn, Lanza-Kaduce, and Radosevich, 1979; Matsueda, 1982). Yet, for each of the dyadic relationships involving these variables, other theoretical perspectives and much empirical evidence suggest the appropriateness of reversing this causal order. For example, social learning theory proposes that associating with delinquents, or more precisely, people who hold and reinforce delinquent values, increases the chances of delinquent behavior (Akers, 1977). Yet, as far back as the work of the Gluecks (1950) this specification has been challenged. Arguing that "birds of a feather flock together," the Gluecks propose that youths who are delinquent seek out and associate with others who share those tendencies. From this perspective, rather than being a cause of delinquency, associations are the result of delinquents seeking out and associating with like-minded peers.

An attempt to resolve the somewhat tedious argument over the temporal priority of associations and behavior is less productive theoretically than capitalizing on the interactive nature of human behavior and treating the relationship as it probably is a reciprocal one. People often take on the behavioral repertoire of their associates but, at the same time, they often seek out associates who share their behavioral interests. Individuals clearly behave this way in conventional settings, and there is no reason to assume that deviant activities, such as delinquency, are substantially different in this regard.

Similar arguments can be made for the other two relationships among the delinquency variables. Most recent theories of delinquency, following the lead of social learning theory, posit that delinquent associations lead to the formation of delinquent values. Subcultural theories, however, especially those that derive from a cultural deviance perspective (Miller, 1958) suggest that values precede the formation of peer groups. Indeed, it is the socialization of adolescents into the "lower-class culture" and its particular value system that leads them to associate with delinquent peers in the first place. This specification can also be derived from a social control perspective as demonstrated in Weis and Sederstrom's social development model (1981) and Burkett and Warren's social selection model (1987).

Finally, the link between delinquent values and delinquent behavior restates, in many ways, the basic social psychological question of the relationship between attitudes and behavior. Do attitudes form behavior patterns or does behavior lead to attitude formation? Social psychological research, especially in cognitive psychology and balance models (for example, Festinger, 1957; Brehm and Cohen, 1962) points to the reciprocal nature of this relationship. It suggests that people indeed behave in a manner consistent with their attitudes, but also that behavior is one of the most persuasive forces in the formation and maintenance of attitudes.

Such a view of the relationship between delinquent values and behavior is consistent with Hindelang's findings:

This general pattern of results indicates that one can "predict" a respondent's self approval [of illegal behaviors] from knowledge of that respondent's involvement/non-involvement [in delinquency] with fewer errors than vice-versa. (1974: 382)

It is also consistent with recent deterrence research which demonstrates that the "experiential effect," in which behavior affects attitudes, is much stronger than the deterrent effect, in which attitudes affect behavior (Paternoster, Saltzman, Chiricos, and Waldo 1983).

Although each of these relationships appears to be reciprocal, the predicted strengths of the associations are not of equal strength during the early adolescent period (see Figure 44.1). Beliefs that delinquent conduct is acceptable and positively valued may be emerging, but such beliefs are not fully articulated for 11- to 13-year-olds. Because of their emerging quality, they are viewed as more effect than cause, produced by delinquent behavior and associations with delinquent peers. As these values emerge, however, they have feedback effects, albeit relatively weak ones at these ages, on behavior and associations. That is, as the values become more fully articulated and delinquency becomes positively valued, it increases the likelihood of such behavior and further reinforces associations with like-minded peers.

Summary. When attention is focused on the interrelationships among associations with delinquent peers, delinquent values, and delinquent behavior, it appears that they are, in fact, reciprocally related. The world of human behavior is far more complex than a simple recursive one in which a temporal order can be imposed on interactional variables of this nature. Interactional theory sees these three concepts as embedded in a causal loop, each reinforcing the others over time. Regardless of where the individual enters the loop, the following obtains: delinquency increases associations with delinquent peers and delinquent values; delinquent values increase delinquent behavior and associations with delinquent peers; and associations with delinquent peers increases delinquent behavior and delinquent values. The question now concerns the identification of factors that lead some youth, but not others, into this spiral of increasing delinquency.

Figure 44.1
A Reciprocal Model of Delinquent Involvement at Early Adolescence[a]

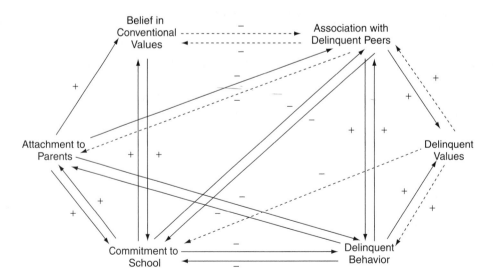

[a] Solid Lines represent stronger effects; dashed lines represent weaker effects.

Social Control Effects

As indicated at the outset of this essay, the premise of interactional theory is that the fundamental cause of delinquency is the attenuation of social controls over the person's conduct. Whenever bonds to the conventional world are substantially weakened, the individual is freed from moral constraints and is at risk for a wide array of deviant activities, including delinquency. The primary mechanisms that bind adolescents to the conventional world are attachment to parents, commitment to school, and belief in conventional values, and their role in the model can now be examined.

During the early adolescent years, the family is the most salient arena for social interaction and involvement and, because of this, attachment to parents has a stronger influence on other aspects of the youth's life at this stage than it does at later stages of development. With this in mind, attachment to parents is predicted to affect four other variables. Since youths who are attached to their parents are sensitive to their wishes (Hirschi, 1969: 16–19) and, since parents are almost universally supportive of the conventional world, these children are likely to be strongly committed to school and to espouse conventional values. In addition, youths who are attached to their parents, again because of their sensitivity to parental wishes, are unlikely to associate with delinquent peers or to engage in delinquent behavior.

In brief, parental influence is seen as central to controlling the behavior of youths at these relatively early ages. Parents who have a strong affective bond with their children, who communicate with them, who exercise appropriate parenting skills, and so forth, are likely to lead their children towards conventional actions and beliefs and away from delinquent friends and actions.

On the other hand, attachment to parents is not seen as an immutable trait, impervious to the effects of other variables. Indeed, associating with delinquent peers, not being committed to school, and engaging in delinquent behavior are so contradictory to parental expectations that they tend to diminish the level of attachment between parent and child. Adolescents who fail at school, who associate with delinquent peers, and who engage in delinquent conduct are, as a consequence, likely to jeopardize their affective bond with their parents, precisely because these behaviors suggest that the "person does not care about the wishes and expectations of other people..." (Hirschi, 1969: 18), in this instance, his or her parents.

Turning next to belief in conventional values, this concept is involved in two different causal loops. First, it strongly affects commitment to school and in turn is affected by commitment to school. In essence, this loop posits a behavioral and attitudinal consistency in the conventional realm. Second, a weaker loop is posited between belief in conventional values and associations with delinquent peers. Youths who do not grant legitimacy to conventional values are more apt to associate with delinquent friends who share those views, and those friendships are likely to attenuate further their beliefs in conventional values. This reciprocal specification is supported by Burkett and Warren's findings concerning religious beliefs and peer associations (1987). Finally, youths who believe in conventional values are seen as somewhat less likely to engage in delinquent behavior.

Although belief in conventional values plays some role in the genesis of delinquency, its impact is not particularly strong. For example, it is not affected by delinquent behavior, nor is it related to delinquent values. This is primarily because belief in conventional values appears to be quite invariant, regardless of class of origin or delinquency status, for example, most people strongly assert conventional values (Short and Strodtbeck, 1965: ch. 3). Nevertheless, these beliefs do exert some influence in the model, especially with respect to reinforcing commitment to school.

Finally, the impact of commitment to school is considered. This variable is involved in reciprocal loops with both of the other bonding variables. Youngsters who are attached to their parents are likely to be committed to and succeed in school, and that success is likely to reinforce the close ties to their parents. Similarly, youths who believe in conventional values are likely to be committed to school, the primary arena in which they can act in accordance with those values, and, in turn, success in that arena is likely to reinforce the beliefs.

In addition to its relationships with the other control variables, commitment to school also has direct effects on two of the delinquency variables. Students who are committed to succeeding in school are unlikely to associate with delinquents or to engage in substantial amounts of serious repetitive delinquent behavior. These youths have built up a stake in conformity and should be unwilling to jeopardize that investment by either engaging in delinquent behavior or by associating with those who do.

Low commitment to school is not seen as leading directly to the formation of delinquent values, however. Its primary effect on delinquent values is indirect, via associations with delinquent peers and delinquent behavior (Conger, 1980: 137). While school failure may lead to a reduced commitment to conventional values, it does not follow that it directly increases the acceptance of values that support delinquency.

Commitment to school, on the other hand, is affected by each of the delinquent variables in the model. Youths who accept values that are consistent with delinquent behavior, who associate with other delinquents, and who engage in delinquent behavior are simply unlikely candidates to maintain an active commitment to school and the conventional world that school symbolizes.

Summary. Attachment to parents, commitment to school, and belief in conventional values reduce delinquency by cementing the person to conventional institutions and people. When these elements of the bond to conventional society are strong, delinquency is unlikely, but when they are weak the individual is placed at much greater risk for delinquency. When viewed from an interactional perspective, two additional qualities of these concepts become increasingly evident.

First, attachment to parents, commitment to school, and belief in conventional values are not static attributes of the person, invariant over time. These concepts interact with one another during the developmental process. For some youths the levels of attachment, commitment, and belief increase as these elements reinforce one another, while for other youths the interlocking nature of these relationships suggests a greater and greater attenuation of the bond will develop over time.

Second, the bonding variables appear to be reciprocally linked to delinquency, exerting a causal impact on associations with delinquent peers and delinquent behavior; they also are causally effected by these variables. As the youth engages in more and more delinquent conduct and increasingly associates with delinquent peers, the level of his bond to the conventional world is further weakened. Thus, while the weakening of the bond to conventional society may be an initial cause of delinquency, delinquency eventually becomes its own indirect cause precisely because of its ability to weaken further the person's bonds to family, school, and conventional beliefs. The implications of this amplifying causal structure is examined below. First, however, the available support for reciprocal models is reviewed and the basic model is extended to later developmental stages. . . .

Developmental Extensions

The previous section developed a strategy for addressing one of the three major limitations of delinquency theories mentioned in the introduction—namely, their unidirectional causal structure. A second limitation is the nondevelopmental posture of most theories which tend to provide a cross-sectional picture of the factors associated with delinquency at one age, but which do not provide a rationale for understanding how delinquent behavior develops over time. The present section offers a developmental extension of the basic model.

Middle Adolescence

First, a model for middle adolescence, when the youths are approximately 15 or 16 years of age is presented. This period represents the highest rates of involvement in delinquency and is the reference period, either implicitly or explicitly, for most theories of delinquent involvement. Since the models for the early and middle adolescent periods have essentially the same structure and causal relationships (Figure 44.1), discussion focuses on the differences between them and does not repeat the rationale for individual causal effects.

Perhaps the most important difference concerns attachment to parents which is involved in relatively few strong relationships. By this point in the life cycle, the most salient variables involved in the production of delinquency are likely to be external to the home, associated with the youth's activities in school and peer networks. This specification is consistent with empirical results for subjects in this age range (Johnson, 1979: 105; and Schoenberg, 1975, quoted in Johnson). Indeed, Johnson concludes that

> an adolescent's public life has as much or more to do with his or her deviance or conformity than do 'under-the-roof' experiences. (1979: 116)

This is not to say that attachment to parents is irrelevant; such attachments are involved in enhancing commitment to school and belief in conventional values, and in preventing associations with delinquent peers. It is just that the overall strength of parental effects are weaker than at earlier ages when the salience of the family as a locus of interaction and control was greater.

The second major change concerns the increased importance of delinquent values as a causal factor. It is still embedded in the causal loop with the other two delinquency variables, but now it is as much cause as effect. Recall that at the younger ages delinquent values were seen as emerging, produced by associations with delinquent peers and delinquent behavior. Given their emergent nature, they were not seen as primary causes of other variables. At midadolescence, however, when delinquency is at its apex, these values are more fully articulated and have stronger effects on other variables. First, delinquent values are seen as major reinforcers of both delinquent associations and delinquent behavior. In general, espousing values supportive of delinquency tends to increase the potency of this causal loop. Second, since delinquent values are antithetical to the conventional settings of school and family, youths who espouse them are less likely to be committed to school and attached to parents. Consistent with the reduced saliency of family at these ages, the feedback effect to school is seen as stronger than the feedback effect to parents.

By and large, the other concepts in the model play the same role at these ages as they do at the earlier ones. Thus, the major change from early to middle adolescence concerns the changing saliency of some of the theoretical concepts. The family declines in relative importance while the adolescent's own world of school and peers takes on increasing significance. While these changes occur, the overall structure of the theory remains constant. These interactive variables are still seen as mutually reinforcing over time.

Later Adolescence

Finally, the causes of delinquency during the transition from adolescence to adulthood, about ages 18 to 20, can be examined. At these ages one should more properly speak of crime than delinquency, but for consistency we will continue to use the term delinquency in the causal diagrams and employ the terms delinquency and crime interchangeably in the text.

Two new variables are added to the model to reflect the changing life circumstances at this stage of development. The more important of these is commitment to conventional activities which includes employment, attending college, and military service. Along with the transition to the world of work, there is a parallel transition from the family of origin to one's own family. Although this transition does not peak until the early 20s, for many people its influence is beginning at this stage. Included in this concept are marriage, plans for marriage, and plans for childrearing. These new variables largely replace attachment to parents and commitment to school in the theoretical scheme; they represent the major sources of bonds to conventional society for young adults.

Both attachment to parents and commitment to school remain in the model but take on the cast of exogenous variables. Attachment to parents has only a minor effect on commitment to school, and commitment to school is proposed to affect only commitment to conventional activities and, more weakly, delinquent behavior.

The other three variables considered in the previous models—association with delinquent peers, delinquent values, and delinquent behavior—are still hypothesized to be embedded in an amplifying causal loop. As indicated above, this loop is most likely to occur among adolescents who, at earlier ages, were freed from the controlling influence of parents and school. Moreover, via the feedback paths delinquent peers, delinquent values, and delinquent behavior further alienate the youth from parents and diminish commitment to school. Once this spiral begins, the probability of sustained delinquency increases.

This situation, if it continued uninterrupted, would yield higher and higher rates of crime as the subjects matured. Such an outcome is inconsistent with the desistance that has been observed during this age period (Wolfgang, Thornberry, and Figlio, 1987). Rates of delinquency and crime begin to subside by the late teenage years, a phenomenon often attributed to "maturational reform." Such an explanation, however, is tautological since it claims that crime stops when adolescents get older, because they get older. It is also uninformative since the concept of maturational reform is theoretically undefined.

A developmental approach, however, offers an explanation for desistance. As the developmental process unfolds, life circumstances change, developmental milestones are met (or, for some missed),

new social roles are created, and new networks of attachments and commitments emerge. The effects of these changes enter the processual model to explain new and often dramatically different behavioral patterns. In the present model, these changes are represented by commitment to conventional activity and commitment to family.

Commitment to conventional activity is influenced by a number of variables, including earlier attachment to parents, commitment to school, and belief in conventional values. And once the transition to the world of work is made, tremendous opportunities are afforded for new and different effects in the delinquency model. Becoming committed to conventional activities—work, college, military service, and so on—reduces the likelihood of delinquent behavior and associations with delinquent peers because it builds up a stake in conformity that is antithetical to delinquency.

Moreover, since the delinquency variables are still embedded in a causal loop, the effect of commitment to conventional activities tends to resonate throughout the system. But, because of the increased saliency of a new variable, commitment to conventional activities, the reinforcing loop is now set in motion to *reduce* rather than increase delinquent and criminal involvement.

The variable of commitment to family has similar, albeit weaker, effects since the transition to the family is only beginning at these ages. Nevertheless, commitment to family is proposed to reduce both delinquent associations and delinquent values and to increase commitment to conventional activity. In general, as the individual takes on the responsibilities of family, the bond to conventional society increases, placing additional constraints on behavior and precluding further delinquency.

These changes do not occur in all cases, however, nor should they be expected to since many delinquents continue on to careers in adult crime. In the Philadelphia cohort of 1945, 51 percent of the juvenile delinquents were also adult offenders, and the more serious and prolonged the delinquent careers were, the greater the odds of an adult career (Wolfgang et al., 1987: ch. 4).

The continuation of criminal careers can also be explained by the nature of the reciprocal effects included in this model. In general, extensive involvement in delinquency at earlier ages feeds back upon and weakens attachment to parents and commitment to school (see Figure 44.1). These variables, as well as involvement in delinquency itself, weaken later commitment to family and to conventional activities (Figure 44.1). Thus, these new variables, commitment to conventional activities and to family, are affected by the person's situation at earlier stages and do not "automatically" alter the probability of continued criminal involvement. If the initial bonds are extremely weak, the chances of new bonding variables being established to break the cycle towards criminal careers are low and it is likely that criminal behavior will continue. . . .

Structural Effects

Structural variables, including race, class, sex, and community of residence, refer to the person's location in the structure of social roles and statuses. The manner in which they are incorporated in the interactional model is illustrated here by examining only one of them, social class of origin.

Although social class is often measured continuously, a categorical approach is more consistent with the present model and with most theories of delinquency that incorporate class as a major explanatory variable—for example, strain and social disorganization theories. For our purpose, the most important categories are the lower class, the working lower class, and the middle class.

The lower class is composed of those who are chronically or sporadically unemployed, receive welfare, and subsist at or below the poverty level. They are similar to Johnson's "underclass" (1979). The working lower class is composed of those with more stable work patterns, training for semiskilled jobs, and incomes that allow for some economic stability. For these families, however,

the hold on even a marginal level of occupational and economic security is always tenuous. Finally, the middle class refers to all families above these lower levels. Middle-class families have achieved some degree of economic success and stability and can reasonably expect to remain at that level or improve their standing over time.

The manner in which the social class of origin affects the interactional variables and the behavioral trajectories can be demonstrated by comparing the life expectancies of children from lower- and middle-class families. As compared to children from a middle-class background, children from a lower-class background are more apt to have (1) disrupted family processes and environments (Conger, McCarty, Wang, Lahey, and Kroop, 1984; Wahler, 1980); (2) poorer preparation for school (Cloward and Ohlin, 1960); (3) belief structures influenced by the traditions of the American lower class (Anderson, 1976; Miller, 1958) and (4) greater exposure to neighborhoods with high rates of crime (Braithwaite, 1981; Shaw and McKay, 1942). The direction of all these effects is such that we would expect children from lower-class families to be *initially* less bonded to conventional society and more exposed to delinquent values, friends, and behaviors.

As one moves towards the working lower class, both the likelihood and the potency of the factors just listed decrease. As a result, the initial values of the interactional variables improve but, because of the tenuous nature of economic and social stability for these families, both the bonding variables and the delinquency variables are still apt to lead to considerable amounts of delinquent conduct. Finally, youths from middle-class families, given their greater stability and economic security, are likely to start with a stronger family structure, greater stakes in conformity, and higher chances of success, and all of these factors are likely to reduce the likelihood of initial delinquent involvement.

In brief, the initial values of the interactional variables are systematically related to the social class of origin. Moreover, since these variables are reciprocally related, it follows logically that social class is systematically related to the behavioral trajectories described above. Youngsters from the lowest classes have the highest probability of moving forward on a trajectory of increasing delinquency. Starting from a position of low bonding to conventional institutions and a high delinquency environment, the reciprocal nature of the inter-relationships leads inexorably towards extremely high rates of delinquent and criminal involvement. Such a view is consistent with prevalence data which show that by age 18, 50 percent, and by age 30, 70 percent of low SES minority males have an official police record (Wolfgang et al., 1987).

On the other hand, the expected trajectory of middle-class youths suggests that they will move toward an essentially conforming life-style, in which their stakes in conformity increase and more and more preclude serious and prolonged involvement in delinquency. Finally, because the initial values of the interactional variables are mixed and indecisive for children from lower-working-class homes, their behavioral trajectories are much more volatile and the outcome much less certain.

Summary. Interactional theory asserts that both the initial values of the process variables and their development over time are systematically related to the social class of origin. Moreover, parallel arguments can be made for other structural variables, especially those associated with class, such as race, ethnicity, and the social disorganization of the neighborhood. Like class of origin, these variables are systematically related to variables such as commitment to school and involvement in delinquent behavior, and therefore, as a group, these structural variables set the stage on which the reciprocal effects develop across the life cycle.

Discussion Questions

1. Give three examples of reciprocal causal effects from Thornberry's model. What does Thornberry mean by an "amplifying causal structure" or a "spiral of increasing delinquency"?
2. Describe how Thornberry's model changes from early to late adolescence (what variables decrease or increase in importance, what new variables enter the model).
3. Why are some adolescents able to desist from delinquency in early adulthood, while others continue to engage in crime?
4. Why does Thornberry state that lower class children "have the highest probability of moving forward on a trajectory of increasing delinquency"?

45. Control Balance Theory

Charles R. Tittle

Control balance theory is perhaps the most complex and ambitious of the major integrated theories. The theory draws on many individual theories of crime, includes a large number of variables, and describes a complex set of relationships among these variables. The theory seeks to explain a broad range of criminal and deviant acts, with six broad categories of crime and deviance being described. A distinguishing feature of the theory is that it seeks to explain not only whether people will engage in crime but also the type of crime or deviance they will commit. And while the theory focuses on the explanation of individual crime and deviance, it can also explain rates of deviance in social groups.

At the core of the theory is the concept of control balance, which strongly influences both the predisposition for deviance and the constraints against (costs of) deviance. As Tittle (1995: 142) states,

> *The central premise of the theory is that the amount of control to which people are subject relative to the amount of control they can exercise affects their general probability of committing some deviant acts as well as the probability that they will commit specific types of deviance. Deviant behavior is interpreted as a device, or maneuver, that helps people escape deficits and extend surpluses of control.*

In particular, people with control deficits (subject to more control than they can exercise) or control surpluses (subject to less control than they can exercise) are more likely to engage in deviance, with such deviance being a means to reduce their deficits or extend their surpluses. The extent of their control deficit or control surplus influences the type of deviance they will engage in (see also Tittle, 2001).

Whether such individuals engage in deviance depends, however, on several factors, including the individual's predisposition for deviance (which is influenced by the degree of control imbalance), situational provocations that are debasing or humiliating, the opportunity to engage in deviance, and the constraints against or costs of deviance (which is influenced by the degree of control deficit or surplus). Also, a number of "contingencies" (e.g., moral beliefs, ability to commit the deviant act) can influence the likelihood and nature of deviance. The best way to understand the theory is to relate these concepts to the example that Tittle uses throughout the selection.

It is important to note that Tittle (2004) recently revised the theory. As indicated below, control balance theory not only explains the occurrence of deviant acts, but also has something to say about the types of deviance that are committed. Tittle (1995) originally classified deviant acts into several categories, such as "defiance," "predation," "exploitation," and "plunder." He has now abandoned that classification, and instead classifies deviant acts according to their "control balance desirability" (Tittle, 2004). The control balance desirability of a deviant act depends on (1) the extent to which the

Copyright © 2001. Reprinted by permission of Roxbury Publishing Company.

act enhances the individual's level of control over the long term, and (2) the extent to which the act is "impersonal" ("can be done without direct, hands-on action by the individual") (Tittle, 2004: 405). To use an example from Tittle (2004: 406), a deviant act like the "massive underpricing of a company's product to drive a competitor out of business" is quite high in control balance desirability. If successful, this act is likely to increase the control of the company over the long term (by driving the competitor out of business) and it is impersonal—since the company executives do not have to personally confront anyone outside the company. Tittle describes how different deviant acts might be ranked according to their "control balance desirability." And he begins to describe how a range of factors, including the individual's level of control imbalance, influence the control balance desirability ranking of the deviant act that is selected. For example, individuals with control surpluses are more likely to engage in deviant acts that are high in control balance desirability. Among other things, such individuals have the resources to get others to perform their deviant acts.

Tittle (2004) has also come to assign a more central role to the individual's level of self-control. He argues that individuals who experience control imbalances generally act in a rational manner. In particular, they attempt to maximize the control balance desirability of the deviant acts they select. Individuals who are low in self-control, however, are more likely to act in an irrational manner. They have trouble controlling their emotions, and often respond to provocations by engaging in deviant acts that have little prospect for increasing their long-term levels of control. An individual who is low in self-control, for example, might punch the co-worker who insulted her rather than covertly starting a smear campaign to get the co-worker fired.

The recent revisions in control balance theory are not described in the selection below. Rather, this selection focuses on the core parts of Tittle's theory—the role of control imbalances in producing deviance and the factors which influence the effect of control imbalances on deviance. At the same

time, this selection does point to some of the factors that influence the type of deviance selected—including the seriousness of the deviant act.

References

Tittle, Charles R. 1995. *Control Balance: Toward a General Theory of Deviance*. Boulder, CO: Westview.

——. 2001. "Control Balance." In Raymond Paternoster and Ronet Bachman (eds.), *Explaining Criminals and Crime*, pp. 315–334. Los Angeles: Roxbury.

——. 2004. "Refining Control Balance Theory." *Theoretical Criminology* 8: 395–428.

———

Suppose you ask a question in this class and your teacher says, "That is the stupidest question any student has ever asked; how did you get into college anyway?" How do you imagine it would make you feel, and what do you think you would do about it? If you are like most people, you would probably feel humiliated, become conscious of your inability to control what happens, and you would want to show the teacher and the other students that you are not the lowly nincompoop implied by the teacher's remark. But what could you do?

An Illustrative Overview

There are several things you might do if you were humiliated by a professor. For one thing, you might make up your mind to study really hard, to "ace" the next test, to succeed in life, and later, after having succeeded, contact that teacher and recall the put-down. Such a response could be called "conformity." However, you might not be able to do those things, and if you did, it would take years; the other students who witnessed the debasement probably would not learn about your triumph; and before too long the pain of the moment would fade, causing you to lose that motivation to succeed in life.

A quicker, more satisfying reaction would be to slug the professor. We'll call this reaction "predation." An assault is not hard to do, and it would overcome your humiliation while giving you a feeling of control. The problem, of course, is that slugging the professor would probably cause you a lot more trouble than it is worth. The teacher may slug you back, the police may arrest you, the university may expel you, and your future plans to go to law school may be jeopardized; in any case you probably wouldn't get credit for the course. So, you probably won't take that kind of drastic action.

You might also start to denigrate the teacher to your friends, give her a poor mark on the student evaluations at the end of the term (even though in other respects this is an excellent teacher), be sullen and uncooperative during the rest of the semester, show contempt when she tries to make a joke in class, or possibly even make loud, disruptive noises. Such actions constitute a form of deviance (usually noncriminal) called "defiance." This, too, is easy to accomplish, and though it will be less gratifying than having slugged the teacher, it will at least help restore your sense of dignity and give you a measure of control over your own destiny. But there is also a potential cost associated with this conduct—you are not likely to do well in the class and the poor grade may affect your future. This cost, however, is much less than that associated with punching the teacher.

Still another possibility is simply to capitulate. In this maneuver, you decide that nothing you can do will help overcome your sense of degradation. You imagine that anything you might do will be met with a response by the teacher that produces even more humiliation and accentuates your lack of control. So you sit quietly, do everything the teacher asks or implies, stop imagining any other possibilities, and accept a permanent state of subordination in that class. If you do this, it is "submission," which may or may not be deviant, depending on how surrender of the human spirit is viewed in your social context. Submission, of course, is not satisfying but it may reflect your feelings of helplessness, and it

at least allows you to get through the semester, perhaps even with a good grade.

If you are from a wealthy, influential family you might have other options. One is to get somebody else to commit predation on your behalf ("exploitation"). For instance, you could ask your father to threaten to stop donating money to the university, or you could ask him to make trouble with the Board of Regents unless that teacher is disciplined or fired. Perhaps you could hire a private detective to gather dirt for jeopardizing the teacher's marriage. You might even employ some thugs to assault the teacher. All of these acts would restore your sense of control, and if you are highly positioned socially, it would be easy to do with little possibility that it would be costly to you. The teacher may not even learn you are responsible for those bad consequences, and the chances that the police will find out who assaulted the teacher or hired the thugs is slight. In other words, on balance, some of these things might be an advantageous response. The trouble is, you probably are not socially situated so as to make it possible.

An additional rare possibility, which would be conceivable only if you are exceptionally wealthy or powerful and are attending a private university owned by your family, or one that you could buy, would be to shut down the school. That way all the teachers could be dismissed, and you could establish a different school staffed with hand-picked professors whom you liked or who would do your bidding. Such deviant reactions (they are deviant because they violate normative expectations in such a way as to be socially unacceptable) that involve pursuing personal goals through broad scale actions with almost no regard for the consequences they have for others is called "plunder."

A final, almost unheard of reaction to your humiliation at the hands of the teacher might be to adopt a completely decadent lifestyle. In doing so, you would ignore all social rules and live a life of complete selfishness that shows utter disregard for the social system that produced your debasement. If you did this, you would lose all sense of direction in your life; you would pursue any and all impulses, including any whimsical pleasures, desires, and cruelties; and your actions would be completely without awareness or concern for others. Of course, you could resort to such decadence only if you were unbelievably wealthy or powerful so that you did not have to worry about sustenance or about what others might think or do about your behavior.

The Causal Process

Although there are many ways to deal with a teacher's humiliating response to a question, not all of the possibilities are equally likely. What influences what you are actually likely to do? According to control balance theory, the most important thing is the extent to which a possible response promises to overcome your sense of humiliation, weighed against the potential costly consequences of committing that act or acts. The greater the value of the act for extending your sense of control (thereby countering feelings of degradation) relative to the potential consequences of your actions (magnitude and potentiality of counter-controlling responses), the greater the chances that you will do it. This balancing of the control you might gain from deviant behavior against the control that will likely be directed back at you is called "control balancing." According to the theory, how the calculation turns out largely determines what you will do when you are provoked.

The control balancing process is similar for all people in all provocative situations, but it does not always unfold in the same way. For one thing, some people start with a lot more relative control than do other people. Those people with a lot of control can contemplate doing more serious things without worrying so much about what will happen in return. For example, if you are from a wealthy and influential family, your response to the hypothetical insulting teacher is probably going to be different from that of a student from a low-income family. That is because the potential counter controls that a wealthy student's deviant actions might elicit are less potent than those for a student with less initial control. In addition, no matter what a person's chances of stimulating counter control, that person may do no deviance because he is inhibited by moral considerations. Perhaps such a student has been taught from an early age to respect teachers and, as a result, has internalized the belief that it would be wrong to misbehave in a classroom. Conditions, such as morally based respect for teachers, that intervene into the control balancing process, are called "contingencies."

Control balance theory, therefore, postulates that there is a fundamental underlying process that leads to deviant behavior and that people's concerns about control are central to it. The process begins with some situational provocation, usually one that stimulates feelings of humiliation, that calls up an individual's awareness of his or her relative control potentiality. The theory contends that the likely outcome depends on how the provoked individual's ability to exercise control compares to the control that is likely to be exercised back if he or she commits various acts of deviance. However, because this underlying process of balancing is affected by a number of other things, criminal or deviant behavior results when a peculiar set of conditions converge.

Key Conditions

The most important condition is the person's *control ratio*, or

> the extent to which an individual can potentially exercise control over circumstances impinging on him, relative to the potential control that can be exercised by external entities and conditions against the individual.

Other conditions must also come together for deviance to occur: (1) a predisposition toward being motivated for deviance, (2) situational provocation that reminds a person of a control imbalance, (3) the transformation of predisposition into actual motivation for deviance, (4) opportunity for deviant response, and (5) the absence or relative weakness of constraint, so that the mental process of "control balancing" will result in a perceived gain in control. Altogether, then, there are six important conditions involved in deviant behavior. Each is considered separately, and then we will see how they fit together.

Control Ratio

Everybody has a global, *general control ratio* that roughly reflects their *typical* ability to exercise control relative to being the object of control. This global control ratio reflects all of one's statuses, roles, personal and physical characteristics, organizational contacts, and interpersonal relationships. All people also have numerous *situational control ratios* that represent their ability in specific circumstances to exercise control relative to being controlled.

A person's general control ratio suggests his or her average probability of being able to control rather than being controlled. Situational control ratios, however, focus on concrete contexts, such as at home, in a work situation, on a date, at school, or on the athletic field. An individual's control ratio, then, is not fixed; it varies from place to place, from time to time, and from situation to situation. Yet in general, and in any given context, one's control ratio conceivably can be estimated empirically.

Control ratios depend on individual characteristics as well as social or organizational variables. For example, almost all students exercise less control than that to which they are subject; they have a general control deficit—a ratio less than one. Because most students are relatively young, they have little control over adults, even though adults can exercise much control over them; because students are subordinates in classes and other university contexts, they have little control over professors and administrators, although professors and administrators have a lot of

control over them; because most students do not have occupations or careers, they have relatively few economic resources that might enable them to control commodities and services, even though economic circumstances exercise a great deal of control over them; and in interpersonal relationships, students may or may not have a favorable balance of control, depending on many things.

Despite the fact that most students have general control deficits, some specific students may have control surpluses in their group of residential friends (because of being highly respected), and they might have large surpluses of control in dating relationships (because somebody is in love with them or because they are exceptionally attractive and pleasant). Moreover, students who generally have control deficits may on occasion see those ratios boosted or lowered. Thus, a solitary student confronting a large number of professors may have a large control deficit, but if numerous students confront one professor, because of the shared collective control inherent in large numbers, each student's control ratio may be enhanced. Similarly, although students may generally have control deficits, the magnitude of those deficits may vary from course to course. In one class, a student may impress the professor with her intelligence or diligence, thereby gaining control from the professor's willingness to assume that student has some degree of mastery of the material. In another class, the student may have less control because the professor has low tolerance for any student mistakes.

Deviance grows from a process involving several sequential steps. Control ratios are important for all of those steps. You'll see later why that is true, and I will outline how the control ratio's influence is played out, but for now you should remember five things about control ratios: (1) control ratio is the key concept and variable in control balance theory, (2) some control ratios may consist of equal parts of control to be exercised and to be suffered; that is, they may be about equal to one, (3) control ratios may be unbalanced, reflecting either a deficit (a ratio less than one) or a surplus (a ratio greater than one), (4) control ratios are not entirely fixed because they may change as individuals change locales and social statuses or assume new roles; nevertheless, they can be characterized as more or less stable, and (5) individuals differ with respect to their control ratios.

Predisposition to Be Motivated

Although one's control ratio is the most important variable in explaining the probability and form of deviance a person is likely to commit, it does not work alone. In fact, it is only when a series of variables, including the control ratio, converge in particular ways that deviant behavior occurs. First, one has to be predisposed toward deviant motivation. Almost anyone may have such predisposition, but it does not become obvious without some blockage of a person's basic goals. Predisposition stems from the convergence of three inputs: (1) desire for autonomy, (2) an unbalanced control ratio, and (3) blockage of goals.

Autonomy Seeking

A necessary element in all deviant behavior, because it fuels the balancing process, is an underlying urge for autonomy. Such a desire is probably instilled in us as infants. It is expressed as an urge to escape control exercised against us and to extend our control over other people and circumstances. Because infants must depend for all their needs on others and on circumstances over which they have no control, they come to resent it. That resentment causes them to want to escape dependency. In addition, because caregivers are the first important people in everybody's lives, infants identify with caregivers; that is, they want to be like them. Because caregivers are controllers, identification with them produces a desire to extend control over others. Hence, everybody has a latent desire to escape the control that is arrayed against them and to extend their own control. . . .

Control Ratios and Predisposition

Desire for autonomy is one thing that affects predisposition for deviant motivation, but predisposition also depends on unbalanced control ratios. The greater the imbalance in the control that one can exercise relative to that to which he is subject, the greater will be the likelihood of that person's predisposition toward becoming motivated for deviance. Because everybody desires autonomy, unbalanced control ratios are latent sore spots that can, under certain conditions, flare into motivation for deviance. This is not to say that those with balanced control ratios are never motivated for deviance. Those with unbalanced control are simply more likely to become motivated, and so their degree of predisposition is greater.

Think back to the student humiliated by the teacher. That student, as all people presumably do, generally desires autonomy. She wants to escape control from others and from environmental constraints; in other words, the student wants to be a master of her own fate. In addition, she probably has a control imbalance—most likely a deficit, although some students, because of family or personal circumstances, may have a surplus. The professor's remarks would not matter to the student if that student did not desire autonomy, and it probably would not matter as much if the professor were dealing with somebody of equal control, say another professor of similar rank and stature. A putdown between equals has less force because it implies almost certain tit for tat, and it does not humiliate like an insult from a person of either lesser or greater control potential.

Goal Blockage

As noted in the paragraphs above, predisposition to become motivated for deviance depends on a desire for autonomy and on a control imbalance. In addition, predispositions are linked to blockages of human goals. If a person were, without restraint or barrier, accomplishing all of his or her goals, including the goal of exercising control, then the issue of deviance would almost never arise. If all of the goals of the student in our example were being accomplished, she would probably not be a classroom student in the first place, would not be asking questions of the professor, and would not be in a position to become humiliated and then contemplate a response.

Convergence to Produce Predisposition

Thus, the degree of predisposition for deviant motivation depends on how three things come together; the three things consist of a constant and two variables. The constant is the desire for autonomy that everybody has. The variables are (1) the extent to which the person's impulses (or goals) are blocked and (2) an imbalance of control. When these three things converge for an individual, that person is then in a state of readiness to experience motivation for deviant behavior.

Motivation

Provocation
Although many people are predisposed, they only occasionally actually become motivated for deviant behavior. Motivation occurs when a person becomes acutely aware of his control imbalance and realizes that deviant behavior can change that imbalance, either by overcoming a deficit or by extending a surplus. The conditions that transform predisposition into actual motivation exist in situations that a person may encounter. Those conditions consist of provocations and things that cause people who experience them to feel debased or humiliated. Sometimes predisposed people encounter situations that vividly remind them of their control imbalance. Such situational provocations may include, but are not limited to, the following: (1) somebody tells an individual what to do, especially in a commanding, harsh tone, (2) a person is jilted by a boyfriend or girlfriend, (3) bills arrive

on top of other bills that have piled up, (4) an individual's authority is questioned, or some rights a person thought she had are questioned, (5) an individual is pushed while waiting in line, (6) a person is stopped by the police, (7) someone is denied admission to a club, (8) an individual is hungry but is denied food because he has no money, or (9) a student gets a sharp or hostile reaction from a professor (as happened to our hypothetical student at the beginning of this essay).

All such situations, and many more, remind people of what their control imbalances are. For most students, these kinds of events would remind them that they have deficits of control. A few students, however, would be reminded that they have control surpluses; being reminded of a control surplus usually occurs when a person realizes that superior control is not at that moment producing the advantages that the person would normally expect. Situational provocations, then, alert the predisposed person to a control imbalance that otherwise she would have been only vaguely aware of, and situational provocations stimulate the alerted individual to search for some mechanism that might help change the imbalance. When a person wants to try to change a control imbalance quickly, deviant behavior often comes to mind.

Debasement
Acute awareness of a control imbalance, however, is usually not enough to motivate deviance. There must also be some negative emotion generated by the situation—a feeling of being debased, humiliated, or denigrated that intensifies the thought that deviance is a possible response to the provocations. Negative emotions produced by situational provocations are inside the person, but they grow out of external circumstances. How potential provocations are interpreted depends partly on individual characteristics. Sometimes provocation is unusual and directly humiliating in a way that would debase just about anybody; such was the case with our example of the

professor denigrating the student's intellect. At other times, however, provocation of some specific individuals stems from ordinary, routine events that ordinarily would not provoke most people or generate emotions of debasement. For instance, students routinely take examinations in college classes. Because it is an expected, everyday occurrence, taking an exam usually does not provoke acute awareness of a control imbalance. Occasionally, however, an individual student, say an older person who has returned to school or a teacher who has decided to obtain an advanced degree, will find examinations humiliating. Such people often think that being tested is beneath their dignity. To them, mere announcement of an exam may activate awareness of a control imbalance and evoke a feeling of debasement.

Convergence to Generate Motivation

Predisposed people—those for whom a desire for autonomy has converged with a control imbalance and some goal blockage—can sometimes become motivated to commit deviant acts. They do so when situations remind them of a control imbalance in a humiliating way. Motivation can be said to exist when deviant behavior comes to be perceived as a means to alter a control imbalance, thereby permitting the person to overcome debasement or humiliation. Motivation to commit deviance, therefore, is a variable. It may not occur at all, it may develop moderately, or it may be intense.

Opportunity

Although motivation depends somewhat on predisposition and is an essential element of deviant conduct, motivation does not always lead to deviant behavior; whether it does or not depends on other variables.

One of them is simple opportunity. Opportunity means that circumstances are such that a potential deviant act is possible. No matter how strongly motivated people are to steal automobiles,

they cannot do it unless there are automobiles to be stolen, and they cannot do it if the automobiles within their purview are impossible to steal. All deviant behavior requires opportunity; and according to control balance theory, when motivation is strong and there is opportunity, some form of deviance is highly likely. When an individual becomes acutely aware of his or her control imbalance, grasps the idea that deviance will help, and in addition is situated so that opportunity to commit one or another of those potentially helpful deviances exists, then we can expect that individual to commit some form of deviance.

Seriousness and Control Balancing

Because opportunity for a variety of deviant acts is usually omnipresent, motivated people have a high probability of doing some deviance. However, they will not commit just any specific kind of deviance that one might imagine; instead, they will commit one of a set that is reasonable for them, given their control ratio, degree of motivation, and quality of opportunity. If we could measure all, or most, forms of deviance that a motivated person might potentially commit (that is, for which there are opportunities) we would expect them to commit some of those acts but not others (how they choose among the possibilities will be discussed shortly). Even though the specific acts likely to be committed are contingent on several simultaneously operating variables, the theory predicts that some form of deviance will be committed (as opposed to conforming behavior) when a person has become motivated. For any particular specific deviant act, say vandalism, the theory does not predict that a motivated person will commit it, even with good opportunity to do so. The reason has to do with the control balancing process, which hinges on possible counter controlling responses.

A potential deviant—a person with motivation and opportunity—contemplates committing forms of deviance that hold the promise of producing the greatest effect—that is, those kinds that most quickly and effectively lead to short-term change in control. However, those deviances with the greatest potential payoff are also the ones that will most likely bring forth counter controlling responses. The degree to which a given deviant act is likely to provoke counter control reflects the "seriousness" of the act. Any person with an urge to do something about his or her control ratio will, therefore, contemplate the most serious form of deviance for which there is an opportunity. However, because the most serious forms of deviance activate the strongest counter control, resorting to that serious act may not be a realistic means of altering a particular person's control imbalance. In fact, for some people, the potential counter control that would be activated by serious acts of deviance would actually cause them to end up with less relative control than that with which they started.

Because of this, a motivated individual will tend to avoid those acts of deviance that appear too costly, given his or her control ratio (and various risk factors). For example, those with high control surpluses can contemplate, and are likely to commit, serious deviant acts that have great value for extending their control surpluses. But those with high control deficits are likely to avoid serious deviant acts, even though such acts would be especially useful for altering their control ratios. So, although motivated persons will do some kind of deviance, the exact kind they are likely to do depends on the seriousness of the potential acts possible in the specific context as well as on their specific control ratios.

The motivated person with a substantial control deficit will abandon the idea of very serious deviant acts as a way of altering the control imbalance. Instead of a very serious deviant response, such as slugging somebody, the individual with a moderate control deficit will slide down the scale of seriousness in search of a less serious deviant act, such as vandalizing an automobile. By contrast, a person with a large surplus of control can realistically contemplate very serious deviant acts (but of a different order called "autonomous deviance") to

extend her control after having become motivated. These more serious acts might include buying and shutting down the school in our example of the humiliated student. However, a person with a small surplus of control can only contemplate a less serious autonomous act, such as hiring someone to find dirt on the professor.

Constraint

The control balancing process by which individuals decide what forms of deviance to use in altering a control imbalance involves an additional, very important variable called "constraint." Constraint is present to a greater or lesser extent in situations where deviance might be possible. It refers to the likelihood or perceived likelihood that potential control will actually be exercised. Constraint is made up of three components: (1) the familiar control imbalance, which influences practically all of the variables in the causal process specified by control balance theory; (2) situational risk, or the specific chances of discovery and activation of potential counter-controlling responses (which are affected by things like lighting, presence of observers, physical evidence, and chance); and (3) seriousness, which rests on the emotional feelings of victims and others as well as on the perceived harm implied by particular acts of deviance (remember that seriousness is the amount of potential counter control for a given deviance in a particular situation). Together these variables represent the costs associated with specific acts of deviance; it is those costs that motivated individuals must take into account in seeking a solution to their "control problem."

Control Balancing

The import of constraint will become clearer if you think about the hypothetical student with whom we began our discussion. That student is predisposed toward deviant motivation by virtue of an unbalanced control ratio, a blockage of her goals (to get the question answered, to make an impression on the professor or other students, or whatever), and her basic desire for autonomy that everybody shares. The student becomes motivated toward deviance by the provocative situation in the classroom where, in asking a question and receiving an insulting response, she realizes that the professor, and probably a lot of other people and circumstances as well, exercise more control over her than she can exercise in return. Moreover, that realization is accompanied by an emotion of having been denigrated, which inspires the thought that various types of deviance, such as slugging the professor, becoming sullen, hiring a private detective, and so on, will help change her control ratio and restore her lost dignity. There is, of course, opportunity for several of these options, no matter who the student is, and there is opportunity for a few of the options only for some select subset of students who might be in this situation. Thus, according to the theory, such a student is likely to do something deviant.

Exactly what she will do depends partly on constraint. The student will want to do serious forms of deviance because serious deviance will most dramatically alter her control imbalance and overcome the denigration. But the more serious the acts, the greater the potential counter control that might be activated; hence, some students can contemplate doing more serious things in response to their humiliation than can other students. In addition, risk factors, which are greater for some students than for others and for some deviant acts than for other deviant acts, have to be taken into account. Therefore, the acts that a given person can realistically contemplate depend on the individual's control ratio, the seriousness of the act, and situational variables like risk (chances of actually being found out). Moreover, the likelihood of a person committing the most serious forms of deviance depends partly on the strength of motivation, which in turn is linked to the nature of the provocation and the degree of debasement experienced by the person. Finally, how a person actually acts—even when motivation is strong, opportunity is present, and constraint is small—is influenced by various contingencies, such as

moral feelings, personal self-control, and social affiliations with members of the audience that might witness the acts.

In short, the deviance-generating process is complicated and highly conditional; that is, it depends on a number of variables. Those variables are identified in the theory, and how they come into play is spelled out. Therefore, despite the complexity, one can use the theory to explain what occurs and to predict what probably will occur, provided there are good indicators of the relevant variables.

So far you have been told what the main variables in the theory are, but the role of "contingencies" has not yet been explicated. Before considering contingent variables, you need to contemplate a diagram of the causal process. Figure 45.1 uses arrows to illustrate the inter-connection of various influences

Figure 45.1
Causal Linkages of Control Balance Theory

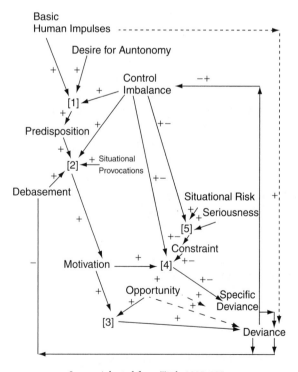

Source: Adapted from Tittle 1995, 189.

in the unfolding of deviance. To trace the process as it has been described above, start in the upper left-hand corner. Note that the first juncture in the process is indicated by a bracketed 1. That nexus, where a blockage of basic human impulses, a desire for autonomy, and a control imbalance come together is the "predisposition" we discussed before.

In examining the diagram, note that some of the arrows are darker and wider than others; this signifies importance or strength of influence. Consider the first nexus where the arrow for a control imbalance is slightly larger and darker than the other arrows. A control imbalance is highlighted because it is the most important of the three influences on predisposition. Observe also that the diagram includes some dotted arrows. They are used to acknowledge that some connections among the variables are possible, even though they are not specifically accounted for within the explanatory scheme of the theory. For instance, blockage of basic human impulses sometimes leads directly to deviance. This might occur when a very hungry person impulsively steals food—not because of the need to alter a control imbalance but simply to avoid starvation. Similarly, opportunity is sometimes so great that deviance results even in the absence of motivation. Finally, be cognizant of the arrows that go backward to some of the variables. This signifies that deviance has a reverse effect on some of the variables. According to the theory, deviance reduces the feelings of debasement that gave rise to deviant motivation in the first place, and it may increase or reduce the control imbalance at the heart of the sequence of influences leading to deviant behavior. These effects are shown by the reverse arrows.

While Figure 45.1 depicts the flow of influences ultimately leading to deviant outcomes, it does not convey the cognitive and emotional processes underlying the interconnection of the variables. For instance, the emotional feeling that an individual experiences when he is humiliated or debased must be imagined; it cannot be pictured. Similarly, the underlying control balancing

process—weighing gain from deviance against cost from constraint—that goes on in nexus [4] must be understood from the earlier qualitative account because it cannot be diagrammed.

You can grasp the import of the theory more fully by considering Figures 45.2 and 45.3. Figure 45.2 depicts the idea that, taking into account the various causal linkages of the theory, as well as the contingencies that we will discuss later, the average overall probability of some form of deviance depends on the magnitude of a control imbalance, conceived as either a deficit or a surplus. Notice that in the middle of the first row of the figure is the word *Balanced*, while to the left is a *minus* and to the right is a *plus*. Below that is the Probability of Deviance. In the middle, where control ratios are more or less balanced (the person exercises as much control as that to which he is subject), we expect low levels of deviance, indicated by the center point of the arrowed V. As a control imbalance increases in the surplus direction (*plus*, indicating more control exercised than is experienced) or in the deficit direction (*minus*, indicating less control exercised than is experienced), the probability of some unspecified kind of deviance increases (note that this probability refers to some among all possible types of deviance, not a given, particular form of deviance).

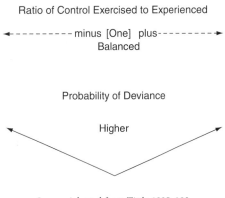

Figure 45.2
Control Imbalance and
Probabilities of Deviance

Ratio of Control Exercised to Experienced

◀ – – – – – – – – – minus [One] plus – – – – – – – – – ▶
Balanced

Probability of Deviance

Higher

Source: Adapted from Tittle 1995, 183.

Figure 45.3
Continua Representing Variations in Control Ratio and Predicted Forms of Deviance
Associated with Positions on Those Continua

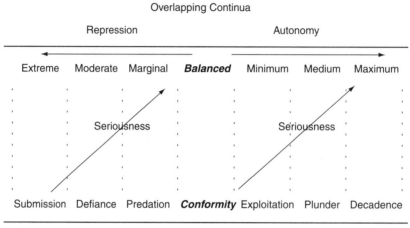

Source: Adapted from Tittle 1995, 189.

Figure 45.3 shows how the seriousness of potential deviant behaviors interacts with control imbalances to generate various probabilities of actual behavior. In the figure, the arrows extending outward from the middle Balanced zone signify continua of increasing control imbalance—a deficit to the left and a surplus to the right. There are also two slanted arrows representing increasing degrees of seriousness, but note that seriousness is not a single continuum from one side of the figure to the other. Instead, there are two different continua, one for seriousness of "repressive" deviance—that associated with control deficits—and another for seriousness of "autonomous" deviance—that associated with control surpluses. The two general categories of deviance, repressive and autonomous, are regarded as qualitatively different (Tittle 1997).

Figure 45.3 shows that on the deficit side, the seriousness of likely deviance decreases as the extent of a control deficit increases. Thus, the most serious forms of repressive deviance are most likely to be committed by those with the smallest control deficits. Those with the greatest deficits are likely to do

the least serious deviance because that is the only kind of deviance they can realistically contemplate doing. Individuals with small control deficits, on the other hand, can imagine getting away with more serious deviant acts; they probably will not face overwhelming possibilities of counter control. On the opposite, autonomous side of the diagram, the most serious deviance is likely to be committed by those with the greatest control surplus—again because they can anticipate extending their control with the least chance of counter control. And those with relatively small control surpluses can imagine getting away with only the least serious forms of autonomous deviance.

Explaining Specific Types of Deviance

The argument that increasingly serious forms of deviance, either of the repressive or the autonomous types, are most likely for those with smaller deficits or larger surpluses of control will be more salient if you imagine that the continua of seriousness are subdivided into categories, each encompassing approximately one-third of each continuum. These subdivided categories can then be identified with types of deviance that are likely to be committed by individuals with the specified degree of control imbalance.

To meaningfully subdivide the continua, however, one must assume that the various kinds of deviance supposedly falling in the zones of the continua are, in fact, characterized by the degrees of seriousness implied by the zone wherein they lie. Presently there are no data concerning the seriousness (as defined in the theory) of all potential acts of deviance relative to each other. Identification of specific types of deviance likely to occur in the various zones of seriousness is, therefore, somewhat problematic. Earlier, when I suggested that students experiencing humiliation at the hand of a teacher might resort to one or another form of deviance, I was speculating that predation is more serious than defiance and that exploitation is less serious than plunder. I really do not know that, so it is actually more accurate to say that those students would most likely resort to the most serious forms of deviance possible, given their control ratios and other conditions. Nevertheless, because it is interesting to speculate, those types of deviance that I assume are most likely to be committed by individuals with the associated control ratios are shown at the bottom of the diagram.

Things Explained

Conformity

In the middle of Figure 45.3, corresponding to the balanced zone of control ratios, is conformity, which in the theory is taken to mean *behavior consistent with social norms that is undertaken with full awareness of possible alternative, nonacceptable behavior.* When people can exercise about as much control as that to which they are subject (when their control ratios are about one), they are less likely to experience the conditions leading up to deviant motivation, and even when they do become motivated for deviance, they are less

likely to do it because of the more or less equal possibility of counter controlling responses. Counterposed to conformity are the various forms of deviance. They will be described in seesaw fashion, moving out from the center of the diagram from one side to the other.

The Least Serious Autonomous Deviance

On the surplus side of the balanced zone, in the first third of the autonomous continuum, are assumed to be acts of exploitation in which *individuals or groups use third parties as intermediaries or use structural or organizational arrangements to coerce, manipulate, or extract property from individuals or groups to benefit the exploiter without regard for the desires or welfare of the exploited.* Exploitation includes activities like corporate price fixing, profiteering from manufacturing processes that endanger workers, influence peddling by political figures, contract killings, employment of religious injunctions to solicit financial contributions for the personal use of evangelists, and, of course, the various exploitative acts committed against the professor by one of our hypothetical insulted students—which, you will recall, includes (1) having a parent threaten to cease donating money to the university unless the professor is fired, and (2) hiring a private detective to gather dirt for revenge.

Though such acts are probably generally regarded as quite serious, they are probably among the least serious forms of autonomous deviance. According to the theory, such acts will be most characteristic of those with the lowest control surpluses. Remember that those with minimum control surpluses are most liable for these acts because, even though such individuals might desire to do more serious things in order to extend their control when provoked, they must take into account the potential counter control that their actions would stimulate. These exploitative acts, of course, are not generally possible at all for people with control deficits.

The Most Serious Repressive Deviance

On the opposite side of the balanced zone, in the first third of the repressive continuum out from the center, we are likely to see acts of predation. They involve *direct physical violence, manipulation, or property extraction by an individual or group for the benefit of the predator, who acts without regard for the desires or the welfare of the individual or group that is the object of predation.* Predation includes theft, rape, homicide, robbery, assault, fraud, price gouging by entrepreneurs, coercive pimping, sexual harassment, and even acts like parental use of guilt to elicit child attention. Recall that in the case of the humiliated student, slugging the professor would qualify as predation. Predatory acts are assumed to be the most serious forms of repressive deviance, and they are most likely to be undertaken by people with relatively small deficits of control—because, given that their control deficits are not great, they can anticipate being able to manage the counter control that is likely to result.

Moderately Serious Autonomous Deviance

The second approximate third of the autonomous continuum encompasses acts that are assumed to be more serious than exploitation; they are characterized as "plunder." Plunderous behavior is that in which *individuals or organizations selfishly pursue their own ends with little awareness or regard for much else, particularly how their behaviors might affect others.* The acts included in this category are things like autocratic behaviors of medieval kings and nobles who destroyed peasant fields while hunting foxes, oppressive taxation of poverty-stricken peoples to provide wealth to corrupt rulers, massive pollution by giant oil companies with accompanying price increases to recover costs of cleanup, attempted genocide directed against racial or ethnic groups by powerful segments of the population, unrealistic taxes or work requirements imposed by occupying armies or slave holders,

or the arrogant destruction of forests and animals by early explorers. In the hypothetical case of a provoked student, described at the beginning of this essay, recall that plunder implies things like buying and shutting down the university. Clearly only those with a considerable control surplus can afford to do such things.

Moderately Serious Repressive Deviance

In contrast, the second third of the repressive continuum is assumed to include acts in which the *individual perpetrator expresses contempt for, or hostility toward, a norm, a set of norms, or toward the individual, group, or organization with which that norm is associated.* Such acts are called "defiance," and they include youthful violation of curfews, vandalism, mocking denigrations of company officials by striking workers, sullenness by a marital partner, exaggerated obedience by employees, political protests, and in the case of the angered student, denigration of the teacher to other students and being loud and disruptive or sullen in class. Those with substantial, but not overwhelming, control deficits are likely to commit defiance, although they would prefer to do more serious things. The reason they do not actually commit the more serious acts is because they cannot realistically expect to handle the consequences that more serious deviance would imply for them.

The Most Serious Autonomous Deviance

Extremely serious autonomous deviance, that in the last third of the continuum out from the middle, is assumed to consist of *random, impulsive acts guided by no consistent or rational life organization, reflecting the perpetrators' momentary whims.* This zone might include excessive or unusual forms of sexual expression, such as group sex with children, cruel debauchery, humiliation of people for entertainment, and nonsensical pleasure-seeking or destruction, as in sadistic torture. Only those with very large control surpluses can be decadent and imagine getting away with it.

The Least Serious Repressive Deviance

Those with the greatest control deficits are likely to *lose all sense of personal autonomy, as well as the ability to visualize alternatives to obedience.* Consequently, they basically give up and become submissive. They adopt passive, unthinking, slavish patterns of obedience to the expectations, commands, or anticipated desires of others. Such behaviors might include eating slop on command, helping repress others to please power holders, allowing oneself to be physically abused, humiliated, or sexually degraded, or as in the case of our student exemplar, conforming to routinized patterns of the class without contemplating or questioning whether there is an alternative. Because the surrender of all efforts toward personal autonomy is probably regarded as unacceptable in many modern societies, including the United States, it is a form of deviance within those societies, albeit perhaps the least serious form. Remember, however, that this cannot be known for sure until survey data are collected to ascertain whether, and to what degree, submissive behavior is regarded as unacceptable.

Submission is especially interesting, partly because it has a different rationale than do the other forms of deviance described previously (Braithwaite 1997). In all of the other types of deviance, an individual or a group uses deviance in an active way. In those cases, deviance serves a purpose and, in that sense, can be said to be instrumental or functional. Submission, however, is passive; it represents almost complete capitulation to superior control and cession of imaginative contemplation. Submission, therefore, is qualitatively different from other forms of deviance. It is not adopted in order to overcome a control imbalance, but instead represents surrender to superior control.

In addition, submission is not the same as conformity. External manifestations might appear similar—those conforming and those submitting are not causing any trouble and they are ostensibly following social rules. Adhering to social expectations with full volition and with ability to visualize the possibility of doing something different (conformity) is a far cry from obedience born of demoralizing defeat. In using control balance theory to account for documented patterns of behavior, such as variations by gender, race, or social class, one must be careful to recognize the distinction between conformity and submission.

Finally, although the theory is designed to explain deviance, and in that effort also explains submission (as well as conformity, which is the residual category), it is important to note that submission is not necessarily deviant in all societies. In some societies, submission is normative (nondeviant), at least for some categories of people, such as women in Muslim contexts. But here one should be reminded that the theory predicts submissive type behavior when an individual or group is confronted with overwhelming control, without regard for the deviant or nondeviant status of submission.

Contingencies

So far, the underlying causal process of control balancing, along with the sequence and convergence of events involved in deviance, have been presented. The theory contends that these basic processes are always at work in such a way that they produce typical outcomes. However, the theory is not deterministic; it does not assert that under various circumstances such and such form of deviance will inevitably occur. For instance, although people with substantial, but not overwhelming, control deficits will probably commit some forms of defiance from time to time, all people with a modest control deficit are not invariably slated for defiance. As you learned earlier, a given person must be provoked and debased, have opportunity for various kinds of defiance, and not face too much constraint, which is at least partly determined by characteristics of the situation. But even then, neither defiance nor any other kind of deviance may occur. That is because a number of other variables impinge on the control balancing process to affect how fully it unfolds.

Conditions that may intervene into the control balancing process are called "contingencies." There are a lot of them, which, for convenience, can be classified as either personal, organizational, or situational in character. Among the personal contingencies are perceptual accuracy, moral feelings, habits, personality, ability to commit the deviance at issue, desire to do things that compete with deviance as alternatives, and previous deviance. Depending on these variables, a particular individual in a given set of circumstances will manage the events, feelings, and thoughts identified in control balance theory somewhat differently. For instance, whether a situation is provocative—that is, whether it brings to mind in an acute way a person's control imbalance—and whether it implies debasement depends partly on perceptual characteristics of the individual. What one person finds routine, such as being asked to wait in a line, another finds provoking. And what some experience as debasing simply rolls off the backs of others. Using our student example, some individuals to whom a professor responds caustically will not take umbrage. They might perceive it as a learning moment, and rather than being demeaned or humiliated, they may perceive that they have done themselves proud by being bold enough to ask a question in the first place. Furthermore, such perceptual differences enter into interpretation of opportunity and assessment of constraint.

In similar ways, the other personal contingencies noted above, such as moral commitments, affect how the control balancing process unfolds and the extent to which it produces the outcomes specified earlier. But there are other contingencies besides characteristics of individuals. Various kinds of organizational arrangements that exist in specific situations in which deviance might be a possibility, as well as those in which the individual is generally enmeshed, are relevant. Subcultural affiliations represent one of the most important organizational contingencies, at least for young people.

Imagine that the hypothetical student we have been using as an example is well integrated into a student subculture that shares and promotes the idea that respect for students on the campus must be enhanced, and that a number of her subcultural peers are also in the class. Such a person will be more easily provoked and more thoroughly humiliated than someone with a similar control ratio who is not part of such a subculture. Moreover, in contemplating potential counter control that might be stimulated by a deviant act, a subculturally-involved student will feel more capable of resisting than would a student with a similar general control ratio who is not enmeshed within a supportive peer network. Finally, the student's response to the professor's putdown may be emboldened by a desire to enhance her stature among the other members of the subculture. In that case, potential counter control from authorities is less relevant than potential control from peers. As a result of all of this, the control balancing process will manifest itself somewhat differently, and with less force, for a subcultural participant than for a student who is not in such a subculture.

Finally, there are some situational contingencies that come into play. Although opportunity, risk, and provocation are part of the fundamental control balancing process, they also vary situationally in ways that may affect the "normal" control balancing process. Some opportunities are better than others, the chances of misbehaviors being discovered vary enormously from one context to the other, and the degree of provocation implicit in given situations is not equal. Where opportunity is maximum, risk is highest, and provocation is most intense, the control balancing process will transpire with greatest efficiency. But when either opportunity or risk or provocation is less than maximum, one can expect outcomes to be affected. How they are affected can be spelled out, and from such theorizing, one can derive more precise hypotheses than would be possible by focusing exclusively on the central causal process of the theory.

One strength of control balance theory is its explicit recognition of contingencies of various kinds. The theory attempts to specify the direction and, in some cases, the likely magnitude of their effects on the causal processes at work (see Tittle 1995, chapter 8). The theory, then, provides explanation and prediction of deviance and of submission, even when submission is not deviant, by reference to a central causal process. In that balancing process, individuals weigh the possible gain in control that would be obtained from deviant behavior against potential counter control that the deviance is likely to stimulate. Control balancing is embedded within networks of converging conditions, and the fullness with which the theoretical process unfolds is affected by particular specified contingencies that may influence any or all of the variables and conditions in the theoretical chain of causes.

Background of the Theory

Control balance is a relatively new theory (Tittle 1995). It was developed as an exemplar to illustrate a particular method of theory building—called "theoretical integration"—involving the merging of parts of preexisting theories. It grew out of a conviction that all extant theories are in one way or another too narrow, too exclusively focused on one or another causal element, too imprecise, or that they lack the ability to spell out a full causal process. The method that led to its development specifies that theories should do the following: (1) focus on abstract rather than concrete commonalities of different behaviors (in this case, seeing disparate acts as having an underlying purpose of advancing one's relative control); (2) be focused around a central causal process (in this instance, control balancing) into which various inputs (largely incorporated in other theories already in the arena) can flow; and (3) articulate how various components of the theory interlink in causal sequences to produce specific outcomes. In addition, the particular mode of theoretical integration that led to

control balance implies that a theory must contain statements about how contingencies that are not part of the theory itself affect the operation of the causal processes in the theory.

Hypotheses and Evidence

As you have seen, control balance attempts to do all of the things that a theory should ideally do. Its internal structure, therefore, appears to be an advancement, yet theories must do more than exhibit good technical structure. Above all, they must explain the phenomena within their domains, which in the case of control balance mainly includes *behaviors that the majority of a given group regards as unacceptable or that typically evokes a collective response of a negative type (called deviance)*. "Explaining" means that a theory must answer questions of "why" and "how" for a critical audience of scientists. Scientists insist that theories produce intellectual satisfaction—satisfy their curiosities about why and how—and they want them to be consistent with empirical reality. Finding out if a theory works empirically involves two things: (1) logically assessing the adequacy with which the theory handles known facts, and (2) ascertaining how well it holds up in empirical tests of specific hypotheses derived from the theory.

This theory seems to account for variations between sexes, ages, races, places of residence, those more or less bonded socially, and socioeconomic categories in certain criminal, delinquent, and deviant activities that have been measured (see Tittle 1995, chapter 9). Space limitations preclude a discussion here showing how that is so, but it is important to note the difficulty of assessing whether the theory "fits the facts," given that the "facts" themselves are often problematic and the existing data do not correspond with the concepts set forth in the theory. Applying the theory to explain familiar variations in demographic distributions of deviance requires assumptions about the average overall control ratios of those occupying specific single statuses. Because there are currently no data suitably reflecting control ratios among those in single statuses, much less the general control ratios for people who occupy multiple statuses, such assumptions may be inaccurate. In addition, assumptions about control ratios based on single statuses, even if they were correct and were good estimators of general control ratios, ignore the individual distinctions in control ratios that characterize different people with similar demographic statuses. That is why it is a mistake, for example, to use femaleness as a proxy measure of a control deficit (see Jensen 1999; Jensen and Westphal 1998).

Furthermore, the theory's domain is far wider than the range of deviances covered in extant data sources; as a result, focusing only on specific, currently measured offenses is likely to underestimate the theory's power. For example, the theory suggests that, in general, people with modest control deficits are likely to engage in some form of defiance. Because more females than males are probably a little more likely to have modest control deficits (this is an assumption, since actual measures of control ratios by sex have not been undertaken), one would expect them to engage a bit more frequently in defiance. To check this out, one would need to have measures of most forms of defiance that females and males respectively might have an opportunity to commit—in order to see if, overall, females commit more kinds of defiance more frequently than males. But current measures of defiance are extremely limited. They most often concern things like vandalism, drug use, and mental illness, and they rarely include those kinds of defiance that are most likely available to females (such as sullenness, crying, withholding sexual favors, or refusal to perform certain household or school duties). So, if one looks only at available data about defiance and confines comparisons to those few offenses that have been studied, one is likely to draw erroneous conclusions about the theory (Tittle 1999).

Not only is the compatibility of the theory with known variations in deviance somewhat uncertain, but at this point there are too few direct tests to judge the empirical adequacy of the theory (at this writing only Piquero and Hickman 1999). If one takes account of the various stages in the theoretical process leading to control balancing and ultimately to deviance, and also makes allowance for the various contingencies that may intrude, the theory yields hundreds of hypotheses that can be tested. Some of those hypotheses are especially provocative because they predict outcomes that are not obvious from conventional thinking. For instance, conventional thinking suggests that the most oppressed people will be the ones most likely to turn to acts like theft, assault, and homicide. But control balance theory suggests that predation will be more likely among those with relatively small control deficits than among those with great control deficits. The theory also suggests that the relationship between its causal variables and different outcomes is not linear—a prediction that is unusual in conventional thinking, which assumes linearity in most causal effects.

The most important, and the most general, hypotheses to be derived from the theory are as follows: (1) the greater a control imbalance, in either direction from central point of balance, the greater the total probability of deviance, and (2) the type of deviance most likely to occur depends on the control ratio of the person and the seriousness of the acts—with control deficits being associated negatively with seriousness of the likely act and control surpluses being associated positively with seriousness of the potential act. Given these rich empirical possibilities, there may soon be a body of direct evidence bearing on the theory. . . .

Conclusion

Control balance theory portrays deviant behavior as emerging from situations where an individual becomes aware of, and is made to feel humiliated by, a control imbalance. To overcome the imbalance and the feelings it generates, the individual resorts to deviant behavior. However, the type of deviance that results represents a compromise between the potential gain in control implied by the deviant behavior and the potential counter-controlling consequences of the contemplated act. Exactly how this process plays out is influenced by numerous contingencies.

Discussion Questions

1. What is a person's "control ratio"? Describe someone with a large control deficit and someone with a large control surplus.
2. What is the control balancing process?
3. Tittle states that the outcome of the control balancing process is affected by several things. In particular, he states that several conditions must converge if deviance or crime is to result. What are these conditions? Why is the person's "control ratio" the most important of these conditions?
4. List and give examples of the major types of deviance described by Tittle. What determines the type of deviance individuals engage in?
5. Tittle's integrated theory draws on several individual theories discussed in this text, including strain, control, learning, and deterrence/rational choice theories. Discuss how these theories are represented in Tittle's theory.
6. Certain types of deviance, especially defiance and predation, are especially high among young people. How would Tittle's theory explain this?
7. Drawing on Tittle's theory, what policies would you recommend for the control of deviance (see Tittle, 2001: 331–333)?

46. Social Support and Crime

Francis T. Cullen

This selection by Cullen illustrates a rather different approach to theoretical integration. Unlike Thornberry, Cullen does not select concepts from different theories and then describe the relationships between them. Rather, he points to a common theme that is implicitly or explicitly treated in several theories, ranging from the early theories of the Chicago school (see Part III) to the recent theoretical work of feminist and peacemaking criminologists. The theme is that social support is implicated in crime. Cullen draws on these different theories in an effort to elaborate on that theme. In doing so, he presents 13 propositions regarding social support. Among other things, he argues that social support has a direct effect on crime; that it influences other variables which affect crime, like the level of social control; that it conditions the impact of certain variables on crime (e.g., strain is more likely to lead to crime when social support is low); and that it plays a critical role in the prevention of crime and the rehabilitation of offenders. Cullen applies the concept of social support to both micro-level and macro-level questions (e.g., why the United States has such a high crime rate), and also uses it to shed light on developmental issues (e.g., the desistance from crime in early adulthood).

The concept of social support represents an important addition to criminology. Even though numerous theories make implicit or explicit reference to social support, Cullen is the first to draw explicit attention to the central role this concept may play in crime. In doing so, he introduces a new variable into mainstream criminology. Support is related to, but distinct from, concepts such as social control and social disorganization. Second, the concept of social support moves us toward a rather different approach to reducing crime. Current policies focus largely on the control of crime, often through very punitive policies. Cullen's theory of social support, however, suggests a more humanitarian approach (Cullen et al., 1999).

Cullen's theory is compatible with much data on crime (as described in his article; see also Cullen and Wright, 1997). Preliminary empirical tests also provide some evidence in favor of the theory. In one study based on a sample of 1,775 adolescents and their parents interviewed for the National Survey of Families and Households, Wright (1995) found that structural factors, such as poverty and broken homes, increase delinquency mainly by diminishing the amount of support that parents are able to supply their children. In another study based on the National Longitudinal Survey of Youth, Wright and Cullen (2001) reported that social support reduces delinquent involvement both directly and in combination with parental control (that is, when parents both support and control their children).

Reprinted from Francis T. Cullen, "Social Support as an Organizing Concept for Criminology: Presidential Address to the Academy of Criminal Justice Sciences" in *Justice Quarterly* 11(4). Copyright ©1994 by the Academy of Criminal Justice Sciences. Reprinted by permission of the Academy of Criminal Justice Sciences.

References

Cullen, Francis T. and John Paul Wright. 1997. "Liberating the Anomie-Strain Paradigm: Implications From Social-Support Theory." In Nikos Passas and Robert Agnew (eds.), *The Future of Anomie Theory*, pp. 187–206. Boston: Northeastern University Press.

Cullen, Francis T., John Paul Wright, and Mitchell B. Chamlin. 1999. "Social Support and Social Reform: A Progressive Crime Control Agenda." *Crime and Delinquency* 45: 188–207.

Wright, John Paul. 1995. *Parental Support and Juvenile Delinquencey: A Test of Social Support Theory*. Unpublished Ph.D. dissertation, University of Cincinnati.

Wright, John Paul and Francis T. Cullen. 2001. "Parental Efficacy and Delinquent Behavior: Do Control and Support Matter?" *Criminology* 39: 601–629.

M y intention is to argue that notions of social support appear in diverse criminological writings....

What is lacking, however, is an attempt to integrate these diverse insights on social support into a coherent criminological paradigm. In the sociology of mental illness, for example, considerable progress has been made in this direction (Lin, Dean, and Ensel 1986; Vaux 1988). But in criminology the insights linking social support to crime remain disparate, and are not systematized so far as to direct theoretical and empirical investigation. Indeed, I can offer one (nonetheless significant) indicator of the latency of this concept: virtually no introductory or theoretical textbook lists "social support" in its index....

My goal, then, is to argue that social support, if approached systematically, can be an important organizing concept for criminology. In the pages ahead, I will discuss propositions that might form the parameters, in a preliminary way, for a criminological paradigm, which draws on existing knowledge to illuminate new research vistas.

What Is Social Support?

... Lin (1986:18) defines social support as "the perceived or actual instrumental and/or expressive provisions supplied by the community, social networks, and confiding partners." Dissection of this definition reveals three major dimensions of support. The first is the distinction between the objective delivery and the perception of support. Taking perceptions into account is important because it leads to the insight that people do not receive support in a mechanical way but interpret, appraise, and anticipate it in the context of social situations (see Matsueda 1992).

Second, although different typologies exist, social support is usually divided into two broad rubrics: instrumental and expressive. According to Lin (1986:20), "the instrumental dimension involves the use of the relationship as a means to a goal, such as seeking a job, getting a loan, or finding someone to babysit." Vaux (1988:21) suggests that "instrumental functions may be served through the provision of goods or money (material aid or financial assistance) and through providing information, making suggestions, and clarifying issues (advice and guidance)."

The expressive dimension, again according to Lin (1986:20), "involves the use of the relationship as an end as well as a means. It is the activity of sharing sentiments, ventilating frustrations, reaching an understanding on issues and problems, and affirming one's own as well as the other's worth and dignity." Vaux (1988:21) notes that the "affective functions" of support "include meeting the needs for love and affection, esteem and identity, and belonging and companionship. These needs are met respectively through emotional support, feedback and social reinforcement, and socializing."

Third, Lin's definition indicates that support occurs on different social levels. Micro-level support can be delivered by a confiding individual, such as a spouse or a best friend. But social support also can be viewed as a property of social networks and of communities and larger ecological units in which individuals are enmeshed.

A fourth dimension, not discussed by Lin, must be added: whether the support is delivered by a formal agency or through informal relations (Vaux 1988). Informal social support would occur through social relationships with others who lack any official status relative to the individual. Formal social support might be provided by schools, governmental assistance programs, and—perhaps most interesting to us—the criminal justice system.

The Ecology of Social Support

In the past decade, scholars have shown a renewed interest in studying the social ecology of crime, as did Shaw and McKay (1942) (Bursik and Grasmick 1993a; Byrne and Sampson 1986; Reiss and Tonry 1986). This research has shown that crime rates vary across nations and, within a single nation, across communities. It is noteworthy, if unsurprising, that the United States has higher rates of serious crime, especially violent offenses, than other Western industrialized nations (Adler 1983; Archer and Gartner 1984; Currie 1985; Messner and Rosenfeld 1994; also see Lynch 1995). This finding prompts my first proposition:

1. *America has higher rates of serious crime than other industrialized nations because it is a less supportive society.*

I am not claiming that Americans, as individuals, are ungenerous in giving their money to charity or their time to voluntary organizations; quite the opposite appears to be the case (Wuthnow 1991). Even so, I assert that American society is not *organized*, structurally or culturally, to be socially supportive. This conclusion receives confirmation from several sources, which makes interrelated or complementary points.

First, Braithwaite (1989:100) observes that societies differ in their "communitarian" quality—that is, in the extent to which "individuals are densely enmeshed in interdependencies which have the special qualities of *mutual help and trust*" (emphasis added). With a mobile, heterogenous, urban population, the United States is low in communitarianism. Accordingly the structural basis for creating and sustaining supportive social relations is weak.

Second, numerous commentators—often referred to as communitarians—have documented the corrosive effects of America's culture of excessive individualism (Bellah et al. 1985, 1991; Coles 1993; Etzioni 1993; Reich 1988; Wuthnow 1991). In the influential *Habits of the Heart*, Bellah et al. (1985) decry in particular "utilitarian individualism"—the dominance of individual self-interest in the pursuit of desired, usually material ends (also see Messner and Rosenfeld 1994). "We have committed," says Bellah et al. (1985:285), "what to the republican founders of our nation was the cardinal sin: we have put our own good, as individuals, as groups, as a nation, above the common good." Building a "good society," in which concern for community and mutuality of support dominate, awaits a fundamental "transformation of American culture" (Bellah et al. 1985:275–96, 1991).

Wuthnow (1991) notes that even compassion is "bounded" by the culture of individualism. Compassionate behavior is managed by being segmented into limited roles (e.g., a few hours of volunteer work). If pursued so extensively that it interferes with a person's self-interest, such behavior is regarded as an unhealthy obsession (1991: 191–220). As a result, while "some of the work—the work that can be divided up into limited commitments—is accomplished, much of it remains to be done" (1991: 220)....

In short, Wuthnow suggests that the demand for support in America exceeds the supply. This observation leads to a corollary to the first proposition: *The more a society is deficient in the support needed, the higher its crime rate will be.*

Third, Currie (1985, 1989, 1993) makes perhaps the most compelling case that support is low in America and is linked inextricably to the country's high violent crime rate. As Currie points out, America's past and recent economic development has disrupted the traditional "private cushions" provided by networks of social support. Unlike other Western nations, however, America's welfare state has been stingy, if not mean-spirited, in the support it offers to the casualities of the social dislocation and wide inequalities bred by this development (also see Block et al. 1987). The cost of undermining the delivery of support, argues Currie, is an inordinately high rate of violent crime. . . .

Currie also challenges attempts to relate America's high crime rate to a weakness in control. Because other Western nations are more socially integrated, the argument goes, they are better able to exercise informal controls over their citizens (Adler 1983; Bayley 1976). Although this view may have merit, it overlooks the role of support in reducing crime. Japan offers an instructive example. Currie (1985:46) notes that previous analyses have neglected "the ways in which Japanese society is more *supportive* than ours, not simply more 'controlling'" (author's emphasis). In particular, he points both to Japan's "private mechanisms of social obligation" and to Japan's efforts to limit inequality and to provide lifetime job security to most workers (also see Beirne and Messerschmidt 1991:608–609).

As I will discuss again later, the broader point here is that criminologists often confound the effects of informal control with those of social support. These concepts are not necessarily rivals in explaining criminal behavior; in reality, support and control may be mutually reinforcing in reducing crime. Still the distinction between the two is important both for achieving theoretical precision and because their policy implications can differ dramatically. . . .

The social ecology of support and crime varies not only across but also within nations (Currie 1985). Thus I offer a second proposition:

2. The less social support there is in a community, the higher the crime rate will be.

This thesis is buttressed by several pieces of evidence. Admittedly, quantitative research on communities and crime has not systematically explored the relationship of social support to crime (Bursik and Grasmick 1993a; Byrne and Sampson 1986; Reiss and Tonry 1986; but see Zuravin 1989). Nonetheless, variables employed in various studies may be viewed as operationalizing the concept of support.

First, there is evidence that governmental assistance to the poor tends to lessen violent crime across ecological units (DeFronzo 1983; Messner 1986; see Rosenfeld 1986). Thus, contrary to conservatives' claims that welfare corrodes individual initiative and fosters irresponsibility, including lawlessness (Ellwood 1988; Murray 1984; but see Block et al. 1987), it appears that state support buffers against criminogenic forces (also see Currie 1985, 1989, 1993).

Second, research reveals that crime rates are higher in communities characterized by family disruption, weak friendship networks, and low participation in local voluntary organizations (Sampson 1986a, 1986b; Sampson and Groves 1989). Sampson interprets these findings as an indication that such communities are unable to exert informal social control over their residents (also see Bursik and Grasmick 1993b). Although this perspective may have merit, it is unclear why these variables are measures of control and not of support. It is telling that the mental illness literature uses neighborhood interaction and participation in voluntary organizations to assess "community and network support" (Lin, Dumin, and Woelfel 1986). Further, high rates of family disruption may operationalize not only adults' ability to exert surveillance over youths but also the availability to youths of both adult support networks and the opportunity to develop intimate relations. In short, existing ecological studies can be interpreted as containing measures of social support and, in turn, as showing that support reduces rates of criminal involvement. . . .

Quantitative and ethnographic research on the "underclass" or the "truly disadvantaged" also is relevant to the social ecology of crime and support. This research documents the powerful social forces—deindustrialization, joblessness, persisting racial segregation, migration to the suburbs—that have created socially and economically isolated inner-city enclaves (Devine and Wright 1993; Jencks and Peterson 1991; Lemann 1991; Massey and Denton 1993; Sullivan 1989; Wilson 1987). This trend, which has been described as a continuing process of social and cultural "disinvestment" in these neighborhoods, has enormous social consequences (Hagan 1993a; Short 1990, 1991).

The literature essentially documents the erosion of community social institutions and of their ability to provide social support. Wilson (1987:144) notes, for example, that the departure of many middle-class families from inner-city neighborhoods reduced the "social buffer" or human capital needed to" absorb the shock or cushion the effect of uneven economic growth and periodic recessions." Similarly, in his review of Anderson's (1990) *Street Wise*, an ethnography of the Philadelphia neighborhood of "Northton," Hagan (1993a:329) shows how "structural and cultural disinvestment" has frayed the supportive relations between adults and youths that previously protected youths against crime. . . .

In short, my thesis is that both across nations and across communities, crime rates vary inversely with the level of social support. The social ecologists of crime have largely overlooked this possibility, but (as I hope I have revealed) their work contains evidence favoring the social support thesis and offers important clues for future investigation. In the next section I explore ways in which the presence or absence of support is implicated in individuals' involvement in crime.

Support and Crime

Since the inception of American criminology, interest in the criminogenic effects of family life has ebbed and flowed (Wilkinson 1974). Over the past decade, attention has increased once again, in part because of the American family's beleaguered status (Sykes and Cullen 1992) and in part because of the emergence of salient criminological findings showing that the pathway to serious adult criminality begins in childhood (Loeber and Le Blanc 1990: Nagin and Farrington 1992; Nagin and Paternoster 1991; Sampson and Laub 1993).

This renewed interest has prompted not only numerous empirical studies on family correlates of crime (Loeber and Stouthamer-Loeber 1986; Wells and Rankin 1991) but also widely read theoretical frameworks. Although these theories differ fundamentally, they emphasize the criminogenic role that the family plays by the way it exercises or instills *control* (Colvin and Pauly 1983; Gottfredson and Hirschi 1990; Hagan 1989; Regoli and Hewitt 1994; Wilson and Herrnstein 1985). These perspectives are earning a measure of empirical confirmation (see, for example, Akers 1994; Burton et al. 1994; Grasmick et al. 1993; Hagan 1989; Hagan, Gillis, and Simpson 1990; Messner and Krohn 1990); thus I will not argue against their value. At the same time, as a result of criminologists' emphasis on control, virtually no theoretical attention has been paid to how family-related social support, or its absence, is involved in crime causation. Accordingly I offer my third proposition:

3. The more support a family provides, the less likely it is that a person will engage in crime.

We have considerable evidence that parental expressive support diminishes children's risk of criminal involvement. . . .

The firmest empirical evidence, however, can be drawn from Loeber and Stouthamer-Loeber's (1986) comprehensive meta-analysis of family correlates of delinquency: factors indicating a lack of parental support clearly increase delinquent involvement. (Also see Feldman's [1993:196] discussion of "positive parenting.") Loeber and Stouthamer-Loeber conclude that delinquency is related inversely to "child-parent involvement, such as the amount of intimate communication, confiding, sharing of activities, and seeking help" (1986:42). Similarly, their analysis indicates that measures of parental rejection of children, such as "rejection, not warm, lack of love, lack of affection, less affectionate," were "consistently related to delinquency and aggression" (1986:54; also see Sampson and Laub 1993:119). These "support" elements, moreover, were among the most powerful family factors related to delinquency; their effects exceeded those of parental criminality, marital discord, parental absence, parental health, and family size (1993:120–23). . . .

In contrast to expressive support, criminological research contains few empirical studies on the impact of instrumental family support on crime (see, for example, Loeber and Stouthamer-Loeber 1986). It is premature to conclude that instrumental support is as salient as expressive support, and possibly these forms of support vary in their effects across the life cycle. In any case, the literature contains some clues as to the importance of instrumental family support. Thus, if we revisit Glueck and Glueck (1950:129–30), we discover that delinquents were more likely than nondelinquents to have parents who "had not given any thought to the boys' futures." Further, as noted above, family-based networks are an important source of entry into the job market; this, in turn, can undermine continued involvement in crime (Sullivan 1989; also see Curtis 1989: 155).

Finally, any discussion of families and crime must be careful to avoid what Currie (1985:185) calls the "fallacy of autonomy—the belief that what goes on inside the family can usefully be separated from the forces that affect it from the outside: the larger social context in which families are embedded for better or for worse." Indeed, large social forces have transformed many American families in ways that often have reduced their capacity to support children (see, for example, Hewlett 1991; Wilson 1987). For example, adolescents today are much less likely than in the past to eat evening meals with parents or to spend time at home (Felson 1994:104; Messner and Rosenfeld 1994:103); the potential time that parents have to spend with children is declining (Hewlett 1991: 90–92); and "less than 5 percent of all families have another adult (e.g., grandparent) living in the home, compared to 50 percent two generations ago. This reduces the backup support that might otherwise be available to working parents" (Panel on High-Risk Youth 1993:56).

Most disconcerting, however, is the concentration of forces that have ripped apart families of the underclass, or the "truly disadvantaged" (Devine and Wright 1993; Wilson 1987), and have made inner-city youths vulnerable to crime, drugs, and an array of unhealthy behaviors (Currie 1985, 1993; Panel on High-Risk Youth 1993). The Panel on High-Risk Youth states,

> Perhaps the most serious risk facing adolescents in high-risk settings is isolation from the nurturance, safety, and guidance that comes from sustained relationships with adults. Parents are the best source of support, but for many adolescents, parents are not positively involved in their lives. In some cases, parents are absent or abusive. In many more cases, parents strive to be good parents, but lack the capacity or opportunity to be so.(1993:213)

Accordingly I offer this as a corollary to my third proposition: *The more support is given to families, the less crime will occur.* As Rivara and Farrington (forthcoming) observe, "increased social support to families can take the form of information (e.g., parenting programs), emotional support (e.g., home visitors), provision of material needs (e.g., food stamps, housing) or instrumental help (e.g., day care)." They also note that the "most successful interventions appear to be those which offer more than one type of social support service, thereby affecting a number of risk factors for the development of delinquency and violence" (forthcoming; also see Farrington 1994). Echoing this theme, Currie (1989:18–19, 1993:310–17) argues persuasively that the government should institute a "genuinely supportive national family policy," including, for example, child care, family leaves, and special programs for families at risk for mistreating children.

Currie's (1985, 1989, 1993) analyses and the above discussion on changing levels of support within the American family lead to a second corollary: *Changes in levels of support for and by families have contributed since the 1960s to increases in crime and to the concentration of serious violence in high-risk inner-city neighbor-hoods.* This statement contradicts the thinking of Murray (1984), who blames the "generous revolution" of the Great Society programs for eroding individual responsibility and for fostering criminal and other deviant behaviors (see Lemann 1991; Lupo 1994).

Beyond the family, Krohn (1986) contends that social networks may provide a "web of conformity" (also see Sampson and Laub 1993). Krohn emphasizes how dimensions of networks operate to control behavior; scholars in the sociology of mental illness study how these characteristics of networks are an important source of social support (Lin et al. 1986; Vaux 1988). In short, the web of conformity involves not only constraints but also supports (Sullivan 1989; also see Zuravin 1989). This point leads to my fourth proposition:

4. The more social support in a person's social network, the less crime will occur.

Social support theorists have examined most extensively how supports mitigate the effects of strain or "stress." The relationships are complex, but social supports can prevent stresses from arising or can lessen negative consequences if stresses should emerge (House 1981; Vaux 1988). These findings are important in light of the recent revitalization of strain theory, particularly empirical research linking strain to criminal behavior (Agnew 1985a, 1989; Agnew and White 1992; Burton and Cullen 1992; Farnworth and Leiber 1989; McCarthy and Hagan 1992; Vaux and Ruggiero 1983)....

The remaining issue, largely ignored by strain theorists (Cullen 1984), is how people respond to this range of stressful conditions. Building on the social support literature (e.g., Vaux 1988), Agnew (1992) suggests that the ability to cope with criminogenic strains is contingent on access to supports. "Adolescents with conventional social support," he observes, "should be better able to respond to objective strains in a nondelinquent manner" (1992:72). This contention suggests my fifth proposition:

5. Social support lessens the effects of exposure to criminogenic strains.

In their important reassessment of Glueck and Glueck's longitudinal data, Sampson and Laub (1993) study not only sources of the stability of crime across the life course but also the "turning points" at which offenders depart from the criminal "pathway." Their analysis shows that during adulthood, job stability and attachments to spouse contribute to desistance from crime. They interpret these findings as indicating that "adult social bonds" provide offenders with social capital which subjects them to "informal social controls" (1993:140–43). "Adult social ties," they observe, "create interdependent systems of obligation and restraint that impose significant costs for translating criminal propensities into action" (1993:141).

I will not take issue with the control theory set forth by Sampson and Laub, but I observe that their *Crime in the Making* also contains insights on the salience of adult *social supports*. Thus Sampson and Laub (1993:141) take note of the "social capital invested by employers and spouses," not simply that invested by offenders. With regard to marriage, for example, life histories on offenders in Glueck and Glueck's sample reveal that this investment took the form of wives' providing "material and emotional *support*" (Sampson and Laub 1993:205, 220, emphasis added; also see Vaux 1988: 173). Two points follow from this observation.

First, marital and employment "social supports" may reduce crime by increasing social capital and thus expanding the basis for informal social controls. Second, these social supports may exert independent (main) effects on crime not by facilitating control but by reducing other sources of crime (e.g., lessening emotional difficulties, relieving strains, transforming deviant identities). More broadly, I offer my sixth proposition:

6. Across the life cycle, social support increases the likelihood that offenders will turn away from a criminal pathway.

I do not mean to confine this proposition to the role of adult social supports in crime desistance. In particular, accounts of at-risk youths suggest that supports can trigger their turning away from crime (see also Dubow and Reid 1994). Such supports may involve a youth's special informal relationship with an adult (e.g., teacher, coach), participation in a mentorship program (Kuznik 1994; Panel on High-Risk Youth 1993:213–14), or placement in a community program (Curtis 1989:154–60).

Commentary on impoverished juveniles at risk for crime also frequently emphasizes the sense of isolation felt by these youths. The Panel on High-Risk (1993:217), for example, notes that "young people from high-risk settings" often "confront the emotional pain and feelings of hopelessness that can interfere with positive development." Echoing this theme, Curtis (1989:158) observes that inner-city minority youths think "the cards are stacked hopelessly against them. These youths believe that fate will not permit them to 'make it 'in any legitimate form."

This isolation might be viewed as a detachment from social bonds that lessens control and increases criminal involvement, but another process also may be operating. These youths may perceive that they will always lack the instrumental and expressive supports needed to change the circumstances in which they are enmeshed. This possibility leads to my seventh proposition:

7. Anticipation of a lack of social support increases criminal involvement.

Thus far I have concentrated on how *receiving* support diminished criminality, but it also seems important to consider how *giving* support affects involvement in crime. The logic of writings from the peacemaking/humanist and feminist perspectives suggests that providing support should reduce criminal propensities (McDermott 1994). Pepinsky (1988), in fact, regards crime as the opposite of "responsiveness" to others. Further, in *The Call of Service*, Coles (1993) tells how the experience of supporting others can transform selves, inculcate

idealism, foster moral purpose, and create long-standing interconnections—all of which would seem anti-criminogenic.

I know of no systematic empirical investigation of the link between giving support and crime, but some insights can be gleaned from the research. Sampson and Laub (1993: 219–20), for example, note that the offenders in their study were likely to desist from crime when they were devoted to their spouses and children, and were "financially responsible not only to their spouses, but also to parents and siblings if the need arose." That is, as offenders assumed a role as providers of expressive and instrumental support, their involvement in crime ceased. . . .

Lynne Goodstein (personal communication, January 2, 1994) offers another pertinent insight: "Women's traditional responsibility for the delivery of social support and nurturance to others (children, elders, partners) and the dramatically lower crime rates for women is an interesting association." Although this association is open to differing interpretations, it suggests that the experience of providing support creates sentiments (e.g., compassion), identities, role expectations, and problem-solving skills that are generally incompatible with the "seductions of crime" (Katz 1988; also see Gilligan, Ward, and Taylor 1988).

In any event, these various considerations lead to my eighth proposition:

8. Giving social support lessens involvement in crime.

Finally, Albert Cohen (personal communication, January 29, 1994) has alerted me to the need to consider the broader concept of "differential social support." To this point, I have largely explored the role of supports in making conformity possible. Cohen, however, observes

that social support is equally important to non-conformity, to crime. Indeed, the burden of much of the literature on causation is that associations, the situation of company, provide much of the support that makes it possible to break the law, more effectively to thwart the justice process and reduce the "hurtfulness" and other consequences of punishment.

Indeed, insights on support for crime are evident in the literature on peers and co-offending (Reiss 1988), on the acquisition and performance of criminal roles (Cloward 1959; Steffensmeier 1983), and on the organizational conditions that make corporate crime possible (Hills 1987; Sutherland 1949). Differential social support also might operate in situational contexts. As shown by Richard Felson (1982: Felson and Tedeschi 1993), "third parties" to interpersonal conflict can support the escalation of violence or can mediate tensions and diminish subsequent aggression. These observations lead to my ninth proposition:

9. Crime is less likely when social support for conformity exceeds social support for crime.

In a related vein, Ronald Akers (personal communication, January 1994) has cautioned that social supports are likely to be most effective when they are linked to "conformity-inducing outcomes." The *source* of the support may be particularly important. For instance, support from conformist sources may not only address criminal risk factors (e.g., strain) but also provide an opportunity for prosocial modeling (Andrews and Bonta 1994:202–205). Conversely, support from criminal friends (e.g., comfort in the face of a stressful life event) may be counteracted if these associations also expose youths to criminogenic influences.

On this point, the research on the effects of marriage provides relevant data. Although the findings are not fully consistent (Sampson and Laub 1993), we find some evidence that marriage—conceptualized here as a social support—reduces crime only if spouses are not themselves deviant or criminal (Farrington, Ohlin, and Wilson, 1986: 56; West 1982:100–104). Thus I offer this corollary to Proposition 9: *Social support from conformist sources is most likely to reduce criminal involvement.*

Support and Control

As stated earlier, recent advances in criminological theory have been dominated by attempts to link control with crime. I have tried to show that these perspectives overlook social support and potentially confound the effects of control and with the effects of support. Now I wish to make a different, but related, argument, which is set forth in my tenth proposition:

10. Social support often is a precondition for effective social control.

The criminological literature contains numerous illustrations of this proposition. Braithwaite's (1989) influential theory of "reintegrative shaming," however, is perhaps the most noteworthy example (also see Braithwaite and Muford 1994; Makkai and Braithwaite 1994). In brief, Braithwaite contends that legal violations often evoke formal and informal attempts at "shaming," which he defines as "all processes of expressing disapproval which have the intention or effect of invoking remorse in the person being shamed and/or condemnation by others who become aware of the shaming" (1989:9). Braithwaite observes, however, that shaming takes two general forms. Disintegrative shaming is criminogenic; as labeling theory would predict, it stigmatizes, excludes, and ensures the exposure of offenders to criminogenic conditions. Reintegrative shaming, in contrast, achieves conformity. After the act is condemned, attempts are made "to reintegrate the offender back into the community of law-abiding or respectable citizens through words or gestures of forgiveness or ceremonies to decertify the offender as deviant" (1989:100–101). Even if repeated efforts are required, the goal is to avoid exclusion and thus to embed the offender in conventional, accepting relationships (Braithwaite and Muford 1994).

In the language of the social support paradigm, Braithwaite is asserting that control can be effective only in the context of support (see Sherman 1992). Further, the very likelihood that reintegrative shaming will be used depends on the extent to which the larger society is supportive, or, as Braithwaite puts it, "communitarian." Not surprisingly, shaming in the United States tends to be disintegrative (also see Benson 1990).

A related insight can be gained from the correctional literature. It appears that family support of offenders during and after incarceration improves chances of successful completion of parole supervision (Farrington et al. 1986:147; Wright and Wright 1992:54). In short, control with support is more effective than control by itself.

The family socialization literature also offers useful information. Wilson and Herrnstein (1985:237–40) argue that "restrictive" parenting is important in detecting and discouraging rule transgressions and thus in teaching that behavior has consequences. But restrictiveness is most effective when coupled with parental warmth. "A warm parent," they state, "is approving and supportive of the child, frequently employs praise as a reinforcement for good behavior, and explains the reasons for rules" (1985:237). In this case, warmth (support) empowers restrictiveness (control): when children care about their parents, obedience is rewarding and disobedience is unrewarding (1985:239)....

Good Criminology and the Good Society

Over the past decade, an increasing number of voices have joined in a national conversation about the requirements for what Robert Bellah and his colleagues call the "Good Society" (Bellah et al. 1991; also see Bellah et al. 1985; Coles 1993;

Etzioni 1993; Reich 1988; Wuthnow 1991). Fundamental to this ongoing conversation is a critique of the excessive individualism in the United States, which too often degenerates into a politics justifying either the crass pursuit of rights or materialistic self-aggrandizement. In this context, there is a lack of attention to the public good, service to others, and an appreciation for our need for connectedness. Accordingly there is a call to revitalize our common bonds and to build a society supportive of all its citizens.

I realize the risk in linking one's criminology to a larger social agenda: regardless of how crime is affected, attempts to build a Good Society certainly should stand or fall on their own merits (Felson 1994:12–13). Still, it is equally misguided to assume that criminological ideas have no consequences (Bohm 1993; Lilly et al. 1989). A criminology that emphasizes the need for social supports thus may have the potential to make a difference.

Indeed, if the social supports paradigm proves to be "Good Criminology," it will provide empirical grounds for suggesting that an important key to solving the crime problem is the construction of a supportive social order—the Good Society. Accordingly this paradigm may present an opportunity to challenge the current hegemony of punitive policy in criminal justice. It may prompt us to consider that the cost of a nonsupportive society, exacerbated by mean-spirited or neglectful public policies, is a disgraceful level of crime and violence (Currie 1985). And, hopefully, it may provide the basis for criminal justice and public policies which help to create a society that is more supportive and hence safer for its citizens.

Discussion Questions

1. What is social support (describe the major types of support in your response)? What types of questions would you ask someone

to measure the social support they receive? How does social support differ from social control?

2. Why does the United States provide less social support than many other industrialized

nations? Why do some communities and families provide less social support than others?

3. Describe the different ways in which low social support might contribute to crime. Consider social support as a direct cause of crime, and as an indirect cause (which influences other variables which cause crime), and as a conditioning variable (which influences the effect of other variables on crime).

4. Describe how the concept of social support is related to any two of the other theories discussed in this volume (e.g., do these theories make implicit or explicit reference to social support; would a more explicit consideration of social support strengthen these theories—for example, by shedding additional light on the causes of the independent variables in these theories or on the factors that influence the effects of these variables on crime).

47. Why Criminals Offend: A General Theory of Crime and Delinquency

Robert Agnew

This selection by Agnew illustrates yet another strategy for developing an integrated theory of crime, one that lists those concrete variables that have relatively large direct effects on crime and then describes how these variables work together to affect crime. Agnew begins by noting that most crime theories and research are based on a rather simple idea—crime is most likely when the constraints against crime are low and the motivations for crime are high. Agnew then describes the major constraints against and motivations for crime, drawing on many of the crime theories described in previous chapters of this book. Next, Agnew argues that many specific variables affect or index these constraints and motivations. These variables can be grouped into five clusters organized by life domain; the self (consisting of the personality traits of irritability and low self-control), the family (poor parenting practices and no/poor marriages), school (negative school experiences and limited education), peers (peer delinquency), and work (unemployment and "bad jobs"). The variables in each life domain affect both the constraints against and the motivations for crime.

The five life domains form the core of Agnew's theory. Agnew then describes how these life domains work together to affect crime. You should note that many of his arguments draw on other theories in this book. Agnew argues that the effect of each life

domain on crime varies over the life course (e.g., work has a larger effect on crime among adults than adolescents). Also, these life domains have reciprocal effects on one another (e.g., poor parenting leads to peer delinquency, which in turn leads to poor parenting). These arguments draw heavily on Thornberry's interactional theory (Chapter 44). In addition, crime affects the five life domains (e.g., crime sometimes leads to unemployment and work in bad jobs). Also, prior crime may sometimes lead directly to subsequent crime. The effects of crime, however, depend on how others react to the crime and the characteristics of the criminal. These arguments draw heavily on the recent research on labeling, deterrence, and rational choice theories here (see Parts VII and X). Further, the life domains interact in affecting crime and one another (e.g., the effect of poor parenting on crime depends on the level of peer delinquency). These types of interaction or conditioning effects receive strong emphasis in Cullen's social support theory (Chapter 46) and Tittle's control balance theory (Chapter 45). Finally, Agnew notes that the larger social environment affects the individual's standing on the life domains—an argument emphasized in several different theories.

So while Agnew takes a rather different approach to constructing an integrated theory of

Adapted with permission from *Why Do Criminals Offend? A General Theory of Crime and Delinquency,* copyright © 2005 by Oxford University Press.

crime, one that focuses on the concrete variables that have large, direct effects on crime, his work clearly builds on that of previous theories. Agnew's theory has not yet been tested, although it is compatible with much previous research (see Agnew, 2005).

Reference

Agnew, Robert. 2005. *Why Do Criminals Offend? A General Theory of Crime and Delinquency.* New York: Oxford University Press.

The general theory presented below focuses on the major, direct causes of crime. These causes are grouped into five clusters, organized by life domain: the self (composed of the personality traits of irritability and low self-control), the family (poor parenting practices, no/bad marriages), the school (negative school experiences, limited education), peers (peer delinquency), and work (unemployment, bad jobs). The theory then advances several general propositions which describe how these clusters are related to one another and how they work together to affect crime. The key arguments of the general theory are as follows:

Crime Is Most Likely When the Constraints Against Crime Are Low and the Motivations for Crime Are High

While there are scores of crime theories and thousands of studies testing these theories, a rather simple idea underlies most of these theories and studies: Crime is most likely when the constraints against crime are low and the motivations for crime are high (e.g., Gold 1963; Sheley 1983; Tittle 1995). Further, there are only a few broad constraints and motivations that we need to consider. Most refer to features of the individual's social environment, particularly the family, school, peer, and work environments. Others refer to the individual's personality traits, which influence how individuals perceive, experience and respond to their social environment.

The Constraints Against Crime
The constraints against crime refer to those factors that hold individuals back or restrain them from committing crime. There are several major types of constraints: You don't engage in crime because you might be caught and punished (external control). You have a lot to lose if you are punished (stake in conformity). And you believe that crime is wrong and are a thoughtful, caring person who does not like risky activities (internal control).

External control. External control refers to the likelihood that others will detect and sanction criminal behavior. When people think of external control they usually think of the police arresting someone and the court sending that person to prison or jail. Being arrested and incarcerated, however, is only one of many examples of external control. Other examples include your parents grounding you for your misbehavior, your friends shunning you, school official expelling you, and employers firing you. Individuals are high in external control to the extent that others: 1) set clear rules for them that prohibit crime and related behaviors; 2) monitor their behavior to detect rule violations; and 3) consistently sanction their rule violations in a meaningful manner, although such sanctions should not be overly harsh or abusive—which may anger and alienate the recipient.

Stake in conformity. External control refers to the likelihood that individuals will be caught and punished by others if they deviate. Some individuals, however, are more fearful of detection and punishment than others. One reason for this is they have a lot to lose if they are caught and punished. That is, they have a large "stake in conformity" or investment in conventional society, which may be jeopardized by crime. For example, they have good jobs that may be lost if they engage in crime. Individuals have a large stake in conformity to the extent that: 1) they have strong emotional bonds to conventional others, like parents, spouses, teachers, and employers; 2) they engage in positively-valued activities with conventional others or receive positive benefits from interacting with conventional others, including material benefits, emotional support, and information; 3) they are doing well in school, like school, expect to get an advanced education, or have already obtained an advanced education; 4) they have "good" jobs that they like or they expect to get such jobs; and 5) they have an excellent reputation among conventional others. All of these things may be jeopardized by crime. As a result, individuals with a strong stake in conformity are less likely to engage in crime.

Internal control. Many individuals refrain from crime even when they are in tempting situations where there is little likelihood that their criminal behavior will be detected and punished. One reason for this is that they believe that crime is wrong or immoral. Such individuals have typically been taught this belief from an early age by parents, teachers, neighbors, religious figures, and others. Eventually, they come to accept or "internalize" this belief and it becomes a major constraint against crime. Also, some individuals have a set of personality traits that increase their awareness of and responsiveness to the above constraints. Such individuals are thoughtful, care about the feelings and rights of others, are good tempered, have an aversion to risky activities, and have little need for the immediate gratification of their desires (see Gottfredson and Hirschi 1990; Grasmick et al. 1993). As a consequence, they are able to exercise much self-control when tempted to engage in crime.

The Motivations for Crime

The motivations for crime refer to those factors that entice or pressure individuals to engage in crime. These motivations may be grouped into two broad categories (see Reckless 1961). One category focuses on those factors that *entice or pull* individuals into crime, with rational choice theory, the routine activities perspective, and especially social learning theory focusing on motivations of this type (see Akers 1998). Another category focuses on those factors that *pressure or push* individuals to engage in crime, with strain theory focusing on motivations of this type (see Agnew 1992, 2001b).

Factors that entice individuals into crime. Many individuals learn to engage in crime from others. These others include peers and gang members, who often deliberately teach individuals to engage in crime. These others may also include parents, who often inadvertently (but sometimes deliberately) teach their children to engage in crime. Individuals are taught to engage in crime in three major ways: they are *reinforced for crime, exposed to successful criminal models,* and *taught beliefs favorable to crime.* As a result of such learning, individuals come to view crime as a desirable or appropriate response in certain circumstances. They are thus enticed or pulled into crime.

Factors that pressure individuals to engage in crime. Strain theory argues that a major motivation for crime is negative treatment by others. Someone treats you in a way you do not like. You experience a range of negative emotions, like anger and frustration. These negative emotions create pressure for corrective action, and you *may* respond with crime—particularly if you lack the ability or desire to cope in a legal manner. Crime may allow you to reduce or escape from your negative treatment; for example, you may assault the people who harass you, run away from the parents who abuse you or steal the money you cannot get through legal channels. Crime may allow you to satisfy your desire for revenge against those who have mistreated you or related targets; for example, you may "get back" at your teachers by vandalizing your school. And crime may allow you to alleviate your negative emotions; for example, you may take illegal drugs to feel better.

A Range of Individual and Social Variables Affect the Constraints Against and the Motivations for Crime

Most of the above constraints and motivations are quite broad and encompass many specific causes of crime. For example, numerous variables index or directly affect the individual's stake in conformity; variables such as the individuals's emotional bonds to parents and teachers, grades, educational and occupational goals, and type of job. I next list the *specific* variables that index or directly affect the constraints against and motivations for crime. These variables constitute the leading causes of crime.

A large number of such variables can be listed. To keep things manageable, I focus on those variables which likely have relatively moderate to large *direct* effects on crime. This still includes a good number of variables, but it is possible to group these variables into a smaller number of categories or clusters. Indeed, there have already been several attempts to do so. The most common way to group the causes of crime is by the type of constraint or motivation they index. Those variables indexing external control are grouped together, those indexing stake in conformity are grouped together, and so on. There is, however, a major problem with grouping variables in this manner. Many variables index or affect more than one type of constraint or motivation. For example, low grades indexes both stake in conformity and strain. Being abused by parents indexes stake in conformity, strain, and exposure to criminal models.

An alternative strategy for grouping the causes of crime into a smaller number of categories. I group the causes into clusters organized around the life domains of self (personality traits), family, school, peers, and work. These domains represent the major spheres of life and they encompass all of the direct causes of crime. Other domains—like the individual's biological state, the community in which the individual lives, and the individual's position in the larger social system (as indexed by class, sex/gender, age, and race/ethnicity)—affect crime primarily through their effect on these domains. Grouping the causes of crime into life domains allows us to ensure that each cause is part of one and only one category. For examples, low grades falls into just one category, the school domain, even though it affects both the constraints against and the motivations for crime. Further, there is good reason to believe that the variables in each life domain are strongly associated with one another. This is because the variables in each domain are caused by many of the same factors and have large causal effects on one another (see Agnew 2005).

The key variables in each of the five life domains are as follows.

Self (Super-Personality Traits of Irritability and Low Self-Control)

Individuals who possess the super-trait of "low self-control" are impulsive, giving little thought to the long-range consequences of their behavior; like exciting, risky, high-energy activities; do not have much ambition or motivation; and do not feel bound by conventional rules and norms. In everyday language, those low in self-control might be described as "wild" or "out of control." (Note that this definition of "self-control" is more narrow than that of Gottfredson and Hirschi (1990), whose definition of self-control encompasses the above traits and irritability, as defined below.)

Individuals who possess the super-trait of "irritability" are more likely to experience events as aversive; attribute these events to the malicious behavior of others (believe that others are "out to get them"); experience intense emotional reactions to these events, especially anger; and respond to these events in an aggressive or antisocial manner. They also show little concern for the feelings and rights of others, and tend to have an antagonistic or adversarial interactional style. In everyday language, irritable people might be described as "mean" or "nasty" or "having a short fuse."

Family (Poor Parenting and No/Poor Marriages)

The key family variables impacting delinquency are poor parental supervision and discipline, weak bonds between the parent(s) and juvenile, family conflict and child abuse, the failure of parents to provide social support, and having criminal parents and siblings. Other family variables, like divorce/separation and family size, affect delinquency primarily through their effect on these key variables.

When juveniles become adults, the above poor parenting variables become less relevant to the explanation of crime. For adults, those family factors most likely to cause crime include the failure to marry or divorce/separation. And, if married, they include negative bonding to spouse/partner, negative bonding to children, family conflict, poor spouse/partner supervision, having a criminal spouse or partner, and low social support.

School (Negative School Experiences and Limited Education)

The key school variables impacting delinquency are negative bonding to teachers and school, poor academic performance, little time on homework, low educational and occupational goals, poor supervision and discipline, negative treatment by teachers, and low social support from teachers. The school research has of course focused on juveniles, since most adults are not in school. Nevertheless, it is reasonable to suppose that crime will be higher among adults with limited educations. I should note, however, that much of the effect of education on crime is probably indirect. In particular, education influences the constraints against and motivations for crime primarily through its effect on the individual's work, marital life, and peer associations.

Peers (Peer Delinquency)

The key peer variables impacting delinquency are having close friends who engage in crime; having frequent conflicts with and being abused by peers; and spending much time with peers in unstructured, unsupervised activities. Peer delinquency is much less common among adults. Nevertheless, some adults are high in peer delinquency, especially adults who are unmarried, unemployed, or employed in "bad jobs." Peers may play a major role in the lives of such adults.

Work (Unemployment and Bad Jobs)

The key work variables affecting crime are unemployment; poor supervision/discipline; negative bonding to work; poor work performance; poor working conditions, including pay and benefits; and having criminal co-workers.

The Relative Importance of the Life Domains at Different Stages in the Life Course

The five life domains—self, family, school, peers, and work—generally have large effects on the individual's level of offending. Some life domains, however, have larger effects than others. It is difficult to compare effect sizes without taking account of the individual's stage in life. For the sake of simplicity, I divide the individual's life into three stages: childhood, adolescence, and adulthood. Irritability/low self-control and poor parenting have the largest effects on crime among children; irritability/low self-control and peer delinquency have the largest effects among adolescents; and irritability/low self-control, peer delinquency, no/bad marriages, and unemployment/bad jobs have the largest effects among adults (see Agnew 2005).

The Web of Crime: The Life Domains Affect One Another

The life domains not only affect crime, they affect one another as well (this section draws heavily on Thornberry, 1987). For example, individuals with the traits of irritability and low self-control are more likely to experience poor parenting, partly because they upset their parents—who respond by employing harsh disciplinary techniques or withdrawing from them. Poor parenting practices, in turn, contribute to irritability and low self-control. Problems in the

Figure 47.1
The Mutual or Reciprocal Effects of the Life Domains on One Another

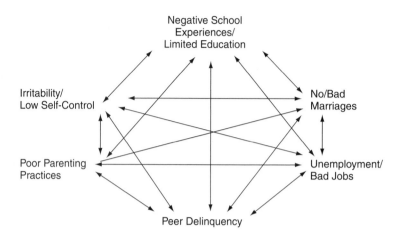

life domains, then, tend to mutually reinforce or contribute to one another. This argument is illustrated in Figure 47.1, which resembles a spider's web to some extent.

Many criminals are trapped in this web. That is, their personality traits and family, school, peer, and work experiences are all conducive to crime and they all work to mutually reinforce one another. These criminals tend to offend at high rates. Some do manage to escape from this web when they make the transition to adulthood, usually because they get involved in good marriages and become bonded to decent jobs. Those who do not escape continue to offend at high rates well into their adult years.

Irritability/low self-control. The traits of low self-control and irritability increase the likelihood that individuals will experience poor parenting, fail to marry or become involved in bad marriages, have a range of negative school experiences, obtain little education, associate with delinquent peers, be unemployed, and work in "bad jobs" when they are employed. These effects occur for four reasons: people with these traits devote little effort to conventional pursuits and sometimes prefer to be in environments conducive to crime (e.g., associating with delinquent

peers), they often fail at conventional pursuits and are forced into environments conducive to crime (e.g., bad jobs), they provoke negative reactions from others and thereby create environments conducive to crime (e.g., harsh/abusive parenting), and they are more likely to perceive given environments in ways conducive to crime.

Poor parenting and no/bad marriages. The family variables tend to have relatively moderate to large effects *on the other life domains,* with parenting practices during the childhood years being especially important.

Negative school experiences. Negative school experiences increase low self-control/irritability (small/moderate effect), poor parenting practices (small/moderate effect), peer delinquency (large effect during adolescence and adulthood), unemployment/bad jobs (large effect), and no/bad marriages (small/moderate effect).

Peer delinquency. Peer delinquency affects low self-control/irritability (small/moderate effect), poor parenting practices (small/moderate effect), negative school experiences (large effect), no marriage/bad marriage (large effect), and unemployment/bad jobs (large effect). These effects are most pronounced during the adolescent years, when there is much variation in peer delinquency and peers play a central role in the lives of individuals. Peer delinquency becomes much less common among adults, but may still have a large effect on certain adults.

No/bad jobs. Few children are involved in paid work in the United States, and work plays only a small to moderate role in the lives of most adolescents. Work, however, occupies a central role in the lives of adults and has a large effect on the other domains at this time.

So each life domain directly affects crime and indirectly affects crime through its effects on the other domains. Criminals who offend at high rates usually develop irritability/low self-control and experience poor parenting in childhood. It is difficult to say which comes first, the traits or the poor parenting. But the traits and poor parenting mutually reinforce one another: irritability/low self-control fosters poor parenting, which in turn fosters irritability/low self-control. As the child becomes older, irritability/low self-control and poor parenting lead to problems in school and to association with delinquent peers. These school and peer problems, in turn, reinforce poor parenting and irritability/low self-control (as well as one another). While some individuals are able to escape from this web of crime when making the transition to adulthood, many others remain trapped—although poor parenting is replaced by marital problems and negative school experiences are replaced by bad jobs. Such individuals continue to offend at high rates well into their adult lives.

Not all criminals, however, are high-rate, chronic offenders. Most criminals, in fact, tend to limit their offending largely to the adolescent years. The social and biological changes associated with adolescence often contribute to irritability/low self-control, poor parenting, negative school experiences, and peer delinquency during the adolescent years. So for a few years, some individuals become trapped in this web. However, they are not as deeply immersed in the web as the chronic offenders described above and so they have a much easier time escaping from it when they reach adulthood.

Crime Affects Its 'Causes,' and Prior Crime Directly Affects Subsequent Crime

We have now examined most of the major direct causes of crime. But there is one important cause that we have overlooked. Studies suggest that engaging in crime at one point in time substantially increases the likelihood of offending at a later point in time. Any general theory of crime, then, must model and explain the large effect of *prior crime* on *subsequent crime*.

I argue that prior crime affects subsequent crime largely because of its effects on the five life domains. In particular, engaging in crime often (but not always) contributes to irritability/low self-control, poor parenting, bad marriages, negative school experiences, peer delinquency, unemployment, and bad jobs. Prior crime also has a *direct effect* on subsequent crime. Most studies suggest that prior crime affects subsequent crime even after we take account of the effect of prior crime on the life domains. This is because prior crime may directly impact certain of the constraints against and motivations for crime. Engaging in crime may reduce the fear of external sanctions, increase certain types of strain that do not involve the life domains, and provide certain benefits to the individual—like money and status.

The argument that prior crime increases the likelihood of subsequent crime draws heavily on labeling theory. According to this theory, individuals who are labeled criminals by others are more likely to engage in crime. This is because others treat these individuals as "criminals" or "bad people." In particular, conventional others reject them and employers do not want to hire them. Eventually, the labeled individuals end up associating with one another. The result of being labeled a criminal, then, is a reduction in the constraints against crime and an increase in the motivations for crime. Labeling theorists tend to focus on individuals who have been "formally labeled" criminals by the police and courts; that is, individuals who have been arrested and officially sanctioned. But a number of labeling theorists also examine individuals who have been "informally labeled" criminals by parents, teachers, and others (e.g., Matsueda 1992). But whatever the focus, labeling theorists argue that being labeled a criminal increases the likelihood of further crime by reducing the constraints against and increasing the motivations for crime.

I also argue that people like parents and employers may become aware of the individual's crime and label the person a "criminal." They may then treat the person in a negative manner—thereby contributing to poor parenting, bad marriages, negative school experiences, peer delinquency, unemployment, and bad jobs. In addition, I move beyond labeling theory and argue that prior crime may increase the likelihood of subsequent crime *even if others never find out about the prior crime or label the individual a criminal.* For example, prior crime may increase the likelihood of subsequent crime if individuals make a lot of money from their crime. This occurs even if the prior crime does not become known to others; in fact, this effect is more likely to occur if the crime does not become known to others. Prior crime may also increase the likelihood of subsequent crime because engaging in crime makes individuals realize that the risk of external sanction is low (see Stafford and Warr 1993). This effect is also more likely if the individual's prior crime remains unknown to others. So I argue that prior crime increases the likelihood of subsequent crime for a number of reasons, some derived from labeling theory and some not.

Having said all this, I should note that while engaging in crime generally increases the likelihood of further crime, it does not always lead to further crime. In some cases, prior crime has no effect on further crime or actually reduces the likelihood of further crime. Criminologists have devoted much effort in recent years to figuring out why this is so. Drawing on the work of several criminologists, I argue that the effect of prior crime on subsequent crime depends on 1) how others react to the crime, and 2) the characteristics of the criminal (Braithwaite 1989, 2002; Sherman 1993, 2000; Stafford and Warr 1993).

The Effect of Prior Crime on Subsequent Crime Depends on the Reaction to Crime and the Characteristics of the Criminal

How others react to the crime. There are four key ways in which others might react to the individual's crime: others may 1) *fail to respond to the crime;* 2) respond in a *harsh/rejecting* manner; 3) respond in a manner that is *approving/supportive of the crime;* and 4) respond in a manner that *firmly rejects the crime, but is accepting of the person.* The first three responses increase the likelihood that prior crime will lead to subsequent crime, while the fourth response reduces the likelihood. I should note that individuals may experience more than one type of response; for example, they may experience a harsh/rejecting response from their parents and an "approving/supportive of the crime" response from their peers.

The type of response experienced is largely determined by the individual's standing on the five life domains (this section draws heavily on Braithwaite 1989). The three types of responses that lead to further crime are most likely when individuals possess the traits of irritability and low self-control and are in social environments conducive to crime (poor parenting, no/bad marriages, negative school experiences, peer delinquency, unemployment/bad jobs). There are several reasons for this. First, such individuals are less likely to have their crime detected since they are poorly supervised by others (which of course contributes to the failure to respond to crime). Second, such individuals are more likely to be labeled "criminals" by conventional others if their crime is detected. That is because they fit the stereotype of a "criminal" or "bad person"; they are irritable and "out of control," come from "bad" families, are doing poorly in school, associate with other criminals, etc. This labeling increases the likelihood of a "harsh/rejecting" response to their crime. Third, other individuals like parents do not care about these people, do not know how to properly sanction them, and lack the skills and resources to address their problems. This increases the likelihood of the "failure to respond" and "harsh/rejecting" responses. Finally, such individuals are, by definition, more likely to have delinquent friends. This increases the likelihood of an "approving/supportive of the crime" response by peers.

The characteristics of the criminal. The effect of prior crime on subsequent crime not only depends on how others react to the crime, but also on the characteristics of the criminal. Two individuals may commit the same crime and experience similar reactions from others, but they may respond quite differently to their crime and these reactions. The first individual, for example, may derive much pleasure from their crime (e.g., thrills, excitement) and may be angered by the negative reactions of others. The second individual may derive little pleasure from their crime and may be quite anxious about the negative reactions of others. Prior crime is obviously more likely to lead to subsequent crime in the case of the first individual. What determines this difference in reaction? The same factors that influence how others respond to the individual's crime also influence how the individual responds to his or her own crime and to the reactions of others. That is, the individual's response is influenced by his or her standing on the five life domains.

Imagine individuals who are high in irritability, low in self-control, experience poor parenting, have negative school experiences, and are high in peer delinquency. Such individuals are more likely to react to their crime in ways that increase the likelihood of further crime. Most notably, they are more likely to benefit from their crime. For example, they find crime exciting. And they have a range of problems for which crime is often an effective solution—especially given their limited coping skills and low social support. Now imagine that these individuals receive one of the three responses to crime that increase the likelihood of further crime (failure to respond to crime, harsh/rejecting response, approving/supportive of the crime response). They are also more likely to react to these responses with further crime. Take, for example, the harsh/rejecting response. They are less likely to be deterred by the negative reactions of others (see Sherman 1993, 2000). Being low in self-control, they are less concerned about the negative consequences of crime. They also have less to lose from crime. In addition, they are more likely to become angry at the negative reactions of others and respond with crime, because they have an irritable disposition and are otherwise disposed to crime because of their standing on the life domains.

So prior crime tends to increase the likelihood of subsequent crime, especially among individuals whose standing on the life domains is conducive to crime.

The Causes of Crime Interact in Affecting Crime and One Another

The core proposition of the general theory is that the five life domains cause individuals to engage in crime. But that is not always the case. While the factors in each life domain increase the likelihood that individuals will engage in crime, they do not cause everyone to engage in crime. For example, individuals who experience poor parenting are more likely than others to engage in crime, but not all individuals who experience poor parenting engage in crime. Poor parenting practices, then, lead to crime among some people but not others. How can we explain this fact?

I argue that the effect of each life domain on crime is influenced or conditioned by the individual's standing on the other life domains. So, for example, the effect of poor parenting on crime depends on whether individuals are irritable and low in self-control, have negative school experiences, are high in peer delinquency, etc. Poor parenting is more likely to lead to crime among irritable individuals, those low in self-control, and those in aversive social environments. The same is true for the effect of the other life domains on crime.

General principle: A cause is more likely to lead to crime when other causes are present. If we apply this principle to the life domains, it means that a life domain is more likely to lead to crime when the other life domains are conducive to crime. For example, poor parenting is more likely to lead to crime when peer delinquency is high (and less likely when peer delinquency is low). This general principle, then, allows us to predict how the different life domains will interact with one another in affecting crime. Irritability/low self-control, for example, should be more likely to lead to crime when individuals experience poor parenting, school problems, peer delinquency, and/or work problems.

To understand the basis for this general principle, you must remember that the variables in each life domain affect both the constraints against and the motivations for crime. For example, individuals who experience poor parenting are lower in external control, have a lower stake in conformity, experience more strain, are lower in social support, are more often exposed to aggressive models and beliefs, and are more likely to be reinforced for aggressive behavior. The same is more or less true for the other life domains. Given these facts, a cause is more likely to increase crime when other causes are present because the individual is: 1) freer to engage in crime (because their constraints against crime are lower), 2) more likely to cope with strains in a criminal manner (because they are experiencing other strains, are lower in conventional social supports, have fewer coping skills/resources, etc.), and 3) more likely to view crime as a desirable or appropriate response (because of

their exposure to criminal models, beliefs favorable to crime, and reinforcements for crime).

The life domains interact in affecting one another. The life domains not only affect crime, they also affect one another—with problems in one domain increasing the likelihood of problems in the other domains. But problems in one domain do not always lead to problems in the other domains. For example, irritability and low self-control increase negative school experiences for some people, but not for others. The explanation for this parallels that given above: the effect of one life domain on another is influenced or conditioned by the remaining life domains. So the life domains interact in affecting one another. For example, irritability/low self-control is more likely to lead to negative school experiences among those who experience poor parenting.

The Causes Tend to Have Contemporaneous and Nonlinear Effects on Crime and One Another

The general theory makes a number of assertions: the life domains affect crime, the life domains affect one another, crime affects the life domains, and prior crime affects subsequent crime. But very little has been said about the timing and form of these effects. Do the causes have an immediate effect on crime and one another or do they have a delayed effect? For example, does poor parenting have an immediate effect on crime or does it take some time before poor parenting leads to crime? Also, do the causes have a linear or a nonlinear effect on crime and one another? A linear effect is one where a given increase in a causal variable always leads to the same amount of change in a dependent variable like crime. For example, a one-unit increase in irritability always leads to two additional crimes per year on average. Linear effects can be plotted on a graph with a straight line, as shown in Figure 47.2a. Nonlinear

Figure 47.2a
The Effect of Irritability on Crime: Linear Effect

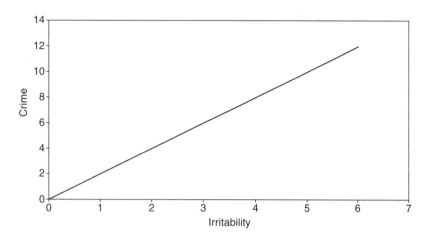

Figure 47.2b
The Effect of Irritability on Crime: NonLinear Effect

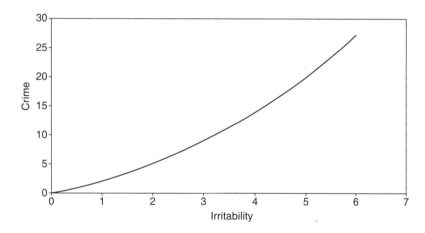

effects cannot be plotted with a straight line, rather they must be plotted with a curved or zig-zagged line. For example, it might be the case that as irritability increases it has an increasingly larger effect on crime, as shown in Figure 47.2b.

Effects are largely contemporaneous in nature, although each cause has a large, lagged effect on itself. The causes have largely contemporaneous effects on crime and one

another, although each cause also has a large, lagged effect on itself. "Contemporaneous effects" refer to effects that occur within a relatively short period of time. In certain cases, a cause may have an immediate effect on crime, as when a provocation by peers leads to immediate retaliation. In other cases, it may take somewhat longer for a cause to affect crime. For example, poor parental supervision may not immediately result in crime, but may lead to an increase in crime over the course of several weeks. While there is no precise definition of "contemporaneous," I somewhat arbitrarily define contemporaneous effects as those that occur within a few months' time.

Why do the life domains have largely contemporaneous effects on crime? Each life domain, you will recall, measures the constraints against and the motivations for crime (i.e., it measures the individual's external control, stake in conformity, internal control, level of strain, and reinforcements/models/beliefs favorable to crime). The life domains have largely contemporaneous effects on crime because crime is largely a function of current constraints and motivations rather than those experienced in the past. Individuals, in particular, are most responsive to the controls, strains, and reinforcements they are currently experiencing. When contemplating crime, for example, individuals consider the likelihood of being caught and punished at that time, not the likelihood that existed a year ago. Or they take account of their current beliefs regarding crime, not their beliefs a year ago.

The causes not only have largely contemporaneous effects on crime, but on one another as well. For example, our current experiences in school are more strongly affected by our current traits and environmental experiences than by our past traits and experiences. The same applies to the effects of crime on the life domains. For example, parenting practices are more strongly influenced by our current levels of crime than by our prior levels (although crime that results in official sanction may sometimes have lasting effects).

While effects are largely contemporaneous in nature, each cause has a large lagged effect on itself. For example, poor parenting at Time 1 has a strong effect on poor parenting at Time 2. The life domains, then, are self-perpetuating to some extent. There are several reasons for this, including the force of habit.

Effects are nonlinear. Most research in criminology implicitly assumes that causes have a linear effect on crime. That is, it assumes that a given increase in a causal variable always results in the same amount of change in crime. But there is reason to believe that the causes have a nonlinear effect on crime. In particular, as a cause increases it should have an increasingly larger effect on crime (see Figure 47.2b). This is the case because most causes must pass a certain threshold point before they start to have a meaningful effect on crime. The logic behind this threshold effect is most easily illustrated with respect to strains or stressors. Moving from a state of no strain to one of mild or moderate strain will not cause most people to engage in crime. Mild strains do not produce much anger and they are easily ignored or dealt with through legal coping methods. After a certain threshold point is reached, however, strains begin to generate some anger, they are less easily ignored, and they begin to tax legal coping efforts. It is at this point when strains become more likely to generate crime. The further one moves beyond the threshold point, the more likely strains are to generate crime, contributing to a nonlinear effect of the type shown in Figure 47.2b.

It is also the case that as the level of the life domains increase they have increasingly larger effects on one another. For example, mild to moderate levels of irritability may not be sufficient to cause parents to dislike their children and treat them harshly. Levels of irritability may have to pass a certain threshold point before this happens. Likewise, one can use these arguments to claim that as crime increases in frequency and seriousness it has an increasingly larger effect on the life domains. For example, minor levels of crime may not cause conventional peers to reject the juvenile. Crime may have to pass a certain threshold point before peer rejection occurs.

An Overview of the General Theory

This discussion of the timing and form of causal effects completes my presentation of the core part of the general theory of crime. It may be useful to pause and summarize the major points made so far:

1. Crime is caused by five clusters of variables, organized into the life domains of self (irritability/low self-control), family (poor parenting practices, no/bad marriages), school (negative school experiences, limited education), peers (peer delinquency), and work (unemployment, bad jobs). The effect of the life domains on crime often varies over the life course.

2. The variables in each domain increase crime by reducing the constraints against crime and increasing the motivations for crime. The constraints against crime include external control, stake in conformity, and internal control. The motivations for crime include strain, reinforcements for crime, exposure to successful criminal models, and beliefs favorable to crime.

3. Each life domain affects the other domains, although some effects are stronger than others and effect sizes often change over the life course. These effects are such that problems in one domain contribute to problems in another; for example, irritability/low self-control contributes to poor parenting, which in turn contributes to irritability/low self-control. Problems in the domains, then, tend to mutually reinforce one another (the "web of crime"). And each domain has both a direct effect on crime and an indirect effect through the other domains.

4. Prior crime has a direct effect on subsequent crime and an indirect effect, through the life domains. These effects are conditioned or influenced by the individual's standing on the life domains. Prior crime is most likely to lead to further crime when the individual is high in irritability, low in self-control, and in social environments conducive to crime.

5. The life domains interact in affecting crime and one another. A given life domain is more likely to increase crime or negatively affect another life domain when the remaining life domains are conducive to crime.

6. The life domains have nonlinear and largely contemporaneous effects on crime and one another, although each life domain has a large lagged effect on itself. Likewise, crime has a nonlinear and largely contemporaneous effect on the life domains.

The general theory of crime up to this point is summarized in Figure 47.3. This figure does not include a causal arrow for each of the many effects in the theory. Rather, I employ certain simplifying devices. The left side of the model lists the five life domains and crime in a box (measured over the same period of time). The arrows going up and down the sides of the box refer to the fact that the life domains and crime have contemporaneous effects on one another; that is, the five life domains affect crime, the five domains affect one another, and crime affects the five domains. The zigzagged sides of the box refer to the fact that these effects are nonlinear. The "x"s within the box refer to the fact that the life domains and crime interact with one another in their effects. The box on the right side of the figure can be interpreted in the same way, except that the life domains and crime in this box are measured at a later period of time. The heavy lines from the first box to the second refer to the fact that crime and each life domain has a strong lagged effect on itself—although this effect is conditioned by the other life domains and crime (as indicated by the "x"s at the start of each arrow).

This model may appear complex on one level— positing many different effects and making a number of claims about the form and timing of these effects. But the model is quite simple on another level. As indicated above, a few simple arguments are sufficient to generate the model in Figure 47.3. It is, however, important to note that this is a "bare bones" model. I do not attempt to list the reasons why the causes affect crime and one another. Such reasons, however, are easily

Figure 47.3
The General Theory of Crime: Core Model

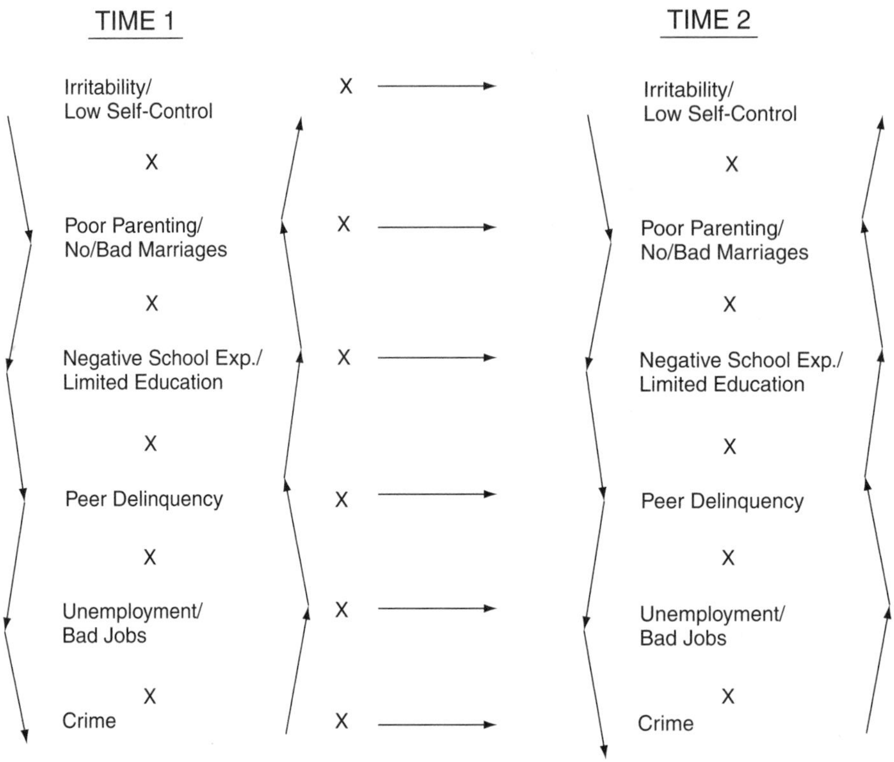

TIME 1   TIME 2

Irritability/   X ————→   Irritability/
Low Self-Control   Low Self-Control

        X   X

Poor Parenting/   X ————→   Poor Parenting/
No/Bad Marriages   No/Bad Marriages

        X   X

Negative School Exp./   X ————→   Negative School Exp./
Limited Education   Limited Education

        X   X

Peer Delinquency   X ————→   Peer Delinquency

        X   X

Unemployment/   X ————→   Unemployment/
Bad Jobs   Bad Jobs

        X   X
Crime   X ————→   Crime

described: the causes affect crime by impacting the constraints against and the motivations for crime listed earlier. And the causes affect one another for similar reasons. The model also does not describe differences in effect sizes. These differences change over the life course, so separate models for childhood, adolescence, and adulthood would be necessary to properly describe differences in effect sizes. Again, however, it is easy to describe the major features of such models.

Incorporating Outside Factors Into the General Theory

A range of "outside" factors affect the individual's standing on the life domains. It would be difficult to incorporate all such factors into the general theory without seriously threatening the simplicity or parsimony of the theory. For that reason, the general theory focuses on the effects of age, sex, race/ethnicity, parent's SES, and community characteristics. These key variables have large direct effects on all or most of the life domains. In particular, the life domains are more likely to be conducive to crime when individuals are in the adolescent years, are male (with the exception of work/unemployment), are African American or members of certain other race/ethnic groups, have parents who are low in SES, and reside in poor, inner-city communities. These facts allow the general theory to explain group differences in crime rates, with such differences being due to the fact that groups differ in their standing on the life domains. That is, the members of some groups are more likely than the members of other groups to have traits conducive to crime, experience family problems, have negative school experiences, be high in peer delinquency, and/or have work problems. For example, males are more likely than females to be irritable and low in self-control, experience poor parental supervision and harsh discipline, have weak family ties as adults, and be high in peer delinquency. And this is the major reason why males have higher crime rates than females.

Conclusion

I believe that the general theory provides a "reasonably complete" explanation of individual offending. In particular, the theory reflects the major crime research and captures the essential arguments of the major crime theories, including biological, psychological, social control, self-control, strain, social learning, social support, and labeling theories. I further believe that the general theory organizes this research and these theories into a "unified whole." In particular, the general theory is much more than a patchwork of different theories. The general theory integrates the major theories and research on the causes of crime in ways that go well beyond the common strategy of claiming that the variables associated with one theory cause the variables associated with another theory (e.g., poor parental supervision causes association with delinquent peers). As a result, each theory is entwined in multiple ways with every other theory. Finally, I believe that the general theory provides a clear and concise answer to the question of "why do criminals offend?"—although you, the reader, are the final judge in this area.

Discussion Questions

1. Describe the major constraints against and motivations for crime. What theories does Agnew draw on when listing these constraints and motivations?
2. Agnew groups the variables that have relatively large, direct effects on crime into five life domains. Briefly describe these life domains. Select any one of these domains and describe how it indexes or affects the constraints against and motivations for crime.
3. What does Agnew mean by the "web of crime"?
4. Prior crime sometimes increases the likelihood of subsequent crime. Describe the different reasons why this occurs, and describe the circumstances under which prior crime is most likely to increase subsequent crime.
5. Describe what Agnew means when he states that (a) "the causes of crime interact in affecting crime and one another," (b) "the causes tend to have contemporaneous effects on crime and one another," and (c) "the causes tend to have nonlinear effects on crime and one another."
6. Briefly describe the key points of Agnew's general theory. What traditional crime theories does Agnew draw on in his general theory?
7. Drawing on Agnew's theory, explain why males have higher crime rates than females.

PART XV

Putting Theory to Work: Guiding Crime Control Policy

Most, if not all, of the criminologists in this book developed their theories in the hope that they would allow us to better control crime. In fact, many of these criminologists have discussed the crime control implications of their theories in detail (see especially Barlow and Decker, 2010). Further, certain of these criminologists have had much success in influencing crime control policy. This is the case with Beccaria, whose work fundamentally altered Western legal systems and inspired our current efforts to "get tough" on crime (see Chapter 1 and Part X). This is also the case with several contemporary criminologists. Braithwaite's work on reintegrative shaming contributed to the development of the restorative justice movement, which has transformed the justice system in several countries (Chapter 21 and Part VI). The work of Chesney-Lind and other feminist criminologists led the police and court system to take family violence and other crimes more seriously (Part IX). Cornish and Clarke's work on rational choice theory provided the foundation for a range of situational crime prevention approaches (Chapters 33, 35, 49). And Wilson and Kelling's work on "Broken Windows" changed the nature of policing in many cities (Chapter 36 and Part XI). Many of the theories presented in this book are therefore of more than academic interest; they have had a large impact on crime control policies.

This is not to imply, however, that crime control policies are always or largely based on crime theories. A host of factors influences our response to crime, including popular perceptions of what works (e.g., "of course punishment reduces crime"), views on what is "just" or appropriate (e.g., "murderers deserve to be executed"), political considerations (e.g., not wanting to appear "soft" on crime), the lobbying efforts of various groups, and cost considerations (e.g., Becket and Sasson, 2000; Garland, 2001; Haggerty, 2004; Lynch, 2007; Ren et al., 2008; Tonry, 2004, 2008b; Useem and Piehl, 2008; Western, 2006). These factors sometimes lead policymakers to employ crime control initiatives that are ineffective or even counterproductive. Examples include "scared straight"-type programs, boot camps, and efforts to try juvenile offenders as adults (see below). Nevertheless, crime theories and research sometimes have an impact on efforts to control crime. In fact, many criminologists, including several in this book, are now involved in efforts that are starting to change our current approach to controlling crime (e.g., Cullen, 2005; Petersilia, 2008).

Since the early 1970s, efforts to control crime in the United States have focused on increasing the certainty and, especially, the severity of punishment. The most notable consequence of this "get tough" approach has been a fivefold increase in the rate of imprisonment, leaving the United States with the highest rate of incarceration in the world. This approach draws on classical and deterrence theories, which argue that individuals choose to engage in crime when they believe that the benefits of doing so outweigh the costs (see Chapter 1 and Part X). Increasing the certainty and severity of punishment raises the cost of crime and should therefore deter people from engaging in crime. This approach also draws on the claim by some criminologists that it is *not* possible to rehabilitate offenders (see below). Given this claim, it is argued that serious offenders should be locked up for long periods so they cannot commit crimes in the larger society. Many criminologists, however, have come to question our efforts to "get tough" on crime.

There is little doubt that imprisoning large numbers of offenders stops some crime, but it is claimed that get-tough efforts are of limited effectiveness and have a range of negative consequences, including negative effects on those who are locked up and the communities from which they come. One reason for the limited effectiveness of these efforts is that they fail to address most of the major causes of crime, as described in this text. In particular, most criminologists state that crime is not simply a matter of choice, but is strongly influenced by a range of individual and environmental factors. Such factors include low self-control, strains of various types, the failure of families and communities to exercise effective control, exposure to others who foster crime, and features of the larger environment—such as poverty and high rates of inequality. Current efforts to get tough on crime do little to address such factors; in fact, they sometimes make them worse.

Further, it is claimed that well-designed and implemented rehabilitation and prevention programs can address these causes. Such programs attempt to alter individual traits and change the nature of the individual's environment, particularly the family, school, peer, and work environments. Less commonly, such programs try to change the communities in which people live and the larger society. These arguments are beginning to have some effect, and there seems to be an increased emphasis on rehabilitation and prevention over the last few years—although efforts to control crime are still dominated by get-tough approaches.

This introduction begins by describing the origins of our current efforts to control crime by increasing the certainty and severity of punishment, highlighting the theoretical foundations of such efforts. It then describes the criticisms of such efforts, particularly those based on the theories in this book. Next, it describes the responses to these criticisms, including theoretically driven efforts to punish in a more effective manner and to increase the emphasis placed on rehabilitation and prevention.

Getting Tough on Crime

Rehabilitation was the guiding philosophy of the criminal justice system from the 1800s until the early 1970s. This does not mean that the criminal justice system made a serious effort to rehabilitate all or even most offenders. There was a large gap between philosophy and practice, and offenders frequently received little in the way of meaningful rehabilitation services. Nevertheless, the stated goal of the system was rehabilitation. As Lipsey and Cullen (2007: 302) indicate, rehabilitation is "distinguished from correctional sanctions by the centrality of interactions with offenders aimed at motivating, guiding, and supporting constructive change in whatever characteristics or circumstances engender their criminal behavior or subvert their prosocial behavior."

Prevention differs from rehabilitation in that prevention programs try to stop individuals from becoming offenders in the first place. Many of the same programs, however, are used for prevention and rehabilitation purposes. Job training programs, for example, are used to prevent high-risk individuals such as high-school dropouts from becoming involved in crime, and they are also used to reduce the future offending of prison inmates. Prevention programs have never played a large role in crime control efforts, except for a brief period in the 1960s and early 1970s, during the heyday of the "War on Poverty."

The War on Poverty was initiated by President Kennedy and implemented by his successor, President Johnson (see Empey et al., 1999). A major purpose of the War on Poverty was to reduce crime by increasing the opportunities for people to achieve monetary success through legal channels. Certain of the programs that made up the War on Poverty, for example, provided educational assistance and job training to people in disadvantaged communities. This approach was partly rooted in the strain theories of Merton (Chapter 13) and Cloward and Ohlin (1960), who argue that crime results from the inability to achieve monetary goals through legal channels. And certain strain theorists were involved in the development of the War on Poverty. Most of the programs that were part of the War on Poverty have since been dismantled, but a few remain, such as Project Head Start (a preschool enrichment program) and Job Corps (a jobs training program).

Beginning in the early 1970s, however, the crime control strategies of rehabilitation and prevention came under heavy attack. There were several reasons for this (for overviews and extended discussions, see Becket and Sasson, 2000; Currie, 1998; Garland, 2001; Haggerty, 2004; Lynch, 2007; Ren et al., 2008; Tonry, 2004, 2008a; Useem and Piehl, 2008; Western, 2006). Rising crime rates in the 1960s and early 1970s caused many to question the effectiveness of rehabilitation and prevention. This questioning was reinforced by several studies in the 1970s and 1980s that claimed that rehabilitation was largely ineffective. The best known of these studies, the "Martinson Report," examined a range of rehabilitation programs and concluded that "with few and isolated exceptions the rehabilitative efforts that have been reported so far have had no appreciable effect on recidivism [or reoffending]" (Martinson, 1974: 25).

Further, the political climate of the country became more conservative. In line with this shift, politicians argued that crime was *not* rooted in such things as poverty and racism. Rather, criminals were said to be responsible for their behavior, and punishment was said to be the best way to reduce crime. Consider this quote from former President Reagan:

Choosing a career in crime is not the result of poverty or an unhappy childhood or of a misunderstood adolescence; it is the result of a conscious, willful choice made by some who consider themselves above the law, who seek to exploit the hard work and, sometimes, very lives of their fellow citizens.... The crime epidemic is [not] some sociological phenomenon... It is, instead, a cumulative result of too much emphasis on the protection of the rights of the accused and too little concern for our government's responsibility to protect the lives, homes, and rights of our law-abiding citizens... [T]he criminal element now calculates that crime really does pay. (Quoted in Beckett and Sasson, 2000: 61–62)

Certain criminologists also argued that crime was a matter of choice and was best controlled through punishment (see Dilulio, 1995–1995; Ren et al., 2008; Wilson, 1975). Some also argued that offenders choose crime because of their "moral poverty." In the words of Bennett et al. (1996: 56):

Moral poverty is the poverty of being without loving, capable, responsible parents and adults who teach you right from wrong; the poverty of being without parents and other authorities who habituate you to feel joy at others' joy, pain at others' pain, satisfaction when you do right, remorse when you do wrong; the poverty of growing up in the virtual absence of people who teach morality by their own everyday example and who insist that you follow suit.

This moral poverty was said to produce "super-predators," that is, "vicious," "remorseless," "uncaring," and "radically impulsive" individuals who readily succumb to the "temptations of crime." Further, Bennett et al. went on to argue that moral poverty is not rooted in economic poverty but rather in the decline in moral standards in the United States and the associated increase in such things as single-parent families. And the solution to moral poverty was said to be a re-imposition of moral standards, including "a full-scale, concentrated, intense effort at combating drugs and crime."

Some argue that this conservative shift was partly a reaction to the civil rights, antiwar, and other political movements in the 1950s and 1960s. Many felt threatened by the changes occurring in American society and were attracted to those who promised to crack down on crime and other "lawlessness." Politicians, in turn, were often eager to exploit the fears of these people. This argument, it should be noted, is compatible with critical criminology (Part VIII), which states that the members of more powerful groups use the criminal justice system—including the police, courts, and corrections—to maintain their privileged position and control those seen as a threat, such as African Americans (e.g., Tonry, 2008a).

Conservative criminologists and policymakers argued that increased punishment would reduce crime for several reasons. The first derive from the classical school of criminology (Chapter 1 and Part I), deterrence theory, and rational choice theory (Part X). As indicated above, many viewed crime as the result of a deliberate choice, based on the belief that "crime really does pay." Increasing the severity of punishment would therefore deter punished individuals from engaging in further crime (specific deterrence). And increasing the certainty and severity of punishment would deter potential offenders in the larger population from crime (general deterrence). This would occur by ensuring that the costs of crime outweighed the benefits.

It was also argued that increasing the number of people imprisoned and the length of their confinement would reduce crime through what is known as an "incapacitation effect." This effect refers to the fact that imprisoned offenders cannot commit crimes in the larger community. Several criminologists, drawing on the "Martinson Report" and other studies, claimed that it was not possible to rehabilitate offenders (e.g., Wilson, 1975). Given our supposed inability to rehabilitate, it was argued that it was necessary to lock up those who were not deterred from crime in order to protect society. As Wilson (1975: 235) stated: "Wicked people exist. Nothing avails except to set them apart from innocent people."

Partly as a result of such arguments, there was a dramatic shift in our crime control policies. Beginning in the early 1970s and continuing through today, the strategies of rehabilitation and prevention were deemphasized. Instead, the focus shifted to increasing the certainty and, especially, the severity of punishment. For example, laws were passed that imposed mandatory prison terms on convicted drug offenders, that imposed life sentences on individuals upon their third conviction for a serious crime ("three strikes and you're out"), that abolished or limited parole, and that made it much easier to try serious juvenile offenders as adults. Many offenses that used to result in minor sanctions, particularly drug offenses, now resulted in imprisonment (Mauer and King, 2007a). And the length of prison sentences for many crimes increased.

Fewer than 200,000 people were imprisoned in the early 1970s, a rate of about 100 per 100,000 people in the United States. This rate had been roughly stable since 1925. About 1.6 million people are imprisoned as of mid-year 2007 (Sabol and Couture, 2008). Another 780,000 people are confined in jail (Sabol and Minton, 2008), making the total rate of incarceration about 770 per 100,000. This compares with a rate of about 50 to 150 in most other Western nations (see Nagin et al., 2009; Western, 2006).

Rates of incarceration are particularly high for certain groups. About one in six African American men has been incarcerated, and, if current trends continue, about one in three African American males born today will spend time in prison (Mauer and King, 2007b; Western, 2006). Further, not only are more people serving more time in prison, but prison inmates have also become less likely to participate in rehabilitation programs (Useem and Piehl, 2008: 111–113; Vieraitis et al., 2007: 592). Petersilia (2008) reports that in California—the state with the largest prison population in the United States—nearly half of all prisoners released in 2006 did not participate in *any* work or rehabilitation program while incarcerated.

In addition to sending more people to prison for longer terms, a range of new "intermediate sanctions" was developed. These sanctions are "intermediate" between regular probation (limited supervision in the community) and prison. That is, they provide more control and punishment than regular probation but less than prison. Intermediate sanctions include intensive probation supervision (frequent meetings with probation officers, regular drug tests, etc.); home confinement, often enforced with electronic monitoring; and boot camps (short stays in military-style prison camps). While these sanctions were partly designed to reduce the high cost of imprisonment, they often did not serve this function. That is because these sanctions were frequently used *in place of* regular probation, rather than *in place of* imprisonment.

These get-tough strategies continue to dominate the criminal justice system. This stems in part from the theoretical basis of these approaches; many criminologists, policymakers, and people in the general public find much appeal in deterrence and related theories. It also stems from the sometimes-grand claims made about the effectiveness of these strategies. There has now been a fair amount of research evaluating these claims, and, as discussed next, there is good reason to question the utility of get-tough approaches.

Challenging Get-Tough Approaches

The research on specific and general deterrence is summarized in Part X. As indicated, there is little evidence that punishing offenders or punishing them more severely reduces their level of subsequent offending (for overviews, see Lipsey and Cullen, 2007; Nagin et al., 2009; Tonry, 2008b). To give a few examples: intermediate sanctions such as boot camps and intensive probation supervision are not more effective than less severe alternatives such as regular probation (MacKenzie, 2006). Trying juveniles as adults, which subjects them to more severe punishments, is not more effective than trying juveniles in juvenile court (Redding, 2008). Harsher prison conditions are not more effective than less harsh conditions (Chen and Shapiro, 2007). And imprisonment is not more effective than less severe alternatives in reducing subsequent crime (Nagin et al., 2009). In fact, studies sometimes find that the administration of punishment or of more severe punishment increases the likelihood of subsequent offending.

These findings regarding specific deterrence are a surprise to many people. But they can be explained in terms of the crime theories presented in this text. Specific deterrence assumes that offenders are rational, taking account of the costs and benefits of crime before acting. As indicated in earlier chapters, however, there is good *reason to question the rationality of many offenders*. Offenders often possess traits such as low constraint and negative emotionality (Chapter 5). As a consequence, they frequently act on the spur of the moment and in anger, giving little thought to the long-term consequences of their behavior. Offenders also commit their crimes in response to strain (see Part V) or pressure from others (see Part VI), which also causes them to ignore or minimize the threat of punishment.

Related to this, *punishment does little to address most causes of crime*, including those individual traits discussed in Part II and the many environmental factors discussed in the other parts of this text. Punishment, for example, does little to reduce strain, minimize the social learning of crime, or increase control. In fact, *punishment may make many of these causes worse*. This is the central point of labeling theory (Part VII). Punishment by the criminal justice system often increases strain. For example, it makes it more difficult for individuals to find decent work. Punishment often reduces control. For example, it often weakens ties to conventional others, such as family members, and to conventional institutions, such as work. Punishment promotes the social learning of crime. Punished individuals are frequently placed in prisons and jails, where they are isolated from conventional others and forced to associate with other criminals—who often reinforce crime, model crime, and teach beliefs favorable to crime. And, upon their release, offenders often find that conventional others are reluctant to associate with them, so they often associate with criminal others.

Finally, the *criminal justice system does not punish in an effective way*. Research on social learning and control theories (Parts IV and VI) suggests that punishments are most effective when individuals are closely monitored and their rule violations are consistently sanctioned in a meaningful, but not overly harsh, manner. The probability that crimes will result in official sanction, however, is generally low. For example, Dunford and Elliott (1984) examined the number of delinquent acts that adolescents self-reported for a two-year period, and they discovered that only 7 percent of the youth reporting between 101 and 200 delinquent acts were arrested and that only 19 percent of those self-reporting over 200 delinquent acts were arrested. As a consequence, punished offenders may feel that they can get away with crime in the future. In fact, some data suggest that punished offenders do not increase their estimates of the certainty of punishment and may even reduce them (Pogarsky and Piquero, 2003). Further, punished offenders are often treated in a harsh manner and subject to severe sanctions, which may prompt further crime through the

process of defiance (see Chapter 21). In sum, there are several reasons why specific deterrence is not an effective crime control strategy.

The research on general deterrence is somewhat more encouraging. As indicated in Part X, studies suggest that increasing the certainty of punishment reduces offending in the general population. However, the reduction is modest in size, and the certainty of punishment typically has a smaller effect on crime than many of the other causes discussed in this book (e.g., association with criminal peers, beliefs regarding crime, self-control). Further, it is often difficult to increase the certainty of punishment. Most get-tough efforts, in fact, have focused on increasing the severity of punishment, which is easily done. Policymakers simply pass laws increasing the penalty for various crimes. The cost of such laws may ultimately be quite high, as new prisons are constructed and staffed, but the laws themselves are easily enacted. Increasing the severity of punishment, however, has little effect on deterring offenders—particularly when the certainty of punishment is low (see Part X).

Given the difficulties with deterrence, one can perhaps understand the appeal of incapacitation as a crime control strategy. Locking offenders up for long periods of time seems certain to reduce crime, even if the act of locking them up has no specific or general deterrent effect. Initially, it was claimed that this strategy would stop a great deal of crime. The first studies on the effectiveness of incapacitation as a crime control strategy were based on surveys of prison inmates. These inmates were asked about the number of crimes they committed each year when free. Based on these reports, it was estimated that incapacitation would stop much crime from occuring. For example, if the average inmate committed 10 crimes per year when free, it was estimated that imprisoning 100,000 additional inmates would stop a million crimes each year.

We now know that such estimates are greatly exaggerated. There are several reasons for this, some having to do with the theories in this text.

First, many offenders commit their crimes in groups (see Part IV). Incapacitating an offender may not affect the amount of crime committed by the group. Second, when one offender is locked up, another offender may emerge to take that person's place. This may be especially true for crimes such as drug selling, with new drug sellers quickly emerging to replace those who are imprisoned. Third, studies of crime and the life course indicate that offending often declines sharply after adolescence and young adulthood (see Part XII). Many offenders may already be "aging out of crime" by the time they are imprisoned, so incarceration does not stop much crime. Finally, as we lock up more and more offenders, we become increasingly likely to lock up low-rate offenders—who commit little crime each year when free.

More recent studies have attempted to estimate the size of the incapacitation effect in ways that avoid the above concerns (for overviews and selected studies, see Andrews and Bonta, 2006; Kovandzic and Vieraitis, 2006; MacKenzie, 2006; Pratt and Cullen, 2005; Spelman, 2006; Western, 2006; Zimring, 2007). Some studies examine the relationship between incapacitation and crime rates in a sample of states or communities, taking account of other factors that may affect the crime rate. In particular, such studies determine whether states or communities with higher incarceration rates have lower crime rates. Other studies examine changes in incarceration and crime rates over time, in an effort to determine whether increases in incarceration are associated with reductions in crime, again taking account of other influences on crime. Estimates of the amount of crime stopped by incarceration vary across studies, with one recent review estimating that a 10 percent increase in the incarceration rate may be associated with a 2 to 4 percent reduction in crime (Stemen, 2007: 5). Further, as the incarceration rate increases, reductions in crime become smaller since we are imprisoning more low-rate offenders (see especially Liedka et al., 2006; Useem and Piehl, 2008). The effect of

incarceration, then, is not insignificant; but it is not as large as many initially claimed.

Further, certain researchers have argued that incarceration has several negative consequences that may ultimately undermine the reduction in crime that it causes. Most notably, incarceration may increase the likelihood that released inmates engage in crime for reasons related to labeling theory (see Part VII; Nagin et al., 2009). There is good evidence that imprisonment has certain negative effects on offenders, such as reduced employment prospects (Pager, 2003; Western, 2002, 2006). And certain studies suggest that imprisonment does increase the likelihood of subsequent crime, although not all studies show this (see the review in Nagin et al., 2009). We are now at a point where close to 700,000 inmates are being released from prison each year (Useem and Piehl, 2008). If many such individuals return to the community with a greater disposition for crime, this may undermine the incapacitation effect (see Vieraitis et al., 2007, for data suggesting that this is beginning to occur). Another negative consequence of incarceration is its high cost. It costs approximately $30,000 per year to confine an offender, and many government agencies have come to spend a large share of their budgets on incarceration (Moore, 2009; Petersilia, 2008). Such money is often diverted from education and other social services, and the consequences of this diversion may ultimately lead to higher crime rates. As Cullen (Chapter 46) and others argue, spending on social support services reduces crime for several reasons.

Chapter 48 in this volume, by Todd Clear, points to yet another possible negative consequence of high rates of incarceration. Clear points out that "imprisonment has been concentrated among poor, minority males who live in improvised neighborhoods." He argues that such neighborhoods suffer from a host of problems as a result of their high incarceration rates. Such problems include family disruption, the reduced earnings of those with prison records, and negative attitudes toward the criminal justice system. These problems, in turn, reduce the ability and willingness of residents to exercise effective social control over one another. That is, high rates of incarceration lead to a breakdown in community controls or to social disorganization (see Part III). Not surprisingly, Clear argues that we should sharply reduce the number of people who are incarcerated and, as an alternative, make use of "community justice programs" and increase social support of various types (see Chapter 46).

Clear's arguments are intriguing. Incarceration has been promoted as a way to make poor communities safe, but Clear contends that our high rates of incarceration have the opposite effect. Clear and others have begun to examine the effects of incarceration on communities. Certain research supports Clear's arguments, suggesting, for example, that high rates of incarceration in a community contribute to family disruption and, ultimately, lead to higher rates of crime (Clear, 2007; Clear et al., 2003). Other research, however, has been less supportive of Clear's arguments, suggesting that incarceration has both negative and positive effects and that, on balance, it may reduce community crime rates (see Lynch and Sabol, 2004). Additional research will hopefully allow us to determine whether the reduction in crime caused by incarceration is outweighed by its criminogenic effects. For now, however, it is clear that the consequences of incarceration are varied and that it does not result in the large reduction in crime that many originally claimed.

Responding to the Criticisms of Get-Tough Approaches: More Effective Sanctioning

Some criminologists have responded to the above criticisms of get-tough approaches by exploring ways to sanction more effectively. Much attention has focused on increasing the certainty of punishment, the critical factor in deterring crime. Most notably, criminologists have suggested new strategies of policing that better target those areas or persons at high risk for crime. One such strategy is called "hot spots" policing. Research suggests that most areas of a community have little or no crime, while other areas—called "hot spots"—have much crime. In one study, researchers discovered that less than 3 percent of the addresses in a city accounted for more than half of all calls to the police (Sherman and Weisburd, 1995). Some of these addresses—such as those associated with bars or convenience stores—produced hundreds of calls to the police each year. Further, crime is more likely to occur on certain days and times of the day at these addresses (e.g., weekend evenings). Research indicates that substantially increasing police patrols at these hot spots results in a moderate reduction in crime both in and around the hot spots. Further, there is no evidence that crime is displaced to other areas (Weisburd et al., 2006). The police do not have the resources to "crack down" on all hot spots at the same time, but crime reductions still result if they rotate their crackdowns in an unpredictable manner.

Another strategy for increasing the certainty of punishment cracks down on those individuals at high risk for engaging in certain crimes. For example, the police in Boston knew that youth gangs were responsible for most of the juvenile homicides in that city. Further, the police, working with community leaders, were able to identify these youth gangs and most of the members in them. The police delivered a clear message to these gang members: stop the violence or face intensive police scrutiny. The police indicated that they would saturate the areas in which the gangs congregated, place severe restrictions on those gang members on probation, and severely punish any gang members who violated the law. This threat was backed up on several occasions. The result was a substantial reduction in youth homicide (Braga et al., 2008). Other cities have also successfully implemented this approach (e.g., McGarrell et al., 2006). Unfortunately, this approach cannot be used with most crimes, since high-risk offenders are less easily identified and monitored. (For another example of an effort to increase the certainty of punishment, see Chapter 36 by Wilson and Kelling.)

Yet another initiative—the restorative justice approach—aims to sanction in a more effective manner, one that reduces the negative effects of punishment and better addresses certain of the causes of crime. The restorative justice approach was partly inspired by the work of Braithwaite. As indicated in Chapter 21, Braithwaite argues that the criminal justice system often sanctions individuals in a way that labels them as criminals, isolates them from conventional others and institutions, and contributes to the development of criminal groups. The restorative justice approach promotes what Braithwaite calls "reintegrative shaming." Offenders are held accountable for their crimes and, through a conference that includes the victim(s) and community representatives, are led to appreciate the harm they have caused. This serves to undermine those beliefs justifying or excusing crime (see Part IV). Offenders then participate in the development of a plan to repair that harm. The plan frequently includes an apology and community service but typically avoids incarceration. After the harm is repaired, the offender is forgiven, frequently at a special gathering. Steps are also taken to preserve or strengthen the offender's bond with conventional others and institutions (see Bazemore and Umbreit, 2004; Braithwaite, 2002). Research suggests that this approach is more effective in preventing subsequent offending than are traditional criminal justice sanctions (Bonta et al., 2006; Braithwaite, 2002; McGarrell and Hipple, 2007; Sherman and Strang, 2007).

Still other researchers have drawn on rational choice and routine activities theory to develop a range of creative strategies for increasing the costs and/or reducing the benefits of crime. These strategies fall under the rubric of "situational crime prevention." Chapter 35, by Clarke, describes the logic behind situational crime prevention and gives some examples of this approach. The selection by Felson in Chapter 49 discusses the approach in more detail and provides numerous examples. At the heart of this approach is the idea that it is often quite difficult to change the offender's disposition for crime. As Felson states in Chapter 49: "Do not try to improve human character. You are certain to fail." However, it is often possible to alter the characteristics of situations and, in doing so, prevent much crime. Situations can be altered so that crime is more difficult to commit (e.g., burglar bars on windows), is more risky (e.g., video cameras in stores), is less rewarding (e.g., reducing the amount of cash in registers), and is less easily excused (e.g., making employees aware of the harm caused by employee theft).

These steps, in essence, increase the costs of particular crimes and/or lower the benefits. These steps, however, move well beyond traditional efforts to deter crime—which focus on increasing the likelihood and/or severity of official sanctions. Situational crime prevention efforts may increase several "costs" of crime in addition to the likelihood and severity of official sanction. For example, efforts may be made to increase the likelihood of informal sanctions (e.g., sanctions by parents and teachers) and the moral costs of crime (e.g., the guilt resulting from crime). Also, situational crime prevention attempts to reduce the benefits of crime as well. A wide range of situational approaches has been employed, and, as Felson points out, some have been quite successful at reducing the extent of particular types of crime (also see Clarke and Eck, 2005).

The successes of situational crime prevention, however, do not mean that it is fruitless to attempt to "improve human character" or alter those factors that create a predisposition for crime. According to many criminologists, these factors can be altered and it is critical to do so if we are to substantially reduce crime. It is unlikely that we can alter situations to the point where predisposed individuals are substantially less likely to engage in *all or most* forms of crime. Among other things, predisposed individuals will seek out or create situations conducive to crime.

Delinquent youth, for example, will find ways to associate with other delinquent youth away from adults. Further, as noted in Parts II and X, predisposed individuals often minimize the costs and maximize the benefits of crime in particular situations. Any complete attempt to control crime must therefore also focus on those factors that create a predisposition for crime.

Responding to the Criticisms of Get-Tough Approaches: Placing More Emphasis on Rehabilitation and Prevention

Given the limitations of get-tough approaches, many criminologists argue that efforts to rehabilitate offenders and prevent crime should receive much more emphasis than is now the case. This argument is beginning to have some effect. Certain states are backing away from get-tough approaches, such as boot camps and increased sanctions for certain crimes, and are placing more emphasis on rehabilitation and prevention (e.g., Jacobson, 2006; Petersilia, 2008). These actions are partly motivated by financial and political considerations. Many states can no longer afford to build and maintain new prisons. Also, the public demand for get-tough approaches has declined, perhaps because crime is no longer the major political issue it once was (Jacobson, 2006). At the same time these actions also stem from increasing evidence that carefully chosen and implemented rehabilitation and prevention programs can reduce crime, are cost effective, and are favored by the public.

There have been several major analyses of the effectiveness of rehabilitation and prevention programs since the "Martinson Report." These analyses consider many more programs than Martinson, including many recent programs. And they employ more sophisticated techniques to examine the effectiveness of these programs. One such technique is meta-analysis, which allows researchers to group programs together—all programs or particular types of programs—and estimate their overall effect on subsequent offending (Boruch and Petrosino, 2004). Researchers can also determine whether the effectiveness of programs is influenced by certain factors, such as the type of offenders who participate in the program (e.g., high versus low risk) or whether the program is run in the community or in prison.

The more recent and best reviews conclude that certain rehabilitation and prevention programs are effective at reducing crime (e.g., Andrews and Bonta, 2006; Blueprints for Violence Prevention website at http://www.colorado.edu/cspv/blueprints/; Campbell Collaboration Crime and Justice Group website at http://camp.ostfold.net/crime and justice/index.php; Catalano, 2007; Cullen, 2002, 2007; Farrington and Welsh, 2007; Greenwood, 2006; MacKenzie, 2006; Sherman et al., 2002; see especially Lipsey and Cullen, 2007, who conduct a review of the reviews). In particular, well-designed and implemented programs can reduce rates of crime 50 percent or more (Lipsey and Cullen, 2007). Well-designed programs have several characteristics, the most important of which is that they address the known causes of crime. That is, they address those causes described in this text, including strain, low control, association with criminal others, and low self-control. The most effective programs are also intensive, lasting several months or longer and employing a range of techniques to reduce offending (e.g., direct instruction, demonstrations, role playing with feedback). They focus on individuals at high risk for offending. It does not make sense to focus on low-risk individuals, since these offenders will refrain from crime regardless of whether they participate in the program. And they are run in the community, although prison-based programs can also be effective.

Chapter 50 by Farrington and Welsh describes some of the more effective prevention programs, all of which address one or more of the leading causes of crime. In particular, these programs focus on individual traits, the family, the school, peer groups, and the community. You will notice that the causes addressed by these programs are intimately related to the theories in this book. For example, these causes include impulsiveness, one of the individual traits listed in Part II and a major component of low self-control (Chapter 19); poor parental supervision, a major variable in social control and social learning theories (Parts IV and VI); and association with delinquent friends, perhaps the central variable in differential association and social learning theories (Part IV).

It is important to note that Farrington and Welsh draw on the life-course research (Part XII) to argue that it is best to address these causes early in life—before individuals have started to offend. Interventions early in life are said to be more effective since children are more receptive than adults to efforts designed to promote their well-being. Also, early interventions prevent individuals from embarking upon a path that may eventually lead to long-term, serious offending (the type of persistent offending described in the chapters in Part XII). Early interventions, for example, may prevent the sorts of family problems that later lead to problems in school and association with delinquent peers—which in turn contribute to work and marital problems in adulthood. In support of this argument, life-course theories and research suggest that several childhood factors—including individual traits and family experiences—predict offending later in life (see Part XII). Interventions later in life, however, may also reduce offending; and many of the programs that Farrington and Welsh describe have been successfully used to rehabilitate adolescent and adult offenders.

The advocates of prevention and rehabilitation also note that many programs are cost effective. That is, they frequently save more money than they cost (e.g., Aos et al., 2001; Caldwell et al., 2006; Farrington and Welsh, 2007; Welsh et al., 2001). For example, one study estimated that several rehabilitation programs for juvenile offenders save $5 to $10 for each dollar of taxpayer cost (Aos et al., 2001). These savings stem from the crime and other problems such programs prevent (e.g., school dropout, unemployment). Many rehabilitation and prevention programs are also more cost effective than get-tough approaches, particularly imprisonment (e.g., Greenwood, 2006). That is, it is cheaper to prevent a crime through rehabilitation and prevention programs than it is through imprisonment. Finally, the public generally supports rehabilitation and prevention: in fact, the public has become increasingly supportive in recent years, although many people *also* support certain get-tough approaches (e.g., Bishop, 2006; Cullen et al., 2000; Jacobson, 2006). In sum, there is very good reason to believe that addressing the causes of crime described in this book should be at the heart of our efforts to control crime.

References

Andrews, D. A. and James Bonta. 2006. *The Psychology of Criminal Conduct*, 4th edition. Cincinnati, OH: LexisNexis.

Aos, Steve, Polly Philips, Robert Barnoski, and Roxanne Lieb. 2001. *The Comparative Benefits and Costs of Programs to Reduce Crime*. Olympia: Washington State Institute for Public Policy.

Barlow, Hugh D. and Scott H. Decker. 2010. *Criminology and Public Policy*. Philadelphia: Temple University Press.

Bazemore, Gordon and Mark Umbreit. 2004. "Balanced and Restorative Justice." In Albert R. Roberts (ed.), *Juvenile Justice Sourcebook*, pp. 467–510. New York: Oxford University Press.

Beckett, Katherine and Theodore Sasson. 2000. *The Politics of Injustice*. Thousand Oaks, CA: Pine Forge.

Bennett, William J., John J. DiLulio, Jr., and John P. Walters. 1996. *Body Count: Moral Poverty and How to Win America's War Against Drugs and Crime.* New York: Simon and Schuster.

Bishop, Donna M. 2006. "Public Opinion and Juvenile Justice Policy: Myths and Misconceptions." *Criminology and Public Policy* 4: 653–664.

Bonta, James, Rebecca Jesseman, Tanya Rugge, and Robert Cormier. 2006. "Restorative Justice and Recidivism." In Dennis Sullivan and Larry Tifft (eds.), *Handbook of Restorative Justice*, pp. 108–120. New York: Routledge.

Boruch, Robert. F. and Anthony Petrosino. 2004. "Meta-analyses, Systematic Reviews, and Research Syntheses," In Joseph Wholey, Harry Hatry, and Kathryn Newcomer (eds.), *Handbook of Practical Program Evaluation*, pp. 176–204. San Francisco: Jossey-Bass.

Braga, Anthony A., Glenn L. Pierce, Jack McDevitt, Brenda J. Bond, and Shea Cronin. 2008. "The Strategic Prevention of Gun Violence Among Gang-Involved Offenders." *Justice Quarterly* 25: 132–162.

Braithwaite, John. 2002. *Restorative Justice and Responsive Regulation.* Oxford, UK: Oxford University Press.

Caldwell, Michael F., Michael Vitacco, and Gregory J. Van Rybroek. 2006. "Are Violent Delinquents Worth Treating?" *Journal of Research in Crime and Delinquency* 43: 148–168.

Catalano, Richard F. 2007. "Prevention Is a Sound Public and Private Investment." *Criminology and Public Policy* 3: 377–398.

Chen, M. Keith and Jesse M. Shapiro. 2007. "Do Harsher Prison Conditions Reduce Recidivism?" *American Law and Economic Review* 9: 1–29.

Clarke, Ronald V. and John E. Eck. 2005. *Crime Analysis for Problem Solvers.* Washington, DC: Office of Community Policing Services, U.S. Department of Justice.

Clear, Todd R. 2007. *Imprisoning Communities: How Mass Incarceration Makes Disadvantaged Neighborhoods Worse.* New York: Oxford University Press.

Clear, Todd R., Dina Rose, Elin Waring, and Kristin Scully. 2003. "Coercive Mobility and Crime: A Preliminary Examination of Concentrated Incarceration and Social Disorganization." *Justice Quarterly* 20: 33–64.

Cloward, Richard A. and Lloyd E. Ohlin. 1960. *Delinquency and Opportunity.* New York: Free Press.

Cullen, Francis T. 2002. "Rehabilitation and Treatment Programs." In James Q. Wilson and Joan Petersilia (eds.), *Crime*, pp. 253–289. Oakland, CA: ICS Press.

Cullen, Francis T. 2005. "The Twelve People Who Saved Rehabilitation: How the Science of Criminology Made a Difference." *Criminology* 43: 1–42.

Cullen, Francis T. 2007. "Making Rehabilitation Corrections' Guiding Paradigm." *Criminology and Public Policy* 6: 717–728.

Cullen, Francis T., Bonnie S. Fisher, and Brandon K. Applegate. 2000. "Public Opinion About Punishment and Corrections." In Michael Tonry (ed.), *Crime and Justice: A Review of Research* Volume 27, pp. 1–79. Chicago: University of Chicago Press.

Currie, Elliott. 1998. *Crime and Punishment in America.* New York: Owl Books.

DiLulio, John J., Jr. 1995–1995. "Comment on Douglas S. Massey's Getting Away with Murder: Segregation and Violent Crime in Urban America." *University of Pennsylvania Law Review* 143: 1275–1284.

Dunford, Franklyn W. and Delbert S. Elliott. 1984. "Identifying Career Offenders Using Self-Report Data." *Journal of Research in Crime and Delinquency* 21: 57–86.

Empey, LaMar T., Mark C. Stafford, and Carter H. Hay. 1999. *American Delinquency.* Belmont, CA: Wadsworth.

Farrington, David P. and Brandon C. Welsh. 2007. *Saving Children from a Life of Crime.* New York: Oxford University Press.

Garland, David. 2001. *The Culture of Control.* Chicago: University of Chicago Press.

Greenwood, Peter. 2006. *Changing Lives: Delinquency Prevention as Crime Control Policy.* Chicago: University of Chicago Press.

Haggerty, Kevin D. 2004. "Displaced Expertise: Three Constraints on the Policy Relevance of

Criminological Thought." *Theoretical Criminology* 8: 211–231.

Jacobson, Michael. 2006. "Reversing the Punitive Turn: The Limits and Promise of Current Research." *Criminology and Public Policy* 5: 277–284.

Kovandzic, Tomislav V. and Lynne M. Vieraitis. 2006. "The Effect of County-Level Prison Population Growth on Crime Rates." *Criminology and Public Policy* 5: 213–244.

Liedka, Raymond V., Anne Morrison Piehl, and Burt Useem. 2006. "The Crime-Control Effect of Incarceration: Does Scale Matter?" *Criminology and Public Policy* 5: 245–276.

Lipsey, Mark W. and Francis T. Cullen. 2007. "The Effectiveness of Correctional Rehabilitation: A Review of Systematic Reviews." *Annual Review of Law and Social Science* 3: 297–320.

Lynch, James P. and William J. Sabol. 2004. "Assessing the Effects of Mass Incarceration on Informal Social Control in Communities." *Criminology and Public Policy* 3: 267–294.

Lynch, Michael J. 2007. *Big Prisons, Big Dreams: Crime and the Failure of America's Penal System.* New Brunswick, NJ: Rutgers University Press.

MacKenzie, Doris Layton. 2006. *What Works in Corrections.* New York: Cambridge University Press.

Martinson, Robert. 1974. "What Works? Questions and Answers About Prison Reform." *Public Interest* 35: 22–54.

Mauer, Marc and Ryan S. King. 2007a. *A 25-Year Quagmire: The War on Drugs and Its Impact on American Society.* The Sentencing Project, available at www.sentencingproject.org.

Mauer, Marc and Ryan S. King. 2007b. *Uneven Justice.* The Sentencing Project, available at www.sentencingproject.org.

McGarrell, Edmund F., Steven Chermak, Jeremy M. Wilson, and Nicholas Corsaro. 2006. "Reducing Homicide Through a 'Lever-Pulling' Strategy." *Justice Quarterly* 23: 214–231.

McGarrell, Edmund F. and Natalie Kroovand Hipple. 2007. "Family Group Conferencing and Re-Offending Among First-Time Juvenile Offenders: The Indianapolis Experiment." *Justice Quarterly* 24: 221–246.

Moore, Solomon. 2009. "Study Shows High Cost of Criminal Corrections." *New York Times*, March 3, A13.

Nagin, Daniel S., Francis T. Cullen, and Cheryl Lero Jonson. 2009. "Imprisonment and Reoffending." In Michael Tonry (ed.), *Crime and Justice: A Review of Research*, Volume 38, pp. 115–200. Chicago, University of Chicago Press.

Pager, Devah. 2003. "The Mark of a Criminal Record." *American Journal of Sociology* 108: 937–975.

Petersilia, Joan. 2008. "Influencing Public Policy: An Embedded Criminologist Reflects on California Prison Reform." *Journal of Experimental Criminology* 4: 335–356.

Pogarsky, Gregg and Alex R. Piquero. 2003. "Can Punishment Encourage Offending? Investigating the 'Resetting' Effect." *Journal of Research in Crime and Delinquency* 40: 95–120.

Pratt, Travis C. and Francis T. Cullen. 2005. "Assessing Macro-Level Predictors and Theories of Crime: A Meta-Analysis." In Michael Tonry (ed.), *Crime and Justice: A Review of Research*, Volume 32, pp. 373–450. Chicago: University of Chicago Press.

Redding, Richard E. 2008. *Juvenile Transfer Laws: An Effective Deterrent to Delinquency?* Washington, DC: U.S. Department of Justice, Office of Juvenile Justice and Delinquency Prevention.

Ren, Ling, Jihong Zhao, and Nicholas P. Lovrich. 2008. "Liberal Versus Conservative Public Policies on Crime: What Was the Comparative Track Record During the 1990s?" *Journal of Criminal Justice* 36: 316–325.

Sabol, William J. and Heather Couture. 2008. *Prison Inmates at Midyear 2007.* Washington, DC: U.S. Department of Justice, Office of Justice Programs.

Sabol, William J. and Todd D. Minton. 2008. *Jail Inmates at Midyear 2007.* Washington, DC: U.S. Department of Justice, Office of Justice Programs.

Sherman, Lawrence W., Denise Gottfredson, Doris MacKenzie, John Eck, Peter Reuter, and Shawn Bushway. 2002. *Evidence-Based Crime Prevention.* London: Routledge.

Sherman, Lawrence and Heather Strang. 2007. *Restorative Justice: The Evidence.* London: The Smith Institute.

Sherman, Lawrence W. and David Weisburd. 1995. "General Deterrent Effects of Police Patrol in Crime 'Hot Spots': A Randomized, Controlled Trial." *Justice Quarterly* 12: 625–648.

Spelman, William. 2006. "The Limited Importance of Prison Expansion." In Alfred Blumstein and Joel Wallman (eds.), *The Crime Drop in America*, pp. 97–127. New York: Cambridge University Press.

Stemen, Don. 2007. *Reconsidering Incarceration*. New York: Vera Institute of Justice.

Tonry, Michael. 2004. *Thinking About Crime: Sense and Sensibility in American Penal Culture*. New York: Oxford University Press.

Tonry, Michael. 2008a. "Crime and Human Rights." *Criminology* 46: 1–34.

Tonry, Michael. 2008b. "Learning from the Limitations of Deterrence Research." In Michael Tonry (ed.), *Crime and Justice: A Review of Research*, Volume 37, pp. 279–308. Chicago: University of Chicago Press.

Useem, Bert and Anne Morrison Piehl. 2008. *Prison State: The Challenge of Mass Incarceration*. New York: Cambridge University Press.

Vieraitis, Lynne M., Tomislav V. Kovandzic, and Thomas B. Marvell. 2007. "The Criminogenic Effects of Imprisonment: Evidence from State Panel Data, 1974–2002." *Criminology and Public Policy* 6: 589–622.

Weisburd, David, Laura A. Wyckoff, Justin Ready, John E. Eck, Joshua C. Hinkle, and Frank Gajewski. 2006. "Does Crime Just Move Around the Corner? A Controlled Study of Spatial Displacement and Diffusion of Crime Control Benefits." *Criminology* 44: 549–592.

Welsh, Brandon C., David P. Farrington, and Lawrence W. Sherman. 2001. *Costs and Benefits of Crime Prevention*. Boulder, CO: Westview.

Western, Bruce. 2002. "The Impact of Incarceration on Wage Mobility and Inequality." *American Sociological Review* 67: 526–546.

Western, Bruce. 2006. *Punishment and Inequality in America*. New York: Russell Sage Foundation.

Wilson, James Q. 1975. *Thinking About Crime*. New York: Vintage Books.

Zimring, Franklin E. 2007. *The Great American Crime Decline*. New York: Oxford University Press.

48. Imprisoning Communities

Todd R. Clear

It seems reasonable to suppose that imprisoning offenders would reduce crime and that communities with the highest proportion of imprisoned offenders would experience the largest reductions in crime. Conservative criminologists and policy-makers have made this claim. DiLulio (1994: 15), for example, stated that "No group of Americans would stand to benefit more from policies that keep convicted felons, adults and juveniles, behind bars for all or most of their terms than crime-plagued inner-city Americans and their children." In the selection below, however, Todd Clear makes the opposite argument.

Clear contends that the very high rates of incarceration that characterize many disadvantaged, largely African American communities increase the crime in those communities. Clear does not deny that incapacitating offenders stops some crime, although he claims that the incapacitation effect is small. He argues, however, that very high rates of incarceration increase community crime rates for several reasons—and this increase outweighs the reduction in crime that results from incapacitation.

Clear notes that in some highly impoverished communities as many as one-fifth of all adult men are incarcerated on any given day. This is said to disrupt families. For example, it leads to more single-parent families, it reduces parental supervision, and it removes parental role models. The high rate of incarceration also creates economic problems; there are fewer employed

residents in the community, both because many people are incarcerated and because those with prison records have trouble finding decent employment upon their release. Also, the money spent on prisons means there is less money to invest in local communities, including money for schools and jobs. Finally, the high rate of incarceration reduces both respect for the legal system and levels of political participation. Many residents, in fact, are unable even to vote because of their criminal records.

All of these effects reduce levels of control. Parents are less able to effectively supervise their children, teach them that crime is wrong, and instill self-control. Likewise, adults in the community are less able and/or willing to exercise control over one another. If the adults are not imprisoned, they are struggling with economic problems, have little "stake in conformity" or investment in conventional society, and are weakly attached to or even hostile toward the legal system. Further, they are unable to secure resources from the larger community, such as money for better schools. High rates of incarceration, in short, are a major source of social disorganization in the community (see Part III).

Clear (2007) presents much evidence in support of these arguments in his book Imprisoning Communities, *although not all evidence is supportive. Most notably, studies on the overall effect of incarceration on community crime rates have*

Reprinted from Todd R. Clear, *Imprisoning Communities: How Mass Incarceration Makes Disadvantaged Neighborhoods Worse.* Copyright © 2007 by Oxford University Press; reprinted by permission.

produced mixed results (see Clear, 2007; Lynch and Sabol, 2004). Some studies indicate that high rates of incarceration increase community crime rates, while other studies find the opposite. These mixed results reflect the fact that it is very difficult to accurately estimate the effect of incarceration on community crime rates. One must take account of the fact that community crime rates may affect incarceration rates and that both incarceration rates and community crime rates may be influenced by the same third variables, such as poverty (see the discussion in Clear, 2007: 166–174). These things are not easily done. Nevertheless, Clear gives us good reason to question what to many is a straightforward proposition: if you lock up a lot of offenders from a community, that community will experience a reduction in crime.

Clear concludes his selection with some policy recommendations. He describes how we might reduce the incarceration rate and thereby reduce the negative effects of high incarceration rates on communities. As an alternative to incarceration, he recommends a form of "community justice" that is quite similar to the restorative justice approach advocated by Braithwaite and others (see Part VII and Chapter 21). Community justice, however, also involves efforts to strengthen the ability of families and neighborhood groups to exercise effective control. For example, it involves efforts to improve local school systems.

References

Clear, Todd R. 2007. *Imprisoning Communities: How Mass Incarceration Makes Disadvantaged Neighborhoods Worse.* New York: Oxford University Press.

DiLulio, John J., Jr. 1994. "The Question of Black Crime." *Public Interest* 117 (Fall): 3–32.

Lynch, James P. and William J. Sabol. 2004. "Assessing the Effects of Mass Incarceration on Informal Social Control in Communities." *Criminology and Public Policy* 3: 267–294.

Prison populations have grown mostly through society's locking up ever-increasing numbers of young men, especially black men, largely from impoverished places. The concentration of imprisonment of young men from disadvantaged places has grown to such a point that it is now a bedrock experience, a force that affects families and children, institutions and businesses, social groups and interpersonal relations. With its isolation of people from poor places, incarceration does more damage than good, including increases in crime. In this way, incarceration has become part of its own dynamic. Imprisonment has grown to the point that it now produces the very social problems on which it feeds. It is the perfect storm.

Uninformed public sentiments and practiced political interests have created a malignant foundation for our crime-prevention policy. Legislative changes lean only in the direction of ever-growing punitiveness, drawing more and more young people—especially black men—into the system's clutches. The system clutches them; indeed, people who get caught up in the penal system stay there longer, are subjected to more controls, and suffer a greater chance of failure than ever before in history. Faced with this situation, policy makers think only of becoming more strict and more punitive, more damaging, for an ever wider range of misbehaviors, drawing into the storm an ever larger group. As that group grows, the ripple effects of the damage also grow, crossing the social networks of those poorer communities and extending into future generations. Crime goes up, crime goes down; yet in a weirdly disconnected fashion, prison populations increase regardless....

This chapter makes four central points:

The extraordinary growth in the U.S. prison system, sustained for over 30 years, has had, at best, a small impact on crime.

The growth in imprisonment has been concentrated among poor, minority males who live in impoverished neighborhoods.

Concentrated incarceration in those impoverished communities has broken families, weakened the social-control capacity of parents, eroded economic strength, soured attitudes toward society, and distorted politics; even, after reaching a certain level, it has increased rather than decreased crime.

Any attempt to overcome the problems of crime will have to encompass a combination of sentencing reforms and philosophical realignment.

Incarceration and Crime

As a general rule, Americans believe that sending people to prison, especially men, prevents crime. This belief in the crime-prevention power of prison has a good dose of apparent face validity. After all, men behind prison walls cannot commit crimes against society. As a kind of proof, there is the all-too-common news story of a violent crime committed by a person recently released from prison. It seems an unassailable fact that at least *this* crime could have been prevented had the person never been allowed to get out. And if we can just make the prison experience *tough* enough, then surely people will think twice about committing the crimes that put them at risk of going there . . . .

In fact, however, the scientific evidence about the relationship between incarceration and crime is by no means uniformly supportive of the prison's capacity to reduce crime. The face validity of incapacitation—if you lock up a person who is actively committing crimes, you prevent the further crimes he would have committed—begins to evaporate upon close inspection. Many crimes still occur, because the person who is now behind bars is replaced by someone else. Almost everyone who goes to prison is eventually released, but the prospects for most of them to live crime-free have been *damaged* by the effects of their prison stay. Moreover, concrete practical and legal limits on punishment establish a surprisingly low ceiling for the potential deterrent power of a prison sentence. A child who is exposed to a parent or sibling who went to prison has an *increased*, rather than a decreased, risk of incarceration, and this testifies to the weakness of the deterrent effect of the sanction.

The limited capability of prisons to prevent crime is surely one of the reasons that, in the 33 years that prison populations have been rising continuously, trends in crime rates have been anything but systematic: they went up in the 1970s; down, then up in the 1980s; and up, then down in the 1990s. Today's headlines raise the fear that after a decade-long drop in crime, the trend may turn upward again (Frieden 2006), even as prison populations continue to rise. There is a puzzling discontinuity between imprisonment rates, which have increased every year since 1973, and crime rates, which have been up and down during that time and are, today, about what they were in 1970, when the prison population was at its lowest level in a generation.

This discontinuity is not discussed very much in the substantial social science literature assessing the impact of prisons on crime rates. Some studies, especially older ones, suggest that the impact is substantial. An equivalent body of studies, many of them more recent, find little or no impact on crime. As weaknesses in the earlier methodology are corrected by newer studies' more careful designs, the results show smaller connections between incarceration and crime prevention. Today, an overwhelming majority opinion is emerging that prison use has probably reduced crime, but only by a marginal amount. Scholars also tend to agree that additional growth in prison populations will produce ever-decreasing marginal returns in public safety (for reviews, see Spelman 1994, 2000). . . .

Black Males

That black men have been put behind bars at higher rates than any other group is not a new observation. But their rate of incarceration, always high, has been growing more rapidly than that for any other subgroup of males, and this is especially true for black high school dropouts. Sociologist

Bruce Western has shown that, in the last 25 years, black high school dropouts have been almost five times more likely to go to prison than white high school dropouts, and that this difference in incarceration rates has been growing (Western 2006). . . .

The main vehicle for the different rate of incarceration for black males is the drug laws. This situation is not because black males are more likely to use drugs. Black high school seniors report using drugs at a rate that is only three-quarters that of white high school seniors, and white students have about three times the number of emergency room visits for drug overdose; this discrepancy in rates has remained steady (or grown) for over a decade (Western 2006, citing Johnston et al. 2004). Blacks, however, are much more likely than whites to be arrested for drug crimes. At the beginning of the incarceration boom (1970), blacks had twice the arrest rate for drugs as whites. As the drug war intensified with a nationwide trend toward mandatory prison sentences for people convicted of drug crime, the arrest rate for blacks grew much more rapidly than for whites, reaching a peak arrest rate in 1989 that was *four* times that of whites. The gap between white and black arrests has declined since then, but the remaining disparity still makes blacks two and a half times more likely than whites to be arrested for drug crimes (Western 2006): Today's laws ensure that most of these arrests will result in some form of incarceration. . . .

Poor, urban black men, especially school dropouts, live in neighborhoods that have been crushed by poverty. They are the men of those neighborhoods—the fathers, brothers, uncles, and sons. When they go to prison, they join many of their neighbors who have already taken that route. Collectively, over time, their high rates of incarceration become the standard for the neighborhood. Sociologist Peter St. Jean has concluded, on the basis of a nearly five-year ethnography, that these men become "part of a cultural attitude which seemed to treat incarceration as a rite of passage". . . .

Damage to Communities

There is a steadily growing body of literature that sheds light on the consequences of high rates of incarceration for individuals from the poorest communities. The level of concentration is substantial: studies estimate that in some of the most impoverished locations, as many as one-fifth of adult men are behind bars on any given day (Lynch and Sabol 2004a). Because these men stay behind prison bars for only a couple of years at a time (jail terms are much shorter, typically much less than a year), they cycle back into their communities, only to be replaced by other cohorts. Many who leave prison come back in a few months. The cycling of these young men through the prison system becomes a dynamic of the poor neighborhoods, so that a family is hardly ever without a son, uncle, or father who has done prison time (Clear, Rose, and Ryder 2001).

The effects on the individual of going to prison are well-documented. Ex-prisoners earn less money during their lifetimes, find it harder to stay employed, are less likely to marry, and suffer a range of medical and psychological problems (see Western, Patillo, and Weiman, 2004). This is important ecologically as well, because the ubiquity of prison touches *almost everybody* in these neighborhoods. Every family has a member who has limited labor-market options; every family knows someone struggling to stay out of jail, many mothers are raising children whose fathers have a prison record. For children in these neighborhoods, merely having a parent or brother who has gone to prison elevates their risk of doing the same; in this way, incarceration serves as its own breeding ground.

Prison is thus woven into the fabric of these communities, with its stark implications for social networks, social capital, and, ultimately, informal social control. Men who are behind bars are the missing links in the social network of those who remain behind. Since these networks have limited strength to begin with, the widespread reality of prison undermines their ability to provide social capital. And neighborhoods with lots of men behind bars are places with especially low endowments of social capital. Because prison saps the limited economic and interpersonal resources of families with a loved one behind bars (Braman 2004), both the families and the neighborhood stay impoverished.

Another consequence of this dynamic is that there are also diminished levels of informal social control when so many members of a community are behind bars or between prison stays. Child-rearing is less likely to implant delinquency-resistant self controls (Weatherburn and Lind 2001), and the pro-social attitudes that usually insulate youths against breaking the law are less likely to develop when they are raised in places where a lot of men go to prison (Crutchfield 2005). Since a neighborhood's level of *informal* social control is far more important for overall public safety than is formal social control, deficits in informal social controls that result from high levels of incarceration are, in fact, criminogenic. The high incarceration rates in poor communities destabilize the social relationships in these places and help cause crime rather than prevent it (Rose and Clear 1998; Clear et al. 2003).

Because over 90 percent of prisoners are men, the social effects of concentrated incarceration are easily seen when a lot of men go to prison from a particular place. But the smaller number of women who cycle in and out of prison from these same neighborhoods does not mean that their *impact* is as small as their numbers. The role women play in their social networks, social capital, and informal social controls, especially in very poor urban neighborhoods, is thought to be more important, per person, than men. Thus, those much smaller levels of incarceration for women seem to produce the same destabilizing results as for men, with an equivalent pattern of increased crime (George and Lalonde 2005)....

The Lack of Strategic Options

The most commonly suggested reforms in today's penal landscape are unlikely to have much to do with the growth of incarceration, whether they are adopted or not. Rehabilitation programs, even if they become wildly successful, will reduce prison return rates only at the margin. The same goes for the new interest in "reentry programs." Three decades of experience with "alternatives to incarceration" suggest that they, likewise, will not reduce the size of the prison population. These are each good ideas, worth our investment on grounds of humaneness and practicality, but they are largely irrelevant to the central need to slow the growth of incarceration....

Communities, Coercive Mobility, and Public Safety

The concentration of young, disadvantaged males of color in prisons has been the subject of substantial empirical work and policy commentary. Their concentration in impoverished, minority neighborhoods has not received the same amount of attention. This is unfortunate, because neighborhoods, "places," matter. Neighborhoods are the building blocks for community life, and community life is an important wellspring for a good quality of life. Clearly, however, the nature and quality of community life varies from one neighborhood to another. That is one reason there has been a resurgence of interest in the influence of neighborhood and community contexts (Gephart and Brooks-Gunn 1997)....

A Framework for Identifying the Community Effects of Concentrated Incarceration

The consequences of imprisonment to the community are embedded in three important legitimate systems of neighborhood order: family, economic, and political....

Familial Systems

Communities that contribute greater numbers of people to incarceration experience higher rates of family disruption, single-parent families, and births to young, single adults (Lynch and Sabol 1992). This close association suggests a plausible hypothesis that one is, in part, a product of another (or at least that they are mutually reinforcing phenomena). Disruptions are numerous: parenting is interrupted, role models are removed, families move and change school districts, mothers go on welfare, children receive less supervision, the number of single-parent families increases, incarceration experiences are models for children, and so forth. This chain of negative effects on the family—the socialization unit of private social control—contributes to a gradual reduction of social capital within the community. None of these changes by itself "causes" delinquency, but such disruptions are associated with earlier and more active delinquent careers. Their effects would be expected to be additive and, in more extreme levels of removal of males, interactive. Moreover, these occur in addition to the destabilizing effects of crime.

Economic Systems

The microeconomics of concentrated incarceration and reentry create neighborhoods of (mostly) men who have depleted their labor-market prospects in places where labor markets are weak to begin with. Imprisonment in large numbers ravages the supplies of local human capital and leaves a gap in employable residents. Prior to incarceration, most prisoners are an economic resource to their neighborhoods and immediate families. For example, in impoverished neighborhoods, a work-age male generates economic activity from a variety of endeavors, including off-the-books work, intermittent illicit drug trade, theft, welfare, and part-time employment. When he goes to prison, some of this economic activity is taken up by others who replace him, and some is not. When he comes back from prison, his legitimate labor-market prospects are even more bleak than they were before.

Also, the macroeconomics of crime policy damage inner-city communities by shifting government funding away from improving those communities and toward penal institutions instead. Once they are arrested and incarcerated, these people's economic value is transformed and transferred into penal capital—the demand for salaried correctional employees to provide security. It is also transferred to the locality of the prison, where the penal system's employees reside. The harsh budgetary politics of the 1990s have corresponded to equally harsh punitive politics, in which correctional expenditures have grown by billions of dollars annually while money to support schools, supplement tuition, provide summer jobs for teens, and so forth was cut. The latter funds had provided meager support for communities already hard hit by crime and justice, but the funds became more meager still. Whatever role these social programs play in propping up informal networks of social control is eliminated with the depletion of funding. A neighborhood experiencing economic loss as a result of increased incarceration will also experience an increase in crime.

Political Systems

The overwhelming presence of the American criminal justice system in these impoverished communities goes a long way to defining the meaning of the state for this segment of society. The state is most likely encountered as a coercive agent of control rather than a fair agent of justice; and when this perception is true, people are less likely to conform their behavior to the requirements of the law (Tyler 1990). Most minority-group children can tell stories of racism in the criminal justice system, and validation of these tales is apparent to the eye. This is one of the reasons it is no surprise that many inner-city young people define the power of the state as a nemesis to be avoided rather than an ally to be cultivated. In the community, disillusionment with the political structure often erodes residents' feelings of empowerment and reduces their willingness to participate in local politics. As a result, the call for citizen involvement may fall on deaf ears.

Furthermore, there has been a systematic move to bar people who have felony convictions or who have been to prison from political participation (Uggen and Manza 2005). Laws that disenfranchise citizens with felony convictions have disparate impact on African Americans, many of whom are already alienated from politics. These laws make certain that inner-city areas with many disenfranchised residents are underrepresented in the vote. One result is that policies friendly to inner-city constituencies have disproportionally poor political payoff for those who run for office. . . .

The Impact of Incarceration on Community Safety

The coercive mobility hypothesis holds that high rates of incarceration, concentrated in poor communities, will destabilize social networks in those communities, thereby undermining informal social control and leading to more crime. A conceptual model of this hypothesis is provided by figure 48.1, below.

This figure posits that incarceration will tend to suppress crime through incapacitation and deterrence. Given what we know about the impact of incarceration on crime, we would expect these effects to be small. We would also expect that, as levels of incarceration grow in impoverished communities, there will be a negative effect on the community's economic structure, family stability, parental capacity, and pro-social beliefs. Each of these effects would also be small. There will also be crimes committed by those now in reentry from prison. It is easy to see how these latter effects, even if small, might in the aggregate outweigh the impact of deterrence and incapacitation. This is the coercive mobility hypothesis, . . . after a certain point, high incarceration rates concentrated in impoverished communities will cause crime to increase rather than decrease. . . .

The Obvious Need: Sentencing Reform

Any solution begins with a recognition of two threshold points: First, programmatic tinkering has not reduced the prison population to date, and it will never have much effect, even under the most optimistic assumptions. Second, to overcome mass incarceration requires that we incarcerate fewer people. There is no getting around it. If the problem is mass imprisonment, then the solution is to change the laws that send people to prison and sometimes keep them there for lengthy terms. Thus, we need to consider the points discussed below.

The Number of Entries and Their Length of Stay Fully Determine the Prison Population
There are two points of leverage for controlling the size of the prison population. This conclusion follows from the simple fact that two variables fully determine the number of prisoners in any prison system: the number of people who go in, and how long they stay (Frost 2006). It follows that the best way to influence the prison population on a major scale is to change either, or both, of these numbers. The choices are not subtle.

Mandatory Sentencing
Eliminating mandatory prison terms across the board would have a substantial impact on the prison population. Much of this impact would involve having fewer people serving time for drug-related crime. There is substantial public support for our dealing differently with drug crime. For instance, a large minority favors decriminalization of some drugs. . . .

Sentence Length
In the last 30 years, the average time served by people going to prison has almost doubled, and the amount of time they are under parole

Figure 48.1
The impact of concentrated incarceration on poor communities and crime. The figure shows coercive mobility—the impact of incarceration on communities

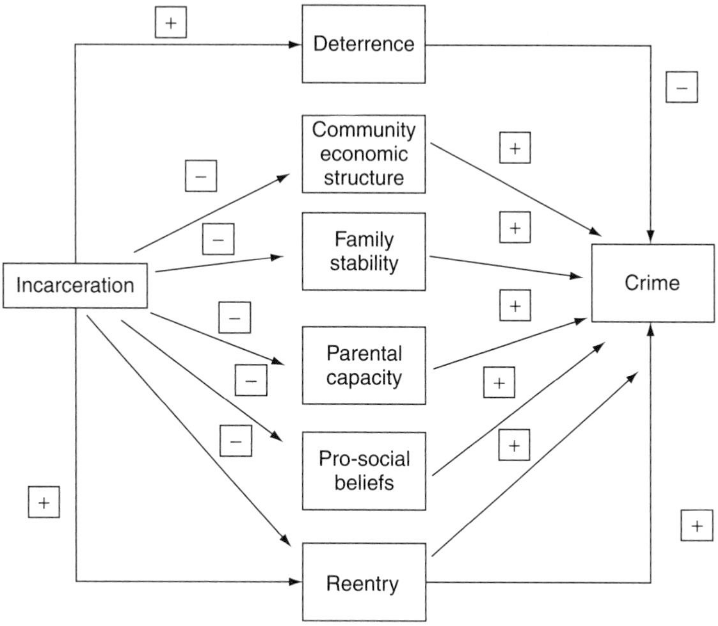

Source: Clear, Rose, Waring, and Scully 2003.

supervision has also increased. This has meant that the system maintains a growing prison population through length-of-stay decisions and post-release failure rates. . . .

Length of stay in the United States could be rolled back considerably and leave the country with a smaller prison population and a punitive policy more in line with other Western democracies. Because decreased length of stay does *not* lead to increased chance of failure (if anything, the relationship is the opposite), and almost everyone going to prison gets out anyway, we can reduce sentence lengths substantially without increasing crime rates. For example, if the average length of stay, which today is 30 months for new court commitments, were instead 20 months or even 24 months, the prison population would drop as a consequence, with little long-term crime increase. . . .

Toward a New Philosophy of Penal Justice: The Idea of Community Justice

Community justice is an emerging paradigm that proposes a rethinking of the aims of the criminal justice system. It sets as a central criterion that the justice system contribute to the quality of life in communities—to help make the places where people work, live, and raise their families, *good* places to do these things. . . .

Because community justice is an idea with a variety of expressions, it is, necessarily, a broad concept that cannot be covered under a single umbrella statement. There are three core elements of all versions of community justice, however. First, there is an emphasis on restoration. Victims' losses are restored, those who are convicted of crime likewise may expect to be able to be restored if they take appropriate action, and the community peace that was fractured by the crime is, for want of a better term, restored. Second, there is an emphasis on maintaining those who are convicted of crimes within their communities. This enables both them and their loved ones to keep their community ties, and it eases post-penalty restoration to community life. Third, purely punitive sanctions, such as solitary confinement, are deemphasized in favor of ameliorative sanctions such as community service. For these reasons, community justice, in whatever form it takes, is an idea that proposes minimal use of imprisonment. It is a philosophy that provides a philosophical pathway out of the current morass.

How would it work? What would our community justice strategies entail?

Community Justice Strategies

Community justice initiatives could thrive under a regime of reduced imprisonment. They could also contribute to reductions in imprisonment. They will have three elements: (1) a focus on high-incarceration places; (2) attention to norms and values in those places; and (3) attempts to improve schools, jobs, and housing as targets....

Norms and Values

Community justice can be described as a series of programs, but that description fails to capture the central ethic. Community justice tries to restore these places' informal social-control mechanisms so that they may perform functions that have been taken over by formal social control agencies in the face of their breakdown. This entails strengthening the social-control capacity of families and neighborhood groups, as well as improving the effectiveness of schools and increasing the vibrancy of the private sector's presence....

Targets: Schools, Jobs, and Housing

A third aspect of community justice is the desire to strengthen the social support provided by informal social controls. The thesis is that, in strong communities, these institutions of informal social control are a main source of public safety, but in high-incarceration communities, they do not perform that function effectively.

Inner-city schools in impoverished neighborhoods are notoriously poor at educating, socializing, and preparing young people for adult roles. One in five adult African Americans lacks a high school degree—twice the rate of white youths—and in impoverished neighborhoods, the picture is worse. As was shown in chapter 5, lack of a high school diploma is one of the factors that most distinguishes the prison population from nonprisoners. Poor inner-city schools are so problem-stricken that they have trouble retaining their youth. The result is high rates of truancy and school dropout—factors that serve as "a pipeline to prison" (Losen and Wald 2003).

The failure of schools in poor, mostly minority inner-city neighborhoods is a precursor to a lifetime of troubles in the labor market for most residents. Unemployment among men in poor neighborhoods is a double negative for the places they live: first, these men fail to bring the economic and network resources to their intimates—assets that most other young men provide through bridging to work; second, they are a drain on the already thin financial and personal resources of those around them, as these men seek support for their own lives.

Public housing is a staple of these high-incarceration neighborhoods. Public housing need not be problem housing, but it often is. All of the so-called million-dollar blocks in Brooklyn—places where over a million dollars was being spent annually in incarcerating residents of that block—are public housing blocks (Cadora, Swartz, and Gordon 2002). When there are problems in public housing, they often take the form of gangs, drug markets, and violence. These problems persist, even though people with criminal records are prohibited from living in some types of public housing, and getting arrested can subject a public-housing resident to immediate eviction.

These are the problems. And there is plenty of evidence of the benefits of overcoming these problems. Children who finish school, even in poor neighborhoods, compared to those who do not finish, are less likely to become involved in *both* juvenile and adult crime (Hawkins et al. 2000). Despite having juvenile records or criminal records as youth, young men in their late twenties and older who are provided with job opportunities, even if marginal, become involved in crime less frequently in adulthood (Uggen 2000). People who leave inadequate public housing in impoverished urban areas to live in places with higher quality housing and better schools achieve more positive school and economic outcomes (Polikoff 2004). Men who survive crime-free for seven years past their most recent criminal conviction no longer look more likely to commit a crime than do other adult males their age (Kurlychek, Brame, and Bushway 2006). . . .

The funds needed for the agenda of community justice, strengthening the informal social-control capacities of poor communities already exist. They are tied up in the inefficiencies of prison and therefore are unavailable for other priorities. But by shifting these funds to community justice initiatives, two goals are accomplished. First, the community-development programs receive the resources they need to strengthen poor communities. Second, and just as important, money spent in the community prevents the collateral damage that otherwise comes from locking up so many residents. Community justice can be a solution that does not require new funds. . . .

Discussion Questions

1. Clear argues that incarceration does not reduce crime by a large amount. Why?
2. Clear states that high levels of incarceration increase community crime rates for several reasons. Describe these reasons, being sure to note the effects of incarceration on "familial systems," "economic systems," and "political systems."
3. Clear contends that high rates of incarceration reduce informal control in a community. Describe the ways in which his argument is similar to and different from that of the social disorganization theorists in Part III. Be sure to discuss his concept of "coercive mobility."
4. Clear argues that rehabilitation programs will not solve the problems he describes. Why? What solutions does he propose?
5. Clear draws on control and social disorganization theory to explain why high incarceration rates increase community crime rates. What arguments might strain and social learning theorists make about the effects of high incarceration rates on communities?

49. Preventing Crime in Everyday Life

Marcus Felson

The likelihood that individuals will engage in crime is a function of their predisposition for crime and the situations they encounter. Most of the theories in this text focus on those factors that increase the individual's predisposition for or general willingness to engage in crime. Such factors include low self-control; weak bonds to conventional others, such as parents, and to conventional institutions, such as work; beliefs favorable to crime; and association with criminal peers. Rehabilitation and prevention programs try to alter such factors and thereby reduce the individual's predisposition for crime. Sometimes, however, this is not easily done (although see Chapter 50 by Farrington and Welsh). In this chapter, Felson argues that we should reduce crime by altering the situations that individuals encounter.

Individuals who are predisposed to crime are more likely to engage in crime in some situations than in others. Rational choice theory (Chapters 33 and 35) and routine activities theory describe the types of situations most favorable to crime. At the most general level, these are situations where the costs of crime are low and the benefits are high. Or, in the words of routine activities theory, these are situations where capable guardians are absent and attractive targets for crime are present. Rational choice and routine activities theorists have devoted much

attention to the types of situations favorable to parti*cular types of crime, such as household burglaries and violence at sporting events. And they have argued that we can substantially reduce the extent of such crimes by altering these situations so as to increase the costs of crime and/or reduce the benefits. Also, we can reduce the likelihood that individuals will encounter situations that are favorable to crime.*

As indicated in the introduction, these efforts at "situational crime prevention" move well beyond traditional efforts to deter crime. Traditional efforts at deterrence focus on increasing one particular cost of crime, punishment by the criminal justice system. Situational crime prevention attempts to increase a range of costs, including informal sanction and "moral costs." Also, it aims to lower the benefits of crime. Chapter 49 by Felson describes the tactics of situational crime prevention: alter situations so that engaging in particular types of crime is difficult, risky, unrewarding, and/or inexcusable. And Felson describes several successful applications of situational crime prevention, focusing on crimes such as car theft, the criminal use of telephones, and violence at soccer games. Chapter 35 by Clarke provides further discussion of the logic and methods of situational crime prevention, as well as several additional examples of its successful application.

Reprinted from Marcus Felson. 2002. *Crime and Everyday Life*. Thousand Oaks: Sage Publications.

Situational Crime Prevention

Situational crime prevention offers society the best chance for a quick and inexpensive way to reduce crime slice by slice.... Clarke and his associates adopted the following policy:

- Do not worry about academic theories. Just go out and gather facts about crime from nature herself (i.e., by observing, interviewing offenders, etc.). (This is not to say you should throw all your education to the wolves. It merely tells you that science has to gather facts and learn from them.)
- Focus on very specific slices of crime, such as vandalism against telephones or soccer violence. Even the crime of "vandalism" would be far too broad!
- Do not try to improve human character. You are certain to fail.
- Try to block crime in a practical, natural, and simple way, at low social and economic cost.
- Do small-scale experiments, especially looking for natural environments to study each slice of the crime prevention puzzle.
- Use very simple statistics and charts that let you see each comparison quite directly....

Clarke seeks to accomplish prevention by making each criminal act appear

- Difficult
- Risky
- Unrewarding
- Inexcusable

That breaks down crime into components that can then be explored—exactly what science is all about. The last of the four is closely linked to "neutralization theory," which considers how offenders excuse their own actions. (Removing these rationalizations or excuses helps prevent crimes. Supermarkets often train their employees in the different types of theft in order to remove the idea that "minor pilfering" is not stealing.)

Preventing Property Crime

A good deal of this chapter presents specific examples of successful situational prevention. I have selected these to tell a story. I include crime prevention methods that were discovered accidentally, those involving criminologists, and others involving people who never heard of situational crime prevention but did it anyway. Whether planned or not, people have acquired a variety of crime prevention experience well worth sharing.

Trouble on Double-Deck Buses

Our illustration of situational prevention begins with the problem of vandalism against Britain's traditional red double-deck buses. The Home Office researchers (Clarke, 1978) learned that most of the vandalism was on the upper deck, usually in the back row, where supervision was least likely to occur.

They also learned that the traditional British bus conductor had a major role in preventing vandalism. A bus conductor would ascend the stairs to the upper deck to collect fares and thus serve as a guardian against the crime of vandalism.

Because some companies had removed the conductor to save money, whereas other companies had not, this was a natural experiment. Those buses with conductors had less vandalism, but they also had more assaults on conductors. This is an instance of how crime prevention can sometimes backfire, solving one crime but leading to another. This example also establishes that situational crime prevention is far from obvious, sometimes producing unexpected results.

Correcting the Criminal Use of Telephones

Ronald Clarke and associates are developing a growing literature on the criminal side of telephones and what to do about it.... They have shown that obscene phone calls can be thwarted by caller identification services; drug transactions are impaired by pay phones that only call out; fraudulent international calls from pay phones are impossible when phones exclude common paths for the fraud; and stolen or cloned cell phones can be designed to fail for anybody but the owner. Clarke, Kemper, and Wyckoff (2001) documented more than $1.3 billion in cell phone fraud losses during 1995 to 1996. Six technical changes were designed to cut off fraud quickly:

1. Computer profiling to detect strange call patterns
2. Personal identification numbers (PINs)
3. Precall validation by computers
4. Operator checks
5. Radio wave checks
6. Encrypted checks of each phone

These adjustments resulted in a 97 percent cut in cell phone fraud.

Telephones are important facilitators in drug transactions. Mangai Natarajan, Ronald Clarke, and Mathieu Belanger, in ongoing work, are paying close attention to the use of telephones for doing illegal work. Some localities have thwarted outdoor retail drug dealing by having pay phones

• Moved inside of businesses for extra supervision
• Programmed to call out but not receive calls
• Removed entirely

Car Theft Is Preventable

The interesting case of steering wheel locks preventing car theft already was offered in the Chapter 8 discussion on displacement. Additional information about thwarting motor vehicle theft is found in several studies (Brown, 1995; Brown and Billing, 1996; Southall and Ekblom, 1985). Clarke and Harris (1992) listed numerous technical changes that the auto industry can contribute to help reduce auto theft. Several of these are already common in cars today. Many cars have better security locks for steering columns, doors, and

the hood. Door buttons today are more difficult to pull up with a clothes hanger. Window glass is often harder to break. Many models make it difficult to leave your keys in the ignition. Smart keys, elimination of external keyholes, and electronic immobilization after break-ins are no longer confined to the most expensive models. Manufacturers have improved some of those models listed as most stolen by the Highway Loss Data Institute. . . . Tremendous strides in car tape player security have combined with lower fence values, thereby interfering with their theft. The time it takes to steal a car has increased, and the pure amateur has more problems than ever. Brown and Billing (1996) show that more secure cars lead to less theft in Britain, and the American auto industry experience shows that cars with disastrous theft problems can be redesigned for crime prevention and their good names restored. By the time you read this, a new design will have been developed, probably for a model that got into the national media as thieves' favorite.

On the other hand, many new cars have expensive airbags, which are quickly pried out and sold for about $1,000 for installation in cars at repair shops, and computers that provide new targets. This illustrates what Ekblom refers to as an "arms race" between offenders and forces of crime control. Crime is never permanently prevented, but neither do we get anywhere against crime when we do not try.

Beyond the automobile industry, inexpensive technology already exists to put a personal identification number into every new and valuable electronic item, such as a television set or videocassette recorder. The product would not work outside your home unless you entered the right number. It would lose its value to a thief. It also should be possible to program something within your electrical system so an appliance removed from your home would not work elsewhere without punching in the code. Industry could make a major contribution to society by designing and selling more products that go kaput when stolen (see Felson, 1997).

A Serendipitous Finding About Motorcycle Theft

American motorcyclists keep complaining about having to put on their helmets and campaigning to stop helmet laws. If they only knew. Wherever helmet safety laws were enacted and enforced, thefts of motorcycles went down greatly.

To understand why, note that many motorcycle thefts are for joyriding and occur on the spur of the moment. The likely offender usually does not have a big motorcycle helmet with him at the time he sees a shiny motorcycle. When Germany enacted and enforced its motorcycle helmet law, thefts went down and stayed down, with no indication of displacement to other vehicle theft (Mayhew, Clarke, and Eliot, 1989).

We see that significant crime prevention can occur completely without planning. Even a very simple change in the law can have a great impact. Because wearing a helmet is highly visible behavior, it provides tangible evidence that the law is being followed and that the motorcycle probably is not stolen. . . .

Music and Control

People are not only influenced by what they see but also by what they hear. Young people generally do not like classical music and will go away when it is played. That's far better than nightsticks and imprisonment. Music is also suitable for calming people down, as wise disc jockeys well know. When the music stops, crowds in bars are rowdiest. The type of dancing also has a major influence on their behavior, with wilder dancing making people bump and, sometimes, fight. Yet the topic of music and crime has been little studied. Psychology students with expertise in perception and human factors are especially likely to break new ground in explaining how music provides cues that affect criminal behavior.

Situational Degeneration

Not only can crime situations be improved, but they can also be exacerbated. Thus, a store manager can remove crime control measures and cause shoplifting to rise. A homeowner can let well-trimmed bushes grow up, to the benefit of local burglars. A car manufacturer can cut costs by putting in cheaper steering wheel locks. One of the challenges of crime science is to put situational prevention and *situational degeneration* within the same intellectual framework. There is no better place to start than the study of violence.

Preventing Violent Crime

It is quite a mistake to think that situational prevention applies only to property crime. Understanding situational features of violence has grown considerably in recent years. The greatest source of progress stems from recognizing that violence is goal oriented and responds to cues from physical settings. As Chapter 3 explained, a book by James Tedeschi and my brother, Richard Felson (1994), shows us that all violence is goal oriented. A person might use violence (a) to get others to comply with wishes, (b) to restore justice as he perceives it, or (c) to assert and protect his self-image or identity. (As we shall see, these goals often make violence highly amenable to situational prevention as well.) A simple robbery starts out with the robber demanding your money and using or threatening force to get it. The robber is simply getting you to comply with his wishes—receiving your money without an argument. But if you challenge the robber in front of his co-offender, he may harm you to assert and protect his own identity (the third reason for violence). That is why it is best not to have a big mouth when someone is pointing a gun at you (see situational degeneration, above). It's also best not to go around giving people grievances against you; they may decide to restore justice. Fights between drunken young males usually occur as attempts to assert and protect identity. Road rage is often an effort to meet the second goal, restoring justice. Domestic violence can meet all three purposes (see R. Felson, in press).

Even with predatory violence, although generally oriented toward the first purpose—gaining compliance—offenders will sometimes seek to protect identity or restore justice. For example, youths angry at the store owner who yelled at them may rob him not only for loot but also to retaliate and punish. Remember, all these evaluations are based on the *offender's viewpoint*. To understand violent or nonviolent crime, we cannot be distracted by our own moral outrage, or by the legal code, or by objective facts about what a person *ought* to think of others. If the guy in the bar hit you because he *thinks* you insulted him, the fact that he heard you wrong is entirely beside the point.

You might readily guess that alcohol plays a major role in violence. It gives people big mouths and big ears. Big mouths help people make aggressive statements that provoke others into fights. Alcohol makes bigger ears by getting people to hear things that were not said. Managing alcohol is part of preventing violence.

Sports Events and Revelry

Speaking of alcohol, British football (soccer) has an unfortunate pattern of serious—and sometimes fatal—violence. Many fans arrive hours before a game, get drunk, and then commit acts of violence, many against fans of the visiting team. Because most of those involved in the violence do not own cars and therefore take buses to the games, the government arranged for these buses to arrive at the game later than in the past, allowing only a few minutes to buy a ticket and no time to get drunk. The effect was a reduction in football violence (Clarke, 1983).

Sweden also has a problem with alcohol-related violence, especially on one day each year. Midsummer's Eve (usually June 21) is the longest day of the year. In much of Sweden, this day has 24 hours of light. It is the most important holiday of the year. Swedes are usually reserved people, but they make an exception on Midsummer's Eve. A common behavior pattern is to get drunk and run wild. People also start bonfires, which sometimes get out of hand and burn more than intended. Moreover, many assaults occur on Midsummer's Eve. The crowds are far larger and wilder than anything police can handle, so deterrence loses its credibility. A more sensible policy was planned by Swedish authorities: They provided bonfires in designated and advertised locations and sought to

channel the holiday spirit into these settings. Their efforts paid off by reducing assaults and other illegal behavior (see Bjor, Knutsson, and Kuhlhorn, 1992).

Compared with events like football games in Britain, American sports venues usually are not bad. The probable reason is that American teams try to sell a lot of tickets to families and business groups. This results in people of mixed ages and both sexes. Even in hockey, with its violence on the ice, there is reasonable peace in the stands. We all know of exceptions, but the rule remains.

American sports venues try to prevent people from bringing in their own bottles. This probably is so that they can sell more drinks, but they also use security justifications. They generally sell soft drinks and beer to the larger crowd, with hard drinks sold only within the corporate boxes. Beer sales are cut off later in the game, when some fans are a bit too drunk. Security people with binoculars keep an eye on the crowd to see if there are fights or if fans are getting dangerous. They then cut off the beer sales in that section or even start watering down the beer. Because beer is highly profitable to management, cutting off beer sales reduces proceeds, but it clearly enhances safety. Watering the beer gets the heavy drinkers to complain, but management is glad to give them their money back and have the drinking dwindle.

To prevent conflicts and fights when people are going out of a stadium, the strategy is to keep people moving, whether in cars or on foot, so they have little time to linger or to get mad. A well-managed stadium looks for bottlenecks where crowds cannot move, relieving the traffic problem quickly as a service to customers and as a way to prevent trouble.

Cruising

In many European and Hispanic nations, young people walk around the center of town on weekend evenings. The United States version of this activity is cruising in cars. Cruising creates traffic jams and interferes with business. The automobile spreads adolescent activity over more space and makes it harder to prevent trouble; thus, vandalism and assaults become more serious (see Felson, Berends, Richardson, and Veno, 1997; Wikstrom, 1995). Many U.S. cities have enacted special cruising ordinances or enforce traffic and parking ordinances more heavily in trying to control cruising.

As explained by authors John Bell and Barbara Burke (1992), the city of Arlington, Texas, found that cruising by more than 1,000 cars was creating a major traffic jam on its main street for hours at a time. Ambulances could not get to hospitals, and little else in the way of normal city business could happen. Conventional traffic control methods were doing little good.

City Councilman Ken Groves learned that teenagers wanted two things: an unstructured and unsupervised environment in which to mingle, and restrooms. He speculated that if these were provided, most teenagers would act reasonably. A "cruising committee" was formed to link local agencies, business, the University of Texas at Arlington, and teenage representatives.

The committee devised a plan for the city to lease a large parking lot from the university and open it to cruisers on weekend nights while providing unobtrusive police protection, portable restrooms, and cleanup the next morning. Within two weekends, the new cruising area was in use by 1,000 parked or circling cars. The program channeled cruising into a smaller and safer area and pleased both teenagers

and adults, while providing the gentle controls of a few police officers on the side.

The lesson of the program is that a crime problem may be related to another problem; solve the other problem, and the crime problem takes care of itself. In this case, the problem was to provide youths with an outlet for a social need in the context of the local situation. When this was done, the related crime problems dissipated. . . .

Conclusion

Situational prevention offers a broad repertoire for preventing crime here and now, rather than there and eventually. It is verifiable, clear, simple, and cheap. It is available to people of all income groups, seldom treading on civil liberties (see Felson and Clarke, 1997b). Situational prevention bypasses the hardliners and softheads. Its idealism is not utopian because it has found practical ways to do the right thing. Most often it applies to a narrow slice of crime, but sometimes it can be mass-produced effectively. . . .

Situational prevention (broadly speaking) offers us our best chance to minimize crime, without interfering substantially or negatively with people's lives. As the repertoire of prevention methods continues to grow, we have a means for slicing away at crime.

Discussion Questions

1. Felson begins Chapter 49 by offering the following advice to those who want to engage in situational crime prevention: "Do not worry about academic theories." Do you think any of the theories presented in this book point to situational factors that might increase or decrease the likelihood of crime? For example, consider general strain theory (Chapter 16), social learning theory (Chapter 11), and routine activities theory (Chapter 34).

2. Consider the deviant act of cheating on exams. What are some ways in which we might make this act more difficult, risky, unrewarding, and inexcusable?

3. Can you think of any types of crime for which effective situational crime prevention may be difficult to implement?

4. Do you think some types of offenders may be more (or less) responsive to situational crime prevention than other types (see the discussion of deterrence in Part X)?

50. Saving Children from a Life of Crime

David P. Farrington and Brandon C. Welsh

This text lists numerous causes of crime, including strain, low control, and association with others who teach crime. As indicated in the introduction, any meaningful effort to reduce crime must address these causes. But exactly how is this to be done? How, for example, does one go about teaching juveniles to exercise self-control or training adults to be better parents? Farrington and Welsh answer such questions in Chapter 50. Drawing on the best research, they identify a range of prevention programs that have shown some success in altering those traits and environmental factors that cause crime.

They focus on prevention rather than rehabilitation because, as they state in the chapter, "prevention is better than cure." And they focus on prevention programs that are implemented early in the life course because children are more receptive to change than are adults. Also, early prevention can stop individuals from embarking on a path that leads to frequent and serious crime (see Part XII on crime and the life course). It should be noted, however, that many of the programs they describe have also been used to reduce crime among criminal offenders.

These programs focus on individual, family, peer, school, and community factors; with each program addressing one or more of the leading causes of crime. Farrington and Welsh focus on specific causes or "risk factors" for crime, such as impulsivity and poor parental supervision, but you

should be able to relate these programs to many of the theories described in this text. Most of the programs, for example, attempt to alter traits conducive to crime (Part II), increase one or more forms of control (Part VI), or reduce the social learning for crime (Part IV). Many also reduce certain forms of strain, such as harsh and erratic parental discipline.

As noted in the introduction, prevention programs of the type described by Farrington and Welsh are also cost effective, typically saving several times the amount they cost. These savings result from the multiple problems they prevent. For example, as Farrington and Welsh point out, preschool programs not only reduce crime but also reduce educational, economic, and family problems. Further, such programs are favored by most people in the general public. There is good basis, then, for Farrington and Welsh's recommendation for the development of a "comprehensive national prevention strategy for America."

The Need for Early Prevention

In medicine and public health, it is widely accepted that prevention is better than cure. The same is true of offending. Public health prevention is often based on identifying and tackling key risk factors. For example, smoking, lack of exercise, and a fatty diet are important

Reprinted from David P. Farrington and Brandon C. Welsh, *Saving Children from a Life of Crime*. Copyright © 2007 by Oxford University Press; reprinted by permission.

risk factors for heart attacks, and these risk factors can be tackled by media campaigns encouraging people to smoke less, exercise more, and eat more healthily. . . .

Two separate but interrelated developments inform this book's focus on the importance of early intervention policy and programs to improve children's life chances and prevent them from embarking on a life of crime.

 First, after decades of rigorous study in the United States and across the Western world—using prospective longitudinal studies—a great deal is now known about early risk factors for delinquency and later criminal offending. . . .

Early risk factors that are most strongly associated with delinquency and later criminal offending can be found at the individual, family, and environmental levels.

Among the most important individual factors that predict offending are low intelligence and attainment, personality and temperament, empathy, and impulsiveness. The strongest family factor that predicts offending is usually criminal or antisocial parents. Other quite strong and replicable family factors that predict offending are large family size, poor parental supervision, parental conflict, and disrupted families. At the environmental level, the strongest factors that predict offending are growing up in a low socioeconomic status household, associating with delinquent friends, attending high-delinquency-rate schools, and living in deprived areas.

The second development is the growing body of high-quality scientific evidence on the effectiveness of early intervention programs designed to tackle these risk factors and from which evidence-based conclusions can be drawn. Many early intervention trials have reached the point at which delinquency can be measured, and others have carried out long follow-ups. In addition, recent systematic literature reviews and meta-analyses of early intervention programs provide scientific evidence that a wide range of programs in different domains (individual, family, school, and community) can be effective

and others promising in preventing delinquency and later offending.

For example, at the individual level, preschool intellectual enrichment and child skills training programs are effective in preventing delinquency and later offending. Results are also highly favorable and robust for these programs' impacts on other important life-course outcomes, such as education, government assistance (e.g., welfare), employment, income, substance abuse, and family stability. At the family level, parent education plus daycare services and parent management training programs are particularly effective in preventing delinquency and later offending. Among environmental approaches, a number of school-based interventions are effective in preventing delinquency among youths in middle school and high school, while after-school and community-based mentoring programs hold promise as efficacious approaches. . . .

Understanding Risk-Focused Prevention

There are many possible ways of classifying crime prevention programs. One of the first efforts drew upon the public health approach to preventing diseases and injuries (Brantingham and Faust, 1976; Moore, 1995). This divides crime prevention activities into three categories: primary, secondary, and tertiary. Primary prevention involves measures targeted on the whole community to prevent the onset of delinquency. Secondary prevention focuses on intervening with children and youth who are at risk for becoming offenders because of the presence of one or more risk factors. Tertiary prevention involves measures targeted on offenders. . . .

Another influential classification scheme distinguishes four major prevention strategies (Tonry and Farrington, 1995). Developmental prevention refers to interventions designed to prevent the development of criminal potential in individuals, especially those that target risk and protective factors discovered in studies of human development (Tremblay and Craig, 1995). Community prevention refers to interventions designed to change the social conditions and institutions (e.g., families, peers, social norms, clubs, organizations) that influence offending in residential communities (Hope, 1995). Situational prevention refers to interventions designed to prevent the occurrence of crimes by reducing opportunities for offending and increasing its risk and difficulty (Clarke, 1995). Criminal justice prevention refers to traditional deterrent, incapacitative, and rehabilitative strategies that law enforcement and criminal justice system agencies operate. The term "risk-focused prevention" is now used more generally than "developmental prevention," but the two terms have essentially the same meaning....

Individual Prevention

Individual-based prevention programs target risk factors for delinquency and later offending that are found within the individual. As we discussed in chapter 3, some of these risk factors include low intelligence and attainment, low empathy, impulsivity, and hyperactivity. These programs are targeted on the child. As noted by Greg Duncan and Katherine Magnuson (2004, p. 94), "individual interventions focus directly on the person whose development is targeted, and can occur very early in life, as with intensive preschool education." This is distinguished from family-based interventions, which are directed at both the child and parent or caregiver.

Early childhood prevention programs have wide appeal across a large spectrum of constituencies (Karoly et al., 1998). The reasons for the widespread support can be found in any number of areas, from developmental theory to prevention science to the welfare of children. These programs help society's most vulnerable members. They have as explicit aims the betterment of children's immediate learning and social and emotional competencies, as well as the improvement of children's success over the life-course. In addition, they are implemented at a time when children are most impressionable and hence receptive to intervention (Duncan and Magnuson, 2004). With a primary emphasis on improving school readiness, providing families in need with various other services, and reaching about half of all impoverished children (Currie, 2001), Head Start is considered the nation's most important early childhood program (Ripple and Zigler, 2003)....

The most rigorous methods of systematic and meta-analytic reviews find that two main types of individual-based programs—preschool intellectual enrichment and child skills training—are generally effective in preventing delinquency or later criminal offending (Farrington and Welsh, 2003; Lösel and Beelmann, 2003, 2006)....

Preschool Intellectual Enrichment

Preschool intellectual enrichment programs are generally targeted on the risk factors of low intelligence and attainment. As noted by Duncan and Magnuson (2004, p. 105), "Child-focused early-education intervention programs are designed to provide economically disadvantaged children with cognitively stimulating and enriching experiences that their parents are unlikely to provide at home." Improved cognitive skills, school readiness, and social and emotional development are the main goals of these programs (Currie, 2001). Some of the key features of these programs include the provision of the following (Duncan and Magnuson, 2004, pp. 105–106).

- Developmentally appropriate learning curricula
- A wide array of cognitive-based enriching activities
- Activities for parents, usually of a less intensive nature, so that they may be able to support the school experience at home....

Child Social Skills Training

Social skills training or social competence programs for children are generally targeted on the risk factors of impulsivity, low empathy, and self-centeredness. As noted by Carolyn Webster-Stratton and Ted Taylor, this type of individual-based program is designed to "directly teach children social, emotional, and cognitive competence by addressing appropriate social skills, effective problem-solving, anger management, and emotion language" (2001, p. 178). A typical program includes one or more of these elements and is highly structured, with a limited number of sessions, this lasting for a relatively short period of time (Lösel and Beelmann, 2003). . . .

One of the most successful early skills training programs to have measured the effects on crime is the Montreal Longitudinal-Experimental Study of the psychologist Richard Tremblay and his colleagues (1995, 1996). This program combined child skills training and parent training. Tremblay and his colleagues (1996) identified disruptive (aggressive/hyperactive) boys at age 6 (from low socioeconomic neighborhoods in Montreal) and randomly allocated over 300 of these to experimental or control conditions.

Between ages 7 and 9, the experimental group received training designed to foster social skills and self-control. Coaching, peer modeling, role playing, and reinforcement contingencies were used in small group sessions on such topics as "how to help," "what to do when you are angry," and "how to react to teasing." In addition, the children's parents were trained using the parent management training techniques developed by Gerald Patterson (1982) at the Oregon Social Learning Center. Parents were taught how to provide positive reinforcement for desirable behavior, to use nonpunitive and consistent discipline practices, and to develop family crisis management techniques. By age 12 (3 years after treatment), the experimental boys committed significantly less burglary and theft, were significantly less likely to get drunk, and were significantly less likely to be involved in fights than the controls. . . .

The effectiveness of preschool intellectual enrichment and child skills training programs is not limited to the prevention of delinquency and later offending. Results are highly favorable and robust for impacts on other important life-course outcomes, such as education, government assistance (e.g., welfare), employment, income, substance abuse, and family stability. This should not come as a surprise to many, given that the original impetus of the majority of these programs was to first and foremost improve early childhood outcomes well before delinquency or crime could be measured. Indeed, the desirable impact on delinquency and offending outcomes could be considered spinoff benefits. The noncrime benefits are also apparent from cost-benefit analyses of individual-based programs. . . .

Family Prevention

Family-based prevention programs target risk factors for delinquency and later offending that are associated with the family, such as poor child-rearing, poor supervision, and inconsistent or harsh discipline (see chapter 4 for other family risk factors). Broadly speaking, family-based prevention programs have developed along the lines of two major fields of study: psychology and public health. When delivered by psychologists, these programs are often classified into parent management training, functional family therapy, or family preservation (Wasserman and Miller, 1998). Typically, they attempt to change the social contingencies in the family environment so that children are rewarded in some way for appropriate or prosocial behaviors and punished in some way for inappropriate or antisocial behaviors.

Family-based programs delivered by health professionals such as nurses are typically less behavioral, mainly providing advice and guidance to parents or general parent education. Home visiting with new parents, especially mothers, is perhaps the most popular form of this type of family intervention. In the early 1990s, Hawaii became the first state to offer free home visits for all new mothers. A small number of other states, with Colorado at the forefront, have more recently implemented more intensive but targeted versions of home visiting programs with the aim of eventually providing universal coverage (Calonge, 2005)....

A recent meta-analysis found that two main types of family-based programs—general parent education (in the context of home visiting and parent education plus daycare services) and parent management—are effective in preventing delinquency or later criminal offending (Farrington and Welsh, 2003)....

Parent Education: Home Visiting

Home visiting with new parents, especially mothers, is a popular, although far from universal, method of delivering the family-based intervention known as general parent education. The main goals of home visiting programs center around educating parents to improve the life chances of children from a very young age, often beginning at birth and sometimes in the final trimester of pregnancy. Some of the main goals include the prevention of preterm or low-weight births, the promotion of healthy child development or school readiness, and the prevention of child abuse and neglect (Gomby, Culross, and Behrman, 1999, p. 4). Home visits very often also serve to improve parental well-being, linking parents to community resources to help with employment, educational, or addiction recovery. Home visitors are usually nurses or other health professionals with a diverse array of skills in working with families. In the words of Deanna Gomby, Patti Culross, and Richard Behrman (p. 5),

> home visitors can see the environments in which families live, gain a better understanding of the families' needs, and therefore tailor services to meet those needs. The relationships forged between home visitors and parents can break through loneliness and isolation and serve as the first step in linking families to their communities....

Parent Education Plus Daycare

A small number of parent education programs that include daycare services for the children of the participating parents have also measured delinquency. As noted in chapter 7, daycare programs are distinguished from preschool programs, in that the daycare programs are not focused on the child's intellectual enrichment or necessarily on readying the child for kindergarten and elementary school, but serve largely as an organized form of childcare to allow for parents (especially mothers) to return to work. Daycare also provides children with a number of important benefits, including social interaction with other children and stimulation of their cognitive, sensory, and motor control skills. In the United States and some other Western countries, daycare services are available to children as young as 6 weeks old (Michel, 1999)....

Parent Management Training

Many different types of parent training have been used to prevent and treat child externalizing behavior problems and delinquency (Wasserman and Miller, 1998). Parent management training refers to "treatment procedures in which parents are trained to alter their child's behavior at home" (Kazdin, 1997, p. 1349). The Oregon psychologist Gerald Patterson (1982) developed behavioral parent management training. His careful observations of parent-child interaction showed that parents of antisocial children were deficient in their methods of child-rearing. These parents failed to tell their children how they were expected to behave, failed to monitor their behavior to ensure that it was desirable, and failed to enforce rules promptly and unambiguously with appropriate rewards and penalties. The parents of antisocial children used more punishment (such as scolding, shouting, or threatening) but failed to make it contingent on the child's behavior.

Patterson attempted to train these parents in effective child-rearing methods, namely, noticing what a child is doing, monitoring behavior over long periods, clearly stating house rules, making rewards and punishments contingent on behavior, and negotiating disagreements so that conflicts and crises do not escalate. His treatment was shown to be effective in reducing child stealing and antisocial behavior over short periods in small-scale studies. . . .

Both general parent education and parent management training programs also produced a wide range of other important benefits for families, from improved school readiness and school performance on the part of children to greater employment and educational opportunities for parents, to greater family stability in general. This mirrors our finding for child-focused early interventions. Again, this may not come as a surprise, because the original impetus of the majority of these programs was to improve family outcomes well before child delinquency or offending could be measured. This is evidenced in the cost-benefit analysis of the Elmira nurse home visitation program performed by Greenwood and his colleagues (2001). An analysis of the distribution of benefits accrued to government, which exceeded program costs by a ratio of 4.1 to 1, revealed that 57 percent of these benefits were due to a reduction in welfare costs, 23 percent were due to tax revenue from increased employment income, 20 percent were due to a reduction in juvenile and criminal justice costs, and less than 1 percent were due to a reduction in health care services. . . .

While beyond the scope of this chapter and the book in general, it is noteworthy that various family-based interventions, parent management training included, have also demonstrated evidence of effectiveness in preventing delinquency and offending among adjudicated populations, both juvenile and adult. In our meta-analysis, we found that the most effective family-based approach was multisystematic therapy (MST), an increasingly popular multimodal intervention that is designed for serious juvenile offenders (Henggeler, Schoenwald, Borduin, Rowland, and Cunningham, 1998). The particular type of treatment is chosen according to the needs of the young person, and it may include individual, family, peer, school, and community interventions (including parent training and skills training). . . .

Peer, School, and Community Prevention

Peer, school, and community prevention programs target environmental-level risk factors for delinquency and later offending. These risk factors include associating with delinquent friends; attending high delinquency-rate schools, which have high levels of distrust between teachers and students, low commitment to the school by students, and unclear and inconsistently enforced rules; and growing up in a poor, disorganized neighborhood.

School-based prevention programs have become increasingly popular in recent years. This is due in part to increased attention to school crime that has come about in response to high-profile school shootings and other violent incidents. Most of the programs that have been set up in the wake of these tragic events focus on the safety of students within schools; fewer focus on the prevention of delinquency in the wider community. Less can be said about early intervention programs targeted on peer risk factors to prevent delinquency. However, peer-based programs have been used extensively to help children resist peer influences to initiate drug use. Community-based prevention covers a wide array of programs, including after-school, mentoring, and youth and resident groups. These programs hold wide appeal among the public and political leaders alike, but are often among the first programs to lose funding in times of federal or state budget cuts (Butterfield, 2003). This state of affairs has hampered the knowledge base on the effectiveness of this type of early intervention. . . .

Peer-Based Programs

Peer-based programs to prevent delinquency and offending are ostensibly designed with two related aims: to reduce the influence of delinquent friends and increase the influence of prosocial friends. Teaching children to resist antisocial peer pressures that encourage delinquent activities can take many forms, including modeling and guided practice. Peers must be older, preferably in their later teens, and influential; such peers are sometimes known as high-status peer leaders.

Unfortunately, we have not found any systematic or meta-analytic review that has investigated the effects of peer-based programs on delinquency or later offending. The reviews that have been completed to date have focused on substance use. For example, a large-scale meta-analysis of 143 substance use prevention programs by Nancy Tobler (1986) concluded that programs using peer leaders were the most effective in reducing smoking, drinking, and drug use....

School-Based Programs

Schools are a critical social context for crime prevention efforts, from the early to the later grades (Elliott, Hamburg, and Williams, 1998). All schools work to produce vibrant and productive members of society. According to the Maryland criminologist Denise Gottfredson and her colleagues (2002b, p. 149), "students who are impulsive, are weakly attached to their schools, have little commitment to achieving educational goals, and whose moral beliefs in the validity of conventional rules for behavior are weak are more likely to engage in crime than those who do not possess these characteristics." The school's role in influencing these risk factors and preventing delinquency in both school and the wider community (the focus here) differs from situational and administrative measures taken to make the school a safer place (e.g., through metal detectors, police in school, or closed-circuit television surveillance cameras)....

In contrast to peer-based intervention strategies, there have been a number of comprehensive, evidence-based reviews on the effectiveness of early school-based programs to prevent delinquency and offending....

Four types of school-based programs as effective in preventing delinquency....

Community-Based Programs

More often than not, community-based efforts to prevent delinquency and later offending are some combination of developmental prevention, with its focus on reducing the development or influence of early risk factors or "root causes"—for delinquency and later offending (Tremblay and Craig, 1995), and situational prevention, with its focus on reducing opportunities for crime (Clarke, 1995). Unlike these two general crime prevention strategies, there is little agreement in the academic literature on the definition of community prevention and the types of programs that fall within it (Bennett, 1996). Tim Hope (1995, p. 21) defined community crime prevention as "actions intended to change the social conditions that are believed to sustain crime in residential communities." Local social institutions (e.g., community associations, churches, youth clubs) are usually the means by which these programs are delivered, in an attempt to address delinquency and crime problems (Hope, 1995, p. 21).

The most rigorous reviews of the effectiveness of community-based crime prevention find that two main types of programs—after-school and community-based mentoring—can be classified as promising in preventing delinquency or later criminal offending. Promising programs are those where the level of certainty from the available scientific evidence is too low to support generalizable conclusions, but where there is some empirical basis for predicting that further research could support such conclusions (Farrington et al., 2002b, p. 18).

After-school programs. This type of program is premised on the belief that providing prosocial opportunities for young people in the after-school hours can reduce their involvement in delinquent behavior in the community. After-school programs target a range of risk factors for delinquency, including alienation and association with delinquent peers. There are many different types of after-school programs, including recreation-based programs, drop-in clubs, dance groups, and tutoring services....

Community-based mentoring. This type of program usually involves nonprofessional adult volunteers spending time with young people at risk for delinquency, dropping out of school, school failure, and other social problems. Mentors behave in a "supportive, nonjudgmental manner while acting as role models" (Howell, 1995, p. 90). In many cases, mentors work one-on-one with young people, often forming strong bonds. Care is taken in matching the mentor and the young person....

Successful School-Based Programs

School and discipline management. One example of an effective program that used school and discipline management to improve the school environment to prevent delinquent and criminal behavior is Project PATHE (Positive Action Through Holistic Education; Gottfredson, 1986). This project was implemented in four middle schools and three high schools in Charleston County, South Carolina. The main elements included increasing shared decision-making in schools, increasing the competence of teachers, increasing the academic competence of students (e.g., through teaching study skills), and improving the school climate (e.g., through a school pride campaign). By increasing students' sense of belonging and usefulness, the project sought to promote a positive school experience....

Classroom or instructional management. One of the most important early school-based prevention experiments was carried out in Seattle by David Hawkins and his colleagues (1991). They implemented a multicomponent program (known as the Seattle Social Development Project) combining parent training, teacher training, and skills training. About 500 first-grade children (aged 6) in 21 classes were randomly assigned to be in experimental or control classes. The children in the experimental classes received special treatment at home and a school that was designed to increase their attachment to their parents and their bonding to the school, in accordance with the assumption that delinquency is inhibited by the strength of social bonds. In addition, the treated children were trained in interpersonal cognitive problem-solving. Their parents were trained to notice and reinforce socially desirable behavior in a program called "Catch Them Being Good." Their teachers were trained in classroom management, for example, to provide clear instructions and expectations to children, to reward children for participation in desired behavior, and to teach children prosocial (socially desirable) methods of solving problems....

Reorganization of grades or classes. One example of an effective program that used the reorganization of grades or classes to improve the school environment to prevent criminal and other problem behaviors is Student Training Through Urban Strategies (STATUS), which was evaluated by Denise Gottfredson (1990). The main component of the program was referred to as "school-within-a-school" scheduling, whereby high-risk students were brought together for a 2-hour period each day to receive an "integrated social studies and English program which involved a law-related education curriculum and used instructional methods emphasizing active student participation"....

Increasing self-control or social competency using cognitive behavioral or behavioral instructional methods. General instruction of students is the most common school-based delinquency prevention strategy. It involves a wide range of functions, including "to teach [students] factual information, increase their awareness of social influences to engage in misbehavior, expand their repertoires for recognizing and appropriately responding to risky or potentially harmful situations, increase their appreciation for diversity in society, improve their moral character" (Gottfredson et al., 2002a, p. 63, box 4.3). The addition of a cognitive-behavioral dimension (e.g., the use of cues, feedback, rehearsal, role-playing) seems to be crucial to the efficacy of self-control or social competency instruction programs.

One example of an effective program that used this individually focused school-based strategy to reduce delinquency is Responding in Peaceful and Positive Ways (RIPP) by Albert Farrell and Aleta Meyer (1997). Targeted at sixth-grade students, mostly African-American children from low-income families, in six public middle schools in Richmond, Virginia, RIPP involved an 18-session violence prevention curriculum, divided into seven instructional topics: building trust; respect for individual differences; the nature of violence and risk factors; anger management; personal values; precipitants and consequences of fighting; and nonviolent alternatives to fighting (Farrell and Meyer, 1997, p. 980). Almost 1,300 students participated in the program. . . .

Successful Community-Based Programs

After-school programs. The Boys and Girls Clubs of America (BGC) plays an important role in the provision of after-school services for children and youths. Founded in 1902, the BGC is a nonprofit organization with a membership of more than 1.3 million young people nationwide. The clubs provide programs in six main areas: cultural enrichment; health and physical education; social recreation; personal and educational development; citizenship and leadership development; and environmental education. Steven Schinke, Mario Orlandi, and Kristin Cole (1992) evaluated the impact of BGCs in public housing sites in five cities. The usual services of BGCs, which include reading classes, sports, and homework assistance, were offered, as well as a program to prevent substance abuse, known as SMART Moves (Self-Management and Resistance Training). This program targets the pressures that young people face to try drugs and alcohol. It also provides education to parents and the community at large to assist young people in learning about the dangers of substance abuse and strategies for resisting the pressures to use drugs and alcohol (p. 120). . . .

Community-based mentoring. Big Brothers Big Sisters (BBBS) of America is a national youth mentoring organization that was founded in 1904 and is committed to improving the life chances of at-risk children and teens. One BBBS program brought together unrelated pairs of adult volunteers and youths ages 10 to 16. Rather than trying to address particular problems facing a youth, the program focused on providing a youth with an adult friend. The premise behind this is that the "friendship forged with a youth by the Big Brother or Big Sister creates a framework through which the mentor can support and aid the youth" (Grossman and Tierney, 1998, p. 405). The program also stressed that this friendship needs to be long lasting. To this end, mentors met with youths on average three or four times a month (for 3 to 4 hours each time) for at least 1 year. . . .

A Comprehensive National Prevention Strategy for America

We believe the time is right for the U.S. federal government to mount a national prevention strategy. Its focus should be on intervening early to save children from a life of crime. Its prevention plans should be grounded in the leading scientific evidence on the causes of offending and what works to prevent delinquency and later offending. It should also be comprehensive. We discuss these and the other main elements of a proposed national strategy here.

The national strategy needs to have a clear vision of intent. The vision should be that early prevention of delinquency and later offending saves lives. It saves lives by diverting the very children who may embark on a life of crime and endure its consequences—incarceration, various social ills that face offenders later in life, injury, even death—and producing instead productive, law-abiding citizens.

This vision may be grand, but it need not be viewed as unrealistic. The scientific evidence on the early causes of crime establishes that identifying at an early age those children who are at greatest risk for offending is no guarantee that they will not later become criminals. Likewise, the scientific evidence on the efficacy of early prevention programs establishes that prevention work is not a panacea for keeping children out of a life of crime. But in each case, the scientific evidence, as we have shown, provides guidance on the most important early crime risk factors to target and demonstrates that impressive results can be achieved by using a number of early prevention programs that target these risk factors....

Discussion Questions

1. Why do Farrington and Welsh place so much emphasis on *early prevention?*
2. Describe the differences among primary, secondary, and tertiary prevention, as well as among developmental, community, situational, and criminal justice prevention. Give examples of each type of prevention.
3. Select any two of the prevention programs described by Farrington and Welsh (e.g., preschool intellectual enrichment, child social skills training, parent education, community-based mentoring). Drawing on the theories in this text, indicate what causes of crime these programs address.
4. Drawing on the theories in this text, are there any causes of crime *not* addressed by the programs that Farrington and Welsh describe?
5. There is good reason to believe that certain prevention and rehabilitation programs are able to substantially reduce offending, are cost effective, and have much public support. Given this, why is it that we do not make greater use of such programs and instead focus on "get-tough" approaches?